'*The Spanish Holocaust* is as polemical as it is well-pondered. Preston tells truths that many are not interested in hearing, and he does so in great detail, with scholarly rigour, and in an accessible, efficient prose. He is driven as much by a thirst for knowledge as by affection and respect for his subject. He has produced an indispensable, important book'
The Volunteer

'Fascinating ... Unflinchingly, Preston sifts through the pillage, torture, and mass executions of this bleak chapter in Spanish history'
New Yorker

'An important resource that has changed historiography on the period ... [Preston] has written a text that is masterly and authoritative in scope, seeking to place the extermination of the Spanish during this period in an analysis of genocide ... his scholarship in revealing the criminals is commendable, and his narrative remains highly deserving of praise. The book is incredibly detailed'
Reviews in History

'Preston's knowledge is deep and encyclopaedic, and his status as the foremost historian of this period is incontestable ... *The Spanish Holocaust* is the culmination of a truly outstanding career. To his peerless scholarship, Preston adds dynamic prose and a deeply humane feeling for those caught in events they did nothing to deserve or to bring about. Although no historical work is ever definitive, *The Spanish Holocaust* will come as close to that as possible. In terms of attention to detail and synthesis, this surely is a book that will stand the test of time'
Times Higher Education

'Breathtaking history ... Preston's work is a powerful intervention in a Spanish discussion. Its significance transcends the events it brings to light, and suggests some basic re-evaluations of recent European history ... Superb'
The New Republic

'Preston's command of detail is unequalled'
Daily Telegraph

D0368081

PAUL PRESTON is the world's foremost historian on twentieth-century Spain and the author of many books, including the standard biographies of General Franco and King Juan Carlos and *The Spanish Civil War*, hailed by *The Times* as 'the definitive work'. He is an Emeritus Professor of the London School of Economics, a Fellow of the British Academy and lives in London. *The Spanish Holocaust* was shortlisted for the 2012 Samuel Johnson Prize and named *Sunday Times* History Book of the Year.

From the reviews of *The Spanish Holocaust*:

'Preston goes well beyond previous historians in his magisterial but chillingly meticulous record of slaughter systematically tearing down the self-serving left-wing and (especially) right-wing myths about the conflict ... Exhaustively researched and masterfully written ... the result is a book of extraordinary moral and emotional power, a classic of historical scholarship and a deeply affecting record of man's inhumanity to man'   DOMINIC SANDBROOK, *Sunday Times*

'Monumental, rigorous and unflinching ... important and opportune in ways that reach far beyond the purely academic ... Preston's contribution is a major one, both in tracing the fundamentalist origins of the military coup that unleashed the killing and in reconstructing its complex consequences ... Preston's study is history as a public good, a substitute for the truth and reconciliation process that has not taken place in Spain'   *Independent*

'Anyone who supposes that Franco's regime was only mildly despotic and repressive should read this wonderful book'   *Daily Express*

'Paul Preston's account of the torture and slaughter of thousands of civilians and captives during and after the Spanish civil war vividly describes events that we would unhesitatingly describe as war crimes or crimes against humanity ... drawing on meticulous research over many years, Preston leaves no room for doubt that the events he describes were ... crimes so appalling that they negate our humanity. He wept at times as he prepared what he calls "an extremely painful book to write". Readers will weep too'   *Financial Times*

'Paul Preston is the outstanding scholar of Spain's civil war, and *The Spanish Holocaust* is unquestionably his opus magnus. For the first time, the horror of the Spanish conflict has been placed in its appropriate historical context. As documented by Preston in this moving, brilliantly rendered account, Spain was not only the scene-setter for World War Two, but also the proving ground for the campaigns of mass-murder that became its ghastly hallmark. A deeply important, powerful work of history'
JON LEE ANDERSON

'Only in democratic Spain, with the end of censorship and the opening up of archives and mass graves, have Spanish historians been able to provide us with the truth: that the Right killed about three times as many people as the Left. It is upon their research that Preston has based his meticulously compiled account … [he] has done his subject proud'
Spectator

'Chillingly powerful … made compelling through the energy of the writing and the author's novelistic eye for detail … the ultimate importance of Preston's relentless and impeccable research is a reminder of the evil unleashed by Franco'
Literary Review

'No one can doubt the scholarship that underpins Preston's account of the extra-judicial murders, executions and torture that General Franco and his forces carried out … a formidable book by Britain's pre-eminent historian of Spain'
Financial Times

'Staggeringly detailed, powerful and affecting … a history of rare emotional power, which alters our view of one of the most symbolic conflicts of the last century'
Sunday Times

'As one would expect from Preston, one of the hardest-working academics I have ever come across, there is no shortage of horror drawn from years of painstaking personal research … I cannot think of a Spanish historian who has managed, as Preston has done, to give such a detailed account of the appalling abuse and loss of life committed on both sides during the civil war'
The Tablet

'Magisterial … an essential reference for anything written on the subject for years to come'
New York Times

THE SPANISH HOLOCAUST

*Inquisition and Extermination
in Twentieth-Century Spain*

PAUL PRESTON

Harper
Press

FOR GABRIELLE

Harper*Press*
An imprint of HarperCollins*Publishers*
77–85 Fulham Palace Road
Hammersmith, London W6 8JB
www.harpercollins.co.uk

This Harper*Press* paperback edition published 2013

7

First published in Great Britain by Harper*Press* in 2012

A catalogue record for this book is
available from the British Library

ISBN 978-0-00-638695-7

Typeset in Minion by G&M Designs Limited,
Raunds, Northamptonshire
Printed and bound in Great Britain by
Clays Ltd, St Ives plc

CONTENTS

LIST OF ILLUSTRATIONS

PROLOGUE

Behind the lines during the Spanish Civil War, nearly 200,000 men and women were murdered extra-judicially or executed after flimsy legal process. They were killed as a result of the military coup of 17–18 July 1936 against the Second Republic. For the same reason, perhaps as many as 200,000 men died at the battle fronts. Unknown numbers of men, women and children were killed in bombing attacks and in the exoduses that followed the occupation of territory by Franco's military forces. In all of Spain after the final victory of the rebels at the end of March 1939, approximately 20,000 Republicans were executed. Many more died of disease and malnutrition in overcrowded, unhygienic prisons and concentration camps. Others died in the slave-labour conditions of work battalions. More than half a million refugees were forced into exile and many were to die of disease in French concentration camps. Several thousand were worked to death in Nazi camps. The purpose of this book is to show as far as possible what happened to civilians and why. All of what did happen constitutes what I believe can legitimately be called the Spanish holocaust.

I thought long and hard about using the word 'holocaust' in the title of this book. I feel intense sorrow and outrage about the Nazis' deliberate attempt to annihilate European Jewry. I also feel intense sorrow and outrage about the lesser, but none the less massive, suffering undergone by the Spanish people during the Civil War of 1936–9 and for several years thereafter. I could find no word that more accurately encapsulates the Spanish experience than 'holocaust'. Moreover, in choosing it, I was influenced by the fact that those who justified the slaughter of innocent Spaniards used an anti-Semitic rhetoric and frequently claimed that they had to be exterminated because they were the instruments of a 'Jewish–Bolshevik–Masonic' conspiracy. Nevertheless, my use of the word 'holocaust' is not intended to equate what happened within Spain with what happened throughout the rest of continental Europe under German occupation but rather to suggest that it be examined in a broadly comparative context. It is hoped thereby to suggest parallels and resonances that will lead to a better understanding of what happened in Spain during the Civil War and after.

To this day, General Franco and his regime enjoy a relatively good press. This derives from a series of persistent myths about the benefits of his rule. Along with the carefully constructed idea that he masterminded Spain's economic 'miracle' in the 1960s and heroically kept his country out of the Second World War, there are numerous falsifications about the origins of his regime. These derive from the initial lie that the Spanish Civil War was a necessary war fought to save the country from Communist take-over. The success of this fabrication influenced much writing on the Spanish Civil War to depict it as a conflict between two more or less equal sides. The issue of innocent civilian casualties is subsumed into that concept and thereby 'normalized'. Moreover, anticommunism, a reluctance to believe that officers and gentlemen could be involved in the deliberate mass slaughter of civilians and distaste for anti-clerical violence go some way to explaining a major lacuna in the historiography of the war.

The extent to which the rebels' war effort was built on a prior plan of systematic mass murder and their subsequent regime on state terror is given relatively little weight in the literature on the Spanish conflict and its aftermath. The same may be said of the fact that a chain reaction which fuelled retaliatory mass assassinations within the loyalist zone was set off once the exterminatory plans of the military rebels began to be implemented from the night of 17 July 1936. The collective violence in both rearguards unleashed by brutal perpetrators against undeserving victims justifies the use of the word 'holocaust' in this context not just because of its extent but also because its resonances of systematic murder should be invoked in the Spanish case, as they are in those of Germany and Russia.

There were two rearguard repressions, one each in the Republican and rebel zones. Although very different, both quantitatively and qualitatively, each claimed tens of thousands of lives, most of them innocent of wrongdoing or even of political activism. The leaders of the rebellion, Generals Mola, Franco and Queipo de Llano, regarded the Spanish proletariat in the same way as they did the Moroccan, as an inferior race that had to be subjugated by sudden, uncompromising violence. Thus they applied in Spain the exemplary terror they had learned in North Africa by deploying the Spanish Foreign Legion and Moroccan mercenaries, the Regulares, of the colonial army.

Their approval of the grim violence of their men is reflected in Franco's war diary of 1922, which lovingly describes Moroccan villages destroyed and their defenders decapitated. He delights in recounting how his teenage bugler boy cut off the ear of a captive.[1] Franco himself led twelve Legionarios on a raid from which they returned carrying as trophies the bloody heads of twelve tribesmen (*harqueños*).[2] The decapitation and mutilation of prisoners was common. When General Miguel Primo de Rivera visited Morocco in 1926, an entire battalion of the Legion awaited inspection with heads stuck on their bayonets.[3] During the Civil War, terror by the African Army was similarly deployed on the Spanish mainland as the instrument of a coldly conceived project to underpin a future authoritarian regime.

The repression carried out by the military rebels was a carefully planned operation to eliminate, in the words of the director of the coup, Emilio Mola, 'without scruple or hesitation those who do not think as we do'.[4] In contrast, the repression in the Republican zone was hot-blooded and reactive. Initially, it was a spontaneous and defensive response to the military coup which was subsequently intensified by news brought by refugees of military atrocities and by rebel bombing raids. It is difficult to see how the violence in the Republican zone could have happened without the military coup which effectively removed all of the restraints of civilized society. The collapse of the structures of law and order as a result of the coup thus permitted both an explosion of blind millenarian revenge (the built-in resentment of centuries of oppression) and the irresponsible criminality of those let out of jail or of those individuals never previously daring to give free rein to their instincts. In addition, as in any war, there was the real military necessity of combating the enemy within.

There is no doubt that hostility intensified on both sides as the Civil War progressed, fed by outrage and a desire for revenge as news of what was happening on the other side filtered through. Nevertheless, it is also clear that, from the first moments, there was a level of hatred at work that sprang forth ready formed from the army in the North African outpost of Ceuta on the night of 17 July 1936 or from the Republican populace on 19 July at the Cuartel de la Montaña barracks in Madrid. The first part of the book explains how those enmities were fomented. Polarization ensued from the right's determination to block the reforming ambitions of the democratic regime established in April 1931, the Second Republic. The obstruction of reform led to an ever more radicalized response by the left. At the same time, rightist theological and racial theories were elaborated to justify the intervention of the military and the destruction of the left.

In the case of the military rebels, a programme of terror and extermination was central to their planning and preparations. Because of the numerical superiority of the urban and rural working classes, they believed that the immediate imposition of a reign of terror was crucial. With the use of forces brutalized in the colonial wars in Africa, backed up by local landowners, this process was supervised in the south by General Queipo de Llano. In the significantly different regions of Navarre, Galicia, Old Castile and León, deeply conservative areas where the military coup was almost immediately successful and left-wing resistance minimal, the application of terror under the supervision of General Mola was disproportionately severe.

The exterminatory objectives of the rebels, if not their military capacities, found an echo on the extreme left, particularly in the anarchist movement, in rhetoric about the need for 'purification' of a corrupt society. In Republican-held areas, the underlying hatreds deriving from misery, hunger and exploitation exploded in a disorganized terror, particularly in Barcelona and Madrid. Inevitably, the targets were not just the military personnel identified with the revolt but also the wealthy, the bankers, the industrialists and the landowners who were regarded as the instruments of oppression. It was directed too, often with greater ferocity, at the clergy who were seen as the cronies of the rich, legitimizing injustice while the Church accumulated fabulous wealth. Unlike the systematic repression unleashed by the rebels as an instrument of policy, this random violence took place despite, not because of, the Republican authorities. Indeed, as a result of the efforts of successive Republican governments to re-establish public order, the left-wing repression was restrained and was largely at an end by December 1936.

Two of the bloodiest episodes in the Spanish Civil War, which are closely interrelated, concern the siege of Madrid by the rebels and the capital's defence. Franco's Africanista forces, the so-called 'Column of Death', left a trail of slaughter as they conquered towns and villages along their route from Seville to the capital. Having thus announced what Madrid could expect if surrender was not immediate, the consequence was that those responsible for the defence of the city made the decision to evacuate right-wing prisoners, particularly army officers who had sworn to join the rebel forces as soon as they could. The implementation of that decision led to the notorious massacres of right-wingers at Paracuellos on the outskirts of Madrid.

By the end of 1936, two differing concepts of the war had evolved. The Republic was on the defensive both against Franco and against enemies within. Such enemies included not just the burgeoning rebel fifth column, dedicated to spying, sabotage and spreading defeatism and despondency. Threats to the international image of the Republic and indeed to its war effort were also seen in the revolutionary ambitions of the anarchist movement, consisting of its trade union, the Confederación Nacional del Trabajo, and its activist wing, the Federación Anarquista Ibérica. The anti-Stalinist Partido Obrero de Unificación Marxista was equally determined to make a priority of revolution. Both thus became targets of the same security apparatus which had put a stop to the uncontrolled repression of the first months. On the rebel side, the rapid advance of the African columns was replaced by Franco's deliberately ponderous war of annihilation through the Basque Country, Santander, Asturias, Aragon and Catalonia. His war effort was conceived ever more as an investment in terror which would facilitate the establishment of his dictatorship. The post-war machinery of trials, executions, prisons and concentration camps consolidated that investment.

The intention was to ensure that establishment interests would never again be challenged as they had been from 1931 to 1936 by the democratic reforms of the Second Republic. When the clergy justified and the military implemented General Mola's call for the elimination of 'those who do not think as we do', they were not engaged in an intellectual or ethical crusade. The defence of establishment interests was assumed to require the eradication of the 'thinking' of progressive liberal and left-wing elements. They had questioned the central tenets of the right which could be summed up in the slogan of the major Catholic party, the CEDA (Confederación Española de Derechas Autónomas – or Spanish Confederation of Autonomous Right-Wing Groups) – 'Religion, Fatherland, Family, Order, Work, Property', the untouchable elements of social and economic life in Spain before 1931. 'Religion' referred to the Catholic Church's monopoly of education and religious practice. 'Fatherland' meant no challenge to Spanish centralism from the regional nationalisms. 'Family' denoted the subservient position of women and the prohibition of divorce. 'Order' meant no toleration of public protest. 'Work' referred to the duties of the labouring masses. 'Property' meant the privileges of the landowners whose position must remain unchallenged. Sometimes, the word 'hierarchy' was included in the list to emphasize that the existing social order was sacrosanct. To protect all of these tenets, in the areas occupied by the rebels, the immediate victims were not just schoolteachers, Freemasons, liberal doctors and lawyers, intellectuals and trade union leaders – those who might have propagated ideas. The killing also extended to all those who might have been influenced by their ideas: the trade unionists, those who didn't attend Mass, those suspected of voting in February 1936 for the left-wing electoral coalition, the Popular Front, and the women who had been given the vote and the right to divorce.

What all this meant in terms of numbers of deaths is still impossible to say with finality, although the broad lines are clear. Accordingly, indicative figures are frequently given in the book, drawing on the massive research carried out all over Spain in recent years by large numbers of local historians. However, despite their remarkable achievements, it is still not possible to present definitive figures for the overall number of those killed behind the lines, especially in the rebel zone. The objective should always be, as far as is possible, to base figures for those killed in both zones on the named dead. Thanks to the efforts of the Republican authorities at the time to identify bodies and because of subsequent investigations by the Francoist state, the numbers of those murdered or executed in the Republican zone are known with relative precision. The most reliable recent figure, produced by the foremost expert on the subject, José Luis Ledesma, is 49,272. However, uncertainty over the scale of the killings in Republican Madrid could see that figure rise.[5] Even for areas where reliable studies exist, new information and excavations of common graves see the numbers being revised constantly, albeit within relatively small parameters.[6]

In contrast, the calculation of numbers of Republican victims of rebel violence has faced innumerable difficulties. Nineteen-sixty-five was the year in which Francoists began to think the unthinkable, that the Caudillo was not immortal, and that preparations had to be made for the future. It was not until 1985 that the Spanish government began to take belated and hesitant action to protect the nation's archival resources. Millions of documents were lost during those crucial twenty years, including the archives of the Franco regime's single party, the fascist Falange, of provincial police headquarters, of prisons and of the main Francoist local authority, the Civil Governors. Convoys of trucks removed the 'judicial' records of the repression. As well as the deliberate destruction of archives, there were also 'inadvertent' losses when some town councils sold their archives by the ton as waste paper for recycling.[7]

Serious investigation was not possible until after the death of Franco in 1975. When researchers began the task, they were confronted not only with the deliberate destruction of much archival material by the Francoist authorities but also with the fact that many deaths had simply been registered either falsely or not at all. In addition to the concealment of crimes by the dictatorship was the continued fear of witnesses about coming forward and the obstruction of research, especially in the provinces of Old Castile. Archival material has mysteriously disappeared and frequently local officials have refused to permit consultation of the civilian registry.[8]

Many executions by the military rebels were given a veneer of pseudo-legality by trials, although they were effectively little different from extra-judicial murder. Death sentences were handed out after procedures lasting minutes in which the accused were not allowed to speak.[9] The deaths of those killed in what the rebels called 'cleansing and punishment operations' were given the flimsiest legal justification by being registered as 'by dint of the application of the declaration of martial law' ('por aplicación del bando de Guerra'). This was meant to legalize the summary execution of those who resisted the military take-over. The collateral deaths of many innocent people, unarmed and not offering any resistance, were also registered in this way. Then there were the executions of those registered as killed 'without trial' in reference to those who were discovered harbouring a fugitive, and so were shot just on military orders. There was also a systematic effort to conceal what had happened. Prisoners were taken far from their home towns, executed and buried in unmarked mass graves.[10]

Finally, there is the fact that a substantial number of deaths were not registered in any way. This was the case with many of those who fled before Franco's African columns as they headed from Seville to Madrid. As each town or village was occupied, among those killed were refugees from elsewhere. Since they carried no papers, their names or places of origin were unknown. It may never be possible to calculate the exact numbers murdered in the open fields by squads of mounted Falangists and extreme right-wing monarchists of the so-called Carlist movement. It is equally impossible to ascertain the fate of the thousands of refugees from Western Andalusia who died in the exodus after the fall of Málaga in 1937 or of those from all over Spain who had taken refuge in Barcelona only to die in the flight to the French border in 1939 or of those who committed suicide after waiting in vain for evacuation from the Mediterranean ports.

Nevertheless, the huge amount of research that has been carried out makes it possible to state that, broadly speaking, the repression by the rebels was about three times greater than that which took place in the Republican zone. The currently most reliable, yet still tentative, figure for deaths at the hands of the military rebels and their supporters is 130,199. However, it is unlikely that such deaths were fewer than 150,000 and they could well be more. Some areas have been studied only partially; others hardly at all. In several areas, which spent time in both zones, and for which the figures are known with some precision, the differences between the numbers of deaths at the hands of Republicans and at the hands of rebels are shocking. To give some examples, in Badajoz, there were 1,437 victims of the left as against 8,914 victims of the rebels; in Seville, 447 victims of the left, 12,507 victims of the rebels; in Cádiz, 97 victims of the left, 3,071 victims of the rebels; and in Huelva, 101 victims of the left, 6,019 victims of the rebels. In places where there was no Republican violence, the figures for rebel killings are almost incredible, for example Navarre, 3,280, La Rioja, 1,977. In most places where the Republican repression was the greater, like Alicante, Girona or Teruel, the differences are in the hundreds.[11] The exception is Madrid. The killings throughout the war when the capital was under Republican control seem to have been nearer three times those carried out after the rebel occupation. However, precise calculation is rendered difficult by the fact that the most frequently quoted figure for the post-war repression in Madrid, of 2,663 deaths, is based on a study of those executed and buried in only one cemetery, the Almudena or Cementerio del Este.[12]

Although exceeded by the violence exercised by the Francoists, the repression in the Republican zone before it was stopped by the Popular Front government was nonetheless horrifying. Its scale and nature necessarily varied, with the highest figures being recorded for the largely Socialist south of Toledo and the anarchist-dominated area from the south of Zaragoza, through Teruel into western Tarragona.[13] In Toledo, 3,152 rightists were killed, of whom 10 per cent were members of the clergy (nearly half of the province's clergy).[14] In Cuenca, the total deaths were 516 (of whom thirty-six, or 7 per cent of the total killed, were priests – nearly a quarter of the province's clergy).[15] The figure for deaths in Republican Catalonia, according to the exhaustive study by Josep Maria Solé i Sabaté and Joan Vilarroyo i Font, was 8,360. This figure corresponds closely to the conclusions reached by a commission created by the Generalitat de Catalunya (the Catalan regional government) in 1937. Part of the efforts of the Republican authorities to register deaths, it was led by a judge, Bertran de Quintana, and investigated all deaths behind the lines in order to instigate measures against those responsible for extra-judicial executions.[16] Such a procedure would have been inconceivable in the rebel zone.

Recent scholarship, not only for Catalonia but also for most of Republican Spain, has dramatically dismantled the propagandistic allegations made by the rebels at the time. On 18 July 1938 in Burgos, Franco himself claimed that 54,000 people had been killed in Catalonia. In the same speech, he alleged that 70,000 had been murdered in Madrid and 20,000 in Valencia. On the same day, he told a reporter there had already been a total of 470,000 murders in the Republican zone.[17] To prove the scale of Republican iniquity to the world, on 26 April 1940 he set up a massive state investigation, the Causa General, 'to gather trustworthy information' to ascertain the true scale of the crimes committed in the Republican zone. Denunciation and exaggeration were encouraged. Thus it came as a desperate disappointment to Franco when, on the basis of the information gathered, the Causa General concluded that the number of deaths was 85,940. Although inflated and including many duplications, this figure was still so far below Franco's claims that, for over a quarter of a century, it was omitted from editions of the published résumé of the Causa General's findings.[18]

A central, yet under-estimated, part of the repression carried out by the rebels – the systematic persecution of women – is not susceptible to statistical analysis. Murder, torture and rape were generalized punishments for the gender liberation embraced by many, but not all, liberal and left-wing women during the Republican period. Those who came out of prison alive suffered deep lifelong physical and psychological problems. Thousands of others were subjected to rape and other sexual abuses, the humiliation of head shaving and public soiling after the forced ingestion of castor oil. For most Republican women, there were also the terrible economic and psychological problems of having their husbands, fathers, brothers and sons murdered or forced to flee, which often saw the wives themselves arrested in efforts to get them to reveal the whereabouts of their menfolk. In contrast, despite frequent assumptions that the raping of nuns was common in Republican Spain, there was relatively little equivalent abuse of women there. That is not to say that it did not take place. The sexual molestation of around one dozen nuns and the deaths of 296, just over 1.3 per cent of the female clergy, is shocking but of a notably lower order of magnitude than the fate of women in the rebel zone.[19] That is not entirely surprising given that respect for women was built into the Republic's reforming programme.

The statistical vision of the Spanish holocaust is not only flawed, incomplete and unlikely ever to be complete. It also fails to capture the intense horror that lies behind the numbers. The account that follows includes many stories of individuals, of men, women and children from both sides. It introduces some specific but representative cases of victims and perpetrators from all over the country. It is hoped thereby to convey the suffering unleashed upon their own fellow citizens by the arrogance and brutality of the officers who rose up on 17 July 1936. They provoked a war that was unnecessary and whose consequences still reverberate bitterly in Spain today.

PART ONE

*The Origins of Hatred
and Violence*

1

Social War Begins, 1931–1933

On 18 July 1936, on hearing of the military uprising in Morocco, an aristocratic landowner lined up the labourers on his estate to the south-west of Salamanca and shot six of them as a lesson to the others. The Conde de Alba de Yeltes, Gonzalo de Aguilera y Munro, a retired cavalry officer, joined the press service of the rebel forces during the Civil War and boasted of his crime to foreign visitors.[1] Although his alleged atrocity was extreme, the sentiments behind it were not unrepresentative of the hatreds that had smouldered in the Spanish countryside over the twenty years before the military uprising of 1936. Aguilera's cold and calculated violence reflected the belief, common among the rural upper classes, that the landless labourers were sub-human. This attitude had become common among the big landowners since a series of sporadic uprisings by hungry day-labourers in the regions of Spain dominated by huge estates (*latifundios*). Taking place between 1918 and 1921, a period of bitter social conflict known thereafter as the *trienio bolchevique* (three Bolshevik years), these insurrections had been crushed by the traditional defenders of the rural oligarchy, the Civil Guard and the army. Previously, there had been an uneasy truce within which the wretched lives of the landless day-labourers (*jornaleros* or *braceros*) were occasionally relieved by the patronizing gestures of the owners – the gift of food or a blind eye turned to rabbit poaching or to the gathering of windfall crops. The violence of the conflicts had outraged the landlords, who would never forgive the insubordination of the *braceros* they considered to be an inferior species. Accordingly, the paternalism which had somewhat mitigated the daily brutality of the day-labourers' lives came to an abrupt end.

The agrarian oligarchy, in an unequal partnership with the industrial and financial bourgeoisie, was traditionally the dominant force in Spanish capitalism. Its monopoly of power began to be challenged on two sides in the course of the painful and uneven process of industrialization. The prosperity enjoyed by neutral Spain during the First World

War emboldened industrialists and bankers to jostle with the great land-owners for political position. However, with both menaced by a militant industrial proletariat, they soon rebuilt a defensive alliance. In August 1917, the left's feeble revolutionary threat was bloodily smothered by the army. Thereafter, until 1923, when the army intervened again, social ferment occasionally bordered on undeclared civil war. In the south, there were the rural uprisings of the 'three Bolshevik years'. In the north, the industrialists of Catalonia, the Basque Country and Asturias, having tried to ride the immediate post-war recession with wage-cuts and lay-offs, faced violent strikes and, in Barcelona, a terrorist spiral of provoca-tions and reprisals.

In the consequent atmosphere of uncertainty and anxiety, there was a ready middle-class audience for the notion long since disseminated by extreme right-wing Catholics that a secret alliance of Jews, Freemasons and the Communist Third International was conspiring to destroy Christian Europe, with Spain as a principal target. In Catholic Spain, the idea that there was an evil Jewish conspiracy to destroy Christianity had emerged in the early Middle Ages. In the nineteenth century, the Spanish extreme right resurrected it to discredit the liberals whom they viewed as responsible for social changes that were damaging their interests. In this paranoid fantasy, Freemasons were smeared as tools of the Jews (of whom there were virtually none) in a sinister plot to establish Jewish tyranny over the Christian world.

As the nineteenth century drew to a close, such views were expressed with ever increasing vehemence. They were a response to the kaleido-scopic processes of rapid economic growth, social dislocation, regional-ist agitations, a bourgeois reform movement and the emergence of trade unions and left-wing parties. An explanation for the destabilization of Spanish society and the attendant collapse of the relative certainties of a predominantly rural society was found in a deeply alarming, yet some-how comforting, assertion that shifted the blame on to an identifiable and foreign enemy. It was alleged that, using Freemasons as their willing intermediaries, the Jews controlled the economy, politics, the press, literature and the entertainment world through which they propagated immorality and the brutalization of the masses. Such views had long been peddled by *El Siglo Futuro*, the daily newspaper of the deeply reac-tionary Carlist Traditionalist Communion. In 1912, the National Anti-Masonic and Anti-Semitic League had been founded by José Ignacio de Urbina with the support of twenty-two Spanish bishops. The Bishop of Almería wrote that 'everything is ready for the decisive battle that must be unleashed between the children of light and the children of darkness, between Catholicism and Judaism, between Christ and the Devil'.[2] That there was never any hard evidence was put down to the cleverness and colossal power of the enemy, evil itself.

In Spain, as in other European countries, anti-Semitism had reached even greater intensity after 1917. It was taken as axiomatic that socialism was a Jewish creation and that the Russian revolution had been financed by Jewish capital, an idea given a spurious credibility by the Jewish origins of prominent Bolsheviks such as Trotsky, Martov and Dan. Spain's middle and upper classes were chilled, and outraged, by the various revolutionary upheavals that threatened them between 1917 and 1923. The fears of the elite were somewhat calmed in September 1923, when the army intervened again and a dictatorship was established by General Miguel Primo de Rivera. As Captain General of Barcelona, Primo de Rivera was the ally of Catalan textile barons and understood their sense of being under threat from their anarchist workforce. Moreover, coming from a substantial landowning family in Jérez, he also appreciated the fears of the big southern landowners or *latifundistas*. He was thus the ideal praetorian defender of the reactionary coalition of industrialists and landowners consolidated after 1917. While Primo de Rivera remained in power, he offered security to the middle and upper classes. Nevertheless, his ideologues worked hard to build the notion that in Spain two bitterly hostile social, political and, indeed, moral groupings were locked in a fight to the death. Specifically, in a pre-echo of the function that they would also fulfil for Franco, these propagandists stressed the dangers faced from Jews, Freemasons and leftists.

These ideas essentially delegitimized the entire spectrum of the left, from middle-class liberal democrats, via Socialists and regional nationalists, to anarchists and Communists. This was done by blurring distinctions between them and by denying their right to be considered Spanish. The denunciations of this 'anti-Spain' were publicized through the right-wing press and the regime's single party, the Unión Patriótica, as well as through civic organizations and the education system. These notions served to generate satisfaction with the dictatorship as a bulwark against the perceived Bolshevik threat. Starting from the premise that the world was divided into 'national alliances and Soviet alliances', the influential right-wing poet José María Pemán declared that 'the time has come for Spanish society to choose between Jesus and Barabbas'. He claimed that the masses were 'either Christian or anarchic and destructive' and the nation was divided between an anti-Spain made up of everything that was heterodox and foreign and the real Spain of traditional religious and monarchical values.[3]

Another senior propagandist of the Primo de Rivera regime, José Pemartín, linked, like his cousin Pemán, to the extreme right in Seville, also believed that Spain was under attack by an international conspiracy masterminded by Freemasonry, 'the eternal enemy of all the world's governments of order'. He dismissed the left, in generalized terms, as 'the dogmatists deluded by what they think are modern, democratic and European ideas, universal suffrage, the sovereign parliament, etc. They are beyond redemption. They are made mentally ill by the worst of tyrannies, ideocracy or the tyranny of certain ideas.' It was the duty of the army to defend Spain against these attacks.[4]

Despite his temporary success in anaesthetizing the anxieties of the middle and ruling classes, Primo de Rivera's dictatorship did not last. His benevolent attempt to temper authoritarianism with paternalism inadvertently alienated landowners, industrialists, the Church hierarchy and some of the elite officer corps of the army. Most dramatically, his attempts to reform military promotion procedures ensured that the army would stand aside when a great electoral coalition of Socialists and middle-class Republicans swept to power on 14 April 1931. After the dictator's departure in January 1930, one of the first to take up the defence of establishment interests was Dr José María Albiñana, an eccentric Valencian neurologist and frenetic admirer of Primo de Rivera.

The author of more than twenty novels and books on neurasthenia, religion, the history and philosophy of medicine and Spanish politics, and a number of mildly imperialist works about Mexico, Albiñana was convinced that there was a secret alliance working in foreign obscurity in order to destroy Spain. In February 1930, he distributed tens of thousands of copies of his *Manifiesto por el Honor de España*. In it, he had declared that 'there exists a Masonic Soviet which dishonours Spain in the eyes of the world by reviving the black legend and other infamies forged by the eternal hidden enemies of our fatherland. This Soviet, made up of heartless persons, is backed by spiteful politicians who, to avenge offences against themselves, go abroad to vomit insults against Spain'. This was a reference to the Republicans exiled by the dictatorship. Two months later, he launched his 'exclusively Spanish Nationalist Party' whose objective was to 'annihilate the internal enemies of the fatherland'. A fascist image was provided by its blue-shirted, Roman-saluting Legionaries of Spain, a 'citizen volunteer force to act directly, explosively and expeditiously against any initiative which attacks or diminishes the prestige of the fatherland'.[5]

Albiñana was merely one of the first to argue that the fall of the monarchy was the first step in the Jewish–Masonic–Bolshevik conspiracy to take over Spain. Such ideas would feed the extreme rightist paranoia that met the establishment of the Second Republic. The passing of political power to the Socialist Party (PSOE – Partido Socialista Obrero Español) and its urban middle-class allies, the lawyers and intellectuals of the various Republican parties, sent shivers of horror through right-wing Spain. The Republican–Socialist coalition intended to use its suddenly acquired share of state power to implement a far-reaching programme to create a modern Spain by destroying the reactionary influence of the Church, eradicating militarism and improving the immediate conditions of the wretched day-labourers with agrarian reform.

This huge agenda inevitably raised the expectations of the urban and rural proletariats while provoking the fear and the determined enmity of the Church, the armed forces and the landowning and industrial oligarchies. The passage from the hatreds of 1917–23 to the widespread violence that engulfed Spain after 1936 was long and complex but it began to speed up dramatically in the spring of 1931. The fears and hatreds of the rich found, as always, their first line of defence in the Civil Guard. However, as landowners blocked attempts at reform, the frustrated expectations of hungry day-labourers could be contained only by increasing brutality.

Many on the right took the establishment of the Republic as proof that Spain was the second front in the war against world revolution – a notion fed by numerous clashes between the forces of order and workers of the Confederación Nacional del Trabajo (CNT), the anarchist union. Resolute action against the extreme left by the Minister of the Interior, Miguel Maura, did not deter the Carlist newspaper *El Siglo Futuro* from attacking the government and claiming that progressive Republican legislation was ordered from abroad. It declared in June 1931 that three of the most conservative ministers, the premier, Niceto Alcalá Zamora, Miguel Maura and the Minister of Justice, Fernando de los Ríos Urruti, were Jews and that the Republic itself had been brought about as a result of a Jewish conspiracy. The more moderate Catholic mass-circulation daily *El Debate* referred to de los Ríos as 'the rabbi'. The Editorial Católica, which owned an influential chain of newspapers including *El Debate*, soon began to publish the virulently anti-Semitic and anti-Masonic magazines *Gracia y Justicia* and *Los Hijos del Pueblo*. The editor of the scurrilously satirical *Gracia y Justicia* was Manuel Delgado Barreto, a one-time collaborator of the dictator General Primo de Rivera, a friend of his son José Antonio and an early sponsor of the Falange. It would reach a weekly circulation of 200,000 copies.[6]

The Republic would face violent resistance not only from the extreme right but also from the extreme left. The anarcho-syndicalist CNT recognized that many of its militants had voted for the Republican–Socialist coalition in the municipal elections of 12 April and that its arrival had raised the people's hopes. As one leading anarchist put it, they were 'like children with new shoes'. The CNT leadership, however, expecting the Republic to change nothing, aspired merely to propagate its revolutionary objectives and to pursue its fierce rivalry with the Socialist Unión General de Trabajadores (UGT), which it regarded as a scab union because of its collaboration with the Primo de Rivera regime. In a period of mass unemployment, with large numbers of migrant workers returning from overseas and unskilled construction workers left without work by the ending of the great public works projects of the dictatorship, the labour market was potentially explosive. This was a situation that would be exploited by the hard-line anarchists of the Federación Anarquista Ibérica (FAI) who argued that the Republic, like the monarchy, was just an instrument of the bourgeoisie. The brief honeymoon period came to an end when CNT–FAI demonstrations on 1 May were repressed violently by the forces of order.[7]

In late May, a group of nearly one thousand strikers from the port of Pasajes descended on San Sebastián with the apparent intention of looting the wealthy shopping districts. Having been warned in advance, the Minister of the Interior, Miguel Maura, deployed the Civil Guard at the entrance to the city. They repelled the attack at the cost of eight dead and many wounded. Then, in early July, the CNT launched a nationwide strike in the telephone system, largely as a challenge to the government. It was defeated by harsh police measures and strike-breaking by workers of the Socialist UGT who refused to join the CNT in what they saw as a sterile struggle. The Director General of Security, the sleek and portly Ángel Galarza of the Radical-Socialist Party, ordered that anyone seen trying to damage the installations of the telephone company should be shot. Maura and Galarza were understandably trying to maintain the confidence of the middle classes. Inevitably, their stance consolidated the violent hostility of the CNT towards both the Republic and the UGT.[8]

For the Republican–Socialist cabinet, the subversive activities of the CNT constituted rebellion. For the CNT, legitimate strikes and demonstrations were being crushed by dictatorial methods indistinguishable from those used by the monarchy. On 21 July 1931, the cabinet agreed on the need for 'an urgent and severe remedy'. Maura outlined a proposal for 'a legal instrument of repression' and the Socialist Minister of Labour, Francisco Largo Caballero, proposed a decree to make strikes illegal. The two decrees would eventually be combined on 22 October into the Law for the Defence of the Republic, a measure enthusiastically supported by the Socialist members of the government not least because it was perceived as directed against their CNT rivals.[9] It made little difference to the right, which perceived the violent social disorder of the anarchists as characteristic of the entire left, including the Socialists who denounced it and the Republican authorities who crushed it.

What mattered to the right was that the Civil Guard and the army lined up in defence of the existing economic order against the anarchists. Traditionally, the bulk of the army officer corps perceived the prevention of political and economic change as one of its primordial tasks. Now, the Republic would attempt to reform the military, bringing both its costs and its mentalities into line with Spain's changed circumstances. A central part of that project would be the streamlining of a massively swollen officer corps. The tough and uncompromising colonial officers, the so-called Africanistas, having benefited from irregular and vertiginous battlefield promotions, would be the most affected. Their opposition to Republican reforms would inaugurate a process whereby the violence of Spain's recent colonial history found a route back into the metropolis. The rigours and horrors of the Moroccan tribal wars between 1909 and 1925 had brutalized them. Morocco had also given them a beleaguered sense that, in their commitment to fighting to defend the colony, they alone were concerned with the fate of the Patria. Long before 1931, this had developed into a deep contempt both for professional politicians and for the pacifist left-wing masses that the Africanistas regarded as obstacles to the successful execution of their patriotic mission.

The repressive role of both the army and the Civil Guard in Spain's long-standing social conflicts, particularly in rural areas, was perceived as central to that patriotic duty. However, between 1931 and 1936, several linked factors would provide the military with pervasive justifications for the use of violence against the left. The first was the Republic's attempt to break the power of the Catholic Church. On 13 October 1931, the Minister of War, and later Prime Minister and President, Manuel Azaña, stated that 'Spain has ceased to be Catholic.'[10] Even if this was true, Spain remained a country with many pious and sincere Catholics. Now, the Republic's anti-clerical legislation would provide an apparent justification for the virulent enmity of those who already had ample motive to see it destroyed. The bilious rhetoric of the Jewish–Masonic–Bolshevik conspiracy was immediately pressed into service. Moreover, the gratuitous nature of some anti-clerical measures would help recruit many ordinary Catholics to the cause of the rich.

The religious issue would nourish a second crucial factor in fostering right-wing violence. This was the immensely successful propagation of theories that left-wingers and liberals were neither really Spanish nor even really human and that, as a threat to the nation's existence, they should be exterminated. In books that sold by the tens of thousands, in daily newspapers and weekly magazines, the idea was hammered home that the Second Republic was foreign and sinister and must be destroyed. This notion, which found fertile ground in right-wing fear, was based on the contention that the Republic was the product of a conspiracy master-minded by Jews, and carried out by Freemasons through left-wing lack-eys. The idea of this powerful international conspiracy – or *contubernio* (filthy cohabitation), one of Franco's favourite words – justified any means necessary for what was presented as national survival. The intel-lectuals and priests who developed such ideas were able to connect with the *latifundistas'* hatred for the landless day-labourers or *jornaleros* and the urban bourgeoisie's fear of the unemployed. The Salamanca land-owner Gonzalo de Aguilera y Munro, like many army officers and priests, was a voracious reader of such literature.[11]

Another factor which fomented violence was the reaction of the land-owners to the Second Republic's various attempts at agrarian reform. In the province of Salamanca, the leaders of the local Bloque Agrario, the landowners' party, Ernesto Castaño and José Lamamié de Clairac, incited their members not to pay taxes nor to plant crops. Such intransigence radicalized the landless labourers.[12] Across the areas of great estates (*lati-fundios*) in southern Spain, Republican legislation governing labour issues in the countryside was systematically flouted. Despite the decree of 7 May 1931 of obligatory cultivation, unionized labour was 'locked out' either by land being left uncultivated or by simply being refused work and told to *comed República* (literally 'eat the Republic', which was a way of saying 'let the Republic feed you'). Despite the decree of 1 July 1931 imposing the eight-hour day in agriculture, sixteen-hour working days from sun-up to sun-down prevailed with no extra hours being paid. Indeed, starvation wages were paid to those who were hired. Although there were tens of thousands of unemployed landless labourers in the south, landowners proclaimed that unemployment was an invention of the Republic.[13] In Jaén, the gathering of acorns, normally kept for pigs, or of windfall olives, the watering of beasts and even the gathering of firewood were denounced as 'collective kleptomania'.[14] Hungry peasants caught doing such things were savagely beaten by the Civil Guard or by armed estate guards.[15]

Their expectations raised by the coming of the new regime, the day-labourers were no longer as supine and fatalistic as had often been the case. As their hopes were frustrated by the obstructive tactics of the *latifundistas*, the desperation of the *jornaleros* could be controlled only by an intensification of the violence of the Civil Guard. The ordinary Civil Guards themselves often resorted to their firearms in panic, fearful of being outnumbered by angry mobs of labourers. Incidents of the theft of crops and game were reported with outrage by the right-wing press. Firearms were used against workers, and their deaths were reported with equal indignation in the left-wing press. In Corral de Almaguer (Toledo), starving *jornaleros* tried to break a local lock-out by invading estates and starting to work them. The Civil Guard intervened on behalf of the owners, killing five workers and wounding another seven. On 27 September 1931, for instance, in Palacios Rubios near Peñaranda de Bracamonte in the province of Salamanca, the Civil Guard opened fire on a group of men, women and children celebrating the successful end to a strike. The Civil Guard began to shoot when the villagers started to dance in front of the parish priest's house. Two workers were killed immediately and two more died shortly afterwards.[16] Immense bitterness was provoked by the case. In July 1933, on behalf of the Salamanca branch of the UGT landworkers' federation (Federación Nacional de Trabajadores de la Tierra), the editor of its newspaper *Tierra y Trabajo*, José Andrés y Mansó, brought a private prosecution against a Civil Guard corporal, Francisco Jiménez Cuesta, on four counts of homicide and another three of wounding. Jiménez Cuesta was successfully defended by the leader of the authoritarian Catholic party, the CEDA, José María Gil Robles. Andrés y Mansó would be murdered by Falangists at the end of July 1936.[17]

In Salamanca and elsewhere, there were regular acts of violence perpetrated against trade union members and landowners – a seventy-year-old beaten to death by the rifle butts of the Civil Guard in Burgos, a property-owner badly hurt in Villanueva de Córdoba. Very often these incidents, which were not confined to the south but also proliferated in the three provinces of Aragon, began with invasions of estates. Groups of landless labourers would go to a landowner and ask for work or sometimes carry out agricultural tasks and then threateningly demand payment. More often than not, they would be driven off by the Civil Guard or by gunmen employed by the owners.[18]

In fact, what the landowners were doing was merely one element of unequivocal right-wing hostility to the new regime. They occupied the front line of defence against the reforming ambitions of the Republic. There were equally vehement responses to the religious and military legislation of the new regime. Indeed, all three issues were often linked, with many army officers emanating from Catholic landholding families. All these elements found a political voice in several newly emerged political groups. Most extreme among them, and openly committed to the earliest possible destruction of the Republic, were two monarchist organizations, the Carlist Comunión Tradicionalista and Acción Española, founded by supporters of the recently departed King Alfonso XIII as a 'school of modern counter-revolutionary thought'. Within hours of the Republic being declared, monarchist plotters had begun collecting money to create a journal to propagate the legitimacy of a rising against the Republic, to inject a spirit of rebellion in the army and to found a party of ostensible legality as a front for meetings, fund-raising and conspiracy against the Republic. The journal Acción Española would also peddle the idea of the sinister alliance of Jews, Freemasons and leftists. Within a month, its founders had collected substantial funds for the projected uprising. Their first effort would be the military coup of 10 August 1932. And its failure would lead to a determination to ensure that the next attempt would be better financed and entirely successful.[19]

Somewhat more moderate was the legalist Acción Nacional, later renamed Acción Popular, which was prepared to try to defend right-wing interests within Republican legality. Extremists or 'catastrophists' and 'moderates' shared many of the same ideas. However, after the failed military coup of August 1932, they would split over the efficacy of armed conspiracy against the Republic. Acción Española formed its own political party, Renovación Española, and Acción Popular did the same, gathering a number of like-minded groups into the Confederación Española de Derechas Autónomas.[20] Within a year, the ranks of the 'catastrophists' had been swelled by the creation of various fascist organizations. What all had in common was that they completely denied the democratic legitimacy of the Republic. Despite the legalist façade of Acción Popular and the CEDA, its leaders would frequently and unrestrainedly proclaim that violence against the Republic was perfectly justifiable.

Barely three weeks after the establishment of the new regime, at a time when the government was notable mainly for its timidity in social questions, Acción Nacional had been created as 'an organization for social defence'. It was the creation of Ángel Herrera Oria, editor of the militantly Catholic (and hitherto monarchist) daily *El Debate*. A shrewd political strategist, Herrera Oria would be the brains behind political Catholicism in the early years of the Second Republic. Acción Nacional brought together two organizations of the right that had combated the rising power of the urban and rural working class for the previous twenty years. Its leaders came from the Asociación Católica Nacional de Propagandistas, an elite Jesuit-influenced organization of about five hundred prominent and talented Catholic rightists with influence in the press, the judiciary and the professions. Its rank-and-file support would be found within the Confederación Nacional Católico-Agraria, a mass political organization which proclaimed its 'total submission to the ecclesiastic authorities'. Established to resist the growth of left-wing organizations, the CNCA was strong among the Catholic smallholding peasantry in north and central Spain.[21]

Acción Nacional's manifesto declared that 'the advance guards of Soviet Communism' were already clambering on the ruins of the monarchy. It denounced the respectable bourgeois politicians of the Second Republic as weak and incapable of controlling the masses. 'They are the masses that deny God and, in consequence, the basic principles of Christian morality; that proclaim, against the sanctity of the family, the instability of free love; that substitute private property, the basis and the motor of the welfare of individuals and of collective wealth, by a universal proletariat at the orders of the State.' In addition, there was 'the lunacy of Basque and Catalan ultra-nationalism, determined, irrespective of its sweet words, to destroy national unity'. Acción Nacional unequivocally announced itself as the negation of everything for which, it claimed, the Republic stood. With the battle cry 'Religion, Fatherland, Family, Order, Work, Property', it declared that 'the social battle is being waged in our time to decide the triumph or extermination of these eternal principles. In truth, this will not be decided in a single combat; what is being unleashed in Spain is a war, and it will be a long one.'[22]

By 1933, when Acción Popular had developed into the CEDA, its analysis of the Republic was even less circumspect: 'the rabble, always irresponsible because of their lack of values, took over the strongholds of government'. Even for Herrera Oria's legalist organization, the Republic was created when 'the contagious madness of the most inflamed extremists sparked a fire in the inflammable material of the heartless, the perverted, the rebellious, the insane'. The supporters of the Republic were sub-human and, like pestilent vermin, should be eliminated: 'The sewers opened their sluice gates and the dregs of society inundated the streets and squares, convulsing and shuddering like epileptics.'[23] All over Europe, endangered elites were mobilizing mass support by stirring up fears of a left presented as 'foreign', a disease that threatened the nation and required a crusade of national purification.

Both at the time and later, the right-wing determination to annihilate the Republic was justified as a response to its anti-clericalism. However, as had been amply demonstrated by its enthusiastic support for the dictatorship of Primo de Rivera, the right hated the Republic for being democratic long before it was able to denounce it for being anti-clerical. Moreover, those who opposed the Republic on religious grounds also cited social, economic and political grounds, especially in opposition to regional autonomy.[24]

Nevertheless, the religious issue was the occasion of intense conflict, both verbal and physical. On Sunday 10 May 1931, the inaugural meeting of the Circulo Monarquico Independiente in the Calle Alcalá ended with loudspeakers provocatively blaring out the Royal Anthem. Republican crowds returning from an afternoon concert in Madrid's Parque del Buen Retiro were outraged. There was a riot; cars were burned and the offices of the monarchist newspaper *ABC* in neighbouring Calle Serrano were assaulted. The fierce popular reaction spilled over into the notorious church burnings which took place in Madrid, Málaga, Seville, Cádiz and Alicante from 10 to 12 May. This suggested how strongly ordinary people identified the Church with the monarchy and right-wing politics. The Republican press claimed that the fires were the work of provocateurs drawn from the scab union, the Sindicatos Libres. Indeed, it was claimed that, to discredit the new regime, young monarchists had distributed leaflets inciting the masses to attack religious buildings.[25]

Even if there were agents provocateurs involved, many on the left were convinced that the Church was integral to reactionary politics in Spain and physical attacks were carried out in some places by the more hotheaded among them. In many villages in the south, priests had stones thrown at them. For those on the right, the identity of the true culprits mattered little. The church burnings confirmed and justified their prior hostility to the Republic. Nevertheless, Miguel Maura, the Minister of the Interior, commented bitterly: 'Madrid's Catholics did not think for a second that it was appropriate or their duty to make an appearance in the street in defence of what should have been sacred to them.' There were serious clashes in many small towns (*pueblos*) where the faithful protected their churches from elements intent on profaning them. Later in May, when the provisional government decreed an end to obligatory religious education, there were many petitions in protest.[26]

While most of Spain remained peaceful, from the earliest days of the Republic an atmosphere of undeclared civil war festered in the *latifundio* zones of the south and in other areas dominated by the CNT. Miguel Maura claimed that, in the five months from mid-May 1931 until his resignation in October, he had to deal with 508 revolutionary strikes. The CNT accused him of causing 108 deaths with his repressive measures.[27] This was demonstrated most graphically by the bloody conclusion to a period of anarchist agitation in Seville. As the culmination of a series of revolutionary strikes, the anarchist union called a general stoppage on 18 July 1931. This was directed not just at the local employers but also at the CNT's local rivals in the Socialist Unión General Trabajadores. There were violent clashes between anarchist and Communist strikers on the one hand and blacklegs and the Civil Guard on the other. At the cabinet meeting of 21 July, the Socialist Minister of Labour, Francisco Lárgo Caballero, demanded that Miguel Maura take firm action to end the disorders which were damaging the Republic's image. When the Prime Minister, Niceto Alcalá Zamora, asked if everyone was agreed that energetic measures against the CNT were called for, the cabinet assented unanimously. Maura told Azaña that he would order artillery to demolish a house from which anarchists had fired against the forces of order.[28]

Meanwhile, on the night of 22–23 July 1931, extreme rightists were permitted to take part in the repression of the strikes in Seville. Believing that the forces of order were inadequate to deal with the problem, José Bastos Ansart, the Civil Governor, invited the landowners' clubs, the Círculo de Labradores and the Unión Comercial, to form a paramilitary group to be known as the 'Guardia Cívica'. This invitation was eagerly accepted by the most prominent rightists of the city, Javier Parladé Ybarra, Pedro Parias González, a retired lieutenant colonel of the cavalry and a substantial landowner, and José García Carranza, a famous bullfighter who fought as 'Pepe el Algabeño'. Arms were collected, and the Guardia Cívica was led by a brutal Africanista, Captain Manuel Díaz

Criado, known as 'Criadillas' (Bull's Balls). On the night of 22 July, in the Parque de María Luisa, they shot four prisoners. On the following after-noon, the Casa Cornelio, a workers' café in the neighbourhood of La Macarena, was, as Maura had promised Azaña, destroyed by artillery fire. Elsewhere in the province, particularly in three small towns to the south of the capital, Coria del Río, Utrera and Dos Hermanas, strikes were repressed with exceptional violence by the Civil Guard. In Dos Hermanas, after some stones had been thrown at the telephone exchange, a lorry-load of Civil Guards arrived from Seville. With the local market in full swing, they opened fire, wounding several, two of whom died later. In total, seventeen people were killed in clashes in the province.[29]

Azaña's immediate reaction was that the events in the park 'looked like the use of the *ley de fugas*' (the pretence that prisoners were shot while trying to escape) and he blamed Maura, commenting that 'he shoots first and then he aims'. Azaña's reaction was influenced by the fact that Maura had recently hit him for accusing him of revealing cabinet secrets to the press. Two weeks later, he learned that the cold-blooded application of the *ley de fugas* was nothing to do with Maura but had been carried out by the Guardia Cívica on the orders of Díaz Criado.[30] The murders in the Parque de María Luisa and the shelling of the Casa Cornelio were the first in a chain of events leading to the savagery of 1936. Díaz Criado and the Guardia Cívica would play a prominent role both in the failed military coup of August 1932 and in the events of 1936.

The events in Seville and the telephone strike were symptomatic of clashes between the forces of order and the CNT throughout urban Spain. In Barcelona, in addition to the telephone conflict, a strike in the metallurgical industry saw 40,000 workers down tools in August. The activist FAI increasingly advocated insurrection to replace the bourgeois Republic with libertarian communism. Paramilitary street action directed against the police and the Civil Guard was to be at the heart of what the prominent FAI leader Juan García Oliver defined as 'revolu-tionary gymnastics'. This inevitably led to bloody clashes with the forces of order and with the more moderate Socialist UGT. The consequent violence in Barcelona, Seville, Valencia, Zaragoza and Madrid, although directed against the government, was blamed by the right on the Republic.[31]

The unease thereby fomented among the middle classes was consoli-dated among Catholics by the anti-clericalism of the Republic. Little distinction was made between the ferocious iconoclasm of the anarchists and the Republican–Socialist coalition's ambition to limit the Church's influence to the strictly religious sphere. Right-wing hostility to the Republic was mobilized fully, with clerical support, in the wake of the parliamentary debate over the proposed Republican Constitution. The text separated Church and state and introduced civil marriage and divorce. It curtailed state support for the clergy and ended, on paper at least, the religious monopoly of education. The proposed reforms were denounced by the Catholic press and from pulpits as a Godless, tyrannical and atheistic attempt to destroy the family.[32] The reaction of a priest from Castellón de la Plana was not uncommon. In a sermon he told his parishioners, 'Republicans should be spat on and never spoken to. We should be prepared to fight a civil war before we tolerate the separation of Church and State. Non-religious schools do not educate men, they create savages.'[33]

The Republic's anti-clerical legislation was at best incautious and at worst irresponsible, perceived on the right as the fruit of Masonic-inspired hatred. Republicans felt that to create an egalitarian society, the power of the Church education system had to be replaced with non-denominational schools. Many measures were easily sidestepped. Schools run by religious personnel continued as before – the names of schools were changed, clerics adopted lay dress. Many such schools, especially those of the Jesuits, tended to be accessible only to the children of the rich. There was no middle ground. The Church's defence of property and its indifference to social hardship inevitably aligned it with the extreme right.[34]

Substantial popular hostility to the Republic's plans for changes in the social, economic and religious landscape was garnered during the so-called revisionist campaign against the Constitution. Bitter right-wing opposition to the Constitution passed on 13 October was provoked by plans to advance regional autonomy for Catalonia and to introduce agrarian reform.[35] Nevertheless, it was the legalization of divorce and the dissolution of religious orders – seen as evil Masonic machinations – that raised Catholic ire.[36] During the debate on 13 October 1931, the parliamentary leader of Acción Popular, José María Gil Robles, declared to the Republican–Socialist majority in the parliament, the Cortes, 'Today, in opposition to the Constitution, Catholic Spain takes its stand. You will bear responsibility for the spiritual war that is going to be unleashed in Spain.' Five days later, in the Plaza de Toros de Ledesma, Gil Robles called for a crusade against the Republic.[37]

As part of the campaign a group of Basque Traditionalists created the Association of Relatives and Friends of Religious Personnel. The

Association attracted considerable support in Salamanca and Valladolid, towns notable for the ferocity of the repression during the Civil War. It published an anti-Republican bulletin, *Defensa*, and many anti-Republican pamphlets. It also founded the violently anti-Masonic and anti-Semitic weekly magazine *Los Hijos del Pueblo* under the editorship of Francisco de Luis, who would eventually run *El Debate* in succession to Ángel Herrera Oria. De Luis was a fervent advocate of the theory that the Spanish Republic was the plaything of an international Jewish–Masonic–Bolshevik conspiracy.[38] Another leading contributor to *Los Hijos del Pueblo* was the integrist Jesuit Father Enrique Herrera Oria, brother of Ángel. The paper's wide circulation was in large part a reflection of the popularity of its vicious satirical cartoons attacking prominent Republican politicians. Presenting them as Jews and Freemasons, and thus part of the international conspiracy against Catholic Spain, it popularized among its readers the notion that this filthy foreign plot had to be destroyed.[39]

The idea that leftists and liberals were not true Spaniards and therefore had to be destroyed quickly took root on the right. In early November 1931, the monarchist leader Antonio Goicoechea declared to a cheering audience in Madrid that there was to be a battle to the death between socialism and the nation.[40] On 8 November, the Carlist Joaquín Beunza thundered to an audience of 22,000 people in Palencia: 'Are we men or not? Those not prepared to give their all in these moments of shameless persecution do not deserve the name Catholic. We must be ready to defend ourselves by all means, and I don't say legal means, because all means are good for self-defence.' Declaring the Cortes a zoo, he went on: 'We are governed by a gang of Freemasons. And I say that against them all methods are legitimate, both legal and illegal ones.' At the same meeting, Gil Robles declared that the government's persecution of the Church was decided 'in the Masonic lodges'.[41]

Incitement to violence against the Republic and its supporters was not confined to the extreme right. The speeches of the legalist Catholic Gil Robles were every bit as belligerent and provocative as those of monarchists, Carlists and, later, Falangists. At Molina de Segura (Murcia) on New Year's Day 1932, Gil Robles declared: 'In 1932 we must impose our will with the force of our rightness, and with other forces if this is insufficient. The cowardice of the Right has allowed those who come from the cesspools of iniquity to take control of the destinies of the fatherland.'[42] The intransigence of more moderate sections of the Spanish right was revealed by the inaugural manifesto of the Juventud (youth movement) de Acción Popular which proclaimed: 'We are men of the right … We will respect the legitimate orders of authority, but we will not tolerate the impositions of the irresponsible rabble. We will always have the courage to make ourselves respected. We declare war on communism and Freemasonry.' In the eyes of the right, 'communism' included the Socialist Party and Freemasonry signified the various Republican liberal parties and their regional variants known as Left Republicans.[43]

Justification for hostility to the Republic could easily be found in its efforts to secularize society. Distress had been caused by the fact that municipal authorities were forbidden to make financial contributions to the Church or its festivals. In January 1932, Church cemeteries came under municipal jurisdiction. The state now recognized only civil marriage, so those who had a Church wedding also had to visit a registry office. Burial ceremonies were to have no religious character unless the deceased, being over the age of twenty, had left specific instructions to the contrary, something involving complicated bureaucracy for relatives.[44]

In May 1932, during the feast of San Pedro Mártir in Burbáguena (Teruel), a brass band played in the town square, thereby deliberately clashing with the religious music being sung in the church in honour of the saint. In Libros (Teruel), a dance was organized outside the parish church while a mass was being said in honour of the Virgen del Pilar.[45] In Seville, fear of attack led to more than forty of the traditional fraternities (*cofradías*) withdrawing from the Holy Week procession. Their members were predominantly militants of Acción Popular and of the Carlist Comunión Tradicionalista and their gesture popularized among right-wing Catholics the phrase 'Seville the martyr', despite the fact that every effort was made by Republican authorities to see the processions go ahead. Vociferous complaints came from the same men who were also prominent in employers' and landowners' organizations. In the event, only one *cofradía* marched and was the target of insults and stones. Some days later, on 7 April 1932, the Church of San Julián was burned down.[46]

Some local municipalities removed crucifixes from schools and religious statues from public hospitals as well as prohibiting the ringing of bells. Such measures went beyond official government policy, which was that municipal permission was required for public ceremonies. Perceived as persecution, they caused ordinary Catholics to see the Republic as their enemy. In many villages in the province of Salamanca, there were street protests and children were kept away from school until the crucifixes were returned. Ordinary Catholics were upset when, in late September 1932, the ringing of church bells was prohibited in Béjar for mass, weddings or funerals. Elsewhere, many left-wing *alcaldes* (mayors) levied a local tax on bell-ringing.[47] In Talavera de la Reina (Toledo), the Mayor imposed fines on women wearing crucifixes. In the socially conflictive province of Badajoz, numerous incidents, such as the prohibition of funeral processions, incited hatred. In Fuente de Cantos, the Mayor imposed a tax on bell-ringing of 10 pesetas for the first five minutes and 2 pesetas for every minute thereafter. In Fregenal de la Sierra, bell-ringing was forbidden altogether and a tax levied on Catholic burials. There were church burnings in several villages. In Villafranca de los Barros, the Socialist majority of the town council voted in April 1932 for the removal of the statue of the Sacred Heart from the main square.[48]

Religious frictions were quickly exploited by the right. Processions became demonstrations, pilgrimages became protest marches, and Sunday sermons became meetings which often provoked anti-clerical reactions, sometimes violent.[49] It was but a short step from the rhetoric of persecution and suffering to the advocacy of violence against Republican reforms portrayed as the work of a sinister foreign Jewish–Masonic–Bolshevik plot.[50] In later years, Gil Robles would admit that he had deliberately set out to push his audiences towards conflict with the authorities. In April 1937, when Acción Popular was being dissolved and incorporated by Franco into his new one-party state, Gil Robles claimed proudly that the reserves of mass rightist belligerence which he had built up during the Republic made possible the victory of the right in the Civil War. He saw this 'splendid harvest' as the fruit of his own propaganda efforts. He was still taking pride in this achievement when he published his memoirs in 1968.[51]

Gil Robles's rhetoric during the Republic reflected the feelings and the fears of his most powerful backers, the big landowners or *latifundistas*. Their outrage at the sheer effrontery of landless labourers in daring to take part in the revolutionary upheavals of 1918–21 reflected their sense of social, cultural and indeed near-racist superiority over those who worked their estates. That the Republican–Socialist coalition should declare its intention to improve the daily lot of the wretched day-labourers implied a sweeping challenge to the very structures of rural power. The hostility of the landowners towards the new regime was first manifested in a determination to block Republican reforms by any means, including unrestrained violence. The hatred of the *latifundistas* for their *braceros* would find its most complete expression in the early months of the Civil War when they would collaborate enthusiastically with Franco's African columns as they spread a wave of terror through south-western Spain.

The Republic's attempts to streamline the officer corps had provoked the hostility of many officers but especially of the Africanistas. General José Sanjurjo, Director General of the Civil Guard and a prominent African veteran, was one of the first officers publicly to identify the subject tribes of Morocco with the Spanish left – a transference of racial prejudice which would facilitate the savagery carried out by the Army of Africa during the Civil War. Sanjurjo blurted this out in the wake of the atrocity at the remote and impoverished village of Castilblanco in Badajoz, when villagers murdered four Civil Guards in an outburst of collective rage at systematic oppression. The Socialist landworkers' union, the Federación Nacional de Trabajadores de la Tierra (FNTT), had called a forty-eight-hour strike in the province to protest against the landowners' constant infractions of the Republic's social legislation. On 31 December 1931, in Castilblanco, urged on by the Mayor, Civil Guards opened fire on a peaceful demonstration by strikers, killing one man and wounding two others. Shocked, the infuriated villagers turned on the four Civil Guards and beat them to death. For the left, the events of Castilblanco were the result of the area's long history of appalling economic deprivation.[52]

Sanjurjo was furious because the obligation to go to Castilblanco forced him to miss a big society wedding banquet in Zaragoza.[53] On 2 January 1932, when he arrived in the village, now occupied by a substantial detachment of Civil Guards, the officer in charge indicated the hundred or so prisoners with the words: 'Here are the murderers, just look at their faces!' Sanjurjo burst out, 'But haven't you killed them yet?' The prisoners were severely mistreated. For seven days and nights, they were kept stripped to the waist and, in temperatures below freezing, forced to stand with their arms upright. If they fell, they were beaten with rifle butts. Several died of pneumonia. Speaking to journalists at the funeral of the murdered guards, Sanjurjo compared the workers of Castilblanco to the Moorish tribesmen he had fought in Morocco, commenting, 'In a corner of the province of Badajoz, Rif tribesmen have a base.' He declared mendaciously that after the colonial disaster at the battle of Annual in July 1921, when nine thousand soldiers had died, 'even in Monte Arruit, when the Melilla command collapsed, the corpses of Christians were not mutilated with such savagery'.[54]

This prejudice was echoed in the national and local press by journalists who never actually visited Castilblanco. The monarchist daily *ABC* remarked that 'the least civilized Rif tribesmen were no worse'.[55] Right-wing journalists described the landless labourers of Extremadura as 'these Rif tribesmen with no Rif' and as 'Berbers, savages, bloodthirsty savages and Marxist hordes'. In general terms, the local newspaper reports of Castilblanco reflected the belligerently racist attitudes of the rural elite. The inhabitants of Castilblanco, and by extension the rural prole-tariat as a whole, were presented as an inferior race, horrible examples of racial degeneration. It was common for them to be described as sub-human and abnormal. Colourfully exaggerated descriptions pandered to the ancestral fears of the respectable classes: the allegation that a woman had danced on the corpses recalled the witches' Sabbath.[56] The often explicit conclusion was that the rural proletariat should be disciplined in the same way as the colonial enemy in Morocco, and there were calls for the Civil Guard to be reinforced with crack motorized units.[57]

Over the course of the week following the incident at Castilblanco, the bloody revenge of the Civil Guard saw eighteen people die. Three days after Castilblanco, they killed two and wounded three in Zalamea de la Serena (Badajoz). Two days later, a striker was shot dead and another wounded in Calzada de Calatrava and one striker was shot in Puertollano (both villages in Ciudad Real), while two strikers were killed and eleven wounded in Épila (Zaragoza), and two strikers killed and fifteen wounded, nine seriously, in Jeresa (Valencia). On 5 January 1932, there took place the most shocking of these actions, when twenty-eight Civil Guards opened fire on a peaceful demonstration at Arnedo, a small town in the northern Castilian province of Logroño.

One of Arnedo's main sources of employment was a shoe factory, owned by Faustino Muro, a man of extreme right-wing convictions. Towards the end of 1931, he sacked several of his workers for failing to vote for monarchist candidates in the elections of April and others for belonging to the UGT. The case was put before the local arbitration committee, which declared in favour of the workers, but Muro refused to give them back their jobs. A public protest meeting was held in front of the Ayuntamiento (town hall). Without apparent motive, the Civil Guard opened fire, shooting dead a worker, a twenty-six-year-old preg-nant mother, her two-year-old son and three other women bystanders. Bullet wounds were suffered by a further fifty townspeople, including many women and children, some of them babes-in-arms. Over the next few days, a further five died of their wounds and many had to have limbs amputated, among them a five-year-old boy and a widow with six chil-dren.[58] The inhabitants of Arnedo would suffer further in the early months of the Civil War. Forty-six would be murdered between late July and early October 1936, including some who had been wounded in 1932.[59]

Azaña observed in his diary that Spanish public opinion was now divided between those who hated the Civil Guard and those who revered it as the last-ditch defender of the social order.[60] After Arnedo, Sanjurjo declared that the Civil Guard stood between Spain and the imposition of Soviet communism and that the victims were part of an uncultured rabble that had been deceived by malicious agitators.[61] His words after Castilblanco and the Civil Guard's revenge reflected the way in which the cruelty and savagery of the Moroccan wars was imported into Spain and used against the working class. Sanjurjo, however, was not the first person to note the link. The Asturian miners' leader, Manuel Llaneza, wrote after the repression of the revolutionary general strike of 1917 of 'the African hatred' with which the military columns had killed and beaten workers and wrecked and looted their homes.[62]

Unfortunately for the Republican–Socialist coalition, for an increasing number of middle-class Spaniards the excesses of the army and the Civil Guard were justified by the excesses of the CNT. On 18 January 1932, there was an insurrection by miners who took over the town of Fígols in the most northerly part of the province of Barcelona. The movement spread to the entire region of northern Catalonia. The CNT immediately declared a solidarity strike. The only place outside Catalonia where there was any significant response was Seville. There, the CNT, with the backing of the Communist Party, called a general strike on 25 and 26 January. The strike was total for the two days and public services were maintained by the Civil Guard. The accompanying violence convinced the Socialists that there were agents provocateurs in the anarchist movement working to show that the government was incapable of maintaining order. On 21 January, Azaña also declared in the Cortes that the extreme right was manipulating the anarchists. He stated that those who occupied factories, assaulted town halls, uprooted railway tracks, cut telephone lines or attacked the forces of order would be treated as rebels. His response was to send in the army, apply the Law for the Defence of the Republic, suspend the anarchist press and deport the strike leaders from both Catalonia and Seville. Inevitably, CNT hostility against the Republic and the UGT intensified to a virtual war.[63]

There were other fatal incidents involving the Civil Guard throughout the months following Arnedo. As part of the 1 May 1932 celebrations at the village of Salvaleón in Badajoz, a meeting of FNTT members from other towns and villages in the province was held at a nearby estate. After speeches by several prominent Socialists including the local parliamentary deputies Pedro Rubio Heredia and Nicolás de Pablo, a workers' choir from the village of Barcarrota sang the 'Internationale' and the 'Marseillaise'. The crowd dispersed, many to attend a dance held in Salvaleón. Afterwards, before returning to Barcarrota, the choir went to sing outside the home of the Socialist Mayor of Salvaleón, Juan Vázquez, known as 'Tío Juan el de los pollos' (Uncle John the Chicken Man). This late-night homage infuriated the local commander of the Civil Guard whose men opened fire, killing two men and a woman, as well as wounding several others. In justification of his action, the commander later claimed that a shot had been fired from the crowd. Arrests were made, including the deputy Nicolás de Pablo and Tío Juan, the Mayor of Salvaleón. Pedro Rubio would be murdered in June 1935, Nicolás de Pablo at the end of August 1936 and Juan Vázquez in October 1936 in Llerena.[64]

Sanjurjo was relieved of the command of the Civil Guard in January 1932 and appointed Director General of the Carabineros (frontier guards). He, and many others, assumed that he was being punished because of his stance after Castilblanco.[65] As a result, he was fêted by the extreme right. Eventually in August 1932, he led an abortive military coup. It was briefly successful only in Seville, where it was enthusiastically supported by the local right. During the so-called 'Sanjurjada' (the Sanjurjo business), the plotters arrested the most prominent Republicans in Seville, including the Mayor, José González Fernández de Labandera. When he had heard of the coup attempt on 10 August, Labandera had immediately gone to the town hall and ordered all the town councillors, heads of parties and unions to attend. He had already created a Committee of Public Salvation (Comité de Salvación Pública) when Major Eleuterio Sánchez Rubio Dávila arrived, sent by Sanjurjo to take over as Mayor. Labandera had refused and a perplexed Sánchez Rubio Dávila withdrew. He returned shortly afterwards with a unit of the Republican anti-riot police, the Assault Guards, and arrested Labandera who, as he was taken away, shouted, 'Last decree of the Mayor, declaration of a general strike of all public services.' The declaration of the strike virtually guaranteed the failure of the coup and saved his life, but the local right would take its revenge when the Civil War started. Labandera was shot on 10 August 1936.

Among the civilian participants in the coup were many of those who had been involved in the Guardia Cívica responsible for the events in the

Parque de María Luisa in July 1931. There is no sign that they were deterred by their failure in 1932. Indeed, several of them, along with the officers involved, would be prominent in the events of the summer of 1936.[66] Sanjurjo was tried for treason on 25 August in the Military Section of the Supreme Court. The acting president of the court, Mariano Gómez González, had no choice but to issue the death sentence, but he recommended a pardon with the sentence reduced to expulsion from the army.[67] Plutarco Elías Calles, the Mexican President, sent a message to Azaña: 'If you wish to avoid widespread bloodshed and make the Republic live, shoot Sanjurjo.' In cabinet, Azaña successfully argued in favour of Mariano Gómez's recommendation. No one was shot, and Sanjurjo and others were imprisoned and eventually released.[68]

Despite loud protests about the allegedly excessive prison sentences meted out, the right was sufficiently emboldened by the relatively feeble punishments to intensify preparations for a successful venture next time.[69] The prison regime could hardly have been more easygoing. The man intended to lead Sanjurjo's coup in Cádiz was Colonel José Enrique Varela, the most highly decorated officer in the army. Although he had not gone into action, his involvement in the conspiracy saw him arrested and jailed in the same prison which held the principal Carlist elements in the coup – Manuel Delgado Brackembury and Luis Redondo García, the leader of the city's militant Carlist militia group or Requeté. They, and the Carlist leader Manuel Fal Conde who visited him, entranced Varela with their ideas for organized popular violence against the regime. Varela was entirely converted to Carlism after being transferred with Redondo to the prison at Guadalajara.[70]

Unfortunately, the left became over-confident, seeing the Sanjurjada as the equivalent of the Kapp putsch of March 1920 in Berlin. Since Sanjurjo, like Kapp, had been defeated by a general strike, many believed that the defeat of the Sanjurjada had strengthened the Republic as Kapp's failure had strengthened Weimar. Nothing was done to restructure guilty units. In contrast, the right learned much from Sanjurjo's fiasco, especially that a coup could not succeed without the collaboration of the Civil Guard and that the Republican municipal authorities and trade union leaders had to be silenced immediately.

Above all, the conspiratorial right, both civilian and military, concluded that they must never again make the mistake of inadequate preparation. In late September 1932, a conspiratorial committee was set up by Eugenio Vegas Latapie and the Marqués de Eliseda of the extreme rightist group Acción Española and Captain Jorge Vigón of the General

Staff to begin preparations for future success. The theological, moral and political legitimacy of a rising against the Republic was argued in the monarchist journal *Acción Española*. The group operated from the Biarritz home of the monarchist aviator and playboy Juan Antonio Ansaldo. Considerable sums of money were collected from rightist sympathizers to buy arms and to finance political destabilization for which unnamed elements of the CNT–FAI were put on the payroll. A substantial amount was also spent each month on the services of a police inspector, Santiago Martín Báguenas. He had been a close collaborator of General Emilio Mola, who had headed the Dirección General de Seguridad (the General Directorate of Security) in the last months of the monarchy. Martín Báguenas was now hired to provide an intelligence service for the conspirators and he in turn employed another of Mola's cronies, the even more corrupt policeman Julián Mauricio Carlavilla. Another of the principal objectives of the new committee was the creation of subversive cells within the army itself, a task entrusted to Lieutenant Colonel Valentín Galarza Morante of the General Staff.[71]

Galarza Morante had been involved in the Sanjurjada, but nothing could be proved against him. Azaña saw him as one of the most dangerous of the military conspirators because of knowledge acquired in years of meddling in the Ministry of War.[72] Galarza would be the link between the monarchist conspirators and the clandestine association of army officers, the Unión Militar Española (UME), created at the end of 1933 by the retired Colonel Emilio Rodríguez Tarduchy, a close friend of General Sanjurjo and one of the first members of the fascist party, Falange Española. Members of the UME would play a crucial role in the military rebellion of 1936.[73] Tarduchy was soon succeeded by a captain of the General Staff, Bartolomé Barba Hernández, an Africanista friend of Franco who had appointed him as a member of his teaching staff at the Academia Militar General in Zaragoza.[74]

The defeat of Sanjurjo did nothing to calm social hatred in the south and the behaviour of the Civil Guard did much to exacerbate it. In late 1932, near Fuente de Cantos in the south of Badajoz, a left-wing meeting in the nearby fields was broken up by the Civil Guard and a local union leader, Julián Alarcón, detained. To teach him a lesson, they buried him up to his neck and left him until his comrades could return and dig him out.[75]

In mid-December 1932, in Castellar de Santiago in the province of Ciudad Real, the Civil Guard stood immobile while local landowners and their retainers ran riot. The principal source of local employment was the olive harvest. There were few large estates and the smaller farmers who grew olives had trouble paying their workers a decent wage and preferred to employ workers from outside the province or women, who were traditionally paid less. After protests from the local Socialist workers' society, the Casa del Pueblo, an agreement had been negotiated with the landowners not to use women and outside workers while local men remained idle. However, encouraged by the Agrupación Nacional de Propietarios de Fincas Rústicas (the Association of Rural Estate-Owners), an aristocratic pressure group, local farmers united to confront what was perceived as the temerity of the workers and ignored the agreement. The Mayor, under pressure from the landowners, did nothing to implement the agreements and simply tried to absent himself from the conflict by going to the town of Valdepeñas.

On 12 December, his car was stopped by a group of unemployed day-labourers who tried to make him return and do his job. Someone in his car fired a shot, hitting Aurelio Franco, the clerk of the Casa del Pueblo, and a fight started. Stones were thrown and the Mayor was hurt. The landowners and their armed guards then rampaged through workers' houses, smashing furniture and threatening their wives and children. Aurelio Franco and two other union officials were pulled out of their houses and shot in front of their families. The Civil Guard witnessed the incidents but did not intervene. The FNTT newspaper, *El Obrero de la Tierra*, commented that what had happened in Castellar de Santiago 'represents in its extreme form the barbarity of a moneyed class that believes that it owns people's lives and livelihoods. Utterly out of control, the local bosses revealed the real nature of the class that they represent because they turned that place into a corner of Africa.' A general strike was called in the province. Nevertheless, the local landowners continued to ignore working agreements and no one from the Castellar post of the Civil Guard was punished for dereliction of duty.[76]

Demonstrating the Civil Guard's support for employers determined to block Republican social legislation, the events at Castellar de Santiago were surpassed less than one month later. Now dominated by the extremist FAI, the anarchist movement launched an ill-prepared insurrection on 8 January 1933. It was suppressed easily in most of Spain, but in the small village of Casas Viejas (Cádiz) a savage repression ensued. With the best land around the village used for breeding fighting bulls, the inhabitants faced year-round unemployment, near-starvation and endemic tuberculosis. The writer Ramón Sender wrote of the poor being maddened with hunger like stray dogs. When the FAI declaration of libertarian communism reached the local workers' centre, the villagers hesitantly obeyed. Assuming that all of Cádiz had followed the revolutionary call, they did not expect bloodshed and naively invited the local landowners and the Civil Guard to join the new collective enterprise. To their bewilderment, the Civil Guard replied to the offer with gunfire. Many fled the village, but some took refuge in the hut of the septuagenarian Curro Cruz, known as Seisdedos. Inside with Seisdedos were his two sons, his cousin, his daughter and son-in-law, his daughter-in-law and his two grandchildren. They and a few other villagers were armed only with shotguns loaded with pellets. A company of Assault Guards arrived under the command of Captain Manuel Rojas Feijespan. During a night-long siege, several were killed as machine-gun bullets penetrated the mud walls of the hovel. Rojas ordered the Guards to set fire to the hut. Those who tried to escape were shot down. Another twelve villagers were executed in cold blood.[77]

The immediate reaction of the rightist press was favourable, echoing its customary applause for the Civil Guard's repression of the rural proletariat.[78] However, when they realized that political capital could be made, rightist groups cried crocodile tears and echoed anarchist indignation. Before the full details of the massacre were known, all three Socialist ministers, especially the moderate Indalecio Prieto, had given Azaña their support for the anarchist rising to be suppressed.[79] However, despite their hostility to the anarchists, the Socialists could not approve of the gratuitous brutality displayed by the forces of order. To make matters worse, the officers responsible claimed falsely that they had been acting under orders. They were backed up to devastating effect by the future leader of the Unión Militar Española. Captain Barba Hernández was on duty the night of 8 January 1933. When the scandal broke out, he defended his friend Captain Rojas Feijespan by claiming that Azaña had personally given the order 'shoot them in the belly'. Seized upon by the right-wing press, the fabrication did immense damage to the Republican–Socialist coalition.[80] Casas Viejas and its repercussions brought home to the Socialist leadership the cost of participation in the government. They saw that the defence of the bourgeois Republic against the anarchists was sacrificing their credibility with the Socialist masses.

There was further violence during the campaign for the re-run municipal elections on 23 April 1933. There were to be elections in twenty-one towns in the province of Badajoz, the most important being Hornachos. On that day, the Mayor of Zafra, José González Barrero, headed a demonstration in Hornachos of three hundred Socialists and

Communists. Red flags were flown and revolutionary chants heard. Initially, on the orders of the Civil Governor, the Civil Guard stood back. However, local rightists, who were running in the elections as the Anti-Marxist Coalition, approached Rafael Salazar Alonso, one of the Radical deputies for the province, who was in Hornachos on that day. Since there was no telephone line to Hornachos, Salazar Alonso drove to the nearby town of Villafranca de los Barros where he telephoned the Minister of the Interior and called for the Civil Guard to be given the freedom to open fire. In his own account, he was still in Villafranca de los Barros when that happened. Other sources suggest that, in fact, he was present when, after stones were thrown and a shot fired, the Civil Guard in Hornachos began to shoot at the crowd. Four men and one woman were killed and fourteen people wounded. Forty workers were arrested, several of whom were badly beaten.[81] It was widely believed that Salazar Alonso was responsible for the action of the Civil Guard in Hornachos on that day.[82]

The pugnacious and provocative Salazar Alonso was a man given to extreme enthusiasms who, prior to 1931, had been a fiery, anti-clerical Republican but had undergone a dramatic change after falling under the spell of the landed aristocracy of Badajoz. In consequence, he threw himself into the service of reactionary interests with the zeal of a convert and played an important role in the genesis of violence in southern Spain. According to Pedro Vallina, a celebrated doctor of anarchist beliefs, Salazar Alonso was ferociously ambitious and had adopted anti-clericalism as a way of rising to prominence within the Radical Party. He had been born and brought up in Madrid. In his father's home town, Siruela in Badajoz, he had married the daughter of a wealthy landowner. He had made his early career manifesting radical views, but once he secured a seat in parliament he moved rapidly to the right. During his lightning visit to Villafranca de los Barros on 23 April 1933, he met Amparo, the wife of another even wealthier landowner, a man much older than herself. He abandoned his own wife and children and began an affair with Amparo, who began to visit him in Madrid. The austere and idealistic Dr Vallina was confirmed in his view that Salazar Alonso was 'one of the most shameless and cynical men I have ever known'. Even the head of the Radical Party, the corrupt Alejandro Lerroux, commented wistfully that Salazar Alonso 'frequented palaces where I had never been other than on official business'.[83] Eventually, both because of and despite the adulterous nature of his relationship with Amparo, he would abandon Freemasonry and become a pious Catholic.[84]

Throughout the spring and summer of 1933, evidence mounted that the Republic's social laws were simply being ignored. Official labour exchanges and the arbitration committees known as mixed juries were bypassed and work offered only to men who would tear up their union cards. Land was withdrawn from cultivation. There were ever more cases of landowners shooting at workers. A meeting of the national committee of the UGT was held in mid-June to consider the drift to anarchist and Communist organizations of members frustrated by Socialist efforts to maintain worker discipline in the face of provocation.[85]

Workers – especially in the countryside – were being forced into increasing militancy by the employers' refusal to comply with social legislation. As long as the Socialists had a presence in the government and could offer the prospect of reform, the unions would still respond to calls for discipline and patience. However, for some time, Alcalá Zamora had been seeking an opportunity to get the Republican–Socialist coalition out of power. This was partly because of discomfort with the Socialists and personal incompatibility with Manuel Azaña. In early September, despite a parliamentary vote of confidence for Azaña, the President invited the corrupt leader of the Radical Party, Alejandro Lerroux, to form a government. Unable to face parliament without certain defeat, he governed with the Cortes closed. Landowners were quickly delighted by the forbearing stance of the new Ministers of Agriculture, Ramón Feced Gresa (a property registrar by profession) and of Labour, Ricardo Samper (a Radical from Valencia). The new Minister of the Interior, Manuel Rico Avello, named several reactionary civil governors who permitted most of the Republic's social legislation to be more or less ignored. To the detriment of local workers, cheap labourers were brought into the southern provinces from Galicia. Infractions of the law were not punished.[86] Inevitably, the dwindling Socialist faith in bourgeois democracy was further undermined.

The appalling conditions in the southern countryside were revealed by the famous Socialist writer and playwright María Lejárraga, on a visit to a village in La Mancha. On her arrival, she discovered that the local Socialists had been unable to find a hall for her meeting. After frantic negotiations, they persuaded a local farmer to let them use his barnyard. After the pigs and hens were shooed away, the meeting began, illuminated only by the light of a hissing acetylene lamp. In the front row sat a number of wretched women, each with one or more children on her lap:

their misshapen heads connected to their skeletal bodies by stick-like necks, their bellies swollen, their little legs twisted into incredible shapes like those of a rag doll, their mouths gulping in air for want of better nourishment. This is the Spain that we found when the Republic was born. Behind the thin and prematurely aged women – who can ever tell whether a woman in the Castilian or Andalusian countryside is twenty-five or two hundred and fifty years old? – stood the men, the oldest supporting their frailty by leaning on the wall at the back.[87]

During the first two years of the Republic, the left had been appalled by the vehemence of opposition to what they regarded as basic humanitarian legislation. After the elections of November 1933, however, the flimsy foundations of a socially progressive Republic laid down in that period were to be ruthlessly torn up as the right used its victory to re-establish the repressive social relations obtaining before 1931. That the right should have the opportunity to do so was a cause of great bitterness within the Socialist movement. In large part, it was their own fault for having made the elemental mistake of rejecting an electoral alliance with the Left Republican forces and thus failing to take advantage of the electoral system. They now believed that the elections had no real validity. The Socialists had won 1,627,472 votes, almost certainly more than any other party running alone could have obtained. With these votes, they had returned fifty-eight deputies, while the Radical Party, with only 806,340 votes, had obtained 104 seats. According to calculations made by the secretariat of the Partido Socialista Obrero Español, the united right had gained a total of 212 seats with 3,345,504 votes, while the disunited left had won ninety-nine seats with 3,375,432 votes.[88] That the right gained a parliamentary seat for fewer than 16,000 votes while left-wing seats 'cost' more than 34,000 was certainly galling, although that did not alter the fact that the main factor in determining the results was the party's own tactical error in failing to take advantage of a system which favoured coalitions.

However, the Socialists had other, more substantial reasons for rejecting the validity of the elections. They were convinced that in the south they had been swindled out of parliamentary seats by electoral malpractice. In villages where one or two men were the sole source of employment, it was relatively easy to get votes by the promise of a job or the threat of dismissal. For many workers on the verge of starvation, a vote could be bought for food or a blanket. In Almendralejo (Badajoz), a local aristocrat bought votes with bread, olive oil and chorizo. In many villages of Granada and Badajoz, those who attended left-wing meetings were beaten by the landowners' estate guards while the Civil Guard stood by. The new Civil Governors named by the Radicals were permitting 'public order' to be controlled by armed thugs in the service of the landowners. Sometimes with the active assistance of the Civil Guard, at other times simply with its benevolent neutrality, they were able to intimidate the left. In the province of Granada, Fernando de los Ríos and other candidates faced violent disruption of their campaign. In Huéscar, De los Ríos was met with a volley of rifle-fire and, in Moclín, his car was stoned by rightists. At Jérez del Marquesado, the local *caciques* (bosses) hired thugs whom they armed and filled with drink. De los Ríos was forced to abandon his planned meeting when he was warned that they planned an attempt on his life. At the remote village of Castril, near Huéscar, a meeting being addressed by María Lejárraga and De los Ríos was disrupted by the simple device of driving into the crowd some donkeys laden with logs. In Guadix, their words were drowned out by the persistent ringing of the nearby church bells. In the province of Córdoba, in Bujalance, the Civil Guard tore down left-wing election propaganda. In Montemayor, Encinas Reales, Puente Genil and Villanueva del Rey, Socialist and Communist candidates were prevented by the Civil Guard from giving election speeches. On the eve of the elections, there was an attempt on the life of the moderate Socialist leader Manuel Cordero. In Quintanilla de Abajo (Valladolid), local workers demonstrated against a fascist meeting. The Civil Guard searched them and, when one said that his only weapons were his hands, they broke his arms with rifle butts.[89]

Given the scale of unemployment in the province of Badajoz, nearly 40 per cent, and the consequent near-starvation of many of its inhabitants, it was inevitable that the election campaign should be marked by considerable violence. In a relatively short time, the Socialist deputy Margarita Nelken had won genuine popularity by vehemently expressing her deep concern for the landworkers and their families. In consequence, she became a target for right-wing hatred. Her passionate speeches at meetings throughout the province drew loud applause. The meetings were often suspended by the local authorities or, if they went ahead, interrupted by hecklers. Her principal opponent, the Radical champion of the local landowners, Rafael Salazar Alonso, larded his attacks on her with sexual insults. A local thug known as Bocanegra was released from prison, allegedly at the behest of Salazar Alonso, in order that he might inflict beatings on her, on another Socialist candidate, Juan-Simeón Vidarte, and on Dr Pedro Vallina, the immensely popular anarchist physician. Vidarte was also the victim of two assassination attempts in the province. In Hornachuelos (Córdoba), the Civil Guard lined up the women of the village at gunpoint and warned them not to vote. In Zalamea de la Sierra (Badajoz), local rightists shouting '¡Viva el Fascio!' opened fire on the Casa del Pueblo, killing a worker.[90]

On the day after the election, Margarita Nelken sent a telegram to the Ministry of Labour protesting that a group of thugs led by the Radical Mayor of Aljucén in Badajoz had opened fire on groups of workers, killing one, seriously wounding two and wounding several more.[91] Margarita was herself manhandled at gunpoint after a speech in the Casa de Pueblo of Aljucén. At voting stations, Civil Guards obliged workers to exchange their voting slips for ones already marked in favour of right-wing candidates. There was significant falsification by the right – votes bought with food and/or blankets, intimidation of voters, repeat voting by truckloads of right-wing sympathizers and the 'misplacing' of boxes of votes from places with known left-wing majorities. The consequence was that the PSOE won only the three seats allotted to the minority block for the province – Margarita Nelken, along with fellow Socialists Pedro Rubio Heredia and Juan-Simeón Vidarte.[92]

Throughout the south, glass voting urns and the louring presence of the *caciques*' thugs made the secret ballot irrelevant. In some provinces (particularly Badajoz, Málaga and Córdoba), the margin of rightist victory was sufficiently small for electoral malpractice to have affected the results. In Granada, there were nine towns where the rightist majority was an implausible 100 per cent, two where it was 99 per cent and a further twenty-one where it was between 84 and 97 per cent. After the elections, the Minister of Justice resigned, in protest at the level of electoral falsification.[93] Across the south, the landowners returned to the semi-feudal relations of dependence that had been the norm before 1931.

2

Theorists of Extermination

Africanista officers and Civil Guards were the most violent exponents of right-wing hostility towards the Second Republic and its working-class supporters. They received encouragement and justification in the murderous hostility to the left peddled by numerous politicians, journals and newspapers. In particular, several influential individuals spewed out a rhetoric which urged the extermination of the left as a patriotic duty. They insinuated the racial inferiority of their left-wing and liberal enemies through the clichés of the theory of the Jewish–Masonic–Bolshevik conspiracy. The presentation at the beginning of 1933 of the draft law prohibiting schools run by religious orders was a useful trigger. On 30 January, at a mass meeting in the Monumental Cinema in Madrid, the Carlist landowner José María Lamamié de Clairac, a parliamentary deputy for Salamanca, denounced the law as a satanic plot by the Freemasons to destroy the Catholic Church.[1] The Law was approved on 18 May. On 4 June, Cándido Casanueva, Lamamié's fellow deputy for Salamanca, responded by telling the Women's Association for Civic Education: 'You are duty bound to pour into the hearts of your children a drop of hatred every day against the Law on Religious Orders and its authors. Woe betide you if you don't!'[2] The following day, Gil Robles declared that 'the Freemasonry that has brought the Law on Religious Orders to Spain is the work of foreigners, just like the sects and the Internationals'.[3]

The idea of an evil Jewish conspiracy to destroy the Christian world was given a modern spin in Spain by the dissemination from 1932 onwards of one the most influential works of anti-Semitism, *The Protocols of the Elders of Zion*. Published in Russia in 1903 and based on German and French novels of the 1860s, this fantastical concoction purveyed the idea that a secret Jewish government, the Elders of Zion, was plotting the destruction of Christianity and Jewish world domination.[4] The first Spanish translation of *The Protocols* had been published in Leipzig in 1930. Another translation was made available in Barcelona in 1932 by a Jesuit publishing house which then serialized it in one of its magazines. Awareness and approval of *The Protocols* was extended through the enormously popular work of the Catalan priest Juan Tusquets Terrats (1901–98), author of the best-seller *Orígenes de la revolución española*. Tusquets was born into a wealthy banking family in Barcelona on 31 March 1901. His father was a descendant of Jewish bankers, a committed Catalan nationalist and a friend of the plutocrat Francesc Cambó. His mother was a member of the fabulously wealthy Milà family, the patrons of Gaudí. His secondary education took place in a Jesuit school, then he studied at the University of Louvain and the Pontifical University in Tarragona, where he wrote his doctorate. He was ordained in 1926 and was soon regarded as one of the brightest hopes of Catalan philosophy. Renowned for his piety and his enormous culture, he became a teacher in the seminary of the Catalan capital, where he was commissioned to write a book on the theosophical movement of the controversial spiritualist Madame Helena Blavatsky. In the wake of its success, he developed an obsessive interest in secret societies.[5]

Despite, or perhaps because of, his own remote Jewish origins, by the time the Second Republic was established Tusquets's investigations into secret societies had developed into a fierce anti-Semitism and an even fiercer hatred of Freemasonry. In a further rejection of his family background, he turned violently against Catalan Nationalism and gained great notoriety by falsely accusing the Catalan leader Francesc Macià of being a Freemason.[6] Working with another priest, Joaquim Guiu Bonastre, he built up a network of what he called 'my faithful and intrepid informers'. His ostentatious piety notwithstanding, Tusquets was not above spying or even burglary. One of the principal lodges in Barcelona was in the Carrer d'Avinyó next to a pharmacy. Since Tusquets's aunt lived behind the pharmacy, he and Father Guiu were able spy on the Freemasons from her flat. On one occasion, they broke into another lodge and started a fire, using the ensuing confusion to steal a series of documents. These 'researches' were the basis for the regular, and vehemently anti-Masonic, articles that Tusquets contributed to the Carlist newspaper *El Correo Catalán* and for his immensely successful book *Orígenes de la revolución española*. This book was notable both for popularizing the notion that the Republic was the fruit of a Jewish–Masonic conspiracy and for publishing the names of those he considered its most sinister members. He later alleged that, in retaliation for his writings, the Freemasons twice tried to assassinate him. From his account, it seems that they did not try very hard. On the first occasion, he cheated death simply by getting into a taxi. On the second, he claimed, curiously, that he was saved by an escort provided by the anarcho-syndicalist newspaper *Solidaridad Obrera*. This alleged benevolence on the part of the anarchists was all the more implausible given their own passionate anti-clericalism.[7]

Tusquets used *The Protocols* as 'documentary' evidence of his essential thesis that the Jews were bent on the destruction of Christian civilization. Their instruments were Freemasons and Socialists who did their dirty work by means of revolution, economic catastrophes, unholy and pornographic propaganda and unlimited liberalism. He condemned the Second Republic as the child of Freemasonry and denounced the President, the piously Catholic Niceto Alcalá Zamora, as both a Jew and a Freemason.[8] The message was clear – Spain and the Catholic Church could be saved only by the destruction of Jews, Freemasons and Socialists – in other words, of the entire left of the political spectrum. *Orígenes de la revolución española* sold massively and also provoked a noisy polemic which gave even greater currency to his ideas. His notion that the Republic was a dictatorship in the hands of 'Judaic Freemasonry' was further disseminated through his many articles in *El Correo Catalán* and a highly successful series of fifteen books (*Las Sectas*) attacking Freemasonry, communism and Judaism.

The second volume of *Las Sectas* included a complete translation of *The Protocols* and also repeated his slurs on Macià. The section entitled 'their application to Spain' asserted that the Jewish assault on Spain was visible both in the Republic's persecution of religion and in the movement for agrarian reform via the redistribution of the great estates.[9] Made famous by his writings, in late 1933 Tusquets was invited by the International Anti-Masonic Association to visit the recently established concentration camp at Dachau. He remarked that 'they did it to show what we had to do in Spain'. Dachau was established as a camp for various groups that the Nazis wished to quarantine: political prisoners (Freemasons, Communists, Socialists and liberal, Catholic and monarchist opponents of the regime) and those that they defined as asocials or deviants (homosexuals, Gypsies, vagrants). Despite his favourable comments at the time, Tusquets would claim more than fifty years later that he had been shocked by what he saw. Certainly the visit did nothing to stem the flow and the intensity of his anti-Semitic and anti-Masonic publications.[10]

Tusquets would come to have enormous influence within the Spanish right in general and specifically over General Franco, who enthusiastically devoured his anti-Masonic and anti-Semitic diatribes. He produced a bulletin on Freemasonry that was distributed to senior military figures. Franco's most powerful collaborator, his brother-in-law Ramón Serrano Suñer, would later praise Tusquets's contribution to 'the creation of the atmosphere which led to the National uprising'.[11] However, Tusquets did more than just develop the ideas that justified violence. He was involved in the military plot against the Republic through his links with Catalan Carlists. He and his crony Joaquim Guiu participated in conspiratorial meetings of the Unión Militar Española, which was powerful in Barcelona. In late May 1936, he would approach the private secretary to the Catalan millionaire Francesc Cambó to request financial assistance for the forthcoming coup d'état. Although Cambó, as a friend of Tusquets's father, had written and congratulated him on the success of Orígenes de la revolución española, he did not provide finance for the coup.[12] From the early 1930s, Tusquets and Joaquim Guiu had assiduously compiled lists of Jews and Freemasons. Their search for the enemy extended to societies of nudists, vegetarians, spiritualists and enthusiasts of Esperanto. When Tusquets finally became a collaborator of Franco in Burgos during the Civil War, his files on alleged Freemasons would provide an important part of the organizational infrastructure of the repression.[13]

Endorsement of The Protocols also came from the founder of the ultra-right-wing monarchist theoretical journal Acción Española, the Marqués de Quintanar. At an event held in his honour at the Ritz, Quintanar alleged that the disaster of the fall of the monarchy came about because 'The great worldwide Jewish–Masonic conspiracy injected the autocratic Monarchies with the virus of democracy to defeat them, after turning them into liberal Monarchies.'[14] Julián Cortés Cavanillas, also of the Acción Española pressure group, cited The Protocols as proof that through Masonic intermediaries the 'evil offspring of Israel', the Jews, controlled the anarchist, Socialist and Communist hordes. That the new Republican–Socialist government contained Freemasons, Socialists and men thought to be Jewish was proof positive that the alliance of Marx and Rothschild had established a bridgehead in Spain.[15] Reviewing with total seriousness a French edition of The Protocols as if it were empirical truth, the Marqués de Eliseda implied with a veiled reference to Margarita Nelken that Castilblanco had been masterminded by the Jews.[16]

Other influential writers in Acción Española were the lay theologian Marcial Solana and Father Aniceto de Castro Albarrán, the senior canon of Salamanca Cathedral. They, and Father Pablo Leon Murciego, produced theological justifications for the violent overthrow of the Republic. They argued that it was a Catholic duty to resist tyranny. Solana used St Aquinas to justify the assertion that the tyrant was any oppressive or unjust government. Since power ultimately rested with God, an anti-clerical constitution clearly rendered the Republic tyrannical.[17] In 1932, Castro Albarrán, at the time rector of the Jesuit University of Comillas, had written a book on the right to rebellion. Although it was not published until 1934, an extract was presented in *Acción Española* which reinforced Solana's incitements to rebellion and specifically attacked the legalism of *El Debate*. Castro Albarrán, through his articles and sermons, would become the principal theological apologist of the military rising. He later summed up his views in his 1938 book *Guerra santa* (Holy War).[18] He, Solana and others argued that violence against the Republic was justified because it was a holy rebellion against tyranny, anarchy and Moscow-inspired Godlessness. In 1932, Father Antonio de Pildain Zapiain, deputy for Guipúzcoa and canon of Vitoria Cathedral, declared in the Cortes that Catholic doctrine permitted armed resistance to unjust laws. Similar arguments were central to a controversial book published in 1933 by Father José Cirera y Prat.[19]

The writings of Castro Albarrán and Cirera horrified more moderate clerics such as Cardinal Eustaquio Ilundain Esteban of Seville and Cardinal Vidal i Barraquer of Tarragona. Vidal was distressed by the arrogance with which Castro Albarrán presented as Catholic doctrine partisan ideas which ran counter to Vatican policy on coexistence with the Republic. He protested to Cardinal Pacelli, the Papal Secretary of State, who ordered that the *nihil obstat* (seal of ecclesiastical approval) be removed from the book and tried to have it withdrawn from circulation. The book was serialized in the Carlist press, and the newly appointed Primate of All Spain, Archbishop Isidro Gomá of Toledo, expressed his approval to members of Acción Española.[20] Gomá's predecessor in Toledo, Cardinal Pedro Segura y Sáenz, exiled in Rome, was presented by the Carlist newspaper *El Siglo Futuro* as the archetype of Catholic intransigence to the Republic. He would later be found actively encouraging the Carlist leadership as their armed militia or Requetés trained for insurrection against the Republic.[21]

General Franco was a subscriber to *Acción Española* and a firm believer in the Jewish–Masonic–Bolshevik *contubernio* (filthy concubinage). Significantly, among the many other senior military figures sharing such views was General Emilio Mola, the future director of the military coup of 1936. The tall, bespectacled Mola had the air of a monk-ish scholar, but his background was that of no-nonsense veteran of the African wars. Born in Cuba in 1887, the son of a captain of the Civil Guard, a harsh disciplinarian, he rose to military prominence serving with the Regulares Indígenas (Native Regulars – locally recruited mercen-aries) during the African wars. His memoirs of Morocco, wallowing in descriptions of crushed skulls and bloated intestines, suggest that he had been utterly brutalized by his African experiences.[22] In February 1930 in the wake of the fall of the dictatorship, Mola was appointed Director General of Security. He quickly took to police work. Until the collapse of the monarchy fourteen months later, he devoted himself to crushing labour and student subversion as he had crushed tribal rebellion in Morocco.[23] To this end, he created a crack anti-riot squad, physically well trained and well armed, and a complex espionage system. This so-called Sección de Investigación Comunista used undercover policemen to infil-trate opposition groups and then act as agents provocateurs. The network was still substantially in place in 1936 when Mola employed it in the preparation of the military uprising.[24]

Mola over-estimated the menace of the minuscule Spanish Communist Party, which he viewed as the tool of sinister Jewish–Masonic machinations. This reflected the credence that he gave to the fevered reports of his agents, in particular those of Santiago Martín Báguenas and of the sleazy and obsessive Julián Mauricio Carlavilla del Barrio. Mola's views on Jews, Communists and Freemasons were also coloured by information received from the organization of the White Russian forces in exile, the Russkii Obshche-Voinskii Soiuz (ROVS, Russian All-Military Union) based in Paris. Thereafter, even when he was no longer Director General of Security, he remained in close contact with the ROVS leader Lieutenant General Evgenii Karlovitch Miller. Miller was, like the Nazi racial theorist Alfred Rosenberg, a Baltic German. Their hatred of communism reflected the fact that the Bolshevik revolution saw them lose their families, property, livelihood and homeland. Believing that the Jews had masterminded the revolu-tion, they were determined to prevent them doing the same in western Europe.[25]

When the Republic was established, convinced that he would be arrested for his work in defence of the monarchy, Mola went into hiding. Then on 21 April 1931, he gave himself up to the Minister of War, Manuel Azaña. Four days earlier, General Dámaso Berenguer had been arrested for his role in the Moroccan wars, as Prime Minister and later as Minister of War during the summary trial and execution of the two pro-Republican rebels Captains Fermín Galán and Ángel García Hernández. The arrests of Mola and Berenguer fed the right-wing perception of the Republic as vindictive.[26] In the eyes of the Africanistas, Berenguer was being persecuted for his part in a war in which they had risked their lives, and for following military regulations in court-martial-ling the mutineers Galán and García Hernández. Similarly, they saw Mola as a hero of the African war who, as Director General of Security, had merely been doing his job of controlling subversion. The Africanistas were enraged that officers whom they admired were persecuted while those who had plotted against the Dictator were rewarded. The arrests gave Africanistas like Manuel Goded, Joaquín Fanjul, Mola and Franco a justification for their instinctive hostility to the Republic. They regarded the officers who received the preferment of the Republic as the lackeys of Jews and Freemasons, weaklings who pandered to the mob.

Awaiting trial for his use of excessive force against a student demon-stration on 25 March, Mola was imprisoned in a 'damp and foul-smell-ing cell' in a military jail.[27] Azaña arranged on 5 August for this to be changed to house arrest, but, unsurprisingly, seeing his recent targets now in positions of power, Mola nurtured a rancorous hostility to the Republic and a personal hatred of Azaña. The paranoid reports sent him by Carlavilla and the dossiers supplied by the ROVS convinced him that the triumph of the democratic regime had been engineered by Jews and Freemasons. In late 1931, in the first volume of his memoirs, he wrote of the threat of Freemasonry: 'When, in fulfilling my duties, I investigated the intervention of the Masonic lodges in the political life of Spain, I became aware of the enormous strength at their disposal, not through the lodges themselves but because of the powerful elements that manipu-lated them from abroad – the Jews.' *Acción Española* celebrated the appearance of the book with a rapturous nine-page review by Eugenio Vegas Latapié, one of the journal's founders and a fierce advocate of violence against the Republic.[28]

By the time that Mola came to write the second volume of his memoirs, he was more explicit in his attacks on Freemasons and Jews. He himself implied that this was because, in addition to the reports of General Miller, he had read both the work of Father Tusquets and *The Protocols of the Elders of Zion*. Thus Mola wrote that the coming of the Republic was a reflection of the hatred for Spain of the Jews and Freemasonry:

What rational motives exist to explain why we Spaniards excite the hatred of the descendants of Israel? Fundamentally three: the envy produced in them by any race that has a fatherland of its own; our religion for which they feel unquenchable revulsion because they blame it for their dispersion throughout the world; the memory of their expulsion, which came about not, as is often claimed, because of a King's whim but because the people demanded it. These are the three points of the Masonic triangle of the Spanish lodges.[29]

In December 1933, Mola wrote the conclusion to his bitterly polemical book *El pasado, Azaña y el porvenir* (The Past, Azaña and the Future), in which he gave voice to the widespread military animosity towards the Republic in general and towards Azaña in particular. Mortified by what he perceived as the unpatriotic anti-militarism of the left, he attributed it to various causes, mainly to the fact that:

decadent nations are the favourite victims of parasitical international organizations, used in their turn by the Great Powers, taking advantage of the situation in weak nations, which is where such organizations have most success, just as unhealthy organisms are the most fertile breeding ground of the virulent spread of pathological germs. It is significant that all such organizations are manipulated if not actually directed by the Jews ... The Jews don't care about the destruction of a nation, or of ten, or of the entire world, because they, having the exceptional ability to derive benefit from the greatest catastrophes, are merely completing their programme. What has happened in Russia is a relevant example and one that is very much on Hitler's mind. The German Chancellor – a fanatical nationalist – is convinced that his people cannot rise again as long as the Jews and the parasitical organizations that they control or influence remain embedded in the nation. That is why he persecutes them without quarter.[30]

Morose and shy, Mola was not previously noted for his popularity. With this best-seller, he found himself an object of admiration among the most reactionary military and civilian elements.[31]

Since 1927, both Mola and Franco had been avid readers of an anti-Communist journal from Geneva, the *Bulletin de l'Entente Internationale contre la Troisième Internationale*. While he was Director General of Security, Mola's agents concocted inflated reports about the alleged threat from the Comintern, as the Third International was known. Mola passed these dubious reports to the Entente in Geneva where they were incorporated into the bulletin and sent back to Spain to Franco and other military subscribers as hard fact. The Entente had been founded by the Swiss rightist Théodore Aubert and a White Russian émigré, Georges Lodygensky. Its publications were given a vehemently anti-Semitic and anti-Bolshevik turn by Lodygensky and praised the achievements of fascism and military dictatorships as bulwarks against communism. Enjoying close contacts with Antikomintern, an organization run from Josef Goebbels's Ministry of Information, the Entente skilfully targeted influential people and supplied them with reports which purported to expose plans for forthcoming Communist offensives. The material from the Entente devoured by Franco, Mola and other officers portrayed the Second Republic as a Trojan horse for Communists and Freemasons determined to unleash the Godless hordes of Moscow against Spain and all its great traditions.[32] For the Spanish extreme right and for many of their allies abroad, the Second Republic was an outpost of the Elders of Zion.[33]

One of the most prominent leaders of the Spanish fascist movement, Onésimo Redondo Ortega, was a fervent believer in *The Protocols*. Redondo had studied in Germany and was also close to the Jesuits. He was much influenced by Father Enrique Herrera Oria, brother of the editor of *El Debate*, Ángel Herrera Oria. Father Herrera had encouraged Onésimo in the belief that communism, Freemasonry and Judaism were conspiring to destroy religion and the fatherland and recommended that he read the virulent anti-Jewish and anti-Masonic tract by Léon Poncins, *Las fuerzas secretas de la Revolución. F∴M∴ – Judaismo*, 'F∴M∴' signifying, of course, 'Freemasonry'. Thus becoming aware of *The Protocols*, Onésimo translated and published an abbreviated text in his newspaper *Libertad* of Valladolid, a version later reissued with notes explicitly linking its generalized accusations to the specific circumstances of the Second Republic.[34]

The ultra-right-wing press in general regarded *The Protocols* as a serious sociological study. Since there were few Jews in Spain, there was hardly a 'Jewish problem'. However, Spanish 'anti-Semitism without Jews' was not about real Jews but was an abstract construction of a perceived international threat. Anti-Semitism was central to integrist Catholicism and harked back to Judas Iscariot's betrayal of Jesus Christ and to medieval myths and fears about Jewish ritual killings of children. Now, it was given a burning contemporary relevance by fears of revolution. The notion that all those belonging to left-wing parties were the stooges of the Jews was supported by references to the left-wingers and Jews fleeing from Nazism who found refuge in the Second Republic. As far as the Carlist press was concerned, the few incoming Jews were the advance guard of world revolution and intended to poison Spanish society with pornography and prostitution.[35] Opposed to urbanism and industrialism, to liberalism and capitalism, all ideologies associated with Jews and Freemasons, the Carlists aspired to destroy the Republic by armed insurrection and to impose a kind of rural Arcadian theocracy.[36]

Conservative intellectuals argued that through various subversive devices the Jews had enslaved the Spanish working class. One alleged consequence of this subjugation was that the Spanish workers themselves came to possess oriental qualities. The Spanish radical right began to see the working class as imbued with Jewish and Muslim treachery and barbarism. The most extreme proponent of this view was the late nineteenth-century Carlist ideologue Juan Vázquez de Mella. He argued that Jewish capital had financed the liberal revolutions and was now behind the Communist revolution in order, in union with the Muslim hordes, to destroy Christian civilization and impose Jewish tyranny on the world. Even King Alfonso XIII believed that the rebellion of tribesmen in the Rif was 'the beginning of a general uprising of the entire Muslim world instigated by Moscow and international Jewry'.[37] Carlist ideologues took these ideas seriously, arguing that 'the four horsemen of the Apocalypse, Judaism, Communism, Freemasonry and Death', already controlled Britain, France and Australia and soon Spain would fall under their dominion.[38]

The books of Vázquez de Mella and other Carlist ideologues were eagerly devoured by Colonel José Enrique Varela during his imprisonment after the Sanjurjada. Contrasting the success of the Primo de Rivera coup of 1923 and the failure of Sanjurjo in 1932, the dynamic and courageous Varela was convinced that a successful military rising needed substantial civilian support. He was persuaded that this could be found in the fierce Carlist militia, the Requeté. Although he resisted calls to lead an exclusively Carlist uprising on the grounds that this required someone more senior such as Franco, Varela undertook to turn the Requeté into an effective citizen army. Since he was still under police surveillance, on his trips to the Carlists' northern heartland of Navarre he took the pseudonym 'Don Pepe'. Day-to-day training was supervised by the National Inspector of the Requeté, the retired Lieutenant Colonel Ricardo de Rada, who also would train the Falangist militia.[39] Similarly, in 1934 another of the officers involved in the Sanjurjada, the Civil

Guard Captain Lisardo Doval, would train the paramilitary squads of the Juventud de Acción Popular (the youth movement of Gil Robles's Catholic party, the CEDA).

Carlists, theologians and Africanista officers were among those who through their writings and speeches fomented an atmosphere of social and racial hatred. Another was Onésimo Redondo. Although hardly a national figure, he merits attention both as one of the founders of Spanish fascism and because it was largely due to his ideas that his home town, Valladolid, experienced greater political violence than other Castilian provincial capitals. As a young lawyer, Onésimo Redondo had been involved in Acción Nacional (as Acción Popular was originally called), the Catholic political group founded on 26 April 1931 by Ángel Herrera Oria and principally supported by Castilian farmers. In early May, he set up its local branch in Valladolid and headed its propaganda campaign for the forthcoming parliamentary elections. On 13 June, Onésimo launched the first number of the fortnightly, and later weekly, anti-Republican newspaper *Libertad*. After the Republican–Socialist coalition won a huge majority on 28 June, Onésimo rejected democracy, broke with Acción Nacional and, in August, founded a fascist party, the Juntas Castellanas de Actuación Hispánica (the Castilian Hispanic Action Groups).[40]

On 10 August, he published a fiery proclamation in *Libertad* expressing his commitment to the traditional rural values of Old Castile, to social justice and to violence. He wrote: 'The historic moment, my young countrymen, obliges us to take up weapons. May we know how to use them to defend what is ours and not to serve politicians.' For him 'nationalism is a movement of struggle, it must include warlike, violent activities in the service of Spain against the traitors within'.[41] Certainly, Onésimo Redondo and the Juntas brought a tone of brutal confrontation to a city previously notable for the tranquillity of its labour relations.[42] Onésimo called for 'a few hundred young warriors in each province, disciplined idealists, to smash to smithereens this dirty phantom of the red menace'. His recruits armed themselves for street fights with the predominantly Socialist working class of Valladolid. He wrote of the need to 'cultivate the spirit of violence, of military conflict'. The meetings of the Juntas were held in virtual clandestinity. Over the next few years, his enthusiasm for violence grew progressively more strident.[43]

The numerical weakness of the Juntas obliged Onésimo to seek links with like-minded groups. Accordingly, his gaze fell upon the first overtly fascist group in Spain, the tiny La Conquista del Estado (the Conquest of the State) led by Ramiro Ledesma Ramos.[44] Originally from Zamora, Ledesma worked in a post office in Madrid. An enthusiastic disciple of German philosophy, he had founded his group in February 1931 in a squalid room in a Madrid office block. The light had not been connected and the only furniture was a table. The ten participants signed a manifesto he had written entitled 'The Conquest of the State'. A newspaper of the same name was launched on 14 March. Despite public indifference and police harassment, it survived for a year.[45] In the first number of *Libertad*, Onésimo Redondo had referred favourably to Ledesma Ramos's newspaper: 'We approve of the combative ardour and the eagerness of *La Conquista del Estado*, but we miss the anti-Semitic activity which that movement needs be effective and to go in the right direction.'[46] Although Redondo translated Hitler's *Mein Kampf*, his anti-Semitism drew more on the fifteenth-century Castilian Queen Isabel la Católica than on Nazism. Anti-Semitism was a recurring theme in his writings. In late 1931, for instance, he described the co-educational schools introduced by the Second Republic as an example of 'Jewish action against free nations: a crime against the health of the people for which the traitors responsible must pay with their heads'.[47]

In October 1931, Onésimo met Ledesma Ramos in Madrid. Over the next few weeks, in several meetings in Madrid and Valladolid, they negotiated the loose fusion of their two groups as the Juntas de Ofensiva Nacional Sindicalista (the Groups of National Syndicalist Offensive or JONS). Launched on 30 November 1931, the JONS adopted the red and black colours of the anarcho-syndicalist CNT and took as its badge the emblem of the Catholic kings, the yoke and arrows. It was anti-democratic and imperialist, demanding Gibraltar, Morocco and Algeria for Spain and aspiring to 'the extermination, the dissolution of the anti-national, Marxist parties'. To this end, 'national-syndicalist militias' were to be created 'in order to oppose red violence with nationalist violence'. Ledesma Ramos argued that political violence was legitimate and advocated the creation of armed militias along the lines of the Italian Fascist Squadri to prepare for insurrection or coup d'état.[48] By way of practice, the JONS squads assaulted left-wing students and, in June 1933, sacked the Madrid offices of the Association of Friends of the USSR.[49]

In Valladolid, Onésimo devoted ever more time to the conversion of his forty-odd followers into warriors of what he now called 'organized anti-communist militias'. Soon they would be involved in bloody clashes with left-wing students and workers in the University and in the streets of Valladolid. Pistols were being bought and much time was spent on training. Already by the spring of 1932, Onésimo Redondo was writing about the civil war to come – 'The war is getting nearer; the situation of violence is inevitable. There is no point in rejecting it. It is stupid to flee from making war when they are going to make war on us. The important thing is to prepare to win, and, to win, it is necessary to seize the initiative and go on to the attack.' On 3 May 1932, a pitched battle was fought with the left in the main square of Valladolid after which more than twenty people were hospitalized. Onésimo himself was sentenced to two months in prison for the excesses of *Libertad*.[50]

Imprisonment did nothing to mellow Onésimo Redondo. His article in the fascist monthly *JONS* in May 1933 reflected the growing virulence of his thought and echoed Sanjurjo's identification of the Spanish working class with the Arabs:

Marxism, with its Mohammedan utopias, with the truth of its dictatorial iron and with the pitiless lust of its sadistic magnates, suddenly renews the eclipse of Culture and freedoms like a modern Saracen invasion ... This certain danger, of Africanization in the name of Progress, is clearly visible in Spain. We can state categorically that our Marxists are the most African of all Europe ... Historically, we are a friction zone between that which is civilized and that which is African, between the Aryan and the Semitic ... For this reason, the generations that built the fatherland, those that freed us from being an eternal extension of the Dark Continent, raised their swords against attacks from the south and they never sheathed them ... The great Isabel ordered Spaniards always to watch Africa, to defeat Africa and never be invaded by her again. Was the Peninsula entirely de-Africanized? Is there not a danger of a new kind of African domination, here where so many roots of the Moorish spirit remained in the character of a race in the vanguard of Europe? We ask this important question dispassionately and we will answer it right away by underlining the evident danger of the new Africanization: 'Marxism'. Throughout the world, there exists the Jewish or Semite conspiracy against Western civilization, but in Spain it can more subtly and rapidly connect the Semitic element, the African element. It can be seen flowering in all its primitive freshness in our southern provinces, where Moorish blood lives on in the subsoil of the race ... The follower of Spanish Marxism, especially the Andalusian, soon takes the incendiary torch, breaks into manor houses and farms, impelled by the bandit subconscious, encouraged by the Semites of Madrid; he wants bread without earning it, he wants to laze around and be rich, to take his pleasures and to take his revenge … and the definitive victory of Marxism will be the re-Africanization of Spain, the victory of the combined Semitic elements – Jews and Moors, aristocrats and plebeians who have survived ethnically and spiritually in the Peninsula and in Europe.[51]

By linking Marxism as a Jewish invention and its alleged threat of a 're-Africanization' of Spain, Redondo was identifying Spain's two archetypal 'others', the Jew and the Moor, with the Republic. His conclusion, shared by many on the right, was that a new Reconquista was needed to prevent Spain from falling into the hands of the modern foes. His views on the legitimacy of violence were similar to those of the Catholic extreme right exemplified by the writings of Castro Albarrán.[52]

Anti-Semitism could be found across most of the Spanish right. In some cases, it was a vague sentiment born of traditional Catholic resentment about the fate of Jesus Christ, but in others it was a murderous justification of violence against the left. Curiously, the virulence of Onésimo Redondo constituted something of an exception within Spain's nascent fascist movement. Ledesma Ramos regarded anti-Semitism as having relevance only in Germany.[53] The Falangist leader, José Antonio Primo de Rivera, had little or no interest in the 'Jewish problem' except when it came to the Jewish–Marxist influence over the working class. Nevertheless, the Falangist daily Arriba claimed that 'the Judaic–Masonic International is the creator of the two great evils that have afflicted humanity: capitalism and Marxism'. José Antonio Primo de Rivera shared with other rightists a belief that violence was legitimate against a Republic that he perceived as influenced by Jews and Freemasons.[54] He approved of attacks by Falangists on the Jewish-owned SEPU department stores in the spring of 1935.[55]

The identification of the working class with foreign enemies was based on a convoluted logic whereby Bolshevism was a Jewish invention and the Jews were indistinguishable from Muslims and thus leftists were bent on subjecting Spain to domination by African elements. Thus hostility to the Spanish working class was presented as a legitimate act of Spanish patriotism. According to another of the Acción Española group, the one-time liberal turned ultra-rightist Ramiro de Maeztú, the Spanish nation had been forged in its struggles against the Jews (arrogant usurers) and the Moors (savages without civilization).[56] In one of his articles, the monarchist leader José Calvo Sotelo neatly encapsulated the racist dimension of the anti-leftist discourse when he referred to the

Socialist leader Francisco Largo Caballero as 'a Moroccan Lenin'.[57] José Antonio Primo de Rivera also shared this association of the left with the Moors. In his reflections in prison in 1936, he interpreted all of Spanish history as an endless struggle between Goths and Berbers. The spirit of the former lived on in monarchical, aristocratic, religious and military values while that of the latter was to be found in the rural proletariat. He denounced the Second Republic as a 'new Berber invasion' signifying the demolition of European Spain.[58]

Gil Robles, if less explicitly than Sanjurjo or Onésimo Redondo, also conveyed the view that violence against the left was legitimate because of its racial inferiority. His frequent use of the word 'reconquest' linked enmity towards the left in the 1930s to the central epic of Spanish nationalism, the battle to liberate Spain from Islam between 722 and 1492. During his campaign for the elections of November 1933, on 15 October in the Monumental Cinema of Madrid, he declared: 'We must reconquer Spain … We must give Spain a true unity, a new spirit, a totalitarian polity … For me there is only one tactic today: to form an anti-Marxist front and the wider the better. It is necessary now to defeat socialism mercilessly.' At this point, Antonio Goicoechea, the leader of the extreme rightist Acción Española group, was made to stand and received a tumultuous ovation. Gil Robles continued his speech in language indistinguishable from that of the conspiratorial right:

> We must found a new state, purge the fatherland of judaizing Freemasons … We must proceed to a new state and this imposes duties and sacrifices. What does it matter if we have to shed blood! … We need full power and that is what we demand … To realize this ideal we are not going to waste time with archaic forms. Democracy is not an end but a means to the conquest of the new state. When the time comes, either parliament submits or we will eliminate it.[59]

Gil Robles's speech was described by *El Socialista* as an 'authentic fascist harangue'. On the left, it was perceived as the real policy of his ostensibly moderate mass party, the CEDA (Confederación Española de Derechas Autónomas). Certainly, his every sentence had been greeted by ecstatic applause. Fernando de los Ríos, Minister of Education and Fine Arts since October 1931, a moderate Socialist and a distinguished professor of law, had suffered anti-Semitic abuse for his policy of toleration for Jewish schools and his expressions of sympathy for the Sephardic community in Morocco. He pointed out that Gil Robles's call for a purge of Jews and Freemasons was a denial of the juridical and political postulates of the Republic.[60] CEDA election posters declared that Spain must be saved from 'Marxists, Freemasons, Separatists and Jews'. The entire forces of the left – anarchists, Socialists, Communists, liberal Republicans, regional nationalists – were denounced as anti-Spanish.[61] Violence against them was therefore both legitimate and indeed an urgent patriotic necessity.

The intensified vehemence of Gil Robles was matched in the pages of *El Debate* by the views of Francisco de Luis, who had succeeded Ángel Herrera Oria as editor. Like Onésimo Redondo, De Luis was an energetic evangelist of the Jewish–Masonic–Bolshevik conspiracy theory. His magnum opus on the subject was published in 1935 with an ecclesiastical imprimatur. In it, enthusiastically quoting Tusquets, the *Protocols*, the Carlist press and General Mola, he argued that the purpose of Freemasonry was to corrupt Christian civilization with oriental values. His premise was that 'the Jews, progenitors of Freemasonry, having no fatherland of their own, want no man to have one'. Having freed the masses of patriotic and moral impulses, the Jews could then recruit them for the assault on Christian values. In his interpretation, Catholics faced a struggle to the death because 'inside every Jew there is a Freemason: cunning, deceitful, secretive, hating Christ and his civilization, thirsting for extermination. Freemasons and Jews are the begetters and controllers of socialism and Bolshevism.'[62]

Other than in the sheer scale of their impact, there was little difference between the pronouncements of Francisco de Luis and Onésimo Redondo and those of a friend, and one-time subordinate of General Mola, the policeman Julián Mauricio Carlavilla del Barrio. Born on 13 February 1896 into a poor rural family in New Castile, in Valparaíso de Arriba in Cuenca, the young Carlavilla worked as an agricultural labourer and as a shepherd before spending three years as a conscript soldier in Morocco only because he couldn't buy himself out. On his return to Spain, he passed the entry examinations for the police and, on 9 July 1921, was posted to Valencia. Only eleven months later, he was transferred to Zaragoza after complaints from the Civil Governor of Valencia to the Director General of Security that Carlavilla's behaviour was bringing the police into disrepute. Thereafter, he was sent in rapid succession to Segovia and Bilbao before ending up in Madrid in October 1923. In November 1925, he was transferred to Morocco, where he made contacts with military figures that would stand him in good stead later in his career. Nevertheless, just over one year later, he was sent back to the Peninsula after accusations of irregularities including pocketing fines and selling protection for prostitutes. Nevertheless, Carlavilla eventually rose, in 1935, to the rank of *comisario* (inspector).[63]

Initially, he specialized in undercover work, infiltrating left-wing groups where he would then act as an agent provocateur. He did this on his own initiative, without informing his superior officers. His efforts included provoking, and later claiming credit for frustrating, assassination attempts against both Alfonso XIII and General Primo de Rivera during the opening of the great exhibition in Seville in May 1929.[64] When General Mola became Director General of Security in early 1930, Carlavilla informed him of his clandestine activities, which he described as 'my role as catalyst within the highest circle of the revolutionaries'.[65] On Mola's orders, Carlavilla wrote a detailed report on the supposed activities of the Communist Party in Spain. A wild mixture of fantasy and paranoia, the report was sent by Mola at the end of 1930 to the influential anti-Communist organization in Geneva, the Entente Internationale contre la Troisième Internationale. The contents were fed into the bulletins that the Entente sent to subscribers, including General Franco. The report formed the basis of Carlavilla's first book, *El comunismo en España*.[66]

Carlavilla was involved in the Sanjurjo coup, his role being to prevent the police discovering the nascent conspiracy.[67] Between 1932 and 1936, he wrote a series of best-sellers, using the pseudonym 'Mauricio Karl'.[68] The first, *El comunismo en España*, described the various Socialist, anarchist and Communist elements of the working-class movement as the enemy of Spain that would have to be defeated. The second and third, *El enemigo* and *Asesinos de España*, argued that the enemies masterminding the left-wing assassins of Spain were the Jews who controlled Freemasonry, 'their first army', the Socialist and Communist Internationals, and world capitalism. Spanish greatness in the sixteenth and seventeenth centuries was the fruit of the expulsion of the Jews, and further greatness would require a repetition. Since there were hardly any Jews to be expelled from Spain, it was their lackeys, the Freemasons and the left, that must be eliminated. The only hope of stopping the destruction of Christian civilization and the establishment of the empire of Israel lay in joining German Nazism and Italian Fascism in defeating the 'sectarians of Masonic Jewry'. Carlavilla claimed that General Primo de Rivera, who died of natural causes, had been poisoned by a Jewish Freemason and that the Catalan financier, Francesc Cambó, was both Jewish and a Freemason.

One hundred thousand copies of the third of his books, *Asesinos de España*, were distributed free to army officers. It ended with a provocative challenge to them. Describing Jews, left-wingers and Freemasons as vultures hovering over the corpse of Spain, he wrote: 'The Enemy howls with laughter while the nations that serve Zion play diplomatic dice for the cadaver's land. Thus the Spain once feared by a hundred nations faces such a fate because her sons no longer know how to die or how to kill.'[69] Carlavilla was expelled from the police in September 1935 as a result, according to his official record, 'of serious offences'. He would later claim that his dismissal was persecution for his anti-Masonic revelations.[70]

In addition to his criminal activities, Carlavilla was an active member of the conspiratorial group Unión Militar Española. Initially, his role was centred on the writing and distribution of propaganda in favour of a military coup. However, he was also believed to have been involved in plots to kill both the distinguished law professor and PSOE parliamentary deputy Luis Jiménez Asúa and Francisco Largo Caballero. In May 1936, on the orders of the UME, he was implicated in an assassination attempt on Manuel Azaña. As a result, he was obliged to flee to Portugal. All these plans seem to have been masterminded by Mola's crony, Inspector Santiago Martín Báguenas, who had been working since September 1932 for the monarchist–military plotters. The foiled attempts also involved the same Africanista, Captain Manuel Díaz Criado, who had instigated the shootings in the Parque de María Luisa in Seville in July 1931. In Lisbon, Carlavilla linked up with the exiled General Sanjurjo and remained on the fringes of the military plot. Shortly after the outbreak of war, he went to Burgos where he was welcomed on to the staff of General Mola. Carlavilla worked for a time there alongside Father Juan Tusquets.[71]

Collectively, the ideas of Tusquets, Francisco de Luis, Enrique Herrera Oria, Onésimo Redondo, Mola, Carlavilla, the Carlist press and all those who alleged the existence of a Jewish–Masonic–Bolshevik plot justified the extermination of the left. The reforms of the Republic and the violent anarchist attacks on the Republic were taken equally as evidence that the left was the ungodly anti-Spain. Accordingly, the brutality of the Civil Guard in crushing strikes and demonstrations, military conspiracy and the terrorist activities of fascist groups were all deemed to be legitimate efforts to defend the true Spain.

3

The Right Goes on the Offensive, 1933–1934

In the wake of their electoral victory in November 1933, the right went on to the offensive just as the unemployment crisis reached its peak. That December there were 619,000 out of work across Spain, 12 per cent of the total workforce. Given Spain's lack of social welfare schemes, these figures, although much lower than those in Germany and Italy, signified widespread and immense physical hardship. With the Socialist leader Francisco Largo Caballero no longer at the Ministry of Labour, there was no protection even for those in work. In Jaén, for instance, the new Radical Civil Governor set aside existing agreements on working conditions. In the case of the *turno riguroso* (the strict rotation of work among unemployed labourers), during the olive harvest, the owners were left free to give work only to the cheapest, non-union labour. The consequence was large numbers of families on the verge of starvation.[1] Worsening conditions saw rank-and-file pressure on union officials for militant action particularly in agriculture, metal industries and construction, all of which were represented by substantial groups within the UGT. In the agrarian south, the number of unemployed was dramatically higher than in industrial areas. The worst-hit provinces were Jaén, Badajoz and Córdoba, where the number of unemployed was 50 per cent above the national average. Once landowners began to ignore social legislation entirely and take reprisals for the discomforts of the previous two years, unemployment rose even further. By April 1934 it would reach 703,000.[2]

In opposition, Largo Caballero responded to rank-and-file distress with empty revolutionary slogans. However, the fact that he had no concrete plans for an insurrection did not diminish middle-class fears provoked both by his statements and by the anarchist commitment to revolutionary violence. In fact, when, on 8 December 1933, the CNT naively called for another nationwide uprising, the Socialists ostentatiously stood aside. In the event, only a few traditionally anarchist areas responded to the call. Despite CNT supporters in Asturias and most of

Andalusia standing aside, there was a sporadic wave of violent strikes, some trains were derailed and Civil Guard posts assaulted. In Galicia, the Rioja, Catalonia and Alicante, the insurrectionists were easily suppressed and several hundred prisoners were taken. Throughout Spain, 125 people were killed, sixteen from the forces of order, sixty-five anarchists and forty-four innocent bystanders.[3]

On 9 December at Bujalance in the highly conflictive province of Córdoba, there was an echo of Casas Viejas. Tempers were running high because the landowners were flouting agreements on wages and conditions. Anarchist peasants took over parts of the town and tried to seize the town hall. The Civil Guard replied by attacking any houses whose doors were not left open. In thirty-six hours of fighting, a Civil Guard, two anarchists, four innocent civilians, including a woman, an eight-year-old child and an elderly landowner, were killed. Two alleged ringleaders were captured in nearby Porcuna and shot by the Civil Guard 'while trying to escape'. Two hundred prisoners were taken, many of whom were badly beaten by the Civil Guard. The Civil Governor, Mariano Jiménez Díaz, blamed the events in Bujalance on the landowners for ignoring the work agreements and amassing firearms.[4]

The scale of social hatred in Córdoba can be deduced from the testimony of a union leader from Baena:

> The same owners who would spend 400,000 pesetas on a shawl for the statue of the Virgin or on a crucifix for the Church stinted the olive oil for the workers' meals and would rather pay a lawyer 25,000 pesetas than an extra 25 cents to the day-labourers lest it create a precedent and let the workers get their way. In Baena, there was a *señorito* [master] who put cattle in the planted fields rather than pay the agreed wages to the reapers. A priest who had a farm, when the lad came down to get olive oil, had made dents in the tin jug so that it would hold less oil.

The union official from Baena went on to comment on the intransigence of the employer class when it came to getting any improvement in the awful situation of the farm labourers:

> They had power, influence and money; we only had two or three thousand day-labourers behind us and we constantly had to hold them back since the desperation of being unable to feed their children turns men into wild animals. We knew that the employers, well protected by the forces of order, were not bothered if there were victims, because they

just bribed the officials to change the paperwork and make black white. In fact, they were happy to see violence because it was a welcome warning to any rebels of the danger of leaving the straight and narrow.

His own experience as a young man was revealing:

The few times (two or three) that I went with a committee to discuss conditions with the employers, the only issue on the table was wages; there was no question of negotiating food or working hours, since everything was considered to be included in the clause 'Usage and customs of the locality', which simply meant to work until your back broke, from sun-up to sun-down, or for hours expanded by the arse-licking foremen from when you could just about see until it was too dark to see a thing. I remember in one heated discussion a *cacique* called me a 'snot-nosed kid recently out of the shell' and said that if my father knew how stupid I was, he wouldn't throw down fodder for me. This exhausted my patience and I got up and said to him as seriously as I could: 'It is true, Señor, that on many occasions I have had to eat, not cattle feed, but the remnants of fried bread that you throw out for your dogs, a very Christian deed in a town where the workers' children are dying of hunger.'[5]

There were a number of violent incidents involving the CNT in the western region of Extremadura, an area dominated by large estates or *latifundios*. In the province of Cáceres, two churches were set alight in Navalmoral de la Mata.[6] However, since the Socialist Landworkers' Federation (FNTT) was not involved, the more southerly province of Badajoz was largely unaffected with the exception of Villanueva de la Serena. There, an infantry sergeant, Pío Sopena Blanco, together with eight other anarchists like himself, took over an army recruiting office, killing two Civil Guards and wounding another. They were surrounded but, instead of waiting for them to surrender, the building was bombarded with heavy machine-guns and artillery by combined units of the Civil Guard, Assault Guards and the army. Pío Sopena and two others were killed in the attack and the six others were shot in cold blood. Although local Socialists were not involved, the Mayor and the officials of the Casa del Pueblo (workers' club) were arrested. The Casas del Pueblo in Villanueva and five other *pueblos* were shut down.[7]

These violent incidents involving the CNT diverted attention from the growing problem of malnutrition. This was not only because landowners were slashing wages and refusing work to union members but also because of price rises in basic necessities. After the new Radical government removed price control on bread, the cost had risen by between 25 and 70 per cent. Demonstrations of starving women, children and old people calling for bread became a frequent sight.[8] At the end of 1933, then, the Socialist leaders faced a rising tide of mass militancy, fed by the employers' offensive and bitterness at the perceived unfairness of electoral defeat. Dismayed by the right's determination to destroy what they regarded as basic humanitarian legislation, ever more members of the trade union movement and the Socialist Youth (Federación de Juventudes Socialistas) had come to believe that bourgeois democracy would never allow the introduction of even a minimal social justice, let alone full-blown socialism. Fearful of losing support, Largo Caballero reacted by heightening his revolutionary tone still further. In mid-January 1934, he declared that to transform society it was necessary to arm the people and disarm the forces of capitalism – the army, the Civil Guard, the Assault Guards, the police and the courts: 'Power cannot be taken from the hands of the bourgeoisie simply by cheering for Socialism.'[9]

This strident rhetoric was not backed by any serious revolutionary intentions, but, replayed via the right-wing press, it could only provoke middle-class fears. Largo Caballero's verbal extremism pandered to rank-and-file dissatisfactions but aimed also to pressure President Alcalá Zamora into calling new elections. It was dangerously irresponsible. If the President did not respond to pressure, the Socialists would be forced either to fulfil Largo Caballero's threats or back down and lose face with their own militants. Since there was little possibility of implementing his threats, the consequence could benefit only the right.

Largo Caballero's ill-considered rhetoric reflected both the aggressive assault on social legislation that had followed the right-wing electoral victory and fears of fascism. He felt that he had to respond to workers' delegations from the provinces that came to Madrid to beg the Socialist Party (PSOE) leadership to organize a counter-offensive.[10] At the same time, he and others suspected that not only the Republic's legislation but also their own persons were in danger from a possible fascist coup. On 22 November, the outgoing Minister of Justice, Fernando de los Ríos, informed the PSOE executive committee of plans being prepared for a rightist coup involving the arrest of the Socialist leadership.[11] Throughout November and December, the Socialist press frequently published material indicating that Gil Robles and the CEDA had fascist ambitions. Reprinted documents included the CEDA's plans for a citizen militia to combat revolutionary activity on the part of the working class. Others showed that, with the connivance of the police, the CEDA was assembling files on workers in every village, with full details of their 'subversiveness', which meant their membership of a union. The appearance of the uniformed militias of the CEDA's youth movement (the Juventud de Acción Popular) was taken as proof that preparations were afoot to establish fascism in Spain.[12]

Inevitably, within the Socialist Youth and among the younger, unskilled union members there was a great surge of enthusiasm for revolution. Largo Caballero was happy to go along with their demands lest they drift towards the more determinedly revolutionary CNT. Although, at a joint meeting of the union (UGT) and party (PSOE) executives on 25 November, revolutionary proposals were defeated, the moderate Indalecio Prieto reluctantly agreed on the need for 'defensive action'. The two executives compromised with a declaration urging workers to be ready to rise up and oppose 'reactionary elements in the event that they went beyond the bounds of the Constitution in their public determination to annul the work of the Republic'. A joint PSOE–UGT committee was set up to prepare this 'defensive action'.[13] The lack of Socialist participation in the CNT insurrection two weeks later showed that reformist habits prevailed over the new revolutionary rhetoric. The CEDA's support for the assault on unionized labour together with its declared determination to smash socialism and to establish a corporativist state made it, for most Spanish leftists, indistinguishable from the Italian Fascist Party or the early Nazi Party. The Socialist leadership wanted to avoid the errors made by their German and Italian comrades, but they had no real intention of actually organizing a revolution. Instead, they hoped that threats of revolution would calm rank-and-file frustration and restrain right-wing aggression.

No Socialist organizations had participated in the CNT action, although a few individual militants had done so, believing it to be the 'defensive action' agreed on 26 November.[14] In the Cortes, Prieto condemned 'this damaging movement'. Yet, when both Gil Robles and the monarchist leader Antonio Goicoechea enthusiastically offered to help the government crush subversion, Prieto reacted angrily. It disturbed him that the 'enemies of the Republic' supported the regime only when the proposal was for the repression of the working class. By their determination to silence the workers' organizations, Prieto perceptively told the deputies of the right, 'you are closing all exits to us and inviting us to a bloody conflict'.[15]

On 16 December, Lerroux formed a government with the parliamentary support of the CEDA. Three days later, Gil Robles made a policy
statement in the Cortes which explained that, in return for CEDA votes,
he expected an amnesty for those imprisoned for Sanjurjo's coup of
August 1932 and a thorough revision of the religious legislation of the
Constituent Cortes (so called because it was the parliament that elaborated and approved the Republican Constitution). Most alarming for the
left were his demands for the repeal of the reforms which had most
benefited the landless peasantry – the laws of municipal boundaries and
of obligatory cultivation, and the introduction of the eight-hour day and
of mixed juries (arbitration committees). He also demanded a reduction
of the area of land subject to expropriation under the agrarian reform
bill and denounced the socializing concept of settling peasants on the
land. Most alarming for the left was his statement that his ambition was
to lead a government and change the Constitution: 'We are in no hurry,
we want other proposals to fail so that experience will show the Spanish
people that there can only be one solution, an unequivocally right-wing
solution.' Behind the measured tone, there lay a dramatic threat that, if
events showed that a right-wing evolution was not possible, the Republic
would pay the consequences. Not surprisingly, the Socialists regarded
this as a fascist speech.[16] In reply, Indalecio Prieto made it clear that, for
the Socialists, the legislation that Gil Robles aimed to repeal was what
made the Republic worth defending. He threatened that the Socialists
would defend the Republic against Gil Robles's dictatorial ambitions by
unleashing the revolution.[17] In the exchange could be seen the seeds of
the violent events of October 1934.

The appalling dilemma faced by the PSOE executive was revealed by
Fernando de los Ríos when he visited the ex-Prime Minister Manuel
Azaña on 2 January 1934. Azaña noted in his diary:

He recounted to me the incredible and cruel persecutions that the
workers' political and union organizations were suffering at the hands
of the authorities and the employers. The Civil Guard was daring to do
things it had never dared do before. It was impossible to restrain the
exasperation of the masses. The Socialist leaders were being overwhelmed. Where would it all end? In a great misfortune, probably. I was
aware of the barbaric policy followed by the government and of the way
the landowners were reducing the rural labourers to hunger and of the
retaliations and reprisals against other workers. I know the slogan 'Let
the Republic feed you' [Comed República]. But all of this and much

more that De los Ríos told me, and the government's measures, and the policy of the Radical–CEDA majority in the Cortes, which aimed only to undo the work of the Constituent Cortes, did not make it advisable, nor justifiable, for the Socialist Party and the UGT to launch themselves into a movement of force.

Azaña told De los Ríos categorically that it was the duty of the Socialist leadership, even at the risk of their own popularity, to make their follow-ers see that an insurrection would be madness. His reason was that 'there was no reason to expect the right to react calmly or even to limit their reaction to the re-establishment of law and order. In fact, they would abuse their victory and would go far beyond what was happening already and what they were announcing.' Shortly afterwards, De los Ríos reported Azaña's prophetic words to the PSOE executive committee. However, given the employers' intransigence, it was impossible for them to tell their rank and file to be patient.[18]

PSOE offices received reports from all over Andalusia and Extremadura about provocations from owners and Civil Guards alike. The new government appointed several conservative provincial govern-ors in the south, a move which was soon reflected in the law being flouted with impunity and an increase in the 'preventive brutality' of the Civil Guard. In El Real de la Jara, in the sierra to the north of the prov-ince of Seville, the local landowners had refused to employ union labour. A subsequent strike lasted several months and, in December 1933, some starving workers found with acorns stolen from pig troughs were savagely beaten by the Civil Guard. The Civil Governor suspended the village Mayor when he protested to the local Civil Guard commander about these abuses. In Venta de Baúl (Granada) the armed guards of the *cacique*, a member of the CEDA, beat up local union leaders.[19]

In Fuente del Maestre, Fuente de Cantos, Carmonita and Alconchel (Badajoz), it was the Civil Guard which did the beating when hungry workers were caught collecting windfall olives and acorns. Elsewhere in Badajoz, to prevent labourers being able to alleviate their hunger in this way, the owners took pigs into the fields to eat the fallen crops. Some *yunteros* (ploughmen) who had started to plough an abandoned estate were imprisoned and the Civil Guard occupied the Casa del Pueblo in nearby Hornachos. In contrast, nothing had been done about the deaths in the same town nine months earlier. In many *pueblos*, especially in Badajoz, Jaén and Córdoba, landowners ignored regulations about rotat-ing jobs among those registered at the local labour exchange. They would give work only to those who had voted for the right and systematically refused jobs to members of the FNTT. In Almendralejo, during the grape and olive harvests, despite massive local unemployment, two thousand outside labourers were brought in. In Orellana la Vieja and Olivenza, the owners employed only women and children, who were paid a fraction of the wage normally paid to men.[20]

Wages had dropped by 60 per cent. Hunger was breeding desperation and hatred was building up on both sides of the social divide. In Priego de Córdoba, a delegation of union members who had had no work for four months asked the Mayor to intervene. He replied that he could not oblige anyone to give them work and advised them to go on their knees to beg the landowners for jobs. And the problem was not confined to the south. A union official from Villanueva del Rebollar in the Castilian province of Palencia wrote, 'The *caciques* should be careful about their foolhardiness. Our patience is wearing thin.' The FNTT executive made several appeals to the new Minister of Labour, Ricardo Samper, for the implementation of existing social legislation but it was to no avail.[21]

In late December 1933, a draft law had already been presented to the Cortes for the expulsion of peasants who had occupied land in Extremadura the previous year. In January 1934, the law of municipal boundaries was provisionally repealed. The CEDA also presented projects for the emasculation of the 1932 agrarian reform, by reducing the amount of land subject to expropriation, and for the return of land confiscated from those involved in the August 1932 military rising. Clashes between the Civil Guard and the *braceros* increased daily.[22]

Throughout January, long and often bitter discussions between the PSOE and the UGT leaderships about a possible revolutionary action in defence of the Republic culminated in the defeat of the cautious line. The leadership of the UGT passed to Largo Caballero and the younger elements who supported his 'revolutionary' rhetoric. With the PSOE, its youth movement – the Federación de Juventudes Socialistas – and now the UGT all in the hands of those advocating a radical line, a joint committee was immediately established to make preparations for a revolutionary movement. PSOE, UGT and FJS organizations in each province were sent seventy-three naive instructions for the creation of militias, the acquisition of arms, the establishment of links with sympathetic members of the army and the Civil Guard and the organization of technicians to run basic services. The replies received made clear the absurdly optimistic nature of these goals and, apart from the flurry of communications generated by the committee, little or no practical action was taken.[23]

However, the various communications were anything but clandestine. Indeed, revolutionary rhetoric from the self-proclaimed 'Bolshevizers' was loudly indiscreet and provided ample evidence for right-wing exaggeration about the dangers of revolutionary socialism. The raucous radicalism of the younger Socialists would be used throughout the spring and summer of 1934 to justify harsh repression of strikes that were far from revolutionary in intent. The anything but secret plan was for the revolutionary movement to be launched in the event of the CEDA being invited to participate in government. There was no link between the vaguely discussed 'revolutionary moment' and the needs and activities of the workers' movement. Indeed, no thought was given to ways of harnessing the energies of organized labour for the projected revolution. Rather, the trade unionist habits of a lifetime saw Largo Caballero persuade the new UGT executive on 3 February to do nothing to stop any conventional strike action which was then treated by the authorities as subversive.[24]

One of the most far-reaching consequences of Largo Caballero's confused swerve to the left would be visited upon the rural proletariat. At a meeting of the national committee of the landworkers' union, the Federación Nacional de Trabajadores de la Tierra, on 30 January 1934, the moderate executive committee resigned and was replaced in its entirety by young radicals led by the representative of Navarre, Ricardo Zabalza Elorga.[25] The new secretary general Zabalza was a tall, handsome, bespectacled and rather shy thirty-six-year-old union official. He was born in Erratzu in the north of Navarre. The poverty of his family had obliged him, aged fifteen, to emigrate to Argentina. There, he had worked in appalling conditions which had impelled him to become a trade unionist. Always committed to self-education, he had managed to become a schoolteacher and eventually a headmaster. He returned to Spain in 1929. Living in Jaca in the Pyrenees, he had become an enthusiastic activist of the UGT. In 1932, he had moved to the Navarrese capital, Pamplona, where he worked hard to establish a local FNTT branch. The right in Navarre was among the most dominant and brutal of any province in Spain and had blatantly flouted Republic social and labour legislation. After the electoral victory of the right-wing coalition, in Navarre, as in the south, the local landlords refused work to union members and ignored existing social legislation.[26]

The new Radical government was impelled, both by the inclinations of its more conservative members and by its dependence on CEDA votes, to defend the interests of the landowners. Its arrival in power just as the strength of fascism was growing in Germany and Italy fostered the belief within the Socialist movement that only a revolutionary insurrection could prevent the establishment of a right-wing dictatorship. Within the FNTT, Zabalza began to advocate a general strike in order to put a stop to the employers' offensive. Older heads within the UGT were opposed to what they saw as a rash initiative which might, moreover, weaken a future rising against a possible attempt to establish an authoritarian state. Suspicion of the right's intentions had intensified with the appointment at the beginning of March of the thirty-nine-year-old Rafael Salazar Alonso as Minister of the Interior.

Salazar Alonso hastened to convene those of his subordinates responsible for public order and outline his 'anti-revolutionary' plans. The head of the Civil Guard was Brigadier General Cecilio Bedia de la Cavallería. In charge of the police and the Assault Guards was the Director General of Security, Captain José Valdivia Garci-Borrón, a crony of Alejandro Lerroux and a man of strong reactionary instincts. Valdivia reassured Salazar Alonso that they could rely implicitly on the head of the Assault Guards, the hard-line Africanista Lieutenant Colonel Agustín Muñoz Grandes, a man who would rise to be Vice-President in Franco's government. Valdivia reported equally favourably on the Civil Guard Captain Vicente Santiago Hodson, the fiercely anti-leftist head of the intelligence service founded by General Mola and a colleague of the sinister Julián Mauricio Carlavilla. To have such reactionary individuals at his command well suited Salazar Alonso's repressive ambitions.[27] Salazar Alonso made it clear to a delighted General Bedia de la Cavallería that the Civil Guard need not be inhibited in its interventions in social conflicts.[28] It was hardly surprising that, when a series of strikes by individual unions took place in the spring of 1934, Salazar Alonso seized the excuse for heavy-handed action. One after another, in the printing, construction and metallurgical industries, the strikes led at best to stalemate, and often to ignominious defeat.

The right could hardly have been more pleased with Salazar Alonzo. On 7 March he declared a state of emergency and closed down the headquarters of the Socialist Youth, the Communist Party and the anarcho-syndicalist CNT. His energy was applauded by Gil Robles, who declared that, as long as the Minister of the Interior thus defended the social order and strengthened the principle of authority, the government was assured of CEDA support. A series of articles in *El Debate* stressed that this meant severe measures against what the paper called the 'subversion' of workers who protested against wage cuts. When the CEDA press demanded the abolition of the right to strike, Lerroux's government responded by announcing that strikes with political implications would be ruthlessly suppressed. For both the right-wing press and Salazar Alonso, all strikes were deemed to be political. On 22 March *El Debate* denounced stoppages by waiters in Seville and by transport workers in Valencia as 'strikes against Spain', and called for anti-strike legislation as draconian as that of Fascist Italy, Nazi Germany and Salazar's Portugal. The government extended its repressive armoury by expanding the Civil Guard and the Assault Guard and by re-establishing the death penalty, which had been abolished in 1932.[29]

Not everyone on the right was as contented as Gil Robles. The co-creator of the fascist JONS (Juntas de Ofensiva Nacional Sindicalista), Onésimo Redondo, found comfort neither in the right's electoral success of November 1933 nor in the efforts of Salazar Alonso. In January 1934, he wrote: 'Get your weapons ready. Learn to love the metallic clunk of the pistol. Caress your dagger. Never be parted from your vengeful cudgel!' 'The young should be trained in physical struggle, must love violence as a way of life, must arm themselves with whatever they can and finish off by any means the few dozen Marxist swindlers who don't let us live.'[30]

The weakness of the JONS impelled Onésimo and Ramiro Ledesma Ramos to seek like-minded partners. This led, in mid-February 1934, to the fusion of the JONS with the Falange Española, the small fascist party led by the aristocratic José Antonio Primo de Rivera.[31] Neither Redondo nor Ledesma Ramos was bothered that, two months before its official launch on Sunday 29 October 1933, Falange Española had accepted funding from the most conservative sectors of the old patrician right. The agreement known as the Pacto de El Escorial made by José Antonio Primo de Rivera with the monarchists of Renovación Española tied the Falange to the military conspiracy against the Republic.[32] The monarchists' were ready to finance the Falange because they saw its utility as an instrument of political destabilization.

Redondo and Ledesma Ramos were probably reassured by the fact that, when recruiting started for the Falange, new militants had been required to fill in a form which asked if they had a bicycle – a euphemism for pistol – and were then issued with a truncheon. The training of the Falange militia had been placed in the hands of the veteran Africanista Lieutenant Colonel Ricardo de Rada, who was also the National Inspector of the Requeté and heavily involved in conspiracy against the Republic.[33] In his inaugural speech, José Antonio declared the new party's commitment to violence: 'if our aims have to be achieved by violence, let us not hold back before violence ... The dialectic is all very well as a first instrument of communication. But the only dialectic admissible when justice or the Fatherland is offended is the dialectic of fists and pistols.'[34] Although violence was becoming a commonplace of the politics of Spain in the 1930s, no party exceeded the Falange in its rhetoric of 'the music of pistols and the barbaric drumbeat of lead'. The representation of political assassination as a beautiful act and death in street-fighting as a glorious martyrdom was central to the funeral rituals which, in emulation of the practice of the Italian Fascist Squadristi, followed the participation of Falangists in street violence.[35]

The merger of the Falange and the JONS, under the interminable name of Falange Española de las Juntas de Ofensiva Nacional Sindicalista, was announced in Valladolid on 4 March 1934 at the Teatro Calderón. Coachloads of Falangists from Madrid and the other Castilian provinces converged on Valladolid. The local left had declared a general strike, and mounted police in the streets outside held back hostile workers. Inside the theatre, bedecked with the black and red flags of FE de las JONS, a forest of stiffly outstretched arms greeted the orators with the fascist salute. The provocative speeches delivered by Onésimo and José Antonio Primo de Rivera fired up the audience to rush out and fight the workers in the streets. Shots were fired and, at the end of the day, with many broken heads on both sides, there was one Falangist dead. Those leftists involved who could be identified would be shot by the rebels during the Civil War.[36]

Shortly after these events in Valladolid, a joint delegation of Alfonsine and Carlist monarchists would arrive in Rome on 31 March seeking financial help and weaponry for their attempts to overthrow the Republic. The delegation included Antonio Goicoechea, now head of the recently created party Renovación Española, which advocated the return of King Alfonso XIII, General Emilio Barrera, of the conspiratorial Unión Militar Española, and Antonio Lizarza Iribarren, the recruiter for the Carlist Requeté. Mussolini offered financial assistance to the tune of 1.5 million pesetas and 20,000 rifles, 20,000 hand grenades and 200 machine-guns which were delivered via Tripoli and Portugal. Arrangements were also made for several hundred Requetés (Carlist militiamen) to be trained by the Italian Army as instructors.[37] Under its newly elected leader, Manuel Fal Conde, the Carlist movement (the Comunión Tradicionalista) was creating a full-scale citizen army. For the Carlist youth organization, 'sick of legality', violence was seen as a

quintessential part of the Carlist way of life. The result of the efforts of
Rada and Colonel José Enrique Varela was that, by the spring of 1936,
the Comunión Tradicionalista could offer the military conspirators a
well-trained, well-armed force of 30,000 'red berets'. With 8,000 men in
Navarre and 22,000 in Andalusia and elsewhere, the Requeté constituted
a crucial military contribution to the rising.[38]

On 22 April 1934, the youth organization of the CEDA, the Juventud
de Acción Popular, organized a fascist-style rally at Philip II's monastery
of El Escorial, a choice of venue that was a provocatively anti-Republican
gesture. In driving sleet, 20,000 gathered in a close replica of the Nazi
rallies. They swore loyalty to Gil Robles 'our supreme chief' and chanted,
'¡Jefe! ¡Jefe! ¡Jefe!' – the Spanish equivalent of *Duce*. The JAP's nineteen-
point programme was recited, with emphasis on point two, 'our leaders
never make mistakes', a direct borrowing from the Italian Fascist slogan
'Il Duce sempre ha raggione.' Luciano de la Calzada, CEDA deputy for
Valladolid, spoke in Manichaean terms identical to those that would be
used by the Francoists during the Civil War. He asserted that 'Jews, heret-
ics, Protestants, admirers of the French revolution, Freemasons, liberals
and Marxists' were 'outside and against the Fatherland and are the
anti-Fatherland'.[39]

In April 1934, the monarchist aviator and playboy Juan Antonio
Ansaldo had joined the Falange at the invitation of José Antonio. He was
given the task of organizing terrorist squads. José Antonio particularly
wanted reprisals for left-wing attacks on the vendors of the Falange
newspaper, *F.E.* Ansaldo's efforts to arrange more violent activities by the
so-called 'Falange of Blood' were welcomed by the leaders of the JONS.
Ledesma Ramos wrote: 'His presence in the party was of undeniable
utility because he mobilized that active, violent sector which the reactionary spirit produces everywhere as one of the most fertile ingredients
for the national armed struggle. Remember what similar groups meant
for German Hitlerism especially in its early stages.' On 3 June, two thousand armed *escuadristas* gathered at Carabanchel aerodrome outside
Madrid. A bus company which had refused to take a further three
hundred to the meeting had two of its coaches destroyed by fire.[40]

In fact, the right, at this stage, had little need for a violent fascist party.
The CEDA's landed backers had achieved a great victory with the definitive repeal of the law of municipal boundaries. The position of the CEDA
had been strengthened on 25 April 1934 when Lerroux offered to resign
in protest at Alcalá Zamora's delay in signing the amnesty for those
imprisoned after the Sanjurjada. It had not occurred to Lerroux that the

President might accept his offer. When he did, Lerroux felt obliged, to avoid the possibility of Alcalá Zamora calling new elections, to give permission to Ricardo Samper to form a government. He did so in the confidence that Samper's indecisiveness would let him continue to govern from the shadows. Lerroux's support for the amnesty and the general rightwards trend of the Radical Party saw its deputy leader, Diego Martínez Barrio, leave, taking with him nineteen of its most liberal parliamentary deputies. Thus the Radical Party shifted even further to the right and was left even more dependent on Gil Robles. This made possible the repeal of the law of municipal boundaries on 23 May.[41]

Coming just before the harvest was due to start, this allowed the owners to bring in Portuguese and Galician labour to undercut the wages of local workers who already faced starvation. The last vestige of protection that left-wing landless labourers had for their jobs and their wages was that provided by the Socialist majorities on many town and village councils. Socialist mayors were the only hope that rural workers had of landowners being obliged to observe social legislation or of municipal funds being used for public works to provide some employment. When the Radicals came into power in late 1933, Lerroux's first Minister of the Interior, Manuel Rico Avello, removed thirty-five of them. Salazar Alonso began to remove many more, usually on flimsy pretexts such as 'administrative irregularities' – which often referred to debts inherited from their monarchist predecessors. As soon as he took up office, in response to petitions from local *caciques*, he ordered provincial civil governors to remove mayors who 'did not inspire confidence in matters of public order' – which usually meant Socialists. The legally elected mayor would then be replaced by a 'government delegate', usually a local conservative nominee.

Some of Salazar Alonso's most drastic interventions were in Extremadura, which was partly explained by his infatuation with the local aristocracy. In his memoirs, he admitted removing 193 southern town councils over the next six months. The procedure was that, after a denunciation of some irregularity, however small or implausible, a 'delegate' of the Civil Governor, accompanied by the Civil Guard and representatives of the local right, would expel the Socialist mayor and councillors. The majority of the 'delegates' were either *caciques* or their appointees. The idea was to put an end to a situation in which Socialist councils endeavoured to ensure the implementation of social legislation, particularly work-sharing. Once the change had taken place, the new mayors did nothing to protect workers, either from the capricious employment policies of the *caciques* or from the attacks of their retainers and the Civil Guard.[42]

Two significant cases of the removal of popular mayors in the province of Badajoz were those of José González Barrero of Zafra and Modesto José Lorenzana Macarro of Fuente de Cantos. González Barrero was a moderate Socialist, respected even by local conservatives because he owned a local hotel and served at Mass. He was widely regarded as an efficient and tolerant Mayor. However, Salazar Alonso, who well remembered their clash at Hornachos some months earlier, was determined to have him removed. Within ten days of his own appointment as Minister of the Interior, he had sent as inspector to Zafra one of his cronies, Regino Valencia, who predictably elaborated a series of charges to justify the suspension of González Barrero. The most serious was that improper methods had been used to raise funds for a road-building scheme to create work for the local unemployed. While in Zafra, Regino Valencia had admitted that the charges were flimsy and that he had been pressured by Salazar Alonso to come up with the required findings or else lose his job. The consequence was that, on 26 May 1934, the entire town council was removed and replaced by another, hand-picked and unelected. Its composition revealed the close links between the Radical Party and the landholding elite in the province. The new Mayor was an ex-member of Primo de Rivera's Unión Patriótica and looked after the considerable interests in Zafra of the Duque de Medinaceli.[43]

In Fuente de Cantos, the Socialist Mayor, Modesto José Lorenzana Macarro, was known for his humanity and for the efforts that he made to improve the town, particularly in terms of water supplies. He had used municipal funds to buy food to alleviate the hunger of the families of the unemployed. In June 1934, he was removed on the grounds of misuse of these funds.[44] As both cases showed, the intention was to diminish the protection afforded to the landless poor by Socialist town councils. The shameless illegality by which the democratic process was ignored, and the long-term consequences of giving the landowners free rein, massively intensified the festering social hatred in the southern countryside. José Lorenzana was to be murdered in September 1936. José González Barrero would be murdered in April 1939.

With tension in the countryside growing by the day, the right in most provinces used every means possible to pressurize the Civil Governor. In the provincial capitals, right-wingers, well dressed and well spoken, were able to honour the governor with lunches and dinners and, with the press on their side, were able to muster considerable influence. When that influence was converted into official acquiescence in the slashing of wages and discrimination against union labour, hungry labourers were reduced to stealing olives and other crops. Landowners and their representatives then complained loudly about anarchy in the countryside to justify the intervention of the Civil Guard. Even *El Debate* commented on the harshness of many landlords while still demanding that jobs be given only to affiliates of the Catholic unions which had emerged in the wake of the elections. To meet the twin objectives of cheap labour and the demobilization of left-wing unions, Acción Popular created Acción Obrerista in many southern towns. It was a right-wing association backed by the local owners which was thus able to hand out jobs, at well below the wage levels agreed in the wage agreements, to those prepared to renounce membership of the Socialist FNTT.[45]

The result was an intensification of hardship and hatred. In Badajoz, starving labourers were begging in the streets of the towns. Rickets and tuberculosis were common. The monarchist expert on agrarian matters, the Vizconde de Eza, said that in May 1934 over 150,000 families lacked even the bare necessities of life. Workers who refused to rip up their union cards were denied work. The owners' boycott of unionized labour was designed to reassert pre-1931 forms of social control and to ensure that the Republican–Socialist challenge to the system should never be repeated. In villages like Hornachos, this determination had been revealed by physical assaults on the Casa del Pueblo. A typical incident took place at Puebla de Don Fadrique, near Huéscar in the province of Granada. The Socialist Mayor was replaced by a retired army officer who was determined to put an end to what he saw as the workers' indiscipline. He surrounded the Casa del Pueblo with a detachment of Civil Guard, and as the workers filed out they were beaten by the Guards and by retainers of the local owners.[46]

The response of the FNTT was an illuminating example of how the newly revolutionized Socialists were reacting to increased aggression from the employers. The FNTT newspaper, *El Obrero de la Tierra*, had adopted a revolutionary line after the removal on 28 January 1934 of the union's moderate executive. The paper asserted that the only solution to the misery of the rural working class was the socialization of the land. In the meantime, however, the new executive adopted practical policies every bit as conciliatory as those of their predecessors. The FNTT sent to the Ministers of Labour, Agriculture and the Interior a series of reasoned appeals for the application of the law regarding obligatory cultivation, work agreements, strict job rotation and labour exchanges, as well as protests at the systematic closures of the Casas del Pueblo. That was in the third week of March. When no response was received, and, indeed, the persecution of left-wing workers began to increase prior to the harvest, a respectful appeal was made to Alcalá Zamora – also to no avail. The FNTT declared that thousands were slowly dying of hunger and published long, detailed lists of villages where union members were being refused work and physically attacked. In the province of Badajoz, the FNTT calculated that there were 20,000 workers unemployed and that they and their families were dying of starvation. There were five hundred union members in prison.[47]

Finally, in a mood of acute exasperation, the FNTT reluctantly decided on a strike. The first announcement of a possible strike was accompanied by an appeal to the authorities to impose respect for the work agreements and for equitable work-sharing.[48] The UGT executive committee advised the FNTT against calling a general strike of the peasantry for three reasons. In the first place, the harvest was ready at different times in each area, so any single date for the strike would lead to problems of co-ordination. Secondly, a general strike, as opposed to one limited to large estates, would cause hardship to leaseholders and sharecroppers who needed to hire one or two workers. Thirdly, there was concern that the provocative actions of the owners and the Civil Guard could push the peasants into violent confrontations which they could only lose. At a series of joint meetings throughout March and April, the UGT executive tried to persuade the FNTT leadership to move to a narrower strategy of staggered, partial strikes. The UGT pointed out that a nationwide peasant strike would be denounced by the government as revolutionary and risked a terrible repression, and Largo Caballero made it clear that there would be no solidarity strikes from industrial workers.[49]

The FNTT leadership was caught between two fires. Zabalza and his comrades were fully aware of the dangers but they were under extreme pressure from a hungry rank and file pushed beyond endurance by the constant provocation of *caciques* and Civil Guard. For example, at Fuente del Maestre in Badajoz, union members returning from celebrating May Day in the country were singing the 'Internationale' and shouting revolutionary slogans. When stones were thrown at the houses of the richer landowners, the Civil Guard opened fire, killing four workers and wounding several more. A further forty were imprisoned.[50] In the province of Toledo, FNTT affiliates found it almost impossible to get work.

Those who did find a job had to accept the most grinding conditions. The agreement on wages and conditions had decreed 4.50 pesetas for an eight-hour day. The owners were in fact paying 2.50 pesetas for sun-up to sun-down working. In parts of Salamanca, wages of 75 céntimos were being paid.[51]

The desperation of the hungry workers in the face of what they saw as the stony-hearted arrogance of the landowners led to minor acts of vandalism. The throwing of stones at landowners' clubs (*casinos*) in several villages was redolent of impotent frustration. It came as no surprise when the FNTT executive told the UGT that it could no longer resist their rank and file's demand for action and could not just abandon them to hunger wages, political persecution and lock-out. As *El Obrero de la Tierra* declared, 'All of Spain is becoming Casas Viejas.' On 28 April, the FNTT had appealed to the Minister of Labour to remedy the situation simply by enforcing the existing laws. When nothing was done, the FNTT national committee decided on 12 May to call strike action from 5 June. The strike declaration was made in strict accordance with the law, ten days' notice being given. The manifesto pointed out that 'this extreme measure' was the culmination of a series of useless negotiations to persuade the relevant ministries to apply the surviving social legislation. Hundreds of appeals for the payment of the previous year's harvest wages lay unheard at the Ministry of Labour. All over Spain, the work conditions agreed by the mixed juries were simply being ignored and protests were repressed by the Civil Guard.[52]

The preparation of the strike had been legal and open and its ten objectives were hardly revolutionary. There were two basic aims: to secure an improvement of the brutal conditions being suffered by rural labourers and to protect unionized labour from the employers' determination to destroy the rural unions. The ten demands were (1) application of the work agreements; (2) strict work rotation irrespective of political affiliation; (3) limitation on the use of machinery and outside labour, to ensure forty days' work for the labourers of each province; (4) immediate measures against unemployment; (5) temporary take-over of land scheduled for expropriation by the Institute of Agrarian Reform, the technical body responsible for the implementation of the 1932 agrarian reform bill, so that it could be rented to the unemployed; (6) application of the law of collective leases; (7) recognition of the right of workers under the law of obligatory cultivation to work abandoned land; (8) the settlement before the autumn of those peasants for whom the Institute of Agrarian Reform had land available; (9) the creation of a credit fund to help the collective leaseholdings; and (10) the recovery of the common lands privatized by legal chicanery in the nineteenth century. The FNTT leader Ricardo Zabalza was hoping that the threat of strikes would be sufficient to oblige the government to do something to remedy the situation of mass hunger in the southern countryside. Certainly, the prospect of a strike led the Minister of Labour to make token gestures, calling on the mixed juries to elaborate work contracts and on government labour delegates to report the employers' abuses of the law. Negotiations were also started with FNTT representatives.[53]

Salazar Alonso, however, was determined not to lose his chance to aim a deadly blow at the largest section of the UGT. In his meetings with the head of the Civil Guard General Cecilio Bedia and the Director General of Security Captain Valdivia, he had started to make specific plans for the repression of such a strike.[54] Accordingly, just as Zabalza's hopes of compromise negotiations between the FNTT and the Ministers of Agriculture and Labour were coming to fruition, Salazar Alonso issued a decree criminalizing the actions of the FNTT by declaring the harvest a national public service and the strike a 'revolutionary conflict'. All meetings, demonstrations and propaganda connected with the strike were declared illegal. Draconian press censorship was imposed. *El Obrero de la Tierra* was closed down, not to reopen until 1936. In the Cortes debate on Salazar Alonso's tough line, the CEDA votes, along with those of the Radicals and the monarchists, ensured a majority for the Minister of the Interior. Nevertheless, the points raised in the debate starkly illuminated the issues at stake.

José Prat García, PSOE deputy for Albacete, in a reasoned speech to the Cortes, pointed out the anti-constitutional nature of Salazar Alonso's measures. He reiterated that the FNTT had followed due legal process in declaring its strike. The application of existing legislation would have been sufficient to solve the conflict, claimed Prat, but Salazar Alfonso had rejected a peaceful solution and resorted to repression. The Minister replied aggressively that, because the FNTT's objective was to force the government to take action, the strike was subversive. When he stated, falsely, that the government was taking steps against owners who imposed hunger wages, José Prat replied that, on the contrary, he had frustrated all attempts at conciliation, by overruling the negotiations between the FNTT and the Ministers of Labour and Agriculture. Prat concluded by stating that the strike aimed only to protect the rural labourers and to end situations such as that in Guadix (Granada) that had reduced workers to eating grass. José Antonio Trabal Sanz, of the

Catalan Republican Left, declared that Salazar Alonso seemed to regard the wishes of the plutocracy and the national interest as synonymous. Cayetano Bolivar, Communist deputy for Málaga, claimed that the government's provocation was closing the doors of legality and pushing the workers to revolution. When Bolivar mentioned the workers' hunger, a right-wing deputy shouted that he and the rest of the majority were also hungry and the debate ended.[55]

As his early preparations made with Bedia and Valdivia revealed, conciliation had not been uppermost in Salazar Alonso's mind. His measures were now swift and ruthless to weaken the left in advance of the conflict. Workers' leaders were rounded up before the strike had started. Other liberal and left-wing individuals in the country districts were arrested wholesale. On 31 May, José González Barrero, the recently removed Mayor of Zafra, was arrested on trumped-up charges. The Mayors of Olivenza and Llerena, also in Badajoz, were likewise arrested, as were numerous union officials, schoolteachers and lawyers, some of whom were beaten or tortured. Salazar Alonso had effectively militarized the landworkers when he had declared the harvest a national public service. Strikers were thus mutineers and were arrested in their thousands. Even four Socialist deputies, including Cayetano Bolívar, visiting prisoners in Jaén, were detained – in violation of the Constitution.[56]

In the prison of Badajoz, with a normal capacity of eighty prisoners, six hundred were held in appalling conditions. There was similar overcrowding in the prisons of Almendralejo, Don Benito and other towns in the province. In addition to those arrested, several thousand peasants were simply loaded at gunpoint on to cattle trucks and deported hundreds of miles away from their homes and then left to make their own way back penniless and on foot. On 4 July, two hundred starving peasants from Badajoz who had been imprisoned in Burgos reached Madrid and congregated in the Puerta del Sol where they were violently dispersed by the police. The FNTT paid for them to return home, where many were rearrested.[57]

Workers' centres were closed down and many town councils, especially in Badajoz and Cáceres, were removed, and the Mayor and councillors replaced by government nominees. The strike seems to have been almost complete in Jaén, Granada, Ciudad Real, Badajoz and Cáceres, and substantial elsewhere in the south. In Jaén and Badajoz, there were violent clashes in many villages between strikers and the permanent workers, the armed guards of the large estates and the Civil Guard. However, neither there nor in other less conflictive provinces could the strikers stop the owners drafting in outside labour, with Civil Guard protection, from Portugal, Galicia and elsewhere. The army was brought in to use threshing machines and the harvest was collected without serious interruption. The CNT did not join in the strike, which limited its impact in Seville and Córdoba although that did not protect anarchist workers from the subsequent repression. Although most of the labourers arrested on charges of sedition were released by the end of August, emergency courts sentenced prominent workers' leaders, including González Barrero, to four or more years of imprisonment.[58]

The Casas del Pueblo were not reopened and the FNTT was effectively crippled until 1936. In an uneven battle, the FNTT had suffered a terrible defeat. In several provinces, the remaining Socialist town councils were overturned and replaced by the *caciques'* nominees. In Granada, the Civil Governor was removed at the behest of local landowners because he had made an effort to ensure that the remaining labour legislation was implemented after the strike.[59] In the Spanish countryside, the clock had effectively been put back to the 1920s by Salazar Alonso. There were no longer any rural unions, social legislation or municipal authorities to challenge the dominance of the *caciques*. The CEDA was delighted.[60]

By choosing to regard a strike of limited material objectives as revolutionary, Salazar Alonso was able to justify his attack on Socialist councils. As has already been noted, he claimed that, by the end of the conflict, he had removed only 193 of them. However, the real figures were much higher. In Granada alone, during the period that the Radicals were in power, 127 were removed. In Badajoz, the figure was nearer 150.[61] By his aggressively brutal action during the peasant strike, the Minister of the Interior had inflicted a terrible blow on the largest union within the UGT and left a festering legacy of hatred in the south. Local landowners were quick to reimpose more or less feudal conditions on workers whom they regarded as serfs. Wages were slashed and work given only to non-union workers regarded as 'loyal'.

Shortly after entering the Ministry of the Interior, Salazar Alonso had crushed strikes in the metal, building and newspaper industries on the grounds that they were political. He had done so despite pleas from labour leaders that all these disputes had social and economic origins and were not meant to be revolutionary.[62] In the summer of 1934, he had managed to escalate the harvest strike and smash the FNTT. Despite his success, Salazar Alonso was still some way from his long-term goal of destroying any and all elements that he considered to be a challenge to the government.

This was clear from a letter that he wrote to his lover Amparo at the end of July:

> You can imagine what I'm going through. It could be said that this is the beginning of a revolutionary movement much more serious than the more frivolous might think. Conscious of the enormous responsibilities I bear, I am totally dedicated to the task of crushing it. It's true that the campaign against me is building up. There are wall slogans saying 'Salazar Alonso just like Dollfuss' [the Austrian Chancellor who had repressed a revolutionary strike in Vienna in February]. The extremist press attacks and insults me, calls for me to be assassinated. I'm calmer than ever. I work ceaselessly. I'm organizing things. Today I had meetings with the Chief of Police, the Director General of Security, the head of the Assault Guard, and the Inspector General of the Civil Guard. I'm preparing everything carefully, technically just like the officer in charge of a General Staff. Needless to say, I don't sleep. Even in bed I continue to plan my anti-revolutionary organization. Public opinion is turning in my favour. People believe in me, they turn to my puny figure and they see the man of providence who can save them.[63]

Salazar Alonso referred to Amparo as his muse and to himself as the chieftain, using the word later adopted by Franco, 'Caudillo'. He painted for her the self-portrait of a brilliant general about to go into battle against a powerful enemy. However, the nearest that Largo Caballero's PSOE–UGT–FJS liaison committee had come to creating militias was to make a file-card index of the names of men who might be prepared to 'take to the streets'. The lack of central co-ordination was demonstrated by Largo Caballero's acquiescence in the erosion of the trade union movement's strength in one disastrous strike after another. Young Socialists took part in Sunday excursions to practise military manoeuvres in the park outside Madrid, the Casa del Campo, armed with more enthusiasm than weapons, activities easily controlled by the police. Desultory forays into the arms market had seen the Socialists lose their scarce funds to unscrupulous arms-dealers and had produced only a few guns. The police were fully informed about the purchases, either by spies or by the arms-dealers themselves, and often arrived at Casas del Pueblo and Socialists' homes with precise information about weapons hidden behind false walls, under floorboards or in wells. The one attempt at a major arms purchase, carried out by Indalecio Prieto, was a farcical failure. Only in the northern mining region of Asturias, where small arms were pilfered from local factories and dynamite from the mines, did the working class have significant weaponry.[64]

On 10 June, while the peasants' strike was taking place in the south, Ansaldo's Falangist terror squads were involved in violent incidents in Madrid. They attacked a Sunday excursion of the Socialist Youth in El Pardo outside the capital. In the subsequent fight, a young Falangist was killed. Without waiting for authorization from José Antonio, Ansaldo requisitioned the car of Alfonso Merry del Val and set off to retaliate. Opening fire on other young Socialists returning to Madrid, they killed Juanita Rico and seriously wounded two others.[65] Margarita Nelken accused Salazar Alonso of covering up the Juanita Rico murder, and that of another Socialist, in the knowledge that they were carried out by Falangist terror squads.[66] Throughout the summer, Ansaldo was planning to blow up the Socialist headquarters in Madrid. Fifty kilos of dynamite was stolen and a tunnel dug from the sewers into the basement of the Casa del Pueblo. Ansaldo's men murdered one of their squad suspected of being a police informer. Before the explosive device was ready, on 10 July, the police discovered large quantities of guns, ammunition, dynamite and bombs at the Falange headquarters. Eighty militants, mainly Jonsistas and Ansaldo's men, were detained, but only for three weeks.[67] Although José Antonio formally expelled Ansaldo in July, the hit squads continued to carry out reprisals against the left with equal frequency and efficiency. In fact, Ansaldo went on working with them.

For Gil Robles and Salazar Alonso, the adventurism of the Falange was an irrelevance. The Socialists' empty revolutionary threat had played neatly into their hands. Their readiness to take advantage of that rhetoric to alter the balance of power in favour of the right had been illustrated brutally during the printers' and landworkers' strikes. Gil Robles knew that the leadership of the Socialist movement, dominated by followers of Largo Caballero, had linked its threats of revolution specifically to the entry of the CEDA into the cabinet. He also knew that, thanks to Salazar Alonso, the left was in no position to succeed in a revolutionary attempt. Constant police activity throughout the summer dismantled most of the uncoordinated preparations made by the revolutionary committee and seized most of the weapons that the left had managed to acquire. Gil Robles admitted later that he was keen to enter the government because of, rather than in spite of, the reaction that could be expected from the Socialists: 'Sooner or later, we would have to face a revolutionary coup. It would always be preferable to face it from a position of power before the enemy were better prepared.'[68]

A linked element of Gil Robles's strategy in the late summer of 1934 was the expansion of the militia of the Juventud de Acción Popular under the banner of 'civilian mobilization'. Essentially, with the forthcoming revolutionary showdown in mind, its purpose was strike-breaking and the guaranteeing of essential public services.[69] The man he chose to organize the 'civilian mobilization' and to train the paramilitary units was Lisardo Doval, the Civil Guard officer expelled from the service for his part in the Sanjurjo coup attempt of August 1932.[70]

During the summer of 1934, political tension was heightened by a conflict over Catalonia which was skilfully manipulated by Gil Robles in such a way as to provoke the left. The right deeply resented the Republic's granting of regional autonomy to Catalonia in 1932. This was reflected in the decision of the Tribunal of Constitutional Guarantees on 8 June to overrule a measure by the Catalan parliament to lengthen leases for smallholders. This delighted big landowners in Catalonia and elsewhere. Presenting the law unchanged to the parliament on 12 June, the President of the Generalitat (the Catalan regional government), Lluís Companys, described the Tribunal's decision as yet another centralist attempt to reduce the region's autonomy by 'the lackeys of the Monarchy and of the monarchist-fascist hordes'.[71]

Salazar Alonso opposed those in the cabinet who favoured a compromise solution. Both the Left Republicans and many Socialists regarded Catalonia as the last remaining outpost of the 'authentic' Republic. The anti-Catalan statements being uttered by the CEDA left little doubt that Catalan autonomy would be under threat if the CEDA joined the government. Gil Robles spoke provocatively at an assembly organized by the Catalan landowners' federation in Madrid on 8 September. The assembly, like others held by the CEDA's agrarian financiers, argued for a restriction of union rights, the strengthening of the forces of authority and, more specifically, the crushing of the Generalitat's 'rebellion'.[72]

On the following day, the Juventud de Acción Popular held a fascist-style rally at Covadonga in Asturias, the site of the battle in 722 considered to be the starting point for the long campaign to reconquer Spain from the Moors. The choice of venue symbolically associated the right-wing cause with the values of traditional Spain and identified the working class with the Moorish invaders. Local Socialists declared a general strike and tried to block the roads to Covadonga, but the Civil Guard ensured that the rally went ahead as planned. The leader of the Asturian branch of Acción Popular, the retired army officer José María Fernández Ladreda, cited the reconquest of Spain as he introduced Gil Robles, who spoke belligerently of the need to crush the 'separatist rebellion' of the Catalans and the Basque nationalists.[73] The wily Gil Robles knew only too well that such language, threatening key achievements of the Republican–Socialist coalition of 1931–3, would confirm the left in its determination to prevent the CEDA coming to power.

Salazar Alonso knew, as did Gil Robles, that the entry of the CEDA into the government was the detonator that would set off the Socialists' revolutionary action and justify a definitive blow against them. On 11 September, at a deeply conflictive cabinet meeting, Salazar Alonso proposed a declaration of martial law precisely in order to provoke a premature outbreak of a revolutionary strike. Both the Prime Minister, Ricardo Samper, and the Minister of Agriculture, Cirilo del Río Rodríguez, protested at such irresponsible cynicism. The Minister of War, Diego Hidalgo, called for Salazar Alonso's resignation.

Later that evening, Salazar Alonso wrote once more to his lover Amparo recounting what had happened earlier in the day. He made it clear that he thought the CEDA should join the government and that his objective was to provoke a reaction by the left precisely in order to smash it.

> I explained the revolutionaries' plan. I examined the Catalan question, pointing out objectively and honestly all the circumstances, the possibilities and the consequences of our decisions ... The situation is serious. I couldn't permit any action that was thoughtless or not properly prepared. I had to consider what was necessary to justify declaring martial law ... The Government, opposed by the revolutionary left, lacks the backing of the parliamentary group [the CEDA] on whose votes it relies ... Was this the Government with the authority to provoke the definitive revolutionary movement?[74]

In his published account of his role, Salazar Alonso wrote: 'The problem was no less than that of starting the counter-revolutionary offensive to proceed with a work of decisive government to put an end to the evil.' He aimed not just to smash the immediate revolutionary bid but to ensure that the left did not rise again.[75]

Not long afterwards, Gil Robles admitted that he was aware of and indeed shared Salazar Alonso's provocative intentions. He knew that the Socialists were committed to reacting violently to what they believed would be an attempt to establish a Dollfuss-type regime. He too was fully aware that the chances of revolutionary success were remote.

Speaking in the Acción Popular offices in December, he recalled complacently:

> I was sure that our arrival in the government would immediately provoke a revolutionary movement … and when I considered that blood which was going to be shed, I asked myself this question: 'I can give Spain three months of apparent tranquillity if I do not enter the government. If we enter, will the revolution break out? Better let that happen before it is well prepared, before it can defeat us.' This is what Acción Popular did: precipitated the movement, confronted it and implacably smashed the revolution within the power of the government.[76]

The Minister of War, Diego Hidalgo, eventually came around to the point of view of Gil Robles and Salazar Alonso. At the end of September, he organized large-scale army manoeuvres in León, in an area contiguous, and of similar terrain, to Asturias, where he suspected the revolutionary bid would take place.[77] When the cabinet discussed cancelling the manoeuvres, Hidalgo argued that they were necessary precisely because of the imminent revolutionary threat. Certainly, once the revolutionary strike did break out in Asturias in early October, the astonishing speed with which the Spanish Foreign Legion was transported from Africa to Asturias suggests some prior consideration of the problem. As Hidalgo later admitted in the Cortes, three days before the manoeuvres started, he had ordered the Regiment No. 3 from Oviedo not to take part and to remain in the Asturian capital because he expected a revolutionary outbreak.[78] In any case, Gil Robles had secured confidential assurances from senior military figures that the army could crush any leftist uprising provoked by CEDA entry into the cabinet.[79]

On 26 September, Gil Robles made his move with a communiqué stating that, in view of the present cabinet's 'weakness' regarding social problems, and irrespective of the consequences, a strong government with CEDA participation had to be formed. In a sinuous speech in the Cortes on 1 October, claiming to be motivated by a desire for national stability he introduced an unmistakable threat: 'we are conscious of our strength both here and elsewhere'. After the inevitable resignation of the cabinet, President Alcalá Zamora entrusted Lerroux with the task of forming a government, acknowledging the inevitability of CEDA participation, but hoping that it would be limited to one ministry. Gil Robles insisted on three in the knowledge that this would incite Socialist outrage.[80]

Gil Robles's provocation was carefully calibrated. His three choices for the cabinet announced on 4 October were José Oriol y Anguera de Sojo (Labour), Rafael Aizpún (Justice) and Manuel Giménez Fernández (Agriculture). Anguera de Sojo was an integrist Catholic (his mother was being considered by the Vatican for canonization), an expert on canon law and lawyer for the Benedictine Monastery of Montserrat. He had been the public prosecutor responsible for a hundred confiscations and numerous fines suffered by *El Socialista*. Moreover, as a Catalan rightist, he was a bitter enemy of the Esquerra Republicana de Catalunya, the ruling party in the Generalitat. As a hard-line civil governor of Barcelona in 1931, his uncompromising strike-breaking policies had accelerated the CNT move to insurrectionism. The choice of Anguera could hardly have been more offensive. The Esquerra sent a deputation to see Alcalá Zamora and plead for his exclusion. Gil Robles refused point-blank the President's suggestions.[81] Aizpún, CEDA deputy for Pamplona, was close to the Carlists. Giménez Fernández, as deputy for Badajoz, was inevitably assumed to be as faithful a representative of the aggressive landlords of that province as Salazar Alonso had been and likely, as Minister of Agriculture, to intensify the awful repression that had followed the harvest strike. The suppositions about the Minister were wrong, since he was a moderate Christian Democrat, but those about the Badajoz landlords were right. Because of his relatively liberal policies, Giménez Fernández was rejected as a candidate for Badajoz in the 1936 elections and was forced to run in Segovia.[82]

The Socialists had every reason to fear that the new cabinet would implement Salazar Alonso's determination to impose reactionary rule. After all, on 222 of the 315 days of Radical government until the end of July, the country had been declared to be in a state of emergency, which meant the suspension of constitutional guarantees. Sixty of the ninety-three days on which there was constitutional normality had been during the electoral period of late 1933. Press censorship, fines and seizures of newspapers, limitation of the freedom of association, declaration of the illegality of almost all strikes, protection for fascist and monarchist activities, reduction of wages and the removal of freely elected Socialist town councils were seen as the establishment of a 'regime of white terror'. These were the policies that Gil Robles, in his speech of 1 October, had denounced as weak. It was impossible to avoid the conclusion that he intended to impose more repressive ones.[83]

In the last few days of September, still hoping to persuade the President to resolve the crisis by calling elections, the Socialist press had resorted to desperate – and empty – threats. *El Socialista* implied that preparation for the revolutionary action was well advanced: 'We have our army waiting to be mobilized, and our international plans and our plans for socialism.'[84] At the end of the month, the paper's editorial asked rhetorically: 'Will it be necessary for us to say now, stating the obvious, that any backward step, any attempt to return to outmoded policies will inevitably face the resistance of the Socialists?'[85] Clearly, Julián Zugazagoitia, the thoughtful director of *El Socialista*, knew full well that the Socialist movement was utterly unprepared for a revolutionary confrontation with the state. If his editorials were not senseless irresponsibility – and Zugazagoitia, a faithful supporter of Prieto, was no extremist – they have to be seen as a last-ditch threat to the President.

Largo Caballero's revolutionary committee made no preparations for the seizure of power and the 'revolutionary militias' had neither national leadership nor local organization. He placed his hopes on revolutionary bluster ensuring that Alcalá Zamora would not invite the CEDA into the government. Just before midnight on 3 October, when news reached the committee that a government was being formed with CEDA participation, Largo Caballero refused to believe it and ordered that no action be taken to start the movement. Even once the truth of the news could no longer be ignored, only with the greatest reluctance did he accept that there was no choice and the threatened revolution had to be launched.[86]

Throughout 1934, the leaders of the PSOE and the CEDA had engaged in a war of manoeuvre. Gil Robles, with the support of Salazar Alonso, had enjoyed the stronger position and he had exploited it with skill and patience. The Socialists were forced by their relative weakness to resort to vacuous threats of revolution and were finally manoeuvred into a position in which they had to implement them. The results were catastrophic.

After defeat in strike after strike in the first nine months of 1934, Socialist intentions in the events that began on the morning of 4 October 1934 were necessarily limited. The objective was to defend the concept of the Republic developed between 1931 and 1933 against the authoritarian ambitions of the CEDA. The entry of the CEDA into the cabinet was followed by the existence for ten hours of an independent Catalan Republic; a desultory general strike in Madrid; and the establishment of a workers' commune in Asturias. With the exception of the Asturian revolt, which held out against the armed forces during two weeks of fierce fighting and owed its 'success' to the mountainous terrain and the special skills of the miners, the keynote of the Spanish October was its half-heartedness. There is nothing about the events of that month, even those in Asturias, to suggest that the left had thoroughly prepared a rising. In fact, throughout the crisis, Socialist leaders were to be found restraining the revolutionary zeal of their followers.[87]

To allow the President time to change his mind, on 4 October the UGT leadership gave the government twenty-four hours' notice of a peaceful general strike in Madrid. Anarchist and Trotskyist offers of participation in a revolutionary bid were brusquely rebuffed. Accordingly, the new government was able with considerable ease to arrest workers' leaders and detain suspect members of the police and the army. Without instructions to the contrary, Socialist and anarchist trade unionists in Madrid simply stayed away from work rather than mounting any show of force in the streets. The army took over basic services – conscripts were classified according to their peacetime occupations – and bakeries, right-wing newspapers and public transport were able to function with near normality. Those Socialist leaders who managed to avoid arrest either went into hiding, as did Largo Caballero, or went into exile, as did Prieto. Their followers were left standing on street corners awaiting instructions and within a week the strike had petered out. All the talk of a seizure of power by revolutionary militias came to nothing. Hopes of collaboration by sympathizers in the army did not materialize and the few militants with arms quickly abandoned them. In the capital, some scattered sniper fire and many arrests were the sum total of the revolutionary war unleashed.[88]

In Catalonia, where anarchists and other left-wing groups collaborated with the Socialists in the Workers' Alliance, events were rather more dramatic. Many of the local committees took over their villages and then waited for instructions from Barcelona, which never came.[89] In the Catalan capital, ill prepared and reluctant, Companys proclaimed an independent state of Catalonia 'within the Federal Republic of Spain' in protest against what was seen as the betrayal of the Republic. The motives behind his heroic gesture were complex and contradictory. He was certainly alarmed by developments in Madrid. He was also being pressured by extreme Catalan nationalists to meet popular demand for action against the central government. At the same time, he wanted to forestall revolution. Accordingly, he did not mobilize the Generalitat's own forces against General Domingo Batet, the commander of military forces in Catalonia. The working class had also been denied arms. Accordingly, Batet, after trundling artillery through the narrow streets, was able to negotiate the surrender of the Generalitat after only ten hours of independence, in the early hours of 7 October.[90] The right in general, and Franco in particular, never forgave Batet for failing to make a bloody example of the Catalans.[91]

Asturias was a different matter. Once the news of the CEDA entry into the government reached the mining valleys in the late afternoon of 4 October, the rank-and-file workers took the lead. There, the solidarity of the miners had overcome partisan differences and the UGT, the CNT and, to a much lesser degree, the Communist Party were united in the Workers' Alliance. It is illustrative of the fact that Socialist leaders had never really contemplated revolutionary action that, even in Asturias, the movement did not start in the stronghold of the party bureaucracy, at Oviedo, but was imposed upon it by outlying areas – Mieres, Sama de Langreo and Pola de Lena. Similarly, in the Basque country, the workers seized power only in small towns like Eibar and Mondragón. Mondragón was an exception, but in Bilbao and the rest of the region rank-and-file militants waited in vain for instructions from their leaders. Throughout the insurrection, the president of the Asturian mineworkers' union, Amador Fernández, remained in Madrid, and on 14 October, without the knowledge of the rank and file, tried to negotiate a peaceful surrender.[92]

The uncertainty demonstrated by the Socialist leadership was in dramatic contrast to the determination of Gil Robles. Indeed, his behaviour, both during and immediately after the October revolt, sustained his later admission that he had deliberately provoked the left. While Socialist hesitation on 5 October suggested a quest for compromise, the new Radical–CEDA government manifested no desire for conciliation and only a determination to crush the left. Gil Robles made it clear at a meeting with his three ministers that he had no faith in either the Chief of the General Staff, General Carlos Masquelet, whom he regarded as a dangerous liberal, or General Eduardo López Ochoa, who was put in charge of restoring order in Asturias. At the cabinet meeting on 6 October, however, their proposal to send Franco to take over operations in Asturias was overruled and the views of Alcalá Zamora, Lerroux and his more liberal cabinet colleagues prevailed.[93] However, in the event Franco was able to play a role that ensured that the rebellion would be repressed with considerable savagery.

Gil Robles demanded the harshest policy possible against the rebels. On 9 October, he rose in the Cortes to express his support for the government and to make the helpful suggestion that parliament be closed until the repression was over. Thus the anticipated crushing of the revolution would take place in silence. No questions could be asked in the Cortes and censorship was total for the left-wing press, although the right-wing newspapers were full of gruesome tales – never substantiated – of leftist barbarism. The new Minister of Agriculture, Manuel Giménez Fernández, one of the few sincere social Catholics within the CEDA, struck a dissident note when he told the staff of his Ministry on 12 October, 'the disturbances which have taken place against the state have not started on the rebels' side of the street but on ours, because the state itself has created many enemies by consistently neglecting its duties to all citizens'.[94] The violence on both sides during the events of October and the brutal persecution unleashed in the wake of the left-wing defeat would deepen existing social hatreds beyond anything previously imagined.

Initially, because of Franco's reputation as a ferocious Africanista, President Alcalá Zamora rejected the proposal to put him formally in command of troops in Asturias. Nevertheless, the Minister of War, the Radical Diego Hidalgo, insisted and gave Franco informal control of operations, naming him his 'personal technical adviser', marginalizing his own General Staff and slavishly signing the orders drawn up by him.[95] The Minister's decision was highly irregular but understandable. Franco had detailed knowledge of Asturias, its geography, communications and military organization. He had been stationed there, had taken part in the suppression of the general strike of 1917 and had been a regular visitor since his marriage to an Asturian woman, Carmen Polo. To the delight of the Spanish right, and as Alcalá Zamora had feared, Franco responded to the miners in Asturias as if he were dealing with the recalcitrant tribesmen of Morocco.

Franco's approach to the events of Asturias was coloured by his conviction, fed by the regular bulletins he received from the Entente Anticommuniste of Geneva, that the workers' uprising had been 'carefully prepared by the agents of Moscow' and that the Socialists, 'with technical instructions from the Communists, thought they were going to be able to install a dictatorship'.[96] That belief justified for Franco and for many on the extreme right the use of troops against Spanish civilians as if they were a foreign enemy.

With a small command unit set up in the telegraph room of the Ministry of War in Madrid, Franco controlled the movement of the troops, ships and trains to be used in the suppression of the revolution.[97] Uninhibited by the humanitarian considerations which made some of the more liberal senior officers hesitate to use the full weight of the armed forces against civilians, Franco regarded the problem with the same icy ruthlessness that had underpinned his successes in the colonial wars. One of his first decisions was to order the bombing and artillery shelling of the working-class districts of the mining towns. Unmoved by the fact that the central symbol of rightist values was the reconquest of Spain from the Moors, he shipped Moroccan mercenaries to Asturias, the only part of Spain where the crescent had never flown. He saw no contradiction about using them because he regarded left-wing workers with the same racist contempt which had underlain his use of locally recruited mercenary troops, the Regulares Indígenas, against the Rif tribesmen. Visiting Oviedo after the rebellion had been defeated, he spoke to a journalist in terms that echoed the sentiments of Onésimo Redondo: 'This war is a frontier war and its fronts are socialism, communism and whatever attacks civilization in order to replace it with barbarism.'[98] Without apparent irony, despite Franco's use in the north of colonial forces, the right-wing press portrayed the Asturian miners as puppets of a foreign, Jewish–Bolshevik conspiracy.[99]

The methods used by the colonial army, just as in Morocco, were aimed at paralysing the civilian enemy by terror. The African Army unleashed a wave of brutality that had more to do with their normal practice when entering Moroccan villages than any threat from the defeated Asturian rebels. The troops used left-wing prisoners as human shields to cover their advances. Innocent men, women and children were shot at random by the Moroccan units under the command of Franco's crony, Lieutenant Colonel Juan Yagüe Blanco. This contributed to the demoralization of the poorly armed revolutionaries. More than fifty male and female prisoners, many of them wounded, were interrogated and immediately shot in the yard of Oviedo's main hospital and their bodies burned in the crematorium oven. Several more were executed without trial in the Pelayo barracks. Other prisoners were tortured and women raped. In the mining village of Carbayín, twenty bodies were buried to hide evidence of torture. Houses and shops were looted of watches, jewellery and clothing, while anything not portable was smashed.[100]

The behaviour of the colonial units provoked serious friction between General López Ochoa, on the one hand, and Franco and Yagüe, on the other. The austere López Ochoa had been placed in operational command of the forces in Asturias. He believed, rightly, that for Franco (below him in seniority) to have been placed in overall charge of the suppression of the rebellions of 1934 was improper, since its only basis was his friendship with Diego Hidalgo. Franco, Yagüe and many on the right were concerned that López Ochoa, as a Republican and a Freemason, would try to put down the rising with as little bloodshed as possible. Their suspicions were justified. Although he condoned the use of trucks of prisoners as a cover for his advances, López Ochoa did, in the main, conduct his operations with moderation. Yagüe sent an emissary to Madrid to complain to both Franco and Gil Robles about his humanitarian treatment of the miners. All three were infuriated by López Ochoa's pact with the miners' leader Belarmino Tomás, holding back the Legionarios and Regulares to permit an orderly and bloodless surrender.[101] Franco's mistrust of López Ochoa was matched by his confidence in Yagüe and his approval for the summary executions following the captures of Gijón and Oviedo.[102]

On one occasion, Yagüe threatened López Ochoa with a pistol.[103] Some months later, López Ochoa spoke with Juan-Simeón Vidarte, the deputy secretary general of the PSOE, about his problems in restraining the murderous activities of the Foreign Legion:

One night, the legionarios took twenty-seven workers from the jail at Sama. They shot only three or four because, as the shots echoed in the mountains, they were afraid that guerrillas would appear. So, to avoid the danger, they acted even more cruelly, decapitating or hanging the prisoners. They cut off their feet, their hands, their ears, their tongues, even their genitals! A few days later, one of my most trusted officers told me that there were legionarios wearing wire necklaces from which dangled human ears from the victims of Carbayín. I immediately ordered their detention and execution. That was the basis of my conflict with Yagüe. I ordered him to take his men from the mining valleys and confine them in Oviedo. And I held him responsible for any deaths that might take place. To judge the rebels, there were the courts of justice. I also had to deal with the deeds of the Regulares of the *tabor* [battalion] from Ceuta: rapes, murders, looting. I ordered the execution of six Moors. It caused me problems. The Minister of War, all excited, demanded explanations: 'How can you dare order anyone to be shot without a court martial?' I answered: 'I have subjected them to the same procedures to which they subjected their victims.'[104]

The events of October 1934 escalated the hostility between the left and the forces of order, particularly the Civil Guard and parts of the army. The Asturian rebels knew that, to control the mining valleys, they had to overcome the Civil Guard. Accordingly, they assaulted various local barracks to neutralize them prior to an attack on the capital city of the province, Oviedo. These episodes were violent and protracted. The bloodiest took place in Sama de Langreo, seventeen miles east of Oviedo, and in Campomanes, fifty miles to the south. In Sama, the battle raged for thirty-six hours and thirty-eight Civil Guards were killed. In the battle at Campomanes, twelve Civil Guards were killed and seven wounded.[105] In total, the casualties of the Civil Guard in Asturias were eighty-six dead and seventy-seven wounded. The Assault Guards lost fifty-eight dead and fifty-four wounded. The army lost eighty-eight dead and 475 wounded. Other security forces lost twenty-four dead and thirty-three wounded. These figures may be compared with the nearly two thousand civilian dead, the large majority of them working class.[106]

October 1934 saw only sporadic clashes elsewhere in Spain. However, there were casualties in Albacete, at both Villarobledo and Tarazona de la Mancha, during assaults on the town halls and other public buildings. In Villarobledo, four people were killed as order was restored by the Civil Guard, which suffered no casualties. In Tarazona, earlier in the summer, the Socialist Mayor had been removed from his post by the Civil Governor of Albacete, the Radical José Aparicio Albiñana. Now, his right-wing replacement was badly wounded in the struggle. Aparicio Albiñana responded to the situation by sending in reinforcements of the Civil Guard. One Civil Guard and several municipal policemen were killed during the defence of the town hall. The rest of the province was hardly affected by the revolutionary movement.[107]

In the province of Zaragoza, the call for a general strike was ignored by the CNT and therefore a failure. However, there were bloody confrontations in Mallén, Ejea de los Caballeros, Tauste and Uncastillo in the area known as Las Cinco Villas, one of the parts of Aragon where social conflict was fiercest during the Republican years. It was a cereal-producing area of huge holdings, where a few landlords held many properties and the local day-labourers depended for survival on their access to common lands which had been enclosed by legal subterfuge in the nineteenth century. The bitterness of the election campaigns of November 1933 and the June harvest strike had contributed to the intensification of class hatred in the area and this was reflected in clashes on 5 and 6 October.[108] In Mallén, one Civil Guard was killed and another wounded and a villager shot dead. In Ejea, a Civil Guard and a villager were wounded. In Tauste, a revolutionary committee took over the village and the Civil Guard barracks was attacked. The revolutionaries were crushed by a regiment of the army which fired on them with machine-guns and an artillery piece. Six villagers were killed.[109]

The most violent events in Cinco Villas took place at Uncastillo, an isolated village of barely three thousand inhabitants. In the early hours of the morning of Friday 5 October, emissaries arrived from the UGT in Zaragoza with instructions for the revolutionary general strike. The mild-mannered Socialist Mayor of Uncastillo, Antonio Plano Aznárez, told them that it would be madness. He was no revolutionary, but rather an unusually cultivated man adept at navigating the complex bureaucratic mechanisms of the agrarian reform. He had earned the hatred of the local landowners by dint of his success in introducing equitable job-sharing, in establishing reasonable working conditions, in recovering some common lands that had been taken from the village by legal subterfuges in the previous century and in improving the local school. Now, however, contrary to his advice, the urgings of the men from Zaragoza were enthusiastically taken up by the local labourers, many of whom were unemployed and whose families were starving.

At 6.00 a.m., when the strikers demanded the surrender of the village Civil Guard barracks, the commander, Sergeant Victorino Quiñones, refused. Plano himself spoke to Quiñones who said that his men were loyal to the Republic but would not surrender. Their conversation was cordial and Plano, albeit without much hope of success, undertook to try to dissuade his neighbours. In fact, as he left the barracks, the strikers surrounding the building opened fire and in the subsequent gunfight two of the seven Guards were killed, Sergeant Quiñones and another badly wounded and yet another blinded. The two remaining Guards fought on until the arrival of reinforcements. Antonio Plano came out of his house with a white flag and tried to talk to them but, when they opened fire, he fled into the surrounding countryside. In the course of the fighting, the home of one of the most powerful landowners, Antonio Mola, was assaulted when he refused to hand over arms to some of the strikers. In the subsequent skirmish, his niece was wounded and Mola shot dead one of the attackers who had burned down his garage and destroyed his car. The others were trying to burn him out when the Civil Guard arrived and drove them off. One of the many wounded strikers died on 8 October.[110]

In all of Spain, Civil Guard casualties in combating the insurrection of October 1934 were 111 killed and 182 wounded, the bulk of which were in Asturias.[111] The memory of this would influence the part played by the Civil Guard in the Civil War. More immediately, it had a profound effect on the way in which the revolutionaries were punished. Once the Asturian miners had surrendered, the subsequent repression was overseen by the forty-four-year-old Civil Guard Major Lisardo Doval Bravo, who had a record of bitter hostility to the left in Asturias. Indeed, he was widely considered in Civil Guard circles as an expert on left-wing subversion in Asturias. He had served in Oviedo from 1917 to 1922 and, having reached the rank of captain, he had commanded the Gijón garrison from 1926 until 1931. He earned notoriety for the ferocity with which he dealt with strikes and disorder. On 15 December 1930, during the failed general strike which was intended to bring down the dictatorship of General Berenguer, he had been involved in a bloody incident in Gijón. The strikers attempted to remove from the wall of a Jesuit church a plaque in honour of the Dictator General Miguel Primo de Rivera. The Jesuits opened fire on the demonstrators, killing a worker and wounding another. In response, the mob set the church ablaze and the Civil Guard was called. Doval led a cavalry charge against the workers. Afterwards, he authorized the savage beating of strikers in his quest to identify the ringleaders. In April 1931, he planned to repel a workers' attack on his barracks with banks of machine-guns. A man who knew him well, the conservative Republican Antonio Oliveros, editor of the Gijón newspaper *El Noroeste*, wrote: 'In my opinion, Doval is a man of exceptional talents in the service of the State. Brave to the point of irresponsibility, his concept of duty leads him to the worst excesses and that accounts for his frequent abuse of suspects when trying to get proof of guilt.'[112]

Doval was subsequently involved in the abortive Sanjurjo coup in Seville in August 1932. Although suspended for his part therein, he had benefited from the amnesty for the conspirators passed on 24 April 1934. Until 19 September that year, when he was posted to Tetuán, he had been on secondment training the JAP militia. On 1 November, Doval was appointed 'Special Delegate of the Ministry of War for Public Order in the Provinces of Asturias and León'. The appointment was made by Diego Hidalgo on the specific recommendation of Franco, who was fully aware of Doval's methods and his reputation as a torturer. They had coincided as boys in Ferrol, in the Infantry Academy at Toledo and in Asturias in 1917.[113] With an authorization signed by Hidalgo himself, Doval was given carte blanche to bypass any judicial, bureaucratic or military obstacles to his activities in Asturias. His fame as a crusader against the left had made him immensely popular among the upper and middle classes of the region.

As Franco knew he would, Doval carried out his task with a relish for brutality which provoked horror in the international press.[114] It was not long before there were reports of his abuses. The Director General of Security, the deeply conservative José Valdivia Garci-Borrón, on 15 November, sent one of his subordinates, Inspector Adrover, to investigate. Adrover was violently expelled from Asturias by Doval. In view of this and of the stream of information about Doval's excesses, Captain Valdivia pressed the new Minister of the Interior, the Radical Eloy Vaquero, for Doval's removal. On 8 December, the special powers were revoked and five days later he was posted back to Tetuán.[115]

Meanwhile in Zaragoza, after the suppression of the uprising in Uncastillo, the fugitive Mayor Antonio Plano was captured and badly beaten by Civil Guards. Back in the village, 110 men were arrested and tortured by the Civil Guard before being taken to the provincial capital for trial.[116] The achievements of Plano's time as Mayor were overturned. Over the next year or so, the Civil Guard in Uncastillo took its revenge. Numerous detentions and beatings on the slightest pretext led to the new right-wing Mayor making an official complaint. Unsurprisingly, an official investigation found no grounds for action. The trial of 110 villagers accused of participation in the events of 5–6 October took place throughout February and March 1935. It was heavily weighted in favour of the Civil Guard and of the local *cacique*, Antonio Mola. The prosecution's aim was to place the blame for everything firmly on the Mayor. To achieve this, the highly respected and conciliatory Plano was portrayed as a hate-fuelled traitor to the Republic. His defence lawyer pointed out that, if the Civil Guard could not stop the revolutionary events, it was absurd to have expected Plano to do so single-handed.

Nevertheless, the judgment of the court on 29 March 1935 was that Plano had been the ringleader and was guilty of military rebellion. Accordingly, he was condemned to death. Fourteen villagers, including the deputy Mayor, were sentenced to life imprisonment. Forty-eight villagers were given sentences ranging from twenty-five to twelve years. When the sentences were announced, confrontations between villagers and Civil Guards became increasingly bitter. After the victory of the left-liberal Popular Front coalition in the elections of February 1936, Antonio Plano and the others were amnestied and he was reinstated as Mayor and revived his reforms.[117] The local *caciques* were furious and their revenge when the Civil War started would be terrible.

4

The Coming of War,
1934–1936

The hopes of Gil Robles and Salazar Alonso had been fulfilled. While the military action in the north was still in train, there had been nationwide round-ups of workers' leaders on a massive scale. On 11 October 1934, the CEDA daily, *El Debate*, reported that in Madrid alone there were already two thousand prisoners. Jails were soon full in areas where there was no revolutionary activity but where landowners had problems with their day-labourers. Workers' clubs, the Casas del Pueblo, were closed down in towns and villages in every part of the country. The Socialist press was banned. On 8 October, in Alicante, a huge crowd demanded the liberation of the many prisoners being brought to the Castillo de Santa Bárbara. There were clashes with the police and José Alonso Mallol, the ex-Civil Governor of Seville and Asturias, and a number of other prominent Republicans were arrested. In the same session of 9 October in which Gil Robles had proposed the closing of parliament, the CEDA voted an increase in the forces of order and the re-establishment of the death penalty. At total of 1,134 Socialist town councils were simply removed and replaced by unelected right-wing nominees. There were many provincial capitals among them, including Albacete, Málaga and Oviedo.

The most scandalous case was that of Madrid, where the town council and its Republican Mayor, Pedro Rico, were suspended, falsely accused of failing to combat the strike. Control was briefly assumed by the head of the Agrarian Party, José Martínez de Velasco, as government delegate. He was replaced on 19 October by Salazar Alonso himself, who had been dropped from the new government because Lerroux felt that the presence of three CEDA ministers was already provocative enough. A week later, he took the title of *alcalde* (mayor).[1] In Málaga, the man chosen to lead the management committee that replaced the elected council was Benito Ortega Muñoz, a liberal member of the Radical Party. As a city councillor, he had successfully opposed the attempts of more left-wing Republicans to remove crosses from the municipal cemetery. That, together with his acceptance of the position of unelected Mayor in October 1934, would lead to his murder in 1936.[2]

The repression in Asturias after October 1934 was a major stepping-stone from the terror of Morocco to the wartime terror exercised against the civilian population of the Republic. With Franco in overall command, the brutal Juan Yagüe leading the African forces and the sadistic Doval in charge of 'public order', Asturias saw the elaboration of the model that would be applied in southern Spain in the summer of 1936. The right applauded the actions of Franco against what was perceived as the 'passions of the beast', 'the pillaging hordes' and 'the rabble unleashed'. As well as the 111 Civil Guards killed, thirty-three clergy, including seven seminary students, lost their lives.[3] It was not surprising then that spine-chilling exaggerations of the revolutionaries' crimes abounded. One of the leaders of Acción Española, Honorio Maura, described the miners as 'putrefaction, scum, the dregs of humanity', 'repugnant jackals unfit to be Spaniards or even humans'. They were portrayed as murderers, thieves and rapists, with female accomplices described as 'brazen women who incited their cruelties. Some were young and beautiful but their faces reflected moral perversion, a mixture of shamelessness and cruelty.'[4]

For the right, the use of the African Army against 'inhuman' leftists was entirely justified. Inevitably, within Spain and abroad, there was loud criticism of the use of Moorish troops in Asturias, the cradle of the Christian reconquest of Spain. José María Cid y Ruiz-Zorrilla, parliamentary deputy for the right-wing Agrarian Party for Zamora and Minister of Public Works, responded with a declaration of double-edged racism: 'For those who committed so many acts of savagery, Moors were the least they deserved, because they deserved Moors and a lot else.'[5] A book published by the Oviedo branch of Ángel Herrera Oria's Asociación Católica Nacional de Propagandistas (ACNP) suggested in similar terms that the crimes committed against clerics by the revolutionaries were Moorish in character and deserved to be punished by exposure to Moorish atrocities.[6] In the majority of Catholic writing about the events of October 1934, it was a commonplace that the revolution was an attack on Catholicism and that the suffering of religious personnel was analogous to the suffering of Christ at the hands of the Jews.[7]

In contrast to Asturias, the October rebellion in Catalonia was put down without savagery, thanks to the moderation and professionalism of Domingo Batet Mestres, the general commanding the Catalan Military Region. The Catalan government, the Generalitat, had found itself caught between extreme nationalists pushing for a separate Catalonia and a right-wing government in Madrid determined to curtail regional autonomy. The President, Lluís Companys, rashly declared independence on 6 October, in an attempt to forestall revolution. General Batet responded with patience and good sense to restore the authority of the central government and thereby prevented a potential bloodbath. Specifically, he bypassed Franco, who was advising the Minister of War Diego Hidalgo on the repression in Catalonia as well as Asturias. To Franco's fury, Batet would deal only with Hidalgo and the Prime Minister, Lerroux. As the senior officer, he ignored Franco's recommendation that he use the Foreign Legion to impose punishment on Catalonia like that inflicted by Yagüe on Asturias. Instead, he used a small number of troops to secure the surrender of the Generalitat with a minimum of casualties. Batet also prevented the bombardment of Barcelona by warships sent by Franco.[8]

When Batet explained in a radio broadcast how he had conducted operations, he did so in a regretful and conciliatory tone that was far from the vengeful spirit of the right. In parliament, José Antonio Primo de Rivera fulminated that Batet was 'a general that didn't believe in Spain' and that his broadcast had 'made us blush with shame'.[9] Two years later, Franco would take his revenge for Batet's moderation. In June 1936, Batet was to be given command of the VI Military Region, whose headquarters were in Burgos, one of the nerve centres of the uprising of 18 July. Faced with the virtually unanimous decision of his officers to join the rising, Batet would bravely refuse to join them. His commitment to his oath of loyalty to the Republic would guarantee his trial and execution. Franco maliciously intervened in the judicial process to ensure that Batet would be executed.[10]

Now, despite the triumph of the government, there were numerous civilians and army officers preparing to destroy the Republic. Onésimo Redondo was trying to build up an arsenal of small arms. He hired a sports ground on the banks of the Río Pisuerga where he would drill and train the local Falange militia. On Sundays, he led parades through Valladolid itself or other towns of the province. During October 1934, there had been bloody clashes in Valladolid between Falangists and picketing railway workers. In the aftermath, Onésimo Redondo distributed a pamphlet in which he advocated that Azaña, Largo Caballero, Prieto and Companys be hanged.[11]

The activities of Onésimo Redondo and others on the extreme right showed that they were oblivious to the successes of a firmly right-wing government. Pushed by them or genuinely alarmed at what he perceived to be the moderate scale of the post-October repression, José Antonio Primo de Rivera committed the Falange to armed struggle to overthrow the democratic regime.[12] In early 1935, he had several meetings with Bartolomé Barba Hernández of the Unión Militar Española and an agreement was reached which also established links with the Carlists through Colonel Ricardo de Rada, who was training the militias of both groups. There was a surge in UME membership among junior officers after October 1934.[13]

In mid-June 1935, at a meeting of the Falange executive committee, the Junta Política, at the Parador in the Sierra de Gredos north of Madrid, the 'official and binding decision was taken to proceed to holy civil war to rescue the Fatherland'. José Antonio reported on his contacts with the UME. He then put forward a plan for an uprising to take place near the Portuguese frontier at Fuentes de Oñoro in the province of Salamanca. An unnamed general, possibly Sanjurjo, would acquire 10,000 rifles in Portugal which would then be handed over to Falangist militants who would proceed to a 'march on Madrid'.[14] With the left already cowed by the repression and the most right-wing elements of the military in positions of power, there was no backing from senior military figures. Probably to José Antonio's relief, the idea was dropped.[15] The only practical consequence of the decision to move to armed struggle was the bid by José Antonio to get weapons from Barba Hernández's UME.[16]

In fact, the successive defeats of both the June harvest strike and the October rising had left political and social tension at an all-time high. This was especially true in the south. The new Minister of Agriculture, the CEDA deputy for Badajoz, Manuel Giménez Fernández, hoped to alleviate the situation by implementing his social Catholic beliefs. Outraged landowners ensured that his aspirations came to naught. The rural population of Extremadura had suffered a long process of pauperization. While large landowners had been able to ride out crises of poor harvests and drought, the smaller owners had ended up in the hands of usurers (often the richer landowners). They had been forced to mortgage, and then lost, their farms. The problem was particularly acute for the *yunteros* or ploughmen who owned a *yunta* (yoke) of mules and rented land to farm.

A long-simmering hostility came to a head in November 1934. It had started in 1932, when the local landlords had systematically refused to grant leases to the *yunteros*, instead turning their land over to pasture for cattle. Their objective had been to force the *yunteros* to sell their oxen and tools and reduce them to the status of day-labourers. In desperation, in the autumn of 1932, the *yunteros* launched a series of invasions of the estates of the most recalcitrant landlords. With some ceremony, flags, bands and families, they would enter the estates at dawn and begin to plough the land. There was little violence and, when confronted by armed retainers or the Civil Guard, the *yunteros* would usually withdraw peacefully. Finally, on 1 November 1932, the Republican–Socialist coalition temporarily legalized the occupations for one year for 15,500 peasants in Cáceres and 18,500 in Badajoz, a measure renewed in 1933 for a further year. Big landowners in Badajoz, Cáceres and Salamanca, especially cattle-breeders, reacted with intense hostility to the ploughing of pasture.[17]

In late 1934, the issue of what to do about the 34,000 *yunteros* settled in November 1932 became urgent. The CEDA now had the opportunity to put into practice its much vaunted aim of combating revolution with social reform. As skilled farmers, with their own tools and animals, the *yunteros* of Extremadura were potential recruits for the social Catholic movement. They could easily have been converted into share-cropping smallholders.[18] However, Giménez Fernández encountered the local right demanding their immediate eviction.[19] Without attacking the agrarian problem at its root, the measures he proposed between November 1934 and March 1935 did attempt to mitigate some of its more appalling consequences. He met only the hostility of the extreme right and, in his own party, the CEDA, little solidarity and much vicious personal abuse. The bitter determination of landowners to bury his Law for the Protection of *Yunteros* and Small Farmers was revealed when he was visited on 16 October 1934 by a group of landowners from Cáceres accompanied by the three CEDA and four Radical deputies for the province and by Adolfo Rodríguez Jurado, CEDA deputy for Madrid and president of the landowners' pressure group, the Agrupación Nacional de Propietarios de Fincas Rústicas. The ferocity of their objections was reflected in Giménez Fernández's diary entry that more than one of them was a 'fascist decided on sabotage'.[20]

In January 1935, Giménez Fernández's Law on Access to Ownership offered tenants the chance to buy land they had worked for twelve years. Mild as it was, the project provoked a parliamentary coalition of ultra-rightist deputies, led by the Carlist José María Lamamié de Clairac (Salamanca) and four CEDA deputies, Mateo Azpeitia Esteban (Zaragoza province), Cándido Casanueva y Gorjón (Salamanca), Luis Alarcón de la Lastra (Seville province) and, most ferociously of all, Rodríguez Jurado. They were virulent in their hostility to the idea of peasants being given access to property.[21]

Luis Alarcón de la Lastra was an artillery officer and Africanista who had left the army rather than take the oath of loyalty to the Republic. He was also an aristocrat, holding the titles of Conde de Gálvez and Marqués de Rende, and owned considerable property around Carmona, the area of Seville province with one of the greatest concentrations of large estates. He had become a CEDA deputy for Seville in 1933 but failed to gain a seat in the February 1936 elections. He would rejoin the army at the beginning of the Spanish Civil War and serve in Yagüe's African columns commanding the artillery that bombarded numerous towns. By 1938, he was commander of the artillery of the Moroccan Army Corps. At the end of March 1939, Franco rewarded him by naming him Civil Governor of Madrid and five months later Minister of Industry and Commerce.[22]

Now, in session after session in the Cortes, Alarcón, Lamamié and the CEDA ultras stripped away the progressive features of Giménez Fernández's law on rural leases and added clauses that permitted a spate of evictions. Gil Robles stated that only concessions made in a Christian spirit could prevent the revolution, yet stood back and watched his Minister being called a 'white bolshevik' and 'a Marxist in disguise'. Moreover, Gil Robles placed Giménez Fernández's fiercest enemies on the parliamentary committee examining the drafts of his laws. Lamamié de Clairac showed just how far his Catholic faith went when he declared that 'if the Minister of Agriculture goes on quoting Papal Encyclicals in support of his projects, I can assure him that we will end up becoming Greek orthodox'.[23] When he next provoked a cabinet crisis, Gil Robles quietly dropped Giménez Fernández.

On 3 July 1935, Giménez Fernández's successor, Nicasio Velayos Velayos, a conservative member of the Agrarian Party from Ávila, presented what came to be known as the 'agrarian counter-reform'. It was so reactionary that it was denounced by José Antonio Primo de Rivera as well as by various Left Republicans and Radicals. Its most dramatic change was to drop the Inventory of Expropriable Property. This permitted landowners to avoid expropriation by putting their properties in other names. Henceforth, only those who wanted their property compulsorily purchased had to undergo expropriation. Moreover, compensation would be decided case by case by tribunals consisting of landowners, who would ensure that it would be at full market value.[24] In Extremadura, the local landowners began to evict the *yunteros*. In the village of Fregenal de la Sierra in Badajoz, one landowner alone evicted twenty families.[25]

The consequent level of social tension in Badajoz was starkly revealed on 10 June 1935 when the twenty-six-year-old Socialist deputy for the province, Pedro Rubio Heredia, was shot dead in a restaurant by Regino Valencia, who worked for Salazar Alonso. It will be recalled that Regino Valencia had carried out the 'inspection' which led to the removal of José González Barrero as Mayor of Zafra. Rubio's funeral was attended by thousands of members of the FNTT. At Valencia's trial, on 27 June, he was defended by Manuel Baca Mateos, a CEDA deputy for Seville, who claimed that the death had come about as a result of a fight. The Socialist Juan-Simeón Vidarte, acting for the victim's family, proved to the satisfaction of the court that the attack had been unprovoked. Valencia was sentenced to twelve years and a day in prison. He then appealed to the Supreme Court, where he was defended by Rafael Salazar Alonso in person. Vidarte wrote later: 'knowing as I and the entire province did, that he [Salazar Alonso] was behind the murder, this hard-faced cheek shocked and disgusted me'. At the unsuccessful appeal at the end of December 1935, there was uproar when Vidarte said that Salazar Alonso should have been wearing not lawyer's robes but convict's overalls.[26]

Despite being made Mayor of Madrid, Salazar Alonso's political fortunes had plummeted since his removal from the Ministry of the Interior at the beginning of October 1934. Aware that the inclusion of three CEDA ministers in his cabinet would provoke fury on the left, Lerroux felt that he could not keep Salazar Alonso on. It was a gesture to secure President Alcalá Zamora's approval for the new cabinet.[27] In the parliamentary debate on the revolutionary events in Asturias and Catalonia and their subsequent repression, the ex-Prime Minister Ricardo Samper declared that responsibility for what had happened lay with Salazar Alonso. Utterly mortified, Salazar Alonso got up and walked out of the Cortes.[28]

Given that both in his private letters to Amparo and in his memoirs, Salazar Alonso boasted of provoking the workers' uprising, his distress can have derived only from the fact that all had not turned out as well as he had hoped. The post-October repression brought a semblance of social peace, but violence was not far from the surface. The south was badly hit by drought in 1935, unemployment rose to more than 40 per cent in some places and beggars thronged the streets of the towns. The hungry agricultural labourers and the well-to-do rural middle and upper classes regarded each other with fear and resentment. The right-wing campaign for the elections of February 1936 prophesied that a left-wing victory would mean 'uncontrolled looting and the common ownership of women'. Even without such apocalyptic provocation, natural disaster intensified social tension. After the prolonged drought of 1935, early 1936 brought fierce rainstorms that ruined the olive harvest and damaged wheat and barley crops. Across Andalusia and Extremadura, during the election campaign, the owners offered food and jobs to those who would vote for the right. To refuse could mean a beating or loss of work. In both urban and rural areas of unemployment, the local branches of Acción Popular began to open soup-kitchens and to distribute blankets to the poor. In many places, the right set out to buy votes.[29]

In most southern provinces, the Casas del Pueblo were still closed sixteen months after the October revolution. In Granada, for example, the Republican newspapers mysteriously disappeared en route from Granada to outlying towns and villages, while the CEDA paper *Ideal* always got through. *Ideal* called on right-wingers to abandon their 'suicidal inertia', recommending a few beatings to keep the left quiet. In many provinces, *caciques* hired thugs who, often with the assistance of the Civil Guard, prevented the dissemination of left-wing propaganda. Republican posters were ripped down at gunpoint; Republican orators were turned away from villages by roadblocks or simply arrested. Rumours were spread that the peasants could not vote unless they had special documentation.[30]

The atmosphere was captured with all its bitterness by Baldomero Díaz de Entresotos who was the land registrar in Puebla de Alcocer in the area in north-east Badajoz known as La Siberia Extremeña. Highly sympathetic to fascism, Díaz de Entresotos was affronted by the fact that a taxi firm in Castuera used second-hand cars to carry the local working class at reasonable prices. A landowner commented to him:

> what we don't need are elections and tolerance. It's all well and good that we used to have such things when it was all kept between ourselves, just to decide whether liberals or conservatives or so-and-so or so-and-so would be in charge. But now, when it's about law and order or revolution, we don't need all this drivel about parliament and democracy. The answer here is to force this rabble to submit, by whatever means, if necessary cutting off their heads before they cut off ours.

One of Díaz de Entresotos's close friends was a landowner, Alfonso Muñoz Lozano de Sosa, who was also an infantry lieutenant serving with the Assault Guards. On election day, 16 February, he came to Puebla de Alcocer with a machine-pistol. The village was also visited on that day by Ricardo Zabalza, the secretary general of the landworkers' union, the FNTT, who was a Socialist candidate for Badajoz. Zabalza was eating alone at the local inn, with his head down, deeply aware of the hostility of his fellow middle-class customers. Díaz de Entresotos had lunch with Lieutenant Muñoz and wrote later of his visceral hatred of Zabalza (on the basis of this one sighting and without ever actually meeting him). Zabalza, a schoolmaster, was invariably neatly and cleanly dressed. However, such was Díaz de Entresotos's paranoid loathing of the left that he saw only an abomination:

> Zabalza looked just like what he was. Unkempt and repulsive, as befitted his damaging activities. He went around the villages advising riot and plunder. It was rumoured that, during the peasants' strike of 1934, he had put a bomb on a railway line. I had no idea if this fact [*sic*] was true but, looking at this grim and dirty man, it seemed perfectly likely. How many times that day did I gaze on Muñoz's machine-pistol, dwelling on the pleasure it would give me to open fire on that disgusting flesh!

When the election results began to come in, Muñoz commented ominously, 'This has to be settled with bullets.'[31] Their desire to see Zabalza dead would be satisfied four years later when he was executed by firing squad in a Francoist prison.[32]

The narrowness of the left-wing electoral victory reflected the polarization of Spanish society. The working masses, especially in the countryside, were in no mood for compromise after the so-called 'two black years' of vindictive right-wing government from 1933 to 1935. Both the rural and urban working classes demanded reparation for the post-October repression and the swift implementation of the reform programme elaborated by the leaders of the Popular Front electoral coalition. Considerable alarm ran through the middle classes when crowds gathered at prisons in Asturias and elsewhere calling for the release of those imprisoned after October 1934 and when groups of labourers presented themselves for work at the large estates. In many rural towns, there were attacks on the *casinos* (landowners' clubs). In others, churches were burned in reprisal for their priests having justified the repression and using their pulpits for right-wing propaganda during the electoral campaign.

The new Prime Minister Manuel Azaña was horrified by the violence of popular agitation and rapidly embarked on a programme of conciliation. On 20 February 1936, his first cabinet meeting approved the return of the elected town councils and decreed an amnesty for those imprisoned after October 1934. The following day, Azaña made a radio broadcast to the nation in which he undertook to 'heal the wounds caused in recent times' and promised that his government would not seek revenge for the injustices of the last two years. He was confident that the popular ferment was a temporary phenomenon, fruit of the euphoria that accompanied the electoral victory. With a view to calming the agitation, on 29 February his cabinet issued a decree obliging employers to readmit workers sacked because of their ideology or for participating in strikes after 1 January 1934 and to compensate them with their pay for a minimum of thirty-nine days or a maximum of six months. The immediate reaction of a huge group of employers' organizations was to issue a statement that this constituted a 'true economic catastrophe'. In the short term, it appeared that the right in general expected from Azaña, as the dramatist Ramón del Valle Inclán put it, 'what the sick expect from cod-liver oil'.[33]

However, Azaña faced debilitating problems. Despite his broadcast, the rural agitation continued. He was deeply depressed by news of events in Yecla in the north of Murcia, where seven churches, six houses and the property registry had been set alight.[34] His ability to control the situation was severely undermined by the refusal of Francisco Largo Caballero to permit Socialist participation in the cabinet. Distrustful of Republican moderation, he had been prepared to support the electoral coalition only to secure political amnesty for the victims of the repression. Embittered by right-wing obstruction of reform between 1931 and 1933, Largo Caballero believed that only an exclusively Socialist cabinet could transform Spanish society. His overconfident view was that the Left Republicans should pursue their own programme and effectively exhaust themselves in carrying out the bourgeois stage of the revolution. They would then either make way for a Socialist cabinet or be engulfed by a fascist uprising which would itself trigger a successful revolution.

On 3 April 1936, Largo Caballero was interviewed by the American journalist Louis Fischer and he told him complacently: 'The reactionaries can come back into office only through a coup d'état.'[35] He was just mouthing revolutionary platitudes, but unfortunately the counterfeit nature of his revolutionary rhetoric was not perceived as such among the middle and upper classes. While their fears of revolution were intensified by right-wing propaganda, Largo Caballero's policy prevented both revolution and strong government. It eventually ensured instead that an ineffectual Republican government would be in power while the military conspiracy was prepared.

The tension was such that Azaña felt obliged to calm things down. He wrote to his brother-in-law: 'every night the left feared a military coup aimed at preventing communism. The right feared that the Soviet was on the horizon. I've never seen such panic or such a stupid situation. The Socialists have organized an intelligence system based on concierges, cleaners and chauffeurs, and they get all the below-stairs gossip.' With the stock market falling and the streets deserted, on 3 April, Azaña made the first of only two major speeches to the new Cortes. In it, he mentioned the agitations and disturbances that had taken place in the countryside, stating that his cabinet had to deal with what he called 'a national ulcer'.

Referring to the excesses of the first six weeks of his government, he asked: 'can the masses, provoked and ill treated, those forced to starve for two years, those coming out of prison, be asked to behave, as we try to do, without resentment for the injustices which we remember only too well? We had to expect, and the Government did expect ... that the first explosion of popular anger would see excesses that would undermine political authority and damage the Government.' While condemning violent abuses, he also denounced those who sought to make political capital from them. He recognized that the tendency of Spaniards to resolve problems by violence engendered 'a presumption of catastrophe'. 'Many people are going around depressed,' he declared, 'imagining that Spain is going to wake up having been turned into a Soviet.' While understanding how apolitical individuals might harbour such fears, he found it intolerable that the politically aware should foment panic in such a way as to create the atmosphere necessary for a coup d'état.

Azaña put the disorder into its proper context and went on to declare that his government aimed to remedy the disequilibrium at the heart of Spanish society. He acknowledged that this could mean harming the interests of those who benefited from 'this horrendous imbalance', adding that 'we come to break up any abusive concentration of wealth wherever it may be'. While he did not expect an entire social class to commit suicide, he called on the wealthy to make sacrifices rather than face the consequences of the desperation provoked by social injustice. He ended prophetically, more so than he knew at the time, declaring that this was the last chance for the Republic because, if the redistribution of wealth he was advocating was opposed as the reforms of 1931–3 had been, then there would be no legal way forward. Astonishingly, the reaction to this ultimatum was widespread relief from the Communists to the extreme right. The stock market began to rise again and Azaña was regarded as a national hero.[36]

Although lacking Socialist participation, Azaña's new government was determined to proceed rapidly with meaningful agrarian change. The task was rendered all the more difficult because of a rise in unemployment by the end of February 1936 to 843,872, or 17 per cent of the working population.[37] The new Minister of Agriculture, Mariano Ruiz-Funes, announced his commitment to rapid agrarian reform. The resurgent landworkers' union intended to make him keep his word. After the harsh rural repression of the previous two years, in 1936 the FNTT began to expand at a vertiginous rate. Its militant leadership was in no mood to tolerate delays from the government or obstruction from the big landowners.

Immediately after the elections, Ricardo Zabalza had written to Ruiz-Funes urging him to expedite the return of land to the leaseholders evicted in 1935 and to re-establish the mixed juries (arbitration committees) and the decree of obligatory cultivation. In a letter to the Minister of Labour, Enrique Ramos, Zabalza requested the introduction of a scheme for placing unemployed workers with landowners. A third letter, to Amós Salvador, Minister of the Interior, called for the disarming of the *caciques*. Seriously alarmed by the quantity of weapons held by landowners and their retainers, and by the support that they enjoyed from the Civil Guard, the FNTT soon called upon members to form militias to prevent a repetition of the persecution of 1934 and 1935. Before the Cortes opened in mid-March, peasant demonstrations all over Spain supported Zabalza's requests.[38] The FNTT's demands were not revolutionary but they still constituted a major challenge to the balance of rural economic power. Moreover, the events of the previous two years had exacerbated rural class hatred to a point which made the peaceful introduction of the desired social legislation highly unlikely. The economic situation ensured that the reforms, which were essential to alleviate the misery of the landless peasants, could not be absorbed by the owners without a significant redistribution of rural wealth. Constant rain between December 1935 and March 1936 had seriously damaged the grain harvest and reduced the profit margins of growers large and small. This natural disaster simply reinforced the reluctance of owners and workers alike to be conciliatory.

Anticipating the FNTT's demands, CEDA propaganda had predicted that left-wing electoral success would be the prelude to the most hair-raising social disasters. Thus defeat on 16 February implied that landed and religious interests could not be defended legally and only violence would suffice. The Chief of the General Staff, Francisco Franco, believed that a left-wing election victory was the first stage of a Comintern plan to take over Spain. He had been convinced by the bulletins that he received from the Geneva Entente Internationale contre la Troisième Internationale, bulletins which in turn drew on inflated reports from Mola's crony, the corrupt policeman Mauricio Carlavilla. From the early hours of 17 February, Gil Robles had been working with Franco to have martial law declared to overthrow the results. They managed to get several garrisons to do so, but their efforts foundered when the Director General of the Civil Guard, Sebastián Pozas Perea, remained loyal to the Republic.

On 8 March, Franco and other senior generals met in Madrid to put in train the most extreme violence of all, a military coup. They agreed to make General Emilio Mola overall director of the conspiracy and Colonel Valentín Galarza Morante his liaison chief.[39] This was hardly surprising. In May 1935, when Gil Robles had become Minister of War, he had appointed Franco Chief of the General Staff and they had quietly established Mola in a secluded office in the Ministry of War to prepare operational plans for the use of the colonial army against the left on mainland Spain.[40] Mola was then made general in command of Melilla and shortly afterwards military commander of the entire Moroccan protectorate. Franco ensured that reliable reactionaries were posted to the command of many units in Morocco and in Spain itself. He boasted later that these officers were key pawns in the coup.[41]

In the meantime, Andalusia and Extremadura were facing bitter conflict because the landowners had flouted agreements on wages and working conditions and evicted the *yunteros*. After the elections, watched by seething rightists, joyful peasants paraded through the towns flying their union banners and red flags. The rural middle classes were appalled by such signs of popular jubilation and by attacks on *casinos*. Labour legislation began to be reinforced and, in the south, workers were 'placed' on uncultivated estates. Those imprisoned after the 1934 harvest strike and the October events were released and returned to their towns and villages, to the chagrin of the local Civil Guards who had arrested them. In Andalusian towns, demonstrators attacked right-wing centres and clubs.[42]

The announcement of Azaña's decrees of 20 February 1936 had been greeted cautiously, but their implementation provoked howls of outrage. The right-wing mayors imposed in 1934 by Salazar Alonso were unceremoniously expelled from the town councils of Badajoz and the deposed Socialists reinstated. Moreover, Salazar Alonso himself, the erstwhile champion of the Badajoz *latifundistas*, was a ruined man. In 1934, he had been heavily involved in the gambling fraud which eventually destroyed the Radical Party. He was one of several prominent Radicals who took bribes to help legalize the use of a rigged roulette wheel in Spanish casinos. The scandal that ensued in 1935 was called 'Estraperlo', from the names of the machine's inventors, Strauss and Perlowitz. Salazar Alonso had been given a gold watch and 100,000 pesetas (about £35,000 in present-day values), and both his undersecretary at the Minister of the Interior, Eduardo Benzo, and the Director General of Security, José Valdivia, were paid 50,000 pesetas. Despite authorizing the use of the roulette wheel, Salazar Alonso, regarding the bribe as insufficient, arranged for a police raid when it was inaugurated at the San Sebastián casino. To get their revenge, the inventors leaked documents on the case to President Alcalá Zamora. In October 1935 in the subsequent parliamentary debate, Salazar Alonso was exonerated by 140 votes to 137, thanks to the support of the CEDA. When this was announced, José Antonio Primo de Rivera shouted, '¡Viva el Estraperlo!'[43] Although he was still Mayor of Madrid, Salazar Alonso's political career was over. During the February 1936 election campaign, his speeches in Badajoz were interrupted by shouted witticisms about roulette wheels and gold watches. He was defeated and immediately claimed that the results had been falsified. He told Lerroux that he had serious financial problems (despite receiving his full ministerial salary, as did all ex-ministers). He became president of the right-wing newspaper *Informaciones* in April 1936.[44] In the early days of the Civil War, he went into hiding, was eventually arrested, summarily tried by a people's tribunal and shot.

Feeling vulnerable, the richest local landowners abandoned their mansions. Throughout the entire south, Republican agrarian legislation was being revived. Mixed juries returned and obligatory cultivation of fallow land was reimposed. A variant of the legislation on municipal boundaries was activated, thereby preventing the local landowners from bringing in cheap outside labour to break union action. In many villages, the restored town councils decreed that municipal employees should be given back-pay to the date when they had been deposed. Workers were assigned to estates whose owners were expected to pay them. Needless to say, the possessing classes were outraged by the perceived injustice of such measures and by the impertinence of those that they expected to be subservient and respectful. Tension was exacerbated in some villages by mayors who prohibited traditional religious processions.[45]

Landowners' resentment at the ending of peasant servility often took the form of violent assaults on union leaders. In the province of Cáceres, between February and June, nine men died at the hands either of local Falangists or of the Civil Guard.[46] Right-wing violence was directed at those who were required to be submissive but were now assertively demonstrating their determination not to be cheated out of reform. In Salamanca, historically social conflict was endemic because the predominant activity of cattle-breeding required little manpower. The consequent unemployment was increased further because much arable land was also given over to hunting grounds. Although there were areas of smallholdings, to the west and south of the province, especially around Ledesma and Ciudad Rodrigo, land tenure was dominated by huge estates, the *latifundios*. The prospect in the spring of 1936 of a renewed push for a division of the great estates saw desperate efforts by the big landowners to block the reform. They quickly turned to violence and made contact with the military conspirators. Such was the case of Gonzalo de Aguilera, who simply shot his labourers.[47]

Of the six victorious right-wing candidates in the February elections in Salamanca, Gil Robles, Cándido Casanueva, Ernesto Castaño and José Cimas Leal of the CEDA, and the Carlists José María Lamamié de Clairac and Ramón Olleros, three were implicated in soliciting the votes of the province's wheat-growers by offering to buy up their surplus stocks. After scrutinizing the results, the committee on electoral validity, the Comisión de Actas, disqualified three, Castaño, Lamamié de Clairac and Olleros, and gave their parliamentary seats to the candidates with the next highest number of votes. Right-wing seats in Granada were also disqualified because of blatant electoral falsification. Claiming to be the target of persecution, the CEDA's deputies withdrew en masse from the Cortes – although its value as a pulpit of propaganda saw them return quickly. The President of the Cortes, the conservative Republican Diego Martínez Barrio, believed that the right-wing reaction to the loss of the fraudulently gained seats heralded a turn to violence. Castaño, a prominent landowner, went to Valladolid, the headquarters of the VII Military Region to which Salamanca belonged, to advocate a military rising against the Republic.[48] Gil Robles was in touch directly with General Mola while his faithful deputy, Cándido Casanueva, acted as the CEDA liaison with Generals Goded and Fanjul.[49] Gonzalo de Aguilera may have been an extreme case, yet he was anything but an unrepresentative figure of the Salamanca landowning class.

Another local landowner, Diego Martín Veloz, was equally active in seeking military aid. He had tried hard to persuade the officers of the Salamanca garrison to join Sanjurjo's coup in August 1932. The swarthy, pistol-toting Martín Veloz had been born in Cuba in 1875. He served as a soldier in the Philippines and Cuba and had been frequently arrested for violent indiscipline. After being invalided out of the army, he had returned penniless to the area to the east of Salamanca known as La Armuña. In the provincial capital, he had earned a living as a street vendor of items ranging from contraband watches to sheep. He had been a bouncer in a casino until he killed a client in a fight. His luck turned when he discovered an aptitude for gambling. Having made a fortune in Monte Carlo, he bought land and buildings in Salamanca. Investing in gambling and prostitution, he became the key figure in the brothels, casinos and gambling dens of Salamanca, Valladolid, Zamora and Palencia. He invested his profits in property and made a fortune, becoming one of the richest men in Salamanca. He owned a large area of the provincial capital and came to be known as 'The boss [el amo] of Salamanca'. His antics ranged from the infantile, such as once breaking up a Corpus Christi procession by unleashing a string of donkeys into its midst, to the bloody, killing several men in gunfights. On one occasion, finding an army officer destitute in the street, he entered a gambling den and at gunpoint took up a collection for the unfortunate wretch. On another, refused entry to a club, he set off fireworks around the door.[50]

First in Santander and later in Salamanca, he acquired a reputation as a thug. He was tried for murder in Santander and was absolved only after numerous senior military figures spoke on his behalf. This imposing, not to say gargantuan, figure was famous for his voracious appetites, both gastronomic and sexual. For a time fabulously rich, and wildly open-handed, Martín Veloz had cultivated friends in the military, inviting them to orgiastic parties at his estate in La Armuña, and paying off their debts. He was as notorious for the violence of his temper as he was for his generosity to his friends. Among his cronies were Generals Primo de Rivera, Queipo de Llano and Goded and Gonzalo de Aguilera. When the government began to close down his casinos, he built a political base, buying the newspaper La Voz de Castilla and creating the Farmers and Cattle-Breeders League, a party with widespread support throughout the province. His political factotum was Cándido Casanueva, the notary who was his link to Gil Robles. It was claimed that Martín Veloz bought votes for Casanueva, just as it was later alleged that Casanueva bought votes for Gil Robles. Martín Veloz's own power base was Peñaranda de Bracamonte, east of Salamanca.[51]

As a powerful *cacique*, he had secured a parliamentary seat in 1919 and had been involved in numerous violent incidents in the Cortes. He threatened other deputies, including Indalecio Prieto, and once drew a gun on a rival from Salamanca. After the dictator Primo de Rivera had closed down casinos and gambling dens, Martín Veloz suffered financial difficulties and faced bankruptcy by the time the Second Republic was established. Nevertheless, he remained in contact with his military friends and during the Sanjurjada vainly tried to get the Salamanca garrison to rise. In the spring of 1936, he and Cándido Casanueva collaborated with the local military in the preparation of the uprising. In particular, Martín Veloz went to great lengths to persuade his friend Gonzalo Queipo de Llano to take part. He invited him to his estate at the end of May 1936 and harangued him on the need for a coup. Moreover, when the war began, Martín Veloz, like other landowners of Salamanca, would put enormous energy into recruiting peasants for the rebel forces.[52]

In the province of Toledo, violence was kept under control by the Civil Governor, who ordered the Civil Guard not to shoot unless under attack. He also ordered the confiscation of all firearms and 10,000 shotguns were collected. This well-intentioned measure was severely damaging to the peasantry, who relied on their shotguns for hunting. The guns that were kept in Civil Guard posts were either destroyed or distributed to rightists when the military coup took place.[53] On 9 March, in Escalona in the north-west of Toledo, local Falangists shot four Socialist landworkers and wounded twelve more. On 5 March, in Quintanar de la Orden in the south of the province, thugs in the pay of the local *cacique* assaulted the house of the Socialist Mayor and pistol-whipped his wife and two small sons. They then tried to kill his elder daughter by throwing her down a well. In neither case were the perpetrators arrested.[54]

Under pressure from the FNTT, on 3 March Ruiz-Funes issued a decree permitting the *yunteros* of Extremadura to reoccupy land that they had worked before being evicted. Its legal implementation would be complex and clearly take some time. But the *yunteros* were desperate and spring planting was a matter of urgency. Just before the new Cortes met, the FNTT called for a massive mobilization of the peasantry on Sunday 15 March to remind the Popular Front deputies of their electoral promises. The demands of the demonstrators were the immediate hand-over of land with credit for peasant collectives, the return of common lands, work for the unemployed, strict observation of agreed wages, working conditions and work-sharing, release of the remaining prisoners and the disarming of extreme rightists.[55]

The call was obeyed in much of Castile and the north and throughout the south. Banners bearing these demands and red flags headed processions of labourers giving clenched-fist salutes and chanting the battle cry of the Asturian miners, 'Unite, Proletarian Brothers!' Díaz de Entresotos, who witnessed this and other demonstrations in Mérida, revealed his bitterness at the turning of the tables: 'From the pavement, with desolation in their eyes and infinite anguish in their hearts, respectable folk watched the demonstrators pass. I was eaten up with a desperate suppressed rage. My head was bursting with murderous thoughts and I would have given my life to be able to kill that scum whose very presence constituted a humiliation and a challenge.'[56]

The 15 March demonstration was a success in numerous villages of Cáceres, León, Zamora and Salamanca and even in Navarre, Valladolid and Burgos. In Salamanca, there were processions in many small towns. In most places, despite the anger of the local right, there were no major incidents. However, in the small village of Mancera de Abajo near Martín Veloz's power base, Peñaranda de Bracamonte, the demonstration was attacked by right-wing thugs. A young Communist and a child were shot dead and, in the subsequent tumult, a local landowner was stabbed to death. The burial of the Communist in the provincial capital saw a massive turn-out of the left, led by the Mayor of Salamanca, Casto Prieto Carrasco of Azaña's party, Izquierda Republicana. The outrage of the local right was inflamed further when, fearful of further disturbances, the new Civil Governor, Antonio Cepas López, also of Izquierda Republicana, prohibited religious processions scheduled for Holy Week. Over the following months, there were a number of clashes between Falangists and leftists during which innocent bystanders were hurt.[57]

A major escalation took place at dawn on 25 March 1936. In torrential rain, more than 60,000 landless peasants occupied 1,934 mainly cattle-rearing estates in Badajoz and proceeded to carry out symbolic acts of ploughing. The initiative had been meticulously organized by the FNTT whose officials had arranged which families were to go to each estate. It was the union's intention that the estates be cultivated as collectives.[58] In order to forestall violence, the Ministry of Agriculture quickly legalized the occupations and settled 50,000 families. In Cádiz, Toledo, Salamanca and the sierra of Córdoba, labourers also invaded estates, although on a smaller scale. Toledo saw the highest proportion of estates expropriated, and was third, behind Badajoz and Cáceres, in the proportion of peasants settled. This was reflected in the vengeance wreaked on the peasantry when the Francoist columns arrived early in the Civil War. When the Ministry declared the occupied estates 'of public utility', the landowner was guaranteed compensation in relation to potential rent. Nevertheless, this spontaneous imposition of agrarian reform infuriated the local owners, who sent in their armed retainers to reoccupy the estates. When the mixed juries sent workers to estates left fallow, they refused to pay their wages. It was a complex situation, with many of the smaller farmers facing real difficulties in paying unwanted workers. Inevitably, crop thefts increased. When the harvest was imminent, the owners refused to negotiate wage and working conditions with local branches of the FNTT. Those who refused to pay the workers were first fined and, if they still refused, in a few cases arrested.[59]

Faced with incontrovertible evidence that the agrarian reforms of the Republic would be combated with violence, the FNTT echoed Zabalza's call for the creation of people's militias, complaining that:

> the government policy of disarming all citizens is a joke. In fact, this means handing us over helpless to our enemies. For the last two years, the Civil Guard has been disarming us while leaving untouched the arsenals of the fascist elements, and when we speak of fascists, we mean the CEDA as well as the Falange. We know only too well that it is the Cedistas and other landowners who pay the Falangist squads. Thus, we face, armed to the teeth, all the landowners, their lackeys, their paid thugs, the shotgun-toting clergy, and backing them up, the Civil Guard, the bourgeois judiciary and government agronomists.[60]

One of the factors that did most to increase social tension during the spring of 1936 was anti-clericalism. Religious hatred was most intense in the towns and villages where the clergy had been vocal in support of the CEDA and of the post-1934 repression. Revenge sometimes took the form of the newly reinstated mayors preventing Catholic burials, baptisms and weddings or charging for bells to be rung. In Rute in southern Córdoba, the Socialist Mayor fined the parish priest for carrying the viaticum through the streets without having applied for a licence to do so. In several places, religious statues and monumental crucifixes were destroyed. This was especially true in Andalusia and the Levante where there was a rash of church burnings and the tombs of clergy were profaned. In several villages in La Mancha, religious processions were interrupted and the faithful harassed by young workers as they left Mass. In Santa Cruz de Mudela, in the south of Ciudad Real, in mid-March, an attempt to set fire to the parish church was prevented by the Civil Guard. Over the next two months, the Mayor closed two Catholic schools, prohibited Catholic burials, prevented children from wearing their first Holy Communion outfits in the village and even hung religious medals from the collars of dogs that he loosed among people leaving Sunday Mass. In Cúllar de Baza in Granada, in June, the Mayor allegedly broke into the church at night and dug up the body of the recently deceased parish priest in order to bury him in the civil cemetery. These were extreme cases. In most places, the Holy Week processions went ahead without incident and manifestations of anti-clericalism diminished after the end of May. Nevertheless, the religious clashes that did take place were an important factor in the political polarization and the incitement of violence. There were instances of trigger-happy clergy (*curas trabucaires*). In Cehegín (Murcia), when his residence was surrounded, the parish priest opened fire on demonstrators, killing one of them. In Piñeres (Santander), a priest shot at villagers and wounded one. The parish priest of Freijo (Orense) possessed a Winchester rifle, a Mauser pistol and a Remington revolver.[61]

Confrontation intensified greatly when work conditions were negotiated in April. The landowners were angered that the Popular Front town councils intended to impose substantial fines on those who flouted the agreements reached by the mixed juries.[62] The agreements were largely ignored in Badajoz, Córdoba, Ciudad Real, Málaga and Toledo. Throughout Badajoz, the owners refused to hire workers and used machinery to bring in the harvest by night. In Almendralejo in the south of the province, a prosperous area, more than two thousand men had no work because the local owners refused to employ FNTT members. Moreover, the unity of the landlords was maintained by threats that any of their number who negotiated with the union would be killed. Nevertheless, the Civil Governor ordered the arrest of four of the richest owners. The tension in the town would explode into bloody violence when the Civil War broke out.[63] In Zafra, the reinstated Mayor, José González Barrero, chaired a mixed committee of landowners and workers which arranged for the placing of unemployed labourers in the area. When the Francoist column entered Zafra on 7 August, four of the five worker representatives on the committee were murdered.[64]

During the cereal harvest in Jaén, the owners brought in non-union-ized labour from Galicia and elsewhere. This scab labour was protected by the Civil Guard, which also colluded as the owners armed their own estate guards. When the owners in Badajoz bypassed local unions by importing cheap labour from Portugal or using machinery, migrant labourers were assaulted and machines sabotaged. With the harvest on the verge of ruin, the local authorities arranged for it to be brought in by non-union labour under police protection. Seeing this as an affront to their property rights, the owners refused the wages demanded and ordered their armed guards to expel the workers from the fields. In some cases, crops were destroyed by the owners to thwart the workers. The Association of Rural Estate-Owners claimed that landowners were faced with annihilation or suicide. In Carrión de los Condes to the north of Palencia, the president of the Casa del Pueblo was hanged by local land-owners. In many parts of Córdoba, the workers' organizations tried to impose the strict rota of workers to be placed on estates. In Palma del Río, there was serious conflict when one of the principal landowners, Félix Moreno Ardanuy, refused to pay the workers 'placed' on his estates. He was imprisoned and ordered to pay the 121,500 pesetas owed. When he refused, the town council confiscated 2,450 of his pigs, cows and horses. His son and other local Falangists then rioted in the town. When the military rebels took the town, his revenge would be ferocious. In Palenciana, in the south of Córdoba, a guard interrupted a meeting in the Casa del Pueblo and attempted to arrest the speaker. A scuffle ensued and he was stabbed to death. His comrades opened fire, killing one worker and wounding three more.[65]

In the province of Seville, the Civil Governor, José María Varela Rendueles, noticed that landowners called for the Civil Guard to expel those who had invaded estates only after they had brought in the harvest. Thus, when the Civil Guard had done its work, the owners had had their crops collected free of charge.[66] Conflict between the forcibly imposed workers and the landowners in Seville was particularly acute. The smaller towns of fewer than 10,000 inhabitants were dominated by the FNTT, while the larger ones were in the hands of the CNT. In one of the latter, Lebrija, on 23 April, anarchist labourers, protesting that they had not been paid enough, were confronted by the local Civil Guard commander, Lieutenant Francisco López Cepero. Stones were thrown, the commander fell and he was beaten to death by the mob. This was the prelude to the burning down of two churches, three convents, the headquarters of Acción Popular and the houses of several landowners.[67] The conflict in the countryside was utterly disorganized and lacked any co-ordinated revolutionary plan for the seizure of power. That, however, did not diminish the alarm of the rural middle and upper classes.

Violence was not confined to rural areas. Indeed, it is unlikely that the situation in the countryside would alone have secured sufficient support for a military coup. The plotters needed to mobilize urban popular opinion and that required the provocation of violence in the streets, especially those of Madrid. The capital, where diplomats and newspaper correspondents were stationed, would be used to convince international opinion that all of Spain was a victim of uncontrolled violence. Provocation was to be undertaken by the Falange, whose leader José Antonio Primo de Rivera had no inhibitions about violence against the left. Irked by the ebullience of Madrid workers celebrating the Popular Front victory in Madrid, he commented to his friend Dionisio Ridruejo: 'With a couple of good marksmen, a demonstration like that can be dissolved in ten minutes.' José Antonio resented the fact that it was taken for granted that the Falange would accept 'the role of guerrillas or the light cavalry of other craftier parties'. As he said to Ridruejo, 'Let's hope that they finally wise up. We are ready to take the risks, no? Well, let them, at least, provide the money.'[68]

In fact, the undermining of government authority by street violence went hand in hand with the military conspiracy for which it provided the justification. Having gained only 0.4 per cent of the vote in the February elections (about 45,000 votes), it was obvious that the Falange had little popular support. José Antonio was already committed to a violent seizure of power and, as his comments to Ridruejo showed, he was ready to contribute a Falangist strategy of tension to the wider conspiracy.[69] Within a month of the elections, there were armed attacks in Madrid on prominent left-wing and liberal politicians. Numerous incidents were provoked in which Falangists and left-wingers fought in the streets of the capital. On 11 March, a Falangist law student, Juan José Olano, was shot dead. The following day, in reprisal, a three-man Falangist hit squad, almost certainly acting with José Antonio's knowledge, tried to kill the Socialist law professor Luis Jiménez Asúa. Jiménez Asúa survived but his police bodyguard was killed. On the day of his funeral, the left reacted by setting fire to two churches and the offices of the Renovación Española newspaper *La Nación*, which belonged to one of the Falange's backers, Manuel Delgado Barreto. The consequence was that, on 14 March, the Director General of Security, José Alonso Mallol, ordered José Antonio and other members of the senior leadership of FE de las JONS to be arrested for illegal possession of weapons.[70]

Azaña was shocked that Largo Caballero had expressed no concern about Jiménez Asúa – a stark indication of Socialist divisions. Nevertheless, in reprisal for José Antonio's arrest, on 16 March, Largo Caballero's house was fired upon by a Falangist terror squad. This prompted a cunning display of hypocrisy from Gil Robles. On 17 March, he went to see the Minister of the Interior, Amós Salvador, to protest about the disorder, citing the attack on Largo Caballero's home as a symptom. The CEDA also tabled a debate on the subject in the Cortes, blaming the government and the left.[71] Knowing that the army was not yet ready to seize power and aware that full-scale obstruction of Azaña's government could only lead to an all-Socialist government, Gil Robles devoted his energies to building up the atmosphere of fear. The objective was that the middle classes, terrified by the spectre of disorder, would eventually turn to the army as their only saviour.

José Antonio was detained on a technicality because his involvement in the attempt on Jiménez Asúa's life could not be proven. However, there is little doubt that he approved of it. The erstwhile leader of the Falange action squads, Juan Antonio Ansaldo, visited him in his Madrid prison, the Cárcel Modelo, to discuss plans to get the three would-be assassins out of Spain. Ansaldo got them to France, but they were arrested and extradited back to Spain. On 8 April, they were tried for the murder of the bodyguard and the attempted murder of Jiménez Asúa. Their leader, Alberto Ortega, was sentenced to twenty-five years' imprisonment and his two accomplices to six years each. At the highest level of the Falange – which meant the imprisoned leadership – a decision was taken to respond with a revenge attack on the judge, Manuel Pedregal, who was shot dead on 13 April as a deadly warning to judges in any future trials of Falangists.[72] On 12 April, José Antonio called off a plan elaborated by the Falange action squads to murder Largo Caballero at the hospital where his wife was terminally ill. Since he visited her without his escort, it was regarded as simple for Falangists disguised as medical staff to kill him in the deserted corridor outside her room. José Antonio explained to a friend that his caution derived from the belief that the Falange would be destroyed by the consequent left-wing backlash. He was also uneasy about the public impact of the murder of a sixty-six-year-old man visiting his dying wife.[73]

Two days later, there took place an incident which played into the hands of the Falange and of the Unión Militar Española. In Madrid's broad Avenida de la Castellana, there was a military parade to commemorate the fifth anniversary of the founding of the Republic. A loud explosion and the sound of machine-gun fire near the presidential platform alarmed the assembled dignitaries and their police escorts. In fact, the noises came from powerful fireworks placed by Falangists. Then, as the Civil Guard marched past, jeers and chants were heard. These included 'Down with the Civil Guard!' and '¡UHP!' (Uníos, Hermanos Proletarios – Unite, Proletarian Brothers), recalling the brutal Asturian repression. Shots were fired and, in the mêlée, a Civil Guard lieutenant in plain clothes, Anastasio de los Reyes López, was fatally wounded by unknown assailants. Subsequently, the left-wing press claimed that he had been shot as a result of a 'fascist provocation'. Whoever the culprit was, the right was successful in squeezing the greatest advantage from the incident.[74]

The government tried to have Reyes buried discreetly but the head of his unit, Lieutenant Colonel Florentino González Vallés, turned the funeral into a massive anti-Republican demonstration. Fernando Primo de Rivera, José Antonio's brother, met representatives of the UME to discuss the role of Falangists and was told that they were expected to carry guns. Flouting government orders to the contrary, González Vallés, himself a Falangist sympathizer, ordered, in an anti-Republican gesture, that the funeral procession should follow the same route as the 14 April military parade. Despite this illegality, Gil Robles and Calvo Sotelo led the cortège. As it came down the Castellana, several shots were fired at the procession. It is not known if the culprits were leftists or right-wing agents provocateurs. When the Falangists tried to turn the procession into an attack on the Cortes, there was a clash with Assault Guards in which Andrés Sáenz de Heredia, a cousin of José Antonio, was killed. Thereafter, the commander of the Guards, Lieutenant José del Castillo Sáenz de Tejada, received death threats.[75] The UME saw the events of 16 April as a boost for recruitment. Prieto commented: 'Yesterday, it was shown that fascism has taken hold really strongly in our military organizations.'[76]

Disorder was certainly on the increase during the spring of 1936, but its scale was greatly inflated by the right-wing press and in the parliamentary speeches of Gil Robles and Calvo Sotelo, which placed the blame exclusively on the left. However, only two groups stood to benefit, even in theory, from the proliferation of indiscriminate lawlessness – the extreme left of the anarchist movement and the 'catastrophist' right who backed military conspiracy. The Popular Front tactic imposed by

Moscow meant that Communists had no plans to undermine public order and seize power. In the Socialist Party, both *El Socialista*, the newspaper of the Prieto wing, and *Claridad*, the mouthpiece of Largo Caballero, warned their readers to ignore rightist provocation.[77] None of the Popular Front parties had any need to provoke violence in order to take power. The creation of an atmosphere of turmoil and disorder could, on the other hand, justify the use of force to establish a dictatorship of the right. It is difficult to distinguish between provocation and reprisal in street fights between Communists or Socialists and Falangists or members of Gil Robles's youth movement, the JAP. However, it is noteworthy that José Antonio's close friend Felipe Ximénez de Sandoval boasted that, in the violence following Reyes's funeral procession, 'the mortuary welcomed, for every one of ours, ten of theirs'.[78]

Significantly, wealthy conservatives who had previously financed Gil Robles to defend their interests were now switching funds to the Falange and the scab union, the Sindicatos Libres. In March, *ABC* had opened a subscription for a hitherto unknown Federación Española de Trabajadores, behind which could be discerned Ramón Sales, the self-styled fascist agent provocateur who had become famous in the political gangsterism of 1919–23. By late April the fund had reached 350,000 pesetas, donated by aristocrats, landowners, industrialists and many anonymous 'fascists' and Falangists. Since the money was never used for trade union purposes and a substantial number of those arrested for acts of violence were members of the Sindicatos Libres, the left had no doubts that this was a fund to finance agents provocateurs. Professional gunmen were being hired by the right and their operations were designed to provoke the widest repercussions.[79]

The attacks on Jiménez de Asúa and Largo Caballero were clearly among those aimed at provoking reprisals. The most successful operation of this kind was carried out in Granada on 9–10 March. A squad of Falangist gunmen fired on a group of workers and their families, wounding many women and children. The local CNT, the UGT, the Partido Comunista de España (PCE) and the Partido Sindicalista united in calling a general strike in the course of which there was considerable violence. Two churches and the offices of both the Falange and Acción Popular were set on fire, and the ACNP newspaper, *Ideal*, was destroyed. Throughout the day, Falangist snipers fired from rooftops on left-wing demonstrators and also on firemen to stop them controlling the fires. In Granada and elsewhere, incidents were often caused by strangers who disappeared as quickly as they had appeared. When the military rebels took power at the beginning of the Civil War, some of the most radical anarchists and Communists in Granada revealed themselves as Falangist agents provocateurs. Throughout Spain, leftist municipal authorities worked hard to maintain order. They were not helped by the fact that conservative members of the judiciary sympathized with Falangist activities. Judges who did take a strong line against rightist gunmen were, in their turn, selected as targets.[80]

On 15 April, when Azaña presented his moderate programme of government to the Cortes, Calvo Sotelo declared that any cabinet that relied on PSOE votes was effectively under Russian dominance. Less stridently, Gil Robles produced a masterpiece of hypocrisy. He patronizingly recognized Azaña's good intentions and denied that the conflictive situation in the countryside owed anything to CEDA policies. Forgetting the humiliation to which Giménez Fernández had been subjected, he claimed that his party was committed to the elimination of social injustice and to the equitable redistribution of wealth. He went on to endorse Calvo Sotelo's claim that the government was impotent before a wave of disorder caused entirely by the left. Blaming the violence of agents provocateurs on governmental weakness, he said that his followers were already taking up arms in self-defence. He declared that he would soon have to tell them to expect nothing from legality and to join parties that offered them 'the lure of revenge'. In apocalyptic terms, he issued a dire warning: 'Half the nation will not resign itself to die. If it cannot defend itself by one path, it will defend itself by another ... When civil war breaks out in Spain, let it be known that the weapons have been loaded by the negligence of a government which has not been able to fulfil its duty towards groups which have stayed within the strictest legality.' He ended with a resounding battle cry: 'It is better to know how to die in the street than to be trampled on as a coward.'

Gil Robles was effectively threatening war if the Popular Front did not drop its commitment to thorough reform of the social and economic structure. Because parliamentary speeches could not be censored, Gil Robles and Calvo Sotelo larded theirs with exaggerations of disorder. They knew that, reported in full in the press, their predictions of doom would generate an atmosphere of terror among sectors of the middle and upper classes, who would look to the army for salvation. Gil Robles's remarks in the Cortes of 15 April and his assiduous attendance at the funerals of Falangist gunmen projected the impression that political violence was the exclusive responsibility of the left. Behind his rhetoric of concern for public order, the CEDA was organizing motorized machine-gun assault groups and, as the spring wore on, ever more right-ist youths arrested for acts of violence were members of the Juventud de Acción Popular.[81]

Gil Robles admitted in his memoirs that the principal function of the CEDA was to make propaganda in parliament and to act as a shield for more violent groups. He quoted approvingly a comment that the perpetrators of right-wing terrorism in the spring of 1936 were 'of the highest nobility and spiritual quality'. In a newpaper interview, he expressed approval of those who left the CEDA 'to take the path of violence, believing it to be the way to solve national problems'.[82] Almost immediately after the elections, the majority of one of key sections of the CEDA, the Derecha Regional Valenciana, had rejected the moder-ation of their leader, Luis Lucia, in favour of direct action. Under the leadership of the party's secretary general, José María Costa Serrano, the DRV was collecting arms and organizing a clandestine militia. Links were established with the local Falange, Renovación Española and the Unión Militar Española. The DRV's youth section drilled and held shooting practice. Throughout the spring, at least 15,000 members of JAP joined the Falange. Nothing was done to dissuade them and no efforts were made to recruit replacements. Many of those remaining with the CEDA were in active contact with groups committed to violence. And, when the war broke out, thousands of CEDA members joined the Carlists.[83]

As confrontation in the countryside increased, fears of military conspiracy abounded. On 1 May, the moderate Socialist Indalecio Prieto laid out the problem in a speech at Cuenca, where there was a by-elec-tion. He went to Cuenca 'worried about an imminent fascist uprising about which I had been making warnings to no avail other than to bring upon myself abuse and contempt'. It was thought prudent for him to have an armed escort provided by a group of the Socialist Youth known as the Motorizada. On the eve of his arrival, there had been fighting between local leftists and rightists and ashes were still blowing about from the burning of the *casino*, the local landowners' club.[84] He under-lined the uncertainty provoked by disorder and the attendant dangers of a military coup. In a passionately patriotic speech, he laid out a plan for social justice based on well-planned economic growth to be imple-mented by a strong government. He denounced right-wing provocation and left-wing agitation – 'what no nation can sustain is the attrition of its government and of its own economic vitality while being forced to live with unease, nerves and anxiety'.[85]

An opportunity to strengthen the government arose in early May with the impeachment of Alcalá Zamora and his replacement as President by Manuel Azaña. It was widely hoped that a combination of a strong President and an equally strong Prime Minister could defend the Republic against military subversion. However, when Azaña asked him to form a government, Prieto made the tactical error of twice consulting the PSOE parliamentary group of which Largo Caballero was president. At meetings on 11 and 12 May, Largo Caballero and his followers opposed him and he capitulated quietly. Despite their opposition, Prieto could have formed a government with the support of the Republican parties and about a third of PSOE deputies. However, he was not prepared to split the PSOE.[86]

By blocking the plan for a Prieto-led government, Largo Caballero had effectively destroyed the last chance of avoiding civil war. A powerful argument in favour of a coup used within the officer corps was that Largo Caballero, once in power, would dissolve the army. Prieto realized, as his rival apparently did not, that attempts at full-scale revolutionary social change would drive the middle classes to fascism and armed counter-revolution. Instead, Prieto, ever the pragmatist, was convinced that the answer was to restore order and accelerate reform. He had plans to remove unreliable military commanders, to reduce the power of the Civil Guard, to appoint a trusted officer as Director General of Security and to disarm the fascist terror squads.[87] Largo Caballero prevented this and ensured that the strongest party of the Popular Front could not participate actively in using the apparatus of the state to defend the Republic. Azaña turned to his fellow Left Republican Santiago Casares Quiroga, who lacked the stature to deal with the problems he was called upon to solve. Prieto wrote later, 'My role was thus reduced to constantly issuing warnings about the danger, and trying to ensure that, within our camp, naive and blind obstinacy, typical of a lamentable revolutionary infantilism, did not go on creating an atmosphere favourable to fascism because that was all that absurd acts of disorder brought about.'[88]

On 19 May, Casares Quiroga, Azaña's successor as Prime Minister, presented his programme to the Cortes. Gil Robles responded with a virtuoso display of ambiguity. As on 15 April, an apparent appeal for moderation was in reality a justification of violence. Without mentioning names, he dwelled gloatingly on Azaña's failure to get a broadly based Popular Front government under Prieto, stating that the Republican government was 'reduced to the sad role, in relation to those groups [pointing to the Socialist benches], of being today the servant, tomorrow the victim'. Regarding Casares Quiroga's declared hostility to fascism, he pointed out that disorder made fascist solutions relevant. While criticizing fascism in theory because of its foreign origins and its elements of state socialism, he justified the violence of those denounced as fascists, saying that there was no other way for them to defend their interests. He had nothing to say about how the present political disorder had been incited by the repressive and vindictive policies carried out by Radical–CEDA cabinets. Declaring that democracy was dead, he praised the trend to fascism as growing out of 'a sense of patriotism, perhaps badly focused but profoundly hurt to see that the rhythm of politics is dictated not by great national interests but by you [turning to the Socialist deputies] with orders from Moscow'. It was an endorsement of the flight of the JAP masses into the Falange. Ending with a provocative challenge to Largo Caballero's followers, he made a sarcastic reference to 'you ferocious revolutionaries who do nothing but talk'.[89]

Gil Robles's denunciations of the breakdown of public order were seen on the left as a hypocritical attempt to discredit the government and justify a military coup. Those speeches also fed on the Falangist strategy of tension, directed from prison by José Antonio Primo de Rivera. After his arrest, his party went underground and the bloody cycle of provocation and reprisal was intensified dramatically. On 7 May, ripples of the Reyes funeral three weeks earlier could be seen in the murder, by a joint UME–Falangist squad, of Captain Carlos Faraudo, the Republican engineers officer who drilled the Socialist militias. The following day, there was a failed attempt on the life of the conservative Republican ex-Minister José María Álvarez Mendizábal. José Antonio told his friend Felipe Ximénez de Sandoval: 'I don't want any more Falangists in jail. I will use all my authority as Jefe Nacional [national leader] of the Falange to expel anyone who comes here without a good reason, such as having killed Azaña or Largo Caballero.' The consequent disorder was the basis of the appeals of Gil Robles and Calvo Sotelo for military intervention.[90]

Within the government apparatus, the man most concerned by the links between military conspiracy and Falangist violence was the Director General of Security, José Alonso Mallol. Since being appointed in February, Alonso Mallol had worked tirelessly to combat Falangist terrorism and to monitor the activities of hostile officers. One of his innovations was to place telephone taps on the houses and the barracks where the coup was being hatched. José Antonio's correspondence with the conspirators was also intercepted. By May, Alonso Mallol was able to give President Azaña and the Prime Minister Casares Quiroga a list of more than five hundred conspirators whom he believed should be arrested immediately. Fearful of the possible reactions, Azaña and Casares failed to act and the coup went ahead.[91]

In fact, as José Antonio boasted to the monarchist Antonio Goicoechea on 20 May 1936, being in prison was no impediment to directing the Falange's role in the preparations for civil war. From his cell, he liaised with Carlists and with Renovación Española.[92] He had already met General Mola on 8 March to offer the services of the Falange. Also in early March, José Antonio's friend Ramón Serrano Suñer had put him in touch with other senior military figures including Yagüe, Mola's key to the participation of the Moroccan Army.[93] The role of the Falange would be to carry out acts of terrorism to provoke left-wing reprisals, the two things combining to justify right-wing jeremiads about disorder. From prison, José Antonio issued on 20 May the first of three clandestine leaflets with the title *No Importa. Boletín de los Días de Persecución* (No Matter. Bulletin of the Days of Persecution). Urging his followers to intensify their attacks on leftists, he wrote on 6 June, 'Tomorrow, when brighter days dawn, the Falange will receive the laurels earned by being first in this holy crusade of violence.' In the same issue, there was a call for the assassinations of the judge who had sent him to prison and of the Socialist parliamentary deputy for Cáceres, Luis Romero Solano, for his part in the arrest of José Luna, the Falange leader in Extremadura.[94]

The principal orchestrator of the coup, General Mola, had been posted to Navarre in March. The government hoped thereby to neutralize him but, confident of the most influential officers in Morocco and of his police network, he still held the key strands of the rebellion. It was assumed that Mola would have few dealings with the deeply reactionary local Carlists. In fact, within three days of his arrival in Pamplona on 14 March, local officers introduced him to B. Félix Maíz, a thirty-six-year-old local businessman who was to be his liaison with the Carlists. Discovering a shared enthusiasm for *The Protocols of the Elders of Zion*, they hit it off immediately. To Maíz's delight, Mola, who was still receiving paranoiac anti-Communist reports from the White Russians in Paris, told him that 'we confront an enemy that is not Spanish'. Maíz, who took *The Protocols* as genuine, believed that a war to the death was imminent between Christians and the stooges of the Jews 'the great beast – tightly knit hordes emerging from the swamp of evil'. His view of the political situation was even more disturbing: 'all over Spain, there are gangs of creatures injected with rabies who are seeking Christian flesh in which to sink their teeth'.[95]

The fantasies of Maíz were merely an extreme version of a carefully prepared fiction intended to justify the military coup and the subsequent repression. 'Secret documents' were concocted to 'prove' that a Soviet take-over in Spain was imminent. A kind of Spanish equivalent to *The Protocols of the Elders of Zion*, these 'documents' were intended to generate fear and indignation, not least because they contained blacklists of right-wingers intended to be murdered as soon as the alleged Communist take-over was completed.[96] Such inventions presented a military coup as a patriotic act to save Spain from the assault masterminded by the dark hand of Judaism. With such a view of the enemy, it was but a short step to Mola's first secret instructions to his fellow conspirators, issued in April. He wrote, 'It has to be borne in mind that the action has to be violent in the extreme so as to subdue as soon as possible the enemy which is strong and well organized. It goes without saying that all leaders of political parties, societies and trade unions not part of the movement will be imprisoned and exemplary punishment carried out on them in order to choke off any rebellion or strikes.'[97] Mola, as a hardened Africanista, placed a high value on the value of terror in paralysing opponents. However, it was not just a question of gaining power but also the first step to 'purifying' Spain of the noxious elements of the left.

José Antonio was transferred to the prison in Alicante on the night of 5 June, and he immediately sent an emissary to Pamplona to reassure Mola that he remained committed to the coup and to offer four thousand Falangists as a shock force for the first days of the uprising.[98] In a further testimony to the links between the military and street violence, the monarchist politician Antonio Goicoechea wrote on 14 June to the Italian government on behalf of the Falange, Renovación Española and the Comunión Tradicionalista to request funding for terrorist squads. Commenting that the military coup was well advanced, he wrote of 'the unavoidable need to organize the atmosphere of violence'.[99]

Despite mounting rural violence, the FNTT managed to maintain the discipline of its members, even after a bloody incident at the end of May near the town of Yeste in the south of Albacete. The fraudulent enclosure of communal lands by local *caciques* had condemned the peasants to desperate poverty. Many had lost their livelihood as a result of the construction of a reservoir near by in 1931, which took fertile land out of production and prevented local woodmen transporting timber via the Rivers Tus and Segura. In the spring of 1936, the efforts of the newly restored Republican–Socialist town council to place unemployed workers on estates had met with furious resistance. On 28 May, a group of workers and their families from the hamlet of La Graya cut down trees for charcoal and then began to plough on an estate called La Umbría. Once common land, La Umbría now belonged to the most powerful *cacique*, Antonio Alfaro. On his instructions, twenty-two Civil Guards arrived.

Most of the villagers fled but six remained. After beating them, the Civil Guards took them to La Graya, where they were further mistreated. At dawn the next day, a crowd of labourers from surrounding hamlets followed as the prisoners were being taken to the nearby town of Yeste to ensure that they would not be shot 'trying to escape' (the *ley de fugas*). The crowd swelled and, as they reached Yeste, it was agreed that the prisoners should be released into the custody of the Mayor. When the crowd pressed forward to greet the prisoners, a Civil Guard panicked and fired a shot. In the ensuing mêlée, a Civil Guard was killed. His companions opened fire on the crowd and then pursued fleeing peasants into the surrounding hills, killing seventeen people, including the deputy Mayor, and wounding many more. Fearing that the Civil Guards would return and burn La Graya, many villagers took refuge in nearby hamlets. Fifty FNTT members were arrested, including the Socialist Mayor of Yeste.[100] Yeste and other clashes could have led to bloodshed on a large scale. However, the FNTT leadership restrained the rank and file, urging them to put their faith in the government's accelerated agrarian reform. Faced with the new determination of the Popular Front, the large landowners began to look to the military for their protection.

A similar scale of belligerence from the landowners was revealed in Badajoz when the Civil Governor took the extraordinary step on 20 May of closing the provincial headquarters of the Association of Rural Estate-Owners which was co-ordinating efforts to sabotage the harvest and to mount a lock-out of unionized labour.[101] It was to no avail; many landowners preferred to let the cereal harvest rot in order to impose discipline on the workers. To their fury, the Civil Governor decreed that the workers should bring in the harvest and keep part of the crop in lieu of wages.[102] In the province of Cáceres, a systematic policy of provocation was carried out by well-armed Falangists. Among the rightists arrested there for public order offences in the spring and summer of 1936 were several members of the JAP.[103]

It was a short step from the exasperation of starving labourers to disorder. The scale of hunger in rural Spain in 1936 is almost unimaginable today. On 21 April, the Civil Governor of Madrid was informed that the only available protein for peasants in the province was lizards and that children were fainting from malnutrition in their schools. The Civil Governor of Ciudad Real reported that in the south of the province peasants were living off boiled weeds. In Quintanar de la Orden in Toledo, men and women were found lying in the streets having collapsed from inanition. In many villages, and not only in the south, hunger provoked mass invasions of estates to steal crops or livestock. Attacks on food shops were not uncommon. In Fuente de Cantos in Badajoz, in May 1936, a meeting to discuss local unemployment was addressed by the local Socialist leader. Appalled by the evident distress of the men, women and children of his audience, he called on them to follow him to where there was food for all. He led them to one of the estates of the biggest owner in the area, the Conde de la Corte. The estate was largely given over to the pasture of pigs and sheep. The starving townspeople fell upon the pigs and, after killing them with sticks and knives, returned to Fuente de Cantos, bloodstained and staggering under the weight of the slaughtered pigs. Further to the north of Badajoz, in Quintana de la Serena, day-labourers entered an estate, stealing sheep to feed their families.[104]

In the very different conditions of conservative Old Castile, it was more difficult to stir up disorder. Segovia was a predominantly agrarian province where the organized working class was relatively tiny, its exiguous strength resting mainly on railway workers.[105] In the provincial capital, a clash on 8 March was provoked when members of the JAP and a few Falangists attacked workers enjoying a Sunday dance. A workers' protest march was fired upon by JAP snipers. This provoked a left-wing attack on the headquarters of Acción Popular. Despite the JAP's involvement in gun-related incidents, most clashes did not go beyond verbal insults. In the town of Cuéllar to the north of the province, building labourers who refused to join the union were prevented from working by UGT members. In the village of Otero de los Herreros, in the south, workers returning from a demonstration made a local Falangist kiss their red flag. The 'victim' later led the local repression and organized the shaving of the heads of left-wing girls.

Although there were some minor anti-clerical incidents, with firecrackers placed at the door of the convent of the Carmelite Fathers, Holy Week celebrations in the first week of April went ahead in most churches in the provincial capital. Segovia's right-wing newspaper, *El Adelantado*, even commented on the respect shown by non-Catholics to those taking part in the various ceremonies and religious services. In June, however, the ecclesiastical authorities suspended the traditional Corpus Christi procession, instead holding a solemn celebration within the Cathedral. The reason was simply outrage that the left should have the effrontery to put up its posters and organize demonstrations with flags flying and slogans shouted. Despite the relative calm, the tensions were later used to justify the repression.[106] In fact, as early as April, the military plotters in Segovia had called upon the local Falangist leader, Dionisio Ridruejo, to have his men, few as they were, ready to take part in the coup.[107]

At a national level, on 16 June, in the Cortes, Gil Robles screwed up the tension with a denunciation of the government in the guise of a call for 'the speedy adoption of measures to end the state of subversion in which Spain is living'. Superficially couched as an appeal for moderation, his speech was essentially a declaration to middle-class opinion that nothing could be expected from the democratic regime. Knowing that the army's preparations were well advanced, he read out a catalogue of disorder alleged to have taken place since the elections. He placed the entire responsibility on the government for his list of 269 murders, beatings, robberies, church-burnings and strikes (statistics to which, on 15 July, he would add another sixty-one dead). Some of it was true, some of it invention and all dispensed in bloodcurdling terms. He gave no indication that the right had played any part in what he described or that many of the dead were workers killed by the Civil Guard or other forces of order. In contrast, he protested about the imprisonment of Falangist and JAP terrorists and the imposition of fines on recalcitrant employers. As long as the government relied on the votes of Socialists and Communists, thundered Gil Robles, there could never be one minute's peace in Spain. He ended by declaring that 'today, we are witnessing the funeral of democracy'.[108]

There has been considerable debate about the accuracy of Gil Robles's figures. The most exhaustive recent study, by Eduardo González Calleja, reached the figure of 351 dead. Significantly, the highest figures – sixty-seven for Madrid, and Seville with thirty-four – were reached in cities where Falangist gunmen were at their most active. The next highest are Santander with twenty-three and Málaga with twenty. Other southern provinces produced substantial numbers, such as Granada with fourteen, Murcia with thirteen, Córdoba with eleven, Cáceres with ten and Huelva with eight. Other highly conflictive provinces produced surprisingly low figures, such as Jaén with one, Badajoz and Cádiz each with four and Almería with three. However, focus on numbers of fatal victims, important though it is, misses the wider issue of the daily violence of grinding poverty and social abuse. Another study, by Rafael Cruz, claims that 43 per cent of all deaths were caused by the forces of order. They were the result of overreaction in repressing pacific demonstrations, the victims of which were almost exclusively of the left. Those same forces of order were to support the military uprising despite the fact that the highest number of deaths was in March and that thereafter the level of fatalities gradually diminished.[109]

Disorder was frequent but sporadic and hardly universal. A picture of total anarchy was being painted in the press and the speeches of Gil Robles and others by simply grouping together as 'social disorders' all brawls, fights and strikes, however insignificant. Incidents were magnified and statistics inflated. In Madrid, the American Ambassador Claude Bowers was told tales of uncontrolled mobs butchering monarchists and feeding their bodies to pigs.[110] Fear of violence and disorder was generated by what was read about other places. Some of those who expressed their disgust at the breakdown of law and order also spoke of their relief that, thankfully, it had not reached their own towns.[111]

The statistics are meaningless without their social context. For instance, in Torrevieja (Alicante) in early March, it was reported that 'extremists' had burned down a hermitage, a hotel, the club of the Radical Party and the municipal registry. What happened was that shots were fired from the hotel balcony on a peaceful demonstration complete with brass band that was passing and one of the demonstrators was wounded. This provoked the attack on the hotel and the other crimes. Among those arrested and accused of responsibility for the shooting were the owner of the hotel, the parish priest and two of his brothers and a teacher from the town's Catholic school.[112]

As late as 1 July, Mola complained that 'there have been efforts to provoke violence between right and left that we could use as an excuse to proceed but so far – despite the help of some political elements – it has not fully materialized because there are still idiots who believe in coexistence with representatives of the masses who dominate the Popular Front'.[113] The perfect conditions for a coup may not have been achieved to Mola's satisfaction, but the violence of right-wing gunmen, incendiary speeches by Calvo Sotelo and Gil Robles and the gloss put on events by the rightist media had gone a long way towards pushing the middle classes into the arms of the military conspirators.

Gil Robles's public pronouncements should be seen in the light of his clandestine support of the military conspiracy, which he described as 'a legitimate resistance movement against the anarchy which threatened the very life of the country'. At the end of May, he advised the American journalist Edward Knoblaugh to take his holidays in early July so as to be back in time to cover the military coup.[114] On 27 February 1942, he sent from Lisbon a signed declaration to the Francoist authorities about his role in the coup, stating that he had 'co-operated with advice, with moral stimulus, with secret orders for collaboration, and even with economic assistance, taken in appreciable quantities from the party's electoral funds'. This last was a reference to 500,000 pesetas which he gave to Mola, confident that its original donors would have approved of his action. Part of the money was used to pay the Falangists and Carlist Requetés who joined the military rebels in Pamplona on 19 July.[115] Gil Robles also tried to help Mola in negotiating the terms of the Carlist role in the uprising. In early July, he accompanied the owner of *ABC*, Juan Ignacio Luca de Tena, to Saint Jean de Luz, in a vain attempt to persuade the Carlist leader, Manuel Fal Conde, to drop his demand for the rebels to carry the monarchist flag and adopt the monarchist anthem.[116]

Throughout June and July, Gil Robles instructed provincial CEDA leaders that, on the outbreak of the rising, all party members were to join the military immediately, party organizations were to offer full collaboration, youth sections were to join the army and not form separate militias, party members were not to take part in reprisals against the left, power struggles with other rightist groups were to be avoided, and the maximum financial aid was to be given to the authorities. Only the instruction about reprisals was ignored, and CEDA members were prominent in the repression, especially in Granada and the cities of Old Castile. The first section of the CEDA to join the rising was the Derecha Regional Valenciana. Its moderate Christian Democrat leader Luis Lucia had been marginalized by the secretary general, José María Costa Serrano. When General Mola was finalizing civilian participation in June, Costa Serrano offered 1,250 men for the early moments of the rising and promised 10,000 after five hours and 50,000 after five days. Alongside local sections of the Falange, Renovación Española and the Carlists, the radical wing of the DRV was placed by Costa Serrano under the orders of the military junta. At the beginning of the war, Lucia issued a statement condemning the coup. As a right-wing politician, he went into hiding from the anarchists only to be caught and imprisoned in Barcelona. Nevertheless, in 1939 he was tried and sentenced to death by the Francoists for the alleged offence of military rebellion. His sentence was later commuted to thirty years in prison.[117]

Military intervention came to seem an ever more urgent necessity in the eyes of landowners as a result of the Socialist campaign for the recovery of common lands which enjoyed the support of the Minister of Agriculture, Mariano Ruiz-Funes.[118] The rhetoric of the landowners, and that of their press, generated an apocalyptic sense of utter catastrophe. On 10 July, *ABC* lamented that 80 per cent of the land would be in the hands of municipalities and that there would be towns where private property would disappear.[119] The younger members of landowning families joined the Falange. Anticipating the coup, many owners moved into their homes in the larger towns of the province, or to Madrid or Seville, or, in the case of the very rich, even to Biarritz or Paris, where they contributed finance and expectantly awaited news of the military plot. Behind them they left gangs of Falangists who attacked local Socialists with the protection of the Civil Guard. In Don Benito, the Civil Guard helped local Falangists when they firebombed the Casa del Pueblo.[120] The FNTT frequently complained that the victims of the Civil Guard were always workers and denounced the stockpiling of arms by the landowners. It was claimed that, in Puebla de Almoradiel in the south of Toledo, the local right had two hundred shotguns, three hundred pistols and more than fifty rifles.[121] When workers tried to collect unpaid wages from the landowners, they were often confronted by the Civil Guard. Those who had made such demands were invariably among the victims of the right-wing columns that captured their towns in the early months of the Civil War.[122]

The hatred between the landless peasants and the owners and their administrators was part of daily life in the south. One major landowner from Seville, Rafael de Medina, wrote of 'the incomprehension of the haves and the envy of the have-nots', of those who walked in rope sandals (*alpargatas*) and those who travelled by car. As he and his father drove past labourers walking along a country road, they noted their 'grim-faced look, of such profound contempt and such outright bitterness, that it had the force of a thunderbolt'. Medina always carried a pistol at meetings to discuss working conditions with union leaders.[123]

The hatred was explained by the Civil Governor of Seville, José María Varela Rendueles. Many of the really big owners, dukes, counts and even very rich non-aristocratic owners, lived in Paris or Biarritz or Madrid. They visited their lands occasionally to hunt and to show them off to their friends. While there, their contempt for the labourers was manifest. They, like the less grand landowners who lived on their estates, would often laughingly take advantage of the wives, sisters and daughters of their labourers. Their administrators ran the estates, hiring and firing arbitrarily, ignoring the law. After the abuses of 1933–5, the return of left-wing town councils after the February 1936 elections saw a reversal of fortunes. The prevailing spirit was one not of conciliation but of outright hatred. As Varela Rendueles put it, the landless labourers wanted to follow the example of their 'betters': 'all they wanted to do was to repeat the barbaric lessons that they had been taught'.[124]

A key element of the hatred between the rural poor and the rich, Varela Rendueles noted, was the way in which proletarian women were used and abused. Baldomero Díaz de Entresotos expressed the patronizing and exploitative attitude of the rural middle classes when he wrote indignantly of those who tried to break free of the prostitution into which they had been forced:

> You lived off the romantic adventures of the *señorito* … Those *señoritos*, once your friends, used to live for you just as you lived for them. You think they stole municipal funds? I don't think so but if they did the people's money returned to the people as represented by pretty proletarian women. The *señoritos* were unable to stay away. At siesta time, they came to your whorehouses, sat in their shirtsleeves in the shade of trailing vines and left you banknotes on the beer crates. They livened up the tedium of your nights with wine and music. They were real democrats. Is there any greater democracy than to sleep in the arms of the daughters of the people? Generous, truly Andalusian, *señoritos*.[125]

The perception and empathy with which Varela Rendueles interpreted rural tensions was rare. In notes for his unfinished autobiography, General Sanjurjo made the revealing comment: 'In reality, the agrarian problem in the name of which so many mistakes are made to the detriment of landowners and against the overall economy of Spain, exists only in Madrid on the lips of demagogues who use it as a way of exciting and manipulating the rural population. The agrarian problem was an invention of people like Margarita Nelken.'[126]

Mola had complained on 1 July that the planned spiral of provocation and reprisal had not persuaded public opinion to consider a military uprising legitimate. Less than two weeks later that goal was reached. On the evening of 12 July, Falangist gunmen murdered a lieutenant of the Assault Guards, José del Castillo Sáenz de Tejada.[127] This crime derived much of its catastrophic impact from the fact that, two months earlier, on 7 May, Castillo's friend Captain Carlos Faraudo de Miches had been shot dead by a Falangist squad. On that same day, the Prime Minister and Minister of War, Santiago Casares Quiroga, showed his adjutant,

Major Ignacio Hidalgo de Cisneros of the air force, a right-wing blacklist of fourteen members of the Unión Militar Republicana Antifascista, which had been created in late 1935 to combat the activities of the UME. Faraudo was number one, Castillo number two and Hidalgo de Cisneros fourth.[128]

After Faraudo's murder, calls for reprisals had been silenced. However, when Castillo was also assassinated, fellow Assault Guards from the Pontejos barracks just behind the Dirección General de Seguridad in Madrid's Puerta del Sol were determined on revenge. In the early hours of the following day, they set out to take revenge on a prominent right-wing politician. Failing to find Gil Robles who was holidaying in Biarritz, they kidnapped Calvo Sotelo and, shortly after he got into the truck, one of them shot him. His body was then taken to the municipal cemetery where it was discovered the next morning.[129] Republican and Socialist leaders were appalled and the authorities immediately began a thorough investigation. For the right, it was the opportunity to launch the coup for which the lengthy preparations were on the point of fruition.

At Calvo Sotelo's burial, Antonio Goicoechea swore to 'imitate your example, avenge your death and save Spain'. Even more bellicose was the speech made to the standing committee of the Cortes on 15 July by the Conde de Vallellano, on behalf of the Carlists and Renovación Española. Vallellano, referring rather inaccurately to 'this unprecedented crime in our political history', claimed that Calvo Sotelo had opposed all violence. Accusing the Popular Front deputies collectively of responsibility, he announced the monarchist abandonment of parliament. In what was to be his last parliamentary intervention, Gil Robles expressed his agreement with Vallellano and blamed both the violence of recent months and the assassination on the government. Knowing full well the objectives of the imminent military uprising, he declared that the parties of the Popular Front would be the first victims of the coming backlash.[130]

PART TWO

Institutionalized Violence in the Rebel Zone

5

Queipo's Terror:
The Purging of the South

The assassination of Calvo Sotelo seemed to confirm the direst predictions of the right-wing press, and the military conspirators pressed ahead. Yet only six weeks earlier, Mola, at his headquarters in Pamplona, had been so depressed by fear that the coup might fail and be followed by the revenge of the left-wing masses that he contemplated resigning his command and retiring to Cuba. He was assailed by doubts about the crucial participation of Spain's Moroccan forces – the locally recruited mercenaries of the Native Regulars (Regulares Indígenas) and the two sections into which the Spanish Foreign Legion (Tercio de Extranjeros) was organized. Mola's alarm had been triggered on 2 June 1936 when the Prime Minister and Minister of War, Santiago Casares Quiroga, removed a key conspirator, Lieutenant Colonel Heli Rolando de Tella, from command of the First Legion based in Melilla on the Mediterranean coast of Spanish Morocco. Even more worrying was the fact that, the next day, Casares Quiroga sent for Lieutenant Colonel Juan Yagüe, who had been placed in overall charge of the uprising in the colony.[1]

While waiting to hear Yagüe's fate, Mola enjoyed a major stroke of luck on 3 June. The Director General of Security, José Alonso Mallol, swooped on Pamplona with a dozen police-filled trucks to search for arms. However, the plotters, warned in advance by Mola's collaborator, the police superintendent Santiago Martín Báguenas, ensured that no evidence was found.[2] They were even more fortunate two weeks later when Yagüe was left in post. Having practised extraordinary brutality during the repression in Asturias in October 1934, Yagüe was bitterly hated on the left. He in turn had ample reason to resent the Republic, having been demoted in 1932 from lieutenant colonel to major by Azaña's military reforms, which had reversed many of the rapid promotions enjoyed by the Africanistas. Humiliated by losing eighty-two places in the seniority list, he had had to wait a year before being restored to the rank of lieutenant colonel.[3] Yagüe commanded the Second Legion in Ceuta on the southern side of the Straits of Gibraltar. Loudly indiscreet in his hostility to the government, he enjoyed the unquestioning loyalty of the tattooed mercenaries under his command.

Leading Socialists had repeatedly warned Casares Quiroga that it was dangerous to leave Yagüe in post. Yet, when he arrived on 12 June, he was offered a transfer either to a desirable post on the Spanish mainland or to a plum position as a military attaché in Rome. Yagüe replied curtly that he would burn his uniform rather than leave the Legion. To Mola's relief, Casares weakly acquiesced and let him return to Morocco. After their meeting, Casares said to his adjutant, Ignacio Hidalgo de Cisneros, 'Yagüe is a gentleman, a perfect officer, and I am sure that he would never betray the Republic. He has given me his word of honour and his promise as an officer that he will always loyally serve the Republic. And men like Yagüe keep their word.' It was a major political error.[4]

In the event, Mola was persuaded by senior Carlists to stay aboard and, regaining his resolve, began to make every effort to ensure the rising's success. Nevertheless, in the second week of July, during the fiesta of San Fermín, Mola was again plunged into despair by news brought to Pamplona by his younger brother Ramón. The thirty-nine-year-old Ramón, an infantry captain in Barcelona, was Emilio's liaison with the plotters there. The Generalitat's security services had uncovered the plans for the rising in Catalonia and a deeply pessimistic Ramón begged his brother to desist. Emilio replied that it was too late and ordered Ramón to return to Barcelona. It was a virtual death sentence. When the coup failed, as Ramón had predicted, he shot himself. This contributed to the further brutalization of Mola. In contrast, he would be unmoved by the fact that the President of the Generalitat, Lluís Companys, saved the life of his father, the eighty-three-year-old retired General of the Civil Guard Emilio Mola López.[5]

The first of Mola's secret instructions, issued in April, echoed the practice of the Africanistas against the Rif tribesmen, calling for extreme violence to shock the left into paralysis. Throughout the army as a whole, commitment to the conspiracy was far from unanimous. If it had been, it is unlikely that there would have been a civil war. Thus, Mola's third secret instruction ordered the immediate execution of officers who opposed, or refused to join, the coup. The fifth instruction, of 20 June, had declared that 'the timid and the hesitant should be warned that he who is not with us is against us and will be treated as an enemy'.[6] Thus the first victims executed by the military rebels would be fellow army officers.

On 24 June, Mola sent specific instructions to Yagüe. He urged three main principles: extreme violence, tempo and high mobility: 'Vacillations lead only to failure.'[7] Six days later, Yagüe received a more detailed set of twenty-five instructions about the organization of the repression. They included the following: use Moorish forces; delegate control of public order and security in the cities to the Falange; arrest all suspect authorities; eliminate all leftist elements (Communists, anarchists, trade unionists, Masons and so on); shut down all public meeting places; prohibit all demonstrations, strikes and public and private meetings.[8] These instructions were the blueprint for the repression unleashed on Spain's Moroccan territories on the night of 17 July. By sheer force of personality, Yagüe entirely dominated the overall commander of forces in Morocco, General Agustín Gómez Morato. Between 5 and 12 July, in the Llano Amarillo in the Ketama Valley, manoeuvres involving 20,000 troops from the Legion and the Regulares saw Yagüe's tent become the epicentre of the African end of the conspiracy as he briefed the principal rebel officers. The manoeuvres concluded with Falangist chants.[9]

On 17 July, at Melilla, headquarters of the Second Legion, the general in command, Manuel Romerales Quintero, having refused to join the plotters, was arrested and shot for his 'extremist ideas'. The rebels, headed by Colonel Luis Solans-Labedán, very soon had nearly one thousand prisoners in a concentration camp. When the overall commander General Gómez Morato flew to Melilla, he was immediately arrested. In Tetuán, in the western half of the Protectorate, Colonel Eduardo Sáenz de Buruaga and Lieutenant Colonel Carlos Asensio Cabanillas detained the acting High Commissioner, Arturo Álvarez Buylla, who was shot some time later. On the night of 17–18 July, the rebels shot 225 soldiers and civilians in Morocco.[10]

Among the first of them was one of the most brilliant officers in the Spanish forces, Captain Virgilio Leret Ruiz, a thirty-four-year-old pilot and an aeronautical engineer of genius, the commander of the Atalayón seaplane base at Melilla. He had opposed the rebels, been detained and shot after a summary trial. His wife Carlota O'Neill, a left-wing feminist, dramatist and journalist, was arrested and separated from her daughters Carlota and Mariela. Many other wives and daughters of Republicans were seized, raped and tortured by Falangists. This was central to the reign of terror initiated by Luis Solans. In late September, a gang of Falangists came to the prison with the intention of killing all the female detainees to celebrate the rebel capture of Toledo. The director of the prison reprimanded them, saying, 'it's outrageous to kill them all at once. When you want to kill women, by all means come and get them, but one at a time.' They left with several victims who were never seen again. After eighteen months in prison, Carlota O'Neill was court-martialled, accused of speaking Russian, of subversion and of responsibility for her husband's actions on 17 July 1937. Nevertheless, she was sentenced to 'only' six years.[11]

Having secured their Moroccan base, the rebels' next objective was Cádiz, the crucial port where the African Army would disembark. At 1.00 a.m. on 18 July, the military commander of Cádiz, Brigadier General José López-Pinto, assured the Civil Governor, Mariano Zapico, of his loyalty to the Republic. Three hours later, he declared for the rebels, imposed martial law and ordered the release of Brigadier General José Enrique Varela Iglesias. Arrested by the Republican authorities on 17 July rightly suspected of military conspiracy, Varela would play a central role in the rebel cause. The civilian plotters in Cádiz were led by a prominent landowner, José de Mora-Figueroa, the Marqués de Tamarón. Mora-Figueroa was head of the Falange in Cádiz; his brother Manuel, a naval officer, led its militia. In liaison with one of the key plotters in Seville, Ramón de Carranza, a retired naval captain, who was also Marqués de Soto Hermoso, the Mora-Figueroa brothers had been busy purchasing and stockpiling weapons.

Now, López Pinto and Varela were quickly joined by Mora-Figueroa's Falangists. The Republican authorities took refuge in the town hall and the offices of the Civil Governor. They were defended by several hundred sparsely armed civilian Republicans and about fifty Assault Guards. López Pinto and Varela had about three hundred soldiers, fifty-odd Falangists and Carlist Requetés and a dozen Civil Guards. The buildings were subjected to artillery bombardment but held out until the arrival from Ceuta, late on the night of 18 July, of the destroyer *Churruca* and a merchant steamer carrying a unit of Regulares.[12] Thereafter, the coup was certain of success in the city.

One after another the following morning, the town hall, the Civil Governor's offices, the telephone exchange, the main post office and the headquarters of left-wing parties and trades unions surrendered virtually without resistance. All those within were detained and numerous members of the town council murdered without even a semblance of a trial. The Mayor, Manuel de la Pinta Leal, was not in Cádiz at the time of the coup and thus in no position to oppose it. Nevertheless, he was arrested in Córdoba in September, taken to Cádiz and shot. Over the days following the capture of Cádiz, the Civil Governor, the President of the provincial assembly (Diputación) and numerous officers who had refused to join the rebellion were accused of military rebellion. While detained, they wrote statements pointing out the absurdity of the accusations, since they were obeying the orders of the legal government and had merely defended themselves. Before any trials could take place, they and several others, including a Socialist parliamentary deputy and the town-hall lawyer, were simply taken from prison and murdered on or about 16 August, on the orders of General Gonzalo Queipo de Llano, rebel commander of the south.[13]

The annihilation of less prominent leftists took place as follows. The rebels first closed off the narrow tongue of land that connected Cádiz to the rest of Spain. Groups of Falangists, Civil Guards and Regulares then searched and looted houses. Liberals and leftists, Freemasons and trade unionists, were arrested en masse. Some were shot directly in the street. Others were taken to Falange headquarters in the Casino where they were subjected to sadistic torture. They were forced to ingest a litre of castor oil and industrial alcohol mixed with sawdust and breadcrumbs. In acute abdominal pain, they were savagely beaten. A so-called 'Tribunal of Blood' was established and each day would select twenty-five of the detainees for execution. Over six hundred of those arrested in Cádiz were executed in the next five months and more than one thousand in the course of the war. A further three hundred would be executed between the end of the war and 1945. These figures do not include those who died in prison as a result of torture.[14]

The conquest of the remainder of the province was carried out with the enthusiastic collaboration of the local landowning class, many of whose younger elements had already joined the Falange or the Requeté. In Alcalá de los Gazules, to the east of Cádiz, local Falangists and Civil Guards took control of the town immediately, murdering the Mayor and town councillors, along with fifty others. In the surrounding villages, Popular Front Committees had been formed. They had detained those rightists known to support the coup and began to distribute grain and cattle among the families of landless labourers. The local landlords responded immediately by providing horses for a mounted squad to recover their property. Moving south-west, through Roche and Campano between Chiclana and Conil, the squad recaptured numerous estates that had been occupied by peasant families. Men, women and children were seized and taken back to Alcalá de los Gazules, many to be killed.[15]

After the fall of Cádiz, José Mora-Figueroa took his men to Jérez de la Frontera where the rising had triumphed immediately thanks to the decisive action of the military commander, another scion of a local landowning family, Major Salvador de Arizón Mejía, the Marqués de Casa

Arizón, director of the army's horse-breeding and training establishment. He and his brother, Captain Juan de Arizón Mejía, used the horses
from their unit to ride out in columns to take control of the surrounding
areas.[16] Mora-Figueroa also organized mounted groups with friends and
their employees, which he put at the disposal of the military authorities
in Cádiz.[17] The aim was not just to crush opposition to the rising but also
to reverse the agrarian conquests of the previous years.

Most of the other principal towns of the province fell quickly. On 19
July, Salvador Arizón Mejía sent troops from Jérez to seize the port of
Sanlúcar de Barrameda in the north. Supporters of the Popular Front
held them off until, on 21 July, a force of Regulares entered the town,
killing twelve citizens including nine in one house. Executions began
immediately, although a few leftists escaped in small boats. Eighty people
were shot over the next five months.[18] In Rota, nothing happened on 18
July. The following day, having been deceived into believing that the
Civil Guard and Carabineros were loyal, the town's anarchists, Socialists
and Communists joined in declaring a general strike and establishing an
anti-fascist committee. Falangists and other rightists were detained and
roads into the town barricaded. When the Civil Guard declared in favour
of the rebels, the anti-fascist committee surrendered without a fight.
Despite the absence of left-wing violence, the Falange and the Civil
Guard set about the systematic annihilation of the town's relatively few
liberals and leftists. They were tortured and forced to drink castor oil,
and over sixty were shot at night, their ears cut off as trophies.[19]

The ambience in Jérez itself could be deduced from a broadcast on
Radio Jérez on 24 July by the monarchist intellectual José María Pemán.
He sang a hymn of praise to the war against what he called 'hordes of
barbarian invaders'. The implicit comparison of the working-class left
with the Berber invaders of 711 was emphasized when he declared, 'The
war with its flashes of gunfire has opened our eyes. The idea of political
alternation has been replaced for ever by that of extermination and
expulsion, which is the only valid response against an enemy which is
wreaking more destruction in Spain than any ever caused by a foreign
invasion.'[20]

An experienced Africanista, Captain Mariano Gómez de Zamalloa,
arrived in Jérez from Ceuta to take overall charge of the landowners'
mounted columns.[21] The recovery of estates in the surrounding area
seized by leftists fell to the column led by the Marqués de Casa Arizón.
Another column was organized by José Mora-Figueroa's brother Manuel,
with the scions of other aristocratic and landowning families and of

sherry magnates, like the Duque de Medina-Sidonia and Estanislao Domecq y González. The self-styled Tercio Mora-Figueroa was made up initially of three hundred young rightists, Falangists, sons of landowners and workers from the Catholic unions.

As if on a hunting party, Mora-Figueroa and his men, accompanied by Civil Guards and Requetés, set out eastwards towards Arcos de la Frontera, where his family owned land. Despite the fact that Arcos had fallen without violence, a terrible repression was unleashed which saw the deaths of eighty-six Republicans.[22] The column attacked villages to the north-east of Cádiz still in Popular Front hands and recaptured estates occupied by their workers. From Arcos, Gómez de Zamalloa's column of Regulares and Mora-Figueroa's men moved on to Algodonales and Olvera, where the repression was fierce.[23] On 13 August, Mora-Figueroa's group reached Villamartín, which had been under the control of the Civil Guard since 19 July. There had been a few isolated incidents of left-wing violence but the repression was disproportionately severe. The landowners of Villamartín were determined to annihilate all members of trade unions and of the Socialist and Republican parties and any Republican who had held any elected office.

Despite the protests of the parish priest, men and women were tortured and shot without trial for reasons as capricious as having advocated improved working conditions or for having taken part in a carnival involving a spoof funeral of Gil Robles and songs ridiculing the right. One seventeen-year-old was shot because his father was a Socialist and a sixteen-year-old because his anarcho-syndicalist father had fled. Altogether four teenagers were murdered. A couple aged seventy-three and sixty-three were shot because their anarcho-syndicalist son had also escaped. Married couples were shot, their young children left to starve. In another case, Cristóbal Alza and his wife were arrested, their heads were shaved and they were given castor oil. Believing that they were now safe, they stayed in the town but were arrested again. Cristóbal's brother Francisco pleaded for their lives with the Captain of the Civil Guard, who replied that he would spare only one and that Francisco must choose. He chose his brother. Between July 1936 and February 1937, a total of 102 men and nine women were executed in Villamartín.[24] Three women were murdered in Bornos, two in Espera, one in Puerto Serrano, one in Arcos de la Frontera, at least ten in Ubrique and five in Olvera.[25]

These first killings were carried out under the umbrella of the proclamation of martial law, the Bando de Guerra, based on that issued by Queipo de Llano on 18 July. In every town and province across Western

Andalusia, although the wording might vary slightly, the sweeping terms of the edict (*bando*) effectively decreed that anyone who opposed the rising would be shot.[26] Those who carried out the killings could then claim airily that they were 'applying the Bando de Guerra'. With no judicial basis, men were taken out and shot, their bodies left by the roadside to rot. In fact, Queipo de Llano had no authority to issue such an edict.[27]

Queipo de Llano wrote to López Pinto on 4 August urging him to speed up the process of eliminating the left in Cádiz. With the first African columns having left Seville for Madrid on 2 and 3 August, he wrote: 'This will be over soon! It won't last more than another ten days. By then it is crucial that you have finished off all the gunmen and communists in your province.' When a new judge made inquiries about the progress of the trial of the prominent Republicans in Cádiz, he was informed that it had been shelved 'as a result of the death of the individuals concerned by dint of the application to them of the edict of martial law of 18 July 1936'.[28]

Queipo de Llano's letter reflected a key moment in the repression. The towns and villages of Cádiz, Huelva and Seville and much of Córdoba and Granada had fallen to the insurgents. The population of this territory was predominantly Republican, Socialist and anarcho-syndicalist in its sympathies. To prevent any rebellion in the rear as the columns moved north, the repression was to be intensified. Prisoners were to be killed. Two days after sending the letter, Queipo de Llano backed up its sentiments by posting the retired Lieutenant Colonel Eduardo Valera Valverde to be Civil Governor of the province of Cádiz. Valera was instructed to 'proceed with greater energy'. In Sanlúcar de Barrameda the occupying forces began more systematic executions from 8 August. In Puerto Real, near the provincial capital, the Mayor had prevented anti-clerical disturbances and the burning of a convent on the night of 18 July. Nevertheless, he had been arrested the following day. He was a bookseller, a moderate Republican of Azaña's Izquierda Republicana. Despite pleas on his behalf by the Mother Superior of the convent, he was killed without any trial on 21 August. Two months later, his bookshop, already ransacked by Falangists, was confiscated.[29]

In the meantime, in the villages between Villamartín and Ubrique, such as Benamahoma, the Mora-Figueroa column arrested the mayors and imposed new town councils. Using Olvera as their base, they advanced over the provincial border into Seville and conquered the town of Pruna on 18 August, and the villages of Villanueva de San Juan and Algámitas four days later. The local landowners and right-wingers who had been placed in protective custody by the Popular Front authorities claimed that the column had arrived just in time to save them from horrendous atrocities. It was not explained why the left had waited so long before contemplating such atrocities.[30]

The repression in Benamahoma was undertaken by a notorious gang known as the 'Lions of Rota', consisting of self-declared Falangists led by Fernando Zamacola, a man from Galicia with a record of assault and armed robbery. At a post-war investigation into Zamacola's crimes, it was revealed that more than fifty people had been executed including several women. The town postman was shot along with his fifteen-year-old son. Members of the Lions testified that Juan Vadillo, the local commander of the Civil Guard, had ordered the shootings to cover up the appalling beatings inflicted on those arrested. As well as murders, there was also considerable theft of the property of those detained and sexual abuse of the wives of men who had fled or been shot. These women were forced to clean the Civil Guard barracks and the offices of the Falange and made to dance at parties organized by Zamacola's men. As well as cases of head-shaving and the use of castor oil, several were raped by both Vadillo and Zamacola.[31] Zamacola was awarded Spain's highest military decoration, the Gran Cruz Laureada de San Fernando.[32]

Meanwhile, Mora-Figueroa's column made daily expeditions to mop up after the troops who conquered the smaller towns to the north of the province, Ubrique, Alcalá del Valle and Setenil. Many local Republicans and trade unionists had fled to the sierra around Ubrique, fearing reprisals. However, when on 24 July a light aeroplane dropped leaflets announcing that anyone without blood on their hands had nothing to fear, many of them returned. Most of these trusting souls, including the Mayor, were shot in the course of the following weeks. A member of Izquierda Republicana, the Mayor owned a prosperous bakery and olive press. By providing cheap bread for the poor, he had earned the enmity of the local oligarchy. He was tortured and forced to hand over substantial sums of money before being shot. At least 149 people were executed in Ubrique.[33]

In nearby Alcalá del Valle, the local Civil Guard had handed over its guns to a rapidly created Comité de Defensa. Weapons held by local rightists were confiscated and several of the men were imprisoned but none was physically harmed. The parish church was requisitioned as the Comité's headquarters, its altar, statues and religious images destroyed. The town was briefly occupied on 25 August by a force of twenty Civil

Guards and Manuel Mora-Figueroa's Falangists. After it had been driven off, a group of anarchist militia arrived from Ronda in the neighbouring province of Málaga and began to loot the houses of local right-wingers until they were stopped by the Comité de Defensa. On 18 September, the town was finally reoccupied by rebel units including Mora-Figueroa's column. The repression in Alcalá del Valle was sweeping, aiming to eradicate left-wing individuals, organizations and ideas. Knowing what the columns had done in nearby towns, many inhabitants of Alcalá del Valle had already fled. These included those who had held posts in Republican parties, trade unions or institutions. The victims were thus those who had stayed confident that, being guilty of no crimes, they had nothing to fear. There was no pretence of trials. Twenty-six men and four women were picked up off the street or from their houses, tortured and then shot.[34]

While the various paramilitary forces purged the province of Cádiz, a similar process was taking place in Seville. There the right-wing victory was attributed by Gonzalo Queipo de Llano to his personal daring and brilliance. Within a year of the events, he claimed that he had captured the city against overwhelming odds with the help of only 130 soldiers and fifteen civilians. In a radio broadcast on 1 February 1938, he made an even wilder exaggeration, declaring that he had taken the city with fourteen or fifteen men.[35] He claimed that he been opposed by a force of over 100,000 well-armed 'communists'. In fact, the defeated workers had had between them only eighty rifles and little ammunition and were armed, if at all, with hunting shotguns, ancient pistols and knives.[36]

Far from being an act of spontaneous heroism, the coup had been meticulously planned by a major of the General Staff stationed in Seville, José Cuesta Monereo, and was carried out by a force of four thousand men. The commander of the Seville Military Region, General José de Fernández Villa-Abrille, and his senior staff were aware of what was being hatched. They did nothing to impede the plot, despite the pleas of the Civil Governor, José María Varela Rendueles.[37] Nevertheless, Queipo had them arrested and tried for military rebellion. The majority of the Seville garrison were involved in the coup, including units of artillery, cavalry, communications, transport and the Civil Guard. This is clear even from the lists included in the hymn of praise to Queipo composed by the journalist Enrique Vila.[38] After artillery bombardment, this large force seized the telephone exchange, the town hall and the Civil Governor's headquarters, blocked the main access routes into the centre and then applied indiscriminate terror.[39]

The subsequent crushing of working-class resistance was undertaken by Major Antonio Castejón Espinosa. According to Castejón himself, with fifty Legionarios, fifty Carlist Requetés, fifty Falangists and another fifty Civil Guards, they immediately began the bloody suppression of the workers' districts of Triana, La Macarena, San Julián and San Marcos. Castejón's artillery was organized by Captain Luis Alarcón de la Lastra, the CEDA deputy and landowner from Carmona, who had immediately placed himself under the orders of Queipo.[40] The Falangists came mainly from the Círculo de Labradores, the rich landowners' club. Civilian participation in the rising was organized by prominent members of the Círculo like Ramón de Carranza, Pedro Parias González and the bull-fighter Pepe el Algabeño (José García Carranza). Queipo de Llano rewarded them by making Carranza Mayor and Parias Civil Governor of Seville. Pepe el Algabeño, who had been the target of an assassination attempt by anarchists in Málaga in March 1934, headed a group of bull-fighters who placed themselves at the disposal of Queipo de Llano.[41] On the morning of 19 July, armed gangs led by Carranza imposed what he called 'brutal punishment' on working-class districts around the city.[42]

Despite artillery bombardment, the working-class districts resisted doggedly. Finally, Queipo's forces, using women and children as human shields, were able to enter and begin the repression in earnest. Women and children, as well as their menfolk, were were put to the sword. After the subjugation of Triana, the new Mayor Carranza strode through the streets with a megaphone ordering that all pro-Republican and anti-fascist graffiti be cleaned from the walls. He set a ten-minute deadline, after which the residents of any house whose walls carried slogans would be shot. With fathers, husbands, brothers and sons dead or dying in the streets around them, the surviving men, women and children began frantically scrubbing at the walls while the victorious rebels gloated.[43] For his final attack on La Macarena, on 22 July, Queipo used aircraft to bomb and strafe the district. He published a warning in the press demanding that weapons be thrown into the street and windows and doors be covered in white sheets to 'avoid the damage that could be caused by air attacks and the forces of the Army'.[44]

On 16 August, the bodies of two Falangists were found in Triana. In reprisal, seventy men from the surrounding streets were arrested at random. They were shot in the cemetery without any form of trial two days later.[45] When the actor Edmundo Barbero reached Seville in August, he would find the city (and many of its inhabitants) entirely plastered in Falangist symbols. Triana, La Macarena, San Julián and San Marcos were full of the rubble of houses destroyed by the artillery barrages. Barbero was appalled by the terror-stricken faces and the fact that all the women wore black, despite Queipo's prohibition of public mourning, incessantly and threateningly repeated in the press and on the radio. Elsewhere, in the *pueblos*, Falangist patrols ensured that no houses carried emblems of mourning and that laments of grief could not be heard.[46]

After the initial slaughter, a more systematic repression began. On 23 July, Queipo de Llano issued another edict which stated that any strike leaders caught would be shot along with an equal number of strikers chosen at the discretion of the military authorities. Anyone who disobeyed his edicts was to be shot without trial. The following day, Queipo issued his sixth edict, which stated that 'on discovering acts of cruelty against individuals in any town or village, the leaders of the Marxist or Communist organizations that exist there will be shot. In the event of them not being found, an equal number of their members, arbitrarily selected, will be shot without this prejudicing the sentences that will be passed against the guilty ones.'[47] This edict was used to justify the execution of large numbers of men, women and children who were innocent of any 'acts of cruelty'.

To take charge of the process, Queipo de Llano chose an Africanista, the infantry Captain Manuel Díaz Criado. He had served with the Foreign Legion in the 1920s and organized the Guardiá Cívica that murdered four workers in the Parque de María Luisa in Seville in 1931; he had also been involved in Carlavilla's attempt to murder Azaña in May 1936. On 25 July, Queipo gave Díaz Criado the title of Military Delegate for Andalusia and Extremadura with the power of life and death over the people of the region. He chose as his right-hand man an equally brutal Civil Guard, Sergeant Major José Rebollo Montiel. Rebollo supervised the torture and interrogation of prisoners. Díaz Criado was described by Edmundo Barbero as 'a cruel and sadistic drunk'.[48] On his orders, the working-class districts of Triana and La Macarena were stripped of their male populations. Among hundreds of prisoners taken and herded into the provincial prison were children and old men. Most were quickly taken out and shot without any pretence of judicial procedure. Others were taken to rot in the fetid prison ship *Cabo Carvoeiro*.[49]

When working-class leaders could not be found, members of their families were taken as hostages. The Communist leader of the Seville dockworkers, Saturnino Barneto Atienza, went into hiding and eventually reached the Republican zone. His sister, his wife, his infant daughter and his mother-in-law were detained in inhuman conditions for the duration of the war. His seventy-two-year-old mother, Isabel Atienza, a devout Catholic, was arrested and interrogated. On 8 October, she was forced to witness a shooting in the cemetery and then, seriously disturbed, was taken to a square near her home and shot. Her body was left in the street for a day.[50] On the night of 10 August, a number of murders were committed to commemorate the anniversary of General Sanjurjo's failed military coup in 1932. Among the victims were the Andalusian intellectual Blas Infante and the Republican Mayor José González Fernández de Labandera, who had helped foil the Sanjurjada.

Queipo de Llano gave Díaz Criado unlimited powers and would hear no complaints against him. Díaz Criado himself refused to be bothered by details concerning the innocence or previous good deeds of his victims. On 12 August, the local press was issued a note prohibiting intercessions in favour of those arrested. It stated that 'not only those who oppose our cause, but also those who support them or speak up for them will be regarded as enemies'.[51] Díaz Criado was widely regarded as a degenerate who used his position to satisfy his bloodlust, to get rich and for sexual gratification. The head of Queipo's propaganda apparatus, Antonio Bahamonde, whose disgust at what he witnessed eventually led to his defection, was appalled by Díaz Criado. He wrote:

> Criado usually arrived around six in the evening. In an hour or less, he would go through the files, signing death sentences (about sixty per day) usually without hearing the accused. To anaesthetize his conscience or for whatever reason, he was always drunk. As dawn broke every day, he was to be seen, surrounded by his courtiers in the restaurant of the Pasaje del Duque, where he dined every night. He was an habitual client of the night clubs where he could be seen with admiring friends, flamenco singers and dancers, sad women trying to appear gay. He used to say that, once started, it was all the same to him to sign one hundred or three hundred death sentences and the important thing was to 'cleanse Spain of Marxists'. I have heard him say: 'Here, for decades to come, no one will dare move.' He did not receive visits; only young women were allowed into his office. I know cases of women who saved their loved ones by submitting to his demands.[52]

Francisco Gonzálbez Ruiz, one-time Civil Governor of Murcia, had similar recollections of Díaz Criado: 'in the small hours, after an orgy, still accompanied by prostitutes, and with unimaginable sadism, he would haphazardly apply his fateful mark "X2" to the files of those who were thus condemned to immediate execution'.[53] One of Díaz Criado's closest friends was a prostitute known as Doña Mariquita who had hidden him when he was on the run after his attempt to kill Azaña. Knowing this, many people paid her to intercede for their loved ones. Edmundo Barbero was present at gatherings in the early hours of the morning at which Díaz Criado, Sergeant Rebollo and Doña Mariquita would discuss the sexual and financial offers made on behalf of prisoners. On one such occasion, a bored Díaz Criado decided to take those present to a dawn execution. To his irritation, they arrived just as the echoes of the shots were dying away. However, he was mollified when the commander of the firing squad offered the women of the party his gun for them to finish off the dying. A sergeant of the Regulares then proceeded to remove gold teeth from the dead by bashing their heads with a stone.[54]

Bahamonde saw Díaz Criado drunk in a bar, signing death sentences. One of the few who survived to tell the tale later was the last Republican Civil Governor of Seville, José María Varela Rendueles. Díaz Criado began his interrogation with the words: 'I have to say that I regret that you have not yet been shot. I would like to see your family in mourning.' He said the same to Varela Rendueles's mother some days later. Díaz Criado falsely accused Varela Rendueles of distributing arms to the workers. The only 'proof' that he could produce was a pistol once known to have been in Varela Rendueles's possession found on a worker shot resisting the coup. The pistol had been stolen when Varela Rendueles's office was looted. However, only after his successor as Civil Governor, Pedro Parias, had corroborated this did Díaz Criado grudgingly withdraw the accusation.[55] Díaz Criado's slipshod manner inevitably led to problems.

According to the usually reliable Bahamonde, 'A friend of General Mola was shot, despite the fact that Mola himself had taken a great interest in his case, even telephoning Díaz Criado personally. Since he usually just signed the death sentences after barely flicking through the files, Díaz Criado failed to notice that on the day in question he had signed the death sentence of Mola's friend.'[56] Even so, Queipo tolerated Díaz Criado's excesses; but, in mid-November 1936, Franco himself insisted on his removal. The immediate trigger had been that he had accused the Portuguese Vice-Consul in Seville, Alberto Magno Rodrigues, of espionage. Given the scale of Portuguese help to the rebel cause, and the efforts of Salazar's government to secure international recognition for Franco, the accusation was acutely embarrassing. Moreover, it was absurd since

Rodrigues was actually compiling information about German and Italian arms deliveries at the request of Franco's brother, Nicolás. An enraged Queipo de Llano was forced to apologize to Rodrigues in front of Nicolás Franco. Now known as the 'Caudillo', Franco personally signed Díaz Criado's posting to the Legion on the Madrid front, where he employed his brutal temperament against the soldiers under his command.[57]

Díaz Criado's replacement by the Civil Guard Major Santiago Garrigós Bernabéu brought little relief to the terrorized population. Indeed, it was fatal for those who had been saved by the bribery of Doña Mariquita or by sexual submission to Díaz Criado himself. Francisco Gonzálbez Ruiz commented on the situation: 'since some fortunate ones were saved by the opportune intervention of a female friend or by dint of paying a goodly sum, of course, when Díaz Criado was sacked, his successor felt the need to review the cases. Because the procedure followed had been corrupt, those who had been freed were now shot. Needless to say, nothing could help the thousands of innocents already dead.'[58]

One reason for which people were executed was having opposed the military coup of 10 August 1932. Among those murdered on these grounds were the then Mayor, José González Fernández de Labandera, the first Republican Mayor of Seville in April 1931 and Socialist deputy at the time, Hermenegildo Casas Jiménez, the then Civil Governor, Ramón González Sicilia, and the President of the Provincial Assembly, José Manuel Puelles de los Santos. After Puelles, a liberal and much loved doctor, had been arrested, his clinic was ransacked and he was murdered on 5 August. A similar fate awaited numerous other municipal and provincial officials.[59]

As soon as the 'pacification' of Cádiz and Seville was under way, Queipo de Llano could turn his attention to the neighbouring province of Huelva. Initially, because of the firm stance of the Civil Governor, Diego Jiménez Castellano, the Mayor, Salvador Moreno Márquez, and the local commanders of the Civil Guard, Lieutenant Colonel Julio Orts Flor, and of the Carabineros, Lieutenant Colonel Alfonso López Vicencio, the coup failed. Arms were distributed to working-class organizations but every effort was made to maintain order. Local rightists were detained for their safety and their weapons confiscated. Given the chaos and the hatred provoked by the uprising, it is a tribute to the success of the measures implemented by the Republican authorities that the number of right-wingers assassinated by uncontrolled elements in Huelva was limited to six.

Such was the confidence of the Madrid government that, on 19 July, the newly appointed Minister of the Interior, General Sebastián Pozas Perea, cabled the Civil Governor, Jiménez Castellano, and Lieutenant Colonel Orts Flor: 'I recommend that you mobilize the miners to use explosives to annihilate these terrorist gangs. You can be confident that the military column advancing triumphantly on Córdoba and Seville will shortly wipe out the last few seditious traitors who, in their last throes, have unleashed the most cruel and disgusting vandalism.' In response to this wildly over-optimistic telegram, the text of which would later be falsified by the rebels, it was decided to send a column from the city to attack Queipo de Llano in Seville. The column consisted of sixty Civil Guards, sixty Carabineros and Assault Guards plus about 350 left-wing volunteers from various towns, including Socialist miners. It was accompanied by two of Huelva's parliamentary deputies, the Socialists Juan Gutiérrez Prieto and Luis Cordero Bel.

In fact, the police, the Civil Guard and the army in Huelva were heavily infiltrated by conspirators. One of the most untrustworthy, Major Gregorio Haro Lumbreras of the Civil Guard, was placed in command of the force being sent to attack Queipo. Haro had been involved in the Sanjurjada and was in close touch with José Cuesta Monereo, who had planned the military coup in Seville. To prevent his real plans being frustrated by the workers in the column, Haro Lumbreras and his men had left for Seville several hours before the civilian volunteers. Along the sixty-two miles separating the two cities, his force was swelled by Civil Guards from other posts. On reaching Seville, Haro Lumbreras liaised with Queipo and Cuesta Monereo then retraced his steps to set up an ambush of the militias coming from Huelva. On 19 July, at a crossroads known as La Pañoleta, his men opened fire on the miners with machine-guns. Twenty-five were killed and seventy-one were taken prisoner, of whom three soon died of their wounds. The remainder, including the Socialist deputies, escaped. Haro's men suffered no casualties apart from one man who broke his leg getting out of a truck. The prisoners were taken to the hold of the prison ship *Cabo Carvoeiro* anchored in the River Guadalquivir. At the end of August, they would be 'tried' and found guilty of the surrealistic crime of military rebellion against 'the only legitimately constituted power in Spain'. The sixty-eight prisoners were then divided into six groups, taken to six areas of Seville where working-class resistance had been significant, and shot. Their bodies were left in the streets for several hours to terrorize further a population which had already seen more than seven hundred people executed since Queipo de Llano's triumph.[60]

Huelva itself would not fall for another ten days. In the meantime, the conquest of the territory between Huelva and Seville was carried out by columns organized by the military and financed by wealthy volunteers with access to cars and weaponry. After taking part in the suppression of the working-class areas of Seville, a Carlist column organized by a retired Major Luis Redondo García attacked small towns to the south-east of Seville.[61] Another typical column was put together by the wealthy land-owner Ramón de Carranza. He had been involved in the preparations for the coup and, with a group of friends, some from the Aero Club and the landowners' *casino*, had taken part in the repression of the working-class districts of Triana and La Macarena. Queipo rewarded him by making him Mayor of Seville. Carranza was the son of the *cacique* of Cádiz, Admiral Ramón de Carranza, the Marqués de Villapesadilla, who owned 5,600 acres in estates near Algeciras and in Chiclana.[62] From 23 July until late August, Carranza alternated his administrative duties with the leadership of a column that occupied the towns and villages in the Aljarafe region to the west of Seville.

It was no coincidence that in many of these municipalities extensive properties were owned by Carranza and other wealthy members of the column such as his friend Rafael de Medina. Their itineraries were often dictated by the location of their estates. In most villages, a Popular Front committee had been set up, with representation of all Republican and left-wing groups, usually under the chairmanship of the mayor. They arrested known sympathizers of the military rebels and confiscated their weapons. This was an area of big estates, producing wheat and olives, with large areas of cork oaks around which cattle, sheep, goats and pigs grazed. The committees centralized food supplies and, in some cases, collectivized estates. The owners had a burning interest in the recovery of the farms that now fed their left-wing enemies.

Carranza's column moved into the Aljarafe, attacking towns and villages such as Saltares, Camas, Valencina, Bollullos and Aznalcázar. Armed with mortars and machine-guns, they met little resistance from labourers armed only with hunting shotguns or farm implements. At one of the first villages reached, Castilleja, Medina liberated estates belonging to his friend the Marqués de las Torres de la Presa. In Aznalcázar, the Socialist Mayor, who, according to Medina's own account, handed over the *pueblo* with great dignity and grace, was taken to Seville and shot. Moving on to Pilas and Villamanrique, the column recaptured estates owned by Medina himself and his father. Eventually, on 25 July, they went as far as Almonte in Huelva. As each village fell, Carranza would arrest the municipal authorities, establish new town councils, shut down trade union offices and take truckloads of prisoners back to Seville for execution.[63]

On 27 July, Carranza's column reached one such town, Rociana in Huelva, where the left had taken over in response to news of the military coup. There had been no casualties but a ritual destruction of the symbols of right-wing power, the premises of the landowners' association and two clubs, one used by the local Falange. Twenty-five sheep belonging to a wealthy local landowner were stolen. The parish church and rectory had been set alight, but the parish priest, the sixty-year-old Eduardo Martínez Laorden, his niece and her daughter who lived with him had been saved by local Socialists and given refuge in the house of the Mayor. On 28 July, Father Martínez Laorden made a speech from the balcony of the town hall: 'You all no doubt believe that, because I am a priest, I have come with words of forgiveness and repentance. Not at all! War against all of them until the last trace has been eliminated.' A large number of men and women were arrested. The women had their heads shaved and one, known as La Maestra Herrera, was dragged around the town by a donkey, before being murdered. Over the next three months, sixty were shot. In January 1937, Father Martínez Laorden made an official complaint that the repression had been too lenient.[64]

When Gonzalo de Aguilera shot six labourers in Salamanca, he perceived himself to be taking retaliatory measures in advance. Many landowners did the same by joining or financing mixed columns like that of Carranza. They also played an active role in selecting victims to be executed in captured villages. In a report to Lisbon, in early August, the Portuguese Consul in Seville praised these columns. Like the Italian Consul, he had been given gory accounts of unspeakable outrages allegedly committed against women and children by armed leftist desperadoes. Accordingly, he reported with satisfaction that, 'in punishing these monstrosities, a harsh summary military justice is applied. In these towns, not a single one of the Communist rebels is left alive, because they are all shot in the town square.'[65] In fact, these shootings reflected no justice, military or otherwise, but rather the determination of the landowners to put the clock back. Thus, when labourers were shot, they were made to dig their own graves first, and Falangist *señoritos* shouted at them, 'Didn't you ask for land? Now you're going to have some, and for ever!'[66]

The atrocities carried out by the various columns were regarded with relish by Queipo de Llano. In a broadcast on 23 July, he declared, 'We are determined to apply the law without flinching. Morón, Utrera, Puente Genil, Castro del Río, start digging graves. I authorize you to kill like a dog anyone who dares oppose you and I say that, if you act in this way, you will be free of all blame.' In part of the speech that the censorship felt was too explicit to be printed, Queipo de Llano said, 'Our brave Legionarios and Regulares have shown the red cowards what it means to be a man. And incidentally the wives of the reds too. These Communist and anarchist women, after all, have made themselves fair game by their doctrine of free love. And now they have at least made the acquaintance of real men, not wimpish militiamen. Kicking their legs about and squealing won't save them.'[67]

Queipo de Llano's speeches were larded with sexual references. On 26 July, he declared: '*Sevillanos!* I don't have to urge you on because I know your bravery. I tell you to kill like a dog any queer or pervert who criticizes this glorious national movement.'[68] Arthur Koestler interviewed Queipo de Llano at the beginning of September 1936: 'For some ten minutes he described in a steady flood of words, which now and then became extremely racy, how the Marxists slit open the stomachs of pregnant women and speared the foetuses; how they had tied two eight-year-old girls on to their father's knees, violated them, poured petrol on them and set them on fire. This went on and on, unceasingly, one story following another – a perfect clinical demonstration in sexual psychopathology.' Koestler commented on the broadcasts: 'General Queipo de Llano describes scenes of rape with a coarse relish that is an indirect incitement to a repetition of such scenes.'[69] Queipo's comments can be contrasted with an incident in Castilleja del Campo when a truckload of prisoners was brought for execution from the mining town of Aznalcóllar, which had been occupied on 17 August by Carranza's column. Among them were two women tied together, a mother and her daughter who was in the final stages of pregnancy and gave birth as she was shot. The executioners killed the baby with their rifle butts.[70]

The most important of the columns carrying out Queipo's bidding was commanded by the stocky Major Antonio Castejón Espinosa. After taking part in the repression of Triana and La Macarena in Seville itself, and prior to setting out on the march to Madrid, Castejón made a number of rapid daily sorties to both the east and west of the city. In its war on the landless peasantry, Castejón's column drew on the training and experience of the Legion and the Civil Guard and had the added advantage of the artillery directed by Alarcón de la Lastra. Fulfilling Queipo's threats, to the east the column conquered Alcalá de Guadaira, Arahal, La Puebla de Cazalla, Morón de la Frontera, reaching Écija before moving south to Osuna, Estepa and La Roda, advancing as far as Puente Genil in Córdoba, seventy-five miles from Seville. To the west, at Valencina del Alcor, just outside Seville, Castejón's forces liberated the estate of a rich retired bullfighter, Emilio Torres Reina, known as 'Bombita'. 'Bombita' himself enthusiastically joined in the fighting and the subsequent 'punishment' of the prisoners. Castejón went as far as La Palma del Condado in Huelva, thirty-four miles from Seville. First the town was bombed, which provoked the murder of fifteen right-wing prisoners by enraged anarchists. On 26 July, La Palma was captured in a pincer action by the columns of both Castejón and Carranza, who bitterly disputed the credit of being first.[71]

When forces of the Legion sent by Queipo de Llano finally took Huelva itself on 29 July, they discovered that the Mayor and many of the Republican authorities had managed to flee on a steamer to Casablanca. The city fell after brief resistance in the Socialist headquarters (the Casa del Pueblo). Seventeen citizens were killed in the fighting and nearly four hundred prisoners were taken. Executions began immediately. Corpses were regularly found in the gutters. Still basking in the glory of the massacre of the miners at La Pañoleta, Major Haro Lumbreras was named both Civil and Military Governor of Huelva. Those Republican civil and military authorities who had not managed to escape – the Civil Governor and the commanders of the Civil Guard and the Carabineros – were put on trial on 2 August, charged with military rebellion. Haro testified against his immediate superior, Lieutenant Colonel Orts Flor, who had organized the miners' column sent to Seville.

To inflate his own heroism, and inadvertently revealing his own obsessions, Haro claimed that the orders from General Pozas passed on by Orts which had instigated the expedition were to 'blow up Seville and fuck the wives of the fascists'. Unsurprisingly, the accused were found guilty and sentenced to death. Numerous conservatives and clerics whose lives had been saved by the Civil Governor, Diego Jiménez Castellano, sent telegrams to Seville on 4 August desperately pleading for clemency. Queipo de Llano replied: 'I regret that I cannot respond to your petition for pardon for the criminals condemned to death, because the critical situation through which Spain is passing means that justice cannot be obstructed, for the guilty must be punished and an example made of them.' Diego Jiménez Castellano, Julio Orts Flor and Alfonso López Vicencio were shot shortly after 6.00 p.m. on 4 August.[72]

With Huelva itself in rebel hands, the process began, as it had in Cádiz and Seville, of columns being sent out to mop up the remainder of the province. Carranza's column was involved in the taking of nearby towns to the south like Lepe, Isla Cristina and Ayamonte. Many of the Republicans who were arrested and taken to Huelva for trial were murdered along the way.[73] In the north, the rebels already had a bridgehead in the town of Encinasola, where the rising had triumphed immediately. The right could count on support from Barrancos across the Portuguese frontier.[74] With considerable bloodshed, a major role in the capture of towns and villages to the east and north of the capital was played by Luis Redondo's column of Carlists from Seville. The mining towns of the north were centres of obdurate resistance, holding out for some weeks despite artillery bombardment. Higuera de la Sierra fell on 15 August. Zalamea la Real on the edge of the Riotinto mining district fell the next day. The capture of these villages was followed by indiscriminate shootings.[75]

The savagery increased as the columns entered Riotinto. The inhabitants had fled from the village of El Campillo. Finding it deserted, Redondo gave the order to burn it to the ground. Queipo de Llano broadcast the absurd lie that the local anarchists had burned twenty-two rightists alive and then set fire to their own homes. An air raid on Nerva on 20 August killed seven women, four men, a ten-year-old boy and six-month-old girl. One right-winger had been killed before the arrival of Redondo. The Communist Mayor ensured that twenty-five others who were in protective custody were unharmed, despite the popular outrage after the bombing raid. When the village was taken, Redondo's men executed 288 people. In Aroche, ten right-wingers were killed and, when Redondo's column arrived on 28 August, despite the fact that many leftists had fled north towards Badajoz, his men executed 133 men and ten women. The town's female population was subjected to humiliation and sexual extortion. Reports of this terror ensured that resistance elsewhere would be dogged. The siege of El Cerro de Andévalo lasted over three weeks and required the contribution of three columns of Civil Guards, Falangists and Requetés. There the local CNT committee or Junta had protected the nuns in a local convent but were unable to prevent attacks on church property. The repression when the town fell on 22 September was ferocious. In nearby Silos de Calañas, women and children were shot along with the men. Large numbers of refugees now headed north towards the small area in Badajoz still not conquered by the rebels.[76]

Meanwhile, in Moguer to the south of the province, and in Palos de la Frontera to the east of the provincial capital, members of the clergy and local rightists had been taken into protective custody. In Moguer, as news filtered through of the repression in Seville, on 22 July the parish church was set on fire and a retired lieutenant colonel of the army was murdered after his house was attacked and looted by a large mob. The Mayor, Antonio Batista, managed to prevent any further deaths. In Palos, the Socialist Mayor, Eduardo Molina Martos, and the PSOE deputy Juan Gutiérrez Prieto tried unsuccessfully to stop the local CNT burning down church buildings including the historic monastery of La Rábida but did prevent any executions. On 28 July, Palos was captured by the Civil Guard without opposition and, on 6 August, Falangists from Huelva began a series of extra-judicial executions.

Gutiérrez Prieto, a talented and highly popular lawyer, was captured in Huelva on 29 July and tried on 10 August. In addition to military rebellion, he was accused of responsibility for virtually every action of the left in the province and sentenced to death. Numerous conservatives and ecclesiastical dignitaries interceded on his behalf. To counteract these pleas, Haro Lumbreras made a statement to the press which echoed the sexual obsessions of his distortion of General Pozas's orders. No right-wingers had been harmed in Palos, yet he stated:

The enemy who burns alive entire families, who crucifies and burns alive the Bishop of Sigüenza in a town square, who cuts open the bellies of pregnant women, who murders innocent children, who steals, attacks buildings, burns, stains the honour of defenceless virgins, throws two hundred and fifty people into pits in Constantina and then throws in dynamite to finish them off, cannot and must not plead for mercy before those who would be his first victims if he got the chance.

Gutiérrez Prieto was shot on 11 August. To silence opposition to his execution, thirty inhabitants of Palos, including his uncle, were shot, along with twelve people from other towns. In Moguer, the arrival of the rebels unleashed a sweeping and well-planned repression that saw the homes of Republicans looted and women raped and claimed the lives of 146 people, including women and twelve-year-old boys. More than 5 per cent of the adult male population was murdered.[77]

In the light of Haro Lumbreras's declaration, it is worth recalling that the total number of right-wingers assassinated in the province from 18 July until it was totally in rebel control was forty-four, in nine locations.

A further 101 died in armed clashes with the defenders of the Republic. The subsequent repression was of a different order of magnitude, not a vengeful response to prior left-wing violence but the implementation of a plan for extermination. In seventy-five of Huelva's seventy-eight towns, a total of 6,019 were executed.[78] In the days between the military coup and the fall of Huelva to the rebels, the Republican authorities had made every effort to protect those rightists arrested in the immediate wake of the military coup. There had been calls for serenity and respect for the law from the Civil Governor, the Mayor, Salvador Moreno Márquez, and Republican and Socialist parliamentary deputies for the province. One hundred and seventy-eight local extreme rightists, including Falangists and the most hated landowners and industrialists, were arrested. All were safe and well when the city was conquered. However, during the previous eleven days, six people were murdered. This was the only excuse that Haro Lumbreras needed to launch a bloody repression. There were nightly shootings without even the farce of a 'trial'. Many of those of the right who had been saved by the Republican authorities protested. Haro was eventually removed on 6 February 1937 when it came to light that he had misappropriated donations of jewellery and money made to the rebel cause. Specifically, it appeared that he had used these funds to pay for the services of prostitutes. Evidence was produced showing that, over the previous fifteen years, he had frequently been guilty of theft and other abuses of his position. When he left Huelva, his luggage, carried in three trucks, consisted of ninety-three trunks and suitcases. After serving in Zaragoza, Teruel and Galicia, he became head of the Civil Guard in León. He was killed on 16 February 1941 by one of his junior officers. It was rumoured that the young man's wife had been the unwilling object of Haro's attentions.[79]

In Seville, as in Huelva, the 'the red terror' was a much exaggerated justification for the repression, often no more than a contrived and feeble excuse. That the savagery visited upon the towns conquered by Spanish colonial forces was a repetition of what they did when they attacked a Moroccan village was proudly recognized by the rebels themselves. The first town taken by Castejón's column was Alcalá de Guadaira to the south-east of the provincial capital. His official chronicler, Cándido Ortiz de Villajos, said of Castejón's men recently arrived from Morocco that it was as if 'they had brought with them, as well as the determination to fight for the salvation of Spain, the deadly, terrible, fatal and efficacious principles of the justice of the Qur'an'.[80] The crimes during the four days of the so-called 'red domination' were cited to justify the repression carried out by the column. Among these 'crimes' was the death on the night of 17 July of Agustín Alcalá y Henke, one of the town's principal olive-producers. A moderate and socially conscious Catholic, Alcalá y Henke had a long-term rivalry with another land-owner, Pedro Gutiérrez Calderón, a supporter of the military uprising. Moreover, other employers had been infuriated when Alcalá y Henke had urged them to meet the demands of striking workers in the olive industry. He was shot by an unknown assassin. Many believed that he had been eliminated for betraying the employers' interests and/or as an expendable victim to justify the imminent coup. When news of the military coup reached the town, a Popular Front Committee established under the chairmanship of the Mayor immediately appealed for calm. Since the local Civil Guard had pledged its loyalty to the Republic, it was not disarmed.[81]

However, against the wishes of the Committee, the anarchist CNT–FAI organized a militia force. Two churches, a convent and seminary were set on fire and some religious images destroyed. Three private houses and three right-wing clubs had been searched and property thrown into the street – a situation eagerly exploited by criminal elements. Between 19 and 21 July, the Committee had detained thirty-eight right-wingers for their own protection. None was harmed and there were no more deaths after Alcalá y Henke. Anarchist efforts to burn the municipal jail were successfully repelled. When Castejón's column reached Alcalá de Guadaira in the early evening of 21 July, it was joined by the local Civil Guard. The town fell after a successful artillery bombardment by Alarcón de la Lastra. In the words of his enthusiastic chronicler, 'all the Communist leaders were killed while Castejón punished or rather liberated the town of Alcalá'. 'Punishment' was the Africanista euphemism for savage repression. The alleged 'Communist leaders' were actually four unconnected individuals. Three were shot by the advancing column: two of them young men who had come from Seville to buy bread and the third an agricultural labourer who ran in panic when he saw the Legionarios. The fourth was Miguel Ángel Troncoso, the head of the local police, who, according to his son, was shot in the town hall by Castejón himself. None could be remotely described as Communist leaders. Thirteen men captured in the town hall were taken to Seville, where at least six of them would be killed. Alcalá de Guadaira was then left in the hands of local rightists and a process of revenge began which saw the murders of a further 137 men. Another 350 were imprisoned and tortured, many of whom died. The belongings of the murdered and imprisoned were stolen by the new masters of the town.[82]

In Carmona, to the east of Seville, local landowners bitterly resented the intense pressure put on them to accept work and wage agreements with their labourers. When news arrived of the coup, the Mayor was on official business in Madrid. A Defence Committee was set up with representatives of the Socialist and Communist parties, the CNT and the moderate liberal party Unión Republicana – the latter being the Municipal Police chief, Manuel Gómez Montes. The commander of the Civil Guard, Lieutenant Rafael Martín Cerezo, and Gómez Montes helped the Popular Front Committee gather available weapons and assign groups to defend the roads leading into the town. A convent was ransacked, but the nuns were evacuated unharmed.

On 21 July, a company of Regulares, accompanied by a local right-winger, Emilio Villa Baena, attempted to take the town. Initially repelled, the Moorish mercenaries took refuge in the town theatre with nineteen hostages. They then sent Villa Baena and three prisoners to negotiate a truce. Just as he began to negotiate with members of the Committee, Villa Baeza was shot by an anarchist from Constantina. The column withdrew back to Seville using the other sixteen hostages as human shields. The Committee now searched the houses of the town's rightists and, in one of them, found six cases of pistols. Eighteen right-wingers were locked in the cellars of the town hall. A landowner was shot dead when he tried to flee over the rooftops. That night, in his broadcast, Queipo de Llano gave a wildly exaggerated account of these events, followed by a horrifying threat:

> Faithful to their usual tactics, the Regulares repelled the aggression with such terrible violence that they left about one hundred dead and wounded among their aggressors. This madness is suicidal since I guarantee that Carmona will soon be punished as the treachery of its citizens deserves … the outrages they have committed against men and women of the right must be severely punished. Things have been done in Carmona that call for exemplary punishments and I will impose them in a way that will make history and will ensure that Carmona will long remember the Regulares.[83]

The following day, after first being bombed three times, the town was attacked by two substantial columns commanded by Major Emilio Álvarez de Rementería, accompanied by the bullfighter Pepe el Algabeño.

The first, equipped with two artillery pieces and a section of machine-gunners, consisted of Regulares, Legionarios and Civil Guards, the second of Falangists. Cannon and machine-gun fire dispersed the poorly armed defenders and the town was captured quickly. That day, twelve were killed, their demise later registered as 'violent death'. Over two hundred people fled. Lieutenant Martín Cerezo was arrested and shot and his replacement set about avenging the two deaths of Emilio Villa and Gregorio Rodríguez. Over the next four months, he ordered the executions of 201 men, some of them barely in their teens and others past retirement, and sixteen women. There were no trials and the only 'legal' veneer was an airy reference to the edict of martial law. Where men had fled, their relatives were shot. In many cases, after the heads of families were killed, their houses were confiscated and their wives and young children thrown on to the street. Another seventeen people from Carmona were executed in Seville and Málaga. Large numbers of men were conscripted into the rebel forces.[84]

The victims were largely selected by the local *caciques*, because they were known to be Republicans or union members or had shown dis-respect. One man was shot because he was the bill poster who had stuck up left-wing election posters in February 1936. As in virtually every conquered town in the south, women had their heads shaved, were given castor oil to make them soil themselves and, led by a brass band, were paraded around the streets to be mocked.[85] The perpetrators of the murders and the other abuses included Civil Guards and estate employ-ees who had swiftly joined the Falange. Their motives ranged from psychotic enjoyment to money, some boasting of being paid 15 pesetas for every killing. For others, involvement reflected gratitude for patron-age received or shared religious views, as well as shared fears and anger. They all perceived savagery as 'services for the Fatherland'. Men and women, and many teenagers, were arrested either by the Civil Guard or by the Falangists. Sometimes, victims were picked up at random, or because these thugs coveted their wife or their property, or simply because they were bored or drunk. Sometimes those arrested were shot immediately, sometimes taken to jail where they were beaten and tortured before being eventually murdered. After the shootings, the *caciques*, the recent Falangist converts and the younger landowners would meet in a bar and comment with satisfaction that there would be no more wage claims from those just despatched. On one occasion, unable to find a young man who in fact was hiding under the floor of his parents' shack, they burned down the dwelling with all three inside.[86]

When the parish priest of Carmona protested at the murders, he was told that those executed had been found guilty by a tribunal consisting of the local landowners. When he pointed out that this did not constitute any kind of legal process, he was threatened. By 1938, those responsible experienced sufficient guilt to feel the need to falsify the circumstances of the murders committed in 1936. Witness statements to the 'tribunal' were fabricated, apparently 'justifying' the shootings. Many deaths were registered as having been caused by 'military operations in the town'. Nevertheless, there were more executions when those who had fled came back at the end of the war.[87]

In Cantillana, a wealthy farming community to the north-east of Seville, there had been little history of social tension despite stark inequalities in landownership (four men owned more than 24 per cent of the land, and one of them over 11 per cent, while three-quarters of the farmers owned only 6 per cent). In the wake of the military coup, an Anti-Fascist Popular Front Defence Committee administered the town under the Socialist Mayor. The nearest to revolutionary drama was the use of clenched-fist salutes and greetings such as 'Salud camarada'; firearms were confiscated from landowners and fines were imposed on those who refused to take on unemployed labourers. To guarantee the feeding of the town, wheat and cattle were requisitioned without compensation. The owners were furious but otherwise unmolested. Rich and poor alike were given rations as was the local Civil Guard contingent, which had been confined to its barracks. Only one man was arrested on suspicion of being in cahoots with the military conspirators. A few houses were looted and, on 25 July, the parish church was set alight although the priest was unharmed.

A substantial column of Legionarios, Falangists and Requetés sent by Queipo de Llano was gradually moving north-eastwards up the Valley of the Guadalquivir, taking town after town. They appeared in Cantillana at midday on 30 July. After the usual artillery bombardment, they entered the town unopposed. The defenders had only a few shotguns and soon the surrounding fields were thronged with people fleeing. Despite having been well treated, the local Civil Guard commander began the first of around two hundred executions without trial. Large numbers of townspeople were imprisoned and, over the next few months, more than sixty people including three women and the Mayor would be taken away and shot in Seville. After the Civil War, the parish priest of Cantillana was removed in punishment for a sermon in which he said: 'If the church is damaged, it can be repaired; if statues have been burned, they can be replaced; but the husband or son who has been killed can never be replaced.'[88]

In his broadcast of 30 August, Queipo declared that the search for Republican criminals would go on for ten or twenty years. He also claimed that, in the rebel zone, there had been no atrocities. With no sense of irony, he reiterated his view that any killing done according to his edict was therefore legal: 'We might shoot someone who committed crimes but no one could possibly say that in any town, anywhere, a single person had been murdered. Those responsible have been shot without hesitation. This was done following the dictates of the edict not for the fun of killing like they did, with the greatest cruelty, burning people alive, throwing them into wells and dynamiting them, putting out people's eyes, cutting off women's breasts.'[89]

In fact, what is known of such broadcasts by Queipo de Llano derives from the following day's press reports, together with occasional snippets noted down by those who heard them. Comparisons, when possible, between the two suggest that the texts printed by the press were a pale reflection of the obscenity of the originals. Newspaper editors knew better than to print the more outrageous incitements to rape and murder. Indeed, there was concern that Queipo's excesses might be damaging to the rebel cause abroad. Accordingly, the instinctive self-censorship of the press was reinforced on 7 September when Major José Cuesta Monereo issued detailed instructions regarding foreign sensibilities. Most of his fourteen points were routine, to prevent the publication of sensitive military information. However, they specifically ordered that the printed version of the radio broadcasts be expurgated: 'In the broadcast chats by the General, any concept, phrase or insult, even though accurate, and doubtless the result of excessive zeal in the expression of his patriotism, whose publication is not appropriate or convenient, for reasons of discretion that will easily be appreciated by our intelligent journalists, shall be suppressed.' Similarly, in the reporting of the repression, specific details of the slaughter were prohibited. Instead, journalists were obliged to use euphemisms like 'justice was carried out', 'a deserved punishment was inflicted', 'the law was applied'.[90]

The censorship may well have been designed to limit awareness of Queipo's incitement to the sexual abuse of left-wing women, but the extent to which the rebels considered it legitimate could be seen from what happened in Fuentes de Andalucía, a small town to the east of Seville. It had surrendered without resistance, on 19 July, to Civil Guards. With the help of Falangists and other right-wingers, a Guardia Cívica (a right-wing volunteer police force) was created which set about rounding up the town's leftists. The houses of those arrested were looted as many of the Falangists stole sewing machines for their mothers and girlfriends. On 25 July, the Socialist Mayor and three Communist councillors were shot. It was the beginning of a massacre. In one case, that of a family called Medrano, the parents were arrested, and their three children, José aged twenty, Mercedes aged eighteen and Manuel aged sixteen, were shot. The family's shack was burned down and the fourth child, Juan, aged eight, was abandoned to his fate. A truckload of women prisoners was taken to an estate outside the town of La Campana further north. Among them were four young girls, aged between eighteen and fourteen. The women were obliged to cook and serve a meal for their captors who then sexually assaulted them before shooting them and throwing their bodies down a well. When the Civil Guard returned to Fuentes de Andalucía, they marched through the town waving rifles adorned with the underwear of the murdered women.[91]

It will be recalled that on 23 July Queipo had made his most explicit incitement to rape. The following day, he commented with relish on the savagery inflicted by Castejón's column when it captured Arahal, a small town of 12,500 inhabitants to the south of Carmona. When news of the military rebellion reached Arahal, thirty-six local right-wingers had been locked up in the town hall. On 22 July, when a Socialist town councillor went to release them, thirteen left but twenty-three preferred to remain, fearful that it was a ruse to shoot them. With the town being bombarded with artillery, some armed men from Seville then set fire to the building and twenty-two of the rightists were burned to death, only the priest escaping with his life. When Castejón's column entered Arahal, they reacted to this atrocity with an orgy of indiscriminate violence. Accounts of the numbers of the town's inhabitants killed vary wildly from 146 to 1,600. Young women considered to be of the left were repeatedly raped. The Socialist Mayor, a seventy-one-year-old cobbler, who had worked hard to prevent violence, was shot.[92]

Further south, in Morón de la Frontera, the local Republican elements had created a Defence Committee as soon as they heard news of the rising in Morocco. They detained those prominent rightists thought to support the rebels. Since the Civil Guard local commander pretended that he and his men were loyal to the Republic, they were allowed to go about their business. A tense peace was broken when a group of armed anarchists, unconnected with the Committee, attempted to take a judge to join the other prisoners. He had a pistol and shot one of the anarchists who, before dying, shot the judge. The Civil Guard intervened, shooting one anarchist and wounding another. Hoping for the arrival of help from Seville, the lieutenant took the right-wing prisoners and their families into the barracks, which was then besieged by the local left. The commander announced that he would surrender and that his men would lay down their arms. It was a lie. They came out using the rightist civilians as a shield and then broke through the besiegers, aiming to capture the town hall. In the subsequent fight, several Civil Guards and rightists lost their lives. When the Civil Guard barracks were searched, two guards were found dead, handcuffed together, which suggested that they had been killed for opposing the actions of the Lieutenant.[93]

When Castejón's column arrived, it was fiercely resisted. Castejón's revenge was fierce. Corpses that littered the streets were left to be eaten by pigs. Shops and houses were looted and women violated. In a radio broadcast, Queipo de Llano crowed with delight:

> An example has been made of Morón that I imagine will serve as a lesson to those towns who still foolishly maintain their faith in Marxism and the hope of being able to resist us. Just as in Arahal, in Morón there was a group of heedless men who had committed unequalled acts of savagery, attacking right-wing individuals who had not provoked them. And I have heard that in various towns the Marxists have right-wing prisoners against whom they plan to commit similar barbarities. I remind them all that, for every honorable person that dies, I will shoot at least ten; and there are already towns where we have gone beyond that figure. And the leaders should not hold out hope of saving themselves by flight, since I will drag them from out of the ground, if necessary, to implement the law.[94]

Castejón himself explained how he took these towns: 'I employed an encircling movement which enabled me to punish the reds harshly.'[95] The rural proletariat was no match for the military experience of the battle-hardened Legionarios. However, as Castejón revealed, it was a question not simply of seizing control but of imposing a savage repression. In the case of the next town conquered, La Puebla de Cazalla east of Morón, refugees from there and Arahal had given bloodcurdling accounts of what had happened when Castejón's column had arrived. Moreover, on 30 July, a rebel aircraft dropped leaflets threatening that the town would be bombed if it did not surrender immediately. Accordingly, no resistance was offered. Nevertheless, the repression that followed was unremitting. The crimes of the left had consisted of sacking the parish church and the headquarters of Acción Popular, requisitioning and distributing food and arresting forty-six local rebel sympathizers. No deaths occurred while the town was in the hands of the Popular Front Committee. Indeed, anarchists from Málaga had been prevented from killing the prisoners. Now, the occupying troops looted houses. Before cursory military trials started, over one hundred people were murdered. More than one thousand men, from a town of nine thousand inhabitants, were forcibly mobilized into the rebel army. To replace them, women and older men were used as slave labour.[96]

Similarly, as Queipo had threatened, when Castejón's column reached the prosperous railway junction and market town of Puente Genil in south-western Córdoba, the repression was indiscriminately ferocious. For once, the events that had followed the initial coup in the town provided some kind of excuse. The numerous forces from the town's three Civil Guards barracks, supported by local Falangists, members of Acción Popular and landowners, had declared for the rebellion on 19 July, seizing the Casa del Pueblo and taking many prisoners. They were opposed by a combination of the local leftists and loyal security forces from Málaga. In fierce fighting over the next four days, around 250 left-wing workers and twenty-one Civil Guards were killed and fifteen wounded. A further fifty left-wing hostages were executed by the Civil Guards on 22 July.

Although the rebellion was defeated by 23 July, sporadic sniper fire saw further left-wing deaths. This intensified the hatred behind the brutal reprisals that were now taken by the left. While a revolutionary committee set about distributing food, the surviving Civil Guards were executed along with many of those who had supported the military coup – landowners, money-lenders, right-wingers and, inevitably, the clergy. Among the atrocities committed, a seventy-year-old man and his wife were burned alive. Although a rich landowner, Manuel Gómez Perales, paid a ransom of 100,000 pesetas for his liberty, he and his four sons were murdered. In justification of the even greater scale of subsequent revenge, the rebel newspaper La Unión stated that there had been seven hundred victims, although official Francoist sources eventually claimed 154. Exhaustive modern research has identified only 115. There were instances of victims being tortured and mutilated and of women dancing with corpses. Many houses were looted and forty-five burned down. Seven churches were destroyed. Ten clergymen were murdered, although three others, who had shown sympathy with the plight of the local working class, were saved. Two teams arrayed in ecclesiastical robes played football with the head of a statue of the Virgin Mary.[97]

One week later, on 1 August, a substantial column of around 1,200 Legionarios, regular troops, Requetés and Falangists reached Puente Genil from Seville under the command of Castejón and Major Haro Lumbreras. Ramón de Carranza also arrived with his column. Enjoying artillery and air support, they quickly overcame the town's fierce resistance. Messages had been sent to Puente Genil threatening that one hundred lives would be taken in reprisal for every right-wing victim of the 'red domination'. When the scale of the attack was realized, many tried to flee towards Málaga. Troops were deployed, according to Castejón himself, 'to prevent the flight of refugees and to increase the scale of the killing'. Regarding his own forces, he said: 'Once inside the town, the repression started in earnest.' The killing was indiscriminate and many of the victims were not at all political, merely people who had fled in terror.

Numerous women were raped before being shot. Men were taken off the street or pulled from their houses to be tortured and shot. Five hundred and one people were killed on that first day. Castejón returned to Seville on the same evening and the 'clean-up operation' continued for months afterwards. It took the lives of many who were anything but leftists, including several lawyers and doctors. The president of the Red Cross was shot 'for having given medicines to the reds'. In his broadcast that evening, Queipo de Llano praised Castejón, saying that 'the repression has been harsh but not nearly as harsh as it should have been and indeed will be'. At least another thousand people were executed over the following months, many as acts of petty vengeance against workers who had stood up to the owners in the previous years.[98]

On 3 August, Castejón was ordered by Franco to join the march on Madrid. His advance would see the 'cleansing' of numerous *pueblos* along the way. The purging elsewhere in the province of Seville continued at the hands of Ramón Carranza, whose column was now incorporated into a larger force under Major Francisco Buiza Fernández-Palacios. On Friday 7 August, this column set off from the provincial capital in a north-easterly direction. Fully equipped with artillery, it numbered 1,200. Its first target was Lora del Río, a relatively tranquil town where the bulk of the working class was Socialist and the Mayor a moderate Republican. There, the Captain of the Civil Guard and his men, together with the parish priest and about eighty local right-wingers, had greeted the news of the military uprising enthusiastically. They gathered arms and set up headquarters in the Civil Guard barracks on 19 July.

Meanwhile, the left had formed a liaison committee consisting of Socialist and Republican members who began to requisition and distribute food. Meat was plentiful since the committee permitted the slaughtering of the fighting bulls being bred on local farms. On each of the next three days, the Civil Guard Captain led a parade of the rightists around the town reading out an edict in favour of the military uprising. To avoid bloodshed, the Mayor ordered them to desist. They ignored him and finally, on the evening of 22 July, when they paraded again, they were confronted by the liaison committee. Four of the rightists were wounded and all the marchers barricaded themselves in the Civil Guard barracks. After a short siege, they surrendered, against the loud protests of the Captain, who was shot. The following day, house searches began and the majority of the town's right-wingers were imprisoned. The funds of local banks and valuables from the church were put into safe-keeping but there were also cases of blatant robbery. On 1 August, anarchists arrived from Constantina to the north and, overcoming the protests of the committee, began to shoot the prisoners. Over the next four days, they executed ninety, including the parish priest and his assistant, five Falangists and twenty Civil Guards. Many of those murdered were active supporters of the military rising, but others were simply known rightists who had provoked the enmity of local workers.[99]

Artillery and air bombardment of the town began on the evening of 7 August. Virtually no resistance was offered when Lora del Río was occupied the next day by Buiza's column. Large numbers of citizens fled. In the words of *ABC*, 'the town's military saviours imposed exemplary justice'. A cavalry captain, the Carlist Carlos Mencos López, was left in charge of the 'pacification'. Houses were systematically looted – the prelude to methodical confiscation of the goods and property of the town's Republicans. In revenge for the crimes of the anarchists from Constantina, people were shot that day on the basis of simple denunciations. That night, there was a great orgy with drink provided by grateful wine-producers. An eyewitness reported that many recently widowed women were used to meet 'the sexual excesses of that collectivity without women [the Legionarios] in an orgy begun by the conservative *señoritos*'. Then 'trials' were mounted in which the witnesses were relatives of the victims. On 10 August, Ramón Carranza arrived with his column. A further three hundred labourers, including some women, were 'tried' without defence. They were accused of 'crimes' ranging from having a

Republican flag to having expressed admiration for President Roosevelt. Domestic servants were accused of criticizing their employers. All were found guilty. Over the next days, they were loaded on to the town's only truck and taken to the cemetery on the outskirts where all, including two pregnant girls, were shot.[100]

Juan Manuel Lozano Nieto was the son of a man murdered by the rebels despite having taken no part in the left-wing atrocities. Seventy years after the events in Lora, Lozano Nieto, by now a Catholic priest, wrote a measured account of them. In his book, he explained why even those who were not seeking revenge for an executed relative took part in the murders of the left. Some were simply trying to save themselves. Others, of lower-middle-class origin, were desperate to differentiate themselves from the landless labourers. Others were interested in enriching themselves with the property of those they killed. There were cases of the simple theft of the shops or cattle of the wealthier executed Republicans and the clothes and household goods of the more humble. Then there were simple degenerates, who killed for money or for alcohol, while others were involved for sexual gratification.[101] According to his dispassionate account, between six hundred and one thousand men young and old, women and children were slaughtered in the repression in Lora. Entire families were eliminated or left without means of support. Children were left without parents. Women were abused and humiliated, subjected to the standard rebel practice of their heads being shaved except for a tuft of hair to which was tied a ribbon with monarchist colours.[102]

Between 5 and 12 August, the forces of Carranza and Buiza had taken the village of El Pedroso, and the towns of Constantina and Cazalla de la Sierra. In Constantina, the atrocities of the local anarchists were avenged threefold. Three hundred inhabitants were executed and a further three thousand fled.[103] In Cazalla de la Sierra, under the anarchist-dominated revolutionary committee, the parish church was sacked and set alight, the Civil Guard detained, food requisitioned and distributed and numerous right-wingers detained. Forty-one civilians and twenty-three Civil Guards were shot during the night of 5–6 August in retaliation for Buiza's first attack on the town.[104] When he took the town at his second attempt a week later, a tribunal consisting of officers from his force and local rightists was set up to try those considered responsible for the crimes committed. Seventy-six, including several women, were shot over the following weeks.[105]

The near racist contempt of the southern landowners for their peasants had found an echo in the Africanistas. Their belief in their right of arbitrary power over the tribes of Morocco was comparable to the sense of near-feudal entitlement of the *señoritos*. An easy identification of interest saw both regard the proletariat as a subject colonial race. Before 1936, explicit parallels had been drawn between the workers of southern Spain and the Rif tribesmen. Now, the 'crimes' of the reds in resisting the military uprising were seen as equivalent to the 'crimes' of the tribesmen who massacred Spanish troops at the battle of Annual in 1921 and nearly captured Melilla. The role of the African columns in 1936 was likened to that of the Legionarios who relieved Melilla.[106]

The relationship between the landowners and their military saviours was illustrated when Queipo de Llano asked Ramón de Carranza's friend Rafael de Medina to raise money for the rebel cause. After years of anguished complaints that agriculture was in ruins as a result of Republican reforms, it might have been expected that Medina's fund-raising efforts would meet with difficulty. On his first day, three olive exporters in Alcalá de Guadaira gave 1 million pesetas between them. Later the same day, in Dos Hermanas, one landowner asked what the money was for. When told that it was hoped to buy aircraft, he asked how much an aeroplane cost. When Medina replied, 'About one million pesetas,' without hesitating the *latifundista* wrote him a cheque for the full amount.[107] Landowners often formed and financed their own units, such as those led by Carranza or the Mora-Figueroa brothers.

Thereafter, several of the various volunteer forces were formalized as a kind of landowners' cavalry usually known as the Volunteer Mounted Police. These units included both landowners and those of their employees specialized in horse-breeding and training. Polo ponies were used as well as working horses. As if taking part in a sport or hunting expeditions, they carried out a continuous campaign against the left in the south. Such groups were to be found throughout most of Andalusia and Extremadura. In Lucena in Córdoba, the local landowners funded a squad of expert horsemen to 'defend property' and pursue leftists who had fled into the countryside. The group was notorious for its cruelty, its pillaging and its many sexual crimes and was known locally as 'the death squad'. In September 1936, for example, they crossed the iron bridge over the River Genil and entered Cuevas de San Marcos in Málaga. Many of the inhabitants who fled into the surrounding countryside, for no reason other than fear, were rounded up and shot. After such expeditions, the death squad would return to Lucena with lorries loaded with furniture, bedding, sewing machines, books, clocks and other household items.[108]

The *caciques* and the army could call upon support for their repressive activities from a substantial social group. Those at the top provided money and weapons but there was no shortage of willing volunteers to do their dirty work. Those who went out searching for leftists, murdering and raping, torturing and interrogating, and those who denounced their neighbours were a heterogeneous group. Some were landowners or local businessmen, some were their sons. Others of whatever social class were hoping to save themselves from a dubious past by manifesting enthusiasm for the killing. Others enjoyed the opportunity to kill and rape without hindrance. Others again welcomed the chance to steal or buy cheaply the coveted property of their neighbours. There were also the silent accomplices who looked on, perhaps appalled, perhaps delighted. As the suffocating atmosphere of fear intensified, despite the legitimizing sermons of the clerics, the terror was based on an all-pervading moral corruption.

Sometimes, however, the intensity of the repression was not sufficient for Queipo de Llano. Córdoba had fallen within a matter of hours to the city's military commander, the Artillery Colonel Ciriaco Cascajo Ruiz, with help from the Civil Guard.[109] With the city of Córdoba isolated within a province that remained loyal to the Republic, a group of Falangists went to Seville to get arms. Their leader was asked by Queipo how many they had shot in Córdoba. When he replied, 'None,' Queipo was outraged and thundered: 'Well, until you shoot a couple of hundred there'll be no more arms for you!' Queipo was dissatisfied because Cascajo was ordering 'only' five executions per day. The municipal authorities and leading Republicans who had taken refuge in the building of the Civil Governor were murdered. Among other victims were four parliamentary deputies for Andalusia and Manuel Azaña's nephew, Gregorio Azaña Cuevas, a state lawyer, who had gone to attend a meeting about the proposed autonomy statute for Andalusia along with another of those arrested, Joaquín García Hidalgo Villanueva, a Freemason and journalist who had been Socialist deputy for the city between 1931 and 1933. García Hidalgo, a diabetic, was taken to prison. There he was tortured and force-fed sugar. He died in a diabetic coma on 28 July.

After an inspection by Queipo on 5 August, the rate of executions speeded up. Bruno Ibáñez, a brutal major of the Civil Guard, was put in charge of the terror. In the first week, he arrested 109 people from lists given him by landowners and priests. They were shot out on the roads and in the olive groves. The Socialist Mayor Manuel Sánchez Badajoz, a number of town councillors and a much loved parliamentary deputy, Dr

Vicente Martín Romera, were taken to the cemetery at dawn on 7 August and, by the light of car headlights, shot with seven others. Within a few days, with the midsummer heat at its height, the numbers of shootings and the corpses left in the streets caused a minor typhoid epidemic. It has been calculated that more than 11,500 people were killed in the province of Córdoba between 1936 and 1945.[110]

A young Falangist lawyer recalled: 'The basement of Falange head-quarters in which people were held was like a balloon which was blown up in the afternoon and was empty the following morning. Each day there were executions in the cemetery and along the roads leading out of the city.' He saw Bruno Ibáñez one day at a bullfight: 'As he came out of the ring people cringed. To get out of his way, people would have incrusted themselves in the walls if they could. Everyone was electrified with terror and fear. Don Bruno could have shot all Córdoba, he was sent there with carte blanche. It was said that his whole family had been wiped out by the reds in some town in La Mancha. Whether it was true or not, he was a prejudiced, embittered man.' He organized book burn-ings and imposed a programme of religious films and Nazi documentar-ies in local cinemas.[111] A note issued by Bruno Ibáñez on 1 October 1936 stated that 'Those who flee are effectively confessing their guilt.'[112]

The repression in the wider province was equally brutal. In the small town of Lucena, 118 men and five women were shot.[113] One of the most significant rebel atrocities took place in Baena, a hilltop town to the south-east of Córdoba on the road to Granada. During the spring of 1936, and indeed before, the town had seen considerable social hatred between its landless labourers and its landowners. The local bosses had systematically flouted the Republic's labour legislation, bringing in cheap labour from outside and paying starvation wages. The commander of the town's Civil Guard detachment, Lieutenant Pascual Sánchez Ramírez, an ex-Legionario, had built up a considerable arsenal of weap-ons and had been arming the local landowners and giving local Falangists official status as 'special sworn-in guards' (guardias jurados). On the night of 18 July, he seized control of the Casa del Pueblo. The next morn-ing, he issued an edict of martial law and, with the sworn-in Falangists, occupied the town hall, the telephone exchange and other key buildings, into which they took hostages.

The rural labourers of the local CNT advanced on the town armed only with axes, sickles, sticks and a few shotguns. After a clash on the outskirts of the town, in which one Civil Guard and eleven workers died, they were driven off by a force of Civil Guards and right-wing civilians.

The next day, 20 July, the workers returned to find the centre of the town defended by well over two hundred Civil Guards, Falangists and landowners distributed among several strategically chosen buildings that dominated the town. They threatened to kill a number of hostages they were holding in the town hall, including a woman at an advanced stage of pregnancy. The workers cut off their water, electricity and food supplies. Effectively controlling the town, the anarchists declared libertarian communism, abolished money and requisitioned food and jewellery as a first step towards common ownership of property. Coupons were issued for food. The revolutionary committee detained prominent members of the middle class in a nearby old people's residence and ordered that none be harmed. A church and a convent where the rebels had established themselves were seriously damaged in the fighting and the parish priest killed. Moreover, in acts of revenge for personal grudges, eleven right-wingers were murdered before the town was captured by the military rebels. Sánchez Ramírez rejected proposals for a truce, fearing that surrender would lead to his death and that of his men.[114]

On 28 July, just as the besieged Civil Guards were about to give up, a large rebel relief column left Córdoba under the orders of Colonel Eduardo Sáenz de Buruaga. It consisted of Civil Guards, Legionarios and Moorish Regulares, equipped with artillery and machine-guns. The workers, with virtually no firearms, were unable to put up much resistance and the column suffered only four wounded in taking Baena street by street. The Regulares led the assault, killing indiscriminately and looting. Survivors found in the street or in houses along the way were rounded up and taken to the town-hall square. The official Civil Guard account of the events in Baena admitted that 'the slightest denunciation would see the accused shot'. Sáenz de Buruaga took refreshment in a café with one of his men, Félix Moreno de la Cova, the son of a rich landowner from Palma del Río. Meanwhile, Sánchez Ramírez, blind with rage, organized a massacre that echoed his experience in Morocco. First he killed the five male hostages detained in the town hall. Then he had lines of prisoners – many of whom had nothing to do with the CNT union or the events of the previous week – lie face down in the square. Completely beside himself, he insisted on shooting most of them himself. The occupying forces aided by local rightists continued to bring in more prisoners to replace those being shot.

ABC referred to these extra-judicial killings as the application of 'exemplary punishment' to 'all leading elements' and of 'the rigour of the law' to anyone found with arms. The paper's final comment was 'it is certain that the town of Baena will never forget the scenes of horror created by so many murders committed there and the activities of the liberating forces'. Nevertheless, despite *ABC*'s comments, Sáenz de Buruaga's forces captured neither union leaders nor individuals with arms. Nearly all of these had withdrawn to the old people's residence where the right-wing prisoners were being kept. The 'so many murders' were largely the consequence of Sáenz de Buruaga's irresponsibility in going for a drink while Sánchez Ramírez conducted the massacre.

The many leftists who fled and packed into the residence used the hostages as shields in the hope that this would restrain Sáenz de Buruaga's pursuing forces. It did not and many were found dead by the windows, shot with munitions possessed only by the attackers. Most of the anarchists who had taken refuge there fled, but a few stayed until the last moment, murdering many of the remaining hostages in reprisal for the executions in the square. In total, eighty-one hostages were killed. Many local people were convinced that, but for the massacre organized by Sánchez Ramírez, the hostages would have survived. Nevertheless, the discovery of their corpses led to a further massacre in an orgy of revenge so indiscriminate that several right-wingers were also victims. Masses of left-wing prisoners were shot, including an eight-year-old boy.[115] On 5 August, with Sáenz de Buruaga's column having gone to Córdoba, Baena was attacked unsuccessfully by anarchist militia. This in turn intensified the rhythm of executions within the town.[116]

On the night of 31 July, Queipo de Llano felt the need to justify, in his nightly broadcast, the repression in Baena, by referring to 'real horrors, monstrous crimes that cannot be mentioned lest they bring shame on our people, and that produced after the fall of Baena, the punishment that is natural when troops are possessed by the indignation provoked by such crimes'.[117] Two months later, the middle classes of Baena hosted a ceremony at which Sáenz de Buruaga presented Sánchez Ramírez with the military medal in the still bloodstained square. Nearly seven hundred people were killed by, or on the orders of, Sánchez Ramírez, Sáenz de Buruaga and, over the next five months, the man named as military judge. This was the leading local landowner, Manuel Cubillo Jiménez, whose wife and three young sons were among those killed in the residence by gunfire from the forces of Sáenz de Buruaga. He was implacable in his desire for revenge. Many townspeople fled eastwards to the Republican-held province of Jaén. The women who remained were subjected to various forms of sexual abuse and humiliation, from rape to head-shaving and being forced to drink castor oil. Over six hundred children were left orphaned, including cases of toddlers left to fend for themselves.[118]

The events in Baena fitted well into the overall thinking behind the military uprising. The point was made expressively by José María Pemán, who declared that 'this magnificent conflict which is bleeding Spain is taking place on a plane that is both supernatural and wondrous. The flames of Irún, Guernica, Lequeitio, Málaga or Baena burn the stubble to leave the land fertilized for the new harvest. We are going to have, my fellow Spaniards, land clean and levelled on which to lay imperial stones.'[119]

Initially, the rebel columns of each Andalusian province had concentrated on occupying nearby towns and villages, the choice of which depended less on military criteria than on the desire of landowners to liberate their estates from left-wing occupations. At the beginning of August, in order to impose a strategic vision of operations, a more central control was imposed on the columns. With numerous towns and villages of Córdoba still in Republican hands, General Varela was sent to undertake their conquest. Although no column would henceforth be permitted to act on its own initiative, their activities continued to reflect the prejudices and objectives of the landowners. One of the first objectives for Varela was the relief of Granada, which remained isolated and besieged by government forces. This was achieved on 18 August. A second objective was the complete occupation of Seville and Cádiz prior to an attack on Málaga. Thus the beautiful hilltop town of Ronda became an intermediate target of the highest importance.[120]

Significantly, among Varela's staff could be found the Falangist bullfighter and landowner Pepe el Algabeño, the great *latifundista* Eduardo Sotomayor and Antonio Cañero, a famous *rejoneador* (horse-back bullfighter). The estate-owners who bred fighting bulls loathed the day-labourers who wanted to plough the pastures for crops. Among them, there were several retired bullfighters who, after their successes in the ring, had bought land and become bull-breeders.[121] Nevertheless, the enthusiasm of the *latifundistas* for the brutal repression of landless labourers would eventually take its toll on the productive capacity of the great estates. The military authorities were sufficiently concerned to take up the question and call for there to be left sufficient workers to ensure agricultural production.[122]

Virtually every town and village of Cádiz had been conquered by 18 September. Despite exhaustive efforts to inflate the figures, the Francoist authorities could claim that, in the areas in Republican hands since the military coup of 18 July, only ninety-eight people had been killed, the majority in response to news of the rightist violence in other *pueblos*.[123] This contrasts with the 3,071 people executed by the rebels within the province. There were executions in every *pueblo* of Cádiz, whether or not there had been any deaths at the hands of Republicans. The principal victims were those who had played any role in Republican institutions, political parties or trade unions. Anyone known to have taken part in any strike action over the previous ten years or known to sympathize with Republican ideas such as schoolteachers or Freemasons was a likely target.[124]

With Cádiz entirely in Francoist hands, Manuel Mora-Figueroa's forces were joined by those of his brother José, and the augmented column began to make incursions into the province of Málaga. They conquered numerous villages as they moved uphill to the sierra dominated by the historic town of Ronda, perched alongside the *tajo* or gorge in which the River Gaudalevin runs more than three hundred feet below. Famous for its Roman and Arab bridges and its exquisite eighteenth-century bullring, Ronda had suffered a pitiless repression at the hands of anarchists led by a character known as 'El Gitano'. Initially, the CNT committee had maintained a degree of order although churches were sacked and images destroyed, but soon there were murders being carried out by anarchists from Málaga and also by locals. However, there is no substance to the claim, first made by Queipo in a broadcast on 18 August and popularized by Ernest Hemingway's novel *For Whom the Bell Tolls*, that large numbers of prisoners were killed by being thrown into the *tajo*. The many rightist victims were shot in the cemetery. Francoist sources claim that victims of the red terror from Ronda and the nearby *pueblos* of Gaucín and Arriate numbered over six hundred. On 16 September, when Varela took the town, the defenders fled and his forces suffered only three casualties in the assault. His men stopped and interrogated anyone found in streets and shot many of them. Over half of the population fled towards Málaga.[125] Under the new authorities, those of the town's defenders who had not fled were subjected to a bloody repression and the theft of their property.[126]

Mora-Figueroa set up headquarters in Ronda. There his forces were joined by a group of young socialites from Sanlúcar under the leadership of another scion of a sherry-producing family, Pedro Barbadillo Rodríguez. After the capture of each *pueblo*, large numbers of prisoners were taken back to Ronda for execution.[127] In response to the intensity of the repression in Western Andalusia, many men, fearing for their lives, fled to the hills and lived by stealing cattle and crops. Mounted patrols of Civil Guards and Falangists of the Mora-Figueroa column devoted considerable time to hunting them down and killing them, particularly after the fall of Málaga in February 1937.[128]

Queipo de Llano placed the 'legal' supervision of the repression throughout all of Andalusia and Extremadura in the hands of the military judge, Francisco Bohórquez Vecina. The utterly arbitrary nature of Bohórquez's proceedings was starkly revealed on 28 May 1937, in a set of complaints sent to General Varela by Felipe Rodríguez Franco, a prosecutor of the Cádiz provincial court. He had been removed from his post for ignoring the illegal instructions issued to members of the summary courts martial by Bohórquez. Rodríguez Franco alleged that these instructions were that 'all the agents and scrutineers of the Popular Front in the 1936 elections should be tried, with decisions as to their guilt to be made on the basis of the impression that their faces made on the judges during their interrogation. All red militiamen, as a general rule, should be tried and shot.' Bohórquez laid down the percentage of sentences of different kinds that should be passed and even made an *a priori* rule about proof, saying that one witness for the prosecution was enough for a guilty verdict. Varela acknowledged receipt but nothing was done.[129]

Events in Granada were significantly different from those in Cádiz, Córdoba and Seville. The military commander, General Miguel Campins, had arrived in Granada only on 11 July and was not party to the conspiracy. Loyal to the Republic, he refused to obey Queipo's order to declare martial law. However, Campins did send a telegram putting himself under the orders of his friend General Franco, whose deputy he had been at the Zaragoza Military Academy. Campins was arrested by rebel officers and it was alleged that his hesitation had led to the coup failing in Jaén, Málaga and Almería. Queipo declared on the radio that, if he had been less of a coward, he would have committed suicide.[130] Campíns was tried in Seville for 'rebellion' on 14 August and shot two days later. Franco sent letters asking that mercy be shown to Campins, but Queipo tore them up.[131]

In the meantime, the main centre of resistance, the working-class district of the Albaicín, was forced to surrender after artillery and bombing attacks. Varela reached Loja west of the city on 18 August, and opened a line of contact with Seville. Granada was still threatened by loyalist forces.[132] The consequent sense of insecurity, along with feeble Republican bombing raids, intensified the brutality of the repression

ABOVE Franco in Seville with the brutal leader of the 'Column of Death', Colonel Juan Yagüe, prior to its march on Madrid.

LEFT Yagüe's artillery chief, the landowner from Carmona, Luis Alarcón de la Lastra.

RIGHT General Emilio Mola, the implacable director of the military coup.

LEFT General Gonzalo Queipo de Llano making one of his incendiary radio broadcasts.

RIGHT Gonzalo de Aguilera, the landowner and army officer who justified rebel policies of extermination to the foreign press. He later lost his mind and murdered his own sons.

ABOVE Virgilio Leret, the first Republican officer to be shot by the rebels, seen here with his wife, the feminist, Carlota O'Neill, who was imprisoned and separated from their daughters, Carlota and Mariela.

ABOVE RIGHT Amparo Barayón, murdered because she was a feminist and married to the left-wing novelist Ramón Sender.

BELOW A Coruña, Anniversary of the foundation of the Second Republic, 14 April 1936. From right to left, the Civil Governor, Francisco Pérez Carballo, his wife, the feminist Juana Capdevielle Sanmartín, the head of the Galician military region, General Enrique Salcedo Molinuevo, the Mayor Alfredo Suárez Ferrín. In the second row, with beard, the Military Governor, General Rogelio Caridad Pita. All five were executed by the military rebels.

RIGHT José González Barrero, Mayor of Zafra, was imprisoned in May 1934 on trumped-up charges and is seen here in Alicante jail. He was murdered in April 1939.

BELOW Modesto José Lorenzana Macarro, Mayor of Fuente de Cantos, was fraudulently removed in June 1934 and murdered in September 1936.

BELOW RIGHT Ricardo Zabalza, secretary general of the FNTT and Civil Governor of Valencia during the war, seen here with his wife Obdulia Bermejo, to whom he was introduced by Margarita Nelken. Zabalza was executed in February 1940.

LEFT Mourning women after Castejón's purge of the Triana district of Seville, 21 July 1936.

ABOVE. Queipo de Llano (foreground) inspects the 5º Bandera of the Legion in Seville on 2 August 1936. From right to left, (by car) Major José Cuesta Monereo who planned the coup in the city, (in shirt-sleeves) Major Antonio Castejón Espinosa who led the columns that brutally purged the towns and villages of the province and Captain Manuel Díaz Criado, who organized the repression in the city.

BELOW The landowner and aristocrat, Rafael de Medina Villalonga, in white, leads the column that has captured the town of Tocina, 4 August 1936.

ABOVE Trucks taking miners captured in the ambush at La Pañoleta for execution.

RIGHT Utrera, 26 July 1936. Townsfolk taken prisoner by the column of the Legion which captured the town.

BELOW Lorca's gravediggers – all were left-wing prisoners obliged under threat of death to dig graves, including that of Lorca. Among them is Antonio Mendoza Lafuente (3rd from right, 2nd row), president of a Masonic lodge in Granada.

ABOVE Regulares examine their plunder.

BELOW After a village falls, the column moves on with stolen sewing machines, household goods and animals.

ABOVE A firing squad prepares to execute townspeople in Llerena.

BELOW Calle Carnicerías (Butchery Street) in Talavera de la Reina. This photo which records a massacre committed by Franco's columns was published by his propaganda services as a non-existent Republican atrocity in Talavera la Real.

RIGHT Mass grave near Toledo.

ABOVE Pascual Fresquet (centre left) with his 'death brigade' in Caspe.

ABOVE The seizure of the Iglesia del Carmen in Madrid by militiamen.

LEFT Arms and uniforms of the Falange found by militiamen in the offices of the monarchist newspaper ABC.

carried out by the newly appointed Civil Governor. The forty-five-year-old Comandante José Valdés Guzmán was a deeply reactionary Africanista as well as an early member of the Falange. The painful legacy of a serious wound suffered in Morocco together with lifelong intestinal problems had left him with an ulcerous disposition. He had been posted to Granada in 1931 as head of the military administration. He harboured a deep loathing of the local left after the events of 9–10 March when Falangist gunmen had fired on a group of workers and their families and thus provóked a joint general strike of all of the unions of the city. The right now took full-scale revenge for the consequent violence, when the offices of both the Falange and Acción Popular had been set on fire.[133]

Numerous doctors, lawyers, writers, artists, schoolteachers and, above all, workers were murdered. Much of the dirty work was carried out by the large numbers of newly recruited Falangists who played a key role in locating and denouncing suspects.[134] When control of the city centre was assured, Valdés allowed the Falangist 'Black Squad' to sow panic among the population. The group was led by prominent local rightists and was made up of a mixture of convinced fanatics, paid thugs and men anxious to hide a left-wing past. Leftists were forcibly seized from their homes at night and shot in the cemetery. One of their leaders, Juan Luis Trescastro Medina, declared that, on expeditions to surrounding villages, he was prepared to slit the throats of any reds including breast-feeding babies.[135] After the fall of Loja, Queipo sent a contingent of Regulares which took part in atrocities in the *pueblos*. In the course of the war, more than five thousand civilians were shot in Granada, many at the cemetery. The cemetery's caretaker went mad and, on 4 August, was committed to an asylum. Three weeks later, his replacement and his family moved from the lodge at the cemetery gates because the shots and the cries and screams of the dying had made it unbearable for them. Large numbers of people from all over the Alpujárras were buried in a common grave in a canyon near Órgiva.[136]

One of the most celebrated victims, not just in Granada but in all of Spain, was the poet Federico García Lorca. Years later, the Francoists were to claim that Lorca had died because of an apolitical private feud related to his homosexuality. In fact, Lorca was anything but apolitical. In ultra-reactionary Granada, his sexuality had given him a sense of apartness which had grown into deep empathy for those on the margins of respectable society. In 1934, he had declared: 'I will always be on the side of those who have nothing.' His itinerant theatre La Barraca was inspired by a sense of social missionary zeal. Lorca regularly signed anti-fascist manifestos and was connected with organizations such as International Red Aid. Since he was an immensely famous and popular poet and playwright, his politics and his sexuality provoked the loathing of the Falange and the rest of the right.

In Granada itself, he was closely connected with the moderate left. His views were well known and it had not escaped the notice of the town's oligarchs that he thought that the Catholic conquest of Moorish Granada in 1492 had been a disaster. Flouting a central tenet of Spanish right-wing thinking, Lorca believed that the conquest had destroyed a unique civilization and created 'a wasteland populated by the worst bourgeoisie in Spain today'. Recent research has also added another element which was resentment of the success of Lorca's father, Federico García Rodríguez. He had become rich, buying and selling land in Asquerosa to the north-west of Granada (now renamed Valderrubio). To the annoyance of other landowners, he paid his employees well, lent his neighbours money when they were in danger of foreclosure and even built homes for his workers. His friendship with the Socialist Minister, Fernando de los Ríos, was another reason for resentment. Among his political and economic rivals were the lawyer and businessman Juan Luis Trescastro Medina and Horacio Roldán Quesada of Acción Popular. Roldán Quesada had hoped to marry the poet's sister Concha, but she had married Manuel Fernández Montesinos, who became Mayor of the city.[137]

When rightists hunting for 'reds' began to look for him, Lorca took refuge in the home of his friend the Falangist poet Luis Rosales. On 16 August, at the home of the Rosales family, Lorca was seized by Civil Guards who were accompanied by the sinister Ramón Ruiz Alonso, a one-time deputy for the local CEDA, Trescastro and another member of Acción Popular, Luis García-Alix Fernández. Ruiz Alonso, who had hitched his cart to the Falange, harboured grudges against both Lorca and the Rosales brothers.[138] Lorca was ludicrously denounced by Ruiz Alonso to Valdés as a Russian spy, communicating with Moscow via a high-powered radio. Valdés sent a message to Queipo de Llano asking for instructions. The reply was 'Dale café, mucho café' – 'give him coffee' being slang for 'kill him'.[139] Federico García Lorca was shot at 4.45 a.m. on 18 August 1936 between Alfacar and Víznar to the north-east of Granada.[140]

Trescastro later boasted that he personally had killed the poet and others, including the humanist Amelia Agustina González Blanco. 'We were sick to the teeth of queers in Granada. We killed him for being a queer and her for being a whore.' On the day after the poet's death, Trescastro entered a bar and declared: 'We just killed Federico García Lorca. I put two bullets in his arse for being a queer.'[141] Murdered with Lorca were a disabled primary school teacher, Dióscoro Galindo, and two anarchists who had fought in the defence of the Albaicín.[142] The cowardly murder of a great poet was, however, like that of the loyal General Campins, merely a drop in an ocean of political slaughter.

A prominent figure in the right-wing support for the coup, the banker and lawyer José María Bérriz Madrigal, wrote to the head of his bank who had been on holiday in Portugal, on 18 August: 'The way forward is to win or die killing rogues. The army wants to destroy by the roots the noxious plant that was consuming Spain. And I think they're going to do it.' On 22 August, he wrote approvingly: 'Lots more shootings, union leaders, schoolteachers, small-town officials and doctors are going down by the dozen.'[143] The following day, the American poet and novelist Baroness de Zglinitzki, a firm rebel supporter, commented with less enthusiasm that the executions were 'increasing at a rate that alarmed and sickened all thinking people'.[144]

The victims referred to by Bérriz included the brilliant journalist and editor of the Republican daily *El Defensor*, Constantino Ruiz Carnero. In its pages, he had satirized Ruiz Alonso as the honorary worker who lived in considerable luxury and wore silk pyjamas. Ruiz Carnero had been Mayor for two weeks after the Popular Front election in February 1932.[145] Seven other men who had been Republican mayors, including the present incumbent, Lorca's brother-in-law Dr Manuel Fernández-Montesinos, were also shot. Ten professors of the University, five of whom had protested about Falangist disorders, were shot. Among them was the thirty-two-year-old rector of the University, the brilliant Arabist Salvador Vila Hernández, a close friend of the philosopher Miguel de Unamuno. Vila's arrest in Salamanca on 7 October was the last straw that led to Unamuno's famous 'you will win but you will not convince' ('venceréis pero no convenceréis') speech. Vila's German Jewish wife, Gerda Leimdörfer, was arrested with him and taken to Granada. He was shot on 22 October, but the intervention of the distinguished composer Manuel de Falla managed to save Gerda's life only after she had been forcibly baptized. Gerda Leimdörfer's parents, Jewish refugees, were deported to Nazi Germany. A friend of both Vila and Lorca, the architect Alfonso Rodríguez Orgaz, went into hiding and the Falange arrested his girlfriend, Gretel Adler, to use as bait to catch him. When this did not work, she was murdered. On 26 November, Unamuno wrote in his notebook: 'In Granada, poor Salvador Vila has been shot by the Falangists, degenerate Andalusians with the passions of syphilitic perverts and frustrated eunuchs.'[146]

The outrages in Granada were seen by the local bourgeoisie as acceptable because they were perceived as less appalling than the atrocities that they were told were being committed by the Republicans elsewhere. Their perception of events elsewhere was fed by Queipo de Llano's broadcasts. Thus they included the notion that people were flung from the cliff at Ronda, that men were impaled alive on stakes then forced to watch as their wives and daughters 'were first raped before their eyes, then drenched with petrol and burned alive', that nuns were exposed naked in the shop windows at Antequera, that priests had their stomachs cut open and filled with quicklime, that nuns were raped and priests tortured on the streets of Barcelona, that the sea around Málaga was full of the headless bodies of all those who were not anarchists, that in Madrid 'famous doctors, lawyers, men of science and letters, actors and artists' were being shot as fast as they could be caught. Baroness de Zglinitzki believed Queipo's broadcasts to the extent of writing that the Republican government, 'composed of anarchists, jailbirds and Russians, were determined to exterminate every man of brains and outstanding ability in Spain'.[147]

Republican Málaga was a rich source of Queipo's horror stories. After sustained bombing raids by Italian aircraft and bombardment by rebel warships, on Monday 8 February 1937 the city was occupied by columns of rebel and Italian troops.[148] For months, Queipo had been threatening in broadcasts and in leaflets dropped on the city to inflict bloody revenge for the repression during the seven months that Málaga had been in the hands of the CNT–FAI-dominated Public Safety Committee.[149] His threats merely confirmed the spine-chilling tales brought by thousands of refugees about the savagery unleashed by the Regulares and the Legion when they entered their *pueblos* in Cádiz, Seville, Córdoba and Granada. The collapse of Antequera on 12 August and of Ronda on 17 September had seen Málaga flooded by desperate and hungry women, children and old people. With food scarce, many suffering serious illness, they had to be accommodated in the Cathedral and other churches as part of a huge relief operation mounted by the parties of the left. This humanitarian effort was presented by the occupiers as vicious desecration and uncontrolled anti-clericalism.[150]

Despite the ease of the victory and the lack of resistance encountered, Queipo showed no mercy. Civilians were not allowed to enter the city for

a week while hundreds of Republicans were shot on the basis of denunciations. Many rightists emerged claiming that they had escaped death
at the hands of the 'reds' only because they had not had time to kill them.
One of Queipo de Llano's officials commented sarcastically: 'In seven
months, the Reds didn't have enough time. Seven days is more than
enough for us. They really are suckers.'[151]

Thousands of arrests were made. As the prisons overflowed, concentration camps had to be opened at Torremolinos and Alhaurín el Grande.
After the immediate slaughter, the repression was organized by the newly
appointed Civil Governor, Captain Francisco García Alted, a Civil Guard
and Falangist. It was implemented by Colonel Bohórquez, under the
overall jurisdiction of General Felipe Acedo Colunga, chief prosecutor
of the Army of Occupation, as the rebel forces now called themselves.
Trials were no longer justified by the application of the edict of martial
law but rather on the pseudo-legal basis of 'urgent summary courts
martial'. The scale of the repression carried out is revealed by a report by
Bohórquez in April 1937. In the seven weeks following the capture of
Málaga, 3,401 people had been tried of whom 1,574 had been executed.
In order to try so many people in such a short time, a large team of
prosecutors had been brought from Seville. The trials, often of several
people at once, provided no facilities for the accused's defence and rarely
lasted for more than a few minutes.[152]

Even before the occupiers began the executions, tens of thousands of
terrified refugees fled via the only possible escape route, the 109 miles
along the coast road to Almería. Their flight was spontaneous and they
had no military protection. They were shelled from the sea by the guns
of the warships *Cervera* and *Baleares*, bombed from the air and then
machine-gunned by the pursuing Italian units. The scale of the repression inside the fallen city explained why they were ready to run the
gauntlet. Along the roughly surfaced road, littered with corpses and the
wounded, terrified people trudged, without food or water. Dead mothers
were seen, their babies still suckling at their breasts. There were children
dead and others lost in the confusion as their many families frantically
tried to find them.[153]

The reports of numerous eyewitnesses, including Lawrence
Fernsworth, the correspondent of *The Times*, made it impossible for
rebel supporters to deny one of the most horrendous atrocities perpetrated against Republican civilians. It has been calculated that there were
more than 100,000 on the road, some with nothing, others carrying
kitchen utensils and bedding. It is impossible to know accurately but the

death toll seems to have been over three thousand. The Canadian doctor Norman Bethune, his assistant Hazen Size and his English driver, the future novelist T. C. Worsley, shuttled back and forth day and night for three days, carrying as many as they could. Bethune described old people giving up and lying down by the roadside to die and 'children without shoes, their feet swollen to twice their size crying helplessly from pain, hunger and fatigue'. Worsley wrote harrowingly of what he saw:

> The refugees still filled the road and the further we got the worse was their condition. A few of them were wearing rubber shoes, but most feet were bound round with rags, many were bare, nearly all were bleeding. There were seventy miles of people desperate with hunger and exhaustion and still the streams showed no signs of diminishing ... We decided to fill the lorry with kids. Instantly we were the centre of a mob of raving shouting people, entreating and begging, at this sudden miraculous apparition. The scene was fantastic, of the shouting faces of the women holding up naked babies above their heads, pleading, crying and sobbing with gratitude or disappointment.[154]

Their arrival brought horror and confusion to Almería. It was also greeted by a major bombing raid which deliberately targeted the centre of the town where the exhausted refugees thronged the streets. The bombing of the refugees on the road and in the streets of Almería was a symbol of what 'liberation' by the rebels really meant.

6

Mola's Terror: The Purging of Navarre, Galicia, Castile and León

In his proclamation of martial law in Pamplona on 19 July 1936, Mola declared: 'Re-establishing the principle of authority demands unavoidably that punishments be exemplary in terms of both their severity and the speed with which they will be carried out, without doubt or hesitation.'[1] Shortly afterwards, he called a meeting of the mayors of the province of Navarre and told them: 'It is necessary to spread terror. We have to create the impression of mastery, eliminating without scruples or hesitation all those who do not think as we do. There can be no cowardice. If we vacillate one moment and fail to proceed with the greatest determination, we will not win. Anyone who helps or hides a communist or a supporter of the Popular Front will be shot.'[2]

Such instructions imply a degree of insecurity on the part of the conspirators desperate to impose control as soon as possible before mass resistance to the coup developed. Thus over half of the executions carried out by the rebels between 18 July 1936 and 1945 took place in the first three months after their seizure of power in each area. Both the short- and long-term objectives of the terror would be more easily accomplished in conservative smallholding areas such as Galicia, Old Castile and Navarre. Terror was the chosen method for the annihilation of everything that the Republic signified, whether specific challenges to the privileges of landowners, industrialists, the clerics and soldiers or a general rejection of subservience by rural and urban workers and, most irksome for the right, women. This was what Sanjurjo, Franco, Gil Robles, Onésimo Redondo and others meant when they railed against the Jewish–Masonic–Bolshevik threat of 'Africanization'. The rhetoric of the need to eradicate such foreign poisons, which always had clerical advocates like Tusquets and Castro de Albarrán, would soon be taken up by the majority of the Church hierarchy. At the beginning of September, José Álvarez Miranda, the Bishop of León, called the Catholic faithful to join the war against 'Soviet Jewish–Masonic laicism'.[3]

On 31 July, after being told that the French press had suggested that Prieto had been appointed to negotiate with the rebels, Mola exploded: 'Negotiate? Never! This war can end only with the extermination of the enemies of Spain.' Again on 9 August, he boasted that his father, who was a crack shot with a rifle, used his wife for his frequent imitations of William Tell. The unfortunate woman was made to balance pieces of fruit on her head and hold others in her hand as targets for her husband to show off his skill. Mola told his secretary, José María Iribarren, that 'A war of this kind has to end with the domination of one side and the total extermination of the defeated. They've killed one of my brothers but they'll pay for it.'[4] This was a reference to his brother Ramón, who had committed suicide when the rising failed.

In the areas of Spain where the military coup met little or no resistance, the war aims of the rebels were starkly revealed. The execution of trade unionists, members of left-wing parties, elected municipal officials, Republican functionaries, schoolteachers and Freemasons, who had committed no crimes, have been called 'preventive assassinations'. Or, as the commander of the Civil Guard in Cáceres defined it: 'the sweeping purge of undesirables'.[5]

In Navarre, Álava, the eight provinces of Old Castile, the three of León, the four of Galicia, two-thirds of Zaragoza and virtually all of Cáceres, the coup was successful within hours or days. In these predominantly right-wing, Catholic areas, the excuses used for the slaughter in Andalusia and Badajoz – alleged left-wing atrocities or a threatened Communist take-over – were not plausible. Essentially, the 'crime' of those executed was to have voted for the Popular Front, or to have challenged their own subordination as workers or as women.[6]

The intention of the rebels was to uproot the entire progressive culture of the Republic. This was made clear in a series of draft decrees prepared by Mola for the Unión Militar Española. 'It is a conclusively demonstrated lesson of history that peoples fall into decadence, misery and ruin when their governments are infiltrated by parliamentary democratic systems, inspired by the erroneous doctrines of Jews, Freemasons, anarchists and Marxists ... All those who oppose the victory of the Movement to save Spain will be shot after summary judgement as miserable assassins of our sacred Fatherland.' The destruction of the Republic by armed violence was justified by the claim that it was illegitimate, based on electoral falsification, and that its political leaders were thieving parasites who had brought only anarchy and crime.[7]

The first step towards establishing a military dictatorship was the establishment of a National Defence Junta. A thin legal veneer was provided by its first decree, on 24 July 1936, which claimed 'full state powers', something repeated in subsequent decrees. Decree no. 37 of 14 August declared that the Republic was guilty of armed rebellion against the legitimate government of the Junta. On 28 July, an edict of martial law placed military law above civil law across the entire territory in the hands of the rebels. It thereby unified the various edicts issued in different places which had seen the military arbitrarily assume the right to punish opposition to its actions with summary execution. All those who supported the legitimate Republic either morally or by taking up arms were declared guilty of military rebellion, liable to court martial and subject to the death penalty or long jail terms. This was justified by the sophistry that the rebels' own military rebellion was carried out in the name of 'the highest moral and spiritual values of religion and the Fatherland, threatened by the perversity of the pseudo-politicians in the pay of the triple Judaeo-Masonic lie: Liberalism, Marxism and Separatism. That is why the term military rebellion can be applied only to the red camp. Regarding our side, we must speak of Holy Rebellion.'[8] Thus the rebels always referred to themselves as 'nacionales' (usually translated as 'Nationalists'), implying that the Republicans were somehow not Spanish and therefore had to be annihilated as foreign invaders.

In some cases, such as Segovia, the local military authorities went further, referring to 'the Madrid government, which since 19 July has been in armed rebellion against the Army, which found itself obliged to assume the responsibility of power to prevent chaos taking hold of the country'.[9] A decree of 31 August 1936 permitted any officer to be a judge, prosecutor or defender in a trial. Officers were thus obliged to fight the enemy on the battlefield and also in the courtroom, where the enemy had even less opportunity to fight back. So wide was the range of the offences deemed to be military rebellion that, in 1937, a handbook was issued to assist officers in the conduct of 'trials'. The author, a military lawyer, recognized that 'in view of the number of proceedings in progress, the consequence of the glorious deeds with which our army, valiantly supported by the true Spanish people, is astounding the world, those who have to act in such trials are facing many difficulties'.[10]

On 20 July, Mola was given the news that a lorry full of Republicans fleeing the Navarrese capital Pamplona had been captured on the road to Bilbao. Without hesitation, he barked into the telephone: 'Shoot them immediately by the roadside!' Aware of the deathly hush that this outburst had provoked, Mola had second thoughts and instructed his aide to rescind the order, saying to the rest of the room: 'Just so you can see that even in such serious times, I am not as bloodthirsty as the left thinks.' At that, one of the officers present said: 'General, let us not regret being too soft.' Three weeks later, on 14 August, Mola would be heard saying, 'A year ago, I would have trembled at having to authorize a firing squad. I wouldn't have been able to sleep for the sorrow of it. Now, I can sign three or four every day without batting an eyelid.'[11]

It was in Navarre that Mola had been able to feel totally confident of success. The wealthy landowners whose properties had been occupied in October 1933 by thousands of landless labourers were thirsting for revenge. Moreover, from the very first, the rebels enjoyed massive popular support from the deeply Catholic local population. According to two apologists of the Carlist militia, the Requeté, 'what was threatened was not just the peaceful digestion and the sleep of the powerful' but an entire value system.[12] Mola's instructions were transcribed and distributed by Luis Martínez Erro, the son of the manager of the Pamplona branch of the Banco de Bilbao who liaised between the conspirators and the local bourgeoisie. Luis Martínez Erro owned a shop in the city selling religious objects. There and in the clerical outfitters of Benito Santesteban, conspiratorial priests, hungry for news of the uprising, had lingered among the racks of cassocks and the shelves of chalices and statues of the Virgin. Among them was the Bishop of Zamora, Manuel Arce Ochotorena, who had been on holiday in Pamplona. On his last visit just before the rising, to order some cassocks, he said to Santesteban, 'if you send me rifles instead of cassocks that would be best of all!' The Navarrese clergy had close contact with military and Carlist conspirators. Except for the Basque clergy, most Spanish priests and religious sided with the rebels. They denounced the 'reds' from their pulpits and adopted the fascist salute. All over Spain, they blessed the flags of rebel regiments, and some – especially Navarrese priests – hastened to the front.[13]

Indeed, they urged their congregations to fight and some were among the first to join rebel columns. Cartridge belts slung over their cassocks, rifles in hand, they joyfully set off to kill reds. So many did so that the faithful were left without clergy to say Mass or hear confessions and the ecclesiastical authorities had to call some of them back.[14] Peter Kemp, a British volunteer with the Requeté, spoke admiringly of Father Vicente, the company chaplain. 'He was the most fearless and the most bloodthirsty man I ever met in Spain; he would, I think, have made a better soldier than priest. "Hola, Don Pedro!" he shouted to me. "So you've come to kill some Reds! Congratulations! Be sure you kill plenty!'" When not occupied with spiritual duties, he would be in the thick of the action. The role of minister of Christ caused him dreadful frustrations. He would point out targets to Kemp, urging him to shoot them. 'It seemed to me that he could barely restrain himself from snatching my rifle and loosing off ... Whenever some wretched militiaman bolted from cover to run madly for safety, I would hear the good Father's voice raised in a frenzy of excitement: "Don't let him get away – Ah! *Don't* let him get away! Shoot, man, shoot! A bit to the left! Ah! *that's* got him," as the miserable fellow fell and lay twitching.'[15]

Unlike those who went to the front, the tall, wild-eyed clerical outfitter Benito Santesteban stayed in Pamplona, like a rapacious carrion crow, devoting himself instead to purging the rearguard of leftists, liberals and Freemasons. He later boasted that he had killed 15,000 reds in Navarre, and more in San Sebastián, Bilbao and Santander. The province's left-wing minority faced immediate extermination at the hands of the fanatical enthusiasts of the rising. In the first months in Pamplona, early-morning executions attracted large crowds and with them stalls selling hot chocolate and *churros* (fried dough fingers). Many were taken as hostages and shot in reprisal when the death of a Carlist was reported.[16] Others were seized at night by the Falangist squad known as 'Black Eagle' and murdered on the outskirts of the city. Santesteban's boast was a wild exaggeration and he was also known to have saved individuals.[17] Nevertheless, many prisoners taken to the Requeté headquarters in the monastery of Los Escolapios were never seen again. In this ultra-conservative province, 2,822 men and thirty-five women were assassinated. A further 305 people died of mistreatment or malnutrition in prison. One of every ten who had voted for the Popular Front in Navarre was murdered.[18]

Whereas bombing raids or news of atrocities elsewhere often provoked mob violence in the Republican zone, the terror in the rebel zone was rarely 'uncontrolled'. An illustrative example took place in Pamplona on Sunday 23 August. The Bishop of Pamplona, Monsignor Marcelino Olaechea Loizaga, presided over a huge procession in honour of the Virgin of Santa María la Real. On the same day, the *Diario de Navarra* published his description of the rebel war effort as a crusade. While the ceremony was taking place, fifty-two detainees were taken from Pamplona prison by a group of Falangists and Requetés. At a large cattle farm on the outskirts of the village of Caparros, the majority of the prisoners, including the local Socialist leader Miguel Antonio Escobar Pérez, were shot. One escaped. Since Monsignor Olaechea sent six priests (including the future Bishop of Bilbao, Antonio Añoveros) to hear the condemned prisoners' confessions and give them spiritual consolation, there can be no doubt that he was aware of what was happening. When the priests took longer than expected, the impatient Falangists went ahead and shot those waiting in order to get back to Pamplona in time to take part in the last part of the religious ceremony.[19]

Another massacre took place on 21 October 1936 near Monreal, a small town south-east of Pamplona. Three days earlier, in the town of Tafalla, after the funeral of a Requeté lieutenant killed in battle, an enraged crowd went to the local prison to lynch the one hundred men and twelve women detained there. When the Civil Guard prevented bloodshed, a delegation secured written authorization from the military authorities. Three days later, at dawn, sixty-five of the prisoners were taken to Monreal and shot by Requetés. Those prisoners still alive were given the coup de grâce by Luis Fernández Magaña, the deputy parish priest of Murchante, a distant town far to the south of the province. He had left his congregation to go to war.[20]

The repression in Navarre was especially ferocious in the area known as the Ribera, along the River Ebro. The Socialist landworkers' union, the FNTT, had been strong there before the war and this was reflected in the scale of the killing. In the small town of Sartaguda, for example, with 1,242 inhabitants, there were eighty-four extra-judicial executions – 6.8 per cent of the population. In Peralta, eighty-nine of the 3,830 inhabitants (2.3 per cent of the population) were killed. Sartaguda was widely known in northern Spain as 'the town of widows'. When the very young, the very old and almost all women are excluded, the scale of the terror can be imagined. The figures suggest that around 10 per cent of the male working class were murdered. Republican women were, of course, molested and humiliated in various ways. Family networks in the area were close, so these killings reverberated throughout the province and beyond.[21]

Father Eladio Celaya, the seventy-two-year-old parish priest of the village of Cáseda, was notable for his benevolent concern for his parishioners whose campaign for the return of common lands he had supported. On 8 August, he went to Pamplona to protest at the diocesan offices about the killings. He was told to go home because nothing could be done. Because of his efforts to prevent the violence, he was murdered on 14 August 1936 and his head cut off. Father Celaya was not the only Catholic priest murdered by the ultra-religious Navarrese. Father Santiago Lucus Aramendia was a captain in the military chaplaincy corps and a lawyer. He was known to be a Republican, to sympathize with the Socialists and to have advocated land redistribution. He had taken refuge in the Convento del Carmen de Vitoria but was seized by Carlists and taken to Pamplona. On 3 September 1936, Carlists from his home town of Pitillas murdered him in nearby Undiano. He was given the last rites by a priest who accompanied the assassins, the same Luis Fernández Magaña from Murchante who was involved in the massacre at Monreal.[22]

Eventually, even Monsignor Olaechea was sufficiently shocked by the slaughter to speak out in a sermon delivered on 15 November. He appealed for 'No more blood! No more blood other than that which God wants to be shed on his behalf on the battlefields to save our Fatherland. No more blood other than that decreed by the courts of justice, serenely considered and scrupulously debated.' This homily, despite justifying the judicial executions, found no echo elsewhere in the Church. In the prevailing atmosphere, it represented considerable courage on the Bishop's part.[23]

It would be from Pamplona that Cardinal Isidro Gomá, Archbishop of Toledo and Primate of All Spain, would broadcast on Radio Navarra on 28 September 1936 to celebrate the 'liberation' of Toledo, 'the city of the most Christian Spanish empire'. He proclaimed the rebel capture of Toledo to be the high point of the 'clash of civilization with barbarism, of the inferno against Christ'. He thundered against 'the bastard soul of the sons of Moscow' and 'Jews and the Freemasons who poisoned the nation's soul with absurd doctrines, Tartar and Mongol tales dressed up as a political and social system in the dark societies controlled by the Semite International'.[24]

The neighbouring province to the south, Logroño, suffered a similar level of repression. Like Navarre, it was largely conservative, albeit with a considerable degree of underlying social tension. As in Navarre, there were rural tensions and a number of strikes by rural labourers, but the easy domination of the right was symbolized by what had happened at Arnedo in January 1932. The position of the province's landowners was not seriously challenged by the anarchist insurrections of January and December 1933 in the wine-producing towns of the Rioja Alta. The weakness of the left ensured that, in 1934, both the harvest strike of June and the revolutionary movement of October had a limited impact in Logroño.[25]

Nevertheless, the subsequent repression left a legacy of bitterness which found expression both in the campaign for the elections of February 1936 and in the celebration of the Popular Front victory. On 14 March that year, in complicated circumstances, Assault Guards intervened in a clash between Falangists and workers. Three workers were killed and another six wounded. In reprisal, several religious schools, the premises of the local right-wing newspaper and the headquarters of the Falange, the Carlists and the CEDA were attacked. A few days later, in country districts, there were land invasions by unemployed labourers attempting to speed up agrarian reform. Throughout May, there was a construction strike in Logroño. In other clashes set off by agents provocateurs, a Carlist died in Haro on 16 April and two Falangists died in Nájera on 14 June.[26]

On 19 July, the coup triumphed in Logroño when the Civil Governor refused to distribute arms to the left. A general strike collapsed when a column of 1,800 men under Colonel Francisco García Escámez travelled through the night in trucks, buses and cars from Pamplona. As they crossed the two bridges over the Ebro, a military band greeted their entry into Logroño. The Mayor, Dr Basilio Gurrea Cárdenas, a dental surgeon, was immediately arrested. He was a moderate Republican and a friend of Mola, who had been his patient during the many years he had spent in Logroño. Mola refused to intervene in Gurrea's case and he was executed in Logroño on 7 August.[27] García Escámez quickly crushed the feeble resistance of unarmed leftists in towns such as Calahorra and Alfaro. Thereafter, the repression throughout the province was undertaken by columns of Civil Guards and a heterogeneous mixture of civilians. A remarkably high number of the Falangists and Requetés who took part in the killing had, prior to the war, been members of the CNT or UGT, or of Republican parties. Several had taken part in the anarchist insurrection of December 1933. It is impossible to say who among them had been agents provocateurs or were simply trying to hide a left-wing past. Some of their victims were shot; others were flung from high bridges into rivers.[28] There were also cases of Republicans thrown from bridges across the Ebro in Burgos and the Tagus as it passed through Cáceres. The corpses caused public health problems.[29]

Logroño was a small, tranquil city at the centre of the Rioja wine trade. As Civil Governor, Mola appointed an artilleryman, Captain Emilio Bellod Gómez, telling him, 'be harsh, very harsh', to which he replied: 'Don't worry, General, that is exactly what I will do.' The bulk of the executions, mostly extra-judicial, took place from 19 July until Bellod's replacement six months later. More formal military trials began only after his departure. Beatings and torture, imprisonment and death were the fate of leftists. There were women murdered and the wives of executed leftists had their heads shaved, were forced to drink castor oil and were frequently subjected to other forms of sexual humiliation. In the capital, Logroño, the provincial prison was soon full to bursting and a jai-alai (pelota) court and a commercial training school were converted into prison annexes. The municipal cemetery was soon equally full and, similarly, the corpses of those executed had to be accommodated outside the town of Lardero, to the south of Logroño. By the end of December, there had been nearly two thousand executions in the province, including more than forty women. In the course of the war, 1 per cent of the total population was executed. As in Navarre, the worst-hit places were the towns along the banks of the River Ebro where the Popular Front had gained most votes, such as Logroño with 595, Calahorra with 504, Haro with 309, Alfaro with 253 and Arnedo with 190.[30] A notable feature of the repression was the scale of support it enjoyed in the small towns and villages from Catholic smallholding farmers infuriated by the wage demands of the FNTT.[31]

The experience of Republican prisoners in Logroño is known in large part thanks to the survival of one of them, Patricio Escobal, the municipal engineer in Logroño and a member of Azaña's Izquierda Republicana party. Although most of his fellow party members were murdered, Escobal survived prison, despite appalling mistreatment, because he had been a famous footballer, a distinguished captain of Real Madrid and a member of Spain's Olympic silver-medal team of 1920. The potential scandal if he was murdered restrained his persecutors. Thus he lived to write his memoirs.[32]

In La Rioja there were cases of the clergy trying to restrain the perpetrators. There were eighty-three villages where, in part as a result of their priests' action and, crucially, because of a pre-existing level of tolerance between right and left, there were no deaths. Unfortunately, there were another ninety-nine towns and villages where extra-judicial killings did take place. To intervene against the killing required great bravery. Father Antonio Bombín Hortelano, a Franciscan monk from Anguciana just outside Haro, was murdered by Falangists because, in his sermons, he had criticized the rich and spoken out about social injustice. Other priests who went to see the Civil Governor, Emilio Bellod, to plead for mercy on behalf of parishioners were thrown out of his office. Sadly, there is no evidence to sustain recent claims that the Bishop of Calahorra protested to Bellod about the arbitrary executions.[33]

One of Mola's closest and most reliable collaborators was the bluff, luxuriantly moustachioed Major General Andrés Saliquet Zumeta. Without a posting during the Republic, Saliquet lived in Madrid but cultivated close connections with the ultra right in the dour Castilian city of Valladolid. Saliquet was the key liaison between the military conspirators and Onésimo Redondo's followers.[34] Falangists were involved daily in violent clashes with the left in the provincial capital and in other small towns. A cycle of provocation and reprisal created a climate of terror. A local journalist, Francisco de Cossío, wrote of the Falange: 'on a daily basis, we witnessed heroic retaliations based on the law of an eye for an eye'. In mid-June, Falangists armed with machine-pistols assaulted several taverns where left-wingers were known to congregate. Bombs were placed at the homes of prominent leftists and in various workers' clubs (Casas del Pueblo). Leftist reprisals were swift: Falangists were attacked and the Carlist Traditionalist Centre sacked.[35]

By the eve of the military uprising, Valladolid was a city seething with hatred. The Republican Civil Governor, Luis Lavín Gautier, faced enormous difficulty in containing street clashes between right and left since the local forces of order sympathized with Onésimo Redondo. Even before General Saliquet arrived to co-ordinate the rising, the unity of the Falange, the local police, Assault Guards, Civil Guard and army units ensured its early success. Lavín's orders that the workers be armed were disobeyed and guns were distributed to the Falange instead. The general strike declared by the left-wing unions was quickly and brutally smashed. A delighted Cossío reported seeing a leading Socialist 'run like a hare down a city centre street looking for somewhere to hide'. Hundreds of Socialists took refuge with their families in the cellars of their headquarters in the Casa del Pueblo. After the building had been briefly shelled with artillery, they surrendered.[36] Most of the women and all of the children were allowed to go free, but 448 men were arrested. According to official figures, nearly one thousand Republicans, Socialists and anarcho-syndicalists were arrested in the city, of whom a relatively small number had taken part in armed resistance. The Civil Governor Lavín, the city's Socialist Mayor, Antonio García Quintana, and the province's only Socialist deputy, Federico Landrove López, were all arrested and shot.

Subsequently, as the first city in the mainland where the coup was successful, Valladolid came to be known as 'the capital of the uprising'.[37]

On Sunday 19 July, within twenty-four hours of the coup, Onésimo Redondo, who had been imprisoned after a bomb attack on the main police station on 19 March, was freed from jail in Ávila. He returned to Valladolid and quickly made contact with General Saliquet. Having secured the General's permission to deploy the Falangist militias, Redondo set up headquarters in the Cavalry Academy, sending squads of armed Falangists all over the province to crush left-wing resistance. He was tireless in implementing his commitment to the extermination of Marxism. His first radio broadcast, on 19 July, was typically intransigent: 'There will be no peace until our victory is total. We can have no qualms and nothing must stand in our way. We have no relatives, no children, no wives, no parents; only the Fatherland.' Declaring that the economic life of the city should go on as normal, he threatened that 'the lives of workers and shop-assistants will depend on their conduct. And hidden subversives, if there are any left, will be hunted down by the vigilant eyes of our Falangists.'[38]

Elsewhere, the rebels did not have it as easy as in Valladolid. Franco and the African Army were blockaded in Morocco by the Republican fleet. Anarchist forces from Barcelona were moving virtually unopposed towards Zaragoza. The overall leader of the coup, General Sanjurjo, had been killed when his plane crashed on take-off for Spain and command was assumed by Mola when he reached the neighbouring Castilian city of Burgos on 20 July. The hope of rebel forces that they would capture Madrid had come to nothing. Faced with an acute shortage of ammunition, they had been held at the sierras to the north of the capital. Mola himself was plunged into a depression by this accumulation of reverses. His spirits were somewhat revived by a visit to Zaragoza on 21 July to consult with General Miguel Cabanellas. At Cabanellas's suggestion, they decided to create a provisional rebel government, the Junta de Defensa Nacional. Its formation was announced by Mola in Burgos on 23 July.[39]

This lay behind the stark reality of the repression in Valladolid. Despite the rapid success of the coup, the city witnessed a pitiless assault on the local left. The slaughter was accelerated as a result of the death of Onésimo Redondo in a clash with Republican forces at Labajos, in the province of Segovia on 24 July. When other Falangists reached Labajos, unable to find those who had killed their leader they shot a local worker and took a further five back to Valladolid where they would be executed in September.[40] A requiem Mass for Onésimo at Valladolid Cathedral on 25 July was celebrated with the pomp normally reserved for national heroes. All shops in the city were closed. Redondo's coffin, covered by a monarchist flag, was carried on a carriage pulled by six white horses. The procession was led by Falangist squads and followed by a military band and girls carrying huge wreaths of flowers. The atmosphere was heavy with a thirst for rapid revenge. After the ceremony, an emotional crowd 'elected' by acclamation Onésimo's brother, Andrés, to be the Falangist Territorial Chief of León and Old Castile. Fully prepared to maintain the same violent policies as his brother, later that night of 25 July Andrés Redondo declared on local radio that 'all Falangists have sworn to avenge his death'.[41]

Years later, Onésimo Redondo's widow, Mercedes Sanz Bachiller, spoke of her conviction that her husband's death had intensified the subsequent repression. In fact, the process of revenge against the left in Valladolid was already well under way and would gather momentum over the next few months. Large numbers of Socialist workers from the railway engineering works were herded into the tram company garages. Those who, having obeyed the union order to strike on Saturday 18 July, had not returned to work by Tuesday 21 July were shot, accused of 'abetting rebellion'. Throughout the late summer and autumn, anyone who had held a position in a left-wing party, municipality or trade union was subject to arrest and the likelihood of being *paseado* – that is to say, seized by Falangists, taken out and shot – or subjected to summary court martial. For many, their crime was simply to carry a membership card of a trade union or left or liberal organization. General Saliquet's edict of martial law, published at dawn on 19 July, effectively passed a death sentence on all those who had not actively supported the uprising. 'Crimes' subject to summary trial and immediate execution included 'rebellion' (either action in defence of the Republic or failure to support the rebels) and extended to disobedience, disrespect, insult or calumny towards both the military and those who had been militarized (thus including Falangists). Men were arrested on suspicion of having their radio dials set to stations broadcasting from Madrid. Court martials were set up and firing squads began to function. In addition to the 448 men arrested on 18 July, one thousand more would be detained in August and September.[42]

While awaiting trial, the prisoners in Valladolid, as in most other places, were kept in appalling conditions. Because the local prison had neither the space nor the resources to look after so many inmates, two repair sheds at the tram depot were used to house prisoners. The acute overcrowding, malnutrition and the lack of basic hygiene facilities led to many deaths from sickness. In the prison, more than six prisoners were squeezed into individual cells. They were forced into icy showers and then, while still wet and shivering, made to run a gauntlet of guards who beat them with truncheons or rifle butts. Responsibility for food, clothing and laundry fell upon their families, an acute hardship given that, by dint of the arrest and imprisonment, the families had already been deprived of their principal breadwinner.[43]

Estimates of the scale of the repression in the province of Valladolid have varied wildly, as high as 15,000 but none lower than 1,303. Exact figures are impossible since many deaths were not recorded. The most recent local study places the figure at over three thousand.[44] There were 1,300 men and women tried between July and December 1936, often in large groups. Such 'trials' consisted of little more than the reading of the names of the accused and the charges against them, followed by the passing of sentence. Although most of those accused of military rebellion were likely to face the death penalty or prison sentences of thirty years, they were given no chance to defend themselves and were not even permitted to speak. On most weekdays, several courts martial were held, rarely lasting more than one hour. All 448 men detained after the surrender of the Casa del Pueblo were tried together accused of the crime of military rebellion. Forty were sentenced to death, 362 to thirty years' imprisonment, twenty-six to twenty years' imprisonment, and nineteen were found not guilty. The selection of the forty to be executed was made on the basis of their having held some position of responsibility in the local Socialist organizations. The one woman condemned to death had her sentence commuted to thirty years' imprisonment, although at least sixteen other women were executed in Valladolid. There were other cases in which fifty-three, seventy-seven and eighty-seven accused were 'tried' at once. In some cases, the 'crime' was simply to be a Socialist member of parliament, as was the case with Federico Landrove and also with José Maesto San José (deputy for Ciudad Real) and Juan Lozano Ruiz (Jaén) who were captured on the outskirts of Valladolid.[45]

Prisoners condemned by court martial were taken out in the early hours of the morning and driven in trucks to the Campo de San Isidro on the outskirts of the city. This became such a regular occurrence that coffee and *churro* stalls were set up for the spectators. Each evening in the Casino, members of distinguished local families, educated middle-class Catholics, would remind each other not to miss the following day's show. Guards had to be assigned to hold back the crowds that thronged to watch and shout insults at the condemned. So shocking did this seem that the newly appointed Civil Governor of the province issued a communiqué reprimanding those who had turned the shootings into an entertainment. Declaring bizarrely that the repression should reflect 'noble feelings and generosity towards the defeated', he deplored the presence of small children, young girls and married women at the executions. The terror had become 'normal' and no one dared condemn it for fear of being denounced as a red.[46] Similarly, in Segovia, middle-class ladies attended military trials, laughing and cheering when death sentences were passed. Executions in the provincial capital were praised as 'a good bullfight'. In the tiny village of Matabuena, to the north-east of Segovia, the inhabitants were forced to watch executions.[47]

At least, the 616 executions carried out in Valladolid as a result of summary wartime courts martial were registered.[48] In contrast, the unofficial murders carried out by the so-called Falangist 'dawn patrols' are impossible to quantify. These killings were significantly more widespread if rather less public. Executions were often extremely inefficient. Having augmented their courage with brandy, the squads often wounded rather than killed prisoners, who were then left to a slow death agony. Corpses were sometimes just dumped by the roadside, at other times buried in shallow common graves. On occasion, wounded prisoners were buried alive. The murders of prisoners were often carried out quite arbitrarily by Falangists who would arrive at the tram sheds or the bullring just before dawn. Macabre humour might see a victim selected simply because it was his saint's day. On the basis of data from those towns and villages in the province for which it is possible to reconstruct what happened, it has been calculated that at least 928 people were murdered by the patrols. The total number is likely to be significantly higher. The random killings caused public health scares for fear that rotting corpses might be affecting the water supply.[49] Certainly, by any standards, the scale of the repression was totally disproportionate to the fighting in the city on 18 and 19 July. At the end of the war, there were still three thousand detainees in the provincial prison, of whom 107 died as a result of the appalling conditions.[50]

The influence of Onésimo Redondo was felt far beyond Valladolid. On 23 July, a group of his most hot-headed followers carried his message to Salamanca. Initially, when news of the rising had reached Salamanca, the Civil Governor, Antonio Cepas López, the Mayor, Casto Prieto Carrasco (both of Izquierda Republicana), and the Socialist deputy, José Andrés y Manso, had been assured by the military commander, General Manuel García Álvarez, that the forces stationed in the province were loyal to the Republic. Accordingly, they refrained from calling a general strike. In fact, when García Álvarez learned during the night that Valladolid had risen, he ordered local garrisons to support the military coup. Before dawn on 19 July, machine-guns were set up in the principal squares of Salamanca. At about 11.00 a.m., a company of mounted soldiers entered the Plaza Mayor and their Captain read out the 'edict' declaring martial law that had been drawn up by General Saliquet. The square was crowded, mainly with people who had just come out of Mass in the Church of San Martín. The edict's last words, a hypocritical cry of '¡Viva la República!', were echoed by the majority of the crowd. However, someone shouted '¡Viva la revolución social!' and fired a shot, wounding a corporal. The military unit opened fire on the crowd and four men and a young girl were killed. The terror had begun.[51]

The town hall, the Civil Governor's offices, the post office, the telephone exchange and the railway station were occupied by troops. Imprisoned Falangists were released. Prieto Carrasco and Andrés y Manso tried vainly to organize resistance. However, since there were few available weapons and local left-wingers had no experience in their use, their efforts were in vain. They, along with the town's relatively few left-wingers, liberals and those who went on strike, were arrested. A similar fate was met by the resistance in other towns in the province like Ciudad Rodrigo, Ledesma and Béjar. In Béjar, the only industrial town in the province, the local Civil Guard did not dare declare for the rebellion. Nonetheless, the town fell on 21 July with the arrival of a column of Falangists and regular troops. Four hundred people were arrested and a dozen women had their heads shaved and were paraded through the streets. In Salamanca itself, General García Álvarez named two of his officers as Mayor and Civil Governor. Apart from the rector of the University, Miguel de Unamuno, the bulk of the members of the new town council were nominees of local landowners or of the rebel military. Unamuno believed naively that his presence would be a guarantee of civility on the part of the new rulers. In fact, the town council was merely a cover of 'legality'. The new Mayor simply exercised his authority as he would a military command.

In keeping with Mola's instructions about the need for rapid, exemplary terror, the left was quickly crushed with notable brutality. The new Civil Governor ordered the removal of all Socialist town councils in the province and their replacement by 'patriotic elements'. Since there had been virtually no violence in Salamanca in the months preceding the military coup, most liberals and leftists made no attempt to flee.

Nevertheless, there was a witch-hunt of liberals, leftists and trade unionists.

Falangists, Carlists and members of the CEDA created a Guardia Cívica, paramilitary units which carried out a virtually uncontrolled repression that opened the way to personal vendettas and naked criminality. Cattle-breeders formed a mounted column known as the 'hunters' battalion'. Armed Falangist columns swooped on villages and took away those denounced as leftists. They also patrolled the border with Portugal to prevent the flight of their prey. Little by little, in towns across the province strikers were arrested and either shot or imprisoned. After interrogation and torture, some just 'disappeared', while others were transferred to the provincial prison. Many of those imprisoned would die of illnesses contracted in the unhygienic conditions of a building designed for one hundred prisoners but housing over two thousand during the war, twelve or more to cells intended for one or two men. The indiscriminate repression led to the collapse of public services and left local schools without teachers. All over the province, the Civil Guard hunted down the mayors who had refused to apply the edict of martial law or had declared a general strike against the coup. In villages where there was no Civil Guard post, General García Álvarez ordered local rightists to take over the town council.[52]

Things worsened dramatically after the arrival of Onésimo Redondo's followers together with a unit of troops led by Franco's friend, the notorious Civil Guard Comandante Lisardo Doval. On 23 July, the Falangists reached Salamanca in a state of heightened passion after being harangued by Onésimo at the battle front. The Falangist flag was raised over the town hall and they demanded the names of all leftists who had been imprisoned; shortly afterwards the so-called *sacas* began, whereby men were dragged from the prison and shot in the nearby countryside. In fact, during the spring of 1936, the local right had already prepared blacklists of leftists and liberals who were to be eliminated when the time came. Both the Mayor, Dr Casto Prieto Carrasco, and Andrés y Manso, were moderates. A professor of radiology in the Faculty of Medicine, Prieto Carrasco was a kindly and unworldly man, who preferred moral rearmament to armed struggle. He had reacted to being appointed interim Civil Governor in 1931 by inviting his monarchist predecessor to dinner. Nevertheless, he was loathed by the Catholic right in Salamanca. As Mayor in 1933, he served an expropriation order on the Catholic Hospital of the Holy Trinity on the grounds that it provided inadequate medical care for its patients. Prieto Carrasco had acted throughout in an even-handed manner.[53] Andrés y Manso, a schools inspector and professor in the teachers' training college, who also had a law degree, was a man renowned for his honesty and rectitude. That counted for nothing. He had edited *Tierra y Trabajo*, the newspaper of the FNTT in Salamanca. In the eyes of the rebels, he, like the Mayor, was a subversive and he too had to be killed.[54]

Both men had stayed in Salamanca believing that, since they had committed no crimes, they had nothing to fear. In fact, they were both arrested on 19 July 1936 and confined in the provincial prison. There were sixty-five inmates when they arrived and more than four hundred a week later.[55] On 29 July, Carrasco Prieto and Andrés y Manso were pulled from prison by the local chief of the Falange, Francisco Bravo, accompanied by those who had come from Valladolid seeking revenge for the death of Onésimo Redondo. The bodies of the two men were found in a ditch twenty-three miles from Salamanca, at La Orbada on the road to Valladolid. It has frequently been alleged that they had been killed in the ritualized spectacle of a mock bullfight.[56] The Protestant pastor, Atilano Coco, was shot on 9 December because, as with other pastors who were detained, tortured and shot, it was assumed that to be a Protestant was to support the Popular Front. On 10 September in San Fernando in Cádiz, another Protestant pastor, Miguel Blanco Ferrer, was shot for refusing Catholic baptism.[57]

The philosopher Miguel de Unamuno was furious with himself for having initially supported the military uprising. On 1 December 1936, he wrote to his friend Quintín de Torre about life in Salamanca: 'It is a stupid regime of terror. Here people are shot without trial and without any justification whatsoever. Some because it is said that they are Freemasons, and I have no idea what that means any more than do the animals who cite it as a reason to kill. There is nothing worse than the marriage of the dementality [*sic*] of the barracks with that of the sacristy. To which is added the spiritual leprosy of Spain, the resentment, the envy, the hatred of intelligence.'[58]

Two weeks later, he wrote to him again: 'How naive and irresponsible I was ... You say that Salamanca is more tranquil because the Caudillo is here. Tranquil? No way. Here there is no battlefield shooting or taking of prisoners, but instead the most bestial persecution and unjustified murders. Regarding the Caudillo – I suppose you mean poor General Franco – he controls none of this repression, this savage rearguard terror. He just lets it happen. The rearguard repression is in the hands of that monster of perversion, poisonous and rancorous, General Mola.' He went on with disgust: 'Obviously, the dogs, and among them some hyenas, of this rabble, have no idea what Freemasonry nor anything else is. They imprison and they impose fines, which is just another name for theft, and even confiscate property and say they judge then execute. They also shoot without any trial.'[59] He singled out Father Tusquets as one of those who had done most to justify the violence.[60]

Throughout the province, leftists were denounced by their neighbours and hunted down by Falangists. One of the most notorious groups was led by the belligerent landowner and retired army officer Diego Martín Veloz, who had a substantial arsenal in his house.[61] Martín Veloz threw himself tirelessly into the uprising. He was one of the civilians most trusted by the military. Indeed, when he walked the streets or appeared in the Gran Hotel, he was saluted by officers. In the first days of the war, it appears that he briefly joined the column of troops which advanced into Ávila under the leadership of Major Lisardo Doval.[62]

Martín Veloz's activities in Ávila were short lived and he was soon to be found back in Salamanca. He had been named President of the Provincial Assembly of Salamanca by his friend General Miguel Cabanellas, on 28 July 1936. Declaring that 'he was not prepared to stay in the post because he had military duties to fulfil', he resigned four days later to devote himself to leading a column of local members of the landowners' party, the Bloque Agrario, of Acción Popular and of the Falange. They rampaged throughout the area east of Salamanca known as La Armuña, organizing recruits for the rebel forces and purging Republicans. Martín Veloz's success in the former enterprise was no doubt linked to his ruthlessness in the latter. In an echo of what was happening in the *latifundio* areas of Andalusia and Extremadura, he led groups of Falangists, some of them very recent converts, in a vicious campaign of repression in La Armuña. In villages like El Pedroso, La Orbada, Cantalpino and Villoria, where there had been no notable incidents of violence before the military coup, men were shot and women raped. After having their heads shaved, the widows and sisters of those shot were made to parade through the streets of their villages.[63]

It was typical of Martín Veloz's volatile personality that he found no difficulty in combining acts of cruelty against the many with benevolent acts of clemency for friends. One example was that of José Delgado Romero, a Republican and the village doctor of El Pedroso, whom he saved from execution by Falangists. Others were the distinguished liberal politician Filiberto Villalobos and the Socialist Manuel Frutos.[64] He helped some acquaintances to reach the Portuguese frontier or the

Republican lines, allegedly by dressing them as women. Others he hid on his estate. He was even reconciled to his lifelong enemy Miguel de Unamuno, allegedly paying him three visits during which he agreed with the philosopher's denunciations of the atrocities being perpetrated in the province. It was also claimed that he prevented a scheme by local Falangists to bury the remains of José Andrés y Manso under the entrance to Salamanca cemetery so that all who entered would walk on his grave.[65] Nevertheless, the widow of Andrés y Manso made reference to Veloz 'with his Falangist hordes, razing to the ground the humble homes of the Salamanca countryside'. His column was involved in the ferocious repression in Cantalpino and El Pedroso. On 24 August, twenty-two men and one woman were murdered in Cantalpino, numerous women were raped and nearly one hundred women forced to parade through the village with their heads shaved.[66] Martín Veloz died of illness in Salamanca on 12 March 1938.[67]

The Falangist Ángel Alcázar de Velasco was struck by the dreadful silence of the peasants who brought their produce to market in Salamanca. 'You could see that they had neither bread nor justice. Almost all those villagers in their flat berets were in mourning and yet the black they wore was not for anyone killed at the front.' They brought their products either on donkeys or on their own backs to a sordid back-street market far from the gloating glances of the landowners sitting with army officers at the terraces of the cafés in the squares: 'Placing their wares on the floor of a little market-place that was like a medieval souk, they worked in silence, in the silence of terror. They worked with that fear which inundates the very soul, terrified that to annoy the boastful victors in the slightest would mean being accused of opposing the regime (and everybody knew that any accusation meant inevitable captivity, and sometimes mysteriously prolonged captivity).'[68]

Any guilt that might have been felt by the killers anywhere in rebel Spain was assuaged by the justifications provided by the senior clergy. In mid-August, Aniceto de Castro Albarrán, the senior canon of Salamanca Cathedral, declared on Radio Nacional:

Ah! When one knows for certain that to kill and to die is to do what God wishes, the hand does not waver when firing a rifle or pistol, nor does the heart tremble when facing death. Is it God's will? Is it God's will that, if necessary, I should die and, if necessary, that I should kill? Is this a holy war or a miserable military coup? The brave men who today are rebels are the men of the deepest religious spirit, the soldiers who

believe in God and in the Fatherland, young men who take communion
daily. Our battle cry will be that of the crusaders: It is God's will. Long
live Catholic Spain! Up with the Spain of Isabel la Católica![69]

The Bishop of Ávila issued instructions to his diocesan priests which
suggest complicity in the execution of prisoners without trial: 'When
dealing with one of the frequent and deplorable cases of the unexpected
discovery in the countryside of the corpse of a person apparently of
revolutionary sympathies, but without official confirmation of them
having been condemned to death by the legitimate authorities, then
simply record that "the corpse appeared in the countryside ... and was
given ecclesiastical burial". However, parish priests must make sure to
avoid any suggestion that could reveal the author or the cause of this
tragic death.'[70] Certificates of good conduct issued by priests could save
a life. The refusal by a priest to certify that someone was a practising
Catholic was the equivalent of a denunciation. Those priests who did
sign certificates to save a parishioner from death or imprisonment were
chastised by their superiors. The Archbishop of Santiago de Compostela
noted that scandal was provoked by such acts of Christian charity. He
ordered the priests of his diocese not to sign certificates for anyone who
belonged to 'anti-Christian Marxist societies'. All others should be
considered 'without timidity or hesitations born of humane
considerations'.[71]

The Bishop of Salamanca, Monsignor Enrique Plá y Deniel, in a celebrated pastoral letter, declared the military rebellion to be a religious
crusade. Issued on 28 September, his text, 'The Two Cities', based on St
Augustine's notion of the cities of God and of the Devil, thundered that
'Communists and Anarchists are sons of Cain, fratricides, assassins of
those whom they envy and martyr merely for cultivating virtue.' In early
1942, Enrique Plá y Deniel became Archbishop of Toledo. In his farewell
sermon in Salamanca Cathedral, he gave thanks that the city he was
leaving had never suffered any violence at the hands of the 'reds'.
Accordingly, as Indalecio Prieto noted, the victims lost their lives simply
for being Republicans or Socialists. José Sánchez Gómez, the popular
bullfight critic of the local newspaper *El Adelanto*, was executed for the
crime of being a friend of Indalecio Prieto.[72]

The first victims in Salamanca, as elsewhere, were those who opposed
the military coup and prominent local left-wing politicians or union
leaders. Schoolteachers and university lecturers were favoured targets.
The repression soon embraced those who had helped the Popular Front,

by distributing leaflets or by acting as stewards in meetings. In some cases, those who had supported centrist groups were put on trial, accused of taking votes away from the right. The victims, as in so many places, had been denounced by those who coveted their property or their womenfolk. This was especially the case with those who owned businesses. When trials became the norm, the victims who had money were frequently blackmailed by those named as their defenders. In fact, the 'defenders' rarely did more than act as court reporters. Nevertheless, there was a racket run by Lieutenant Marciano Díez Solís. The accused was told that a punitive sentence awaited him but that Díez Solís could get it reduced for a price. Díez Solís was finally stopped, not for extorting money, but because it was discovered that he was homosexual and had tried to blackmail some of his victims into having sex with him.[73]

The prevailing mentality among the rebel military authorities was revealed during an exchange in General Mola's headquarters in Burgos on 7 August 1936 between the recently appointed Provincial Governor, Lieutenant Colonel Marcelino Gavilán Almuzara, and the renegade Republican lawyer Joaquín del Moral. Del Moral asserted that 'Spain is the country where cowardice wears the nicest clothes. Fear in Spain is dressed up as resolving conflict, tolerance of the differences between people, coexistence and formulas. No one dared face up to the fundamental problems of the Fatherland.' Gavilán agreed, saying: 'we must get rid of all that drivel about the Rights of Man, humanitarianism, philanthropy and other Masonic clichés'. A lively conversation followed on the need to exterminate in Madrid 'tram workers, policemen, telegraph-operators and concierges'. One of those present suggested that the notice in apartment buildings that read 'Speak to the concierge before entering' should be changed to 'Kill the concierge before entering'.[74]

Joaquín del Moral was perhaps typical of those who manifested an extreme hatred of the left in order to cover up their own short-lived Republican past. A lawyer, he had been a Freemason and, after the fall of the Primo de Rivera dictatorship, had joined a Republican party. He wrote virulent articles against the monarchy, but never achieved political office. In consequence, deeply embittered and blaming his failure on what he assumed to be electoral fraud, he turned against the Republic and wrote poisonous diatribes against those more successful than himself. Prieto was 'the plutocrat', Azaña 'the cave-dweller' and Francesc Macià 'the paranoid old grandfather'. Those who held more than one paid position in the government were 'illiterate parasites'. Suspected of complicity in the preparation of the Sanjurjada in 1932, Del Moral had been arrested in Bilbao. He was retained as defence lawyer by four of the military conspirators. He then wrote a book applauding the Sanjurjo coup, denouncing the trial and imprisonment of the ringleaders as sadistic persecution and describing Azaña as an ignorant coward for his efforts to reform the army. Del Moral thereby clinched a relationship with the plotters of 1936. Documentary proof of this was found when his apartment in Madrid was searched in August that year by the militia group known as 'Los Linces de la República' (the lynxes of the Republic).[75]

In July 1936, finding himself in Burgos, it had been easy for Del Moral to attach himself to Mola's entourage. Having detailed knowledge of the Republican and Socialist movements, he assumed the task of selecting those for arrest and also of compiling lists of those to be seized from the prison in Burgos to be shot. He was notorious for his prurient enjoyment of the executions. Each morning, he would take groups of his friends to watch the condemned beg for mercy before being shot. General Cabanellas protested about these distasteful dawn excursions to Franco who, typically, just let Del Moral know about the complaints. Del Moral then wrote to Cabanellas in an effort to secure his patronage. The General told his own son: 'I replied that I regretted ever having met him, that he has done nothing but damage, that I had learned with disgust of his passion for watching executions and of the pleasure he derived from producing misery and that I regarded him as a wretch.' Cabanellas's views were shared by Mola's private secretary and by the Falangist Maximiano García Venero, who wrote of Del Moral's 'inhuman viciousness'.[76]

Despite the distaste with which Del Moral was regarded by some, he was rewarded for his murderous zeal and soon found himself propelled ever further upwards. After Franco had been declared head of the rebel state on 1 October 1936, seven commissions, embryonic ministries, were set up under the governmental structure initially called the Junta Técnica. The second of these was the Justice Commission. Within it, over the next three weeks, various departments were set up, including the High Court of Military Justice and the Inspectorate of Prisons. Joaquín del Moral was made Inspector of Prisons.[77]

The vindictiveness of the military high command and the senior clergy took its toll throughout most of Castile and León. The weakness of the working class in most of the region facilitated the rapid annihilation of opposition. In Soria, a profoundly conservative province whose capital was a town of only 10,098 inhabitants, three hundred local people were executed along with others brought from Guadalajara. Soria had seen no violence during the years of the Republic and there was no resistance to the military coup. The arrival of Requetés on 22 July was the trigger for the killing. The wives of those murdered were forced to sign documents stating that their husbands had simply disappeared.[78] In neighbouring Segovia, there was also no resistance yet there were 217 illegal executions during the war and a further 175 as a result of sentences passed by military tribunals. Another 195 men died in prison.[79]

All the local military forces in Segovia had long been committed to the coup. Unaware of this, the Civil Governor, Adolfo Chacón de la Mata, of the centrist Republican party Unión Republicana, informed representatives of the left-wing parties that he had full confidence in the local garrisons and refused to have arms distributed to the workers. At 10.00 a.m. on Sunday 19 July, Chacón de la Mata was arrested by army officers and Civil Guards. Half an hour later, martial law was declared. The main post, telephone and telegraph office, the town hall and the Casa del Pueblo were occupied by troops. The left, without leaders or weapons, and totally outnumbered, was unable to resist beyond some sporadic pacific strike action.[80] Chacón de la Mata was tried in Valladolid on 13 October on charges of 'military rebellion', sentenced to death and shot on 5 December.

In the wider province, there were strikes in the towns along the main railway line. Although largely unarmed, apart from a few hunting shotguns, local workers took advantage of the absence of the Civil Guard in the provincial capital to establish Popular Front Committees in their villages. However, when the Civil Guard returned, accompanied by Falangists and Japistas, they took over without a shot being fired. Leftists were disarmed and arrested. Many others, including municipal councillors and schoolteachers, and individuals who were neither left-wing nor politically active, were shot out of hand. Individuals who showed a lack of enthusiasm for the new authorities were forced to drink castor oil. In El Espinar to the south of the province, there were uneven clashes between Civil Guards and poorly armed workers. Of eighty-four workers involved, thirty-two were subsequently tried and shot. According to the Francoist authorities, there was soon almost total tranquillity in the province. Nevertheless, arrests continued of liberals and leftists who had remained confident that nothing would happen to them because they had done nothing.[81]

In all cases, the terror – acts of robbery, torture, sexual violation and murder – was carried out by Falangists under the loose supervision of the new Civil Governor, a Civil Guard major. The military authorities provided institutional justification, turning a blind eye, giving permission or even issuing direct orders to murder individuals known, or merely assumed, to be supporters of the Republic. In Segovia, as in all of rebel Spain, the military recruited civilian vigilantes to carry out what one of the Falange's leaders later described as 'the dirty work'. Even after a town or village had been 'purged', killing continued on the basis of denunciations of those who had been imprisoned earlier or even to 'celebrate' some anniversary or other.[82] In Segovia, it was recognized publicly that 'mobile units of Falangists, under the direct orders of the Civil Governor, who has provided their itinerary, are moving around the province disarming Marxist elements' and preventing any disturbance of public order. When San Rafael in the south of the province was taken, the prisoners shot included two seventeen-year-old girls. In Segovia itself, the bulk of the victims were workers and members of the liberal professions known to have liberal or progressive views.[83]

The Casa del Pueblo of each town was looted and often requisitioned but first scoured for membership lists of left-wing parties or unions. Discovery of a name could lead to murder. Equally, Falangist groups executed people simply on the basis of accusations that they were Republicans, Freemasons, Marxists or simply opposed to the military coup. No judicial procedures were carried out to ascertain the validity of the accusations. Once arrested in a village, allegedly to enable them to make a statement before judicial authorities, some men were simply murdered en route to the provincial capital. Others were first taken to the local Falange headquarters, tortured, forced to drink castor oil and beaten. Frequent use was made of the *ley de fugas*, known locally as 'the greyhound or rabbit race'. Men supposedly being transferred from one prison to another were set down from the truck transporting them and told that they were free to go. When they ran, they were shot in the back. Some of the killings were carried out by very young adolescents. There were cases of entire families being executed, usually with the children shot first in order to intensify the suffering of the parents. Bodies were generally left where they fell as part of the terror. Subsequently, letters were delivered to the homes of men already shot, demanding information as to their whereabouts or requiring them to present themselves for military service.[84]

When the columns arrived, the landowners seized the opportunity to take revenge for Republican reforms. Labourers regarded as subversive were denounced. Individuals of little political significance were shot in several *pueblos*, such as Navas de Oro where Falangists murdered five individuals virtually at random. There, a *cacique* offered a huge sum of money to thugs to cut off the head of the left-wing Mayor. The sons of *caciques*, wearing recently acquired Falangist uniforms, were prominent in the repression. The Falange in Segovia swelled from a mere thirty members before 18 July to several hundred in a matter of months. Progressive country schoolmasters, believed to have poisoned the minds of the workers with liberal ideas, were a particular target in Segovia. In some places, the local villagers prevented the murder of the school-teacher or some other well-liked Republican. The few towns where committees of the Popular Front had been able to maintain power for a few days saw especially vicious repression, despite the fact that there had been no violence against, or even arrests of, right-wingers.[85]

In Palencia, an equally conservative province where the resistance was minimal, it has been estimated by local historians that the total of those executed was around 1,500, or 0.72 per cent of the population. Among the executed were the Civil Governor, the Mayor and the miners and other leftists who had led a failed attempt to combat the coup in the provincial capital. They were accused of military rebellion. Mineworkers in the northern towns were the most numerous casualties in Palencia, although in more southerly towns like Carrión de los Condes, Astudillo and Osorno the repression was also fierce. Throughout the province, the number of people executed ranged from 1.1 to 3.3 per cent of the population. Mola's edict of martial law was used to justify the repression. Those who did not hand over any arms in their possession within two hours were shot. Those who did were detained and executed.[86]

The situation in the neighbouring province of León was almost identical. There was little resistance against the coup but considerable repression, especially in the mining districts in the north and in the three other principal towns, Ponferrada near the border with Ourense, and La Bañeza and Astorga towards the border with Zamora.[87] Despite early enthusiasm for the coup, the Bishop of León, Monsignor José Álvarez Miranda, was so appalled by the scale of killing that he began to intercede with the local military on behalf of some of the prisoners, including Manuel Santamaría Andrés, Professor of Literature at the Instituto de León. Santamaría was imprisoned at the end of July, in the notorious San Marcos prison, simply because he was a prominent member of Azaña's Izquierda Republicana party. On 4 September, along with the Civil Governor and twenty-nine other Republicans, he was sentenced to death. His wife and family went to Burgos and successfully interceded for his sentence to be commuted to imprisonment. The news of this concession reached León before they did and when they returned, they were met with a hail of bullets. The commutation was revoked in response to protests by the military authorities. All thirty-one were shot on 21 November 1936. The Bishop was fined the enormous sum of 10,000 pesetas for his temerity in questioning a military tribunal.[88]

In Zamora, the coup triumphed easily, although railway workers maintained a resistance movement which would continue until the late 1940s. In both the provincial capital and the other principal town, Toro, the prisons were soon overflowing. Beatings, torture and mutilation and the rape of female prisoners were frequent. As elsewhere, the targets were Socialists, trade unionists, Republican officials and schoolteachers. Local historians calculate that more than 1,330 people were murdered in the province. Between 31 July 1936 and 15 January 1937, a total of 875 bodies were buried in the cemetery of San Atilano, registered simply as 'found dead' or 'executed after sentence'.[89]

Perhaps the most extreme example of the impact on the innocent of the repression in Zamora, as in so many places in Castile and León, was that of Amparo Barayón, the wife of Ramón J. Sender, world-famous novelist and anarchist sympathizer. Sender and his wife and two children were on holiday in San Rafael in Segovia at the beginning of the war. He decided to return to Madrid and told Amparo to take the children to her native city of Zamora where he was sure they would be safe. In fact, on 28 August 1936, she was imprisoned along with her seven-month-old daughter, Andrea, after protesting to the Military Governor that her brother Antonio had been murdered earlier the same day. This thirty-two-year-old mother, who had committed no crime and was barely active in politics, was mistreated and eventually executed on 11 October. Her crime was to be a modern, independent woman, loathed because she had escaped the stultifying bigotry of Zamora and had children with a man to whom she was married only in a civil ceremony.

Amparo was not alone in her suffering. Kept in below-zero temperatures, without bedding, other mothers saw their babies die because, themselves deprived of food and medicines, they had no milk to breast-feed them. One of the policemen who arrested Amparo told her that 'red women have no rights' and 'you should have thought of this before having children'. Another prisoner, Pilar Fidalgo Carasa, had been arrested in Benavente because her husband, José Almoína, was secretary of the local branch of the PSOE. Only eight hours before her detention and transport to Zamora, she had given birth to a baby girl. In the prison, she was forced to climb a steep staircase many times each day in order to be interrogated. This provoked a life-threatening haemorrhage. The prison doctor, Pedro Almendral, was called. He refused to prescribe anything either for Pilar or for her baby and told her that the best cure for her was death. Numerous young women were raped before being murdered.[90]

Burgos, where there had been relatively little social conflict before the war, fell immediately to the rebels. In the provincial capital, the Republican authorities were detained immediately, among them the Civil Governor and the General in command of the military region, Domingo Batet Maestre. As a Catalan and for his moderation in repressing the rebellion of the Generalitat in October 1934, Batet was a marked man. The extreme centralist right despised him because he avoided the exemplary slaughter that they considered appropriate for use against the Catalans. When he refused to join the rising, he was arrested. Because of their long-standing friendship, Mola prevented his immediate execution. However, Franco intervened in Batet's subsequent trial to ensure that he was sentenced to death and executed.[91]

Burgos saw around four hundred extra-judicial murders between August and October 1936 and a further one thousand in the wider province. Overall, in Burgos, there were more than 1,700 people either murdered by the rebels or who died of mistreatment in the massively overcrowded prisons. The old prison of Santa Águeda had been built for two hundred but held nearly one thousand; the central Penal de Burgos, built for nine hundred, held three thousand prisoners. Those awaiting execution were union leaders, Republican officials, schoolteachers and those who had voted for the Popular Front. These included children and women, some pregnant, shot on the bizarre grounds of 'right of representation' which meant that they were executed in substitution for their husbands who could not be found. Another 5,500 people suffered beatings, torture and/or imprisonment. By 2007, some 550 bodies had been exhumed from unmarked graves.[92]

Throughout most of Old Castile, the violence was carried out by groups of recently recruited Falangists and the younger members of other right-wing groups, students, the younger sons and permanent employees of landowners. There, as elsewhere, men joined for money, to curry favour with the powerful or to blur a left-wing past. Just as in the Republican zone, there were criminal elements that enjoyed the grisly opportunities for violence and rape.[93] They were egged on and often financed by landowners and helped with denunciations and information by local villagers, either out of fear or because they had in some way felt threatened by Republican legislation. With vehicles and weapons provided by the military authorities, legitimized by the Church, these groups acted with impunity. In the minds of the local conservative establishment, which included poor small farmers as well as rich landowners, the enemies were those who had disturbed the traditional structure. That meant the trade unionists who had encouraged landless labourers to negotiate for better wages and working conditions, the left-wing municipal officials who had supported them or the schoolteachers who had disseminated subversive and secular ideas that persuaded the poor to question the established order. Those who, to a large extent, formed the social basis of Republicanism were among the first targets of the repression.[94]

Although the rising succeeded very quickly in Ávila, the repression was severe. By the early hours of the morning of 19 July, the provincial capital was in the hands of the Civil Guard, the Popular Front authorities had been detained and Onésimo Redondo and eighteen of his followers had been released from the provincial prison. The Civil Governor, the Republican writer and friend of Azaña, Manuel Ciges Aparicio, was shot on 4 August. There was greater resistance in the small towns and villages. Columns of Civil Guards, soldiers and Falangists from the provincial capital quickly took Navalperal on 21 July and Las Navas the following day. Then, the arrival of a militia column from Madrid under Lieutenant Colonel Julio Mangada saw various villages change hands over the following weeks. However, when, in the course of August, they were occupied by rebel forces, the repression was especially severe. This was in no small part the consequence of the arrival from Salamanca of the column led by the notorious Civil Guard Lisardo Doval. The death of Onésimo Redondo at the village of Labajos in a clash between Falangists and Mangada's men would also contribute to the ferocity of the repression in Ávila. Throughout the ensuing months and for long afterwards, corpses would be found on country roads. Well over six hundred people were executed in the province.[95]

In the course of the operations in Ávila, the village of Peguerinos was captured on 30 August by a unit of Regulares accompanied by Falangists. The atrocities that they committed gained particular notoriety. Two Republican nurses insisted on staying to look after the wounded in an improvised field hospital set up in the village church. The hospital was shelled, the wounded bayoneted and the nurses and a number of other women were raped by the Moors and Falangists. Houses were looted and many set on fire. When the village was retaken, the two nurses and a fourteen-year-old girl who had also been sexually assaulted were discovered in a state of collapse.[96]

For the families of those executed or murdered, the suffering did not end with the loss of their menfolk. Gruesome details of the executions would reach them from members of the squads, who often boasted publicly of killing a particular individual. They would recount with relish how prisoners had begged for water or how fear had made them lose control of their bowels. Frequently, the surviving families of executed left-wingers were subjected to punitive fines. A notable case was that of Eduardo Aparicio Fernández, a bank manager in Ciudad Rodrigo and a man of broadly liberal views. He was arrested on 15 December 1936, along with seven others. In the early hours of the morning of the next day, all eight were taken from their cells, on the basis of an order for their release from the local military commander. They were brought to a nearby estate, shot and buried in a shallow grave. Eduardo Aparicio's family was given permission for him to be buried in the cemetery in Béjar on 24 December. At the end of the war, twenty-eight months after his death, Eduardo Aparicio was called for trial on a charge of political responsibilities. The judge demanded that his widow reveal where he was since he had been 'released' from prison on 15 December 1936. The accusations against him were that he had worn a red tie, had announced the news of Calvo Sotelo's murder in the Ciudad Rodrigo Casino and was a member of the Socialist Party. The third charge was demonstrably untrue. On the basis of the first two, the deceased was sentenced to a fine of 500 pesetas, which had to be paid by his widow.[97]

For all families, the death of a loved one without proper burial and ritual was traumatic. To be able to visit a grave, leave flowers or meditate permits some reconciliation with the fact of loss. This was denied to almost all the families of those killed in the repression. The theft of the dignity of the dead caused intense pain. In the deeply Catholic areas, like Castile and Navarre, the experience was especially painful. Those brought up there, Catholics practising or not, believed that, after death, the body would be buried and the soul pass on to heaven, purgatory or hell. Most Catholics would assume that their loved ones would go to purgatory, the halfway house, where they would purge their sins in order to continue on to heaven. Friends and relatives on earth could hasten this process by prayer, lighting candles in church, or paying for Masses to be said. In Castile, there even existed fraternities dedicated to praying for the dead. All such spiritual comfort was denied to the families of Catholics killed in the repression. For the families of all the victims, Catholic or not, mourning and the support of their community were replaced by insult, humiliation, threats and economic hardship.

To some extent, this was just an organic part of the process as hatred escalated. However, it also had an official dimension. Within days of the uprising succeeding, all Civil Governors and senior police officials who had not been totally committed to the uprising were removed from their posts. The edict of 28 July, whereby martial law was declared in all of Spain by the rebel Junta de Defensa, ratified all the previous local impositions of martial law. It stated that 'Any functionaries, authorities or corporations that do not lend the immediate aid demanded either by my authority or by my subordinates for the re-establishment of order or the implementation of the provisions of this edict, will be immediately suspended from their positions, without prejudice to the corresponding criminal proceedings against them which will be pursued by the wartime authorities.'[98] Among those immediately hit were schoolteachers. Large numbers were sacked and many jailed. The charges against them were often as trivial as to have worn a red tie, to have been a reader of a Republican newspaper or to have been a Freemason, an atheist or an anti-fascist.[99]

From his first headquarters in Burgos, Mola made a number of radio broadcasts in all of which he underlined his commitment to merciless continuation of the repression. On 31 July, on Radio Pamplona, he declared: 'I could take advantage of our present favourable circumstances to offer the enemy some negotiated settlement; but I do not want to. I want to defeat them to impose my, and your, will upon them and to annihilate them. I want Marxism and the red flag of Communism to be remembered in history as a nightmare but as a nightmare that has been washed clean by the blood of patriots.'[100] On 15 August, speaking on Radio Castilla of Burgos, he stated: 'There will be no surrender nor anything other than a crushing and definitive victory.'[101] On 28 January 1937, he spoke on Radio Nacional from Salamanca. After denying categorically that there were any German volunteers fighting with the rebels, he went on to denounce the Republic's leaders as 'traitors, arsonists, murderers and bank-robbers'.[102]

On 20 August, Mola moved his headquarters to the town hall in Valladolid, where he would remain for two months. While there, he went to Salamanca to receive a visit from Colonel Juan Yagüe, who was congratulated for the bloodshed in Badajoz. When it was time for Yagüe to leave, a cheering crowd gathered around his convoy of cars. Mola embraced him and called him 'my favourite pupil'.[103]

Although Yagüe was not involved, an Africanista ferocity was unleashed on Galicia. Even in comparison with the provinces of Old Castile, the repression throughout Galicia was massively disproportionate to the limited scale of resistance.[104] Indeed, the repression there was comparable to that in Navarre and La Rioja, where the presence of militant Carlism constituted something of an explanation. In Galicia, however, albeit a highly conservative region, the extreme right was not prominent before the military coup. In the course of 20 July, the rebels took over the region. The only places where there was any significant resistance were A Coruña, Vigo and Ferrol, but it was sporadic and had been crushed well before the end of the month. In Vigo, when the edict of martial law was read out, the crowd protested and twenty-seven people died when troops opened fire.[105]

The first few days after the coup saw relatively few deaths, just over one hundred. Thereafter the pace of executions increased with more than 2,500 in the five months from 1 August to the end of December. Recent research identified the total number of executions in Galicia as 4,560, including seventy-nine women. Of these 836 were the result of trials; the rest were extra-judicial murders. The worst of the repression was in A Coruña with nearly 1,600 executions and in Pontevedra with nearly 1,700. In these two Atlantic provinces, the Popular Front had won, albeit with a predominance of moderate left-of-centre Republican deputies. In Lugo, where the centre party had won, there were 418 deaths, of which two-thirds were the victims of extra-judicial murders. In Orense, where Renovación Española and the CEDA triumphed, there were 569.[106] The experience of Galicia shows that, as in Castile, the rebels aimed not just to defeat the left but to eradicate an ideal and to terrorize the population into subservience.

Between February and July 1936, throughout Galicia there had been intense civilian collaboration with the military conspirators. In the beautiful medieval Cathedral city of Santiago de Compostela, members of the JAP and the Falange were trained in military barracks and, in Orense, local elements of Renovación Española were in close contact with the Civil Guard. In Galicia, in comparison with most of Spain, there was relatively little disorder other than some fatal street fights between Falangists and Socialists in Santiago, Vigo, Ourense and Ferrol. In every province, when news of the rebellion arrived, the Republican authorities were confident, indeed complacent. The workers' unions, especially the CNT, tried to organize resistance, but the Civil Governors, fearful of revolution, refused to distribute arms. In the bustling port of A Coruña, the Governor, the twenty-six-year-old law professor Francisco Pérez Carballo, obeying messages from Madrid to maintain calm, put his confidence in the Civil Guard. He was also swayed by the fact that the head of the Galician Military Region (VIII), General Enrique Salcedo Molinuevo, was not a partisan of the coup. When he refused to declare martial law without news from his friend Sanjurjo, Salcedo was arrested and eventually executed by the conspirators, along with the other key commanders, the Military Governor of A Coruña and the commander of the naval arsenal in Ferrol, both of whom remained loyal. Pérez Carballo was forced to surrender after an artillery bombardment of the Civil Governor's building. His calls for calm had persuaded the majority of local authorities throughout the province to assume that a general strike would be enough to foil the coup.[107]

Accordingly, resistance was minimal and in inverse proportion to the ferocity of the repression. The establishment of martial law in A Coruña prompted resistance in the naval base at Ferrol. A mutiny by sailors on the warships *España* and *Cervera* was crushed. Both the town hall and the Casa del Pueblo surrendered after artillery bombardment and false promises that there would be no reprisals. On 26 July, the executions began of the sailors who had opposed the rising. On 3 August, the Admiral in charge of the base was tried and sentenced to death for the 'offence of abandoning his post'. Captain Victoriano Suances of the Civil Guard, who was put in charge of public order, supervised a particularly savage repression, with Falangist squads given free rein to eliminate Republicans.[108]

Columns of troops and Civil Guards moved out from A Coruña and Ferrol to organize the 'pacification' of the towns and villages of the province. Although there were few examples of church-burnings in Galicia, in Betanzos retreating anarchists set fire to the Convento de San Francisco. In consequence, the repression was all the more intense. In Curtis, to the east of A Coruña, sporadic resistance was smashed with ferocity. Throughout the province, the Falange suddenly found itself overflowing with new recruits from among the unemployed and petty criminals.[109]

In A Coruña itself, Lieutenant Colonel Florentino González Vallés, of the Civil Guard, was made Delegate for Public Order. He was the pro-Falange officer who had organized the anti-Republican demonstration by the Civil Guard after the funeral of Anastasio de los Reyes in Madrid. He was punished by being arrested and held briefly before being posted to A Coruña, where he played a crucial role in the uprising. Now, he conducted a particularly vicious repression making full use of the newly swollen Falange. He ordered the Civil Governor, Francisco Pérez Carballo, to be shot on 24 July, along with the commander of the Assault Guards and his second-in-command. There was no kind of trial. Pérez Carballo's death was initially inscribed in the registry as 'executed'. Since this implied, as assumed by the press, an official trial and sentence, it was later altered to death as a result of 'internal haemorrhage'.[110] Their executions were followed by those of large numbers of workers and school-teachers, as well as of some of the most distinguished doctors, lawyers, writers and professors of Galicia. Trials of the remaining Republican authorities began at the beginning of August. Their crime was dual, to have supported the Republic before 20 July and not to have supported the uprising on that date. Extra-judicial murders were carried out by Falangist groups with names like the 'Knights of Santiago' or the 'Knights of Coruña'. The latter gang's role in what was called 'the repression and pacification of the zones of the province attacked by subversive elements' was overseen by Lieutenant Colonel Benito de Haro Lumbreras, brother of Gregorio who had achieved notoriety in Huelva. To cover up the torture and/or disappearance of prisoners, it was claimed that they had been shot while trying to escape – in application of the *ley de fugas*. The places where bodies were left, next to crossroads or bridges, were care-fully chosen for the terror to have greatest impact. Many bodies were just thrown into the sea and their appearance in fishing nets and traps augmented the sensation of ubiquitous terror.[111]

After the arrest of Francisco Pérez Carballo, his wife, the thirty-one-year-old Juana María Clara Capdevielle Sanmartín, a well-known femin-ist intellectual, was alleged to have urged her husband to arm the work-ers and to have helped organize the resistance. No proof of this was ever put forward. She was already bitterly hated by the local right, assumed to dominate her husband and to have dangerous opinions. When the fighting began, Pérez Carballo had made her go and stay in the home of a pharmacist friend whose family, aware that she was pregnant, had kept her husband's death from her. Left alone one day, she phoned the Civil Governor's office for news of him. González Vallés told her her husband was well and that he would send a car for her to join him. The car took her directly to prison. After a week, she was released and took refuge with the family of another friend in Vilaboa outside A Coruña. Some days later, on the orders of González Vallés, Juana Capdevielle was detained by the Civil Guard on 17 August, taken to A Coruña and handed over to a Falangist squad. She was murdered the next day. Her assassins apparently discussed whether to poison her to provoke a miscarriage or to fling her into the sea, deciding finally to shoot her. Her body was found far to the east of A Coruña in Rábade in the province of Lugo. She had been shot in the head and chest and had recently had a miscarriage.[112]

Rumours abounded to the effect that Juana Capdevielle had been raped. It was common in Galicia for Republican women to be raped, to be beaten, to have their heads shaved, to be made to drink castor oil, to be detained and separated from their children. María Purificación Gómez González, the Republican Mayoress of A Cañiza in the south of Pontevedra, the only female mayor in Galicia, was arrested, summarily tried and condemned to death. Her execution was postponed because she was pregnant, and her sentence commuted to life imprisonment. She served seven years in the notorious prison of Saturrarán (Vizcaya) until released on conditional liberty in 1943.[113]

Those tried by court martial in A Coruña were usually executed by firing squad in the early hours of the morning. Nevertheless, it was common for there to be crowds of spectators. However, they did not compare with the spectacle mounted on 23 October 1936 when eight young conscripts were shot after being accused of plotting to rebel against their superior officers. They were paraded through the city in mid-afternoon and executed before a huge crowd. Their stentorian shouts of '¡Viva la República!' as they stood before the firing squad undermined the effect being sought.[114]

The repression in Galicia was notable for the high level of denunciations by parish priests, the Falange or hostile neighbours. In country districts, this was perhaps a reflection of the resentments provoked by poverty. There were also cases of denunciations of professional rivals such as led to the arrest and subsequent murder in A Coruña of Dr Eugenio Arbones, a distinguished obstetrician who had been a Socialist deputy in 1931 but had been now retired from politics for some years. His 'crime' was to have treated men wounded by the military rebels.[115]

A more striking case was that of José Miñones Bernárdez, a popular lawyer, banker and businessman from A Coruña who was elected deputy for Unión Republicana in the February 1936 elections. In the immediate aftermath of the elections, when there were riots in response to right-wing voting fraud, he had been acting Civil Governor. With remarkable courage, he had prevented the burning of two convents and a Jesuit church and protected a number of right-wingers. In gratitude, the Compañía de María granted his children and descendants free education in perpetuity. In response to the assassination of Calvo Sotelo, he called upon his fellow deputies of Unión Republicana to renounce their participation in the Popular Front. He returned from Madrid to A Coruña on 18 July, convinced that he was in no danger, having always been fair in his treatment of both left and right. This was demonstrated by the fact that, on 19 July, he appealed for military protection for the local electricity generating company of which he was managing director and he also successfully persuaded a convoy of workers to refrain from going to A Coruña to oppose the coup. Nevertheless, he was arrested, accused of military rebellion, condemned to pay a fine of 1 million pesetas and shot on 2 December. The reasons behind his death lay in his home town of Corcubión, where his family had incurred the hatred of the local commander of the Civil Guard.[116]

Santiago was quickly taken, with military trials beginning as early as 26 July. Five men, tried for crimes such as using the clenched-fist salute or shouting 'Long live Russia', were sentenced to life imprisonment. Murders began on 14 August; many of those who had been sentenced to imprisonment were taken from the jail illegally and shot. One of the victims was Eduardo Puente Carracedo, well known in the town for his fierce anti-clericalism. This derived from the fact that a young cousin of his, made pregnant by a canon of the Cathedral, had died when she was obliged to have a (necessarily illegal) abortion. Thereafter, Eduardo Puente would interrupt religious processions (on one occasion with a donkey bearing a crucifix). If the canon in question was taking part, Puente would attempt to hit him. Detained in the early days of the war, Puente was seized from the local prison; on 28 June 1937 he was murdered, and his body dumped under a bridge. The registry recorded the deaths of those murdered as the consequence of 'internal haemorrhage', 'cardiac arrest' or 'organic destruction of the brain'.[117]

On 3 October 1936, Father Andrés Ares Díaz, the parish priest of the tiny hamlet of Val do Xestoso near Monfero, in the province of A Coruña, was shot by a group of Falangists and Civil Guards. He had been denounced for refusing to donate to the rebels the funds collected for the religious festival of Los Remedios, scheduled for the first Sunday of September but suspended by the military authorities. He was accused of belonging to International Red Aid, arrested and taken to the village of Barallobre, near Ferrol, where he was obliged to make his confession to the parish priest there, Antonio Casas. It was hoped that the distressing sight of his fellow priest about to be shot might pressure Father Casas into admitting that he had helped Republicans escape. Casas had provoked suspicion because of his efforts to stop the repression in Barallobre. After making his confession, Father Ares handed over 200 pesetas and his watch to Father Casas. Andrés Ares was then taken to the cemetery and executed at 11 p.m. There was no trial, although the commander of the firing squad is alleged to have shouted, 'On the orders of Suances!', a reference to the Delegate for Public Order in Ferrol, Victoriano Suances. Although Father Casas was interrogated on several occasions, he escaped arrest and death because of the protest by Cardinal Gomá about the execution of Basque priests by the rebels.[118]

In the province of Lugo, east of A Coruña, the rising triumphed quickly without violence. The feeble attempt by the Civil Governor, Ramón García Núñez, to make the Civil Guard distribute arms had been ignored. The substantial local organization of the Falange and the local clergy were closely involved in the conspiracy. The military commander, Colonel Alberto Caso Agüero, had reluctantly declared martial law but made no arrests. Then a column arrived led by Captain Molina, who brusquely informed Caso: 'Colonel, the time for Vaseline is over. If we do not act energetically, we will lose control.' Caso himself was detained and the Civil Governor, the Mayor and most of the city's prominent Republicans were arrested. They were all tried in mid-October, condemned to death and shot at the end of the month. All working-class organizations were banned. There was little resistance except in the towns in the south of the province like Quiroga and Becerreá where, according to a priest, the population was notable for its 'lack of subordination'. In Monforte, an important railway junction, where the working class was Socialist, the Civil Guard, helped by Falangists, crushed the resistance.[119]

In the years before the war, violence in Ourense, Galicia's only inland province, was minimal. Even during the events of October 1934, and despite the unity shown by Socialists, Communists and anarchists, the general strike was defeated without significant bloodshed. In the elections of February 1936, Ourense registered the most notable conservative victories in Galicia with the province won by Renovación Española and the CEDA. The Popular Front was left without representation. The only violence provoked during the spring was the work of Falangists who killed four people on 8 June. On 18 July, the Civil Governor refused to arm the workers and all resistance melted away as soon as the edict of martial law was read out. There was some sporadic resistance in the Valdeorras area to the east of the province, in the course of which a Civil Guard was killed, the only casualty suffered by the rebels. A thirteen-year-old boy was shot because he had criticized the brutality of the Civil Guard. Despite this peaceful history, extra-judicial murders and trials quickly started in parallel. The *ley de fugas* was applied and bodies were thrown into the River Miño. Falangists were recent recruits with no real ideological commitment, some just paid thugs or men trying to hide a left-wing past, but all under the orders of the military. In a conservative, rural society, it was easy to find passive support for the repression of left-wingers.[120] Throughout Galicia, the usual routine was that men would be detained, then 'freed', taken to outskirts and shot, their bodies left in places where they would be seen and the message of terror spread.[121]

On the Portuguese border, in Galicia's coastal province of Pontevedra, the Civil Governor, like his counterparts elsewhere, refused to arm the workers. As in Ourense, there was a high level of collaboration in the repression in poor rural communities. Indeed, the military authorities issued a statement on 9 August that unsigned denunciations would not be pursued and eventually threatened to impose fines on those who made false accusations. Perhaps the most striking death in Pontevedra was that of Alexandre Bóveda Iglesias, founder of the Galician Nationalist Party, a conservative Catholic greatly admired by Calvo Sotelo. General Carlos Bosch y Bosch, the commander of the VIII Military Region, dismissed a plea for clemency, saying, 'Bóveda is not a Communist but he is a Galician Nationalist which is worse.'[122] In the prosperous fishing port of Vigo, the complacency of the Republican authorities facilitated the military take-over. The Mayor, a moderate Socialist businessman, had accepted assurances of loyalty from the military commander and had prevented the arming of the workers. Nevertheless, along with other Republican figures, he was tried and executed for military rebellion. Seven young men were shot for listening to a Madrid radio station. The repression in the province was organized by the military authorities and implemented by the Civil Guard and civilian squads. Under the umbrella of general instructions from the military authorities, local *caciques* were able to remove subversive elements. People could be shot without trial for having arms or for harbouring a fugitive or merely for making an unfavourable comment about the progress of the rebel war effort.[123] Great notoriety was gained by two groups known as the 'Dawn Brigades' organized by Dr Víctor Lis Quibén, deputy for Renovación Española. Several hundred prisoners died in the infamous concentration camp on the Isle of San Simón, in the Ría de Vigo near Redondela, some as a result of the appalling conditions, others shot by Falangists.[124]

While this rebel repression had proceeded in Spain's north-western corner, similar horrors were taking place far to the south and the east outside the Spanish peninsula. In the Canary Islands where the rebellion had triumphed immediately, there were no deaths at the hands of Republicans. Nevertheless, in the course of the war, it has been estimated that as many as 2,500 people were killed by the rebels.[125] It has been reckoned that more than two thousand people were executed in the Balearic Islands. In Mallorca alone, despite having an extremely weak workers' movement, there were at least 1,200 and probably as many as two thousand executed. The initial coup provoked a general strike as a result of which large numbers of workers were arrested and imprisoned.[126] The bulk of them were killed after Alberto Bayo's ill-fated attempt to retake the island for the Republic in mid-August. Prisoners captured by the rebels were immediately executed. They included five nurses, all aged between seventeen and twenty, and a French journalist.[127]

Bayo's attack was beaten off by rebel forces assisted by Italian air support and Italian troops led by Mussolini's viceroy, Arconovaldo Bonacorsi, the self-styled Conde Rossi. A homicidal maniac, Bonacorsi tutored the local Falange in unleashing a savage repression against the civilian population of the island. The French Catholic author Georges Bernanos was appalled as he watched lorryloads of men seized from their villages and taken to be shot. He was told by military contacts that more than two thousand people had been killed. He blamed the ferocity of the repression on Bonacorsi and the acquiescence of the Bishop of Mallorca, Josep Miralles.[128] One of the most significant victims of the repression in Mallorca was Alexandre Jaume i Rosselló, a distinguished intellectual from a wealthy bourgeois family of great military tradition. He was the first Socialist parliamentary deputy for the Balearic Islands. For this 'treachery', in a military trial on 13 February 1937, he was absurdly accused of trying to establish a Soviet dictatorship in Mallorca. He was condemned to death and shot on 24 February against the wall of the cemetery of Palma.[129]

The victims included several women and a priest. Among the most celebrated was Aurora Picornell i Femenies, known as 'La Pasionaria Mallorquina' and married to the future Communist leader, Heriberto Quiñones. She was murdered by Falangists on 5 January 1937 at the cemetery of Porreres, along with four other women. Perhaps the most famous was Matilde Landa, who, after lengthy psychological torture, committed suicide in Mallorca on 26 September 1942.[130] On 8 June

1937, Father Jeroni Alomar Poquet was shot in the cemetery of Palma because of his loud protests at the imprisonment of his brother Francesc, a member of the middle-class Catalanist party, the Esquerra Republicana de Catalunya. Another priest, Father Antoni Rosselló i Sabater, arrested because of links with Father Alomar and because his brother was the Republican Mayor of Bunyola, was sentenced to thirty years in prison.[131]

As the death toll mounted throughout rebel Spain, in September 1936 the monarchist poet José María Pemán coincided in Pamplona with General Cabanellas, who was still head of the Junta. Cabanellas requested his help in drafting a decree to forbid the wearing of mourning. His reasoning was twofold. In the case of the widows and bereaved mothers of rebels, the gesture of not wearing black would proclaim that 'the death of someone fallen for the Fatherland is not a black episode but a white one, a joy that should overcome any sorrow'. For the mothers, widows and fiancées of executed Republicans, forbidding the wearing of mourning 'would put an end to that sort of living protest and dramatic testimony that, when we conquer any town, we see in the squares and on the street corners – those black and silent figures that in reality represent protest as much as sorrow'.[132] Cabanellas was right that Republican mourning implied a protest since it signified solidarity with the recently eliminated family member. However, a decree forbidding Spanish women in rural areas to wear mourning would have been impractical because most older or widowed women wore black dresses as a matter of course. Moreover, the Catholic womenfolk of the rebel dead could not be deprived of their right to mourn their heroic loved ones. The issue was how to deprive the mothers, sisters, wives and fiancées of liberal and left-wing men of the opportunity to mourn and express that solidarity. In the south, Queipo simply issued a decree prohibiting mourning. In the north, it had to be done through more informal social pressures and fear of further reprisals.

Sometimes, after a man had been taken away at night, family members would bring food for him to the jail only to be told brutally that 'where he has gone, he won't be needing it'. The agony would often never end. They would see, as did Mola's secretary, José María Iribarren, while walking in Burgos, children playing at capturing a Republican then shooting the 'prisoner' who had refused, as the game required, to shout the rebel slogan '¡Viva España!'[133] Women whose menfolk had 'disappeared' could never remarry since, without an official death certificate, they were not legally widows. They had no right to administer the property registered in the names of their husbands. It is doubtful that Mola cared about, or was even aware of, the wider consequences of the terror that he had initiated.

PART THREE

The Consequence of the Coup: Spontaneous Violence in the Republican Zone

Far from the Front:
Repression behind the Republican Lines

Once the military rebellion had provoked the collapse of many instruments of the state, in every city not conquered by the insurgents, power in the streets was assumed by the armed workers who had contributed to the defeat of the rising. Committees set up by working-class unions and parties created their own autonomous police forces and detention centres, known as *checas* (in a misuse of the name of the early Soviet security service). In the chaos created by the disappearance of most of the conventional structures of law and order, there was also an element of sheer criminality. This reflected long-standing resentments of years of social injustice, but it was also born of the unleashing of the worst instincts of those who took advantage of the removal of social restraints. The problem was exacerbated by the opening of the prisons and the release of thousands of common criminals.

In the first months, the application of justice was usurped by the committees and for a time ceased to be a function of the state. Moreover, there was a wave of killing which sprang from a variety of motives. The 'justice' of the committees against supporters of the coup, revenge by non-unionized workers for the brutality of labour relations and the activities of common criminals all combined in a tumultuous process that seemed to the rest of the world an orgy of violence. The targets included rebel army officers and the clergy, those prominent in the old establishment, landowners and businessmen, and those who had participated in the repression that followed the events of October 1934. Under the umbrella of 'popular justice' against those responsible for the coup, crimes with no political motive, of robbery, kidnapping, extortion, rape and murder, were also committed. As these were brought under control, there would be other acts of revenge for bombing raids and for the atrocities committed by the rebels transmitted in the bloodcurdling tales brought by refugees. Eventually too, there would be the legal violence carried out by the instruments of state organized to combat the 'enemy within', the supporters of the military rising who carried out acts of sabotage and espionage.

A new overarching revolutionary power never replaced the Republican authorities. However, for the first months, the central government and the Catalan Generalitat, the autonomous regional government, could do no more than maintain a veneer of institutional continuity. Their orders were often ignored. Rather, the first priority had to be to persuade the more moderate elements of the left-wing parties and unions to collaborate in putting an end to uncontrolled violence – an especially difficult task in the case of the anarchist movement. At the same time, it was necessary to create a legal framework to encompass the spontaneous, and often mutually contradictory, actions of the committees and *checas*. Eventually, it would be recognized by many on the left, though by far from all of the anarchists, that the conduct of a modern war required a central state. There would be no end to the internal violence until the Republican state had been rebuilt, and that would take time. Meanwhile, the Republican authorities were deeply embarrassed by the situation which undermined their efforts to secure diplomatic and material support from Britain and France.

The most damaging element of the violence, exploited to the full by supporters of the rebels abroad, was constituted by attacks on the clergy. Anti-clericalism was explicitly advocated by both the anarchist Confederación Nacional del Trabajo and the anti-Stalinist Partido Obrero de Unificación Marxista. Andreu Nin, the POUM leader, told a meeting in Barcelona at the beginning of August that the working class had resolved the problem of religion by not leaving a single church standing.[1] The anarchists were less confident and saw the Church as a powerful enemy still. At best, priests were suspected of persuading their female parishioners to vote for the right, at worst of using the confessional to seduce them. The hatred deriving from that perceived sexual power of the clergy was revealed in the statement that 'the Church must disappear for ever. Churches will no longer be used for filthy pimping.'[2] The loudly proclaimed Catholicism of the possessing classes was another trigger for anti-clericalism. There was little Christian charity about the attitude of industrialists to their workers or of landowners to their tenants and day-labourers. Inevitably, anarchists, Socialists and Communists were united in suspecting that the attraction of the Catholic Church for the wealthy was the fact that it preached patience and resignation to those struggling for better wages and working conditions. Thus the assassination of priests and the burning down of churches were given an idealistic veneer by anarchists as the prior purification necessary for the building of a new world, as if it was that easy to eliminate religion.

On 24 July, the Canadian journalist Pierre van Paassen interviewed the anarchist leader Buenaventura Durruti in the CNT metalworkers' union headquarters in Barcelona. When Van Paassen remarked that 'you will be sitting on top of a pile of ruins even if you are victorious', Durruti replied, 'We have always lived in slums and holes in the wall … We are not in the least afraid of ruins. We are going to inherit the earth. The bourgeoisie may blast and ruin its own world before it leaves the stage of history. We carry a new world here in our hearts.'[3] The process of building a new world involved the liberation of common criminals perceived as victims of bourgeois society. Released into cities in which the instruments of public order had disappeared, these men, and others, committed crimes under the guise of revolutionary justice. A specific case which underlined the ambiguous relationship between anarchism and crime was that of the journalist Josep Maria Planes. He was murdered on 24 August by anarchists outraged by a series of articles that he had written under the title 'Gangsters in Barcelona', linking the activist wing of the anarchist movement, the Federación Anarquista Ibérica, with organized crime.[4]

In Barcelona, Lluís Companys, the President of the Generalitat, had refused to issue arms, but weapons depots were simply seized by workers. Over 50,000 guns were in the hands of anarchist militiamen. In the course of 19 July, the rebel troops were defeated by a curious alliance of predominantly anarchist workers and the local Civil Guard which, decisively, had stayed loyal. By the time General Manuel Goded had arrived by seaplane from the Balearic Islands to lead the rebellion, the coup was already defeated in Catalonia. He was arrested and obliged to broadcast an appeal to his followers to lay down their arms. The manner of the rebel defeat left a confused relationship between the institutions of the state and the power which had passed into the hands of the CNT–FAI. The immediate consequence was a breakdown of law and order. Barcelona was a port city with a large lumpenproletariat made up of dock labourers and many rootless immigrants subject to the insecurity of casual work. There is no doubt that theft, vandalism and common criminality found free rein behind a façade of revolutionary ideals, although the scale was exaggerated by both the foreign press and diplomats sympathetic to the rebels.

The Portuguese Consul in Barcelona reported 'acts of pillage and barbarism committed by the hordes that do whatever they like, ignoring the orders of their respective political bosses'. Referring to 'the indescribably refined cruelty of the assaults carried out by authentic cannibals on religious personnel of both sexes', he claimed that nuns were raped and then dismembered, and that not a single church or convent in the entire region remained standing.[5] Although the apocalyptic terms of this report can be discounted, it is certainly the case that in Barcelona shops, especially jewellers, and cafés were looted, money was extorted from merchants, the houses of the wealthy vandalized and churches desecrated. Religious and military personnel were the principal targets of left-wing anger.[6]

In the first days after the military coup, the events in Catalonia saw newspapermen flocking from around the world. Some of their initial reports were gratuitously lurid. A Reuters despatch alleged that bodies were piled in the underground stations and that 'The victorious Government civilian forces, composed of Anarchists, Communists and Socialists, have burned and sacked practically every church and convent in Barcelona.' It went on: 'The mob, drunk with victory, afterwards paraded the streets of the city attired in the robes of ecclesiastical authorities.'[7] Over the next few days the stories became ever gorier. The reign of terror was described under the sub-heading 'Priests Die Praying. The mob is uncontrollable and class hatred rules'. According to this account, 'Priest are being dragged with a prayer on their lips from their monasteries to be shot – in the back – by firing squads. Some of them have had their heads and arms hacked off after death as a final vindictive act.'[8]

Journalists who knew Spain well wrote more sober accounts of what was happening. Lawrence Fernsworth, the experienced correspondent of both *The Times* of London and the *New York Times*, accepted the popular view that anti-clerical outrage had been provoked because some military rebels and their civilian sympathizers had been allowed to install machine-guns in church bell-towers to fire on the workers. This was denied by the Generalitat's security chief, Federico Escofet Alsina, although it was widely believed by many on the streets of Barcelona. Certainly, Joan Pons Garlandí, a prominent member of the Esquerra Republicana de Catalunya (ERC), claimed that there were isolated cases of snipers firing from church towers. On 23 and 24 July, *La Humanitat*, the newspaper of the ERC, claimed that machine-guns were firing from churches. However, Escofet's contention is supported by the fact that no trial was ever held in Catalonia of any priest or monk accused of firing from church premises. In contrast, it has been alleged that anarchists would go into a church firing their guns in the air and then claim that the shots had been aimed at them, thereby seeking to justify the arrest of the priest and destruction of the church.[9]

Although probably not in response to sniper fire, there were numerous arson attacks on churches, but, as Fernsworth also noted, the Catalan government made every effort to save those that it could, such as the Cathedral. The Capuchin church in the central avenue, the Passeig de Gràcia, was saved because the Franciscan friars were noted for their close relation to the poor. In describing the terror, Fernsworth stressed that the Catalan Generalitat was not responsible and laboured incessantly to save property and lives: 'Persons in official positions risked the anger of extremists, and consequently their lives, to save priests, nuns, bishops and certain other Spanish nationals by getting them aboard foreign ships or across the frontier.'[10]

On the evening of 19 July, the last rebels, the Cavalry Regiment No. 9 under Colonel Francisco Lacasa, had taken refuge in the Monastery of the Barefoot Carmelites in the great Avinguda Diagonal that divides the city in two from west to east. Persuaded that Lacasa's wounded men were in desperate need of attention, the Prior let the monastery be used as a hospital, but the Colonel turned it into a fortress, placing machine-guns at strategic points. When an emissary arrived from the Generalitat's public order chief, Federico Escofet, Lacasa said that he would surrender only to the Civil Guard. This condition was accepted by Escofet, but, in the consequent delay, the building was surrounded by a mass of people, the majority bearing arms captured the day before. Ever more nervous, the defenders opened fire on the crowd. When the commander of the Civil Guard, Colonel Antonio Escobar Huerta, arrived, the rebels began to file out. As he tried to supervise their detention, he was held down by elements from the crowd and was unable to intervene as the rebel officers and four of the monks were murdered. Despite Escobar's heroic efforts to protect the monks and soldiers, he was executed by the Francoists in 1940.[11]

Escofet wrote later that the appearance on the streets of thousands of armed people posed an insuperable public order problem.[12] This underlines the difference between the repression in the two war zones – repression from below in the Republican zone and repression from above in the rebel zone. Escofet also commented on the fact that, in the raids on the homes of the wealthy and the property of the Church, theft was confined to a criminal minority, acknowledging the honesty and romanticism of many anarchists who handed in money and jewels.[13]

The victory of the working-class forces posed a significant problem for President Companys, who was leader of the bourgeois party, the Esquerra Republicana de Catalunya. He confronted it with considerable skill. On 20 July, in the immediate wake of the rebel defeat, he received in the Palace of the Generalitat a delegation from the CNT–FAI, consisting of Buenaventura Durruti, Juan García Oliver and Ricardo Sanz. According to García Oliver, Companys said:

> Today you are masters of the city and of Catalonia because you alone have defeated the military fascists and I hope you will not mind if I remind you that you were not denied the help of the few or the many loyal men of my own party and of the Civil Guards and Mossos d'Esquadra [the local police] … You have won and everything is in your power; if you do not need or want me as President of Catalonia, tell me now and I will become just one more soldier in the struggle against fascism. If, on the other hand, you believe that, in my post, with the men of my party, my name and my prestige, I can be useful in the struggle that is over today in this city but which we do not know how and when it will end in the rest of Spain, then you can count on me and on my loyalty as a man and a politician.

Some doubt has been thrown on García Oliver's accuracy by Federico Escofet. However, it is clear that with apparent candour and some cunning exaggeration, Companys disarmed the delegation. Taken by surprise, and with no practical plans, they agreed to Companys staying on.[14]

In another salon of the Palace, representatives of all the other Popular Front parties of Catalonia were waiting on the outcome of the meeting. When Companys brought in the CNT–FAI delegation, they were all persuaded to join in creating the Central Anti-Fascist Militia Committee. The CCMA's ostensible task was to organize both the social revolution and its military defence. Its secretary general, Jaume Miravitlles, was charged with drawing up a set of rules defining the powers and responsibilities of each department. However, he never did so, a failure that contributed to the chaotic and conflictive record of the CCMA and to the eventual reassertion of the powers of the Generalitat. Indeed, within a matter of days, Companys had ordered the Interior Minister (Conseller de Governació), Josep Maria Espanya i Sirat, to re-establish public order in the towns and villages of Catalonia. On 2 August, Companys entrusted the government to Joan Casanovas, the President of the Catalan parliament. Unfortunately, Casanovas could not muster the necessary level of energy or authority that Companys had hoped for to put an early end to the duality of power.

On 20 July, the principal rebel officers arrested in Barcelona had been taken by Civil Guards and CNT militants to the castle of Montjuich. Six days later they were transferred to the abandoned ocean liner *Uruguay*, a rust bucket converted into a prison ship. At first, they were treated well, allowed to sit on deck and read novels from the ship's library. This easy treatment was curtailed because of their adolescent behaviour. They insisted on greeting passing Italian naval vessels by standing to attention and giving the fascist salute. To boats full of leftists who had come to gawp and threaten them, they responded by sticking out their tongues and other more expressive gestures. Although they were prevented from going on deck, they were allowed to receive food parcels from family and friends. On 11 August, the leaders, Generals Manuel Goded and Álvaro Fernández Burriel, were tried by court martial on board the ship. They had as defence counsel a retired officer who was also a lawyer. Both were found guilty and sentenced to death and were shot by a firing squad the next day, at Montjuich. Over the following days, other rebels were tried and executed. Nevertheless, many survived, including Goded's son, Manuel.[15]

The spontaneous decision of Durruti, Sanz and García Oliver to join in creating the Central Anti-Fascist Militia Committee was accepted after some discussion by the rest of the CNT leadership. They were ill prepared, both ideologically and temperamentally, to improvise state institutions capable of simultaneously organizing both a revolution and a war. Essentially, Companys had offered them a great face-saving device. For the moment, the workers seemed to be in control. At first, the Generalitat would give legal form to the wishes of the Central Anti-Fascist Militia Committee, but the lack of political expertise within the CNT saw the CCMA gradually reduced to being a sub-committee of the Generalitat and then dissolved altogether. Companys had effectively ensured the continuity of state power and, in the long term, the eventual taming of the revolution by manoeuvring the CNT into accepting responsibility without long-term institutionalized power.[16]

In the short term, however, the CNT was set on clearing the ground for the building of the new world. Its mouthpiece, *Solidaridad Obrera*, justified violence against priests and capitalists. The wave of criminality that had engulfed Barcelona was acknowledged and rationalized:

there is nothing like the whiff of gunpowder to unleash all the instincts lurking inside man. At the same time, the upheaval reached a point where control was lost over those people interested only in the satisfaction of their selfish and vengeful instincts. They and they alone are responsible this week for the things (and not as many as has been claimed) that have been perpetrated in Barcelona that the Confederación Nacional del Trabajo and, alongside it, all the organizations which have participated in the revolution, would rather had not happened. Nevertheless, we cannot join the chorus of those shedding crocodile tears who, when all is said and done, bear the responsibility, not just for the fascist uprising but also for having kept the people for years on end in a condition of permanent destitution and an even more lasting ignorance. Inevitably, the outcome could hardly have been different. What has happened to the exploiting bourgeoisie, to the obscurantist clergy and to the greedy shopkeepers is that they have had to reap the consequences of the seeds they themselves sowed.[17]

Three days later, on 1 August, the national committee of the CNT issued a manifesto which declared that 'no rifle should be silent as long as there exists a single fascist in Spain'.[18]

That anarchist violence would continue uncontrolled was ensured by the fact that, under the CCMA, the Departament d'Investigació which was responsible for public order was headed by the FAI extremist Aurelio Fernández Sánchez. He secured the removal of the efficient Federico Escofet as head of security because of his determination to control the FAI. In every town and village, there was created a defence or revolutionary anti-fascist committee the bulk of which were dominated by members of the CNT or the FAI. Fernández delegated power to 'control and security teams', known as Patrulles de Control, of which seven hundred were created within a week. Their composition reflected the fact that most committed anarchists were repelled by the idea of acting as policemen and preferred to fight at the battle front. Thus the armed members of the patrols were made up of a mixture of extremists committed to the elimination of the old bourgeois order and some recently released common criminals. In the main, they acted arbitrarily, searching and often looting houses, arresting people denounced as right-wing and often killing them. As a result, by early August, over five hundred civilians had been murdered in Barcelona. Aurelio Fernández authorized an assault on the prison ship *Uruguay* which saw many right-wing prisoners murdered.[19]

Sometimes, when the defence committees of given localities wanted some criminal act carried out, they would arrange for it to be done by patrols from other towns on a reciprocal basis. A so-called 'ghost car' would arrive from a neighbouring town or district equipped with black-lists that can only have been provided by local elements. This accounts for the impunity with which outsiders could arrive, burn a church and arrest or kill local people. There were many motorized squads or brigades whose vehicles reflected the FAI's penchant for luxury saloons. They were often headed by men with criminal records, usually for armed robbery, appointed by Aurelio Fernández. Among the more notorious were the one-time bank robber Joaquim Aubí, alias 'El Gordo', who drove the ghost car of Badalona; Josep Recasens i Oliva, alias 'El Sec de la Matinada', whose group operated in Tarragona; Jaume Martí Mestres from Mora la Nova, whose group was active in the villages along the banks of the River Ebre; and Francesc Freixenet i Alborquers who dominated the area around Vic in the north of the province of Barcelona. Freixenet, with his accomplices Pere Agut Borrell and Vicenç Coma Cruells, known as 'the cripple of the road to Gurb', ran a fleet of six ghost cars, maintained by his family's garage and paid for by the municipality. Their main targets were members of the clergy.[20]

One of the most feared of such itinerant groups was led by Pascual Fresquet Llopis and operated in the so-called 'death's-head car'. Fresquet was twenty-nine years old and known for his violent temper. He had been imprisoned in the early 1930s for armed robbery and intimidated or murdered recalcitrant industrialists on the instructions of the FAI.[21] At the beginning of the war, he joined the anarchist column from Barcelona led by the charismatic ex-carpenter Antonio Ortiz of the FAI. Ortiz's base was Caspe in the south of Zaragoza, a small town which had initially been taken for the rebels by Captain José Negrete at the head of forty Civil Guards. The fact that Negrete had used Republican women and children as human shields ensured that, after the town was occupied on 25 July by Ortiz's column, the reprisals would be ferocious with fifty-five local rightists executed before the month was out. The prominent part played by Fresquet's group led Ortiz to give them the title of 'brigada de investigación' with carte blanche to hunt down fascists. Their death's-head car was actually a black, thirty-five-seat charabanc decorated with skulls. The brigade had a skull embroidered on their caps and a metal skull-badge pinned to their chests.[22]

In early August, Fresquet flushed out some of the remaining right-wingers of Caspe. Before dawn, his men ran into the streets firing shots and shouting rebel slogans. Optimistic that the town was being taken by rebel forces from Zaragoza, four or five rightists came out of hiding, brandishing weapons. They were immediately detained and shot.

Thereafter, Fresquet's group, known as the 'Death Brigade', spread terror through the area of Lower Aragon, Teruel and Tarragona. They moved eastwards, first to Fabara where they killed fifteen right-wingers, and then north to Riba-roja d'Ebre where they killed eight people on 5 September and another eight at Flix in Tarragona the following day. They then headed south to Mora d'Ebre where the local committee prevented them killing anyone.[23]

From Mora d'Ebre, they moved west to Gandesa where, on the night of 12 and the morning of 13 September, they executed twenty-nine rightists. Fresquet had the red and black flag of the FAI flown over the town hall and then harangued the town's inhabitants as he declared libertarian communism. In the afternoon of 13 September, they went east to Falset, at the base of the steep wine-growing Priorat area in Tarragona, where an identical sequence of events was seen. Arriving in the bus and two large black cars, Fresquet and about forty-five of his men immediately detained the local ERC–UGT anti-fascist committee and sealed off roads into the town. Between nightfall and the following morning, on the basis of lists prepared by local members of the FAI, they arrested and executed twenty-seven right-wingers in the cemetery. Fresquet then assembled the entire population of the village and, under the black and red flag of the FAI, made a speech from the balcony of the town hall. He justified the killings by saying that his squad had been asked to come and 'impose justice'. The local FAI had indeed called him in to accelerate the imposition of libertarian communism and immediately there began massive confiscations of land.[24]

The next stop of the Death Brigade was Reus. However, the local anti-fascist committee had been warned of their arrival. Led by Josep Banqué i Martí of the Partit Socialista Unificat de Catalunya (PSUC, the Catalan Communist Party), Communists, Socialists and even anarchists agreed to act in concert. On arrival, Fresquet himself went first to the headquarters of the committee and told Banqué that his column had come to carry out a purge of fascists. As Banqué was telling him that his services were not required, Fresquet was informed by one of his lieutenants that their convoy had been surrounded by local militiamen in the main square, La Plaça de Prim. The Death Brigade was forced to leave and a bloodbath like those at Gandesa and Falset prevented. Eventually, in late October 1936, the CNT would clamp down on the activities of Fresquet because they were bringing the organization into disrepute. By that time, Fresquet's busload of killers had executed around three hundred people.[25] As Josep Maria Planes had pointed out in the articles for which he was murdered, it was difficult to distinguish between idealistic revolutionary fervour and plain criminality. The Patrulles de Control all over Catalonia were also giving the CNT a bad name but little was done precisely because they were being administered by Aurelio Fernández, an extremely senior figure in the movement.

Under his overall control, the Central Patrol Committee was run by its secretary general, another FAI member, Josep Asens Giol. Asens, aided by Dionís Eroles i Batlle, would issue orders for investigation and detention. Until they were dissolved after the events of May 1937, the patrols took exclusive responsibility for rooting out pro-rebel elements in the rearguard. Behind this function, crimes were committed for personal gain, revenge or class hatred by the notorious group known as 'Eroles's Boys'. There were a few of the patrols controlled by other parties such as those run out of the Hotel Colón by the PSUC. There were also numerous completely separate autonomous groups with their own private prisons or *checas*. Fernández, Asens and Eroles had no qualms about using criminal elements, believing them to be victims of bourgeois society. Together, they presided over a network of terror throughout Catalonia. It has been alleged that Aurelio Fernández and one of his closest collaborators, Vicente Gil 'Portela', were guilty of sexual crimes. Another sinister FAI figure was Manuel Escorza del Val, head of the CNT–FAI counter-espionage service who used his units to eliminate any perceived enemies of the movement.[26]

Escorza's Investigation Committee, as it was called, was set up in August. The portrayal of revolutionary terrorism in the right-wing press throughout Europe, together with diplomatic protests, brought pressure from the Madrid government, from the Generalitat and from the Comité Central de Milicias Antifascistas for an end to the 'disorder'. The CNT leadership was fearful that complaints about disorder could be a device to generate a desire for a return to the old state structures and initially set up Escorza's committee to investigate the excesses. Operating from the wheelchair to which he was confined by paralysis, Escorza was described by García Oliver as 'that lamentable cripple, of mind as well as of body'. The secretary of the CCMA and later Generalitat press chief, Jaume Miravitlles, remembered him as 'the implacable and incorruptible Robespierre of the FAI'. In contrast, Miravitlles's colleague, Joan Pons Garlandí, regarded Escorza as 'head of the uncontrolled elements of the FAI'. The anarchist Federica Montseny, later to be Spain's first ever female minister, described Escorza as the Felix Dzerzhinsky of the Spanish revolution. The brutality of his methods provoked in her 'considerable anxiety not to say anguish'. From his office on the top floor of CNT headquarters in the Via Laetana, he used his huge file-card index to pursue rightists and criminals from within the ranks of anarchism.[27]

An early example of Escorza's work was the case of Josep Gardenyes Sabaté, a notoriously violent and uncontrollable thug. He had not been amnestied when the Popular Front came to power but, on 19 July, had been released along with other common criminals. With a group of comrades, he became an FAI 'expropriator' guilty of murder and looting. As early as 30 July, the CNT–FAI issued a statement that anyone undertaking unauthorized house searches and acts that compromised the new revolutionary order would be shot. Some days afterwards, on 3 August, Gardenyes and some members of his gang were detained and executed without trial. This caused outrage within certain sectors of the anarcho-syndicalist movement.[28]

Gardenyes enjoyed cult status within the movement, having earned his spurs during the period of unrestrained gangsterism between 1918 and 1923. He was one of the most prominent of the so-called 'men of action', specializing in fund-raising by armed robbery. He was a committed and ideological anarchist, blacklisted by Barcelona employers for his efforts. Having been exiled then imprisoned during the Primo de Rivera dictatorship, he was released as a result of the amnesty to celebrate the establishment of the Second Republic in April 1931 and soon returned to robbery. Some of his comrades found his behaviour too extreme and he was expelled from the movement. After his release from prison, he joined the Patrulles de Control and soon reverted to old habits, allegedly stealing jewels from a house that was being searched.

Gardenyes's execution was the response of the CNT–FAI leadership to demands for an end to the revolutionary terrorism. His execution was carried out by a group led by Manuel Escorza, and the body was dumped on the outskirts of Barcelona. It was rumoured that Gardenyes struggled to the last, some of his fingernails being left in the car that took him on his final journey.[29] The Madrid-based anarchist Felipe Sandoval, a notorious and vicious killer in his own right, described Escorza to his own Francoist interrogators as 'a twisted figure, physically and morally a monster, a man whose methods disgusted me'.[30]

The activities of Escorza did nothing to reassure the moderate elements alarmed by anarchist atrocities. The Generalitat's efforts to save lives were more effective. Safe-conducts were issued to Catholics, businessmen, right-wingers, middle-class individuals and clergy. Passports were made available for well over 10,000 right-wingers to embark on foreign ships in the port of Barcelona. Passports with false names were issued for people whose real identities might have put them in danger. In 1939, the French government reported that in the course of the civil war, in collaboration with the Generalitat, its Consulate in Barcelona had evacuated 6,630 people, of whom 2,142 were priests, monks and nuns, and 868 children. On 24 August 1936, Mussolini's Consul in Barcelona, Carlo Bossi, reported that 4,388 Spaniards had been evacuated in Italian warships.[31]

Few of the beneficiaries showed gratitude. One of them was the wealthy financier Miquel Mateu i Pla, who, on reaching the rebel zone, formed part of Franco's staff. After Barcelona was occupied in 1939, on the recommendation of Father Juan Tusquets, Franco appointed Mateu as Mayor. Mateu's policies suggested that he wished to take revenge on the entire population for his discomfort at the hands of the FAI.[32]

A difference between the practice in Catalonia and that in the rebel zone was the way in which the corpses of the victims of extra-judicial violence were treated. In Barcelona, the relatives of the victims were able to ascertain the fate of their loved ones. The Red Cross, the municipal sanitation services or the staff of the judiciary took the corpses found in the streets to the hospital clinic where they were photographed and numbered. To avoid any such investigations, the FAI patrols established crematoriums in order to dispose of the bodies of their victims. Sometimes the bodies would be burned with gasoline, others dissolved in lime. At other times, bodies were concealed in wells or buried in remote spots.

While the Patrulles de Control ruled the streets in Barcelona, as elsewhere, to be identified as a priest, a religious, a militant Catholic or even a member of a pious society was to be in danger of death or prison – a consequence of the Church's traditional identification with the right. During the events of October 1934, there had been isolated physical attacks on priests in Barcelona. Further south, in Vilanova i la Geltrú, the Church of the Immaculate Conception was looted and destroyed. All but two of the churches of Vilafranca del Penedès were set alight. During the spring of 1936, there were cases of stones being thrown at priests in the streets, parish residences being assaulted and religious ceremonies being violently disrupted.[33] During the war, the FAI's persecution of religious personnel in Catalonia intensified.

Churches were sacked and burned to the ground. Initially, priests in cassocks were murdered on the street. Later, priests and those who assisted in ecclesiastical functions, sacristans and parish administrators, as well as the most notably pious lay Catholics, were arrested, principally by the FAI. They were executed after interrogation in the *checa* to which they had been taken. Many priests fled or went into hiding. A post-war report compiled by the Diocese of Barcelona ascertained that many of the abuses against both clergy and churches, although organized by local extremists, were actually carried out by elements from outside. There were many places where the local faithful opposed the assaults on their churches but sometimes, in order to save the clergy, had to accept, or even collaborate in, setting fire to the church. Equally, there were many cases where the local Popular Front Committee prevented the murder of the clergy and facilitated their escape. In Valls, a small town in Tarragona, the altars of most churches were destroyed and the buildings used as garages and agricultural warehouses. One especially valuable seven-teenth-century altar was saved by local FAI members who were descend-ants of the sculptor who had built it. Nevertheless, twelve priests were murdered in the town.[34]

According to the diocesan report, there were many towns, such as Granollers or Sitges, where the local committee organized anti-clerical excesses. In the case of Vilanova i la Geltrú, since the local right had played no part in the military coup and was caught unawares, left-wing reprisals were less ferocious than in other places. Nonetheless, trucks loaded with armed men arrived from Barcelona and forced religious personnel to leave their churches, monasteries and convents. Religious buildings were looted but none burned to the ground. Nevertheless, all public liturgical practice was curtailed. The Property Registry was sacked and much documentation burned. The town was under the control of a CNT militia committee. There were other uncontrolled elements that moved around in another ghost car looting houses and making un-authorized arrests. Many murders were committed by elements who came from outside but had links with leftists within the town. Of those killed by the patrols in Vilanova i la Geltrú, only four were priests. In contrast, over half of those killed in Lleida in the five weeks following the military uprising were clergy. In the entire course of the war, 65.8 per cent of the clergy of the dioceses of Lleida met violent deaths. The left-wing association of the Church with fascism was strengthened by papal declarations to the effect that fascism was the best weapon with which to defeat proletarian revolution and defend Christian civilization.[35]

The notion of purification by fire, of clearing the ground of the legacy of previous Spanish history, underlay much of the violence perpetrated by idealistic anarchists. However, it was also used as a justification of the activities of the common criminals who had been released from jail and joined the CNT–FAI's patrols and *checas*. Individuals jailed for armed robbery and murder may have been simply criminals or even psychopathic monsters, but there were plenty of otherwise humanitarian anarchists who glorified them as heroes of the social struggle.[36]

Even without the recently freed prisoners, it would have been impossible to keep the groundswell of long-repressed anti-clerical feeling entirely in check once the restraints were off. Churches and convents were sacked and burned everywhere in the Republican zone except the Basque Country. Many were put to profane use as prisons, garages or warehouses. Acts of desecration – the shooting of statues of Jesus Christ and saints, the destruction of works of art, or the use of sacred vestments in satires of religious ceremonies – were usually symbolic and often theatrical. The most reliable study of religious persecution during the Civil War, by Monsignor Antonio Montero Moreno, calculated that 6,832 members of the clergy and religious orders were murdered or executed. Many others fled abroad. The popular hatred of the Church was the consequence both of its traditional association with the right and of the ecclesiastical hierarchy's open legitimization of the military rebellion.

Despite the murder of clergy, including nearly three hundred female religious, the propaganda stories of naked nuns forced to dance in public and gang-raped by Republican militiamen were wild exaggerations. One celebrated post-war account, published under the name of Fray Justo Pérez de Urbel, the mitred Abbot of the monastery of the Valle de los Caídos, was entirely invented by his ghost writer, Carlos Luis Álvarez, a journalist who used the pseudonym 'Cándido'.[37] In 1936, Spain had just over 115,000 clergy, of whom about 45,000 were nuns, 15,000 monks and the remainder lay priests. The latest figure for the deaths of nuns in the war is 296, just over 1.3 per cent of the female clergy present in the Republican zone. This contrasts dramatically with the figures for male clergy killed, 2,365 monks and 4,184 secular priests – over 30 per cent of the monks and 18 per cent of the lay clergy in Republican territory.[38]

Although still shocking, the figures for confirmed sexual molestation are also extremely low, even taking into account the reluctance of victims to speak out. After exhaustive research, Montero Moreno concluded that, even if threatened, nuns were normally protected from sexual abuse, if not from death. Nuns belonging to orders devoted to social work such as the Little Sisters of the Poor were those most likely to escape any kind of persecution. The diocesan archivist of Barcelona,

Father José Sanabre Sanromá, assembled details of all the female religious murdered. Almost all were killed in the first few days. Sanabre
Sanromá made no mention of sexual crimes in the Barcelona dioceses.
Those incidents that did take place, such as the sexual torture and
murder of five nuns in the village of Riudarenes in Girona between 22
and 25 September, were the exception. The most frequently cited reason
for this is the widespread male conviction that young women could have
entered convents only as a result of coercion or deception. In contrast,
male religious personnel were singled out for symbolic and often
barbaric tortures which often involved sexual humiliation. This reflected
burning resentment of the Church's overwhelming privileges and its
power to control everyday lives, especially those of women.[39]

Anti-clerical violence was firmly combated by key figures in the
Generalitat, despite the enormous risks involved in doing so. Jaume
Miravitlles, for instance, hid groups of priests and religious in the dressing rooms of Barcelona Football Club while they awaited passage out of
Catalonia. Josep Maria Espanya, the Interior Minister, Joan Casanovas as
both Prime Minister until late September and as President of the Catalan
Parliament, and Ventura Gassol, the Conseller de Cultura, all made
heroic efforts. Azaña commented in his notes: 'Gassols has saved many
priests. And the Archbishop.'[40] This was a reference to Cardinal Francesc
Vidal i Barraquer, the Archbishop of Tarragona. The Bishop of Girona
was given an escort out of the city and sent to Italy and the Bishops of
Tortosa, La Seu d'Urgell and Vic were also saved. In his report of 24
August, the Italian Consul, Carlo Bossi, noted the facilities granted by
Josep Maria Espanya to ensure the evacuation of numerous religious
communities including those of the Abbey of Montserrat. He noted that
obstacles were placed on the issuing of passports by the head of the local
police, who was from the PSUC. Nevertheless, he could report on 11
September that a further 996 religious personnel had been evacuated in
Italian vessels.[41]

On 20 July, the delegate of the Generalitat in Tarragona urged Cardinal
Vidal i Barraquer to abandon the episcopal palace, but he rejected the
advice. However, as the city's churches began to go up in smoke, he
agreed that the palace and the nearby seminary should be converted into
a military hospital. A large group of heavily armed anarchists arrived
from Barcelona on the afternoon of 21 July. They released all the
common criminals from the city's prison, then looted and set fire to first
the monastery of Santa Clara, then the contiguous convent and orphanage run by the Barefoot Carmelites. Ordinary citizens stopped them

burning the libraries of the churches. Still the Cardinal refused to move. Finally, he agreed to leave when he was told that, if he delayed any further, he could be got out only at the cost of considerable bloodshed. On 21 July, he took refuge in the Monastery of Poblet in the interior halfway to Lleida. An anarchist patrol from Hospitalet in the south of Barcelona appeared and at gunpoint forced him to go with them. They were driving towards Hospitalet so that he could be put on trial when their car ran out of petrol. A unit of Assault Guards arrived and freed him. He was taken to Barcelona where the Generalitat arranged with Carlo Bossi for him to go into exile in Italy.[42]

Despite the rescue of Cardinal Vidal i Barraquer, eighty-six members of the clergy, fifty-eight secular priests and twenty-eight religious were murdered in the provincial capital of Tarragona between 23 July and 22 December, when the repression was brought under control. One-third of these were killed in the first ten days, a further third in the following three weeks of August and the remainder over the next four months. In the entire province, 136 clergy were murdered.[43] Vidal i Barraquer's Vicar General, Salvador Rial i Lloberas, was captured on 21 August by a group of CNT railwaymen and tried by a spontaneous tribunal. Its president declared that Rial was automatically sentenced to death since 'the proletariat had agreed to exterminate all priests'. He was offered his life if he would reveal where the diocesan funds were hidden. When he refused, he was imprisoned without food or water in a minuscule store-room on the prison ship *Río Segre* in Tarragona harbour. As he continued to refuse to reveal the location of the funds, he was about to be shot when jurisdiction was taken away from the local militiamen by the creation of people's courts (*jurats populars*) on 24 August.[44]

What happened to the clergy in Tarragona was representative of the entire region. In general terms, the greatest number of murders of religious personnel in Catalonia took place between 19 July and the end of September 1936. Thereafter, the functioning of people's courts with some minimal judicial guarantees meant that the clergy were usually given prison sentences. The reactionary Bishop of Barcelona, Dr Manuel Irurita Almandoz, was less fortunate than Cardinal Vidal i Barraquer. On 21 July, when a patrol searched the bishop's palace, he had gone into hiding in the home of Antoni Tort, a piously Catholic jeweller, who had also given refuge to four nuns. On 1 December, a patrol from Poble Nou searched the jeweller's workshop and discovered Dr Irurita. Although Irurita claimed to be a simple Basque priest, the militiamen concluded that he was someone important. It is believed that he was shot in

Moncada, along with Antoni Tort, on 4 December. Nevertheless, rumours circulated that he had been rescued. He was certainly the object of negotiations for a prisoner exchange carried out in 1937 by the Basque priest Alberto de Onaindia. It was also claimed widely that he was seen in Barcelona in 1939. Doubts were not resolved by DNA tests carried out in 2000 and speculation continues.[45]

Thus, behind a rhetoric of revolutionary justice, acts of violence were being perpetrated and not just against the clergy. The violence reflected popular outrage at the military coup and its attempt to destroy the advances made by the Republic. Revenge was taken against the sections of society on whose behalf the military was acting. So hatred of an oppressive social system found expression in the murder or humiliation of parish priests who justified it, of Civil Guards and policemen who defended it, of the wealthy who enjoyed it and of their agents who implemented it. In some cases, the acts did have a revolutionary dimension – the burning of property records and land registries in the countryside or the occupation of the homes of the rich in the big cities. Although there were also criminal acts, murder, rape, theft and the settling of personal scores, for some the liquidation of the old ruling class was seen as a revolutionary act within a new morality, as it had been in France, Mexico and Russia. The targets of 'revolutionary justice' were 'proven fascists', which meant right-wingers of any kind who could be supposed to support the coup. Accordingly, landowners, bankers, factory owners, shopkeepers, senior personnel, engineers and technicians in factories and even workers thought to be too close to the bosses were likely to be condemned by any of the many tribunals that were set up by factory or neighbourhood committees in the towns or village committees in the countryside.

The initial rage against the military rebels and a desire to punish them for the bloodshed that they had caused soon combined with a determination to consolidate the revolution by eliminating all those supposed to be its enemies. Equally, news of military reverses and the arrival of the corpses of the fallen provoked outbursts of vengeful executions.[46] A different kind of violence was sparked by the rivalries – sometimes ideological, sometimes personal – between the various political parties and militia groups. On the one hand, Companys's Esquerra and the PSUC sought to rebuild a judicial system, thus offering captured political opponents constitutional guarantees, while the anarchists saw the immediate physical annihilation of the enemy, without any due process, as the basis of a new utopian revolutionary order.

Initially, most local committees put enormous energy into confiscating motor vehicles, radios and typewriters, requisitioning the headquarters of right-wing organizations and the mansions of the wealthy and placing patrols on the roads in and out of towns. This latter activity ensured that journeys of any distance became interminable as papers were demanded at every turn. Theft and vandalism during house searches were not uncommon.[47] While most local committees were concerned with the collectivization of agriculture and the eradication of rebel elements, there were others that were unequivocally criminal. Typical examples in Girona were the Comitè d'Orriols whose members committed particularly violent acts of banditry, and those from Riudarenes. Along the frontier, at Portbou, La Jonquera and Puigcerdà, there were elements of the FAI that carried out the systematic extortion of those who wanted to cross into France. Many were murdered after giving up their valuables. These frontier patrols also facilitated the smuggling of property stolen by the FAI patrols in Barcelona, sometimes for private benefit, sometimes for arms purchases.[48]

A priority for the anarchists was to secure reparation for the perceived injustice of sentences passed by monarchist and Republican courts before 18 July 1936. The first step had to be the destruction of judicial records. The anarchist leadership, including Diego Abad de Santillán, one of the leaders of the CCMA militias, believed that the people's justice had no need of lawyers or judges. Accordingly, on 11 August, they sent an armed squad to take control of the Palace of Justice in Barcelona. Their excuse for entering the building was that they had come to search for arms. The radical anarchist lawyer and journalist Ángel Samblancat witnessed the consequent stand-off between the Civil Guards protecting the Palace and the patrol whose leader announced that they had come to arrest 'the scoundrels who combat the revolution from behind their barricades of files and indictments'.

At this point, Samblancat went to inform the CNT representatives on the CCMA. They explained that they had sent the first patrol because 'that nest of vipers has to be fumigated whether the Generalitat likes it or not'. It was then suggested that he take over the Palace and they instructed him to get substantial reinforcements and return to the building to clear out 'rogues' still there. This he did and the professional jurists were evicted. The official announcement in the press at the time claimed that Samblancat had been sent to prevent uncontrolled elements destroying material archived there. Since this was far from the anarchists' intention, it is reasonable to assume that it was the cover used to secure the approval of the other members of the CCMA for the operation.[49] Several judges were murdered. The proceedings were legitimized on 17 August 1936, when the Generalitat dismissed all judicial personnel and set up a revolutionary body, known as the Oficina Jurídica, run initially and briefly by Samblancat.[50]

On 28 August, Samblancat resigned and was replaced by the anarchist lawyer Eduardo Barriobero. He declared that all crimes were social in origin and boasted of destroying hundreds of tons of judicial records from before 19 July 1936. Huge quantities of paper were burned on the sidewalk of the Passeig de Sant Joan. Barriobero claimed that he renounced a salary but was later accused of using his position to accumulate considerable wealth. He took on as assistants two members of the FAI prisoners' aid committee, José Batllé i Salvat and Antonio Devesa i Bayona, who both had prison records, having been sentenced to twelve and fourteen years respectively for armed robbery. Large amounts of money held in escrow in relation to cases under consideration simply disappeared. Certificates of anti-fascist reliability were sold. Sixty anarchist militiamen were on the payroll of the Oficina. People that they arrested had money extorted from their families for their release. Huge fines were imposed for possession of religious artefacts, the money disappearing into the pockets of Barriobero's men. According to Pons Garlandí, Barriobero worked in cahoots with Aurelio Fernández, Escorza and Eroles.[51]

During the period that Barriobero and his CNT cronies ran the justice system, the Generalitat was largely impotent in terms of public order. The only active step that it was able to take towards stopping spontaneous 'justice' was the creation, on 24 August, in each of the four Catalan provinces, of people's courts composed of three magistrates and twelve jurors from workers' unions and left-wing parties. This was partly a reaction to the central government's introduction of popular tribunals by decrees of 23 and 25 August in response to the murder of prisoners at the Cárcel Modelo of Madrid. The Generalitat's establishment of its own version, the *jurats populars*, was accepted by the CNT.[52] Their mission was initially the repression of fascism, but it was quickly expanded to include crimes of rebellion and sedition. In general, the lack of juridical training of their members meant that proceedings were often shambolic. Much time was wasted as jurors, witnesses, the accused and even the public were given free rein to speak at length. Overall, there was a tendency towards leniency. Sentences were usually extreme, either absolution or the death penalty, with most of the latter generally commuted to imprisonment.[53]

By mid-September, in response to the ineffectiveness of the dual system of power, President Companys had decided that the Central Anti-Fascist Militia Committee had to be dissolved. The fear and unpopularity generated by the Patrulles de Control made this slightly easier. Believing that the initiative should come from the CCMA itself, Companys first broached the idea with a CNT–FAI delegation consisting of Durruti, García Oliver and Aurelio Fernández. They agreed and, on 26 September, a new coalition government was formed, under Josep Tarradellas, including CNT ministers (*consellers*). This did not immediately put an end to the abuses of the patrols. In fact, because of the arrogance and sectarianism with which the CNT *consellers* behaved, they quickly provoked the enmity of other left-wing groups. In particular, the Conseller de Defensa ensured that the bulk of the arms purchased by the Generalitat ended up in anarchist hands. Similarly, the way Josep Joan i Domènech, the CNT Minister of Supply, organized the requisitioning of food provoked conflict in the Catalan countryside and the hostility of the PSUC. This would fester until it caused a mini-civil-war in Catalonia in May 1937.[54]

One of the major issues facing Tarradellas's government was the growing concern about Eduardo Barriobero's probity. In mid-September, seven Falangists had been discovered hiding in his home in Madrid. It was alleged that his wife took money to hide them. When Barriobero himself was interviewed in Barcelona, he denied all knowledge of the matter.[55] The problem was resolved when the Oficina Jurídica was dissolved on 20 November by the new Minister of Justice, Andreu Nin, the leader of the POUM, who exposed the abuses of Barriobero. Having been chosen by Tarradellas as the only man likely to be able to challenge the power of the CNT, Nin had Barriobero, Batlle and Devesa arrested and tried for theft. Evidence was discovered that they had been crossing the frontier and depositing money in French banks. Nin's achievement was to reinstate conventional justice and put an end to the arbitrary 'justice' of the CNT–FAI.[56]

The Generalitat's opposition to uncontrolled violence is further evidenced by the major investigation that was begun in April 1937 into the assassinations in the first months of the war and the clandestine cemeteries where the victims were buried. The president of the high court of Barcelona, Josep Andreu i Abelló, set up a special court and, as a result of its investigations throughout Catalonia, the corpses of many missing persons were located and their assassins identified. Among those arrested was Dionís Eroles, accused of involvement with a clandestine cemetery in Cerdanyola, although he was released on bail. Aurelio Fernández was also arrested, albeit for offences related to the extortion of individuals arrested by the patrols. There were numerous trials of those accused of murder and robbery. After the mini-civil-war in Barcelona in May 1937, witnessed by George Orwell, the CNT presented these trials as Communist revenge on the anarchists and the POUM, but they had started one month before. Moreover, on 2 August that year, FAI gunmen made an unsuccessful attempt on the life of Andreu i Abelló. Subsequent investigation suggested that Eroles was behind the attempt, although nothing was proven. Nevertheless, it is the case that atrocities committed by members of the PSUC and the Esquerra were not pursued with the same vigour as those of the anarchists. When the denunciations had come from those whose houses or land had been confiscated, the accused were released. Nevertheless, those found guilty of murder and looting were punished.[57]

Not long after the creation of Tarradellas's government, major problems quickly became apparent in the Ministry of Internal Security. The new Minister, Artemi Aiguader i Miró of the Esquerra, inherited much of the personnel of the old Departament d'Investigació of the CCMA, including Aurelio Fernández, Dionís Eroles, Manuel Escorza and Josep Asens. Inevitably, there was tension bordering on violence as Aiguader's first chief of police, Andreu Revertés i Llopart of the ERC, tried to restrain the patrols. In late November 1936, he was falsely accused of plotting against the Generalitat by Aurelio Fernández and Eroles. He was imprisoned and later murdered. Aiguader then chose as his chief of police Eusebio Rodríguez Salas, 'El Manco', a PSUC member. Rodríguez Salas was as enthusiastic as his predecessor about controlling the FAI. Aurelio Fernández physically attacked him in Aiguader's office and the Conseller himself had to intervene, pistol in hand, to prevent a serious crime. The freedom given by Eroles to the FAI patrols led to conflict with the Civil Guard.[58]

Outside Barcelona, uncontrolled terror was the norm for a brief period. The columns of anarchists who flooded from the city in requisitioned vehicles left a trail of slaughter in their wake. As they passed through towns and villages en route to Aragon, they executed anyone considered to be a fascist, which meant clergy and practising Catholics, landowners and merchants. In the province of Lleida, army officers, the Civil Guard and local right-wing groups had initially controlled the city. However, under pressure from a general strike and demoralized by news of the defeat of the rising in Barcelona, the rebels surrendered on 20 July.

The POUM was the dominant force in the province of Lleida and co-operated with the CNT and UGT in creating a Committee of Public Safety, but it did little to prevent either the destruction by fire of the majority of the city's churches or a wave of assassinations. On the night of 25 July, twenty-six army and Civil Guard officers were pulled from the local prison and shot and the Cathedral was set on fire. A Claretian priest, fourteen seminarists of the same order and a dozen civilians were also murdered. It has been suggested that this atrocity was triggered by the arrival that day of the column led by Durruti. As the dominant force in the city, the POUM appointed a shoemaker, Josep Rodés Bley, as Commissar of Public Order. When Aurelio Fernández sent an emissary to organize Patrulles de Control, the two combined to impose a wave of criminality on the city. On 5 August, twenty-one detainees, including the Bishop of Lleida, Dr Salvi Huix Miralpeix, were loaded on to a truck to be transferred to Barcelona. The truck was ambushed and they were shot in the cemetery. It has been suggested that the ambush was mounted by another column from Barcelona, 'Los Aguiluchos de la FAI' (the Young Eagles of the FAI) led by Juan García Oliver and, if anything, more violent than Durruti's men.

On the night of 20 August, seventy-three priests and religious and several civilians were shot in the cemetery. By the end of October, more than 250 people had been murdered. This was over half of all of the deaths in Lleida during the entire war. The high incidence of terror was closely related to the fact that Lleida saw considerable traffic of anarchist columns en route to the Aragon front. Several of the civilian victims had been prominent in the repression after the events of October 1934.[59] Elsewhere in the province, the POUM take-over saw harvests left to rot and factories abandoned. Those who pointed out that the economy had to be organized were denounced as reactionaries. This was particularly the case in Balaguer, to the north-east of the provincial capital, where, after murdering thirty-five people, seventeen of them on 5 August, the POUM committee seemed most concerned with leading the good life in the requisitioned homes of the wealthy.[60]

As early as 25 July, a joint declaration of the Catalan regional committee and the Barcelona Federation of the CNT had issued a statement declaring that 'It is ignoble, unworthy and detrimental to the interests of the labouring class to besmirch the triumph with looting and pillage, the arbitrary ransacking of homes and other irresponsible acts.' With either innocence or hypocrisy, it was claimed that the CNT and the FAI would impose severe measures against those caught by the Patrulles de Control committing such acts. Since such activities continued, some days later, an even more unbelievable declaration was issued to the effect that house searches, arbitrary arrests and executions had nothing to do with the CNT–FAI and were the work of those in the pay of fascists.[61]

Nevertheless, even those who were neither hypocrites nor innocents denounced the violence and the destruction unconditionally. The influential anarchist thinker Joan Peiró made a distinction between legitimate revolutionary violence and what he called 'inopportune bloodshed'. He wrote in late August 1936: 'If the cruelly exploitative bourgeoisie fall exterminated by the holy anger of the people, the neutral spectator will find therein an explanation for the killing. And the same is true if those exterminated are *caciques*, clerics devoted to extremist political activities or reactionaries. The revolution is the revolution, and it is only logical that the revolution should involve bloodshed.' Then, having justified the 'holy anger of the people', he went on to denounce those who wasted time and petrol by burning down and looting churches and the summer homes of the rich while 'the fat cats who deserve to be strung up from the lamp-posts of the riverside' get away.[62]

The views of Peiró about gratuitous violence were echoed in Tarragona, if not in Lleida. Elements of Tarragona's anti-fascist committee successfully opposed the summary execution of those considered to be fascists. Nevertheless, the fact that the Civil Guard and the Assault Guard had been posted to the battle front rendered it difficult at first to control the more bloodthirsty militiamen. Moreover, news of atrocities in the rebel zone would provoke reprisals. Nevertheless, local Esquerra Republicana, UGT and POUM leaders denounced terrorism and criminality. The atrocities committed in the town were the work of three gangs consisting of members of the Libertarian Youth and the FAI. Those of them not criminals released from jail on 22 July were unskilled, and often unemployed, manual labourers, on the margins of society. Provided with weapons, they committed acts of theft, extortion and murder in the name of revolution.[63]

The moment of what Peiró had called 'the holy anger of the people' passed and the wider needs of the war effort ensured that, by the end of August, *Solidaridad Obrera* could be found calling for an end to spontaneous violence against the perceived enemies of the people.[64] Yet that same *Solidaridad Obrera* published an article calling for the elimination of Manuel Carrasco i Formiguera, a prominent member of the Catalanist Christian Democrat party Unió Democràtica de Catalunya. He worked in the early months of the war as a legal adviser to the Finance Ministry of the Generalitat – work which would subsequently be used by the Francoists to justify his execution. In that post, he had opposed various attempts by anarchists and others to get access to the frozen bank accounts of people who had been assassinated or had gone into exile. These included the fortune of Miquel Mateu i Pla, whom the Generalitat had helped escape. In other cases, there were attempts to cash cheques that had been extorted from wealthy individuals arrested by the patrols or efforts by the committees that had confiscated businesses to get access to the funds of their owners. One such refusal, to the committee running the newspaper *Diari de Barcelona*, saw Carrasco denounced in its pages on 15 December as a fascist assassin. Two days later, an article in *Solidaridad Obrera* by Jaume Balius, a member of the FAI who was also a wealthy, and fanatical, Catalan separatist, denounced Carrasco for his Catholic faith. In fact, Carrasco was a conservative of common sense and humanity as well as a deeply pious Catholic. Balius's denunciation was effectively an invitation for him to be assassinated. On the evening following its appearance, a FAI patrol came looking for him at his home.[65] Since the authorities could not guarantee his safety, Carrasco was forced to flee his beloved Catalonia to work on behalf of the Generalitat in the Basque Country. Captured by the Francoists, Carrasco was tried and executed by firing squad on Easter Saturday, 9 April 1938.[66]

By November 1936, Peiró had hardened his line and could be found courageously denouncing the terrorism and theft which had plunged Catalonia into bestiality and brought the revolution into disrepute:

> Here, for too long, there has been no law but that of the strongest. Men have killed for the sake of killing, because it was possible to kill with impunity. And men have been murdered not because they were fascists, nor enemies of the people, nor enemies of our revolution, nor anything remotely similar. They have been killed on a whim, and many have died as a result of the resentment or grudges of their killers. When the popular violence erupted, the killers and thieves took advantage and they continue stealing and killing and bring shame on those who risk their lives at the front.

Peiró's indignation about the abuses of the revolutionary context intensified throughout the autumn of 1936. He commented that 'in certain areas around the province of Barcelona, and especially in Lleida, the scale of bloodshed has been terrifying. And how many committees around Catalonia have had to order the execution of "revolutionaries" who took advantage of the situation sometimes to steal and other times to murder in order to prevent the discovery of their theft?' Peiró believed that it was in the interests of the anarchist movement to make public denunciations of these abuses. In one of his articles he wrote of a leader of the anti-fascist committee of a village near Mataró. The individual in question had furnished his house with the proceeds of his robberies. 'This "revolutionary", who boasts of having liquidated God and the Virgin Mary, has made "his own revolution", to acquire not only furnishings worthy of a prince, but also clothes, carpets, works of art and jewellery.' For Peiró, the reason why so many were fighting and dying at the front was to eliminate theft and violence, not to encourage it. Obviously, the thieves and murderers were hardly those who could be trusted to build a new world.[67]

Nor, however, could such trust be placed in many members of the CNT–FAI. A notorious occasion when anarchist intruders from outside were resisted took place on 23 January 1937 with a bloody clash in La Fatarella, a hilltop village in the Terra Alta region of Tarragona. A long-running conflict between poor smallholders and hungry landless labourers who favoured collectivization was ignited by the arrival of elements of the FAI from Barcelona. They tried forcibly to collectivize the smallholdings of the local peasantry but were expelled by them. Claiming that the rebel fifth column had risen in La Fatarella, these anarchists called for reinforcements from Barcelona and Tarragona. Large numbers of anarchist patrols were sent from elsewhere in Tarragona and also from Barcelona – among them the group of Joaquim Aubí 'El Gordo' who ran the ghost cars of Badalona. A villager managed to telephone the Generalitat, but the various delegates sent either arrived too late or did nothing. One of them was Aurelio Fernández, and in his presence the FAI militia killed thirty of the smallholders who were opposing their policy of collectivization and sacked La Fatarella. In CNT sources, the smallholders were referred to as 'rebels' and it was falsely alleged that a monarchist uprising was being planned in the village.[68] The extremist Jaume Balius wrote: 'the revolution must purge the rearguard. We suffer from too much legalism. He who is not with the workers is a fascist and should be treated as such. Let us not forget the case of La Fatarella.'[69]

Anarchist violence was as likely to be directed against the Communists as against the clergy, the middle classes or the smallholding peasantry. The relatively ineffective efforts of the Generalitat to control the excesses of the CNT–FAI were reflected in the timidity shown by Josep Tarradellas, the first minister since the end of September. In mid-September,

President Companys told Ilya Erhenburg that he was outraged by the terror inflicted by the anarchists on the Communists and expressed surprise that the PSUC did not respond in kind.[70] However, Companys was significantly reinforced by the arrival, on 1 October, of the Russian Consul Vladimir Antonov-Ovseenko. His first report to Moscow gave the measure of the problem. He complained that the CNT was recruiting so indiscriminately that it contained ever more right-wing provocateurs and criminal elements from the lumpenproletariat. He reported that, in late July, the CNT had taken advantage of the outbreak of the war to kill over eighty workers on the pretext that they were scabs. Certainly, among them was Ramón Sales, the head of the scab union, the Sindicatos Libres.

Anarchist victims also included the president of the UGT in the port of Barcelona, Desiderio Trillas Mainé, who was shot dead on 31 July along with two others, all three members of the PSUC. The excuse used was that, being able to choose who got work on the docks, he had favoured UGT members. In fact, the motive was more to do with his opposition to a CNT port strike in January 1934.[71] Subsequently, in a village near Barbastro in Huesca, twenty-five members of the UGT were murdered by anarchists in a surprise attack. In Molins de Rei near Barcelona, workers in a textile factory went on strike in protest against arbitrary dismissals by the FAI committee. A delegation trying to take the workers' complaints to Barcelona was forced off the train. Those who did manage to get through were too frightened to return.[72]

An even more extreme example of FAI activity was the extortion of the Marist Order carried out by Aurelio Fernández. Having already suffered the deaths of fourteen of their number, senior elements of the order met with Aurelio Fernández and Eroles on 23 September 1936 to propose a ransom for the surviving members. It was agreed that, for 200,000 francs, to be paid in two instalments, their safe passage into France would be guaranteed. When the first half of the money was paid to Fernández, 117 novices were allowed to cross the frontier at Puigcerdà on 4 October, but all those over the age of twenty-one were detained. Thirty were taken to Barcelona, allegedly to join another seventy-seven monks of the order who were awaiting passage by sea to Marseilles. In fact, all 107 were held in the prison of Sant Elíes. Meanwhile, the treasurer of the order returned to Barcelona with the second instalment of the ransom. He was imprisoned and the money handed over to Aurelio Fernández. On the same evening, forty-four of the monks in Sant Elíes were shot. A brother of one of those imprisoned persuaded Aurelio Fernández to release him and then informed the Generalitat of the situation. It took an intervention by President Companys to save the lives of the remaining sixty-two. Anarchist sources have claimed that the entire operation was carried out with the complicity of Tarradellas.[73]

The bitter hostility between the CNT and the Communists fed off the fact that the anarchists hoarded substantial quantities of weaponry including machine-guns. In a report to the Comintern on 19 September, the secretary general of the French Communist Party, Maurice Thorez, claimed that, in Barcelona, 'the anarchists have seized virtually all the weapons in Catalonia and they keep them, not just for their columns, but for use against other working-class groups. Since the military insurrection, they have assassinated several Communist militants and trade unionists and committed atrocities in the name of what they call libertarian communism.' Similarly, André Marty, the Comintern overseer of the volunteers of the International Brigades, commented that the anarchists' superiority in weapons meant that, in the short term, compromise was necessary but 'we will get even with them'.[74]

Some of the most violent clashes between Communists and anarchists took place in the Valencian region. This was in part a reflection of the repressive violence that had already occurred both in the city and in many towns and villages of its three provinces. Self-styled patrols and committees had eliminated those they considered to be fascists. Many Popular Front Committees would sanction land seizures, attacks on churches or the burning of the property registries but they could not always control individuals who, as happened in Catalonia, murdered priests, landowners and municipal and judicial functionaries. Not untypical was the case of Llíria, to the north-west of Valencia, where a moderate committee found itself under threat from FAI patrols from the capital. Others in danger included smallholders who did not want their farms collectivized. Again, as in Catalonia, the killing was often done by groups from elsewhere on a reciprocal basis by those ashamed to murder people from their own town. In Castellón, the killing was shared between 'La Desesperada', a group from Izquierda Republicana, and 'Los Inseparables' of the CNT–FAI.[75]

In the fertile Valencian countryside, there had been few problems when CNT and UGT members occupied land belonging to rebel supporters, many of whom had been assassinated in the first wave of disorder. However, when the anarchists tried to impose collectivization forcibly, they were resisted by smallholders old and new. The anarchists would arrive at a village, whether in Catalonia, Aragon or Valencia, and oblige the town crier to declare 'libertarian communism' and the abolition of money and property. Thus considerable violence was provoked by CNT columns trying to impose the collectivization of land wherever they passed. Many of the members of the columns were urban workers who propounded purist anarchist aspirations without any understanding of the specific conditions of each place.

This explains the extraordinary case of the province of Zaragoza, where only forty-four of its towns and villages were in Republican territory. With 742 victims, this small area of Zaragoza, approximately one-third of the province, had the highest number of victims per capita in the Republican zone – 8.7 per cent of the population. Eight of the forty-four towns had no victims at all and a further eight between one and two. The towns with the greatest number of victims, such as Caspe, had not experienced significant social disorder before 18 July 1936 but were all ones occupied by the anarchist columns from Barcelona and Valencia. It was the militiamen of these columns who detonated the process whereby churches were set alight, clergy and right-wingers murdered and land forcibly collectivized. Most of these things, however, could not have happened without assistance from local anarchists. Victims were more likely where right-wingers had collaborated with the military coup, as was the case in Caspe, or where there had been social conflict before 18 July, as in Fabara. Where neither condition pertained, the local committee was able to ensure that there were no deaths. This was the case in Bujaraloz, Lécera, Mequinenza and Sástago, as well as many small villages. One hundred and fifty-two people of the province's 742 victims were murdered by the anarchists elsewhere, and taken to Teruel, Huesca, Lleida or Barcelona to be killed.[76]

The pattern of violence beginning when the anarchist columns arrived, sometimes with the collaboration of the local committees, was repeated in Huesca, the northernmost province of Aragon. The highest indices of anti-clerical violence were in the east. In the small town of Barbastro, the Bishop Florentino Asensio and 105 priests were murdered, 54 per cent of a total of 195. The provincial capital lost thirty-one of its 198 priests, 16 per cent of the total. In numerous villages, the parish priest was murdered after being forced to watch parodies of the Mass and offered life if he renounced God. As was not uncommon in Aragon, the bodies of murdered priests were frequently soaked in gasoline and burned.[77] In most of the province, no nuns were killed. At worst, they were threatened and obliged to leave their convents. However, at Peralta de la Sal in the east of the province, which fell in the diocese of Lleida, on 1 October 1936 three nuns were raped and murdered. Numerous lay

Catholics, including at least eight women, were assassinated by anarchists in Huesca.[78]

In the southernmost Aragonese province, Teruel, the repression was also set off by the arrival of anarchist columns. Having detained rightists and clergy identified by local militants, the leaders of the Ortiz Column would often organize a crude public trial. In communities like La Puebla de Híjar or Alcorisa, the population was obliged to assemble in the village square. Prisoners were brought out one by one on to the balcony of the town hall and the villagers asked to vote on whether they should live or die. The scale of the repression would depend on the will and determination of the local anti-fascist committee to prevent killings. In tiny villages like Azaila, Castel de Cabra and Vinaceite, the committee managed to ensure that there would be no executions. In other towns and villages such as Alcañiz, Calanda, Albalate del Arzobispo, Calaceite, Muniesa or Mora de Rubielos, the committee gave the names of those to be executed to the anarchist occupiers. In others, such as La Puebla de Valverde, the initiative came entirely from the anarchists of the notorious 'Iron Column' from Valencia (Columna de Hierro) who killed those who opposed their collectivization.[79]

Idealistically motivated collectivization was usually greeted enthusiastically by the landless labourers but met fierce resistance from smallholders. Some of the anarchist columns were accused of looting, abuse of women and large-scale theft of crops. In the villages of Valencia, growers were given worthless vouchers in exchange for requisitioned livestock. Their wheat and orange harvests were seized and taken to Valencia for export by the CNT. In late August, at Puebla de Valverde in Teruel, tens of thousands of cured hams were requisitioned 'for the revolution'. The worst culprits in looting came from the self-styled Iron Column.[80]

The origins of the Column can be traced to an earlier episode at Puebla de Valverde in late July. What happened there underlined the contrast between the naive innocence of Republican militias and what they were up against. It also goes some way to explaining the reasons for the subsequent brutality of the anarchists involved. On 25 July, a Republican expedition was organized to recover Teruel, which had been taken by a small number of rebels. Surrounded by the loyal provinces of Tarragona, Castellón, Valencia, Cuenca and Guadalajara, it was assumed, reasonably, that Teruel would succumb easily. There were two columns, one from Valencia, consisting of Carabineros (frontier guards), Civil Guards and some anarchist militia, and another from Castellón, consisting of Civil Guards and a larger number of militiamen. Overall command was entrusted to a fifty-six-year-old colonel of the Carabineros, Hilario Fernández Bujanda, who led the column from Valencia, accompanied by Major Francisco Ríos Romero of the Civil Guard. The column from Castellón was led by Francisco Casas Sala, the Izquierda Republicana parliamentary deputy for the city and, at his prompting, his friend, a retired army engineer, Major Luis Sirera Tío. In trucks and buses, 180 militiamen left Castellón at 8.15 p.m., to be followed shortly afterwards by two companies of Civil Guards.

The two columns joined together at Sagunto. Anarchist attacks on the town's churches and the properties of local right-wingers severely undermined the commitment of the Civil Guards in the columns. According to one of their officers, they were merely biding their time until they could rebel, aware that to do so in a town like Sagunto would be suicidal. They moved off at dawn on 27 July. Some hours later, they reached Segorbe, where the force was joined by more Civil Guards from the local garrison and from Cuenca. The town was entirely in the hands of the CNT–FAI. The situation there, with evidence that members of the column were stealing, clinched the determination of the Civil Guard officers to change sides as soon as an opportunity arose. Setting off towards Teruel at dawn on 28 July, the force totalled approximately 410 Civil Guards, some Carabineros and an indeterminate number of militiamen, ranging from 180 to 600. The imprecision over numbers reflects the fact that new volunteers joined and others dropped out along the way. Whatever their number, all were recent volunteers, totally untrained, and many without weapons. Among them were several local politicians from Castellón.[81]

As they neared Teruel, the columns split up. Casas Sala led one group, the bulk of the militiamen and a small contingent of Civil Guards, to capture Mora de Rubielos further to the north. Fernández Bujanda headed directly for Teruel with the Carabineros and Civil Guards and about fifty militiamen. En route, they stopped to rest overnight at the tiny village of Puebla de Valverde, south-east of Teruel. Using the excuse of looting by some of the militiamen, the Civil Guards made their move. They surrounded the resting militiamen and, in a battle lasting barely twenty minutes, murdered most of them, the Carabineros and between fifty and sixty inhabitants of the town. When the news reached Mora de Rubielos, the other column hastened to Puebla de Valverde. Casas Sala halted the trucks outside the village, believing that he could negotiate a solution. When he and Major Sirera entered the village alone, they were quickly overpowered. The bulk of the militiamen abandoned them to their fate and fled back to Castellón. On 30 July, the Civil Guards took Casas Sala, Colonel Fernández Bujanda and about forty-five other prisoners to Teruel, where they were executed without trial the following day. Their deaths were inscribed in the town registry as caused by 'internal haemorrhage'. The reinforcement of the tiny garrison at Teruel by the treacherous Civil Guards guaranteed its immediate survival for the rebels.[82]

When the survivors carried back the news of the massacre to Sagunto, there was a wave of outrage. Twelve people were murdered in the port on 21 August and a further forty-five some days later in Sagunto itself. When the Column regrouped, its members insisted that the remaining Civil Guards in the town be disarmed to prevent them fleeing to Teruel. A compromise was reached whereby their weapons were handed over and the Civil Guards placed in the custody of the Communist Party. Nevertheless, the lieutenant in command was assassinated on 23 September.[83]

According to an article in the Republican press, before the expeditionary force set out, Colonel Fernández Bujanda had stated that he wanted only officers of proven loyalty. Concerned about one of the Civil Guards, he offered him the chance to drop out. The officer refused and begged Fernández Bujanda to let him join those going to Teruel and so prove his loyalty to the Republic. Fernández Bujanda was so impressed that he placed the officer in command of the Civil Guards in the expedition. Although unnamed in the article, the officer in question was clearly Major Ríos Romero. If the story is true, it explains why, after reaching Teruel with his men, and commanding the firing squad that shot Colonel Fernández Bujanda, Ríos Romero committed suicide.[84]

The survivors of the episode at Puebla de Valverde were among those who formed the Iron Column. Founded by José Pellicer Gandía, the Column was a hard-line anarchist group. It was composed largely of construction workers and dock labourers from Valencia and metalworkers from Sagunto. However, it also included substantial numbers of common criminals who, on being released from the prison of San Miguel de los Reyes in Valencia, had been offered the chance of 'social redemption'. According to the Communist Minister Jesús Hernández, many Falangists, including the Marqués de San Vicente, took refuge in the Column. The POUM theorist Juan Andrade described the Iron Column as entirely undisciplined and consisting of both committed revolutionaries and 'shady and depraved individuals', driven by their basic instincts and an urge for vengeance. The ex-prisoners desired revenge on the society that had imprisoned them. Others sought vengeance against rebel supporters for what had happened at Puebla de Valverde.[85]

In consequence, members of the Iron Column often just left the front to go to Valencia and other towns of the region where they were responsible for wreaking terror. The criminal records of the Civil Governor's offices were burned. Policemen were murdered. The scale of robbery and vandalism committed in the Valencian rearguard by the Iron Column led both Communists and Socialists to deem it to be as much of an enemy as the fifth column. In clashes with its militants, there were numerous cases of prominent militants of the PCE and the UGT being assassinated. In late September, with the excuse of raising funds to buy arms for the front, members of the column left their posts and carried out robberies and other crimes in Castellón, Valencia and Gandía. The Bank of Spain, police headquarters, the Palace of Justice and the Treasury delegation in the provincial capital were sacked and their documentation burned. Shops, especially jewellers, were looted. Hostelries of all kinds were stripped of alcohol and cigarettes and their clients robbed. The secretary of the Valencian UGT, Josep Pardo Aracil, was murdered on 23 September. It was widely believed that the assassin was one of the more prominent leaders of the Column, Tiburcio Ariza González, 'El Chileno'.

On 2 October, the provincial prison in Castellón was assaulted by the Columna de Hierro and at least fifty-three detainees murdered. The arrival of Ricardo Zabalza as Civil Governor of Valencia in early October was a major step towards the re-establishment of order. The Republican authorities, with the support of Socialists and Communists, created the Guardia Popular Antifascista, which began to clamp down on the violence. In one bloody clash, Tiburcio Ariza was killed. Ariza had served prison sentences for drug dealing, extortion, rape, theft and running prostitutes. He was shot by UGT members of the GPA in a shoot-out when they tried to arrest him for the murder of Pardo Aracil.[86]

Ariza's funeral on 30 October saw the decisive showdown between anarchists and Communists in Valencia. The leaders of the Iron Column called on their militiamen and those of other CNT columns to abandon the front in Teruel to attend the burial of their comrade and make those responsible for his death pay. Knowing this, the authorities decided, contrary to usual practice with public funerals, to take the cortège down the narrow Plaza de Tetuán, where both the PCE offices and the local Republican military headquarters were located. A bloody battle ensued.

The Communists claimed that shots had been fired from an armoured truck that led the procession. Fire was returned by militants in the PCE building and by soldiers in the military headquarters. A later statement by the Columna de Hierro alleged that there had been a trap and that crossfire had come first from machine-guns set up in both buildings. Certainly, the memoirs of Carlos Llorens, a Communist eyewitness, suggest that the Guardia Popular Antifascista had prepared an ambush. The members of the Iron Column fled, abandoning their banners and the corpse of Tiburcio Ariza. Around thirty people were killed, either shot or else drowned trying to escape by swimming across the River Trubia. The anarchists were set on bloody revenge, but further violence was prevented when the CNT leadership, which was about to join Largo Caballero's government, persuaded the columns to return to the Teruel front. In many respects, the events of October 1936 in Valencia antici-pated what would happen in Barcelona in May 1937.[87]

In Alicante, the round-up of local right-wingers began immediately after the defeat of the uprising in the city. Many of the military personnel arrested were transferred to the prison ship *Río Sil*, whose passengers were to be murdered in Cartagena in mid-August. Corpses began to appear on beaches and in the fields. Many house searches were merely an excuse for robbery. Militia groups, and among them many recently released common criminals, were largely responsible for the wave of kill-ings and other abuses. However, the murders of several prominent Republicans indicated that Falangist hitmen were operating under cover of the prevailing confusion. As early as 28 July, the Civil Governor published an edict: 'anyone who, whether or not they belong to a polit-ical entity, carries out acts against life or property, is threatened with the immediate application of the maximum penalty, since such criminals will be regarded as rebels at the service of the enemies of the Republic'. Moreover, by the end of August, even the CNT newspaper *El Luchador* felt obliged by the 'monstrous' occurrence of house searches for theft, arrests and murders based on personal grudges to adopt an 'authoritar-ian and statist' stance and to express a determination to put an end to such abuses. It was to little avail. The biggest massacre took place on 29 November 1936 when forty-nine right-wingers were shot against the walls of the cemetery in reprisal for a bombing raid.[88]

Moving further south, in the province of Murcia, the death toll was much lower than in Valencia or Catalonia. This was a reflection of the lesser presence of the FAI. As elsewhere, the bulk of the violence took place in the early months of the war. The deaths of 84 per cent (622) of the total number of rightists killed in the city (740) took place between 18 July and 31 December 1936. Unusually, however, there were relatively few deaths in the immediate wake of the coup – eighteen in the remainder of July, only two of them in the naval port of Cartagena, the province's second city. This reflected the fact that on 21 July the Popular Front Committee issued a manifesto in which it declared: 'Those who feel and understand what the Popular Front is and what it represents at this moment, must scrupulously respect people and property.' Nevertheless, complaints about the house searches and arrests carried out by extremist militia groups saw the Popular Front Committee in Cartagena issue an edict, on 13 August, banning unauthorized house searches, the confiscation of property and arrests. It declared that anyone contravening the edict would be shot. Since the activities of the militias continued, a further edict was issue on 12 September threatening that further house searches would be punished by execution without trial.[89]

The numbers of assassinations rocketed, with over three hundred deaths in August. Most of these were of military personnel in Cartagena. The naval and army officers who had risen in Cartagena were held on a prison ship, *España No. 3*. In another, the *Río Sil*, were held the Civil Guards who had taken part in the unsuccessful uprising in Albacete. With tension building up in response to news of the massacres in the south, crowds of militiamen and sympathizers gathered daily on the quayside demanding 'justice' – in other words, their execution. While being transferred to the city's prison on the morning of 14 August, ten of the Civil Guards were murdered after provoking the crowd and then trying to escape. To prevent further assassinations, both ships put to sea. However, bloody events were triggered around 1.00 p.m. when the battleship *Jaime I* arrived in port carrying three dead and eight wounded crewmen as a result of being bombed by rebel planes in Málaga. The ship's anarchist-dominated revolutionary committee linked with the port's anarchist militias in demanding revenge. That night, the crew of the *Río Sil* threw overboard fifty-two of the nearly four hundred Civil Guards. On the *España No. 3*, ninety-four naval officers and fifty-three army, Civil Guard and Carabinero officers, 147 prisoners in total, were shot and then thrown overboard. Another five were shot the next morning.[90]

Thereafter, as will be seen below, the creation and operation of the so-called People's Courts (Tribunales Populares) gradually reduced the scale of executions. During the worst month of the war, August 1936, nearly 70 per cent of the executions were of military personnel involved in the coup. Indeed, in the worst year, 1936, more than 40 per cent of the deaths were of army and naval officers. Over the entire war, military personnel constituted 31 per cent of the total rearguard executions in Murcia, although they constituted 66 per cent of those killed in Cartagena. The next most numerous group of victims were priests and religious, around 9 per cent of the total, followed by a similar number of property-owners, industrialists and rightists in general.[91]

Rebel bombing attacks frequently led to popular reprisals in the Republican zone. In Málaga, this was a frequent occurrence in response to bombs dropped by a rebel seaplane. The city was largely in the hands of the CNT–FAI-dominated Committee of Public Safety. Approximately five hundred right-wingers had been detained by various militia groups working on its orders and were held in the city's Cárcel Nueva. These groups, which had names like 'Death Patrol', 'Dawn Patrol', 'Lightning Patrol' and 'Pancho Villa', were predominantly anarchist, and included common criminals released in the immediate wake of the uprising. On 22 August, a furious crowd gathered after thirty women, children and old people were killed and many more wounded in a bombing raid. To appease the mob, the Committee drew up a list of sixty-five prisoners, who were taken out and shot. On 30 August, after another visit from the seaplane, a further fifty-three prisoners were selected and shot; on 20 September another forty-three; the following day, a further seventeen; on 24 September ninety-seven. In fact, 25 per cent (275) of all the right-ists killed in the city of Málaga (1,110) while it remained in Republican hands met their fates in reprisals for bombing raids.[92] Similarly, the bulk of killings in both Guadalajara and Santander were in response to bomb-ing attacks on both cities.[93]

One of those murdered in Málaga was the seventy-year-old Benito Ortega Muñoz. He had been sought by FAI militiamen, who wanted revenge for the fact that he had been imposed as Mayor after the uprising of October 1934. He had gone into hiding and they had arrested his eldest son, Bernardo, who was shot when he refused to reveal his father's hiding-place. Finally, Benito was denounced by a household servant and arrested by an FAI patrol on 11 August. Even though, as Mayor, he had acted fairly, he was among those shot on 30 August despite an attempt to save him by the then Mayor, Eugenio Entrambasaguas of Unión Republicana, who made constant efforts to stop the assassinations being carried out by the various patrols. Nevertheless, when Málaga was occu-pied by the Francoists, Entrambasaguas was condemned to death and shot.[94]

The victims of the rebels in the south inevitably were those who had been prominent in the social war that had festered throughout the first half of the decade, but also included many innocent members of their families and others whose only crime was to have belonged to a union or voted for the Popular Front. In those parts of Andalusia where the coup had failed, such as Málaga, the targets of left-wing vengeance were priests, landowners and their agents, foremen and guards as well as Civil Guards, right-wing militants and army officers. In Jaén, where the rising had been defeated by the local peasantry, there were widespread land seizures and acts of revenge for the daily brutality of the previous years. As in so many places, the bulk of the killing took place in the first five months of the war and was at its height during August and September 1936. Despite public statements by successive Civil Governors, Luis Ruiz Zunón and José Piqueras Muñoz, that crimes against persons and property would be inflexibly punished, social hatred led to savage violence. In the course of September and October, in the town of Martos, to the west of the provincial capital and near the rebel-held zone, 159 rightists were murdered, including nine priests and twelve women, among them three nuns, the only ones killed in the entire province. There is evidence that some corpses were dismembered and decapitated.[95]

There were significant differences in the social structures of rural Andalusia, the Levante and Catalonia and also within those regions. Nevertheless, there were striking similarities in the origins and practice of repression. In all cases, the degree of bitterness of the pre-1936 class struggles was a key determinant of the scale of violence. Bombing raids and tales carried by terrified refugees from the rebel zone had a huge impact everywhere. In this regard, a revealing case is that of Elche near Alicante, a large town of about 46,000 inhabitants. There, the first assassination did not take place until 18 August 1936, when news of the massacre of Badajoz arrived, and the last two murders were in reprisal for a sustained bombing raid on the night of 28 November 1936. The fact that the CNT had fewer than four hundred militants in the town might account for the fact that the overall figure for extra-judicial executions in Elche, sixty-two, was very low for a town of its size. Relatively low too was the total number of clergy assassinated – four priests. The bulk of the murders have been attributed to members of the Communist Party.[96] In Alicante itself, the largest single atrocity, with thirty-six deaths, took place when the provincial prison was attacked after the sustained bombing of 28–29 November 1936. The bombing had been a deliberate, and previously announced, reprisal for the execution of José Antonio Primo de Rivera eight days earlier.[97]

The correlation between CNT–FAI strength and the nature of extra-judicial repression is far from clear. Two other towns in Alicante with similar populations of around 45,000, Orihuela and Alcoy, offer puzzling comparisons. In Alcoy, in the north of the province, where the CNT was dominant, there were one hundred murders of which twenty were clergy. Anarchist anti-clericalism saw the most important church in Alcoy not burned down but demolished stone by stone and the materials reused to build an Olympic-size swimming pool. In Orihuela, in the Socialist-dominated south of the province, the total number of assassinations was low at forty-six. Yet, despite a marginal CNT presence, as in Elche, twenty-five of those murdered were members of the clergy. The killers responsible were identified as young men not affiliated to any party, although it has been plausibly suggested that they might have been working on instructions from the Socialist Committee.[98]

In general, anti-clericalism tended to be more acute where anarchism was stronger, but there were also dramatic examples of anti-clerical violence where the PSOE was the dominant force, in Orihuela, Castilla-La Mancha and Asturias. The south-east of Toledo in Castilla-La Mancha had one of the highest indexes of extra-judicial deaths per head of the population. This contrasted with the north of the province where one hundred villages saw minimal rearguard violence, forty-seven with no deaths at all and fifty-three with between one and five. The difference is explained by the high levels of illiteracy in the south of the province and the especially conflictive social context in the large estates there. Equally dramatic were the figures for the much larger anarchist-dominated area from the south of Zaragoza, through Teruel into the Terra Alta and Priorat regions of Tarragona.[99] Nevertheless, whatever the differences and similarities, one thing remains clear. Had the basic norms of social coexistence not been torn asunder by the military coup, the bloodshed in the Republican rearguard would never have taken place on the scale seen.

Revolutionary Terror in Madrid

The military uprising, ostensibly against a non-existent Communist take-over plot, provoked a collapse of the structures of law and order. To make matters worse, in an effort to convince the Great Powers to support the Republic, the cabinet formed on 19 July was made up exclusively of middle-class liberals and thus neither respected nor, initially, obeyed by the left-wing parties and unions that defeated the uprising. An outburst of revolutionary fervour and an orgy of killing would demonstrate once more that Spain's harshly repressive society had produced a brutalized underclass. The key events that underlay the violence in Republican Madrid took place in the first two days. The opening of the prisons saw hundreds of common criminals released, among them sadists and psychopaths who were only too willing to use the political chaos as a shield for their activities. Moreover, they had ample motives to seek revenge against the magistrates and judges who had put them in jail. In fact, out of fear of reprisals or because of their sympathy with the coup, many judicial functionaries went into hiding. More than one hundred judges were murdered.[1]

A central factor in the violence was the distribution of arms in the wake of the defeat of the military uprising. On the evening of 19 July, the General in charge of the coup in the capital, Joaquín Fanjul, took command of the troops and Falangist volunteers gathered in the Montaña barracks near the Plaza de España. He was unable to lead them out because the building was surrounded by a huge crowd of civilians together with about one hundred Civil Guards and a few Assault Guards. Fanjul's men opened fire with machine-guns. Those with rifles replied. Early the following morning, an even larger crowd converged on the barracks, accompanied now by two artillery pieces, albeit with few shells. Cannon fire and a bomb dropped by a loyalist aircraft saw a white flag extended through a window. The flag may have been waved by one of the many pro-Republican soldiers among Fanjul's forces, but the crowd advanced in expectation of an immediate surrender. Many were killed or wounded when they were met by a burst of machine-gun fire. The outraged throng pulled back but, when a second white flag appeared, swarmed forward only to be greeted once more by the rattle of the machine-guns. Finally, just before noon, the now infuriated mob broke in. Weapons were distributed and a massacre ensued at the hands of the pro-Republican conscripts from within and the militiamen from outside. A giant left-winger hurled officers from the windows. Some officers committed suicide and Falangists who had joined the rebels inside were shot.[2]

On that brilliantly sunny Monday morning, 20 July, an English nurse, Mary Bingham de Urquidi, saw defeated soldiers being shot while a baying crowd howled abuse. She counterpointed her gruesome tale with evidence of the humanity of some of the Republicans. She saw a ten-year-old boy beg for the life of his father who was about to be shot. His plea that he and his father were Republicans was successful. The mob was moved on by Republican soldiers and numerous corpses could be seen. Mary Bingham seemed unaware that many of the bodies were of Republican civilians killed while attacking the barracks.[3] In contrast, the firmly pro-rebel Ambassador of Chile, Aurelio Núñez Morgado, described the events at La Montaña as 'the start of the Madrid massacre'. Certainly many of the weapons distributed when the barracks was taken would be used over the next five months in the repression.[4]

In the course of 19 July, some churches were burned, often because rebel supporters had been storing arms there and now had fired from the towers on groups of workers. Other churches were left intact because their parish priest had opened them and invited the militiamen to see that there were no fascists inside. The art treasures therein were thus saved.[5] In the first few days, what was called 'popular justice' was meted out spontaneously and indiscriminately against anyone denounced as a rightist. However, in Madrid, as had happened in Barcelona and Valencia, virtually every left-wing political party and trade union soon established its own squads, the *checas*, to eliminate suspected fascists. At headquarters set up in requisitioned buildings, they often had private prisons where detainees were interrogated. Executions usually took place on the outskirts of the city. In Madrid, there were nearly two hundred of these squads, if those set up by recently freed common criminals are included. The principal *checas* run by left-wing parties and unions numbered about twenty-five.[6] Considered to be warriors in the social war, criminals were often accepted into anarchist rearguard militias. Although far from having a monopoly of the worst excesses, the anarchists were the most prominent in the bloodshed in Madrid. Their *checas* often took the names given respectively to CNT and PCE neighbourhood headquarters and cells – the anarchists using 'Libertarian Atheneum' and the Communists using the name 'Radio'.

The ability of the forces of order to control the *checas* was severely circumscribed. Many policemen, Assault Guards and Civil Guards supported the military rebellion and had either crossed the lines or else been arrested. Many others were often suspect, and the Assault Guards and Civil Guards who remained loyal had to be deployed at the front. The consequent decimation of the various police forces facilitated the activities of the rearguard militia groups. Nevertheless, the government began almost at once to take faltering steps to put a stop to the theft, extortion and murder being committed by some *checas*, although it would be five months before anything like full control was established. The new Minister of the Interior, General Sebastián Pozas Perea, had been Inspector General of the Civil Guard until 19 July. He had worked frantically, albeit in vain, to limit the spread of the rebellion within the corps.[7] Now he worked equally hard and equally unsuccessfully to stop the *checas* carrying out arrests and house searches.[8]

The targets of the self-appointed *checas* and militia groups were not only the active supporters of the military coup. Many totally innocent individuals were arrested and sometimes murdered, as one middle-class detainee wrote later, simply for owning a business, for having opposed a strike, for having expressed support for the suppression of the Asturian rising, for belonging to the clergy or 'for being rude to the maid's boyfriend or to the lout of a doorman'. Concierges would often tip off a *checa* on the basis of the arrival of an unknown visitor or an unusual package, or because an occupant of the building never left home. Suspicion was enough.[9] Antonio Machado, the fervently pro-Republican poet, was arrested in the early days of the war in a café in the Glorieta de Chamberí because a militiaman mistook him for a priest.[10]

The Consul of Norway, the pro-rebel German Felix Schlayer, compiled a similar list of likely innocent victims of the *checas*, adding landowners resident in Madrid murdered by labourers from their estates and eccentric aristocrats, too old to have played any part in the uprising. Henry Helfant, the commercial attaché of the Romanian Embassy, considered that Schlayer was pro-Nazi.[11] Although Schlayer collaborated with the fifth column, passing information about troop movements to the rebels besieging the capital and, after leaving Republican Spain, spending time in Salamanca, he was a valuable eyewitness. One of the names on his list was that of the last descendant of Christopher Columbus, the Duque de Veragua, whose murder by an unknown *checa* sent shockwaves around the Latin American embassies. As in the rebel zone, denunciations were often motivated by nothing more than a desire to avoid a debt or by sexual jealousy. Crimes of theft and murder were frequently committed in the name of revolutionary justice. Often corpses were found with notes pinned to their clothing bearing the words 'Justicia del Pueblo'.[12]

Some responsibility for the violence must fall on a significant part of the anarcho-syndicalist leadership. At the end of July, the principal anarchist daily in Madrid, *CNT*, carried the banner headline 'Popular Justice. The Fascist Murderers Must Fall'. The passionate article went on to dismiss the Republican authorities as if they were as much the enemy as the rebels:

> Faced with a judiciary and courts that stink of rot and whose spirit and whose laws are purely bourgeois, the people must take control of justice for itself ... the Republic was and is bourgeois, strictly conservative and authoritarian. Having survived the events that we have just survived, and with the popular forces in the street, with the weapons of their free will in their hands, there is no other law and no other authority than that of the people. This is justice: what the people want, what the people order, what the people impose. The Spanish people must smash its enemies, both at the front and in the rearguard. We must destroy the thousand-year-old enemy who hides in the administration, in the laws of the State, in the banks and in the management of companies. The murderers of the people have to fall! They pululate in industry, in commerce, in politics, in the courts. That is where fascism hides ... it is necessary to purify with fire. Exactly. We must burn much, MUCH, in order to purify everything.[13]

As in Barcelona, for many anarchists in the capital, destruction of churches and the assassination of the representatives of the old order, whether clergy, police or property-owners, were steps towards the creation of a new world. Overall control of CNT groups, both front-line militias and rearguard *checas*, was exercised in Madrid by the CNT–FAI Defence Committee. Its secretary and mastermind was a twenty-eight-year-old waiter from Jaca in Huesca, Eduardo Val Bescós, who had overall control of the militas and the *checas*. The volatile Amor Nuño Pérez, secretary of the Madrid Federation of the CNT, ran the *checas* on a day-to-day basis. Manuel Salgado Moreira ran the investigation units.

Cipriano Mera commanded front-line militia units which operated out of the Cine Europa, headquarters of one of the most notorious *checas*. The CNT militia units that controlled the roads out of Madrid were under the direct command of Eduardo Val.[14]

Before the Civil War, the intelligent and elusive Val – 'as silent as a shadow', in the words of a comrade – had run the CNT–FAI 'action groups' in Madrid. This fact was not known by most of the rest of the anarcho-syndicalist leadership. Indeed, according to both Durruti's close friend Ricardo Sanz and Gregorio Gallego, the leader of the regional organization of the Federación de Juventudes Libertarias (the anarchist youth movement), Val was as little known at the end of the war as he had been before 1936. Gallego wrote of the taciturn Val:

> Professionally, he was an elegant waiter, smiling and amiable. When, in evening dress, he served table in the great political banquets organized at the Ritz and Palace hotels, nobody suspected that behind his gentle, slightly ironic smile lurked the man who pulled the secret strings of the terrorist groups. By nature, he was mysterious, elusive and little given to revealing anything. Many militants accused him of being a chameleon and there were those who thought he had bourgeois aspirations because of his stylish way of dressing and his refined manners. Nevertheless, as soon as the war started, he squeezed himself into a pair of overalls and the elegant cove turned himself into a scruffy wretch. Was it just another mask to permit him to pass unnoticed? I think so, because he got through the war without anyone really knowing him … Upon this man, fiercely private, secretive, more violent and daring than anyone could imagine, rested the security of the Castilian CNT.[15]

Some anarchists were appalled by the *paseos* (people 'being taken for a ride' that culminated in their murder), but many others favoured the elimination of enemy supporters both as an opportunity to build a new world and as a necessary part of the war effort. For most elements of the Popular Front, the annihilation of the enemy within was a central wartime imperative. *Política*, the daily newspaper of Azaña's middle-class party Izquierda Republicana, expressed outrage that rightists had been released because some Republican had intervened on their behalf. Arguing that neither friendship nor family ties should hinder the purging of the rearguard, the paper threatened to publicize the names of those involved in future cases.[16] The Communists and the anarchists were both ruthless in wanting to root out the enemy within. Eventually, however, the Communists would come to see the anarchists as damaging the war effort and would turn on them, somewhat later than in Barcelona, and thus open a new phase of the repression.

More urgent incitements to violence came in the form of bombing raids and news of atrocities committed by the rebels. Both the bombings and the tales of the refugees were pervasively toxic in their effects, producing outbursts of mass fury that the Republican authorities were often unable to contain. In Madrid, on the night of 7 August, in reprisal for the first bombing raid, a number of rightist prisoners were assassinated. In response to the violence in general and to these murders, the moderate Socialist Indalecio Prieto made a much publicized radio broadcast. Prieto was effectively prime minister in the shadows from 20 July to 4 September while apparently serving merely as adviser to the cabinet led by the liberal Republican Professor José Giral. From a large office in the Navy Ministry, he worked untiringly to give direction to the shambles that was Giral's government. On 8 August, he declared:

> Even if the terrible and tragic reports about what has happened and is still happening in areas dominated by our enemies are really to be believed, even if day after day we receive lists of the names of comrades, of beloved friends, whose commitment to an ideal ensured their death at the hands of traitors, do not, I beg you, I entreat you, do not imitate their behaviour. Meet their cruelty with your pity, meet their savagery with your mercy, meet the excesses of the enemy with your generous benevolence. Do not imitate them! Do not imitate them! Be better than them in your moral conduct! Be better than them in your generosity.[17]

Prieto referred to this broadcast in a speech made in Chile near the end of the war: 'I ask you to show me a single word of mercy pronounced by the rebels. I ask you to show me, if there are none from the military rebels, words of mercy from the civilian elements that supported the insurgency. And lastly, I ask, with even more justification, that you show me, because I don't know of any, a single word, similar to mine, pronounced in public before the bloodthirsty crowds, by a representative of the Catholic Church in the Francoist zone.'[18] Felix Schlayer later testified to Prieto's efforts to stop the violence.[19] One way in which the Republic tried to save lives was its tolerance of the questionable legality with which several embassies, including Schlayer's, rented buildings in which refuge was given – sometimes at a price – to rebel supporters. Similarly, efforts to permit those under threat to leave Spain had no equivalent on the rebel side.[20] After the war, the only embassy to offer asylum to defeated Republicans was that of Panama. It was raided by Falangists and those who had sought asylum therein were seized.

Prieto's appeal on 8 August was supported by Socialists and Republicans of the centre-left who also expressed concern that round-ups by extremist militiamen were netting respectable citizens. However, it fell on deaf ears as far as most of the left was concerned.[21] This was especially true of the Socialist youth who were drawing ever closer to the Communist Party. They had been attacking Prieto since 1934. Now, one of the most prominent adult followers of Largo Caballero, Carlos Baraibar, editor of the left-Socialist daily *Claridad*, published a firm editorial two days after Prieto's speech, with the title 'About a Speech. Neither brothers nor compatriots'. In it, while recognizing Prieto's generosity and good faith, he argued that it was impossible to regard as brothers those who had taken up arms against the Republic and were murdering workers in order to enslave them in a dictatorship. He referred to 'the feudal landowners, the warlike and anti-Christian clergy, the military barbarians who lead the campaign, the pseudo-intellectuals who justify them, and the bankers who finance them'.[22]

On the same day, in the Communist Party daily, Dolores Ibárruri replied to Prieto in similar terms:

> We must exterminate them! We must put an end once and for all to the threat of a coup d'état, to military intervention! There has been too much blood spilt for us to forgive while the horrendous crimes, the multiple murders committed coldly, sadistically weigh on us like blocks of lead … We must not agree to a single one being pardoned; and if at any time we should feel weakness then let the memory of our comrades burned alive, of the children murdered, of the men mutilated, be the spur that strengthens us in the hard but necessary work of liquidating the enemies of democracy and the Republic.[23]

Similar sentiments emanated from the Communists' militia, the so-called Fifth Regiment. Under the headline 'Pity? Mercy? No!', its mouthpiece, *Milicia Popular*, declared: 'The struggle against fascism is a battle of extermination. Pity would be an encouragement to the fascist bandits. Where they pass, they sow death, sorrow, misery. They rape our women. They burn our houses … Pity? Mercy? No; a thousand times no.'[24]

One of Prieto's closest allies, Julián Zugazagoitia, the editor of *El Socialista*, decided not to print personal accusations of the kind that in the anarchist press often led to assassinations. 'We worked', he wrote later, 'to build up popular confidence and to strengthen the authority of the government.' Marcelino Domingo, the president of Azaña's moderate Izquierda Republicana, was interviewed in *Milicia Popular*. Pointing out that the international standing of the Republic was in the hands of the militiamen, he said that they must establish a reputation 'for their daring but also for their civic feelings; for their determination to annihilate the enemy on the field of battle but also for their religious respect for the rights of the adversary when he is no longer a combatant but a prisoner … It is important for each militiaman to have medals for heroism on his chest but it is even more important that he be able hold his head high and show that his hands are clean.' The impact of his words was no doubt diluted by the details of rebel atrocities reported elsewhere in the paper.[25]

There were no such ambiguities in the rebel zone where the working class and the liberal bourgeoisie were either exterminated or terrified into near total passivity. In contrast, despite the crisis of state authority provoked by the military coup and the consequent extra-judicial abuses, the Republican authorities tried to curb extremist atrocities and to rebuild the state. The militias of the most left-wing parties and trade unions were determined to annihilate the representatives of the Church, the army, the upper class and the non-liberal bourgeoisie. In other words, they aimed to create a revolutionary society to combat the military/fascist state. However, the Republican establishment and the bulk of the Socialist and Communist parties stood out against it because they understood that the Republic needed the backing of the Western democracies and that required law and order. Accordingly, they tried to recreate the structures that would permit a multi-class democracy. However, the determination of the extremists rendered the task immensely difficult.

There was widespread terrorism for a period of about five months which gradually diminished over the subsequent four months. Hatred of the clergy was fanned by evidence of the exorbitant wealth of the Church and also by examples of clergy seen fighting on the rebel side.[26] There were frequent reports in the Republican press about the wealth found during searches of monasteries, convents and other ecclesiastical properties. In early August, it was claimed that, when the Bishop's palace in Jaén was searched, 8 million pesetas in cash was found. When the Bishop's sister, Teresa Basulto Jiménez, was arrested, she allegedly had 1 million pesetas concealed in her corsets. On 18 August, it was reported that in the offices of the Madrid diocese there had been found nearly 17 million pesetas' worth of government bonds and a further million in cash and jewels. The following day, a search of the Madrid branch of Credit Lyonnais discovered two safe-deposit boxes belonging to the Sisters of Charity of St Vincent de Paul – sometimes known as the Little Sisters of the Poor. They contained 340,000 pesetas in cash, 60 million pesetas' worth of shares, the deeds of ninety-three properties in Madrid worth another 100 million pesetas, a quantity of gold ingots and three kilos of gold coins, some of great numismatic value. One day later, it was reported that, in a Carmelite convent in the Calle de Góngora in Madrid, works of art worth 1 million pesetas had been found.[27]

Reports of exorbitant ecclesiastical wealth were based on claims from the militia groups carrying out the searches. They further intensified popular anti-clericalism by confirming age-old clichés. A similar boost came from the belief that, in the early days of the rising, Church premises were used by rebel supporters to store weapons and also as a refuge from which snipers could operate. A moderate Republican army officer, José Martín Blázquez, claimed that six monks fired on the crowd from the church tower in the Montaña barracks.[28] The Civil Governor of Almería, Juan Ruiz Peinado Vallejo, recalled that, on 23 July, his offices were fired on from a nearby monastery by three priests.[29] In general, however, outside of Navarre, there is only limited evidence of priests taking part in fighting.

Despite dogged international propaganda about nuns being molested, there is substantial anecdotal evidence of nuns being protected. The English nurse Mary Bingham recounted examples of nuns being looked after by Assault Guards. Many nuns had been arrested in the first days when militiamen had entered the convents. Jesús de Galíndez, of the Basque Nationalist Party's delegation in Madrid, found little difficulty in securing their release and finding safe refuge for them. There were cases of convents and their cloistered nuns being 'socialized', by which they were left to function as before except that, alongside the mother superior, there was a supervisor named by the authorities and their work consisted of making uniforms and blankets.[30]

The official stance of the CNT was that nuns should not be molested in any way but that their communities were to be dissolved. The nuns thereby 'liberated' should work in collectivized workshops or as nurses in military hospitals. They could also choose protective detention in prison or return to live with family members. There were cases of ex-nuns marrying their 'liberators'.[31] When Cardinal Gomá returned to Toledo after the city fell to the rebels, he found his cellar drunk dry and his crucifixes damaged. However, the nuns who served in the episcopal palace assured him that they had been well treated during the two months that it had been occupied by thirsty militiamen.[32]

The collapse of the apparatus of the state inevitably facilitated violence of all kinds, whether in the name of revolutionary justice or of personal satisfaction. In Madrid, as elsewhere, the judiciary was bypassed by 'revolutionary' tribunals spontaneously set up by political parties, trade unions or individual militia groups. Because of the frequency of the *paseos*, as early as 28 July the Portuguese Chargé d'Affaires reported that the corpses left in the streets of Madrid were provoking fears of an epidemic.[33]

Prominent among those in danger of losing their lives in the Republican zone were army officers who had taken part in the failed coup. That was the usual punishment for mutiny. However, they were not the only ones at risk. The potential stance of all officers was being investigated by a rapidly created committee under the presidency of Captain Eleuterio Díaz-Tendero Merchán. A Socialist and a Freemason, and somewhat embittered by his being only a captain at the age of fifty-four, he was one of the founders of the Unión Militar Republicana Antifascista, of which he became president. In the spring of 1936, he had built up a file-card system on the officer corps which included the conspirators' own lists of officers they could trust not to betray their plans. Now, on the basis of the file-cards and interviews, the committee classified officers by an A (anti-fascist), R (Republican), I (indifferent) or F (fascist). Those classified as 'fascist' or as 'indifferent' and refusing to fight for the Republic were arrested.[34] In prison, they were given the opportunity to recant their rightist views, fulfil their oath of loyalty and fight against the rebels. Few accepted the chance and, guilty of mutiny, virtually guaranteed their own eventual execution.[35]

The trial of the leading rebels in Madrid, General Joaquín Fanjul and Colonel Fernández de la Quintana, began on 15 August in the Cárcel Modelo, in the presence of foreign journalists and photographers. The judge was the distinguished jurist and acting president of the Supreme Court Mariano Gómez González, who had presided at the trial of General Sanjurjo in 1932. Scrupulously fair, Gómez ensured that due legal process was observed at Fanjul's trial.[36] Fanjul, himself a trained lawyer, undertook his own defence. His defence was that he was obeying the orders of General Mola. When it was pointed out that Mola was not his superior officer, Fanjul admitted that, in obeying such orders, he had recognized Mola's position as head of the military uprising. One of the witnesses against him was Ricardo Zabalza, who had found the declaration of martial law signed by Fanjul at the press where it had been printed. Fanjul and Fernández de la Quintana were both found guilty and sentenced to death on 16 August. They were executed at dawn the following day. The anarcho-syndicalist newspaper *CNT* thundered: 'The shooting of these military traitors symbolizes the death of an entire class. What a pity that this is no more than a metaphor!'[37]

A victim of the popular rage fuelled by such inflammatory journalism was General Eduardo López Ochoa, commander of government forces in Asturias in 1934. After the Popular Front electoral victory, he was arrested, accused of ordering the execution without trial of twenty civilians in the Pelayo barracks in Oviedo. These charges were never proven. Far from being a rightist, López Ochoa was loathed by the military conspirators as a Freemason, for having negotiated with the Asturian miners in order to avoid bloodshed and for ordering exemplary punishment for those members of Yagüe's African columns guilty of atrocities.[38]

López Ochoa was awaiting trial in the military prison in Burgos until, in the late spring, his wife had secured his transfer to the Hospital Militar in Carabanchel in the south of Madrid. For his role in Asturias, the Republican authorities expelled him from the army on 11 August, news of which may have triggered his death. On the next day, the Madrid anarchist daily, *CNT*, published an editorial demanding that the leaders of the failed coup in Barcelona, Generals Manuel Goded and Álvaro Fernández Burriel, be shot. The headline, 'The People's Justice. There can be mercy for no one', could well have been a reply to Prieto's earlier appeal. The article declared that 'this is no time for Christian sentiments which were only ever applied to the high-flying evil-doers in cahoots with the Church and never to the people'.[39]

The government tried to have General López Ochoa transferred to somewhere safer but was prevented twice by anarchists surrounding the hospital. A third attempt, on 17 August, saw him being taken out in a coffin drugged with morphine to appear dead, when the ruse was discovered. He was later alleged to have been dragged from the coffin by an anarchist called Manuel Muñoz de Molino and shot in the gardens of the hospital. His head was severed and carried around the streets on a pole, with a card reading: 'This is the butcher of Asturias'.[40] When one of the many militiamen accused of being involved was interrogated after the war, he claimed, almost certainly having been tortured to do so, that they were acting on the orders of the Ministry of War. The Chilean

Ambassador, Aurelio Núñez Morgado, had been informed that López Ochoa was in danger but reached the military hospital in Carabanchel too late. Núñez Morgado later made the utterly baseless claim that General Pozas had authorized the handing over of López Ochoa to his eventual assassins, members of the Libertarian Atheneum of Carabanchel.[41]

On the same day as the murder of López Ochoa, a much greater atrocity took place. In Jaén, with the provincial prison bursting at the seams, other captured right-wingers were held in the Cathedral. There were around eight hundred prisoners bunking down in the various naves and chapels. The problems of feeding them were acute and trucks bringing them food were regularly attacked. They had every reason to fear for their lives. Already on the night of 30 July, forty-eight right-wingers had been massacred by an armed mob that assaulted the prison at Úbeda. The Civil Governor, Luis Ruiz Zunón, was anxious to avoid similar bloodshed in Jaén itself. Ruiz Zunón secured permission from the Director General of Prisons in Madrid, Pedro Villar Gómez, himself from Jaén, to transfer several hundred to the prison at Alcalá de Henares. However, Manuel Muñoz Martínez, the Director General of Security, claimed, when interrogated in 1942, that he had not been informed of the plan and therefore had been unable to arrange adequate security.

At dawn on 11 August, a first expedition of 322 detainees from the provincial prison were taken in trucks to the railway junction at Espelúy north of the capital where they were put on a train. It would appear that someone in Jaén tipped off extremists further north that the train was coming. At each station along the way, stones and insults were hurled by hostile mobs. On reaching Atocha station in the capital, eleven of the prisoners, prominent landowners and right-wing figures including two priests, were murdered. The remaining 311, a third of whom required medical attention, reached Alcalá de Henares. Early in the morning of the following day, there was a second expedition of 245 captives from the Cathedral and from the recently conquered town of Adamuz (north-east of Córdoba). Among them was the sixty-seven-year-old Bishop of Jaén, Manuel Basulto Jiménez, his sister Teresa and the Dean of the Cathedral chapter, Felix Pérez Portela.

When the train reached the station of Santa Catalina Vallecas in the south of Madrid, it was stopped by anarchist militiamen who uncoupled the locomotive. The station master and the commander of the Civil Guard escort telephoned the Director General of Security, Manuel Muñoz, and told him that the anarchists had set up three machine-guns and threatened to shoot the Civil Guards if they did not leave. Muñoz allowed the Civil Guards to leave because, he claimed later, the government's authority was a fiction that would crumple if the forces of order were overwhelmed in a clash with the armed people. When the guards withdrew, 193 of the prisoners were executed in groups of twenty-five. In the course of the carnage, the Bishop fell to his knees and began to pray. His sister, Teresa Basulto, shouted at one of the militiamen, 'This is an outrage. I'm just a poor woman.' 'Don't worry,' he replied, 'we'll get a woman to shoot you,' and she was shot by an anarchist named Josefa Coso. Two days later, devastated by the denouement of an initiative intended to avoid bloodshed, Luis Ruiz Zunón resigned as Civil Governor.[42] A further 128 prisoners were seized from the provincial prison of Jaén between 2 and 7 April 1937 and shot in reprisal for a series of rebel bombing raids.[43]

The assassination of López Ochoa and of the prisoners from Jaén revealed the scale of the task facing the Republican authorities. The Director General of Prisons, Pedro Villar Gómez, a moderate Republican, was as affected as Ruiz Zunón by 'the trains of death'. Overwhelmed by atrocities being committed in the prisons of Madrid by militiamen who freed and armed common prisoners and abducted rightists, he resigned in September. As a landowner in Quesada in the east of Jaén, he had seen his own property confiscated. Moreover, his son Bernardo Villar was an artillery captain who had joined the military rebels in Córdoba. Perceiving himself to be hated by both sides, Villar Gómez went into exile in France. His absence was just one more factor in the subsequent escalation of the outrages in the capital's prisons.[44]

Juan García Oliver, the anarchist who was to become Minister of Justice in November 1936, justified atrocities on the grounds that 'the military uprising destroyed all social restraints because it was carried out by those classes that usually maintained the social order. Accordingly, efforts to re-establish a legal equilibrium saw the spirit of justice revert to its most distant and pure form: the people: *vox populi, suprema lex.* And the people, while the abnormality continued, created and applied its own law and procedure, the *paseo*.'[45] Uncontrolled acts of reprisal and revenge, responses to offences real and imagined, were not confined to high-profile atrocities like the murders of López Ochoa or of the passengers on the train from Jaén. Corpses found strewn along roadsides at dawn were the gruesome products of midnight *paseos* which could equally have been the work of militia patrols or of private enterprise hoodlums.

Both General Sebastián Pozas Perea and Manuel Blasco Garzón, who, on 19 July, became respectively Ministers of the Interior and of Justice, were simply swamped by the enormity of the task facing them. At the end of July, the Director General of Security, José Alonso Mallol, resigned in frustration at the impotence of the apparatus of the state to prevent uncontrolled criminals and militia groups taking the law into their own hands.[46] To replace Alonso Mallol, Pozas had turned to the forty-eight-year-old Manuel Muñoz Martínez, a retired army major from Chiclana just outside Cádiz. Muñoz had represented Cádiz in the Cortes as a Left Republican deputy.[47] Described by the Chilean diplomat Carlos Morla Lynch as 'tall and terse, very dark, very hard and very obstinate', he was, by most accounts, a mediocre individual.[48] He was also distracted by fears for his own family in Cádiz.

When Muñoz first went to the Dirección General de Seguridad (DGS – Security Headquarters), he found the building completely deserted. Attempting to rebuild the apparatus of law and order, Muñoz faced the unreliability of the police, the Civil Guard and the Assault Guards. Those that could be relied upon were needed at the front.[49] An indication of the consequent impotence was his ineffectual announcement that *porteros* (concierges) would be held responsible for any searches and arrests carried out in their buildings by unauthorized personnel.[50]

Muñoz's basic problem in trying to rebuild his department's central role in public order was that every party and trade union had squads that autonomously carried out house searches, arrests and executions. The most numerous and the most disorganized were the anarchist ones. The one run by the Madrid branch of the Socialist Party was more efficient and was soon given official status. It was known as the CIEP because it used the file-card system built up by the party's Electoral Information Committee (Comisión de Información Electoral Permanente). Its principal leaders, who went on to play important roles, were Julio de Mora Martínez and two professional policemen who were also Socialists, Anselmo Burgos Gil and David Vázquez Baldominos. Julio de Mora would later become head of the Departamento Especial de Información del Estado (DEDIDE – Special State Intelligence Department). Burgos Gil would lead the bodyguards of the Soviet Ambassador. In June 1937 Vázquez Baldominos would be made chief of police in Madrid.[51]

Aware of their own impotence and in a first desperate attempt to regain some vestige of control, General Pozas and Muñoz agreed that it was necessary to get the left-wing parties and unions involved in supporting the DGS. The result was the creation on 4 August of the

Comité Provincial de Investigación Pública. Muñoz's declared objective was 'to contain the assassinations and excesses being committed in Madrid because of the lack of authority and control over the armed masses'. The scale of the problem was revealed when, four days later, Enrique Castro Delgado, the commander of the most highly disciplined militia unit, the Communist Fifth Regiment, was obliged to announce that any of its members found to have carried out unauthorized arrests and/or house searches would be expelled.[52] It was perhaps no coincidence that two battalions of the Fifth Regiment shared the premises of the most important Communist *checa*, known as 'Radio 8'.[53]

By creating the Comité Provincial de Investigación Pública (CPIP), Muñoz was placing law and order in the capital in the hands of a committee composed of thirty representatives of the left-wing parties and trade unions. It was dominated by the CNT–FAI, whose representatives were Benigno Mancebo Martín and Manuel Rascón Ramírez. They would later acquire notoriety for their role in the *sacas* – the removal and subsequent assassination of prisoners. The same was true of Arturo García de la Rosa, the representative of the Communist-dominated United Socialist Youth (Juventudes Socialistas Unificadas). These poachers turned gamekeepers operated initially out of the Círculo de Bellas Artes located in the capital's great Calle Alcalá at number 42. At the first meeting, Muñoz said that he simply could not trust the staff of the DGS and that, once it had been properly purged of rebel supporters, he would bring in members of the CPIP as 'provisional police officers' to fill the gaps. Nevertheless, his statement that all arrests must be made in collaboration with the police was rejected out of hand by some delegates, who made it clear that they reserved the right to shoot those considered 'indisputably fascist and dangerous'. Muñoz was alleged to have smiled and to have said that some things did not need to be spelled out.

The Committee designated six tribunals to function round the clock with two of them working eight-hour shifts each day. These tribunals, under the overall supervision of Benigno Mancebo and consisting of men without any legal training or experience, sometimes themselves criminals, undertook the arrest, trial and sentencing of suspects. The men responsible for arresting suspects were able, with credentials provided by the DGS, to enter any premises, seize any property they considered questionable and arrest anyone they thought suspicious. Mancebo made decisions on the basis of statements from the employees or domestic servants of those detained. He was merciful with those said to have treated their staff well. Those found guilty by these tribunals would be taken to prison. Often, militiamen from the Committee or some independent *checa* would go to the prisons with an order of liberation on DGS notepaper. As the man left the prison, usually between midnight and dawn, he would be picked up by militiamen, driven away and shot. Among those given DGS badges and identification papers were common criminals such as the notorious Felipe Emilio Sandoval Cabrerizo, a fifty-year-old anarchist who used the sobriquet 'Dr Muñiz'.[54]

Not long after the creation of the CPIP, Muñoz was so concerned by the continuing wave of *paseos* that he turned to the CNT leadership for help. He was particularly appalled by the spectacle of large numbers of corpses being found each morning in the Pradera de San Isidro, the popular park to the south-west of the city. Muñoz knew that David Antona, the secretary of the Regional CNT, was hostile to the *paseos*. Through Antona, he was able to meet some young CNT leaders, including Gregorio Gallego, in the hope of securing their help in putting an end to the *paseos*. They told him it was impossible since that would involve them taking on their own comrades from the CPIP and the other *checas*. When Gallego discussed the meeting with Eduardo Val and Amor Nuño, who ran the anarchist *checas*, Val was critical of uncontrolled violence, but he may have been making a distinction between that and the violence that he did control. Nuño expressed approval of the *paseos*, saying 'instant justice strengthens the revolutionary morale of the people and commits it to the life-and-death struggle in which we are involved'.[55]

On occasions, Muñoz would telephone the Círculo de Bellas Artes to order the arrest of a given individual, only for the anarchists to refuse. With ample reason not to trust the anarchists of the CPIP, Manuel Muñoz assigned to the Dirección General de Seguridad two somewhat more reliable armed units which would operate largely, although not exclusively, on his own orders. One such squad, consisting mainly of Assault Guards, was headed by Captain Juan Tomás de Estelrich. Thanks to an imaginative journalist of *Heraldo de Madrid*, the squad came to be known as 'Los Linces de la República' (the Lynxes of the Republic). Operating out of the ex-royal palace, it was used, on the specific orders of the DGS, for the arrest of named individuals and the confiscation of valuables. Many of its operations took place in small towns and villages outside Madrid in the provinces of Toledo and Ávila, where they shot local rightists. The unit would de dismantled in December 1936. After the war, several of its members were accused of murdering some of those arrested.[56]

The other group was known as the 'Escuadrilla del Amanecer' (the Dawn Squad) because of its practice of arrests and house searches from 1.00 a.m. until dawn. Like the Lynxes, it consisted mainly of Assault Guards, although it was more directly responsible to Muñoz and operated out of the DGS.[57] It made important arrests such as those of the great liberal politician Melquíades Álvarez and Dr José María Albiñana, who had founded the diminutive Spanish Nationalist Party in 1930. It acquired a reputation for its ruthlessness and often worked in collaboration with the CPIP and some of the anarchist *checas*, including the group led by the notorious killer Felipe Sandoval at the Cine Europa.[58] After the war, members of the Escuadrilla del Amanecer were tried for theft, murder and sexual crimes. The most notorious case was that of María Dolores Chicharro y Lamamié de Clairac, the nineteen-year-old daughter of a Carlist. Despite her family's beliefs, Dolores's only crime seems to have been her beauty. She was arrested in April 1937, gang-raped and then murdered in the Casa de Campo.[59]

Obviously, the overlap between police and parallel police organizations opened up considerable opportunities for corruption and abuse. The wages of those who worked in the CPIP were paid from money confiscated during house searches. Three weeks after its creation, the CPIP was obliged to issue a statement insisting that no unauthorized house searches were to be carried out, that only weapons, compromising documents and valuables of use to the war effort were to be confiscated and that everything taken was to be handed in to the CPIP.[60] Accordingly, all the left-wing political parties and unions jointly announced that detentions or house searches could be carried out only by agents or militiamen carrying documentation from the DGS or the CPIP. Citizens were instructed to denounce to the authorities any attempts at either without such authorization.[61]

As might have been expected, this did not deter some of the groups ostensibly undertaking security functions, even those linked to the CPIP. In part to counter the disproportionate anarchist influence in the CPIP, on 5 August General Pozas ordered the reorganization of the criminal investigation section of the police, the Cuerpo de Investigación y Vigilancia. As a result, about one hundred men, the majority Socialists, were sworn in as temporary police officers. On the recommendation of the PSOE's executive committee, Agapito García Atadell was appointed to head a unit supposedly under the supervision of a professional policeman, the commander of the Criminal Investigation Brigade, Antonio Lino. García Atadell was a thirty-four-year-old typesetter from Galicia who claimed later to be a close friend of Indalecio Prieto. This was far from the truth and was not why he was recommended for the job. He certainly knew Prieto but merely because he had been part of his armed escort during the February election campaign. He would betray the trust placed in him. Through his nefarious activities, he was to become the most celebrated example of a man turned into a criminal by the temptations of his role.[62]

The García Atadell Brigade, and another set up at the same time under the command of Javier Méndez, a career policeman, effectively operated on their own initiative. The authority of their supervisor Antonio Lino was no more than nominal. García Atadell established his forty-eight men in the confiscated palace of the Condes de Rincón on Madrid's grand Paseo de la Castellana.[63] Méndez set up headquarters in the Gran Vía above the Cafetería Zahara and the press regularly recorded the arrests of spies, saboteurs, snipers, Falangists and other rebel supporters by his unit. García Atadell went to some trouble to ensure that ever more flattering accounts of the exploits of his own men were published almost daily. These legitimate duties in rearguard security usually led to the discovery of weapons and large sums of money and valuables as a result of denunciations by the *porteros* and cleaners of buildings in upper-class areas. Considerable amounts of money and valuables were handed over to the authorities by García Atadell, although part of the booty remained in his hands and those of his two closest cronies, Luis Ortuño and Pedro Penabad.[64]

Antonio Lino, who was secretly a rebel supporter, later alleged that the militiamen brought in by García Atadell and Méndez included 'common thieves, gangsters and murderers'. He claimed that he and other professional policemen did not dare come out of their offices unless armed. According to Lino, Méndez was corrupt and responsible for the deaths of numerous policemen, although it is likely that Méndez was uncovering the treachery of rebel supporters within the force. Lino, fearful that his own rebel sympathies were about to be exposed, eventually took refuge in the Mexican Embassy.[65] When García Atadell fell into rebel hands, he tried to put himself in a favourable light by claiming that he had often helped Lino neutralize Méndez, who used to tip off the CPIP about suspect policemen. He also boasted that he had arranged for Lino's family to be given refuge in the Mexican Embassy. This is plausible since he ran a racket with an attaché at the Embassy whereby right-wingers arrested by his men could buy sanctuary there.[66]

While it was certainly the case that there were criminal elements at work in the Republican rearguard, some of the robberies and other abuses were the work of right-wing agents provocateurs. In pursuit of its legitimate duties, the Atadell Brigade uncovered an organization that provided Republican uniforms so that its members could carry out night-time shootings with impunity. García Atadell himself felt obliged to issue a statement that only men carrying an identity card with his signature were authentic members of his unit.[67] Given the mix of official functions and abuse, it is extremely difficult to estimate the scale of the crimes committed by the Atadell Brigade. When he fell into rebel hands in November 1936, he tried to ingratiate himself with his interrogators by exaggerating the number of robberies and murders and claiming that they were all approved by the Republican authorities.

He admitted that the brigade carried out many executions on its own initiative after nightly judgments reached by a 'sentencing committee'. This consisted of the so-called 'control committee' which administered the overall operation, augmented with a different rank-and-file militia-man each day. The prisoners were sentenced to death or imprisonment or freed. In the cases of dispute, Atadell had the casting vote. In Atadell's version, the hundred or so persons sentenced to death were immediately driven to the outskirts of Madrid and shot. One of the committee's members, Ángel Pedrero, who later attained prominence in the Republican security services, denied any knowledge of such executions throughout interrogation and torture and at his trial on 20 February 1940. Nevertheless, he was sentenced to death by garrotte vil for involve-ment in at least fifteen of the Atadell Brigade's killings as well as for his role in the Republic's military counter-intelligence organization from 1937 to 1939.[68]

The majority of the brigade's prisoners were handed over to the DGS, along with confiscated valuables and weapons. Some of the more import-ant, however, were kept as hostages in the brigade's Rincón Palace. In some cases, they were held until they paid a ransom or bought the pass-ports that enabled them to escape to the rebel zone. In others, they were murdered to cover up the theft of their property. Several others, such as the Duquesa de Lerma, were saved. Indeed, in gratitude, the Duquesa later travelled from San Sebastián to Seville to speak at Atadell's trial. Atadell also 'graciously extended his protection' to people from his native village of Viveiro in Lugo. Life in the Palace gave an insight into García Atadell's bizarre mentality. His exquisite treatment of some aristocratic prisoners perhaps suggested an ostentatious desire to show off, an impression confirmed by the tawdry arrangements in the Palace itself. He often received visitors in a dressing gown. The reception hall was staffed by attractive typists wearing diaphanous, low-cut dresses in pastel shades and others dressed like French maids in lace aprons. The gateway into the garden was crowned by an arch of coloured lightbulbs that spelled out the name 'Brigada García Atadell'.[69]

On 24 September 1936, Atadell made his most famous celebrity arrest – that of a forty-three-year-old widow, Gonzalo Queipo de Llano's sister, Rosario. Virtually the entire Republican press carried the story that she had said, 'Kill me but don't make me suffer,' to which it was alleged that Atadell replied, 'Madame, we neither murder nor execute. We are more human than those who shoot workers en masse.' Heraldo de Madrid accompanied a big piece on the arrest headlined 'The Humanization of the War' with a photo of Atadell and Rosario. The text compared 'the decency, the nobility, the chivalry of the chief of the people's investigation militias' with 'the ignoble and inhuman conduct, the sheer abjection of the way the war is carried out by the rebels'. Rosario allegedly thanked him for 'his kindness and consideration'.[70]

The press version implied that Rosario had been located as a result of brilliant detective work – 'with the diligence that is the hallmark of this brigade, Atadell personally carried out the investigation that unearthed this person's hiding-place'. This was contradicted by Ángel Pedrero who, in his post-war interrogation, revealed that she had contacted the brigade through a friend, to ask for protection. This is confirmed by Rosario's own post-war account that, weary of living in clandestinity and terrified that she might be caught by anarchist 'uncontrollables', she gave herself up to Atadell. She hoped, rightly, that she might thereby be looked after for a potential prisoner exchange.[71] According to the press, she was handed over to the Dirección General de Seguridad and, after processing, sent to a women's prison. However, García Atadell told his interrogators in Seville that he kept her in great comfort in the Rincón Palace until 20 October when Manuel Muñoz, three of whose sons were being held by General Queipo de Llano, requested that she be transferred to his custody.[72] Rosario Queipo de Llano was not the only woman to give herself up to Atadell in the hope of avoiding a worse fate at the hands of the FAI.[73]

The wealth of the right in general and of the Catholic Church in particular was a significant factor in the repression. The need to finance the Republican war effort led to official sanction of confiscations. Most importantly, reports of its existence fuelled much class hatred. At the end of August, the Dawn Squad searched the home of the banker Manuel Muguiro and found bonds, cash and jewels to the value of 85 million pesetas. Felipe Sandoval's *checa* from the Cine Europa took part in this operation. Muguiro claimed in his defence that the valuables had been given him for safe-keeping by various religious orders. A raid on the home of the treasurer of another order recovered a more modest haul of 1,800,000 pesetas.[74]

It was, however, not only in religious hands that vast wealth was found. Some days earlier, the Dawn Squad found over 100 million pesetas in gold coins, foreign banknotes and jewellery in the home of another banker. The proceeds were deposited in the Banco de España. The Lynxes searched the house of the lawyer César de la Mora and found clocks, watches, Manila shawls, 300 kilos of silver, 3 million pesetas in shares and gold jewellery to the value of 25,000 pesetas, as well as an enviable wine cellar. César was the uncle of Constancia de la Mora, the future Republican press chief. In mid-September, security forces searched the home of the Marqués de San Nicolás de Mora and found 100 million pesetas' worth of cash, jewels and bonds. Similar reports of fortunes being found in the homes or bank deposit boxes of aristocrats were frequent and no doubt served to justify some of the repression. The reports were usually accompanied by a statement that the proceeds of the search had been handed over to the authorities. Occasionally, arrests were made of individuals who engaged in common theft in the guise of militiamen.[75]

One of the most notorious groups involved in the repression was headed by Felipe Sandoval, a criminal with a record of armed robbery who had spent long periods in prison. A bitter hatred of the bourgeoisie developed during a harsh childhood as an illegitimate child in Madrid had been intensified by his prison experiences. He was badly disfigured after a savage beating received on Christmas Eve 1919, when police, Civil Guards and soldiers swept through the Cárcel Modelo of Barcelona to avenge a strike, leaving many dead and crippled. He had been imprisoned in late 1932 for a series of armed robberies. In 1935, the Communist Enrique Castro Delgado, himself a political prisoner for his part in the left-wing rebellion of October 1934, was a fellow inmate: 'Sandoval was a professional thief and, some said, a murderer. Taciturn, with a strange look. And an aquiline nose that had nothing human to it. And thin, pale hands dangling from really long arms. He walked hunched over, frequently coughing and spitting.' In the opinion of Eduardo de Guzmán who came to know him well in a Francoist prison after the war, Sandoval was a man without ideas or ideology: 'He is not a worker rebelling against injustice who seeks ethical reasons to feed his rebellion and finds in them the strength to put up with prison and torture. He is no more than a vulgar racketeer, a common criminal.'[76]

Sandoval was still serving his sentence for armed robbery, and suffering from tuberculosis, when the military uprising found him in the sick bay of the Cárcel Modelo in Madrid. Considered a violent criminal, he was not released immediately, but within two weeks he was free. He presented himself to Amor Nuño, the secretary of the Madrid Federation of the CNT, who ordered him to join the so-called Checa del Cine Europa. Nuño was in operational control of the anarchist *checas*. The Cine Europa in the Calle Bravo Murillo was also the headquarters of the CNT militias. Its *checa* worked closely with the CPIP. Sandoval was soon running a squad dedicated to rooting out snipers and saboteurs. His group sped around Madrid in a black Rolls-Royce nicknamed 'El Rayo' (lightning). The group's members included other recently released criminals. On the direct orders of Eduardo Val, it carried out numerous assassinations, including prisoners seized from the Cárcel de Ventas. Among the victims, on 14 and 17 September, were three prison functionaries and, on 7 November, a prison doctor, Gabriel Rebollo, murdered like others in revenge for Sandoval's own experiences in jail.[77]

The Checa del Cine de Europa was one of the most notorious in Madrid, and among its members the thirty-six-year-old Santiago Aliques Bermúdez was the man responsible for the execution of prisoners. Along with an ex-bullfighter known as 'El Bartolo', Aliques led what was called the 'defence group' which is said to have committed several hundred murders of men and women, mostly in places on the outskirts of Madrid. Aliques was a common criminal with a long record of prison sentences for armed robbery. Among those murdered by his group were many women, several of whom were raped. Their only crime was to have been the wives and daughters of rightists. Indicative of the casually vicious way in which the Aliques gang went about its business was the murder of a woman because she had criticized the workers during a pre-war construction strike. Similarly, an old lady whose brother was a priest was arrested and executed for possessing religious medals. Even more gruesome was the case of the victim forced to dig his own grave by Aliques, who then killed him with the same pick he had had to use.[78]

Despite the complaints of corpses being seen on the streets, most of those killed were identified quickly, carefully registered by the Republican authorities and their relatives informed. In addition, on most days, the

Gaceta de Madrid carried lists of unidentified corpses, with a physical description of the deceased and the place where they had been found. Moreover, in the Dirección General de Seguridad, there was an office where boxes of photographs of the corpses were kept for relatives of the missing to check.[79] This was part of the Republican authorities' efforts, albeit with uneven results, to put an end to the atrocities. That the government was not ignoring the repression was clear from the frequent public condemnation thereof, a phenomenon that had no equivalent in the rebel zone.

Among those who worked to limit the repression was the delegation of the Basque Nationalist Party (Partido Nacionalista Vasco – PNV) in Madrid. One of its most energetic members was Jesús de Galíndez, who wrote later that 'only by condemning one's own excesses can one condemn those of the enemy; only by exposing the crude reality does one have the right to accuse'. He was successful, with considerable official help, in rescuing large numbers of Basques and also non-Basque clergy. The intercessions of Galíndez and his colleagues and safe conducts issued by the PNV delegation saved numerous priests, nuns and right-wingers as well as legitimate Basque nationalists.[80]

The humanitarian efforts of Galíndez and others were a drop in the ocean. More than eight thousand supposed rebel supporters were killed in Madrid between 18 July and the end of December 1936. About 50,000 civilians were killed in the entire Republican zone in the course of the war. It is difficult to find a simple explanation. Some, such as those killed in the biggest massacre of prisoners, at Paracuellos del Jarama, during the siege of Madrid, were victims of decisions based on an assessment of their potential danger to the Republican cause. Some were executed as enemy supporters. Although concern about the enemy within existed from the earliest part of the war, anxiety grew more intense as Franco's columns drew nearer to Madrid and refugees flooded into the city carrying bloodcurdling stories of the massacre that had followed the capture of Badajoz by Juan Yagüe's African column, on 14 August. In many respects, what happened at Badajoz had been meant as a message to Madrid – just as Guernica would be a message to the people of Bilbao – 'this is what will happen to you if you do not surrender'. The arrival of the terrified refugees provoked demands for revenge against the rebel supporters imprisoned in Madrid.

Hostility focused on the Cárcel Modelo in the Argüelles district of Madrid. There were approximately five thousand detainees in the prison, including over one thousand army officers who had been involved in the thwarted uprising in the Montaña barracks, Falangists and other rebel supporters, as well as some common criminals and a number of Communists and anarchists who had not been released at the beginning of the war, having been imprisoned for violent crimes. Whereas Madrid's other four prisons, San Antón, Porlier, Duque de Sesto and Las Ventas, were in the hands of militiamen, the Cárcel Modelo remained under the vigilance of Assault Guards and prison functionaries. For that reason, a number of political personalities had been placed there, some under arrest, some voluntarily, for their own safety. The prison consisted of five wings or galleries, like a star or a cog, around the main courtyard or patio. Each gallery had two hundred individual cells and a wide, rectangular central paved area, also known as a patio. However, by the late summer of 1936, there were five prisoners per cell.[81]

The right-wing prisoners would gather in the courtyard and the patios and rejoice openly at news of the advances of rebel troops. On various pretexts – to prevent them enjoying the sight of German aircraft bombing the city, when a prisoner was about to be executed or when militiamen arrived to take one away – they were often confined to their cells.[82] Some of the younger Falangists would shout insults and fascist slogans through the windows at passing militiamen. Such provocative behaviour worried prisoners like Ramón Serrano Suñer, Franco's brother-in-law. Some Republican newspapers published indignant articles about the prisoners which drew the attention of the CPIP. One especially provocative piece referred to:

> various priests and military chaplains, with few exceptions, sleek and fat as befits their profession. They are dressed haphazardly, many in pyjamas, some in militia overalls, shirts of every colour of the rainbow, cotton and khaki trousers, wrinkled, too long or too short. Unshaved, they are hardly distinguishable from ordinary prisoners. Their previously elegant air was provided by their uniforms or suits. They speak little, meditate a lot and sob a bit ... Other galleries hold more fascists involved in the rising and others who were arrested before it took place, such as the Falangist leaders Ruiz de Alda and Sánchez Mazas.

It then named the founder of the Agrarian Party and ally of Gil Robles, José Martínez de Velasco, the conservative Republican and friend of President Azaña, Melquíades Álvarez and Dr José María Albiñana, founder of the Spanish Nationalist Party.[83]

Even more specific was an article from *El Sindicalista*, reprinted in *Claridad*, protesting that many warders in the Cárcel Modelo were rebel sympathizers. Thus it was alleged that extreme rightists, such as Manuel Delgado Barreto (a right-wing newspaper editor and early sponsor of the Falange), were living comfortably and able to communicate with whomsoever they liked. It ended with a provocatively rhetorical question: 'Will it be necessary for the people's militias to do here what they have already done in Barcelona, widening their activities to take in the Cárcel Modelo? What simply cannot be permitted is that things go on in the Cárcel Modelo as they have up to now. Not a day longer! Not an hour longer!'[84] The next day, two right-wing prison guards disappeared. Several were dismissed and then arrested.[85]

On 15 August, agents of the DGS, accompanied by militiamen of the CPIP, entered the prison to search right-wing prisoners for hidden weapons and compromising documents. The militiamen insulted and threatened the prisoners, from whom they stole money, watches, rings, pens and other personal possessions. Some militiawomen also came and harangued the common prisoners with speeches to turn them against the politicals.[86] Rumours that Falangists in the Cárcel Modelo were planning to escape saw the CPIC, with authorization from Manuel Muñoz, send two teams of militiamen to the prison, led by Sandoval 'el Dr Muñiz' and Santiago Aliques Bermúdez. They arrived in the afternoon of 21 August and, as well as interrogating the army officers and right-wing politicians, stole their money, watches, religious medals and other valuables, even, in some cases, shoes and clothes.[87]

In the early hours of the morning of 22 August, the rebels carried out an air raid on Madrid, causing severe damage in Argüelles, where the prison was located. This provoked an appalling incident that saw more than thirty men murdered. On that afternoon, while Sandoval, Aliques and their men continued their search, the common criminals rioted and demanded their release, threatening to kill the right-wing inmates. Sandoval addressed the common prisoners and promised their release if they joined the CNT. Some of them set fire to the wood-store of the bakery in the cellar of the second gallery. At the same time, a hail of bullets from a machine-gun, previously set up by other anarchists on a nearby rooftop, was aimed at the right-wing inmates of the first gallery. Eleven were wounded and six were killed, including José Martínez de Velasco. It was later alleged that the fire and the machine-gun salvo were not an unfortunate coincidence but had been carefully choreographed by Sandoval's men. The difficulties of access to this wood-store also suggested a degree of collusion between the militiamen and the common prisoners.[88]

A rumour spread that the aviator and adventurer Julio Ruiz de Alda, one of the founders of the Falange, had bribed prison officials to permit right-wingers to escape under cover of the fire. Large numbers of angry militiamen entered the prison with the firemen who were responding to the fire alarm. Meanwhile, attracted by the talk of a fascist break-out, a huge crowd had gathered in the surrounding streets. The Minister of the Interior, General Pozas, arrived accompanied by a city councillor, Ángel Galarza Gago (who would replace him two weeks later). However, after vain efforts to halt the train of events, they quickly departed. The DGS, Manuel Muñoz, also appeared. With the crowd baying for the release of the common prisoners and threatening to invade the prison to lynch the fascist detainees, he telephoned for help from the political parties. Then he went to the Ministry of War and got permission from the Prime Minister, José Giral, to release the common prisoners.

However, when Muñoz returned to the prison, he discovered that Sandoval had already let two hundred common prisoners escape. As helpless as Pozas had been, Muñoz claimed he was unwell and returned to his office. While some of the released inmates looted the prison food store, the militiamen went through the prison registry and selected about thirty of the rightists, among them well-known liberals and conservatives as well as army officers and Falangists. They were taken down to the cellars and, after a brief 'trial' before a hastily convened 'tribunal', shot. The dead included prominent Falangists Ruiz de Alda and Fernando Primo de Rivera (brother of the party's founder, José Antonio), Dr Albiñana, two one-time ministers from Lerroux's Radical Party, Ramón Álvarez Valdés and Manuel Rico Avello (both of whom were in protective custody), and Melquíades Álvarez. The latter had been the mentor of Azaña, who was shattered by the news of his death. Among the lesser-known victims was Mola's agent, the policeman Santiago Martín Báguenas, who had been involved in provoking disorder during the spring. The militiamen had picked out three left-wing defectors to the Falange – Enrique Matorras Páez, who had previously been a prominent member of the Communist Party in Seville, Sinforiano Moldes, who had left the CNT and started up a scab building workers' union, and an ex-CNT gunman named Ribagorza. Another, Marciano Pedro Durruti, escaped the same fate because his brother Buenaventura, the founder of the FAI, had managed to secure his release.[89]

Further to Muñoz's appeal, Giral arranged for the principal parties to send representatives to try to calm the crowds.[90] The future Socialist Prime Minister, the distinguished physiologist Dr Juan Negrín, had already rushed to the Cárcel Modelo in a vain attempt to prevent bloodshed. One of his colleagues wrote of his courageous attempt to save lives:

> Negrín hastened to put a stop to the murderous fury and, at the same time, to try to save the life of the father of Elías Delgado, the head porter at his laboratory. Elías's father had risen through the ranks of the army to become an officer, which is why he was in the Cárcel Modelo. The determination of Dr Negrín to prevent the inevitable was useless since Elías's father was already dead when he arrived. Negrín's outspoken fury when he found out nearly led to the perpetrators killing him too.[91]

The prison officials could only look on helplessly while the militiamen went through prisoners' files seeking out additional victims. Around 10 p.m. on 22 August, the lawyer of the prison officers' union appealed to the British Chargé d'Affaires in Madrid, George Ogilvie-Forbes, to do something to prevent further killing. Ogilvie-Forbes immediately went to the Ministry of Foreign Affairs where he saw the Minister, Augusto Barcia Trelles. On the verge of tears, Barcia confessed the government's impotence. Juan-Simeón Vidarte, a senior member of the Socialist Party who had gone to the prison, was appalled to see the crowd outside baying for blood, having been infuriated by the earlier bombing raid and by the refugees' horror stories. A long and tense night ensued before the violence died down.[92] It took the combined efforts of a unit of Assault Guards and the Socialist squad known as the 'Motorized Brigade', which was closely associated with Prieto. Led by Enrique Puente, the men of the Motorized Brigade were fiercely opposed by anarchist militia, some of whom, according to Sandoval, were led by Amor Nuño.[93]

A prison official who was one of the right-wing sympathizers denounced by *Claridad* was Juan Batista, whose brother was a Falangist. In November 1933, Batista had been involved in the prison break of the millionaire smuggler Juan March and was known for helping imprisoned Falangists.[94] Now, fearing for the lives of the inmates and for his own family, he sought help from an anarchist who had once been his prisoner but who was now working hard to counter the indiscriminate violence in the Republican zone. The man to whom he turned was Melchor Rodríguez García, a forty-three-year-old anarchist from Seville, a disciple of the humanist Dr Pedro Vallina whom he had met in prison.

Melchor had been a bullfighter until he was gored and then worked as a skilled panel-beater and cabinet-maker. He would be credited with saving thousands of lives and helping stop the repression behind the Republican lines. He had begun by requisitioning the Palace of the Marqués de Viana in the old part of the city. He did so at the request of the Marqués's administrator, who was anxious to save the Palace, its many treasures and its staff. Rodríguez was accompanied by a group of friends who, he later claimed to his Francoist interrogators, were apolitical. They went by the name of 'Los Libertos' (the Freed Slaves). At his eventual trial, Melchor would be accused of using the Palacio de Viana as a *checa*, when in fact it was used to give refuge to many right-wingers, clergy, officers and Falangists. Indeed, his humanitarian activities eventually earned him the nickname 'the Red Angel'. On the night of 22 August, to the fury of Sandoval, but helped by Enrique Puente, Melchor Rodríguez managed to save Juan Batista, and fifteen members of his family who had taken refuge in the prison. Thereafter, Batista became Melchor Rodríguez's secretary.[95]

The Republican government reacted in a way that was in stark contrast to the official encouragement of atrocities in the rebel zone. Indalecio Prieto visited the prison and, appalled by the Dantesque scenes that were reported to him, said that 'the brutality of what has happened here means quite simply that we have lost the war'.[96] Late on the night of 22 August, the government took steps to put a stop to irregular 'justice'. At the suggestion of Vidarte, and with the backing of Prieto, Giral's government set up 'special courts against rebellion, sedition and crimes against State security', known as Tribunales Populares, under the reluctant authority of the acting president of the Supreme Court, Mariano Gómez. With remarkable courage, Gómez had a tribunal set up and working in the prison by 9.00 a.m. on 23 August. It was hoped that the new tribunals would temper the revolutionary excesses, although they had only a limited effect in the first weeks of their existence.[97]

Two reporters from *El Socialista*, Fernando Vázquez Ocaña and Manuel Pastor, had managed to gain access to the interior of the prison on the evening of 22 August and what they found resembled an abattoir. One of the patios was strewn with corpses. They returned to the newspaper's offices shaking with indignation. On the basis of what they recounted, the editor Julián Zugazagoitia and his senior staff composed a strongly worded condemnation which was published in a prominent position under the headline 'An Unavoidable Moral Imperative'. Zugazagoitia was determined to help the government emerge from the position into which it had been placed by the extremists who had taken justice into their own hands, writing, 'to judge those who have transgressed, we have the law. As long as we have it, we must respect it. With the law, everything is legitimate; without it, nothing is.' On the same day, Izquierda Republicana also condemned violence in the rearguard.[98]

Among those most appalled was the President of the Republic, Manuel Azaña. On the morning of 24 August, his brother-in-law, the playwright Cipriano Rivas Cherif, found him shocked and horrified by what he called 'the hammer blow', almost unable to speak. 'They've murdered Melquíades!' he said, and after a silence, 'This cannot be, this cannot be! I am sickened by the blood. I have had as much as I can take; it will drown us all.' He felt 'despair', 'horror', 'dejection', 'shame'. 'In mourning for the Republic', he considered resigning.[99] In his novel, *La velada en Benicarló*, drawing upon this experience, Azaña has one of his characters hear the screams of agony of political prisoners being shot at night in a cemetery.[100]

The massacre was only one among the many human tragedies concerning prisoners. An extraordinary case was that of Rafael Salazar Alonso. Given his record as Minister of the Interior in 1934, Salazar Alonso was a marked man. Fearing that various militia groups were after him, he went into hiding at the beginning of the war. At first he was in the Portuguese Embassy but, when the Chargé d'Affaires had to leave Madrid, Salazar had gone to the house of a friend called Cámara. In the hope of forcing them to reveal his hideout, a Communist militia group had arrested his sixteen-year-old daughter, Carmencita, and his wife, Cecilia, whom he was in the process of divorcing. In return for their freedom, Cecilia revealed Cámara's address, but when the militiamen got there, he had already moved on. He hid briefly in the flat of an ex-lover, Irene Más, who had taken refuge with her husband and son in Melchor Rodríguez's Palacio de Viana. Now, fearful that Salazar would be arrested, Irene arranged for him to be given sanctuary by one of her neighbours. Irene visited him every day. Her outraged husband arranged for him to surrender himself to Melchor Rodríguez.[101]

Salazar Alonso was arrested on 31 August 1936 by three members of Melchor Rodríguez's Libertos. He recalled in his prison diary that all three, Melchor Rodríguez and two others, were 'three splendid fellows, all three perfect gentlemen, who were completely horrified by the violence'. He remained in the Palacio de Viana for three days, well fed and treated with courtesy by Melchor Rodríguez. Other anarchists sent by Eduardo Val interrogated Salazar Alonso. They wanted to know about double agents that he had infiltrated into the FAI while he was Minister of the Interior in 1934 and were keen to shoot him. To avoid further problems, Melchor Rodríguez, at the suggestion of Salazar Alonso himself, spoke with the Minister of Justice, Manuel Blasco Garzón, and arranged for him to be taken into custody. On 2 September, Melchor conveyed him to the Cárcel Modelo where he was handed over to Manuel Muñoz, and to Mariano Gómez, the president of the Supreme Court.[102]

Once transferred to the Cárcel Modelo, Salazar Alonso was allowed visits, although the only people who actually came were, on one occasion, the Chilean Ambassador Aurelio Núñez Morgado, various lawyers and a woman from Villafranca de los Barros, Amparo Munilla. Irene Más did not visit, but Amparo came almost every day. Her courage and commitment in doing so was extraordinary. She had given birth to a son on 2 August. Five days later, Amparo, along with her baby and a daughter, had been arrested by militiamen. In a book written by another daughter, it is claimed that during her week-long detention, she was repeatedly raped by these men, who were allegedly led by the Socialist Mayor of Villafranca de los Barros, Jesús Yuste, and the deputy Mayor, Manuel Borrego. However, on 7 August, Yuste and Borrego were still in Extremadura. Borrego would be executed by the rebels in Mérida some days later and Yuste remained fighting Franco's columns in the south. Even more damaging to her daughter's allegations is a post-war letter to the Francoist authorities about her experiences, written by Amparo Munilla herself. Amparo's only reference to maltreatment is to being threatened with death if she did not reveal the hiding place of Salazar Alonso and other friends. This she bravely refused to do. She was detained in four different places including the Dirección General de Seguridad and the Checa de Bellas Artes and was released on 14 August.

Since her husband was also in danger, on the same day that Salazar Alonso entered the Cárcel Modelo the family sought safe refuge in the Norwegian Legation, where the Consul, Felix Schlayer, sheltered many rebel supporters. Despite the danger, Amparo regularly left the safety of the Legation in order to visit the man many assumed was her lover. She wrote to Salazar Alonso often and brought him books and a wristwatch. His prison diary, in which there is not a word about Irene Más, reveals his desperation on the days that Amparo did not visit or write. The diary entries leave no doubt of his intense feelings for her. Her deep regard for him was revealed when, at enormous risk, she even appeared at his trial on his behalf.[103]

Mariano Gómez, who presided over the Tribunal Popular operating in the Cárcel Modelo, was an experienced Republican magistrate. He was also personally opposed to the death penalty, on which he had been writing a book. Despite the extraordinary wartime circumstances, he made every effort to put a stop to judicial decisions being made on the basis of passion and hatred. Instead, he tried to impose due legal process.[104] This ensured that the trial of Salazar Alonso, and of many others, would be significantly different from the procedures pertaining in the military trials within the rebel zone, where those accused were given no facilities for their defence. Initially, the moderate Republican Juan Botella Asensi, a distinguished lawyer who had been Minister of Justice in late 1933, had offered to defend Salazar Alonso but later withdrew the offer. The reasons for his change of heart are not known, but possibly derived from the fact that Salazar Alonso had broken his Masonic oaths.[105] Nevertheless, Salazar Alonso was provided with the services of two lawyers and was also given the indictment to help him prepare his defence. Accused of implication in the military plot, his trial began on 19 September.

The first day consisted of four hours of questioning by the prosecution, largely concentrated on statements made in his book *Bajo el signo de la revolución*. This demonstrated his role in provoking the Asturian uprising of October 1934 with a view to crushing the labour movement. However, the prosecution could produce no proof of any involvement in military conspiracy. There followed statements from defence witnesses. With the exception of the intervention by Amparo Munilla, which moved him greatly, he was disappointed by his witnesses, who seemed mainly concerned to distance themselves from him. On the following day, he opened his defence. He pointed out that thorough searches of his home and those of his friends had found no evidence that he was involved in any way in the military conspiracy. The prosecutor admitted that this was the case. Indeed, the Republican press had commented on the fact that his fascist friends had not kept him informed of the date of the uprising. Nevertheless, Salazar Alonso was found guilty and the prosecutor successfully requested the death sentence.[106]

The final decision was passed for approval to the government which had been formed barely three weeks earlier. Azaña, as President, regarded the death penalty for Salazar Alonso as 'an outrage', but the cabinet was deeply divided. The two extremes were explained by Indalecio Prieto, who said:

It is likely that there is no one among you who feels such unquenchable loathing towards Salazar Alonso as I do. After building his career on extreme demagoguery, he let himself be seduced by the blandishments of the right and went over to them, presenting as his qualifications the vicious persecution carried out against us when he was Minister of the Interior. However, in the records of the trial, there appears no proof of the indictment that he had participated in the military uprising. Therefore, I vote in favour of pardon.

Prieto's intervention swayed the cabinet, which voted by seven votes to six in favour of the death sentence being commuted to life imprisonment.

Mariano Gómez was informed immediately. Shortly afterwards, while the cabinet was still in session, Gómez appeared and asked to speak to Prieto. He told him that, although he had received Salazar Alonso's file with the cabinet's decision:

I have informed no one because I am sure that as soon as it is made public, there will be a terrible riot in the prison which will start with the shooting of the prisoner. The Government, without sufficient means to impose its decision, will be unable to save his life and, defeated on this issue, its remaining authority will crumble. But this is not the worst. The Tribunal Popular, I am sure, will refuse to continue working and, after Salazar Alonso, perhaps this very night, all the political prisoners will die riddled with bullets.

Prieto explained why he had voted as he had done. Gómez was in complete agreement but repeated that the decision could cost over one hundred lives. Accordingly, Prieto went back into the cabinet, explained what Gómez had said and changed his vote. Salazar Alonso was executed on the morning of 23 September.[107]

Salazar Alonso was executed – despite not being guilty of the crime of which he had been accused – because of his part in the provocation of both the peasant strike of June 1934 and the Asturian uprising of October. His role as Minister of the Interior was believed to have caused untold suffering and many deaths and so brought civil war nearer. That he was not accused of this was clearly a legal error which exposed the contradictions between conventional justice and popular justice. The extraordinary episode of Prieto's volte-face over Salazar Alonso illustrated the continuing weakness of the government in the face of the armed militias. As Manuel Muñoz had been with the anarchists who hijacked the trainload of prisoners from Jaén, the moderates were totally inhibited by fear of a confrontation between the forces of order and the revolutionary militias.

Nevertheless, despite what had happened in the case of Salazar Alonso, the newly instituted tribunals functioned relatively well and increasingly reconciled public opinion to the idea that the Republic could administer justice in the interests of the people. The Colegios de Abogados (Bar Associations) in each provincial capital invigilated procedures and ensured that prisoners were ably defended. Sessions of the tribunals were attended by substantial audiences. There was often applause and even cheering when, if the accused were found not guilty, the president of the tribunal made a speech praising the generosity of popular justice. A remarkable example took place in mid-September in Madrid with the not-guilty verdicts reached against three officers accused of an offence committed at the battle front. Addressing the jury, the president said: 'Every day I feel greater pride in chairing this people's court, which has to be inexorable with traitors to the Republic but which has its heart full of justice and mercy for those who have done their duty.' One of the accused, on behalf of all three, then thanked the tribunal and the jury, shouting 'Long Live the Republic! Long Live the Popular Front! Long Live the People's Tribunal!'[108]

Throughout September and October, piecemeal measures to control the *checas* and centralize the militias would continue to be introduced but with relatively little effect. Only when the war was on the doorstep in early November and the militias had other priorities could a central control be imposed. The will to reimpose order had been there all along among the Republicans and moderate Socialists. However, the Communists would provide the singleminded ruthlessness that made a significant difference. Even then, a price would be paid in blood in terms of the fate of thousands of prisoners.

Meanwhile, the moderate Socialists and the Basque nationalists were in the forefront of efforts to put a stop to rearguard outrages. Along with Prieto and Zugazagoitia, Dr Juan Negrín opposed with equal fervour the repression on either side. His friend Marcelino Pascua recounted Negrín's foolhardiness. Throughout the late summer of 1936 'he made every effort, at serious risk to himself but with considerable success, to save people in Madrid who for various reasons including personal vendettas were afraid for their lives. This involved rash acts of daring which came as no surprise to his friends who were fully aware of his personal bravery.'[109] Having become Minister of Finance in the government of Largo Caballero on 4 September 1936, Dr Negrín showed no inclination to restrain his temerity in trying to put a stop to the repression. His efforts to prevent the nightly *paseos* outraged the anarchist *checas*. One group even went into the Finance Ministry in Madrid to threaten him. In the ensuing confrontation, they were prevented from killing him only by the intervention of the security staff of the Ministry.[110]

Equally strenuous efforts to put a stop to arbitrary arrests and executions were made by Jesús Galíndez of the Basque delegation in Madrid and by Manuel Irujo Olla, the piously Catholic Basque, who became Minister without Portfolio in the new cabinet. He made desperate efforts for humanitarian values to prevail behind the lines: 'I have held conversations with both political and trade union organizations of the extreme left. I have made every effort for the Government of the democratic Republic and for all anti-fascists to show that we are a generous and high-minded people. I am certain that any attempt on another life is more pernicious than a battle; more is lost with a crime than with a defeat.' The efforts of the Basques were principally aimed at helping their compatriots, many, if not most, of whom were Catholics. However, their protection also extended to more than 850 monks, nuns and members of the lay clergy, Basques or otherwise.[111]

The Basque efforts were rendered immensely difficult by the fact that, in the wake of the events of 22–23 August in the Cárcel Modelo, control of the prisons had passed completely to the militiamen of the CPIP. *Sacas* and the murder of detainees on the outskirts of the city became ever more frequent throughout September and October. The release of common prisoners had seen many of them swell the ranks of the militias. Armed and with papers that seemed to grant them the authority of the Dirección General de Seguridad, they were able to vent their resentments on the prison officials who had previously been their jailers.[112]

In response, in mid-September, the government took another halting step towards the taming of the *checas*. The new Minister of the Interior, Ángel Galarza, had been the state prosecutor who launched the ill-advised 'responsibilities' case against those who had served as ministers during the Primo de Rivera dictatorship. In 1933, he had joined the Socialist Party and earned notoriety for the violence of his rhetoric in the Cortes. The majority of the PSOE executive regarded him as an opportunist who had little interest in controlling the abuses of the *checas*.[113] However, on 16 September, he introduced a decree signed by

President Azaña creating the Rearguard Security Militias (Milicias de Vigilancia de Retaguardia – MVR). The preamble implicitly recognized that the creation of the CPIP six weeks earlier had been a failure. It stated that the MVR were being established because of 'the imperative need to regulate the services of law and order in the rearguard'. The proposed change was justified by the statement that 'since the militia groups that had been collaborating with the police had no clearly defined function or a co-ordinated organization, it had been difficult to prevent their infiltration by the enemy to disrupt their work and bring the organizations into disrepute'. This was an accurate representation of the weaknesses of the CPIP, while sugaring the pill for the militia groups by throwing the blame for atrocities on the enemy within.

The decree proposed to fuse all of the militia groups run by parties and unions into a temporary police corps. It stated that any autonomous groups that continued to carry out the functions of security now attributed to the MVR would be regarded as 'facciosos', enemy agents. To encourage the militia groups to join the MRV, it was stated that those who served would be given preference for eventual incorporation into the regular police forces. Like the creation of the Comité Provincial de Investigación Pública only a month and a half earlier, the measure was another step towards the centralization of the parallel police constituted by the *checas*.[114] In the short term, it changed little other than give a veneer of legitimacy to some left-wing groups and patrols from the CPIP, but there were still others operating outside the MVR.

Despite Galarza's measure, the tempo of the repression in Madrid was about to increase. This was inevitable as the rebel columns drew nearer and the bombing of the city became more frequent. The danger was given a name by General Mola, who famously stated that there were four columns poised to attack Madrid but that the attack would be initiated by a fifth column already inside the city. The exact date on which Mola made the remark is not known but it was almost certainly in the first days of October.[115] At this stage, there was no properly structured fifth column, but nocturnal snipers, saboteurs and agents provocateurs were active. As Geoffrey Cox, the British newspaper correspondent, wrote later: 'Secret radio, couriers, men who slipped across the lines in darkness, saw to it that many of the Government's closest secrets were revealed to the rebels.'[116]

Republican politicians started making references to the speech from early October. In popular parlance and political rhetoric, the term 'fifth columnist' came to denote any rebel supporter, real or potential, active or imprisoned. It was first used as a device to raise awareness and popular passion by Dolores Ibárruri 'Pasionaria', who wrote:

> That traitor Mola said that he would launch 'four columns' against Madrid, but that only the 'fifth column' would begin the offensive. The 'fifth column' is the one which lurks within Madrid itself and which, despite all measures, continues to move in the darkness. We sense its feline movements; its dull voice is to be heard in rumours, stories and outright panic. This enemy must be crushed immediately while our heroic militia is fighting outside Madrid … The law of war is a brutal one, but we must adopt it without sentimentality, with neither aggressiveness nor weakness. We cannot sink to the sadism of the fascists. We will never torture prisoners. Nor will we humiliate the wives of traitors, nor murder their children. But we will inflict lawful retribution rapidly and impressively, so as to tear out the very roots of treachery.[117]

The diplomatic corps had long since been concerned about the situation and was now alarmed by the escalation implicit in Pasionaria's article. The British Chargé d'Affaires in Madrid, George Ogilvie-Forbes, co-ordinated appeals to the Spanish Foreign Ministry for something to be done about the growing number of killings and the dangerous situation in the prisons. On 1 October, he reported that 125 had been murdered on the previous Saturday (26 September). He was convinced that the article was an incitement to murder because, in the twenty-four hours following its publication on Saturday 3 October, there were two hundred murders in Madrid. On 5 October, Ogilvie-Forbes visited the Foreign Minister, Julio Álvarez del Vayo, and told him that, two days earlier, he had been in the University City and seen the bodies of at least fifteen men and women. Although reluctant to believe that the authorities had anything to do with the killings, Ogilvie-Forbes protested that they were guilty of permitting them. Álvarez del Vayo 'blushed to the roots of his hair', assured him that the government would do everything possible to stop them and arranged for him to visit the Minister of the Interior.

The deleterious effect on Republican Spain's international status caused by news of the killings was exacerbated by the fact that the British were convinced, or chose to believe, that 'executions of civilians by the rebels have been relatively few and carried out with a certain show of justice'. On 6 October, Ogilvie-Forbes met Ángel Galarza, who told him that the constant killings and the situation in the prisons were the consequence of the fact that it had been necessary to use the bulk of the Assault

Guards as front-line troops, leaving security in the hands of militia groups.[118] Nevertheless, he responded to diplomatic concerns by issuing a decree imposing a curfew between 11 p.m. and 6 a.m. on all those who did not belong to the official Rearguard Security Militias. Moreover, within three weeks of creating the MVR, Galarza was obliged to issue a statement prohibiting all house searches other than those specifically ordered by the Director General of Security, withdrawing all identity cards previously issued by the CPIP and requiring the left-wing organizations to give the names of the militiamen authorized to join the MVR.[119]

The difference in international perception of the repression in both zones was one of the most difficult problems faced by the Republic. There were plenty of diplomats and journalists in Republican cities to report what was happening. In contrast, so far, most of the atrocities were carried out by Franco's columns in small country towns. Moreover, rebel commanders ensured that unsympathetic foreign newspaper correspondents were not present. Winston Churchill's reaction to the situation in Republican Spain was representative of the perception of events in upper-class and official circles. When the new Spanish Ambassador, Pablo de Azcárate, arrived in London in early September 1936, he was introduced by his friend Lord David Cecil to Churchill. Although Azcárate arrived with a reputation as a highly respected functionary of the League of Nations, a red-faced Churchill angrily rejected his outstretched hand and stalked off muttering, 'Blood, blood …' In an article in the *Evening Standard* on 2 October 1936, entitled 'Spain: Object Lesson for Radicals', Churchill wrote:

The massacre of hostages falls to a definitely lower plane; and the systematic slaughter night after night of helpless and defenceless political opponents, dragged from their homes to execution for no other crime than that they belong to the classes opposed to Communism, and have enjoyed property and distinction under the Republican constitution, ranks with tortures and fiendish outrages in the lowest pit of human degradation. Although it seems to be the practice of the Nationalist [rebel] forces to shoot a proportion of their prisoners taken in arms, they cannot be accused of having fallen to the level of committing the atrocities which are the daily handiwork of the Communists, Anarchists, and the P.O.U.M., as the new and most extreme Trotskyist organization is called. It would be a mistake alike in truth and wisdom for British public opinion to rate both sides at the same level.[120]

Republican leaders were expected to maintain civilized social relations within Madrid despite seething popular resentment of those who bombed their city and despite the activities of snipers and saboteurs. Thus Julián Zugazagoitia, the faithful ally of Prieto, continued to use his position as editor of the daily *El Socialista* to campaign for discipline in the rearguard and for respect on the battlefield for the lives of opponents. Typical of the ethical tone adopted by the paper was his editorial of 3 October 1936, headed 'Moral Obligations in War'. He wrote: 'The life of an adversary who surrenders is unassailable; no combatant can dispose of that life. But that is not how the rebels behave. No matter. It is how we should behave.'[121]

However, such pleas for moderation paled in the context of the desperation that engulfed the city. The political commissar of the Communist Fifth Regiment, Comandante Carlos Contreras (the pseudonym of the Italian Communist, and Soviet agent, Vittorio Vidali), showed that he was more concerned with eliminating the enemy within than placating diplomats without. Five days after Pasionaria's speech, he made an even more explicit analysis of Mola's remarks for those who would take responsibility for eliminating the fifth column. 'General Mola has been kind enough to point out to us where the enemy is to be found. The Government of the Popular Front has already taken a series of measures aimed at cleansing Madrid rapidly and energetically of all those doubtful and suspect elements who could, at a given moment, create difficulties for the defence of our city.'[122] 'Fifth column' was soon the generalized term for rebel supporters who found themselves in the Republican zone.[123] On 21 October, the united Socialist and Communist Youth, the Juventudes Socialistas Unificadas, issued a declaration that 'the extermination of the "fifth column" will be a huge step in the defence of Madrid'.[124]

As the circle closed around Madrid, bombing raids on the undefended city intensified and triggered popular fury. Appeals for the population to be mobilized in defence of the city were increasingly accompanied by demands for the elimination of fifth columnists. Given the intensity of the fear that stalked the streets, such appeals served to stoke up the fires of hatred against the perceived enemy within.[125] The sense of urgency was notable in the rearguard activities of the *checas*. The most feared of them all was the CPIP, which had come to be known popularly as 'la Checa de Fomento'. This was because, on 26 August, the CPIP had moved its ever-growing operations out of the overcrowded Círculo de Bellas Artes to more spacious premises at Calle Fomento no. 9. From then until it was disbanded by Santiago Carrillo on 12 November, its activities against suspected fifth columnists reached a level of frenzy.[126]

In mid-September, it and several other *checas* had begun systematic *sacas* – the seizing and murder of detainees from the four main prisons. The first *sacas*, though frequent, were usually of relatively few prisoners at a time taken from the Cárcel de Ventas and San Antón and murdered in Aravaca. The Cárcel de Porlier was run by a group of four Communists whose abuses finally led to them being arrested in December. Nevertheless, on their watch, before November, there were frequent individual *sacas* but none of substantial numbers of prisoners. At the end of October, the scale increased dramatically and both anarchists and Communists were involved. On the 29th of that month, fifty rightists were taken from the Checa de Fomento and executed in Boadilla del Monte. In all the prisons, the militiamen usually arrived equipped with letters of authorization from the Comité Provincial de Investigación Pública. On 31 October, CPIP agents came to the Cárcel de Ventas with an order signed by Manuél Muñoz for the transfer of thirty-two prisoners to Chinchilla, far to the south-east in the province of Albacete. Twenty-four of them, including the right-wing thinker Ramiro de Maeztu and the founder of the JONS, Ramiro Ledesma Ramos, were shot in the cemetery of Aravaca on the outskirts of Madrid. On 1 and 2 November, over seventy more were taken from Ventas. About half reached Chinchilla and half were murdered in Aravaca cemetery. At least one of these *sacas* was carried out by militiamen from the Checa del Cine Europa led by Eduardo Val himself. On 4 November, a further fifty-six were killed in the prison at Carabanchel. Not all of those murdered in Aravaca and Boadilla were the victims of the anarchists. There was at least one Communist 'radio' involved as well.[127]

Paradoxically, as the *sacas* accelerated, the activities of one of the most famous *checas* began to wind down. The García Atadell Brigade had concealed many criminal acts behind their own much lauded fight against the fifth column. Since Atadell and many of his men came from the Socialist printing union, it had been easy for them to place articles about their exploits in the Republican press. This was particularly true of *Informaciones*, the newspaper now run by their fellow trade unionists. In any case, praise for the struggle against the enemy within was considered to be an important morale-booster.[128] This could be deduced from an editorial in *El Socialista* which proudly declared García Atadell and his men to be Socialists with the vocation of policemen fighting for a common cause. Zugazagoitia, the editor, was unaware of the Brigada's nefarious activities when he wrote: 'Atadell should be judged not on his past – a limpid, transparent past as a righteous Socialist – but rather on his present. His work, more than useful, is necessary. Indispensable.' The article went on to sing a hymn of praise for the detailed preparation and precision of his pre-dawn raids. It ended with a tone redolent of Zugazagoitia's views: 'Bad faith, resentment and envy all press to find expression in illegal activities which, for the honour of all and the prestige of the Republic, must be frustrated.'[129]

In fact, García Atadell's brigade had carried out many legitimate activities on a daily basis. These included searching Franco's Madrid apartment and finding there weapons, including a machine-pistol, and correspondence with other conspirators. More notably, his group was credited with the break-up of espionage rings, the capture of a clandestine radio station, the arrests of Falangists, saboteurs and snipers and the foiling of a plan to assassinate Azaña, Largo Caballero, Prieto and Pasionaria. Newspaper articles about these triumphs cannot be taken as official endorsement of García Atadell's criminal activities. Press references to confiscated cash and valuables usually specified that they had been handed in at the Dirección General de Seguridad.[130] García Atadell later reiterated to his interrogators that large amounts of money and jewellery were handed in as well as claiming to have saved many lives. One of the most curious cases was the 'rescue' of Lourdes Bueno Méndez, the missing daughter of a conservative Republican officer who, because of alleged links with the Nazis, had been arrested by Communists from a *checa* known as 'Radio Oeste'. García Atadell located her at the end of September and took her to the Dirección General de Seguridad, where she was held for another two and a half months. His interest in the case was probably based on the payment of a reward by her family.[131] García Atadell also claimed that he believed that, in recognition of his achievements, he would eventually have been made Director General of Security.[132]

However, in the second half of October, just when it might have been thought that his services would be in greatest demand, his group began to fade from public view. Questions were being asked about his activities and the whereabouts of confiscated valuables. Ironically, on 26 October, Ogilvie-Forbes had a conversation with García Atadell and explained the dreadful impact that news of the arrests, murders and robberies was having on the Republic's international situation. Atadell, who was at the time about to flee with his own ill-gotten gains, agreed wholeheartedly and blamed the disorder exclusively on the anarchists.[133] According to

Rosario Queipo de Llano, the number of detainees brought to Atadell's headquarters had begun to diminish greatly by the end of October.[134] He was clearly already planning his get-away. On 27 October, he met with two of his closest cronies, Luis Ortuño and Pedro Penabad, and made plans for flight. He later claimed that this was because Madrid was about to fall to the rebels and also because his life had been threatened by the Communists and the FAI in revenge for his efforts to prevent their atrocities. The three gathered together several suitcases full of money and valuables and, accompanied by García Atadell's wife, Piedad Domínguez Díaz, an ex-nun, headed for Alicante. There they acquired false Cuban passports and took ship for Marseilles. In Marseilles they bought tickets on a boat to La Habana on 19 November.[135]

Their plans backfired thanks to the film director Luis Buñuel. In his memoirs, he recalled García Atadell as illustrating 'the complexity of the relations that we had at times with the fascists'. Buñuel was in Paris working for the Republican Embassy as part of the anti-rebel espionage network run by the artist Luis Quintanilla. A French trade unionist, who worked in a hotel, reported to him that a Spaniard was about to take ship for South America with a suitcase full of stolen valuables. Buñuel informed the Ambassador, Luis Araquistain, who told the government in Valencia. Attempts were made to extradite him, but it was too late. Accordingly, Araquistain was authorized by the government to pass the information, via a neutral embassy, to the rebel representation in the French capital. Since the ship carrying García Atadell and his cronies had to put in at Vigo and Santa Cruz de Tenerife, it was assumed that it would be possible for the rebel authorities to arrest them there.[136]

In fact, the rebel leadership at Burgos was unable to get the agreement of the French government to the arrest of a passenger on a French ship and so it left Vigo without incident. Since both Burgos and Valencia shared the desire to see García Atadell brought to justice, however, Paris agreed. In Las Palmas, García Atadell and Penabad were arrested. After initial interrogation in the Canary Islands, they were transferred to Seville for further interrogation.[137] From 19 December, García Atadell was held for seven months in the maximum-security wing of Seville Provincial Prison until his execution by garrotte in July 1937. As García Atadell fled Madrid and headed to his eventual downfall, the most notorious period of the activities of the *checas* was about to begin.

PART FOUR

Madrid Besieged: The Threat and the Response

The Column of Death's
March on Madrid

Even before the bulk of his African troops arrived in Spain, either by sea, as part of the so-called 'victory convoy', or in the airlift made possible by German and Italian aircraft, Franco had already, on 2 August 1936, flown to Seville. The march on Madrid was to begin that day with the first column sent northwards to Mérida in the province of Badajoz. Under the command of the tall, grey-haired and red-faced Lieutenant Colonel Carlos Asensio Cabanillas, a hardened Africanista, it consisted of two battalions of the Foreign Legion and two battalions of Moorish Regulares. In trucks provided by Queipo de Llano, it advanced fifty miles in the first two days. Asensio was followed on 3 August by Castejón's column which advanced somewhat to the east and on 7 August by a third under Lieutenant Colonel Heli Rolando de Tella. Castejón travelled in the limousine of the Marqués de Nervión, a prominent landowner. The ultimate goal of these columns was Madrid. However, the use of three columns advancing on a wide front made it clear that an equally central objective was to destroy the left in towns and villages along the way.[1]

The unwritten orders were unambiguous: 'to smash the cruel rabble with a great hammer blow that would paralyse them'.[2] Accordingly, as the three columns moved rapidly north from Seville in early August, they used the techniques of terror which had been the regular practice of the Africanistas against the subject population of Morocco. After they crossed the Sierra Morena, word of their tactics spread a wave of fear before them. The labourers that opposed them, inexperienced and armed only with shotguns, ancient blunderbusses, knives and hatchets, hardly merited the label of 'militiamen'. With the advantage of total air superiority provided by Savoia-81 flown by Italian air-force pilots and Junkers Ju-52 flown by Luftwaffe pilots, and equipped with artillery, the crack shock units of the Spanish colonial army took villages and towns in the provinces of Seville and Badajoz. The number of casualties among the Republican volunteers far exceeded those among the African columns. No prisoners were taken. Militiamen captured along the way were simply shot.

In Badajoz, there was a desperate and vain attempt by the provincial Popular Front Defence Committee to co-ordinate the hastily assembled militias. Two parliamentary deputies, the Socialist José Sosa Hormigo and the Communist Pedro Martínez Cartón, together with Ricardo Zabalza, the FNTT leader, organized militia groups which tried, with little success, to hinder the progress of the African columns. Eventually, Zabalza led a substantial group (named 'Columna Pedro Rubio' in memory of the PSOE deputy murdered in 1935) through the rebel lines to Madrid to join Republican forces. The columns of Sosa Hormigo and Martínez Cartón were soon swollen with men fleeing from the African columns. This did nothing for their military efficacy but intensified their readiness to kill right-wingers found in villages not yet in rebel control.[3]

This undermined the endeavours of the Republican government to forestall atrocities. A stream of telegrams from Madrid on the evening of 19 July naively urged left-wing organizations to have faith in the loyalty of the Civil Guard and the army. On 20 July, the Popular Front Committees of towns within the Republican zone received orders from the Madrid government that 'there should be no breakdown of law and order for any reason whatsoever' and that measures should be taken 'to prevent anyone taking advantage of the understandable nervousness of the population to commit offences against law-abiding persons or to take justice into their own hands'. Strikes were forbidden, by agreement with the Unión General de Trabajadores. On 28 July, the Civil Governors of each province passed on even stricter instructions from Madrid to local Popular Front Committees requiring them to announce that 'the death penalty will be applied against anyone, whether belonging to a political entity or not, who attacks the life or property of others, since such crimes will be considered as acts of rebellion in the service of the enemy'. On 29 July, mayors were ordered not to touch the bank accounts of right-wingers in their towns.[4]

No such restraint was imposed upon the rebel columns. Moving north into Badajoz, with relative ease, they took El Real de la Jara, Monesterio, Llerena, Fuente de Cantos, Zafra and Los Santos de Maimona. In addition to raping and looting, the men of the columns of Asensio, Castejón and Tella annihilated real or supposed Popular Front sympathizers that they found, leaving a trail of bloody slaughter as they went. It was no coincidence that Badajoz was the province where the spontaneous occupations of estates in the spring of 1936 had seemed to end the injustice of the landholding system. The Africanistas' execution of captured peasant volunteers was jokingly referred to as 'giving them agrarian reform'.[5]

In fact, everywhere in the rebel zone where the Republic had decreed expropriations or legalized land occupations, the columns helped the owners take back the land. Previously neglected land had usually been improved by the laborious removal of stones, stubble and bracken and the clearing of ponds and streams. Moreover, the harvest was awaiting collection. Those who had carried out the improvements received no compensation for their labour, nor for the crops, stores, seeds, animals and tools that were pillaged along with the land. In most cases, they had already fled or been killed or imprisoned by the rebel forces. The repression was especially brutal against the men and women who had benefited from land redistribution under the Republic. They would be between 70 and 80 per cent of the total executed in Badajoz.[6]

A startling example of the relationship between the columns and the landowners concerns the *cacique* of Palma del Río, in the province of Córdoba, Félix Moreno Ardanuy. He bred fighting bulls which limited the amount of work on his estates. He refused to cultivate his land, using the slogan 'Comed República' (Let the Republic feed you). After the Popular Front elections, many labourers were placed on his estates, but he refused to pay them. When war broke out, Félix Moreno was in his palatial home in Seville. The anarchist committee of Palma del Río collectivized the land and rationed food supplies until fields could be tilled and the harvest came in. Moreno's fighting bulls were killed for food and the villagers tasted red meat for the first time in their lives. The news infuriated Moreno. When a rebel column captured the town on 27 August, he drove behind in a black Cadillac accompanied by the other prominent landowners of the area. The village menfolk who had not fled were herded into a large cattle-pen. For each of his slaughtered bulls, he selected ten to be shot. As desperate men pleaded with him on the grounds that they were his godson, his cousin or linked to him in some way, he just looked ahead and said, 'I know nobody.' At least eighty-seven were shot on that day and twice that many over the following days.[7]

In early October 1936, a delegation of southern landowners went to Burgos to persuade Franco's embryonic government, the Junta Técnica del Estado, to overturn the land redistribution of the previous years. Among them was Adolfo Rodríguez Jurado, the president of the Association of Rural Estate-Owners and the president of the Federation of Landowners of Badajoz. Arguing that left-wing labourers should not enjoy the benefits of landholding, they called for all land distributed by the Republic to be returned to its original owners and insisted that they should not have to pay for the work carried out by the settlers in preparing the land for sowing. Their identification with the rebel cause was trumpeted loudly: their appeal ended with the words 'we landowners, farmers and cattlemen place ourselves unconditionally at the orders of the glorious army, the saviour of the Patria, and we are ready to take on any sacrifices asked of us'.[8]

In a real sense, the *latifundistas*' representatives were merely seeking legal consolidation of what the African columns were doing. In Llerena, there was a substantial concentration of Civil Guards, the town's garrison having been reinforced on 21 July by that of Zafra and the one from Azuaga to the east. The commander from Azuaga, Lieutenant Antonio Miranda Vega, convinced the Socialist Mayor of Llerena, Rafael Matrana Galán, and the Popular Front Committee that his force of Civil Guards was loyal to the Republic and ready to fight the columns moving up from the south. The road into Llerena from the south crossed a bridge over two deep gullies. On 4 August, Miranda Vega offered to take a joint force of Civil Guards and militiamen to destroy the bridge and block Castejón's column. On reaching the bridge, the Civil Guard overpowered the workers, loaded them on to lorries and then drove south towards the advancing rebel forces. At El Ronquillo in the north of the province of Seville, they met up with Castejón's forces. Before joining them on their march northwards, the prisoners from Llerena were shot.

The Mayor, Rafael Maltrana, having escaped at the bridge by jumping from a truck taking the prisoners to be executed, had managed to return to Llerena. Castejón's forces easily annihilated the sporadic opposition on the road northwards. At dawn the following day, Llerena was encircled, then shelled. As the Moors, Legionarios and Civil Guards closed the circle advancing into the town, the defenders retreated to the main square. Armed only with shotguns and crude home-made bombs, they took refuge in the town hall, a school and the church. The town hall and the school were reduced by the use of hand grenades and those defenders found alive were bayoneted. The church was bombarded with artillery, then set alight. One hundred and fifty Republicans were killed, while Castejón lost two dead and twelve wounded. According to the right-wing journalist who accompanied the columns, Manuel Sánchez del Arco, the Moors were so impressed by the bravery with which the defenders of Llerena died that they commented, 'the revolutionaries here not like

Jews', a remark redolent of the prejudices of their officers. A small band of militiamen led by Rafael Maltrana managed to escape.[9]

In each of the towns and villages along the route of the African columns, the streets were left littered with the bayoneted corpses of those unfortunate enough to have been in their way. The first town reached by Castejón where a significant left-wing atrocity had been committed was Fuente de Cantos. In fact, it was one of the few where the local right suffered violence. There, nearly seventy right-wingers had been arrested on 18 July. The next day, groups of masked leftists from surrounding villages, armed with shotguns, locked fifty-six of them in the town church. Despite the desperate efforts of the Mayor, Modesto José Lorenzana Macarro, to stop them, the church was soaked with petrol and set alight. Twelve people died. Lorenzana was more successful on 4 August. As Castejón's column approached, the town was bombed and a twenty-year-old woman was killed. When an enraged mob attempted a further assault on over ninety right-wing prisoners in the town jail, Lorenzana risked his own life. Pistol in hand, he confronted the would-be assassins saying, 'there have already been enough deaths in this town', at which one of the thwarted crowd quipped prophetically, 'Well, you watch out, because those whose lives you're saving now will be the ones who kill you.' However, aware of the consequences of the earlier massacre, most of the town's leftists, including Lorenzana, fled. Fuente de Cantos was virtually empty when the column arrived. When it moved on, Castejón left, on Franco's orders, a company of Regulares under the command of the Civil Guard Captain Ernesto Navarrete Alcal, to undertake the repression in the area. Between 6 August and 30 December, for each one of the victims in the church at Fuente de Cantos, twenty-five supposed leftists were shot without trial. Among them were sixty-two women, several of them pregnant and many raped before being shot.[10] Thereafter, Navarrete was accused by local members of the Falange of stealing vehicles, works of art, crops and other property. The scale of his requisitions, including several tons of grain, was such that they occupied various warehouses.[11]

A large column of Republican militia led by professional army officers was sent from Badajoz in an effort to halt the Africanista advance. On 5 August, near Los Santos de Maimona, they mounted a desperate defensive action but were overwhelmed by the better-trained, better-armed column of Asensio with its artillery and air support. To weigh the odds further, disloyal army officers had disabled the Republican artillery pieces. The rebel columns suffered four dead; the defenders about 250.

Before moving to Zafra, in the early hours of the morning of 7 August, Castejón sent twenty Falangists and twenty Carlist Requetés to carry on the repression in Los Santos de Maimona. Neither there nor in Zafra had any right-wingers been killed. In Los Santos de Maimona, the parish priest, Ezequiel Fernández Santana, pleaded vainly with the Falangists on behalf of the chosen victims. One hundred were shot in the immediate aftermath of the fall of the town. Many more suffered imprisonment, harassment, confiscation of their goods and fines.

Despite considerable class tension in Zafra, during the five months between the elections of February and the arrival of Castejón's column, the Mayor, José González Barrero, had worked hard to restrain left-wing reprisals for the social abuses of 1933–5. There were some assaults on right-wingers and he was obliged to evacuate several religious communities. However, at considerable risk to his own life, he managed to ensure that no blood was shed. After the military coup, González Barrero presided over the town's Popular Front Committee which imprisoned twenty-eight known supporters of the uprising. He prevented two attempts by radical elements to kill these prisoners. Nevertheless, in Zafra, which fell on 6 August virtually without resistance, as in Los Santos de Maimona, the repression was every bit as ferocious as in Fuente de Cantos. Forty people were shot on the first day of the military occupation of Zafra, and two hundred in total over the next months. At the end of the war, González Barrero found himself in Madrid. After Franco had announced that those without blood on their hands had nothing to fear, believing himself totally innocent, he returned home, was arrested and interned in the concentration camp of Castuera and executed at the end of April 1939.[12]

In all these towns, the occupying troops raped working-class women and looted the houses of leftists. Francoist officers admitted that Moroccan mercenaries were recruited with promises of pillage and that, when a town was captured, they were given free rein for two hours.[13] Moorish soldiers and Legionarios selling radios, clocks, watches, jewellery and even items of furniture became a common sight in the towns of the south. The Falangist elements that undertook the repression after the columns had moved on also looted at will.[14] When the columns moved northwards from Zafra, the deputy parish priest of the Church of La Candelaria, Juan Galán Bermejo, decided to join them as a chaplain. Thereafter, this tall, wavy-haired priest, with a large pistol in his belt, distinguished himself by the bloodthirsty ruthlessness with which he participated in the repression. On one occasion, discovering four men and a wounded woman in a cave near the border of Badajoz with Córdoba, he forced them to dig their own graves before shooting them and burying them wounded but still alive. He later boasted of personally killing more than one hundred leftists.[15]

From Zafra, the next towns on the road to Mérida were Villafranca de los Barros and Almendralejo. Bypassing Villafranca on the night of 7 August, Asensio's column moved on towards Almendralejo. Since there had been no assassinations of rightists in Villafranca, the inhabitants felt reasonably secure. However, angry leftists fleeing from the terror of the columns arrived with news of the slaughter, only too ready to exorcize their fears and hatred on the rightists found in the towns as yet unconquered. On the morning of 8 August, retreating militiamen tried to burn a church in Villafranca where fifty-four right-wing prisoners were being held but were foiled by the local Popular Front Committee. Nevertheless, as punishment for the unsuccessful attempt, the inhabitants of the town suffered a savage repression when, on the next day, Asensio sent back a detachment from Almendralejo to occupy Villafranca. Despite the fact that the more prominent leftists had already fled, they arrested several hundred people and shot fifty-six of them. More than three hundred were shot over the next three months. Inevitably, this had an impact on the repression in the Republican zone. In revenge for what happened in their town, individuals from Villafranca were involved in killings in Madrid and eastern Extremadura.[16]

Asensio's column was experiencing considerable trouble controlling Almendralejo despite having subjected the town to artillery and air bombardment. Militiamen threatened to burn down the building holding right-wing prisoners if Asensio's men entered the town. When they breached the outskirts, twenty-eight of the prisoners were killed. Reinforced by Castejón's column, Asensio now advanced into the centre. Forty leftists had taken refuge in the parish church, so Asensio set fires, to which wet straw and sulphur were added, to force them out with the noxious fumes. When that failed, what was left of the church after repeated shelling was burned down. All resistance was at an end by 10 August and several hundred prisoners were taken.[17] According to contemporary press reports, more than one thousand people including one hundred women were shot in what the Portuguese press called 'this accursed town'. Local historians investigating the repression during occupation and the following three months have been able to confirm the names of over four hundred men and of sixteen women but conclude that the number of both sexes executed was certainly much higher. After the shootings, many women were raped and others had their heads shaved and were forced to drink castor oil. Many men were given the choice 'to Russia or the Legion', 'Russia' signifying execution. They usually chose recruitment into the Legion. Local right-wingers organized mounted patrols to search the surrounding countryside for escaped leftists.[18]

This deliberate savagery constituted what one scholar has called 'education through terror'. The aim was literally to bury for once and for all the aspiration of the landless peasants to collectivize the great estates. Using the excuse of the 'red terror', irrespective of whether there had actually been any crimes against the local conservatives, a vengeful bloodbath was unleashed by the rebel columns. In places where rightists had been protected by the Popular Front Committee, it was claimed that the columns had arrived just in time to prevent atrocities. Members of the Popular Front Committee found in a village would be shot. A similar fate awaited members of left-wing trade unions and many totally apolitical individuals unfortunate enough to be in the way. The 'crimes' of those executed were often unrelated to atrocities. The local right was outraged that, since the elections of February 1936, left-wing councils, in agreement with the Casas del Pueblo, had obliged the principal landowners to give jobs to unionized labour, forced them to pay wages outstanding since 1934 and prohibited religious ceremonies.[19] During the spring and summer of 1936, wealthy middle- and upper-class inhabitants of the towns and villages of the rural south faced insults and impertinence from those that they regarded as their inferiors. This intolerable challenge to their social and economic status lay behind the approval of many conservatives for the brutality of the African columns.[20]

The *latifundio* system of sprawling estates, the dominant mode of landholding in Andalusia, Extremadura and Salamanca, made it easier for the owners to think of the *bracero* (labourer hired by the day) as subhuman and a 'thing' to be punished or annihilated for daring to rebel. To the owners, the entire experience of the Second Republic constituted a 'rebellion'. After the bloodshed at Almendralejo, Franco ordered the columns of Asensio and Castejón to join together and press on to attack Mérida and Badajoz. With the local right reluctant to see him go until the left had been definitively eliminated from the town, Castejón requested units of the Civil Guard and armed Falangists and Carlists to finish the 'cleansing'.[21]

Franco now gave overall field command of the three columns to Lieutenant Colonel Juan Yagüe Blanco.[22] Ramón Serrano Suñer described

Yagüe as 'Chunky, tall, with a leonine mane and the look of a hunting animal – a short-sighted one – he was an intelligent man but led, at times blinded, by his temper. A bully and a rebellious braggart, he often suffered cyclical depressions, perhaps the result of an improperly healed wound, which made his actions inconsistent and incoherent.' Born in San Leonardo in Soria on 9 November 1891, he attended the infantry academy in Toledo at the same time as Franco. He was a typical Africanista having, for eighteen of his twenty-six years as a soldier before 1936, served in Morocco where his impulsive bravery saw him wounded three times, frequently decorated and promoted to the rank of lieutenant colonel by 1928. His role in Asturias established the bespectacled Yagüe, with his mane of grey hair, as the Africanista most feared by the left.[23]

Franco ordered Yagüe to mount a three-pronged attack on Mérida, the old Roman town on the road to Cáceres, and an important communications centre between Seville and Portugal. Mérida was subjected to fierce air and artillery bombardment. Yagüe chose as his senior artillery commander Captain Luis Alarcón de la Lastra, the landowning Africanista from Carmona. Mérida fell on 11 August, at a cost of nine rebels and 250 defenders left dead. The defence had been based naively on an antique cannon aimed across the Roman bridge over the River Guadiana. In the event, demoralized by an artillery bombardment, the poorly armed defenders were no match for the machine-guns of Asensio's troops. The usual bloody repression took place. Those leftists who were unable to escape took refuge in the cellar of the Casa del Pueblo. They were obliged to file out one by one and were shot as they emerged. In the following days, house after house was searched, mass arrests were made and more men were shot and women were sexually humiliated.[24]

The repression in Mérida went on for months at the hands of Falangists under the overall charge of a sinister Civil Guard, Manuel Gómez Cantos. After acquiring a reputation for perverse brutality in various southern postings, especially in Málaga, he had been posted to Villanueva de la Serena in the north-east of Badajoz. On 19 July, he had led an uprising of the town's Civil Guard garrison. After a bloody victory, helped by local Falangists, Gómez Cantos detained members of the town council and of the Casa del Pueblo and other leftists. When Republican relief forces neared the town, he led his men and his prisoners to Miajadas in the rebel-dominated province of Cáceres. The hostages were taken to the provincial capital where some were shot and others taken back for execution in Villanueva when it was captured in 1938. In

Miajadas, Gómez Cantos was joined by a substantial number of other rebel Civil Guards.[25]

Thereafter, he rose to a point where he had a virtually free hand in the repression. He was promoted to major on 11 August. In Mérida, he supervised nightly executions of men held in the Casino, which had been turned into an improvised prison. One of his prisoners was a liberal Republican, Dr Temprano. Each day for a month, Gómez Cantos would walk around the town centre with the doctor, taking note of anyone who greeted him. The doctor's friends were thus identified and then arrested. Gómez Cantos himself shot the doctor. In February 1938, Queipo de Llano would send Gómez Cantos as Delegate for Public Order for Badajoz. Despite the fact that the repression under his predecessors had virtually eliminated the left, he had the idea of having a stripe of red paint brushed on to the jacket of anyone suspected of left-wing sympathies.[26]

On reaching Mérida, Franco's forces had advanced 125 miles in a week. The battle experience of the African Army in open scrub easily explains the success of Asensio and Castejón. The scratch Republican militia would fight desperately as long as they enjoyed the cover of buildings or trees. However, they were not trained in elementary ground movements or even in the care and reloading of their weapons. Bunched near roads, seemingly unaware of better positions on nearby hill slopes, they made easy targets. The accumulated terror that accompanied the advance of the Moors and the Legionarios, a terror amplified after each victory, ensured that even the rumoured threat of being outflanked would send them fleeing, abandoning their equipment as they ran. John T. Whitaker of the *New York Herald Tribune* commented, 'Marching with these Moors, I watched them flank, dislodge, and annihilate ten times their numbers in battle after battle. Individual heroism among untrained soldiers is not enough against professionals supported by aircraft.'[27]

Franco was fully aware of the columns' superiority over untrained and poorly armed militias and he and his chief of staff, Colonel Francisco Martín Moreno, planned their operations accordingly. Intimidation and terror, euphemistically described as 'castigo' (punishment), were specified in written orders.[28] Martín Moreno summed up the situation in an order of 12 August, in which he observed:

The quality of the enemy that faces us, with neither discipline nor military training, lacking trained leaders, and short of arms, ammunition and support services, means that, in combat, resistance is generally feeble ... Our superiority in weaponry and our skilful use thereof permits us to achieve our objectives with very few casualties. The psychological impact of mortars or the accurate use of machine-gun fire is enormous on those who don't have such weapons or don't know how to use them.[29]

The use of terror was neither spontaneous nor an inadvertent side-effect. The Legion as well as the Regulares mutilated casualties, cutting off ears, noses, sexual organs and even heads. Such practices, along with the massacres of prisoners and the systematic rape of working-class women, were permitted by the rebel officers in Spain as they had been in Morocco by Franco and others. As had been the case in Asturias in 1934, they were useful in several ways. They indulged the bloodlust of the African columns, they eliminated large numbers of potential opponents and, above all, they generated a paralysing terror among others.[30] The rebels were sufficiently uneasy about what they were doing to feel the need to conceal it. On or around 13 August, General Queipo de Llano was interviewed in Seville by the immensely sympathetic correspondent of the London *Daily Mail*, Harold Cardozo. Queipo de Llano assured the British journalist that:

> Except in the heat of battle or in the capture by assault of a position, no men are shot down without being given a hearing and a fair trial in strict accordance with the rule of procedure of our military courts. The trials are held in public and those only are condemned to death who have personally taken part in murders and other crimes punishable according to our military code by death, or who by their position of authority are responsible for having allowed such crimes to be committed. I have taken thousands of prisoners, and today more than half of them are at liberty.[31]

However, Harold Pemberton, the correspondent of the equally pro-rebel *Daily Express*, reported that, after the capture of Mérida, members of the Legion tried to sell him and his photographer 'Communist ears as souvenirs'.[32]

After the occupation of Mérida, Yagüe's troops turned south-west towards Badajoz, the principal town of Extremadura, on the banks of the River Guadiana near the Portuguese frontier. If the columns had hastened onwards to Madrid, the Badajoz garrison could not seriously have threatened them from the rear. Francoist military historians have implied that Yagüe turned to Badajoz on his own initiative. If this had been the case, he would have been in serious trouble with Franco, who made all the major daily decisions, which were then implemented by Yagüe. Franco personally supervised the operation against Mérida and, on the evening of 10 August, received Yagüe in his headquarters to discuss the capture of Badajoz and the next objectives. He wanted to knock out Badajoz to unify the two sections of the rebel zone and leave the left flank of the advancing columns covered by the Portuguese border. It was a strategic error, contributing to the delay which allowed the government to organize its defences. However, Franco, as he showed repeatedly during the war, was more concerned with a total purge of all conquered territory than with a quick victory.[33]

One of the first villages after Mérida was Torremayor. There, the Popular Front Committee had ensured that there was no violence. No rightists had been imprisoned, no atrocities committed, and Yagüe's troops passed by without incident.[34] Midway between Badajoz and Mérida lay the contiguous towns of Lobón, Montijo and Puebla de la Calzada. When news of the military conspiracy had reached all three, Defence Committees had been set up with representatives of all the left-wing parties and trade unions. Local 'militias' were created and armed with the few hunting shotguns possessed by workers or confiscated from the rich. In Puebla de la Calzada, the 'militia' had thirty-three members; in Montijo, it was one hundred strong. In all three towns, the Committees arrested those wealthy members of the local population who supported the military uprising. In Puebla de la Calzada, many of the sixty-six men detained were landowners who had refused to pay workers placed on their estates. Nineteen were property-owners, twelve were farmers and four were owners of small factories. All were well treated, their families being allowed to bring them food, tobacco, mattresses and blankets. Those who paid the wages owing to their labourers were released. The Committee ensured that no prisoners were killed but, when Yagüe's column arrived at dawn on 13 August, the prisoners claimed falsely that they were about to be burned alive in the village church. In Montijo, fifty-six rightists were detained in a convent. Their families were allowed to bring them food, but the prisoners were obliged to work in the fields and some were mistreated by their guards. Nevertheless, when some militiamen from Badajoz tried to burn down the convent, the town's Committee prevented them.[35]

Faced with Yagüe's three thousand hardened mercenaries, many left-wingers of both Puebla de la Calzada and Montijo fled, some to join in the defence of Badajoz, others east towards Don Benito. When Yagüe received the surrender of the villages, he named a right-wing committee to run each and gave them the following instruction: 'leave no left-wing leader alive'. Falangists sacked the Casa del Pueblo of Puebla de la Calzada, burning most of its contents other than membership lists. Despite the efforts of the president of the new Committee, once of the CEDA and now of the Falange, twenty-nine men and one woman were shot. She, along with other female trade unionists and wives of leftists, was taken to the town square where they all had their heads shaved and were forced to drink castor oil. After being made to witness her execution, the others were then slowly paraded back to their homes, soiling themselves as they went. In addition to this systematic humiliation, most of them found it extremely difficult to find work again.

To lure back those who had fled, the new administrations of both towns issued a statement that those not guilty of 'crimes of blood' could safely return home. Once again, those who naively returned were arrested and shot. In Montijo, a major religious festival was arranged on 28 August, the culmination of which was the exhibition of the town's remaining left-wingers and trade union leaders who were forced at gunpoint to ask forgiveness for their grave sins. At dawn on 29 August, fourteen of them, including the Mayor Miguel Merino Rodríguez, were shot. His land was confiscated and his widow and six children were left in extreme poverty. The shootings went on for years thereafter and claimed well over one hundred victims.[36]

On 2 September in nearby Torremayor where, it will be recalled, no violence had occurred, a group of Falangist thugs arrived. They burst into the houses of the president of the Popular Front Committee, of its secretary, a schoolteacher, and of the president of the Casa del Pueblo. After searching the houses and stealing money and jewellery, the Falangists took the three men away and murdered them. When she heard the news, the seriously ill wife of the schoolteacher died, leaving two daughters, one aged twenty-one months and the other four years. Her brother, a senior Falangist in Seville, endeavoured to get some sort of pension for the children. This was refused because their father was not officially dead. An inquiry then revealed that the Falangists had taken the three men to the local Civil Guard post where a 'tribunal' consisting of their leader and two Civil Guards had condemned the men to death. The parish priest of Torremayor then accompanied them to the cemetery where they were shot. The Falangists said that they were obeying the instructions left by Yagüe in Lobón, Montijo and Puebla de la Calzada to shoot all left-wingers 'responsible for the anarchic state in which Spain found itself'. The death of the schoolteacher was finally registered, but no action was taken against the Falangists.[37]

After capturing Puebla de la Calzada, Montijo and Lobón, Yagüe's troops proceeded westwards to Talavera la Real. There, too, eighty-two local rightists had been arrested by the Popular Front Committee. They had been paraded through the town streets and insulted. Many were forced to pay outstanding wages to workers. Fifty-nine were detained in a church, the other twenty-three in the municipal storehouse. When Yagüe's troops were on the point of entering the town, an attempt by drunken militiamen to burn the church down was prevented by two local leftists. Others, together with members of the committee, fled, taking with them twenty-three rightist prisoners. Half a mile outside Talavera, they shot them, killing twenty-one. Not surprisingly, one of the two survivors took part in the subsequent repression in which, according to local estimates, nearly 250 people were shot.[38]

Yagüe's column moved on to Badajoz. The military coup had failed there. This was thanks in part to the decisive action of the Popular Front Defence Committee led by the Civil Governor Miguel Granados Ruiz, the Socialist deputy Nicolás de Pablo and the Mayor Sinforiano Madroñero. The Committee had quickly ordered the arrest of more than three hundred rebel supporters and organized the creation and (utterly inadequate) arming of militia groups. The rebel failure in Badajoz also reflected indecision and divisions among the local military commanders and the fact that in Badajoz, unlike other southern cities, there was a group of firmly pro-Republican officers. On 26 July, the Madrid government sent Colonel Ildefonso Puigdengolas Ponce de León to take over the defence of the town. Wearing the blue overalls of the militia and fresh from overcoming the uprising in Guadalajara and Alcalá de Henares, Puigdengolas was welcomed as a hero by the left in Badajoz. He arrested some of the more suspect officers and began training the militias.[39]

Before the arrival of Yagüe's forces, there was little violence against rightists in Badajoz. This was largely thanks to the efforts of both the Mayor, Sinforiano Madroñero, and the head of the police, Eduardo Fernández Arlazón. Although later condemned to death by the Francoists, Fernández Arlazón's sentence was commuted to thirty years' imprisonment in recognition of numerous testimonies from grateful rightists. Prior to a failed uprising by the local Civil Guard garrison on 6 August, the only fatal incident in the town took place on 22 July when militiamen killed Feliciano Sánchez Barriga, an extreme rightist land-owner who had been the liaison between the military conspirators and the local Falange. The Bishop of Badajoz, José María Alcaraz Alenda, was evicted peacefully from his palace, permitted to take the Holy Sacrament from the tabernacle and also provided with a bodyguard. When casualties started to mount after daily rebel bombing raids began on 7 August, and in the wake of the Civil Guard uprising on the previous day, there were reprisals. Ten men were killed in total, the victims being two army officers, two retired Civil Guards, two religious and four prominent rightists. In one case, the victim was a man who had been on a rooftop signalling to the attacking aircraft. The gang responsible for these murders was in no way connected with the Defence Committee and most of its members were either killed in Yagüe's attack or else escaped. Most right-wing prisoners arrested by the Committee were unharmed. That, however, did not prevent the massacre carried out in reprisal for the 'red terror'.[40]

When Yagüe's forces encircled the walled city, their reputation had preceded them. Badajoz had been flooded with refugees and, since the daily bombings had begun, the atmosphere in the city was of doom-laden anticipation. On 13 August, a rebel aircraft flew over the city and dropped thousands of leaflets carrying a dire warning signed by Franco. It read 'Your resistance will be pointless and the punishment that you will receive will be proportionate. If you want to avoid useless bloodshed, capture the ringleaders and hand them over to our forces ... Our triumph is guaranteed and, to save Spain, we will destroy any obstacles in our way. It is still time for you to mend your ways: tomorrow it will be too late.' The leaflet clearly signalled the massacre to come.[41]

The defenders commanded by Puigdengolas numbered approximately 1,700, of whom about one-third were soldiers and the remainder poorly armed militiamen, some from the town itself and others who had fled there from the advancing columns. Recruitment of volunteers for the defence of the city had begun only on 4 August after the fall of Llerena. A few were armed with rifles, but ammunition was scarce. Many had only scythes and hunting shotguns. Most of the regular troops garrisoned there had been called away to reinforce the Madrid front. As the air and artillery bombardments took their toll, there had been a constant trickle of desertions. Certainly the real numbers of defenders were a fraction of those implied in rebel sources. Yagüe's forces were altogether more numerous than the handful of heroes lauded in the same literature. The united columns of Castejón and Asensio had 2,500 soldiers, as well as many Requetés and Falangists who had joined them on their passage from Seville. Moreover, several of Colonel Puigdengolas's officers were of dubious loyalty and did what they could to obstruct defensive preparations, hiding weapons and misdirecting guns.[42]

In the early hours of 14 August, bombing attacks were mounted and the city was heavily pounded by Alarcón de la Lastra's artillery. At about 9.00 a.m., Puigdengolas, Nicolás de Pablo, the Mayor, and other members of the Defence Committee fled to Portugal. In the course of the morning, after their flight, numerous officers went over to the attackers. By midday, despite the desperate courage of the civilian militia, the walls of Badajoz were breached by ferocious attacks from Castejón's troops. Their task was facilitated by the small fifth column of regular officers among the defenders. Several of these abandoned their defensive positions and gathered by the town prison in order to join the right-wing detainees there in greeting their 'liberators'. One of those released was Regino Valencia, the friend of Salazar Alonso and murderer of the PSOE deputy, Pedro Rubio Heredia. As the Legionarios and Regulares advanced into the centre, they killed anyone in their path, including those who had thrown down their weapons and had their hands up.[43] Many militiamen fled into the Cathedral, where some were bayoneted in the aisles and others on the steps of the high altar. One man who hid in a confessional box was shot dead where he knelt by Father Juan Galán Bermejo, the priest from Zafra who had become a chaplain with the Legion. With his heavily brillantined hair, his swagger stick and pistol, Father Galán was carefully building a reputation for cruelty.[44]

The Legionarios and Regulares, and the Falangists who had accompanied them, unleashed an orgy of looting in shops and houses, most of which belonged to the very rightists who were being 'liberated'. 'It is the war tax they pay for salvation,' a rebel officer told the American journalist Jay Allen. Anything portable – jewellery and watches, radios and typewriters, clothing and bales of cloth – was carried off through streets strewn with corpses and running with blood. Hundreds of prisoners were rounded up and herded to the bullring. As night fell, drunken Moors and Falangists were still entering houses in the working-class districts, looting, raping women, dragging men out either to shoot them on the spot or to take them to the bullring. Many corpses were sexually mutilated. At the bullring, machine-guns were set up on the barriers around the ring and an indiscriminate slaughter began. On the first afternoon and evening, eight hundred were shot in batches of twenty. In the course of the night, another 1,200 were brought in. There were many innocent non-political civilians, men and women, Socialists, anarchists, Communists, middle-class Republicans, simple labourers and anyone with the bruise of a rifle recoil on their shoulders. No names were taken, no details checked. At 7.30 in the morning, the shootings began again. The screams of the dying could be heard many streets away. Accounts by survivors indicate that soon the firing squads were manned by Civil Guards.[45]

Over the next three days, as Yagüe's columns prepared to move northwards, the Moors set up stalls to sell the watches, jewellery and furniture that they had looted. Yagüe himself stole a limousine belonging to the moderate Republican Luis Plá Alvarez. Together with his brother, Plá owned a thriving transport and automobile sales business. The two men had used their influence to save the lives of numerous right-wingers and had sheltered several religious in their homes, many of whom wrote appeals in their favour. They were taken out into the countryside by Civil Guards on 19 August, told that they were free to go and shot 'while trying to escape'. Their businesses and goods were seized.[46] Bishop Alcaraz Alenda had interceded on their behalf, but Yagüe told his messenger: 'Tell the Bishop that they have already been shot this morning along with others so that the Bishop may live.'[47] By the second day, cheering right-wing spectators were permitted to watch and to insult the prisoners. Even if there was not, as was later alleged in the Republican press, a simulacrum of a bullfight, men were certainly treated as if they were animals. With their amused officers looking on, Moorish troops and Falangists goaded the prisoners with bayonets. Franco's General Staff and the Portuguese border police were working in close collaboration. Accordingly, hundreds of refugees attempting to flee into Portugal were turned back.[48] The scenes in the bullring were witnessed by Portuguese landowners invited as a reward for handing over fleeing leftists.[49]

Although there had been few killings of rightists in Badajoz, the intense rhythm of killings was maintained for months. After the departure of Yagüe, the repression was supervised by the new Military Governor, Colonel Eduardo Cañizares, and Lieutenant Colonel Manuel Pereita Vela, sent from Seville by Queipo de Llano on 18 August as commander of the Civil Guard and Delegate for Public Order. It has been suggested that Pereita was responsible for a further 2,580 deaths before he was replaced on 11 November 1936. His successor, Manuel Gómez Cantos, reported that Pereita had accumulated a fortune on the basis of property, including land and cattle, confiscated from his victims. Egged on by a Falangist landowner from Olivenza, Pereita began to order arrests on the basis of the most frivolous or malicious denunciations, or the slightest hint of leftist or liberal leanings. Those arrested were usually shot, without any investigation. The Falange, swollen with the young scions of the landowning class, eagerly joined in the carnage. Prisoners were brought in from other parts of Extremadura, as the local right seized the opportunity to put an end for ever to the threat of agrarian reform. Young women who had served in the houses of the wealthy as maids and seamstresses were sexually abused as punishment for having attempted to form a union in the spring of 1936. Female members of other trades suffered equally.[50]

On Tuesday 18 August, four hundred men, women and children were taken by cavalry escorts from Caia in Portugal to Badajoz. Nearly three hundred of them were executed. Expeditions of Falangists were given free rein to enter Portugal in search of Spanish refugees. Jay Allen described the scene in Elvas:

> This very day (August 23) a car flying the red and yellow banner of the Rebels arrived here. In it were three Phalanxists (Fascists). They were accompanied by a Portuguese lieutenant. They tore through the narrow streets to the hospital where Senor Granado [sic], Republican Civil Governor of Badajoz, was lying. The Fascists ran up the stairs, strode down a corridor with guns drawn, and into the governor's room. The governor was out of his mind with the horror of the thing. The director of the hospital, Dr. Pabgeno, threw himself over his helpless patient and howled for help. So he saved a life.[51]

Among the many liberals, leftists, Freemasons and others brought back to be shot were the Mayor, Sinforiano Madroñero, and two Socialist deputies, Nicolás de Pablo and Anselmo Trejo. Dragged through the streets, their clothes ripped, their flesh bruised, they were executed as the culmination of an elaborate ceremony on 30 August, after a procession with a band and a field Mass. Colonel Cañizares informed Antonio Bahamonde, Queipo de Llano's head of press and propaganda, that the later executions were accompanied by a military band playing the royal anthem and the Falangist hymn. Many spectators came from nearby Portugal and applauded frenetically as the executed fell. Nevertheless, many ordinary Portuguese families took in refugees from Badajoz and Huelva and several Portuguese army officers saved Spanish lives.[52] In mid-October, 1,435 refugees were sent to Republican Spain in a boat from Lisbon to Tarragona.[53]

The historian Francisco Espinosa Maestre has demonstrated that the total number of casualties suffered by Yagüe's men in the attack on Badajoz was 185, of whom 44 were killed and 141 wounded. The disproportion with the Republican casualties could hardly have been greater.[54] Estimates of those killed in the subsequent repression vary from 9,000 to 'between two and six hundred'. Many of those executed in the days following the initial massacre were either militiamen who had come to help defend the city, refugees who had fled there or prisoners brought there from other towns. Since they were shot without trial, their bodies disposed of in common graves or else incinerated, there is no record of them. Nevertheless, an exhaustive study by Dr Espinosa Maestre has shown that the number is at least 3,800. He has demonstrated that, even limiting the comparison to the small number of the known victims whose deaths were registered, there were more executions in Badajoz between August and December 1936 than in Huelva and Seville combined, despite the fact that Huelva's population was 12.5 per cent larger than that of Badajoz and Seville's more than 600 per cent. Moreover, in both Seville and Huelva, it was possible to compare the names in the city registries with the names of those buried in their respective cemeteries. In both cities, in addition to those inscribed in the registry, the cemeteries have records of unnamed corpses. In the case of Huelva, there were five times as many unknown as named dead; in the case of Seville, nearly six times as many. Extrapolating from this data for Badajoz, where there are no records of the unnamed dead buried in the cemetery, Espinosa Maestre calculates that the total number of killed in the city might have been around 5.5 times the number of the named dead.[55]

In the intense summer heat, the piles of corpses constituted a major public health risk. They were thrown on to lorries that ran back and forth to the municipal cemetery. Since neither the local sanitation services nor private mortuaries could cope with the bodies, they were soaked in petrol, set alight and then buried in large common graves. Throughout the long hot summer, the stench of the burned corpses permeated the night. Left-wing women who were not shot or raped after the capture of the town were subjected to systematic humiliation. Their heads were shaved and they were forced to drink castor oil, on the grounds that 'their tongues were dirty'.[56]

Yagüe had prevented correspondents from entering the town with the troops. However, in the early hours of the morning of 15 August, several journalists, mainly Portuguese, and two French, Marcel Dany of the

Havas Agency and Jacques Berthet of *Le Temps* of Paris, arrived from Elvas. As they drove into the town they could see a column of smoke from the cemetery and were assailed by a sickly sweet stench. They witnessed what Mário Neves of the *Diário de Lisboa* called 'a scene of desolation and dread'. Neves managed to interview Yagüe and asked him if it were true, as he had heard, that two thousand men had already been shot in the course of the night. Yagüe replied, 'Oh, not quite that many.' A priest who acted as guide for Neves, Dany and Berthet took them to the cemetery to see the great piles of corpses being burned. Some were completely carbonized, but there emerged arms and legs so far untouched by the flames. Seeing the horrified looks of the journalists, the priest explained: 'They deserved this. Moreover, it is a crucial measure of hygiene.' It was not clear whether he referred to the killings or to the disposal of the corpses. Another Portuguese journalist, Mario Pires of the *Diário de Notícias*, was so disturbed by the executions he had witnessed that he had to be interned in a mental institution in Lisbon. Castejón told Jorge Simões of the *Diário da Manhã* that 1,500 defenders had been killed, both in the fighting and afterwards. Simões wrote that 1,300 had been shot by the Legion in the first twenty-four hours after the conquest. Two days later, Felix Correia of the *Diário de Lisboa*, the journalist closest to Queipo de Llano, wrote that 1,600 had been executed. Yagüe himself commented on 15 August, 'After the final clean-up tomorrow, everything will be ready for a more extended operation. Now, with the Muscovites liquidated, this is a Spanish city once more.'[57]

On 17 August, the cameraman René Brut of Pathé newsreels arrived and was able to film piles of bodies, for which act of courage he was later imprisoned and threatened with death by the insurgent authorities.[58] Some days later, Franco sent a telegram to Queipo de Llano with instructions for the strict control of photographers, 'even those from Nationalist newspapers', although this was to conceal the delivery of German and Italian war material as much as to hide the atrocities committed by his columns.[59] It was the beginning of a massive campaign by the rebel authorities and their foreign supporters to deny that the massacre at Badajoz had taken place. Their cause was not helped when Yagüe cheerfully boasted to the journalist John Whitaker, 'Of course, we shot them. What do you expect? Was I supposed to take four thousand Reds with me as my column advanced racing against time? Was I expected to turn them loose in my rear and let them make Badajoz Red again?' In a town of 40,000 people, the killings may have reached nearly 10 per cent of the population.[60]

According to Yagüe's biographer, in 'the paroxysm of war' it was impossible to distinguish pacific citizens from leftist militiamen, the implication being that it was perfectly acceptable to shoot prisoners. Another semi-official military historian of the rebel war effort, Luis María de Lojendio, later mitred Abbot of the monastery of the Valle de los Caídos, not only claimed that the defending forces were greater but also managed to explain away the deaths among them with pious sophistry:

> A really criminal war is that in which chemical or technological mechanisms destroy human life pointlessly. But this was not the case in Badajoz. The material advantage, the fortress and the barricades, lay with the Marxists. The men of Lieutenant Colonel Yagüe triumphed because of that indubitably spiritual superiority which maintains in combat the will to win, the virtues of sacrifice and discipline. The streets of Badajoz were sown with corpses. Well, war is a hard and cruel spectacle.[61]

The savagery unleashed on Badajoz reflected both the traditions of the Spanish Moroccan Army and the outrage of the African columns at encountering solid resistance and, for the first time, suffering serious casualties. It was part of a deliberate attempt to paralyse the enemy, as well as to reward the men of the column with an orgy of rape, looting, killing and alcohol. It had a past, a colonial tradition. It had a present, as a reflection of the determination of the landowners to crush the rural proletariat once and for all. It also had a future. In late August, as the Basque towns of Irún and Fuenterrabía were being shelled from the sea and bombed from the air, the rebels dropped pamphlets threatening to deal with the population as they had dealt with the people of Badajoz. In consequence, panic-stricken refugees headed for France.[62] The events of Badajoz were also meant as a message to the inhabitants of the capital as to what would happen when the columns reached Madrid.

The speed with which the African columns had progressed left many towns and villages still unconquered to the west of the line of their advance and between Badajoz and Cáceres. In these places, desperate refugees gathered. Following the pattern of what had happened in Seville and Huelva, before setting off for Madrid Yagüe organized small columns of local rightists, landowners, their sons and faithful retainers, Falangists, Requetés and a sprinkling of Civil Guards, under the command of an officer. They spread out from Badajoz to the surrounding villages where they implemented a brutal repression. Irrespective of whether local rightists had been killed or merely suffered preventive detention, men and women were shot without the slightest pretence of a trial. Among the more enthusiastically brutal leaders of such columns were the Civil Guard Captain Ernesto Navarrete Alcal and two Africanistas, Lieutenant Colonel Francisco Delgado Serrano and the Major of Regulares Mohammed ben Mizzian. Among the civilian volunteers were not only local Falangists of more or less recent vintage but also contingents from Vigo and Valladolid, who had run out of victims in their provinces of origin.

Between 19 and 29 August, these rebel columns captured dozens of towns and villages in the western part of the province of Badajoz. It was often the case that the Defence Committee of these villages had arrested local rightists and confiscated their weapons. In most cases they were insulted, in some forced to pay outstanding wages to day-labourers. Later accounts record their indignation at such humiliations which were sometimes no more than the Committee insisting that their own families, as opposed to their servants, delivered their food. Sometimes, the able-bodied prisoners were obliged to undertake physical labour ranging from road-mending to agricultural tasks. There was outrage expressed later that they had been forced to clean their prison, a church or a warehouse, and dispose of their own excrement. More irksome was the requisition of cows, sheep and pigs to be rationed to feed the workers. Olive oil, hams, chorizos and other food were also collected from the houses of the rich.[63] In some villages, the rightist prisoners were beaten and, in others, murdered. The cases where this happened were greatly outnumbered by those where the local authorities prevented atrocities being committed by militiamen from other villages bent on revenge for the horrors committed by the African columns.

The subsequent revenge was wildly disproportionate. Where there had been murders of right-wingers, those killed in reprisal were rarely the perpetrators, who had usually fled. The executions were justified on the specious grounds that the left had intended to kill all the prisoners but had not done so thanks to the arrival of the column. Similarly, although there were generalized allegations of sexual abuse of right-wing women prisoners, specific accusations tend to centre on intentions which had been thwarted by members of the Defence Committees. The leftist authorities did not have a programme of extermination like that of the military rebels. Landowners who had sought confrontation with their workers by denying them jobs and often wages, supporters of the Falange and of the military coup and rabidly right-wing priests were in the hands of the left in many towns and villages across the south of Spain. In most places, the bulk of them were not harmed.[64]

An appalling exception was Azuaga in the east of the province of Badajoz. The local working class, consisting of miners and agricultural day-labourers, was already deeply radicalized. From 1931 to the summer of 1936, landowners had belligerently blocked the Republic's agrarian measures, such as the decree of municipal boundaries, which protected workers from the import of cheap outside labour. The levels of unemployment and hunger had led to a degree of social tension that raised fears that the town might see clashes like those of Castilblanco or Casas Viejas. Aware that the military uprising heralded a brutal repression, local anarchist leaders demanded that the workers be armed. In the course of 19 July, in clashes with the town's Civil Guard unit, sixteen civilians and one Civil Guard were killed. On 21 July, Lieutenant Antonio Miranda Vega, commander of Azuaga's substantial Civil Guard detachment, concluded that he could not win, abandoned the town and took his men to Llerena, where, as was seen earlier, he played a crucial part in the fall of the town to Castejón's column.

The withdrawal of the Civil Guard opened the way to the tragic events that unfolded in Azuaga. Following Miranda's departure, a Revolutionary Committee was formed and, under its control, the town remained peaceful for two weeks. Things changed with the fall of Llerena on 5 August. Many refugees arrived with horror stories of the repression unleashed there. Then, as happened when refugees from elsewhere had reached Llerena, Almendralejo and Fuente de Cantos, a wave of indignation swept the town. The committee ordered the arrest of rebel sympathizers. At dawn on 8 August, twenty-eight of them were taken to the cemetery on the outskirts and shot. They included three priests, three retired Civil Guards, three lawyers and most of the town's landowners and businessmen. Another two were shot on 10 August. A factor in the killings was that Azuaga was constantly swelled by refugees and militiamen from other towns such as Cazalla de la Sierra and Guadalcanal (Seville), Granja de Torrehermosa (Badajoz) and Peñarroya (Córdoba). Those from outside had no compunction about venting their rage on strangers. Thus the arrival of a contingent of miners from Peñarroya on 20 August was the prelude to a further nine deaths, eight of whom, including four children aged from two to five, were from the closely related Vázquez and Delgado families.

Another atrocity took place on 31 August at the hands of a small group of militiamen returning, embittered, from a disastrous attempt to retake Llerena. Their column had been bombed and strafed by German aircraft and nearly wiped out. A detachment of Falangists had finished off the wounded. The dead were not buried. Instead, the stomachs of the corpses were split open with bayonets, filled with petrol and ignited. The few that survived vented their anger by executing thirty-three land-owners and businessmen. On 8 September, another priest was murdered. The last murders committed in Azuaga while it was still in Republican hands were the work of the militia group headed by Rafael Maltrana, the Mayor of Llerena. He controlled an area between Azuaga to Fuenteovejuna (Córdoba) where, on 22 September, his group loaded on to seven trucks fifty-seven men, including five priests and seven Franciscan monks. Six miles east of Azuaga, the first six trucks stopped and forty-three prisoners including the five lay priests were shot. The seventh truck carrying the remaining fourteen prisoners, among them the seven monks, carried on to Azuaga, where they were shot by Maltrana's militiamen.

Two days later, after a sustained artillery bombardment, Azuaga was easily conquered by two columns of Regulares under the command of Major Alfonso Gómez Cobián, fresh from victory over a column of eight thousand refugees. In Azuaga as elsewhere, the repression was implac-able. In justification, Gómez Cobián reported that 175 rightists had been hacked to death with hatchets. This was an exaggeration of the eighty-seven people who had been shot in and around Azuaga. However, the Franciscan Father Antonio Aracil provided documentation of horren-dous tortures inflicted on the clergy.[65]

In contrast, in Fuente del Maestre to the west of the road traversed by the African columns, the Defence Committee managed to restrain the local left and there were only two deaths among the prisoners. After the fall of Los Santos de Maimona on 5 August, and with the African columns approaching, the Committee had fled and the prisoners were released. However, several hundred armed leftists arrived and took over Fuente del Maestre, rearrested the prisoners and killed a further eleven men. A column of Regulares appeared, led by Lieutenant Colonel Francisco Delgado Serrano, and a massive repression began. Over three hundred people were shot, including nearly twenty women. Most of the men were agricultural labourers. Many women considered to be leftist were raped and virtually all had their heads shaven and were forced to drink castor oil.[66] In Barcarrota, where there was only one right-wing victim, those shot after the town was occupied on 25 August included all those prominent Socialists and municipal officials who had not managed to flee. Among them were Joaquín and Juan Sosa Hormigo, brothers of the parliamentary deputy José. Joaquín was shot on 24 October 1936 and Juan on 10 January 1937 after horrific torture. When Juan's body was exhumed years later, it was discovered that his arms and legs had been pulled from his torso.[67]

Inevitably, as the rebel 'cleaning up' operations proceeded, there were ever more refugees in flight. Some were fleeing southwards from Badajoz and Mérida towards others who had fled northwards into Badajoz from the repression in Huelva. The occupation by the Carlist columns of Luis Redondo of the mining towns of the sierra in the north of Huelva provoked a substantial exodus. Already as towns and villages along the road from Seville to Badajoz had been taken by the African columns, many had fled westwards. The result was that a large number of desperate refugees came together in an ever shrinking pocket of the western part of Badajoz. They were cut off to the east by the Seville–Mérida road and to the north by the Mérida–Badajoz road, to the south by the advancing columns, and to the west by the Portuguese frontier. By mid-September, several thousand people including children, as well as the old and infirm, had congregated between Jérez de los Caballeros and Fregenal de la Sierra. Many were in Valencia del Ventoso, where the local population did its best to feed them at rapidly organized soup kitchens.

When Fregenal fell on 18 September, faced with the prospect of being driven into rebel hands the remnants of the Defence Committees of several towns convened at Valencia del Ventoso. The organization was assumed by municipal and union leaders including José Sosa Hormigo, the Socialist deputy for Badajoz, the Mayor of Zafra, José González Barrero, and the Mayor of Fuente de Cantos, Modesto José Lorenzana Macarro, who had escaped the night before his town fell on 5 August.[68] They decided to undertake a forced march towards Republican lines, dividing this desperate human mass into two groups. The first contingent consisted of about two thousand people, the second of approximately six thousand. The first had a dozen men armed with rifles and about one hundred with shotguns, the second about twice as many. These exiguous forces had to protect two lengthy columns of horses, mules and other domestic animals and carts containing whatever possessions the refugees had managed to grab from their homes before taking flight. Young children, women with babes in arms, others pregnant, and many old people made up the bulk of the columns. It is impossible to say exactly how many refugees marched. The two contingents together have come to be known as 'la columna de los ocho mil' (the column of the eight thousand), although they seem to have marched separately.

The first, smaller column, led by José Sosa Hormigo, successfully crossed the road from Seville to Mérida between Los Santos de Maimona and Fuente de Cantos. They then headed for Valencia de las Torres north of Llerena and reached Castuera in the Republican zone. The larger, slower column crossed the main road further south between Monesterio and Fuente de Cantos. Inevitably, the column spread out and broke up into several groups, the aged and those with young families moving much more slowly than others. It had been a particularly hot summer, streams were dry and there was little water. The dust clouds thrown up by the progress of the refugees made it easy for rebel reconnaissance aircraft to pinpoint their position. Queipo de Llano's headquarters in Seville was fully informed of the movements, the civilian composition of the columns and their sparse armament. Nevertheless, preparations were made to attack them as if they were well-equipped military units.

A force of five hundred well-armed soldiers, Civil Guards and Falangist and Carlist militia under the command of Major Alfonso Gómez Cobián prepared an elaborate ambush between Reina and Fuente del Arco, about twenty miles to the east of the main road. Machine-guns were placed among the trees of a hill overlooking the route. When the refugees were within range, they opened fire. Many were killed and wounded by the fusillades of bullets. More than two thousand were taken prisoner and transported to Llerena. A smaller refugee group that was straggling behind was met by a unit of soldiers flying a Republican flag. They believed that they had reached safety when, in fact, they had fallen into the hands of rebel troops under the command of Captain Gabriel Tassara. They were lured to Fuente del Arco, where they were detained. Some who tried to escape were shot on the spot. The remainder were loaded on to a goods train and taken to Llerena.

When Gómez Cobián's ambush took place, many hundreds scattered into the surrounding countryside. Families were separated, some never to meet again. Some wandered in the unfamiliar territory for weeks, living off the land as best they could. Many were killed or captured by search parties of Civil Guards and mounted Falangists. Of the rest, some went back to their villages and an uncertain fate and a few hundred made it through to the Republican zone. In Llerena, where the prisoners taken by Gómez Cobián and Tassara were held, a massacre took place over the next month, with prisoners machine-gunned each morning in the bullring. Some prisoners were obliged to dig their own graves before being shot. Others were brought back to their places of origin for execution after right-wingers came from their *pueblos* to identify them. Many women were raped. Since the perpetrators were married men from well-known local families, considerable efforts were made to conceal their crimes. Many Andalusian prisoners were taken to Seville and imprisoned in the bilges of the ship *Cabo Carvoeiro*, moored in the Guadalquivir river. With inadequate food and water, in the baking heat of the late summer, few survived.[69]

In his nightly broadcast on 18 September, Queipo de Llano boasted about what he described as a great military victory by Gómez Cobián over what he called 'an enemy force'. After accusing the components of the refugee column of cowardice for letting themselves be defeated by five hundred soldiers, he spoke of the prisoners including many wounded. He ended with sinister overtones. 'There are also numerous women, some schoolteachers and other educated professionals.'[70]

Before the ambush, when the larger refugee column had got about ten miles beyond the Seville–Mérida road, it was joined by a man fleeing from Fuente de Cantos. He told the Mayor, Lorenzana Macarro, that his wife and five daughters had been arrested by the occupying forces. Ignoring the frantic protests of his father and numerous friends, Lorenzana left the column, half crazed with fear that, because he had failed to stop the massacre of rightists in the town church on 19 July, revenge would be taken on his wife and daughters. He hoped that if he gave himself up he might be able to save them. After some days wandering in the countryside, he was captured by a patrol of mounted Falangists. Along with a number of prisoners from the refugee column, Lorenzana was brought into Fuente de Cantos. Once on the outskirts, he was tied to the tail of a horse. He fell and was dragged around the town square. He was beaten, then tied to a chair outside the Ayuntamiento, where local rightists kicked him, spat on him and insulted him. He was then shot against the wall of the church. Lorenzana's battered corpse was left all night in the town square. The following day, his body was taken around all the streets of the town on the municipal rubbish cart, ending at the local cemetery, where it was burned. His wife and daughters were then released from prison.[71]

The repression continued throughout the province. One of the devices used to capture leftists was broadcasts of 'edicts of pardon' to the effect that those who gave themselves up voluntarily would face no reprisals. Those naive enough to do so rarely lived to tell the tale. A typical case took place at Olivenza, near the Portuguese border. Many rightists had been detained and demands made on the landowners among them for wages unpaid since 1932. The Socialist Mayor, Ignacio Rodríguez Méndez, ensured that no prisoners were killed and, to avoid a bloodbath, negotiated the peaceful surrender of the town on 17 August. After Olivenza was taken, the new authorities issued a declaration which returned working conditions to their pre-1936 level and also stated that 'all those who are not charged with acts involving bloodshed ... can return to their homes certain that our open arms are waiting to receive them'. Over the months following, 130 people from Olivenza and surrounding towns were executed in the town.[72] In nearby Valverde de Leganés, there had been no violence before it fell to the rebels but more than one hundred men had fled for fear of the repression. On 2 January 1937, five men who handed themselves over to a patrol of mounted Falangists were taken to a farm and shot. The Falangists then went to the homes of three of them and stole the domestic animals on which their widows and children depended for their livelihood.[73]

In the meantime, Yagüe's forces had long since moved on, accompanied by foreign correspondents. Harold Cardozo, the enthusiastic *Daily Mail* correspondent with Castejón's column, reported on the fate awaiting any captured militiamen. They faced 'a ten-minute trial, a drive in a motor-lorry, accompanied by a priest, to some outlying barracks, a volley and a grave full of quicklime'.[74] From Badajoz, Castejón had set off back towards Mérida in order to take the road to Madrid through the province of Cáceres. By 27 August 1936, Tella's column had reached the bridge across the Tagus at Almaraz and shortly afterwards arrived at Navalmoral de la Mata in the north of Cáceres. Later that day, Castejón, Tella and Asensio merged their columns before the last town of importance on the way to Madrid, Talavera de la Reina in the province of Toledo. In two weeks, they had advanced 190 miles.[75]

In the course of the advance, Queipo de Llano outdid even his own record in misogynist remarks on 29 August when he referred to the capture between Navalmoral de la Mata and Talavera de la Reina of Republican women. Gloating over the savagery of the repression, he fed widespread fears that women were given to Moroccan mercenaries for gang rape, remarking with relish, 'Great quantities of munitions, ten trucks and many prisoners, including women, have fallen into our hands. The Regulares will be delighted and Pasionaria will be really jealous.' The sexual comment appeared in *ABC* but was censored in the other Seville paper, *La Unión*.[76] It was shortly after this broadcast that Queipo de Llano's chief of staff, Major Cuesta Monereo, issued orders to the press not to publish the exact words of the broadcasts because 'they are not appropriate and their publication is not convenient'. A journalist who read transcripts of the complete broadcasts observed later, 'they were nauseating. The published versions were censored to eliminate their crudity.'[77]

Queipo's verbal excesses were often excused as the result of his being drunk, although efforts were made to suggest that he was teetotal. The Bloomsbury Group exile Gerald Brenan, who lived near Málaga, referred to 'his whisky voice'. Brenan's wife, the writer Gamel Woolsey, wrote:

> I am told that he does not drink at all, but he has the mellow loose voice
> and the cheerful wandering manner of the habitual drinker. He talks for
> hours always perfectly at ease, sometimes he stumbles over a word and
> corrects himself with a complete lack of embarrassment, speaks of
> 'these villainous Fascistas' and an agonized voice can be heard behind
> him correcting him, 'No, no, mi General, Marxistas.' 'What difference
> does it make' – says the general and sweeps grandly on.[78]

The actor Edmundo Barbero recalled this notorious occasion on which Queipo revealed his contempt for the Falange, referring to 'the fascist scum', only to be corrected nervously by the hushed whisper of one of his staff 'Marxist scum'. Major Cuesta Monereo revealed years later that Queipo was not teetotal but was not supposed to drink because he was an alcoholic with serious liver problems. Cuesta wrote: 'How often did I, who do not drink, take a glass out of his hand just as he was about to raise it because I knew the damage it would cause him.' On the occasion of the fall of Toledo, without realizing that the microphone was still live, at the end of his programme Queipo de Llano shouted: 'Bring wine for fuck's sake!'[79]

The columns reached Talavera de la Reina on 3 September.[80] The American journalist John T. Whitaker, who travelled with them, gained the confidence of Varela, Yagüe, Castejón and other officers. They helped him avoid the rigid controls imposed on the majority of correspondents from the democracies who were transported to the front only after a battle and escorted by Franco's propaganda staff. Such limits were rarely imposed on the newsmen from Nazi Germany and Fascist Italy. Whitaker took a room in Talavera as his base for visits to the front. There he established a relationship with José Sainz, the provincial head of the Falange in Toledo. Sainz showed him a neatly kept notebook, saying: 'I jot them down. I have personally executed 127 red prisoners.' Of his two months at Talavera de la Reina, Whitaker wrote:

I slept there on an average of two nights a week. I never passed a night there without being awakened at dawn by the volleys of the firing squads in the yard of the *Cuartel*. There seemed no end to the killing. They were shooting as many at the end of the second month as in my first days in Talavera. They averaged perhaps thirty a day. I watched the men they took into the *Cuartel*. They were simple peasants and workers, Spanish Milquetoasts. It was sufficient to have carried a trade-union card, to have been a Freemason, to have voted for the Republic. If you were picked up or denounced for any one of these charges you were given a summary, two-minute hearing and capital punishment was formally pronounced. Any man who had held any office under the Republic was, of course, shot out of hand. And there were mopping-up operations along the roads. You would find four old peasant women heaped in a ditch; thirty and forty militiamen at a time, their hands roped behind them, shot down at the crossroads. I remember a bundle in a town square. Two youthful members of the Republican assault guards had been tied back to back with wire, covered with gasoline and burned alive.

On 21 September, Yagüe's forces captured the town of Santa Olalla. Whitaker was appalled by the shooting of captured militiamen in the main street:

I can never forget the first time I saw the mass execution of prisoners. I stood in the main street of Santa Olalla as seven trucks brought in the militiamen. They were unloaded and herded together. They had that listless, exhausted, beaten look of troops who can no longer stand against the steady pounding of the German bombs. Most of them had a soiled towel or a shirt in their hands – the white flags with which they had signalled their surrender. Two Franco officers passed out cigarettes among them and several Republicans laughed boyishly and self-consciously as they smoked their first cigarette in weeks. Suddenly an officer took me by the arm and said, 'It's time to get out of here.' At the edge of this cluster of prisoners, six hundred-odd men, Moorish troopers were setting up two machine guns. The prisoners saw them as I saw them. The men seemed to tremble in one convulsion, as those in front, speechless with fright, rocked back on their heels, the color draining from their faces, their eyes opening with terror.[81]

The repression in Talavera was as brutal as anything that had taken place further south. Itinerant workers from Galicia were shot along with militiamen. An eyewitness, at the time a child, recalled a massacre in the prophetically named Calle de Carnicerías (Butchery Street) on 3 September. A large number of Republican prisoners with their hands tied behind their backs were being herded down the street by Regulares. When one tried to escape, the Moors just shot the entire group. The bodies were left there for three days, some wounded but not yet dead. The terrified neighbours were locked in their houses listening to the agonized groans and screams of the dying. Eventually, the municipal rubbish carts collected them.[82] So numerous were the victims in Talavera de la Reina that, for health reasons, the corpses were soaked in petrol and burned.[83] As part of the operation to justify the massacre at Badajoz, Luis Bolín, the head of Franco's propaganda apparatus, published photographs of the rebel killings at Talavera de la Reina, presenting them as left-wing atrocities encountered by the columns at Talavera la Real, between Mérida and Badajoz. In fact, Antonio Bahamonde, Queipo's propaganda chief, recounted how the corpses of both battle casualties and executed men and women were frequently mutilated and then photographed to fabricate evidence of Republican atrocities.[84]

Noel Monks of the *Daily Express* wrote: 'In Talavera, because not much was going on at the front, one was fed on a steady diet of atrocity propaganda; the things the Reds did as they fell back into Madrid. And the strange thing was that the Spanish troops I met – Legionaires, Requetés and Falangists – bragged openly to me of what *they'd* done when they took over from the Reds. But they weren't *atrocities*. Oh no, señor. Not even the locking up of a captured militia girl in a room with twenty Moors. No, señor. That was fun.'[85] According to Edmund Taylor of the *Chicago Tribune*, a militia girl captured near Santa Olalla was locked in a big room with fifty Moors.[86] John T. Whitaker witnessed a scene on the road to Madrid similar to those related by Monks and Taylor. He knew that gang rape was a frequent occurrence:

These 'regenerators' of Spain rarely denied, too, that they deliberately gave white women to the Moors. On the contrary, they circulated over the whole front the warning that any woman found with Red troops would meet that fate. The wisdom of this policy was debated by Spanish officers in a half-dozen messes where I ate with them. No officer ever denied that it was a Franco policy. But some argued that even a Red woman was Spanish and a woman. This practice was not denied by El

Mizzian, the only Moroccan officer in the Spanish Army. I stood at the cross-roads outside Navalcarnero with the Moorish major when two Spanish girls, not out of their teens, were brought before him. One had worked in a textile factory in Barcelona and they found a trade-union card in her leather jacket. The other came from Valencia and said she had no politics. After questioning them for military information, El Mizzian had them taken into a small schoolhouse where some forty Moorish soldiers were resting. As they reached the doorway an ululating cry rose from the Moors within, I stood horrified in helpless anger. El Mizzian smirked when I remonstrated with him. 'Oh, they'll not live more than four hours,' he said.[87]

The rising in Toledo was initially successful. The Socialist Domingo Alonso, one-time parliamentary deputy and editor of *El Heraldo de Toledo*, was shot and his wife and daughter seized as hostages. Many other Republicans were arrested. After the arrival of an army column from Madrid, the rebel leader Colonel José Moscardó ordered his forces into the Alcázar, the huge fortress that dominates both Toledo and the River Tagus which curls around it.[88] About one thousand Civil Guards from around the province and Falangists retreated into the impregnable building with around six hundred non-combatants, mainly their wives and children, together with an unknown number of leftists as hostages. There has been bitter debate about the numbers of the latter. The civilian in charge of the siege, Luis Quintanilla, was told by Major Manuel Uribarri Barrutell that there were more than five hundred. At the other extreme, Colonel Moscardó never admitted to more than sixteen. In a numerical list of various categories of those present in the Alcázar, including those killed and wounded during the siege, the semi-official military historian of the war, Manuel Aznar, included the figure of fifty-seven 'disappeared'. This figure is additional to the number of those named as present, given in official lists, and thus it could well refer to the hostages who were shot. The Austrian sociologist Franz Borkenau saw the photographs of twenty hostages displayed in the militia refectory, while several scholars have calculated that there were at least fifty hostages. Francoist sources do not mention the fate of the sixteen hostages admitted by Moscardó.[89]

For all, the circumstances were appalling – cooped up in the dank cellars, with no light and little food or water. Another reason why Quintanilla came to count all of the women and children as hostages was the fact that Moscardó consistently refused offers to evacuate them all to a place of safety.[90] They served, some willingly, others not, as a kind of human shield, since their existence seriously inhibited the Republican attackers. Allegedly, women and children were forcibly placed next to windows. Among them were several servant girls, one of whom escaped and, before she died from her mistreatment, claimed that she had been raped by eight or nine officers in the Alcázar.[91] Moscardó's recently discovered correspondence indicates that he did release a small number of hostages.[92] Moscardó also made a deal with the attackers whereby, in return for the families of the besieged being safeguarded, the Legion and the Regulares would not commit the excesses that had characterized the conquest of other towns.[93] Unlike the Army of Africa, the Republicans kept their word.

Franz Borkenau commented after his visit in early September: 'The town has always been very Catholic and anti-socialist, the administration and the militia feel themselves surrounded by passive resistance and treason.'[94] The repression was considerable while Toledo was in the Republican zone, leading to 222 assassinations – an appalling figure, yet no clergy felt the need to take refuge in the Alcázar other than the five nuns who already worked in the infirmary. Of the nearly 1,500 clergy in Toledo, a relatively small number were killed and they included eighteen Carmelite monks accused of fighting alongside the Civil Guard. The town's substantial population of nuns was evacuated to Madrid without incident. Nevertheless, after a bombing raid on 23 August, anarchist militiamen seized and murdered sixty-four right-wing prisoners, including twenty-two clergy. In contrast, the wives and children of the principal leaders of the coup in Toledo were not molested in any way.[95] Huge amounts of time, energy and ammunition had been squandered by the Republican militia in a vain effort to take the strategically unimportant fortress. The resistance of the besieged garrison had thus become a symbol of heroic rebel resistance. On 21 September, Franco's columns had reached Maqueda, a junction where the road from Talavera de la Reina divided to go north-east to Madrid or south-east to Toledo. Rather than send the columns on to Madrid, Franco ordered them to turn to Toledo, to relieve the besieged Alcázar.

On the day after this fateful decision was taken, Franco was visited by a delegation of his monarchist supporters, including one of the most prominent theorists of the uprising, Eugenio Vegas Latapié, and the poet and intellectual José María Pemán. Vegas Latapié took the risk of expressing his concerns about the scale of the repression in the insurgent zone. Although believing, erroneously, that it was on a smaller scale than in the Republican zone, Vegas Latapié told Franco in unequivocal terms that it was a moral issue, fundamental 'for those of us who claimed to be fighting out of religious motives'. He told Franco that 'it was normal and even necessary that summary courts function with rigorous and severe criteria, provided that the accused are allowed to defend themselves fully and freely. To act otherwise, to seize a citizen indiscriminately, no matter how much an adversary he might be, and just shoot him was a crime against morality and was, moreover, the quickest way of discrediting us politically.' As Vegas noted later, Franco 'knew very well what was happening and didn't give a damn'. He listened impassively and with total indifference changed the subject to talk about the imminent attack on Toledo.[96]

By diverting his troops to Toledo, Franco deliberately lost an unrepeatable chance to sweep on to the Spanish capital before its defences were ready. He was in no hurry to end the war before the captured territories had been purged and he was aware that an emotional victory and a great journalistic coup would strengthen his position within the rebel zone. By 26 September, the rebel columns were at the gates of Toledo. The Jesuit chronicler Father Alberto Risco described the passage of the Moroccan Regulares of El Mizzian through the outlying districts: 'with the breath of God's vengeance on the blades of their machetes, they pursue, they destroy, they kill … and intoxicated with blood, the column moves on'. The following day, the African columns entered the city centre along what Risco called 'their path of extermination'. Large numbers of refugees trying to flee on foot, on bicycles, in cars and in trucks were bombarded by artillery.[97]

Luis Bolín ensured that no correspondents were permitted to enter Toledo for two days during the bloodbath that followed its occupation. Father Risco wrote with relish of 'a second day of extermination and punishment'. It was hardly surprising that Bolín would not want newspapermen reporting the atrocities taking place while, in the words of Yagüe, 'we made Toledo the whitest town in Spain'.[98] What the journalists witnessed, when they were allowed in on 29 September, shocked them deeply. Webb Miller of the United Press saw pools of fresh blood which denoted a mass execution only just before the reporters arrived. At many other places, he saw pools of clotted blood, often with a militia cap lying next to them. John Whitaker reported that 'The men who commanded them never denied that the Moors killed the wounded in the Republican hospital. They boasted of how grenades were thrown in among two hundred screaming and helpless men.' Whitaker was referring to the

Tavera Hospital, housed in the hospice of San Juan Bautista on the outskirts of Toledo. Webb Miller also reported on what happened there, claiming that two hundred militiamen were burned to death when the grenades were thrown in. As in Badajoz, most of the shops had been looted as a 'war tax'. At the maternity hospital, more than twenty pregnant women were forced from their beds, loaded on to a truck and taken to the municipal cemetery where they were shot. The hostages in the Alcázar had already been shot. Webb Miller told Jay Allen that, after he saw what the rebels did to the wounded and to the nurses and the doctors in the hospital in Toledo, 'he came close to going off his rocker'.[99] Father Risco describes men and women committing suicide to avoid capture by the African columns. Those who were taken in the house-to-house searches, he commented, 'had to die'. They were rounded up and conveyed to different town squares where they were shot in groups of twenty or thirty.[100] More than eight hundred people were shot and then buried in a mass common grave in the municipal cemetery. Nothing more was known of the executed hostages.[101]

An insight into the behaviour of the columns during the march on Madrid is provided by the extraordinary experience of one of its chaplains, Father Fernando Huidobro Polanco. A thirty-four-year-old Jesuit from Santander, he had spent the last few years pursuing theological studies in Portugal, Germany, Holland and Belgium. He regarded the Republic as a pigsty and, while still in Belgium, he wrote in justification of the massacre of Badajoz that it was an isolated event provoked by the atrocities of the reds.[102] In late August, the Superior General of the Society of Jesus, Father Wlodimiro Ledochowski, a keen sympathizer of the rebels, granted Huidobro's request to return to Spain. On reaching Pamplona, he discovered that there was a surfeit of priests keen to join the rebels and so he went on to Valladolid, where he briefly served with the Falangist militia. From there, he went to Franco's headquarters in Cáceres and was granted an audience. Franco said: 'A warning, Father. You and your companions should do all you can for the good of Spanish soldiers, but, for various common-sense reasons, refrain from trying to convert the Moors.' Huidobro wanted to join the Foreign Legion as a chaplain, so Franco sent him to see Yagüe at Talavera de la Reina. On 8 September, Yagüe agreed.[103]

The slight, bespectacled Huidobro, a one-time pupil of Heidegger, was initially received with ribaldry by the brutal Legionarios whose spiritual welfare he had come to tend. His bravery impressed some, but others were irritated by his efforts to persuade them to make confession, to stop gambling and to avoid prostitutes. During the advance on Madrid, and particularly in Toledo, Father Huidobro witnessed a number of atrocities. His efforts to prevent the shooting of prisoners or, as his biographer put it, 'to save them from the just fury of his men', did not endear him to the merciless Legionarios. He tried to justify what he saw: 'our style is clean. Our procedures are different from theirs. They shoot, they torture, they exterminate. But they are criminals. We, because we are Christians and gentlemen, know how to fight.' In this spirit, he gave prior absolution to the men of his unit before they went into action. However, he found their savagery disturbing since it damaged the image of the cause in which he fervently believed. He tried to protect the wounded and, when he could, attended to the spiritual needs of those about to be shot.[104]

Accordingly, in the lull that followed the fall of Toledo, he wrote down his reflections on the issue in two papers for 'the military authorities' and for the Military Legal Corps. Both papers were sent to the military authorities on 4 October. Under the heading, 'On the Application of the Death Penalty in the Present Circumstances. Rules of Conscience', he proposed that the 'justice' being exercised should not lead to excesses that besmirched the honour of the army. He argued against 'the war of extermination advocated by some' on the grounds that it would create lasting hatreds that would make the war last longer and impede reconciliation, deprive Spain of labour for its reconstruction and damage the country's international reputation. He asserted that 'Every wholesale condemnation, wherein no effort is made to ascertain if there are innocents among the crowd of prisoners, is to commit murder, not perform an act of justice ... To kill those who have thrown down their arms or surrendered is always a criminal act.'

In the paper sent to the Military Legal Corps, he justified the death penalty for leftist murderers of women, priests and the innocent, and for Communists, or those 'who, through the medium of a newspaper, a book or a pamphlet, have agitated the masses'. However, he suggested that membership of a left-wing trade union such as the CNT or UGT deserved not death but prison or a labour camp. He went on to denounce as murder the execution of those whose guilt had not been proven. His final words would not have endeared him to his readers: 'the procedure being followed is deforming Spain and ensuring that instead of being a chivalrous and generous people, we are turning into a people of murderers and informers. The things that are happening make those of us who have always considered ourselves above all else to be Spaniards begin to be ashamed that we were born in this land of implacable cruelty and endless hatred.'[105]

It took great courage to stand up against the blanket savagery of the Legion. He sent both papers to many officers and to other chaplains and they were seen by both Castejón and Varela. Castejón was outraged. In front of other chaplains, he commented that Huidobro's papers were 'a kick in the teeth'.[106] On 14 November 1936, when the army was on the outskirts of Madrid, Father Huidobro wrote to Varela to say that his glorious name should not be stained by the bloodletting that some junior officers were planning in order to teach the Madrileños a lesson. If a massacre were to take place, Huidobro feared that Varela's name would go down in history 'as monstrous and linked to the most cruel and barbaric deed of modern times'. After his forces had failed to take Madrid, Varela replied on 3 December from Yuncos in Toledo, congratulating Huidobro on his sentiments and claiming to share them.[107]

Father Huidobro had also written on 4 October to Lieutenant Colonel Carlos Díaz Varela, adjutant to General Franco, asking him to hand on to the Generalísimo copies of his two papers. Given Franco's more pressing concerns, Díaz Varela passed Father Huidobro's reflections to Yagüe, who commanded the division to which Huidobro's unit belonged. Since the atrocities were part of a deliberate policy, Yagüe did nothing. Frustrated, Huidobro continued to make a nuisance of himself. He wrote a letter to Franco drawing his attention to:

> the haste with which the execution takes place of people whose guilt is not only not proven but not even investigated. This is what is happening at the front, where every prisoner is shot, irrespective of whether he was deceived or forced to fight or even if he has sufficient capacity to understand the evil of the cause for which he was fighting. This is a war with neither wounded nor prisoners. Militiamen are shot for the mere fact of being militiamen without being given a chance to speak or to be questioned. Thus many are dying who do not deserve such a fate and who could mend their ways.

Since he was describing the usual practice of the Army of Africa, it was obvious that nothing would be done. Nevertheless, his letter, for all its naivety, constituted an astonishing act of courage.[108]

He wrote again to Díaz Varela on 10 November 1936 describing as 'iniquitous and criminal' the general order that anyone found with arms should be summarily shot. He called instead for them to be taken prisoner, interrogated and then, if 'guilty', sent to punishment camps. He asserted that 'the limitless executions on a scale never before seen in history' provoked the dogged resistance of the desperate Republicans who knew that there was no point in surrender. He went on to draw conclusions about the reaction in Madrid to the massacre that followed the fall of Toledo: 'If they knew that in Toledo the wounded were murdered in the hospitals, would they need to know anything more about our harsh barbarity? Already some say that when we reach Madrid, we should shoot the wounded in the hospitals. We are falling back into barbarism and we are corrupting people's morals with so much irresponsible killing. Previously, no one was killed until their guilt had been proved; now people are killed in order to hide their innocence.' Huidobro begged Díaz Varela to raise the matter with Franco and had the temerity to suggest that he might go public: 'Up to now, I have made my observations prudently and without raising my voice. Now the time has come to cry out. I do not fear either the right or the left but only God.' He ended in dramatic terms: 'I have witnessed murders, as we all have, and I do not want the new regime to be born with blood on its hands.'[109]

Díaz Varela finally replied on 25 November to say that Franco had been appalled to hear about the excesses that Huidobro had denounced and was determined to punish all those responsible. It goes without saying that nothing was done. Himself in hospital after being wounded, Huidobro knew that the shootings were continuing on the same scale but chose to believe that Franco was sincere. Over the next months, Huidobro became ever more vocal about the need for an eventual reconciliation of both sides. A number of officers told him that if he continued to preach his message 'they're going to shoot you'. On 11 April 1937, Huidobro was killed at Aravaca on the outskirts of Madrid, allegedly by shrapnel from an exploding Russian shell. This detail helped initially when, in 1947, the process was put in train by the Jesuits for his beatification and canonization. Huidobro had saved lives and lived a thoroughly Christian existence. However, in the course of the thorough investigation of the case instituted by the Vatican, it emerged that he had been shot in the back by one of the Legionarios of his own unit, tired perhaps of the preaching of his chaplain. When it was discovered that Huidobro had been killed by the Francoists and not by the reds, the Vatican shelved his case.[110]

10

A Terrified City Responds:
The Massacres of Paracuellos

Franco once claimed that he would never bomb Madrid, but already in September 1936, there were major raids. He ensured, however, that the Barrio de Salamanca, the wealthiest neighbourhood, would be spared. Accordingly, its streets were crowded and, at night, people who could not get into Metro stations for shelter slept on the pavements of the Barrio's great boulevards, Salamanca, Velázquez, Goya and Príncipe de Vergara. The raids on the rest of the city, far from undermining the morale of the Madrileños, did exactly the opposite and also provoked a deep loathing of the rebels, a loathing whose immediate targets were those assumed to be their supporters within the capital. This included both as yet un-detected members of the fifth column and right-wingers already in prison. In the paranoia of the siege, they were indiscriminately regarded as 'fifth columnists'.

Hatred was intensified when a rebel aircraft inundated the city with leaflets announcing that ten Republicans would be shot for every prisoner killed in Madrid. The acrimony was whipped up by the Republican daily *La Voz*, which announced that 'it is estimated that Madrid, if it falls, will be the terrifying theatre of one hundred thousand sacrificial victims'. On the basis of what had been done in the south by the African columns, it was believed that anyone who had been a member of any party or group linked to the Popular Front, had held a government post or was an affiliate of a trade union would be shot. 'After a final orgy of blood, when the barbaric revenge of the enemies of freedom has been consummated, with the most significant men of the bourgeois left and the proletarian left murdered, twenty-two million Spaniards would suffer the most atrocious and humiliating slavery.'[1] Another Republican daily, *Informaciones*, reported that Queipo de Llano had told a British journalist that half of Madrid's population would be shot by the victorious rebels.[2]

However, in terms of propagating fear and hatred, nothing could equal what happened a fortnight after *La Voz*'s hair-raising prediction.

On 16 November, the diplomats still in Madrid were shown the horribly mutilated corpse of a Republican pilot. On the previous day, he had crash-landed behind the Francoist lines near Segovia. He was beaten to death and his body dragged around the streets of the town. His captors had then taken the trouble to dismember him, place his body parts in a box, attach a parachute, load the box on to an aircraft, fly to Madrid and drop it over the aerodrome at Barajas. In the box was a paper which said, 'this gift is for the head of the red air force so that he knows the fate that awaits him and all his bolsheviks'.[3]

In the claustrophobia generated by the siege, the daily terror had long since found expression in a popular rage which focused on the prison population. A potent mixture of fear and resentment inevitably fuelled the actions of the many militia groups that operated in Madrid, whether independent vigilante groups or 'official' groups such as the Rearguard Security Militias (Milicias de Vigilancia de Retaguardia – MVR) created in mid-September or those still operating within the Comité Provincial de Investigación Pública. This had been starkly demonstrated by both the events in the Cárcel Modelo on 22 August and subsequent *sacas* from the prisons. Neither ordinary citizens nor political leaders made any significant distinction between the active 'fifth column' and the nearly eight thousand imprisoned rightists. At this stage, the fifth column was far from being the organized network that it became in 1937 and the exploits of snipers, saboteurs and defeatists were relatively random. However, among those detained as rebel supporters were many, especially the army officers, who were considered potentially very dangerous.

As Franco's columns advanced ever nearer to the capital, to generalized hatred of rightists there was added a much more specific concern about the presence in Madrid's prisons of so many experienced right-wing officers who had already categorically refused invitations, individual and collective, to honour their oath of loyalty to the Republic and fight in defence of the city. On a razor's edge between survival and annihilation, the Republican military and political authorities were determined that these men should not be permitted to form the basis of new units for the rebel columns. This would be the most crucial factor in the eventual fate of prisoners throughout November 1936.

Already, on 1 November, this problem had been discussed at a tense meeting of the War Commissariat – the body set up two weeks earlier under the chairmanship of the Minister of Foreign Affairs, the Socialist Julio Álvarez del Vayo. The War Commissariat's purpose was to invigilate the loyalty of the new Popular Army created when 'all armed and organ-ized forces' had been placed under the command of the Minister of War, the beginning of the militarization of the militias.[4] When the question of the prisoners was raised on 1 November, Álvarez del Vayo left the meeting to go and seek advice from Largo Caballero. He returned to say that the Prime Minister had ordered the Minister of the Interior, Ángel Galarza, to arrange the evacuation of the prisoners; but little was done over the next five days.[5]

On 2 November, a group of anarchists had visited the Cárcel de San Antón, a converted convent, and picked out the file-cards of the four hundred army officers detained there. The youngest had been interro-gated and offered the chance to fight for the Republic. They all refused, which constituted mutiny. On 4 November, Getafe to the south fell and, on the same day, between thirty and forty officers were 'tried' by a Tribunal Popular. Having reaffirmed that they abjured their oath of loyalty, at dawn on 5 November they were removed from the prison and shot. Another forty were taken later the same day and also shot on the outskirts of the capital. The following day, a further 173 were evacuated in three batches. The first and the third, each of fifty-nine prisoners, reached Alcalá de Henares safely. The fifty-five prisoners of the second convoy were executed at Paracuellos, halfway to Alcalá. These evacu-ations on 6 November, but not the murders, were authorized by the Director General of Security, Manuel Muñoz, who had also ordered others from the Cárcel de Ventas between 27 October and 2 November.[6]

As a result of the tribunals conducted by agents of the CPIP, from late October onward the rhythm of *sacas* accelerated. The illegality of this deeply distressed senior Republicans. Luis Zubillaga, the secretary general of the Bar Association, and Mariano Gómez, the acting president of the Supreme Court, took the extraordinary step of seeking the help of the anarchist Melchor Rodríguez, whose efforts to save many rightists had already earned him the suspicion of his comrades. The incorpor-ation into the government, on 4 November, of four anarchist ministers, Juan López (Commerce), Federica Montseny (Health), Juan Peiró (Industry) and Juan García Oliver (Justice), led Zubillaga and Gómez to hope that some official support might be given to Melchor's humanitar-ian efforts. In fact, García Oliver had been one of the founders of the FAI along with Durruti. His record of frequent imprisonment for terrorist acts made him a remarkable choice. The logic behind it was the hope that he might be able to persuade the anarchist rank and file that the implementation of justice could be left to the state. Zubillaga and Gómez wanted him to appoint Melchor Rodríguez to the post of Director General of Prisons, vacant since the resignation of Pedro Villar Gómez in late September. However, given the threat to Madrid posed by Franco's columns, the protection of prisoners was not a priority for García Oliver.

García Oliver refused to appoint Melchor Rodríguez as Director General of Prisons without first checking with the regional and national committees of the CNT, which were deeply implicated in the repression and thus highly suspicious of Melchor Rodríguez. Accordingly, García Oliver appointed two trusted CNT stalwarts who had accompanied him from Barcelona, Juan Antonio Carnero as Director General and Jaume Nebot as Inspector General of Prisons.[7] Rather than to prevent atrocities, the task given by García Oliver to Nebot was to locate and destroy the criminal records of all members of the CNT or the FAI who had ever been jailed.[8]

Advancing through the University City and the Casa de Campo, by 6 November the rebels were only two hundred yards from the largest of the prisons, the Cárcel Modelo, in the Argüelles district. Francoist officers later claimed that advance units of Regulares organized snatch squads on that day and managed to get inside the Cárcel Modelo and rescue some prisoners. Such raids would lead to the stationing of units of the International Brigades at the prison.[9] Most of the approximately two thousand army officers incarcerated there had already shown that they were ready, indeed anxious, to join the besieging forces by rejecting calls to fight for the Republic. Their resolve can only have been hardened by the successful rescue attempts. Indeed, they made no secret of their delight at the developments outside, threatened their jailers and trumpeted their intentions of joining their rebel comrades as soon as they could.[10] That would have constituted a massive reinforcement for Franco's forces.

In this context, the necessary decision for Largo Caballero's cabinet to leave for Valencia was finally taken in the early afternoon of 6 November.[11] The variations in the memoir material are such that exact timings of events on that day can be established only approximately. Not long after the fateful meeting finished, probably some time between 4.00 and 5.00 p.m., the Under-Secretary of War, General José Asensio Torrado, met Generals Sebastián Pozas, the Chief of Operations of the Army of the Centre, and José Miaja Menent, head of the 1st Military Division. After a lengthy discussion, he gave each a sealed envelope emblazoned with the words 'Top Secret. Not to be opened until 6 a.m. tomorrow'. Given the urgency of the situation, as soon as Asensio left for Valencia, both generals ignored the instruction and opened the envelopes. They discovered that each contained the orders meant for the other. Pozas was ordered to set up a new headquarters for the Army of the Centre at Tarancón on the road to Valencia. Miaja was placed in charge of the defence of the capital and ordered to establish a body, to be known as the Junta de Defensa, which would have full governmental powers in Madrid and its environs. Had they complied with the instruction not to open the envelopes and gone back to their respective headquarters, they would have seen their orders when they were many miles apart, with catastrophic consequences for the defence of the city. Whoever sealed the envelopes was probably a rebel sympathizer.[12]

The view of the cabinet and the large numbers of functionaries who fled to Valencia was that the capital was doomed and that the Junta was there merely to administer the inevitable defeat. In the event, under intolerable pressure and against all odds, it was to preside over a near miraculous victory.[13] Miaja's awesome task was to organize Madrid's military and civil defence at the same time as providing food and shelter for its citizens and the refugees who thronged its streets. In addition, he had to deal with the violence of the *checas* and the activities of the fifth column.[14] The Junta de Defensa was thus a localized mini-government. Its 'ministers' were known as Councillors and their deputies would be chosen from all those parties that made up the central government. However, it was to the Communists that Miaja would turn first in search of help. And they were ready and waiting.

Immediately after the cabinet meeting earlier in the afternoon, the two Communist ministers, Jesús Hernández and Vicente Uribe, reported the government's evacuation to the top brass of the Partido Comunista de España, Pedro Checa and Antonio Mije. Checa (whose name was totally unconnected with the *checas*) was the PCE organization secretary. He and Mije were effectively leading the Party in the frequent absences of its seriously ill secretary general, José Díaz. The implications were discussed and plans made. Astonishingly, among those participating were two young leaders of the Juventudes Socialistas Unificadas, Santiago Carrillo Solares and José Cazorla Maure, who were, theoretically at least, members of the Socialist Party and not of the Communist Party, for membership of which they would not formally apply until the next day. Their presence at the meeting demonstrates that they were actually already in the highest echelons of the PCE.

Late in the afternoon, Checa and Mije negotiated with Miaja the terms of the Communist participation in the Junta de Defensa. A grateful Miaja eagerly accepted their offer that the PCE run the two 'ministries' or Councils (Consejerías) of War and Public Order in the Junta. He also accepted their specific nominations of Antonio Mije as War Councillor with Isidoro Diéguez Dueñas as his deputy and of Carrillo as Public Order Councillor with Cazorla as his deputy. Thus, as Carrillo recalled later, 'on that same night of 6 November, I began to undertake my responsibilities along with Mije and others'. Mije, Carrillo and Cazorla then went to see the Prime Minister to seek a statement to explain the government's departure to the people of Madrid. Largo Caballero denied that the government was about to leave despite the pile of suitcases outside his office. Deeply disillusioned by the lies of their broken hero, they went back to the Central Committee of the PCE.[15]

Several sources have confirmed that Carrillo was able to name his subordinates in the Public Order Council and assign them tasks immediately after this meeting with Miaja late on 6 November. A sub-committee, known as the Public Order Delegation, was set up under the JSU's elegant intellectual Segundo Serrano Poncela. He was given responsibility for the work in Madrid of the Dirección General de Seguridad.[16] Ramón Torrecilla Guijarro, one of the members of the Public Order Delegation, told his interrogators after he had been captured by the Francoists in 1939 that the nominations of Carrillo and of Serrano Poncela had taken effect on the night of 6 November. Torrecilla further revealed that he and the other members of the Delegation met and took decisions from the very early hours of 7 November. Another member, Arturo García de la Rosa, confirmed this in an interview with the Irish historian Ian Gibson.[17] The anarchist Gregorio Gallego highlighted the Communists' ability to hit the ground running: 'we realized that the operation was far too well prepared and manipulated to have been improvised'.[18]

It had been nearly 9.00 p.m. when Miaja sat down with his aide de camp and his secretary to give some thought to the problem of how to create the Junta de Defensa. While they were still sifting the names of possible councillors, the Communist delegation had arrived and successfully pitched for the War and Public Order Councils. Because the Communists had already decided on the personnel, those two Councils were able to function immediately. Having been left to hold the city as best he could, most of the rest of Miaja's time on the night of 6–7 November was dedicated to trying to ascertain the forces and weaponry available to him. At 7.00 in the morning of 7 November, Miaja went to the office of the Commissar General of War hoping to make contact with other political leaders. Hitherto, there had been a daily meeting in the Ministry of War to discuss the progress of the conflict. Now, Miaja discovered that most of those he wanted to meet had fled to Valencia along with the government. Thus only gradually throughout the morning was he able to assemble the rest of the personnel of the Junta. According to various eyewitnesses, it was not until 11 a.m. that the final list was drawn up. It consisted largely of young representatives of the various parties and trade unions.[19]

The first official meeting of the hastily formed Junta de Defensa was not until the late afternoon of 7 November. However, there can be no doubt that, from late the previous evening, overall operational responsibility for the prisoners lay with three men: Santiago Carrillo Solares, his deputy José Cazorla Maure and Segundo Serrano Poncela, who was effectively Director General of Security for Madrid. Key decisions about the prisoners were clearly taken in the vacuum between the departure of the government for Valencia on the evening of 6 November and the formal constitution of the Junta de Defensa twenty-four hours later. However, it is inconceivable that those decisions were taken in isolation by three inexperienced young men aged respectively twenty-one (Carrillo), thirty (Cazorla) and twenty-four (Serrano Poncela). The authorization for their operational decisions, as will be seen, had to have come from far more senior elements. Certainly, it required the go-ahead from Checa and Mije who, in turn, needed the approval of Miaja and probably of the Russian advisers. In the terror-stricken city, the aid provided by the Russians in terms of tanks, aircraft, the International Brigades and technical experience ensured that their advice would be sought and gratefully received. The implementation of the operational decisions also required, and indeed would receive, assistance from the anarchist movement.

Thus, the authorization, the organization and the implementation of what happened to the prisoners involved many people. However, Carrillo's position as Public Order Councillor, together with his later prominence as secretary general of the Communist Party, saw him accused of sole responsibility for the deaths that followed. That is absurd, but it does not mean that he had no responsibility at all. The calibration of the degree of that responsibility must start with the question of why a twenty-one-year-old member of the Socialist Youth should have been given such a crucial and powerful position. In fact, Carrillo was not entirely who he seemed to be at the time. Late on the night of 6 November, after the meeting with Miaja, Carrillo, along with Serrano

Poncela, Cazorla and others, was formally incorporated into the Communist Party. They were not subjected to stringent membership requirements. In what was hardly a formal ceremony, they simply informed José Díaz and Pedro Checa of their wishes and were incorporated into the party on the spot.[20]

The brevity of the proceedings indicates that Carrillo was already an important Communist 'submarine' within the Socialist Party. In prison after the miners' uprising in Asturias in October 1934, as secretary general of the Socialist Youth Movement (Federación de Juventudes Socialistas), he began to advocate its merger with the numerically smaller Communist equivalent, the Unión de Juventudes Comunistas. This was noted by Comintern agents and Carrillo was identified as a candidate for recruitment. The most senior Comintern representative in Spain, the Argentinian Vittorio Codovila, arranged for him to be invited to Moscow to discuss the potential unification of the FJS with the UJC. On being released from prison after the elections of 16 February 1936, he had immediately applied for a passport to travel to Russia. It represented a dazzling prospect for him. After a year incarcerated with Largo Caballero, Carrillo, like other prominent members of the Socialist Youth, sensed that the PSOE was yesterday's party. The Socialist leadership of middle-aged men rarely allowed young militants near powerful positions in its sclerotic structures. Carrillo now went to Moscow as the guest of the KIM, the Communist International of Youth, on 3 March. The KIM was closely watched by the Russian intelligence service, the NKVD (the People's Commissariat for Internal Affairs). Thus it is highly likely that Carrillo, who had already been identified for grooming as a potential Comintern star, was thoroughly vetted in Moscow and would have been obliged to convince his bosses of his loyalty to the Soviet Union.

On his return to Spain, Carrillo took part in a meeting of the Communist Party Central Committee on 31 March, at which he suggested that the Socialist Youth seek membership of the KIM and that the PSOE unite with the PCE and join the Comintern. Attendance at Central Committee meetings was a privilege not normally extended to outsiders.[21] In his memoirs, Carrillo made the even more startling admission that by early November 1936, although still formally a member of the Socialist Party, he was attending meetings of the PCE's Politbureau, an indication of great seniority.[22] With the help of Codovila, in April 1936, he secured an agreement to unite the Socialist and Communist youth movements (FJS and the UJC) as the United Socialist Youth (Juventudes Socialistas Unificadas). In some areas of Spain, although not all, unification took place immediately. In September, Carrillo would be named secretary general of the new youth movement, which was in some places a Communist organization. In general terms, the JSU constituted a massive advance of Communist influence at the expense of the Socialist Party. By this time, if Carrillo was not already a member of the PCE, he was very close to being so.

When Serrano Poncela began to run the Public Order Delegation, in the early hours of 7 November, he was able to use orders for the evacuation of prisoners left by the DGS, Manuel Muñoz, before leaving Madrid for Valencia.[23] The German Felix Schlayer, a fervent supporter of the rebels, claimed that the director of the Cárcel Modelo had shown him the order for the prisoner release which was signed by Vicente Girauta Linares, overall head of the police and Muñoz's second-in-command. Moreover, Schlayer believed that Girauta had signed the document on the spoken instruction of Muñoz. It is possible that, rather than actually signing orders, Muñoz told his deputy to draw up the necessary document. Schlayer also claimed to have been told later that Muñoz's action was the price that he paid to Communist militiamen who were preventing him joining the rest of the government in Valencia. No proof of this has come to light.[24] In any case, evacuation orders were not the equivalent of specific instructions for murder – as was shown by the safe arrival of some evacuated prisoners at their destinations.

Whoever signed the orders, in the midst of administrative collapse and widespread popular panic, the evacuation of eight thousand prisoners seemed impossible. Nevertheless, Carrillo's Public Order Council would undertake the task.[25] In the event, the evacuation became a massacre. It is the purpose of the rest of this chapter to elucidate, within the limits of the available evidence, what happened, who made the decision for it to happen and who carried it out.

Among those pushing for the evacuation – not necessarily the execution – of the prisoners were the Republican military authorities, General Miaja and his chief of staff, Vicente Rojo, the senior Russians present in Madrid and the Communist hierarchy. Given the crucial military assistance being provided by the Soviet personnel, and their own experience of the siege of St Petersburg in the Russian Civil War, it was natural that their advice should be sought. The most senior of the Soviet military personnel were Generals Ian Antonovich Berzin, the overall head of the Soviet military mission, and Vladimir Gorev. Berzin, along with Soviet diplomats, had gone to Valencia with the government, while Gorev, officially the military attaché but actually Madrid station chief of Soviet Military Intelligence (GRU), remained. Gorev would thus play a crucial role, alongside Rojo, in the defence of Madrid. Also present and involved was Mikhail Koltsov, the *Pravda* correspondent, perhaps the most powerful Russian journalist of the day. He was close to Stalin himself, although in Madrid, when not concentrating on his journalistic tasks, he seems to have been acting on Gorev's instructions.[26]

Other influential figures in the defence of Madrid were the senior Comintern personnel, the Argentinian Vittorio Codovila and the Italian Vittorio Vidali. Under the pseudonym 'Carlos Contreras', Vidali had played a crucial role in the founding of the Fifth Regiment which later became the core of the Republic's Popular Army. He was the Fifth Regiment's political commissar and his obsession with the need to eliminate rebel supporters within Madrid was reflected in numerous articles and speeches. Like their Spanish comrades, the Russian and Comintern officials were all alarmed to hear reports that the prisoners were already crowing about their imminent liberation and their incorporation into the rebel forces. Gorev, Berzin and other Russian advisers, including Vidali, insisted that it would be suicidal not to evacuate dangerous prisoners. Given the desperate situation of the siege, this was a view shared by Vicente Rojo and Miaja.[27]

Miaja quickly established a close relationship with one of the key players in the organization of the fate of the prisoners, José Cazorla.[28] The taciturn Cazorla was equally determined to eliminate rebel supporters. For this task, as will be seen, he drew upon the advice of Russian security personnel. Every bit as concerned as Miaja about the prisoners was the forty-two-year-old and recently promoted Lieutenant Colonel Vicente Rojo. He regarded the fifth column as 'an operational column with sufficient force and capacity to attack organized troops in the rear'. He was convinced that it was not made up only of spies, saboteurs and agitators but constituted a tightly woven network capable of influencing every aspect of the struggle, a network that had been organized long before the outbreak of war. At the beginning of November, he feared that it was capable of playing a decisive role in the fate of the capital. Accordingly, wrote Rojo, the military authorities had to take the decision to eliminate it.[29] In November 1936, this was an over-pessimistic assessment of the operational capacity of the fifth column, which would not reach that level for many months yet. Nevertheless, Rojo's view was an indication of the fear shaping Republican action and was quite reasonable, given the many times that accurate information about Republican movements had reached the rebels and the increase of sniping as the rebel forces were moving into the capital's western approaches.

There has been considerable speculation that Mikhail Koltsov played a key role in determining the fate of the prisoners. This is based on the entry in his diary for 7 November in which he described how, in the early hours of the morning, Pedro Checa took the decision to send militiamen to the prisons after pressure from 'Miguel Martínez', a supposedly Latin American Comintern agent with sufficient influence to give advice at the highest level. It has been widely assumed that 'Miguel Martínez' was none other than Koltsov himself because some of the activities attributed in his diary to 'Miguel Martínez' are known to have been carried out by Koltsov himself. Moreover, at a meeting in Moscow in April 1937, Stalin jokingly called Koltsov 'Don Miguel'. However, it is probable that 'Miguel Martínez' was a composite personality invented by Koltsov in order to include material in his published diary that he could not attribute directly to his informants.

In his memoirs, Vicente Rojo refers to a foreign Communist, 'Miguel Martínez', who helped Contreras organize the Fifth Regiment. Rojo knew Koltsov and had no reason not to mention him by name. Accordingly, it is clear that, for Rojo, 'Miguel Martínez' was someone other than Koltsov, almost certainly a Spanish-speaker who worked with Vidali at the Fifth Regiment and went by the name of 'Camarada Miguel'. The only man fitting this description was an NKVD operative named Josif Grigulevich.[30] In the very small NKVD presence in Spain, of fewer than ten operatives, some were 'legal' – that is to say, declared to the Spanish Foreign Ministry and having diplomatic cover – and some (two or three) were 'illegal', that is to say, working undercover. An example of the first would be Lev Lazarevich Nikolsky, the acting NKVD station chief in Madrid who went by the name Aleksandr Orlov, and of the second Josif Grigulevich. Nikolsky/Orlov was in Spain to advise on the creation of security services and to liquidate foreign Trotskyists.

Josif Romualdovich Grigulevich was a twenty-three-year-old Lithuanian who spoke fluent Spanish as a result of having lived in Argentina, where he was known as 'Camarada Miguel'. As a member of the NKVD's Special Tasks Administration, Grigulevich was trained in assassination and abductions. In Spain, he helped set up units known as 'special squads', as well as assisting Orlov in the elimination of Trotskyists. Thus, in Koltsov's diary, 'Miguel Martínez' was sometimes Koltsov himself, sometimes Grigulevich, sometimes General Gorev and perhaps sometimes someone else.[31] Gorev was the senior Russian officer actually in Madrid from the evening of 6 November, after the departure of Berzin to Valencia, and Koltsov sometimes acted as his messenger during this period. Gorev later reported to Moscow that 'comrades Koltsov and Karmen were with us, loyally carrying out to the letter all the missions that I entrusted them with in relation to the defence of the city'. This is confirmed by the writer Arturo Barea, who recalled that Koltsov put him in charge of foreign censorship in the besieged city, something that he could have done only on Gorev's authority.[32]

In the case of the meeting with Checa, it is possible that 'Miguel Martínez' was Gorev, Grigulevich or Koltsov himself. The memoirs of the Russian cameraman Roman Karmen suggest that it may actually have been Koltsov. Late on the night of 6 November, Karmen went to the Ministry of War, only to find it already deserted. After wandering around, he finally stumbled into a room containing the Communist leader, Antonio Mije, General Gorev and the chief of the Republican General Staff, Vicente Rojo – three influential individuals all highly concerned about the problem of the prisoners. From the Ministry, he went to PCE headquarters, where he found Koltsov locked in conversation with Pedro Checa.[33] This was almost certainly the encounter described in Koltsov's diary as being between Checa and 'Miguel Martínez'. In Koltsov's version, 'Miguel Martínez' urged Checa to proceed to the evacuation of the prisoners. Koltsov/Miguel Martínez pointed out that it was not necessary to evacuate all of the eight thousand but that it was crucial to select the most dangerous elements and send them to the rearguard in small groups.[34] Accepting this argument, Checa sent three men to 'two big prisons'. Although the two prisons were not named by Koltsov, they were almost certainly San Antón and the Cárcel Modelo, from which there were *sacas* on 7 November. 'Calling out names, they made the fascists come into the patio. This disconcerted and terrified them. They thought that they were about to be shot. They took them in the direction of Arganda.'[35]

In fact, it is highly unlikely that Koltsov would have had the authority to make such a crucial intervention. However, as Gorev's emissary, he might well have been sent to press for action on the evacuation of prisoners. If so, that would establish the link in the decision-making chain between Gorev and the Spanish Communist Party. Since Koltsov's 'diary' was not a diary as such but a book written later on the basis of his notes and *Pravda* articles, it is entirely possible that the meeting, stated there as having been early on 7 November, took place either side of midnight on 6 November. That would certainly make sense given that the prisons were in fact visited by militiamen later on the morning of the 7th.

There is no doubt that, already in the late afternoon or evening of 6 November, the two-man leadership of the PCE had provided Miaja with the public order set-up of the Junta de Defensa under the command of Santiago Carrillo. There is equally no doubt that the Public Order Council had begun to function late that same night and started the process of evacuation of prisoners. It is also clear that both Checa and Mije were in constant touch with the Russians. Karmen witnessed a meeting between Mije, Gorev and Vicente Rojo and another between Koltsov and Pedro Checa. There are no minutes of these meetings, but it is difficult to imagine that they were not concerned with the issue of what to do about the prisoners.

Another senior Communist, Enrique Castro Delgado, commander of the Fifth Regiment, had as his political commissar Vittorio Vidali, an NKVD agent. There can be no doubt, as will be seen, that they discussed the execution of prisoners. The journalist Herbert Matthews wrote later of the massacre of prisoners:

> I believe, myself, that the orders came from the Comintern agents in Madrid because I know that the sinister Vittorio Vidali spent the night in a prison briefly interrogating prisoners brought before him and, when he decided, as he almost always did, that they were fifth columnists, he would shoot them in the back of their heads with his revolver. Ernest Hemingway told me that he heard that Vidali fired so often that the skin between thumb and index finger of his right hand was badly burned.[36]

What Hemingway heard and then told Matthews is hardly reliable evidence. Nevertheless, the Italian Vidali was indeed in Spain as an emissary of the Comintern under the name Carlos Contreras, but he was also an agent of the NKVD. Both Josif Grigulevich (codenamed 'Maks'), who was briefly Vidali's assistant at the Fifth Regiment, and Vidali himself (codenamed 'Mario') belonged to the NKVD Administration for Special Tasks (assassination, terror, sabotage and abductions) commanded by Yakov Isaakovich Serebryansky.[37] Both Vidali and Grigulevich would later be heavily involved in the first attempt to assassinate Trotsky.

In support of Matthews's comment on Vidali/Contreras, there is a remarkable passage in the memoirs of Castro Delgado. Castro described how, on the night of 6 November, after talking to Contreras, he said to someone identified only as Tomás, the head of a special unit: 'The massacre starts. No quarter to be given. Mola's Fifth Column must be destroyed before it begins to move. Don't worry about making a mistake! There are times when you find yourself in front of twenty people knowing that one of them is a traitor but not which one. So you have a problem of conscience and a problem concerning the Party. You understand?' Tomás understood only too well that, to make sure of killing the traitor, some innocent people would have to die. Castro continued, 'Bear in mind that a break-out by the Fifth Column would be a lot to cope with for you and for everyone.' Tomás asked: 'A completely free hand?' Castro replied: 'This is one of those free hands that the Party, at times like this, can deny to no one – least of all you.' Tomás agreed and Castro then turned to Contreras, who had been present throughout, and said: 'Let's get a few hours' sleep. Tomorrow is 7 November. The day of decision. That's what it was for the Bolsheviks and what it will be for us. Are we thinking along the same lines or is there anything that you don't agree about, Commissar?' Contreras: 'We're in agreement.'[38] Since Vidali was the senior partner, it is reasonable to assume that it was his instructions that Castro was giving to Tomás.

On 12 November, an article in the Fifth Regiment's newspaper suggested that Castro Delgado's instructions had been taken to heart:

> In our city, there are still some of Mola's accomplices. While the rebels' evil birds drop their murderous bombs, killing defenceless women and children, the fascist elements of the fifth column throw hand grenades and fire their pistols ... We know only too well what the hordes of Moors and the Legion will do if they get into Madrid. We can have no mercy for the accomplices of those savages. The fifth column must be exterminated! The committees of every apartment block must locate where the fascist, the traitor, the suspect is hiding and denounce them. In a matter of hours, let us exterminate them![39]

The clear implications of the encounter between Contreras/Vidali and Castro Delgado are that elements of both the Fifth Regiment and the NKVD were involved in what happened to the prisoners in November. In the report by Gorev mentioned earlier, he wrote appreciatively of the 'neighbours' (a reference to the NKVD station in Madrid) 'headed by Comrade Orlov who did much to prevent an uprising from within'. A possible break-out of the detained military officers, 'an uprising from within', is exactly what the prisoner evacuation was about. Gorev's report thus suggests that Orlov was involved in the elimination of prisoners, albeit not in the initial decision-making process.[40]

In a revealing interview in 1986, two years before his death, Grigulevich stated that, in Madrid, he had worked under the orders of Santiago Carrillo heading a special squad (the Brigada Especial) of Socialist militants in the Dirección General de Seguridad dedicated to 'dirty' operations.[41] This elite security detachment would be expanded into three special squads in December 1936 when Carrillo was replaced by Cazorla. The initial squad was formed by Grigulevich from what he called 'trusted elements' recruited from members of the Juventudes Socialistas Unificadas who had been part of the unit responsible for the security of the Soviet Embassy in Madrid. It was formally commanded by the Socialist policeman David Vázquez Baldominos.

Grigulevich had arrived in Spain in late September and worked for Contreras for some weeks before beginning to collaborate with Carrillo in late October or early November. Carrillo, Cazorla and the unit's members knew Grigulevich as 'José Escoy', although he was known to others as 'José Ocampo'. This unit was run out of the Dirección General de Seguridad. Grigulevich's assertion is sustained by the record in the Francoist archive, the Causa General, of the post-war interrogations of JSU members of what came to be the three Brigadas Especiales. In the published résumé of the Causa General proceedings, there is a statement that 'Representatives of the [NKVD], calling themselves comrades Coto, Pancho and Leo, backed up by an individual who used the name José Ocampo and several female interpreters, all installed in the Hotel Gaylord, in Calle Alfonso XI ... were directing the activities of the Marxist police of Madrid.'[42]

When questioned after the war, Tomás Durán González, one of the members of the first special squad, provided descriptions which, while not entirely accurate, make it possible to identify these figures. 'Coto', he said, advised on questions of interrogation and investigation. Durán believed him to be the head of the Soviet Technical Investigation Group. He described 'Coto' as being about thirty-five years old, tall, with dark hair sharply parted, cleanly shaven and always dressed in civilian clothes. 'Coto' was rarely in Madrid because he was based in Barcelona. Accordingly, 'Coto' can be identified with certainty as the thirty-seven-year-old Naum Isakovich Eitingon (Leonid Aleksandrovich Kotov), who was the *rezident* in the NKVD sub-station in the Soviet Consulate in Barcelona.

'Pancho' was an NKVD agent described by Durán as being 'about forty-five years old, tall, corpulent, with a red face and wavy blond hair with some streaks of grey combed back'. He also took part in the interrogation and torture of prisoners. This would suggest that 'Pancho' was Senior Major of State Security Grigory Sergeievich Syroyezhkin. The description given by Durán fits photographs of Syroyezhkin. In a separate declaration, the later head of the principal Brigada Especial, Fernando Valentí Fernández, referred to 'Pancho' as 'Pancho Bollasqui'. The ill-remembered Russian surname might have referred to Lev Vasilevsky, Syroyezhkin's deputy and regular companion, since Valentí would often have seen them together.

Durán remembered the man known to him only as 'Leo' as being responsible for the internal security of the Russian Embassy. He was 'tall, slender, about twenty-eight years old, dark'. If Durán's testimony is accurate, he was probably referring to Lev Sokolov, who was indeed in charge of security at the Embassy. 'José Ocampo' (Grigulevich) was described as being about thirty-five years old, with a noticeable Argentinian accent, five feet six inches tall, chunky in build, with a pale complexion, blood-shot eyes and dark wavy hair. He disappeared from Spain after the assassination of Andreu Nin in June 1937.[43]

The NKVD's role in the creation and functioning of the Brigada Especial was confirmed by José Cazorla to his post-war interrogators. He told them that Lev Gaikis, the political counsellor at the Russian Embassy, had introduced him to a Russian whom he had called 'Alexander'. 'Alexander', who offered him help and advice, was almost certainly Orlov, the acting head of the NKVD station. Cazorla also admitted that he and Vázquez Baldominos collaborated closely with 'José Ocampo' (Grigulevich), to whom he had also been introduced by Gaikis. 'Ocampo' and 'Alexander', whom Cazorla now knew as 'Leo' (Lev Nikolsky/Orlov), provided technical advice on what he called counter-espionage matters – in other words, the campaign against the fifth column. 'Pancho' (Syroyezhkin) was also in regular contact with both Cazorla and Vázquez Baldominos.[44] Orlov's main task at this moment was the defence of the Soviet Embassy, and he enjoyed considerable operational discretion. There can be little or no doubt that he would have seen the prisoners as a threat and could have ordered Grigulevich to help Carrillo and Cazorla in resolving the problem via their evacuation and execution.

In the summer of 1937, Orlov told the Republican premier Juan Negrín that 'his service' worked in co-operation with the Republican security apparatus.[45] Moreover, a report written by the Republican police in October 1937 referred to the frequent visits made to Carrillo's office by Russian technicians specializing in security and counter-espionage matters. The report also stated that these technicians had offered their 'enthusiastic collaboration to the highest authority in public order in Madrid', which could have been a reference to Miaja or to Carrillo. If the former, it would mean that Carrillo's activities were covered by Miaja's approval, although his collaboration with the Russians would have happened anyway given the Soviet links with the Communist Party. The report went on to state that Carrillo had directed these technicians to 'the head and the officers of the Brigada Especial', which had to mean David Vázquez Baldominos. This was confirmed by Vázquez Baldominos's successor, Fernando Valentí, to his Francoist interrogators. By following the advice of these experienced technicians, the Brigada achieved maximum efficacy in a new area of police activity made necessary by wartime circumstances. The report stated that 'the collaboration of said technicians was ever more intense until a total mutual understanding between the Spanish and Russian security services was reached'.[46] Grigulevich later described himself as 'the right hand of Carrillo' in the Public Order Council.[47] According to the records of the NKVD's successor organization, the KGB or Committee for State Security, their friendship was so close that years later Carrillo chose Grigulevich to be his son's secular 'godfather'.[48]

It is clear that Miaja, Rojo, Gorev and the senior leadership of the Communist Party were all anxious to see the prisoner question resolved with the greatest urgency. They certainly approved of prisoner evacuations but not necessarily of executions, although it is possible that they approved of them too. What is likely is that, in the meetings immediately following the creation of the Junta de Defensa, they delegated responsibility to the two-man leadership of the PCE. They, who certainly did approve of the execution of prisoners, passed organizational responsibility to Carrillo, Cazorla and Serrano Poncela. To implement their instructions, the trio could draw on members of the JSU who were given posts in the Public Order Delegation headed by Serrano Poncela, which then ran the Dirección General de Seguridad for Madrid. They could also count on assistance from Contreras/Vidali and the Fifth Regiment and from Grigulevich and the Brigada Especial. However, they could do nothing against the will of the anarchist movement which controlled the roads out of Madrid. Given that the anarchists had already seized and murdered prisoners, it was not likely that they would offer insuperable opposition to the Communists. Indeed, the formal agreement of senior elements of the CNT militias was soon forthcoming.

The inaugural session of the Junta began at 6.00 p.m. on 7 November 1936. It was addressed by the newly appointed President, General Miaja, who explained the perilous situation, with the remaining forces short of arms, their morale shattered by constant retreats. There was little in the way of reserves and the Ministry of War was in a state of near collapse.[49] Before the meeting, at around 5.30 p.m., Carrillo, coming out of Miaja's office in the Ministry of War, met a representative of the International Red Cross, Dr Georges Henny, with Felix Schlayer, the Norwegian Consul. Carrillo invited them to meet him in his office immediately after the plenary session. Before returning for that encounter, Schlayer and the Red Cross delegate went to the Cárcel Modelo, where they learned that several hundred prisoners had been taken away. On coming back to the Ministry of War, they were greeted amiably by Carrillo, who assured them of his determination to protect the prisoners and put a stop to the murders. When they told him what they had learned at the Cárcel Modelo, he denied knowledge of any evacuations. Schlayer reflected later that, even if this were true, it raises the question why Carrillo and Miaja, once having been informed by him of the evacuations, did nothing to prevent the others that continued that evening and on successive days.[50]

Later in the same evening, there was a meeting held between unnamed representatives of the Juventudes Socialistas Unificadas who controlled the newly created Public Order Council, and members of the local federation of the CNT. They discussed what to do with the prisoners. Liaison between the two was necessary, despite mutual hostility, since the Communists held sway inside Madrid, controlling the police, the prisons and the files on prisoners, while the anarchists, through their militias, controlled the roads out of the city. The next morning, at a meeting of the CNT's national committee, a detailed report was given on the agreements made at the previous evening's CNT–JSU encounter. The only record of that meeting is the account given in the minutes of the report by Amor Nuño Pérez, the Councillor for War Industries in the Junta de Defensa. Those minutes did not include the names of the other participants at the CNT–JSU meeting. It is reasonable to suppose that, since the meeting took place immediately after the plenary session of the Junta de Defensa, the CNT was represented by some or all of its nominees on the Junta – Amor Nuño, his deputy Enrique García Pérez, Mariano García Carrascales, the Councillor for Information, and his deputy Antonio Oñate, both from the Juventudes Libertarias. It is equally reasonable to suppose that the JSU representatives included at least two of the following: Santiago Carrillo, José Cazorla and Segundo Serrano Poncela. The gravity of the matter under discussion and the practical agreements reached could hardly have permitted them to be represented by more junior members of the JSU. If Carrillo was not there, it is inconceivable that he, as both Public Order Councillor and secretary general of the JSU, was not fully apprised of the meeting, whoever represented the JSU.

Gregorio Gallego, who was present at the CNT meeting, later described Amor Nuño, whom he knew well: 'Amor Nuño, generally speaking, was emotional and temperamental and not much given to thinking. When he did think, which was rare, he didn't trust his own judgement.' Elsewhere, Gallego wrote: 'Amor Nuño, as jumpy as a squirrel, was incapable of being still anywhere. He always wanted to be in on everything without ever committing himself to anything.'[51]

Nuño reported that the CNT and JSU representatives, on the evening of 7 November, had decided that the prisoners should be classified into three groups. The fate of the first, consisting of 'fascists and dangerous elements', was to be 'Immediate execution', 'with responsibility to be hidden' – the responsibility being of those who took the decision and of those who implemented it. The second group, of prisoners considered to be supporters of the military uprising but, because of age or profession, less dangerous, were to be evacuated to Chinchilla, near Albacete. The third, those least politically committed, were to be released 'with all possible guarantees, as proof to the Embassies of our humanitarianism'. This last comment suggests that whoever represented the JSU at the meeting knew about and mentioned the earlier encounter between Carrillo and Schlayer.[52]

The first consignment of prisoners had already left Madrid early in the morning of 7 November, presumably in accordance with the instructions for evacuation issued by Pedro Checa in response to Koltsov/ Miguel Martínez. Thus some prisoners were removed and killed before the formal agreement with the CNT made later that evening. There is no record of any difficulty of their getting through the anarchist militias on the roads out, and that is not surprising since there were CNT–FAI representatives on Serrano Poncela's Public Order Delegation. Nevertheless, the agreement guaranteed that further convoys would face no problems at the anarchist checkpoints on the roads out of the capital and could also rely on substantial assistance in the gory business of executing the prisoners. The strongest CNT controls were posted on the roads out to Valencia and Aragon which the convoys would take. Large flotillas of double-decker buses and many smaller vehicles could not get out of Madrid without the approval, co-operation or connivance of the CNT patrols. Since Carrillo, Cazorla and Serrano Poncela knew this only

too well, it is not plausible that they would have ordered evacuation
convoys without first securing the agreement of the CNT–FAI. This
undermines Carrillo's later assertions that the convoys were hijacked by
anarchists. The grain of truth in those claims resides in the certainty that
the anarchists took some part in the actual killing.

The consequences of the first decisions taken by Carrillo and his
collaborators were dramatic. On the morning of 7 November, there was
a *saca* at San Antón and, in the afternoon, a larger one at the Cárcel
Modelo. At some point that morning, policemen from the Dirección
General de Seguridad and members of the rearguard militias MVR
appeared at the Cárcel Modelo with the orders signed by Manuel Muñoz
for the evacuation of prisoners. They were led by the Inspector General
of the MVR, Federico Manzano Govantes.[53]

This is confirmed by the important testimony of Felix Schlayer. When
he visited the Cárcel Modelo on 6 November, with a view to preventing
possible evacuations, he saw nothing. However, the next morning, when
he returned, he did see a large number of buses outside and was told that
they were for the evacuation of military officers towards Valencia.[54] This
coincides with the graphic description given by Caamaño Cobanela, an
inmate in the Cárcel Modelo, of the prisoners being lined up for evacuation in the early hours of the morning of 7 November. Cobanela is
unequivocal that, having been taken from their cells, the prisoners were
left waiting with their belongings in the patio but, after two hours, were
returned to their cells.

Later in the afternoon, according to the detailed descriptions left by
three prisoners, large numbers were led from their cells in the Cárcel
Modelo. Two men (those sent by Pedro Checa?) with numerous yellow-
ing file-cards from the prison registry were accompanied by militiamen.
They called out names through a loud-hailer and ordered the men to
take all their belongings and wait below. Those named were a mixture of
army officers, priests and civilians, young and old, with no apparent
pattern. They speculated anxiously whether they would be transferred
to other prisons outside Madrid or be killed. They were tied together in
groups and forced to leave all their bags and cases behind. Moreover,
they were searched and any remaining watches, money or valuables
taken from them.[55] They were loaded on to double-decker buses.
Convoys consisting of the buses escorted by cars and trucks carrying
militiamen shuttled back and forth over the next two days.

Their official destinations were prisons well behind the lines, in Alcalá
de Henares, Chinchilla and Valencia. However, only about three hundred

arrived. Eleven miles from Madrid, on the road to Alcalá de Henares, at the small village of Paracuellos del Jarama, the first batch, from San Antón, were violently forced off the buses. At the base of the small hill on which the village stood, they were lined up by the militiamen, verbally abused and then shot. In the evening of the same day, the second batch, from the Cárcel Modelo, suffered the same fate. A further consignment of prisoners arrived on the morning of 8 November. The Mayor was forced to round up the able-bodied inhabitants of the village (there were only 1,600 in total) to dig huge ditches for the approximately eight hundred bodies which had been left to rot. When Paracuellos could cope with no more, subsequent convoys made for the nearby village of Torrejón de Ardoz, where a disused irrigation channel was used for the approximately four hundred victims.[56] There have been numerous assertions that ditches had already been dug.[57] On 8 November, there were more *sacas* from the Cárcel Modelo. By then, news had already reached the prisoners of the first murders in Paracuellos del Jarama and Torrejón de Ardoz.

It is certain that, from approximately 8.00 on the morning of Saturday 7 November onwards, 175 prisoners were taken from San Antón and, later in the afternoon of the same day, more than nine hundred from the Cárcel Modelo. A further 185 to 200 were brought from the Cárcel de Porlier in the Barrio de Salamanca. Another 190 to 200 were taken from the Cárcel de Ventas. On that day, 1,450–1,545 prisoners were removed from Madrid's four jails. Thereafter, there were *sacas*, on 7, 8, 9, 18, 24, 25, 26, 27, 28, 29 and 30 November and 1 and 3 December. The Cárcel Modelo was the prison with the highest number of victims – 970 – but suffered *sacas* only on the first three days. By 16 November, the Francoists were so close that the Carcel Model had to be evacuated and was used as headquarters for the Durruti Column and the International Brigades despite heavy bomb damage. The prisoners were taken to the other Madrid jails, Porlier, Ventas and San Antón, and to Alcalá de Henares. Porlier saw *sacas* on 7, 8, 9, 18, 24, 25 and 26 November and 1 and 3 December. Of these, a total of 405 were murdered in Paracuellos or Torrejón. *Sacas* from San Antón on 7, 22, 28, 29 and 30 November saw a total of four hundred prisoners murdered in Paracuellos or Torrejón. Five other expeditions of prisoners from San Antón, two on 7 November and three more on 27, 28 and 29 November, arrived safely in Alcalá de Henares. From the prison at Ventas, *sacas* on 27, 29, 30 November and 1 and 3 December ended with about two hundred murders at Paracuellos or Torrejón. The total numbers killed over the four weeks following the creation of the Junta de Defensa cannot be calculated with total precision, but there is little doubt that it was somewhere between 2,200 and 2,500.[58]

All these *sacas* were initiated with documentation on Dirección General de Seguridad notepaper indicating that the prisoners were either to be released or to be taken to Chinchilla. When the order was for them to go to Alcalá de Henares, they usually arrived safely. This indicates that 'liberty' and 'Chinchilla' were codewords for elimination.[59] The specific orders for the evacuations of prisoners were not signed by Carrillo, nor by any member of the Junta de Defensa. Until 22 November, such orders were signed by Manuel Muñoz's second-in-command in the Dirección General de Seguridad, the head of the police Vicente Girauta Linares. Until he followed Muñoz to Valencia, Girauta was under the orders of Serrano Poncela, Muñoz's successor for Madrid. Thereafter, the orders were signed either by Serrano Poncela himself, or else by Girauta's successor as head of the Madrid police, Bruno Carreras Villanueva.[60] In the Causa General, there are several documents signed by Serrano Poncela. Its published version reproduces two. The one dated 26 November 1936 read, 'I request that you release the individuals listed on the back of this page,' of whom there were twenty-six named. The document dated 27 November read, 'Please release the prisoners mentioned on the two attached sheets,' which had 106 names. All those on these two lists were assassinated.[61] No explicit orders for the execution have been found.

Important evidence about the responsibility for what happened was provided in the post-war testimony of the Communist and close friend of José Cazorla, Ramón Torrecilla Guijarro. He stated that the entire process was directed by Segundo Serrano Poncela, supervised by members of his Public Order Delegation and implemented by agents of the Dirección General de Seguridad. These 'agents' were the policemen from the DGS and members of the rearguard militias of the MVR led by Federico Manzano Govantes. Torrecilla Guijarro himself admitted that three members of the Delegation, himself, Manuel Rascón Ramírez of the CNT and Manuel Ramos Martínez of the FAI, together with three policemen, Agapito Sainz, Lino Delgado and Andrés Urrésola, went to the Cárcel Modelo after 10 o'clock on the night of 7 November. Their orders from Serrano Poncela were to select prisoners and they began to go through the file-cards dividing them into military men, professionals and aristocrats, workers and those whose profession was unknown.

Between 3.00 and 4.00 a.m., they were about halfway through the task when their boss, Serrano Poncela, arrived. Given the urgency of the situation, he ordered them to prepare those so far selected for loading on to buses. He allegedly said that this was in fulfilment of an order telephoned from Tarancón by the fleeing Minister of the Interior, Ángel Galarza, on 6 November, to which Serrano Poncela added that those preparing the expedition knew that it was for 'definitive evacuation' of the prisoners, which presumably meant death. Accordingly, the categorization process was abandoned. Again, the prisoners had their wrists tied together with cord, usually in twos, and were dispossessed of everything of value. Between 9 and 10 the following morning, 8 November, seven to nine double-decker buses and two large single-deck charabancs arrived. The prisoners were loaded aboard and the expedition set off, escorted by armed militiamen and accompanied by the anarchist Manuel Rascón Ramírez and the three policemen, Sainz, Delgado and Urrésola.[62] In the declarations made by those later interrogated by the Francoist police, there are no references to the convoys on this or any other occasion facing any difficulties from the anarchist militias guarding the roads out of Madrid. This suggests that the deal reached on the evening of 7 November between the CNT and JSU was being implemented. It is probable that Rascón Ramírez went along to ensure easy passage through anarchist checkpoints by confirming that the expedition had CNT–FAI approval.[63]

What happened that morning of 8 November at the Cárcel Modelo seems to have been the standard practice employed during the subsequent *sacas*. From that day, Carrillo had started to publish a series of decrees that would ensure Communist control of the security forces within the capital and put an end to the myriad parallel police forces. On 9 November, Carrillo issued two decrees that constituted a significant step towards the centralized control of the police and security forces. The first required the surrender of all arms not in authorized hands. The second stated that the internal security of the capital would be the exclusive responsibility of forces organized by the Council for Public Order. This signified the dissolution, on paper at least, of all *checas*.[64] Under the conditions of the siege, Carrillo was thus able to impose by emergency decree measures that had been beyond the government. Nevertheless, there was a considerable delay between the announcement of the decree and its successful implementation. The anarchists resisted as long as they could and the Communists never relinquished some of their *checas*.

Shortly after taking up office, Carrillo had called a meeting with representatives of the Comité Provincial de Investigación Pública. He reminded them that, when the CPIP had been created, Manuel Muñoz had said it was a temporary structure while the Dirección General de Seguridad was being purged, after which some of its members would be incorporated into the police. Carrillo declared that the moment had arrived.[65] Accordingly, by his decree of 9 November, he returned the services of security and investigation to the now reformed police and suppressed all those groups run by political parties or trade unions. This meant the end of the CPIP, known as the Checa de Fomento. In fact, several of its members, including Manuel Rascón Ramírez and Manuel Ramos Martínez, were already working with the Public Order Delegation. The treasurer of the Checa de Fomento handed over 1,750,000 pesetas in cash, gold to the value of 600,000 pesetas and 460 chests full of valuable household items, including silver, porcelain, clocks and radios, that had been taken in house searches and from those arrested. Other items of jewellery had been regularly delivered to the Dirección General de Seguridad.[66]

Explicitly included within these reformed services was 'everything relative to the administration of the arrest and release of prisoners, as well as the movement, transfer etc of those under arrest'. They were under the control of the Public Order Delegation, which consisted of eight delegates chaired by Segundo Serrano Poncela with the Sub-Director General of Security, Vicente Girauta Linares, as his second-in-command and technical adviser. It will be recalled that one of the eight delegates, Arturo García de la Rosa, told Ian Gibson that this body began to function in the early hours of the morning of 7 November. This was confirmed by Ramón Torrecilla when interrogated in November 1939, which underlines Carrillo's own admission that his team began to function before they had been officially named by Miaja at 11 a.m. and certainly before the first meeting of the Junta de Defensa in the evening.[67]

Two weeks after the creation of the Public Order Delegation in the DGS, under Serrano Poncela, Vicente Girauta followed Manuel Muñoz to Valencia and was replaced by Bruno Carreras, a member of the CPIP who had been accepted as a professional policeman and rose swiftly to become the inspector in charge of the city's most important police station, the Comisaría de Buenavista. The post carried with it the position of Inspector General (Comisario General) with authority over the other eleven inspectors. This effectively made Carreras second-in-command of the Dirección General de Seguridad.[68] What all of this makes indisputably clear is that all functions of the DGS were controlled by Serrano Poncela. However, it has to be noted that he, in turn, followed the instructions of Carrillo or of his deputy José Cazorla.

The Public Order Delegation took over the activities, and absorbed many of the personnel, of the CPIP. Control of roads in and out of the capital was to be in the hands of the police, the Assault Guards and Rearguard Security Militias (MVR) and co-ordinated by Serrano Poncela's Delegation. The Delegation had a representative in each police station and in each of the principal prisons. According to Carrillo, the only opposition to his centralization measures came from the anarchists. Indeed, the closure of Felipe Sandoval's *checa* in the Cine Europa was resisted and eventually required the intervention of the Assault Guards. Carrillo's measures constituted the institutionalization of the repression under the Public Order Delegation in the DGS. Despite the presence of two CNT–FAI members and the fact that many ex-members of the component groups of the CPIP now became policemen, the Delegation was dominated by the Communists. They were thus able to push forward the reconstruction of the Republican state which had been a crucial necessity since the military coup had shattered the apparatus of government.[69]

Within Serrano Poncela's Delegation, there were three sub-sections. The first dealt with investigation, interrogations and petitions for release. This was headed by Manuel Rascón Ramírez of the CNT. After interrogations had been carried out, this section made recommendations to the Delegation and final decisions were taken by Carrillo. This function was entirely compatible with the decisions taken at the meeting between JSU and CNT members on the evening of 7 November. The second sub-section, headed by Serrano Poncela himself, dealt with prisons, prisoners and prison transfers. According to Rascón, it used the Dawn Squad and small tribunals of militiamen set up in each prison to go through the file-cards of the prisoners. One such group in Porlier prison was run by Felipe Sandoval. The third sub-section dealt with the personnel of the police and other more or less official armed groups in the rearguard. Headed by another close JSU collaborator of Cazorla, Santiago Álvarez Santiago, it evaluated the reliability of existing policemen and also decided which members of the old *checas* could be incorporated into the police. For all these jobs, the Public Order Delegation could draw on the files and personnel of the technical section of the DGS.[70]

The procedures that would be applied to prisoners between 18 November and 6 December were established on 10 November at a meeting of the Public Order Delegation. Serrano Poncela laid down three categories: army officers with the rank of captain and above; Falangists; other rightists. This was roughly similar to what had been agreed at the meeting on 7 November between members of the CNT–FAI and representatives of the JSU, one of whom had almost certainly been Serrano Poncela himself. To supervise the process, Rascón Ramírez of the CNT and Torrecilla Guijarro of the PCE were in charge of appointing those who would in turn select the prisoners to be executed. Rascón and Torrecilla named a 'responsible' and a deputy for each prison who in turn set up a number of three-man tribunals to select the prisoners. When these tribunals had made up their lists, they were taken to Rascón who passed them to Serrano Poncela. He then signed orders for their 'release', which meant their execution. According to Torrecilla, those expeditions of prisoners that arrived safely at their destination consisted of men not listed for execution by the prison tribunals. Serrano Poncela had to report every day to Carrillo in his office in the Junta de Defensa (in the Palace of Juan March in Calle Núñez de Balboa in the Barrio de Salamanca). Carrillo also often visited the office of Serrano Poncela in nearby Calle Serrano.[71]

That 'release' (execution) orders came from Serrano Poncela was confirmed by the declaration of another policeman, Álvaro Marasa Barasa. In fact, the tribunals established after the August events in the Cárcel Modelo had already drawn up lists of candidates to be shot, some of whom had been executed in the course of September and October. Now, agents would arrive at each prison late at night with a general order signed by Serrano Poncela for the 'liberation' of the prisoners listed on the back or on separate sheets. The director of the prison would hand them over and they would then be taken to wherever Serrano Poncela had indicated verbally to the agents. The subsequent phase of the process, the transportation and execution of the prisoners in the early hours of the following morning, was supervised by the Inspector General of the rearguard militias, Federico Manzano Govantes, or his deputy on the day. The actual tasks were carried out each day by different groups of militiamen, sometimes anarchists from the rearguard militias, sometimes Communists from the *checa* in the Calle Marqués de Riscal and sometimes from the Fifth Regiment. The prisoners were obliged to leave all their belongings, which were handed over to Santiago Álvarez Santiago. They were then tied together in pairs and loaded on to buses. Usually, Manuel Rascón or Arturo García de la Rosa went along and delivered the coup de grâce to prisoners not killed when the militiamen fired.[72]

On Monday 9 November, Jesús de Galíndez of the PNV had gone to the Cárcel Modelo to collect some Basque prisoners whose release had been approved by the DGS. This was something that he had been doing regularly over the course of the previous two months. On this day, however, he noted a dramatic change. The prison was now in the hands of militiamen who were reluctant to accept the release orders that he carried. After a fierce argument, they agreed. However, as he left, his driver told him that, while he was waiting outside in the car, a truckload of militiamen had arrived to be greeted by one of the sentries saying, 'Today you can't have any complaints since you've had plenty of meat.' This was understood by Galíndez to be a reference to the shootings that had taken place on Sunday 8 November.[73]

If Galíndez knew what was happening, it is impossible that Carrillo did not. This is demonstrated by the minutes of the meeting of the Junta de Defensa on the night of 11 November. The Councillor for Evacuation, Francisco Caminero Rodríguez (of the anarchist youth), asked if the Cárcel Modelo had been evacuated. Carrillo responded by saying that the necessary measures had been taken to organize the evacuations of prisoners but that the operation had had to be suspended. At this, the Communist Isidoro Diéguez Dueñas, second-in-command to Antonio Mije at the War Council, declared that the evacuation must continue given the seriousness of the problem of the prisoners. Carrillo responded that the suspension had been necessary because of protests emanating from the diplomatic corps, presumably a reference to his meeting with Schlayer. Although the minutes are extremely brief, they make it indisputably clear that Carrillo knew what was happening to the prisoners, if only as a result of the complaints by Schlayer.[74]

In fact, after the mass executions of 7–8 November, there were no more *sacas* until 18 November, after which they continued on a lesser scale until 6 December. Jesús de Galíndez, who was in constant touch with both the DGS and the various prisons as he tried to secure the release of Basque prisoners and members of the clergy, described the procedure that was followed. His account broadly coincides with those of Torrecilla Guijarro and Marasa Barasa. The tribunals would examine the antecedents of the prisoners to decide if they were dangerous – anyone so deemed would be executed. Those who had someone to vouch for them were released. Others remained in prison. Mistakes were made, with evident enemies of the Republic surviving and entirely innocent individuals being executed. Among the survivors were Manuel Valdés Larrañaga, a Falangist who was later Franco's Ambassador to the Dominican Republic, Agustín Muñoz Grandes, who would become Franco's Minister of War and Vice-President, and Raimundo Fernández

Cuesta, one of the principal Falangist leaders and future minister under Franco.[75]

According to a prisoner held in Porlier, one of the tribunals there, known as the 'tribunal de la muerte', was headed by Felipe Sandoval. Since its members were usually drunk, its decisions were largely arbitrary. Elsewhere, the process of selection was more systematic and was facilitated by the exhaustive records held in the Technical Section of the DGS. This consisted of the files on all those arrested since the beginning of the war, with the reasons for the arrest together with details of their fate – release, imprisonment, trial, execution. The Section also held the records of right-wing groups that had been seized by various militia groups. These files had been consolidated into one large archive at the DGS. There was relatively little material on the Falange, which had managed to destroy its records, but the files of Acción Popular, the Carlists and the Unión Militar Española were virtually complete. When the Junta de Defensa was created, the Technical Section's holdings were passed over to Serrano Poncela's Public Order Delegation.[76]

The *sacas* and executions, known collectively as 'Paracuellos', constituted the greatest single atrocity in Republican territory during the war, its horror explained but not justified by the terrifying conditions in the besieged capital. Unlike previous *sacas*, triggered by popular outrage at bombing raids or news brought by refugees of rebel atrocities, these extra-judicial murders were carried out as a result of political-military decisions. They were organized by the Council for Public Order but they could not have been carried out without help from other elements in the rearguard militias. In the immediate aftermath, little was known about the events at Paracuellos and Torrejón on the road to Alcalá de Henares since they were not reported in the press. However, an investigation was initiated by a group of diplomats: the doyen of the diplomatic corps, the Ambassador of Chile, Aurelio Núñez Morgado; the Chargé d'Affaires of Argentina, Edgardo Pérez Quesada; the British Chargé d'Affaires, George Ogilvie-Forbes; Felix Schlayer, the German who, despite his questionable diplomatic status, was recognized by the Republic as Norwegian Chargé d'Affaires; and a representative of the Red Cross, Dr Georges Henny.

The government was bombarded with diplomatic protests, particularly from the two most openly pro-rebel diplomats, Schlayer and Núñez Morgado. Núñez Morgado's sympathy for Franco's cause actually saw him cross the lines to take the Romanian and Argentine representatives to Toledo to address the rebels ostensibly on behalf of the diplomatic corps.[77] Schlayer's position was extremely questionable given his German citizenship and consular post. Ogilvie-Forbes was led to ask 'what exactly is the position of Schlayer, who sometimes calls himself Norwegian Ambassador?'[78] According to the wife of the Reuters correspondent, Julio Álvarez del Vayo was 'most insulting about Schlayer of Norway and has written the Norwegian Government demanding Schlayer's removal'.[79] Despite their blatant hostility to the Republic, the protests of Schlayer and Núñez Morgado led to the Red Cross representative, Georges Henny, being able to prise from the Junta de Defensa a list of 1,600 names of prisoners who had been taken from the Cárcel Modelo, of whom 1,300 had not reached Alcalá de Henares.[80]

Schlayer, accompanied by Henny and Pérez Quesada, had been to Torrejón where they found recently disturbed ground from which protruded arms and legs.[81] An initial report on the first murders sent by Ogilvie-Forbes was minuted by Sir Robert Vansittart, the Permanent Under-Secretary at the Foreign Office: 'This is a ghastly tale of ghastly gangsters in whose hands the so-called "government" ... is a bad joke. I suppose the other side will do as horribly in their turn.'[82] In fact, British diplomats rarely acknowledged atrocities on the rebel side and never saw the differences between what happened in each zone. While the rebel authorities actively sanctioned atrocities throughout the war and after, it was precisely the Republican government's opposition to them that limited them to the first five months of the war. In this context, it is worth noting the comment of the New Zealand journalist Geoffrey Cox: 'The spotlight of publicity which has been turned on these unauthorised executions is, ironically enough, itself a reflection of the antagonism of the Spanish Government towards such deeds. For much of the information has become available only because of the freedom with which the Government has discussed the problem with foreign authorities and with visiting delegations.'[83]

After the mass *sacas* of 7 and 8 November, there was a brief interlude thanks to the anarchist Melchor Rodríguez and Mariano Sánchez Roca, the under-secretary at the Ministry of Justice. Those *sacas* had occurred in the absence of the Minister of Justice, García Oliver, and his Director General of Prisons, Juan Antonio Carnero, who had gone to Valencia with the rest of the government. Appalled by what was happening, the president of the Supreme Court, Mariano Gómez, and the secretary general of the Bar Association, Luis Zubillaga, sent a telegram requesting García Oliver once more to put Melchor Rodríguez in charge of the prisons in Madrid. Sánchez Roca, a labour lawyer who had represented various CNT militants including Melchor Rodríguez, managed to persuade

García Oliver to name Melchor Special Inspector of Prisons. Surprisingly, García Oliver agreed. It is not known whether this had anything to do with the diplomatic protests although, as will be seen, other members of the government had heard about, and were appalled by, the *sacas*. On 9 November, before his appointment was officially announced, Melchor took up the post. By the time his appointment was made official five days later, he would already have resigned.[84]

When Melchor Rodríguez unofficially assumed the post of Inspector General of Prisons, his exact powers were imprecise, not to say debatable. Nevertheless, his first initiative on the night of 9 November was decisive. Melchor's friend, Juan Batista, the administrator of the Cárcel Modelo, had told him that a *saca* of four hundred prisoners was planned. In response, he went to the prison at midnight and ordered that all *sacas* cease and that the militiamen who had been freely moving within the prison remain outside. He forbade the release of any prisoners between 6 p.m. and 8 a.m., to prevent them being shot. He also insisted on accompanying any prisoners being transferred to other prisons. In consequence there were no *sacas* between 10 and 17 November. His next objective was to get the militiamen out and the professional prison functionaries back.[85] He explained his intentions to Schlayer and Henny. On behalf of the diplomatic corps, Schlayer wrote to Melchor Rodríguez to confirm what had been promised:

> That you consider the detainees to be prisoners of war and that you are
> determined to prevent them being assassinated, except as a result of a
> judicial sentence; that you are going to implement the division of the
> prisoners into three categories, in the first those who are considered to
> be dangerous enemies and whom you intend to transfer to other pris-
> ons, such as Alcalá, Chinchilla and Valencia; in the second the doubtful
> ones, those who have been judged by the courts; and in the third, the
> remainder who should be released immediately.[86]

Melchor Rodríguez still had people hidden in the Palacio de Viana, where he had established his headquarters. This fact, plus Melchor's decisive action in the prisons, was provoking tension with the Defence Committee of the CNT, which was heavily implicated in the murders of the prisoners. One of the more hostile anarchist leaders was Amor Nuño, who had made the deal with the Public Order Council for the evacuation and elimination of prisoners. García Oliver and Carnero appeared unex-pectedly in Madrid on 13 November. In a discordant meeting, García

Oliver informed Melchor that he had received reports from the Defence Committee and others about his activities. He made it clear that he did not approve of initiatives to stop the murder of prisoners. Far from being conciliatory, Melchor responded by demanding that those responsible for the killings be punished. When García Oliver told him to be reasonable, Melchor threw his appointment letter at him. Melchor's nomination had been sent to the official *Gaceta* on 12 November but was not published until after the confrontation with García Oliver. After Melchor Rodríguez's resignation, the *sacas* started again.[87] Until he was reappointed in early December, Melchor Rodríguez worked on his own in an effort to stop executions being carried out by the anarchist militias still operating out of the Checa del Cine Europa in defiance of Carrillo's decree of 9 November.[88]

Meanwhile, on 10 November, Manuel Irujo, the Basque Catholic who was Minister without Portfolio in the government of Largo Caballero, heard from his representative in Madrid, Jesus de Galíndez, about both the murders of the previous days and Melchor Rodríguez's initiatives. From Barcelona, where he had gone to see President Azaña, Irujo sent a teletype to General Miaja's office:

> I have received news of lamentable events in the prisons as a result of which a large number of prisoners have been shot, having been taken by militiamen using transfer orders emanating from the Dirección General de Seguridad, and I would like to know the number of victims, the prisons from which they were taken, the names of those who authorized these seizures, and the measures that have been taken by the Junta in response to these events. I need this information to inform the Head of State.

Miaja's ADC replied that he had no knowledge of these events. The following day, 11 November, Irujo and José Giral, who was also a Minister without Portfolio, demanded explanations from the Minister of the Interior, Ángel Galarza. His vague response showed that he knew that prisoners were being removed from the prisons, although he attributed the deaths to the fury of the families of victims of bombing raids.[89]

After speaking to Irujo about the situation, Azaña jotted down in his notebook: 'cabinet tit-bits from Irujo: García Oliver's hard-line stance that the war must be harsh. Shooting of 80 officers after inviting them to serve the Republic. "I'm not sorry for what has been done," exclaims García Oliver according to Irujo … That an Inspector of Prisons from the FAI had prevented the handing over of more prisoners.'[90] This was a reference to Melchor Rodríguez.

In the light of the fact that Azaña, Irujo, Giral and Galarza knew about the *sacas*, a speech made on 12 November by Santiago Carrillo assumes greater significance. Speaking from the microphones of Unión Radio, he made an admission regarding the measures being taken against the prisoners:

> it is guaranteed that there will be no resistance to the Junta de Defensa from within. No such resistance will emerge because absolutely every possible measure has been taken to prevent any conflict or alteration of order in Madrid that could favour the enemy's plans. The 'Fifth Column' is on the way to being crushed. Its last remnants in the depths of Madrid are being hunted down and cornered according to the law, but above all with the energy necessary to ensure that this 'Fifth Column' cannot interfere with the plans of the legitimate government and the Junta de Defensa.[91]

Two days after Carrillo's broadcast, the Junta de Defensa issued a statement under the title 'To counteract a vile campaign':

> News has reached the Junta de Defensa de Madrid that enemy radio has broadcast information taken from foreign newspapers regarding the mistreatment of rebel prisoners. In the light of the attempt to start a campaign, the Councillors find themselves obliged to declare before Spain and the foreign nations that what has been said about this matter is totally untrue. The prisoners are not the victims of mistreatment nor need they fear for their lives. They will all be judged within the law appertaining in each case. The Junta de Defensa does not need to take any further measures and will not only prevent anyone else doing so, but also ensure that those who intervene or have intervened in these cases will do so within the established order and norms.[92]

After the *sacas* began again on 18 November, Schlayer, Núñez Morgado and Henry Helfant (the Romanian commercial attaché) pressed the government to reappoint Melchor, as did Luis Zubillaga of the Bar Association and Mariano Gómez. Finally, on 25 November, García Oliver telephoned Melchor and asked him to come to Valencia. En route three days later, his car was ambushed by a group from the FAI. Nevertheless, he reached his appointment with García Oliver, who offered to make him Delegate for Prisons for Madrid and Alcalá de Henares. Melchor's two conditions for accepting were that men on whom he could rely be made directors of prisons and that those guilty of atrocities be punished. Some days later, Melchor had an interview with the Minister of the Interior, Ángel Galarza, who agreed to support his nomination which was made public on 1 December. On his return to Madrid, Melchor again put a stop to the *sacas*, forced the militia groups out of the prisons and replaced them with Assault Guards. In some cases, he arrested men accused of murder, extortion and blackmail. He was fortunate in being able to count on the full support of the under-secretary at the Ministry of Justice, Mariano Sánchez Roca.[93]

On 1 December 1936, the Junta de Defensa was renamed the Junta Delegada de Defensa de Madrid by order of Largo Caballero. Having led the government to Valencia, the Prime Minister was deeply resentful of the aureole of heroism that had accumulated around Miaja as he led the capital's population in resisting Franco's siege. Thus Largo Caballero wished to restrain what he considered the Junta's excessive independence. In the rearranged body, Amor Nuño moved to the post of Councillor for Transport.[94] Serrano Poncela had already left the Public Order Delegation at some point in early December. He was still there when, on 4 December, he supervised an assault on the Finnish Legation to flush out fifth columnists. Shortly thereafter, his responsibilities were taken over by José Cazorla.

At the end of the war, Serrano Poncela gave Jesús de Galíndez an implausible account of why he had left the Public Order Delegation. He claimed that he had had no idea that the phrases 'transfer to Chinchilla' or 'place in liberty' on the orders that he signed were code meaning execution. The use of such code could have been the way in which those responsible covered their guilt, as agreed at the meeting on the evening of 7 November. Serrano Poncela told Galíndez that the orders were passed to him by Santiago Carrillo and that all he did was sign them. If this were true it would not mean that he was ignorant of what was happening, given his presence in the Cárcel Modelo to supervise the *saca* of 7–8 November. He told Galíndez that, as soon he realized what was happening, he resigned from his post and not long afterwards left the Communist Party.[95] This was not entirely true since he held the important post of JSU propaganda secretary until well into 1938. In an extraordinary letter to the PCE Central Committee, written in March 1939, Serrano Poncela claimed that he had resigned from the Party only once he was in France in February 1939, implying that previously he had feared for his life. He referred to the disgust he felt about his past in the Communist Party. He also claimed that the PCE prevented his emigration to Mexico because he knew too much.[96]

Subsequently, and in reprisal for Serrano Poncela's rejection of the Party, Carrillo denounced him. In an interview with Ian Gibson, Carrillo claimed that he had nothing to do with the activities of the Public Order Delegation and blamed everything on Serrano Poncela. He alleged that 'my only involvement was, after about a fortnight, I got the impression that Serrano Poncela was doing bad things and so I sacked him'. Allegedly, Carrillo had discovered in late November that 'outrages were being committed and this man was a thief'. He claimed that Serrano Poncela had in his possession jewels stolen from those arrested and that consideration had been given to having Serrano Poncela shot.[97] Serrano Poncela's continued pre-eminence in the JSU belies this.

The claim that he personally had nothing to do with the killings was repeated by Carrillo in his memoirs of 1993. He alleged that the classification and evacuation of prisoners was left entirely to the Public Order Delegation under Serrano Poncela. Carrillo went on to assert that the Delegation did not decide on death sentences but merely selected those who would be sent to Tribunales Populares and those who would be freed. His account is brief, vague and misleading, making no mention of executions and implying that the worst that happened to those judged to be dangerous was to be sent to work battalions building fortifications. The only unequivocal statement in Carrillo's account is a declaration that he took part in none of the Public Order Delegation's meetings.[98] However, if Manuel Irujo and José Giral in Valencia knew about the killings and if, in Madrid, Melchor Rodríguez, the Chargé d'Affaires of Argentina, the Chargé d'Affaires of the United Kingdom and Felix Schlayer knew about them, it is inconceivable that Carrillo, as the principal authority in the area of public order, could not know. After all, despite these later claims, he received daily reports from Serrano Poncela.[99]

Cazorla's assumption of the role of Director General of Security for Madrid raises the question of what he had been doing since 6 November 1936 when he was first named Carrillo's deputy in the Council for Public Order. In the Causa General file on Cazorla, it is claimed that he had played both an operational and a supervisory role in the *sacas* from the various prisons. It is alleged that, along with Arturo García de la Rosa, he ran a *checa* in the Calle Zurbano. It is further claimed that he sent instructions to the Public Order Delegation's representatives in each police station ordering the execution of suspect prisoners. Under inter-rogation, Cazorla admitted that he was fully aware of the *sacas* and the subsequent killings, 'with fictitious orders for transfers or release being signed by Serrano Poncela or Bruno Carreras whose job it was'. As Serrano Poncela's deputy, Carreras had chosen as his own assistant the anarchist Benigno Mancebo, who had previously run the Checa de Fomento.[100]

One of the first things that Cazorla did as Director General of Security was to replace Carreras as Inspector General of the Madrid Police. His own nominee was David Vázquez Baldominos, who up to that moment had been running the Brigada Especial with Grigulevich. The substitu-tion of Serrano Poncela by Cazorla coincided with the reappointment of Melchor Rodríguez as Delegate for Prisons and the ending of the *sacas*. Cazorla told his interrogators that, when he took over, the Dirección General de Seguridad was in chaos and the various militia groups involved in policing were more likely to obey their party than the Junta de Defensa. Accordingly, Cazorla started to implement fully the meas-ures taken by Carrillo against the *checas*. The investigation and punish-ment of suspected fifth columnists was tightened up. The large-scale *sacas* stopped and the repression became much more narrowly targeted. Melchor Rodríguez told his interrogators that the previous *sacas* had been ordered by the Dirección General de Seguridad – which would point to Serrano Poncela. Another detainee interrogated by the Causa General, Eloy de la Figuera González, reported that he had heard the anarchist Manuel Rascón who ran the investigation sub-section of the Dirección General de Seguridad ranting furiously about the obstacles placed by Melchor Rodríguez in the way of the *sacas*.[101]

The more precise targeting of fifth columnists was apparent in Galíndez's description of the functioning of the Tribunales Populares. They were presided over by a judge and the jury consisted of two members of each of the Popular Front parties. The accused were given a public defender and allowed to call witnesses on their own behalf. These people's courts were principally for trying those accused not simply of being right-wingers but of active hostility to the Republic (*desafección al regimen*). The maximum sentence was five years in prison. Membership of the Falange got three years; members of Acción Popular were usually fined unless guilty of spreading defeatism or of black marketeering. Those involved in hard-core fifth-column activities like espionage or sabotage would be tried by the Tribunal for Treachery and Espionage or by military courts.[102] On 22 December, the government created work camps for those found guilty of sedition, rebellion and disloyalty.[103] This last was a category that would be used substantially by Cazorla.

Serrano Poncela's last public intervention as Director General of Security was the incident at the Finnish Legation on 4 December, which was provoked by an abuse of the right of asylum. Finland's Ambassador, George Arvid Winckelman, was accredited to both Lisbon and Madrid and understandably preferred to stay in Portugal. In his absence, a Spanish employee of the Embassy, Francisco Cachero, had appointed himself Chargé d'Affaires. He had rented several houses and, for a price, gave refuge to large numbers of fifth columnists. At the 14 November meeting of the Junta de Defensa, it was claimed that these premises housed 2,500 fascists armed with pistols and machine-guns. On 19 November, the Junta ordered the Finnish premises to be put under surveillance.

At the beginning of December, under cover of a rebel bombing raid, home-made bombs were thrown from one of these houses into a nearby militia barracks and snipers fired on militiamen. On 3 December, the Dirección General de Seguridad informed all the foreign embassies that measures would be taken to prevent a repetition. Using the illegal status of the improvised asylum as justification, a police raid on the houses (not on the Finnish Embassy itself) was mounted the next day by José Cazorla and Serrano Poncela using the Brigada Especial commanded by David Vázquez Baldominos. The Republican security forces were met with gunfire. When they finally gained entry, they found maps with targets, an arsenal of guns and hand grenades. It was reported that numerous armed rebel supporters had been found, of whom 387 men and women were arrested.[104] According to official Soviet sources, Grigulevich was involved in organizing this raid, which confirms his links with the Brigada Especial.[105]

Schlayer and Henry Helfant, the commercial attaché of the Romanian Embassy, appealed to Melchor Rodríguez to prevent the execution of prisoners taken in the Finnish raid. Melchor and Helfant went to see Serrano Poncela. After a tense encounter, Serrano agreed that the prisoners should be placed under Melchor's charge.[106] With Madrid's prisons bursting at the seams, Melchor set out on 8 December to see if the prison at Alcalá de Henares had accommodation for them.

On 6 December, the prison at Guadalajara had been attacked by a mob that had killed 282 prisoners.[107] That mob had included nearly one hundred militiamen under the orders of Valentín González, 'El Campesino'. Two days later, in Alcalá de Henares, a furious crowd including some of the same militiamen gathered to seek revenge for those killed and maimed in a bombing raid. Their target was the prisoners held there, many of them as a result of the evacuation from the Cárcel Modelo. Among the more famous prisoners were the Falangist leader, Raimundo Fernández Cuesta, the founder of the Assault Guards, Colonel Agustín Muñoz Grandes, the secretary of the CEDA, Javier Martín Artajo, and the radio personality Bobby Deglané. The recently arrived Melchor Rodríguez, showing greater courage than the prison functionaries who had fled, confronted the mob. Braving threats, insults and accusations of being a fascist, he argued that the prisoners were not responsible for the air raid and that the murder of defenceless men would bring shame on the Republic. His voice raw from making himself heard above the tumult, he said that they would have to kill him to get to the galleries. He also gave them pause by threatening to arm the prisoners. Campesino's militiamen were led away by Major Coca, their commander, and the rest of the crowd drifted after them. Fearing that Coca planned to come back, Melchor went to his headquarters and, in a bitter confrontation with the Major, persuaded him to guarantee the safety of the prisoners. Melchor thereby saved over 1,500 lives.[108]

However, on his return to Madrid on the night of 8 December, Melchor was called before the CNT–FAI Defence Committee and severely criticized by its secretary, Eduardo Val. Melchor managed to calm his critics, but they were suspicious of his claim that he could stop the bombing of Madrid by negotiating with the rebels and offering to prevent any more assassinations of prisoners.[109] Nevertheless, from 12 December, the situation was changing yet again. The Junta de Defensa had decreed that the militarization of all the militias and all their functions were under the control of the new Director General of Security, José Cazorla. In agreement with Cazorla, arrangements were made for young prisoners either to be forcibly conscripted into the Republican Army or, if they chose, to join work battalions building fortifications. It was later alleged that some of those 'released' or 'transferred' were taken to *checas* under the control of Cazorla. Certainly, Cazorla and Melchor Rodríguez did arrange for the release of those against whom there were no charges and of female prisoners over the age of sixty. Melchor Rodríguez also took measures to improve the food in prisons and created an information office where families could find out where prisoners were being held and their state of health. With the help of the Red Cross, he created a hospital service which ended up being used as a centre for fifth columnists. He also organized a party in the Romanian Embassy for recently released detainees.[110] Despite suspicions of his links with the fifth column, Melchor Rodríguez's success in stopping *sacas* raises questions about Santiago Carrillo's inability to do the same.

Subsequently, Francoist propaganda built on the atrocity of Paracuellos to depict the Republic as a murderous Communist-dominated regime guilty of red barbarism. Francoists have even claimed that the number murdered was 12,000.[111] Despite the fact that Santiago Carrillo was only one of the key participants in the entire process, the Franco regime, and the Spanish right thereafter, never missed any opportunity to use Paracuellos to denigrate him during the years that he was secretary general of the Communist Party (1960–82) and especially in 1977 as part of the effort to prevent the legalization of the Communist Party. Carrillo has himself inadvertently contributed to keeping himself in the spotlight by absurdly denying any knowledge of, let alone responsibility for, the killings. However, a weight of other evidence confirmed by some of his own partial revelations makes it clear that he was fully involved.[112]

For instance, in more than one interview in 1977 Carrillo claimed that, by the time he took over the Council for Public Order in the Junta de Defensa, the operation of transferring prisoners from Madrid to Valencia was 'coming to an end and all I did, with General Miaja, was order the transfer of the last prisoners'. It is certainly true that there had been *sacas* before 7 November, but the bulk of the killings took place after that date while Carrillo was Councillor for Public Order. His admission that he ordered the transfers of prisoners after 7 November clearly puts him in the frame.[113] Elsewhere, he claimed that, after an evacuation had been decided on, the vehicles were ambushed and the prisoners murdered by uncontrolled elements. He has frequently insinuated that the killers were anarchists and has stated, 'I can take no responsibility other than having been unable to prevent it.'[114] This would have been hardly credible under any circumstances, but especially so after the discovery that there had been a CNT–JSU meeting on the night of 7 November.

Moreover, Carrillo's post-1974 denials of knowledge of the Paracuellos killings were contradicted by the congratulations heaped on him at the time. Between 6 and 8 March 1937 the PCE celebrated an amplified plenary meeting of its Central Committee in Valencia. Francisco Antón said: 'It is difficult to say that the fifth column in Madrid has been annihilated but it certainly has suffered the hardest blows there. This, it must be proclaimed loudly, is thanks to the concern of the Party and the selfless, ceaseless effort of two new comrades, as beloved as if they were veteran militants of our Party, Comrade Carrillo when he was the Councillor for Public Order and Comrade Cazorla who holds the post now.' When the applause died down, Carrillo rose and praised 'the glory of those warriors of the JSU who can fight in the certain knowledge that the rearguard is safe, cleansed and free of traitors. It is no crime nor is it a manoeuvre [against the CNT] but a duty to demand such a purge.'[115]

Comments made at the time and later by Spanish Communists such as Pasionaria and Francisco Antón, by Comintern agents, by Gorev and by others show that prisoners were assumed to be fifth columnists and that Carrillo was to be praised for eliminating them. On 30 July 1937, in a report to the head of the Comintern Giorgi Dimitrov, the Bulgarian Stoyan Minev, alias 'Boris Stepanov', from April 1937 the Comintern's delegate in Spain, wrote indignantly of the 'Jesuit and fascist' Irujo that he had tried to arrest Carrillo because he had given 'the order to shoot several arrested officers of the fascists'.[116] In his final post-war report to Stalin, Stepanov referred to Mola's statement about his five columns. Stepanov went on to write proudly that the Communists took note of the implications thereof and 'in a couple of days carried out the operations necessary to cleansing Madrid of fifth columnists'. Stepanov explained in more detail his outrage against Irujo. In July 1937, shortly after becoming Minister of Justice, Manuel Irujo initiated investigations into what happened at Paracuellos, including a judicial inquiry into the role of Carrillo.[117] Unfortunately, no trace of this inquiry has survived and it is a reasonable assumption that any evidence was among the papers burned by the Communist-dominated security services before the end of the war.[118]

What Carrillo himself said in his broadcast on Unión Radio and what Stepanov wrote in his report to Stalin were echoed years later in the Spanish Communist Party's official history of its role in the Civil War. Published in Moscow when Carrillo was secretary general of the PCE, it declared proudly that 'Santiago Carrillo and his deputy Cazorla took the measures necessary to maintain order in the rearguard, which was every bit as important as the fighting at the front. In two or three days, a serious blow was delivered against the snipers and fifth columnists.'[119]

What has gone before, like everything written about Paracuellos, is inevitably distorted because of the imbalance of material about the three phases of authorization, organization and implementation. It is possible to know that meetings took place at which evacuation and elimination were almost certainly discussed and authorization almost certainly given. These are the meetings on 6 November of José Miaja with Pedro Checa and Antonio Mije, of Mikhail Koltsov with Checa, and of Mije with Vladimir Gorev and Vicente Rojo. However, there is little or nothing by way of records of those conversations. In contrast, there is a vast quantity of material in the Causa General on the administrative organization of the *sacas* and on what happened at the prisons when militiamen arrived to load the prisoners on to the buses. Nevertheless, there is little material on the actual murders, on the specific parts played in the killing by the anarchists, by the Fifth Regiment or by the Brigada Especial created with the help of Orlov and Grigulevich. Accordingly, there will always be an element of deduction if not speculation about the collective responsibility.

Astonishingly, despite all the other problems of defending the besieged and starving city, the Junta managed to make a priority of controlling the *checas* and centrally co-ordinating the forces of order and security in Madrid. Its efforts in terms of rebuilding the state apparatus went far beyond the ineffective measures of General Pozas and the slightly more energetic efforts to control the *checas* made by Ángel Galarza in October. Nevertheless, the greatest death toll of rebel supporters in the city would take place on the Junta's watch between 7 November and 4 December. Thereafter, there would be little of the indiscriminate violence that marked the early months of the war as the reorganized security forces targeted more specifically those perceived to be undermining the war effort, and the numbers executed plummeted.

PART FIVE

Two Concepts of War

11

Defending the Republic from the Enemy Within

By the end of 1936, the spontaneous mass violence of the early months was no more, although in early February 1937 President Azaña could still note the disgust felt by the Minister of Finance, Juan Negrín, about the atrocities. He suggested that they made Negrín ashamed to be Spanish.[1] Negrín's commitment to ending the uncontrolled violence is corroborated by his friend Mariano Ansó, who recounted that, in Valencia on one occasion, he accosted armed militiamen who had detained a man and were clearly planning to shoot him as a fascist. At enormous risk, and by sheer force of personality, he obliged them to release the man.[2]

From January 1937, repressive violence behind the Republican lines was not uncontrolled and hate-fuelled as it had been in the first weeks of the war. Henceforth, it was largely a question of the Republican state rebuilding itself and, of course, defending itself. Accordingly, it took two principal forms which occasionally overlapped. On the one hand, the security services focused their efforts on the enemy within, the saboteurs, snipers and spies of the fifth column. On the other, there were bitter rivalries over the nature of the war effort. The Communists, many of the Socialists and the Republicans perceived as subversives those on the libertarian and anti-Stalinist left who resisted the creation of a strong state capable of pursuing a centralized war effort. A substantial segment of the anarchist left was concerned with revolutionary goals and was actively hostile to the Republican state. A significant minority was simply involved in criminal activities. Clashes with the security forces were inevitable. This already fraught scenario was further complicated by the fact that, in the case of the Spanish and foreign anti-Stalinists, the Russian security advisers regarded them as Trotskyists who had to be eliminated.

Ever since the Republican government in Valencia, the Madrid Junta and the Catalan Generalitat had all made a determined effort to central-ize the police and security services and disarm the various rearguard militia groups, they had been on a collision course with the anarchists. Anarchist militiamen had violently resisted efforts to collect their weapons or to shut down their control posts on the roads in and out of the capital and on the Catalan–French border. There had been numerous incidents, including one in November 1936 when Antonio Mije, the War Councillor in the Junta, had been prevented from leaving the city on an official mission.[3] There was a long-standing and fierce hostility between the PCE and the CNT. This was fuelled by the assassination by anarchists of prominent Communist union leaders such as Andrés Rodríguez González in Málaga in June and Desiderio Trillas Mainé in Barcelona on 31 July. Similarly, the foiled assassination attempts in Madrid by anarchists from the Checa del Cine Europa on both Vittorio Vidali and Enrique Líster in September had merely intensified the Communist determination to exact revenge.[4]

At the beginning of December 1936, when Serrano Poncela left the Dirección General de Seguridad, his executive responsibilities were taken over by José Cazorla, Carrillo's deputy. Cazorla appointed David Vázquez Baldominos as his police chief. One of his tasks was to expand the Brigada Especial created by Carrillo and Grigulevich. Two more of these special squads were set up, led by two JSU militants, Santiago Álvarez Santiago and José Conesa Arteaga. From the beginning of 1937, all three brigades, under the operational command of Fernando Valentí Fernández, would concentrate on the detention, interrogation and, sometimes, elimination of suspicious elements. This meant not only Francoists but also members of the Madrid CNT, which Cazorla believed to be out of control and infiltrated by the fifth column.[5]

Cazorla was not the only one to believe that the anarchist movement was infested with fifth columnists. Largo Caballero told PSOE executive committee member Juan-Simeón Vidarte that 'the FAI has been infiltrated by so many agents provocateurs and police informers that it is impossible to have dealings with them'.[6] Neither was entirely wrong. The ease with which membership cards of the CNT could be acquired gave the fifth column access to information, an instrument for acts of provocation and relative ease of movement. With CNT accreditation, fifth columnists could also get identity cards for the Republican security services.[7]

A bitter example of the consequent conflict between Communists and anarchists took place in Murcia. Luis Cabo Giorla, the Communist Civil Governor of the province from mid-October 1936 until early January 1937, was fierce in his pursuit of fifth columnists, some of whom had

had CNT credentials since before the outbreak of war. After their defeat in Valencia, elements of the anarchist Iron Column had moved into Murcia and been guilty of pillage and violence against peasants who resisted them. In December, Cabo Giorla appointed Ramón Torrecilla Guijarro, who had played a key role in Paracuellos, as Delegate of the Dirección General de Seguridad in the province. After Cabo Giorla had been replaced by Antonio Pretel, Torrecilla operated ruthlessly on the blanket assumption that anyone not a member of the Communist Party was likely to be a fifth columnist. Detainees were subjected to torture, beatings and simulated executions. Eventually, in April 1937, a CNT campaign backed by the PSOE led to an official investigation, the arrest of Torrecilla and his collaborators and the resignation of Pretel. Torrecilla spent six months in prison and, after his release, joined the security staff of Cazorla, who had become Civil Governor of Albacete. There his obsessive determination to purge the rearguard led to further complaints from non-Communist elements of the Popular Front.[8]

Communist suspicions of the CNT were confirmed by the announcement, by a self-evidently fit Amor Nuño, at the 23 December 1936 session of the Junta Delegada de Defensa, that he was resigning for health reasons. It emerged that, some days before, a meeting of senior militants from the CNT, FAI and the Federación de Juventudes Libertarias had considered expelling him from the anarchist movement and even having him shot. According to Gregorio Gallego, Cipriano Mera, the CNT's front-line military commander, had grabbed Nuño by the neck, shaken him and hurled him against the wall, saying that he deserved to be executed. Nuño's offence derived from his sexual involvement with the daughter of a rebel officer. He had appointed her his secretary and taken her to important meetings where she had been able to listen to secret discussions. Nuño's comrades suspected that she was a rebel spy and that she had him brainwashed. They spared his life but, regarding him as unreliable, made him resign from the Junta de Defensa. He took a lesser post on the secretariat of the CNT's transport union and moved to Barcelona, where he would be arrested for his involvement in the May 1937 conflict. At the end of the war, Nuño would be captured in Alicante and beaten to death by policemen in Madrid.[9]

Amor Nuño was not the only Councillor of the Madrid Junta to resign on 23 December 1936. He was accompanied by Santiago Carrillo, who was replaced on Christmas Day by his former deputy José Cazorla Maure. Carrillo announced that he was leaving to devote himself totally to preparing the forthcoming congress to seal the unification of the

Socialist and Communist youth movements. That may indeed have been his motive, but his replacement was also connected with an incident two days earlier.[10]

At 3 p.m. in the afternoon of 23 December, the Councillor for Supply in the Junta, Pablo Yagüe Esteverá, had been stopped at an anarchist control point when he was leaving the city on official business. Since Carrillo's decree of 9 November, control of roads in and out of the capital had been supervised by the police, the Assault Guards and the rearguard militias (MVR) under the overall co-ordination of the Public Order Council. The anarchists who stopped Yagüe thus had no authority to do so. After they had refused to recognize his credentials as a Councillor of the Junta, Yagüe continued past the roadblock and they shot and seriously wounded him. They then took refuge in the Ateneo Libertario of the Ventas district. Carrillo ordered their arrest, but the police who went to the Ateneo were told that they were under the protection of the CNT's regional committee. Carrillo then sent in a company of Assault Guards to seize them. When this was discussed at the meeting of the Junta later that night, he called for them to be shot.[11]

The report in the Communist press denounced the perpetrators as *incontrolables* in the service of fascism, 'real enemies of the people and of the revolution who, like cruel and heartless highwaymen, murder in cold blood the best defenders of the people'. The PCE called for exemplary punishment and, to avoid a repetition of the crime, for the militia groups outside Madrid to be disarmed. It was claimed that 'certain organizations' were heavily infiltrated by the fifth column, a clear reference to the CNT. The accusation was in fact entirely justified.[12]

The initial response of the anarcho-syndicalist leadership was emollient. It was stated that left-wing unity would be endangered by the accusation that those who shot Yagüe were fifth columnists. Then, on 25 December, three CNTistas were found dead with their union cards stuffed into their mouths. Those murders were avenged by Eduardo Val's Defence Committee, which left three Communists dead with their party cards in their mouths. In reply, two more CNTistas were killed and the PCE press stepped up its campaign for a purge of the CNT. Outraged, the CNT published a list of militants killed by Communists in Málaga, Cabeza de Buey in La Serena (eastern Badajoz), Las Herencias (Ciudad Real), Miguel Esteban and La Guardia (Toledo) and Perales de Tajuña and other towns in Madrid.[13]

Carrillo failed in his demand for the Junta to condemn to death the militiamen responsible for the attack on Yagüe, something which was outside its jurisdiction. He was furious when the case was put in the hands of a state tribunal at which the prosecutor refused to ask for the death penalty when it was claimed that Yagüe had not shown his credentials at the CNT control point. With the Communist press baying for the militiamen's blood, José García Pradas, the editor of the newspaper *CNT*, published a demand that they be released and threatened that, if this did not happen, CNT forces would be withdrawn from the front to release them by force. It was the sort of incendiary comment that convinced many others that the anarchists were irresponsible, if not downright subversive. *CNT* was the mouthpiece of the Defence Committee, run by Eduardo Val, Manuel Salgado Moreira and García Pradas, all three violently anti-Communist. Miaja ordered the suspension of *CNT*, but García Pradas refused to obey. He printed, and was about to distribute, the next issue when Miaja had the paper's offices surrounded by Assault Guards and declared that it was absurd, after the sacrifices made to defend Madrid, for a squabble between anarchists and Communists to provoke its fall. Only Miaja's intervention prevented serious bloodshed. In the event, to the chagrin of the PCE, the tribunal decided that the men who had shot Yagüe had acted in good faith. The immediate reaction of both organizations was an agreement not to let this hostility undermine anti-fascist unity. It was short lived.[14] This war of organizations was symptomatic both of the continuing weakness of the state and of the CNT's exiguous loyalty to the Republic.

Carrillo's successor, José Cazorla, was determined to put an end to parallel police forces. He found it intolerable that many files on rightwingers seized by militia groups in July 1936 had not been handed over to the Dirección General de Seguridad. In consequence, the Tribunales Populares had released many fifth columnists because there was no record of their political affiliations. Cazorla started the job of centralizing files and organizations when he took over the DGS in the capital from Serrano Poncela in December. He saw this as the first step towards his principal goal which was the investigation and punishment of prorebel sabotage and subversion. His zeal in this led to a bitter conflict with the anarchists and anti-Stalinist dissident Communists. The Communists believed that opposition to a tightly centralized war effort constituted sabotage and subversion. Moreover, they had little doubt that some of the rearguard violence was the work of agents provocateurs embedded within the CNT working to discredit the Republic internationally and to spread demoralization.

Another factor poisoning relations between the CNT and the Communists was suspicion of Melchor Rodríguez, who was arranging for more than one hundred prisoners to be released each day. Suspicions that he might have links with the fifth column were intensified when several of those whose release he arranged went over to the rebels, including Colonel Agustín Muñoz Grandes and the Falangist radio personality Bobby Deglané. In a meeting of the Madrid Junta on 8 January 1937, Cazorla complained that Melchor Rodríguez gave prisoners permission to hold pro-rebel demonstrations and have private meetings with members of the diplomatic corps. He called him 'protector of the prisoners' because he treated right-wing detainees as if they were exactly the same as the CNT prisoners of old. On 19 February, Cazorla accused Melchor of opposing his public order policy. He further infuriated the CNT leadership when, in his campaign against sabotage and espionage, he began to investigate the infiltration by fifth columnists of the ineffective secret services run in the Ministry of War by the CNT's Manuel Salgado.[15]

As a result of these investigations, the Brigada Especial led by Santiago Álvarez Santiago arrested over thirty anarchists and Socialists in mid-February. The CNT press protested that anarchist militants deemed to be enemies of the state were being interned as part of a dirty war being carried out by Cazorla's Public Order Council.[16] After shots were fired at a Communist policeman on 23 February, Cazorla reiterated his view that the CNT sheltered fifth columnists and his agents started to rearrest prisoners released by the courts even as they left the building.[17]

Complaints emanated both from diplomats on behalf of rightists and from the CNT on behalf of its militants that those arrested were being sent to punishment battalions in dangerous front-line positions to work on fortifications.[18] Ironically, forced-labour camps were the brainchild of the Minister of Justice, the CNT's Juan García Oliver. Two days after he had taken over his Ministry in November 1936, he had called for the creation of camps where fascists could be used in constructive labour. On 31 December, accompanied by Mariano Gómez, the president of the Supreme Court, he explained in Valencia his idealistic vision of justice. Common criminals, whom he saw not as the enemies of society but as its victims, would find redemption in prison through libraries, sport and theatre. Political prisoners would achieve rehabilitation by building fortifications and strategic roads, bridges and railways, and would get decent wages. García Oliver believed that it made more sense for fascist lives to be saved than for them to be sentenced to death. He established the first camp in Totana, in the province of Murcia. Above its entrance was a huge placard with the words 'Work and Don't Lose Hope'.[19]

On 28 February 1937, the preventive detention of released prisoners saw a major clash between Melchor Rodríguez and Cazorla. Melchor was asked by the under-secretary of Justice, Mariano Sánchez Roca, to help find his nephew, Ricardo Pintado-Fe. Melchor located the young man in a Communist *checa* where he had been held for more than two months and wrote to Cazorla to get him released. Cazorla secured his freedom, but Melchor Rodríguez gave damaging publicity to the detention rather than the release.[20] In fact, Melchor Rodríguez was sacked by García Oliver on 1 March because of growing suspicions about the warmth of his relations with the many detained rightists that he had helped. He was replaced by Julián Fernández, the secretary of the CNT Federation of Madrid Unions. Fernández continued Melchor Rodríguez's policy of preventing the abuse of prisoners, although unlike his predecessor he did not establish controversial links with them.[21]

On 12 March, the second-in-command of the Transport Council of the Madrid Junta, a CNT militant, was murdered and three of his comrades wounded.[22] Four days later in the small town of Villanueva de Alcardete (Toledo), Communist militiamen led by the Mayor assaulted the local CNT headquarters and killed nine men. In an astonishing turn of events, the PCE agreed to a judicial investigation. The Mayors of Villanueva and nearby Villamayor were found guilty of murders, rapes and looting committed since the summer of 1936. The Tribunal Popular of Cuenca condemned the ringleaders to death and imprisoned eight others. Throughout the spring of 1937, there were clashes in several other villages of Ciudad Real, Cuenca and Toledo. Six anarchists were killed in Torres de la Alameda near Madrid. However, the picture presented by anarchist literature of innocent victims of Communist aggression is only part of the story. There was a genuine ideological struggle between anarchists committed to collectivization and the Communist policy of supporting the smallholders in order to improve agricultural production. Some of the clashes derived from local resistance against anarchists from Madrid who requisitioned food without payment.[23]

In mid-March, there were clashes in Vinalesa, north of Valencia, between ostensible left-wingers and Assault Guards. The Ministry of the Interior denounced the infiltration of left-wing organizations by agents provocateurs and instructed all parties and unions to investigate those who had joined their ranks since 16 July 1936 and to surrender all weapons. The Communist press also demanded strong measures against 'those out of control' and those who protected them, calling for the annihilation of the agents provocateurs, who were described as 'new dynamiters', a term deliberately meant to provoke echoes of anarchist terrorists of earlier times.[24]

The enmity reached such heights in mid-April that it provoked the dissolution of the Junta de Defensa. On 14 April, Cazorla announced in *Mundo Obrero* that an important spy-ring in the Republican Army had been dismantled. He revealed that one of those arrested was Alfonso López de Letona, a fifth columnist who had reached a high rank in the General Staff of the 14th Division of the Popular Army, commanded by the anarchist Cipriano Mera. López de Letona was a member of the extreme monarchist party Renovación Española, and had been private secretary of Antonio Goicoechea, its leader. He had been arrested by Salgado's men and persuaded, either by threats or by financial inducements, to act as a double agent. However, Cazorla claimed that López de Letona had become a member of Manuel Salgado's secret services in the Ministry of War on the basis of a recommendation by Mera's chief of staff, Antonio Verardini Díez de Ferreti.[25]

There was no doubt of a connection between López de Letona and Verardini since they had collaborated in an operation mounted by the CNT to flush out fifth columnists. The December 1936 raid on the buildings under the protection of the Finnish Embassy had exposed how the right of asylum was being abused in favour of the fifth column. Accordingly, Eduardo Val and the CNT's Defence Committee had established a fictitious Embassy of Siam, a country that had no diplomatic relations with Spain. With López de Letona as a 'guarantee' to his fifth-columnist contacts, the Embassy made offers of asylum that were eagerly accepted by several enemies of the Republic. Hidden listening devices picked up their conversations and thus gathered intelligence about their networks. When General Miaja learned that some of these rebel supporters had been murdered by Val's men, in early January 1937, he ordered the operation closed down on the grounds that it was illegal and that the struggle against the fifth column should be conducted according to the law.[26] In November 1939, López de Letona would be sentenced to death by the Francoists for his part in the Siam Embassy operation.[27]

Verardini was arrested in early April as a result of an operation by the Brigada Especial led by Fernando Valentí to hunt down a Falangist network founded by Félix Ciriza Zarrandicoechea. Ciriza's principal collaborators were Falangists like himself, who had been tried by

Tribunales Populares but released for lack of proof of their guilt – a stark contrast with the 'judicial' situation of Republicans arrested in the rebel zone. Ciriza's group was large and its activities included demoralization of the population, provocation of discord between left-wing parties and, above all, espionage.[28] When Valentí's men went to arrest a member of the spy-ring, called Manuela Pazos Queija, they found her in bed with Verardini, who was a notorious womanizer. Important documents belonging to secret services of the Ministry of War were discovered in her apartment, presumably brought there by Verardini, who was arrested. Cipriano Mera responded by threatening Miaja that he would bring a truckload of militiamen armed with machine-pistols and hand grenades from the front to break Verardini out of jail. Miaja prevailed on an irate Cazorla to release Verardini. In the evening edition of *CNT* on the same day, García Pradas accused Cazorla of being a fascist agent provocateur.[29]

At Cazorla's behest, *CNT* was banned for two days, failing to appear on 15 and 16 April 1937. On 15 April, what would be the last-ever meeting of the Junta de Defensa was entirely concerned with this bitter conflict. It began at 7.30 p.m. and went on until 2.15 the following morning. With the abstention of the outraged anarchist councillors, the Junta gave Cazorla a vote of confidence. However, a committee of the Republican and Socialist members was nominated to investigate anarchist accusations of irregularities committed by the police and in the prisons.[30]

When *CNT* reappeared on 17 April, the front-page headline called for the immediate dismissal of José Cazorla and demanded that he be investigated by the Ministers of Justice and the Interior. Inside, there was a long article claiming that a majority of the Junta believed Cazorla's note of 14 April about López de Letona and Verardini to be 'unfounded'. With shameless hypocrisy, given the CNT's own record in terms of extra-judicial murders, tortures and *checas*, the article denounced Cazorla's record as Public Order Councillor: 'For some time, murderous activities occurring in Madrid have been denounced in the CNT press. The victims of these actions were sometimes genuinely revolutionary workers, true anti-fascists, and at other times indubitably right-wing elements, against whom implacable action should be taken but always inside the law.' The article ended by claiming that the commission of inquiry set up the previous day had found evidence of 'criminal acts that reveal the existence in Spain of a "chequista" political terrorism against which it is necessary to react, not only from below, but also from above, from the

Government, and especially from the Ministries of the Interior and of Justice, which under no circumstances can allow murders, beatings, arbitrary arrests, and provocations lest the unity that we all need to face the enemy should be drowned in fraternal blood'.[31]

In the same issue, there was also a coruscating article by Melchor Rodríguez denouncing Carrillo, Serrano Poncela and Cazorla. He quoted letters and documents exchanged between Cazorla and himself,

> relative to the deceptions, secret orders and codes given by this Cazorla to the agents under his command for people absolved by the Tribunales Populares apparently to be released from government prisons where they had been detained on his orders, but actually to be taken to clandestine prisons and to Communist militia units, to be used at the front building 'fortifications' ... (in his words). I declare that I am ready to appear before any authorities or committees, with documents, to expose the sinister 'policy' pursued in the Public Order Council first by Santiago Carrillo and Serrano Poncela, and more recently by José Cazorla.

At his trial in 1940, Cazorla was accused of sending right-wing prisoners to the units commanded by Líster and El Campesino ostensibly to work on fortifications when, in reality, they were being sent to be executed.

Melchor Rodríguez went on to use the case of Ricardo Pintado-Fe as an illustration of what he called 'outrages committed by the "Communist" and "Communistoid" hordes with police badges and warrant cards, under the orders of Councillor Cazorla', and of 'how in the "Communist" "*Checas*" converted into clandestine prisons, men and women are held kidnapped for days, weeks and months just on the basis of denunciations real or false, by dint of which all kinds of personal outrages are committed against all elemental laws, whether written or human'.[32]

The ensuing scandal saw confrontation in the cabinet between Communist and Socialist ministers. Largo Caballero, already irritated by Miaja's popularity, silenced the clash by simply closing down the Junta de Defensa on 23 April. He did not bother to inform Miaja, who learned of the decision in the newspapers. The Junta was replaced with a new Madrid town council.[33] Despite anarchist claims that the commission of inquiry set up on 15 April was gathering devastating evidence that Cazorla had run a network of secret prisons in which CNT militants were interrogated, often tortured and sometimes executed, its report was never completed because the dissolution of the Junta deprived it of any jurisdiction over the issues raised. On 25 April, Cazorla, on handing power over to the new national Director General of Security, Wenceslao Carrillo, said he welcomed any investigation that might be carried out. Wenceslao, father of Santiago, praised Cazorla's work in making the streets of Madrid safe. In an article published the following day, Cazorla himself wrote that he had remained silent only while awaiting the conclusions of the investigation and now felt free to comment. He attacked what he called 'the verbal terrorism of those who beg in private and attack in public' – a clear reference to Melchor Rodríguez and the Pintado-Fe case. He went on to defend his record against 'those who having recently infiltrated the CNT–FAI use a union card to hide their murky past and to enable them to work against the interests of the anti-fascist masses'.[34] Two days later, the Communist press published news that a fifth-column network had been discovered using CNT member-ship cards.[35]

An obvious conclusion to be drawn from the clashes between the Communists and the CNT is the extraordinary level of press freedom prevailing in a tense wartime situation. The denunciations in the CNT press of alleged abuses by the police and the prisons are remarkable indi-cations of the maintenance of democratic norms. Even more so were some of the decisions of the popular tribunals. Noteworthy in this regard were the acquittals of the anarchist militiamen who shot Pablo Yagüe and of rebel supporters like Agustín Muñoz Grandes or Bobby Deglané. Even more striking were the condemnations by the tribunals of both anarchists and Communists found guilty of theft or murder. There was no equivalent in the rebel zone and even less was there anything like General Miaja's closure of the Siam Embassy operation as illegal, the Madrid Junta's creation of a committee to investigate anarchist allega-tions of police irregularities or the Republican government's insistence that the struggle against the fifth column be conducted according to the law. For Cazorla, it was deeply frustrating, as he saw it, that so many were getting away with so much because security was so lax.

Random violence was largely under control by the end of 1936 and the new system of popular justice was working relatively well. The proced-ures and the ample facilities provided for the defence of those accused dramatically distinguished Republican justice from the summary trials in the rebel zone. There were increasing numbers of cases of religious personnel being absolved of accusations of disloyalty to the regime.[36] Indeed, certainly before 1938, as was shown by the frequent acquittals that Cazorla tried to reverse with preventative arrests, trials often erred in their leniency. The trial of Captain Ramón Robles Pazos, on 26

January 1937 at an emergency court, and the parallel fate of his elder brother José, accused of espionage on behalf of the fifth column, are illustrative of the workings of both the Republican judiciary and the security services and their Russian advisers.

The thirty-seven-year-old Captain Robles Pazos was a reactionary Africanista officer. At the beginning of the war, he was an instructor at the Infantry Academy housed in the Alcázar of Toledo.[37] He had been in Madrid when his insurrectionary comrades fortified themselves in the Alcázar. On 21 July 1936, on his way to join them, he was arrested in Getafe in the south of the capital and taken to a *checa* in the Paseo de las Delicias. He swore that he was loyal to the Republic, and, after a few hours, was released and ordered to present himself at the Ministry of War. Despite not reporting for military service, he remained free until 16 October when he was arrested by agents from Madrid's principal police station, the Comisaría de Buenavista. Charged with breaking his oath of loyalty to the Republic, he was imprisoned in the Cárcel Modelo. Astonishingly, he escaped the evacuation and subsequent massacre of prisoners on 7, 8 and 9 November. This suggests that someone of considerable influence was looking out for him. And it was scarcely coincidental that, from the end of August, his elder brother José was working in some capacity in the Soviet Embassy.

On 17 November, Ramón was transferred to the prison near the Ventas bullring, where he remained until, on 26 January 1937, he was tried for disloyalty. Again swearing that he was entirely loyal to the Republic, he was released provisionally on condition of appearing before the court on the 15th and 30th of each month. When he failed to do so, he was summoned to stand trial again on 27 February. He then sent an obsequious letter to the president of the court ('that you preside over with such dignity'). In it, he asked the judge to inform 'the comrades of the court' that he would be unable to appear as ordered on the entirely mendacious grounds that he had received orders to join the Republican forces on the Teruel front on 24 February. The court decided on his absolution because of this fictitious service at the front.[38]

In fact, on 28 January, two days after his first trial, Ramón had taken refuge in the Chilean Embassy. Three weeks later, he moved to the French Embassy, from where he wrote his letter of 22 February claiming to be about to fight for the Republic at Teruel. It seems that he was provoked into going into hiding at the Chilean and French embassies because his pretence of loyalty to the Republic was in danger of being exposed. In late December the previous year, his brother José had been arrested and it is likely that Ramón feared what he might, under interrogation, reveal about their contacts. José claimed that he had tried to persuade Ramón to fulfil his military duties, but the security services suspected that he was handing him information from the Soviet Embassy for the fifth column. In January 1938, Ramón managed to get evacuated to France and, after some difficulties, reached the rebel zone in mid-May. He was not subjected to the rigorous investigation applied to most officers who crossed the lines. Indeed, within five weeks, he was incorporated into the rebel forces with the rank of major, a promotion backdated to 10 December 1936, and given command of a unit of Regulares. This was on the basis of favourable reports from fifth columnists of his complete commitment to the rebel cause. He was promoted to lieutenant colonel and decorated several times. In 1942, he fought in Russia as a volunteer with the Blue Division, the force sent by Franco in support of Hitler. Thereafter, he enjoyed a highly distinguished military career, being promoted to brigadier general in 1952, to major general in 1957 and to the highest rank in the Spanish army, lieutenant general, in 1961, and the highest possible postings as Captain-General of the VII (Valladolid) and IX (Granada) Military Regions.[39] These subsequent career achievements suggest that Ramón's links with José were damaging to the Republic.

José had been arrested by the Brigada Especial of Vázquez Baldominos and Grigulevich, the force specialized in counter-espionage. Linking this with the activities of his brother, it is reasonable to suppose that José was suspected of passing important information about Soviet personnel to the fifth column. The international situation obliged the Soviet Union to play down its aid to the Spanish Republic, so any knowledge of Russian activities was sensitive and José Robles, as some kind of liaison officer between Vladimir Gorev and the Republican General Staff, seems to have had high-level access. Rumours flew around Valencia that Robles had been arrested on espionage charges and shot while in Soviet custody. Café gossip had it that he had carelessly let slip military information.[40] The parallel experience of Ramón suggests that more than carelessness was at stake. The internationally renowned journalist and Sovietologist Louis Fischer, who had privileged access to both the Russian hierarchy in Spain and the highest levels of the Spanish government, was convinced that Robles's execution was the work of the Russians.[41]

The novelist John Dos Passos was informed at the United States Embassy that José Robles, his friend from way back, had been seen alive in a prison camp by the American military attaché, Colonel Stephen Fuqua, on 26 March 1937.[42] Robles was executed at some point between then and 22 April. On the morning of that day, Dos Passos told Ernest Hemingway and their friend the novelist Josephine Herbst that he had just learned that Robles had been executed after being tried for giving away military secrets.[43] In 1939, Dos Passos said that he had been told regretfully by 'the then chief of the Republican counter-espionage service' of Robles's death at the hands of 'a special section'.[44] That phrase would suggest David Vázquez Baldominos, as Inspector General of the police and commander of the Brigadas Especiales, but there is far more reason to suppose that Dos Passos's informant was Vázquez Baldominos's secretary, Pepe Quintanilla. Like his brother, the artist Luis Quintanilla, Pepe was in contact with Hemingway, Herbst and Dos Passos. Given his post, Pepe Quintanilla had to know about Grigulevich and the Brigadas Especiales.[45] The contrasting fates of the two brothers underline the difference between the relative laxity of the popular tribunals and the deadly seriousness of the Brigadas Especiales.

The clashes between Cazorla and the CNT in Madrid were merely a reflection of a much wider problem at the heart of Republican Spain. For the Communists, substantial sectors of the PSOE and the bourgeois Republican parties, the war effort was the central priority and that required the full reconstruction of the state. In contrast, the revolutionary elements of the left, the CNT–FAI and the POUM, were determined to collectivize industry and agriculture and opposed state control in economic and military issues even after the Republican debacle at Málaga in February 1937 had starkly revealed the shortcomings of the militia system. The anarchists, despite their occasional rhetoric, also opposed the reorganization of public order. In the eyes of the Republicans, Socialists and Communists, the activities of the CNT and the POUM were on the same spectrum of subversion as those of the fifth column.

Although the conflict in Madrid had been intense, it was restrained by the sense of common struggle imposed by the siege. The definitive clash would come in May 1937 in Barcelona, where the greater distance from any active military front created a qualitatively different context in which both social and political tensions had been mounting for some months. Already throughout late 1936, some of the first revolutionary advances in Catalonia were being clawed back and the regional government, the Generalitat, was recovering powers lost when the military coup left the state apparatus in ruins. The Catalan President, Lluís Companys, of the bourgeois Esquerra Republicana de Catalunya, and the Catalan Communist Party (Partit Socialista Unificat de Catalunya) were trying to re-establish control of the political and military structures of the region. In the POUM newspaper, *La Batalla*, the party leader, Andreu Nin, and his principal theorist, Juan Andrade, denounced the collaboration between the PSUC and the Esquerra as counter-revolutionary and urged the CNT to join the POUM in opposing it with revolutionary committees.[46]

Already in the autumn of 1936, Louis Fischer had told Andrade's wife, María Teresa García Banús, that the Kremlin was determined to exterminate the POUM and urged her to warn her comrades to take precautions.[47] By late 1936 the Comintern delegate to the PSUC, the taciturn and enigmatic Ernö Gerö, codenamed 'Pedro', had already been directing a campaign to remove Andreu Nin from his post as Justice Councillor in the Generalitat.[48] On 11 December, the executive committee of the Comintern sent the following telegram to 'Luis' (Victorio Codovilla, delegate to the PCE), 'Pedro' (Ernö Gerö) and 'Pepe' (José Díaz, the secretary general of the PCE): 'It is necessary to focus on the political liquidation of the Trotskyists, as counter-revolutionaries, as agents of the Gestapo. After the political campaign, get them out of national and local government bodies, ban their press, expel all foreign elements. Try to do so in agreement with the anarchists.'[49]

The following day, 12 December, the PSUC's secretary general, Joan Comorera, set off a cabinet crisis by calling for the removal of Nin from the Generalitat, pointing out that the POUM was a discordant and disloyal element, provoking divisions between the UGT and the CNT. He declared that the POUM, by attacking and insulting the Republic's only powerful ally, the Soviet Union, was effectively guilty of treachery.[50] The Russian Consul General in Barcelona, Vladimir Antonov-Ovseenko, had dinner with Companys that same night and, despite being an old friend of Nin, 'used every argument, Soviet arms, the foreign situation, raw materials and food shipments', to make the same point. Since deliveries were imminent and a food crisis looming, Companys, who was in any case happy to see a more compact cabinet, agreed and Nin was removed in the cabinet reshuffle of 16 December.[51] After he had been arrested six months later, Nin told his interrogators that when the Catalan Prime Minister, Josep Tarradellas, informed him of his removal, he said that the POUM would be persecuted and its leaders eliminated politically and physically.[52]

The POUM's outspoken criticisms of the trial and execution of the old Bolsheviks Kamenev and Zinoviev had drawn the fire of the Soviet advisers. Encouraged by Antonov-Ovseenko, the PSUC denounced the

POUM leadership as 'fascist spies' and 'Trotskyist agents' and called for the Party's extermination.[53] However, hostility to the anti-Stalinist leftists was not just about Russian paranoia. There was a growing conviction among Republicans, Socialists, Communists and numerous foreign observers that the Catalan anarchists were not fully committed to the war effort. The CNT was importing and hoarding weapons in Barcelona against the day when they could make their revolution.[54] In mid-March 1937, several hundred of the more extreme members of the libertarian movement who had opposed the militarization of the militias abandoned the front at Gelsa (Zaragoza) and took their weapons to the Catalan capital. Inspired by the extremist Catalan separatist Jaume Balius Mir, they aimed to create a revolutionary vanguard and oppose the CNT leadership's collaboration with the central government. Even García Oliver considered Balius to be a deranged bohemian. On 17 March, they formed the group known as 'the Friends of Durruti' and, within a matter of weeks, had recruited five thousand CNT members. The new organization was warmly welcomed by Andreu Nin.[55]

Part of the CNT leadership, having accepted participation in the Republican government, was more inclined to agree to the need for the prioritization of the war effort. However, at rank-and-file level, especially in Barcelona, there was intense resistance to the loss of revolutionary power. Many anarchists and POUM militants felt that the sacrifices demanded by the Communists, Socialists and Republicans in favour of bourgeois democracy were pointless since the Western powers saw Franco as a better bet for capitalism than the Republic could ever be. The belief of many in the CNT and POUM that the revolution should have priority was seen as treacherous and subversive by all those who were committed to the war effort.

The tension generated by the Generalitat's efforts to claw back its powers from the revolutionary unions was exacerbated by the economic and social dislocation imposed by the war. By December 1936, the population of Catalonia had been swelled by the arrival of 300,000 refugees. This constituted 10 per cent of the population of the entire region and probably nearer 40 per cent of the population of Barcelona itself. After the fall of Málaga, the numbers soared even more. The strain of housing and feeding the new arrivals had embittered existing conflicts. Until December 1936, during which time the CNT controlled the Supply Ministry, the anarchist solution had been to requisition food at artificially low prices. This provoked shortages and inflation as farmers resisted by hoarding stocks. After the mid-December cabinet crisis, the

PSUC leader Joan Comorera had taken over the supply portfolio and introduced a more market-based approach. This infuriated the anarchists but did not solve the problem. Catalonia also needed to import food but lacked the foreign exchange to buy it. There were bread riots in Barcelona, as well as armed clashes for control of food stores between the CNT–FAI and the PSUC.[56]

In parallel with the conflict over food shortages and collectivization, other outbreaks of violence were generated as the forces of order tried to restrain the anarchist Patrulles de Control. In February 1937, more than thirty members of the National Republican Guard (ex-Civil Guard) were killed. At the beginning of March, the Generalitat dissolved the CNT-controlled Defence Committee and assumed the power to dissolve all local police and militia committees. The Assault Guards and National Republican Guards were merged into a single Catalan police corps whose officers were not permitted membership of any political party or trade union. These measures effectively placed the workers' patrols beyond the law. Ten days later, the central Republican government ordered all worker organizations, committees, patrols and individual workers to hand over their weapons. The Interior Councillor in the Generalitat, Artemi Aiguader of the Esquerra, stepped up the disarming of militia patrols. At the same time, along the French border, there were increasingly bloody clashes between the border police, the Carabineros, and CNT committees over control of customs posts which they had held since July 1936.[57]

On 24 April 1937, anarchists reacted with an attempt on the life of the chief of the Catalan police, Eusebio Rodríguez Salas of the PSUC, who had been appointed by Aiguader. Matters came to a head the next day with the assassination, at Molins de Llobregat, of Roldán Cortada, a member of the PSUC and secretary to Rafael Vidiella, Labour and Public Works Councillor in the Generalitat. Two days later, a huge official procession through the streets of Barcelona accompanying Cortada's coffin was orchestrated as a mass demonstration against the CNT–FAI. At the same time, an extraordinary event took place in the Pyrenean border area of Lleida known as La Cerdanya. The entire area was controlled by the FAI activist and smuggler Antonio Martín Escudero, known as 'el Cojo de Málaga' (the cripple from Málaga). As the virtual viceroy of La Cerdanya, Martín made a fortune by smuggling and also by extorting money from wealthy individuals trying to cross the frontier. Important politicians were detained and threatened by his gunmen. Control of the frontier was of considerable importance to the CNT leadership both for the unfettered export of requisitioned valuables and for the illegal import of arms. Information about the movements of the Carabineros and other government forces was passed to him by the CNT, which controlled telephone communications in Catalonia.

The mayors of local towns were determined to put an end to Martín's reign of terror and finally, in April, they began to get some support from Aiguader and the Generalitat. Informed from Barcelona that forces were gathering against him at the small town of Bellver, Martín led a substantial militia force in an attack on the town. However, in the shooting, the attackers were beaten off and Martín and some of his men were killed.[58] Anarchist literature turned the bandit chieftain into a martyr. The entire episode was rewritten to give the impression that the criminal Martín had not been killed in Bellver by the town's defenders but murdered in Puigcerdà by forces of the Generalitat. Diego Abad de Santillán, the Generalitat's Economy Councillor, twice went with government delegations to look into complaints against Martín and was fully aware of his murky record but turned a blind eye.[59]

The disputes over food supplies and the events in La Cerdanya showed how deep rooted was the conflict between the advocates of revolution and those who believed that priority should be given to the war effort. The notion that its culmination in the so-called 'May events' was a carefully laid Stalinist plot has no basis. The immediate spark that ignited the long-smouldering clashes in May was a twofold initiative of the Generalitat. A decree prohibiting the traditional 1 May rallies to prevent clashes between the CNT and the UGT was seen as a provocation by the CNT rank and file. Then, on 3 May, a raid on the CNT-controlled central telephone exchange in the Plaça de Catalunya was ordered by Artemi Aiguader and carried out by the belligerent police commissioner Rodríguez Salas. Aiguader was following the instructions of Companys, who had been humiliated to learn that a CNT operator had interrupted a telephone call by President Azaña. Clearly the state needed control of the main communication system, but Companys was warned by a CNT Councillor that the anarchist rank and file would resist.[60]

There is no doubt that the anarchists and the POUM were infuriated by the police campaign to disarm the militia patrols over the previous three months. The insurrectionary response to Aiguader's initiative from the CNT suggested some prior preparation. The scale of armament held by the CNT saw the crisis escalate extremely seriously if hardly into a mini-civil war. Anarchist and POUM militias came on to the streets of Barcelona and several other towns. After a cabinet meeting to discuss the situation, one of the anarchist ministers, possibly García Oliver, said:

'This is just the beginning. The attack is going to be full-scale and defini-tive.' Companys declined to pull back the forces surrounding the tele-phone building and seized the opportunity to press home the offensive against the CNT patrols and finally reassert the power of the state.[61]

Barricades went up in the centre of Barcelona. The Friends of Durruti, along with other anarchists and the POUM, confronted the forces of the Generalitat and the PSUC for four days. PSUC headquarters in the Passeig de Gràcia was unsuccessfully attacked by three armoured cars. Working-class districts and the industrial suburbs were in the hands of the anarchist masses, but their lack of co-ordination gave the advantage back to Companys.[62] Although the origins of the crisis lay deep in the wartime circumstances of Catalonia, the Generalitat and the PSUC real-ized that they had to seize the chance to break the power of the CNT. The central government also saw the opportunity to limit the power of the Generalitat. García Oliver and Carlos Hernández Zancajo of the UGT were sent to Barcelona to discuss the situation with the CNT leadership. They were humiliated, kept waiting while the anarchists finished a lengthy dinner. When they requested food, two thin sandwiches were sent out to them. They returned to Valencia without achieving anything.[63]

Such cheap victories aside, the situation exposed the fundamental dilemma of the CNT. The anarchists could win in Catalonia only at the cost of all-out war against other Republican forces. The CNT's Madrid newspaper *Frente Libertario* denounced the revolutionaries as the allies of Hitler, Mussolini and Stalin. García Oliver broadcast from the Generalitat on behalf of the CNT ministers in the central government and called on the incredulous militants to lay down their arms. The bulk of the Catalan anarchist leadership was unwilling to recall CNT militias from Aragon to fight the Generalitat and the central Republican govern-ment. On 7 May, the government in Valencia sent the police reinforce-ments which finally decided the outcome. It did so only in return for the Generalitat surrendering control of the Army of Catalonia and respon-sibility for public order in Catalonia. Several hundred members of the CNT and the POUM were arrested, although the need to get the war industries working as soon as possible limited the scale of the repression. The backdrop to these events was the Francoist advance into the Basque Country. As Manuel Domínguez Benavides, a prominent journalist, wrote, while Euskadi was being bombed, 'the POUM and the FAI organ-ized a bloody revolutionary carnival'.[64]

The events of 3 May took the Russians by surprise. Some of their senior guerrilla advisers were unexpectedly trapped in Barcelona by the fighting. The senior military adviser, General Grigory Shtern, wrote later that, far from being resented as having inspired the events, Russians 'could pass serenely among the barricades of both sides and be greeted by the anarchists with a clenched-fist salute'.[65] If the Russians and the PCE had not planned the entire affair, they certainly leaped at the opportunities presented by it. Having boasted of leading an insurrection which was really the work of elements of the CNT, the POUM would now be the sacrificial goat.[66] Andreu Nin and the rest of the POUM leadership had far exceeded the CNT in the militancy of their revolutionary pronouncements during the crisis. Moreover, since the principal beneficiaries of the events were the military rebels and their Axis allies, there was a strong suspicion among Communists, Socialists and Republicans that there had been an element of fascist provocation behind the activities of the POUM and the CNT. It was a frequent complaint of Cazorla and others that the CNT was porous and easily infiltrated. The internationalist POUM was extremely welcoming to the recruitment of foreign volunteers. Specifically, in January 1937, an operative of the NKVD in Berlin had reported to Moscow that German agents had infiltrated the POUM.[67] Franco boasted to the German Chargé d'Affaires, General Wilhelm Faupel, that 'the street fighting had been started by his agents', which was a reference to attacks on CNT members carried out by elements of the right-wing Catalan nationalist party Estat Català on the night of 2 May on instructions from Salamanca. Similarly, the Italian Foreign Minister Count Ciano boasted to the Francoist Ambassador in Rome that Italian agents had contributed to the disorder. Indeed, there was no shortage of Italians in the CNT, some of whom may well have been infiltrated agents of the Italian secret police, the OVRA.[68]

Shortly after the fighting in Barcelona had ended, Largo Caballero was removed as Prime Minister and not simply because of his mistakes during the crisis. Certainly, President Azaña, who had been besieged in the Palau de les Corts Catalanes during the May events, would never forgive Largo for the delay in arranging his evacuation. The Minister without Portfolio, José Giral of Izquierda Republicana, informed Azaña that the Republicans, the Communists and the Socialists were united in wanting major change. They were frustrated not only by Largo Caballero's ludicrous pretensions of being a great strategist but also by his practice of taking decisions without cabinet discussion. When ministers complained that they were not told what was happening, he would tell them to read the newspapers. All three groups were united in dissatisfaction with Largo Caballero's sympathy with the CNT and his failure to confront the issue of public order. They were equally keen to see the removal of his incompetent Minister of the Interior, Ángel Galarza.

A stormy cabinet meeting on 14 May was provoked by the Communist ministers, with the prior agreement of the Socialists and Republicans. They demanded a change in military strategy and for the POUM to be declared illegal. When the Prime Minister refused, reluctant to punish the POUM when the FAI and the Friends of Durruti were being left unpunished, they left the meeting. Largo Caballero tried to carry on without them only to be astonished when the other ministers supported them.[69] He was forced to resign, and the government was offered to Dr Juan Negrín, a victory for the political forces that had opposed the revolutionary factions. From this point on, the revolutionary achievements of the initial stages of the war would be steadily dismantled, leaving policy to follow the direction dictated by the Republicans and moderate Socialists who took over the key ministries.

The humanitarian concerns which underlay the new Prime Minister's determination to put an end to the terror were closely linked to his perception that atrocities were being used to justify the refusal of the democratic powers to help the Republic. Between September 1936 and May 1937, as Treasury Minister, Negrín had done everything he could to keep the Republic afloat. He had worked hard to ensure that national resources were put at the service of the war effort, whether by sending the Republic's gold reserves abroad to protect their availability for arms purchases or by strengthening the frontier guards (Carabineros) to re-establish state control over foreign exchange and to curb the activities of the many illegal CNT frontier posts on the French–Catalan border. His efforts to stop the illegal repression were put on a different plane by his elevation to the premiership.

In his new cabinet, Negrín appointed as his Minister of the Interior the Basque Socialist Julián Zugazagoitia, who was equally committed to the re-establishment of law and order. Together with the choice of another Basque, Manuel Irujo, as Minister of Justice, this ensured that, despite the Soviet determination to destroy the POUM, there would be no Moscow trials in Spain. A series of other important appointments were made to bring public order under greater control. Another Socialist, Juan-Simeón Vidarte, was named as Zugazagoitia's under-secretary, and his first actions were to disband a squad which had carried out extra-judicial executions on the orders of Ángel Galarza and to close down the notorious prison of Santa Úrsula in Valencia. Another Socialist, Paulino Gómez Saiz, was named Delegate for Public Order for Catalonia, in order to impose greater control over the region. The highly efficient Lieutenant Colonel Ricardo Burillo was made police chief in Barcelona and a professional policeman, Teodoro Illera Martín, was sent to the city as Delegate of the Dirección General de Seguridad. Burillo had been commander of the Assault Guard barracks in Calle Pontejos on 13 July 1936 when Calvo Sotelo was murdered – a crime in which he played no part but for which he would be executed in 1939. He was a Communist but also loyal to Negrín.[70] The one disastrous appointment was that of Colonel Antonio Ortega Gutiérrez as Director General of Security on 27 May 1937. Negrín appointed Ortega believing him simply to be a professional soldier and a Socialist follower of the Minister of Defence, Indalecio Prieto. As he noted later in his draft memoirs, he would never have accepted the recommendation had he known that Ortega's loyalty would be to the PCE rather than to the government.[71]

According to Diego Abad de Santillán, 60,000 weapons were in the hands of leftists in Barcelona, mainly members of the CNT–FAI. On arriving in Barcelona, Vidarte and Burillo began to close down the Patrulles de Control and to confiscate their arms. This process was resisted with considerable violence by the CNT–FAI in the course of which, on 4 June, a sergeant of Carabineros and four Assault Guards were killed. According to Vidarte, a significant role in this resistance was played by Manuel Escorza del Val, who had run the Investigation Committee of the Central Anti-Fascist Militia Committee. Those responsible for the deaths were arrested, but Negrín insisted that there be no executions.[72] Illera dismissed seventy-two policemen of the Generalitat whom he claimed were involved in theft, murder and smuggling, exactly the kind of crimes linked to Antonio Martín Escudero, 'el Cojo de Málaga'. Illera inevitably clashed with the man he had come to replace, Dionisio Eroles Batlló of the FAI, who, until Negrín took over the government, had been the Generalitat's head of public order. Illera also faced fierce opposition from the leader of the CNT–FAI Patrulles de Control, Aurelio Fernández Sánchez.[73]

Negrín was fully aware of Irujo's efforts to stop violence in the Republican rearguard when he had been Minister without Portfolio.[74] Now, on taking up the post of Minister of Justice, Irujo reflected Negrín's attitude to the repression when he declared: 'the *paseos* have finished … There were days when the government did not control the levers of power. It was unable to prevent social crimes. Those times have passed … We must not let the monstrous brutality of the enemy be used to excuse the repugnant crimes committed on our side.'[75] Revolutionary justice was being replaced by conventional bourgeois justice. Trained judges were placed at the head of the Tribunales Populares. One of the first things that Irujo did was to professionalize the prison service to ensure no repetition of the atrocities of November 1936. The prison regime was relaxed in a way unimaginable in the rebel zone. Catholic clergy and religious were released. The Red Cross was allowed full access to prisons.[76] Many civilian prisoners were allowed out on parole for the births, marriages, illnesses or deaths of family members. As a result of these measures, Irujo was for a time denounced by the anarchist press as a Vaticanist caveman and a bourgeois reactionary, but eventually he was congratulated for his work by an anarchist delegation. Similarly, in the Ministry of the Interior, Zugazagoitia would use his position to save the lives of prominent Falangists in Republican custody.

An illustration of the personal ethics of Negrín and Irujo was the extraordinary case of Amelia de Azarola. She was a Basque nationalist and an anti-fascist who was also the wife of, and deeply in love with, Julio Ruiz de Alda, one of the founders of the Falange. She was arrested in August 1936, shortly before he was murdered in the massacre of the Cárcel Modelo. She was tried on 29 March 1937 for 'hostility to the regime'. Both Irujo and Negrín showed up as witnesses at her trial. Irujo knew her as a firm Republican from her native village in Euskadi. Negrín had studied medicine with her at Madrid University and spoke of her activities then as a left-wing student and as a Republican. In consequence, she was found not guilty, but Cazorla refused to release her and had her detained as a hostage for a possible prisoner exchange. She was permitted to work in the women's prison of Alacuás just outside Valencia. After intervention by Negrín, in the autumn of 1937, Dr Azarola was released by the DGS and permitted to return to her home in Barcelona under protective custody and then, in early 1938, she was exchanged and went to Navarre.[77]

The prison at Alacuás where Dr Azarola worked had once been a Jesuit residence, refurbished on the orders of Irujo. Light, airy, with a gymnasium and swimming pool, conditions there were relatively comfortable. Queipo de Llano's sister Rosario arrived there in July 1937, and encountered a distinguished roster of Francoists, including José Antonio Primo de Rivera's sister Carmen, his aunt María Jesús and his sister-in-law Margot Larios, as well as María Luisa Millán Astray, the sister of the founder of the Foreign Legion, Franco's niece, Pilar Jaraiz Franco, a cousin of the Duque de Alba and female relatives of several prominent rebel officers.[78]

Irujo had accepted the post of Minister of Justice on the condition that freedom of conscience would be respected and religious practice legalized. Safe-conducts and identity cards were provided for priests and religious and efforts were made to establish the right to practise the liturgy. He created the Office of Religious Orders and worked tirelessly until he succeeded in arranging for the first public Mass to be said in the Basque Delegation in Valencia, on 15 August 1937, and for the first chapel to be reopened in Barcelona. These achievements provoked strident CNT criticism. Jesús de Galíndez, who worked in the Office of Religious Orders, served as an altar boy at that first Mass. The fifth column tried to undermine the initiative by spreading the rumour that the chapel was deconsecrated and that anyone who attended Mass there would be excommunicated. They realized that, with the churches open, they had lost one of their principal propaganda weapons against the government.[79]

The one thing that Irujo and Zugazagoitia could not do was to control the activities of Lev Lazarevich Nikolsky, the NKVD station chief known as Aleksandr Orlov. Theoretically, Orlov had various tasks – counter-espionage, especially within the International Brigades, the organization of guerrilla and sabotage activities and the creation of a small, elite Republican secret police force to counter internal opposition to the government. This latter was his principal activity and the fruit of this was the Brigadas Especiales. Their initial purpose was to combat the fifth column, but they had soon been turned against those elements of the Spanish left perceived as subversive traitors. On 3 May 1937, Grigulevich led one of the Brigadas Especiales to Barcelona to eliminate, under the cover of the disorder, a number of prominent foreign Trotskyists linked to the POUM.[80] It has been suggested that Grigulevich's group may have been responsible for the murder, on the night of 5–6 May, of the Italian anarchists Camilo Berneri and Francesco Barbieri. Since Berneri constituted a far greater danger to Mussolini than to Stalin, it is possible that this was the work of the Italian OVRA. The CNT's own investigation concluded that Berneri had been killed by members of Estat Català working for the OVRA.[81]

As far as a paranoid Stalin was concerned, Orlov's principal task was the eradication of foreign dissident Communists in Spain. Indeed, Russian security personnel in Republican Spain were much more concerned with this task than with any action against the POUM, which was considered to be the job of the Spanish police. Many eastern Europeans were arrested and imprisoned by agents of a Catalan unit, similar to the Madrid-based Brigadas Especiales, known as the Grup d'Informació. It was part of the secret service of the Generalitat's Defence Council with which Orlov had established links. The arrested Trotskyists were taken to the convent of Santa Úrsula in Valencia, where they were interrogated and tortured by Russians, Germans and east Europeans, all members of their respective Communist parties.[82]

One of Orlov's victims was Mark Rein, the son of the Russian Menshevik leader Rafail Abramovich. Rein had come to Spain as correspondent for several anti-Stalinist publications including the New York Jewish daily, *Forward*. On 9 April 1937, he left the Hotel Continental in Barcelona and was never seen again. He had been abducted and murdered by agents of the Grup d'Informació.[83] Another of Orlov's targets was Andreu Nin, more as a one-time close collaborator of Trotsky than as leader of the POUM. Already, in a report to Moscow in late February 1937, Orlov had noted that the war effort was being undermined by 'inter-party conflicts in which the energy of most people is devoted to winning authority and power for their own party and discrediting others rather than to the struggle against fascism'. After dismissive comments about both Gorev and Berzin, he went on to say:

> the time has come when it is necessary to analyze the threatening situation ... and forcefully present to the Spanish Government (and Party leaders) the full gravity of the situation and to propose the necessary measures – if the Spanish Government really wants help from us: (1) bringing the army and its command into a healthier state of discipline (shooting deserters, maintaining discipline, etc.) and (2) putting an end to the inter-party squabbles. If, in the face of immediate danger, we do not bring the Spanish Government to its senses, events will take a catastrophic turn.[84]

Now, after the May events, Orlov made the elimination of Nin his prime objective and the task was made easier because of the POUM's role during those events. Nin became the object of what was known as a *liter* operation. A *liter* (letter) file was a letter-coded file opened on a person scheduled for assassination who was given a codename. In the case of Nin, this was 'Assistant', a reference perhaps to his one-time work with Trotsky. The file was designated with the letter 'A' for such operations where 'A' stood for an 'active measure' (*aktivka* or direct action, that is assassination). It was presumably no coincidence, if the Communist Minister Jesús Hernández is to be believed, that, on the day following the murder of Nin, a cable sent to Moscow read 'A.N. business resolved by procedure A.'[85]

Orlov's plan was based on two carefully choreographed 'discoveries'. The first involved a bookshop in Girona belonging to a Falangist called José Roca Falgueras. Roca was part of a fifth-column network run out of a small hotel in the town by its owner, Cosme Dalmau Mora. The network had been discovered by the police but kept under observation rather than shut down. One day in May, an elegantly dressed man went into Roca's shop, leaving some money and a message for Dalmau. He asked if he could leave a suitcase that he would pick up some days later. The next day, there was a police raid and the suitcase was found to contain an incriminating collection of technical documents about bomb-making together with plans to assassinate key Republican figures. All were apparently sealed with the stamp of the POUM Military Committee.[86]

The second discovery was initially genuine but was doctored by Orlov to 'demonstrate' the collaboration of the POUM with the Falange. The principal element was a detailed map of Madrid seized when the Brigadas Especiales, led by David Vázquez Baldominos and Fernando Valentí Fernández, broke up a large fifth-columnist network, with the help of Alberto Castilla Olavarría, a paid double agent. Castilla was a Basque of right-wing ideas. The fact that he had taken refuge in the Peruvian Embassy gave him the plausibility to infiltrate the fifth column. He became the liaison between the four Falangist groups that made up the substantial network known as the 'Organización Golfin-Corujo' run by the architect Francisco Javier Fernández Golfin. When the organization was dismantled thanks to Castilla's information, Fernández Golfin had in his possession a street plan of Madrid on which his brother Manuel had drawn details and positions of military installations. This map was part of the group's plans to facilitate the rebel entry into the capital.[87]

Well over one hundred Falangists were arrested by Vázquez Baldominos's squad, although only twenty-seven were tried. Their confessions would play a key part in the complex plot being hatched by Orlov, although it is unlikely that Vázquez Baldominos was party to what Orlov did with the street map. Orlov's elaborate scheme was outlined in a report sent to Moscow on 23 May 1937:

> Taking into consideration that this case, in connection with which the overwhelming majority have pleaded guilty, has produced a great impression on military and government circles, and that it is firmly documented and based on the incontrovertible confessions of

defendants, I have decided to use the significance and the indisputable facts of the case to implicate the POUM leadership (whose [possible] connections we are looking into while conducting investigations). We have, therefore, composed the enclosed document, which indicates the co-operation of the POUM leadership with the Spanish Falange organization – and, through it, with Franco and Germany. We will encipher the contents of the document using Franco's cipher, which we have at our disposal, and will write it on the reverse side of the plan of the location of our weapons emplacements in Casa del Campo, which was taken from the Falangist organization. This document has passed through five people: all the five Fascists who have admitted passing the document to each other for dispatch to Franco. On another seized document we will write in invisible ink a few lines of some insignificant content. It will be from this document that, in cooperation with the Spaniards, we shall begin to scrutinize the document for cryptographic writing. We shall experiment with several processes for treating these papers. A special chemical will develop these few words or lines, then we will begin to test all the other documents with this developer and thus expose the letter we have composed compromising the POUM leadership. The Spanish chief of counter-intelligence department [Vázquez Baldominos] will leave immediately for Valencia where the cipher department of the War Ministry will decipher the letter. The cipher department, according to our information, has the necessary code at its disposal. But if the department cannot decipher the letter for some reason, then we will 'spend a couple of days' and decipher it ourselves. We expect this affair to be very effective in exposing the role POUM has played in the Barcelona uprising. The exposure of direct contact between one of its leaders and Franco must contribute to the government adopting a number of administrative measures against the Spanish Trotskyites to discredit POUM as a German–Francoist spy organization.[88]

According to a police report of late October 1937, the captured document was first examined by the then Director General of Security, Wenceslao Carrillo, by General Miaja and by the recently promoted General Vicente Rojo. At this stage, the damning reverse side of the document had not been 'discovered' since it had not yet been added. Its later 'discovery' was attributed to its being in invisible ink.[89] The police report spoke appreciatively of the invaluable technical help received from foreign (Russian) experts who were given free access to the captured documentation in the office of the Brigada Especial and then allowed to take it back to their own Embassy. Orlov reported to Moscow that the faking of the actual document was carried out by Grigulevich. Valentí told his post-war Francoist interrogators that Grigulevich had had the map for some time. On returning it to the Brigada Especial, he suggested to Vázquez Baldominos that it be chemically tested for messages in invisible ink.

The police report explained how the Russian technicians also supplied the necessary chemical reagents and the electrical plate to heat the document. When the map was heated, there appeared on the reverse a message in code. At this point, Vázquez Baldominos was sent for. Unable to decipher the message, he and Valentí, accompanied by two of the foreign technicians (Orlov and Grigulevich?), took the document to Valencia to the newly appointed Director General of Security, Colonel Ortega. They struggled for nearly eighteen hours in Ortega's office in a vain attempt to decipher the message. Finally, military codebreakers, using a Francoist codebook, were able to interpret the message. All concerned then went to the Russian Embassy in Valencia to draw up a report.[90]

The definitive 'text' of the coded message stated that one of the members of the Fernández Golfín organization had met 'N., the leader of the POUM, who had offered his forces which would constitute crucial support for the victory of the Nationalists'. There was also a letter to Franco outlining the services of the POUM in terms of espionage, sabotage and the provocation of anti-Republican disorder. The message in itself was as implausible as the idea that Nin would use 'N' as his codename. Six months later, in January 1938, an analysis of the message by two calligraphic experts reported that it could not have been written by any member of the network and was a forgery.[91] Now, the report drawn up in the Russian Embassy presented the story of the Fernández Golfín network and the document at face value. It concluded with a recommendation that the POUM be 'extirpated'. Dated 1 June 1937, copies were sent by the counter-espionage service of Vázquez Baldominos's office of the Madrid police to Zugazagoitia and Ortega.[92]

Vázquez Baldominos, Valentí and the Brigada Especial returned to Madrid. Six days later, Ortega sent an order for Valentí and seven members of his Brigada Especial, including Jacinto Rosell Coloma and Andrés Urresola Ochoa, to report to him in Valencia. According to another of the JSU members in the Brigada Especial, Javier Jiménez Martín, the squad was led by 'a Brazilian named José': 'José was someone who we thought was Russian. He spoke Russian and you could really see that he was the almighty power in the organization.' There can be no doubt that the 'Brazilian named José' was Grigulevich.[93] In Valencia, they were ordered by Ortega to go to Barcelona and arrest Andreu Nin. Ortega later admitted that, throughout, he had been following instructions from Orlov.[94] Since Zugazagoitia had never trusted Ortega because he was a Communist and incompetent, he had appointed the Civil Governor of Almería, the Socialist Gabriel Morón Díaz, as Inspector and deputy Director General of Security to watch over Ortega. However, on the day of Nin's arrest, Ortega had got Morón out of the way by sending him to Ciudad Real on a pretext. On 15 June, Valentí and his men, accompanied by Grigulevich, went to Barcelona. On 16 June, Nin, and later that day the other members of the POUM executive, were arrested by local police commanded by Lieutenant Colonel Burillo.[95]

The POUM newspaper, *La Batalla*, had been banned on 28 May. Now the POUM itself was declared illegal and the POUM militia disbanded. The procedure was justified by a communiqué stating that the DGS had seized from POUM HQ 'cyphers, telegrams, codes, documents concerning money and arms purchases and smuggling, and with incriminating documents showing that the POUM leadership, namely Andrés Nin, was mixed up in espionage'. Orlov himself reported to Moscow that the Madrid police considered the falsified document 'absolutely genuine in its double aspects' – that is to say, both regarding the original Falangist plans for rebel occupation of Madrid and the additions in invisible ink.[96] The Catalan President Lluís Companys and his head of propaganda, Jaume Miravitlles, in contrast, thought that the idea of Nin as a fascist spy was absurd and deeply damaging to the Republic. They wrote a letter to the Valencia government to this effect. When Ortega tried to convince Miravitlles by showing him the doctored street map, he burst out laughing saying that it was the first time in history that a spy had signed an incriminating document with his own name.[97]

Nin was taken first to Valencia and then transferred to Madrid.[98] There then arose the problem of how to obey Ortega's order that Nin be kept isolated during his interrogation and in a place suitable for a prisoner of his category. All possible places of confinement in the capital were already occupied by the fifth columnists arrested in the Golfín case. He was kept in the offices of the Brigada Especial until 'one of the senior foreign technicians', no doubt Orlov, offered to hold him in a house at Alcalá de Henares. Vázquez Baldominos accepted Orlov's offer and proposed that several of his agents guard him. Orlov brushed aside the idea as likely to attract unwanted attention and offered to take responsibility for Nin's safety. On 17 June, Vázquez Baldominos signed the order for Nin's transfer to the house and for just two agents to be posted. Orlov undertook to supply their rations.[99]

Before being transferred to Alcalá de Henares, Nin was questioned in Madrid four times by Jacinto Rosell as secretary of the Brigada Especial on 18, 19 (twice) and 21 June. Nothing about Rosell's questions or Nin's answers in the transcript signed by Nin and published by the POUM itself suggests anything other than a legally conducted interrogation without torture. The often unreliable Jesús Hernández claimed that Nin was tortured and interrogated by Orlov and others for several days, in an effort to make him sign a 'confession' of his links with the fifth column. This is highly unlikely; a confession was needed as the basis for a trial and, for that, Nin would have to be seen to be in good physical shape and testify that he had not been tortured. On 21 June, on the orders of Ortega, Vázquez Baldominos sent Rosell and other members of the Brigada Especial to Valencia to collect other POUM prisoners, including Andrade, and escort them to Madrid. At that point, Nin was transferred to Alcalá de Henares.[100] Because Nin had not confessed, there was little prospect of the desired show trial. Thus Orlov took the decision to eliminate him. A charade was choreographed at the house. On 22 June, between 9.30 and 10.00 p.m., in a heavy rainstorm, some men in military uniform arrived headed by a 'captain' and a 'lieutenant' who spoke Spanish with a heavy foreign accent. They presented orders for Nin's hand-over with the forged signatures of Vázquez Baldominos and Miaja. Allegedly, Vázquez Baldominos's agents resisted but were overpowered, tied up and gagged and, in the struggle, the intruders dropped incriminating 'evidence', including banknotes from rebel Spain and German documents. The agents later stated that the 'captain' spoke in a friendly way to Nin and called him 'comrade'. When Vázquez Baldominos began to investigate these events, Orlov could not be contacted.[101]

It is impossible to say whether the struggle took place or was merely reported as having done so, since it may be that there were members of the Brigada Especial whose loyalty was to Orlov rather than to Vázquez Baldominos. What is certain is that a car containing Orlov, Grigulevich, an NKVD driver, a German NKVD agent and two Spaniards had arrived. Between them, they could have knocked out the two guards, seized Nin and left the incriminating documents. What is not in doubt is that Nin was taken away and shot near the main road halfway between Alcalá de Henares and Perales de Tajuña.[102]

The impulse for the elimination of Nin came from the Russians and not from the Republican authorities. On the basis simply of Orlov's mendacious statements to the FBI after his defection, the American historian Stanley Payne has claimed that 'Stalin issued a handwritten order, which remains in the KGB archives, that Nin be killed.'[103] This is highly unlikely. Nevertheless, as has been seen, Nin had been made the target of a *liter* operation. Moreover, once Nin had refused to sign a false confession, Orlov was not about to have him simply released, even if he had not been tortured. Orlov made oblique reference to what happened in his report about 'operation NIKOLAI' sent to Moscow on 24 July 1937. This report describes, 'in the characteristically cryptic terms he used for *liter* operations', the seizing of Nin from the house and his murder. As well as revealing that Grigulevich forged the documents used to incriminate Nin, it underlines the participation in the operation of Orlov himself. Grigulevich's police credentials, as a member of the Brigada Especial, facilitated the passage through controls on the roads.[104]

There is a relevant note in Orlov's files allegedly written by Grigulevich. Transliterated into English, it refers to 'N. from Alcala de Enares in the direction of Perane de Tahunia, half way, 100 metres from the road, in the field. [Present were] BOM, SCHWED, JUZIK, two Spaniards. Pierre's driver VICTOR.' This means that the scene of the crime and where Nin was buried was between Alcalá de Henares and Perales de Tajuña. The executioners were thus Orlov (Schwed), Grigulevich (Juzik), the German NKVD agent Erich Tacke (BOM), the two unidentified Spaniards and Victor Nezhinsky, an NKVD agent. 'Pierre' was Naum Eitingon, head of the NKVD sub-station in Barcelona, and not, as has been suggested, Ernö Gerö.[105]

Shortly after the disappearance of Nin, Negrín was visited by Orlov, who had been introduced to him many months before as 'Blackstone'. Orlov claimed to have come to report on the success of his men in establishing what had happened to Nin. He based his version of Nin being kidnapped by Falangists disguised as International Brigaders on incriminating documents allegedly dropped by them and by Nin himself. Orlov asked Negrín if this was enough proof for him to drop the formal investigation. When Negrín said that it was up to the judicial authorities, Orlov asked him if he was convinced personally. Orlov was mortified to be told by the Premier that the story was so neat as to resemble a cheap detective story. Furiously, he shouted that Negrín had insulted the Soviet Union, at which point he was invited to leave. Some hours later, Negrín was visited by the Soviet Chargé d'Affaires, Sergei Marchenko, who said that he had heard of the disagreeable incident of that morning and had come to express his apologies. He offered to have Orlov punished and, when Negrín replied that the incident was closed, said that Orlov was no longer on the Embassy staff.[106]

When first questioned by Zugazagoitia about what had happened to Nin, Ortega rather gave the game away, saying, 'Don't worry, we'll find him dead or alive.' Zugazagoitia responded that he was not interested in the corpse of Nin and wanted him found alive. Later the same day, questioned further by the Minister, Ortega claimed that Nin was an agent of the Gestapo whose agents had taken him so that he could not be interrogated by the Republic's security services. When Zugazagoitia asked how he knew this, Ortega said it was simply something that had crossed his mind. The Minister immediately told Negrín of his suspicions that Ortega was involved in foul play concerning Nin. Negrín told him to get reports about what exactly had happened. According to Fernando Valentí, Vidarte and Zugazagoitia himself, the latter demanded a report from Vázquez Baldominos, who produced two drafts. In the first 'official' document, he examined three possibilities – that Nin had been kidnapped by Falangists, by Gestapo agents or by the POUM. In the second, secret, report for Zugazagoitia only, he expressed his opinion that the disappearance of Nin was nothing to do with the Gestapo or the Falange but was rather the result of the conflict between the POUM and the PCE encouraged by the various Russians who were operating in the DGS. It is likely that Vázquez Baldominos reached this conclusion after he was unable to locate Grigulevich or Orlov to discuss the case with them. Grigulevich had already returned to Russia. At this point, Vázquez Baldominos thought that Nin was still alive.[107]

The forged documents were published in a book by the non-existent 'Max Rieger', with a preface by José Bergamín demanding the immediate execution without trial of the arrested men. 'Max Rieger' was the collective pseudonym of the French Communist journalist Georges Soria, the recently arrived Comintern delegate, the Bulgarian Stoyan Minev, alias Boris Stepanov, and the Spanish Communist intellectual Wenceslao Roces.[108] This Comintern version was recited parrot-fashion by Ortega when he was questioned by Zugazagoitia's under-secretary, Juan-Simeón Vidarte. The incredulous Vidarte responded: 'Listen, Colonel, are you an idiot or do you think I am?' Jesús Hernández also claimed to have laughed when Orlov had explained his scheme for framing Nin. When Negrín informed Azaña of Orlov's version, the President responded that it was all too neat. In fact, on 29 June, Prieto had already told Azaña about the kidnapping of Nin and shared his conviction that Ortega was both an idiot and a Communist.[109]

At first, Negrín had interpreted Ortega's behaviour as the incompetence of a non-commissioned Carabinero officer promoted beyond his ability. As soon as he was informed that Ortega was a Communist, Negrín and Zugazagoitia agreed that he must be replaced. To minimize friction with the Communist ministers over his removal, they concocted the fiction that he was urgently needed at the front. Morón, the Inspector and deputy Director General of Security, became acting Director General.[110] In response to the international outcry provoked by Nin's disappearance, Negrín authorized Irujo to set up a judicial investigation to investigate the case. Morón is alleged to have said to Zugazagoitia: 'Given that the Prime Minister wants to know the truth, you can tell him that the truth is that the kidnapping of Andrés Nin was planned by the Italian Codovila, Comandante Carlos, [Palmiro] Togliatti and the leaders of the Communist Party, Pepe Díaz among them. The order to torture him was given by Orlov and they have all done their best to satisfy Stalin's desire for the disappearance of the secretary and confidant of the creator of the Red Army. Tell Negrín and if he wants them arrested, I'll have them all in prison tomorrow.' Vidarte's account suggests that Morón's information came from David Vázquez Baldominos.[111] There was an attempt on Vidarte's life. The front axle on his car had been cut and he crashed into an elm tree.[112]

For his inquiry into the case, Irujo gave plenary powers to a state prosecutor, Gregorio Peces Barba del Brío, who had Vázquez Baldominos, Fernando Valentí, Jacinto Rosell Coloma and Andrés Urresola Ochoa arrested. Convinced that Vázquez Baldominos was not the guilty party, a furious Gabriel Morón denounced Irujo as a 'poor lunatic' and immediately had them released, and they were not rearrested. Although Negrín approved of Morón's directness, he felt he had to be replaced.[113] In mid-November he was succeeded by Paulino Gómez Sáiz, who had been highly successful as the government delegate in Catalonia since early June.[114] Negrín, though he supported the sacking of Ortega and had far-reaching suspicions of Orlov, was not prepared to see further revelations undermine the unity of the cabinet. He took the difficult decision to suspend Irujo's investigation because, just as he opposed the unofficial repression, he also believed that the reckless and indeed treasonous rebellion of the POUM could not be tolerated in wartime.

To consolidate the security of the Republican state, a major reorganization of counter-espionage services was made in the summer of 1937. On 12 June, the Special Services Bureau of the General Staff of the Army of the Centre, which had been commanded by the anarchist Manuel

Salgado, was dissolved. In addition to concerns that prisoners had disappeared in suspicious circumstances, there were suspicions that Salgado's staff had been infiltrated by Falangists. In fact, his secretary was the Falangist Antonio Bouthelier España. The functions of the Special Services Bureau were fused with those of the Brigadas Especiales and other groups that worked on internal security to create the Special State Intelligence Department (Departamento Especial de Información del Estado – DEDIDE). Initially led by David Vázquez Baldominos, the new body was entrusted with the eradication of espionage and sabotage in loyalist territory, under the direct orders of the Minister of the Interior, Julián Zugazagoitia.[115] The DEDIDE targeted not only the supporters of Franco but also those on the left, like the POUM, who were considered to be treacherously subversive. There was considerable suspicion of foreigners – both the POUM and the International Brigades were regarded as potential havens for spies, whether of the Axis or, in the more paranoid vision of the NKVD, of Trotsky's Fourth International. The Republic was, in fact, extremely vulnerable to enemy espionage, whether directed by the Gestapo, the OVRA or the ever more sophisticated fifth column.[116] Bilbao fell on 19 June and constant defeat intensified anxiety and paranoia.

Barely six weeks later, on 9 August, a military counter-espionage unit, the Servicio de Investigación Militar (SIM), was created by Prieto in the Ministry of Defence. As it assumed ever more responsibility for collecting political intelligence in – and therefore policing – the rearguard, in late March 1938 the SIM absorbed the DEDIDE.[117] Initially, the SIM was directly responsible to Prieto, who suggested that it had been created on the advice of the Soviet 'technicians'. However, he also claimed that, in the light of the Nin affair, he had hesitated to take the advice for fear of the police acting independently of the government, as had happened with the Communist Antonio Ortega. Keen to place all the Republican special services under his own command, to head the SIM Prieto appointed his friend Ángel Díaz Baza, who, according to Orlov, was a speculator with an interest in night clubs.[118]

The key role of chief of the SIM of the Army of the Centre (Madrid) was initially given to a brilliant young officer, Major Gustavo Durán, at the suggestion of Orlov, via Miaja. Prieto accepted, and later claimed that he knew that Durán was a Communist, but kept him under surveillance by naming Ángel Pedrero García as his deputy. After the dissolution of the García Atadell Brigade, Pedrero, its second-in-command, had served briefly as a police inspector at Chamberí in central Madrid before being transferred, in December, to Salgado's Special Services Bureau in the Ministry of War. His growing importance in military counter-intelligence saw him become SIM chief for the Army of Central Spain in October 1937.[119]

In the decree creating the SIM, Prieto had stipulated that all agents be approved by the Minister himself and that their credentials carry his signature. However, Gustavo Durán proceeded independently and named about four hundred SIM agents. Claiming that they were all Communists, which Durán and Orlov denied, Prieto used the excuse that Durán was needed at the front to suspend him from the SIM after barely two weeks in the job. Orlov intervened on Durán's behalf. Pedrero claimed that Durán also received support from Eitingon and Ivan Maximov, the adviser to the General Staff of the Army of the Centre, other Soviet military advisers and Miaja.[120]

The overall chief of the SIM, Ángel Díaz Baza, hated the role and had soon been replaced on an interim basis by his deputy, Prudencio Sayagués. Seeking a more appropriate long-term appointment, Prieto named Major, later Colonel, Manuel Uribarri Barrutell. On Prieto's own admission, this was a disastrous choice. While at the Toledo front, Uribarri had allegedly been guilty of large-scale looting. Now, at first he followed Prieto's instructions but became increasingly aligned with the Communists.[121] Uribarri eventually defected in April 1938, with a substantial amount of money and jewellery. Negrín seized the opportunity to purge the SIM. On the advice of Zugazagoitia and Paulino Gómez, he appointed a Socialist, Santiago Garcés Arroyo, as head of the SIM to limit the influence of the Communists.[122] By February 1938, only Socialists could get jobs in the SIM.[123]

The Republic, like other democratic societies faced with an existential threat, adopted undemocratic norms such as censorship, internment without trial, suspension of civil liberties, strike bans in essential industries and conscription. To root out fifth-column networks and to get confessions, from May 1938 the SIM carried out illegal arrests and its operatives sometimes used refined tortures, disorientating prisoners with bright lights, constant loud noises and freezing water. Beds and benches were placed at a sharp angle, making sleep or sitting difficult. Floors were scattered with bricks and other geometric blocks to prevent prisoners from pacing up and down and leaving them to stare at the walls, which were curved and covered with dizzying patterns of cubes and spirals which, with special lighting, gave the impression that the walls were moving. These cells were created in Barcelona in the so-called

Checa de Vallmajor or 'Preventorio D', a converted convent, and in the 'Preventorio G' in Carrer Saragossa, both run by the SIM. The psycho-technic designs were the work of a bizarre international adventurer called Alfonso Laurencic, who was part of the Grup d'Informació of the Generalitat's secret intelligence service when it was absorbed by the SIM. A self-proclaimed music-hall pianist and architect, Laurencic was a Frenchman of Austrian parents and Yugoslav nationality, who had served in the Spanish Foreign Legion. He had belonged variously to the CNT, the UGT and the POUM, had made money selling false passports and eventually defrauded the SIM.[124]

Another element of the Republican clamp-down on the anarchist movement was the abolition of their autonomous Council of Aragon, which had been created in early October 1936 in Bujaraloz, under the presidency of Joaquín Ascaso, leader of the Zaragoza construction work-ers and representative of the Ortiz Column. It had had some success in limiting the excesses committed by the militias in Republican Aragon but its principal objective of co-ordinating 'the needs of the war and the rearguard' was never achieved because the leaders of the anarchist columns had been determined to maintain their autonomy. Republicans, Socialists and Communists regarded the Council as an anarchist dicta-torship imposed by the militias. Its closure by the central government in August 1937 was achieved only at the cost of some violence. Land that had been collectivized was returned to its owners and a definitive end was made to the anarchist repression in the region.[125]

The clandestine war of the Russian security services against foreign Trotskyists, however, remained beyond the control of the Republican authorities. In September 1937, Orlov managed to eliminate Erwin Wolf, who had become Trotsky's secretary in Norway. In 1936, Wolf played a key role in refuting the accusations made at the Moscow trials and was a central figure in the International Secretariat which was the predecessor to the Fourth International. He came to Spain to work with Grandizo Munis's Bolshevik-Leninist group. In Barcelona, he was arrested for subversive activity on 27 July 1937, released on the following day but then immediately rearrested. He was officially released on 13 September but was never seen again.[126]

Another prominent Trotskyist who disappeared ten days later was the Austrian Kurt Landau. A one-time collaborator of Trotsky, Landau had a long history of anti-Stalinist militancy in Austria, Germany, France and Spain. Using the pseudonym 'Wolf Bertram', he was secretary of *Der Funke* (the Star), an international Communist opposition group. In

Spain, he worked closely with Andreu Nin and conducted liaison between the POUM and foreign journalists and writers as well as writing virulent polemics against the militarization of the militias and their incorporation into the Republican Army. He had outraged the Soviets with his pamphlet *Spain 1936, Germany 1918*, published in December 1936, which compared the crushing of the revolutionary workers of Germany by the Freikorps in 1918 to Stalinist hostility to the CNT and the POUM in Spain. In consequence, he had been smeared by Soviet propaganda as 'the leader of a band of terrorists' and the liaison agent between the Gestapo and the POUM.[127] Kurt Landau managed to remain at liberty until 23 September 1937 when he was abducted by Soviet agents from his hiding place. Like Rein and Wolf, he was never seen again.[128]

It has been alleged that Stanislav Vaupshasov, a guerrilla-warfare expert, had constructed a crematorium in the basement of a building in Barcelona. He ran it with a Spanish NKVD agent, José Castelo Pacheco. Those targeted for liquidation were lured into the building, killed and their bodies eradicated in a single operation.[129] Whether this is what happened to Rein, Wolf, Landau and some of the other foreigners who disappeared is not known. Manuel Irujo ensured that Nin would be the last Spanish Trotskyist to be murdered, but he was unable to stop the persecution of foreign leftists by the Soviet security services.

While these clandestine abuses were still being perpetrated by the Russians, Negrín and his ministers pressed on with their efforts to regularize the policing and justice functions of the state. In late June 1937, the Special Court for Espionage and High Treason had been created. It reflected Negrín's view that the authority of the state should not be flouted. However, he was totally opposed to any arbitrary form of repression such as that practised in the Francoist zone.[130] With Negrín's approval, Irujo ensured that the Special Court was staffed by judges of impartiality and probity. Many rank-and-file POUM militants were in prison, infuriated at being held alongside fascists and saboteurs. Still not formally charged, they were awaiting trial by the new Special Court. Among them were several foreign anti-Stalinists. One of them, Kurt Landau's wife, Katia, had been arrested by a Brigada Especial operating on Russian orders. Their intention was to flush her husband out of hiding.

When Kurt disappeared, Katia demanded a judicial inquiry. By then, Ortega had been dismissed and Negrín's new Director General of Security, the Basque Socialist Paulino Gómez, tried unsuccessfully to ascertain Kurt's whereabouts. When the authorities were unable to clarify the fate of her husband, Katia led a hunger strike of five hundred inmates in the women's prison in Barcelona. In addition to the investigation by Gómez, an international commission of inquiry went to Catalonia in November 1937 to study conditions in Republican prisons and to look into the disappearance of Andreu Nin, Erwin Wolf, Mark Rein and Kurt Landau. Led by John McGovern (general secretary of the British Independent Labour Party – George Orwell's radical left group which had separated from the Labour Party) and the French pacifist Professor Felicien Challaye, it was permitted to interview Katia in the General Hospital where she was a patient as a result of her hunger strike.[131]

Irujo visited her in hospital and convinced her that the trials would be fair. She was sufficiently impressed to call off the strike. When Irujo sent prosecutors and judges into each prison with the appropriate paperwork, they were applauded by the prisoners who saw them as guarantors against Stalinist illegalities.[132] Everything about the role of the Spanish authorities in the Landau case, particularly the success of Katia's demand for an inquiry and of the hunger strike, contrasted with procedures in the rebel zone. Women in a rebel prison in 1938 could not have gone on hunger strike as there would have been hardly any food for them to reject and, even if they did, no one would have cared, certainly not a minister.

Shortly after taking possession of his ministry, Irujo had commissioned Mariano Gómez, the president of the Supreme Court, to draw up a draft decree to be applied to crimes perpetrated in the Republican zone since the beginning of the war, including all cases of extra-judicial deaths. It also included a revision of the release of common criminals amnestied by García Oliver.[133] On 30 July 1937, Boris Stepanov reported to Dimitrov that the 'fascist Irujo' had tried to arrest Carrillo because of Paracuellos and 'is organizing a system of searches of Communists, Socialists and anarchists, who brutally treated imprisoned fascists. In the name of the law, this minister of justice freed hundreds upon hundreds of arrested fascist agents or disguised fascists. Together with Zugazagoitia, Irujo does everything possible and impossible to save the Trotskyists and to sabotage trials against them. And he will do everything possible to acquit them.'[134] In fact, in the light of opposition from Communists and anarchists alike, Irujo's decree was never fully applied.

Irujo's approach was illustrated by the case of General José Asensio Torrado, who was arrested and charged with sabotage after the precipitate fall of Málaga in February 1937. He was brought to trial in October that year, just as the north was falling, and given a prison sentence. While in prison, Asensio was permitted to write and publish a book defending his position and to send autographed copies to members of the government. The book was openly sold in Barcelona bookshops. Largo Caballero claimed that the arrest and trial of Asensio was provoked by Communist pressure on Prieto. If so, it is testimony to Negrín's independence not only that Asensio was able to publish his book but also that, after appeal, the case was dismissed in July 1938.[135]

As the trend of the war worsened, however, the work of the Special Court expanded beyond Irujo's original intentions. Those found guilty of espionage or sabotage ran the risk of execution, yet far fewer death sentences were passed than were demanded by prosecutors and even fewer were implemented than actually passed. In Catalonia, whose courts were by far the most active, 166 such sentences were carried out between December 1937 and 11 August 1938, although only seven were shot thereafter. Unlike the military courts in the rebel zone, the Special Court often found the accused not guilty. Moreover, many who were found guilty had their sentences reduced or quashed on appeal. Those suspected of more minor fifth-column offences, of defeatist propaganda and black-market activities were interned either in prisons or in the work camps created by García Oliver. As the military situation got worse throughout 1938, deserters and draft-dodgers were imprisoned.[136]

With the fifth column getting more confidently aggressive, the SIM became more ruthless and several notably brutal individuals came to the fore. Ramón Torrecilla was one. Another individual who brought immense disrepute to SIM was Loreto Apellaniz Oden, a former post office official, who became a police inspector in Valencia after running the notorious Checa de Sorní. The Brigada Apellaniz spread terror with its activities in the area around Játiva. He later became a much feared chief of the SIM in Valencia from August 1937 to the end of the war. Accused of robbery, torture and murder, he was alleged to have taken instructions directly from Orlov. He was captured by the Francoists in March 1939 and shot.[137]

From April 1938, the SIM ran six work camps in Catalonia where the conditions were reputed to be harsh and the discipline fierce. There were cases of prisoners shot for trying to escape. Nonetheless, in stark contrast with the rebel zone, literacy and other educational classes were provided and prisoners were freed at the end of their sentences.[138] The largest prison camp in the Republican zone was at Albatera in the province of Alicante. With the mission of draining 40,000 hectares of saltmarshes and converting them to arable production, it had been opened in October 1937.[139] As food shortages became ever more prevalent in the Republican zone, conditions in all the camps also became progressively worse, although they never reached the levels of overcrowding, malnutrition and abuse that characterized the rebel camps.[140]

By March 1938, the Republic was in dire straits, demoralized and suffering badly from a drastic lack of food and armaments. Indeed, so bleak did the prospects seem that Negrín's friend and ally Prieto had come to believe, as did Azaña, that all was lost. Prieto advocated a negotiated peace to avoid the senseless loss of more lives. At tense cabinet meetings on 16 and 29 March, Prieto supported Azaña in proposing a request to the French government to mediate an end to the war. Negrín had reasserted his conviction that the war should go on precisely because he was aware of what would befall the defeated Republic at the hands of the vengeful Francoists. Appalled by the demoralizing impact of Prieto's words and determined that the Republic would continue to resist, Negrín removed Prieto from the Ministry of Defence on 5 April. Ten days later, the rebels reached the Mediterranean.

Resistance meant combat not only at the battle front but also in the rearguard. The determination to follow judicial procedure did not stop the war on spies and saboteurs. A significant success of the SIM took place that April in Barcelona with the discovery and arrest of several fifth-column networks. The British and French diplomatic staff appealed for mercy, but the cabinet voted seven to five for the execution, at the end of June, of ten fifth columnists. The British Chargé d'Affaires, John Leche, commented, 'I fear repercussions on the other side may be serious, and gave the government serious warning to this effect, but the president of the council and his supporters in the Cabinet are pitiless, and now seem to have as little consideration for their people in the hands of Franco as the latter has for his supporters here.' The ten prisoners were shot on the morning of 25 June.[141]

As the battle of the Ebro raged, the militarization of society was intensified. Control of the rearguard became ever more implacable against those suspected of sabotage or espionage. This provoked the severe discomfort of those who felt that the democratic values of the Republic were being compromised by wartime necessities. Thus, on 9 August 1938, there was a cabinet crisis when Negrín forced through approval for the execution of a further sixty-two fifth columnists the following day. Now Minister without Portfolio, Irujo complained of irregularities in the investigation carried out by the SIM. Negrín lost his temper and accused him of 'legalistic drivel'. In contrast to the rebel practice of rarely reporting executions, the full coverage by the Republican press of this decision led to a considerable scandal. President Azaña was mortified. The Francoists replied immediately by executing sixty-six people.[142] The next day, when Irujo said that the SIM had used torture, Negrín undertook to ensure that it ceased forthwith. Irujo resigned, albeit not over this issue. He did so, obliged by an agreement between the Generalitat and the Basque government in exile, in support of Jaume Aiguader's resignation in protest at further limits on the powers of the Generalitat.[143]

In the spring of 1938, the British had set up an exchange commission under Field Marshal Sir Philip Chetwode. Denys Cowan, a former vice-consul to Havana and both a Conservative and a Catholic, was the Commission's liaison officer with the Republican authorities. He arrived in Barcelona on 20 August and immediately met Álvarez del Vayo, Giral, Negrín and Azaña. Two days later, he reported that the Republican government was prepared to go to 'almost any lengths' to exchange all prisoners 'provided they could receive proper reciprocity from the other side'.[144] Indeed, so willing were the Republican ministers that Leche felt the need to protect them from themselves and suggested to the Chetwode Commission that, in view of the Francoists' 'previous intransigence and bad faith it would be better that first proposals should come from them'.[145]

Cowan approached Álvarez del Vayo to seek a suspension of executions, telling him that it would create a better atmosphere for the Republic. Del Vayo passed the proposal to Negrín and the cabinet agreed to suspend executions until 30 September, as the basis for negotiation of a general amnesty on both sides. There was to be no reciprocity from Burgos, merely a radio communiqué stating that Franco's system of justice was so pure that there was no reason to make a similar concession. Nevertheless, to facilitate Chetwode's work, Negrín undertook to maintain the suspension of executions until 11 October. Although the Burgos authorities still refused to reciprocate, Negrín told Cowan just before the 11 October deadline that he would extend the suspension to the end of the month and would authorize no further executions without lengthy prior notice to the Chetwode Commission.

One problem was that there were fewer than three hundred persons under sentence of death in the Republican zone but many thousands in rebel territory. Negrín suggested that all death sentences on both sides be commuted, but Burgos refused. Throughout the period after the Republican suspension of executions, the Francoists continued to implement death sentences. Cowan was inevitably worried that this would provoke Republican reprisals. He reminded Negrín that he had declared that his policy was one of 'clemency ad infinitum'. Negrín responded by undertaking to recommend to the cabinet that there be no reprisals.[146] The moratorium on executions was extended until the end of December. On Christmas Eve 1938, Negrín made a broadcast in which, referring to 'the norms of tolerance and civility that are the essence of our fundamental law', he appealed to Franco to 'stop unnecessary ferocity!' Pointing out that the Republic had suspended executions four months previously, he called on Franco to reciprocate.[147]

In Burgos, Chetwode met the Conde de Jordana, Franco's Foreign Minister, who claimed falsely that 'only those persons were executed by his side who had committed abominable felonies and had been convicted after fair trial in a court of law'. To support this fiction, Jordana produced the chief of Franco's military juridical corps, Lieutenant Colonel Lorenzo Martínez Fuset, who declared that the Burgos regime had executed nobody for their political opinions, or even for taking up arms, but 'only because they had committed crimes which in common law would have been worthy of death'. Accordingly, he said, Franco could not interfere and was prepared to risk Republican reprisals.[148] Chetwode wrote to the Foreign Secretary, Lord Halifax, in mid-November:

> I can hardly describe the horror that I have conceived of Spain since my interview with Franco three days ago. He is worse than the Reds and I could not stop him executing his unfortunate prisoners. And when I managed to get 140 out of the Cuban embassy in Madrid across the lines the other day, having got them across, Franco frankly refused to give anyone for them in spite of his promise. And when he did send people down nearly half of them were not the people he had promised to release but criminals who had been in jail, many of them, since before the war started.[149]

Yet again, Franco reneged on an exchange agreement after the Republican government had already made it possible for many of its prisoners to cross into insurgent territory.[150] Meanwhile, as the war drew to a close, Franco refused to exchange forty or fifty senior officers in return for his supporters in the embassies. According to Chetwode, Franco was gambling, successfully as it turned out, on the Republicans being able to prevent any harm coming to them.[151]

In a speech to the Standing Committee of the Cortes six months after coming to power, Negrín had referred to his own efforts, and those of

Zugazagoitia and Irujo, to maintain legal norms. Essentially, his speech was a hymn of praise to the re-establishment of normality by successive Republican governments.[152] Nevertheless, there had been considerable tension between Negrín and Irujo over the eventual trial of the POUM executive committee members and the investigation into the death of Nin.[153] When the trial took place in October 1938, Irujo was no longer Minister of Justice. The summary procedures of the Special Court saw it referred to jokily as the 'fotomatón' (photo machine). There were complaints that lawyers could not properly represent their clients, that police evidence was given without police witnesses being identified or that the only evidence presented was confessions secured by the SIM. The fact that such complaints could be published and heard constituted another dramatic contrast with the rebel zone.[154]

Irujo had been replaced as Minister of Justice by Negrín's friend the Republican Mariano Ansó. Nevertheless, Irujo remained in the cabinet as Minister without Portfolio, having ensured that any death penalties imposed by the Special Court would have to be ratified by the cabinet. The trial of the seven POUM executive committee members eventually proceeded in an atmosphere of great tension during the final stages of the decisive battle of the Ebro. Nevertheless, it was conducted, as Irujo had promised Katia Landau, with full judicial guarantees. Irujo was in Paris at the time but returned in order to appear in court, as Julián Zugazagoitia also did, as a witness. Their declarations were a crucial element in the prosecutor withdrawing the demand for the death penalty. Two of the accused were acquitted and five given prison sentences. All escaped from Spain at the end of the war.[155]

After defeat on the Ebro, with Franco's forces pouring into Catalonia, the bulk of prisoners held by the Republic were evacuated on 23 January 1939. Thousands crossed the border into France. At Pont de Molins, however, Negrín ordered the transfer of several of the more important ones to the central zone, where they could be used for prisoner exchanges. They included Bishop Anselmo Polanco, who had been captured when Republican forces took Teruel in January 1938. Polanco was first imprisoned in Valencia but was soon moved to Barcelona, where he remained for the rest of the war. He was kept in comfortable circumstances and permitted to carry out his spiritual exercises and to say Mass for his fellow prisoners. The government wanted to avoid the scandal of anything happening to Polanco, but Franco blocked Prieto's efforts via the Red Cross to exchange him for General Rojo's fourteen-year-old son.

As the remnants of the defeated Republican Army headed for an uncertain exile, harassed by rebel supporters within the civilian population, Negrín's orders for the safety of the prisoners were ignored. A truck containing thirty soldiers, under the command of Major Pedro Díaz, arrived at Pont de Molins and took charge of the prisoners, ostensibly in order to transfer them to the port of Roses. The convoy stopped near a ravine at a place called Can de Tretze and the prisoners were shot. Their corpses were soaked in petrol and ignited. The forty-two victims included most of the captured rebel top brass from Teruel: Bishop Polanco and his vicar general, the military commander Colonel Rey d'Harcourt, the head of the Civil Guard and the police chief. Twenty-one Italians and one German who had been taken prisoner at Guadalajara were among those killed. This senseless act of revenge became a symbol of red barbarism. Polanco was eventually beatified by the Vatican in 1995.[156]

After the fall of Catalonia in January 1939 and an exodus of hundreds of thousands of civilians, at the last meeting of the Cortes at Figueras Negrín presented a plan to bring the war to an end in return for Franco observing certain conditions, above all no reprisals.[157] The plan was put to British and French representatives, who replied that the Burgos government was not interested in humanitarian sentiments, peace-making or magnanimity and anyway declared that it punished only common crimes. The hypocrisy thereof was underlined by Negrín's comment that 'in a savage and pitiless civil war like ours, either everything is a common crime or nothing is'. Accordingly, Negrín offered himself as an expiatory victim, letting it be known that he would hand himself over if Franco would accept his symbolic execution in exchange for the lives of the mass of innocent Republican civilians. He did not reveal this offer to the majority of his own cabinet apart from Zugazagoitia.[158]

Negrín's offer was ignored by Franco. The government remained in Spain at the Castle at Figueras until the last units of the Republican army had crossed the French frontier on 9 February. The night before, one of the few colleagues who remained with Negrín, his friend Dr Rafael Méndez, Director General of Carabineros, said to Julio Álvarez del Vayo: 'I don't know what we're doing here. I fear that we will be woken up tonight by Carlist rifle-butts.' Negrín called Méndez aside and said: 'We are not leaving here until the last soldier has crossed the frontier.' Determined to see these Republicans safe from the reprisals of Franco, he watched for eighteen hours until General Rojo arrived to announce that all the Republican troops had crossed into France. Only then did Negrín move on to Toulouse to take a plane back to Alicante. Some ministers thought that he was mad, but as he himself explained: 'If I had not done that then, today I would die of shame.'[159] Back in Spain, he tried to reorganize the military forces of the centre to mount resistance either until a European war started or at least until a massive evacuation could ensure the lowest number of Republican deaths possible. On 16 February, he held a meeting of the military high command in Albacete. Having ascertained that the morale of the ordinary soldier seemed high, he was surprised when senior officers insisted that it was necessary to end the war as soon as possible. Asked why he did not sue for peace, he replied: 'because to beg for peace is to provoke a catastrophe'.[160]

As his friend the American journalist Louis Fischer wrote later, 'Negrín and del Vayo hoped, by holding out a little while longer, to extract a promise of mercy and clemency from Franco and to win time for the flight of those with a price on their heads.'[161] The idea that Franco might guarantee that there would be no reprisals against the defeated was a vain one given his Law of Political Responsibilities, announced on 9 February, by which supporters of the Republic were effectively guilty of the crime of military rebellion, which in Franco's topsy-turvy moral world meant all those who had not supported the military coup of 1936. Negrín was convinced that a fight to the finish was possible and, as a result, had been accused by Prieto of having provoked 'the gigantic hecatomb'. Prieto claimed that a negotiated peace had been possible and blamed the policy of resistance for Francoist vengeance. This revealed either culpable ignorance of what the rebels had been doing in captured territory or else a cynical desire to make political capital for use against Negrín in the coming Republican power struggle in exile. With some bitterness, Negrín reflected on those who just wanted the war to be over, 'without thinking about the millions of unfortunates who could not save themselves'.[162] In the event, his hopes of resistance to save more Republicans would be dashed as much by the coup of Colonel Segismundo Casado in March 1939 as by Franco himself. More in sadness than in anger, he told the Standing Committee of the Cortes that 'We could still have resisted and held on and that was our obligation. It was our obligation to remain to save those who are now going to end up murdered or in concentration camps.' As things had turned out, thanks to Casado, he said, the Republic ended 'in terms of catastrophe and shame'.[163]

12

Franco's Slow War
of Annihilation

In Galicia, Castile, León and Navarre, the areas of the north where there had been virtually no resistance to the coup, the elimination of leftists, trade unionists and supposed supporters of the Republic was immediate and thorough. In the meantime, Franco's African forces and the columns organized by army officers and landowners were bloodily purging the southern countryside. That still left the Basque Country, Santander, Asturias, much of Aragon and all the eastern seaboard in Republican hands. The military coup had failed in most of Guipúzcoa, and the Popular Front parties had created a Defence Junta in San Sebastián. It and the smaller juntas in other towns were largely dominated by the Socialists and Communists. Basque nationalists participated in the hope of maintaining public order. Their priority was to prevent executions of rightists being carried out by the Communists.[1]

The military coup in the profoundly conservative province of Álava was organized by Franco's lifelong friend Camilo Alonso Vega. Except in the north of the province, it met little resistance. A general strike was quickly suppressed and large numbers of armed Carlists and some Falangists gathered in the provincial capital, Gasteiz/Vitoria. Hundreds of CNT members were arrested, some Republicans and Basque nationalists taken as 'hostages' and municipal functionaries and schoolteachers removed from their jobs. On 22 July 1936, an aircraft from Vitoria bombed the village square of Otxandio in the south of Vizcaya, killing eighty-four people, of whom forty-five were children, and mutilating a further 113. In justification, the rebel command in Vitoria announced: 'our aircraft have struck a heavy blow against a group of rebels gathered in the rearguard at Otxandiano'. The repression in Álava was overseen by the military but largely carried out by Carlists and Falangists. Carlists from the neighbouring provinces of Navarre, Logroño and Burgos undertook executions in small towns on the basis of lists provided by the local right. The Church hierarchy replaced parish priests if they were sympathetic to Basque Nationalism and some were even imprisoned.

Often, where the priest was a Carlist, leftists and Basque nationalists could expect little mercy, although there were honourable exceptions. Elsewhere, the Basque clergy did much to save lives. There were 170 executions in Álava of people from the province and another thirty or so in neighbouring areas. More than half of all the killings were extra-judicial.[2]

While the rest of the Basque Country remained under Republican control, anti-clerical violence was relatively limited, significantly less than in many other provinces. Sixty-nine priests died at the hands of leftists, the majority in Vizcaya, while in Guipúzcoa, four clergy were killed. This was the consequence of the lesser influence of the CNT and the committed efforts of Basque nationalists, Republicans and moderate Socialists to prevent bloodshed. Churches were not attacked and religious practices continued without interruption. Nevertheless, right-wingers were in danger. In the industrial town of Rentería, near the provincial capital San Sebastián, the local Carlist leader was arrested and shot. The total number of deaths in Rentería was three. In Tolosa, in the south of the province, right-wingers involved in the military plot were shot and thirteen Carlists were taken to San Sebastián and executed. As in most places, revolutionary committees were established which arrested wealthy holidaymakers along with members of the local bourgeoisie. Moderate Socialists and Basque nationalists tried hard to ensure their safety. The starkest exception was the provincial capital, where 183 people were executed, more than half of the total of 343 people killed in Guipúzcoa while it was under Republican control.[3]

The most notorious incident concerned eighty-six rebel army officers and policemen arrested on 29 July and taken to the provincial assembly. The president of the Defence Junta of San Sebastián addressed a seething mob and announced that the prisoners would be properly tried with judicial guarantees. The War Councillor of the Junta, the local Communist leader Jesús Larrañaga, demanded summary 'justice', and Communist militants assaulted the assembly building and seized the leader of the coup, the Military Governor Colonel León Carrasco Amilibia. They were prevented from shooting him by the Catholic Manuel de Irujo, who was denounced by Larrañaga as a fascist. A second, successful attempt to seize Carrasco saw him murdered that night alongside a railway track. Larrañaga then issued the order for the execution of the prisoners in the provincial prison at Ondarreta beach. As well as the rebel officers, those named included policemen prominent in the repression of strikes in previous years. At dawn the next day, the prison was assaulted. Despite the efforts of Catholic Basque nationalists and Socialists, forty-one rebel army officers and twelve of their civilian supporters were shot. The assassins included militiamen from Galicia thirsting for revenge for the repression unleashed in A Coruña and Ferrol.[4]

Already on 23 July, Carlist troops from Navarre had entered the southern part of Guipúzcoa. Although they encountered no resistance, in Cegama and Segura they sacked the headquarters of Republican parties and the Batzoki (centres) of the PNV (Basque Nationalist Party), whose militants were detained and mistreated. Some were shot and many more subjected to arbitrary fines.[5] In early August, General Mola began a campaign to cut off the Basque Country from the French border. Thus under the Carlists Colonel José Solchaga Zala and Colonel Alfonso Beorleguí y Canet, commander of the Civil Guard in Navarre, large numbers of Requetés set off from Navarre towards Irún and San Sebastián. Beorleguí was a fearless but rather childlike giant. When his column was bombed, he simply opened his umbrella.[6] Irún and Fuenterrabía were being shelled from the sea and attacked daily by German and Italian bombers. They dropped rebel pamphlets threatening to repeat what had been done in Badajoz. San Sebastián was also heavily shelled from the sea and eight civilian right-wingers and five army officers were executed in reprisal.[7] Irún's poorly armed and untrained militia defenders fought bravely but were overwhelmed on 3 September. Thousands of panic-stricken refugees fled across the international bridge from Irún across the River Bidasoa to France. The last defenders, largely anarchists enraged by their lack of ammunition, shot some rightist prisoners in Fuenterrabía and set parts of Irún on fire.[8]

The Basque Country, Santander and Asturias were now cut off from France as well as from the rest of Republican Spain. Rebel forces occupied San Sebastián on Sunday 13 September, too late to prevent the shooting of several right-wing prisoners, including the Carlist ideologue Víctor Pradera and his son Javier. It was the second provincial capital captured from the Republic by rebel troops, and by the end of September virtually all of Guipúzcoa was in Mola's hands.[9] A substantial number of the city's 80,000 inhabitants had fled either towards Vizcaya or else by boat to France. Despite that exodus, the number of executions in San Sebastián would be the highest carried out by the rebels in any Basque city. Mass detentions began immediately, beginning with the wounded Republicans who could not be evacuated from the military hospital. Soon two prisons, at Ondarreta and Zapatari, the offices of the Falange, the San José hospice and the Kursaal cinema were all bursting at the seams with detainees. There is considerable doubt regarding the exact number of executions in the immediate aftermath of the rebel occupation. It is impossible to reach figures for the extra-judicial *paseos* carried out by Requetés or Falangists. Between 1936 and 1943, a total of 485 people were executed as a result of pseudo-trials mounted by the army. Forty-seven of these were women, almost all members of the CNT. Accordingly, if *paseos* are included, according to the exhaustive researches of Pedro Barruso Barés and of Mikel Aizpuru and his team, the total number for the first months is likely to be well over six hundred.[10]

The most notorious executions by the rebels in Guipúzcoa were those of thirteen Basque priests, which were carried out at the behest of the Carlists. In mid-September, Manuel Fal Conde, the Carlist leader, protested to General Cabanellas, the President of the Burgos Junta, about the 'feeble nature' of the military repression in Guipúzcoa compared with that in the south, complaining: 'this leniency is especially notable where the clergy is concerned. The military are afraid of falling foul of the Church.' He repeated his complaints to Cardinal Isidro Gomá, Archbishop of Toledo and Primate of All Spain, and to his deeply reactionary predecessor, the exiled Cardinal Pedro Segura. He urged the use of the rules of martial law to enable the execution of Basque nationalists, including priests. Since the usual practice of extra-judicial executions was inappropriate for priests, he suggested that problems with the Church be avoided by means of a simulacrum of military trial. For Fal Conde to assume that the Church hierarchy would give written approval for the execution of priests is an accurate reflection of the Carlist mentality.[11]

In total, the rebels murdered sixteen priests in the entire Basque region and imprisoned and tortured many more. One of those killed, Celestino Onaindía Zuloaga, was selected because his younger brother Alberto, a canon of the Cathedral of Valladolid, was a friend of the Basque President José Antonio Aguirre, for whom he was a kind of roving ambassador. Another, Father Joaquín Iturricastillo, was shot on 8 November, after being denounced as a dangerous nationalist for criticizing cheek-to-cheek waltzing as contrary to Basque customs. In general, the names of those to be executed appeared in blacklists brought by the Carlists from Pamplona. Executions of priests led to protests to Franco by Cardinal Gomá, who nonetheless justified them to the Vatican as the result of priests engaging in political activity. When Father Alberto Onaindía heard the news of the murder of his brother, he said: 'if this was how the army behaved with the Basque clergy, what would it be like for civilians!'[12]

On 20 January 1937, the Military Governor of Guipúzcoa, Alfonso Velarde, wrote to the Vicar General of Vitoria demanding 'energetic punishment' of Basque nationalist priests. In some twisted logic, he held them responsible for an assault on the prisons of Bilbao in reprisal for a bombing attack two weeks earlier. The letter was accompanied by a list of 189 priests divided into three groups, 'extremists, nationalists and sympathizers', and another list of ninety priests who were allegedly members of the Basque Nationalist Party. After some dispute between the military and ecclesiastical authorities, it was agreed that the clergy of Guipúzcoa should be purged, with twenty-four priests expelled from the province, thirty-one exiled from Spain, thirteen transferred and forty-four imprisoned.[13]

The visceral hatred underlying the repression carried out by the Carlists and the military in the Basque Country is reflected in the memoirs of Jean Pelletier, a French toy manufacturer who was travelling to Bilbao in order to donate gliders to children. On 15 October 1936, he left Bayonne on the trawler *Galerna*, which had been requisitioned by the Basque government to carry mail to Bilbao. It was seized, with the probable collusion of its captain, by six armed rebel trawlers from Pasajes, the port of San Sebastián. The trawlers were crewed by Basque fishermen but controlled by Carlists. The passengers were all imprisoned. Because he had served as a pilot in the French air force during the Great War and his luggage contained the toy gliders, Pelletier was assumed to be selling aircraft to the Basque government. He was severely tortured and nineteen of his fellow passengers, most of whom were entirely non-political, were shot on the night of 18 October. Among them were an eighteen-year-old girl, some old men, a sixteen-year-old boy and the writer 'Aitzol' (Father José Ariztimuño), who was first beaten and tortured. At the last minute Pelletier himself was withdrawn from the group about to board the bus to the cemetery at Hernani where they were to be shot. He was valuable as a hostage. Others were shot at a later date.

When the fall of Madrid was erroneously announced in Guipúzcoa in mid-November, numerous businessmen and shopkeepers were arrested and their money and property confiscated because they had not displayed the requisite patriotic fervour. Several priests were also detained and, to humiliate them, their cassocks were confiscated. Pelletier was kept imprisoned because the Francoist authorities were trying to persuade the French government to pay a high ransom, of the order of a shipload of foodstuffs. After six months, he was released when the Basque government agreed to exchange him for a German bomber pilot.[14]

While the attack on Madrid was the principal rebel preoccupation, the Basque front remained static until late March 1937. Even before the fall of San Sebastián, Mola had initiated secret negotiations with the Basque Nationalist Party. He hoped for a peaceful surrender of Vizcaya in return for a promise not to destroy Bilbao and a guarantee of no subsequent repression. Given what had happened after the captures of Irún and San Sebastián, the PNV leadership was not inclined to believe him. Alberto Onaindía was the principal PNV interlocutor with Mola's representative. He appealed for Mola not to bomb Bilbao on the grounds that to do so would provoke reprisals against the 2,500 imprisoned rightists in the city.[15] On 25 and 26 September 1936, major bombing raids on Bilbao caused dozens of deaths and mutilations of women and children.

As had been predicted, this provoked an outburst of rage from the starving population. Despite the intervention of the local forces of order, anarchists assaulted two prison ships and murdered sixty rightist detainees, including two priests. Greater efforts to prevent similar atrocities were made in the wake of the formation of a Basque government on 7 October, after the Republic had granted regional autonomy the day before. Sporadic bombing raids continued, but nothing had prepared the city for the scale of a sustained attack on 4 January 1937. In response, there was an even more ferocious incursion into the city's four prisons, when 224 right-wingers were killed, mostly Carlists, but also several priests and some Basque nationalists. The main culprits were anarchists, but UGT militiamen sent to put a stop to the killing joined in at one of the prisons. At considerable risk, members of the Basque government went to the prisons and managed to control the carnage before it reached all the prisoners.[16] In contrast with the repression in Madrid and even more so with that throughout the rebel zone, the Basque government accepted responsibility for the atrocities and permitted the families of the victims to hold public funerals. Proceedings to bring the culprits to justice were initiated but had not been completed when Bilbao fell. The remaining prisoners were well treated and released safe and sound before the rebel occupation of Vizcaya. The Tribunal Popular in Bilbao, which had begun to function in October 1936, held 457 trials and issued 156 death sentences, of which nineteen were carried out.[17]

By the end of March 1937, Mola had gathered nearly 40,000 troops for a final assault on Vizcaya. He opened his campaign with a widely publicized threat broadcast on radio and printed in thousands of leaflets dropped on the main towns: 'If your submission is not immediate, I will raze Vizcaya to the ground, beginning with the industries of war. I have ample means to do so.'[18] On 31 March, he arrived in Vitoria to put the final touches to the offensive that was to be launched the following day. To crush enemy morale, he ordered the execution of sixteen prisoners, including several popular local figures, one of whom was the Mayor. This led to protests from the local right.[19] This act of gratuitous violence was followed by a massive four-day artillery and aircraft bombardment of eastern Vizcaya, in which the small picturesque country town of Durango was destroyed: 127 civilians died during the bombing and a further 131 died shortly afterwards as a consequence of their wounds. Among the dead were fourteen nuns and two priests.[20] Four days after the bombing of Durango, Franco met the Italian Ambassador, Roberto Cantalupo, and explained the reasons for such savagery: 'Others might think that when my aircraft bomb red cities I am making a war like any other, but that is not so.' He declared ominously that 'in the cities and the countryside which I have already occupied but still not redeemed, we must carry out the necessarily slow task of redemption and pacification, without which the military occupation will be largely useless'. He went on: 'I am interested not in territory but in inhabitants. The reconquest of the territory is the means, the redemption of the inhabitants the end.'[21]

Increasingly, Mola relied on the air support of the German Condor Legion, whose Chief of Staff and later leader was Lieutenant Colonel Wolfram von Richthofen, who was to mastermind the German *Blitzkrieg* invasion of Poland. Durango saw the beginning of Richthofen's experiments in terror bombing designed to break the morale of the civilian population and also to destroy road communications where they passed through population centres. On the night of 25 April, presumably on Mola's instructions, the rebel radio at Salamanca broadcast the following warning to the Basque people: 'Franco is about to deliver a mighty blow against which all resistance is useless. Basques! Surrender now and your lives will be spared.'[22] The mighty blow was the obliteration of Guernica in one afternoon of relentless bomb attacks. On the day after the bombing, an eyewitness, Father Alberto Onaindía, wrote a passionate letter to Cardinal Gomá: 'I have just arrived from Bilbao with my soul destroyed after having witnessed the horrific crime that has been perpetrated against the peaceful town of Guernica.' He told the Cardinal of 'Three hours of terror and Dantesque scenes. Children and mothers collapsed on the roadside, mothers screaming in prayer, a population of believers murdered by criminals who have not the slightest claim to humanity. Señor Cardinal, for dignity, for the honour of the gospel, for Christ's infinite pity, such a horrendous, unprecedented, apocalyptic, Dantesque crime cannot be committed.' Describing scenes of the sick burned alive, the wounded buried in mounds of ashes, Onaindía appealed to Gomá to intercede, reminding him of international law and 'an eternal law, God's law, that forbids the killing and murder of the innocent. This was trampled underfoot on Monday in Guernica. Which cruel personage coldly planned this horrific crime of burning and killing an entire peaceful town?'

Onaindía's letter ended with a plea to Gomá to prevent the implementation of the rebel threats that Bilbao would be next. Gomá's dismissive reply with its repetition of Mola's threat was a spine-chilling affirmation of the Church's official support for Franco's war of annihilation: 'I regret, as anyone would, what is happening in Vizcaya. I have suffered for months, God is my witness. I particularly regret the destruction of your towns, where the purest faith and patriotism once dwelt. But it was not necessary to be a prophet to foresee what is now happening.' In an angry reference to Basque loyalty to the Madrid government, Gomá fulminated, 'Peoples pay for their pacts with evil and for their perverse wickedness in sticking to them.' He then casually endorsed Mola's threats: 'I take the liberty of replying to your anguished letter with a simple piece of advice. Bilbao must surrender, it has no other choice. It can do so with honour, as it could have done two months ago. Whichever side is responsible for the destruction of Guernica, it is a terrible warning for the great city.'[23]

When the insurgents reached the burned-out remnants of Guernica on 29 April, the Carlist Jaime del Burgo asked a lieutenant colonel of Mola's staff: 'was it necessary to do this?' The officer barked: 'This has to be done with all of Vizcaya and with all of Catalonia.'[24] Although the Caudillo's propaganda service went to great lengths to deny that Guernica had been bombed, there is no doubt that Mola and Franco shared the ultimate responsibility and were pleased with the outcome.[25]

Euskadi was subjected to another six weeks of bombing, against which the defenders had only sporadic air cover. However, dogged Basque resistance in the steep hills held up the rebel advance. As towns fell, the repression was fierce. In Amorebieta on 16 May, the Father

Superior of the Carmelite monastery tried to negotiate with the rebel attackers to limit the repression. He was shot as a Basque nationalist and robbed of a substantial sum of money. The rebels announced in the press that he had been murdered by the red separatists; at the same time they privately informed the Carmelite Order that he had been executed as a spy.[26]

The terror provoked by artillery and aerial bombardment and political divisions within the Republican ranks ensured the gradual collapse of Basque resistance. The death of Mola in an aircraft accident on 3 June made no difference. The Army of the North, under the command of General Fidel Dávila, continued its march on Bilbao. When the city fell on 19 June, 200,000 people were evacuated westwards into Santander, first on trawlers. Then, when the Francoists had taken the port of Bilbao, the refugees fled in cars, lorries, horse carts or on foot. They were bombed and strafed by the Condor Legion along the way.[27] Fifteen women were shot, their deaths announced as suicides.[28] Shops were looted and Falangists from Valladolid were given free rein. The subsequent repression was implemented on the pseudo-legal basis of the 'emergency summary courts martial' which had replaced the application of the edict of martial law since the conquest of Málaga in February. Nearly eight thousand were imprisoned in punishment for their nationalist ambitions, many of whom were forced into work battalions. When executions began, in December following the first trials, there would be several hundred victims of firing squads and at least thirty executed by garrotte vil.[29] Nevertheless, the repression in the Basque Country was, according to the senior military prosecutor Felipe Acedo Colunga, of notably less severity than elsewhere. Two possible reasons for this were the rebels' need for skilled labour to run Basque industries and the fact that the Catholic Church had less need to pursue a vengeful policy in a largely Catholic province.[30] There have been wildly different claims of the number of executions in Vizcaya but the most reliable estimate to date is 916.[31]

Despite these deaths, the Carlist press in Navarre demanded the extermination of Basque nationalists. The newly imposed Falangist Mayor, José María de Areilza, himself a Basque, gloated in victory, declaring on 8 July: 'The revolting, sinister, heinous nightmare called Euskadi has been smashed for ever ... You have fallen for ever, self-seeking, wretched, twisted Basque nationalist toady Aguirre, you who pretended to be someone during eleven months of crime and robbery while the poor Basque soldiers were being hunted down in the villages with lassos like four-legged animals, leaving their pelts scattered over the mountains of Vizcaya.'[32] Areilza was active in the repression, denouncing many individuals who were then imprisoned.

The Basque Army retreated into Santander and stabilized the front along a line that ran south from Ontón on the coast. The rebel forces consolidated in Bilbao and did not pursue the Basques, missing the chance of a rapid sweep through the north as Franco dithered over preparations for the next stage of his war effort. Finally, an advance into Santander was planned through western Vizcaya. However, before it could be launched, the Republic had struck with a diversionary attack at Brunete on the Madrid front. Franco suspended the offensive in the north and sent two Navarrese brigades plus the Condor Legion and the Italian Aviazione Legionaria to Madrid. Despite the relative strategic insignificance of Brunete, Franco deployed massive numerical and technological superiority in order to destroy large numbers of Republican troops. In a bloody war of attrition, Brunete cost more than 20,000 of the Republic's best troops and much valuable equipment, delaying the eventual collapse of Santander by only five weeks.[33]

The defence of Santander was always going to be difficult. The military coup in the province had failed because it was badly planned and poorly executed. Nevertheless, despite the existence of industrial areas such as Torrelavega, Polanco, Astillero, Reinosa and Castro Urdiales, the province and its capital city were deeply conservative.[34] The provincial capital had barely experienced the war. Restaurants and cafés remained open and there were few shortages.[35] However, while the province was under Republican control, nearly 1,300 right-wingers were killed. Considerable responsibility fell on Manuel Neila Martín, bizarrely appointed police chief by the Civil Governor, Juan Ruiz Olazarán. An ex-shop assistant and rifle-shooting champion, Neila became notorious for his cruelty and corruption. He delighted in torturing prisoners, stole from them and accumulated a significant fortune. On 27 December 1936, a sustained German bombing attack on the working-class Barrio del Rey killed forty-seven women, eleven children and nine men, seriously wounding fifty others. A vengeful crowd gathered in the harbour next to a ship, *Alfonso Pérez*, on which there were 980 right-wing prisoners. Hand grenades were thrown into the hold. Then, under the supervision of Ruiz Olazarán and Neila, summary trials were held on deck. Those identified as army officers, priests or militants of right-wing groups were shot. In total, 156 Falangists and other rightists were murdered that night.[36]

Tension was simmering in the city already when the arrival of almost 170,000 refugees caused massive social dislocation. Deep resentment was generated among the local population by dramatic food shortages and the sight of thousands of Basques, including wounded and mutilated soldiers, sleeping in the streets. A number of Basques were murdered by Neila's own *checa*. Revenge attacks were carried out by Basque soldiers. A group of nearly forty Basque priests were rescued from being murdered by anarchists only after payment of a large ransom. The defence of the province was undermined not only by these divisions but also by the fact that neither the Basque nor the Asturian forces felt commitment to the task. Moreover, the second-in-command of these disparate forces, Colonel Adolfo Prada Vaquero, told Azaña that 85 per cent of those from Santander were conscripts of dubious loyalty. On 14 August 1937, an army of 60,000 troops, amply supplied with Italian arms and equipment and backed by the Condor Legion and the Corpo di Truppe Volontarie, began to encircle Santander. In brilliant sunshine, massive air and artillery support as well as numerical superiority ensured a virtual walk-over as they easily brushed aside the disorganized Republican forces and the remnants of the Basque Army. Prada claimed that the lack of resistance was manifested in the fact that the rebel forces advanced faster than on manoeuvres. Santander itself fell on 26 August. The commander of the northern forces, General Mariano Gámir Ulibarri, delayed ordering an evacuation, and so relatively few were able to escape. The Mayor, who remained to surrender the city, was immediately shot.[37]

The consequent repression was notably harsher than in the Basque Country. One of the most striking executions was that of Colonel José Pérez y García Argüelles. He had been Military Governor of Santander on 18 July 1936. Because of his involvement in the coup, he had been condemned to death by a Tribunal Popular, but his sentence had been commuted to imprisonment. When the rebels arrived, he was arrested because his indecision between 18 and 20 July was regarded as contributing to the failure of the coup. He was tried and sentenced to death on 25 October 1937 and executed on 18 November. More than 13,000 people were tried, of whom 1,267 were sentenced to death. A further 739 were murdered in extra-judicial *paseos* and at least 389 died of maltreatment in prison.[38]

In the meantime, the Basque forces, having dropped out of the fight altogether, had gathered at Santoña to the east of Santander. They believed that they would be evacuated to France on the basis of the so-called 'Pact of Santoña' negotiated with the Italians by the Basque

Nationalist Party. This belief was based on an offer made on 23 July by Franco's brother, Nicolás, of no reprisals and facilities for the evacuation of prominent figures if the Basques surrendered. After long delays, during which they might have been able to organize an earlier evacuation, the Basques finally agreed to surrender to the Italians at Santoña on 26 August. In accordance with the agreement made, 473 Basque political and military leaders embarked on two British ships, the SS *Seven Seas Spray* and the SS *Bobie*, under Italian protection. The next day, rebel warships blockaded the port on Franco's orders and Dávila told the Italians to disembark the refugees. They refused and held the prisoners for four days until, on 31 August, Franco personally ordered the Italians to hand them over.[39] After assurances that the surrender conditions would be respected, the Italians relinquished the captives on 4 September. To their horror, summary trials began at once and hundreds of death sentences were passed. Among the victims were the entire General Staff of the Basque Army. The prisoners tried in Santoña were taken to Bilbao for execution in December 1937.[40]

In addition to the executions, a significant element of the repression in the Basque Country was constituted by fines and confiscations. Many doctors, lawyers, architects and engineers had their licences to practise withdrawn. As elsewhere, schoolteachers were a prime target. The Basque President or Lehendakari, José Antonio Aguirre, was fined 20 million pesetas and his property seized. Many businesses and properties were handed over to rebel supporters and bank deposits confiscated. In 1939, the rebels imposed a fine of 100 million pesetas on the shipping magnate Sir Ramón de la Sota, who had died three years earlier. His family was stripped of all of his businesses and his entire property, including forty ships that had been used in the evacuation of Bilbao. A typical case was that of the Abando family. The seventy-seven-year-old businessman Julián de Abando y Oxinaga was arrested, although seriously ill, and hit with a fine of over 1 million pesetas. Two of his sons were arrested with him and condemned to long prison sentences. One of them, the distinguished gynaecologist Dr Juan Blas de Abando y Urrexola, had his clinic confiscated.[41]

Another element of the repression was directed against the Basque language. In his notorious speech when he took over as Mayor of Bilbao, José María de Areilza declared: 'the great shame of the separatist clergy is finished for ever'. The close relationship between the Basque clergy and the people was targeted by the prohibition of the use of Basque language Euskera in all religious activities, whether collective prayer, sermons or the teaching of the catechism. Instructions from the ecclesiastical authorities permitting the use of Euskera were overruled by General Severino Martínez Anido, Franco's head of public order. Priests who spoke to their Euskera-speaking flocks in their native languages were given huge fines.[42]

Among the prisoners taken at Santoña were eighty-one priests from the Corps of Chaplains of the Basque Army, a unique body among the Republican forces, dedicated to providing Mass and the sacraments at the front. Three were condemned to death (although their sentences were later commuted). The others were given sentences ranging from six to thirty years in prison. One of these priests, Victoriano Gondra y Muruaga, was known as 'Aita Patxi' (Father Frank), having taken the name Francisco de la Pasión on joining the Passionist Order. Imprisoned, along with the other Gudaris (Basque soldiers), in the concentration camp at San Pedro de Cardeña near Burgos, he was sentenced with them to forced labour. Learning that an Asturian Communist sentenced to death for trying to escape was married with five children, Aita Patxi offered himself to be shot instead. He was told mendaciously that his request had been accepted and the Asturian pardoned, and subjected to a pretence of execution by firing squad. He learned the next day that the Asturian had been shot at dawn.[43]

In Asturias, the legacy of the repression after October 1934 ensured that the struggle would be extremely bitter. On 18 July 1936, the coup had failed except for the two rebel outposts of the Simancas barracks in Gijón and the city of Oviedo which was taken as a result of the duplicity of Colonel Antonio Aranda. Declaring his loyalty to the Republic, he convinced the local authorities that he approved of arms being distributed to the workers. However, claiming not to have enough weapons and ammunition in Oviedo for them all, he assured the local left-wing forces that he had arranged for supplies in León. On Sunday 19 July, about 3,500 unarmed miners and steelworkers confidently left the city for León, some by train, others in a convoy of trucks. About three hundred were given obsolete weapons with inappropriate ammunition and the entire group continued south, reaching Benavente in Zamora. Meanwhile in Oviedo, Aranda declared for the rebels and other workers awaiting arms were massacred. In Benavente, on 20 July, news reached the militia expedition of Aranda's treachery and they decided to return to Oviedo. Those who had come by train had to return via Ponferrada, a town already in the hands of the Civil Guard. The poorly armed militia fought bravely there but suffered many casualties and retreated back to Asturias, many on foot. By 21 July, the miners travelling by truck from Benavente had returned and besieged Oviedo. The Asturian Popular Front Committee established its headquarters in Sama de Langreo under the presidency of Belarmino Tomás.[44]

In Gijón, the coup had failed in large part because of the indecision of the commander of the Simancas barracks, Colonel Antonio Pinilla Barceló. Besieged by the anarchists who dominated the local committee, Pinilla had overseen by radio the fierce bombardment of the city by the rebel battlecruiser *Almirante Cervera*. On 14 August alone, air attacks and naval artillery made direct hits on the railway station and a hospital leaving fifty-four dead and seventy-eight seriously wounded. Under the umbrella of the consequent popular outrage, a group of FAI militants, accompanied by some Communists, headed to the Church of San José where two hundred right-wing prisoners were being held. They selected the most prominent and murdered them. A second group of militiamen arrived in the evening and took away another batch, including twenty-six priests and religious. Other individuals were shot in the course of the night. In total, 106 right-wing prisoners were killed.[45] The barracks was stormed from 19 to 21 August by the local militia. Facing defeat, Pinilla rejected offers that the lives of the defenders would be respected if he surrendered and requested that the rebel warship fire on the building. Assuming the message to be a trick, the commander of the *Almirante Cervera* did not fire. The barracks was overrun and Pinilla and his men were executed in the ruins.[46]

The siege of Oviedo lasted another two months. Inside the city, Aranda waged war on what he considered to be the internal enemy. He himself claimed that Republican supporters made up half of the city and one of his supporters put the figure at 75 per cent of the population.[47] Aranda also told Webb Miller of the United Press that seven hundred prisoners were held as hostages.[48] Republican sources put the figure at more than one thousand, including the wives of working-class leaders and parliamentary deputies for Asturias. Of many, nothing was ever heard again. Shortly after Aranda had taken over the city, he launched an attack on the loyal Santa Clara barracks of the Assault Guards. In the aftermath, twenty-five militiamen and two Assault Guards were shot. It has been suggested that the repression was limited by the rebels' fears of reprisals if the city fell to the besieging miners. Certainly, Aranda himself kept at some distance from the repression, but an atmosphere of terror was nevertheless maintained by his Delegate for Public Order, Mayor Gerardo Caballero, who had been prominent in the repression after

October 1934. Under his orders, Falangist squads hunted down leftists at night. Corpses were often found in the streets and more than sixty unidentified bodies, including twelve women, were deposited in local cemeteries. During the siege, prisoners were used as human shields.[49]

There could be little doubt that the relative restraint of the repression would change if the relief column from Galicia were to liberate the city. The column had nearly 19,000 men, having been reinforced at the end of September with a *bandera* of the Legion (five hundred men) and eight *tabores* of Regulares (two thousand men). Along the way, any militiamen captured were shot. Moreover, as the column had taken small towns along the way, there were numerous executions without trial of school-teachers, including women, and others assumed to be Republican supporters. After the columns had moved on, squads of Falangists began the bloody task of what was euphemistically called 'cleansing'. One group which operated in small towns like Luarca, Boal, Castropol and Navia murdered many including several young women. The gang was notori-ous for the 'cangrejo' (crab), the green truck in which they transported their victims to the remote areas where they were murdered. In addition to many extra-judicial murders, many people were subjected to the briefest summary trials in which they were sentenced to death for 'mili-tary rebellion'.[50]

The fate of the hundreds of hostages in the Asturian capital was sealed as a result of the arrival, on 17 October 1936, of the Galician column just as Oviedo, without food, water or electricity, was about to fall to the besieging miners. The tenor of the rebel advance was revealed in the joyous comment next day in *ABC* of Seville: 'yesterday the victorious Nationalist columns entered Oviedo after inflicting a real butchery on the red miners who were besieging it'.[51] Three hundred and seventy pris-oners were executed without trial, many while allegedly being trans-ported to prisons further to the west. Two expeditions, of forty-five prisoners in late October and another of forty-six in December, never reached their destination. At the same time, there was the pantomime of military trials. After the shortest procedures, many were immediately executed, among them the Assault Guards who had remained loyal to the Republic, the Civil Governor, the director of the miners' orphanage, the miners' leader and PSOE deputy Graciano Antuña and the rector of the University, Leopoldo Alas Argüelles. The latter was the son of the novelist Leopoldo Alas 'Clarín' whose novel *La Regenta* was a devastating dissection of the provincialism and hypocrisy of Oviedo's high society. A distinguished lawyer, the novelist's son had been deputy Secretary of

Education and a parliamentary deputy in the Constituent Cortes. After a farcical trial, Leopoldo Alas was shot on 20 February 1937. It was believed in the city that he was executed less for his moderate politics than to satisfy the local bourgeoisie's desire for revenge on his father.[52]

After the arrival of the relief column, Republican forces tried to recapture Oviedo. Although remaining dominant in the south and east of the province, their efforts were in vain. Once Santander had fallen, Asturias was in Franco's sights and, to delay his expected onslaught, General Vicente Rojo now launched a ferocious assault aimed at capturing Zaragoza. Republican forces attacked the small town of Belchite. This time Franco did not take the bait as he had at Brunete but began a great three-pronged assault on a now encircled Asturias on 2 September 1937. Under the overall command of General Dávila and led in the field by Generals Antonio Aranda and José Solchaga, troops quickly moved through the rain-swept mountains. Anxious to finish the campaign before the winter, Franco imbued his staff with a greater urgency than was normally the case. Their efforts were greatly facilitated by the fact that the Republicans had virtually no air cover. Although Asturias was geographically a strong defensive redoubt, it was tightly blockaded by sea and remorselessly bombarded from the air. The defenders' morale was shattered as the Germans perfected their ground-attack techniques with forays along the mountain valleys, using a combination of incendiary bombs and gasoline to create an early form of napalm.[53]

After the fall of Santander, the Asturians set up an independent government, sacked the Republican commander, General Gamir, and made Colonel Prada commander of military forces. In Gijón, the repression of the local right had been profound and often gratuitously vindictive, with small businesses and shops confiscated and children and adolescents imprisoned because their parents had been denounced as fascists. Prisoners were transferred to a prison ship docked in the port of El Musel to the west of Gijón. As the war effort disintegrated, the *sacas* increased. Many prisoners were shot, notably near Oviedo and, as the rebels advanced from Santander, in the east of the region, at Cangas de Onís.[54] In the course of the war in Asturias, around two thousand rightist prisoners were murdered. The rebels' revenge when Asturias was occupied saw them kill nearly six thousand Republicans.[55]

When the front collapsed on 21 October, people fled in cars, buses, trucks and on foot to El Musel. As many as could squeezed on to fishing boats and headed for France. Some trawlers got through but others were intercepted by the rebel fleet and forced to sail to Galicia, where the passengers were herded into concentration camps. Groups of Falangists came to seek victims and many were taken back to Gijón or Oviedo for trial. Some were murdered on the spot. Others were forced to enlist in work battalions. Military trials were brief, with the accused given little or no chance to speak.[56]

Back in Gijón, Father Alejandro Martínez was deeply shocked by the ferocity of the repression, which he described as of an 'inopportune rigour, as though a certain species of human being had to be liquidated … The troops sacked and looted Gijón as though it were a foreign city.' The Regulares and Legionarios had the usual licence to pillage and rape and, given the lingering hatred from 1934, did so with especial vehemence. The fifth columnists who had been in hiding during the period of Republican dominance came out hungry for revenge. Colonel José Franco Mussió, a rebel sympathizer, had remained in Asturias in the hope of saving right-wing prisoners and had stayed behind in Gijón rather than flee to the Republican zone. He was tried immediately along with seven other Republican officers and shot on 14 November 1937. At least twenty schoolteachers were shot and many more were imprisoned. In the mining valleys, villagers were subjected to assassinations and beatings. Haystacks were burned at farms to force out those hiding. *Paseos* and the sexual abuse and even mutilation of women were frequent.[57] Of the many atrocities committed, one of the most notorious took place at the Monastery of Valdediós near Villaviciosa. The building had been requisitioned when the Psychiatric Hospital of Oviedo was evacuated there in October 1936. On 27 October 1937, troops of the Brigadas de Navarra arrived. Without motive, they shot six men and eleven women of the staff. They were buried in a large unmarked grave, one of sixty *fosas* in Asturias.[58]

Institutionalized violence was most acute in the mining valleys. In Pola de Lena, more than two hundred people were assassinated, many being forced to dig their own graves. Afterwards, their assassins held a drink-fuelled celebration. When the rebels entered Sama de Langreo, wounded militiamen were loaded on to trucks, taken to the trenches used during the siege of Oviedo, shot and buried there. In the small mining town of San Martín del Rey Aurelio, in the Turón Valley, east of Langreo, at least 261 people were murdered. Near Turón itself, more than two hundred corpses were brought in trucks to a mine shaft known as the Pozo del Rincón.[59] Their unions crushed, those not executed or imprisoned were then forced into slave labour in the mines in penal battalions. Some went into hiding or else became involved in a sporadic guerrilla war often linking up with others on the run from Galicia. For years, the Civil Guard and Falangist patrols hunted them down.

One guerrillero who was caught was Pascual López from Sobrado dos Monxes in A Coruña, whose wife and six children had had no news of him since he fled at the beginning of the war. In June 1939, a man who had served in Franco's forces returned to the village and said that he had seen Pascual in a concentration camp near Oviedo. Pascual's wife packed some food and clothes and sent her thirteen-year-old son Pascualín to find him. It took him two weeks to walk to Oviedo and another to locate the correct camp among those in the area. Although his father told him to go home, Pascualín stayed, stealing food during the day and sneaking into the camp at night to sleep, in the open air, alongside Pascual. In early October, a group of Falangists arrived and selected the Galician prisoners to take for execution in Gijón. The Falangists were on horseback, the prisoners walking. Against his father's orders, Pascualín followed for twelve days, keeping out of sight. Along the way, the oldest who were too weak to keep up were murdered. When they reached El Musel, the remaining prisoners were lined up and shot on a row of rocks used as a sea defence. The youngest of the Falangists, seeing that several were still alive, asked why they had been ordered to aim at the prisoners' legs. Their veteran leader, calling him a novice, explained: 'Because that way they take longer to bleed to death.' Pascual was not dead and his son managed to pull him out of the water and get him into the hills where a bullet was prised out of his leg with a knife. When he had recovered, he sent Pascualín home to Galicia while he rejoined the guerrillas and was killed shortly afterwards.[60]

In Oviedo, as well as the many extra-judicial murders carried out by Falangists between November 1937 and April 1938, a total of 742 people were sentenced to death. In May 1938 alone, 654 people were tried and 260 sentenced to death. When the military courts left Asturias in January 1939 in order to begin the repression in Catalonia, the senior judge praised the police in Oviedo for the speed with which death sentences had been carried out. Altogether, 1,339 people were sentenced to death and all were shot except for fifteen who were executed by garrotte vil. In order to be buried in the cemetery, the prisoner was obliged to confess before a priest and be reconciled with the Church. Only two hundred made their confessions, but a further 102 were able to be buried when their families paid a special fee. In addition to those executed after a trial, another 257 people died in prison as a result of ill-treatment or malnutrition. Approximately one-third of those killed were miners. Many women suffered rape, beatings to reveal the whereabouts of their menfolk, head shaving and imprisonment. At least nine were executed.[61]

The repression was most acute in Gijón since the Republican administration, union and political leaders and the military command had been there. The prison of El Coto which had a capacity for two hundred prisoners soon had nearly 2,500. Nine hundred and three prisoners were tried and shot in the twelve months starting 9 November 1937. There were many other unrecorded cases of prisoners being taken out and shot by groups of Falangists. Beatings and torture were common. The bullring, an old glass factory and a cotton mill were used as improvised prisons. All those who had had any form of political or trade union responsibility were to be eliminated. The military prosecutor in Gijón demanded so many death sentences in such a short time that he was called 'machine-gun'. Ninety-eight were executed in the last two months of 1937 and 849 in 1938. In addition, there were the extra-judicial murders. The director of the cemetery of El Sucu (Ceares) claimed that on many days between seventy and eighty corpses were dumped there. A recently inaugurated monument at El Sucu carries the names of 1,882 men and fifty-two women buried in the common grave between 21 October 1937 and 1951. They include the more than 1,245 from El Coto shot after court martial, the eighty-four who died there from beatings, torture or illness caused by malnutrition, overcrowding and insanitary conditions, others who died in the glass factory and those murdered whose names are known. Seventy per cent of those executed were workers.[62]

On 1 October 1937, after the conquest of the north, all over Spain there was a celebration of the anniversary of Franco's elevation to the headship of state, now consecrated as 'el Día del Caudillo'. In San Leonardo in Soria, Yagüe, dressed in the blue shirt of the Falange, made a speech that provoked wild applause when he spoke of the working class in the following terms: 'They are not bad. The really evil ones are their leaders who deceive them with gilded promises. They are the ones that we must attack until we have entirely exterminated them.' He then described the Falangist new order and prompted laughter and applause when he declared:

> and for those of you who resist, you know what will happen, prison or the firing squad, either will do. We have decided to redeem you and we will redeem you whether you want to be redeemed or not. Do we need you for anything? No, there will never again be any elections, so why

would we need your vote? The first thing to do is to redeem the enemy. We are going to impose our civilization on them and if they don't accept it willingly, we will impose it by force, defeating them as we defeated the Moors when they didn't want our roads, our doctors, and our vaccinations, in a word, our civilization.[63]

Yagüe's speech was a reminder, if one was needed, of what would happen if any more territory fell into rebel hands. Assuming that Franco's next move would be an attack on Madrid, the Republican high command decided on a pre-emptive attack against Teruel, capital of the bleakest of the Aragonese provinces. The insurgent lines there were weakly held and the city was already virtually surrounded by Republican forces. In freezing weather, with the lowest temperatures of the century, savage house-to-house fighting saw the Republicans capture the rebel garrison on 8 January 1938. Enjoying massive material superiority, Franco made a fierce counter-attack. After a debilitating defence, the Republicans had to retreat on 21 February, with Teruel about to be encircled. Franco now launched a huge eastwards offensive at the beginning of March. By the middle of April, his forces had reached the Mediterranean, splitting the Republican zone in two, and occupying all of Aragon.

In fact, much of the region had long been in rebel hands and had suffered a brutal repression. The military coup was successful in most of the province of Zaragoza apart from the salient between Huesca and Teruel. Before the March rebel offensive conquered that remnant, the repression in the province had already seen intense violence.[64] In the first two weeks of July 1936, around eighty Republican officials and the leaders of trade unions and political parties had been arrested and executed. Thereafter, there was a wave of terror with 730 executions in August alone. Nocturnal *paseos* by 'vigilance patrols' of Falangists and Carlists aided the police in this purge of 'undesirables'. The scale of killing was not diminished by the establishment of military courts from September, and 2,578 were shot before 1936 was out. The ferocity of the repression was part of the prior plan of extermination, but was intensified by the fears provoked by the anarchist columns pressing on the east of the province. However, the readiness of civilians to participate in the killing in Zaragoza, as elsewhere, was motivated by sheer bloodlust, by the desire to hide a left-wing past and seek favour with the new regime, by envy or by long-festering resentment.[65]

The proximity of the anarchist columns could be an explanation for a brutal mass execution that took place in Zaragoza at the beginning of

October. In late August, the rebel radio in Zaragoza had announced that recruiting had started for a new unit of the Foreign Legion named after General Sanjurjo. In Navarre, Civil Guard posts received orders to oblige men suspected of left-wing sympathies to appear at the recruiting offices. Summoned to the barracks, they were given the stark choice 'the Legion or the ditch'. In La Rioja, similar calls were made in the local press but, to meet the numbers required, young men were also given a choice between being shot or joining the Sanjurjo unit. Between 2 and 10 September, several hundred young men were transported to Zaragoza for training. On 27 September, they were sworn in and on 1 October sent to the front at Almudévar south of Huesca. However, before they went into action against the anarchist columns from Catalonia, they were ordered to return to Zaragoza, where they were disarmed because the military authorities suspected that many of them planned to desert. Between 2 and 10 October, they were taken in small groups to a field behind the Military Academy in Zaragoza and shot. The bodies were conveyed to the Torrero cemetery and buried in a huge common grave. Two hundred and eighteen of those murdered were from Navarre out of a total of more than three hundred.[66]

Personal hatreds and resentments were much more instrumental in the events in the tiny and remote village of Uncastillo in the far north of the province of Zaragoza, midway between Pamplona and Huesca. There an act of revenge for the events of October 1934 saw 180 people killed. As in other areas of rural Aragon under rebel control, groups of Falangists and Requetés, together with the Civil Guard, entered houses, took goods and detained members of left-wing organizations and unions, as well as their friends and family. These arrests were made on the basis of captured documentation, mere rumours or denunciations from local right-wingers that were often motivated by purely personal resentments deriving from economic or sexual conflicts. The arrests of men, women and adolescents were followed by savage beatings and, often, death. For the 'crime' of having embroidered a Republican flag, two young women, Rosario Malón Pueyo aged twenty-four and Lourdes Malón Pueyo aged twenty, were raped and then murdered, and their corpses burned. That was done away from the village, but many executions were public with the entire village forced to watch.

In many cases, the arrests and assassinations were carried out on the recommendation of the parish priest. In the case of a young woman of nineteen who was pregnant with twins, the village doctor argued that she should be spared, and the Civil Guard accepted his reasoning. With reluctance, the local Falange also agreed, but a priest who was present exclaimed, 'with the animal dead, there is no more rabies', and she was shot.[67] The most prominent victim was the Mayor, Antonio Plano Aznárez. It will be recalled that he was hated by the landowners of the area for his success in improving the working conditions of the day-labourers. He was also held responsible, unjustly, for the revolutionary events of 5–6 October 1935. At first held in Zaragoza, at the beginning of October 1936, Antonio Plano was brought to Uncastillo and imprisoned with his wife Benita and his children Antonio and María in the Civil Guard barracks.

The plan was for him to be assassinated on the second anniversary of the events of October 1934. It was an act not only of revenge for the past but also a warning for the future. Plano represented in the area everything that the Republic offered in terms of social justice and education. He was not only killed but made the object of the most brutal humiliation both before and after his death. As a result of his beatings, he was brought out of the Civil Guard barracks covered in blood. The Civil Guard and Falangists obliged the remaining villagers to come to the square to watch. Plano had been forced to drink a bottle of castor oil. Bloodied and besmirched, he had to be carried on a wooden board. In front of the church, he was shot, to the delight and applause of the right-wingers present. His corpse was then kicked and abused before it was mutilated by one of the Falangists with an axe. A year after his death, he was fined the colossal sum of 25,000 pesetas and his wife a further 1,000. In order for these fines to be paid, the family home and contents were confiscated. There were many similar cases which provided an excuse for the theft of the property of those who had been assassinated. Altogether, 140 leftists were murdered in Uncastillo. Of the 110 who had been tried for the events of 1934, many had fled, but of those who remained, forty-four were executed.[68]

In Teruel in July 1936, the least populated of Spanish provinces, the western part fell immediately to a tiny rebel garrison. Despite the fact that there had been little social conflict in the area, detentions began immediately. The first victims were, as elsewhere, trade union and Republican political leaders and officials. A second wave of violence began in March 1938, with the entry of rebel troops into towns and villages that had been under Republican control. One of the worst incidents in this second wave took place in the small town of Calanda, where around fifty people were killed, including a pregnant woman beaten to death, and numerous others raped. At the end of the war, those who had fled from the province of Teruel when it had been taken by the Francoists faced the choice of either going into exile or returning home. Hoping that the fact that they were guilty of no crimes meant that they would face no problems, many returned home. In Calanda, as they descended from a bus, they were set upon. Tortures, beatings, murders and sexual attacks were organized by the local chief of the Falange and the secretary of the town council. So scandalous were these events that the Civil Governor of the province reported them to the military authorities. In consequence, the perpetrators were tried and imprisoned for eight years.[69] In none of these explosions of repression were all the deaths formally registered. Nevertheless, the names are known of 1,030 people who were executed in Teruel, 889 in the course of the war and 141 afterwards. To these have to be added a further 258 who were taken to Zaragoza for execution. There were many more whose names were not recorded in the civil register or buried in cemeteries. It was not in the interests of their assassins for too much to be known and subsequently the Francoist authorities made a concerted effort to hide the magnitude of the violence in Teruel.[70]

The scale of the repression in Teruel reflects a combination of the basic exterminatory plan of the insurgents and consciousness that the province was vulnerable to Republican attack. Among the first to be arrested from 20 July 1936 were the Mayor, the secretary of the provincial branch of the Socialist Party and the directors of the local secondary school and of the teachers' training college. The wives and families of men who had fled to the Republican zone were detained. For instance, the wife and seventeen-year-old daughter of a Socialist town councillor were arrested and eventually shot. All the detainees were herded into the local seminary where they were kept in appalling conditions of acute overcrowding before being killed. Until 13 August, when the executions began, men and women were used as forced labour, mending roads. They were taken out at dawn in a truck known variously as the 'dawn truck', the 'death truck' or the 'one-way truck'.[71]

One of their destinations was the village of Concud, about two and a half miles from the provincial capital. Here, into a pit six feet wide and 250 feet deep, known as Los Pozos de Caudé, were hurled the hundreds of bodies of men and women, including adolescent boys and girls. Few of them were political militants. Their crime was simply to be considered critical of the military coup, to be related to someone who had fled, to have had a radio or to have read liberal newspapers before the war. Throughout the years of the dictatorship fear prevented anyone from

even going near the pit, although occasionally at night bunches of flowers would be left near by. In 1959, without the permission of the relatives
of those murdered, a lorryload of human remains was taken to Franco's
mausoleum at the Valle de los Caídos. Once the Socialists achieved
power in 1982, people began openly to leave floral tributes. Then in 1983
a local farmer came forward and said that he had kept a notebook with
the numbers of shootings that he heard each night throughout the
Spanish Civil War. They totalled 1,005. Among the unregistered deaths
were Republican prisoners as well as people brought from small villages.
In 2005, the works for the laying of a major gas pipe unearthed remains
which led to the excavation of fifteen bodies. Caudé was only one of
several places in the province where bodies were dumped by the
executioners.[72]

At least two priests were executed by the rebel military authorities in
the province of Teruel. José Julve Hernández was the parish priest of
Torralba de los Sisones. Father Julve was arrested on 25 July 1936, taken
to the prison in Teruel and shot, because one of his relatives was a mayor
of the Popular Front. The second case was that of Francisco Jaime-
Cantín, a Carlist and parish priest of Calamocha. Despite such credentials, in August 1936, some Falangists and Civil Guards arrested his
brother, Castro Pedro, and he was shot on 27 September. When he found
out, Father Jaime-Cantín went to seek information at the Civil Guard
barracks, was himself arrested, taken to Teruel and shot on 12 December.
In these two cases, there was an element of personal revenge. Before the
war, Castro Pedro, a landowner, had been involved in a dispute with the
local branch of the FNTT over an attempt to evict tenants. He lost in the
subsequent court case. When the military coup took place, the judge in
the case was falsely denounced by the two brothers as a dangerous red
and shot on 12 September. However, the judge had a brother who was a
rebel officer. He went to Calamocha and managed to ascertain that the
landowner and the priest had fabricated evidence against the judge.
Thus he had them both executed.[73]

It is difficult to believe that priests could be executed without the tacit
approval of Monsignor Anselmo Polanco, the Bishop of Teruel-
Albarracín, a pious, austere and conservative cleric given to distributing
alms to the poor. Before the war began, he had aligned himself with the
right. Before the elections of February 1936, he wrote a circular to be
read out by all parish priests in which he stated that the struggle was
between 'the defenders of religion, property and the family' and 'the
proclaimers of impiety, Marxism and free love', between 'the two enemy

cities of which St Augustine speaks, the opposed forces of good and evil'.[74] It was not a message likely to endear him to the wretched of the earth.

When the Civil War started, Polanco was outspoken in support of the rebels. On 31 July 1936, in his pastoral letter, he referred to 'the rising of our glorious National Army to save Spain'. On 14 March 1937, denouncing anti-clerical violence in ferocious terms, he referred to 'the Marxist hordes who committed every kind of uncontrolled crime and outrage with holy people and things the prime target of their fury'. He went on to denounce 'the satanic hatred of the atheistic revolutionaries which has spread desolation and piled up debris and ruins everywhere', in short what he called 'Soviet *vandalismo*'.[75]

He rejected proposals for mediation between the two sides on the grounds that the only satisfactory end to the war was the total victory of Franco. Unsurprisingly, he had nothing to say publicly about the massive repression in his own dioceses, although there do exist testimonies to his private distress at the executions. He also made unsuccessful efforts to save some of the parishioners of the poor working-class area of Teruel known as El Arrabal. Indeed, on one occasion, when he went to intercede before the military authorities on behalf of a prisoner, a well-known Falangist said to him: 'If you keep coming here, it will be you we shoot next.'[76]

Whatever Polanco's private feelings, they did not restrain his public enthusiasm for the rebel cause. Among the more than one thousand killings by the right in Teruel during the war, two of the most notorious incidents took place in the central square, the Plaza del Torico. The first was on 27 August 1936. Falangists drove two trucks into the square. From the first, a group of musicians descended and began to play. When a large crowd gathered to listen to the band, Falangists closed the exits to the square and took thirteen prisoners from the second lorry. They included a twenty-year-old girl and the director of the local teacher training college. They were paraded around the square, insulted and ridiculed and then shot. The corpses were removed and the musicians played while the spectators danced in pools of blood – a not uncommon combination of fiesta and horror.[77] It seems that the Bishop was present since he protested to the authorities about the subsequent dance.[78]

The second incident concerned a parade in early August 1937 by a battalion of the Legion, the Bandera Palafox, which was part of the unit named after General Sanjurjo. The Legionarios filed past the Episcopal Palace with human remains on the ends of their bayonets. These

belonged to seventy-eight Republican casualties in a battle for control of
the area around Campillo and Bezas, to the west of Teruel and the south
of Albarracín. The Bandera was composed of the Republicans from
Zaragoza who had enlisted in the Legion to save their own lives and
survived the massacre of October 1936. Bezas fell on 1 August.[79] The
prisoners had been stripped naked then machine-gunned in the village
square before being mutilated. The parade also included a prisoner
loaded with blankets secured with an ox's halter as if he was a beast of
burden. According to Indalecio Prieto, the parade was presided over by
Polanco. He may not have 'presided' formally but he certainly witnessed
the event. The Governor General of Aragon, José Ignacio Mantecón,
discussed the event with Polanco after the capture of Teruel by
Republican troops. The Bishop recounted 'without emotion how he had
watched from the balcony of the Episcopal Palace the parade by the
Legionarios of the Tercio de Sanjurjo who carried on their bayonet
points the ears, noses and other organs of Republican prisoners, describing the scenes as merely the "natural excesses of all Wars"'.[80]

Claims that the Bishop had protested to the rebel military authorities
both about the events in the Plaza del Torico and about the obscene
spectacle mounted by the Legion were made by three priests interrogated by Republican officers. The trio had been detained in the seminary
of Teruel carrying rifles whose barrels were still hot when the town fell
to the Republicans on 8 January 1938. The relaxed nature of the interrogation may be deduced from their ingenuous comment that 'The
bishop didn't protest about the rest of the shootings carried out in
Teruel, about 2,000, because he thought it would be pointless and
anyway, the scandal was much less because those shootings didn't offend
consciences like the ones that took place in public.'[81] In addition to the
three rifle-toting priests captured in the seminary, four diocesan priests
served in the front line, with Polanco's explicit approval, not as chaplains, but as combatants. The Bishop's attitude to the repression might
be deduced from the instructions sent to every parish priest in Teruel on
3 August 1937. In the event that the parish register of deaths had been
destroyed or lost, he instructed that a new one be obtained and that
entries henceforth be made only under the following four categories:
'natural death; murdered by the revolutionaries; killed in battle; shot by
orders of the military authorities'.[82]

When Polanco himself was captured after the fall of Teruel, the then
Minister of Defence, Indalecio Prieto, intervened to prevent his being
shot by militiamen. Prieto gave Father Alberto Onaindía an account of

the Bishop's interrogation. The principal charge against him was that he had signed the Episcopate's Collective Letter of 1 July 1937 in support of Franco, which was deemed to constitute incitement to, and justification of, military rebellion. Asked if he was aware of the Collective Letter, Polanco replied that, having signed it, he could hardly deny that he was. Asked if he would change anything, he said: 'Just the date. We should have written it earlier.' At this, the officer brought the interrogation to a close, saying, 'You, Bishop, are an exemplary Spaniard. Your words imply character and courage. We are all Spaniards here and the sad thing is that you are on one side and we are on the other.' With permission from Prieto, Onaindía visited Polanco in prison, finding him in good spirits, treated with respect and generally well looked after. When Onaindía told him of the rebel repression in the Basque Country, including the execution of priests, Polanco listened coldly but clearly did not want to hear.[83] After all, two parish priests in his own dioceses had been shot by the rebels, presumably with his permission. After some months, thanks to the intervention of both Julián Zugazagoitia and Manuel Irujo, he was given permission to celebrate daily Mass, although he chose to do so only on Sundays and feast days.[84]

Although the military uprising triumphed in two of Huesca's three major towns, the provincial capital and Jaca, the rebels initially controlled only about one-third of the province. The consequent sense of possible Republican attack ensured that the repression would be particularly harsh with just under 1,500 people killed, a figure comparable to the repression carried out by the anarchists in the part of the province under Republican control. In the capital, the military commander, General Gregorio de Benito, had a close relationship with Mola, under whom he had served in Africa. As might have been expected, he ordered the immediate execution of several Freemasons, including the Mayor, and the arrest of the remaining Republican officials. A general strike was quickly put down. Those arrested were members of the Republican middle classes, especially doctors and schoolteachers, members of the UGT (the predominant union in both Jaca and Huesca) and the wives and families of those who had fled. Seventy-four women were executed because they were the wives or mothers of men who had either fled or been shot. After De Benito had gone to take command in Zaragoza, the repression in Huesca was taken over by another Africanista, Colonel Luis Solans-Labedán, who had earned notoriety during the coup in Melilla.[85]

In the provincial capital, arrests, the later *sacas* from the prison and the subsequent murders were carried out by the so-called 'Death Squad'.

The selection of victims had as much to do with personal resentments or envy as with politics. Perhaps the most celebrated victim was the artist and teacher Ramón Acín Aquilué, a member of the CNT renowned for his pacifist views. He was a friend of Federico García Lorca and of Luis Buñuel, whom he had helped make the film *Tierra sin pan*. He was shot on 6 August 1936, his death in Huesca being the local equivalent of the murder of Lorca. Acín's wife, Concha Monrás, was shot on 23 August along with ninety-four other Republicans, including a pregnant woman. No thought was given to the young children of those executed. The best these orphans could expect was to be taken in by relatives or friends of their parents who, in doing so, ran the risk of themselves being denounced.[86] The purging of the left in the smaller towns was carried out by groups of recently recruited Falangists whose victims were often selected by local landowners.

The repression was particularly brutal in Jaca under the direction of Major Dionisio Pareja Arenilla, who received orders from Zaragoza 'to purge once and for all the undesirable elements'. The portly Bishop of Jaca, Juan Villar Sanz, was a cipher who gave free rein to a small clique of reactionary priests. Blacklists were assembled with the help of local bosses both in Jaca itself and in surrounding *pueblos* like Sabiñánigo, Ansó, Canfranc and Biescas. There were no trials. Army columns aided by Falangists detained hundreds of people and the shootings began on 27 July and ran right through the autumn and the following months. One of the most notorious crimes took place on 6 August 1936. An army captain, two Falangists and a Capuchin monk, Father Hermenegildo de Fustiñana, seized two women from Jaca prison, took them out into the countryside and shot them. One, Pilar Vizcarra, aged twenty-eight and pregnant, was the wife of a man shot exactly one week previously; the other, Desideria Giménez of the Socialist Youth, was aged sixteen. The event was presided over by the tall and bony Father de Fustiñana. Chaplain to the local Requetés, he went about the streets ostentatiously carrying a gun. His visits to the prison were dreaded by the detainees, who regarded him as a 'bird of ill omen'. He delighted in the executions and was present at most of them. He offered confession and the last rites to those about to be shot. Then, his shoes caked with blood, he would visit the families of the few that accepted. He kept a list of all those executed, with a note if they had made their confession. More than four hundred people from Jaca and the surrounding villages were shot.[87]

Among those murdered in one of them, Loscorrales to the north-west of the provincial capital, was Father José Pascual Duaso, the parish priest.

He was the third priest murdered in Aragon at the hands of the rebels. During the Republic, there had been tension in the village between the priest and the local left. The most extreme of the local anti-clericals was the Mayor, Antonio Ordás Borderías, a member of the Radical-Socialist Party. The priest had vehemently opposed his efforts to prohibit bell-ringing, religious weddings and funerals. Nevertheless, Father Pascual was a much respected liberal in other ways, having brought food to soldiers hiding after the abortive Republican coup of 1931 in Jaca. He had supported local labourers in disputes over common lands with the wealthier landowners. He also enjoyed the friendship of many local Republicans, including the anarchist secretary of the town council. In February 1936, Ordás was replaced as Mayor by a Socialist.

In July 1936, with Loscorrales in the rebel zone, the new Socialist Mayor was arrested, released after Father Pascual vouched for him, then shot in October. Ordás, who had by now joined the Falange, was re-established as Mayor. However, for his membership of the Radical-Socialist Party and his anti-clerical activities, he was imprisoned in Huesca. In danger of being shot, he was saved by the intervention of a sergeant major in the forces of General Gustavo Urrutia Fernández. The man in question was married to a cousin of Ordás and apparently had considerable influence over Urrutia. Ordás then ingratiated himself with Urrutia, who was a Falangist, by offering to establish the party in the village. Ordás also seized the opportunity to rid himself of those against whom he had grudges. One was Félix Lacambra Ferrer, who had been Mayor during the Primo de Rivera dictatorship. Ordás hated Lacambra because he had made his daughter Sacramento reject him as a suitor. On 15 September 1936, after a denunciation by Ordás, Lacambra was arrested and shot two days later.

Ordás hated Father Pascual even more, regarding him as a dangerous enemy because of what he knew of his left-wing past and because he suspected him, wrongly, of being the cause of his own arrest. First, in a report to the provincial Falange, Ordás denounced Father Pascual as subversive, which led to an unsuccessful request to the Bishop of Huesca that Father Pascual be transferred. Then, at a Mass to commemorate Ordás's being named local chief of the Falange in mid-November, the priest expressed his opposition to Falangist atrocities in the area. Since the authorities did nothing, Ordás decided to accelerate matters. On 21 December, he organized a search of a haystack belonging to the recently murdered Mayor and 'discovered' a pistol and an incriminating document which he had actually written himself. It purported to be a plan

drawn up by the local Socialist landworkers' federation for a purge of
right-wing 'scum' and stated that the priest supported this. The 'discovery' prompted the military authorities to issue a warrant for the priest's
detention. Ordás and two accomplices were given the task of arresting
him, but they simply shot him in his home on 22 December. A cursory
investigation saw Ordás acquitted of guilt after claiming that Father
Pascual had attacked him. The parish priest of nearby Ayerbe was
arrested for trying to send a telegram to the Bishop of Huesca denouncing what had happened. In December 1939, however, the friends and
families of Ordás's victims managed to get the military authorities to
open a more serious investigation into the death of Father Pascual.
Ordás and his two accomplices were arrested on 11 December and held
until 14 February 1942 while the investigation was carried out. The
Falange supported them and, with little prospect of a trial, they were
eventually released, but Ordás never dared return to Loscorrales.[88]

The rebel offensive which had reached the Mediterranean and which
had permitted the completion of the repression in the Republican areas
of Aragon also made major inroads into Catalonia. Sustained Italian
bombing raids on Barcelona on 16, 17 and 18 March 1938 left nearly one
thousand dead and three thousand injured. The working-class districts
where the refugees huddled were especially badly hit. Many of the
victims were women and children. According to the German Ambassador,
the objective was not military but simply to terrorize the civilian population.[89] There is some confusion as to whether the bombings took place
on the orders of Franco or of Mussolini. Whoever issued the command,
after protests from the British, French and American governments and
the Vatican, the raids on the Catalan capital were suspended.[90] However,
as Franco's massively superior forces cut through the disorganized and
demoralized Republicans who were retreating into Catalonia, their
advance was preceded by heavy bombardments of civilian targets by the
Condor Legion.

On 26 March, fifty people were killed in the small town of Fraga. The
next day, it was the turn of Lleida, which was packed with refugees from
Aragon. Lleida had already suffered numerous bombardments, of which
the most terrible took place on 2 November 1937. On that day, nearly
three hundred had been killed. The event is commemorated in one of
the war's most famous photographs, taken by Agustí Centelles, of the
mother of the journalist Josep Pernau weeping over the corpse of her
husband. When the Liceu Escolar was hit, of one class of sixty-three
children, only two survived. Astonishingly, there were no reprisals,

thanks to the swift intervention of the military authorities, including a radio broadcast by Major Sebastián Zamora Medina, one of whose daughters had been killed in the raid and another badly wounded. Throughout late March, the Condor Legion continued its campaign of *Blitzkrieg* attacks, aimed at provoking the flight of the civilian population and facilitating the advance of Yagüe's columns. On Sunday 27 March, a two-hour bombardment by Heinkel 51s left four hundred people dead. Many bodies could not be recovered, given the dangerous state of the buildings. The consequent stench left the city centre uninhabitable for months.[91]

There were further bombing raids in the last three days of March and the first two of April. There were also artillery barrages directed by Luis Alarcón de la Lastra, who now commanded the artillery of the Moroccan Army Corps. Despite a courageous defence by the division led by Valentín González 'El Campesino', Lleida was occupied the following day. Franco's forces found a ghost town. In a city normally of 40,000 inhabitants, barely two thousand were there to greet their conquerors. The Generalitat had organized a massive evacuation of refugees and the bulk of the local population. A Francoist newspaper crowed, 'A few reds who could not flee have take refuge in some houses but they will soon be annihilated.' Shops and houses were looted. One of the first acts of the occupying forces was to remove the records of the deaths from the bombing raids. In Lleida, Gandesa and the towns along the right bank of the Ebro, Corbera, Mora d'Ebre and many others, summary trials and executions began. In Lleida, one of those to be sentenced to death and executed was the director of one of the city's hospitals. His crime was to have organized the evacuation of the hospital despite having been ordered by the fifth column to hand it over complete with all wounded soldiers to the rebels. The director of another hospital, who did obey such orders, was nevertheless dismissed simply because his post made him an employee of the Generalitat de Catalunya.[92]

The depth of anti-Catalan sentiment that had been generated in the rebel zone was inevitably reflected in the repression unleashed there. The entry of the occupiers into any town or village was immediately followed by the prohibition of the Catalan language, despite the fact that many of the inhabitants knew no other. The ban on use of the regional language was extended, as it had been in Euskadi, to all the public activities of the clergy.[93] The extent of a near-racist hatred is illustrated by the fate of Manuel Carrasco i Formiguera, a deeply pious Catholic who was a senior member of the Christian Democrat party, Unió Democràtica de

Catalunya. Denounced in Barcelona by the FAI for his conservative and Catholic views, Carrasco was forced to flee his beloved Catalonia because the Generalitat could not guarantee his safety. He went to work on behalf of the Generalitat in the Basque Country. After an initial visit to Bilbao, where he was received as if he were an ambassador, he returned to Barcelona to collect his family. On 2 March 1937, he set off with his wife and six of his eight children through France. The final part of the journey to Bilbao was from Bayonne by sea. The steamer *Galdames* on which they were travelling was captured by the rebel battlecruiser, *Canarias*. His wife and children were held in four separate prisons.

After five months in jail, Carrasco i Formiguera was tried on 28 August 1937 accused of military rebellion. Prominent Catalans in Franco's circle, men whose lives and fortunes had been saved in Barcelona by Carrasco's intervention, were too frightened by the prevailing anti-Catalanism to speak up on his behalf. In a vengeful atmosphere, charged with anti-Catalan prejudice, no account was taken of his humanitarian efforts or of the fact that Carrasco had defended the Church during the 1931 constitutional debates. The future Mayor of Barcelona, Mateu i Pla, whose fortune had been secured by Carrasco, did nothing to help his defence despite the fact that he was part of Franco's secretariat in Burgos.

Given the military court's insistence on speed, there was little time for Carrasco's defence. In any case, his official advocate, a captain of the medical corps with no juridical training, had already been told that the death sentence had been decided upon before the trial started. Then, for nearly seven and a half months, suffering acute cardiac problems, Carrasco was kept in a freezing cell. Despite energetic efforts to secure a prisoner exchange by José Giral and Manuel Irujo and prominent clergymen, including the Cardinal-Archbishop of Paris, Franco was immovable. One of the Caudillo's senior collaborators commented: 'I know all about Carrasco being an exemplary Christian but his politics are criminal. He has to die!' Carrasco i Formiguera was executed by firing squad on Easter Saturday, 9 April 1938 because he was a Republican and a Catalan nationalist. Franco had chosen the moment that his forces were occupying Catalonia to send a message to the population.[94]

In the days following the occupation of Lleida, the press in the rebel zone gave vent to an ecstatic imperialist rhetoric, rejoicing in the crushing of the 'separatist hydra' by Yagüe's African troops. Republican prisoners who were identified as Catalans were shot without trial. Anyone overheard speaking Catalan was likely to be arrested. The arbitrary brutality of the anti-Catalan repression reached such a scale that Franco himself felt obliged to issue an order that errors must be avoided which might cause regret in the future.[95] The many executions that followed immediately on the occupation of the eastern part of Lleida were not registered. Accordingly, the task for local historians of quantification of those who 'disappeared' between 5 April and 31 May 1938 has been rendered almost impossible. Those who have been identified include eighteen women, of whom two were pregnant and at least two were raped. Seventeen men and five women were shot in Almacelles, north-east of Lleida, on 20 April. In the tiny village of Santa Linya, halfway between Lleida and Tremp, all men of military age were arrested, twenty in all. They were interrogated with questions like: 'How many priests have you murdered?' Nine considered to be Catalan nationalists were taken away and never seen again. The rest were transported to a concentration camp in Valladolid, where three died almost immediately. A high proportion of the executions took place during 'evacuations' or when prisoners were ostensibly being transferred to prison in Barbastro.[96]

The gratuitously savage nature of the repression was demonstrated in the north, near the Pyrenees in El Pallars Sobirà. The area was occupied by the 62nd Division under the command of General Antonio Sagardia, who established his headquarters at the town of Sort. On the grounds that the battle front was near, Sagardía decreed that 'vigilance and cleansing' and the evacuation of 'suspect inhabitants' were crucial, tasks to which he devoted three companies of Civil Guards, aided by Falangists.[97] In consequence, between 15 April and the end of May, sixty-nine civilians from tiny villages previously untouched by the war were murdered. The first were from València d'Aneu, Borén (nine men), Isavarre and Llavorsí (five men and a woman). On 14 May, nine people from Escaló were shot, four men and five women, including a mother and her daughter. The next day, eleven men from Rialb were shot despite being vouched for by the parish priest and local rightists. Their crime was to have belonged to the CNT. On 24 May, nine people were shot at Unarre after being detained for interrogation. Among the five men executed was a seventy-four-year-old shot because his son could not be found and an eighteen-year-old shot instead of his father. Three of the four women were killed because their husbands had fled. One of them was eight months pregnant. Another was her sister-in-law whose seventeen-year-old daughter had asked permission to go as her interpreter since she didn't speak Castilian. The girl was forced to watch her mother being executed and was then herself gang-raped before being shot. Many of the prisoners were badly beaten before being executed and the younger women sexually assaulted.[98]

Entering the south of Catalonia, the Moroccan forces of Colonel Mohammed ben Mizzian captured Batea, Pinell de Brai and Gandesa on 2 April. There, as in the towns along the right bank of the Ebro and through the Terra Alta, Arnes, Corbera, Mora d'Ebre, Ascó, Flix, Tortosa, Amposta and many others, they found houses locked and the streets deserted. Many had fled, but there were both extra-judicial executions and summary trials. As was common with the arrival of African columns, houses were pillaged and women raped.[99]

Although he had Catalonia at his mercy, Franco ordered Yagüe to dig in along the River Segre, much to the frustration and incomprehension of his staff. An offensive against Catalonia, where the Republic's remaining war industry lay, would have brought the war to a speedier conclusion, but Franco had no interest in a quick victory that would still have left hundreds of thousands of armed Republicans in central and southern Spain. Nor did he want to turn to Madrid, since a swift debacle there would have left numerous Republican forces in Catalonia and in the south-east. Either option would have meant an armistice by which some consideration would have to be given to the defeated. As he had made clear to the Italians, Franco's aim remained the gradual but total annihilation of the Republic and its supporters.[100]

Thus, in July, instead of attacking Madrid or Barcelona, he launched a major attack on Valencia. As before, he sought to write in Republican blood the message of his invincibility. In this instance, the cost to his own side was considerable. As his armies moved through the Maestrazgo into Castellón, skilful defence saw the Republican troops inflict heavy casualties on the Francoists while suffering relatively few themselves. Nonetheless, the progress of the rebels, if painfully slow, was inexorable. Castellón, Burriana and Nules were occupied in July after heavy bombing attacks. The rebel entry into the southern part of Tarragona and the province of Castellón was accompanied by a scale of repression on a par with that inflicted on Lleida. In Vinarós, for example, the Church of San Francisco was commandeered by the military as a prison. The acting parish priest, later Cardinal-Archbishop, Vicente Enrique y Tarancón, was appalled by the overcrowded and unhygienic conditions. He was even more appalled by the frequency of executions. When he complained that the accused in military trials were not allowed to defend themselves and that their guilt was simply taken for granted, he was told that there was no time for legal niceties in wartime.[101] The bombing raids were extended to the port cities of the Levante coast – Valencia, Gandía, Alcoy and Alicante. By 23 July 1938, Valencia was under direct threat, with the Francoists less than twenty-five miles away. If Valencia fell, the war would effectively be over.

As defeat became inevitable, the Republican Prime Minister Juan Negrín became ever more determined to fight on, believing that capitulation would simply open the floodgates to mass slaughter. When a senior Republican figure, almost certainly Azaña, suggested that an agreement with the rebels was an inevitable necessity, he responded: 'Make a pact? And what about the poor soldier of Medellín?' At the time, Medellín, near Don Benito, was the furthermost point on the Extremadura front. Since Franco demanded total surrender, Negrín knew that, at best, a mediated peace might secure the escape of several hundred, maybe some thousands, of political figures. However, the great majority of ordinary Republican soldiers and citizens would be at the mercy of the Francoists, who would be pitiless.[102] On 25 July 1938, Medellín and the entire area of La Serena in the province of Badajoz fell to the insurgents. In the following weeks, large numbers of people from the surrounding villages were taken to Medellín and shot and many more transferred to the concentration camp at Castuera. Under the command of the notorious Major Ernesto Navarrete Alcal, it was ruled with his characteristic brutality. The prisoners experienced starvation, overcrowding, slave labour, beatings and frequent *sacas*.[103]

With the insurgents less than twenty-five miles away from Valencia, on the same day that La Serena fell, the Republic mounted a spectacular diversion. In an attempt to restore contact between Catalonia and the rest of Republican Spain, a huge army of 80,000 men crossed the River Ebro. The advance through an immense curve in the Ebro from Flix in the north to Miravet in the south surprised the thinly held rebel lines. Negrín hoped that, if the Republic could fight on for another year, it would find salvation in the general war which he believed to be inevitable. Within a week, the Republicans had advanced twenty-five miles and reached Gandesa, but there they were bogged down as Franco rushed in reinforcements. Knowing that Franco would not consider an armistice, Negrín refused to contemplate unconditional surrender. On 7 August, he said to his friend Juan-Simeón Vidarte: 'I will not hand over hundreds of defenceless Spaniards who fight heroically for the Republic so that Franco can have the pleasure of shooting them like he did in his own Galicia, in Andalusia, in the Basque country and wherever the hooves of Attila's horse have left their mark.'[104]

Franco could have contained the Republican advance across the Ebro and advanced on a near helpless Barcelona. Instead, he seized the opportunity to catch the Republicans in a trap, encircle and destroy them, turning the fertile Terra Alta into their graveyard. With nearly one million men now under arms, he could afford to be careless of their lives. As the battle was moving in his favour, on 7 November, he announced to the vice-president of the United Press, James Miller, 'there will be no mediation because the criminals and their victims cannot live together'. He went on threateningly: 'We have on file more than two million names along with proof of their crimes.'[105] He was referring to the political files and documentation captured as each town had fallen. This information, archived in Salamanca, provided the basis for a massive card index of members of political parties, trade unions and Masonic lodges which in turn would be the database for a policy of institutionalized terror.[106]

By mid-November 1938, at a cost of nearly 15,000 dead and 110,000 wounded or mutilated, the Francoists had pushed the Republicans out of the territory captured in July. The Republic had lost its army. The Francoists would soon sweep further into Catalonia. The war had been prolonged in accordance with Negrín's hope of seeing the democracies wake up to the Axis's aggressive ambitions, but the betrayal of Czechoslovakia at Munich turned the Ebro into a useless sacrifice. After a brief lull for his forces to rest and regroup, in late November Franco began to gather a massive army along a line surrounding the remainder of Republican Catalonia from the Mediterranean to the Ebro and to the Pyrenees. After delays caused by torrential rain, and despite the pleas of the Papal Nuncio for a Christmas truce, the final offensive was launched on 23 December.[107] The Caudillo had new German equipment in abundance, total air superiority and sufficient Spanish and Italian reserves to be able to relieve his troops every two days. The attacking force consisted of five Spanish army corps together with four Italian divisions. A heavy artillery barrage preceded the attack. The shattered Republicans could put up only token resistance.[108]

In the course of the advance, many Republican prisoners were shot as soon as they were captured. There were also many atrocities committed against the civilian population. There were examples of peasants being murdered for no apparent reason other than the fact that they spoke Catalan. On Christmas Eve 1938, when Maials in the far south of Lleida was captured by Regulares, at least four women were raped. In one case, a woman was raped while her husband and seven-year-old son were forced at gunpoint to watch. In another, a woman's father was shot for protesting at her violation. In an isolated country house, a young woman was raped and died when she was stabbed in the stomach with a bayonet. Fifteen minutes later, her mother was raped then shot. In Vilella Baixa in the Priorat, a man was shot for trying to prevent a woman being raped. At another farm outside Callús, in the province of Barcelona, a man who lived with his wife, his daughter and her cousin was shot by some Regulares who raped the three women and then killed them at bayonet point. In the tiny nearby village of Marganell, two women were raped by Regulares who then killed them by placing hand grenades between their legs.[109]

As fear of the Moors saw the roads to Barcelona blocked with terrified refugees, Franco announced his plans for the defeated in an interview given to Manuel Aznar on 31 December 1938. He divided them into hardened criminals beyond redemption and those who had been deceived by their leaders and were capable of repentance. There would be no amnesty or reconciliation for the defeated Republicans, only punishment and repentance to open the way to their 'redemption'. Prisons and labour camps were the necessary purgatory for those who had committed minor 'crimes'. Others could expect no better fate than death or exile.[110] A good example of what redemption by Franco really meant could be found in the experience of Catalonia after the occupation of Tarragona on 15 January 1939. The city was deserted and thousands of refugees were trudging north. An elaborate ceremony was held in the Cathedral involving a company of infantry. The officiating priest, a canon of the Cathedral of Salamanca, José Artero, got so carried away that, during his sermon, he shouted: 'Catalan dogs! You are not worthy of the sun that shines on you!'[111]

In Tarragona, there were the inevitable executions that followed the occupation of the city. The fact that so many people had fled reduced the potential for mass killings but, as people came forward with denunciations, large numbers of arrests were made. Formal military trials began on 16 February 1939. Although they were brief, without any juridical guarantees, the military authorities held them in public and advertised the time and place. The new Francoist Mayor, disconcerted when the population did not react with enthusiasm to this free entertainment, made public appeals to their patriotism in order to ensure that the courts would be full. When death sentences were confirmed, the executions were also held in public. Numerous executions were carried out in the course of 1939 – on 22 April, twenty-three were shot, on 15 July, thirty-one, on 20 October, forty-three, and on 15 November, forty. In each case, the doctor in attendance certified death by 'internal haemorrhage'.[112] The repression in the surrounding area of the Alt Camp was on a similar scale. The trials and subsequent executions took place in Valls. On 17 July forty-one people were executed, on 8 August another forty and on 19 October another forty-four.[113]

When news reached Barcelona, on 23 January 1939, that the Francoists were at the River Llobregat to the south of the city, a colossal exodus began. On the night of 25 January, the Republican government fled northwards to Girona. The President of the Generalitat, Lluís Companys, drove one last time through the centre of a deserted city, as leaflets calling for resistance blew through the streets along with ripped-up party and trade union membership cards.[114] The next morning, the streets were full of smoke from the burning papers of ministries, parties and unions. The young Communist Teresa Pàmies witnessed, on 26 January, horrendous scenes of the fear provoked by the advancing rebels:

> There is one thing I will never forget: the wounded who crawled out of the Vallcarca hospital, mutilated and bandaged, almost naked, despite the cold, they went down to the street, shrieking and pleading with us not to leave them behind to the mercies of the victors. All other details of that unforgettable day were wiped out by the sight of those defenceless soldiers ... The certainty that we left them to their fate will shame us for ever. Those with no legs dragged themselves along the ground, those who had lost an arm raised the other with a clenched fist, the youngest cried in their fear, the older ones went mad with rage. They grabbed the sides of lorries loaded with furniture, with bird cages, with mattresses, with silent women, with indifferent old people, with terrified children. They screamed, they ululated, they blasphemed and cursed those who were fleeing and were abandoning them.

There were around 20,000 wounded Republican soldiers in Barcelona. Their wounds and missing limbs were proof that they had fought and would guarantee that they would be the victims of reprisals.[115]

Four hundred and fifty thousand terrified women, children, old men and defeated soldiers trekked towards France. In numbers and in human suffering, the exodus far exceeded even the horrors seen by Norman Bethune on the road from Málaga to Almería. Those who could squeezed into every kind of transport imaginable. Through bitterly cold sleet and snow, on roads bombed and strafed by rebel aircraft, many others walked, wrapped in blankets and clutching a few possessions, some carrying infants. Women gave birth at the roadsides. Babies died of the cold, children were trampled to death. A witness summed up the horror of that dreadful exodus: 'At the side of the road, a man had hung himself from a tree. One foot had a rope sandal, the other was bare. At the foot of the tree was an open suitcase in which lay a small child that had died of cold during the night.' It is not known how many people died on the roads to France.[116]

Those who fled faced the bleakest future, but it was one that they chose in preference to being 'liberated' by Franco's forces. From 28 January, a reluctant French government allowed the first refugees across the border. At first, they had to sleep in the streets of Figueras, the last town on the Spanish side of the border. Many died in sustained rebel bombing raids.[117] The defeated Republicans, many sick or wounded, were received by the French Garde Mobile as if they were criminals. The women, children and the old were shepherded into transit camps. The soldiers were disarmed and escorted to insanitary camps on the coast, rapidly improvised by marking out sections of beach with barbed wire. Under the empty gaze of Senegalese guards, the refugees improvised shelters by burrowing into the wet sand of the camp at Saint-Cyprien a few miles to the south-east of Perpignan.

Meanwhile, the formal parade into an eerily empty Barcelona was headed by the Army Corps of Navarre, led by General Andrés Solchaga. They were accorded this honour, according to a British officer attached to Franco's headquarters, 'not because they have fought better, but because they hate better – that is to say, when the object of this hate is Catalonia or a Catalan'.[118] A close friend of Franco, Víctor Ruiz Albeniz ('El Tebib Arrumi'), published an article asserting that Catalonia needed 'a biblical punishment (Sodom, Gomorrah) to purify the red city, seat of anarchism and separatism as the only remedy to extirpate these two cancers by implacable thermo-cauterization'. None of the conquering generals or Falangists referred to the crushing of Marxism or anarchism. Their entire discourse was about the conquest of Catalonia by Spain. One officer told a Portuguese journalist that the only solution to the 'Catalan problem' was 'kill the Catalans. It's just a question of time.'[119]

One of the first acts of the occupying forces was to ban the use of Catalan in public. For Ramón Serrano Suñer, Franco's brother-in-law and Minister of the Interior, Catalan nationalism was a sickness that had to be eradicated. He told the Nazi newspaper *Völkischer Beobachter* that the Catalan population was 'morally and politically sick'. The man he appointed as Civil Governor of Barcelona, Wenceslao González Oliveros, announced, in a reversal of Unamuno's famous dictum that the rebels might win (*vencer*) but never convince (*convencer*), that Franco's forces had come 'to save the good Spaniards and to defeat, but not convince, the enemies of Spain'. For González Oliveros, that meant the Catalans. He stated that 'Spain opposed the divisive autonomy statutes with greater ferocity than communism' and that any toleration of any kind of regionalism would lead once more to 'the putrefaction represented by Marxism and separatism that we have just surgically eradicated'.[120]

Within a week, the military secret police was functioning. Newspaper advertisements called for recruits, preference being given to ex-prisoners of the Republican SIM. Large queues of people with denunciations gathered outside the offices of the Occupation Services. In consequence, 22,700 people were arrested in the first eight months.[121] Precisely because so many of those of political or military significance had fled, those killed by the rebels in Catalonia were perhaps fewer than might have been expected. Between those murdered by the occupying troops and those tried and executed, more than 1,700 were killed in Barcelona, 750 in Lleida, 703 in Tarragona and five hundred in Girona. Many more died from mistreatment in prison.[122]

In Catalonia, as in other parts of Spain occupied by the rebels, the repression took many forms and merely to stay alive was a major achievement for many Republicans. Those who had not been executed, imprisoned or exiled lived in an atmosphere of terror. Daily life for the defeated was a question of combating hunger, illness and fear of arrest or of denunciation by a neighbour or by a priest. Rural parish priests were particularly active in denouncing their parishioners. Their contribution to the exacerbation of social divisions suggested a quest for vengeance rather than a Christian commitment to forgiveness or reconciliation. The sheer misery of life for the defeated explains a notable rise in the suicide rate. Considerable cruelty was visited upon women under the rhetorical umbrella of 'redemption'. As well as confiscation of goods and imprisonment as retribution for the behaviour of a son or husband, the widows and the wives of prisoners were raped. Many were forced to live in total poverty and often, out of desperation, to sell themselves on the streets. The increase in prostitution both benefited Francoist men who thereby slaked their lust and reassured them that 'red' women were a fount of dirt and corruption. Soldiers billeted on poor families often abused the unprotected women of the household. Many priests defended the honour of male parishioners and denounced their female victims as 'reds'.[123]

After Catalonia fell, a huge area amounting to about 30 per cent of Spain remained in the hands of the Republic. Negrín still cherished hope of fighting on until a European war started and the democracies at last realized that the anti-fascist battle of the Republic had been theirs too. Franco was in no hurry to go into battle since the repression was a higher priority. In any case, he had reason to believe that the Republic was about to face major divisions that might save him the trouble of fighting in central Spain. His confidence was such that, on 9 February 1939, he published the Law of Political Responsibilities and dashed the hopes of non-Communist Republicans who were prepared to betray Negrín in the hope of a negotiated peace. Retroactive to October 1934, the law declared Republicans guilty of the crime of military rebellion, and was essentially a device to justify the expropriation of the defeated.[124]

On 4 March, Colonel Segismundo Casado, commander of the Republican Army of the Centre, formed an anti-Negrín National Defence Junta, in the hope of negotiating with Franco. He thereby sparked off what was effectively a second civil war within the Republican zone. Although he defeated pro-Communist forces, there was no prospect of a deal with Franco. Troops all along the line were surrendering or just going home. On 26 March, a gigantic and virtually unopposed advance was launched along a wide front. The next day, Franco's forces simply occupied deserted positions and entered an eerily silent Madrid. Tens of thousands of Republicans headed for the Mediterranean coast in the vain hope of evacuation. The war was over, but there would be no reconciliation. Instead, in the areas that had just fallen under Franco's control, Valencia, Alicante, Murcia and Albacete, Almería and eastern Andalusia, and the eastern part of New Castile, a massive wave of political arrests, trials, executions and imprisonment was about to begin.

PART SIX

Franco's Investment in Terror

13

No Reconciliation:
Trials, Executions, Prisons

As Franco had demonstrated by the nature of his war effort and made
explicit in interviews private and public, he was engaged in an investment in terror. With all of Spain in his hands at the beginning of April
1939, the war against the Republic would continue by other means, not
on the battle fronts but in military courts, in the prisons, in the concentration camps, in the labour battalions and even in pursuit of the exiles.
The immediate tasks were the classification and punishment of those
who had gathered in the eastern seaboard, the cleansing of the provinces
that had just fallen and the marshalling of the hundreds of thousands of
prisoners into work battalions. The long-term institutionalization of
Franco's victory required the perfection of the machinery of state terror
to protect and oversee the original investment. For that reason, the
martial law declared in July 1936 was not rescinded until 1948.

That Franco had no inclination to magnanimity and saw the repression as a long-term undertaking was made clear by his speech on 19 May
1939, the day on which he presided over the spectacular Victory Parade
in Madrid. 'Let us not deceive ourselves: the Jewish spirit, which permitted the alliance of big capital with Marxism and which was behind so
many pacts with the anti-Spanish revolution, cannot be extirpated in a
day and still beats in the hearts of many.'[1] The belief that the war had
been against the Jewish–Bolshevik–Masonic conspiracy was reiterated in
his end-of-year message on 31 December 1939. Franco praised German
anti-Semitic legislation, declaring that the persecution of the Jews by the
fifteenth-century Catholic monarchs Ferdinand and Isabel had shown
the Nazis the way:

> Now you will understand the reasons which have led other countries to
> persecute and isolate those races marked by the stigma of their greed
> and self-interest. The domination of such races within society is disturb-
> ing and dangerous for the destiny of the nation. We, who were freed of
> this heavy burden centuries ago by the grace of God and the clear vision

of Ferdinand and Isabel, cannot remain indifferent before the modern flourishing of avaricious and selfish spirits who are so attached to their own earthly goods that they would sacrifice the lives of their children more readily than their own base interests.

In the same speech, he rejected any notion of reconciliation with the defeated:

It is necessary to put an end to the hatreds and passions of our recent war but not in the manner of liberals, with their monstrous and suicidal amnesties, which are more fraud than pardon, but rather with the redemption of sentences through work, with repentance and penance. Anyone who thinks otherwise is guilty of irresponsibility or treason. Such damage has been done to the Patria and such havoc has been wreaked on families and on morality, so many victims cry out for justice that no honourable Spaniard, no thinking being, could stand aside from the painful duty of punishment.[2]

The repressive judicial system applied after 1 April 1939 used both the administrative machinery and the pseudo-legal framework developed throughout the war. On 28 July 1936, the Burgos Junta's declaration of martial law had proclaimed its determination to punish those who, 'blinded by an incomprehensible sectarianism, commit actions or omissions that might prejudice this Movement of Redemption of the Fatherland'. Any such offence was deemed to be a crime of military rebellion and thus subject to summary court martial. The sophistry underlying this legal fiction was that the military had legitimately assumed power on 16 and 17 July (before the actual military uprising) and therefore that the defence of the Republic constituted rebellion. All political activities on behalf of parties of the left or trade unions from the beginning of October 1934 were deemed retrospectively to constitute 'support for military rebellion' on the grounds that they had contributed to the disorder which was said to have provoked the military take-over.[3]

On 15 August 1936 in Burgos, General Mola had declared, in a broadcast on Radio Castilla, 'My words go out to our enemies, since it is only right and proper that they know what to expect lest, when the time arrives for the settling of scores, they have recourse to the legal principle that "no punishment can be imposed on an offender that was not established before the offence was committed".'[4] Franco had reiterated this nonsensical position in an interview given on the first anniversary of the military coup: 'The National Movement was never an uprising. The reds were and are the rebels.'[5]

The absurdity of these declarations was underlined by the author of the Republican Constitution and distinguished criminal lawyer, Luis Jiménez de Asúa, when he described the accusation of military rebellion as 'reverse rebellion', for which 'crime' the accused would receive 'a vice-versa sentence'. Franco's Minister of the Interior, Ramón Serrano Suñer, retrospectively called it 'back-to-front justice'. Jiménez de Asúa observed that 'a more curious reversal of the truth is inconceivable and can only be explained in psychological terms as the projection of guilt'.[6]

The initial basis for the repression was formalized further with a decree issued on 13 September 1936 by the Burgos Junta which outlawed all political parties, trade unions and social organizations that supported the Popular Front and opposed the 'National Movement'. The decree ordered the confiscation of all goods, effects and documents, as well as buildings and other properties of such entities. Also liable were left-wing and liberal parties and trade unions, Freemasons, Jews, the Rotary Club, feminist, vegetarian, nudist, Esperanto and homeopathic societies, Montessori schools and sports clubs. Furthermore, the decree ordered the purging of all public servants, functionaries and schoolteachers who had served the institutions of the Republic. Special tribunals were established to judge those deemed worthy of keeping their livelihood. The human cost was colossal. For instance, when Catalonia was occupied at the end of the war, out of 15,860 public servants, 15,107 lost their jobs.[7] The paranoia that lay behind the blanket denunciation of anything and everything that fell outside right-wing Catholic values was in large part thanks to the anti-Republican campaigns of the right-wing press which had fed off the writings of Juan Tusquets, Mauricio Carlavilla and Onésimo Redondo. Father Tusquets in particular had linked all these peripheral organizations to the Jewish–Masonic–Bolshevik conspiracy.

The fiction that defence of the Republic was a crime of military rebellion was the basis of all the summary courts martial. Except in some cases of famous defendants, the accused were usually denied the possibility of defending themselves. The military would choose the judge, the prosecutor and the defence 'lawyer', this latter always being an officer junior to the judge and prosecutor. Given that the Army Legal Corps simply did not have sufficient personnel to cope with the demands made by the new situation, trials were usually conducted by officers with no legal training whatsoever. Groups of prisoners, unknown to one another and accused of notably different offences, would be tried together en masse. They would have no access to the 'case' against them, which consisted of accusations read out without evidence. Only rarely, after the prosecutor had finished making the 'case', were the accused permitted to confer with the defending officer and consider their defence. If lucky, they were given an hour to prepare their case but not allowed to call witnesses or present any evidence. They were often not permitted to hear the 'case' against them, either because they had already been shot or because, in 'emergency summary trials', the charges were not even read out. In no cases were appeals permitted.[8]

When Juan Caba Guijarro, a CNT member from Manzanares, was tried with nineteen others, the prosecutor stated:

> I do not care, nor do I even want to know, if you are innocent or not of the charges made against you. Nor will I take cognizance of any excuses, alibis or mitigating circumstances that you might present. I must base my accusations, as in previous courts martial, on the files prepared by the investigators on the basis of the denunciations. As far as the accused are concerned, I represent justice. It is not me who condemns them but their own towns, their enemies, their neighbours. I merely give voice to the accusations that others have made discreetly. My attitude is cruel and pitiless and it may appear as if my job is just to feed the firing squads so that their work of social cleansing can continue. But no, here all of us who have won the war participate and it is our wish to eliminate all opposition in order to impose our own order. Considering that there are crimes of blood in all the accusations, I have reached the conclusion that I must demand the death penalty, and I do demand the firing squad for the first eighteen in the list and, for the other two, garrotte vil. Nothing more.

The defence lawyer represented all twenty defendants at the same time, without having had time or opportunity to prepare any kind of defence. He rose and said: 'After hearing the serious charges that have been laid against all those I am here to defend, I can only plead for mercy. Nothing more.' The judge then proceeded to sentence the accused.[9]

Some of those tried by the innumerable military courts were guilty of real crimes in the *checas*, although many such had escaped into hiding or exile. Most were men and women whose crime was simply their failure actively to support the coup. The majority were condemned on the basis of an assumption of guilt, without the need for evidence. In a typical case, that of a railwayman accused of involvement in crimes of blood, the guilty verdict was justified on the grounds that 'although there is no evidence that he took a direct part in looting, theft, arrests or murders, his beliefs make it reasonable to suppose that he did'. Membership of a left-wing committee in a town or village where right-wingers were killed would usually guarantee a death sentence even if the accused knew nothing of the killing or had opposed it. Men and women were condemned to death for participation in crimes not on the basis of direct evidence but because the prosecutor extrapolated from their known Republican, Socialist, Communist or anarchist convictions that 'they must have taken part'.[10]

As territory fell to the rebels, and especially after the end of the war, prisoners were herded into camps, frequently beaten and tortured to reveal the names of other Republicans. Inquiries were made in the prisoners' home towns. If the local report was negative, the camp officials would usually send the prisoner back to his home town to face further investigation and prosecution. By carrying out trials in the town of origin of the detainees, it would ensure that they would be at the mercy of their neighbours who provided the necessary denunciations.[11] Statements by 'reliable' citizens that a suspect was an undesirable or left-wing were sufficient to secure an arrest and usually a trial. Such statements were taken by the military authorities, without further investigation, as trustworthy 'evidence'.

The military instructions for the re-establishment of civilian life in 'liberated areas' invited the local population of occupied territory to present denunciations of criminal acts of which they had been victims during the period of left-wing control.[12] When Catalonia was occupied, 'all good Spaniards' were urged to come forward with information about any crimes or injustices committed 'in the Companys period'.[13] In Los Pedroches in the north-east of Córdoba, 70 per cent of trials were triggered by denunciations from civilians.[14] There and elsewhere, this suggested considerable social support for the Francoists, much more than would have been found in 1936. This was hardly surprising given the scale of both the terror and the anti-Republican propaganda carried out by the victors. Whether a denunciation would fail or prosper frequently depended on the stance of the local clergy.

Denunciations often came from the bereaved relatives of those who had died in the violence that followed the defeat of the military uprising. Their grief and their desire for revenge led to them denouncing people assumed to belong to the same group as the real killers. Any leftist could thus be incorporated into a collectivity presented as the barbaric and depraved 'red horde'. Coincidentally, many of those denounced happened to belong to the unions and parties that had threatened the social, economic and political privileges of the denouncers. Businessmen and landowners keen to recoup the economic losses that their enterprises had suffered during the revolutionary period often denounced their competitors.[15]

From November 1936, increasing numbers of civilian lawyers, judges and even law students had been drafted into the military judicial corps. The main requirement was that they demonstrate right-wing sympathies. Entirely under the vigilance of the military authorities and often fearful for their own safety, even those who had qualms about what was happening had to be harsh in order to guarantee their own survival.[16] At the beginning of 1938, Felipe Acedo Colunga, the senior military prosecutor, produced a report on the activities of the Auditoría de Guerra (War Court) created in November 1936 when the rebels had believed that they were about to capture Madrid. This report argued that the military courts must work pitilessly to clear the ground for the creation of a new state. Acedo Colunga insisted that there should be no equality between prosecution and defence and that the presumed intentions of defendants were every bit as reprehensible as their actual deeds.[17]

Acedo Colunga's report revealed the industrial scale of the work of this one court up to the end of 1938. It had held 6,770 trials and, by trying multiple defendants together, it had been possible to prosecute 30,224 people, of whom 3,189 had been condemned to death.[18] When the Republic finally fell, the military courts intensified their activity. They continued to function in regions long since occupied as well as in the recently conquered areas where they now had to deal with large numbers of captured soldiers and civilians. In Granada, where many who had fled from the rebel-held capital were captured when the eastern part of the province fell, there were 5,500 cases tried in 1939; four hundred defendants were sentenced to death and more than one thousand to life imprisonment. Between 1939 and 1959, a total of 1,001 people in Granada were executed after military trial. A decree of 8 November 1939 multiplied the number of courts martial by creating numerous provisional courts and increasing the size of the military juridical corps.[19]

The repression was facilitated by the betrayal of the Republic perpetrated by the military coup by Colonel Segismundo Casado on 4 March 1939. Casado, commander of the Republican Army of the Centre, hoping to stop further slaughter, formed an anti-Negrín National Defence Junta along with fiercely anti-Communist anarchist leaders such as Cipriano Mera, the Socialist intellectual Julián Besteiro and Miaja. Casado and Besteiro were culpably naive to believe assurances from the fifth column that Franco would contemplate an armistice and that those without blood on their hands had nothing to fear. Widespread hunger and demoralization saw Casado receive unexpectedly wide support. In the subsequent mini-civil war against the Communists, about two thousand people were killed. To the delight of Franco, troops were withdrawn from the front to fight the Communists.[20]

Many Communists were left in prison where they were found by the Francoists and soon executed. This was especially true of the areas in the centre such as Madrid and Guadalajara. In the latter province, it will be recalled that 282 right-wingers had been killed in the local prison in reprisal for a rebel bombing raid on 6 December 1936. The reprisals now were brutal. The Communists left imprisoned by Cipriano Mera, the local military commander, were shot immediately. José Cazorla, the Civil Governor, had been arrested with his wife Aurora Arnaiz and their baby son, who died during their detention. Aurora and Cazorla managed to escape along with Ramón Torrecilla Guijarro, who had been Cazorla's chief of police. After failing to get on board a ship at Alicante, Cazorla and Torrecilla returned to Madrid, where they worked for several months trying to build up the clandestine networks of the PCE. They were arrested by the Francoist forces on 9 August 1939 and interrogated under torture. They were tried on 16 January 1940 and sentenced to death. Cazorla was eventually executed on 8 April that year and Torrecilla on 2 July.[21] Meanwhile, in Guadalajara, a small province of 200,000 people, 822 were executed. There were six thousand prisoners, 3 per cent of the total population and nearer 10 per cent of the adult male population. One hundred and forty-three died in prison because of the appalling conditions, overcrowding, disease and non-existent hygiene. Torture and maltreatment provoked many suicides, some of them faked to conceal beatings that had gone too far. The levels of malnutrition were such that any prisoner without family to bring in food was condemned to die.[22]

In Jaén, in return for the arrested Communists being left in jail, the Francoist command agreed with the Casadista authorities that the victorious troops would enter the city without bloodshed and two hundred Republicans and Socialists be given safe passage to Almería. Those prisoners not released by the warders on their own initiative were shot immediately. The convoy of Republicans and Socialists that was heading for the coast was ambushed en route by Falangists. Some were killed in the fighting, while the majority were captured and taken to Granada to be shot. Four who escaped were picked up later, tried and executed in Jaén. Thereafter in Jaén, 1,984 people were executed after military trial, 425 murdered extra-judicially and a further 510 died in prison.[23]

When he visited recently conquered Almería on 11 April 1939, Queipo de Llano declared that 'Almería must make an act of contrition.' This provoked a Falangist assault on the provincial prison and the murder of at least three prisoners. Formal executions began two weeks later on 25 April; 1,507 people were tried in 1939, another 1,412 in 1940, and 1,717 in 1941 – a total of 6,269 between 1939 and 1945, but the number executed, 375, was the lowest in any Andalusian province. This is because many leftists had protected rightists from the repression and, unusually, the rightists now returned the favour. The squeezing of more than six thousand prisoners into a prison built for five hundred led inevitably to conditions of malnutrition and minimal hygiene. However, this accounts only in part for the notably high level of 227 deaths of prisoners, many of them young men, suspiciously registered as victims of cardiac failure.[24]

Such prison overcrowding was common. In Ciudad Real, in the provincial prison built for one hundred, at any one time the number of prisoners ranged from 1,300 to 2,200. In total, between 1939 and 1943, more than 19,000 passed through the prison and over two thousand were executed.[25] In Murcia too, well over five thousand people were imprisoned and more than one thousand executed. In addition to the usual privations, many prisoners were subjected to beatings. There, as elsewhere, the sexual abuse of women prisoners was notorious.[26] In nearby Albacete, where 920 rightists had met their deaths while the province was under Republican control, the Francoist revenge saw this number doubled. Between 1939 and 1943, more than one thousand Republicans were shot after trial and at least 573 murdered extra-judicially, several after *sacas* by Falangists from the prison at Villarobledo and the castle at Yeste. A further 291 people died in the overcrowded prisons.[27] In the three provinces of the Valencian region, Castellón, Valencia and Alicante, more than 15,000 people were imprisoned, of whom, after interrogation, at the end of 1939 there remained 7,610 still behind bars. A total of 1,165 people died in prison in the years following the Francoist occupation. Together with the more than 4,700 people executed, these figures constitute, in percentage terms, double the scale of the repression in Catalonia. The difference is explained by the escape of hundreds of thousands of potential victims from Catalonia at the end of January 1939.[28]

Much of the suffering undergone in the recently conquered areas was the direct consequence of the Casado coup. Cipriano Mera had made a worthless promise that if the self-styled National Defence Council did not secure an honourable peace his men would fight on. However, while the prisoners were being handed over to the Francoists and others fled to the eastern coast, all the members of Casado's Junta who wished to escape were evacuated from Gandía on the British destroyer *Galatea* in the early hours of the morning of 30 March 1939.[29] Betrayed by Casado's coup, tens of thousands of desperate Republican men, women and children fled from Madrid on 28 March pursued by Falangists. They headed for Valencia and Alicante. They had been promised that there would be ships to take them into exile. In fact, there was no chance of that. The French company normally used by the Republic refused to undertake any evacuation on the grounds that it had had no dealings with Casado, only with Negrín. It also claimed to be owed money. Moreover, the Republican fleet had abandoned Spain and landed in Bizerta in Algeria. Therefore, there was no protection against the rebel fleet blockading the Spanish ports of the eastern Mediterranean, under orders from Franco to permit no refugees to escape.

The last boats to leave, organized by the Socialist Federation of Alicante, were the British steamers *Stanbrook*, *Maritime*, *Ronwyn* and *African Trader* and some fishing boats. They carried 5,146 passengers. The greatest number were on the *Stanbrook*, while the *Maritime* carried only thirty-two important politicians.[30] The very last of the ships to leave Alicante, the *Stanbrook*, precariously carried 2,638 refugees. There were passengers on every inch of the deck and in the holds and its Plimsoll line was well below the surface of the water. Miraculously, its captain, Archibald Dickson, managed to manoeuvre through the rebel gauntlet. The *Stanbrook* reached Oran in Algeria. For nearly a month, the French authorities refused to let Captain Dickson disembark his passengers, though they were short of food and water, in conditions of extreme overcrowding. The French relented only when there was a danger of contagious illnesses spreading, and at last the refugees were taken to internment camps.[31]

Back in Alicante, over the next few days, those who had arrived too late were joined by thousands more refugees from all over the remaining Republican territory. In despair, many committed suicide, some drowning themselves, others shooting themselves.[32] Some ships came into view but, with their captains fearful of interception by the rebel navy, they either left empty or turned back before even reaching the dockside. Having already recognized Franco, neither London nor Paris was prepared to let its navies intervene against the rebel fleet. The refugees waited in vain for three and a half days without food or water. Children died of inanition. The Mexican government offered to take all the refugees, but Franco refused, declaring that they were all prisoners of war and must face the consequences. On Friday 31 March, the city was occupied by Italian forces. There was a repetition of what had happened to the Basque Army at Santoña. The Italians undertook to arrange evacuation if the thousands of Republicans gave up their weapons. After they had done so, the Italians were overruled once more by Franco. When two ships carrying Francoist troops arrived, the majority of the refugees were taken away and the remainder followed the next morning.[33] Families were violently separated and those who protested were beaten or shot. The women and children were transferred to Alicante, where they were kept for a month packed into a cinema with little food and without facilities for washing or changing their babies. The men – including boys from the age of twelve – were taken either to the bullring in Alicante or to a large field outside the town, the Campo de los Almendros, so called because it was an orchard of almond trees.[34]

As the prisoners were marched to the improvised concentration camp, they passed substantial numbers of corpses of men who had been shot 'while trying to escape'. One commented, 'Soon, we'll envy the dead.' They were stripped of valuables and their jackets and coats by the Francoist troops.[35] For six days, 45,000 were kept virtually without food or water, sleeping in mud in the open, exposed to the wind and the rain. On two occasions in six days, they were fed – the first time with a small tin of sardines between four and a small loaf of bread between five and the second with a small tin of lentils between four and a crust of bread between five. The prisoners stripped the trees of the young unripe nuts and then resorted to eating the leaves and the bark. Machine-gun emplacements prevented mass break-outs.[36]

Delegations of rightists came from all over Spain in search of leftists from their villages. On 7 April, 15,000 prisoners were taken to the bullring in Alicante and the castles of San Fernando and Santa Barbara. The remaining 30,000 were packed into cattle trucks and driven to the concentration camp built by the Republicans at Albatera in the southwest of the province. Many died during the journey.[37] The site of the camp had been chosen precisely so that prisoners could work on draining the inhospitable saltmarsh which surrounded it. It was intended to hold a maximum of two thousand prisoners and, during the Republic, had never held more than 1,039. Between its creation and the end of the Civil War, five prisoners had died.[38] Now, there were 30,000 prisoners. Hundreds died of malnutrition, many more were taken for execution in their home towns and many were shot each night for trying to escape.

Food and fresh water were as scarce as they had been in the Campo de los Almendros or the bullring. The prisoners were fed on only four occasions between 11 and 27 April, when they were given approximately sixty-five grams of sardines and sixty grams of bread on 11, 15, 20 and 27 April. Only the youngest and strongest survived as spectres of their former selves, prematurely aged and skeletal. It rained solidly for the first two weeks. Forced to sleep in mud, in soaking-wet clothes, many caught fevers and died. In the open, in mud that got ever deeper as the rain drove in, they were afflicted with plagues of mosquitoes, fleas and other parasites. Since there was no sanitation, many died of malaria, typhus and dysentery. There were few latrines, and the holes over which they were placed were not emptied and soon overflowed. Although there were many doctors among the prisoners, they had no access to medicines. To add to the humiliations of diarrhoea and constipation, many prisoners, tormented by scurvy, mange, fleas and other parasites, could barely remain upright during the daily rituals during which they were kept standing for hours. Twice a day, they had to sing Francoist anthems. Any mistakes with the lyrics were punished with beatings. On a daily basis, when commissions came from towns and villages looking for their enemies, the prisoners were expected to stand often for as long as four hours, being insulted throughout. Those taken away were often shot near by by commissions too impatient to wait until they reached their towns of origin.[39] Such conditions were replicated in camps all over Spain.

Among those in the greatest danger from the Francoists were Republican politicians, political commissars and journalists, all of whom were regarded as keeping alive Republican ideals throughout the war. Perhaps those most hated and sought were members of the SIM or the judiciary, the police or the prison service. The one-time head of the SIM in Madrid, Ángel Pedrero, who was in the Campo de los Almendros with two hundred of his men, remarked prophetically that they were doomed because of what they knew about the fifth column and its betrayals. The empty boasts of those who were claiming to have been fifth columnists would be exposed if Pedrero lived. To justify their exiguous triumphs, they had to exaggerate the horrific sufferings that he was alleged to have imposed upon them. Tens of thousands of others, whose only 'crime' was to have supported the Republic or served in the army, as well as their innocent wives and children, were appallingly treated.[40] Those who tried to escape were shot and the other prisoners were obliged to line up to witness the executions. Very few escape bids were successful and most of those who tried were quickly captured. One of those who managed to get away was Benigno Mancebo, of the CNT, who had supervised the tribunals of the Comité Provincial de Investigación Pública in Madrid. He was picked up in Madrid many months later and executed. In other prisons, the *sacas* were organized according to the date – three to be murdered on the 3rd of the month, seven on the 7th and so on.[41]

The anarchist journalist Eduardo de Guzmán recounted how he was taken to Madrid from Albatera in mid-June 1939 in a group that included Ricardo Zabalza, José Rodriguez Vega, the secretary general of the UGT, and David Antona, who, as secretary of the Madrid CNT, had tried to restrain the *sacas* and was later Civil Governor of Ciudad Real. It will be recalled that, as Civil Governor of Valencia, Zabalza had played a key role in halting the excesses of the anarchist Iron Column. The group was split up, and individuals were detained in any police station that happened to have room. They were packed together with twenty to thirty men in cells meant for two. With non-existent hygiene, they were persecuted by fleas and scabies. They were barely fed, receiving in the morning a quantity of filthy water with some malt that was presented as coffee, and at midday and in the evening a bowl of equally filthy water in which floated the occasional bits of carrot or turnip that was presented as soup or stew. For their survival, they had to depend on food parcels sent in by their families. With their breadwinners dead, in exile, on the run or in jail, the families were impoverished. Excoriated as worthless red scum, their chances of work were minimal. They still sent in food parcels at the cost of going hungry themselves. Many had no family in Madrid, or in whichever town they were imprisoned, but a spirit of solidarity prevailed and the more fortunate shared their parcels with them.

The dreadful conditions were merely the background to the central experience for most prisoners. In the police station in the Calle Almagro, where Eduardo de Guzmán was detained, they were repeatedly subjected to savage beatings for days without actually being asked any questions. It was part of a softening-up process. The beatings were delivered not by professional policemen but by men who had worked in the *checas* but now claimed to have been fifth columnists acting as provocateurs. There were humiliating rituals such as attempts to force them to beat each other up or immersing them in toilets full of faecal matter. Sometimes, the beatings went too far and the prisoner would be killed. There were many cases of prisoners who found a way of committing suicide rather than take the pain. They thereby avoided the risk of breaking down and confessing to something they had or had not done or even worse of becoming an informer. Several did break. In the end, nearly all prisoners would be forced to sign 'declarations' and confessions without being allowed to read them. Thus anyone who happened to be from Vallecas was held responsible for the massacre of rightists on the trains from Jaén, and those from Carabanchel were assumed guilty of the murder of General López Ochoa, even if they had been fighting on a distant front at the time.[42]

In Madrid, Zabalza was tortured but wrote no confession. He was tried on 2 February 1940 and shot at dawn on the 24th. One of the principal charges against him was that he had organized the perfectly legal harvest strike of the summer of 1934. Shortly before he was led out to the firing squad, he wrote to his parents:

> When you read these lines, I will be just a memory. Men who describe themselves as Christians have wished it so and I, who never knowingly did anyone harm, submit myself to this test with the same clear conscience that has ruled my entire life. You in the simplicity of your religious faith will never be able to understand how a man who committed no crime – even the prosecutor recognized that – and against whom there are no accusations of any shameful act should suffer the death that awaits him.[43]

One of the most notable cases of a confession extracted after torture was that of the FAI assassin Felipe Sandoval. Already suffering from advanced tuberculosis, he was beaten mercilessly for days on end. Bones broken in his chest, he would lie groaning in agony, coughing blood. He would be beaten again until he cleaned up the blood. Eventually, after repeated hours of being kicked and punched in the chest and stomach, he began to give up the names of comrades on the run, stating where they were to be found. Under threat of further beatings, and barely able to speak, he was forced to confront his fellow prisoners. He repeated, parrot-fashion, the accusations which his torturers had instructed him to make. Most of the prisoners already regarded Sandoval with disgust but, once they discovered his treachery, this turned into hatred. The general consensus was that his lack of moral fibre proved that, far from being a warrior in the social struggle, he was merely a thief and an assassin. They set about persuading him to commit suicide. Whether in response to their arguments or to his own suffering, finally on 4 July 1939 he threw himself from a window and died in the patio below. The anarchist Amor Nuño, who negotiated the agreement between the CNT and the JSU for the evacuation of prisoners from Madrid that led to the massacre of Paracuellos, was beaten to death in the Dirección General de Seguridad.[44]

When Guzmán and others had finally signed their 'confessions', they were transferred to prisons. In the truck carrying Guzmán, the driver visited nine prisons before he could find one which would admit the prisoners. Eventually, they were allowed into Yeserías in the southern outskirts of the city near Carabanchel. Food was scarce. After each meal, they were obliged to line up in the gallery for at least an hour and sing the Falangist, Carlist and monarchist anthems, 'Cara al Sol', 'Oriamendi' and the 'Marcha Real', with their right arms outstretched in the fascist salute. The ceremony would end with them having to shout '¡Viva Franco! ¡Viva la Falange!' and the ritual chant of '¡España, una, España, grande, España, libre!' Those considered to be singing with insufficient gusto would be taken out and punished by having their heads shaved, being beaten, sometimes even being shot. The most common punishment was for them to be obliged to stand singing, arm outstretched, for four or five hours. Most week nights, those sentenced to death there would be executed.[45]

Eduardo de Guzmán's trial was similar to that of Juan Caba Guijarro. More than thirty prisoners, accused of various 'crimes', were tried at the same time. One defender was named for all of them and they had no chance to talk to him until the eve of the trial. The prior assumption of the court was that all were guilty as charged. It was up to the accused to prove their innocence, but they were not usually allowed to speak. Theoretically, if they were accused of killing a named victim on a specific date in a specific place, and if they had not been in that place at that time, there was the slight possibility that they might be able to be heard and thus prove their innocence. However, it was common for someone to be accused of numerous murders without the victims, the times or the places being specified.[46]

The accusations were based on the declarations that, after weeks of beatings and torture, they had signed but not been allowed to read. Accordingly, the prisoners had little prospect of being found innocent. One of the women recounted to Guzmán the torture that had obliged her to sign a false confession of having participated in murders in the

Checa del Cine Europa. She showed him how her breasts had been horribly deformed as a result of being burned with lighters and matches until sections of flesh had burned away. Her nipples had been ripped off with staplers.[47]

On the day that Guzmán was tried, nearly two hundred men and sixteen women were tried in four trials which lasted little more than two hours. In Guzmán's trial, the proceedings started with the reading by the clerk of the charges against the twenty-nine accused. This was done in a nearly inaudible, mechanical monotone. The fact that the charges were incomprehensible bothered only the accused and their families. The judges, the prosecutor and the defending lawyer gave no sign of being interested. The charges that could be deciphered were wildly disparate, ranging from membership of a *checa* to having set fire to a church, been a political commissar in the Republican army, been an officer or simply been a volunteer. One of Guzmán's fellow defendants was the poet Miguel Hernández, who was accused both of having been a Communist commissar and of having written poems that were injurious to the Francoist cause. Guzmán himself was accused of being an editor of the newspaper *La Tierra* and of being the director of *Castilla Libre*, of insulting the rebel leaders and exaggerating Republican triumphs and of being responsible for the crimes committed by the readers of both newspapers. After the reading of the charges, there was cross-examination by the prosecutor. The prisoners were allowed to answer only yes or no. No witnesses were called. The members of the tribunal then took a recess. When they returned, the prosecutor gave a twenty-minute speech during which he accused the prisoners of being sub-human scum, cowards, criminals, illiterate savages, thieves and murderers.

All of the crimes of the bulk of the prisoners were then attributed to the inspiration of Hernández and Guzmán. The pages of *La Tierra* and *Castilla Libre* were alleged to have caused the electoral victory of the Popular Front in February 1936, the fire and subsequent massacre in the Cárcel Modelo in August that year and the resistance of Madrid in November. The prosecutor seemed unaware or unconcerned that *La Tierra* had closed down in May 1935 and that *Castilla Libre* was not created until February 1937. The defending lawyer, who had not been allowed to speak to any of the prisoners until the previous evening, had not received the files of all twenty-nine, nor those of others that he had to defend later, and had barely had time to skim over them. He basically asked for the accused to be given the sentence inferior to that demanded by the prosecutor – life imprisonment instead of the death penalty, thirty years instead of life imprisonment and so on. When the accused were allowed to speak, they were interrupted as soon as they opened their mouths. When Guzmán tried to point out the prosecutor's error in accusing him of publishing in non-existent newspapers, he was ordered to sit down and told that the court already knew everything he could possibly say.

The entire proceedings had taken less than two hours; indeed, if the recess was counted, less than ninety minutes. In that time, less than three minutes per accused, fifteen of the twenty-nine men had been sentenced to death and the remainder to prison sentences of life or thirty years. One man whose name had not even figured in the list of accusations was sentenced to death for an unspecified crime. One of Guzmán's fellow prisoners, the Communist Narciso Julián, was tried and sentenced to death along with sixteen others in a court martial lasting eleven minutes. In Tortosa, the trials were presided over by the notorious Lisardo Doval. On 10 August 1939, in two trials of fourteen and fifteen men, he barely permitted the prosecutor time to read out the charges. The accused had not met the defence lawyer before. The entire proceedings lasted less than half an hour. In the military court of Tarragona, it was common for twenty to thirty men and women to be tried together.[48]

A factor that facilitated Franco's state terror was the ever-closer collaboration between his security services and those of the Third Reich. This had begun in November 1937, when the authorities in Burgos requested that the German government send a team of experts to instruct the Spanish police in the latest methods for the eradication of communism. A team was assembled under the command of SS Colonel Heinz Jost, head of the Sicherheitsdienst Foreign Intelligence Office, a man who would be sentenced to death at the Nuremberg trials for atrocities committed in Russia. Jost's team reached Valladolid in mid-January 1938 and was attached to Franco's recently created Ministry of Public Order, headed by the seventy-five-year-old General Severiano Martínez Anido. Notorious as Civil Governor of Barcelona in the early 1920s when the infamous *ley de fugas* (the shooting of 'escaping' prisoners) was the norm, Martínez Anido had won Franco's admiration for his implacable imposition of law and order during the Primo de Rivera dictatorship. He wanted to step up the purge of leftists in captured territory and was delighted to have German help in creating the necessary instruments of repression. Jost returned to Germany in February 1938 but left behind a three-man SD team which helped reorganize the Francoist police administration, the political police and the criminal police force. One of its lasting legacies was the analysis and systematization of captured Republican documentation to create a vast repository of political information in Salamanca.[49]

Already before the war, Father Juan Tusquets had been feverishly compiling lists of supposed Jews and Freemasons. In 1937, with his help and the encouragement of the Caudillo himself, the Cuartel General (Franco's headquarters) had been collecting material seized in captured areas from the offices of political parties and trade unions, from Masonic lodges and from the houses of leftists. This had been done principally within the Judaeo-Masonic Section of the Military Information Service under the direction of Father Tusquets and Major Antonio Palau. The documentation was scoured by Tusquets to swell his lists of suspected Freemasons. The task was extended on 20 April 1937 with the additional creation of the Oficina de Investigación y Propaganda Antimarxista, manned by army officers and volunteers. The official objective was 'to collect, analyse, and catalogue all types of propaganda material that has been used by communism and its puppet organizations for its campaigns in our fatherland, with a view to organizing counter-propaganda, both in Spain and abroad'. Accordingly, efforts were made to seize all possible material on all the organizations of the left from conservative Republicans to anarchists, including Freemasons, pacifists and feminists. Limited numbers of copies of printed material were kept and the rest destroyed. More important than the counter-propaganda objective, correspondence and membership and subscription lists were scoured for names to go into a great file-card index of leftists to be arrested and tried.

On 29 May 1937, in a parallel initiative, Franco had named Marcelino de Ulibarri Eguílaz as head of the Delegation of Special Services. Its brief was to 'recover all documentation related to secret sects and their activities in Spain found in the possession of individuals or official entities, storing it carefully in a place far removed from danger where it can be catalogued and classified in order to create an archive that will permit the exposure and punishment of the enemies of the fatherland'.[50] Ulibarri, one of the most prominent Navarrese Carlists, had first met Franco in Zaragoza when he was Director of the General Military Academy. Ulibarri had also been instrumental in promoting the political career of Franco's brother-in-law, Ramón Serrano Suñer, in the city. His nomination was a reward for the part that he had played in facilitating the docile acceptance in April 1937 by the Carlist movement of its fusion with the Falange within Franco's single party, the Falange Española Tradicionalista y de las JONS. The appointment was also in recognition of the obsessive anti-Freemasonry that Ulibarri shared with Franco and, of course, with Father Tusquets. Ulibarri, long an admirer of Father Tusquets, became acquainted with his fellow anti-Masonic campaigner on his frequent visits to Franco's residence in the Episcopal Palace in Salamanca. So fierce was his hatred of Freemasons and Jews that Ulibarri was known among his Carlist comrades as 'the hammer of Freemasonry'.[51]

Within weeks, Ulibarri had set up the Office for the Recovery of Documents. With the Basque Country about to fall into Francoist hands, the ORD's purpose was the systematic seizure and subsequent classification of captured documentation. This task was entrusted to a small group of specially selected Civil Guards. Ulibarri soon argued for the merger of the ORD with the Oficina de Investigación y Propaganda Antimarxista. The determination of the overbearing and authoritarian Ulibarri to centralize all such activities eventually led to a clash with Tusquets.

With the prospect of the fall of Santander and Asturias following on that of the Basque Country, Ulibarri called for the collection of the documentation to be speeded up to permit the greatest efficiency in the subsequent repression. He stated that, in the wake of each victory, the police had to be supplied with 'the documents that indicate the guilt of those persons who are to be tried immediately'. After the victory at Teruel and the subsequent drive through Aragon towards the Mediterranean, huge opportunities were opening up. The desired departmental merger was formalized on 26 April 1938 when, as Minister of the Interior, Serrano Suñer issued a decree creating the Delegación del Estado para la Recuperación de Documentos (DERD). Its purpose was to gather, store and classify all documents emanating from political parties, organizations and individuals 'hostile to or even out of sympathy with the National Movement' in order to facilitate their location and punishment.[52]

The documentation gathered by the Judaeo-Masonic Section of the Military Information Service was passed over to the ORD in the immediate wake of the merger. However, in his efforts to centralize all information on Freemasons, Ulibarri also tried to make Tusquets hand over his personal archive and file-card system which had been swelled by material collected under the auspices of the SIM. Tusquets replied by denying that he had any material and claiming that his papers were in Barcelona. Eventually, however, it appears that Tusquets's archive was put at the disposal of the DERD. Until the occupation of Catalonia in January 1939, Tusquets continued to work in a much reduced Judaeo-

Masonic Section within the Military Information Service.[53]

One of the most influential of Ulibarri's staff was the policeman Eduardo Comín Colomer. In August 1938, all security services in the Francoist zone had been unified under the National Security Service headed by Lieutenant Colonel José Medina. One of its principal departments was the Investigation and Security Police, which in turn was divided into various sections. One of them, Anti-Marxism, consisted of three sub-sections, Freemasonry, Judaism and Publications. Comín Colomer was the head of both the Freemasonry and Judaism offices, as well as producing the *Boletín de Información Antimarxista*. In January 1939, he was seconded to the DERD to be Marcelino de Ulibarri's assistant. There he would play a key role in the classification and sifting of the captured material in preparation for its use by the secret police.[54] The material would become the basis for his own legendary library and also for a stream of books and pamphlets published over the following thirty-five years in which he denounced all elements of the Republican left. During this time, one of his assistants was Mauricio Carlavilla.[55]

DERD search teams followed Franco's troops as they moved across Aragon and into Catalonia. Barcelona was occupied on 26 January 1939 and placed under martial law the following day. DERD operatives started to search the city on 28 January and, by 7 June, had filled fourteen buildings with paper. Two hundred tons of documents were taken by train and truck from Catalonia to Salamanca. Eight hundred tons in total were gathered from all over what had remained of the Republican zone. With the help of the German specialists, this material was converted into a massive index of 80,000 suspected Freemasons, despite the fact that there had been nearer five than ten thousand Freemasons in Spain in 1936 and that fewer than one thousand remained after 1939. These files would facilitate the purges carried out in the 1940s under the infamous Special Tribunal created to implement the Law for the Repression of Freemasonry and Communism of February 1940.[56] Ulibarri was named its first president on 1 September 1940 but was replaced soon afterwards by General Andrés Saliquet, who had presided over the repression in Valladolid.[57]

Tusquets's labours bore fruit in that, in Franco's Spain, to be considered a Freemason was to be guilty of treason. This often meant execution without trial. Before the end of 1936, thirty members of the Masonic lodge Helmanti of Salamanca had been shot. A similar fate awaited thirty members of the Masonic lodge Constancia of Zaragoza, fifteen in Logroño, seven in Burgos, five from Huesca, seventeen in Ceuta, twenty-four in Algeciras, twelve in La Línea, fifty-four in Granada. All the Freemasons of Vigo, Lugo, A Coruña, Zamora, Cádiz, Melilla, Tetuán and Las Palmas were shot. The paranoiac exaggerations of the files accumulated in Salamanca meant that in Huesca, for example, where there were five Freemasons before the outbreak of war, one hundred men were shot after being accused of belonging to a lodge. As late as October 1937, eighty men in Málaga, accused of Freemasonry, were shot.[58]

In April 1938, Reichsführer SS Heinrich Himmler had contacted the Minister of Public Order, General Martínez Anido, to suggest widening the Spanish–German agreement on police co-operation. The Gestapo was interested in repatriating German Jews, Communists and Socialists who had fought in the International Brigades and been captured by Franco's forces. The agreement signed on 31 July permitted the swift exchange of leftists caught by the two security services. International Brigaders were handed over to Gestapo interrogators stationed in Spain, then despatched to Germany without even minimal judicial procedures. Individual cases for repatriation required only the approval of Franco, which was never refused. In return, a programme of training for Franco's political police was headed by SS Sturmbannführer Paul Winzer, the Gestapo attaché at the German Embassy in Salamanca. Martínez Anido died shortly before the end of 1938 and the functions of his Ministry were absorbed by the Ministry of the Interior. As his Director General of Security, Serrano Suñer appointed his crony José Finat y Escrivá de Romaní, the Conde de Mayalde. On Mayalde's suggestion, Himmler was awarded the regime's highest decoration, the Grand Cross of the Imperial Order of the Yoke and Arrows in recognition of his role in the fight against the enemies of Franco's Spain.[59]

Franco got his reward when, after the collapse of France, thousands of Spanish exiles fell into the hands of the Germans. On the very day, 22 June 1940, that the Franco-German armistice was signed in Compiègne, the Spanish Ministry of Foreign Affairs informed the French Embassy in Madrid that Azaña, Negrín and 'other red leaders' had requested visas to leave France for Mexico. Francoist efforts to extradite prominent Republicans from France would meet fewer problems in the German-occupied zone than in the territory of the newly established Vichy regime. Serrano Suñer requested that the French Ambassador, Le Comte Robert Renom de la Baume, inform the Vichy premier, Marshal Philippe Pétain, that Spain was impatiently waiting for France to 'neutralize' the Spanish red leaders currently in its territory. Then, on 24 July, the Spanish government asked the Comte de la Baume to prevent the departure for

Mexico of the seventy-four-year-old ex-Prime Minister, the conservative Manuel Portela Valladares, and several members of the Basque government.[60] The Franco government's interest in Portela's extradition derived from his prominence in the lists of Father Juan Tusquets.

These requests were followed on 27 August by a peremptory demand for the extradition without delay of 636 prominent Republicans believed by the Madrid government to be in Vichy France. Underlying these requests was the threat that, if they were not met, Spain would use its special relationship with Nazi Germany to push its territorial claims to French North Africa. In any case, Marshal Pétain loathed the Spanish Republicans since he considered most of them to be Communists, but he was reluctant to breach the right of asylum. Accordingly, to the intense annoyance of Madrid, Vichy insisted that requests for extradition had to pass through the courts, in accordance with the Franco-Spanish extradition treaty of 1877 and a law of 1927 that required each case to be judged individually. Nevertheless, the Vichy French police, using names and addresses supplied by José Félix de Lequerica, Franco's Ambassador, began to round up prominent Republicans, or at least place them under close surveillance. The French knew that to hand over these men would be to send them to certain death. Serrano Suñer was outraged that several, including Prieto and Negrín, had managed, with the collusion of the French authorities, to escape.[61]

On 1 July 1940, the President of Mexico, Lázaro Cárdenas, informed his Minister Plenipotentiary in France, Luis Ignacio Rodríguez Taboada, that Mexico was prepared to accept all Spanish refugees currently in France. Moreover, he instructed him to inform the French government that, until their transport could be arranged, all Spanish Republicans in France were under the diplomatic protection of Mexico. On 8 July, Rodríguez Taboada was received by Pétain in Vichy. After warning him that the Spaniards were undesirables, Pétain agreed in principle. A joint committee was set up to work out the details and, on 23 August, an agreement was signed by the Mexican government and Vichy. Many Vichy officials viewed this arrangement with suspicion and they, and the Germans in the occupied zone, complied with Spanish requests for many Republicans to be prevented from leaving France. Nevertheless, the Mexican initiative helped thousands of Republicans until November 1942, when the German occupation of Vichy France severed diplomatic relations between the two.[62]

If the Francoist authorities were hindered by the judicial scruples of the Vichy French and the humanitarian efforts of the Mexicans, they had no such problems regarding the Spaniards who found themselves in German-occupied France. In the days following the capture of Paris, groups of Falangists sacked the buildings in which various Spanish Republican organizations had their offices. Their funds and archives were seized and taken to Spain. Lequerica quickly established cordial relations with the Germans, who facilitated the activities of Spanish policemen within the occupied zone. The consequence was that the exiled Republicans' places of residence were searched, their goods, money and documents seized and their persons mistreated even when they had not been arrested or extradited.

In late August 1940, the Conde de Mayalde visited Berlin to discuss the fate of the captured Republican refugees. He was shown the latest police installations and techniques and met Himmler and other top brass of the various German police and security services, including Reinhard Heydrich, the head of the Sicherheitsdienst. Himmler proposed that Spain and Germany exchange police liaison officers who would have diplomatic immunity and the right to arrest citizens of their respective countries. Himmler would thereby be able to increase the Gestapo network in Spain to maintain surveillance of German refugees and the Spaniards would get rapid access to Republican exiles. Mayalde said he would have to consult with his Minister but suggested that Himmler might like to visit Spain himself.

Even before that visit took place, as soon as France fell Franco and Serrano Suñer hastened to take advantage of Himmler's earlier agreement with General Martínez Anido. Officers of the Dirección General de Seguridad were sent to Paris to arrange the extradition from occupied France of several recently arrested Republican leaders. The police attaché at the Paris Embassy, Pedro Urraca Rendueles, was in charge of securing their hand-over and taking them to the Spanish frontier. The Germans arrested prominent figures from lists provided by Lequerica including Lluís Companys Jover, the President of the Catalan Generalitat. On 10 July, in Pyla-sur-Mer, near Arcachon, German police, accompanied by a Spanish agent, had arrested Cipriano Rivas Cherif, Azaña's brother-in-law, along with two close friends of the exiled President, Carlos Montilla Escudero and Miguel Salvador Carreras. The following day, two Socialists, Teodomiro Menéndez, one of the leaders of the Asturian miners' insurrection of October 1934, and the journalist Francisco Cruz Salido, were arrested by the Germans in Bordeaux. On 27 July 1940, the Gestapo arrested in Paris the one-time editor of El Socialista and wartime Minister of the Interior Julián Zugazagoitia Mendieta. All were handed over to the Spanish police in France and taken to Madrid. There were no judicial procedures. According to Franco himself, the Germans delivered the prisoners 'spontaneously'.[63]

Companys had passed up various chances to escape from France because his son Lluís was seriously ill in a clinic in Paris. He was arrested in La Baule-les-Pins near Nantes on 13 August 1940, taken to Paris and detained in La Santé prison. However, on 26 August, La Santé received an order from the Conde de Mayalde requiring that Companys be handed over to Pedro Urraca Rendueles. He was transferred to Madrid in early September and imprisoned in the cellars of the DGS. For five weeks, he was kept in solitary confinement and tortured and beaten. Senior figures of the regime visited his cell, insulted him and threw coins or crusts of dry bread at him. On 3 October, his clothing bloodstained, a heavily manacled Companys was transferred to the Castillo de Montjuich in Barcelona.

Accused of military rebellion, he was subjected to a summary court martial on 14 October. While the military prosecutor prepared his case, Companys was given no opportunity to talk to the officer appointed to 'defend' him nor was he permitted to call witnesses on his own behalf. The defence advocate, an artillery captain, Ramón de Colubrí, pointed out that Companys had saved hundreds of lives of right-wingers in Catalonia, among them several army officers, including himself. At a trial lasting less than one hour, Companys was sentenced to death. The sentence was quickly approved by the Captain General of the IV Military Region, Luis Orgaz. In the early hours of the following day, the deeply Catholic Companys heard Mass and took communion. Refusing to wear a blindfold, he was taken before a firing squad of Civil Guards and, as they fired, he cried 'Per Catalunya!' According to his death certificate, he died at 6.30 a.m. on 15 October 1940. The cause of death was cynically given as 'traumatic internal haemorrhage'.[64]

General Orgaz was displeased by having to sign the death sentence, not for moral or humanitarian considerations but because he resented having to do what he regarded as the dirty work of Falangists. Until the beginning of 1940, all death sentences had required the approval of General Franco. However, there were long delays before he could review the large numbers of pending cases. So, on 26 January that year, to speed up the process, it was decreed that Franco's signature was no longer required. It was further decided that, in cases where those sentenced had been ministers, parliamentary deputies or civil governors or who had held other senior posts in the Republican administration, there could be no appeal for clemency.[65]

Four days after the death of Companys, Heinrich Himmler arrived in Spain. The invitation issued by Mayalde had been confirmed by Serrano Suñer, now newly appointed Foreign Minister. In the view of the British Ambassador, Serrano Suñer wanted to seek 'expert advice on the liquidation of opponents and the capture of political refugees'. Himmler was interested both in police collaboration and in preparing security for the forthcoming meeting between Hitler and Franco on the French border. Arriving on the morning of 19 October 1940, he was treated to a lavishly orchestrated welcome first in San Sebastián and then in Burgos. The streets of both cities were draped with swastika flags. On 20 October, he was greeted in Madrid by Serrano Suñer and senior officials of the Falange. He set up base at the Ritz Hotel, then had a meeting with Serrano Suñer at the Ministry of Foreign Affairs before both moved on to El Pardo to see Franco. Serrano Suñer was particularly interested in the whereabouts of several prominent captured Republicans, just as Himmler was concerned about exiled Germans. They reached an agreement whereby the Gestapo would establish an office in the German Embassy in Madrid and the Sicherheitsdienst would have offices in the main German consulates throughout Spain. German agents would thus operate with full diplomatic immunity. The same privilege would be applied to Spanish agents in Germany and, more importantly, in the German occupied zone of France.[66]

The Conde de Mayalde, who was also Mayor of Madrid, arranged an out-of-season bullfight in Himmler's honour in a swastika-emblazoned Plaza de Ventas and also invited him to a hunting party on his estate in Toledo. Over the next few days, Himmler was taken to the Prado and the Archaeological Museum in Madrid, the historical monuments of Toledo and El Escorial and the Monastery of Montserrat in Catalonia. His visits to the archaeological museum and to Montserrat were linked to his patronage of the SS Deutsches Ahnenerbe (German Ancestral Heritage). Himmler was always on the look-out for the talisman that would win the war. On the basis of Wagner's *Parsifal*, he was convinced that Montserrat was Montsalvat, the mountain where, according to Wolfram von Eschenbach and later Wagner, the Holy Grail was kept. In the magnificent library of Montserrat, he demanded to see the archives on the location of the Holy Grail. When he was informed that he was mistaken, he rudely claimed a Germanic pagan origin for everything to do with Montserrat and declared that Jesus Christ was not Jewish but Aryan.[67]

Alongside these cultural activities, there were visits to prisons and concentration camps. According to one of Serrano Suñer's closest aides,

Ramón Garriga, Himmler was shocked by what he saw. He thought it absurd that hundreds of thousands of able-bodied Spaniards were detained in appalling conditions, many facing the death sentence, at a time when the country was in desperate need of labour for the reconstruction of roads, buildings and houses destroyed during the Civil War. Apparently, he had been impressed by the work carried out by Republican exiles in labour battalions in France. He told Franco and Serrano Suñer that they were wasting valuable resources and that it made more sense to incorporate working-class militants into the new order rather than annihilate them. In his view, the regime should have shot a small number of prominent Republicans, imprisoned some more and let the rest go free under close police vigilance. Himmler made an important distinction between ideological and racial enemies. Franco was not convinced.[68]

While Himmler was still in Spain, the trial began of the other prominent Republicans handed over by the Germans at the end of July. Cipriano Rivas Cherif, Francisco Cruz Salido, Carlos Montilla, Miguel Salvador, Teodomiro Menéndez and Julián Zugazagoitia were charged with military rebellion and tried on 21 October. Recognizing that they had committed no crime, the prosecutor declared that he had no intention of citing concrete facts or calling witnesses since it was clear that they had all contributed to 'inducing revolution'. Their posts before and during the Civil War were considered to be more than sufficient proof. According to the prosecutor, anyone who held a position in a government that organized, tolerated or was impotent to prevent crimes of blood was guilty of those crimes. That Teodomiro Menéndez had retired from politics after October 1934 and, more crucially, that Ramón Serrano Suñer came and spoke on his behalf meant that he escaped the death penalty and was sentenced instead to thirty years' imprisonment. All five of the others were sentenced to death. Several significant Francoists, including the writer Wenceslao Fernández Flórez, the Falangist Rafael Sánchez Mazas and Antonio Lizarra, a leader of the Carlist Requetés, testified that Zugazagoitia, far from tolerating crimes of blood, had saved many lives, particularly of priests and nuns. Amelia de Azarola, the widow of Julio Ruiz de Alda, spoke of Zugazagoitia's efforts on her behalf. It was to no avail. Cruz Salido and Zugazagoitia were executed in the Madrid Cementerio del Este on 9 November 1940, along with fourteen other Republicans. On 21 December, Rivas Cherif, Montilla and Salvador learned that Franco had commuted their sentences to life imprisonment.[69]

There were many victims of the notion that, irrespective of their intentions and efforts, anyone who worked for the government had been impotent to prevent crimes of blood and so was guilty thereof. On 10 July 1940, the man who had been Civil Governor of Málaga from the beginning of the Civil War until mid-September 1936, José Antonio Fernández Vega, had been arrested in France by the Gestapo and brought to Spain along with Companys, Zugazagoitia, Cruz Salido, Cipriano Rivas Cherif, Teodomiro Menéndez and other deputies. He was tried in Málaga in March 1942, accused of responsibility for all the assassinations committed during his period of office. Despite an abundance of testimonies regarding the thousands of people that he had saved and the fact he had been overwhelmed by the local anarchist committees, he was sentenced to death and executed on 18 May 1942.[70]

The procedure for extraditions from Vichy France saw Blas Pérez González, the senior prosecutor of the Supreme Court, prepare arrest warrants that were passed to the Ministry of Foreign Affairs, which then made the corresponding request to Vichy. In November 1940, Lequerica had delivered a list of the names of nearly three thousand Republicans wanted for trial in Spain. The official response of Vichy was lukewarm and made it clear that an individual dossier for each case was required. The majority of extradition demands were unsuccessful since the requests were absurd.

For instance, Ventura Gassol had been the Minister of Culture in the Generalitat and had saved many lives of right-wingers and religious personnel threatened by the extreme left. In consequence, he himself had received death threats from extremist groups and, in October 1936, had been forced into exile in France. Nevertheless, the extradition request accused him of being a common criminal. All those who were the object of extradition demands were arrested and imprisoned until their cases were heard. Gassol remained in prison for three months before his case came to trial. The request was rejected when the French court heard the testimony of one of those whose life he had saved, the Archbishop of Tarragona, Francesc Vidal i Barraquer, himself exiled in Italy.[71] Another extradition that was turned down was that of Federica Montseny, the Minister of Health in the Largo Caballero cabinet.[72]

Frustrated by the legal niceties, Lequerica sometimes took matters into his own hands. One such case was the seizure in Nice on 10 December of Mariano Ansó, who had been Minister of Justice in the government of Negrín. He was arrested by the local police on the basis of instructions apparently emanating from Vichy. The team that came to take him, supposedly to Vichy, consisted of a close friend of Lequerica, an ultra-right-wing French policeman named Victor Drouillet, a White Russian in Lequerica's employ and the police attaché at the Spanish Embassy, Pedro Urraca Rendueles. They planned to take Ansó illegally to Spain. He managed to escape and was, with some difficulty, protected by a local police commissioner in Nice. He spent some time in prison before a judicial hearing denied the Spanish request for his extradition. The same team of Drouillet, Urraca and the White Russian thug were behind the arrest of the conservative Republican Manuel Portela Valladares. They usually confiscated the money and belongings of those they detained, on the pretext that they had been stolen in Spain. Portela was accused of stealing items that actually belonged to him and that he had managed to rescue from his house in Barcelona. They beat him to get him to hand over his property. Old and seriously ill, he considered suicide rather than face prison but was dissuaded by his friends. His case was eventually heard in Aix-en-Provence on 15 September 1941. The request for extradition was rejected on the grounds that the Spanish application had specified no date, place or victim in respect of the supposed crimes. Given that Portela had lived in France since 31 July 1936, the French court regarded the application as dubious. The Spanish authorities immediately presented a second extradition request which was rejected on 25 November 1941.[73]

Another ludicrous extradition request was made for the under-secretary of Justice in the Generalitat, Eduardo Ragasol i Sarrà. A distinguished lawyer in Barcelona, he had been in Madrid when the Civil War broke out and had taken part in the defence of the capital. While there, anarchists had looted his house in Barcelona. After the events of May 1937, the new Catalan Minister of Justice, Pere Bosch i Gimpera, had appointed him his under-secretary. In that position, he had worked for the re-establishment of law and order, imprisoning many extremists. At the end of the war, he went into exile and worked helping Republican refugees and also recruiting Spanish volunteers to join French forces. He was arrested on 7 July 1940 after Lequerica had accused him of holding 'Republican treasure', a reference to the funds taken out of Spain by the Republican government to help pay for the exiles. Over the next year, he was repeatedly arrested by the Vichy police but released each time. Finally, Blas Pérez drew up an extradition request falsely accusing Ragasol of running a parallel police force responsible for numerous murders. It was a striking example of the hypocrisy and vindictiveness that underpinned Francoist 'justice'. Blas Pérez, as a lawyer and professor of law in the University of Barcelona, knew Ragasol personally and himself had escaped from the Catalan capital thanks to the intervention of the Generalitat. Despite the fact that the accusation mentioned no names, dates or places nor provided any proof, a Vichy French court acceded to the Spanish request on 2 August 1941. Until energetic protests from the Mexican government persuaded the Vichy government not to hand Ragasol over to the Francoist authorities, he underwent considerable psychological humiliation and physical mistreatment in prison. Moreover, the threat of extradition and his frequent arrests created great unease within the exile community.[74]

In November 1940, the anarcho-syndicalist Joan Peiró Belis, who had denounced the excesses of the FAI in Catalonia and had been Minister of Industry in Largo Caballero's government, was arrested by the Vichy police in Chabris, in the Loire. He was jailed for three weeks for illegally crossing the demarcation line and then handed over to the Gestapo and taken to Germany. On 19 February 1941, the Germans sent him to Madrid. For two and a half months, he was held in the cellars of the Dirección General de Seguridad. To make him reveal the location in France of the funds used to help Republican refugees, he was badly beaten. Police reports from Barcelona confirmed that Peiró had also saved many lives during the war. Despite both this and the fact that he had combated the extremists in his native Mataró, he was held responsible for crimes there. On 8 April, he was transferred to the provincial prison in Valencia where, for over a year, various leading Falangists offered him his liberty if he would join the regime's official unions, the Vertical Syndicates. Having refused, he was court-martialled on 21 July 1942, accused of stealing millions of pesetas and of organizing the *checas* in Barcelona. Unusually, Peiró had a dedicated defence lawyer, Lieutenant Luis Serrano Díaz. Moreover, many people whose lives he had saved, including senior army officers, the heads of two monastic congregations and Francisco Ruiz Jarabo, Director General of Labour, submitted testimony on his behalf. The founder of the Falange in Barcelona, Luys Gutiérrez Santamarina, spoke eloquently in his defence. The judge warned Serrano Díaz that if he spoke for more than thirty minutes he risked serious punishment. He spoke for an hour and a quarter – an unprecedented defence in a Francoist court martial. It was to no avail. Peiró was found guilty and shot three days later.[75]

One of Peiró's fellow prisoners in Valencia was Dr Joan Peset i Aleixandre. An immensely distinguished bacteriologist and also a lawyer, he had been the rector of the University of Valencia from 1932 to 1934 and a parliamentary deputy for Azaña's Izquierda Republicana in the Popular Front. During the war, he worked as a doctor in military hospitals. When Valencia fell, he was one of the thousands of Republicans whose hopes of evacuation were thwarted and who were captured and taken first to the infamous concentration camp of Albatera and later to that of Portaceli. Although the mild-mannered and kindly Peset had worked hard to prevent killings by the anarchists, he was tried on the basis of accusations from three envious professional rivals. Although none of them could produce any evidence of wrongdoing, they all alleged, in suspiciously similar language, that his position as a celebrated Republican made him responsible for all of the killings in Valencia and Castellón.

Many people, including several nuns and a priest, testified to Peset's efforts in preventing detentions, murders and church burnings by extremists. A court martial on 4 March 1940 found him guilty of military rebellion and condemned him to death but with a recommendation for commutation of the sentence. In protest, the Falange presented the text of an academic lecture on applied psychology in which, en passant, he had denounced the military coup and said that it was a civic duty to oppose it. The court reconvened on 25 March and reaffirmed the death sentence this time without the possibility of commutation. He was condemned not for his crimes, since he had committed none, but for what he represented in terms of the ideals of the Republic. Twenty-eight personalities, religious, military and even Falangist, petitioned for his sentence to be commuted. During the fourteen months that he had to wait for his sentence to be confirmed, he worked as a doctor in the model prison of Valencia. He was shot in the cemetery of Paterna on 24 May 1941.[76]

Another example of the vindictiveness of Francoist 'justice' even with those who had worked hard to stop the repression in the Republican zone was Melchor Rodríguez. His efforts to save right-wingers in Madrid had led some of his anarchist comrades to suspect him of being a traitor. Even his wife became convinced that, at best, he had naively let himself be used by the fifth column and, when he rejected her suspicions, she left him in early 1939. Having been named Mayor of Madrid by Casado's Junta, he surrendered the capital to Franco's troops. Thereafter, he was arrested on 13 April 1939 and tried by court martial in December that year. After an energetic defence by Ignacio Arenillas de Chaves, an extremely competent military lawyer, he was found not guilty. However, the Auditor General of the Military Region of the Centre rejected the verdict and insisted on a retrial.

Melchor Rodríguez was tried again on 11 May 1940 accused of a crime that took place in Madrid at a time when he was in Valencia. A young and inexperienced defender was appointed two days before the trial. He was not permitted to meet his client or given any prosecution documents until the trial had actually started. The prosecutor, Leopoldo Huidobro Pardo, was a Carlist who had suffered frightening experiences in Madrid during the war. This more than accounted for his bitterly hostile attitude towards prominent CNT members. Furthermore, Huidobro's hatred of the left was compounded by his distress at the death of his cousin Father Fernando Huidobro Polanco. He was, of course, unaware that Father Fernando had been shot in the back by a Legionario. However, his life had been saved when he was enabled to take refuge in the Finnish Embassy, something facilitated by Melchor Rodríguez. Nevertheless, he accused Melchor of being a bloodthirsty gunman and demanded the death penalty. However, the pantomime of a trial rigged with false testimonies was ruined by the unscheduled appearance of General Agustín Muñoz Grandes, who spoke on Melchor's behalf and presented a list of over two thousand rightists whose lives he had saved. Among them were many aristocrats and one of the founders of the Falange, Raimundo Fernández Cuesta. Unlike Peiró, Melchor had not been a minister of the Republic and the main witness on his behalf outranked everyone else in the room. The planned death sentence was commuted to twenty years and one day and he was sent on 1 March 1941 to the prison of El Puerto de Santa María in Cádiz. Then Muñoz Grandes, as Captain General of the I Military Region, commuted his sentence to twelve years and a day, which permitted him provisional liberty.[77]

Melchor Rodríguez was one of the few senior elements of the Casado Junta who had remained in Madrid, naively believing that, since he had no blood on his hands, he had nothing to fear. The most senior of all was the Socialist Julián Besteiro, who had been Foreign Minister in the seven-man Junta. Besteiro had done nothing to oppose the military rising and had done more than most to put an end to Republican resistance. He was the only one of the Casado Junta's members to stay in Madrid. The others, including the notorious organizer of the anarchist *checas* of Madrid, Eduardo Val Bescós, managed to escape with Casado to England. It was inevitable that Besteiro would face the full ferocity of the repression since he was a parliamentary deputy, had been president of both the

Socialist Party and its trade union movement, the UGT, and been President of the Constituent Cortes in 1931.

Nevertheless, Besteiro chose wilfully to ignore the revenge being wreaked on captured Republican areas. Instead, he believed assurances from his contacts in the fifth column that Franco guaranteed the life and liberty of those innocent of common crimes. Moreover, although the Casado coup had already undermined the chances of a properly organized evacuation of those in danger, Besteiro refused to allow any government resources to be used for those who needed to flee. His logic was that the national wealth was required in Spain for post-war reconstruction and that Franco would treat those who stayed behind in Spain all the better for safeguarding resources. He facilitated the peaceful surrender of the Republic to the Francoists, in co-operation with the clandestine Falange and the fifth-column organization. He complacently believed that his contribution to shortening the war would incline Franco to use him in the process of post-war reconstruction.

Despite his hope that a shared anti-communism would permit him to be the instrument of reconciliation between the two sides, Besteiro, nearly sixty-nine years old, was arrested and, on 8 July 1939, faced a court martial charged with military rebellion. It was an indication of his importance that his case was in the hands of Lieutenant Colonel Felipe Acedo Colunga, head prosecutor of the court of the Army of Occupation. Acedo Colunga recognized that Besteiro was innocent of any crime of blood, yet demanded the death sentence.[78] In the event, he was sentenced to life imprisonment which was commuted to thirty years of hard labour. At the end of August 1939, he was sent to the prison of Carmona. His health destroyed by lack of adequate food and medical attention, he was forced to undertake hard physical work, scrubbing floors, cleaning latrines. This latter activity led to an untreated septicaemia which caused his death on 27 September 1940.[79] Besteiro was unfortunate that the Francoists, unable to try Azaña, Prieto, Negrín, Largo Caballero and the other major figures who had made it into exile, vented their hatred on him.[80]

Another prominent Republican who fell foul of Francoist vindictiveness was the second wartime Prime Minister, Francisco Largo Caballero. He crossed the French frontier on 29 January 1939 and lived in Paris until two days before the German occupation. Thereafter, the Vichy authorities moved him around and kept him always under surveillance. Blas Pérez prepared the application for his extradition at the end of May 1941. It accused him of direct responsibility for assassinations, theft and looting. Four months passed before the Vichy authorities arrested him on 9 October 1941. Now seventy-one years old, Largo Caballero was imprisoned in harsh conditions in Limoges. The petition from Madrid was heard, on the same day as another for the extradition of Federica Montseny, and both were rejected. Although Montseny was released, Largo Caballero was kept confined in Nyons. Shortly after the German occupation of Vichy France, he was arrested again on 20 February 1943 by the Italian political police and two Gestapo agents. He was interrogated in Lyons before being held in Paris. On 8 July, he was sent to Berlin and then on 31 July imprisoned in the brutal labour camp of Sachsenhausen in Oranienburg. Had he been extradited to Spain, the pressure for him to be shot would have been immense but, in the wake of the fall of Mussolini, Franco did not want to risk an international scandal likely to be greater than that provoked by the execution of Companys. Largo Caballero believed that the Madrid authorities did not request his transfer to Spain because they preferred to see him die in a German camp. In fact, he survived to be liberated by the Soviet forces, but his health was broken and he died in March 1946.[81]

When Blas Pérez compiled the extradition applications to Vichy he drew on a body of 'evidence' from one of the central instruments of the Francoist state project which had first begun to function after the conquest of the north in 1937. This was the Causa General or the 'State proceedings to collect information about criminal acts and other aspects of life in the red zone from 18 July 1936 until the liberation'. It was formalized on 26 April 1940 when the prosecution service of the Supreme Court was instructed to start collecting information on alleged Republican misdeeds. A colossal collection of documents was assembled consisting of transcripts of interrogations of prisoners, denunciations by witnesses and captured documents. It provided 'evidence' for the trials of Republicans and was a central part of the regime's process of self-legitimization. Its published version established, for internal and external consumption, the Manichaean narrative of the Civil War's meaning which underlay the dictatorship's rhetoric until Franco's death.

Its rhetorical message was that heroic Christian martyrs had sacrificed their lives in the struggle against the Anti-Spain of the depraved hordes of Moscow. This provided some solace to the bereaved among the regime's supporters, as did the belief that the guilty would get their comeuppance. A crucial element in the assembly of evidence was the encouragement of denunciations. Not to come forward was to invite suspicion. As the *Diario Montañés* of Santander declared, 'you can forgive what they did to you but you have no right to deprive the justice system of any enemy of the Fatherland'. Any denunciation, however implausible, could lead to arrests, interrogations, torture and often executions. The delegations from villages that came to the prison camps in search of alleged criminals were often accompanied by men or women dressed in mourning. Sometimes, they might identify those guilty of crimes but would happily seize sacrificial victims in the form of anyone from their village who had been a member of the Popular Front Committee or was a trade unionist. This reflected in practical terms the homogenization of guilt which was the underlying message of the Causa General – all of the defeated were guilty of every crime committed during the war in the Republic zone.[82] There were cases of groups of individuals executed for crimes that only one of them could have committed and cases of people executed for crimes that they could not possibly have committed.[83] In general, Francoist 'justice' attributed all deaths to a deliberate policy of the Republican government and the Generalitat. This was simply not true and a projection on to the Republicans of the rebels' own murderous intentions.

The repression of Republicans was not limited to prison and death. They were also subject to a huge state-sponsored programme of extortion based on the Law of Political Responsibilities, announced in Burgos on 9 February 1939. Although the concept had been developed in the rebel zone since the start of the war, the timing left no doubt that a negotiated peace was out of the question. Its first article was as sweeping as it was awkwardly worded: 'The political responsibility is declared of all those persons who, after 1 October 1934 and before 18 July 1936, contributed to the creation or aggravation of the subversion of any kind of which Spain was made a victim, and of those others, who from the second of said dates have opposed or might oppose the National Movement with concrete acts or serious passivity'.[84]

The concept of 'serious passivity' ensured that no Republican would go unpunished and justified the 'legal' persecution of any individual who had not actively fought in the insurgent ranks or else been a fifth columnist. It also permitted the trial and punishment of anyone who had exercised their political and trade union rights under Republican democracy from 1 October 1934 until the conquest of their area by the military rebels. The punishments involved massive fines and/or the confiscation of property ranging from businesses, factories, clinics and houses, via bank savings and shareholdings, to household furniture, crockery and cutlery. The Law was designed not just to punish the defeated but also to pay for the war that had been inflicted upon them. This 'juridical monstrosity' as it has been called was applied retroactively and criminalized activities, from membership of a political party to government service, that were perfectly legal when they were carried out.[85]

Many of the sentences imposed under the Law were applied against people who had long since been executed or gone into exile. In such cases, their fines were passed on to their widows or other relatives if they could be found. A case was brought against the exiled lawyer Eduardo Ragasol i Sarrà. The denunciation which provoked the case came from members of the town council of Caldes de Monbui, north of Barcelona. They wanted to evict his mother from the family property to get hold of it. The Tribunal of Political Responsibilities confiscated the family patrimony in December 1939, although, three years later, his mother managed to get part of the property returned.[86]

A more striking case was that of Josep Sunyol i Garriga, the president of Barcelona football club since 1934, who was executed in August 1936. Sunyol, the wealthy owner of sugar factories in La Rioja, Zaragoza, Málaga and Lleida, had represented Barcelona for Esquerra Republicana in all three Cortes. The dressing rooms of the football club's stadium at Les Corts had been used to hide many religious personnel while the Generalitat made arrangements to evacuate them. At the beginning of the war, Sunyol had been sent to Madrid to liaise with the government of José Giral. On 6 August, he went to the Guadarrama front to the north-west of the capital to see the Alto del León, from which the Republican press had erroneously announced the expulsion of Mola's troops. His car strayed into rebel territory and he and his companions were shot by the roadside. There was no trial. His properties located in the rebel zone were confiscated immediately. On 24 October 1939, the regional Tribunal of Political Responsibilities opened proceedings, charging him with being a Communist and a separatist. Since Josep Sunyol failed to appear to respond to these charges, his father was sentenced to a fine of 5 million pesetas and exclusion from any senior position in the industrial or banking world.[87]

Hardly less extraordinary was the case of Camil Companys i Jover, the youngest of the Catalan President's three brothers. Although his political activity had been negligible, as a precaution he had gone into exile when the rebels occupied Barcelona. He had been obliged to leave behind his wife and five-year-old son and faced acute economic difficulties in France. Before the war, he had been a member of the Catalan Socialist Party and then of Esquerra Republicana, and had served as president of the executive committee of the Barcelona Bar Association. In September 1939, the Tribunal of Political Responsibilities started proceedings against him despite the fact that its preliminary investigations had produced testimony from his parish priest and his neighbours to the effect that he had protected numerous religious during the war. The proceedings continued even after Camil had committed suicide on 20 September 1940 when he heard of the arrest of his elder brother Lluís. His widow, Josefa Pascual, was interrogated one month after his death. On 28 February 1941, the deceased Camil was sentenced to fifteen years' exclusion from professional activity and a fine of 1,000 pesetas, for which Josefa was made liable.[88]

Nothing better illustrated the spirit of the law than Franco's choice of Enrique Suñer Ordóñez as president of the national Tribunal of Political Responsibilities. During the war, as vice-president of the Education and Culture Committee of Franco's first government, Suñer, previously a professor of paediatric medicine at Madrid University, had overseen the purging of schoolteachers. In a book published in 1938, he wrote of the blood shed during the war. He contrasted the blood 'of vile brutes, with worse instincts that those of wild beasts', with the blood that flowed 'from noble Spanish breasts – soldiers and militiamen – generous youth, full of sacrifice and heroism so immense that their wounds raise them to the status of the demigods of Greek myth'. Then he asked: 'And this horrific mortality, must it go without its just punishment? Our spirit rebels against a possible impunity of the pitiless individuals who caused our tragedy. It is just not possible that Providence and man leave without punishment so many murders, rapes, cruelties, pillages and destructions of artistic wealth and the means of production. It is necessary to swear before our beloved dead that the deserved sanctions will be executed with the most holy of violence.'[89]

Suñer regarded Republican politicians as:

horrific, truly devilish men. Sadists and madmen working with professional thieves, fraudsters, armed robbers and murderers have occupied the posts of ministers, under-secretaries, senior civil servants and all kinds of important jobs ... Wild boars and cloven-hoofed beasts running through parliament, in search of sacrificial victims to bite with their fangs or smash with their hooves ... Monsters in the style of Nero, leaders of sects and their agents, murdered the greatest hope of the Fatherland: Calvo Sotelo ... Behind them stand the Freemasons, the socialists, the communists, the Azañistas, the anarchists, all the Jewish leaders of the black Marxism that has Russia for its mother and the destruction of European civilization for its motto. Spain has been before and is again the theatre of an epic combat between Titans and apocalyptic monsters. The programmes laid out in the *Protocols of the Elders of Zion* are beginning to become reality.[90]

The aim of the war, wrote Suñer, was 'to strengthen the race', for which 'it is necessary to bring about the total extirpation of our enemies, of those front-line intellectuals who brought about the catastrophe'.[91] Determined to eliminate any intellectuals who had contributed to the liberal culture of the Republic, Suñer sent many denunciations to the rebel intelligence service, the Servicio de Información Militar. At the end of June 1937, he denounced the family of the distinguished medievalist and philologist Ramón Menéndez Pidal, president of the Spanish Academy. A conservative, Menéndez Pidal had fled into exile, terrified of being the victim of the left. Suñer also denounced Menéndez Pidal's wife, the feminist and philologist María Goyri, who had been the first woman in Spain to earn a university degree (1896) and later a doctorate (1909). Suñer claimed that she had perverted her husband and children and was one of the most dangerous people in Spain.[92]

The machinery of the Tribunal was soon clogged with a massive backlog of cases, not least since the process invited denunciations. The extent to which these were motivated by personal envy or resentment led to expressions of disgust by the military authorities who had to judge them.[93] Unable to cope, Suñer was succeeded in December 1940 by the man who had been first Civil Governor of Barcelona after its capture. The pro-Nazi Wenceslao González Oliveros had immediately embarked on a fierce persecution of Catalan language and culture. He too had difficulty dealing with the huge backlog left by Suñer. In fact, this was inevitable given the extent of the application of the Law of Political Responsibilities as merely part of the ongoing repression. There was a shortage of legally trained personnel that could be hired by the Tribunal. Hundreds of thousands of cases were opened, including against Negrín, Azaña, Largo Caballero, Dolores Ibárruri and many more exiled Republicans. Fines imposed on dead or exiled Republicans were collected by the confiscation of their families' goods. Eventually, the Tribunal collapsed under the weight of its own ambition. The regional Tribunal of Albacete had resolved only 9.25 per cent of its open cases. The Tribunal in Madrid had resolved only 15.51 per cent of the cases that had gone to trial. It had eleven times as many files still awaiting trial. The Law was modified in February 1942 to reduce the number of cases and, in April 1945, the regime declared that the Tribunal had done its job. No more new cases were opened, but 42,000 were still pending. Eventually, in 1966, a general pardon was announced for offences defined as coming under the jurisdiction of the Tribunal.[94]

Systematic persecution would continue in virtually every aspect of daily life well into the 1950s. The mass of the Republican population would suffer from grinding poverty, with families deprived of their menfolk, women forced into prostitution, labouring men forced to take work at miserable wages, schoolteachers deprived of their jobs and a rationing system which intensified social division. The worst hit was the prison population. As early as 15 August 1936, Mola had told his secretary, José María Iribarren, 'prison must be a place of atonement'.[95] Two and a half years later, the decision of the regime to ignore the Geneva Convention on prisoners of war ensured that the prisons and camps which held hundreds of thousands of Republicans would become what one of them called 'cemeteries for the living'.[96] In the north of Lugo, the provincial prison quickly became so full that is was necessary to improvise another. This provisional jail was set up in a decrepit and run-down old convent, known as the Prisión Habilitada de Alfoz. It held more than five hundred prisoners, the majority peasants. It would not have been difficult to escape, but they never tried. Weakened by hunger, their spirits broken, they would not have escaped, in the view of one of them, even if the gates had been left open. After all, outside the walls, all of Spain had been converted into a gigantic prison.[97]

Provincial prisons held between ten and fifteen times more inmates than they had been built for. Temporary prisons were established in converted colleges and schools, convents, hospitals and military barracks. Confusingly, some, such as the charity hospital in the Horta district of Barcelona, were denominated concentration camps. The regime used the term 'concentration camp' in a confused and chaotic manner when referring to detention or classification centres in improvised premises often in old buildings spread over a wide area.[98] These additional premises barely reduced the problem of overcrowding, the scale of which can be deduced from the fact that many detainees were held for more than a year before their first interrogation. On 6 May 1940, Colonel Máximo Cuervo Radigales, the Director General of Prisons, sent a report to Franco complaining about the excessive number of prisoners. It stated that, in round numbers, in addition to those awaiting trial, 103,000 prisoners had already been tried and sentenced, and 40,000 of them had faced trial since 1 April 1939. He estimated that, at the current rate of trials and sentencing, it would take at least three years to deal with the backlog and that only if no new arrests were made. He went on to lament that there were not enough judges from the Military Legal Corps to cope and that the people recruited were not of the required quality.[99]

Franco's rhetoric of the need for the defeated to seek redemption through sacrifice provided a clear link between the repression and the capital accumulation that made possible the economic boom of the 1960s. The destruction of trade unions and the repression of the working class led to starvation wages. This permitted banks, industry and the landholding classes to record spectacular increases in profits. There can be few doubts about the extent to which this was a deliberate policy approved by Franco. This was most starkly obvious in terms of the exploitation of captured Republican soldiers. At first, they were herded into rapidly constructed 'camps' such as those at Castuera in Badajoz, Nanclares de la Oca in Álava or Miranda de Ebro in Burgos. After a crude process of classification aimed at identifying officers and political commissars, who were shot, others were deemed to be usable in the Francoist ranks or, as was the case with a huge number, left to wait until their cases could be clarified.[100] Those deemed suitable for recycling had to redo their military service and were usually sent to work on fortifications, or to punishment or work battalions known as penal columns.[101]

The human cost of forced labour, the deaths and the suffering of the workers and their families were matched by the fortunes made by the private companies and the public enterprises that exploited them. The penal columns provided labour for mines, railway building and the reconstruction of the so-called 'devastated regions'. Stone walls were erected around coal mines in Asturias, the Basque Country and León so that prisoners could be used to dig coal. Many would die from silicosis. More died in the mercury mines of Almadén because of the dangerous conditions. Before the war, no one was permitted to work for more than three hours on two days per week; now, they were forced to work for four and a half hours on three days. In the pyrites mines of Tharsis and Rio Tinto in Huelva, productivity was greater than before 1936 with several thousand fewer workers.[102]

The Militarized Penal Colonies Service was set up on 8 September 1939 for long-term public-works projects such as the hydraulic schemes along the rivers Guadiana, Tagus, Guadalquivir and Jarama. The largest such project was the Canal del Bajo Guadalquivir, dug out over 110 miles and twenty years, a huge irrigation venture in the interests of the same

ABOVE Aurelio Fernández, head of the Patrulles de Control in Barcelona.

ABOVE RIGHT Juan García Oliver, anarchist Minister of Justice in Largo Caballero's cabinet.

RIGHT Ángel Pedrero García, head of the SIM of the Centre zone, seen here in Francoist captivity shortly before his execution.

BELOW The Brigada García Atadell outside their Madrid headquarters, the Rincón Palace. Agapito García Atadell, centre with glasses.

LEFT Santiago Carrillo – addressing a meeting in the Madrid bullring, 5 April 1936.

BELOW Melchor Rodríguez, the anarchist 'red angel' who saved the lives of many right-wing prisoners, in October 1937 with his daughter and his wife who was injured in a rebel bombing raid.

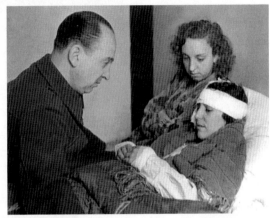

BELOW The wounded Pablo Yagüe receives visitors including José Cazorla, far left, and General Miaja, far right.

RIGHT The cameraman
Roman Karmen and the
Pravda correspondent
Mikhail Koltsov who
acted as messengers for
General Gorev during
the siege of Madrid.

RIGHT Andreu Nin
(head of the POUM)
and Vladimir Antonov-
Ovseenko (Russian
Consul.)

ABOVE Left to right: Josif Grigulevich, (NKVD
assassin, organizer of the Republic's crack
security squads, the Brigadas Especiales,
and almost certainly the murderer of Andreu
Nin), Roman Karmen, then two of the NKVD
staff, Lev Vasilevsky and then his boss, Grigory
Sergeievich Syroyezhkin. Madrid, October 1936.

ABOVE To left, Vittorio Vidali, pseudonym
Carlos Contreras, a member of the NKVD
Administration for Special Tasks
(assassination, terror, sabotage and
abductions) also involved in the execution
of right-wing prisoners, with the journalist
Claud Cockburn.

ABOVE Refugees flee from Queipo's repression in Málaga towards Almería.

LEFT Exhaustion overcomes the refugees from Málaga on the road to Almería.

BELOW The Regulares enter northern Catalonia, January 1939.

ABOVE Republican prisoners packed into the fortress of Montjuich in Barcelona, February 1939.

ABOVE No military threat from those making the long trek to the French border.

RIGHT A crowd of Spanish women and children refugees cross the border into France at Le Perthus.

TOP Recently arrived at
Argelès, women await
classification.

ABOVE The male refugees
are detained at Argelès –
the only facility being
barbed wire.

LEFT Prisoners carry
rocks up the staircase at
the Mauthausen-Gusen
death camp near Linz.

ABOVE A beaming Franco welcomes Himmler to Madrid. On the right, in black uniform, Ramón Serrano Suñer, centre Moscardó with dark glasses.

BELOW Antonio Vallejo-Nájera, head of Franco's psychiatric services. He conducted experiments on prisoners to identify the 'red gene'.

BELOW RIGHT Himmler visits the psycho-technic checa of Alfonso Laurencic in Barcelona.

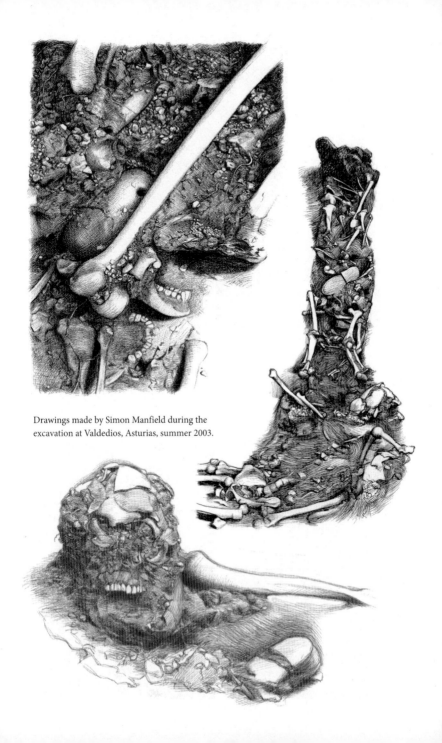

Drawings made by Simon Manfield during the
excavation at Valdedios, Asturias, summer 2003.

landowners who had backed the military coup. Begun in January 1940, it soon involved five thousand prisoners, among them Republican engineers, architects, doctors and accountants as well as carpenters, electricians, plumbers and builders' labourers.[103] Two thousand prisoners were used building mountain roads in the Pyrenees in Navarre. Many more were used on irrigation channels, dams and reservoirs.[104] The great public works could be presented as a programme of retribution that both perpetuated and honoured the sacrifice made by the martyrs in the struggle against Republican depravity.

The most extreme example of the exploitation of Republican prisoners was Franco's personal caprice, the gigantic basilica and towering cross of the Valle de los Caídos. Twenty thousand were employed, and several were killed or badly injured, in the construction of this mausoleum for the Caudillo, a monument to his victory which was intended, in his own words, 'to have the grandeur of the monuments of old, which defy time and forgetfulness'.[105]

The use of prisoners as slave labour was a way of making them pay the costs of their own incarceration and of rebuilding the Spain destroyed by the war. The conditions in the camps and prisons were unsustainable. During the terrible winter of 1940–1, many prisoners died of hunger and the intense cold. Many also died from tuberculosis and typhoid especially during the epidemic in the spring of 1941. Indeed, more died from disease in prison than from execution. In the prison of Córdoba alone, 502 died in 1941.[106] In addition to the use of prisoners as slave labour, there was a variation, given a theological veneer by the Jesuit Father José Agustín Pérez del Pulgar, known as 'the redemption of sentences through work'. This enabled prisoners to shorten their sentences and, at the same time, earn some money for their families. It raised substantial funds for the regime.[107] In October 1938, the Board of Trustees for the Central Trust (Patronato) for the Redemption of Sentences through Work had been established. The work was regarded as reparation for war damage which was blamed on the prisoners, despite being largely caused by rebel artillery and air raids. Indeed, the National Service for the Reconstruction of Devastated Regions established by Serrano Suñer in March 1938 was represented on the Patronato and made full use of the labour pool.[108]

The scheme was also necessary because the prison system was on the verge of collapse. In response to an international commission, in 1954 the Francoist Ministry of Justice admitted that there had been more than 270,719 prisoners in 1940. In fact, these figures referred only to those prisoners who had already been sentenced and there were at least another

100,000 awaiting trial. Nor did they refer to those working in 'militarized penal colonies'. It was hardly surprising that the prisons received constant visits from priests preaching the ideas of Pérez del Pulgar.[109] Sometimes the jobs offered were in primitive workshops established in the prisons themselves, producing clothing, furniture and many other kinds of goods, but more often they were for dangerous jobs in mines, digging railway tunnels and other public works for which the wages were scandalously low. Many prisoners accepted the appalling conditions in order to contribute in some small way to the maintenance of their wives and children and in the hope of being transferred to somewhere nearer their families. When the average daily wage for manual labour was 10 pesetas per day, the prisoners were rented out to private companies for 5 or 6. The government took half and the rest theoretically was paid to the prisoners. However, they did not receive all the money that they were due. One peseta was deducted for the prisoner's exiguous rations, one was placed in a savings account which the prisoner could collect when he was eventually freed and the third, theoretically, was sent to the family. In fact, this latter was distributed, if at all, via the town council where the family lived and often was never handed over. Those under a death sentence were not allowed to participate in the scheme.[110]

In prisons, no newspapers were allowed, even though the only ones existing were those of the totally controlled Falange network, the Press of the Movement. The reason for the prohibition was not to prevent access to already heavily censored news but rather to oblige prisoners to buy the Patronato's own weekly newssheet, *Redención*, which was written by imprisoned Republican journalists. The print run of *Redención* was well over one million copies. A copy cost the same as a commercial newspaper. In theory, no prisoner was obliged to buy it, but visits from family were often conditional on the prisoner being a subscriber to the paper, which placed an intolerable strain on the economies of families already on the verge of starvation.[111]

A British musician arrested on suspicion of espionage was told by the wardress who confiscated her belongings: 'In here, nothing belongs to you except what you've eaten, and then not always, as you're likely to throw up.'[112] That woman's suffering would be relatively mild. The scale of deprivation suffered by the defeated Republican women may be deduced from the fact that, by the third week of April 1939, the women's prison at Ventas in Madrid, designed for five hundred inmates, had more than 3,500 and would eventually hold nearly 14,000. Cells designed for one prisoner held twelve or more. It was common for women to be arrested in lieu of their missing menfolk. Some of the charges against them were self-evidently absurd, ranging from washing clothes or frying eggs for Republican soldiers to having been a cleaner in a Republican hospital.[113] In addition to the horrors of overcrowding, disease and malnutrition, the suffering of women in the prisons had dimensions unknown in the male population. Many of the women arrested were pregnant or had very young children with them. Mothers of children older than three were not allowed to take them into the prison. Often they did not have family to care for them, since they too had been imprisoned, exiled or executed. These mothers suffered the anguish of knowing that their children were alone on the streets. Older women were forced to watch while their sons were tortured and sometimes murdered.[114]

Rape was a frequent occurrence during interrogation in police stations. Transfer to prisons and concentration camps was no guarantee of safety. At night, Falangists took young women away and raped them. Sometimes their breasts were branded with the Falangist symbol of the yoke and arrows. Many were impregnated by their captors. The executions of women sentenced to death who were pregnant were sometimes delayed until they had given birth and their children taken for adoption.[115] Nevertheless, in the prison in Zamora, numerous pregnant women and nursing mothers were shot. On 11 October 1936, Amparo Barayón, the wife of Ramón J. Sender, was told that 'reds had no right to feed children' and her eight-month-old baby daughter Andrea was ripped from her arms and placed in a Catholic orphanage. Utterly distraught, Amparo was shot the next day.[116] From 1937 to 1941, the Franciscan Capuchin friar Gumersindo de Estella served as a chaplain at the prison of Torrero in Zaragoza. In September 1937, he recalled the execution of three young women whose crime had been an attempt to reach the Republican zone. He was appalled not least by their anguished cries when their one-year-old daughters had been dragged from them by the guards. On another occasion in May 1938, he appealed for the execution of a twenty-one-year-old to be halted on the grounds that she was pregnant. The judge replied indignantly: 'Wait seven months for every woman who was to be executed? You know that is just not possible!'[117]

Savage beatings were administered, often to pregnant women, but torture was often more refined. Among the tortures were electric shocks delivered to nipples, genitals and ears. In addition to the pain and humiliation of all of these tortures, the application of electric shocks to the ears caused profound mental problems and headaches that lasted for years afterwards. Many young girls among those arrested were submitted to beatings, torture and sexual harassment. Women in their seventies and eighties were also subject to mistreatment. The mother of Juana Doña was unable to use her hands for two months because of electrical torture.[118] Women were sentenced to death and imprisonment for the crime of military rebellion, yet they were given the status not of political prisoners but of common criminals.[119]

On 5 August 1939 in Madrid, fifty-six prisoners were executed including a fourteen-year-old boy and thirteen women, seven of whom were under the age of twenty-one. They came to be known as the Trece Rosas, thirteen roses whose fate symbolized the cruelty of the Franco regime. They were members of the United Socialist Youth, the JSU. Their capture in the spring of 1939 had been facilitated because the Casado Junta had seized JSU membership lists then left them for the Francoists. The excuse for the executions was a non-existent plot to murder Franco. In reality, it was an act of revenge for the murder on 27 July of a Civil Guard, Major Isaac Gabaldón, his eighteen-year-old daughter and their driver by members of the resistance. Unknown to the car-hijackers who killed him, Gabaldón was head of the Freemasonry and Communism Archive gathered by Marcelino de Ulibarri. Those shot on 5 August were already in prison when the murders took place. The consequent international scandal saw the death penalties imposed on three women in a later trial commuted to lengthy prison sentences, although twenty-seven men were executed on 9 September.[120]

Another victim of the Casado coup was a woman who had just given birth when her husband, arrested and left in prison by Casado's forces, was condemned to death. Evicted from her home, she lived on the streets with her baby daughter, sleeping in doorways and on the steps of the Metro. When a lawyer told her that her husband's sentence could be commuted if she paid a bribe of 10,000 pesetas, she became a thief and ended up in prison with her baby daughter.[121] An example of the brutality inflicted on women was the case of a mother who, when the police came to arrest her, called to her son who was crying. On hearing that his name was Lenin, they picked him up by the legs and killed him by smashing his head against a wall.[122]

Once in jail, the conditions for nursing mothers were horrendous. With no facilities to wash themselves or their children's clothes, they were forced to live in filth and fight a daily battle against rats. In the prison of Ventas, the water to the bathrooms and toilets was cut off. For every two hundred women, there was only one toilet which had to be flushed with dirty water that had been used for cleaning the floors and was then collected in big tins. Paz Azati, a Communist from Valencia, recounted that 'every day on the floor of the Ventas infirmary you would see the corpses of fifteen to twenty children dead from meningitis'. The Communist Julia Manzanal had just given birth to a daughter when she was arrested in Madrid in the spring of 1939. Manzanal's death sentence was commuted to thirty years in prison. Ten months later, her baby died of meningitis.[123] While some women suffered the agony of seeing their babies die, others had them torn from their arms.[124]

After the war, the sequestration of the children of Republican prisoners, not just of those executed, became systematic. Twelve thousand children were taken to religious or state institutions where they were brainwashed. After one woman's husband was shot in front of her and her small daughter, she was arrested and the child taken to a Catholic orphanage. The mother wrote regularly until one day her daughter replied saying, 'Don't write to me any more about papa. I know he was a criminal. I am taking the veil.' Many children were taken from their mothers, put into religious orphanages and brainwashed into denouncing their fathers as assassins. Amparo Barayón's daughter Andrea became a nun. Pilar Fidalgo noted that orphans were obliged 'to sing the songs of the murderers of their father; to wear the uniform of those who have executed him, and to curse the dead and to blaspheme his memory.'[125] In the book signed by the chaplain of the prison in Barcelona, Father Martín Torrent (in reality ghost-written by a near-destitute Luis Lucia), great pride is expressed in the fact that seven thousand indigent children of prisoners found starving on the streets had been taken to religious orphanages. Father Torrent expressed even greater satisfaction that some of them had decided to join the priesthood.[126]

Children were stolen from their mothers in several prisons, most notoriously in Saturrarán in the Basque Country and in the prison for nursing mothers in Madrid. More than one hundred women and over fifty children died of illness in Saturrarán, which was run under the harsh direction of María Aranzazu, known to the prisoners as 'the white panther'. In Madrid, the brutal regime in the improvised prison for nursing mothers was run by María Topete Fernández, a wealthy woman who had herself been imprisoned in the Republican zone. She assuaged her own resentments in the treatment of the mothers and their children. The principal food they received was a thin gruel containing bugs and maggots. If the children regurgitated it, María Topete made them eat their vomit. Separated from them for much of the daytime and at night, the women lived in constant terror of their children being taken from them. Once the children were three years old they could be removed and many were forcibly seized from their mothers. By 1943, more than 10,000 were in religious orphanages.[127] The justification for this policy was provided by the head of the psychiatric services of the rebel army, Major Antonio Vallejo Nágera.

Obsessed with the need for racial cleanliness, Vallejo had written a book in 1934 arguing in favour of the castration of psychopaths.[128] As a member of the army medical corps, he had served in Morocco and spent time in Germany during the First World War visiting prison camps. He also met the German psychiatrists Ernst Kretschmer, Julius Schwalbe and Hans Walter Gruhle, whose work influenced him profoundly. During the Civil War, he was made head of the Psychiatric Services of the rebel army. In August 1938, he requested permission from Franco to set up the Laboratory of Psychological Investigations. Two weeks later, he was authorized to do so. His purpose was to pathologize left-wing ideas. The results of his research gave the delighted military high command 'scientific' arguments to justify their views on the sub-human nature of their adversaries and he was promoted to colonel.[129]

Vallejo's quest for the environmental factors that fostered 'the red gene' and the links between Marxism and mental deficiency took the form of psychological tests carried out on prisoners already physically exhausted and mentally anguished. His team consisted of two physicians, a criminologist and two German scientific advisers. His subjects were captured members of the International Brigades in San Pedro de Cardeña and fifty Republican women prisoners in Málaga, thirty of whom were awaiting execution. In the latter case, starting from the premise that they were degenerate and thus prone to Marxist criminality, he explained 'female revolutionary criminality' by reference to the animal nature of the female psyche and the 'marked sadistic nature' unleashed when political circumstances allowed females to 'satisfy their latent sexual appetites'.[130]

Vallejo's theories were used to justify the sequestration of Republican children and were gathered in a book entitled The Eugenics of Spanishness and the Regeneration of the Race'.[131] More environmental than biological, his eugenic racism postulated that a race was constituted by a series of cultural values. In Spain, these values, the prerequisites of national health, were hierarchical, military and patriotic. Everything that the Republic and the left stood for was inimical to them and therefore had to be eradicated. Obsessed with what he called 'the transcendent task of the cleansing of our race', his model was the Inquisition, which had protected Spain from poisonous doctrines in the past. He advocated 'a modernized Inquisition, with a different focus, other ends, means and organization but an Inquisition nonetheless'.[132] The health of the race required that children be separated from their 'red' mothers.

Authorization for the application of his theories was facilitated by his links with both Franco (whose wife Carmen Polo was a friend of Vallejo's wife) and the Falange.[133] He dedicated his book on the psychopathology of war, which incorporated his work on the links between Marxism and mental deficiency, 'in respectful and admiring homage to the undefeated imperial Caudillo'. Vallejo also had a direct link to the regime organization concerned with war orphans, Auxilio Social, through his friend the psychiatrist Dr Jesús Ercilla Ortega. A close friend of Onésimo Redondo, Ercilla had been one of the founders of the JONS.[134] He was a member of the executive committee of Auxilio Social, its medical adviser and the liaison with other groups. After the war, Ercilla was made clinical direct-or of the Psychiatric Clinic of San José in Ciempozuelos, a hospital offi-cially headed by Vallejo Nágera.[135] Franco himself was enthusiastic about Auxilio Social's work with Republican orphans, seeing it as a major contribution to the long-term 'redemption' of Spaniards from their left-ist errors.[136] A key element in the process was the law of 14 December 1941 which legalized the changing of the names of Republican orphans, of the children of prisoners unable to look after them and of babies taken away (often by force) from their mothers immediately after birth in prison.[137]

As the Second World progressed, conditions for all prisoners wors-ened. Already undernourished, they were forced to give blood transfu-sions for the German Army.[138] Perhaps the most shocking example of the malice that underlay the Francoist treatment of the defeated Republicans was the fate of the Spanish exiles captured in France by the Germans. Some had been fighting in the French forces, others were still in French internment camps. Around 10,000 ended up in German camps, some-thing made possible by the acquiescence of Franco's government when the prisoners were offered by the Germans. Numerous letters were sent in July 1940 from the Spanish Embassy in Paris to the Foreign Ministry asking for instructions regarding the German offer to hand over the pris-oners. When no reply came, the German Embassy in Paris wrote to Madrid in August asking for clarification of the Spanish government's wishes regarding 100,000 Spanish refugees. The only reply that has been found was a list of specific individuals, which led to the extraditions discussed earlier in the chapter. In the absence of other documentation, this alone condemned Republicans to German camps. According to SS Standartenführer August Eigruber, Gauleiter of Oberdonau in Austria, the Germans were told 'by Franco' that, as they had fought for 'a Soviet Spain', the prisoners were not considered to be Spaniards. This is consistent with Franco's public declarations about those Republicans regarded as unredeemable criminals. Accordingly, the Spanish prisoners were treated as stateless persons and transferred from the front-line prisoner-of-war camps (Stalags) to concentration camps. Ninety per cent of the 'Fighters for Red Spain' (Rotspanienkämpfer) were in Mauthausen-Gusen in Austria.[139]

On 20 August 1940, a cattle train left Angoulême. A total of 927 Spanish refugees, 490 of them men, the remainder women and children, were squeezed – forty to fifty per wagon – into twenty wagons each designed for eight horses. They believed that they were being taken to Vichy. They travelled for three days and nights, with room only to stand, without food or water. On 24 August, they reached Mauthausen. The males over the age of thirteen were separated from their families and taken to the extermination camp near by. They were told by the camp commander Franz Ziereis in his 'welcome speech', 'you enter by the door and you will leave by the crematorium chimney'. Three hundred and fifty-seven of the 490 would die in the camp.[140] The women and children were then sent to Spain – they had been put on the train because the Germans did not want French civilians seeing the families being separated. There can be no doubt that the French authorities knew all about Mauthausen. In Spain, the returned women were interrogated and those with no one to vouch for them were imprisoned. The children were put in state orphanages even when there were Republican families willing to look after them.[141]

It was just the beginning. Spanish Republicans ended up facing the whole gamut of horrors in many different Nazi camps, including Buchenwald, Bergen-Belsen, Dachau, Ravensbrück and Sachsenhausen in Germany, and Auschwitz and Treblinka in Poland. In Ravensbrück, there were 101 Spanish women who had belonged to the French resistance.[142] Mauthausen was an extermination camp where those not murdered on arrival were required to work until they died of exhaustion. From the quarry at Mauthausen, an endless chain of men carried stones weighing between 44 and 88 pounds in backpacks up 186 steep steps.[143] About 60 per cent of the Spanish Republicans who died in German camps perished at Mauthausen.[144]

Franco's propagandists presented the executions, the overflowing prisons and camps, the slave-labour battalions and the fate of the exiles as the scrupulous yet compassionate justice of a benevolent Caudillo. In 1964, they launched a highly choreographed, nationwide celebration of the 'Twenty-Five Years of Peace' since the end of the war. Every town and village in Spain was bedecked with posters rejoicing in the purging of the atheistic hordes of the left. The celebrations began on 1 April, with a Te Deum in the basilica at the Valle de los Caídos. This, together with an interview given by Franco to *ABC*, made it clear that the celebrations were not for peace but for victory.[145] This was confirmed eight days later when he told the *Consejo Nacional* that the festivities were a 'commemoration of the twenty-five years of victory'. That the Jewish–Bolshevik–Masonic conspiracy was still on his mind was made clear when he warned his audience of plots and sectarianism coming from Europe, of 'secret machinations, subversive action and the power of occult forces'.[146] The unspoken message of the elaborate celebrations was that the return on Franco's investment in terror could not have been more successful.

Epilogue

The Reverberations

In mid-July 1939, Count Galeazzo Ciano, Mussolini's son-in-law and the Foreign Minister of Fascist Italy, made an official visit to Spain. When his guides proudly took him to see a work gang of Republican prisoners, he remarked to his own officials: 'They are not prisoners of war, they are slaves of war.' On his return to Rome, he described Franco to one of his cronies: 'That queer fish of a Caudillo, sits there in his Ayete palace, in the midst of his Moorish Guard, surrounded by mountains of files of prisoners condemned to death. With his work schedule, he will see about three a day, because that fellow enjoys his siestas.'[1]

There is no evidence that Franco's sleep was ever interrupted by concern for his victims. Indeed, his regime made considerable efforts to ensure that the same tranquillity was enjoyed by all of his collaborators. The consequence is that Spain today is still in the throes of a memory war. There are two sets of historical memory: the homogeneous Francoist one imposed on the country during four decades of dictatorship and the diverse Republican ones, repressed until recent years. The Francoist one was constructed in three stages before, during and after the Civil War. It was based on the need to justify the military coup against the democratically elected government and the planned slaughter that the coup was to entail. During the first stage, before 18 July 1936, the betrayal of the military oath of loyalty to the government was justified by the assertion that Spain had to be saved from the 'Jewish–Bolshevik–Masonic conspiracy' which was allegedly responsible for the greatly exaggerated breakdown of law and order. As the war progressed, the second stage saw the tightly controlled rebel media and the Catholic Church collaborate to publicize and exaggerate atrocities in the Republican zone. Thus was created a deep fear of 'red barbarism', an untrammelled violence allegedly masterminded by Moscow, with a view to destroying Spain and its Catholic traditions. At the same time, the atrocities committed by the rebels and their Falangist and Carlist allies were encouraged as part of the prior plan of extermination and also by way of sealing a covenant of blood among the perpetrators. Thus those guilty of the atrocities would never contemplate any reconciliation with the defeated for fear of the vengeance of their victims.

After the war came the third and most enduring stage. By dint of totalitarian control of the education system and of all the means of public communication, press, radio and the publishing industry, the Franco regime made a powerfully sustained attempt to brainwash its population. An entirely homogeneous and impermeable version of the long- and short-term origins of the Civil War was imposed upon the Spanish people. Through endless reiteration in the press, in schools, in children's textbooks and from church pulpits, a single historical memory was created and disseminated over three and a half decades. The rewriting of history – and denial of the experiences and recollections of both victors and victims – absolved the military rebels of guilt and sanitized the regime abroad. The process inflicted great long-term damage on Spanish society. To this day, its powerful residual effects hamper the ability of mainstream contemporary society to look upon its recent violent past in an open and honest way that could facilitate the necessary social and political closure.

During the years of the dictatorship, the defeated in Spain had no public right to historical memory, living as they did in a kind of internal exile. Only after the death of Franco and the slow reconstruction of democracy did it become possible for there to be a process of recovery of their historical memory. Of course, there were many historical memories among the defeated Republicans and their descendants, differing according to whether their politics were liberal Republican, Socialist, Communist or anarchist but always with some with elements in common deriving from the suffering and loss imposed by the Francoist repression, whether through execution, imprisonment or exile.

When the grandchildren of the victims of the Francoists finally initiated a nationwide movement for the recovery of historical memory in the year 2000, it provoked a near-hysterical rejection by those who denounced their quest as merely 'raking up the ashes'. In the first instance, that was understandable because the coming of democracy, quite properly, had not silenced those who had either benefited from the dictatorship or merely been educated to accept its monolithic version of the nation's historical memory. However, the ferocity of the denunciation of the quest for the recovery of memory reflected something else, something very profound. This is the principal consequence of the process of brainwashing, what in Spain is called sociological Francoism, and it lives on in the democratic Spain of today just as sociological communism exists in the countries of the old Soviet bloc. The venom of the denunciations of the quest for the truth about the repression derives from the fact that there were also many historical memories among the victors and their descendants that have had to be repressed by the need to safeguard a false memory. The recovery of memory is distressing because it challenges the integrity of the reassuringly unified but ultimately false memories upon which the regime was reliant for its survival.

Despite the massive operation to justify the innocent blood shed because of the military rebellion, some of the Caudillo's collaborators seem to have slept uneasily after the war. Inevitably, there is little evidence of the psychological repercussions of all that went before. It is especially difficult to know anything regarding the mental state of those who committed atrocities in the Republican zone. Those who did not escape into exile were either tried during the war itself by the Republican authorities or else afterwards by the Francoists. In the confessions extorted under torture by the Francoist police, such as that of Felipe Sandoval, there are declarations of remorse. However, taking into account the murderous repression which encompassed virtually everyone still in Spain who might have been guilty of something (as well as many who had done no wrong), it is not surprising that there is so little by way of free expressions of guilt. Nevertheless, it would be reasonable to suppose that at least some of those responsible for crimes on both sides might have suffered from post-traumatic stress disorder or guilt.

In contrast to the paucity of evidence from the Republican side, perhaps because the victors were able to enjoy the fruits of their work for decades after the war, rather more of them seem to have reflected on what had happened and others seem to have suffered qualms of conscience. The most significant recognition by a Francoist that what was done, starting long before the military coup, might have been wrong came from Ramón Serrano Suñer, both in numerous interviews and in his memoirs where he described the trials in the rebel zone during the war and in all of Spain after 1939 as 'back-to-front justice' (*la justicia al revés*).[2]

One of the most celebrated cases of remorse was that of the poet Dionisio Ridruejo, who was a friend both of Serrano Suñer and of José Antonio Primo de Rivera and one of the founders of the Falange. In the late 1940s, he became disenchanted with the corruption of the Franco regime and reneged on his past. In the 1960s, he began to write critically about what had happened in the Civil War. He then formed a political association in timid opposition to the regime. An erstwhile comrade, Eugenio Montes, said to Ridruejo: 'When someone like you has led hundreds of compatriots to their deaths, and then reaches the conclusion that the struggle was a mistake, it is just not enough to found a political party. A believer should become a monk; an agnostic should shoot himself.'[3]

A faster change of heart than Ridruejo's came about in the case of Father Juan Tusquets. In the autumn of 1938, on the eve of the great rebel offensive against Catalonia, Franco and Serrano Suñer asked Tusquets to suggest names to head the institutions to be set up by the occupying forces. His advice led to the selection of the future Mayor of Barcelona, Miquel Mateu, and other important appointees.[4] Despite such influence, after the Civil War, Tusquets surprisingly turned his back on preferment, declining both Serrano Suñer's offer of the post of Director General of Press and Propaganda and Franco's invitation for him to become religious adviser to the Higher Council of Scientific Research.[5] Since, in previous years, Tusquets had revelled in his closeness to the epicentres of power and had shamelessly sought to accumulate salaries, the refusal of two such important and well-paid posts is noteworthy.

There are reasons for suspecting that the brutality of the Francoist occupation of Catalonia provoked some remorse in Tusquets for his part in fomenting the hatred that drove it. He began to construct a highly sanitized account of his role in the war and claimed later that he had tried to get people he knew out of concentration camps. This may be true but no evidence has come to light. Moreover, he maintained that he prevented major Catalan treasures such as the Archive of the Crown of Aragon and the Library of Catalonia from suffering the fate of so many other Catalan institutions whose books, documents and papers were seized and taken to Salamanca, a process which he had encouraged.[6] Most implausibly of all, he alleged that it was not himself but his sidekick, Joaquim Guiu, who had been obsessive about Freemasonry.[7] He denied any participation in the repression, claiming mendaciously that he had refused to let his lists of names be used by the military authorities. He denounced his wartime collaborator Mauricio Carlavilla as 'a passionate Nazi' who invented his material.[8] In the light of these untruths, is not unreasonable to speculate that he was ashamed and horrified by the practical consequences of his anti-Masonic and anti-Jewish campaigns. Instead of accepting official preferment, he returned to religious education.

There is some second-hand evidence of the perpetrators of atrocities suffering some sort of psychosomatic illness or other distress as a result of repressed guilt. One of the men involved in the murder of Lorca, for instance, suffered in a way that suggested an element of remorse. Juan Luis Trescastro Medina died as an alcoholic in 1954 having spent years tormented by the memory of the atrocities in which he had been involved.[9] In Lora del Río, one of the town's three most prominent assassins had to leave his home because of the collective hostility of neighbours. When a second died, no one from the town was willing to carry his coffin. The third used to recount with guffaws how those that he shot in the stomach would first jump and then be doubled over. He himself died, doubled over in pain, from stomach cancer. Many fellow citizens decided that this was a form of divine retribution. They saw the same in the case of a trigger-happy assassin who later lost his thumb and trigger-finger in an industrial accident. There were popular claims that other perpetrators, on their deathbeds, were to be heard screaming, 'They're coming to get me!' In Uncastillo in Zaragoza, it was believed that the Falangist who mutilated the corpse of Antonio Plano, the Mayor, lived in similar torment, terrified that he would be murdered in his bed in revenge for what he had done.[10]

It is impossible to say whether some of the exiguous evidence that exists derives from popular fantasy. The construction of the popular memory/mythology of those who suffered the repression may well have been fuelled by a desire to see the later misfortunes of the perpetrators as their just deserts on the basis of 'the punishment fits the crime'. For instance, regarding Fuente de Cantos in Badajoz, there is a persistent belief that two of the men who played a particularly vicious part in the repression died with their consciences tormented by what they had done and by the hatred felt towards them in the town. One was a man notorious for denunciations which led to executions. He lived happily, apparently, during the entire period of the Franco regime, but when it became clear that the dictator was on his deathbed, he began to fear that the left was going to seek revenge and he committed suicide. The other case concerns the local head of the Falange, Sixto Castillón, the man that detained the Mayor José Lorenzana who was shortly afterwards ritually murdered in the town square. The popular recollection of Castillón is of a bestial individual who had killed many people including a child. After the war, he died in Seville. According to the popular legend, he died in an agony of remorse, tortured by fears of reprisals and by visions of the ghosts of his victims, constantly calling out the name of Lorenzana and unable to sleep because of hearing the persistent crying of the child that he had murdered.[11]

More dramatic was a case in Ubrique (Cádiz). Local legend recounts a particularly gruesome tale of apparently psychosomatic illness provoked by guilt. A few days after the military coup, a group of Falangist assassins shot a number of Republican prisoners on the outskirts of the town. Among the first was the twelve-year-old son of a Gypsy named Diego Flores. One of them mocked Flores's distress at witnessing the murder of his son, saying: 'What now? Are you going to put the Gypsy's curse on us?' To which Flores replied: 'Yes, you bastard, I am. May your flesh fall from you in pieces and may you die in atrocious pain.' This man, who became rich from the properties that he stole from his victims, died in the late 1970s from a hideously painful form of leprosy.[12]

In Cantalpino, a village twenty-five miles north-east of Salamanca, where there had been no incidents before the war, rightists murdered twenty-two men and a woman named Eladia Pérez, as well as raping a number of other young women. When they came to bury Eladia, the hole in the ground was not big enough and, rather than dig more, the man who had shot her simply cut off her head with a spade. According to villagers, he was Anastasio González, 'El Cagalubias', who, years later, died delirious, screaming for Eladia to be pulled off him.[13]

Another case of repentance in Salamanca was inadvertently triggered by one of José Antonio Primo de Rivera's friends, Francisco Bravo, who wrote an article in *La Gaceta Regional* of Salamanca in celebration of the coup of 18 July 1936. A couple of days later, an anonymous reply arrived at the newspaper's offices. It came from one of Bravo's collaborators in the repression:

You don't remember me. I was one of your comrades who swallowed the bait of killing people for the sake of it. I killed only five and I couldn't continue participating in all that horror. To this day, I have those five brothers on my mind. Yes, even though it might surprise you, I call them brothers; they were human beings, creatures of God that I killed and I still want to believe that I don't know why I did it. I didn't kill in that way for God or for Spain. I leave it to you, if you're able, if you have a conscience, if you are a believer, to choose the correct adjective for those victims … You should have said more in your article about everything that happened just in the area where you were the head of a Falangist militia. Maybe you've forgotten all that. Your last breath might be peaceful, without regrets, just like someone who did only good and knew nothing about hatred or revenge. Can you tell me that you are such a person? Comrade, I want a quick death. I live as a wreck, followed by the spectre of those whose memory I have been unable to erase for twenty-seven years. Forgive? I doubt that our victims can forgive us.[14]

In the town of Pozoblanco in Córdoba, the repression was particularly virulent. Three of those who took part later committed suicide. Juan Félix, 'El Pichón', threw himself from a moving train. Another, a lawyer, Juan Calero Rubio, killed himself apparently overcome with guilt about his role in the terror. Acting as a military judge, Calero had been responsible for hundreds of death sentences carried out against prisoners from several towns. He had also ordered the torture of many prisoners and had often taken part in the brutal beatings. In 1940, when the death sentence imposed on the postmaster of Villanueva was commuted, he ordered his immediate execution and then claimed that the pardon had arrived too late. The relative of the condemned man, an army officer, who had arranged the pardon, made an official complaint and, while awaiting trial, Calero poisoned himself on 28 August 1940, aged fifty-three. Another man who had taken part in many executions, a lieutenant of the Civil Guard known as 'Pepinillos', shot himself in the head at a dance held in the nearby village of Espiel to celebrate the outbreak of the Civil War.[15] Another example of a suicide allegedly motivated by guilt is that of a man called Ortiz who was one of those responsible for much of the repression in San Fernando in Cádiz. Ortiz hung himself.[16]

The brother of Fernando Zamacola, the leader of the notorious Falangist gang known as the 'Lions of Rota' responsible for numerous atrocities in the province of Cádiz, spoke in the 1950s to the psychiatrist Carlos Castilla del Pino. Referring to the social injustice that prevailed in Franco's Spain, he said: 'And it was for this that we had to kill. Because I have killed. I've left more than one corpse in the ditches at Puerto de Tierra, lots in fact, I don't know exactly how many, but I have killed and I've watched them die, and now those children are driving me mad. I have nightmares about them.'[17]

Segundo Viloria, the man regarded by the family of Amparo Barayón as the person who had actually killed her, was also denounced by Pilar Fidalgo as guilty of multiple sexual crimes against imprisoned women. According to Miguel Ángel Mateos, the official chronicler of Zamora, Viloria was guilty of horrible crimes and worthy of psychiatric study. The Barayón family claimed that Viloria 'died insane in a mental hospital'.[18]

Finally, there is the case of the Conde de Alba de Yeltes, Gonzalo de Aguilera, the landowner from Salamanca who boasted of shooting six of his workers. After the Civil War, he retired from the army as a lieutenant colonel and returned to his estates and his books. He had difficulty readjusting to civilian life, although he became a well-known 'character' in Salamanca. He was an assiduous member of a group (*tertulia*), consisting mainly of doctors, who used to meet at the Café Novelty in the Plaza Mayor. His conversation was considered fascinating even if his irritability did not encourage friendship or intimacy.[19] As he got older, he became increasingly abrasive and bad tempered. He neglected his estates and his house, both of which were badly run down.

He developed persecution mania. His wife Magdalena Álvarez, aged seventy-two, became so afraid of his violent rages that, in late 1963, for her own protection, she asked her two sons to come and live at home at the estate near Matilla de los Caños in the province of Salamanca. The elder son, Gonzalo, aged forty-seven, was a retired cavalry captain who had been seriously wounded in the Civil War. While in hospital, he had fallen in love with Concepción Lodeiro López, a nurse at the military hospital in Lugo. Aguilera had reacted furiously to his son's relationship with a social inferior and had forbidden them to marry. They did so regardless and settled in Lugo, where they had a daughter, Marianela. The younger son, Agustín, a thirty-nine-year-old farmer, also had a difficult relationship with his father. Leaving home, he had settled first in Zamora, where he had married Angelines Núñez. More recently, they had moved to Jérez de la Frontera with their two daughters and young son. Given the inconvenience for their own families and aware of the irascibility of their father, the two sons reluctantly agreed to spend as much time as possible at the estate watching over him.

After a year, things had not improved. The family reluctantly contemplated having Gonzalo declared mentally incapacitated and placing him in psychiatric care. For fear of scandal and with a natural horror of the head of the household being declared insane, they hesitated. Finally, they put the matter in the hands of a lawyer in Salamanca. Because Gonzalo now suffered bronchial problems and rarely attended the gatherings in the café in the Plaza Mayor, it was possible to fabricate the pretext of a visit of two medical friends in order to have him diagnosed. One, a psychiatrist, and another, a doctor, reached the conclusion that Gonzalo was paranoiac and the process began to have him committed. The legal procedure, however, was lengthy and tortuous.

Gonzalo became so difficult that his sons rearranged the house to provide him with a separate apartment with his own television and his books. They hid all the many guns and knives that, as an assiduous hunter, he possessed. He believed himself to have been kidnapped and imprisoned by his family, even writing a letter to this effect to the judicial authorities in Salamanca, at the beginning of August 1964. He had wild fits of rage, shouting threats and insults from his solitary apartment. He would occasionally find weapons and, in mid-August, his sons took a flick-knife away from him.

Before anything could be done, Gonzalo completely lost his mind. After lunch, at four o'clock on the sultry afternoon of Friday 28 August 1964, his younger son Agustín went into the Conde's room to look for some papers. When his father complained of sore feet, Agustín knelt and started to massage them. Don Gonzalo began to abuse his son, pulled out a rusty Colt revolver that he had hidden and shot Agustín without warning. Badly wounded in the chest, Agustín staggered out of the room. His brother Gonzalo, alerted by the sound of gunfire, ran into the room and the Conde shot him full in the chest and in the arm. Stepping over his elder son's corpse, he then set off in search of Agustín in order to finish him off. He found him lying dead at the door of the kitchen. His wife then came out of her room. When she saw him glaring at her while he calmly reloaded his pistol over the body of his son, she locked herself in another room. Since the farm labourers stood back, frightened by the sight of Gonzalo waving his revolver threateningly, she was obliged to escape through a window. The Civil Guard was called by the estate workers and they ordered Gonzalo to throw down his gun and come out with his hands in the air, which, his fury spent, he did.

After surrendering, he sat outside the house for more than three hours, still in his pyjamas, quietly awaiting the investigating judge from Salamanca. His wife, beside herself with grief and rage, screamed at him 'Assassin! Murderer!' Until calmed down by the farm workers, she shouted to the Civil Guards, 'Kill him, he's a savage!' He was arrested and taken to Salamanca by the Civil Guard. They travelled in a car with reporters from the local newspaper, *La Gaceta Regional*. The journalists who interviewed him recounted that, en route, he chatted amiably to the driver. He spoke about various cars that he had had at different times, about the traffic system in France and about the poor state of the roads. He explained: 'I'm talking to put what has happened out of my mind.' When he was told that he was being taken to a psychiatric clinic, he said that psychiatrists are not usually in their right minds and added, 'I called

the ones that visited me village quacks and they got angry with me.'[20]
Detained in the provincial psychiatric hospital in Salamanca, he apparently entertained himself by loudly insulting the nuns who staffed it.[21]
His daughter-in-law, Concepción Lodeiro, and granddaughter, Marianela de Aguilera Lodeiro, escaped the carnage because they had gone to Lugo to make the arrangements for Marianela's wedding. The wife and three children of Agustín were in southern Spain. Gonzalo never stood trial and died in the hospital nearly eight months later on 15 May 1965.[22]

ACKNOWLEDGEMENTS

This book has been many years in the making. The gratuitous cruelty that it recounts ensured that it would be an extremely painful book to write. It was also methodologically difficult because of the sheer scale of a subject covering the different kinds of repression in both zones during the war and in all of Spain afterwards. In fact, it could not have been written without the pioneering efforts of numerous Spanish historians. Their published work is referred to fully in the Notes.

Moreover, in addition to being able to read their books and articles, with many of these historians I had the pleasure and privilege of discussing detailed issues regarding the places and the topics on which they are the experts. Their readiness to share with me ideas and material was one of the most heartening and memorable features of a difficult task. Their names are listed in the Spanish edition of this book.

For a historian living in London, keeping up with the avalanche of information in some way or other related to the various aspects of the subject is a particularly difficult problem. In this regard, I owe special thanks to Javier Díaz and Sussana Anglés i Querol of Mas de las Matas, Teruel. Everyone who works on the question of repression and historical memory is in their debt for the astonishing daily updates on publications and events that they send out from La Librería de Cazarabet and through their bulletin *El Sueño Igualitario*.

I must make particular mention of a group of friends and colleagues with all of whom I have had frequent and fruitful conversations over many years. I am immensely grateful for their help and their friendship: Fernando Arcas Cubero (Málaga), Montse Armengou i Martín (Barcelona), Nicolás Belmonte (Valencia), Julián Casanova (Zaragoza), Ángela Cenarro (Zaragoza), Ian Gibson (Madrid), María Jesús González (Santander), Angela Jackson (Marçà, Tarragona), Rebecca Jinks (London), Father Josep Massot i Muntaner (Baleares), Antonio Miguez Macho (Santiago de Compostela), Father Hilari Raguer (Barcelona), Ángel Viñas (Brussels) and Boris Volodarsky (Vienna).

I must also thank my colleagues in the Cañada Blanch Centre for Contemporary Studies in the London School of Economics: Peter Anderson, Jerry Blaney, Ana de Miguel, Susana Grau, Didac Gutiérrez Peris and Rúben Serem. In all kinds of ways, their support permitted me to make progress on the book while still meeting the heavy demands of university teaching and administration.

With two friends, the interchange of ideas and material has been almost daily. I have learned an enormous amount from them and I am deeply grateful for their friendship and for sharing with me their encyclopaedic knowledge: Francisco Espinosa Maestre (Seville) and José Luis Ledesma (Zaragoza).

Finally, I must thank Linda Palfreeman for her painstaking and insightful reading of the text. I have benefited too from the perceptive comments of Helen Graham, Lala Isla and my wife, Gabrielle, over the many years during which I have been working on the book. However, only Gabrielle knows what the emotional cost has been of daily immersion in this chronicle of inhumanity. Without her understanding and support, the task would have been so much more difficult. Accordingly, the book is dedicated to her.

GLOSSARY

Acción Popular (briefly known as Acción Nacional): 'an organization for social defence' created in 1931 by Ángel Herrera Oria, the editor of *El Debate*, in response to the coming of the Second Republic. It would be the nucleus of the CEDA (q.v.)

Africanistas: Spanish army officers experienced in, and often brutalized by, the colonial war in Morocco

Agrupación Nacional de Propietarios de Fincas Rústicas: National Association of Rural Estate-Owners

alcalde: mayor

ANCP: Asociación Católica Nacional de Propagandistas – an elite Jesuit-influenced organization of about five hundred prominent and talented Catholic rightists with influence in the press, the judiciary and the professions

Ayuntamiento: town council and also the town hall

bracero: unskilled agricultural labourer hired by the day

cacique: a powerful rural boss, usually a landowner but sometimes a money-lender or both

Casa del Pueblo: the main gathering place for the local left wing, sometimes a kind of club, sometimes the headquarters of parties and unions

casino: the main gathering place for the local right wing

Caudillo: literally bandit chieftain, more usually military leader, became Franco's title, the equivalent of Hitler's 'Führer' or Mussolini's 'Duce'

CCMA: Comitè Central de les Milícies Antifeixistes de Catalunya – Central Anti-Fascist Militia Committee, the executive body created on 20 July 1936 to combine the Generalitat (q.v.) and representatives of all the democratic and left-wing forces in Catalonia. It never functioned efficiently and within months the Generalitat had re-established its power

CEDA: Confederación Española de Derechas Autónomas – Spanish Confederation of Autonomous Right-Wing Groups, the principal mass party of the right, created in 1933, led by José María Gil Robles

checas: autonomous police forces and detention centres created in July 1936 in the Republican zone by working-class unions and parties

Civil Governor: the principal authority in any province, appointed by the Ministry of the Interior

CNCA: Confederación Nacional Católico-Agraria – National Catholic Agrarian Confederation, conservative association of smallholders created in 1917. It provided mass support for the CEDA

CNT: Confederación Nacional del Trabajo – National Confederation of Labour, anarcho-syndicalist trade union founded in 1910

CPIP: Comité Provincial de Investigación Pública – Provincial Committee of Public Investigation, created in August 1936 by the Republican Ministry of the Interior in an attempt to control the *checas* (q.v.) of the left-wing parties and trade unions

DEDIDE: Departamento Especial de Información del Estado – State Special Intelligence Department, created in June 1937 to centralize the Republican security and counter-espionage services

DERD: Delegación del Estado para la Recuperación de Documentos – State Delegation for the Recovery of Documents, the Francoist entity created in April 1938 to classify captured documentation from left-wing and liberal political parties, organizations and individuals in order to facilitate their location and punishment

DGS: Dirección General de Seguridad – General Directorate of Security, the national headquarters of the police and security forces

DRV: Derecha Regional Valenciana – the right-wing group of the Valencian region, one of the principal component groups that made up the CEDA (q.v.)

ERC: Esquerra Republicana de Catalunya – the Republican Left of Catalonia, the principal Catalan nationalist party, led by Lluís Companys

FAI: Federación Anarquista Ibérica – Iberian Anarchist Federation, the activist or terrorist wing of the anarchist movement founded in 1927

Falange Española: Spanish fascist party founded by José Antonio Primo de Rivera in October 1933

FE de las JONS: Falange Española de las Juntas de Ofensiva Nacional Sindicalista – the Spanish fascist party created by the merger in February 1934 of the Falange and the JONS (q.v.)

FJS: Federación de Juventudes Socialistas – the youth movement of the Socialist Party, PSOE (q.v.)

FNTT: Federación Nacional de Trabajadores de la Tierra – the Socialist landworkers' union affiliated to the UGT (q.v.)

Frente Popular: Popular Front, wide electoral coalition created in November 1935. It replicated the Republican–Socialist coalition of 1931 with the addition of three small groups – the Spanish Communist Party, the more or less Trotskyist POUM (q.v.) and the Syndicalist Party of the moderate anarchist Ángel Pestaña

Generalitat de Catalunya: the Catalan regional government, established by the autonomy statute of 1932

GRU: Glavnoye Razvedyvatel'noye Upravleniye – Soviet military intelligence

Izquierda Republicana: the Republican Left, the liberal party formed on 2 April 1934 from the merger of three other Republican groups and led by Manuel Azaña

JAP: Juventud de Acción Popular – the youth movement of the CEDA (q.v.)

JONS: Juntas de Ofensiva Nacional Sindicalista – the Juntas of National-Syndicalist Offensive, a tiny but violent fascist group founded by Onésimo Redondo and Ramiro Ledesma Ramos, who provided Spain's fascist insignia, the yoke and the arrows

jornalero: agricultural labourer, paid by the day worked

JSU: Juventudes Socialistas Unificadas – the United Socialist Youth, closely linked to the PCE (q.v.) after it was created in mid-1936 from the fusion of the Socialist and Communist youth movements

KGB: Komitet Gosudarstvennoy Bezopasnosti – Committee for State Security, the Soviet security and intelligence organization, the successor to the NKVD (q.v.)

latifundio: a huge estate found principally in Andalusia and Extremadura

latifundista: the owner of such an estate

Legionario: soldier of the Spanish Foreign Legion or Tercio de Extranjeros (q.v.)

NKVD: Narodnyy Komissariat Vnutrennikh Del – the People's Commissariat for Internal Affairs, Soviet security and intelligence organization

ORD: Oficina de Recuperación de Documentos – Office for the Recovery of Documents, set up on Franco's orders in May 1937 by the Carlist Marcelino de Ulibarri Eguílaz

OVRA: Organizzazione per la Vigilanza e la Repressione dell'Antifascismo – Italian fascist secret police

paseo: taking prisoners for a ride, slang for extra-judicial execution

PCE: Partido Comunista de España – Spanish Communist Party

PNV: Partido Nacionalista Vasco – the conservative and Catholic Basque Nationalist Party which sided with the Republic in 1936

POUM: Partido Obrero de Unificación Marxista – Workers' Marxist Unification Party, founded in late 1935, with the intention of uniting all left-wing forces into a revolutionary communist party opposed to Stalinism and therefore closer to Trotskyism

PSOE: Partido Socialista Obrero Español – the Spanish Socialist Workers Party

PSUC: Partit Socialista Unificat de Catalunya – the Catalan Communist Party

pueblo: small town or village

Regulares Indígenas: Native Regulars, a section of the Spanish colonial army consisting of tribal mercenaries recruited in Morocco

Renovación Española: Spanish Renovation – the extremist monarchist party

Requeté: the Carlist militia. The word denotes both an individual militiaman and the entire corps

ROVS: Russkii Obshche-Voinskii Soiuz – Russian All-Military Union, White Russian anti-Bolshevik organization in Paris with which General Emilio Mola had close ties

saca: the seizing and murder of an individual

SIM: Servicio de Inteligencia Militar – military intelligence service

Tercio de Extranjeros: the Spanish Foreign Legion created on 31 August 1920 (*tercio*, or third, was the name used in the sixteenth century for regiments in the Army of Flanders which had been composed of three groups, pikemen, crossbowmen and arquebusiers)

UGT: Unión General de Trabajadores – the General Union of Workers, Socialist trade union which incorporated many specialized unions of railway, building and other workers

UHP: Uníos, Hermanos Proletarios – Unite, Proletarian Brothers, a slogan coined during the Asturian rising of October 1934 and thereafter used as a chant and as graffiti

UME: Unión Militar Española – clandestine association of army officers devoted to the overthrow of the Republic, created in late 1933 by the retired Colonel Emilio Rodríguez Tarduchy, one of the first members of the Falange Española

UMRA: Unión Militar Republicana Antifascista – organization of Republican army officers committed to foiling the conspiratorial activities of the UME (q.v.). It was founded in late 1935 by Captain Eleuterio Díaz-Tendero Merchán, who would later die in Dachau

yuntero: ploughman owning his own yoke of oxen, usually hired on the same basis as a *jornalero*

NOTES

Prologue

1 Comandante Franco, *Diario de una bandera* (Madrid: Editorial Pueyo, 1922) pp. 129, 177.

2 *El Correo Gallego*, 20 April 1922.

3 José Martín Blázquez, *I Helped to Build an Army: Civil War Memoirs of a Spanish Staff Officer* (London: Secker & Warburg, 1939) p. 302; Herbert R. Southworth, *Antifalange: estudio crítico de 'Falange en la guerra de España: la Unificación y Hedilla' de Maximiano García Venero* (Paris: Ruedo Ibérico, 1967) pp. xxi–xxii; Guillermo Cabanellas, *La guerra de los mil días: nacimiento, vida y muerte de la II República española*, 2 vols (Buenos Aires: Grijalbo, 1973) II, p. 792.

4 Juan de Iturralde (Father Juan José Usabiaga Irazustabarrena), *La guerra de Franco, los vascos y la Iglesia*, 2 vols (San Sebastián: Publicaciones del Clero Vasco, 1978) I, p. 433.

5 The most widely accepted figure for Madrid is 8,815. See Santos Juliá *et al.*, *Víctimas de la guerra civil* (Madrid: Ediciones Temas de Hoy, 1999) p. 412; Mirta Núñez Díaz-Balart *et al.*, *La gran represión: los años de plomo del franquismo* (Barcelona: Flor del Viento, 2009) p. 443; and José Luis Ledesma, 'Una retaguardia al rojo: las violencias en la zona republicana', in Francisco Espinosa Maestre, ed., *Violencia roja y azul: España, 1936–1950* (Barcelona: Editorial Crítica, 2010) pp. 247, 409. The figure of 8,815 is based on that of 5,107 given by General Rafael Casas de la Vega, *El terror: Madrid 1936: investigación histórica y catálogo de víctimas identificadas* (Madrid: Editorial Fénix, 1994) pp. 247, 311–460, to which, without explanation, 3,708 were added by Ángel David Martín Rubio, *Paz, piedad, perdón ... y verdad: la represión en la guerra civil: una síntesis definitiva* (Madrid: Editorial Fénix, 1997) p. 316. In the same work pp. 317–19, 370, 374, and in *Los mitos de la represión en la guerra civil* (Madrid: Grafite Ediciones, 2005) p. 82, Martín Rubio gives the figure of 14,898, again without explanation.

6 For examples, see Jesús Vicente Aguirre González, *Aquí nunca pasó nada: La Rioja 1936* (Logroño: Editorial Ochoa, 2010) p. 8, and Francisco Espinosa Maestre in Núñez Díaz-Balart *et al.*, *La gran represión*, p. 442.

7 Francisco Espinosa Maestre, *La justicia de Queipo: violencia selectiva y terror fascista en la II División en 1936: Sevilla, Huelva, Cádiz, Córdoba, Málaga y Badajoz* (Seville: Centro Andaluz del Libro, 2000) pp. 13–23.

8 See the chapters on Burgos (by Luis Castro) and Palencia (by Jesús Gutiérrez Flores), in Enrique Berzal de la Rosa, ed., *Testimonio de voces olvidadas*, 2 vols (León: Fundación

27 de marzo, 2007) pp. 100–2, 217–18.

9 Julián Casanova, Francisco Espinosa, Conxita Mir and Francisco Moreno Gómez, *Morir, matar, sobrevivir: la violencia en la dictadura de Franco* (Barcelona: Editorial Crítica, 2002) p. 21.

10 For analysis of how deaths were registered, see the chapter by José María García Márquez in Antonio Leria, Francisco Eslava and José María García Márquez, *La guerra civil en Carmona* (Carmona: Ayuntamiento de Carmona, 2008) pp. 29–48; Julio Prada Rodríguez, 'Golpe de Estado y represión franquista en la provincia de Ourense', in Jesús de Juana and Julio Prada, eds, *Lo que han hecho en Galicia: violencia política, represión y exilio (1936–1939)* (Barcelona: Editorial Crítica, 2007) pp. 120–1.

11 Espinosa Maestre, ed., *Violencia roja y azul*, pp. 77–8; Francisco Espinosa Maestre in Núñez Díaz-Balart *et al.*, *La gran represión*, pp. 440–2.

12 Mirta Núñez Díaz-Balart and Antonio Rojas Friend, *Consejo de guerra: los fusilamientos en el Madrid de la posguerra (1939–1945)* (Madrid: Compañía Literaria, 1997) pp. 107–14; Fernando Hernández Holgado, *Mujeres encarceladas: la prisión de Ventas: de la República al franquismo, 1931–1941* (Madrid: Marcial Pons, 2003) pp. 227–46. Other places of execution are now being studied: http://www.memoriaylibertad.org/.htm.

13 For comparative analysis, see José Luis Ledesma Vera, *Los días de llamas de la revolución: violencia y política en la retaguardia republicana de Zaragoza durante la guerra civil* (Zaragoza: Institución Fernando el Católico, 2003) pp. 83–4; Ledesma Vera, 'Qué violencia para qué retaguardia, o la República en

guerra de 1936', *Ayer. Revista de Historia Contemporánea*, No. 76, 2009, pp. 83–114.

14 José María Ruiz Alonso, *La guerra civil en la provincia de Toledo: Utopía, conflicto y poder en el sur del Tajo (1936–1939)*, 2 vols (Ciudad Real: Almud, Ediciones de Castilla-La Mancha, 2004) I, pp. 283–94.

15 Ana Belén Rodríguez Patiño, *La guerra civil en Cuenca (1936–1939)*, 2 vols (Madrid: Universidad Complutense, 2004) II, pp. 122–32.

16 Josep M. Solé i Sabaté and Joan Villarroya i Font, *La repressió a la reraguarda de Catalunya (1936–1939)*, 2 vols (Barcelona: Publicacions de l'Abadia de Montserrat, 1989) I, pp. 11–12; Josep Benet, 'Pròleg', in *ibid.*, pp. vi–vii.

17 Francisco Franco Bahamonde, *Palabras del Caudillo 19 abril 1937–7 diciembre 1942* (Madrid: Ediciones de la Vicesecretaría de Educación Popular, 1943) pp. 312, 445.

18 Ramón Salas Larrazábal, *Los fusilados en Navarra en la guerra de 1936* (Madrid: Comisión de Navarros en Madrid y Seville, 1983) p. 13.

19 Antonio Montero Moreno, *Historia de la persecución religiosa en España 1936–1939* (Madrid: Biblioteca de Autores Cristianos, 1961) pp. 430–4, 762; Gregorio Rodríguez Fernández, *El hábito y la cruz: religiosas asesinadas en la guerra civil española* (Madrid: EDIBESA, 2006) pp. 594–6.

Chapter 1: Social War Begins, 1931–1933

1 He told the British volunteer Peter Kemp and the French correspondent Jean d'Hospital: Peter Kemp, *Mine Were of Trouble* (London: Cassell, 1957) p. 50; Herbert Rutledge Southworth,

Guernica! Guernica!: A Study of Journalism, Propaganda and History (Berkeley: University of California Press, 1977) p. 50.

2 Gonzalo Álvarez Chillida, *El antisemitismo en España: la imagen del judío (1812–2002)* (Madrid: Marcial Pons, 2002) pp. 201–3, 279.

3 José María Pemán, *El hecho y la idea de la Unión Patriótica* (Madrid: Imprenta Artística Sáez Hermanos, 1929) pp. 28–9, 105, 308–9.

4 José Pemartín, *Los valores históricos en la dictadura española*, 2nd edn (Madrid: Publicaciones de la Junta de Propaganda Patriótica y Ciudadana, 1929) pp. 103, 106–7, 683.

5 The manifesto of the PNE is printed in José María Albiñana, *Después de la dictadura: los cuervos sobre la tumba*, 2nd edn (Madrid: CIAP, 1930) pp. 252–9. See also Ismael Saz Campos, *Mussolini contra la II República: hostilidad, conspiraciones, intervención (1931–1936)* (Valencia: Edicions Alfons el Magnànim, 1986) pp. 95–7; Manuel Pastor, *Los orígenes del fascismo en España* (Madrid: Túcar Ediciones, 1975) pp. 38–61; Herbert Rutledge Southworth, *Antifalange: estudio crítico de 'Falange en la guerra de España' de Maximiano García Venero* (Paris: Ediciones Ruedo Ibérico, 1967) pp. 29–30; Julio Gil Pecharromán, *'Sobre España inmortal, sólo Díos': José María Albiñana y el Partido Nacionalista Español (1930–1937)* (Madrid: Universidad Nacional de Educación a Distancia, 2000) pp. 44–51.

6 Juan Tusquets, *Orígenes de la revolución española* (Barcelona: Editorial Vilamala, 1932) pp. 30–44, 137–42; Francisco de Luis, *La masonería contra España* (Burgos: Imprenta Aldecoa, 1935) pp. 153–62; Martin Blinkhorn, *Carlism and Crisis in Spain 1931–1939*

(Cambridge: Cambridge University Press, 1975) pp. 46, 179; Álvarez Chillida, *El antisemitismo*, pp. 181, 334–8.

7 Angeles Barrio Alonso, *Anarquismo y anarcosindicalismo en Asturias (1890/1936)* (Madrid: Siglo XXI, 1988) pp. 314–19; Enrique Montañés, *Anarcosindicalismo y cambio político: Zaragoza, 1930–1936* (Zaragoza: Institución Fernando el Católico, 1989) pp. 47–60; Enric Ucelay Da Cal, *La Catalunya populista: imatge, cultura i política en l'etapa republicana (1931–1939)* (Barcelona: Edicions de La Magrana, 1982) p. 135; Julián Casanova, *De la calle al frente: el anarcosindicalismo en España (1931–1939)* (Barcelona: Editorial Crítica, 1997) pp. 14–17.

8 Miguel Maura, *Así cayó Alfonso XIII*, 1st edn (Mexico City: Imprenta Mañez, 1962) pp. 278–9; Santos Juliá Díaz, *Madrid, 1931–1934: de la fiesta popular a la lucha de clases* (Madrid: Siglo XXI, 1984) pp. 198–207; Casanova, *De la calle al frente*, pp. 21–2; José Manuel Macarro Vera, *La utopía revolucionaria: Sevilla en la segunda República* (Seville: Monte de Piedad y Caja de Ahorros, 1985) p. 124; Eulàlia Vega, *El Trentisme a Catalunya: divergències ideològiques en la CNT (1930–1933)* (Barcelona: Curial Edicions Catalanes, 1980) p. 134.

9 Diary entries for 21 July 1931, Manuel Azaña, *Obras completas*, 4 vols (Mexico City: Ediciones Oasís, 1966–8) IV, pp. 36–7; Eulàlia Vega, *Anarquistas y sindicalistas durante la segunda República: la CNT y los Sindicatos de Oposición en el País Valenciano* (Valencia: Edicions Alfons el Magnànim, 1987) pp. 98–101.

10 Azaña, *Obras completas*, II, pp. 49–58.

11 Arnold Lunn, *Spanish Rehearsal* (London: Hutchinson, 1937) p. 70; Conde de Alba de Yeltes, *Cartas a un sobrino* (n.p., n.d.).

12 Ricardo Robledo and Luis Enrique Espinosa, "'¡El campo en pie!'": política y reforma agraria', in Ricardo Robledo, ed., *Esta salvaje pesadilla: Salamanca en la guerra civil española* (Barcelona: Editorial Crítica, 2007) pp. 23–5.

13 Alejandro López López, *El boicot de las derechas a las reformas de la Segunda República: la minoría agraria, el rechazo constitucional y la cuestión de la tierra* (Madrid: Instituto de Estudios Agrarios, 1984) p. 254.

14 *La Mañana* (Jaén), 16 January 1934.

15 *La Mañana* (Jaén), 1 October 1932, 21, 27 January, 3, 18 February, 5 April 1933; *El Adelanto* (Salamanca), 19 October 1932; *Región* (Cáceres), 24 February 1933; *El Obrero de la Tierra*, 14 January, 4 March 1933, 6, 13, 20 January, 17 February 1934; *El Socialista*, 21 January, 20 April, 1 July 1933. See also Paul Preston, *The Coming of the Spanish Civil War: Reform, Reaction and Revolution in the Second Spanish Republic 1931–1936*, 2nd edn (London: Routledge, 1994) pp. 101–2, 111, 134–5, 140, 148–9, 184–5.

16 *ABC*, 29, 30 September, 3, 4, 7 October 1931.

17 *ABC*, 16, 18, 19, 29 July 1933.

18 *El Socialista*, 29 September, 10, 11 November 1931; López López, *El boicot de las derechas*, pp. 255–7; Manuel Tuñón de Lara, *Tres claves de la segunda República* (Madrid: Alianza Editorial, 1985) p. 52; Casanova, *De la calle al frente*, pp. 39–43.

19 Eugenio Vegas Latapie, *El pensamiento político de Calvo Sotelo* (Madrid: Cultura Española, 1941) pp. 88–92; Eugenio Vegas Latapie, *Escritos políticos* (Madrid: Cultura

Española, 1941) pp. 9–12; Eugenio Vegas Latapie, 'Maeztu y Acción Española', *ABC*, 2 November 1952; Pedro Carlos González Cuevas, *Acción Española: teología política y nacionalismo autoritario en España (1913–1936)* (Madrid: Editorial Tecnos, 1998) pp. 144–5, 165–8, 171–5.

20 Preston, *The Coming of the Spanish Civil War*, pp. 61–6; Paul Preston, 'Alfonsist Monarchism and the Coming of the Spanish Civil War', *Journal of Contemporary History*, Vol. 7, Nos 3/4, 1972.

21 For the ACNP, See A. Sáez Alba, *La otra 'cosa nostra': la Asociación Católica Nacional de Propagandistas* (Paris: Ruedo Ibérico, 1974) pp. ix–xxii; José María García Escudero, *Conversaciones sobre Angel Herrera* (Madrid: Editorial Católica, 1986) pp. 16–20. For the CNCA, see Antonio Monedero Martín, *La Confederación Nacional Católico-Agraria en 1920: su espíritu, su organización, su porvenir* (Madrid: V. Rico, 1921) p. 22, and Juan José Castillo, *Propietarios muy pobres: sobre la subordinación política del pequeño campesino* (Madrid, 1979); Tom Buchanan and Martin Conway, eds, *Political Catholicism in Europe 1918–1965* (Oxford: Oxford University Press, 1996) pp. 8–11.

22 *El Debate*, 7, 9 May 1931; José R. Montero, *La CEDA: el catolicismo social y político en la II República*, 2 vols (Madrid: Ediciones de la Revista de Trabajo, 1977) II, pp. 593–4.

23 José Monge Bernal, *Acción Popular (estudios de biología política)* (Madrid: Imp. Sáez Hermanos, 1936) pp. 114–15, 122.

24 Frances Lannon, *Privilege, Persecution, and Prophecy: The Catholic Church in Spain 1875–1975* (Oxford: Clarendon Press, 1987) pp. 188–9.

25 *La Libertad*, 13 May 1931; *La Voz*, 14 May 1931; Maura, *Así cayó Alfonso XIII* (1st edn), pp. 240–55.

26 Maura, *Así cayó Alfonso XIII* (1st edn), p. 254; Leandro Álvarez Rey, *La derecha en la II República: Sevilla, 1931–1936* (Seville: Universidad de Seville/Ayuntamiento de Seville, 1993) pp. 188–98.

27 Miguel Maura, *Así cayó Alfonso XIII: de una dictadura a otra*, 2nd edn by Joaquín Romero Maura (Madrid: Marcial Pons Historia, 2007) p. 365.

28 Maura, *Así cayó Alfonso XIII* (1st edn) pp. 278–87; diary entry for 21 July, Azaña, *Obras completas*, IV, pp. 37–8.

29 Macarro Vera, *La utopía revolucionaria*, pp. 147–60; Eduardo de Guzmán, *Sevilla la trágica: Ocho días que estremecieron a España* (Madrid: Ediciones Minuesa, 1931) pp. 21, 51–2; Francisco Espinosa Maestre, *La justicia de Queipo: violencia selectiva y terror fascista en la II División en 1936: Sevilla, Huelva, Cádiz, Córdoba, Málaga y Badajoz* (Seville: Centro Andaluz del Libro, 2000) pp. 32–7; Carlos Enrique Bayo and Cipriano Damiano, 'Toreros fascistas: matadores de obreros', *Interviú*, No. 103, 3–9 May 1978, pp. 40–5; Juan-Simeón Vidarte, *Las Cortes Constituyentes de 1931–1933* (Barcelona: Grijalbo, 1976) pp. 76–8; Manuel Tuñón de Lara, *Luchas obreras y campesinas en la Andalucía del siglo XX* (Madrid: Siglo XXI, 1978) pp. 190–203; Dr Pedro Vallina, *Mis memorias* (Madrid and Seville: Libre Pensamiento/Centro Andaluz del Libro, 2000) pp. 247–56.

30 Azaña, diary entries for 24 July, 9 August 1931, *Obras completas*, IV, pp. 43–5, 73. Maura's account of his attack on Azaña was omitted from the first edition of his memoirs. It appears in the 2nd edition by Joaquín Romero Maura: Maura, *Así cayó Alfonso XIII*, pp. 366–7.

31 Casanova, *De la calle al frente*, pp. 49–52; Juan García Oliver, *El eco de los pasos* (Barcelona: Ruedo Ibérico, 1978) pp. 115–36; Macarro Vera, *La utopía revolucionaria*, p. 124; Vega, *El Trentisme a Catalunya*, pp. 68–72, 132–6; Vega, *Anarquistas y sindicalistas*, pp. 57–9, 85–97; Juliá Díaz, *Madrid, 1931–1934*, pp. 172–90; Chris Ealham, *Class, Culture and Conflict in Barcelona 1898–1937* (London: Routledge/Cañada Blanch Studies, 2004) pp. 90–101.

32 *El Debate*, 18, 19 August 1931; Lannon, *Privilege, Persecution, and Prophecy*, p. 181.

33 López López, *El boicot de las derechas*, pp. 252–3.

34 Lannon, *Privilege, Persecution, and Prophecy*, pp. 181–5; Álvarez Rey, *La derecha*, pp. 203–6.

35 José María Gil Robles, *No fue posible la paz* (Barcelona: Ariel, 1968) pp. 55–6.

36 *ABC*, 10 October 1931.

37 *Diario de sesiones de las Cortes Constituyentes* [henceforth *DSCC*], 13 October 1931; Mary Vincent, *Catholicism in the Second Spanish Republic: Religion and Politics in Salamanca 1930–1936* (Oxford: Clarendon Press, 1996) pp. 180–1.

38 Tusquets, *Orígenes*, pp. 30–44, 137–42; Blinkhorn, *Carlism*, pp. 46, 179; Álvarez Chillida, *El antisemitismo*, pp. 181, 334–8.

39 Vincent, *Catholicism*, pp. 183–4; Agustín Martínez de las Heras, 'El discurso antimasónico de *Los Hijos del Pueblo*', in José Antonio Ferrer Benimeli, ed., *La masonería en la España del siglo XX*, 2 vols (Toledo: Universidad de Castilla-La Mancha, 1996) II, pp. 713–50.

40 *El Debate*, 1, 3 November 1931; *El Socialista*, 2 November 1931.

41 *ABC*, 10 November 1931; *El Debate*, 10, 12 November 1931; *El Socialista*, 2 November 1931; Gil Robles, *No fue posible*, pp. 70–1.

42 *La Época*, 2 January 1932.

43 *La Época*, 24 February 1932; Monge Bernal, *Acción Popular*, pp. 223–5.

44 Vincent, *Catholicism*, p. 186.

45 María Pilar Salomón Chéliz, *Anticlericalismo en Aragón: protesta popular y movilización política (1900–1939)* (Zaragoza: Prensas Universitarias de Zaragoza, 2002) pp. 287–8.

46 Álvarez Rey, *La derecha*, pp. 215–35.

47 Vincent, *Catholicism*, p. 185; José María Lama, *Una biografía frente al olvido: José González Barrero, Alcalde de Zafra en la II República* (Badajoz: Diputación de Badajoz, 2000) p. 46.

48 José Luis Gutiérrez Casalá, *La segunda República en Badajoz* (Badajoz: Universitas Editorial, 1998) pp. 128–9; Amparo Cabeza de Vaca, *Bajo cielos de plomo: unas memorias y el diario de Rafael Salazar Alonso* (Madrid: Editorial Actas, 2009) p. 30.

49 Rafael Cruz, *En el nombre del pueblo: República, rebelión y guerra en la España de 1936* (Madrid: Siglo XXI de España Editores, 2006) pp. 51–8

50 *ABC*, 16 June 1932.

51 Letter of 25 April 1937 from Gil Robles to Luciano de la Calzada, *Sur* (Málaga), 28 April 1937; Gil Robles, *No fue posible*, pp. 67–76. Cf. José Gutiérrez Ravé, *Gil Robles, caudillo frustrado* (Madrid: ERSA, 1967) pp. 198–9.

52 Manuel Albar, 'Sobre unos sucesos: el verdadero culpable', *El Socialista*, 2 January 1932. For a description of Castilblanco, see Vidarte, *Las Cortes Constituyentes*, pp. 306–9; Luis Jiménez Asúa, Juan-Simeón Vidarte, Antonio Rodríguez Sastre and Anselmo Trejo, *Castilblanco* (Madrid: Editorial España, 1933). Outspoken in this regard was Margarita Nelken,

see Paul Preston, *Doves of War: Four Women of Spain* (London: HarperCollins, 2002) pp. 297–407.

53 César González-Ruano and Emilio R.Tarduchy, *Sanjurjo (una vida española del novecientos)* (Madrid: Acción Española, 1933) p. 177; Vidarte, *Las Cortes Constituyentes*, pp. 600–1; Jesús Vicente Chamorro, *Año nuevo, año viejo en Castilblanco* (Madrid: Ediciones Albia, 1985) p. 80.

54 *ABC*, 1, 2, 3, 5 January 1932; *El Debate*, 2 January 1932; *La Nación*, 4, 5 January 1932; *El Sol*, 3 January 1932; *La Voz Extremeña*, 5 January 1932; González-Ruano and Tarduchy, *Sanjurjo*, pp. 180–1. See also Francisco Espinosa Maestre, *La columna de la muerte: el avance del ejército franquista de Sevilla a Badajoz* (Barcelona: Editorial Crítica, 2003) p. 498.

55 *ABC*, 2 January 1932.

56 Francisco Valdés, 'Márgenes. El Afincado', *La Voz Extremeña* (Badajoz), 10 January 1932; 'La tragedia de Castilblanco', *El Faro de Extremadura* (Plasencia), 9 January 1932; 'La tragedia de Castilblanco' in *La Opinión* (Trujillo), 7 January 1932; 'Aún quedan tribus', *El Pueblo Manchego* (Ciudad Real), 4 January 1932.

57 'La guerra contra la Guardia Civil', *ABC*, 2 January 1932; *El Imparcial*, 2 January 1932.

58 *El Socialista*, 6 January 1932; *La Rioja*, 6, 8, 9, 10, 12 January 1932; *El Debate*, 6 January 1932; Carlos Gil Andrés, *La República en la Plaza: los sucesos de Arnedo de 1932* (Logroño: Instituto de Estudios Riojanos, 2003) pp. 24–33, 43–9; Edward E. Malefakis, *Agrarian Reform and Peasant Revolution in Spain: Origins of the Civil War* (New Haven: Yale University Press, 1970) pp. 310–11.

59 Gil Andrés, *La República en la Plaza*, pp. 257–72; Jesús Vicente Aguirre

González, *Aquí nunca pasó nada: La Rioja 1936* (Logroño: Editorial Ochoa, 2007) pp. 271–89.

60 Azaña, *Obras completas*, IV, pp. 294–7.

61 Gil Andrés, *La República en la Plaza*, pp. 210–11.

62 Manuel Llaneza, *Escritos y discursos* (Oviedo: Fundación José Barreiros, 1985) pp. 206–14.

63 Vega, *El Trentisme a Catalunya*, pp. 149–54; Macarro Vera, *La utopía revolucionaria*, pp. 198–202; Azaña, *Obras completas*, II, pp. 139–42; Casanova, *De la calle al frente*, p. 55.

64 According to Gutiérrez Casalá, *La segunda República en Badajoz*, p. 153, after being addressed by Margarita Nelken the crowd had intended to attack the Civil Guard barracks in Salvaleón, and a shot was fired by someone in the crowd. In fact Margarita Nelken was not present, and the local version of events claims that the only shots fired emanated from the Civil Guard. I am grateful to Francisco Espinosa Maestre who communicated to me the eyewitness account of Francisco Marín Torrado, a local judge (*juez de paz*), who denied that any shots were fired from the crowd. See also 'Los sucesos de Salvaleón', *El Obrero de la Tierra*, 14 May 1932; José Ignacio Rodríguez Hermosell, *Movimiento obrero en Barcarrota: José Sosa Hormigó, diputado campesino* (Badajoz: Asamblea de Extremadura, 2005) pp. 412.

65 Azaña, diary entry for 8 January 1932, *Obras completas*, IV, pp. 299–301.

66 Espinosa Maestre, *La justicia de Queipo*, pp. 33, 77–9; Antonio L. Oliveros, *Asturias en el resurgimiento español (apuntes históricos y biográficos)* (Madrid: Imprenta Juan Bravo, 1935) p. 276.

67 Pedro-Pablo Miralles Sangro, 'Al servicio de la Justicia y de la República': Mariano Gómez (1883–1951), *Presidente del Tribunal Supremo* (Madrid: Editorial Dilex, 2010) pp. 78–84; Pascual Marzal Rodríguez, *Una historia sin justicia: cátedra, política y magistratura en la vida de Mariano Gómez* (Valencia: Universitat de València, 2009) pp. 153–7.

68 Julio Alvarez del Vayo, *The Last Optimist* (London: Putnam, 1950) p. 228; Manuel Azaña, *Diarios, 1932–1933: 'Los cuadernos robados'* (Barcelona: Grijalbo-Mondadori, 1997) pp. 41–6.

69 Joaquín del Moral, *Lo del '10 de agosto' y la justicia* (Madrid: C.I.A.P., 1933) pp. 99–108.

70 José María Pemán, *Un soldado en la historia: vida del Capitán General Varela* (Cádiz: Escelicer, 1954) pp. 111–20, 126–30; General Francisco Javier Mariñas, *General Varela (de soldado a general)* (Barcelona: Editorial AHR, 1956) pp. 56–64.

71 Juan Antonio Ansaldo, *¿Para qué …? (de Alfonso XIII a Juan III)* (Buenos Aires: Editorial Vasca Ekin, 1951) pp. 47–51.

72 Azaña, diary entry for 29 August 1932, *Diarios, 1932–1933*, p. 53.

73 Antonio Cacho Zabalza, *La Unión Militar Española* (Alicante: Egasa, 1940) pp. 14–16; Vicente Guarner, *Cataluña en la guerra de España* (Madrid, 1975) pp. 64–6; Stanley G. Payne, *Politics and the Military in Modern Spain* (Stanford, Calif.: Stanford University Press, 1967) pp. 293–4.

74 Carlos Blanco Escolá, *La Academia General Militar de Zaragoza (1928–1931)* (Barcelona: Editorial Labor, 1989) p. 71.

75 Cayetano Ibarra, *La otra mitad de la historia que nos contaron: Fuente de Cantos, República y guerra 1931–1939* (Badajoz: Diputación de Badajoz, 2005) pp. 187–8.

76 *El Obrero de la Tierra*, 17, 24 December 1932; María Paz Ladrón

de Guevara, *Reforma agraria y conflicto campesino en la provincia de Ciudad Real (1931–1936)* (Ciudad Real: Diputación Provincial de Ciudad Real, 1993) pp. 97–115.

77 Ramón Sender, *Viaje a la aldea del crimen* (Madrid: Pueyo, 1934) pp. 33–42, 70–130; Francisco Guerra, *Casas Viejas: apuntes de la tragedia* (Jerez: Establecimiento Tipográfico 'El Martillo', 1933); Eduardo de Guzmán, *La tragedia de Casas Viejas, 1933: quince crónicas de guerra, 1936* (Madrid: Ediciones Vosa, 2007) pp. 15–48; Gérald Brey and Jacques Maurice, *Historia y leyenda de Casas Viejas* (Bilbao: Editorial Zero/ZYX, 1976) pp. 65–75; Jerome R. Mintz, *The Anarchists of Casas Viejas* (Chicago: University of Chicago Press, 1982) pp. 189–225; Antonio Ramos Espejo, *Después de Casas Viejas* (Barcelona: Argos Vergara, 1984) pp. 11–25.

78 *El Debate*, 15 January 1932.

79 Manuel Azaña, diary entry for 13 January 1933, *Diarios, 1932–1933*, p. 136.

80 *DSCC*, 3, 23, 24 February, 2, 3 March 1933; *El Debate*, 24 February 1933. On Barba Hernández and Casas Viejas, see *DSC*, 16 March 1933; Azaña, *Obras completas*, IV, pp. 469–71; Guillermo Cabanellas, *La guerra de los mil días: nacimiento, vida y muerte de la II República española*, 2 vols (Buenos Aires: Grijalbo, 1973) I, pp. 274, 494–6; Gabriel Jackson, *The Spanish Republic and the Civil War* (Princeton, NJ: Princeton University Press, 1965) p. 514.

81 Rafael Salazar Alonso, *Bajo el signo de la revolución* (Madrid: Librería de San Martín, 1935) pp. 36–7; Lama, *José González Barrero*, pp. 46–8. According to Gutiérrez Casalá, *La segunda República en Badajoz*, p. 176, Salazar Alonso was present.

82 *Diario de las Sesiones de Cortes* [henceforth *DSC*], 25 January 1934. See also Margarita Nelken, *Por qué hicimos la revolución* (Barcelona: Ediciones Sociales Internacionales, 1936) p. 96.

83 Niceto Alcalá Zamora, *Memorias* (Barcelona: Planeta, 1977) p. 283; *DSC*, 25 January 1934; Nelken, *Por qué hicimos la revolución*, p. 87; Vallina, *Mis memorias*, pp. 226–7; Alejandro Lerroux, *La pequeña historia: apuntes para la historia grande vividos y redactados por el autor* (Buenos Aires: Editorial Cimera, 1945) pp. 149, 245.

84 His love letters to the woman named only as Amparo were seized from his house at the beginning of the Civil War and reprinted in *CNT*, 13 January 1937. The daughter of Amparo Munilla Montero de Espinosa and Francisco Amparo Cabeza de Vaca, from Villafranca de los Barros, refers to her parents' friendship with Salazar Alonso in her memoirs (a book heaving with extreme snobbery and class hatred) but denies categorically that her mother was Salazar's lover – Amparo Cabeza de Vaca, *Bajo cielos de plomo: unas memorias y el diario de Rafael Salazar Alonso* (Madrid: Editorial Actas, 2009) pp. 32, 39, 88.

85 *BUGT*, August–September 1933; *El Obrero de la Tierra*, 12, 20 August, 9 September 1933; *El Debate*, 22, 23, 29 August 1933.

86 *El Debate*, 19 September 1933; *El Obrero de la Tierra*, 16, 23, 30 September 1933; *BUGT*, November 1933; Mario López Martínez, *Órden publico y luchas agrarias en Andalucia* (Madrid: Ediciones Libertarias/Ayuntamiento de Córdoba, 1995) p. 319.

87 María Martínez Sierra, *Una mujer por los caminos de España*, 2nd edn (Madrid: Editorial Castalia, 1989) pp. 81–6.

88 Juan-Simeón Vidarte, *El bienio negro y la insurreción de Asturias* (Barcelona: Grijalbo, 1978) pp. 109–10; Francisco Largo Caballero, *Discursos a los trabajadores* (Madrid: Gráfica Socialista, 1934) Apéndice, pp. 163–6.

89 Antonio Ramos Oliveira, *Politics, Economics and Men of Modern Spain* (London: Victor Gollancz, 1946) pp. 489–91; Nelken, *Por qué hicimos la revolución*, pp. 67–9; Martínez Sierra, *Una mujer*, pp. 133–40; Antonina Rodrigo, *María Lejárraga: una mujer en la sombra* (Madrid: Ediciones Vosa, 1994) pp. 266–7; López Martínez, *Órden publico y luchas agrarias*, pp. 320–4; Francisco Moreno Gómez, *La República y la guerra civil en Córdoba* (Córdoba: Ayuntamiento de Córdoba, 1982) p. 230; *El Obrero de la Tierra*, 31 March 1934.

90 *El Socialista*, 28, 30 October 1933; Gutiérrez Casalá, *La segunda República en Badajoz*, pp. 153, 169, 187, 190; Nelken, *Por qué hicimos la revolución*, pp. 69, 96; Vidarte, *El bienio negro*, pp. 32–5. On his activities in Badajoz, see Vallina, *Mis memorias*, pp. 260–2.

91 Nelken to Pi Sunyer, 21 November 1933, Arxiu Carles Pi Sunyer, Barcelona.

92 Margarita Nelken, 'Las Actas de Badajoz: con el fango hasta la boca', *El Socialista*, 30 November 1933; Nelken, *Por qué hicimos la revolución*, pp. 69–70; Vidarte, *El bienio negro*, pp. 151–2; Gutiérrez Casalá, *La segunda República en Badajoz*, pp. 193–9.

93 Ramos Oliveira, *Politics, Economics*, p. 490; López Martínez, *Órden publico y luchas agrarias*, pp. 326–9.

Chapter 2: The Patriotic Duty to Exterminate the Left

1 *ABC*, 31 January 1933. Many of Lamamié de Clairac's relatives, including his brother (a Jesuit) and his son, were priests and nuns – see Antonio Pérez de Olaguer, *Piedras vivas: biografía del Capellán Requeté José María Lamamié de Clairac y Alonso* (San Sebastián: Editorial Española, 1939) pp. xvi–xviii, 30–3.

2 Antonio Rodríguez de las Heras, *Filiberto Villalobos, su obra social y política 1900–1936* (Salamanca: Centro de Estudios Salmantinos, 1985) p. 193.

3 *ABC*, 6 June 1933.

4 On the genesis of the Protocols, see Norman Cohn, *Warrant for Genocide: The Myth of Jewish World Conspiracy and the Protocols of the Elders of Zion* (Harmondsworth: Pelican Books, 1970).

5 On Tusquets, see Antoni Mora, 'Joan Tusquets, en els 90 anys d'un home d'estudi i de combat', Institut d'Estudis Tarraconenses Ramón Berenguer IV, *Anuari 1990–1991 de la Societat d'Estudis d'Història Eclesiàstica Moderna i Contemporània de Catalunya* (Tarragona: Diputació de Tarragona, 1992) pp. 231–42; José Antonio Ferrer Benimelli, *El contubernio judeo-masónico-comunista: del Satanismo al escándalo del P-2* (Madrid: Ediciones Istmo, 1982) pp. 191–7; Jordi Canal, 'Las campañas antisectarias de Juan Tusquets (1927–1939): una aproximación a los orígenes del contuberio judeo-masónico-comunista en España', in José Antonio Ferrer Benimeli, ed., *La masonería en la España del siglo XX*, 2 vols (Toledo: Universidad de Castilla-La Mancha, 1996) II, pp. 1193–1214; Javier Domínguez Arribas, 'Juan Tusquets y sus ediciones antisectarias (1936–1939)', in José Antonio Ferrer Benimeli, ed., *La masonería española en la época de Sagasta*, 2 vols (Zaragoza: Gobierno de Aragón, 2007) II, pp. 1157–96.

6 On Tusquets's accusations against
Macià, see Juan Tusquets, *Orígenes
de la revolución española* (Barcelona:
Editorial Vilamala, 1932) pp. 150–1;
Juan Tusquets, *Masones y pacifistas*
(Burgos: Ediciones Antisectarias,
1939) pp. 104–5; Hilari Raguer, *La
Unió Democràtica de Catalunya i el
seu temps (1931–1939)* (Barcelona:
Publicaciones de l'Abadia de
Montserrat, 1976) pp. 279–80; Arxiu
Vidal i Barraquer, *Esglesia i Estat
durant la Segona República espanyola
1931/1936*, 4 vols in 8 parts
(Monestir de Montserrat:
Publicacions de l'Abadia de
Montserrat, 1971–90) II, pp. 386,
638, III, p. 935.

7 On the burglary and the alleged
assassination attempts, see Mora,
'Joan Tusquets', pp. 234–5.

8 Tusquets, *Orígenes*, pp. 101, 137.
Alcalá Zamora wrote in protest to
Archbishop Vidal i Barraquer, 26
March 1932, Arxiu Vidal i Barraquer,
Esglesia i Estat, II, pp. 644–6.

9 *Los poderes ocultos en España: los
Protocolos y su aplicación a España –
infiltraciones masónicas en el
catalanismo – ¿El señor Macià es
masón?* (Barcelona: Editorial
Vilamala, Biblioteca Las Sectas,
1932) pp. 35–46; Tusquets, *Orígenes*,
pp. 35–6, 41, 99, 126–7; Jordi Canal,
'Las campañas antisectarias', pp.
1201–7.

10 Joan Subirà, *Capellans en temps de
Franco* (Barcelona: Editorial
Mediterrània, 1996) p. 25; interview
with Lluís Bonada, *Avui*, 28
February 1990.

11 Ignasi Riera, *Los catalanes de Franco*
(Barcelona: Plaza y Janés, 1998) pp.
126–7; Ramón Serrano Suñer,
'Prólogo', in Tusquets, *Masonería y
pacifistas*, p. 7.

12 José del Castillo and Santiago
Álvarez, *Barcelona: objetivo cubierto*
(Barcelona: Editorial Timón, 1958)
p. 146; Hilari Raguer, *Salvador Rial,

vicari del cardenal de la pau*
(Barcelona: Publicacions de l'Abadia
de Montserrat, 1993) p. 40; Joaquín
María de Nadal, *Seis años con don
Francisco Cambó (1930–1936):
memorias de un secretario político*
(Barcelona: Editorial Alpha, 1957) p.
265.

13 Tusquets, *Orígenes*, pp. 51–7, 95–6,
122–6, 170, 177, 207–15. On the
compilation of lists, see also the
'Declaración del testigo Francesc
Casanova a la Causa General,
Provincia de Barcelona, 8 June 1942',
Barcelona, Pieza No. 2, Legajo 1630,
Archivo Histórico Nacional
[henceforth AHN].

14 *Acción Española*, Vol. II, No. 10, 1
May 1932, p. 422.

15 Julián Cortés Cavanillas, *La caída de
Alfonso XIII: causas y episodios de
una revolución*, 7th edn (Madrid:
Librería de San Martín, 1933) pp.
25, 33–4.

16 *Acción Española*, Vol. II, No. 10, 1
May 1932, pp. 434–8.

17 'La resistencia a la tiranía', *Acción
Española*, Vol. VI, No. 34, 1 August
1933, pp. 352–71; No. 35, 16 August
1933, pp. 442–61; No. 36, 1
September 1933, pp. 580–90; No. 37,
16 September 1933, pp. 1–8.

18 'La sumisión al Poder ilegítimo',
Acción Española, 16 October 1933,
pp. 205–28; Aniceto de Castro
Albarrán, *El derecho a la rebeldía*
(Madrid: Cultura Española, 1934);
Aniceto de Castro Albarrán, *Guerra
santa: el sentido católico del
Movimiento Nacional Español*
(Burgos: Editorial Española, 1938)
pp. 77–84.

19 José Cirera y Prat, *El criterio
legitimista frente al confusionismo
actual* (Barcelona: La Hormiga de
Oro, 1933); Frances Lannon,
*Privilege, Persecution and Prophecy:
The Catholic Church in Spain 1875–
1975* (Oxford: Clarendon Press,
1987) p. 187.

20 Vidal i Barraquer to Pacelli, 6 December 1933, Arxiu Vidal i Barraquer, *Esglesia i Estat durant la Segona República espanyola 1931/1936*, IV, Parts 1 and 2, pp. 167–71; Ramón Comas, *Isidro Gomá: Francesc Vidal i Barraquer: dos visiones antagónicas de la Iglesia española de 1939* (Salamanca: Ediciones Sigueme, 1977) pp. 89–94; Ramón Muntanyola, *Vidal i Barraquer: cardenal de la pau*, 2nd edn (Barcelona: Publicaciones de l'Abadia de Montserrat, 1976) pp. 318–19; Mary Vincent, *Catholicism in the Second Spanish Republic: Religion and Politics in Salamanca 1930–1936* (Oxford: Clarendon Press, 1996) pp. 217, 248–9.

21 Santiago Martínez Sánchez, *Los papeles perdidos del cardenal Segura, 1880–1957* (Pamplona: Ediciones Universidad de Navarra, 2004) pp. 289–96.

22 Emilio Mola Vidal, *Obras completas* (Valladolid: Librería Santarén, 1940) pp. 197–8, 200.

23 Carlos Blanco Escolá, *General Mola: el ególatra que provocó la guerra civil* (Madrid: La Esfera de los Libros, 2002) pp. 61–4.

24 *Ibid.*, pp. 79–81, 187–8.

25 Jorge Vigón, *General Mola (el conspirador)* (Barcelona: Editorial AHR, 1957) pp. 57–8, 63–4; B. Félix Maíz, *Mola, aquel hombre* (Barcelona: Planeta, 1976) pp. 25–8, 43–4, 84–6, 238. Evgenii Miller had been a dictatorial Governor General and Commander of the White military forces in the Northern Region Archangel during the Russian Civil War, and then Chief of Staff in Paris of the White Russian Army from 1922 to 1924. Thereafter, he was one of the key figures among the military émigrés between the wars. He was abducted by the NKVD in Paris in 1937 and shot in Moscow in May 1939 on the orders of Lavrentiy Beria. See Vladislav I. Goldin and John W. Long, 'Resistance and Retribution: The Life and Fate of General E. K. Miller', *Revolutionary Russia*, Vol. 12, No. 2, December 1999, pp. 19–40; Paul Robinson, *The White Russian Army in Exile 1920–1941* (Oxford: Clarendon Press, 2002) pp. 174–7, 208–10, 224–5, 236; Marina Gorboff, *La Russie fantôme: l'émigration russe de 1920 à 1950* (Lausanne: Éditions L'Age d'Homme, 1995) pp. 135–6, 151–8; John J. Stepan, *The Russian Fascists: Tragedy and Farce in Exile 1925–1945* (London: Hamish Hamilton, 1878) pp. 18–23. I am grateful to Dr Jonathan Smele for his help on the White Russian connection.

26 Vigón, *General Mola*, pp. 75–6; Carolyn P. Boyd, '"Responsibilities" and the Second Republic, 1931–1936', in Martin Blinkhorn, ed., *Spain in Conflict 1931–1939: Democracy and its Enemies* (London, 1986) pp. 14–39.

27 Mola, *Obras*, pp. 879–80; José María Iribarren, *Mola: datos para una biografía y para la historia del alzamiento nacional* (Zaragoza: Librería General, 1938) pp. 39–40; Manuel Azaña, *Obras completas*, 4 vols (Mexico City: Ediciones Oasís, 1966–8) I, p. 64.

28 *Lo que yo supe: memorias de mi paso por la Dirección General de Seguridad* written in 1931 but not published until January 1933 – Mola, *Obras*, p. 347. Mola's personal loathing of Azaña was underlined in a broadcast from Radio Castilla in Burgos on 15 August 1936 in which he described him as a monstrous degenerate – Mola, *Obras*, p. 1178. See Vegas Latapié's review in *Acción Española*, VI, 31, 16 June 1933.

29 Mola, *Tempestad, calma, intriga y crisis*, reprinted in *Obras*, pp. 574–5.

30 Mola, *Obras*, pp. 1166–7.

31 Blanco Escolá, *General Mola*, pp. 12–13. On his personality, see Guillermo Cabanellas, *La guerra de los mil días: nacimiento, vida y muerte de la II República española*, 2 vols (Buenos Aires: Grijalbo, 1973) I, p. 303.

32 Herbert Rutledge Southworth, *Conspiracy and the Spanish Civil War: The Brainwashing of Francisco Franco* (London: Routledge/Cañada Blanch Studies, 2002) pp. 128–91; Brian Crozier, *Franco: A Biographical History* (London: Eyre & Spottiswoode, 1967) p. 92; George Hills, *Franco: The Man and his Nation* (New York: Macmillan, 1967) p. 157; Luis Suárez Fernández, *Francisco Franco y su tiempo*, 8 vols (Madrid: Fundación Nacional Francisco Franco, 1984) I, pp. 197–8. On the many White Russian émigrés in Switzerland, see Cohn, *Warrant for Genocide*, pp. 243–55.

33 Cohn, *Warrant for Genocide*, p. 268.

34 Enrique Herrera Oria, *Los cautivos de Vizcaya: memorias del P. Enrique Herrera Oria, S.J., preso durante cuatro meses y medio en la cárcel de Bilbao y condenado a ocho años y un día de prisión* (Bilbao: Aldus S.A., 1938) pp. 12–13; *Protocolos de los Sabios de Sión* (Valladolid: Libertad/ Afrodisio Aguado, 1934); Onésimo Redondo, 'El autor y el precursor de los "Protocolos"', 'El precursor de los "Protocolos"', *Obras completas: edición cronológica II* (Madrid: Publicaciones Españolas, 1955) pp. 201–4, 223–6.

35 Cohn, *Warrant for Genocide*, p. 326; Vincent, *Catholicism*, pp. 217–19; Gonzalez Álvarez Chillida, *El antisemitismo: la imagen del judío (1812–2002)* (Madrid: Marcial Pons, 2002) pp. 302–3, 324–5; Martin Blinkhorn, *Carlism and Crisis in Spain 1931–1939* (Cambridge: Cambridge University Press, 1975) p. 179.

36 Martin Blinkhorn, 'Right-wing Utopianism and Harsh Reality: Carlism, the Republic and the "Crusade"', in Martin Blinkhorn, ed., *Spain in Conflict 1931–1939: Democracy and its Enemies* (London: Sage Publications, 1986) pp. 183–205.

37 Álvarez Chillida, *El antisemitismo*, pp. 286–8.

38 Blinkhorn, *Carlism*, pp. 180–1.

39 José María Pemán, *Un soldado en la historia: vida del Capitán General Varela* (Cádiz: Escelicer, 1954) pp. 126–35; Antonio Lizarza Iribarren, *Memorias de la conspiración*, 4th edn (Pamplona: Editorial Gómez, 1969) pp. 32–3, 49–51.

40 José Monge y Bernal, *Acción Popular (Estudios de biología política)* (Madrid: Imp. Saez Hermanos, 1936) pp. 126–32; Javier Jiménez Campo, *El fascismo en la crisis de la Segunda República española* (Madrid: Centro de Investigaciones Sociológicas, 1979) pp. 129–30; José R. Montero, *La CEDA: el catolicismo social y politico en la II República*, 2 vols (Madrid: Ediciones de la Revista de Trabajo, 1977) I, pp. 98, 385; José Luis Mínguez Goyanes, *Onésimo Redondo 1905–1936: precursor sindicalista* (Madrid: Editorial San Martín, 1990) pp. 24–30.

41 Anon. (Javier Martínez de Bedoya), *Onésimo Redondo Caudillo de Castilla* (Valladolid: Ediciones Libertad, 1937) pp. 19–22; Onésimo Redondo, *El Estado Nacional* (Barcelona: Ediciones FE, 1939) pp. 42–3.

42 Ángel de Prado Moura, *El movimiento obrero en Valladolid durante la Segunda República* (Valladolid: Junta de Castilla y León, 1985) p. 135.

43 Anon., *Onésimo Redondo Caudillo*, p. 30.

44 *Ibid.*, pp. 22–7; Tomás Borrás, *Ramiro Ledesma Ramos* (Madrid:

Editora Nacional, 1971) p. 284; Mínguez Goyanes, *Onésimo Redondo*, p. 36.

45 Ramiro Ledesma Ramos, *¿Fascismo en España?*, 2nd edn (Barcelona: Ediciones Ariel, 1968) pp. 77–81; Borrás, *Ramiro Ledesma Ramos*, pp. 216, 248–50; Herbert Rutledge Southworth, 'The Falange: An Analysis of Spain's Fascist Heritage', in Paul Preston, ed., *Spain in Crisis: The Evolution and Decline of the Franco Regime* (Hassocks: Harvester Press, 1976) p. 6; Ferran Gallego, *Ramiro Ledesma Ramos y el fascismo español* (Madrid: Síntesis, 2005) pp. 62–115, 138–77.

46 Anon., *Onésimo Redondo Caudillo*, p. 9.

47 Eduardo Álvarez Puga, *Historia de la Falange* (Barcelona: Dopesa, 1969) p. 25.

48 Roberto Lanzas (Ramiro Ledesma Ramos), 'La violencia política y las insurrecciones', *JONS*, No. 3, August 1933, reproduced in *JONS Antología* (Barcelona: Editora Nacional, 1939) pp. 81–91.

49 Ramiro Ledesma Ramos, 'El "caso" Valladolid', *La Patria Libre*, No. 6, 23 March 1935, reproduced in Ramiro Ledesma Ramos, *Escritos políticos 1935–1936* (Madrid: Herederos de Ramiro Ledesma Ramos, 1988) pp. 255–7; José María Sánchez Diana, *Ramiro Ledesma Ramos: biografía política* (Madrid: Editora Nacional, 1975) pp. 125–6; Mínguez Goyanes, *Onésimo Redondo*, p. 40; Anon., *Onésimo Redondo Caudillo*, pp. 34–5.

50 Anon., *Onésimo Redondo Caudillo*, pp. 40–7, 51–7; Mínguez Goyanes, *Onésimo Redondo*, pp. 42, 170–3.

51 Onésimo Redondo, 'El regreso de la barbarie', *JONS Antología*, pp. 154–9.

52 Eduardo González Calleja, 'La violencia y sus discursos: los límites de la "fascistización" de la derecha española durante el régimen de la II República', *Ayer. Revista de Historia Contemporánea*, No. 71, 2008, pp. 89–90; Eduardo González Calleja, 'Aproximación a las subculturas violentas de las derechas españolas antirrepublicanas españolas (1931–1936)', *Pasado y Memoria. Revista de Historia Contemporánea*, No. 2, 2003, pp. 107–42; Eduardo González Calleja, 'The symbolism of violence during the Second Republic in Spain, 1931–1936', in Chris Ealham and Michael Richards, eds, *The Splintering of Spain: Cultural History and the Spanish Civil War, 1936–1939* (Cambridge: Cambridge University Press, 2005) pp. 23–44, 227–30.

53 Ledesma Ramos, *Escritos políticos*, pp. 44–6; Ledesma Ramos, *¿Fascismo*, p. 302.

54 Sancho Dávila and Julián Pemartín, *Hacia la historia de la Falange: primera contribución de Sevilla* (Jerez: Jerez Industrial, 1938) pp. 24–7.

55 *Arriba*, 18 April, 2 May 1935; Álvarez Chillida, *Antisemitismo*, pp. 342–3; José Antonio Primo de Rivera, *Obras*, 4th edn (Madrid: Sección Feminina de FET y de las JONS, 1966) p. 192.

56 Ramiro de Maeztú, *Defensa de la Hispanidad*, 4th edn (Madrid: Editorial Cultura Española, 1941) pp. 197–9; José Luis Villacañas Berlanga, *Ramiro de Maeztu y el ideal de la burguesía en España* (Madrid: Espasa Calpe, 2000) pp. 350–78.

57 He claimed to be quoting an unnamed acquaintance. José Calvo Sotelo, *La voz de un perseguido*, 2 vols (Madrid: Librería de San Martín, 1933, 1934) II, p. 225.

58 'España: Germanos contra bereberes', in Miguel Primo de Rivera y Urquijo, ed., *Papeles póstumos de José Antonio* (Barcelona: Plaza y Janés, 1996) pp. 160–6.

59 *El Debate*, 17 October 1933.

60 *El Socialista*, 17, 21 October 1933.

61 *CEDA*, 31 October 1933.

62 Tusquets, *Orígenes*, pp. 30–44, 137–42; Francisco de Luis, *La masonería contra España* (Burgos: Imprenta Aldecoa, 1935) pp. 6, 99–102, 158–60, 191; Blinkhorn, *Carlism*, pp.46, 179; Álvarez Chillida, *El antisemitismo*, pp. 181, 334–8.

63 Expediente 1736, Expediente personal de Julián Mauricio Carlavilla del Barrio, Archivo General del Ministerio de Interior; Eduardo Conolly, 'Mauricio Carlavilla: el encanto de la conspiración', *HIBRIS. Revista de Bibliofilia* (Alcoy), No. 23, September–October 2004, pp. 4 ff.

64 He gave his own account of this under the pseudonym Mauricio Karl in *Asesinos de España: marxismo, anarquismo, masonería* (Madrid: Ediciones Bergua, 1935) pp. 60–8, 76–81.

65 Documento 272, expediente de depuración, 1 February 1940, Expediente 1736, Archivo General del Ministerio de Interior. See also Mauricio Carlavilla, *Anti-España 1959: autores, cómplices y encubridores del comunismo* (Madrid: Editorial NOS, 1959) pp. 18, 434–8. In his memoirs, *Obras*, p. 758, General Mola describes the work of an unnamed undercover policeman. Carlavilla, *Anti-España*, p. 436, claims that this was a reference to his activities.

66 Carlavilla, *Anti-España*, p. 439.

67 Documento 272, expediente de depuración, 1 February 1940, Expediente 1736, Archivo General del Ministerio de Interior.

68 Karl, *Asesinos de España*. On Carlavilla, see Southworth, *Conspiracy*, pp. 207, 212–13; Álvarez Chillida, *Antisemitismo*, pp. 320–1. According to Ricardo de la Cierva,

Bibliografía sobre la guerra de España (1936–1939) y sus antecedentes (Barcelona: Ariel, 1968) pp. 115, 140, 365, his name was Mauricio Carlavilla de la Vega. However, in his *partida de nacimiento*, he is registered as 'Julián Mauricio Carlavilla del Barrio'. Moreover, one of his later books, published when he no longer felt the need for a pseudonym, is signed 'Mauricio Carlavilla del Barrio "Mauricio Karl"', *Sodomitas* (Madrid: Editorial NOS, 1956). Mola acknowledged knowing Carlavilla well – Mola, *Obras*, p. 624.

69 Karl, *Asesinos de España*, pp. 21–4, 85–9, 196–207 (on Hitler and Mussolini), 320–1 (army). On Cambó, pp. 74–5; Julio Rodríguez Puértolas, *Literatura fascista española*, 2 vols (Madrid: Ediciones Akal, 1986, 1987) I, p. 309; Maximiano García Venero, *Falange en la guerra civil de España: la unificación y Hedilla* (Paris, Ruedo Ibérico, 1967) p. 309.

70 Carlavilla del Barrio, Expediente 1736, Documento 129, 27 September 1935.

71 Carlavilla del Barrio, Expediente 1736, Documento 272, expediente de depuración, 1 February 1940; *Claridad*, 4 May 1936; Joaquín Arrarás, *Historia de la cruzada española*, 8 vols, 36 tomos (Madrid: Ediciones Españolas, 1939–43) II, 9, p. 503; Guillermo Cabanellas, *Los cuatro generales*, 2 vols (Barcelona: Planeta, 1977) I, p. 274; Juan Ortiz Villalba, *Sevilla 1936: del golpe militar a la guerra civil* (Seville: Diputación Provincial, 1997) pp. 158–9; Edmundo Barbero, *El infierno azul (seis meses en el feudo de Queipo)* (Madrid: Talleres del SUIG (CNT), 1937) p. 39.

Chapter 3: The Right Goes on the Offensive, 1933–1934

1 Francisco Cobo Romero, *Labradores, campesinos y jornaleros: protesta social y diferenciación interna del campesinado jiennense en los orígenes de la Guerra Civil (1931–1936)* (Cordoba: Publicaciones del Ayuntamiento de Córdoba, 1992) pp. 400–5.

2 *Boletín del Ministerio de Trabajo,* January 1935.

3 Enrique Montañés, *Anarcosindicalismo y cambio político: Zaragoza, 1930–1936* (Zaragoza: Institución Fernando el Católico, 1989) pp. 98–100; José María Azpíroz Pascual, *Poder político y conflictividad social en Huesca durante la II República* (Huesca: Ayuntamiento de Huesca, 1993) pp. 161–9; Enrique Pradas Martínez, *La segunda República y La Rioja (1931–1936)* (Logroño: Cuadernos Riojanos, 1982) pp. 139–54; Enrique Pradas Martínez, ed., *8 de diciembre de 1933: insurrección anarquista en La Rioja* (Logroño: Cuadernos Riojanos, 1983) *passim*; Salvador Forner Muñoz, *Industrialización y movimiento obrero: Alicante 1923–1936* (Valencia: Edicions Alfons el Magnànim, 1982) pp. 354–7; José Manuel Macarro Vera, *La utopía revolucionaria: Sevilla en la segunda República* (Seville: Monte de Piedad y Caja de Ahorros de Seville, 1985) p. 368; Joaquín Arrarás, *Historia de la segunda República española*, 4 vols (Madrid: Editora Nacional, 1956–68) II, pp. 251–7; José Peirats, *La CNT en la revolución española*, 2nd edn, 3 vols (Paris: Ediciones Ruedo Ibérico, 1971) I, pp. 77–80; César M. Lorenzo, *Les Anarchistes espagnols et le pouvoir* (Paris: Éditions du Seuil, 1969) pp. 79–80; Roberto Villa, 'La CNT frente a la República: la insurrección revolucionaria de diciembre de 1933', *Historia y Política*, No. 24, 2010.

4 Francisco Moreno Gómez, *La República y la guerra civil en Córdoba* (Córdoba: Ayuntamiento de Córdoba, 1982) pp. 244–8; Manuel Pérez Yruela, *La conflictividad campesina en la provincia de Córdoba 1931–1936* (Madrid: Servicio de Publicaciones Agrarias, 1979) pp. 169–72.

5 Francisco Moreno Gómez, *La guerra civil en Córdoba (1936–1939)* (Madrid: Editorial Alpuerto, 1985) p. 238.

6 Fernando Ayala Vicente, *La violencia política en la provincia de Cáceres durante la Segunda República (1931–1936)* (Brenes: Muñoz Moya Editores Extremeños, 2003) pp. 67–8.

7 Juan-Simeón Vidarte, *El bienio negro y la insurrección de Asturias* (Barcelona: Grijalbo, 1978) pp. 58–9, 70–81.

8 Mario López Martínez, *Órden publico y luchas agrarias en Andalucia* (Madrid: Ediciones Libertarias/Ayuntamiento de Córdoba, 1995) pp. 351–4.

9 Francisco Largo Caballero, *Discursos a los trabajadores* (Madrid: Gráfica Socialista, 1934) pp. 140–2.

10 Francisco Largo Caballero, *Mis recuerdos: cartas a un amigo* (Mexico City: Editores Unidos, 1953) pp. 132–3.

11 Actas de la Comisión Ejecutiva del PSOE, 22 November 1933, Fundación Pablo Iglesias [henceforth FPI], AH 20–2; Francisco Largo Caballero, *Escritos de la República*, ed. Santos Juliá (Madrid: Fundación Pablo Iglesias, 1985) pp. 40–3.

12 *El Socialista*, 26, 28, 30 November, 1, 2, 8, 19, 21 December 1933, 13, 14 January 1934.

13 *Boletín de la UGT*, January 1934; Amaro del Rosal, *1934: el*

movimiento revolucionario de octubre (Madrid: Akal, 1983) pp. 93–150.

14 *El Socialista*, 12 December 1933; Largo Caballero, *Escritos*, pp. 48–50; Amaro del Rosal, *1934: el movimiento revolucionario de octubre* (Madrid: Akal, 1983) pp. 35–93.

15 *DSC*, 12 December 1933.

16 *DSC*, 19 December 1933; *El Debate*, 22 December 1933; *Renovación*, 23 December 1933.

17 *DSC*, 20 December 1933.

18 Diary entry for 1 July 1937, in Manuel Azaña, *Obras completas*, 4 vols (Mexico City: Ediciones Oasis, 1966–8) IV, p. 650; Vidarte, *El bienio negro*, p. 97.

19 *El Obrero de la Tierra*, 6 January 1934.

20 *DSC*, 25 January 1934; Margarita Nelken, *Por qué hicimos la revolución* (Barcelona: Ediciones Sociales Internacionales, 1936) pp. 87–96.

21 *Renovación*, 20 January 1934; *El Obrero de la Tierra*, 23 December 1933, 6, 13, 20 January 1934.

22 *El Debate*, 27 December 1933, 26, 27 January, 8, 25 February 1934; *Renovación*, 6 January 1934; *El Socialista*, 23, 25, 26 January, 2 February 1934; *La Mañana*, 17, 19, 20 January 1934.

23 *BUGT*, January 1934; *El Socialista*, 25, 26, 28, 30 January 1934; *BUGT*, February 1934; Rosal, *1934*, pp. 94–200; Largo Caballero, *Mis recuerdos*, pp. 134–5; Gabriel Mario de Coca, *Anti-Caballero: una crítica marxista de la bolchevización del Partido Socialista Obrero Español* (Madrid: Ediciones Engels, 1936) pp. 133, 137–42; Largo Caballero, *Escritos*, pp. 64–141; Dolores Ibarruri *et al.*, *Guerra y revolución en España*, 4 vols (Moscow: Editorial Progreso, 1967–77) I, pp. 52–7; Santos Juliá Díaz, *Historia del socialismo español (1931–1939)* (Barcelona, 1989) pp. 101–2.

24 Rosal, *1934*, pp. 200–56.

25 *El Obrero de la Tierra*, 3 February 1934.

26 Emilio Majuelo, *Luchas de clases en Navarra (1931–1936)* (Pamplona: Gobierno de Navarra, 1989) pp. 40–61, 206–11, 221 ff. Emilio Majuelo, *La generación del sacrificio: Ricardo Zabalza 1898–1940* (Tafalla: Editorial Txalaparta, 2008) pp. 237–8.

27 On Valdivia and Santiago, see Azaña, *Obras completas*, IV, p. 569; Ministerio de la Guerra, Estado Mayor Central, *Anuario Militar de España 1936* (Madrid: Imprenta y Talleres del Ministerio de la Guerra, 1936) pp. 326, 380. On Muñoz Grandes, see Fernando Vadillo, *Muñoz Grandes, el general de la División Azul* (Madrid: Fundación Don Rodrigo, 1999) pp. 71–8.

28 Rafael Salazar Alonso, *Bajo el signo de la revolución* (Madrid: Librería de San Martín, 1935) pp. 34–5.

29 *El Debate*, 2, 8, 10, 11, 22, 27 March 1934; *El Socialista*, 29 March 1934; *DSC*, 8 March 1934; Pedro Oliver Olmo, *La pena de muerte en España* (Madrid: Editorial Síntesis, 2008) pp. 109–22.

30 Anon., *Onésimo Redondo Caudillo*, pp. 71–2, 82–4.

31 *Ibid.*, pp. 85–90.

32 The only reliable contemporary report of this agreement is Guariglia to MAE, 1 September 1933, in Raffaele Guariglia, *Ambasciata in Spagna e primi passi in diplomazia 1932–1934* (Naples: Edizioni Scientifiche Italiani, 1972) pp. 304–5; Ismael Saz Campos, *Mussolini contra la II República: hostilidad, conspiraciones, intervención (1931–1936)* (Valencia: Edicions Alfons el Magnànim, 1986) pp. 111–12; Pedro Sainz Rodríguez, *Testimonio y recuerdos* (Barcelona: Planeta, 1978) pp. 220–2; José María Gil Robles, *No fue posible la paz* (Barcelona: Ariel,

1968) pp. 442–3; Juan Antonio Ansaldo, *¿Para qué ...? (de Alfonso XIII a Juan III)* (Buenos Aires: Editorial Vasca Ekin, 1951) p. 89.

33 Alejandro Corniero Suárez, *Diario de un rebelde* (Madrid: Ediciones Barbarroja, 1991) pp. 47–50, 66–8.

34 José Antonio Primo de Rivera, 'Discurso de la fundación de Falange Española', *Textos de doctrina política*, 4th edn (Madrid: Sección Femenina, 1966) pp. 61–9.

35 Herbert Rutledge Southworth, *Antifalange estudio crítico de 'Falange en la guerra de España' de Maximiano García Venero* (Paris: Ediciones Ruedo Ibérico, 1967) pp. 26–9; Felipe Ximénez de Sandoval, *'José Antonio' (Biografía apasionada)* (Barcelona: Editorial Juventud, 1941) pp. 204–5, 210–12, 316–17, 330, 358, 437–40; Francisco Bravo Martínez, *Historia de Falange Española de las JONS*, 2nd edn (Madrid: Editora Nacional, 1943) pp. 213–14.

36 Bravo Martínez, *Historia de Falange*, pp. 26–7; Domingo Pérez Morán, *¡A estos, que los fusilen al amanecer!* (Madrid: G. del Toro, 1973) pp. 208–9; Ignacio Martín Jiménez, *La guerra civil en Valladolid (1936–1939): amaneceres ensangrentados* (Valladolid: Ámbito Ediciones, 2000) pp. 13, 41.

37 Colloquio del Capo del Governo con i rappresentanti de la destra spagnola, 31 March 1934, *I Documenti Diplomatici Italiani*, 7th Series, Vol. XV: *18 marzo–27 settembre 1934* (Roma: Istituto Poligrafico e Zecca dello Stato/ Libreria dello Stato, 1990) pp. 64–8; Antonio Lizarza Iribarren, *Memorias de la conspiración*, 4th edn (Pamplona: Editorial Gómez, 1969) pp. 34–41; *How Mussolini Provoked the Spanish Civil War: Documentary Evidence* (London: United Editorial, 1938) *passim*.

38 Javier Ugarte Telleria, *La nueva Covadonga insurgente: orígenes sociales y culturales de la sublevación de 1936 en Navarra y el País Vasco* (Madrid: Editorial Biblioteca Nueva, 1998) pp. 74–8, 266–71; Eduardo González Calleja, 'La violencia y sus discursos: los límites de la "fascistización" de la derecha española durante el régimen de la Segunda República', *Ayer. Revista de Historia Contemporánea*, No. 71, 2008 (3), pp. 98–102; Jordi Canal, *Banderas blancas, boinas rojas: una historia política del carlismo, 1876–1939* (Madrid: Marcial Pons, 2006) pp. 44–6.

39 *El Debate*, 22, 24 April 1934; *El Socialista*, 22, 24 April 1934; José Monge Bernal, *Acción Popular (estudios de biología política)* (Madrid: Imp. Sáez Hermanos, 1936) pp. 258–60.

40 Ansaldo, *¿Para qué?*, pp. 71–3; Ramiro Ledesma Ramos, *¿Fascismo en España?*, 2nd edn (Barcelona: Ariel, 1968) pp. 161–3.

41 *DSC*, 17, 23 May 1934; Nigel Townson, *The Crisis of Democracy in Spain: Centrist Politics under the Second Republic 1931–1936* (Brighton: Sussex Academic Press, 2000) pp. 225–41.

42 *El Debate*, 26 May 1934; *El Socialista*, 24, 25 May 1934; Salazar Alonso, *Bajo el signo*, pp. 121–9; Cobo Romero, *Labradores*, pp. 417–20; López Martínez, *Órden público y luchas agrarias*, pp. 330–45.

43 Lama, *José González Barrero*, pp. 35–6, 52–4, 58; José María Lama, *La amargura de la memoria: República y guerra en Zafra (1931–1936)* (Badajoz: Diputación de Badajoz, 2004) pp. 150–60.

44 For information on Modesto José Lorenzana Macarro, I am grateful to Cayetano Ibarra Barroso for permitting me to use his

forthcoming study of Fuente de Cantos.

45 *El Debate*, 6, 10 May 1934; Cobo Romero, *Labradores*, pp. 409-20.

46 *El Obrero de la Tierra*, 17 February 1934.

47 *El Obrero de la Tierra*, 24 February, 3, 24, 31 March, 14, 21 April 1934.

48 *El Obrero de la Tierra*, 31 March, 7, 14, 21 April 1934.

49 The above account derives from the proceedings of a meeting on 31 July 1934 of the National Committee of the UGT which held a post-mortem on the defeated strike (*Boletín de la Unión General de Trabajadores*, August 1934). See also Vidarte, *El bienio negro*, pp. 152-4.

50 *El Sol*, 2 May 1934; *ABC*, 2 May 1934; *El Obrero de la Tierra*, 5 May 1934; *El Socialista*, 6 May 1934.

51 *El Obrero de la Tierra*, 21 April, 5 May 1934.

52 *El Obrero de la Tierra*, 19 May 1934.

53 *El Obrero de la Tierra*, 26 May 1934; Vidarte, *El bienio negro*, pp. 151-6.

54 Salazar Alonso, *Bajo el signo*, p. 141.

55 *DSC*, 30 May 1934. Cf. Vidarte, *El bienio negro*, pp. 156-9.

56 Paul Preston, *The Coming of the Spanish Civil War: Reform, Reaction and Revolution in the Second Spanish Republic 1931-1936*, 2nd edn (London, Routledge, 1994) pp. 147-53, 245; Paul Preston, 'The Agrarian War in the South', in Paul Preston, ed., *Revolution and War in Spain 1931-1939* (London: Methuen, 1984) pp. 159-81; Vidarte, *El bienio negro*, pp. 151-3.

57 Lama, *José González Barrero*, pp. 65-8; Lama, *La amargura*, pp. 162-7; Paloma Biglino Campos, *El socialismo español y la cuestión agraria 1890-1936* (Madrid, 1986) pp. 464-7; Gabriel Jackson, *The Spanish Republic and the Civil War* (Princeton, NJ: Princeton University Press, 1965) pp. 137-9; Manuel Tuñón de Lara, *Tres claves de la segunda República* (Madrid: Alianza Editorial, 1985) pp. 138-9.

58 *La Mañana*, 6, 8-12 June 1934, shows the thoroughness of the stoppage. See also *El Socialista*, 31 May, 1, 2, 3, 7, 8, 13, 28, 29, 30 June 1934; *El Debate*, 30, 31 May, 6, 7, 10 June 1934; *DSC*, 7, 14 June 1934; *El Obrero de la Tierra*, 13 June 1936; Cobo Romero, *Labradores*, pp. 421-34; Pérez Yruela, *La conflictividad*, pp. 190-6; Moreno Gómez, *La República y la guerra civil en Córdoba*, pp. 268-79; Macarro Vera, *La utopía*, pp. 388-93; Fernando Pascual Cevallos, *Luchas agrarias en Seville durante la segunda República* (Seville, 1983) pp. 91-3. More critical accounts of the FNTT are to be found in Edward E. Malefakis, *Agrarian Reform and Peasant Revolution in Spain: Origins of the Civil War* (New Haven: Yale University Press, 1970) pp. 335-40, and Salazar Alonso, *Bajo el signo*, pp.141 ff.

59 José Antonio Alarcón Caballero, *El movimiento obrero en Granada en la II República (1931-1936)* (Granada, 1990) pp. 409-12.

60 José María Gil Robles, *No fue posible la paz* (Barcelona: Ariel, 1968) p. 129.

61 Alarcón Caballero, *El movimiento obrero en Granada*, p. 132; López Martínez, *Órden público y luchas agrarias*, pp. 340-2; Timothy John Rees, 'Agrarian Society and Politics in the Province of Badajoz under the Spanish Second Republic' (unpublished doctoral thesis, University of Oxford, 1990) p. 274.

62 *El Debate*, 8 March 1934; *El Socialista*, 11, 13, 14, 15 March 1934; *ABC*, 14, 15, 16 March 1934; Salazar Alonso, *Bajo el signo*, pp. 50-73; Torcuato Luca de Tena, *Papeles para la pequeña y la gran historia: memorias de mi padre y mías* (Barcelona: Planeta, 1991) pp. 167-72.

63 Salazar to Amparo, 30 July 1934, reprinted in José García Pradas, 'La conversión ejemplar de un "pobre hombre" que llegó a Ministro de la República', *CNT*, 17 January 1937.

64 Largo Caballero, *Escritos*, pp. 86–110, 115–41, 143–9; Rosal, *1934*, pp. 207–49; Bernardo Díaz Nosty, *La Comuna asturiana: revolución de octubre de 1934* (Bilbao: ZYX, 1974) pp. 105–7; Indalecio Prieto, 'La noche del Turquesa', *Convulsiones de España: pequeños detalles de grandes sucesos*, 3 vols (Mexico City: Ediciones Oasis, 1967–9) I, pp. 109–11; Manuel Grossi, *La insurrección de Asturias (quince días de revolución socialista)* (Barcelona: Gráficos Alfa, 1935) p. 23; Salazar Alonso, *Bajo el signo*, pp. 226–7; Manuel Benavides, *La revolución fue así (octubre rojo y negro) reportaje* (Barcelona: Imprenta Industrial, 1935) pp. 9–20.

65 Miguel Ramos González, *La violencia en Falange Española* (Oviedo: Ediciones Tarfe, 1993) pp. 75–6; Ledesma Ramos, *¿Fascismo en España?*, pp. 163–4; Nelken, *Por qué hicimos la revolución*, pp. 118–19; David Jato, *La rebelión de los estudiantes (apuntes para una historia del alegre S.E.U.)* (Madrid: CIES, 1953) p. 109; Stanley G. Payne, *Falange: A History of Spanish Fascism* (Stanford, Calif.: Stanford University Press, 1967) pp. 57–8.

66 AHN, FC-Tribunal Supremo – Recursos, Legajo 97, 163.

67 Ledesma Ramos, *¿Fascismo en España?*, pp. 169–80; Ansaldo, *¿Para qué?*, pp. 84–6; Ximénez de Sandoval, *'José Antonio'*, pp. 577–82.

68 *El Debate*, 28 September 1934; Gil Robles, *No fue posible*, p. 131.

69 Monge Bernal, *Acción Popular*, pp. 301–3.

70 Antonio L. Oliveros, *Asturias en el resurgimiento español (apuntes históricos y biográficos)* (Madrid: Imprenta Juan Bravo, 1935) p. 277.

71 Text of Companys's speech in Frederic Escofet, *Al servei de Catalunya i de la República*, 2 vols (Paris: Edicions Catalanes, 1973) I, pp. 199–205; Edgar Allison Peers, *Catalonia Infelix* (London: Methuen, 1937) pp. 222–8; Manuel Azaña, *Mi rebelión en Barcelona* (Madrid: Espasa-Calpe, 1935) pp. 28–38.

72 *El Debate*, 7–9 September 1934; *El Socialista*, 7 September 1934; Grandizo Munis, *Jalones de derrota, promesa de victoria* (Mexico City: Editorial Lucha Obrera, 1948) pp. 128–9; Segundo Serrano Poncela, *El Partido Socialista y la conquista del poder* (Barcelona: Ediciones L'Hora, 1935) pp. 119–21.

73 *El Debate*, 11 September 1934; *CEDA*, 15 September 1934; Gil Robles, *No fue posible*, pp. 127–30.

74 *CNT*, 17 January 1937.

75 *El Sol*, 12 September 1934; Salazar Alonso, *Bajo el signo*, pp. 316–20.

76 *CEDA*, Nos. 36–7, December 1934.

77 Maximiano García Venero, *El general Fanjul: Madrid en el alzamiento nacional* (Madrid: Ediciones Cid, 1967) p. 196.

78 *DSC*, 4, 7 November 1934.

79 Ricardo de la Cierva, *Historia de la guerra civil española* (Madrid: Editorial San Martín, 1969) I, pp. 302–3.

80 *El Debate*, 26, 27, 28 September 1934; *El Socialista*, 3, 4 October 1934; José María Gil Robles, *Discursos parlamentarios* (Madrid: Taurus, 1971) pp. 338–43; Gil Robles, *No fue posible*, pp. 134–9; Niceto Alcalá Zamora, *Memorias* (Barcelona: Planeta, 1977) pp. 285–6.

81 Vidarte, *El bienio negro*, p. 233; Coca, *Anti-Caballero*, p. 107. I am grateful to Josep M. Ainaud de Lasarte and Father Hilari Raguer for

their clarifications regarding Anguera de Sojo and his mother. See also Ramon Corts Blay, Joan Galtés Pujol and Albert Manent Segimon, eds, *Diccionari d'història eclesiàstica de Catalunya*, 3 vols (Barcelona: Generalitat de Catalunya/Claret, 1998–2001) III, p. 459.

82 Javier Tusell and José Calvo, *Giménez Fernández: precursor de la democracia española* (Seville: Mondadori/Diputación de Seville, 1990) pp. 52–6.

83 *El Socialista*, 1 August 1934.

84 *El Socialista*, 27 September 1934.

85 *El Socialista*, 30 September 1934.

86 Largo Caballero, *Escritos*, pp. 150–8; Largo Caballero, *Mis recuerdos*, p. 136; Rosal, *1934*, pp. 257–61; Amaro del Rosal, *Historia de la UGT de España 1901–1939*, 2 vols (Barcelona: Grijalbo, 1977) I, pp. 387, 401–2; Julio Alvarez del Vayo, *The Last Optimist* (London: Putnam, 1950) pp. 263–6.

87 Grossi, *La insurrección*, pp. 23, 63; José Canel (José Díaz Fernández), *Octubre rojo en Asturias* (Madrid: Agencia General de Librería y Artes Gráficas, 1935) pp. 31, 43; Vidarte, *El bienio negro*, pp. 267–85, 334.

88 Munis, *Jalones*, pp. 130–40; Joaquín Maurín, *Hacia la segunda revolución: el fracaso de la República y la insurrección de octubre* (Barcelona: Gráficos Alfa, 1935) pp. 144–67; testimony of Madrid CNT secretary Miguel González Inestal to the author; Enrique Castro Delgado, *Hombres made in Moscú* (Barcelona: Luis de Caralt, 1965) pp. 176–83; Andrés Nin, *Los problemas de la revolución española* (Paris: Ruedo Ibérico, 1971) pp. 156–7; Santos Juliá Díaz, 'Fracaso de una insurrección y derrota de una huelga: los hechos de octubre en Madrid', *Estudios de Historia Social*, No. 31, October–December 1984;

Santos Juliá Díaz, *Historia del socialismo español (1931–1939)* (Barcelona: Conjunto Editorial, 1989) pp. 126–9.

89 For an account of the revolutionary events in Lerida, Gerona and other parts of provincial Catalonia where the Alianza Obrera had influence, see J. Costa i Deu and Modest Sabaté, *La veritat del 6 d'octubre* (Barcelona: Tipografia Emporium, 1936) *passim*. For a more recent scholarly account, see Jaume Barrull, *Els fets del 6 d'octubre* (Barcelona: Raval Edicions, 2009).

90 Enric Ucelay da Cal, *La Catalunya populista: imatge, cultura i política en la etapa republicana (1931–1939)* (Barcelona: Edicions de La Magrana, 1982) pp. 208–20; Maurín, *Segunda revolución*, pp. 123–44; Frederic Escofet, *Al servei de Catalunya i de la República*, 2 vols (Paris: Edicions Catalanes, 1973) I: *La desfeta 6 d'octubre 1934*, pp. 109–44; Josep Dencàs, *El 6 d'octubre des del Palau de Governació* (Barcelona: Curial Edicions, 1979) pp. 77–9. Cf. Andrés Nin, 'Los acontecimientos de octubre en Barcelona', *Leviatán*, No. 18, October–November 1935.

91 Hilari Raguer, *El general Batet: Franco contra Batet: crónica de una venganza* (Barcelona: Ediciones Península, 1996) pp. 155–6, 169–71, 276–81.

92 Benavides, *La Revolución fue así*, p. 372; Munis, *Jalones*, p. 154; Ignotus (Manuel Villar), *El anarquismo en la insurrección de Asturias*, 1st edn (Valencia: Tierra y Libertad, 1935) pp. 176–9. On the deaths in Mondragón, see *Diario Vasco*, 30 April 2006.

93 General López Ochoa, *Campaña militar de Asturias en octubre de 1934 (narración táctico-episódica)* (Madrid: Ediciones Yunque, 1936) pp. 26–30; Gil Robles, *No fue posible*,

pp. 140–1; Vidarte, *El bienio negro*, pp. 358–9; César Jalón, *Memorias políticas: periodista, ministro, presidiario* (Madrid: Guadarrama, 1973) pp. 128–31; Coronel Francisco Aguado Sánchez, *La revolución de octubre de 1934* (Madrid: Editorial San Martín, 1972) pp. 188–93.

94 Tusell and Calvo, *Giménez Fernández*, p. 57.

95 Niceto Alcalá Zamora, *Memorias* (Barcelona: Planeta, 1977) p. 296; Vidarte, *El bienio negro*, pp. 290–1.

96 Luis Suárez Fernández, *Francisco Franco y su tiempo*, 8 vols (Madrid: Fundación Nacional Francisco Franco, 1984) I, pp. 268–9; George Hills, *Franco: The Man and his Nation* (New York: Macmillan, 1967) p. 207; Francisco Franco Bahamonde, '*Apuntes' personales sobre la República y la guerra civil* (Madrid: Fundación Nacional Francisco Franco, 1987) pp. 11–12.

97 Francisco Franco Salgado-Araujo, *Mi vida junto a Franco* (Barcelona: Planeta, 1977) pp. 114–16; Joaquín Arrarás, *Franco*, 7th edn (Valladolid: Librería Santarén, 1939) p. 189.

98 Claude Martin, *Franco, soldado y estadista* (Madrid: Fermín Uriarte, 1965) pp. 129–30.

99 See Sebastian Balfour, *Deadly Embrace: Morocco and the Road to the Spanish Civil War* (Oxford: Oxford University Press, 2002) pp. 252–4.

100 Díaz Nosty, *La Comuna asturiana*, pp. 355–69. The literature on the atrocities committed by the African Army in Asturias is considerable. Among the most convincing testimonies are those assembled at the time by two relatively conservative individuals, Vicente Marco Miranda, a Republican prosecutor, and Félix Gordón Ordás, one-time Minister of Industry with the Radical Party.

They are reproduced in Nelken, *Por qué hicimos la revolución*, pp. 172–255. See also Narcis Molins i Fábrega, *UHP: la insurrección proletaria de Asturias*, 2nd edn (Gijón: Ediciones Júcar, 1977) pp. 169–74, 184–7, 196–219; Leah Manning, *What I Saw in Spain* (London: Victor Gollancz, 1935) pp. 167–221; Fernando Solano Palacio, *La revolución de octubre: quince días de comunismo libertario en Asturias* (Barcelona: Ediciones El Luchador, 1936) pp. 176–82.

101 Joaquín Arrarás, *Historia de la segunda República española*, 4 vols (Madrid: Editora Nacional, 1956–68) II, pp. 614, 637–8; Joaquín Arrarás, *Historia de la cruzada española*, 8 vols, 36 tomos (Madrid: Ediciones Españolas, 1939–43) II, 7, p. 259; López de Ochoa, *Campaña militar de Asturias en octubre de 1934*, pp. 37, 71–96; Franco Bahamonde, '*Apuntes' personales sobre la República y la guerra civil*, p. 12; Ramón Garriga, *El general Yagüe* (Barcelona: Planeta, 1985) pp. 59–63; Juan José Calleja, *Yagüe, un corazón al rojo* (Barcelona: Editorial Juventud, 1963) pp. 63–7.

102 On the repression, see *ABC*, 13 October 1934; Ignacio Carral, *Por qué mataron a Luis de Sirval* (Madrid: Imp. Saez Hermanos, 1935) pp. 37–60; Díaz Nosty, *La Comuna asturiana*, pp. 355–72; José Martín Blázquez, *I Helped to Build an Army: Civil War Memoirs of a Spanish Staff Officer* (London: Secker & Warburg, 1939) pp. 12–33.

103 Garriga, *El general Yagüe*, p. 61; Calleja, *Yagüe*, p. 66.

104 Vidarte, *El bienio negro*, pp. 360–2.

105 Aurelio de Llano Roza de Ampudia, *Pequeños anales de 15 días: la revolución en Asturias. Octubre 1934* (Oviedo: Talleres Tipográficos Altamirano, 1935) pp. 206–7; Francisco Aguado Sánchez, *La*

Guardia Civil en la revolución roja de Octubre de 1934 (Madrid: Servicio Histórico de la Guardia Civil, 1972) pp. 135–55, 425, 427; Vidarte, *El bienio negro*, pp. 268–9; Adrian Shubert, *The Road to Revolution in Spain: The Coal Miners of Asturias, 1860–1934* (Urbana and Chicago: University of Illinois Press, 1987) p. 3.

106 Aguado Sánchez, *La Guardia Civil en la revolución roja*, pp. 425–31.

107 José Aparicio Albiñana, *Para qué sirve un gobernador …* (Valencia: La Semana Gráfica, 1936) pp. 98–101, 104–12.

108 Víctor Lucea Ayala, *Dispuestos a intervenir en política: Don Antonio Plano Aznárez: socialismo y republicanismo en Uncastillo (1900–1939)* (Zaragoza: Institución Fernando el Católico, 2008) pp. 214–26.

109 *Ibid.*, pp. 331–4.

110 Aguado Sánchez, *La Guardia Civil en la revolución roja*, pp. 366–70; Lucea Ayala, *Antonio Plano*, pp. 245–65, 318, 322–3.

111 Aguado Sánchez, *La Guardia Civil en la revolución roja*, pp. 425–32.

112 Oliveros, *Asturias en el resurgimiento español*, pp. 274–9.

113 Ramón Serrano Suñer, *Entre el silencio y la propaganda, la Historia como fue: memorias* (Barcelona: Planeta, 1977) p. 52; Aguado Sánchez, *La revolución*, pp. 308–9.

114 Diego Hidalgo, *¿Porqué fui lanzado del Ministerio de la Guerra? Diez meses de actuación ministerial* (Madrid: Espasa Calpe, 1934) pp. 91–3; Manuel Ballbé, *Orden público y militarismo en la España constitucional (1812–1983)* (Madrid: Alianza Editorial, 1983) pp. 372–3; Aguado Sánchez, *La revolución*, pp. 308–9.

115 De la Cierva, *Historia de la guerra civil española*, I, p. 448; Aguado Sánchez, *La revolución*, p. 316.

116 Lucea Ayala, *Antonio Plano*, pp. 265–90.

117 *Ibid.*, pp. 268, 290–330, 349–58, 366–72.

Chapter 4: The Coming of War, 1934–1936

1 *DSC*, 9 October 1934; *La Mañana*, 7, 11 October 1934; *El Debate*, 11 October 1934; Pedro Luis Angosto, *José Alonso Mallol: el hombre que pudo evitar la guerra* (Alicante: Instituto de Cultura Juan Gil-Albert, 2010) pp. 191–2. Total figures for the arrests are difficult to find. The lowest respectable figures are those of Edward E. Malefakis, *Agrarian Reform and Peasant Revolution in Spain: Origins of the Civil War* (New Haven: Yale University Press, 1970) p. 342, who gives 15,000–20,000. Gabriel Jackson, *The Spanish Republic and the Civil War* (Princeton, NJ: Princeton University Press, 1965) p. 161, gives 30,000–40,000; and Henry Buckley, *Life and Death of the Spanish Republic* (London: Hamish Hamilton, 1940) p. 166, gives 60,000. The prisoners' fate is described in Leah Manning, *What I Saw in Spain* (London: Victor Gollancz, 1935) pp. 54–135. See also Ignacio Carral, *Por qué mataron a Luis de Sirval* (Madrid: Imp. Saez Hermanos, 1935), *passim*. On the Ayuntamientos, see *ABC*, 9, 27, 28 October 1934; Rafael Salazar Alonso, *Bajo el signo de la revolución* (Madrid: Librería de San Martín, 1935), p. 129; Juan-Simeón Vidarte, *El bienio negro y la insurreción de Asturias* (Barcelona: Grijalbo, 1978) p. 397; Sandra Souto Kustrín, 'Y ¿Madrid? ¿Qué hace Madrid?' *Movimiento revolucionario y acción colectiva (1933–1936)* (Madrid: Siglo XXI de España Editores, 2004) pp. 243–4, 310.

2 I am grateful to Álvaro Martínez Echevarría y García de Dueñas for

drawing my attention to the case of his great-grandfather.

3 Asociación Católica Nacional de Propagandistas de Oviedo, *Asturias roja: sacerdotes y religiosos perseguidos y martirizados (octubre de 1934)* (Oviedo: Imprenta Trufero, 1935) p. 12; Aurelio de Llano Roza de Ampudia, *Pequeños anales de 15 días: la revolución en Asturias. Octubre 1934* (Oviedo: Talleres Tipográficos Altamirano, 1935), p. 26.

4 ACNP de Oviedo, *Asturias roja*, pp. 60–1; Gil Nuño de Robledal, *¿Por qué Oviedo se convirtió en ciudad mártir?* (Oviedo: Talleres Tipográficos F. de la Presa, 1935) pp. 40–5, 95–104; Antonio M. Calero, 'Octubre visto por la derecha', in Germán Ojeda, ed., *Octubre 1934: cincuenta años para la reflexión* (Madrid: Siglo XXI, 1985) p. 163.

5 *El Noroeste* (Gijón), 26 October 1934, quoted by Bernardo Díaz Nosty, *La Comuna asturiana: revolución de octubre de 1934* (Bilbao: ZYX, 1974) p.359.

6 ACNP de Oviedo, *Asturias roja*, p. 14.

7 Sarah Sánchez, *Fact and Fiction: Representations of the Asturian Revolution (1934–1938)* (Leeds: Maney Publishing for the Modern Humanities Research Association, 2003) pp. 151–2.

8 On the unusual circumstances that gave Franco overall control of the repression, see Paul Preston, *Franco: A Biography* (London: HarperCollins, 1993) pp. 101–5. On the role of Batet, see Diego Hidalgo, *¿Por qué fui lanzado del Ministerio de la Guerra? Diez meses de actuación ministerial* (Madrid: Espasa Calpe, 1934) pp. 65–8; Hilari Raguer, *El general Batet: Franco contra Batet: crónica de una venganza* (Barcelona: Ediciones Península, 1996) pp. 154–86.

9 Raguer, *El general Batet*, pp. 190–4, 201; José Antonio Primo de Rivera, *Obras*, 4th edn (Madrid: Sección Feminina de FET y de las JONS, 1966) p. 306.

10 Raguer, *El general Batet*, pp. 211–37, 239 ff.

11 Ignacio Martín Jiménez, *La guerra civil en Valladolid (1936–1939): amaneceres ensangrentados* (Valladolid: Ámbito Ediciones, 2000) pp. 15–16; Anon. (Javier Martínez de Bedoya), *Onésimo Redondo Caudillo de Castilla* (Valladolid: Ediciones Libertad, 1937) pp. 113–30.

12 Francisco Bravo Martínez, *José Antonio: el hombre, el jefe, el camarada* (Madrid: Ediciones Españolas, 1939) pp. 100–2.

13 Antonio Cacho Zabalza, *La Unión Militar Española* (Alicante: Egasa, 1940) pp. 21–5; José del Castillo and Santiago Álvarez, *Barcelona: objetivo cubierto* (Barcelona: Editorial Timón, 1958) pp. 102–4; Stanley G. Payne, *Politics and the Military in Modern Spain* (Stanford, Calif.: Stanford University Press, 1967) pp. 300–1.

14 Bravo Martínez, *José Antonio*, pp. 159–65; Alejandro Corniero Suárez, *Diario de un rebelde* (Madrid: Ediciones Barbarroja, 1991) p. 120; Raimundo Fernández Cuesta, *Testimonio, recuerdos y reflexiones* (Madrid: Ediciones Dyrsa, 1985) pp. 51–2; Gumersindo Montes Agudo, *Pepe Sainz: una vida en la Falange* (n.p. [Burgos?]: Ediciones Pallas de Horta, 1939) pp. 56–7; Maximiano García Venero, *Falange en la guerra de España: la Unificación y Hedilla* (Paris: Ruedo Ibérico, 1967) p. 66; Rafael Ibáñez Hernández, *Estudio y acción: la Falange fundacional a la luz del Diario de Alejandro Salazar (1934–1936)* (Madrid: Ediciones Barbarroja, 1993) pp. 98–101.

15 Salazar, *Diario*, in Ibáñez Hernández, *Estudio y acción*, p. 36.

16 Cacho Zabalza, *La Unión Militar Española*, pp. 24–5.

17 Francisca Rosique Navarro, *La reforma agraria en Badajoz durante la IIª República* (Badajoz: Diputación Provincial de Badajoz, 1988) pp. 225–42, 265–73; Timothy John Rees, 'Agrarian Society and Politics in the Province of Badajoz under the Spanish Second Republic' (unpublished doctoral thesis, University of Oxford, 1990) pp. 191–2; Malefakis, *Agrarian Reform*, pp. 126–8, 238–43; *El Obrero de la Tierra*, 26 November 1932; Sergio Riesco Roche, 'La aceleración de la Reforma Agraria durante el Frente Popular', in Manuel Ballarín and José Luis Ledesma, eds, *La República del Frente Popular: reformas, conflictos y conspiraciones* (Zaragoza: Fundación Rey del Corral, 2010) pp. 83–96.

18 Malefakis, *Agrarian Reform*, pp. 343–7; Rosique, *Badajoz*, pp. 289–91.

19 Javier Tusell and José Calvo, *Giménez Fernández, precursor de la democracia española* (Seville: Mondadori/Diputación de Seville, 1990) pp. 71–3.

20 *Ibid.*, p. 75.

21 *El Debate*, 24 November, 1, 5, 7, 20, 21 December 1934, 1 January 1935; Carlos Seco Serrano, *Historia de España: época contemporánea*, 3rd edn (Barcelona: Instituto Gallach, 1971) p. 130; Tusell and Calvo, *Giménez Fernández*, pp. 76–85.

22 On Alarcón de la Lastra, see *ABC*, 2 April 1939; Nicolás Salas, *Quién fue Luis Alarcón de la Lastra (1891–1971)* (Seville: Guadalturia, 2010) pp. 147–59, 166–7, 193. On landholding in Carmona, see Pascual Carrión, *Los latifundios en España* (Madrid: Gráficas Reunidas, 1932) pp. 220–2, 227.

23 *El Sol*, 13 December 1934; Alfred Mendizábal, *Aux origines d'une tragédie: la politique espagnole de 1923 à 1936* (Paris: Desclée de Brouwer, n.d. [1937?]) p. 231.

24 Malefakis, *Agrarian Reform*, pp. 358–63.

25 Rosique, *Badajoz*, p. 303.

26 *El Debate*, 14 June 1935; Vidarte, *El bienio negro*, pp. 383–5; José María Lama, *La amargura de la memoria: República y guerra en Zafra (1931–1936)* (Badajoz: Diputación de Badajoz, 2004) p. 156.

27 Alejandro Lerroux, *La pequeña historia: apuntes para la historia grande vividos y redactados por el autor* (Buenos Aires: Editorial Cimera, 1945) p. 302; Salazar Alonso, *Bajo el signo*, pp. 324–31.

28 *DSC*, 15 November 1934; Octavio Ruiz Manjón, *El Partido Republicano Radical 1908–1936* (Madrid: Ediciones Giner, 1976) pp. 464–5.

29 *El Debate*, 3 January 1936; *El Socialista*, 30 January 1936; Claude G. Bowers, *My Mission to Spain* (London: Victor Gollancz, 1954) p. 182; Buckley, *Life and Death*, pp. 190–1; Constancia de la Mora, *In Place of Splendour* (London: Michael Joseph, 1940) p. 207; Luis Enrique Espinosa Guerra, 'De la esperanza a la frustración: la Segunda República', in Ricardo Robledo, ed., *Historia de Salamanca*, Vol. V: *Siglo veinte* (Salamanca: Centro de Estudios Salmantinos, 2001) p. 205; José María Gil Robles, *No fue posible la paz* (Barcelona: Ariel, 1968) p. 544.

30 *Ideal*, 3, 14, 15, 28, 29 January, 11, 12, 14, 16 February 1936; *El Defensor*, 14, 19, 22, 23, 28 January, 1, 6, 11, 15–20 February, 5–7 March 1936; *El Socialista*, 18 January, 9 February, 7 March 1936; Ronald Fraser, *In Hiding: The Life of Manuel Cortes* (London: Allen Lane, 1972) p. 116; Diego Caro Cancela, *La Segunda República en Cádiz: elecciones y*

partidos políticos (Cádiz: Diputación Provincial de Cádiz, 1987) p. 256; Arturo Barea, *La forja de un rebelde* (Buenos Aires: Losada, 1951) pp. 522–9; Francisco Cobo Romero, *Labradores, campesinos y jornaleros: protesta social y diferenciación interna del campesinado jiennense en los orígenes de la Guerra Civil (1931–1936)* (Córdoba: Publicaciones del Ayuntamiento de Córdoba, 1992) pp. 445–6; Francisco Cobo Romero, *De campesinos a electores: modernización agraria en Andalucía, politización campesina y derechización de los pequeños propetarios y arrendatarios: el caso de la provincia de Jaén, 1931–1936* (Madrid: Biblioteca Nueva, 2003) pp. 308–10.

31 Baldomero Díaz de Entresotos, *Seis meses de anarquía en Extremadura* (Cáceres: Editorial Extremadura, 1937) pp. 4, 25–7, 30, 39–40, 48–52.

32 On the imprisonment and execution of Zabalza, see Emilio Majuelo, *La generación del sacrificio: Ricardo Zabalza 1898–1940* (Tafalla: Editorial Txalaparta, 2008) pp. 283–337.

33 *ABC*, 1 March 1936; Santos Juliá Díaz, *Manuel Azaña: una biografía política* (Madrid: Alianza Editorial, 1990) pp. 459–67.

34 Azaña to Rivas Cherif, 17 March 1936, Cipriano de Rivas-Cherif, *Retrato de un desconocido: vida de Manuel Azaña (seguido por el epistolario de Manuel Azaña con Cipriano de Rivas Cherif de 1921 a 1937)* (Barcelona: Grijalbo, 1980) pp. 665–7; Carmen González Martínez, *Guerra civil en Murcia: un análisis sobre el Poder y los comportamientos colectivos* (Murcia: Universidad de Murcia, 1999) pp. 56–7.

35 Louis Fischer, *Men and Politics: An Autobiography* (London: Jonathan Cape, 1941) p. 309.

36 *DSC*, 3 April 1936; Azaña to Rivas Cherif, 4 April 1936, Rivas-Cherif, *Retrato*, pp. 674–5.

37 *Boletín del Ministerio de Trabajo*, April 1936.

38 *El Obrero de la Tierra*, 29 February, 7, 21, 28 March 1936.

39 Preston, *Franco*, pp. 115–18, 122; Del Castillo and Álvarez, *Barcelona: objetivo cubierto*, pp. 143–7.

40 Carlos Martínez de Campos, *Ayer 1931–1953* (Madrid: Instituto de Estudios Políticos, 1970) p. 32; José María Iribarren, *Mola, datos para una biografía y para la historia del alzamiento nacional* (Zaragoza: Librería General, 1938) p. 44; Ricardo de la Cierva, *Francisco Franco: biografía histórica*, 6 vols (Barcelona: Planeta, 1982) II, p. 162.

41 Gil Robles, *No fue posible*, pp. 234–43; Antonio López Fernández, *Defensa de Madrid* (Mexico City: Editorial A. P. Márquez, 1945) pp. 40–3; Francisco Franco Bahamonde, *'Apuntes' personales sobre la República y la guerra civil* (Madrid: Fundación Nacional Francisco Franco, 1987) p. 15.

42 Díaz de Entresotos, *Seis meses*, pp. 60–1; Manuel Pérez Yruela, *La conflictividad campesina en la provincia de Córdoba 1931–1936* (Madrid: Servicio de Publicaciones Agrarias, 1979) pp. 207–9; Arcángel Bedmar González, *Desaparecidos: la represión franquista en Rute (1936–1950)*, 2nd edn (Rute: Ayuntamiento de Rute, 2007) p. 39.

43 Nigel Townson, *The Crisis of Democracy in Spain: Centrist Politics under the Second Republic 1931–1936* (Brighton: Sussex Academic Press, 2000) pp. 315–17; Ruiz Manjón, *El Partido Republicano Radical*, pp. 519–23; *DSC*, 28 October 1935.

44 Ruiz Manjón, *El Partido Republicano Radical*, pp. 569–70, 574–5, 578–60, 672.

45 Pérez Yruela, *La conflictividad campesina*, pp. 204–6; Rees, 'Agrarian Society', pp. 298–300; *El Obrero de la Tierra*, 7 March 1936; Juan Carlos Molano Gragera, *Miguel Merino Rodríguez: dirigente obrero y Alcalde de Montijo* (Badajoz: Diputación de Badajoz, 2002) p. 116; Díaz de Entresotos, *Seis meses*, p. 52; Bedmar González, *Desaparecidos*, pp. 38–9.

46 Julián Chaves Palacios, *Violencia política y conflictividad social en Extremadura: Cáceres en 1936* (Badajoz and Cáceres: Diputación Provincial de Badajoz/Diputación Provincial de Cáceres, 2000) pp. 78–85.

47 Ricardo Robledo and Luis Enrique Espinosa, '"¡El campo en pie!": política y reforma agraria', in Ricardo Robledo, ed., *Esta salvaje pesadilla: Salamanca en la guerra civil española* (Barcelona: Editorial Crítica, 2007) pp. 3–8, 41–3; Julio Aróstegui and Juan Andrés Blanco, 'La República, encrucijada de cambio: Salamanca y las tensiones políticas en los años treinta', in Ricardo Robledo Hernández, ed., *Sueños de concordia: Filiberto Villalobos y su tiempo histórico 1900–1955* (Salamanca: Caja Duero, 2005) pp. 318–31.

48 *DSC*, 31 March, 1, 2 April 1936; *ABC*, 1 April 1936; Diego Martínez Barrio, *Memorias* (Barcelona: Planeta, 1983) p. 314. Castaño played an important role in the preparation of the military uprising of July 1936: Ronald Fraser, *Blood of Spain: The Experience of Civil War 1936–1939* (London: Allen Lane, 1979) pp. 85–6.

49 Gil Robles, *No fue posible*, pp. 719, 728–30, 798. On the roles of both Casanueva and Gil Robles, see Aróstegui and Blanco, 'La República, encrucijada de cambio', pp. 331–3.

50 Indalecio Prieto, *De mi vida: recuerdos, estampas, siluetas, sombras* (Mexico City: Ediciones 'El Sitio', 1965) pp. 183–5; Jaime de Armiñán, *La dulce España: memorias de un niño partido en dos* (Barcelona: Tusquets, 2000) p. 163.

51 On Martín Veloz, see Javier Infante, 'Sables y naipes: Diego Martín Veloz (1875–1938): de cómo un matón de casino se convirtió en caudillo rural', in Robledo, ed., *Esta salvaje pesadilla*, pp. 264–79, 425, 428; José Venegas, *Andanzas y recuerdos de España* (Montevideo: Feria del Libro, 1948) pp. 74–85; Prieto, *De mi vida*, pp. 185–6.

52 Infante, 'Sables y naipes', pp. 264, 274–9; Francisco Blanco Prieto, *Miguel de Unamuno: diario final* (Salamanca: Globalia Ediciones Anatema, 2006) p. 607; Josefina Cuesta Bustillo, 'Un republicano en la inclemencia: Filiberto Villalobos encarcelado, en la Guerra civil española (1936–1938)', in Robledo Hernández, ed., *Sueños de concordia*, pp. 450–1; Prieto, *De mi vida*, pp. 181–92; L. Santiago Díez Cano and Pedro Carasa Soto, 'Caciques, dinero y favores: la restauración en Salamanca', in Robledo, ed., *Historia de Salamanca*: Vol. V: *Siglo Veinte*, pp. 143–4.

53 José María Ruiz Alonso, *La guerra civil en la provincia de Toledo: Utopía, conflicto y poder en el sur del Tajo (1936–1939)*, 2 vols (Ciudad Real: Almud, Ediciones de Castilla-La Mancha, 2004) I, pp. 107, 118.

54 *El Obrero de la Tierra*, 28 March 1936.

55 *El Obrero de la Tierra*, 7, 14, 21, 28 March 1936; Francisco Cobo Romero, *Por la reforma agraria hacia la revolución: el sindicalismo agrario socialista durante la II República y la guerra civil (1930–1939)* (Granada: Universidad de Granada, 2007) pp. 275–82.

56 Díaz de Entresotos, *Seis meses*, p. 61.
57 Santiago López García and Severiano Delgado Cruz, 'Víctimas y Nuevo Estado 1936–1940', in Robledo, ed., *Historia de Salamanca*: Vol. V: *Siglo Veinte*, pp. 221–3.
58 *El Obrero de la Tierra*, 4 April 1936. This issue of the paper was banned by the censorship and is therefore extremely difficult to find. I was able to consult it thanks to the kindness of Francisco Espinosa Maestre.
59 Manuel Tuñón de Lara, *Tres claves de la segunda República* (Madrid: Alianza Editorial, 1985) pp. 172–8; Molano, *Miguel Merino*, pp. 120–3; Rosique, *Badajoz*, pp. 303–5; Rees, 'Agrarian Society', pp. 300–3; Díaz de Entresotos, *Seis meses*, pp. 65–7; Pérez Yruela, *La conflictividad campesina*, pp. 209–10; Ruiz Alonso, *La guerra civil en la provincia de Toledo*, I, pp. 106–10. On the reoccupation of estates, see Francisco Espinosa Maestre, 'La reforma agraria del Frente Popular en Badajoz: los orígenes de la Guerra Civil' (unpublished doctoral thesis, Universidad de Sevilla, 2006) pp. 199–200; Bedmar González, *Desaparecidos*, pp. 38–9.
60 *El Obrero de la Tierra*, 28 March 1936.
61 *La Vanguardia*, 18 March 1936; Bedmar González, *Desaparecidos*, pp. 38–9; Fernando del Rey, *Paisanos en lucha: exclusión política y violencia en la Segunda República española* (Madrid: Biblioteca Nueva, 2008) pp. 511–20; George A. Collier, *Socialists of Rural Andalusia: Unacknowledged Revolutionaries of the Second Republic* (Stanford, Calif.: Stanford University Press, 1987) pp. 143–4; Juan Blázquez Miguel, 'Conflictividad en la España del Frente Popular (febrero–julio de 1936)', *Historia 16*, No. 328, 2003, pp. 86–7; Rafael Cruz, *En el nombre del pueblo: República, rebelión y guerra en la España de 1936* (Madrid: Siglo XXI, 2006) pp. 123–32, 186–7.
62 Malefakis, *Agrarian Reform*, pp. 364–74.
63 *El Obrero de la Tierra*, 13 June 1936; Manuel Rubio Díaz and Silvestre Gómez Zafra, *Almendralejo (1930–1941): doce años intensos* (Los Santos de Maimona: Grafisur, 1987) pp. 236–40.
64 Lama, *La amargura de la memoria*, p. 187.
65 Cobo Romero, *Labradores, campesinos y jornaleros*, pp. 446–8; Rees, 'Agrarian Society', pp. 304–5; Tuñón de Lara, *Tres claves*, p. 183; Pérez Yruela, *La conflictividad campesina*, pp. 210–13; Francisco Moreno Gómez, *La República y guerra civil en Córdoba* (Córdoba: Ayuntamiento de Córdoba, 1983) p. 389; Francisco Moreno Gómez, *1936: el genocidio franquista en Córdoba* (Barcelona: Editorial Crítica, 2008) pp. 173–4.
66 José Manuel Macarro Vera, *Socialismo, República y revolución en Andalucía (1931–1936)* (Seville: Universidad de Seville, 2000) p. 448; José María Varela Rendueles, *Rebelión en Seville: memorias de un Gobernador rebelde* (Seville: Servicio de Publicaciones del Ayuntamiento de Seville, 1982) pp. 65–71.
67 *ABC* (Seville), 25, 26 April 1936; José María García Márquez, *La UGT de Seville: golpe militar, resistencia y represión (1936–1950)* (Córdoba: Fundación para el Desarrollo de los Pueblos de Andalucía, 2008) p. 18.
68 Francisco Sánchez Pérez, 'Un laboratorio de huelgas: el Madrid del Frente Popular (mayo–julio de 1936)', in Marie-Claude Chaput, ed., *Fronts Populaires: Espagne, France, Chili* (Paris: Université Paris Ouest Nanterre La Défense, 2007) pp. 155–72; Dionisio Ridruejo, *Casi unas memorias* (Barcelona: Planeta,

1976) p. 60; *Arriba*, 19 December 1935.

69 Ismael Saz Campos, *Fascismo y franquismo* (Valencia: Publicacions de la Universitat de València, 2004) pp. 70–2.

70 Angosto, *José Alonso Mallol*, pp. 206–10.

71 Azaña to Rivas Cherif, 21 March 1936, in Rivas Cherif, *Retrato*, p. 669; *El Debate*, 18, 19 March 1936. On Amós Salvador, see Manuel Portela Valladares, *Memorias: dentro del drama español* (Madrid: Alianza Editorial, 1988), pp. 197–8; Stanley G. Payne, *Spain's First Democracy: The Second Republic, 1931–1936* (Madison, Wis.: University of Wisconsin Press, 1993) p. 282.

72 Felipe Ximénez de Sandoval, *'José Antonio' (biografía apasionada)* (Barcelona: Editorial Juventud, 1941) pp. 526–7, 546; Juan Antonio Ansaldo, *¿Para qué? de Alfonso XIII a Juan III* (Buenos Aires: Editorial Vasca-Ekin, 1951) pp. 115–19; Corniero Suárez, *Diario*, p. 150; Herbert Rutledge Southworth, *Antifalange: estudio crítico de 'Falange en la guerra de España' de Maximiano García Venero* (Paris: Ediciones Ruedo Ibérico, 1967) p. 95; Juan-Simeón Vidarte, *Todos fuimos culpables* (Mexico City: Fondo de Cultura Económica, 1973) pp. 66–7; Julio Gil Pecharromán, *José Antonio Primo de Rivera: retrato de un visionario* (Madrid: Temas de Hoy, 1996) pp. 439–41, 461.

73 Bravo Martínez, *José Antonio*, pp. 96–9; Corniero Suárez, *Diario*, pp. 154–5.

74 *El Socialista*, 15 April 1936; *ABC*, 15 April 1936; Bowers, *My Mission*, pp. 217–19; Ximénez de Sandoval, *'José Antonio'*, pp. 546–7; Ian Gibson, *La noche en que mataron a Calvo Sotelo* (Barcelona: Argas Vergara, 1982) pp. 25–36.

75 Cacho Zabalza, *La Unión Militar Española*, pp. 24–8; Gibson, *La noche*, pp. 36–53; Gil Robles, *No fue posible*, pp. 674–5; Vidarte, *Todos fuimos culpables*, pp. 90–1.

76 Cacho Zabalza, *La Unión Militar Española*, p. 26; *El Liberal*, 18 April 1936.

77 *El Socialista*, 18, 19 April, 8 May 1936; *Claridad*, 15, 16, 18 April 1936.

78 Ximénez de Sandoval, *'José Antonio'*, pp. 546–7.

79 *ABC*, 4, 5, 11 March, 2, 19, 29 April 1936; Ansaldo, *¿Para qué?*, pp. 77–8; De la Mora, *In Place of Splendour*, pp. 214–15; Buckley, *Life and Death*, p. 129; Stanley G. Payne, *Falange: A History of Spanish Fascism* (Stanford, Calif.: Stanford University Press, 1961) pp. 98–105. On the fascist tendencies of Sales and the Sindicatos Libres, see Colin M. Winston, *Workers and the Right in Spain 1900–1936* (Princeton, NJ: Princeton University Press, 1985) pp. 312–22.

80 Ian Gibson, *El asesinato de García Lorca* (Barcelona: Plaza y Janés, 1996) pp. 60–3; *La Mañana*, 14 March 1936; *Claridad*, 14 April 1936; *El Sol*, 4, 11, 15, 21, 26 March, 6 April 1936.

81 *El Socialista*, 7, 8, 15 March 1936; speech of Rodolfo Llopis, *DSC*, 15 April 1936.

82 Gil Robles, *No fue posible*, pp. 573–5.

83 Payne, *Politics and the Military*, p. 318; Payne, *Falange*, pp. 104–5; Martin Blinkhorn, *Carlism and Crisis in Spain 1931–1939* (Cambridge: Cambridge University Press, 1975) p. 257; Rafael Valls, *La Derecha Regional Valenciana 1930–1936* (Valencia: Edicions Alfons el Magnànim, 1992) pp. 227–31; Ramón Serrano Suñer, *Entre Hendaya y Gibraltar* (Madrid: Ediciones y Publicaciones Españolas, 1947) p. 25.

84 Indalecio Prieto, *Cartas a un escultor: pequeños detalles de grandes sucesos* (Buenos Aires: Editorial Losada, 1961) pp. 93–4.

85 Indalecio Prieto, *Discursos fundamentales* (Madrid: Ediciones Turner, 1975) pp. 255–73.

86 Vidarte, *Todos fuimos culpables*, pp. 117–27; Indalecio Prieto, *Discursos en América con el pensamiento puesto en España* (Mexico City: Ediciones de la Federación de Juventudes Socialistas de España, n.d. [1944]) pp. 29–31.

87 Coronel Jesús Pérez Salas, *Guerra en España (1936 a 1939)* (Mexico City: Imprenta Grafos, 1947) pp. 77–80.

88 Prieto, *Cartas a un escultor*, p. 93; Vidarte, *Todos fuimos culpables*, pp. 93–5, 99–100, 146–7.

89 *DSC*, 19 May 1936.

90 Francisco Bravo Martínez, *Historia de Falange Española de las JONS*, 2nd edn (Madrid: Editora Nacional, 1943) pp. 164–8; Ximénez de Sandoval, 'José Antonio', pp. 539, 548; Southworth, *Antifalange*, pp. 101–2.

91 Angosto, *José Alonso Mallol*, pp. 199, 212–14.

92 Pedro Sainz Rodríguez, *Testimonio y recuerdos* (Barcelona: Planeta, 1978), p. 222.

93 Interview with Ramón Serrano Suñer in *Dolor y memoria de España en el II aniversario de la muerte de José Antonio* (Barcelona: Ediciones Jerarquía, 1939) p. 205; B. Félix Maíz, *Mola, aquel hombre* (Barcelona: Planeta, 1976) p. 238.

94 Bravo Martínez, *José Antonio*, pp. 193–203. See also http://plataforma2003.org/diccionario-falange/diccionario_n.htm#no_importa.

95 B. Félix Maíz, *Alzamiento en España*, 2nd edn (Pamplona: Editorial Gómez, 1952) pp. 23–8, 52–6, 61–3, 67, 162.

96 Herbert Rutledge Southworth, *Conspiracy and the Spanish Civil War: The Brainwashing of Francisco Franco* (London: Routledge/Cañada Blanch Studies, 2002).

97 Felipe Bertrán Güell, *Preparación y desarrollo del alzamiento nacional* (Valladolid: Librería Santarén, 1939) p. 123.

98 Joaquín Arrarás, *Historia de la Cruzada española*, 8 vols, 36 tomos (Madrid: Ediciones Españolas, 1939–43) II, 9, p. 511; Maíz, *Mola*, p. 158; García Venero, *Falange/Hedilla*, pp. 197–8.

99 Ismael Saz Campos, *Mussolini contra la II República: hostilidad, conspiraciones, intervención (1931–1936)* (Valencia: Edicions Alfons el Magnànim, 1986) pp. 166–70.

100 *El Obrero de la Tierra*, 18 April, 1, 16, 23, 30 May, 13, 20, 27 June 1936; *Claridad*, 6, 9, 18 June 1936; Manuel Requena Gallego, *Los sucesos de Yeste (mayo 1936)* (Albacete, 1983) pp. 83–100; Manuel Ortiz Heras, *Violencia política en la II República y el primer franquismo: Albacete, 1936–1950* (Madrid: Siglo XXI de España Editores, 1996) pp. 58–63. There is a remarkably vivid and plausible account of these events in the novel by Juan Goytisolo, *Señas de identidad* (Mexico City: Editorial Joaquín Mortiz, 1969) pp. 130–45. The events at Yeste on 29 May were debated in the Cortes on 5 June.

101 Rees, 'Agrarian Society', pp. 303–4.

102 *El Obrero de la Tierra*, 20 June 1936; Rubio Díaz and Silvestre Gómez, *Almendralejo*, p. 245.

103 Chaves Palacios, *Violencia política y conflictividad social en Extremadura*, pp. 98–111.

104 Souto Kustrín, *Madrid*, p. 333; Blázquez Miguel, 'Conflictividad en la España del Frente Popular (febrero–julio de 1936)', p. 83; Cayetano Ibarra, *La otra mitad de la historia que nos contaron: Fuente de Cantos, República y guerra 1931–1939* (Badajoz: Diputación de

Badajoz, 2005) pp. 200–1; Espinosa Maestre, 'La reforma agraria', pp. 173–4.

105 Felipe Bertrán Güell, *Preparación y desarrollo del alzamiento nacional* (Valladolid: Librería Santarén, 1939) p. 280.

106 Santiago Vega Sombría, *De la esperanza a la persecución: la represión franquista en la provincia de Segovia* (Barcelona: Editorial Crítica, 2005) pp. 11–12, 25–9.

107 Dionisio Ridruejo, *Casi unas memorias* (Barcelona: Planeta, 1976) p. 44.

108 *DSC*, 16 June 1936.

109 *DSC*, 15 July 1936. Eduardo González Calleja, 'La necro-lógica de la violencia sociopolítica en la primavera de 1936', *Mélanges de la Casa de Velázquez*, Vol. 41, No. 1, 2011, pp. 37–60; Blázquez Miguel, 'Conflictividad en la España del Frente Popular (febrero–julio de 1936)', pp. 77–95; Cruz, *En el nombre del pueblo*, pp. 164–70; Stanley G. Payne, 'Political Violence during the Spanish Second Republic', *Journal of Contemporary History*, Vol. 25, No. 2/3, May–June 1990, pp. 269–88; Gabriele Ranzato, 'El peso de la violencia en los orígenes de la guerra civil de 1936– 1939', *Espacio, Tiempo y Forma*, Serie V, No. 20, pp. 159–82.

110 Bowers, *My Mission*, pp. 200–10, 224–8.

111 Sid Lowe, *Catholicism, War and the Foundation of Francoism* (Brighton: Sussex Academic Press, 2010) pp. 120–1.

112 *La Vanguardia*, 5 March 1936.

113 Copias de documentos facilitados por el Tte. Coronel Emilio Fernández Cordón referentes a la preparación y desarrollo del Alzamiento Nacional (Instrucciones del general Mola) SHM/AGL/ CGG/A.31/l.4/C.8, quoted by Alberto Reig Tapia, 'La justificación

ideológica del "alzamiento" de 1936', in José Luis García Delgado, ed., *La II República Española: bienio rectificador y Frente Popular, 1934– 1936* (Madrid: Siglo XXI, 1988) p. 220.

114 H. Edward Knoblaugh, *Correspondent in Spain* (London and New York: Sheed & Ward, 1937) pp. 20–2.

115 Gil Robles, *No fue posible*, pp. 719, 728–30, 789, 798; Ricardo de la Cierva, *Historia de la guerra civil española* (Madrid: Editorial San Martín, 1969) I, pp. 741–3; correspondence between Gil Robles and Mola, 29 December 1936 and 1 January 1937, reprinted in Francisco Franco Salgado-Araujo, *Mi vida junto a Franco* (Barcelona: Planeta, 1977) pp. 202–3; Aróstegui and Blanco, 'La República, encrucijada de cambio', p. 333.

116 Juan Ignacio Luca de Tena, *Mis amigos muertos* (Barcelona: Planeta, 1971) p. 68; Payne, *Politics and the Military*, p. 335; Gil Robles, *No fue posible*, p. 733.

117 Valls, *DRV*, pp. 231–6, 241–2, 246–8; Vicent Comes Iglesia, *En el filo de la navaja: biografía política de Luis Lucia* (Madrid: Biblioteca Nueva, 2002) pp. 350–71, 378–436; Cierva, *La Guerra civil*, I, pp. 743–4.

118 *DSC*, 1, 2 July 1936.

119 Espinosa Maestre, 'La reforma agraria', pp. 248–50.

120 Díaz de Entresotos, *Seis meses*; Rees, 'Agrarian Society', pp. 307–8; Cobo Romero, *Labradores, campesinos y jornaleros*, pp. 447–8; Molano, *Miguel Merino*, pp. 124–5.

121 *El Obrero de la Tierra*, 21 March 1936.

122 Espinosa Maestre, 'La reforma agraria', pp. 224–5.

123 Rafael de Medina Vilallonga, Duque de Medinaceli, *Tiempo pasado* (Seville: Gráfica Sevillena, 1971) pp. 22–3.

124 Varela Rendueles, *Rebelión en Seville*, pp. 65–8.

125 Díaz de Entresotos, *Seis meses*, pp. 73–7.

126 According to a recent biography written by a relative with access to his private papers, Enrique Sacanell Ruiz de Apodaca, *El general Sanjurjo: héroe y víctima: el militar que pudo evitar la dictadura franquista* (Madrid: La Esfera de los Libros, 2004) pp. 160, 264.

127 Ximénez de Sandoval, *'José Antonio'*, p. 548.

128 Gibson, *La noche*, pp. 15–23, 54–8; Manuel Tagüeña Lacorte, *Testimonio de dos guerras* (Mexico City: Ediciones Oasis, 1973) pp. 89, 96–8; Ignacio Hidalgo de Cisneros, *Cambio de rumbo (memorias)*, 2 vols (Bucharest: Colección Ebro, 1964) II, pp. 135–6.

129 Julián Zugazagoitia, *Guerra y vicisitudes de los Españoles*, 2 vols (Paris: Librería Española, 1968) I, pp. 28–32; Indalecio Prieto, *Convulsiones de España: pequeños detalles de grandes sucesos*, 3 vols (Mexico City: Ediciones Oasis, 1967–9) I, pp. 157–63; Vidarte, *Todos fuimos culpables*, pp. 213–17. For a graphic reconstruction of the assassination, see Gibson, *La noche*, pp. 15–22.

130 *DSC*, 15 July 1936.

Chapter 5: Queipo's Terror: The Purging of the South

1 Emilio Estéban Infantes, *General Sanjurjo (un laureado en el Penal del Dueso)* (Barcelona: Editorial AHR, 1958) pp. 254–6; Jorge Vigón, *General Mola (el conspirador)* (Barcelona: Editorial AHR, 1957) pp. 100–3.

2 Vigón, *Mola*, pp. 93–4; José María Iribarren, *Mola, datos para una biografía y para la historia del alzamiento nacional* (Zaragoza: Librería General, 1938) pp. 55–6.

3 Ramón Garriga, *El general Juan Yagüe* (Barcelona: Planeta, 1985) pp. 38–9.

4 Juan-Simeón Vidarte, *Todos fuimos culpables* (Mexico City: Fondo de Cultura Económica, 1973) p. 382; Juan José Calleja, *Yagüe, un corazón al rojo* (Barcelona: Editorial Juventud, 1963) pp. 72–8; Ignacio Hidalgo de Cisneros, *Cambio de rumbo (memorias)*, 2 vols (Bucharest: Colección Ebro, 1964, 1970) II, pp. 131–5; Garriga, *Yagüe*, pp. 76–80; Joaquín Arrarás, *Historia de la cruzada española*, 8 vols, 36 tomos (Madrid: Ediciones Españolas, 1939–43) II, 9, p. 523; B. Félix Maíz, *Alzamiento en España: de un diario de la conspiración*, 2nd edn (Pamplona: Editorial Gómez, 1952) pp. 153–4.

5 José María Iribarren, *Con el general Mola* (Zaragoza: Librería General, 1937) pp. 54–5; Hilari Raguer, *El general Batet: Franco contra Batet: crónica de una venganza* (Barcelona: Ediciones Península, 1996) p. 227.

6 Cabanellas, *La guerra de los mil días: nacimiento, vida y muerte de la II República española*, 2 vols (Buenos Aires: Grijalbo, 1973) I, pp. 304–5.

7 Emilio Mola, 'Directivas para Marruecos, 24.06.1936', reproduced in Servicio Histórico Militar (José Manuel Martínez Bande), *La marcha sobre Madrid* (Madrid: Editorial San Martín, 1968) p. 163.

8 Mohammad Ibn Azzuz Hakim, *La actitud de los moros ante el alzamiento: Marruecos 1936* (Málaga: Editorial Algazara, 1997) pp. 100–3.

9 Julio Martínez Abad, *¡¡17 de julio!! La guarnición de Melilla inicia la salvación de España* (Melilla: Artes Gráficas Postal Exprés, n.d. [1937]) pp. 117–44; Rafael Fernández de Castro y Pedrera, *El alzamiento nacional en Melilla: hacia las rutas de la nueva España* (Melilla: Artes

Gráficas Postal Exprés, 1940) pp.
83–7; Garriga, *Yagüe*, pp. 82–3;
Calleja, *Yagüe*, pp. 80–2.

10 'Informe presentado por el
Delegado del Gobierno en Melilla,
sobre los sucesos del 17 de julio de
1936', anexo documental I, Carlota
O'Neill, *Circe y los cerdos: como fue
España encuadernada; los que no
pudieron huir* (Madrid: Asociación
de Directores de Escena de España,
1997) pp. 511–51, especially pp.
543–50; Fernández de Castro, *El
alzamiento nacional en Melilla*, pp.
139–87; Azzuz Hakim, *La actitud de
los moros*, pp. 25–8; Enrique Arqués,
*17 de julio: la epopeya de Africa:
crónica de un testigo* (Ceuta-Tetuán:
Imprenta África, 1938) pp. 24–9,
36–77; Francisco Sánchez Montoya,
*Ceuta y el Norte de África:
República, guerra y represión 1931–
1944* (Granada: Editorial Natívola,
2004) pp. 286–96; Vicente Moga
Romero, *Las heridas de la historia:
testimonios de la guerra civil
española en Melilla* (Barcelona:
Edicions Bellaterra, 2004) pp.
87–134; Julián Casanova, Francisco
Espinosa, Conxita Mir and
Francisco Moreno Gómez, *Morir,
matar, sobrevivir: la violencia en la
dictadura de Franco* (Barcelona:
Editorial Crítica, 2002) pp. 62–3,
311.

11 On their early life, see Carlota
O'Neill, *Los muertos también hablan*
(Mexico City: Populibros La Prensa,
1973) pp. 58–68, 101–4. On her
experiences in Melilla, see Carlota
O'Neill, *Una mexicana en la guerra
de España* (Mexico City: Populibros
La Prensa, 1964) pp. 18–60, 70–6,
145–57. See also Juan Antonio
Hormigón, 'Un velero blanco en la
bahía: el derrotero de Carlota
O'Neill', introduction to O'Neill,
Circe y los cerdos, pp. 42–54, 74–130,
146–53; Moga Romero, *Las heridas*,
pp. 50–64.

12 José de Mora-Figueroa, Marqués de
Tamarón, *Datos para la historia de la
Falange gaditana: 1934–1939* (Jérez
de la Frontera: Gráficas del
Exportador, 1974) pp. 49–74;
Antonio de Puelles y Puelles, *Por las
rutas del tercio Mora-Figueroa
(recuerdos de la campaña)* (Cádiz:
Imprenta Gades, 1939) pp. 15–16;
Eduardo Juliá Téllez, *Historia del
movimiento liberador de España en
la provincia gaditana* (Cádiz:
Establecimentos Cerón, 1944) pp.
65–7, 76–86; Alfonso Patrón de
Sopranis, *Burlando el bloqueo rojo: el
primer salto del Estrecho (julio del
36)* (Jérez de la Frontera: Tip. Lit.
Jérez Industrial, n.d.) pp. 28–9,
52–3; Antonio Garrachón Cuesta,
*De África a Cádiz y de Cádiz a la
España Imperial por sendas de
heroismo, de justicia, de hermandad
y de amor* (Cádiz: Establecimiento
Cerón, 1938) pp. 119–29.

13 Alicia Domínguez Pérez, *El verano
que trajo un largo invierno: la
represión político-social durante el
primer franquismo en Cádiz (1936–
1945)*, 2 vols (Cádiz: Quórum
Editores, 2005) I, pp. 61–72; Jesús
N. Núñez Calvo, *Francisco Cossi
Ochoa (1898–1936): el último
Presidente de la Diputación
Provincial de Cádiz en la Segunda
República: una muerte sin esclarecer*
(Cádiz: Diputación de Cádiz, 2005)
pp. 73–4; Francisco Espinosa
Maestre, *La justicia de Queipo:
violencia selectiva y terror fascista en
la II División en 1936: Sevilla,
Huelva, Cádiz, Córdoba, Málaga y
Badajoz* (Seville: Centro Andaluz
del Libro, 2000) pp. 67–72.

14 *ABC* (Madrid), 17 April 1937;
Domínguez Pérez, *El verano*, pp.
74–103.

15 Juliá Téllez, *La provincia gaditana*,
pp. 88–90; Fernando Romero
Romero, 'La represión en la
provincia de Cádiz: bibliografía y

cifras', *Ubi Sunt?*, No. 17, Cádiz, May 2005, pp. 27–30.

16 Juliá Téllez, *La provincia gaditana*, p. 101.

17 Jesús Núñez, 'La actuación de las columnas rebeldes en las Sierras de Cádiz y Ronda', http://usuarios. lycos.es/historiaymilicia/html/ guecicadizcolumnas.htm.

18 Eduardo Domínguez Lobato, *Cien capítulos de retaguardia (alrededor de un diario)* (Madrid: G. del Toro, 1973) pp. 19–54, 89–115, 137, 179, 185, 190–5.

19 Mercedes Rodríguez Izquierdo and Pedro P. Santamaria Curtido, eds, *Memoria rota: República, Guerra Civil y represión en Rota* (Cádiz: Ayuntamiento de Rota, 2009) pp. 128–41, 147–52, 206–82.

20 José María Pemán, *Arengas y crónicas de guerra* (Cádiz: Establecimientos Cerón, 1937) pp. 12–13.

21 Hoja de Servicios del teniente general Gómez de Zamalloa, Archivo General Militar de Segovia.

22 Romero, 'La represión en la provincia de Cádiz', pp. 27–30.

23 Hoja de Servicios del teniente general Gómez de Zamalloa, Archivo General Militar de Segovia.

24 Puelles, *Tercio Mora-Figueroa*, pp. 15–17; Mora-Figueroa, *La Falange gaditana*, pp. 74, 129–31; Fernando Romero Romero, *Guerra civil y represión en Villamartín* (Cádiz: Diputación Provincial de Cádiz, 1999) pp. 19–47.

25 Fernando Romero Romero, 'Víctimas de la represión en la Sierra de Cádiz durante la guerra civil (1936–1939)', *Almajar*, No. 2, Villamartín, 2005, pp. 209–40.

26 Julio de Ramón-Laca, *Bajo la férula de Queipo: cómo fue gobernada Andalucía* (Seville: Imprenta Comercial del Diario FE, 1939) pp. 15–18; Eduardo Domínguez Lobato, *Cien capítulos de retaguardia*

(alrededor de un diario) (Madrid: G. del Toro, 1973) pp. 31–3; Romero Romero, *Guerra civil y represión en Villamartín*, pp. 54–5.

27 Joaquín Gil Honduvilla, *Justicia en guerra: bando de guerra y jurisdicción militar en el Bajo Guadalquivir* (Seville: Ayuntamiento de Sevilla Patronato del Real Alcázar, 2007) pp. 82–3, 100–5.

28 Núñez Calvo, *Francisco Cossi Ochoa*, pp. 75–119; Espinosa Maestre, *La justicia de Queipo*, pp. 59–65, Queipo de Llano's letter (underlined in the original) p. 280.

29 Domínguez Lobato, *Cien capítulos*, pp. 19–35; Espinosa Maestre, *La justicia de Queipo*, pp. 191–5, 280; Jesús Núñez, 'El Alcalde "desaparecido" de Puerto Real', *Diario de Cádiz*, 21 August 2005.

30 Puelles, *Tercio Mora-Figueroa*, pp. 17–21, 29; Mora-Figueroa, *La Falange gaditana*, pp. 131–38; Juliá Téllez, *La provincia gaditana*, p. 89.

31 Archivo del Tribunal Militar Territorial No. 2, Sumarios, Legajo 170, doc. 7.385, quoted by Romero Romero, 'Víctimas de la represión en la Sierra de Cádiz durante la guerra civil (1936–1939)', pp. 209–40, especially pp. 215–18; Fernando Romero Romero, 'Falangistas, héroes y matones: Fernando Zamacola y los Leones de Rota', *Cuadernos para el Diálogo*, No. 33, September 2008, pp. 32–8.

32 Carlos Castillo del Pino, *Casa del Olivo: autobiografía (1949–2003)* (Barcelona: Tusquets, 2004) p. 372.

33 On the events in Ubrique, see Alfonso Domingo, *Retaguardia: la guerra civil tras los frentes* (Madrid: Oberón, 2004) pp. 17–33. There are 149 names on a monument unveiled at a ceremony held on 21 January 2005 in the Municipal Cemetery of Ubrique.

34 Fernando Romero Romero, *Alcalá del Valle: República, Guerra civil y*

represión 1931–1946 (Cádiz: Ayuntamiento de Alcalá del Valle, 2009) pp. 99–128, 138–51; Juliá Téllez, *Historia del movimiento liberador*, p. 91.

35 Queipo de Llano's versions, General Queipo de Llano, 'Como dominamos a Sevilla', *Estampas de la Guerra: Album no. 5, Frentes de Andalucía y Extremadura* (San Sebastián: Editora Nacional, 1937) pp. 28–35, and *ABC*, 2 February 1938. Similar versions of the same myth can be found in Antonio Olmedo Delgado and General José Cuesta Monereo, *General Queipo de Llano (ventura y audacia)* (Barcelona: AHR, 1958) and Arrarás, *Historia de la cruzada*. There is an updated version by Nicolás Salas, *Sevilla fue la clave: República, Alzamiento, Guerra Civil (1931–39)*, 2 vols (Seville: Editorial Castillejo, 1992). For an account that casts doubt on Queipo de Llano's heroism, see Manuel Barrios, *El último virrey Queipo de Llano*, 3rd edn (Seville: J. Rodríguez Castillejo, 1990). The myth of Queipo de Llano's epic deed is deftly dismantled by Espinosa Maestre, *La justicia de Queipo*, pp. 45–56. See also Hugh Thomas, *The Spanish Civil War*, 3rd edn (London: Hamish Hamilton, 1977) pp. 210–12.

36 Luis de Armiñán, *Excmo. Sr. General Don Gonzalo Queipo de Llano y Sierra Jefe del Ejército del Sur* (Ávila: Impresora Católica, 1937) p. 28; Juan Ortiz Villalba, *Seville 1936: del golpe militar a la guerra civil* (Seville: Diputación Provincial, 1997) pp. 127–8.

37 José María Varela Rendueles, *Rebelión en Sevilla: memorias de su gobernador rebelde* (Seville: Ayuntamiento de Sevilla, 1982) pp. 73–80, 95–9.

38 Espinosa Maestre, *La justicia de Queipo*, pp. 51–3. Vila published his

lists in his pseudonymous Guzmán de Alfarache, *¡18 de julio! Historia del alzamiento glorioso de Sevilla* (Seville: Editorial F.E., 1937) pp. 72–88, 110–15, 130–7, 153–60, 223–69.

39 Manuel Sánchez del Arco, *El sur de España en la reconquista de Madrid*, 2nd edn (Seville: Editorial Sevillana, 1937) pp. 27–35; Guzmán de Alfarache, *¡18 de julio!*, pp. 91–110.

40 Sánchez del Arco, *El sur de España*, pp. 17–20, 31; Cándido Ortiz de Villajos, *De Sevilla a Madrid: ruta libertadora de la columna Castejón* (Granada: Librería Prieto, 1937) p. 27; Nicolás Salas, *Quién fue Luis Alarcón de la Lastra (1891–1971)* (Seville: Guadalturia, 2010) pp. 166–7.

41 Queipo de Llano, 'Como dominamos a Seville', pp. 32–3, Carlos Enrique Bayo and Cipriano Damiano, 'Toreros fascistas: matadores de obreros', *Interviú*, No. 103, 3–9 May 1978, pp. 40–3.

42 Rafael de Medina Vilallonga, Duque de Medinaceli, *Tiempo pasado* (Seville: Gráfica Sevillena, 1971) pp. 39–40; Ortiz Villalba, *Sevilla 1936*, pp. 116–17.

43 Medina, *Tiempo pasado*, pp. 42–3; Francisco Sánchez Ruano, *Islam y guerra civil española: Moros con Franco y con la República* (Madrid: La Esfera de los Libros, 2004) pp. 171–2.

44 *El Correo de Andalucía*, 22 July 1936.

45 Edmundo Barbero, *El infierno azul (seis meses en el feudo de Queipo)* (Madrid: Talleres del SUIG (CNT), 1937) p. 28; Espinosa Maestre, *La justicia de Queipo*, p. 281.

46 Barbero, *El infierno azul*, pp. 25–8; Richard Barker, *El largo trauma de un pueblo andaluz: República, represión, guerra, posguerra* (Castilleja del Campo: Junta de Andalucía and Ayuntamiento de Castilleja del Campo, 2007) p. 100;

Manuel Ruiz Romero and Francisco Espinosa Maestre, eds, *Ayamonte, 1936: diario de un fugitivo: memorias de Miguel Domínguez Soler* (Huelva: Diputación de Huelva, 2001) p. 83.

47 *ABC* (Seville), 24 July 1936; Ramón-Laca, *Bajo la férula*, pp. 27–9.

48 Ortiz Villalba, *Sevilla 1936*, pp. 158–9; Barbero, *El infierno azul*, p. 39.

49 Espinosa Maestre, *La justicia de Queipo*, pp. 270–7.

50 Ortiz Villalba, *Sevilla 1936*, pp. 233–5; Barbero, *El infierno azul*, pp. 28–9.

51 Ortiz Villalba, *Sevilla 1936*, p. 160.

52 Antonio Bahamonde y Sánchez de Castro, *Un año con Queipo* (Barcelona: Ediciones Españolas, n.d. [1938]) p. 108.

53 Francisco Gonzálbez Ruiz, *Yo he creído en Franco: proceso de una gran desilusión (dos meses en la cárcel de Sevilla)* (Paris: Imprimerie Coopérative Étoile, 1938) pp. 51–2.

54 Barbero, *El infierno azul*, pp. 51–4. *The Times*, 9 December 1936, contains an account of members of the public being invited to attend 'shooting parties'.

55 Varela Rendueles, *Rebelión en Sevilla*, pp. 152–3.

56 Bahamonde, *Un año con Queipo*, pp. 108–10.

57 Memorandum of Vice-Consul to Portuguese Ambassador, 19 November 1936, Pedro Teotónio Pereira, *Correspondência de Pedro Teotónio Pereira para Oliveira Salazar*, Vol. I: *1931–1939* (Lisbon: Presidência do Conselho de Ministros, 1987) pp. 228–9. On the subsequent career of Díaz Criado, see Espinosa Maestre, *La justicia de Queipo*, pp. 105–17.

58 Gonzálbez Ruiz, *Yo he creído en Franco*, pp. 51–2.

59 *ABC* (Madrid), 18 April, 16 June 1937; Ortiz Villalba, *Sevilla 1936*,

pp. 85, 102, 343; Espinosa Maestre, *La justicia de Queipo*, pp. 75–9, 92–4.

60 Francisco Espinosa Maestre, *La guerra civil en Huelva*, 4th edn (Huelva: Diputación Provincial, 2005) pp. 85–103, 137–54; Espinosa Maestre, *La justicia de Queipo*, pp. 140–50.

61 P. Bernabé Copado SJ, *Con la columna Redondo: combates y conquistas: crónica de guerra* (Seville: Imprenta de la Gavidia, 1937) pp. 29–34.

62 Ortiz Villalba, *Sevilla 1936*, pp. 82, 95–8, 115–18, 138–43, 165.

63 Medina, *Tiempo pasado*, pp. 45–59; Alfonso Lazo, *Retrato del fascismo rural en Sevilla* (Seville: Universidad de Sevilla, 1998) p. 14; Barker, *El largo trauma*, pp. 87–8; Espinosa Maestre, *La guerra civil en Huelva*, pp. 104–18.

64 Francisco Espinosa Maestre, 'Vida y muerte en retaguardia: Hinojos y Rociana: dos historias del 36', in *IV Encuentro de poetas y escritores del Entorno de Doñana* (Doñana: Biblioteca Ligustina, 1999) pp. 107–46; Espinosa Maestre, *La guerra civil en Huelva*, pp. 380–1.

65 António de Cértima to MNE, 6 August 1936, *Dez anos de política externa (1936–1947) a nação portuguesa e a segunda guerra mundial*, Vol. III (Lisbon: Imprensa Nacional/Casa da Moeda, 1964) p. 86. For a similar Italian account of alleged red atrocities, on the basis of information provided by the military authorities in Seville, see Curio Mortari, *Con gli insorti in Marocco e Spagna* (Milan: Fratelli Treves Editori, 1937) pp. 231–47.

66 Alfonso Lazo, *Retrato de fascismo rural en Sevilla* (Seville: Universidad de Sevilla, 1998) pp. 11–14; Margarita Nelken, *Las torres del Kremlin* (Mexico City: Industrial y Distribuidora, 1943) p. 259.

67 *La Unión*, 23 July 1936; Ian Gibson, *Queipo de Llano: Sevilla, verano de 1936* (Barcelona: Grijalbo, 1936) p. 164; Arthur Koestler, *Spanish Testament* (London: Victor Gollancz, 1937) p. 34.

68 *ABC* (Seville), 26 July 1936.

69 Koestler, *Spanish Testament*, pp. 34, 84–8.

70 *La Unión*, 18 August 1936; Barker, *El largo trauma*, p. 116.

71 Ortiz de Villajos, *De Sevilla a Madrid*, pp. 21, 30–8, 46–7, 51–2; Espinosa Maestre, *La guerra civil en Huelva*, pp. 122–8; Miriam B. Mandel, *Hemingway's Death in the Afternoon: The Complete Annotations* (Lanham, Md: Scarecrow Press, 2002) p. 82.

72 Espinosa Maestre, *La guerra civil en Huelva*, pp. 147–54; Espinosa Maestre, *La justicia de Queipo*, pp. 129–37, 145–6, 197–200.

73 Espinosa Maestre, *La guerra civil en Huelva*, pp. 161–2; Ruiz Romero and Espinosa Maestra, *Ayamonte, 1936*, pp. 65–103.

74 Manuel Tapada Pérez, *Guerra y posguerra en Encinasola: Aroche, Cumbres Mayores, Cumbres de San Bartolomé y Barrancos* (Seville: Autor, 2000) pp. 44–55; Maria Dulce Antunes Simões, *Barrancos na encruzilhada de la guerra civil de Espanha* (Lisbon: Câmara Municipal de Barrancos, 2007) pp. 173–83; Espinosa Maestre, *La guerra civil en Huelva*, pp. 173–4.

75 Copado, *Con la columna Redondo*, pp. 41–60; Espinosa Maestre, *La guerra civil en Huelva*, pp. 174–227.

76 Copado, *Con la columna Redondo*, pp. 68–94; Luciano Suero Sánchez, *Memorias de un campesino andaluz* (Madrid: Queimada Ediciones, 1982) pp. 78–87; Espinosa Maestre, *La guerra civil en Huelva*, pp. 228–58; *La Unión*, 27 August 1936; Antonio Muñiz, Jesús Berrocal and Nieves Medina, *La historia silenciada: víctimas de la represión franquista en Aroche (Huelva)* (Huelva: Ayuntamiento de Aroche/ Junta de Andalucía, 2007) pp. 140–87.

77 Guillermo A. Molina Domínguez, *Víctimas y desaparecidos: la represión franquista en Palos de la Frontera (1936–1941)* (Huelva: Autor, 2005) pp. 76–90, 106–11, 119–40; Espinosa Maestre, *La justicia de Queipo*, 2nd edn, pp. 138–9, 343–4; Antonio Orihuela, *Moguer – 1936* (Madrid: La Oveja Roja, 2010) pp. 143–205, 211–76.

78 Espinosa Maestre, *La guerra civil en Huelva*, pp. 321–3, 715–16; Francisco Espinosa Maestre, ed., *Violencia roja y azul: España, 1936– 1950* (Barcelona: Editorial Crítica, 2010) pp. 77, 247; Orihuela, *Moguer – 1936*, p. 176.

79 Espinosa Maestre, *La guerra civil en Huelva*, pp. 137–46, 409–31; Espinosa Maestre, *La justicia de Queipo*, pp. 127–8, 151–9.

80 Ortiz de Villajos, *De Sevilla a Madrid*, pp. 45–6.

81 Javier Jiménez Rodríguez, 'La tragedia de todos: odios y violencias durante la guerra civil (1936–1939)', in Arias Castañón, Leandro Álvarez Rey and Javier Jiménez Rodríguez, *Permanencias y cambios en la Baja Andalucía: Alcalá de Guadaíra en los siglos XIX y XX* (Alcalá de Guadaira: Ayuntamiento de Alcalá de Guadaira, 1995) pp. 309–12.

82 Félix J. Montero Gómez, *Alcalá de Guadaira, 21 de julio de 1936: historia de una venganza* (Seville: Ayuntamiento de Alcalá de Guadaíra/Asociación Andaluza Memoria Histórica y Justicia, 2007) pp. 13–14, 449–51, 675–8, 704–10; Jiménez Rodríguez, 'La tragedia de todos', pp. 313–41; Ortiz de Villajos, *De Sevilla a Madrid*, pp. 46–7.

83 *La Unión*, 22 July 1936.

84 Servicio Histórico Militar (José Manuel Martínez Bande), *La campaña de Andalucía*, 2nd edn (Madrid: Editorial San Martín, 1986) p. 71. On the two dead in Carmona, see *Preliminary Official Report on the Atrocities Committed in Southern Spain in July and August, 1936, by the Communist Forces of the Madrid Government* (London: Eyre & Spottiswoode, 1936) pp. 40–2. On the death of Villa and the subsequent repression, Francisco Rodríguez Nodal, *Al paso alegre de la paz 1939* (Carmona: Autor, 2004) pp. 45–58; Antonio Lería and Francisco Eslava, *Carmona tricolor: militancia política y afiliación sindical en la Segunda República* (Carmona: Ayuntamiento de Carmona, 2008) pp. 168–98; Antonio Lería, 'Golpe de estado y Guerra Civil en Carmona', in his *La Guerra Civil en Carmona* (Carmona: Ayuntamiento de Carmona, 2008) pp. 11–26. See also José García Márquez, 'La represión franquista en la provincial de Sevilla: estado de la cuestión', *EBRE 38. Revista Internacional de la Guerra Civil 1936–1939*, Barcelona, No. 2, 2003, pp. 85–97.

85 Ruiz Romero and Espinosa Maestra, *Ayamonte, 1936*, pp. 101–2.

86 For the memories of survivors, see Francisco Rodríguez Nodal, *Caínes del amanecer 1936*, 3rd edn (Carmona: Autor, 2001) pp. 67–71, 81–5, 121, 133–42, 229–36, and the unpublished work by Paqui Maqueda Fernández, 'Como si nunca hubiera ocurrido: un relato por los caminos de la memoria'.

87 Rodríguez Nodal, *Caínes del amanecer*, pp. 89–102, 185–215; Lería and Eslava, *Carmona tricolor*, pp. 207–16.

88 *ABC* (Seville), 31 July 1936; Ramón Barragán Reina, *Cantillana II República: la esperanza rota: la brutal represión franquista en un pueblo Sevilleno* (Brenes: Muñoz Moya Editores Extremeños, 2006) pp. 86–7, 102–52; Antonio Rosado, *Tierra y libertad: memorias de un campesino anarcosindicalista andaluz* (Barcelona: Editorial Crítica, 1979) pp. 121–2.

89 *La Unión*, 31 August 1936.

90 Archivo General Militar, Madrid, Armario 18, Legajo 6, Carpeta 5. I am grateful to Rúben Serém for giving me a copy of this document.

91 José Moreno Romero, *Fuentes de Andalucía: crónicas del siglo XX* (Seville: Edición del Autor, 1999) pp. 112–19.

92 *ABC* (Seville), 24, 25 July 1936. On the rebel version of the events in Arahal, *Preliminary Official Report on the Atrocities*, pp. 31–4; Ortiz de Villajos, *De Sevilla a Madrid*, pp. 52–5. On the subsequent repression in the town, the conservative historian Nicolás Salas, *Sevilla fue la clave*, p. 623, gives the figure of 146, adding, pp. 650–1, that locally the number was considered to be somewhere between 200 and 500. The figure of 1,600 is given in Carmen Muñoz, 'Masacre fascista en Arahal (Sevilla)', *Interviu*, No. 91, 9–15 February 1978, pp. 38–41.

93 José María García Márquez and Miguel Guardado Rodríguez, *Morón: Consumatum Est: 1936–1953: historia de un crimen de guerra* (Morón de la Frontera: Planta Baja, 2011) pp. 61–97; Rosado, *Tierra y libertad*, pp. 122–5.

94 García Márquez and Guardado Rodríguez, *Morón*, pp. 99–206; *La Unión*, 26 July 1936.

95 Ortiz de Villajos, *De Sevilla a Madrid*, pp. 55–7; José María García Márquez, 'La represión franquista en la provincia de Sevilla: estado de la cuestión', in *Ebre 38. Revista Internacional de la Guerra Civil (1936–1939)*, No. 2 (Barcelona:

Publicacions i Edicions de la Universitat de Barcelona, 2004), p. 94.

96 José María García Márquez, *La represión militar en la Puebla de Cazalla* (Seville: Fundación Centro de Estudios Andaluces, 2007) pp. 9, 31–58, 66–84, 201–4.

97 Francisco Moreno Gómez, *La guerra civil en Córdoba (1936–1939)* (Madrid: Editorial Alpuerto, 1985) pp. 110–11, 253–61; Francisco Moreno Gómez, *1936: el genocidio franquista en Córdoba* (Barcelona: Editorial Crítica, 2008) pp. 409–22; *Preliminary Official Report on the Atrocities*, pp. 59–61; Antonio Pérez de Olaguer, *El terror rojo en Andalucía* (Burgos: Ediciones Antisectarias, 1938) pp. 49–53.

98 Ortiz de Villajos, *De Sevilla a Madrid*, pp. 67–70; Moreno Gómez, *La guerra civil en Córdoba*, pp. 261–78; Moreno Gómez, *1936: el genocidio franquista*, pp. 422–36; Queipo's speech in *ABC* (Seville), 2 August 1936.

99 *ABC* (Seville), 9 August 1936; Antonio Montero Moreno, *Historia de la persecución religiosa en España 1936–1939* (Madrid: Biblioteca de Autores Cristianos, 1961) pp. 776, 798; Juan Manuel Lozano Nieto, *A sangre y fuego: los años treinta en un pueblo andaluz* (Córdoba: Almuzara, 2006) pp. 132–74; Leopoldo Nunes, *La guerra en España (dos meses de reportaje en los frentes de Andalucía y Extremadura)* (Granada: Librería Prieto, 1937) pp. 165–8.

100 *ABC* (Seville), 9, 11 August 1936; Lozano Nieto, *A sangre y fuego*, pp. 185–239. An eyewitness account by a reluctant executioner was published anonymously as 'El comienzo: 1936 La "liberación" de Lora del Río', *Cuadernos de Ruedo Ibérico* (Paris), Nos 46–8, July–December 1975, pp. 81–94.

101 Lozano Nieto, *A sangre y fuego*, pp. 200–3, 234–5.

102 *Ibid.*, pp. 215–38, 329–40. The figure of 600 dead was given in the 1938 Civil Guard report to the Delegado de Orden Público, AHN, Fondo de Expedientes Policiales, H-753, 754, 755, quoted by Lozano Nieto, p. 318.

103 *ABC* (Seville), 11 August 1936; *Heraldo de Madrid*, 15 August 1936. The figure of 300 dead and 3,000 fled was given by the Commander of the Civil Guard post of Constantina on 17 October 1938 in a report to the Delegado de Orden Público, AHN, Fondo de Expedientes Policiales, H-754. I am grateful to José María García Márquez for supplying me with this information.

104 José Iglesias Vicente, *Cazalla de la Sierra: los sucesos del verano del 36* (Zafra: Edición del Autor, 2006) pp. 39–78.

105 *ABC* (Seville), 13, 14, 15 August 1936; *La Unión*, 14, 15 August 1936; Iglesias Vicente, *Cazalla de la Sierra*, pp. 79–83, 111–17, 131–5.

106 Manuel Sánchez del Arco, *El sur de España en la reconquista de Madrid*, 2nd edn (Seville: Editorial Sevillana, 1937) pp. 18–20.

107 Medina, *Tiempo pasado*, pp. 61–2, 80–1.

108 Manuel Chaves Nogales, *A sangre y fuego* (Madrid: Espasa Calpe, 2006) pp. 47–72; Arcángel Bedmar González, *Lucena: de la Segunda República a la Guerra Civil* (Córdoba: Imprenta Vistalegre, 1998) pp. 118–19; Arcángel Bedmar González, *República, guerra y represión: Lucena 1931–1939* (Lucena: Ayuntamiento de Lucena, 2000) pp. 190–1; testimony of Juan Manuel Moyano Terrón (Cuevas de San Marcos); José María Pemán, *Mis encuentros con Franco* (Barcelona: Dopesa, 1976) p. 90.

109 Moreno Gómez, *1936: el genocidio franquista*, pp. 55–79.

110 Moreno Gómez, *La guerra civil en Córdoba*, pp. 288–98, 326–7; Moreno Gómez, *1936: el genocidio franquista*, p. 814; Barbero, *El infierno azul*, pp. 9–10, 13, 16–17; Espinosa Maestre, *La justicia de Queipo*, pp. 121–4.

111 Ronald Fraser, *Blood of Spain: The Experience of Civil War 1936–1939* (London: Allen Lane, 1979) pp. 161–4; *ABC* (Seville), 12 October 1936.

112 *ABC* (Seville), 3 October 1936.

113 Bedmar González, *Lucena*, pp. 134–5; Bedmar González, *República, guerra y represión: Lucena*, pp. 167–78.

114 Fernando Rivas Gómez, 'La defensa de Baena – Episodios de la Guardia Civil', *Revista de Estudios Históricos de la Guardia Civil*, Año V, No. 9, 1972, pp. 63–85; Moreno Gómez, *La guerra civil en Córdoba*, pp. 214–23; Moreno Gómez, *1936: el genocidio franquista*, pp. 363–76; Arcángel Bedmar González, *Baena roja y negra: guerra civil y represión (1936–1943)* (Lucena: Librería Juan de Mairena, 2008) pp. 21–37.

115 *ABC* (Seville), 30 July 1936; Moreno Gómez, *La guerra civil en Córdoba*, pp. 225–39; Rivas Gómez, 'La defensa de Baena', pp. 85–8; Moreno Gómez, *1936: el genocidio franquista*, pp. 377–97; Bedmar González, *Baena roja y negra*, pp. 39–70; Félix Moreno de la Cova, *Mi vida y mi tiempo: la guerra que yo viví* (Seville: Gráficas Mirte, 1988) p. 23.

116 Rivas Gómez, 'La defensa de Baena', pp. 88–9; Moreno Gómez, *1936: el genocidio franquista*, pp. 397–8.

117 *ABC* (Seville), 1 August 1936.

118 Moreno Gómez, *1936: el genocidio franquista*, pp. 385, 397–400; Bedmar González, *Baena roja y negra*, pp. 70–155.

119 José María Pemán, *¡Atención! … ¡Atención! … Arengas y crónicas de guerra* (Cádiz: Establecimientos Cerón, 1937) pp. 94–5.

120 Moreno Gómez, *La guerra civil en Córdoba*, pp. 210–12; Barbero, *El infierno azul*, pp. 14, 19–20.

121 Mandel, *Hemingway's Death in the Afternoon*, pp. 163–4, 167–9; Bayo and Damiano, 'Toreros fascistas', pp. 42–3.

122 Servicio Histórico Militar, Cuartel General del Generalísimo, Legajo 273, Carpeta 6, quoted by Espinosa Maestre, *La justicia de Queipo*, p. 287.

123 Ángel David Martín Rubio, *Paz, piedad, perdón … y verdad: la represión en la guerra civil: una síntesis definitiva* (Madrid: Editorial Fénix, 1997) pp. 211–16; Romero Romero, 'Víctimas de la represión en la Sierra de Cádiz durante la guerra civil', p. 210.

124 Romero Romero, 'La represión en la provincia de Cádiz: bibliografía y cifras', pp. 27–30; Domínguez Pérez, *El verano*, I, pp. 79, 88–103; Espinosa Maestre, ed., *Violencia roja y azul*, p. 77.

125 José María Pemán, *Un soldado en la historia: vida del Capitán General Varela* (Cádiz: Escelicer, 1954) pp. 179–82; Gerald Brenan, *Personal Record 1920–1972* (London: Jonathan Cape, 1974) pp. 310–11; J. R. Corbin, *The Anarchist Passion: Class Conflict in Southern Spain 1810–1965* (Aldershot: Avebury Publishing, 1993) pp. 43–4; *Second & Third Reports on the Communist Atrocities Committed in Southern Spain from July to October, 1936, by the Communist Forces of the Madrid Government* (London: Eyre & Spottiswoode, 1937) pp. xxii, 58–61; Carlos G. Mauriño Longoria, *Memorias* (Ronda: private publication by family, n.d. [1937]), pp. 38–59, 66–77, 95–115; Salvador Fernández Álvarez and José María Gutiérrez Ballesteros, *De la gesta española (breviario de la conquista de Ronda)* (Cádiz: Establecimientos Cerón y Librería Cervantes, 1939)

pp. 24, 39–47; Gil Gómez Bajuelo, *Málaga bajo el dominio rojo* (Cádiz: Establecimientos Cerón, 1937) pp. 33–45; Lucía Prieto Borrego and Encarnación Barranquero Texeira, 'Población civil y guerra: Málaga, de la retaguardia al éxodo', in Fernando Arcas Cubero, ed., *Málaga 1937 nunca más: historia y memoria: guerra civil y franquismo en Málaga* (Málaga: Ateneo de Málaga, 2006) (special issue of *Ateneo del Nuevo Siglo*, No. 9, December 2006) pp. 9–14.

126 Espinosa Maestre, *La justicia de Queipo*, pp. 223–31.

127 Puelles, *Tercio Mora-Figueroa*, pp. 17–21, 65–7, 101–2; Mora-Figueroa, *Datos para la historia*, pp. 138–44; Eduardo Juliá Téllez, *Historia del movimiento liberador de España en la provincia gaditana* (Cádiz: Establecimentos Cerón, 1944) p. 89; Eduardo Domínguez Lobato, *Cien capítulos de retaguardia* (Madrid: G. del Toro, 1973) p. 318.

128 Report of Gobernador Militar de Cádiz, quoted in Ángel David Martín Rubio, *Paz, piedad, perdón … y verdad*, pp. 214–16.

129 Espinosa Maestre, *La justicia de Queipo*, p. 50.

130 *La Unión*, 22 July 1936; Bérriz to Rodríguez-Acosta, 13 August 1936, Manuel Titos Martínez, *Verano del 36 en Granada: un testimonio sobre el comienzo de la guerra civil y la muerte de García Lorca* (Granada: Editorial Atrio, 2005) p. 80.

131 Francisco Franco Salgado-Araujo, *Mi vida junto a Franco* (Barcelona: Planeta, 1977) pp.185–8, 348–53.

132 Ángel Gollonet Megías and José Morales López, *Rojo y azul en Granada*, 2nd edn (Granada: Librería Prieto, 1937) pp. 111–25; Martínez Bande, *La campaña de Andalucía*, pp. 99–112.

133 Gollonet Megías and Morales López, *Rojo y azul*, pp. 79–96; Ian

Gibson, *El asesinato de García Lorca* (Barcelona: Plaza y Janés, 1996) pp. 60–3, 69–74.

134 Gollonet Megías and Morales López, *Rojo y azul*, pp. 165–9; Gibson, *El asesinato*, pp. 106–19.

135 Bérriz to Rodríguez-Acosta, 18 August 1936, Titos Martínez, *Verano del 36*, p. 117.

136 Gibson, *El asesinato*, pp. 129–42; Helen Nicholson, *Death in the Morning* (London: Lovat Dickson, 1937) pp. 33–4; Rafael Gil Bracero and María Isabel Brenes, *Jaque a la República (Granada, 1936–1939)* (Granada: Ediciones Osuna, 2009) pp. 225–31, 295–300.

137 Gibson, *El asesinato*, pp. 15–36, 265–6; Miguel Caballero Pérez and Pilar Góngora Ayala, *La verdad sobre el asesinato de García Lorca: historia de una familia* (Madrid: Ibersaf Editores, 2007) pp. 154–5, 168–9, 299, 301–9; Ian Gibson, *El hombre que detuvo a García Lorca: Ramón Ruiz Alonso y la muerte del poeta* (Madrid: Aguilar, 2007) pp. 99–100, 143.

138 Gibson, *El hombre*, pp. 11–39, 89–90; Ian Gibson, ed., *Agustín Penón: diario de una búsqueda lorquiana (1955–56)* (Barcelona: Plaza y Janés, 1990) pp. 190–7, 206–19.

139 Eduardo Molina Fajardo, *Los últimos días de García Lorca* (Barcelona: Plaza y Janés, 1983) pp. 40–50.

140 Until it was definitively established by Manuel Titos in 2005, there had been considerable dispute about the exact date of Lorca's murder. See José Luis Vila-San-Juan, *García Lorca asesinado: toda la verdad* (Barcelona: Planeta, 1975) pp. 160–3; Molina Fajardo, *Los últimos días*, pp. 67–70, 194; Marta Osorio, *Miedo, olvido y fantasía: Agustín Peñón: crónica de su investigación sobre Federico García Lorca*

(1955–1956) (Granada: Editorial Comares, 2001) pp. 295–307, 344–8, 355, 407–9, 667–9; Titos Martínez, *Verano del 36*, pp. 45–64, 122; Gibson, *El hombre*, pp. 141–2.

141 Gibson, *El asesinato*, pp. 265–6; Gibson, *El hombre*, pp. 99–100, 143.

142 Francisco Vigueras Roldán, *Los 'paseados' con Lorca: el maestro cojo y los dos banderilleros* (Seville-Zamora: Comunicación Social Ediciones, 2007) pp. 28–9, 37–50, 133–48; Gibson, *El asesinato*, p. 236; Gollonet Megías and Morales López, *Rojo y azul*, pp. 101–2.

143 Bérriz to Rodríguez-Acosta, 18 August 1936, Titos Martínez, *Verano del 36*, pp. 117–19, 133.

144 Nicholson, *Death in the Morning*, pp. 81–2. Her novel about the Civil War, *The Painted Bed*, reveals her Francoist sympathies.

145 Gibson, *El hombre*, pp. 53, 78–80, 83–8; Francisco Vigueras, *Granada 1936: muerte de un periodista Constantino Ruiz Carnero 1887–1936* (Granada: Editorial Comares, 1998) pp. 179–89, 227–40.

146 Mercedes del Amo, *Salvador Vila: el rector fusilado en Víznar* (Granada: Universidad de Granada, 2005) pp. 123–5, 135–57, 163–9; Molina Fajardo, *Los últimos días*, pp. 286, 423; Miguel de Unamuno, *El resentimiento trágico de la vida: notas sobre la revolución y guerra civil españolas* (Madrid: Alianza Editorial, 1991) p. 57.

147 Nicholson, *Death in the Morning*, pp. 82, 72–3, 99.

148 Martínez Bande, *La campaña de Andalucía*, pp. 169–210.

149 Edward Norton, *Muerte en Málaga: testimonio de un americano sobre la guerra civil española* (Málaga: Universidad de Málaga, 2004) pp. 170–87, 193–208, 225–42; Juan Antonio Ramos Hitos, *Guerra civil en Málaga 1936–1937: revisión histórica*, 2nd edn (Málaga: Editorial

Algazara, 2004) pp. 217–35, 244–72, 283–5; Ángel Gollonet Megías and José Morales López, *Sangre y fuego: Málaga* (Granada: Librería Prieto, 1937); Gómez Bajuelo, *Málaga bajo el dominio rojo*, pp. 81–4; Padre Tomás López, *Treinta semanas en poder de los rojos en Málaga de julio a febrero* (Seville: Imprenta de San Antonio, 1938) pp. 61–6, 93–101; Francisco García Alonso, *Flores del heroismo* (Seville: Imprenta de la Gavidia, 1939) pp. 76–9, 90–103, 129–36.

150 Encarnación Barranquero Texeira and Lucía Prieto Borrego, *Población y guerra civil en Málaga: caída, éxodo y refugio* (Málaga: Centro de Ediciones de la Diputación de Málaga, 2007) pp. 21–99; Encarnación Barranquero Texeira, *Málaga entre la guerra y la posguerra: el franquismo* (Málaga: Editorial Arguval, 1994) p. 202; Bahamonde, *Un año con Queipo*, pp. 125–9.

151 Bahamonde, *Un año con Queipo*, pp. 132–5.

152 *ABC* (Seville), 11, 12 March 1937; García Márquez, *La represión militar en la Puebla de Cazalla*, pp. 126–30; Francisco Espinosa Maestre, *Contra el olvido* (Barcelona: Crítica, 2006) pp. 79–93; Arcas Cubero, ed., *Málaga 1937 nunca más*, passim; Barranquero Texeira, *Málaga entre la guerra y la posguerra*, pp. 215–39; Antonio Nadal, *Guerra civil en Málaga* (Málaga: Editorial Arguval, 1984) pp. 190–2, 217–32; Ramos Hitos, *Guerra civil en Málaga*, pp. 309–36.

153 Barranquero and Prieto, *Población y guerra civil*, pp. 180–209.

154 Dr Norman Bethune, *The Crime on the Road Malaga–Almeria* (n.p.: Publicaciones Iberia, 1937) pp. 8–9; T. C. Worsley, *Behind the Battle* (London: Robert Hale, 1939) pp. 185–8, 197–201; *The Times*, 17, 24 February, 3 March 1937.

Chapter 6: Mola's Terror: The Purging of Navarre, Galicia, Castile and León

1 Emilio Mola Vidal, *Obras completas* (Valladolid: Librería Santarén, 1940) p. 1173.

2 Juan de Iturralde (Father Juan José Usabiaga Irazustabarrena), *La guerra de Franco: los vascos y la Iglesia*, 2 vols (San Sebastián: Publicaciones Clero Vasco, 1978) I, p. 433. See also Hugh Thomas, *The Spanish Civil War*, 3rd edn (London: Hamish Hamilton, 1977) p. 260.

3 Alfonso Álvarez Bolado, *Para ganar la guerra, para ganar la paz: Iglesia y guerra civil 1936–1939* (Madrid: Universidad Pontificia de Comillas, 1995) p. 52.

4 José María Iribarren, *Con el general Mola: escenas y aspectos inéditos de la guerra civil* (Zaragoza: Librería General, 1937) pp. 168–9, 222–3.

5 Josep Fontana, 'Julio de 1936', *Público*, 29 June 2010; Julián Chaves Palacios, *La represión en la provincia de Cáceres durante la guerra civil (1936–1939)* (Cáceres: Universidad de Extremadura, 1995) p. 101.

6 Fernando Mikelarena Peña, 'La intensidad de la limpieza política franquista en 1936 en la Ribera de Navarra', *Hispania Nova. Revista de Historia Contemporánea*, No. 9 (2009) p. 5.

7 José del Castillo and Santiago Álvarez, *Barcelona: objetivo cubierto* (Barcelona: Editorial Timón, 1958) pp. 153–7, 165–9.

8 I. Berdugo, J. Cuesta, M. de la Calle and M. Lanero, 'El Ministerio de Justicia en la España "Nacional"', in Archivo Histórico Nacional, *Justicia en guerra: jornadas sobre la administración de justicia durante la Guerra Civil Española: instituciones y fuentes documentales* (Madrid: Ministerio de Cultura, 1990) pp. 249–53.

9 Santiago Vega Sombría, *De la esperanza a la persecución: la represión franquista en la provincia de Segovia* (Barcelona: Editorial Crítica, 2005) p. 110.

10 José María Dávila y Huguet, *Código de justicia militar: con notas aclaratorias y formularios* (Burgos: Imprenta Aldecoa, 1937) p. 5.

11 Iribarren, *Con el general Mola*, pp. 94, 245.

12 General Luis Redondo and Comandante Juan de Zavala, *El Requeté (la tradición no muere)* (Barcelona: Editorial AHR, 1957) pp. 78–81.

13 Marino Ayerra Redín, *No me avergoncé del evangelio (desde mi parroquia)*, 2nd edn (Buenos Aires: Editorial Periplo, 1959) pp. 29–30.

14 Julián Casanova, *La Iglesia de Franco*, 2nd edn (Barcelona: Editorial Crítica, 2005) pp. 63–5; Iturralde, *La guerra de Franco*, I, pp. 417–23.

15 Peter Kemp, *Mine Were of Trouble* (London: Cassell, 1957) pp. 76, 80.

16 Javier Ugarte Telleria, *La nueva Covadonga insurgente: orígenes sociales y culturales de la sublevación de 1936 en Navarra y el País Vasco* (Madrid: Editorial Biblioteca Nueva, 1998) pp. 86–9; Ayerra Redín, *No me avergoncé del evangelio*, pp. 27–31; Iturralde, *La guerra de Franco*, I, pp. 435–40.

17 Galo Vierge, *Los culpables: Pamplona 1936* (Pamplona: Pamiela, 2009) pp. 148–57.

18 Altaffaylla, *Navarra: de la esperanza al terror*, 8th edn (Tafalla: Altaffaylla, 2004) pp. 718–19; Mikelarena Peña, 'La intensidad de la limpieza política', p. 5.

19 Álvarez Bolado, *Para ganar la guerra*, p. 42; Vierge, *Los culpables*, pp. 33–48; Iturralde, *La guerra de Franco*, I, p. 422; Altaffaylla, *Navarra*, pp. 492–4, 784–90. There are minor discrepancies in these sources (Vierge, 52; Iturralde, 56; Altaffaylla, 52) concerning the exact

numbers assassinated but there is little doubt that a massacre took place.

20 Altaffaylla, *Navarra*, pp. 588–90.

21 Mikelarena Peña, 'La intensidad de la limpieza política', p. 24; Altaffaylla, *Navarra*, pp. 497–508.

22 Josefina Campos Oruña, *Los fusilados de Peralta, la vuelta a casa (1936–1978): operación retorno* (Pamplona: Pamiela, 2008) pp. 296–302; Altaffaylla, *Navarra*, pp. 508, 793; Jesús Equiza, *Los sacerdotes navarros ante la represión de 1936–1937 y ante la rehabilitación de los fusilados* (Madrid: Editorial Nueva Utopía, 2010) pp. 25–8.

23 Hilari Raguer, *La pólvora y el incienso: la Iglesia y la guerra civil española* (Barcelona: Ediciones Península, 2001) pp. 163–4; Ayerra Redín, *No me avergoncé del evangelio*, pp. 136–9.

24 Cardenal Gomá, *Por Dios y por España 1936–1939* (Barcelona: Editorial Casulleras, 1940) pp. 306–15.

25 Carlos Gil Andrés, *Echarse a la calle: amotinados, huelguistas y revolucionarios (La Rioja, 1890–1936)* (Zaragoza: Prensas Universitarias de Zaragoza, 2000) pp. 209–43; Carlos Gil Andrés, *Lejos del frente: la guerra civil en la Rioja alta* (Barcelona: Editorial Crítica, 2006) pp. 3–79; Enrique Pradas Martínez, ed., *8 de diciembre de 1933: insurrección anarquista en La Rioja* (Logroño: Cuadernos Riojanos, 1983) *passim*; Enrique Pradas Martínez, *La segunda República y La Rioja (1931–1936)* (Logroño: Cuadernos Riojanos, 1982) pp. 139–54; Jesús Vicente Aguirre González, *Aquí nunca pasó nada: La Rioja 1936* (Logroño: Editorial Ochoa, 2007) p. 906.

26 Gil Andrés, *Echarse a la calle*, pp. 248–59; María Cristina Rivero Noval, *La ruptura de la paz civil:*

represión en la Rioja (1936–1939) (Logroño: Instituto de Estudios Riojanos, 1992) pp. 32–5; Aguirre González, *Aquí nunca pasó nada*, pp. 583, 907.

27 Joaquín Arrarás, *Historia de la cruzada española*, 8 vols, 36 tomos (Madrid: Ediciones Españolas, 1939–43) III, 13, pp. 498–504; Aguirre González, *Aquí nunca pasó nada*, pp. 55, 63, 66–7, 74, 111–13.

28 Antonio Hernández García, *La represión en La Rioja durante la guerra civil*, 3 vols (Logroño: Autor, 1982) I, pp. 25–31; Rivero Noval, *La ruptura de la paz civil*, pp. 45–51; Gil Andrés, *Lejos del frente*, pp. 86–92, 130–5.

29 Antonio Sánchez-Marín Enciso, *Plasencia en llamas (1931–1939)* (Madrid: Editorial Raíces, 2009) pp. 255–6; Chaves Palacios, *La represión en la provincia de Cáceres*, p. 103.

30 Francisco Bermejo Martín, *La II\u00aa República en Logroño* (Logroño: Ediciones del Instituto de Estudios Riojanos, 1984) pp. 385–90; Patricio Escobal, *Las sacas (memorias)* (Sada-A Coruña: Edicios do Castro, 2005) pp. 83–6; Hernández García, *La represión en La Rioja*, I, pp. 47–60, II, pp. 23–130, 141–73, III, pp. 57–63, 101–37; Rivero Noval, *La ruptura de la paz civil*, pp. 69–79; Gil Andrés, *Lejos del frente*, pp. 107, 212–20, 252; Carlos Gil Andrés, *La República en la Plaza: los sucesos de Arnedo de 1932* (Logroño: Instituto de Estudios Riojanos, 2003) pp. 258–79; Aguirre González, *Aquí nunca pasó nada*, pp. 966–70.

31 Carlos Gil Andrés, 'La zona gris de la España azul: la violencia de los sublevados en la Guerra Civil', *Ayer. Revista de Historia Contemporánea*, No. 76, 2009, pp. 115–41.

32 There have been several editions of his book. The first was Patricio Escobal, *Death Row: Spain 1936* (New York: Bobbs Merrill, 1968).

The most recent and definitive is *Las sacas (memorias)*.

33 Aguirre González, *Aquí nunca pasó nada*, pp. 254–6, 349–50, 891, 936–9; Hernández García, *La represión en La Rioja*, I, p. 48; Antonio Arizmendi and Patricio de Blas, *Conspiración contra el Obispo de Calahorra: denuncia y crónica de una canallada* (Madrid: EDAF, 2008) pp. 10, 164–7, 177.

34 B. Félix Maíz, *Mola, aquel hombre* (Barcelona: Planeta, 1976) pp. 92–3; José María Gil Robles, *No fue posible la paz* (Barcelona: Ariel, 1968) pp. 727, 775.

35 Arrarás, *Historia de la cruzada*, III, 12, p. 308; Vicente Gay, *Estampas rojas y caballeros blancos* (Burgos: Hijos de Santiago Rodríguez Editores, 1937) pp. 47–52; Francisco de Cossío, *Hacia una nueva España: de la revolución de octubre a la revolución de Julio 1934–1936* (Valladolid: Editorial Castilla, 1936) pp. 326–7; Ignacio Martín Jiménez, *La guerra civil en Valladolid (1936–1939): amaneceres ensangrentados* (Valladolid: Ámbito Ediciones, 2000) pp. 24–9, 34; Felipe Bertrán Güell, *Preparación y desarrollo del alzamiento nacional* (Valladolid: Librería Santarén, 1939), pp. 202–18.

36 Cossío, *Hacia una nueva España*, pp. 328–31; Gay, *Estampas*, pp. 115–30; Arrarás, *Historia de la cruzada*, III, 12, pp. 310–21; Francisco J. de Raymundo, *Cómo se inició el glorioso Movimiento Nacional en Valladolid y la gesta heróica del Alto del León* (Valladolid: Imprenta Católica, 1936) pp. 6–39; Francisco de Cossío, *Guerra de salvación: del frente de Madrid al de Vizcaya* (Valladolid: Librería Santarén, 1937) pp. 224–9; Domingo Pérez Morán, *¡A estos, que los fusilen al amanecer!* (Madrid: G. del Toro, 1973) pp. 26–32.

37 Jesús María Palomares Ibáñez, *La guerra civil en la ciudad de Valladolid: entusiasmo y represión en la 'capital del alzamiento'* (Valladolid: Ayuntamiento de Valladolid, 2001) p. 22.

38 *Diario Regional* (Valladolid), 21 July 1936; Raymundo, *Cómo se inició*, pp. 44–6; Anon. (Javier Martínez de Bedoya), *Onésimo Redondo Caudillo de Castilla* (Valladolid: Ediciones Libertad, 1937) pp. 203–8; Arrarás, *Historia de la cruzada*, III, 12, pp. 321–2; Martín Jiménez, *Amaneceres ensangrentados*, pp. 95, 181.

39 José Ignacio Escobar, *Así empezó…* (Madrid: G. del Toro, 1974) pp. 56–7; Guillermo Cabanellas, *La guerra de los mil días: nacimiento, vida y muerte de la II República española*, 2 vols (Buenos Aires: Grijalbo, 1973) I, pp. 631–5; José María Iribarren, *Mola: datos para una biografía y para la historia del alzamiento nacional* (Zaragoza: Librería General, 1938) pp. 130–3; Iribarren, *Con el general Mola*, pp. 135–8.

40 Vega Sombría, *Segovia*, pp. 56–7.

41 Author's interview with Mercedes Sanz Bachiller; *Diario Regional* (Valladolid), 26 July 1936; Cossío, *Hacia la nueva España*, p. 97; José Antonio Girón de Velasco, *Si la memoria no me falla* (Barcelona: Planeta, 1994) p. 42; José Luis Mínguez Goyanes, *Onésimo Redondo 1905–1936: precursor sindicalista* (Madrid: Editorial San Martín, 1990) pp. 101–2; Martín Jiménez, *Amaneceres ensangrentados*, pp. 380–2; Julián Casanova, *La Iglesia de Franco* (Madrid: Ediciones Temas de Hoy, 2001) p. 65; Joan Maria Thomàs, *Lo que fue la Falange* (Barcelona: Plaza y Janés, 1999) pp. 295–6.

42 Martín Jiménez, *Amaneceres ensangrentados*, pp. 32–40, 47–65, 76–89, 182–3; Palomares Ibáñez, *Valladolid*, pp. 133–59.

43 Martín Jiménez, *Amaneceres ensangrentados*, pp. 195–9; Palomares Ibáñez, *Valladolid*, pp. 151–5.

44 The figure of 15,000 is given by Gabriel Jackson, *The Spanish Republic and the Civil War* (Princeton, NJ: Princeton University Press, 1965) p. 535. A more modest 9,000 is shared by César M. Lorenzo, *Les anarchistes espagnols et le pouvoir* (Paris: Éditions du Seuil, 1969) p. 204, and 'a Catholic Deputy' in conversation with the British diplomat Bernard Malley, quoted by Thomas, *The Spanish Civil War*, p. 265. A more reasonable 1,600 derives from a contemporary testimony cited by Iturralde, *La guerra de Franco*, I, p. 448. The semi-official figure of 1,303 derives from Ramón Salas Larrazábal, *Pérdidas de la Guerra* (Barcelona: Planeta, 1971) p. 371, and the local estimate of 3,000 from Enrique Berzal de la Rosa, ed., *Testimonio de voces olvidadas*, 2 vols (León: Fundación 27 de marzo, 2007) I, p. 18, II, pp. 178–9.

45 Martín Jiménez, *Amaneceres ensangrentados*, pp. 199–208; Palomares Ibáñez, *Valladolid*, pp. 145–7. The names of the women shot figure in the lists in Palomares Ibáñez, *Valladolid*, pp. 161–85.

46 Ronald Fraser, *Blood of Spain: The Experience of Civil War 1936–1939* (London: Allen Lane, 1979) pp. 167–8; *El Norte de Castilla*, 25 September 1937, reproduced in Rafael Abella, *La vida cotidiana durante la guerra civil: la España Nacional* (Barcelona: Planeta, 1973) pp. 77, 81–2; Iturralde, *La guerra de Franco*, I, pp. 447–9; Martín Jiménez, *Amaneceres ensangrentados*, pp. 220–5; Palomares Ibáñez, *Valladolid*, p. 139; Dionisio Ridruejo, *Casi unas memorias* (Barcelona: Planeta, 1976) pp. 69–70.

47 Vega Sombría, *Segovia*, pp. 114, 240–1.

48 Palomares Ibáñez, *Valladolid*, pp. 161–85.

49 Martín Jiménez, *Amaneceres ensangrentados*, pp. 226–51; Iturralde, *La guerra de Franco*, I, p. 448.

50 Martín Jiménez, *Amaneceres ensangrentados*, pp. 122, 134, 181–2, 199–218; Palomarez Ibáñez, *Valladolid*, pp. 136–51, 161–85; Jesús María Palomares Ibáñez, *El primer franquismo en Valladolid* (Valladolid: Universidad de Valladolid, 2002) pp. 105–13.

51 Arrarás, *Historia de la cruzada*, III, 12, pp. 429–30.

52 *Ibid.*, pp. 430–1; Santiago López García and Severiano Delgado Cruz, 'Víctimas y Nuevo Estado 1936–1940', and Enrique de Sena, 'Guerra, censura y urbanismo: recuerdos de un periodista', in Ricardo Robledo, ed., *Historia de Salamanca*, Vol. V: *Siglo Veinte* (Salamanca: Centro de Estudios Salmantinos, 2001) pp. 227–37, 325–8; Santiago López García and Severiano Delgado Cruz, 'Que no se olvide el castigo: la represión en Salamanca durante la guerra civil', in Ricardo Robledo, ed., *Esta salvaje pesadilla: Salamanca en la guerra civil española* (Barcelona: Editorial Crítica, 2007), pp. 106–7, 110–17; Luciano González Egido, *Agonizar en Salamanca: Unamuno julio–diciembre 1936* (Madrid: Alianza Editorial, 1986) pp. 48–50; Mary Vincent, *Catholicism in the Second Spanish Republic: Religion and Politics in Salamanca 1930–1936* (Oxford: Clarendon Press, 1996) p. 244; Adoración Martín Barrio, María de los Ángeles Sampedro Talabán and María Jesús Velasco Marcos, 'Dos formas de violencia durante la guerra civil: la represión en Salamanca y la resistencia

armada en Zamora', in Julio Aróstegui, ed., *Historia y memoria de la guerra civil*, 3 vols (Valladolid: Junta de Castilla y León, 1988) II, pp. 367–412.

53 Vincent, *Catholicism in Salamanca*, pp. 56–7; Manuel Sánchez, *Maurín, gran enigma de la guerra y otros recuerdos* (Madrid: Edicusa, 1976) pp. 46–7, 79–80.

54 Arrarás, *Historia de la cruzada*, III, 12, p. 426; Severiano Delgado Cruz and Javier Infante Miguel-Mota, 'Nadie preguntaba por ellos: guerra y represión en Salamanca', in Berzal de la Rosa, ed., *Testimonio de voces olvidadas*, I, pp. 300–17.

55 Robledo, ed., *Esta salvaje pesadilla*, pp. xxiii, 286.

56 Lawrence A. Fernsworth, 'Terrorism in Barcelona Today', *Washington Post*, 10 June 1937; Jaime de Armiñán, *La dulce España: memorias de un niño partido en dos* (Barcelona: Tusquets, 2000) p. 169; Sánchez, *Maurín*, p. 93.

57 Juan Bautista Vilar, 'La persecución religiosa en la zona nacionalista: el caso de los protestantes españoles', in Miguel Carlos Gómez Oliver, ed., *Los nuevos historiadores ante la guerra civil española*, 2 vols (Granada: Diputación de Granada, 2002) II, pp. 169–88; José Casado Montado, *Trigo tronzado: crónicas silenciadas y comentarios* (San Fernando: Autor, 1992) p. 48.

58 Miguel de Unamuno, *Epistolario inédito*, Vol. II: *1915–1936* (Madrid: Espasa Calpe, 1991) pp. 350–1.

59 *Ibid.*, pp. 353–5.

60 Miguel de Unamuno, *El resentimiento trágico de la vida: notas sobre la revolución y guerra civil españolas* (Madrid: Alianza Editorial, 1991) p. 57.

61 Vincent, *Catholicism in Salamanca*, pp. 244–6; Sánchez, *Maurín*, p. 93; González Egido, *Agonizar en Salamanca*, pp. 51–8; De Sena,

'Guerra, censura y urbanismo: recuerdos de un periodista', pp. 325–30. On Martín Veloz, see Javier Infante, 'Sables y naipes: Diego Martín Veloz (1875–1938): de cómo un matón de casino se convirtió en caudillo rural', in Robledo, ed., *Esta salvaje pesadilla*, pp. 265–79.

62 Armiñán, *La dulce España*, pp. 164–5; Arrarás, *Historia de la cruzada*, III, 12, p. 432.

63 Ángel Montoto, 'Salamanca: así fue el terrorismo falangista', *Interviú*, No. 177, 4–10 October 1979, pp. 44–7, 'Salamanca: "así me fusilaron los falangistas"', *Interviú*, No. 180, 25 October 1979, p. 778.

64 Agustín Salgado Calvo, *La grama* (Salamanca: Editorial Alcayuela, 2001), pp. 236, 252, 275, 283 and 291; Infante, 'Sables y naipes', p. 424; Armiñán, *La dulce España*, pp. 168–9.

65 Armiñán, *La dulce España*, p. 164; Emilio Salcedo, *Vida de Don Miguel: Unamuno en su tiempo, en su España, en su Salamanca: un hombre en lucha con su leyenda* (Salamanca: Ediciones Anaya, 1964) p. 413; Blanco Prieto, *Miguel de Unamuno: diario final*, pp. 602, 673, 691, 721.

66 Ángel Montoto, 'Salamanca: así fue el terrorismo falangista'; Infante, 'Sables y naipes', pp. 266, 423; Salgado Calvo, *La grama*, pp. 323–6.

67 The idea that he was killed in action in José Venegas, *Andanzas y recuerdos de España* (Montevideo: Feria del Libro, 1948) p. 103; Indalecio Prieto, *De mi vida: recuerdos, estampas, siluetas, sombras* (Mexico City: Ediciones 'El Sitio', 1965) p. 192. The proof of his peaceful death in Infante, 'Sables y naipes', p. 423.

68 Ángel Alcázar de Velasco, *Siete días de Salamanca* (Madrid: G. del Toro, 1976) pp. 132–3.

69 Ricardo Robledo, '"¡Dios se ha hecho generalísimo nuestro!":

dichos y hechos de Castro Albarrán, magistral de Salamanca (1896–1981)', in Robledo, ed., *Esta salvaje pesadilla*, p. 332.

70 Álvarez Bolado, *Para ganar la guerra*, pp. 80–1.

71 *Ibid.*, pp. 78–9.

72 Indalecio Prieto, *Palabras al viento*, 2nd edn (Mexico City: Ediciones Oasis, 1969) pp. 247–8.

73 López García and Delgado Cruz, 'Víctimas y Nuevo Estado', pp. 241–5, 250–5.

74 Iribarren, *Con el general Mola*, pp. 210–11.

75 Joaquín del Moral, *Lo del '10 de agosto' y la justicia* (Madrid: C.I.A.P., 1933) pp. 9–14, 17–23; Joaquín del Moral, *Oligarquía y 'enchufismo'* (Madrid: Imp. Galo Sáez, 1933) *passim*; *Informaciones*, 27 August 1936.

76 Maximiano García Venero, *Falange en la guerra de España: la unificación y Hedilla* (Paris: Ruedo Ibérico, 1967) pp. 232–3; Cabanellas, *La guerra de los mil días*, II, pp. 849–50.

77 Berdugo *et al.*, 'El Ministerio de Justicia en la España "Nacional"', pp. 257–8.

78 Gregorio Herrero Balsa and Antonio Hernández García, *La represión en Soria durante la guerra civil*, 2 vols (Soria: Autores, 1982) I, pp. 8–9, II, pp. 193–4; Antonio Hernández García, 'Guerra y represión en Soria (1936–1939)', in Berzal de la Rosa, ed., *Testimonio de voces olvidadas*, II, pp. 105–11, 155–62.

79 Vega Sombría, *Segovia*, pp. 351–92; Santiago Vega Sombría, *Tras las rejas franquistas: homenaje a los segovianos presos* (Segovia: Foro por la Memoria de Segovia, 2009) pp. 334–47.

80 Vega Sombría, *Segovia*, pp. 36–41; Bertrán Güell, *Preparación y desarrollo*, pp. 280–1.

81 Vega Sombría, *Segovia*, pp. 41–56, 69; Bertrán Güell, *Preparación y desarrollo*, pp. 281–2.

82 Raimundo Fernández Cuesta, 'Los falangistas realizamos el trabajo sucio: fusilar', in Justino Sinova, ed., *Historia del Franquismo: Franco, su régimen y su oposición*, 2 vols (Madrid: Información y Prensa, 1985) I, p. 23; Ángela Cenarro, 'Matar, vigilar, delatar: la quiebra de la sociedad civil durante la guerra y la posguerra en España (1936–1948)', *Historia Social*, No. 44, 2002, pp. 65–86. On the distribution of weaponry, Chaves Palacios, *La represión en la provincia de Cáceres*, p. 102.

83 J. Cifuentes and P. Maluenda, 'De las urnas a los cuarteles: la destrucción de las bases sociales de la República en Zaragoza', in J. Casanova *et al.*, *El pasado oculto: fascimo y violencia en Aragón (1936–1939)* (Madrid: Siglo Veintiuno de España Editores, 1992) pp. 29–78, 41; Vega Sombría, *Segovia*, p. 88.

84 Vega Sombría, *Segovia*, pp. 88–9, 96–9, 105–6.

85 Vega Sombría, *Segovia*, pp. 69–81, 86, 463; Gay, *Estampas*, p. 153. On the Mayor of Navas de Oro, see Jesús Torbado and Manuel Leguineche, *Los topos* (Barcelona: Librería Editorial Argos, 1977) pp. 138–9.

86 Jesús María Palomares Ibáñez, *La guerra civil en Palencia: la eliminación de los contrarios* (Palencia: Ediciones Cálamo, 2002) pp. 121–44; Jesús Gutiérrez Flores, 'Guerra y represión en Palencia (1936–1939)', in Berzal de la Rosa, ed., *Testimonio de voces olvidadas*, I, pp. 217–22, 227–38, 256–7.

87 Javier Rodríguez González, 'Guerra y represión en León', in Berzal de la Rosa, ed., *Testimonio de voces olvidadas*, I, pp. 160–205; José Cabañas González, *La Bañeza 1936: la vorágine de julio*, Vol. I: *Golpe y represión en la comarca Bañezana* (León: Lobo Sapiens, 2010) pp. 93–120.

88 Rodríguez González, 'Guerra y represión en León', pp. 166–7; José Enrique Martínez Fernández and Isabel Cantón Mayo, *Penumbra vital, literaria y educativa de Manuel Santamaría* (León: Universidad de León, 1997) pp. 59–84. I am indebted to Alejandro Valderas Alonso for drawing my attention to this case.

89 Adoración Martín Barrio, María de los Ángeles Sampedro Talabán and María Jesús Velasco Marcos, 'Dos formas de violencia durante la guerra civil; la represión en Salamanca y la resistencia armada en Zamora', in Julio Aróstegui, ed., *Historia y memoria de la guerra civil*, 3 vols (Valladolid: Junta de Castilla y León, 1988) II, pp. 413–37; Cándido Ruiz González and Juan Andrés Blanco Rodríguez, 'La represión en la provincia de Zamora durante la guerra civil y el franquismo', in Berzal de la Rosa, ed., *Testimonio de voces olvidadas*, II, pp. 244–52, 255–85; Ángel Espías Bermúdez, 'Memorias, Año 1936: hechos acaecidos en Zamora y provincia', *Ebre 38. Revista Internacional de la guerra civil*, No. 2, 2003, pp. 62–84. See also Pilar de la Granja Fernández, *Represión durante la guerra civil y la posguerra en la provincia de Zamora* (Zamora: Instituto de Estudios Zamoranos Florián de Ocampo, 2002) which deals with the eastern town of Puebla de Sanabria.

90 Pilar Fidalgo, *A Young Mother in Franco's Prisons* (London: United Editorial, 1939) pp. 5–10, 15–25; Ramón Sender Barayón, *A Death in Zamora* (Albuquerque: University of New Mexico Press, 1989) pp. 109, 127–46, 164–5; *La Opinión – El Correo de Zamora*, 17 February, 29 March, 3, 4, 5, 6, 7, 8, 24 April 2005; Francisco Espinosa Maestre, 'Amparo Barayón: historia de una

Calumnia', in his *Callar al mensajero: la represión franquista entre la libertad de información y el derecho al honor* (Barcelona: Editorial Península, 2009) pp. 97–136.

91 Hilari Raguer, *El general Batet: Franco contra Batet: crónica de una venganza* (Barcelona: Ediciones Península, 1996) pp. 216–86.

92 Antonio Ruiz Vilaplana, *Doy fe … un año de actuación en la España nacionalista* (Paris: Éditions Imprimerie Coopérative Étoile, n.d. [1938]) pp. 30–48, 61–80, 95–8; Luis Castro, *Capital de la Cruzada: Burgos durante la guerra civil* (Barcelona: Editorial Crítica, 2006) pp. 4–7, 211–22; Luis Castro, 'Burgos', in Berzal de la Rosa, ed., *Testimonio de voces olvidadas*, pp. 101–3, 124–40; Isaac Rilova Pérez, *Guerra civil y violencia política en Burgos (1936–1943)* (Burgos: Editorial Dossoles, 2001) pp. 79–98, 251–65, 383–410; Fernando Cardero Azofra and Fernando Cardero Elso, *La guerra civil en Burgos: fusilados, detenidos y represaliados en 1936* (Burgos: Olivares Libros Antiguos, 2009) pp. 33–7, 51–6; Isaac Rilova Pérez, *La guerra civil en Miranda de Ebro (1936–1939): a la luz de la documentación histórica* (Miranda de Ebro: Fundación Cultural Profesor Cantera Burgos, 2008) pp. 175–213.

93 On recruitment for the Falange, see Julio Prada, 'Ya somos todos uno: la unificación de las milicias en la retaguardia franquista: el caso ourensano', in Segon Congrés Recerques, *Enfrontaments civils: postguerres i reconstruccions*, 2 vols (Lleida: Associació Recerques y Pagés Editors, 2002) II, pp. 1102–3; Joan Maria Thomàs, *Lo que fue la Falange* (Barcelona: Plaza y Janés, 1999) pp. 164–5; Alfonso Lazo, *Retrato de fascismo rural en Sevilla*

(Seville: Universidad de Sevilla Secretariado de Publicaciones, 1998) pp. 32–40.

94 López García and Delgado Cruz, 'Que no se olvide el castigo', pp. 121–6; Arrarás, *Historia de la cruzada*, III, 12, p. 382.

95 María del Mar González de la Peña, 'Guerra y represión en Ávila (1936–1939)', in Berzal de la Rosa, ed., *Testimonio de voces olvidadas*, pp. 25–54.

96 Margarita Nelken, *Las torres del Kremlin* (Mexico City: Industrial y Distribuidora, 1943) pp. 320–1; Henry Buckley, *Life and Death of the Spanish Republic* (London: Hamish Hamilton, 1940) p. 235; Aurora Arnaiz, *Retrato hablado de Luisa Julián* (Madrid: Compañía Literaria, 1996) pp. 40–1; Manuel Tagüeña Lacorte, *Testimonio de dos guerras* (Mexico City: Ediciones Oasis, 1973) pp. 124–7.

97 López García and Delgado Cruz, 'Que no se olvide el castigo', pp. 134–5.

98 Alberto Reig Tapia, *Franco 'Caudillo': mito y realidad* (Madrid: Editorial Tecnos, 1995) pp. 222–3.

99 Palomares Ibáñez, *Valladolid*, p. 127.

100 Julio González Soto, *Esbozo de una síntesis del ideario de Mola en relación con el Movimiento Nacional* (Burgos: Hijos de Santiago Rodríguez Editores, 1937) p. 31.

101 Mola, *Obras*, p. 1179.

102 *Ibid.*, p. 1188; González Soto, *Ideario de Mola*, p. 32.

103 Iribarren, *Con el general Mola*, pp. 297–301; Palomares Ibañez, *Valladolid*, p. 54.

104 Ramón Villares, 'Galicia mártir', in Jesús de Juana and Julio Prada, eds, *Lo que han hecho en Galicia: violencia política, represión y exilio (1936–1939)* (Barcelona: Editorial Crítica, 2007) p. viii; Antonio Miguez Macho, *Xenocidio e represión franquista en Galicia: a violencia de*

retagarda en Galicia na Guerra Civil (1936–1939)* (Santiago de Compostela: Edicións Lóstrego, 2009) pp. 54–9.

105 De Juana and Prada, eds, *Lo que han hecho en Galicia*, p. 143. The figure of twenty-seven is based on research in the Registro Civil de Vigo by Antonio Miguez Macho, which he generously shared with me.

106 Carlos Fernández Santander, *Alzamiento y guerra civil en Galicia (1936–1939)*, 2 vols (Sada-A Coruña: Ediciós do Castro, 2000) I, pp. 13, 85–101. The most reliable, and regularly updated, figures for the repression from Lourenzo Fernández Prieto *et al.*, *Vítimas da represión en Galicia, (1936–1939)* (Santiago de Compostela: Universidade de Santiago/Xunta de Galicia, 2009) pp. 11–23. Regarding Lugo, higher figures have been presented by María Jesús Souto Blanco, 'Golpe de Estado y represión franquista en la provincia de Lugo', in De Juana and Prada, eds, *Lo que han hecho en Galicia*, pp. 90–6.

107 Anon., *Lo que han hecho en Galicia: episodios del terror blanco en las provincias gallegas contados por quienes los han vivido* (Paris: Editorial España, n.d. [1938]) pp. 161–74; Carlos Fernández Santander, *El alzamiento de 1936 en Galicia*, 2nd edn (Sada-A Coruña: Ediciós do Castro, 1982) pp. 67–83; Isabel Ríos, *Testimonio de la guerra civil* (Sada-A Coruña: Ediciós do Castro, 1990) pp. 67–8; Fernández Santander, *Alzamiento y guerra civil*, I, pp. 77–84; Emilio Grandío Seone, 'Golpe de Estado y represión franquista en A Coruña', in De Juana and Prada, eds, *Lo que han hecho en Galicia*, pp. 25–38.

108 Xosé Manuel Suárez, *Guerra civil e represión en Ferrol e comarca* (El Ferrol: Concello de Ferrol, 2002) pp. 69–73; Fernández Santander,

Alzamiento y guerra civil, I, pp. 171–203.

109 Grandío Seone, 'Golpe de Estado', pp. 39–42; Fernández Santander, *Alzamiento y guerra civil*, I, pp. 107–12, 118–21, 130–1; Ríos, *Testimonio*, pp. 69–75; X. Amancio Liñares Giraut, *Negreira na guerra do 36* (Sada-A Coruña: Ediciós do Castro, 1993) pp. 105–9; V. Luis Lamela García, *Crónica de una represión en la 'Costa da Morte'* (Sada-A Coruña: Ediciós do Castro, 1995) pp. 69–76, 154–60, 206–14, 242–57, 271–86.

110 Rafael Torres, *Nuestra señora de la cuneta: vida y muerte de la intelectual republicana Juana Capdevielle y de su amor, Francisco Pérez Carballo, governador civil de La Coruña* (Vigo: Edicións Nigra Trea, 2009) p. 49; *La Voz de Galicia*, 26 July 1936.

111 Grandío Seone, 'Golpe de Estado', pp. 46–57; Emilio Grandío Seoane, *Vixiancia e represión na Galicia da guerra civil: o 'Informe Brandariz' (A Coruña, 1937)* (Sada-A Coruña: Ediciós do Castro, 2001) pp. 64–73; Anon., *Lo que han hecho en Galicia*, pp. 200–1.

112 Carmen Blanco, 'Vida e morte de Juana Capdevielle', *Unión Libre. Cadernos de vida e culturas*, No. 11, 2006, pp. 13–21; Torres, *Nuestra señora de la cuneta*, pp. 15–31, 46–7, 111–22. I am grateful to Antonio Miguel Macho for sharing with me his researches in the Registro Civil of Rábade. See also Luis Lamela García, *Estampas de injusticia: la guerra civil del 36 en A Coruña y los documentos originados en la represión* (A Coruña: Ediciós do Castro, 1998) pp. 71, 83, 106; Fernández Santander, *Alzamiento y guerra civil*, I, pp. 94, 156; Manuel D. Benavides, *La escuadra la mandan los cabos*, 2nd edn (Mexico City: Ediciones Roca, 1976) p. 144.

113 I am grateful to Antonio Miguez Macho for providing me with details of the Causa 432/36 held in Vigo against the Alcaldesa and others from A Cañiza. See also Ángel Rodríguez Gallardo, *Memoria e silencio na Galiza contemporánea* (Ponteareas: Edicións Alén Miño, 2008) pp. 18–19.

114 Luis Lamela García, *A Coruña, 1936: memoria convulsa de una represión* (Sada-A Coruña: Ediciós do Castro, 2002) pp. 118–21; Anon., *Lo que han hecho en Galicia*, pp. 211–12.

115 Anon., *Lo que han hecho en Galicia*, pp. 39–43; Lamela García, *A Coruña, 1936*, pp. 189–92.

116 V. Luis Lamela García, *Pepe Miñones: un crimen en la leyenda (1900–1936)* (Sada-A Coruña: Ediciós do Castro, 1991) pp. 293–309, 337, 340–2, 435–8, 461–3, 469–555; Lamela García, *A Coruña, 1936*, pp. 97–102.

117 José Antonio Tojo Ramallo, *Testimonios de una represión: Santiago de Compostela Julio 1936–Marzo 1937* (Sada-A Coruña: Ediciós do Castro, 1990) pp. 15–70; Fernández Santander, *Alzamiento y guerra civil*, I, pp. 219–29.

118 Maria Xesus Arias and Henrique Sanfiz, *Barallobre no pasado* (Fene: Concello de Fene, 1996) pp. 70–3; *La Opinión* (A Coruña), 4 November 2007; Xosé Manuel Suárez, *Guerra civil e represión en Ferrol e comarca* (El Ferrol: Concello de Ferrol, 2002) pp. 191–2, 264.

119 María Jesús Souto Blanco, *La represión franquista en la provincia de Lugo (1936–1940)* (Sada-A Coruña: Ediciós do Castro, 1998) pp. 222–8, 243–72, 361–423; María Jesús Souto Blanco, 'Golpe de estado y represión franquista en la provincia de Lugo', in De Juana and Prada, eds, *Lo que han hecho en Galicia*, pp. 61–96; Fernández

Santander, *Alzamiento y guerra civil*, I, pp. 233–56; Alfonso Santos Alfonso, *La guerra civil en Lugo años 1937, 1938 y 1939* (Sada-A Coruña: Ediciós do Castro, 1993) pp. 17–74.

120 Julio Prada Rodríguez, *Ourense, 1936–1939: alzamento, guerra e represión* (Sada-A Coruña: Ediciós do Castro, 2004) pp. 21–51, 83–95, 153–99; Julio Prada Rodríguez, 'Golpe de estado y represión franquista en la provincia de Ourense', in De Juana and Prada, eds, *Lo que han hecho en Galicia*, pp. 104–8, 112–20; Fernández Santander, *Alzamiento y guerra civil*, I, pp. 257–74; Julio Prada Rodríguez, *De la agitación republicana a la represión franquista: Ourense, 1934–1939* (Barcelona: Editorial Ariel, 2006) pp. 64–134 *et seq*. The fate of the boy is related by A. Domínguez Almansa, 'De los relatos de terror al protagonismo de la memoria: el golpe de estado de 1936 y la larga sombra de la represión', *Historia, Antropología y Fuentes Orales*, No. 40, 2008, pp. 37–74.

121 Antonio Miguez Macho, *O que fixemos en Galicia: ensaio sobre o concepto de práctica xenocida* (Ourense: Difusora de Letras, Artes e Ideas, 2009) pp. 59–62.

122 Dionisio Pereira, 'A represión franquista na provincia de Pontevedra (1936–1950)', *Unión Libre. Cadernos de Vida e Culturas*, No. 9, 2004, pp. 34–9; Ángel Rodríguez Gallardo, 'Golpe de estado y represión franquista en la provincia de Pontevedra', in De Juana and Prada, eds, *Lo que han hecho en Galicia*, pp. 139–64; Fernández Santander, *Alzamiento y guerra civil*, I, pp. 278–311; V. Luis Lamela García, *Inmolados gallegos: Alexandro Bóveda, Víctor Casas, Telmo Bernárdez, Adrio Barreiro …* (Sada-A Coruña: Ediciós do Castro, 1993) pp. 79–96, 224–99.

123 Anon., *Lo que han hecho en Galicia*, pp. 11–36; Fernández Santander, *Alzamiento y guerra civil*, I, pp. 324–36.

124 Anon., *Lo que han hecho en Galicia*, pp. 51–2; Gonzalo Amoedo López and Roberto Gil Moure, *Episodios de terror durante a guerra civil na provincia de Pontevedra: a illa de San Simón* (Vigo: Edicións Xerais de Galicia, 2006) pp. 135–53.

125 Francisco Espinosa Maestre, ed., *Violencia roja y azul: España, 1936–1950* (Barcelona: Editorial Crítica, 2010) pp. 77–8, suggests, on the basis of unpublished research by Pedro Medina Sanabria, that the figure is as high as 2,600. See also Francisco Espinosa Maestre, 'Informe sobre la represión franquista', in Mirta Núñez Díaz-Balart *et al.*, *La gran represión: los años de plomo del franquismo* (Barcelona: Flor del Viento, 2009) pp. 440–1. For specific cases, see Ricardo García Luis, *La justicia de los rebeldes: los fusilados en Santa Cruz de Tenerife 1936–1940* (Canarias: Vacaguaré/Baile del Sol, 1994) pp. 9–10, 13, 81, 167–9; Alfredo Mederos, *República y represión franquista en La Palma* (Santa Cruz de Tenerife: Centro de la Cultura Popular Canaria, 2005) pp. 47–51, 57–66, 70–144, 179–205; Ricardo García Luis and Juan Manuel Torres Vera, *Vallehermoso 'El Fogueo': toma de conciencia popular, resistencia y represión (1930–1942)*, 2nd edn (Tenerife: Baile del Sol, 2000) pp. 181–214, 224–62, 284–96; Miguel Ángel Cabrera Acosta, ed., *La Guerra Civil en Canarias* (La Laguna: Francisco Lemus, 2000) pp. 28–35, 55–64, 74–7, 103–8, 122–32.

126 See the list of names of people executed in Mallorca in Llorenç Capellà, *Diccionari vermell* (Palma de Mallorca: Editorial Moll, 1989)

pp. 19–184. The most reliable recent estimate is by David Ginard i Féron, 'Les repressions de 1936–1939: una anàlisi comparativa', in Pelai Pagès i Blanch, ed., *La guerra civil als Països Catalans* (Valencia: Publicacions de la Universitat de València, 2007) pp. 256–96. See also Lawrence Dundas, *Behind the Spanish Mask* (London: Robert Hale, 1943) pp. 64–79; Jean A. Schalekamp, *De una isla no se puede escapar: Mallorca '36* (Palma de Mallorca: Prensa Universitaria, 1987) pp. 49–72, 105–7, 113–17; Bartomeu Garí Salleras, *Porreres: desfilades de dia, afusellaments de nit* (Palma de Mallorca: Edicions Documenta Balear, 2007) pp. 195–252; Antoni Tugores, *La guerra civil a Manacor: la guerra a casa* (Palma de Mallorca: Edicions Documenta Balear, 2006) pp. 109–15, 179–91, 204–30.

127 Alberto Bayo, *Mi desembarco en Mallorca (de la guerra civil española)* (Palma de Mallorca: Miquel Font Editor, 1987) pp. 105–6; Josep Massot i Muntaner, *El desembarcament de Bayo a Mallorca, Agost–Setembre de 1936* (Barcelona: Publicacions de l'Abadia de Montserrat, 1987) pp. 334–41.

128 Georges Bernanos, *A Diary of my Times* (London: Boriswood, 1938) pp. 66–7, 76, 142–7, 186, 218–24; Josep Massot i Muntaner, *Georges Bernanos i la guerra civil* (Barcelona: Publicacions de l'Abadia de Montserrat, 1989) pp. 156–217; Josep Massot i Muntaner, *Vida i miracles del 'Conde Rossi': Mallorca, agost–decembre 1936, Málaga, gener–febrer 1937* (Barcelona: Publicacions de l'Abadia de Montserrat, 1989) pp. 104–22; Josep Massot i Muntaner, *Guerra civil i repressió a Mallorca* (Barcelona: Publicacions de l'Abadia de Montserrat, 1997) pp. 210–13; Josep Massot i Muntaner, *El Bisbe Josep*

Miralles i l'Esglesia de Mallorca (Barcelona: Publicacions de l'Abadia de Montserrat, 1991) pp. 123–65.

129 Josep Massot i Muntaner, *Els escriptors i la guerra civil a les Illes Balears* (Barcelona: Publicacions de l'Abadia de Montserrat, 1990) pp. 325–67. For a full biography, see Alexandre Font, *Alexandre Jaume Rosselló (1879–1937)* (Palma de Mallorca: Lleonard Muntaner, 2011).

130 David Ginard i Ferón, *L'Esquerra mallorquina i el franquisme* (Palma de Mallorca: Edicions Documenta Balear, 1994) pp. 113, 144–64, 169–72, 188–9; David Ginard i Ferón, *Matilde Landa: de la Institución Libre de Enseñanza a las prisiones franquistas* (Barcelona: Flor de Viento Ediciones, 2005) pp. 132–4, 185–204; Capellà, *Diccionari vermell*, pp. 131–3; David Ginard i Ferón, *Heriberto Quiñones y el movimiento comunista en España (1931–1942)* (Palma de Mallorca and Madrid: Documenta Balear/Compañía Literaria, 2000) pp. 47–52.

131 Nicolau Pons i Llinàs, *Jeroni Alomar Poquet: el capellà mallorquí afusellat pels feixistes el 1937* (Palma de Mallorca: Lleonard Muntaner, 1995) pp. 62–75; Massot i Muntaner, *El Bisbe Josep Miralles*, pp. 184–97.

132 José María Pemán, *Mis almuerzos con gente importante* (Barcelona: Dopesa, 1970) pp. 152–3.

133 Iribarren, *Con el general Mola*, p. 191.

Chapter 7: Far from the Front: Repression behind the Republican Lines

1 *La Vanguardia*, 2 August 1936.

2 *Solidaridad Obrera*, 15 August 1936.

3 *Toronto Daily Star*, 18 August 1936, reproduced in facsimile in Carlos García Santa Cecilia, ed., *Corresponsales en la guerra de*

España (Madrid: Fundación Pablo Iglesias/Instituto Cervantes, 2006) pp. 104–5. *Ibid.*, pp. 170–1, for a Spanish translation. The location and timing of the interview in Abel Paz, *Durruti en la revolución española* (Madrid: Fundación Anselmo Lorenzo, 1996) pp. 529–31.

4 Xavier Diez, *Venjança de classe: causes profundes de la violència revolucionaria a Catalunya el 1936* (Barcelona: Virus Editorial, 2010) pp. 28–30.

5 Casanova to Lisbon, 3 August 1936, *Dez anos de política externa (1936–1947) a nação portuguesa e a segunda guerra mundial*, Vol. III (Lisbon: Imprensa Nacional/Casa da Moeda, 1964) pp. 69–70.

6 Francisco Gutiérrez Latorre, *La República del crimen: Cataluña, prisionera 1936–1939* (Barcelona: Editorial Mare Nostrum, 1989) pp. 18–20.

7 *Daily Express*, 22 July 1936.

8 *Daily Express*, 27 July 1936.

9 *The Times*, 23, 24 July 1936; Albert Manent i Segimon and Josep Raventós i Giralt, *L'Església clandestina a Catalunya durant la guerra civil (1936–1939)* (Barcelona: Publicacions de l'Abadia de Montserrat, 1984) pp. 34–8; Joan Pons Garlandí, *Un republicà enmig de Faistes* (Barcelona: Edicions 62, 2008) p. 61; Luis Carreras, *The Glory of Martyred Spain: Notes on the Religious Persecution* (London: Burns, Oates & Washbourne, 1939) pp. 19–26.

10 Lawrence A. Fernsworth, 'Terrorism in Barcelona Today', *Washington Post*, 10 June 1937; Lawrence Fernsworth, 'Revolution on the Ramblas', in Frank C. Hanighen, ed., *Nothing But Danger* (New York: National Travel Club, 1939) pp. 28–9, 34–5; Lawrence Fernsworth, *Spain's Struggle for Freedom* (Boston: Beacon Press, 1957) pp.

192–20; Frederic Escofet, *Al servei de Catalunya i de la República*, 2 vols (Paris: Edicions Catalanes, 1973) II, p. 383.

11 Macià Irigoye's account in Albert Manent i Segimon, *De 1936 a 1975: estudis sobre la guerra civil i el franquisme* (Barcelona: Publicacions de l'Abadia de Montserrat, 1999) pp. 16–22; Escofet, *Al servei*, II, pp. 381–4; Vicente Guarner, *Cataluña en la guerra de España* (Madrid: G. del Toro, 1975) pp. 124–5; Josep M. Solé i Sabaté and Joan Villarroya i Font, *La repressió a la reraguarda de Catalunya (1936–1939)*, 2 vols (Barcelona: Publicacions de l'Abadia de Montserrat, 1989) I, pp. 82–3; Jordi Albertí, *El silenci de les campanes: de l'anticlericalisme del segle XIX a la persecució religiosa durant la guerra civil a Catalunya* (Barcelona: Proa, 2007) pp. 195–6; Hilari Raguer, *La pólvora y el incienso: la Iglesia y la guerra civil española* (Barcelona: Ediciones Península, 2001), p. 178.

12 Escofet, *Al servei*, II, pp. 371–2, 382.

13 *Ibid.*, pp. 397–8.

14 José Peirats, *La CNT en la revolución española*, 2nd edn, 3 vols (Paris: Ediciones Ruedo Ibérico, 1971) I, pp. 159–60; Juan García Oliver, *El eco de los pasos* (Barcelona: Ruedo Ibérico, 1978), pp. 176–7; Ángel Ossorio y Gallardo, *Vida y sacrificio de Companys* (Buenos Aires: Editorial Losada, 1943) pp. 170–1; Escofet, *Al servei*, II, pp. 406–8.

15 Hugh Thomas, *The Spanish Civil War*, 4th edn (London: Penguin Books, 2003) p. 390. Manuel Goded, *Un 'faccioso' cien por cien* (Zaragoza: Librería General, 1939) pp. 77–96.

16 Diego Abad de Santillán, *Por que perdimos la guerra: una contribución a la historia de la tragedia española*, 2nd edn (Madrid: G. del Toro, 1975) pp. 62–70; Peirats, *La CNT*, I, pp. 157–72.

17 'Más nobleza que pillaje', *Solidaridad Obrera*, 29 July 1936.

18 *Solidaridad Obrera*, 1 August 1936.

19 García Oliver, *El eco de los pasos*, pp. 181–2, 209–12, 231–3; Abad de Santillán, *Por que perdimos la guerra*, pp. 80–1, 93; Pons Garlandí, *Un republicà*, p. 145; Francisco Lacruz, *El alzamiento, la revolución y el terror en Barcelona* (Barcelona: Librería Arysel, 1943) pp. 118–21, 130–1; Solé and Villarroya, *La repressió a la reraguarda*, I, pp. 94–100; Gregorio Rodríguez Fernández, *El hábito y la cruz: religiosas asesinadas en la guerra civil española* (Madrid: EDIBESA, 2006) pp. 298–311; Gutiérrez Latorre, *La República del crimen*, pp. 36–7, 44–7.

20 Joan Villarroya i Font, *Revolució i guerra civil a Badalona 1936–1939* (Badalona: Mascaró de Proa, 1986) pp. 33–8; Josep M. Cuyàs Tolosa, *Diari de guerra: Badalona, 1936–1939*, 2 vols (Badalona: Museu de Badalona, 2006) I, pp. 144, 206, 249, II, pp. 12–14, 37–8, 57, 82, 353; Solé and Villarroya, *La repressió a la reraguarda*, I, pp. 8, 72–8; Toni Orensanz, *L'Òmnibus de la mort: parada Falset* (Badalona: Ara Llibres, 2008) pp. 135–40, 266–9; Pons Garlandí, *Un republicà*, pp. 88–92; Jordi Piqué i Padró, *La crisi de la reraguarda: revolució i guerra civil a Tarragona (1936–1939)* (Barcelona: Publicacions de l'Abadia de Montserrat, 1998) pp. 147–54; Isidre Cunill, *Los sicarios de la retaguardia (1936–1939): in odium fidei: la verdad del genocidio contra el clero en Catalunya* (Barcelona: Styria, 2010) pp. 111–24.

21 Miguel Íñiguez, *Enciclopedia histórica del anarquismo español*, 3 vols (Vitoria: Asociación Isaac Puente, 2008) I, p. 649; Orensanz, *L'Òmnibus*, pp. 171–5. Juan Giménez Arenas, *De la Unión a Banat: itinerario de una rebeldía* (Madrid: Fundación de Estudios Libertarios Anselmo Lorenzo, 1996) pp. 64–6, relates Fresquet's later bullying in a military unit.

22 Sebastián Cirac Estopañán, *Los héroes y mártires de Caspe* (Zaragoza: Imp. Octavio y Félez, 1939) pp. 23–35, 37–58, 134–6; Fermín Morales Cortés, *Caspe combatiente, cautivo y mutilado: estampas de la revolución* (Caspe: La Tipográfica, 1940) pp. 23–39, 43–50, 57–70, 73–6, 81–9; José Luis Ledesma Vera, *Los días de llamas de la revolución: violencia y política en la retaguardia republicana de Zaragoza durante la guerra civil* (Zaragoza: Institución Fernando el Católico, 2003) pp. 45–6, 53–9, 74–7, 82; Julián Casanova, *Caspe, 1936–1938: conflictos políticos y transformaciones sociales durante la guerra civil* (Zaragoza: Institución Fernando el Católico, 1984) pp. 35–40; José Luis Ledesma Vera, 'Qué violencia para qué retaguardia, o la República en guerra de 1936', *Ayer. Revista de Historia Contemporánea*, No. 76, 2009, p. 106; José Manuel Márquez Rodríguez and Juan José Gallardo Romero, *Ortiz: General sin Díos ni amo* (Barcelona: Editorial Hacer, 1999) pp. 110–13; Orensanz, *L'Òmnibus*, pp. 65–6, 129–31, 191–2.

23 Ledesma Vera, *Los días de llamas*, pp. 141–3; Solé and Villarroya, *La repressió a la reraguarda*, II, pp. 320–1, 324–5; Orensanz, *L'Òmnibus*, pp. 17–19, 100–6.

24 Orensanz, *L'Òmnibus*, pp. 35–7, 41–7, 74–9, 86–90, 112–15, 128, 145–9; Solé and Villarroya, *La repressió a la reraguarda*, II, pp. 314–15, 349–50.

25 Josep Banqué i Martí, *Comunistes i catalans* (Reus: Associació d'Estudis Reusencs, 2004) pp. 116–17; Orensanz, *L'Òmnibus*, pp. 177–9, 190–1, 197–8, 259–63.

26 Pons Garlandí, *Un republicà*, pp. 68–70, 84–6, 90–1, 104–5, 114–16; Solé and Villarroya, *La repressió a la reraguarda*, I, pp. 95–103; César M. Lorenzo, *Los anarquistas españoles y el poder 1868–1969* (Paris: Ruedo Ibérico, 1972) pp. 92–3; Carlos Semprún-Maura, *Revolución y contrarrevolución en Cataluña (1936–1937)* (Barcelona: Tusquets Editor, 1978) pp. 59–65.

27 García Oliver, *El eco de los pasos*, pp. 229–30; Jaume Miravitlles, *Episodis de la guerra civil espanyola* (Barcelona: Editorial Pòrtic, 1972) p. 128; Federica Montseny, *Mis primeros cuarenta años* (Barcelona: Plaza y Janés, 1987) p. 95; Solé and Villarroya, *La repressió a la reraguarda*, pp. 110–13.

28 *Solidaridad Obrera*, 30 July 1936; Baltasar Porcel, *La revuelta permanente* (Barcelona: Planeta, 1978) pp. 126–30; Solé and Villarroya, *La repressió a la reraguarda*, II, p. 91.

29 García Oliver, *El eco de los pasos*, pp. 230–1; Chris Ealham, *Class, Culture and Conflict in Barcelona 1898–1937* (London: Routledge/Cañada Blanch Studies, 2004) p. 176; Porcel, *La revuelta permanente*, pp. 126–9. I am immensely grateful to Chris Ealham for information regarding the death of Gardenyes.

30 Sandoval, 'Informe de mi actuación', AHN, FC-Causa General, 150-1, pp. 211–12.

31 Pons Garlandí, *Un republicà*, pp. 76–84; Hilari Raguer, *Salvador Rial, vicari del cardenal de la pau* (Barcelona: Publicacions de l'Abadia de Montserrat, 1993) pp. 32–4; Solé and Villarroya, *La repressió a la reraguarda*, I, pp. 179–82; Hilari Raguer, *La pólvora y el incienso: la Iglesia y la guerra civil española* (Barcelona: Ediciones Península, 2001) pp. 201–3; Ian Gibson, *Queipo de Llano: Sevilla, verano de 1936* (Barcelona: Grijalbo, 1936) p. 405.

32 Ignasi Riera, *Los catalanes de Franco* (Barcelona: Plaza y Janés, 1998) pp. 127, 172–3.

33 Josep M. Martí Bonet, *El martiri dels temples a la diocesi de Barcelona (1936–1939)* (Barcelona: Arxiu Diocesà de Barcelona, 2008) pp. 37–8, 42–9.

34 Raguer, *La pólvora y el incienso*, pp. 175–9; Ferran Casas Mercadé, *Valls: la guerra civil (quan no hi havia pau ni treva) 1936–1939* (Valls: Institut d'Estudis Vallencs, 1983) pp. 163–72; Martí Bonet, *El martiri dels temples*, pp. 50–4; José Sanabre Sanromá, *Martirologio de la Iglesia en la Diócesis de Barcelona durante la persecución religiosa 1936–1939* (Barcelona: Editorial Librería Religiosa, 1943) pp. 29–35.

35 Martí Bonet, *El martiri dels temples*, pp. 54–5; Francesc Xavier Puig Rovira, *Vilanova i la Geltrú 1936–1939: guerra civil, revolució i ordre social* (Barcelona: Publicacions de l'Abadia de Montserrat, 2005) pp. 65–78, 445–7; Jaume Barrull Pelegrí, *Violència popular i justícia revolucionària: el Tribunal Popular de Lleida (1936–1937)* (Lleida: Edicions de l'Universitat de Lleida, 1995) pp. 36–41.

36 Gregorio Gallego, *Madrid, corazón que se desangra* (Madrid: G. del Toro, 1976) pp. 136–7; Julián Casanova, *De la calle al frente: el anarcosindicalismo en España (1931–1939)* (Barcelona: Editorial Crítica, 1997) pp. 155–9.

37 Fray Justo Pérez de Urbel, *Los mártires de la Iglesia (testigos de su fe)* (Barcelona: AHR, 1956) pp. 182–8; Cándido, *Memorias prohibidas* (Barcelona: Ediciones B, 1995) pp. 147–51.

38 Antonio Montero Moreno, *Historia de la persecución religiosa en España 1936–1939* (Madrid: Biblioteca de

Autores Cristianos, 1961) pp. 430, 762; Rodríguez Fernández, *El hábito y la cruz*, pp. 594–6.

39 The definitive study is by Rodríguez Fernández, *El hábito y la cruz*. See also Montero Moreno, *Historia de la persecución religiosa*, pp. 433–4; Sanabre Sanromá, *Martirologio*, pp. 183–211, 470–1; Julián Casanova, *La Iglesia de Franco*, 2nd edn (Barcelona: Editorial Crítica, 2005) pp. 188–92; Frances Lannon, 'Los cuerpos de las mujeres y el cuerpo político católico: autoridades e identidades en conflicto en España durante las décadas de 1920 y 1930', *Historia Social*, No. 35 (1999), pp. 65–80; Mary Vincent, '"The Keys to the Kingdom": Religious Violence in the Spanish Civil War, July–August 1936', in Chris Ealham and Michael Richards, eds, *The Splintering of Spain: Cultural History and the Spanish Civil War, 1936–1939* (Cambridge, 2005) pp. 86–7.

40 Solé and Villarroya, *La repressió a la reraguarda*, I, pp. 179–86; Raguer, *Salvador Rial*, pp. 34–5; Manuel Azaña, *Apuntes de memoria inéditos y cartas 1938–1939–1940* (Valencia: Pre-Textos, 1990) pp. 128–9; Enrique de Rivas, *Comentarios y notas a 'Apuntes de memoria' de Manuel Azaña* (Valencia: Pre-Textos, 1990) p. 83.

41 Manent and Raventós, *L'Església clandestina*, pp. 46–8; Raguer, *Salvador Rial*, pp. 33–4, 211–14.

42 Ramón Muntanyola, *Vidal i Barraquer: cardenal de la pau*, 2nd edn (Barcelona: Publicaciones de l'Abadia de Montserrat, 1976) pp. 353–85, 401–15; Josep María Tarragona, *Vidal i Barraquer: de la República al franquisme* (Barcelona: Columna Assaig, 1998) pp. 188–201; Piqué i Padró, *La crisi de la reraguarda*, pp. 125–8; Raguer, *Salvador Rial*, pp. 207–12.

43 Piqué i Padró, *La crisi de la reraguarda*, pp. 132–48. The figure of 136 is from Martí Bonet, *El martiri dels temples*, p. 56. Marginally different figures for all the Catalan dioceses are given in Montero Moreno, *Historia de la persecución religiosa*, pp. 763–4.

44 Raguer, *Salvador Rial*, pp. 23–7.

45 Sanabre Sanromá, *Martirologio*, pp. 421–3; Montero Moreno, *Historia de la persecución religiosa*, pp. 416–21; Alberto Onaindia, *Hombre de paz en la guerra* (Buenos Aires: Editorial Vasca Ekin, 1973) pp. 421–9; Martí Bonet, *El martiri dels temples*, pp. 61–3; Vicente Cárcel Ortí, *Caídos, víctimas y mártires: la Iglesia y la hecatombe de 1936* (Madrid: Espasa Calpe, 2008) pp. 447–50, 489; Solé and Villarroya, *La repressió a la reraguarda*, pp. 176–7; Antonio Sospedra Buyé, CP, CR, *La misteriosa muerte del Santo Mártir Obispo de Barcelona Doctor Manuel Irurita y Almandoz* (Barcelona: EGS, 2008) pp. 278–95.

46 Piqué i Padró, *La crisi de la reraguardia*, p. 138.

47 Casas Mercadé, *Valls: la guerra civil*, pp. 159–62.

48 Solé and Villarroya, *La repressió a la reraguarda*, I, pp. 79–81; Rodríguez Fernández, *El hábito y la cruz*, pp. 298–311; Montero Moreno, *Historia de la persecución religiosa*, pp. 526–9; Pons Garlandí, *Un republicà*, pp. 68–70, 86–9, 95.

49 Abad de Santillán, *Por que perdimos la guerra*, pp. 92–3; Samblancat's version in Peirats, *La CNT*, II, pp. 77–81; *Solidaridad Obrera*, 11, 12 August 1936; *La Vanguardia*, 12 August 1936.

50 Eduardo Barriobero y Herrán, *Un tribunal revolucionario: cuenta rendida por el que fue su presidente* (Barcelona: Imprenta y Librería Aviñó, 1937) pp. 39–51, 141–9; Lorenzo, *Los anarquistas españoles*,

p. 93; Solé and Villarroya, *La repressió a la reraguarda*, I, pp. 114–16; Lacruz, *El alzamiento*, pp. 151–9.

51 Barriobero y Herrán, *Un tribunal revolucionario*, pp. 40–7; Marià Rubió i Tudurí, *Barcelona 1936–1939* (Barcelona: Publicacions de l'Abadia de Montserrat, 2002) pp. 113–18; Solé and Villarroya, *La repressió a la reraguarda*, I, pp. 66, 116–21; Pons Garlandí, *Un republicà*, pp. 92, 144; Manuel Benavides, *Guerra y revolución en Cataluña*, 2nd edn (Mexico City: Ediciones Roca, 1978) pp. 197–201.

52 *Solidaridad Obrera*, 30 August 1936.

53 Benavides, *Guerra y revolución*, pp. 196–7.

54 Pons Garlandí, *Un republicà*, pp. 72–4, 117–19; Semprún-Maura, *Revolución y contrarrevolución*, pp. 53–8; Joaquín Almendros, *Situaciones españolas: 1936/1939: el PSUC en la guerra civil española* (Barcelona: Dopesa, 1976) pp. 100–1; Pelai Pagès i Blanch, *Cataluña en guerra y en revolución 1936–1939* (Seville: Ediciones Espuela de Plata, 2007) pp. 170–1.

55 *Informaciones*, 16, 18 September 1936.

56 Eduard Masjuan Bracons, 'Eduardo Barriobero y Herrán i la justícia revolucionària a la Barcelona de 1936', Segon Congrés Recerques, *Enfrontaments civils: postguerres i reconstruccions*, 2 vols (Lleida: Associació Recerques y Pagés Editors, 2002) II, pp. 1024–35. A robust but somewhat disingenuous defence of his activities was mounted by Barriobero himself and by the editor of *Solidaridad Obrera*, Jacinto Toryho. See Barriobero y Herrán, *Un tribunal revolucionario*, pp. 119–20, 147–56, 178–92, 195–205, and Jacinto Toryho, *No eramos tan malos* (Madrid: G. del Toro, 1975) pp. 199–257. For Nin's

role, see Francesc Bonamusa, *Andreu Nin y el movimiento comunista en España (1930–1937)* (Barcelona: Editorial Anagrama, 1977) pp. 293, 309, 426–9; Pelai Pagès i Blanch, *Andreu Nin: una vida al servei de la classe obrera* (Barcelona: Laertes, 2009) pp. 225–7.

57 Solé and Villarroya, *La repressió a la reraguarda*, pp. 12, 217–39; Pons Garlandí, *Un republicà*, pp. 93–5, 169–70; Peirats, *La CNT*, II, pp. 263–4.

58 Pons Garlandí, *Un republicà*, pp. 129–57; Josep Sánchez Cervelló, *¿Por qué hemos sido derrotados? Las divergencias republicanas y otras cuestiones* (Barcelona: Flor del Viento, 2006) pp. 111–14; Enric Ucelay da Cal, 'El complot nacionalista contra Companys', in Josep Maria Solé i Sabaté, ed., *La guerra civil a Catalunya*, Vol. III: *Catalunya, centre neuràlgic de la guerra* (Barcelona: Edicions 62, 2004) pp. 209–12.

59 Escofet, *Al servei*, II, p. 376; Barrull Pelegrí, *Violència popular i justícia revolucionària*, pp. 19–33; Jaume Barrull Pelegrí and Conxita Mir Curcó, eds, *Violència política i ruptura social a Espanya 1936–1945* (Lleida: Edicions de l'Universitat de Lleida, 1994) pp. 67–79; Solé and Villarroya, *La repressió a la reraguarda*, I, pp. 87–8, II, pp. 467–84; Montero Moreno, *Historia de la persecución religiosa*, pp. 369–73; Pons Garlandí, *Un republicà*, pp. 80–3, 89.

60 Tomàs Pàmies and Teresa Pàmies, *Testament a Praga* (Barcelona: Edicions Destino, 1971) pp. 128–31, 135–9; Solé and Villarroya, *La repressió a la reraguarda*, II, pp. 447–9.

61 Peirats, *La CNT*, I, pp. 173–5.

62 Joan Peiró, *Perill a la reraguarda* (Mataró: Edicions Llibertat, 1936) pp. 39–40.

63 Piqué i Padró, *La crisi de la reraguarda*, pp. 149–59.

64 *Solidaridad Obrera*, 30 August 1936.

65 *Solidaridad Obrera*, 17 December 1936; Hilari Raguer, *Divendres de passió: vida i mort de Manuel Carrasco i Formiguera* (Barcelona: Publicaciones de l'Abadia de Montserrat, 1984) pp. 250–8; Josep Benet, *Manuel Carrasco i Formiguera, afusellat* (Barcelona: Edicions 62, 2009) pp. 23–8. On Balius, see Miguel Íñiguez, *Enciclopedia histórica del anarquismo español*, 3 vols (Vitoria: Asociación Isaac Puente, 2008) I, pp. 159–60.

66 Raguer, *Divendres de passió*, pp. 258–78, 334–46, 373–90; Benet, *Manuel Carrasco i Formiguera*, pp. 84–5.

67 Peiró, *Perill a la reraguarda*, pp. 131–2.

68 Josep Termes, *Misèria contra pobresa: els fets de la Fatarella del gener de 1937: un exemple de la resistència pagesa contra la collectivització agrària durant la guerra civil* (Catarroja, Valencia: Editorial Afers, 2005) pp. 53–74, 81–107; Carles Gerhard, *Comissari de la Generalitat a Montserrat (1936–1939)* (Barcelona: Publicacions de l'Abadia de Montserrat, 1982) pp. 487–90; Peirats, *La CNT*, II, pp. 128–9; Pons Garlandí, *Un republicà*, pp. 105–8; Villaroya i Font, *Revolució i guerra a Badalona*, p. 37.

69 Solé and Villarroya, *La repressió a la reraguarda*, I, p. 68.

70 Ehrenburg to Rosenberg, 18 September 1936, Ronald Radosh, Mary R. Habeck and Grigory Sevostianov, eds, *Spain Betrayed: The Soviet Union in the Spanish Civil War* (New Haven: Yale University Press, 2001) pp. 28, 75–6.

71 *La Vanguardia*, 1, 2 August 1936; Peirats, *La CNT*, I, p. 176.

72 Antonov-Ovseenko, 14 October 1936, Radosh, Habeck and Sevostianov, *Spain Betrayed*, pp. 75–7.

73 Solé and Villarroya, *La repressió a la reraguarda*, I, pp. 103–4; Albertí, *El silencí de les campanes*, pp. 260–1; Raguer, *La pólvora y el incienso*, p. 219; Miquel Mir, *El preu de la traïció: la FAI, Tarradellas i l'assassinat de 172 Maristes* (Barcelona: Pòrtic Visions, 2010) pp. 55–140, 222–6. There is a highly tendentious account of this by García Oliver, *El eco de los pasos*, pp. 467–71.

74 Report of Maurice Thorez to Comintern Secretariat, 19 September 1936, Carlos Serrano, *L'Enjeu espagnol: PCF et guerre d'Espagne* (Paris: Messidor/Éditions Sociales, 1987) pp. 182–215; Report of André Marty to Comintern Secretariat, 10 October 1936, Radosh, Habeck and Sevostianov, *Spain Betrayed*, pp. 46, 55.

75 Vicent Gabarda Cebellán, *La represión en la retaguardia republicana: País Valenciano (1936–1939)* (Valencia: Edicions Alfons el Magnànim, 1996) pp. 25–33; J. Daniel Simeón Riera, *Entre la rebellia i la tradició (Llíria durant la República i la guerra civil 1931–1939)* (Valencia: Diputació de Valencia, 1993) pp. 201–10; Vicente Cárcel Ortí, *La persecución religiosa en España durante la segunda República (1931–1939)* (Madrid: Ediciones Rialp, 1990) pp. 211–14.

76 Ledesma Vera, *Los días de llamas*, pp. 9, 83–123.

77 José María Azpiroz Pascual, *La voz del olvido: la guerra civil en Huesca y la Hoya* (Huesca: Diputación Provincial de Huesca, 2007) pp. 441–9; Luisa Marco Sola, *Sangre de cruzada: el catolicismo oscense frente a la guerra civil (1936–1939)* (Huesca: Instituto de Estudios

Altoaragoneses/Diputación Provincial de Huesca, 2009) pp. 114–19; María Pilar Salomón Chéliz, *Anticlericalismo en Aragón: protesta popular y movilización política (1900–1939)* (Zaragoza: Prensas Universitarias de Zaragoza, 2002) pp. 292–301.

78 Marco Sola, *Sangre de cruzada*, pp. 120–2; Montero Moreno, *Historia de la persecución religiosa*, p. 525; Rodríguez Fernández, *El hábito y la cruz*, pp. 316–20.

79 Ester Casanova Nuez, *La violencia política en la retaguardia republicana de Teruel durante la guerra civil* (Teruel: Instituto de Estudios Turolenses de la Diputación de Teruel, 2007) pp. 37–49, 169–77; Abel Paz, *Crónica de la Columna de Hierro* (Barcelona: Virus Editorial, 2001) pp. 50–2.

80 Jesús Hernández, *Negro y rojo: los anarquistas en la revolución española* (Mexico City: La España Contemporánea, 1946) pp. 227–41; Miquel Siguan, 'Els anarquistes valencians al front de Llevant', *Estudis d'Història del País Valencià*, No. 7, 1982, pp. 273–6; Paz, *Columna de Hierro*, pp. 49–52; Aurora Bosch Sánchez, *Colectivistas (1936–1939)* (Valencia: Almudín, 1980) pp. ix–xxxii; Aurora Bosch Sánchez, *Ugetistas y libertarios: guerra civil y revolución en el País Valenciano, 1936–1939)* (Valencia: Institución Alfons el Magnànim, 1983) pp. 43–57; Eladi Mainar Cabanes, *De milicians a soldats: les columnes valencianes en la guerra civil espanyola (1936–1937)* (Valencia: Universitat de València, 1998) pp. 49–50, 54–6.

81 José Ramón Carbonell Rubio, 'La traición de la Puebla: milicianos saguntinos en la columna Fernández Bujanda', in *Braçal* (Sagunto), No. 34, 2006, pp. 69–92; Juan Bautista Mari Clérigues, 'La Guardia Civil en el Alzamiento Nacional: la columna de Puebla de Valverde', *Revista de Estudios Históricos de la Guardia Civil*, No. 2, 1968, pp. 120–1.

82 *La Vanguardia*, 11, 14, 21 August 1936; Mari Clerigues, 'La Guardia Civil en el Alzamiento Nacional: la columna de Puebla de Valverde', *Revista de Estudios Históricos de la Guardia Civil*, No. 2, 1968, pp. 107–126 and No. 3, 1969, pp. 99–118; Joaquín Arrarás, *Historia de la cruzada española*, 8 vols, 36 tomos (Madrid: Ediciones Españolas, 1939–43) IV, 15, pp. 240–2; Ramón Salas Larrazábal, *Historia del ejército popular de la República*, 4 vols (Madrid: Editora Nacional, 1973) I, pp. 307–8; Servicio Histórico Militar (José Manuel Martínez Bande), *La invasión de Aragón y el desembarco en Mallorca* (Madrid: Editorial San Martín, 1989) pp. 89–91; Ángela Cenarro Lagunas, *El fin de la esperanza: fascismo y guerra civil en la provincia de Teruel (1936–1939)* (Teruel: Instituto de Estudios Turolenses de la Diputación de Teruel, 1996) pp. 52–5; Dolores Ibárruri *et al.*, *Guerra y revolución en España 1936–39*, 4 vols (Moscow: Editorial Progreso, 1966–77) I, 171–2; José María Maldonado Moya, *El frente de Aragón: la guerra civil en Aragón (1936–1938)* (Zaragoza: Mira Editores, 2007) p. 64; José Luis Ledesma and José María Maldonado Moya, eds, *La Guerra Civil en Aragón*, 14 vols (Barcelona: Ciro Ediciones/El Periódico de Aragón, 2006) II, p. 82.

83 Manuel Girona Rubio, *Una miliciana en la Columna de Hierro: María 'La Jabalina'* (Valencia: Universitat de València, 2007) pp. 35–7; Carlos Llorens Castillo, *La primera década: una aportación al proceso político e ideológico del franquismo y a la historia del Partido*

Comunista de España (Valencia: Fernando Torres, 1983).

84 *La Vanguardia*, 11, 14 August 1936; Carbonell Rubio, 'La traición de la Puebla', p. 85; Mainar Cabanes, *De milicians a soldats*, pp. 19–20; Ministerio de la Guerra, Estado Mayor Central, *Anuario Militar de España 1936* (Madrid: Imprenta y Talleres del Ministerio de la Guerra, 1936) p. 322.

85 Mainar Cabanes, *De milicians a soldats*, pp. 49–50, 57–8; Siguan, 'Els anarquistes valencians', pp. 276–81; Hernández, *Negro y rojo*, p. 222; Juan Andrade, 'La Columna de Hierro', *La Batalla*, 13 March 1937, reproduced in Juan Andrade, *La revolución española día a día* (Barcelona: Editorial Nueva Era/ Publicaciones Trazo, 1979) pp. 187–8; Paz, *Columna de Hierro*, p. 39; Gabriel Araceli, *Valencia 1936* (Zaragoza: El Noticiero, 1939) pp. 111–15.

86 Gabarda Cebellán, *La represión*, p. 30; Siguan, 'Els anarquistes valencians', pp. 282–4; Mainar Cabanes, *De milicians a soldats*, pp. 72–80; Hernández, *Negro y rojo*, pp. 242–4; Terence M. Smyth, *La CNT al País Valencià 1936–1937* (Valencia: Editorial Eliseu Climent, 1977) pp. 53–7; Paz, *Columna de Hierro*, pp. 70–6; Adolfo Bueso, *Recuerdos de un cenetista*, Vol. II: *De la Segunda República al final de la guerra civil* (Barcelona: Ariel, 1978) p. 220.

87 Mainar Cabanes, *De milicians a soldats*, pp. 80–3; Smyth, *La CNT al País Valencià*, pp. 57–8; Paz, *Columna de Hierro*, pp. 85–9; Carlos Llorens, *La guerra en Valencia y en el frente de Teruel: recuerdos y comentarios* (Valencia: Fernando Torres, 1978) pp. 50–1; Hernández, *Negro y rojo*, pp. 244–8.

88 Vicente Ramos, *La guerra civil (1936–1939) en la provincia de Alicante*, 3 vols (Alicante: Ediciones Biblioteca Alicantina, 1973) I, pp. 133–9; Arrarás, *Historia de la cruzada*, V, 23, pp. 548–60; José Luis Ledesma, 'La "santa ira popular" del 36: la violencia en la guerra civil y revolución, entre cultura y política', in Javier Muñoz Soro, José Luis Ledesma and Javier Rodrigo, *Culturas y políticas de la violencia: España siglo XX* (Madrid: Siete Mares Editorial, 2005) pp. 156–7.

89 Juan Martínez Leal, *República y guerra civil en Cartagena (1931– 1939)* (Murcia: Universidad de Murcia/Ayuntamiento de Cartagena, 1993) pp. 196–201; Carmen González Martínez, *Guerra civil en Murcia: un análisis sobre el Poder y los comportamientos colectivos* (Murcia: Universidad de Murcia, 1999) pp. 158–9.

90 González Martínez, *Guerra civil en Murcia*, pp. 159–61; Martínez Leal, *República y guerra civil en Cartagena*, pp. 203–11.

91 González Martínez, *Guerra civil en Murcia*, pp. 161–8, 197–211; Martínez Leal, *República y guerra civil en Cartagena*, pp. 200–2, 211–12.

92 Arrarás, *Historia de la cruzada*, VI, 24, p. 97; Edward Norton, *Muerte en Málaga: testimonio de un americano sobre la guerra civil española* (Málaga: Universidad de Málaga, 2004) pp. 170–87, 193–208, 225–42; Antonio Nadal, *Guerra civil en Málaga* (Málaga: Editorial Arguval, 1984) pp. 166–7, 170–2, 180–5; Juan Antonio Ramos Hitos, *Guerra civil en Málaga 1936–1937: revisión histórica*, 2nd edn (Málaga: Editorial Algazara, 2004) pp. 222–62.

93 Ledesma, 'La "santa ira popular" del 36', p. 157.

94 Ramos Hitos, *Guerra civil en Málaga*, p. 251.

95 Francisco Cobo Romero, *Conflicto rural y violencia política: el largo*

camino hacia la dictadura: JAÉN, 1917–1950 (Jaén: Publicaciones de la Universidad de Jaén, 1999) pp. 267–78; Luis Miguel Sánchez Tostado, *La guerra civil en Jaén: historia de un horror inolvidable* (Jaén: Junta de Andalucía/Colección Memoria Histórica, 2005) pp. 79–80, 86–7, 97, 133.

96 Eulàlia Vega, *Anarquistas y sindicalistas durante la segunda República: la CNT y los Sindicatos de Oposición en el País Valenciano* (Valencia: Edicions Alfons el Magnànim, 1987) p. 283; Miguel Ors Montenegro, *Elche, una ciudad en guerra (1936–1939)* (Elche: Llibreria Ali i Truc, 2008) pp. 107–11, 120–3, 128–9, 143–5; Montero Moreno, *Historia de la persecución religiosa*, pp. 787, 780, 858, 873.

97 Miguel Ors Montenegro, 'La represión de guerra y posguerra en Alicante 1936–1939' (unpublished doctoral thesis, Universitat d'Alacant, 1993) pp. 51, 67–9.

98 *Ibid.*, pp. 130–3, 337, 342–3. I am grateful to Miguel Ors Montenegro for the anecdote about the fate of the church in Alcoy.

99 For comparative analysis, see Ledesma Vera, *Los días de llamas*, pp. 83–4; Ledesma Vera, 'Qué violencia para qué retaguardia', pp. 83–114. For Toledo, see José María Ruiz Alonso, *La guerra civil en la provincia de Toledo: Utopía, conflicto y poder en el sur del Tajo (1936–1939)*, 2 vols (Ciudad Real: Almud, Ediciones de Castilla-La Mancha, 2004), I, pp. 285–9. For the Terra Alta, see Solé and Villarroya, *La repressió a la reraguarda*, I, pp. 431–3.

Chapter 8: Revolutionary Terror in Madrid

1 Aurelio Núñez Morgado, *Los sucesos de España vistos por un diplomático* (Buenos Aires: Talleres Rosso, 1941) p. 155; Luis Enrique Délano, *Cuatro meses de guerra civil en Madrid* (Santiago de Chile: Editorial Panorama, 1937) pp. 25–6; Glicerio Sánchez Recio, *Justicia y guerra en España: los tribunales populares (1936–1939)* (Alicante: Instituto de Cultura 'Juan Gil-Albert', 1994) pp. 25–7, 36–41.

2 Maximiano García Venero, *El general Fanjul: Madrid en el alzamiento nacional* (Madrid: Ediciones Cid, 1967) pp. 338–44; Arturo Barea, *The Forging of a Rebel* (London: Davis-Poynter, 1972) pp. 528–32; Délano, *Cuatro meses de guerra civil en Madrid*, pp. 12–13; Joaquín Arrarás, *Historia de la cruzada española*, 8 vols, 36 tomos (Madrid: Ediciones Españolas, 1939–43) IV, 17, pp. 403–9, 434–68; José Martín Blázquez, *I Helped to Build an Army: Civil War Memoirs of a Spanish Staff Officer* (London: Secker & Warburg, 1939) pp. 111–17; Julián Zugazagoitia, *Guerra y vicisitudes de los españoles*, 2nd edn, 2 vols (Paris: Librería Española, 1968) I, pp. 69–71; Eduardo de Guzmán, *La muerte de la esperanza* (Madrid: G. del Toro, 1973) pp. 133–73; Luis Romero, *Tres días de julio (18, 19 y 20 de 1936)*, 2nd edn (Barcelona: Ariel, 1968) pp. 414–16, 432–5, 457–62, 469–91, 543–58.

3 Mary Bingham de Urquidi, *Mercy in Madrid: Nursing and Humanitarian Protection during the Spanish Civil War, 1936–37* (Córdoba, Argentina: Ediciones del Sur, 2004) pp. 21–2.

4 Núñez Morgado, *Los sucesos de España*, p. 155.

5 Barea, *The Forging of a Rebel*, pp. 525–8.

6 Causa General, *La dominación roja en España* (Madrid: Ministerio de Justicia, 1945) pp. 83–92; Javier Cervera Gil, *Madrid en guerra: la ciudad clandestina 1936–1939*, 2nd

edn (Madrid: Alianza Editorial, 2006) pp. 64–72; Rafael Casas de la Vega, *El terror: Madrid 1936: investigación histórica y catálogo de víctimas identificadas* (Madrid: Editorial Fénix, 1994) pp. 80–91.

7 Eduardo de Guzmán, *La muerte de la esperanza* (Madrid: G. del Toro, 1973) pp. 60, 101–3.

8 *El Liberal*, 25 July, 1 August 1936.

9 Zugazagoitia, *Guerra y vicisitudes*, pp. 79–82; Jesús de Galíndez, *Los vascos en el Madrid sitiado: memoria del Partido Nacionalista Vasco* (Buenos Aires: Editorial Vasca Ekin, 1945) pp. 16–18; Cervera Gil, *Madrid en guerra*, pp. 59–61; El Preso 831, *Del Madrid Rojo: últimos días de la Cárcel Modelo* (Cádiz: Establecimientos Cerón, 1937) p. 10; David Jato Miranda, *Madrid, capital republicana: del 18 de julio al 6 de noviembre de 1936* (Barcelona: Ediciones Acervo, 1976) pp. 320–1.

10 Andrés Trapiello, *Las armas y las letras: literatura y guerra civil (1936–1939)* (Barcelona: Planeta, 1994) p. 83.

11 Henry Helfant, *The Trujillo Doctrine of the Humanitarian Diplomatic Asylum* (Mexico City: Editorial Offset Continente, 1947) pp. 63, 173, 206; Javier Cervera Gil, 'La radio: un arma más de la Guerra Civil en Madrid', *Historia y Comunicación Social*, No. 3, 1998, p. 282; Felix Schlayer, *Diplomático en el Madrid rojo* (Seville: Espuela de Plata, 2008) p. 42.

12 Schlayer, *Diplomático en el Madrid rojo*, pp. 61–3.

13 *CNT*, 31 July 1936.

14 On Val, see Juan García Oliver, *El eco de los pasos* (Barcelona: Ruedo Ibérico, 1978) pp. 306, 317–320, 323–4, 526. On Nuño, see Declaración de Manuel Rascón Ramírez, AHN, FC-Causa General, 1530, Exp. 4, pp. 124, 127; Sandoval, 'Informe de mi actuación', AHN,

FC-Causa General, 1530-1, Exp. 1, p. 222. On the Cine Europa, see Declaración de Santiago Aliques Bermúdez, AHN, FC-Causa General, 1530-2, pp. 82 ff.

15 Guzmán, *La muerte de la esperanza*, p. 27; Ricardo Sanz, *Los que fuimos a Madrid: Columna Durruti 26 División* (Toulouse: Imprimerie Dulaurier, 1969) p. 107; Gregorio Gallego, *Madrid, corazón que se desangra* (Madrid: G. del Toro, 1976) pp. 151–3.

16 *Política*, 6 August 1936.

17 *El Socialista*, 9 August 1936; *Heraldo de Madrid*, 10 August 1936.

18 Indalecio Prieto, *La tragedia de España: discursos pronunciados en América del Sur* (Mexico City: Fundación Indalecio Prieto/Sitesa, 1995) pp. 38–9.

19 Schlayer, *Diplomático en el Madrid rojo*, pp. 65, 112–13.

20 Ángel Viñas, *La soledad de la República: el abandono de las democracias y el viraje hacia la Unión Soviética* (Barcelona: Editorial Crítica, 2006) pp. 183–4.

21 *Informaciones*, 10 August 1936; *El Liberal*, 14 August 1936.

22 *Claridad*, 10 August 1936.

23 *Mundo Obrero*, 10 August 1936.

24 *Milicia Popular*, 12 August 1936.

25 Zugazagoitia, *Guerra y vicisitudes*, p. 79; *Milicia Popular*, 12 August 1936.

26 José Antonio Balbontín, '¿Qué dice la Iglesia?', *Heraldo de Madrid*, 17 August 1936.

27 *Claridad*, 3, 18, 19, 20 August 1936; *Heraldo de Madrid*, 18 August 1936.

28 Martín Blázquez, *I Helped to Build an Army*, pp. 115, 157.

29 Juan Ruiz Peinado Vallejo, *Cuando la muerte no quiere* (Mexico City: Impr. Azteca, 1967) pp. 188–9.

30 Bingham de Urquidi, *Mercy in Madrid*, p. 27; Galíndez, *Los vascos en el Madrid sitiado*, pp. 112–17; Montero Moreno, *Historia de la persecución religiosa*, pp. 444–7.

31 Gallego, *Madrid, corazón que se desangra*, pp. 109–13.

32 Gomá to De Despujol, 6 October 1936, Archivo Gomá, *Documentos de la guerra civil 1 julio–diciembre*, ed. José Andrés-Gallego and Antón M. Pazos (Madrid: Consejo Superior de Investigaciones Científicas, 2001) pp. 182–4.

33 Declaración de Teodoro Illera Martín, AHN, FC-Causa General, 1505, Exp. 2, pp. 16–17; Riba Tâmega to Lisbon, 28 July 1936, *Dez anos de política externa (1936–1947) a nação portuguesa e a segunda guerra mundial*, Vol. III (Lisbon: Imprensa Nacional/Casa da Moeda, 1964) p. 40.

34 Martín Blázquez, *I Helped to Build an Army*, pp. 121–2, 134; Antonio Cordón, *Trayectoria (recuerdos de un artillero)* (Seville: Espuela de Plata, 2008) pp. 410–11, 429, 454–5, 470, 479–80; Michael Alpert, *El ejército popular de la República 1936–1939* (Barcelona: Editorial Crítica, 2007) pp. 18, 126–7.

35 El Preso 831, *Del Madrid Rojo*, p. 99; Ian Gibson, *Paracuellos: cómo fue* (Barcelona: Argos Vergara, 1983) pp. 166–7, 171.

36 Pedro-Pablo Miralles Sangro, '*Al servicio de la Justicia y de la República': Mariano Gómez (1883–1951), Presidente del Tribunal Supremo* (Madrid: Editorial Dilex, 2010) pp. 94–5; Pascual Marzal Rodríguez, *Una historia sin justicia: cátedra, política y magistratura en la vida de Mariano Gómez* (Valencia: Universitat de València, 2009) pp. 167–70.

37 *Claridad*, 15, 17 August 1936; Juan-Simeón Vidarte, *Todos fuimos culpables* (Mexico City: Fondo de Cultura Económica, 1973) pp. 393–5; Maximiano García Venero, *El general Fanjul: Madrid en el alzamiento nacional* (Madrid: Ediciones Cid, 1967) pp. 361–87;

Jato Miranda, *Madrid, capital republicana*, pp. 313–17.

38 Eugenio Vegas Latapie, *Memorias políticas: el suicido de la monarquía y la segunda República* (Barcelona: Planeta, 1983) pp. 223–4, 276.

39 *CNT*, 12 August 1936.

40 Casa del Pueblo de Carabanchel, AHN, FC-Causa General, 1535, ramo separado 87, pp. 1–3; Hospital Militar de Carabanchel, AHN, FC-Causa General, 1535, ramo separado 111, pp. 1–17; Author's interview with Libertad López Ochoa, in the spring of 2005; Jato Miranda, *Madrid, capital republicana*, pp. 317–19; Pablo Gil Vico, 'Derecho y ficción: la represión judicial militar', in Francisco Espinosa Maestre, ed., *Violencia roja y azul: España, 1936–1950* (Barcelona: Editorial Crítica, 2010) pp. 251–7.

41 Declaración de José Rocamora Bernabeu, AHN, FC-Causa General, 1535, ramo separado 87, pp. 9–10; Núñez Morgado, *Los sucesos de España*, pp. 325–6; *La dominación roja*, p. 59.

42 Declaración de Manuel Muñoz, AHN, FC-Causa General, 1530-1, Exp. 1, p. 302; Padre Carlos Vicuña OSA, *Mártires Agustinos de El Escorial* (El Escorial: Imprenta del Monasterio de El Escorial, 1943) pp. 114–15; Antonio Montero Moreno, *Historia de la persecución religiosa en España 1936–1939* (Madrid: Biblioteca de Autores Cristianos, 1961) pp. 390–5; Capitán Antonio de Reparaz and Tresgallo de Souza (Maximiano García Venero), *Desde el Cuartel General de Miaja al Santuario de la Virgen de la Cabeza* (Valladolid: Afrodisio Aguado, 1937) p. 97; Francisco Cobo Romero, *La guerra civil y la represión franquista en la provincia de Jaén 1936–1950* (Jaén: Diputación Provincial, 1993) pp.

139–44 (trains), 149–50 (Úbeda); Luis Miguel Sánchez Tostado, *La guerra civil en Jaén: historia de un horror inolvidable* (Jaén: Junta de Andalucía/Colección Memoria Histórica, 2005) pp. 89–90 (Úbeda), 136–7 (prison), 141–54 (trains); Arrarás, *Historia de la cruzada*, VI, 25, pp. 132–6; Núñez Morgado, *Los sucesos de España*, pp. 201–2.

43 Sánchez Tostado, *La guerra civil en Jaén*, pp. 203–11.

44 *Ibid.*, pp. 156–60.

45 García Oliver, *El eco de los pasos*, p. 347.

46 Pedro L. Angosto, *José Alonso Mallol: el hombre que pudo evitar la guerra* (Alicante: Instituto Juan Gil-Albert, 2006) pp. 230–5.

47 Declaración de Manuel Muñoz Martínez, AHN, FC-Causa General, 1530-1, Exp. 1, p. 293; *Heraldo de Madrid*, 30 July 1936; *Política*, 31 July 1936; Jesús Lozano, *La segunda República: imágenes, cronología y documentos* (Barcelona: Ediciones Acervo, 1973) p. 455.

48 Diary entry for 24 September 1936, Carlos Morla Lynch, *España sufre: diarios de guerra en el Madrid republicano* (Seville: Editorial Renacimiento, 2008) p. 77.

49 Declaración de Manuel Muñoz Martínez, AHN, FC-Causa General, 1530-1, Exp. 1, pp. 294–5.

50 *Política*, 2, 15 August 1936; *Heraldo de Madrid*, 17 August 1936.

51 AHN, FC-Causa General, 1504, Exp. 5, p. 38; *Heraldo de Madrid*, 15 September 1936; *Gaceta de la República*, 13 June 1937; *ABC*, 11 March 1944; *La dominación roja*, pp. 155–6.

52 Declaración de Manuel Muñoz Martínez, AHN, FC-Causa General, 1530-1, Exp. 1, p. 295; *Heraldo de Madrid*, 8 August 1936; *Política*, 8 August 1936.

53 Cervera Gil, *Madrid en guerra*, p. 66.

54 Declaración de Manuel Rascón Ramírez, AHN, FC-Causa General, 1530, Exp. 4, pp. 127–39; G. Arsenio de Izaga, *Los presos de Madrid: recuerdos e impresiones de un cautivo en la España roja* (Madrid: Imprenta Martosa, 1939) pp. 69–71; *La dominación roja*, pp. 99–104; Casas de la Vega, *El terror*, pp. 105–13; AHN, FC-Causa General, 1520-1, p. 34; Gallego, *Madrid, corazón que se desangra*, pp. 126–7.

55 Gallego, *Madrid, corazón que se desangra*, pp. 87–99.

56 *Checas*: 'Linces de la República', AHN, FC-Causa General, 1532-1, pp. 1–39, 48–74; Declaración de Felipe Marcos García Redondo, AHN, FC-Causa General, 1532-1, pp. 40–7; Declaración de Manuel Muñoz Martínez, AHN, FC-Causa General, 1530-1, Exp. 1, p. 296. *Heraldo de Madrid*, 31 August, 9, 11, 17, 18 September 1936; *El Liberal*, 1, 16 September 1936; *Informaciones*, 31 August, 8, 15, 16, 17 September 1936; *La dominación roja*, pp. 139–41.

57 Declaración de Teodoro Illera Martín, AHN, FC-Causa General, 1505, Exp. 2, pp. 17–20. *La Voz*, 10 August 1936 gives the names of eleven of its then twelve members. See also *Heraldo de Madrid*, 31 August, 9, 12, 14, 15, 18, 23, 24 September 1936; *El Liberal*, 16 September 1936; *Informaciones*, 31 August, 8, 9, 16, 23 September 1936. There has been confusion between García Atadell's Brigada de Investigación Criminal and the Brigada o Escuadrilla del Amanecer. See, for example, José María Varela Rendueles, *Rebelión en Sevilla: memorias de un Gobernador rebelde* (Seville: Servicio de Publicaciones del Ayuntamiento de Sevilla, 1982) p. 186, and Román Gubern and Paul Hammond, *Los años rojos de Luis Buñuel* (Madrid: Ediciones Cátedra,

2009) p. 350. Ángel Pedrero told his interrogators that the García Atadell Brigade had nothing to do with the Escuadrilla del Amanecer: AHN, FC-Causa General, 1520-1, p. 118.

58 *Checas*: 'Brigadilla del Amanecer', AHN, FC-Causa General, 1534-1, pp. 5–10, 52–74; Declaración de Manuel Rascón Ramírez, AHN, FC-Causa General, 1530, Exp. 4, pp. 133, 135, 138.

59 Declaración de Carmelo Olmedo Marín, AHN, FC-Causa General, 1534-1, pp. 3–4, 23–32.

60 Declaración de Manuel Ramírez, AHN, FC-Causa General, 1530, Exp. 4, p. 136; *Informaciones*, 24 August 1936; *La Voz*, 11 September 1936.

61 *La Voz*, 7 September 1936; *Informaciones*, 8 September 1936; *Milicia Popular*, 10 September 1936.

62 Julius Ruiz, 'Defending the Republic: The García Atadell Brigade in Madrid, 1936', *Journal of Contemporary History*, Vol. 42, No. 1, 2007, pp. 97–115; Játo Miranda, *Madrid, capital republicana*, pp. 321–2.

63 AHN, FC-Causa General, 1532-2, pp. 11–15; 1520–1, pp. 7–8, 18, 50; Declaración de Manuel Muñoz, AHN, FC-Causa General, 1530-1, Exp. 1, p. 301; *Gaceta de Madrid*, 7 August; *Informaciones*, 6 August 1936; *Heraldo de Madrid*, 19 August 1936.

64 *Informaciones*, 2, 7, 8, 10, 11, 15, 17, 22 September 1936; *El Socialista*, 27 September, 1 October 1936; *El Heraldo de Madrid*, 10 September 1936; *El Liberal*, 23 August, 16 September 1936; *La Voz*, 29 September 1936; AHN, FC-Causa General, 1520-1, pp. 47–8, 64, 120, 136; Cervera Gil, *Madrid en guerra*, pp. 71–2.

65 Declaración de Teodoro Illera Martín, AHN, FC-Causa General, 1505, Exp. 2, p. 15; Antonio Lino's unfinished memoirs reproduced in Julio de Antón, *Policía y Guardia Civil en la España republicana* (Madrid: Edibeso Wells, 2001) pp. 323–5, and the letter from Lino reproduced in Julio de Antón, 'Las checas policiales', 11 February 2008 accessible at http://historianovel. blogspot.com/2008/02/ las–*checas*–policiales–segn–julio– de.html.

66 AHN, FC-Causa General, 1520-1, pp. 45–7; Ministerio de la Gobernación, *Apéndice I al Dictamen de la Comisión sobre ilegitimidad de poderes actuantes en 18 de julio de 1936* (Barcelona: Editora Nacional, 1939) pp. 179–81.

67 *La Voz*, 17 September 1936; *Heraldo de Madrid*, 17, 19 September, 2 October 1936.

68 AHN, FC-Causa General, 1532-2, 40, pp. 8–15, 24–30; also quoted in declaration of Pedrero, AHN, FC–Causa General, 1520-1, pp. 18–19; Pedrero's denial, 1520-1, pp. 118–19, 148–50.

69 José Ignacio Escobar, *Así empezó* (Madrid: G. del Toro, 1974) pp. 300–9; AHN, FC-Causa General, Declaración de Emilia Donapetri López, 1532-2, pp. 3–5; Declaración de Pedro Penabad, 1532–2, pp. 29–32.

70 *Política*, 24 September 1936; *La Voz*, 25 September 1936; *Heraldo de Madrid*, 25, 28 September 1936; *Informaciones*, 25 September 1936.

71 Atadell's detective work, *Heraldo de Madrid*, 25 September 1936; Pedrero's declaration, AHN, FC-Causa General, 1520-1, p. 119; Rosario Queipo de Llano, *De la cheka de Atadell a la prisión de Alacuas* (Valladolid: Librería Santaren, 1939) pp. 37–44.

72 Declaración de García Atadell, AHN, FC-Causa General, 1520-1, p. 20.

73 Declaración de Emilia Donapetri López, AHN, FC-Causa General, 1532-2, p. 3.

74 Sandoval, 'Informe de mi actuación', AHN, FC-Causa General, 1530-1, Exp. 1, pp. 206–7; *Heraldo de Madrid*, 31 August, 24 September 1936; *Informaciones*, 31 August 1936; *El Liberal*, 1 September 1936.

75 *Política*, 8 August 1936; *Heraldo de Madrid*, 13, 22, 26 August 1936; *Informaciones*, 14, 15, 18 September, 16 October 1936.

76 On the events in the prison in 1919, see Juan García Oliver, *El eco de los pasos* (Barcelona: Ruedo Ibérico, 1978) pp. 31–4. On Sandoval in prison in 1935, see Enrique Castro Delgado, *Hombres made in Moscú* (Barcelona: Luis de Caralt, 1965) pp. 214–15, and in 1939, see Eduardo de Guzmán, *Nosotros, los asesinos (memorias de la guerra de España)* (Madrid: G. del Toro, 1976) pp. 84–5. There is a fascinating biography of Sandoval by Carlos García Alix, *El honor de las injurias: busca y captura de Felipe Sandoval* (Madrid: T Ediciones/No Hay Penas, 2007). The work also exists in cinematic form: Carlos García Alix, *El honor de las injurias* (Madrid: No Hay Penas, 2007).

77 Sandoval, 'Informe de mi actuación', AHN, FC-Causa General, 1530-1, Exp. 1, pp. 201–6, 216, 222. See also AHN, FC-Causa General, 1530-2, pp. 44, 71, 85, 111; *La dominación roja*, p. 221; Cervera Gil, *Madrid en guerra*, p. 67.

78 AHN, FC-Causa General, 1530-2, pp. 12, 18–19, 20–37, 44–5, 58, 84. On his record and subsequent capture, see *ibid.*, pp. 47–9. For denunciations by the relatives of individuals arrested and murdered by *milicianos* from the Cine Europa, see *ibid.*, pp. 87–110, 113–14, 120.

79 Zugazagoitia, *Guerra y vicisitudes*, pp. 78–9; Nora Allwork, unpublished diary, Cañada Blanch Centre, London School of Economics, p. 61; Cervera Gil, *Madrid en guerra*, p. 66.

80 Galíndez, *Los vascos en el Madrid sitiado*, pp. 11, 33–43, 69–72, 108–17.

81 Izaga, *Los presos de Madrid*, pp. 41–4, 76; Ramón Serrano Suñer, *Entre el silencio y la propaganda, la historia como fue: memorias* (Barcelona: Planeta, 1977) pp. 128–9; Casas de la Vega, *El terror*, pp. 123–6; *La dominación roja*, p. 220.

82 Izaga, *Los presos de Madrid*, pp. 55–6, 60–8.

83 *Política*, 8 August 1936; *Heraldo de Madrid*, 10 August 1936.

84 *Claridad*, 14 August 1936; Izaga, *Los presos de Madrid*, pp. 76–8; Serrano Suñer, *Memorias*, p. 133.

85 *Claridad*, 21 August 1936.

86 *La dominación roja*, p. 221; Serrano Suñer, *Memorias*, p. 133.

87 Sandoval, 'Informe de mi actuación', AHN, FC-Causa General, 1530-1, Exp. 1, pp. 202–4; Denuncia de Emilio Arenillas Caballero, AHN, FC-Causa General, 1526-1, Exp. 1, pp. 125–31; Declaración de Santiago Aliques Bermúdez, AHN, FC-Causa General, 1530-2, p. 85; Vicuña, *Mártires*, pp. 117–21; Casas de la Vega, *El terror*, pp. 126–7; Cervera Gil, *Madrid en guerra*, pp. 66–7; Alfonso Domingo, *El ángel rojo: la historia de Melchor Rodríguez, el anarquista que detuvo la represión en el Madrid republicano* (Córdoba: Editorial Almuzara, 2009) p. 146.

88 Sandoval, 'Informe de mi actuación', AHN, FC-Causa General, 1530-1, Exp. 1, pp. 203; 1526, Exp. 1, p. 9; *Heraldo de Madrid*, 24 August 1936; Vicuña, *Mártires*, pp. 121–6; Izaga, *Los presos de Madrid*, pp. 91–100; Casas de la Vega, *El terror*, pp. 127–31; Gallego, *Madrid, corazón que se desangra*, pp. 122–4.

89 Declaración de Manuel Muñoz, AHN, FC-Causa General, 1530-1,

Exp. 1, pp. 299–300; *La dominación roja*, pp. 222–5; Casas de la Vega, *El terror*, pp. 131–4; Cervera Gil, *Madrid en guerra*, pp. 86–8; Vicuña, *Mártires*, pp. 126–35; Izaga, *Los presos de Madrid*, pp. 100–12; Serrano Suñer, *Memorias*, pp. 133–8; Manuel Valdés Larrañaga, *De la Falange al Movimiento (1936–1952)* (Madrid: Fundación Nacional Francisco Franco, 1994) pp. 27–33; Gallego, *Madrid, corazón que se desangra*, pp. 128–9. I am grateful to José Cabañas González for information about Marciano Pedro Durruti.

90 Mijail Koltsov, *Diario de la guerra de España* (Paris: Ruedo Ibérico, 1963) pp. 49–50; Vidarte, *Todos fuimos culpables*, pp. 419–20.

91 Testimony of Francisco García Valdecasas in Joan Llarch, *Negrín: ¡Resistir es vencer!* (Barcelona: Planeta, 1985) p. 41.

92 Schlayer commented on Ogilvie-Forbes's démarche, *Diplomático en el Madrid rojo*, p. 103; Ogilvie-Forbes to FO, 23 August 1936, *Documents on British Foreign Policy [DBFP]*, 2nd Series, Vol. XVII (London: HMSO, 1979) pp. 148–9; Zugazagoitia, *Guerra y vicisitudes*, pp. 129–31; Vidarte, *Todos fuimos culpables*, pp. 422–5.

93 Sandoval, 'Informe de mi actuación', AHN, FC-Causa General, 1530-1, Exp. 1, p. 216; Declaración de Manuel Muñoz, AHN, FC-Causa General, 1530-1, Exp. 1, p. 300.

94 Cervera Gil, *Madrid en guerra*, p. 105; Valdés Larrañaga, *De la Falange al Movimiento*, p. 71.

95 AHN, FC-Causa General, Caja 1530-2, pp. 4 (Melchor Rodríguez), 24 (Salvador Urieta); Cervera Gil, *Madrid en guerra*, p. 108; Domingo, *El ángel rojo*, pp. 135–51. On the relationship with Dr Vallina, see Domingo, *El ángel rojo*, pp. 39–41.

96 Serrano Suñer, *Memorias*, p. 138.

97 *Gaceta de Madrid*, 24, 26 August 1936; *El Liberal*, 23 August 1936; *Claridad*, 24, 28 August 1936; Vidarte, *Todos fuimos culpables*, pp. 425–6; Marzal Rodríguez, *Mariano Gómez*, pp. 170–5; Miralles Sangro, *Mariano Gómez*, pp. 102–11; Manuel Azaña, *Obras completas*, 4 vols (Mexico City: Ediciones Oasis, 1966–8) IV, pp. 850–1; Guillermo Cabanellas, *La guerra de los mil días: nacimiento, vida y muerte de la II República española*, 2 vols (Buenos Aires: Grijalbo, 1973) II, p. 816; Sánchez Recio, *Justicia y guerra*, pp. 15–16; Franz Borkenau, *The Spanish Cockpit* (London: Faber & Faber, 1937) pp. 125–6; Ronald Fraser, *Blood of Spain: The Experience of Civil War 1936–1939* (London: Allen Lane, 1979) pp. 175–6.

98 Zugazagoitia, *Guerra y vicisitudes*, pp. 129–30; *El Socialista*, 23 August 1936; *Política*, 23 August 1936.

99 Azaña, *Obras completas*, IV, pp. 625–6, 851; Manuel Azaña, *Apuntes de memoria inéditos y cartas 1938–1939–1940*, ed. Enrique de Rivas (Valencia: Pre-Textos, 1990) pp. 113–15; Cipriano de Rivas-Cherif, *Retrato de un desconocido: vida de Manuel Azaña (seguido por el epistolario de Manuel Azaña con Cipriano de Rivas Cherif de 1921 a 1937)* (Barcelona: Grijalbo, 1980) pp. 344–7; Santos Martínez Saura, *Memorias del secretario de Azaña* (Barcelona: Planeta, 1999) pp. 610–13.

100 Azaña, *La velada en Benicarló* in *Obras completas*, III, p. 395.

101 Monteiro to Riba Tâmega, 20, 22 August 1936, *Dez anos de política externa*, III, pp. 167, 182–3; Diary entry for 22 September 1936, Carlos Morla Lynch, *España sufre: diarios de guerra en el Madrid republicano* (Sevilla: Editorial Renacimiento, 2008) p. 76. On Salazar's surrender to Melchor Rodríguez, see

Declaración de Pilar Revilla López in AHN, FC-Causa General, 1530-2, pp. 38–9; Domingo, *El ángel rojo*, pp. 153–5.

102 AHN, FC-Causa General, 1530-2, pp. 42–3; *ABC*, 2 September 1936; Domingo, *El ángel rojo*, pp. 156–8.

103 Schlayer, *Diplomático en el Madrid rojo*, p. 75; Amparo Cabeza de Vaca, *Bajo cielos de plomo: unas memorias y el diario de Rafael Salazar Alonso* (Madrid: Editorial Actas, 2009) pp. 72–3 and 235 (militiamen), 82–7; Salazar Alonso, Prison diary, entries for 8, 9, 12, 14, 16, 18, 20, 22 September, in Cabeza de Vaca, *Bajo cielos de plomo*, pp. 123–55. Amparo Munilla's letter to the Juzgado Militar de Sevilla, in 'La Causa Contra el Teniente Coronel Arturo Dalías Chartres, por injurias al Jefe del Estado y estafa' (Archivo del Tribunal Militar Territorial Segundo, Seville). Both for the letter and for the information about Yuste and Borrego, I am indebted to Francisco Espinosa Maestre.

104 Miralles Sangro, *Mariano Gómez*, pp. 93, 112; Indalecio Prieto, *Convulsiones de España: pequeños detalles de grandes sucesos*, 3 vols (Mexico City: Ediciones Oasis, 1967–9) III, p. 314.

105 Francoist sources have claimed implausibly that there was an element of Masonic vengeance underlying Salazar Alonso's trial – Izaga, *Los presos de Madrid*, pp. 128, 131; *La dominación roja*, p. 340. The accusation is echoed in Cabeza de Vaca, *Bajo cielos de plomo*, pp. 161–2 and 169 (letter from Salazar Alonso to Amparo relating how he broke with Freemasonry).

106 Salazar Alonso, Prison diary, entries for 18–22 September, 'Notas sobre su propia defensa', in Cabeza de Vaca, *Bajo cielos de plomo*, pp. 337–50; see also pp. 131, 143–59; *ABC*, 20 September 1936; Núñez

Morgado, *Los sucesos de España*, pp. 176–9; *Heraldo de Madrid*, 28 August 1936.

107 Azaña, *Obras completas*, IV, pp. 877–8; Prieto, *Convulsiones de España*, III, pp. 315–16; Miralles Sangro, *Mariano Gómez*, pp. 112–15; Cabeza de Vaca, *Bajo cielos de plomo*, p. 159.

108 Sánchez Recio, *Justicia y guerra*, pp. 20–1; *El Socialista*, 18 September 1936.

109 Santiago Álvarez, *Negrín, personalidad histórica: documentos* (Madrid: Ediciones de la Torre, 1994) p. 280; Enrique Moradiellos, *Don Juan Negrín López* (Barcelona: Ediciones Península, 2006) pp. 177–80.

110 AHN, FC-Causa General, 1520-1, pp. 44–5; Anon., *García Atadell: hombre símbolo* (Bilbao: Editora Nacional, n.d.) p. 17

111 *Heraldo de Madrid*, 17 October 1936; Galíndez, *Los vascos en el Madrid sitiado*, pp. 20–2, 27–9, 34–7; El Preso 831, *Del Madrid rojo*, pp. 93–4.

112 Cervera Gil, *Madrid en guerra*, pp. 88–9.

113 Vidarte, *Todos fuimos culpables*, p. 655.

114 *Heraldo de Madrid*, 16, 22 September 1936; *Gaceta de Madrid*, 17 September 1936; *Política*, 18 September 1936; Declaración de Manuel Ramírez, AHN, FC-Causa General, 1530, Exp. 4, pp. 137–8.

115 Cervera Gil, *Madrid en guerra*, pp. 145–6; Cabanellas, *La guerra de los mil días*, II, p. 685, dates the broadcast on 7 August. Mola did not broadcast on that day, although he did so on 15 August and again on 13 September – see José María Iribarren, *Con el general Mola: escenas y aspectos inéditos de la guerra civil* (Zaragoza: Librería General, 1937) pp. 251–2, 358. For published texts of these two

speeches, see Emilio Mola Vidal, *Obras completas* (Valladolid: Librería Santarén, 1940) pp. 1177–84. The journalist Noel Monks, *Eyewitness* (London: Frederick Muller, 1955) p. 71, refers to a press conference on 7 November but this is certainly an error. According to Carlos Contreras, *Milicia Popular*, 10 October 1936, Mola's press conference took place a few days earlier, which might suggest 7 October.

116 Geoffrey Cox, *Defence of Madrid* (London: Victor Gollancz, 1937) p. 175.

117 *Mundo Obrero*, 3, 5 October 1936.

118 Edmond (Geneva) to FO, 29 September 1936; Ogilvie-Forbes to FO, 1, 6, 8 October 1936; Memorandum on the execution of civilians and prisoners of war by adherents of either party in Spain, 13 October 1936, *DBFP*, 2nd Series, Vol. XVII, pp. 336–7, 348, 366, 406–8; Ángel Viñas, *El escudo de la República: el oro de España, la apuesta soviética y los hechos de mayo de 1937* (Barcelona: Editorial Crítica, 2007) pp. 35–7.

119 *La Voz*, 6 October 1936; *Informaciones*, 6, 10 October 1936; *Gaceta de Madrid*, 7, 9 October 1936; *Heraldo de Madrid*, 7 October 1936; *ABC*, 9 October 1936.

120 Pablo de Azcárate, *Mi embajada en Londres durante la guerra civil española* (Barcelona: Ariel, 1976) pp. 26–7; Winston S. Churchill, *Step by Step* (London: Odhams Press, 1939) pp. 54–7.

121 *El Socialista*, 3 October 1936.

122 Carlos Contreras, 'En defensa de Madrid: la quinta columna', *Milicia Popular*, 10 October 1936.

123 *El Liberal*, 10, 16 October 1936.

124 *Heraldo de Madrid*, 21 October 1936.

125 *Milicia Popular*, 8 October 1936.

126 Casas de la Vega, *El terror*, p. 114.

127 Declaración de Manuel Rascón Ramírez, AHN, FC-Causa General, 1530, Exp. 4, p. 142; Declaración de Manuel Muñoz, AHN, FC-Causa General, 1530-1, Exp. 4, p. 298; Declaración de Santiago Magariños, AHN, FC-Causa General, 1526-1, Exp. 2, p. 102; Declaración de Santiago Aliques Bermúdez, AHN, FC-Causa General, 1530-2, p. 83. For examples, see the reproductions in *La dominación roja*, Annex IV, following p. 108; Casas de la Vega, *El terror*, pp. 137–42, 155–8, 163–7; Gibson, *Paracuellos*, pp. 136–7, 151–2, 166–9; Domingo, *El ángel rojo*, p. 170; José Luis Ledesma, 'Un retaguardia al rojo: las violencias en la zone republicana', in Espinosa Maestre, ed., *Violencia roja y azul*, pp. 225–6.

128 Rivas Cherif, *Retrato*, p. 344; Jato Miranda, *Madrid, capital republicana*, pp. 320 ff.

129 *El Socialista*, 27 September 1936.

130 *Informaciones*, 14, 17, 21, 24, 27, 28, 31 August, 2, 7, 8, 9, 10, 11, 14, 15, 16, 17, 23 September 1936; *Política*, 15 August, 3, 13, 17, 18, 20, 24 September 1936; *Heraldo de Madrid*, 8 August, 2, 3, 4, 5, 8, 12, 14 September 1936; *La Voz*, 3, 8, 15 September 1936; *El Liberal*, 13 September 1936. Ruiz, 'Defending the Republic', pp. 100–2, suggests that Atadell's activities were a known quantity. Cervera Gil, *Madrid en guerra*, pp. 71–2, suggests that they were not.

131 Declaración de Lourdes Bueno Méndez, AHN, FC-Causa General, 1532-2, p. 112; *Heraldo de Madrid*, 29 September 1936; *Mundo Obrero*, 30 September 1936; *La Voz*, 1 October 1936.

132 AHN, FC-Causa General, 1520-1, pp. 21–3.

133 Viñas, *El escudo*, p. 41. File in The National Archives [henceforth TNA], FO 371/20545.

134 Queipo de Llano, *De la cheka de Atadell*, p. 68.

135 AHN, FC-Causa General, 1532-2, pp. 16–19; 1520-1, pp. 23–7; Declaración de Emilia Donapetri López, AHN, FC-Causa General, 1532-2, pp. 5–6.

136 Luis Buñuel, *Mi último suspiro: memorias* (Barcelona: Plaza y Janés, 1982) p. 164; Luis Quintanilla, *'Pasatiempo': la vida de un pintor (memorias)* (Sada-A Coruña: Ediciós do Castro, 2004) p. 403; Román Gubern and Paul Hammond, *Los años rojos de Luis Buñuel* (Madrid: Ediciones Cátedra, 2009) pp. 350–1. Buñuel gave a slightly different version to Ricardo Muñoz Suay in 1961, saying that he personally sent an anonymous telegram to the Francoist authorities denouncing García Atadell – see *Conversaciones de Max Aub con Muñoz Suay*, Fundación Max Aub, Segorbe, Archivo, Fondo ADU, Caja 19–2/1, pp. 6–7. On the extradition attempts, see *Heraldo de Madrid*, 14 November 1936; *Informaciones*, 26 November 1936.

137 Varela Rendueles, *Rebelión en Sevilla*, p. 187.

Chapter 9: The Column of Death's March on Madrid

1 Carlos Asensio Cabanillas, 'El avance sobre Madrid y operaciones en el frente del centro', in *La guerra de liberación nacional* (Zaragoza: Universidad de Zaragoza, 1961) pp. 160–2; Servicio Histórico Militar (José Manuel Martínez Bande), *La marcha sobre Madrid* (Madrid: Editorial San Martín, 1968), pp. 24–30; Manuel Sánchez del Arco, *El sur de España en la reconquista de Madrid*, 2nd edn (Seville: Editorial Sevillana, 1937) pp. 61–4.

2 Juan José Calleja, *Yagüe, un corazón al rojo* (Barcelona: Editorial Juventud, 1963) pp. 90–1.

3 José Ignacio Rodríguez Hermosell, *Movimiento obrero en Barcarrota: José Sosa Hormigo, diputado campesino* (Badajoz: Asamblea de Extremadura, 2005) pp. 130–1; María de la Luz Mejías Correa, *Así fue pasando el tiempo: memorias de una miliciana extremeña*, ed. Manuel Pulido Mendoza (Seville: Renacimiento, 2006) pp. 67–9, 40–1; Ramón Salas Larrazábal, *Historia del Ejército popular de la República*, 4 vols (Madrid: Editora Nacional, 1973) I, pp. 252–3; Francisco Espinosa Maestre, *La columna de la muerte: el avance del ejército franquista de Sevilla a Badajoz* (Barcelona: Editorial Crítica, 2003) pp. 15–16, 34, 43, 161, 187.

4 Gobernador Civil de Badajoz a Ayuntamiento de Barcarrota, 19, 20, 28, 29 July 1936 in Archivo Municipal de Barcarrota, (Secretaría-Registro, Caja 53). I am indebted to José Ignacio Rodríguez Hermosell for providing me with copies of these telegrams. See also Rodríguez Hermosell, *José Sosa Hormigo*, pp. 131–2.

5 Francisco Moreno Gómez, 'La represión en la España campesina', in José Luis García Delgado, ed., *El primer franquismo: España durante la segunda guerra mundial* (Madrid: Siglo XXI, 1989) p. 192. The link between land reform and the subsequent repression was made by the Federación Socialista de Badajoz in a pamphlet published in Madrid in 1938, *El fascismo sobre Extremadura*, reprinted in 1997. Page references are to *El fascismo sobre Extremadura* (Badajoz: Federación Socialista de Badajoz, 1997) pp. 29–30, 47–9.

6 Carlos Barciela, Ramón Garrabou and José Ignacio Jiménez Blanco, eds, *Historia agraria de la España contemporánea*, 3 vols (Barcelona:

Editorial Crítica, 1986) III, pp. 298–405; Juan Martínez Alier, *La estabilidad del latifundismo* (Paris: Ediciones Ruedo Ibérico, 1968) pp. 52–4; Francisco Espinosa Maestre, 'La reforma agraria del Frente Popular en Badajoz: los orígenes de la Guerra Civil' (unpublished doctoral thesis, Universidad de Sevilla, 2006) pp. 283–9, 304–21.

7 Francisco Moreno Gómez, *La guerra civil en Córdoba (1936–1939)* (Madrid: Editorial Alpuerto, 1985) pp. 375–82; Larry Collins and Dominique Lapierre, *Or I'll Dress You in Mourning* (London: Weidenfeld & Nicolson, 1968) pp. 62–9, 82–99; Félix Moreno de la Cova, *Mi vida y mi tiempo: la guerra que yo viví* (Sevilla: Gráficas Mirte, 1988).

8 Espinosa Maestre, 'La reforma agraria', pp. 308–10.

9 Julia Vela Alburquerque, Manuel Martín Burgueño and Julián González Ruiz, *Diego Vela González: biografía* (Llerena: Tipografía Grandizo, 2009) pp. 28–39; Juan-Simeón Vidarte, *Todos fuimos culpables* (Mexico City: Fondo de Cultura Económica, 1973) pp. 363–7; Sánchez del Arco, *El sur de España*, pp. 66–9; Cándido Ortiz de Villajos, *De Sevilla a Madrid: ruta libertadora de la columna Castejón* (Granada: Librería Prieto, 1937) pp. 76–81; Espinosa Maestre, *La columna*, pp. 12–15.

10 Espinosa Maestre, *La columna*, pp. 17–19; Sánchez del Arco, *El sur de España*, pp. 70–2; José Luis Gutiérrez Casalá, *La guerra civil en la provincia de Badajoz: represión republicano-franquista* (Badajoz: Universitas Editorial, 2004) pp. 99–106. For information on the events in Fuente de Cantos, I am deeply indebted to information supplied by Cayetano Ibarra Barroso. See also his superb study of the town, Cayetano Ibarra, *La otra mitad de la historia que nos contaron: Fuente de Cantos, República y guerra 1931–1939* (Badajoz: Diputación de Badajoz, 2005) pp. 294–304, 322–51. For the names of those shot, see pp. 527–41, 553–56, 571–3.

11 Cayetano Ibarra, *Fuente de Cantos*, pp. 304–7; Espinosa Maestre, 'La reforma agraria', pp. 292–4.

12 *Diáro de Noticias*, 10, 14 August 1936; Francisco Pilo Ortiz, *Ellos lo vivieron: sucesos en Badajoz durante los meses de julio y agosto de 1936 narrados por personas que los presenciaron* (Badajoz: Edición del Autor, 2001) pp. 42–4; José María Lama, *Una biografía frente al olvido: José González Barrero, Alcalde de Zafra en la segunda República* (Badajoz: Diputación de Badajoz, 2000) pp. 83–126, 136–8; Ortiz de Villajos, *De Sevilla a Madrid*, pp. 82–3; Espinosa Maestre, *La columna*, pp. 21–3, 29–31.

13 Francisco Sánchez Ruano, *Islam y guerra civil española: moros con Franco y con la República* (Madrid: La Esfera de los Libros, 2004) pp. 165–7, 185; María Rosa de Madariaga, *Los moros que trajo Franco: la intervención de tropas coloniales en la guerra civil* (Barcelona: Ediciones Martínez Roca, 2002) pp. 296–9. For an example, see Manuel Velasco Haro, *Los Corrales: referencias históricas de un pueblo andaluz*, 2 vols (El Saucejo, Seville: Manuel Velasco Haro/Imprenta Gracia, 2000) II, pp. 611–12.

14 Antonio Bahamonde y Sánchez de Castro, *Un año con Queipo* (Barcelona: Ediciones Españolas, n.d. [1938]) p. 96; Antonio Bahamonde, *Memoirs of a Spanish Nationalist* (London: United Editorial, 1939) pp. 91–2; Manuel Rubio Díaz and Silvestre Gómez Zafra, *Almendralejo (1930–1941):*

doce años intensos (Los Santos de Maimona: Grafisur, 1987) p. 276.

15 Bahamonde, *Un año con Queipo*, pp. 66–8; José María Lama, *La amargura de la memoria: República y guerra en Zafra (1931–1936)* (Badajoz: Diputación de Badajoz, 2004) pp. 487–92; Vidarte, *Todos fuimos culpables*, pp. 370–1.

16 Martínez Bande, *La marcha sobre Madrid*, p. 32; Espinosa Maestre, *La columna*, pp. 31–3, 420–3. On the revenge, see Espinosa Maestre, 'La reforma agraria', p. 270.

17 Asensio Cabanillas, 'El avance sobre Madrid', pp. 162–4; Leopoldo Nunes, *La guerra en España (dos meses de reportaje en los frentes de Andalucía y Extremadura)* (Granada: Librería Prieto, 1937) pp. 183–90; Espinosa Maestre, *La columna*, pp. 33–4; Juan Carlos Molano Gragera, *Miguel Merino Rodríguez: dirigente obrero y Alcalde de Montijo (1893–1936)* (Badajoz: Diputación de Badajoz, 2002) p. 136.

18 *Diário de Notícias*, 14 August 1936; *Washington Post*, 15 August 1936; *O Seculo*, 14, 17, 18 August 1936; Rubio Díaz and Gómez Zafra, *Almendralejo*, pp. 253–83, 272, 288, 400; Espinosa Maestre, *La columna*, pp. 332–6.

19 Bernal, 'Resignación de los campesinos andaluces', p. 148; Espinosa Maestre, *La columna*, pp. 39–44.

20 Alberto Oliart, *Contra el olvido* (Barcelona: Tusquets Editores, 1998) p. 137.

21 Espinosa Maestre, *La columna*, p. 38.

22 Archivo General Militar, Ávila, ZN, Armario 6, Legajo 337, Carpeta 17.

23 On Yagüe's early career, see Ramón Garriga, *El general Yagüe* (Barcelona: Planeta, 1985) pp. 7– 42; Calleja, *Yagüe*, pp. 19–58. Ramón Serrano Suñer, *Entre el silencio y la propaganda, la Historia como fue: memorias* (Barcelona: Planeta, 1977) p. 232.

24 Calleja, *Yagüe*, pp. 94–6; Sánchez del Arco, *El sur de España*, pp. 74–7; Ortiz de Villajos, *De Sevilla a Madrid*, pp. 86–90.

25 Jacinta Gallardo Moreno, *La guerra civil en La Serena* (Badajoz: Diputación Provincial, 1994) pp. 67–8, 150–6; Pedro José Masa Redondo, 'Guerra civil y represión en la zona de Miajadas', in Julián Chaves Palacios *et al.*, *Guerra y represión: las fosas de Escurial y Miajadas (1936–2009)* (Mérida: Asamblea de Extremadura, 2010) pp. 79–91; Pilo Ortiz, *Ellos lo vivieron*, pp. 33–6. On Gómez Cantos, see Francisco Espinosa Maestre, *La justicia de Queipo: violencia selectiva y terror fascista en la II División en 1936: Sevilla, Huelva, Cádiz, Córdoba, Málaga y Badajoz* (Seville: Centro Andaluz del Libro, 2000) pp. 167–72; Jesús Mendoza, 'Gómez Cantos, el exterminador', *La Aventura de la Historia*, No. 11, 1999, pp. 22–31.

26 Oliart, *Contra el olvido*, pp. 81–2, 127–8, 134–5; Espinosa Maestre, *La columna*, p. 460; Francisco Espinosa Maestre, 'Francisco Marín Torrado: vida y muerte de vencidos', *Cuadernos para el Diálogo*, April 2009, No. 40, pp. 81–3; Abdón Mateos, *Historia del antifranquismo* (Barcelona: Flor del Viento, 2011) p. 140.

27 Harold G. Cardozo, *The March of a Nation: My Year of Spain's Civil War* (London: Right Book Club, 1937) pp. 160–2; John T. Whitaker, *We Cannot Escape History* (New York: Macmillan, 1943) p. 100.

28 Martínez Bande, *La marcha sobre Madrid*, pp. 165–70.

29 Espinosa Maestre, *La columna*, p. 56.

30 Comandante Franco, *Diario de una bandera* (Madrid: Editorial Pueyo, 1922) pp. 197–8. See also

Madariaga, *Los moros*, pp. 133–4, 296–9, 305–18; Gustau Nerín, *La guerra que vino de África* (Barcelona: Editorial Crítica, 2005) pp. 285–8; Sebastian Balfour, *Deadly Embrace: Morocco and the Road to the Spanish Civil War* (Oxford: Oxford University Press, 2002) pp. 253–6; Sánchez Ruano, *Islam y guerra civil*, pp. 357–63, 373–5.

31 Cardozo, *The March*, p. 56.

32 *Daily Express*, 28 August 1936.

33 Joaquín Arrarás, *Historia de la cruzada española*, 8 vols, 36 tomos (Madrid: Ediciones Españolas, 1939–43) VII, 28, pp. 24–6; Manuel Aznar, *Historia militar de la guerra de España (1936–1939)* (Madrid: Ediciones Idea, 1940) p. 103; and Martínez Bande, *La marcha sobre Madrid*, pp. 34–5, all attribute the decision to Yagüe. Calleja, *Yagüe*, p. 97, makes it clear that there was full consultation with Franco.

34 Espinosa Maestre, *La justicia de Queipo*, p. 236.

35 Juan Carlos Molano Gragera, *La izquierda en Puebla de la Calzada desde mediados del siglo XIX hasta mediados del siglo XX* (Montijo: Edición del Autor, 2004) pp. 77–82; Molano Gragera, *Miguel Merino Rodríguez*, pp. 130–6; Espinosa Maestre, *La columna*, p. 62.

36 Molano Gragera, *Puebla de la Calzada*, pp. 82–95, 99–100; Molano Gragera, *Miguel Merino Rodríguez*, pp. 136–50.

37 Espinosa Maestre, *La justicia de Queipo*, pp. 231–6.

38 Espinosa Maestre, *La columna*, pp. 59–62; Pilo Ortiz, *Ellos lo vivieron*, pp. 42, 72–81.

39 Espinosa Maestre, *La columna*, pp. 62–73; Rodríguez Hermosell, *José Sosa Hormigo*, pp. 130–1; Calleja, *Yagüe*, pp. 100–1.

40 Espinosa Maestre, *La columna*, pp. 78–84; Pilo Ortiz, *Ellos lo vivieron*, pp. 32–3, 51–70; Francisco Pilo Ortiz, *La represión en Badajoz (14–31 de agosto de 1936)* (Badajoz: Edición del Autor, 2001) pp. 12–15. On the bombings, see Mário Neves, *La matanza de Badajoz* (Badajoz: Editora Regional de Extremadura, 1986) pp. 24, 28–9, 34–5.

41 Alberto Reig Tapia, *Memoria de la guerra civil: los mitos de la tribu* (Madrid: Alianza Editorial, 1999) pp. 146–7.

42 Espinosa Maestre, *La columna*, pp. 76–7, 85–9; Pilo Ortiz, *Ellos lo vivieron*, pp. 40–1; Neves, *La matanza*, pp. 33–7. Calleja, *Yagüe*, p. 101, talks of 5,000 'superiormente armadas'; Hugh Thomas, *The Spanish Civil War*, 3rd edn (London: Hamish Hamilton, 1977) p. 372, gives the figure of 8,000; Nunes, *La guerra en España*, p. 204, claims 12,000. Sánchez del Arco, *El sur de España*, p. 90, writes of the key attack being carried out by ninety men.

43 *Diário de la Manhã*, 16 August 1936; Espinosa Maestre, *La columna*, pp. 89–94; Neves, *La matanza*, pp. 39–41; Sánchez del Arco, *El sur de España*, pp. 82–92; Calleja, *Yagüe*, pp. 101–6; Ortiz de Villajos, *De Sevilla a Madrid*, pp. 93–8; Pilo Ortiz, *Ellos lo vivieron*, pp. 92–8.

44 Hipólito Escolar Sobrino, *No pudimos escapar* (Madrid: Editorial Gredos, 1996) pp. 201–2; Bahamonde, *Un año con Queipo*, p. 67. Cf. Pilo Ortiz, *Ellos lo vivieron*, p. 134.

45 *Diário de Notícias*, 16 August 1936; Neves, *La matanza*, pp. 13, 43–5, 50–1; Jay Allen, 'Slaughter of 4,000 at Badajoz, City of Horrors', *Chicago Daily Tribune*, 30 August 1936; *El fascismo sobre Extremadura*, pp. 63–9; Espinosa Maestre, *La columna*, pp. 95–7; Pilo Ortiz, *Ellos lo vivieron*, pp. 138–44, 149; Julián Márquez Villafaina, *Aquellos días de agosto* (Badajoz: Diputación de Badajoz,

1999) pp. 197–221; Justo Vila Izquierdo, *Extremadura: la guerra civil* (Badajoz: Universitas Editorial, 1983) pp. 54–6; Pilo Ortiz, *La represión*, pp. 38–42. Gutiérrez Casalá, *La guerra civil en la provincia de Badajoz*, pp. 493–6, claims that there were no shootings in the bullring. It has been alleged that a substantial amount of the looting was carried out by local civilians: see Pilo Ortiz, *La represión*, pp. 32–3.

46 On the brothers Plá, see testimony of Luis Plá de Urbina, son of Luis, nephew of Carlos, in *El fascismo sobre Extremadura*, pp. 94–100; Pilo Ortiz, *La represión*, pp. 67–74; Espinosa Maestre, *La columna*, pp. 216–17; Gutiérrez Casalá, *La guerra civil en la provincia de Badajoz*, p. 501, who quotes the farcical claim of a Civil Guard, Manuel Carracedo, that the execution was carried out with the fullest legal guarantees.

47 *Diário de Lisboa*, 21 August 1936. For two slightly different accounts of this episode, see Pilo Ortiz, *La represión*, p. 71, and Francisco Pilo, Moisés Domínguez and Fernando De la Iglesia, *La matanza de Badajoz ante los muros de la propaganda* (Madrid: Libros Libres, 2010) p. 165.

48 *Diário de Notícias*, 15 August 1936; Iva Delgado, *Portugal e a guerra civil de Espanha* (Lisbon: Publicações Europa-América, n.d.) pp. 95–6; Espinosa Maestre, *La columna*, pp. 109–24; Vila Izquierdo, *Extremadura: la guerra civil*, pp. 56–8; Escolar Sobrino, *No pudimos escapar*, pp. 196–7.

49 Espinosa Maestre, 'La reforma agraria', p. 322.

50 Gutiérrez Casalá, *La guerra civil en la provincia de Badajoz*, pp. 490, 494, 500, 730–1, 764; *El fascismo sobre Extremadura*, pp. 78–9, 94–5. For Gómez Cantos's report on Pereita, see Espinosa Maestre, *La justicia de Queipo*, pp. 167–8, 177.

51 Allen, 'Slaughter of 4,000 at Badajoz, City of Horrors'.

52 César Oliveira, *Salazar e a guerra civil de Espanha* (Lisboa: O Jornal, 1987) pp. 169–70; Report of Ministro dos Negócios Estrangeiros, Armindo Monteiro, to Non-Intervention Committee, 22 October 1936, *Dez anos de política externa (1936–1947) a nação portuguesa e a segunda guerra mundial*, Vol. III (Lisbon: Imprensa Nacional/Casa da Moeda, 1964) pp. 463–84; *El fascismo sobre Extremadura*, pp. 73–5; Vila Izquierdo, *Extremadura: la guerra civil*, pp. 58–9; Bahamonde, *Un año con Queipo*, pp. 117–18; Espinosa Maestre, *La columna*, p. 211; Pilo Ortiz, *La represión*, pp. 78–81; Manuel Tapada Pérez, *Guerra y posguerra en Encinasola* (Seville: Autor, 2000) pp. 314, 327–8; Manuel Ruiz Romero and Francisco Espinosa Maestre, eds, *Ayamonte, 1936: diario de un fugitivo: memorias de Miguel Domínguez Soler* (Huelva: Diputación de Huelva, 2001) pp. 131–45.

53 Francisco Espinosa Maestre, 'Barrancos, 1936: el caso del Teniente Seixas y la aventura del *Niassa*', in Maria Dulce Antunes Simões, *Barrancos en la encrucijada de la guerra civil española* (Mérida: Editorial Regional de Extremadura, 2008) pp. 127–53.

54 Calleja, *Yagüe*, p. 106; Neves, *La matanza*, pp. 46, 61; Sánchez del Arco, *El sur de España*, p. 90; Espinosa Maestre, *La columna*, pp. 101–4; Pilo Ortiz, *Ellos lo vivieron*, pp. 123–9.

55 For an excellent summary of the massacre and its implications, see Reig Tapia, *Memoria de la guerra civil*, pp. 138–47. The figure of 9,000 is given in Vila Izquierdo, *Extremadura: la guerra civil*, p. 58; that of 200–600 in Pío Moa

Rodríguez, *Los mitos de la guerra civil* (Madrid: La Esfera de los Libros, 2003) p. 283; the analysis of Espinosa Maestre, *La columna*, pp. 228–34, and *La Justicia de Queipo*, pp. 172–80. The most recent effort to bring down the figures is Pilo, Domínguez and De la Iglesia, *La matanza de Badajoz*, pp. 183–94.

56 Pilo Ortiz, *Ellos lo vivieron*, pp. 150–4; Márquez Villafaina, *Aquellos días*, p. 218.

57 *O Seculo, Diário de Notícias, Diário de la Manhã*, all 16 August 1936; *Diário de Lisboa*, 16, 18 August 1936; Nunes, *La guerra en España*, p. 203; Neves, *La matanza*, pp. 43, 47, 60. On Pires, see the report of the Spanish Ambassador to Portugal, Claudio Sánchez Albornoz, 18 August 1936, in José Luis Martín, ed., *Claudio Sánchez Albornoz: Embajador de España en Portugal, mayo–octubre 1936* (Ávila: Fundación Sánchez Albornoz, 1995) pp. 157–60; Alberto Pena Rodríguez, *El gran aliado de Franco: Portugal y la guerra civil española: prensa, radio, cine y propaganda* (Sada-A Coruña: Ediciós do Castro, 1998) pp. 285–6.

58 On the pro-Francoist propaganda campaign to deny what happened in Badajoz, see Herbert Rutledge Southworth, *El mito de la cruzada de Franco* (Paris, 1963) pp. 217–31; 'A. Journalist', *Foreign Journalists under Franco's Terror* (London: United Editorial, 1937) pp. 6, 17–18.

59 Archivo General Militar (Madrid), Armario 18, Legajo 6, Carpeta 2.

60 John Whitaker, 'Prelude to World War: A Witness from Spain', *Foreign Affairs*, Vol. 21, No. 1, October 1942, pp. 104–6; Calleja, *Yagüe*, pp. 99–109.

61 Martínez Bande, *La marcha sobre Madrid*, pp. 35–41; Sánchez del Arco, *El sur de España*, pp. 82–91; Calleja, *Yagüe*, p. 105; Luis María de Lojendio, *Operaciones militares de la guerra de España* (Barcelona, 1940) pp. 141–4.

62 *The Times*, 29, 31 August, 1, 2, 4, 5 September 1936.

63 Espinosa, 'La reforma agraria', pp. 274–7.

64 Márquez Villafaina, *Aquellos días*, pp. 219–20; Espinosa Maestre, *La columna*, pp. 136–9, 161–76, 181, 253.

65 Manuel Martín Burgueño, 'La guerra civil española en la comarca de Llerena (1) Azuaga', *Torre Túrdula*, No. 5, Llerena, July 2002, pp. 31–5; José Fernando Mota Muñoz, 'Documentos sobre la guerra civil en Llerena', *Torre Túrdula*, No. 6, Llerena, January 2003, pp. 19–21; Bahamonde, *Un año con Queipo*, p. 118. On the massacre of the priests and monks from Fuenteovejuna, see Antonio Montero Moreno, *Historia de la persecución religiosa en España 1936–1939* (Madrid: Biblioteca de Autores Cristianos, 1961) pp. 290–5.

66 Espinosa Maestre, *La columna*, pp. 154–8.

67 Rodríguez Hermosell, *José Sosa Hormigo*, p. 141.

68 *Ibid.*, p. 136; Lama, *La amargura de la memoria*, p. 432.

69 The fate of the columna de los 8,000 is known thanks to the pioneering researches of Francisco Espinosa and José María Lama. They published their initial findings in 'La columna de los ocho mil', *Revista de Fiestas de Reina* (Badajoz), August 2001. See also Espinosa Maestre, *La columna*, pp. 195–9; Lama, *José González Barrero*, pp. 128–30; Ibarra, *Fuente de Cantos*, pp. 281–93. This account is largely based on their work, and also that of Cayetano Ibarra, but reconstructs the end of the story somewhat differently with regard to the respective roles of Gómez Cobián and Tassara, as a result of

the eyewitness accounts gathered in the remarkable documentary film *La columna de los ocho mil* made in 2004 by the Asociación Cultural Mórrimer – regarding which, see the article by one of the producers, Ángel Hernández García, 'La columna de los ocho mil: una tragedia olvidada', *Revista de Fiestas de Reina*, No. 7, August 2005, pp. 103–8. More recently, some fascinating eyewitness accounts have been recorded in Ángel Olmedo Alonso, *Llerena 1936: Fuentes orales para la recuperación de la memoria histórica* (Badajoz: Diputación de Badajoz, 2010) pp. 168–82. Tassara's own inflated version of his 'heroism' was recounted to Rafael de Medina Vilallonga, Duque de Medinaceli, *Tiempo pasado* (Seville: Gráfica Sevillana, 1971) pp. 88–90.

70 *ABC* (Seville), 19 September 1936.

71 Ibarra, *Fuente de Cantos*, pp. 351–8. See also Eduardo Pons Prades, *Guerrillas españolas, 1936–1960* (Barcelona: Planeta, 1977) pp. 317–19.

72 *Correio Elvense*, No. 308, 30 August 1936, reprinted in Luis Alfonso Limpo Píriz, ed., *Olivenza: antología esencial* (Mérida: Editora Regional de Extremadura, 1994) pp. 251–5; Espinosa Maestre, *La columna*, pp. 149–50, 404–6.

73 Espinosa Maestre, *La justicia de Queipo*, pp. 180–4.

74 *Daily Mail*, 22 August 1936.

75 Martínez Bande, *La marcha sobre Madrid*, pp. 45–8; Calleja, *Yagüe*, pp. 111–12; Sánchez del Arco, *El sur de España*, pp. 94–114; Julián Chaves Palacios, *La guerra civil en Extremadura: operaciones militares (1936–1939)* (Mérida: Editora Regional de Extremadura, 1997) pp. 123–37, 153–82.

76 *ABC* (Seville), *La Unión*, both 30 August 1936.

77 Archivo General Militar (Madrid), Armario 18, Legajo 6, Carpeta 5; Eduardo Haro Tecglen, *Arde Madrid* (Madrid: Temas de Hoy, 2000) pp. 159, 163–4.

78 Gerald Brenan, *Personal Record 1920–1972* (London: Jonathan Cape, 1974) p. 297; Gamel Woolsey, *Death's Other Kingdom* (London: Longmans, Green, 1939) pp. 34–5.

79 José Cuesta Monereo, *Una figura para la historia: el general Queipo de Llano* (Seville: Jefatura Provincial del Movimiento de Sevilla, 1969) pp. 11, 25; Edmundo Barbero, *El infierno azul (seis meses en el feudo de Queipo)* (Madrid: Talleres del SUIG (CNT), 1937) pp. 44, 47.

80 Martínez Bande, *La marcha sobre Madrid*, pp. 55–7.

81 Whitaker, *We Cannot Escape History*, pp. 111–12; Whitaker, 'Prelude to World War', pp. 105–6.

82 Memories of Miguel Navazo Taboada, quoted by Espinosa Maestre, *La columna*, pp. 435–7.

83 Pena Rodríguez, *El gran aliado*, p. 271.

84 Photograph no. 3, *Preliminary Official Report on the Atrocities Committed in Southern Spain in July and August, 1936, By the Communist Forces of the Madrid Government* (London: Eyre & Spottiswoode, 1936) after p. 73. Bahamonde, *Un año con Queipo*, pp. 142–3.

85 Noel Monks, *Eyewitness* (London: Frederick Muller, 1955) pp. 78–9.

86 Edmund Taylor, 'Assignment in Hell', in Frank C. Hanighen, ed., *Nothing But Danger* (London: Harrap, 1940) pp. 68–9.

87 Whitaker, 'Prelude to World War', pp. 106–7; Whitaker, *We Cannot Escape History*, pp. 113–14.

88 José María Ruiz Alonso, *La guerra civil en la provincia de Toledo: Utopía, conflicto y poder en el sur del Tajo (1936–1939)*, 2 vols (Ciudad Real: Almud, Ediciones de

Castilla-La Mancha, 2004) I, pp. 161–78; Rafael Casas de la Vega, *El Alcázar* (Madrid: G. del Toro, 1976) pp. 33–77; Antonio Vilanova Fuentes, *La defensa del Alcázar de Toledo (epopeya o mito)* (Mexico City: Editores Mexicanos Unidos, 1963) pp. 189–92; Luis Quintanilla, *Los rehenes del Alcázar de Toledo* (Paris: Ruedo Ibérico, 1967) pp. 82–8.

89 Aznar, *Historia militar de la guerra de España*, p. 212; Franz Borkenau, *The Spanish Cockpit* (London: Faber & Faber, 1937) p. 145; Ruiz Alonso, *La guerra civil en Toledo*, I, pp. 184–8; Herbert Rutledge Southworth, *El mito de la cruzada de Franco*, 3rd edn (Barcelona: Random House Mondadori, 2008) pp. 196–201; Vilanova Fuentes, *La defensa*, pp. 197–9; Sánchez Ruano, *Islam y guerra civil*, p. 203. Lists of names in Comandante Alfredo Martínez Leal, *El asedio del Alcázar de Toledo: memorias de un testigo* (Toledo: Editorial Católica Toledana, 1937) pp. 57, 229–41; Joaquín Arrarás and Luis Jordana de Pozas, *El sitio del Alcázar de Toledo* (Zaragoza: Editorial 'Heraldo de Aragón', 1937) pp. 315–49. Alfonso Bullón de Mendoza y Gómez de Valugera and Luis Eugenio Togores Sánchez, *El Alcázar de Toledo: final de una polémica* (Madrid: Actas Editorial, 1996) p. 109, quote a letter to Moscardó from the Civil Governor which clearly indicates that he, his wife and family were not arrested but entered the Alcázar willingly. 'Declaration del General Moscardó', in Causa General, *La dominación roja en España* (Madrid: Ministerio de Justicia, 1945) p. 316.

90 For pro-Republican versions, see Quintanilla, *Los rehenes*, pp. 75, 85, 99–100, 183–5, 223–32; Vilanova Fuentes, *La defensa*, pp. 180, 191,

197; Isabelo Herreros, *Mitología de la Cruzada de Franco: el Alcázar de Toledo* (Madrid: Ediciones Vosa, 1995) pp. 21–3. There are numerous references in Francoist sources to the existence of hostages. See General Moscardó, *Diario del Alcázar* (Madrid: Ediciones Atlas, 1943) pp. 29, 34, 83, 107, 152; 'Declaración del General Moscardó', *La dominación roja*, p. 318; Alberto Risco SJ, *La epopeya del Alcázar de Toledo*, 2nd edn (Burgos: Editorial Española, 1937) pp. 27, 213–14; D. Muro Zegri, *La epopeya del Alcázar* (Valladolid: Librería Santarén, 1937) pp. 33, 69, 134–5; Martínez Leal, *El asedio*, p. 58. Manuel Aznar, *El Alcázar no se rinde*, 2nd edn (Madrid: Ograma, 1957) pp. 36–7, prints a facsimile declaration by a *miliciano* who believed that there were prisoners who could have been exchanged for Moscardó's son. Two more recent and interesting pro-rebel sources, which opt for the figure of sixteen hostages, are Casas de la Vega, *El Alcázar*, pp. 61–4; Bullón de Mendoza and Togores Sánchez, *El Alcázar*, pp. 81–113.

91 Francisco Largo Caballero, *Mis recuerdos: cartas a un amigo* (Mexico City: Editores Unidos, 1954) pp. 185–6; Southworth, *El mito*, pp. 201–6; Vilanova Fuentes, *La defensa*, p. 198. On the fate of the girl, see Arthur Koestler, *Spanish Testament* (London: Victor Gollancz, 1937) p. 159.

92 Bullón de Mendoza and Togores Sánchez, *El Alcázar*, pp. 125–6, 128.

93 Moscardó, *Diario*, p. 107; Vilanova Fuentes, *La defensa*, pp. 194–5.

94 Borkenau, *The Spanish Cockpit*, p. 145.

95 Ruiz Alonso, *La guerra civil en Toledo*, I, pp. 207–9, 225–6, 279–94; Vilanova Fuentes, *La defensa*, pp. 175–80; Montero Moreno, *Historia de la persecución religiosa*, pp.

307–10. Herreros, *Mitología*, pp. 22–3, 37–8.

96 Eugenio Vegas Latapié, *Los caminos del desengaño: memorias políticas*, Vol. II: *1936–1938* (Madrid: Tebas, 1987) pp. 74–5; Ronald Fraser, *Blood of Spain: The Experience of Civil War 1936–1939* (London: Allen Lane, 1979) p. 168.

97 Risco, *La epopeya*, pp. 216–18.

98 H. R. Knickerbocker, *The Siege of Alcazar: A War-Log of the Spanish Revolution* (London: Hutchinson, n.d. [1937]) pp. 172–3; Webb Miller, *I Found No Peace* (London: The Book Club, 1937) pp. 329–30; Herbert L. Matthews, *The Yoke and the Arrows: A Report on Spain* (London: Heinemann, 1958) p. 176.

99 Miller, *I Found No Peace*, pp. 335–7; Allen to Southworth, 17 January 1964, 7 August 1967, Southworth Papers, Museo de Guernica.

100 Risco, *La epopeya*, pp. 225–6.

101 Herreros, *Mitología*, pp. 77–9, 95; Sánchez Ruano, *Islam y guerra civil*, pp. 204–6.

102 Rafael María Sanz de Diego SJ, 'Actitud del p. Huidobro, S.J., ante la ejecución de prisioneros en la guerra civil: nuevos datos', *Estudios Eclesiásticos*, No. 60, 1985, p. 445.

103 Rafael Valdés SJ, *Fernando Huidobro: intelectual y héroe*, 2nd edn (Madrid: Apostolado de la Prensa, 1966) pp. 292–316; Carlos Iniesta Cano, *Memorias y recuerdos* (Barcelona: Planeta, 1984) pp. 85–8.

104 Valdés, *Huidobro*, pp. 316–40, 496–504; Hilari Raguer, *La pólvora y el incienso: la Iglesia y la guerra civil española* (Barcelona: Ediciones Península, 2001) p. 88; Iniesta Cano, *Memorias*, pp. 97, 99; Sanz de Diego SJ, 'Actitud del p. Huidobro, S.J.', pp. 447–9.

105 Sanz de Diego SJ, 'Actitud del p. Huidobro, S.J.', Apéndice documental [henceforth Huidobro Papers] pp. 464–8, 481–4; Valdés,

Huidobro, pp. 510–21, 542–52; Raguer, *La pólvora y el incienso*, pp. 191–3.

106 Sanz de Diego SJ, 'Actitud del p. Huidobro, S.J.', p. 459.

107 Huidobro to Varela, 14 November, Varela to Huidobro, 3 December 1936, Huidobro Papers, pp. 477–8.

108 Huidobro to Díaz Varela, 4 October 1936, Huidobro to Franco, undated, Huidobro Papers, pp. 469–71.

109 Huidobro to Díaz Varela, 10 November 1936, Huidobro Papers, pp. 472–3.

110 Díaz Varela to Huidobro, 25 November, Huidobro to Díaz Varela, 1 December 1936, Huidobro Papers, pp. 475–6. I am indebted to Hilari Raguer for sharing with me the information about Huidobro's beatification process received in the Archives of the Society of Jesus. The Legion's account of Huidobro's death in Iniesta Cano, *Memorias*, pp. 108–10.

Chapter 10: A Terrified City Responds: The Massacres of Paracuellos

1 *La Voz*, 31 October, 3, 5 November 1936.

2 *Informaciones*, 10 November 1936; *ABC* (Seville), 14, 17 November 1936.

3 *ABC*, 17 November 1936; Mijail Koltsov, *Diario de la guerra de España* (Paris: Ruedo Ibérico, 1963), p. 233; Ignacio Hidalgo de Cisneros, *Cambio de rumbo (memorias)*, 2 vols (Bucharest: Colección Ebro, 1964) II, p. 187.

4 'Por resolución del gobierno y orden del ministro de la Guerra se ha creado el cuerpo de comisarios del ejército, con un comisariado de guerra en cabeza. El comisario general es Julio Álvarez del Vayo. Los subcomisarios son Crescenciano Bilbao (socialista), Antonio Mije (comunista), Angel Pestaña (sindicalista), Roldán (anarquista) y

Pretel (socialista, segundo secretario de la Unión General de Trabajadores). Objetivo del comisariado: "Se crea un Comisariado general de Guerra, cuya principal misión consistirá en ejercer un control de índole político-social sobre los soldados, milicianos y demás fuerzas armadas al servicio de la República, y lograr una coordinación entre los mandos militares y las masas combatientes encaminada al mejor aprovechamiento de la eficiencia de las citadas fuerzas." *Gaceta de Madrid*, 16 October 1936; *La Vanguardia*, 17 October 1936; *Milicia Popular*, 18 October 1936; Koltsov, *Diario*, p. 142.

5 Koltsov, *Diario*, p. 168.

6 Declaración de Antonio Viqueira Hinojosa, AHN, FC-Causa General, 1526-1, Exp. 2, pp. 179–82; Ian Gibson, *Paracuellos: cómo fue* (Barcelona: Argos Vergara, 1983) pp. 136–41; Félix Schlayer, *Diplomático en el Madrid rojo* (Sevilla: Espuela de Plata, 2008) p. 145; Adelardo Fernández Arias (El Duende de la Colegiata), *Madrid bajo el 'terror' 1936–1937 (impresiones de un evadido, que estuvo a punto de ser fusilado)* (Zaragoza: Librería General, 1937) pp. 201–3.

7 AHN, FC-Causa General, 1526, Exp. 5, p. 230, 1530, Exp. 12, p. 5; *ABC*, 9 November 1936; Juan García Oliver, *El eco de los pasos* (Barcelona: Ruedo Ibérico, 1978) pp. 308–9; Pascual Marzal Rodríguez, *Una historia sin justicia: cátedra, política y magistratura en la vida de Mariano Gómez* (Valencia: Universitat de València, 2009) pp. 177–86; Ángel Viñas, *El escudo de la República: el oro de España, la apuesta soviética y los hechos de mayo de 1937* (Barcelona: Crítica, 2007) p. 49; Lluís Alegret, *Joan García Oliver: retrat d'un revolucionari*

anarcosindicalista (Barcelona: Pòrtic, 2008) pp. 168–75.

8 Miguel Íñiguez, *Enciclopedia histórica del anarquismo español*, 3 vols (Vitoria: Asociación Isaac Puente, 2008) II, p. 1202

9 Rafael Casas de la Vega, *El terror: Madrid 1936: investigación histórica y catálogo de víctimas identificadas* (Madrid: Editorial Fénix, 1994) p. 205; Padre Carlos Vicuña OSA, *Mártires Agustinos de El Escorial* (El Escorial: Imprenta del Monasterio de El Escorial, 1943) pp. 159–61.

10 Vicuña, *Mártires*, p. 149; G. Arsenio de Izaga, *Los presos de Madrid: recuerdos e impresiones de un cautivo en la España roja* (Madrid: Imprenta Martosa, 1940) pp. 159–63; David Jato Miranda, *Madrid, capital republicana: del 18 de julio al 6 de noviembre de 1936* (Barcelona: Ediciones Acervo, 1976) p. 655; Causa General, *La dominación roja en España* (Madrid: Ministerio de Justicia, 1945) p. 239.

11 Julio Aróstegui and Jesús A. Martínez, *La Junta de Defensa de Madrid* (Madrid: Comunidad de Madrid, 1984) pp. 54–61; Antonio López Fernández, *Defensa de Madrid: relato histórico* (Mexico City: Editorial A. P. Márquez, 1945) pp. 82–4.

12 López Fernández, *Defensa de Madrid*, pp. 84–9; Koltsov, *Diario*, p. 189.

13 *ABC*, 8 October 1936; Gregorio Gallego, *Madrid, corazón que se desangra* (Madrid: G. del Toro, 1976) pp. 173–80.

14 Helen Graham, *The Spanish Republic at War 1936–1939* (Cambridge: Cambridge University Press, 2002) pp. 168–9; General Vicente Rojo, *Así fue la defensa de Madrid* (Mexico City: Ediciones Era, 1967) pp. 32–6.

15 Aróstegui and Martínez, *La Junta de Defensa*, pp. 62–3; Dolores Ibárruri

et al., Guerra y revolución en España 1936–39, 4 vols (Moscow: Editorial Progreso, 1966–77) II, p. 142; Santiago Carrillo, *Memorias* (Barcelona: Planeta, 1993) pp. 189–90; Gibson, *Paracuellos*, p. 192.

16 For a description of Serrano Poncela, see Aurora Arnaiz, *Retrato hablado de Luisa Julián* (Madrid: Compañía Literaria, 1996) pp. 142–3.

17 Declaración de Ramón Torrecilla Guijarro, AHN, FC-Causa General, 1526-3, Exp. 5, p. 25. See also Gibson, *Paracuellos*, pp. 260–6. García de la Rosa statement in Gibson, *Paracuellos*, p. 45.

18 Gallego, *Madrid, corazón que se desangra*, p. 222.

19 López Fernández, *Defensa de Madrid*, pp. 113–25; Rojo, *Así fue la defensa de Madrid*, pp. 32–5, 247; Koltsov, *Diario*, pp. 185–90.

20 Carrillo, *Memorias*, pp. 186–7. For a rather fanciful account see Enrique Castro Delgado, *Hombres made in Moscú* (Barcelona: Luis de Caralt, 1965) p. 390.

21 According to radio traffic between Madrid and Moscú, intercepted by British intelligence, TNA, HW-26, 5631/Sp., 31 March 1936. I am grateful to Fernando Hernández Sánchez for drawing this document to my attention. See also Max Gallo and Régis Debray, *Demain l'Espagne* (Paris: Éditions du Seuil, 1974) pp. 42–9.

22 Carrillo, *Memorias*, p. 186.

23 Declaración de Manuel Muñoz, AHN, FC-Causa General, 1530-1, Exp. 1, p. 305. This has led to absurd speculation that he was acting on orders from Margarita Nelken. See *La dominación roja*, p. 239; Casas de la Vega, *El terror*, pp. 175, 193–4, 205–6, 234; Carlos Fernández Santander, *Paracuellos del Jarama: ¿Carrillo culpable?* (Barcelona: Argos Vergara, 1983) p. 102.

24 Schlayer, *Diplomático en el Madrid rojo*, pp. 143–4.

25 Helen Graham, *The Spanish Republic at War 1936–1939* (Cambridge: Cambridge University Press, 2002) p. 189.

26 Rojo, *Así fue la defensa de Madrid*, p. 31; Roman Malinovsky in *Bajo la bandera de la España Republicana*, cited by Jato, *Madrid*, pp. 664–5.

27 For such a view, see Jorge M. Reverte, 'Paracuellos, 7 de noviembre de 1936: agentes de Stalin indujeron la matanza de presos sacados de las cárceles de Madrid', *El País*, 5 November 2006.

28 Arnaiz, *Retrato hablado*, p. 35.

29 Rojo, *Así fue la defensa de Madrid*, pp. 43–5.

30 *Ibid.*, p. 214. I am grateful to Ángel Viñas for drawing my attention to this reference.

31 On this point, I am grateful for the advice of Boris Volodarsky. See also Viñas, *El escudo*, pp. 63–8; Paul Preston, *We Saw Spain Die: Foreign Correspondents in the Spanish Civil War* (London: Constable, 2008) pp. 178–83.

32 Sancho (Gorev) report to the Director (Voroshilov), 5 April 1937, Russian State Military Archive (Rossiisky gosudarsvenny voyennyi arkhiv) [henceforth RGVA], f. 35082, op. 1, d. 333, ll. 14–18. See also Frank Schauff, *La victoria frustrada: la Unión Soviética, la Internacional Comunista y la guerra civil española* (Barcelona: Debate, 2008) p. 231; Barea's account in Arturo Barea, *The Forging of a Rebel* (London: Davis-Poynter, 1972) pp. 596–7.

33 Román Karmen, *¡No pasarán!* (Moscow: Editorial Progreso, 1976) pp. 276–8.

34 Koltsov, *Diario*, pp. 191–2.

35 'El Duende Azul' (Caamaño Cobanela), *Emocionario íntimo de un cautivo: los cuatro meses de la*

Modelo (Madrid: Gráfica Administrativa, 1939) p. 225; Gibson, *Paracuellos*, p. 83.

36 Herbert L. Matthews, *Half of Spain Died: A Reappraisal of the Spanish Civil War* (New York: Charles Scribner's Sons, 1973) pp. 120–1.

37 Contreras articles in *Milicia Popular*; Viñas, *El escudo*, pp. 61–2; Alexander I. Kolpakidi and Dmitri P. Prokhorov, *KGB: vsyo o vneshnei razvedke* (Moskva: Olimp, 2002) p. 168, quoted by Boris Volodarsky, 'Soviet Intelligence Services in the Spanish Civil War, 1936–1939' (unpublished doctoral thesis, London School of Economics, 2010) ch. 3.

38 Castro Delgado, *Hombres*, pp. 390–1.

39 *Milicia Popular*, 12 November 1936.

40 Sancho to Director, 5 April 1937, RGVA, f. 35082, op. 1, d. 333, ll. 14–18. I am indebted to Frank Schauff and Boris Volodarsky for their help in securing a copy of this document and to Dr Volodarsky for translating it and also for sharing with me his encyclopaedic knowledge about Orlov and Grigulevich.

41 'V Madride ya rukovodil gruppoi, kotoroi polzovalsya dlya samykh raznykh del' – Grigulevich, interviewed by Shatunovskaya, *Latinskaya Amerika*, No. 3, 1993, pp. 63–9, quoted by Volodarsky, 'Soviet Intelligence Services', ch. 3.

42 *La dominación roja*, pp. 279–80.

43 The descriptions of the three Russians from Declaración de Tomás Durán González in Procedimiento Militar contra José Cazorla Maure, AHN, FC-Causa General, 1525-1, pp. 25–7. The role of 'Pancho' from the Declaración de Antonio Gutiérrez Mantecón in Procedimiento Militar contra José Cazorla Maure, AHN, FC-Causa General, 1525-1, pp. 27–8. The surname 'Bollasqui' of 'Pancho' from the Declaración de Fernando Valentí Fernández in Procedimiento Militar contra José Cazorla Maure, AHN, FC-Causa General, 1525-1, pp. 28–9. I am indebted to Boris Volodarsky for his help in identifying them.

44 Procedimiento Militar contra José Cazorla Maure, AHN, FC-Causa General, 1525-1, pp. 4–5, 11–14, 25, 31–2.

45 Juan Negrín, 'Apuntes Barcelona del 1 al 40', Archivo de la Fundación Juan Negrín, Carpeta 2, pp. 23–4.

46 'Informe sobre la actuación de la policía en el servicio que permitió el descubrimiento en los meses de abril, mayo y junio de la organización de espionaje de cuyas derivaciones surgieron las detenciones y diligencias instruidas contra elementos destacados del POUM', 28 October 1937, FPI, AH 71-6; Declaración de Fernando Valentí Fernández in Procedimiento Militar contra José Cazorla Maure, AHN, FC-Causa General, 1525-1, pp. 28–9. I am grateful to Ángel Viñas for drawing my attention to the 'Informe' and to Aurelio Martín Nájera of the Fundación Pablo Iglesias for providing me with a copy. See also Viñas, *El escudo*, pp. 75–6.

47 'V Madride ya rukovodil gruppoi, kotoroi polzovalsya dlya samykh raznykh del' – Grigulevich, interviewed by Shatunovskaya, *Latinskaya Amerika*, No. 3, 1993, pp. 63–9, quoted by Volodarsky, 'Soviet Intelligence Services', ch. 3.

48 Christopher Andrew and Vasili Mitrokhin, *The Sword and the Shield: The Mitrokhin Archive and the Secret History of the KGB* (New York: Basic Books, 1999) p. 300.

49 Aróstegui and Martínez, *La Junta de Defensa*, pp. 75–6, 292.

50 Schlayer, *Diplomático en el Madrid rojo*, pp. 138–40.

51 Gallego, *Madrid, corazón que se desangra*, pp. 165, 193.

52 The original of the document is in the Archives of the International Institute for Social History, Amsterdam. Jorge Martínez Reverte, *La batalla de Madrid* (Barcelona: Editorial Crítica, 2004) pp. 226–7; Gibson, *Paracuellos*, p. 12.

53 Gibson, *Paracuellos*, pp. 77–84; El Preso 831, *Del Madrid Rojo: últimos días de la Cárcel Modelo* (Cádiz: Establecimientos Cerón, 1937) pp. 257–8; *La dominación roja*, p. 239.

54 Schlayer, *Diplomático en el Madrid rojo*, pp. 133–4.

55 Vicuña, *Mártires*, pp. 168–9; 'El Duende Azul', *Emocionario íntimo*, pp. 256–7; Izaga, *Los presos de Madrid*, pp. 174–84; Gibson, *Paracuellos*, pp. 84–90.

56 Fernández Arias, *Madrid bajo el 'terror'*, pp. 249–52; Gibson, *Paracuellos*, pp. 11–17.

57 Ricardo de la Cierva, *Carrillo miente: 156 documentos contra 103 falsedades* (Madrid: Editorial Fénix, 1994) p. 205.

58 There is considerable debate concerning the exact numbers: see Fernández Santander, *Paracuellos*, p. 47; Adelardo Fernández Arias ('El Duende de la Colegiata'), *La agonía de Madrid 1936–1937 (diario de un superviviente)* (Zaragoza: Librería General, 1938) p. 64. For overall figures, see Gibson, *Paracuellos*, pp. 184–91; Javier Cervera Gil, *Madrid en guerra: la ciudad clandestina 1936–1939*, 2nd edn (Madrid: Alianza Editorial, 2006) pp. 91–3.

59 Declaración de Antonio Viqueira Hinojosa, AHN, FC-Causa General, 1526-1, Exp. 2, pp. 183–6; Gibson, *Paracuellos*, pp. 184–91; Cervera Gil, *Madrid en guerra*, pp. 88–93; Casas de la Vega, *El terror*, pp. 299–303, 311–95; Fernández Arias, *Madrid bajo el 'terror'*, pp. 248–52.

60 Declaración de José Cazorla Maure, AHN, FC-Causa General, 1525-1, pp. 9–10; Declaración de Ramón Torrecilla Guijarro, AHN, FC-Causa General, 1526-3, Exp. 5, p. 25; Gibson, *Paracuellos*, pp. 48, 52, 172.

61 Reproduced in *La dominación roja*, between pp. 51 and 53. Gibson, *Paracuellos*, pp. 144–50.

62 Declaración de Ramón Torrecilla Guijarro, AHN, FC-Causa General, 1526-3, Exp. 5, pp. 26–7; Vicuña, *Mártires*, pp. 169–70; 'El Duende Azul', *Emocionario íntimo*, pp. 261–2; Izaga, *Los presos de Madrid*, pp. 184–90; El Preso 831, *Del Madrid rojo*, pp. 265–8; Gibson, *Paracuellos*, pp. 91–6.

63 Martínez Reverte, *La batalla de Madrid*, p. 246.

64 *Heraldo de Madrid*, 10 November 1936; *La Voz*, 12 November 1936; Vicente Rojo, *Así fue la defensa de Madrid*, p. 35; Gibson, *Paracuellos*, pp. 36–8.

65 Declaración de Manuel Rascón Ramírez, AHN, FC-Causa General, 1526, Exp. 5, pp. 196–7.

66 Declaración de Teodoro Illera Martín, AHN, FC-Causa General, 1505, Exp. 2, pp. 21–2; Casas de la Vega, *El terror*, pp. 114–15; *La dominación roja*, pp. 104–5.

67 Declaración de Ramón Torrecilla Guijarro, AHN, FC-Causa General, 1526-3, Exp. 5, p. 25; Gibson, *Paracuellos*, p. 48.

68 Declaración de Ramón Torrecilla Guijarro, AHN, FC-Causa General, 1526-3, Exp. 5, p. 25. See also Gibson, *Paracuellos*, pp. 260–6. García de la Rosa statement in Gibson, *Paracuellos*, p. 45.

69 *La Voz*, 1, 11 November 1936; *Informaciones*, 10, 11, 12 November 1936; Gibson, *Paracuellos*, pp. 38–45, 49, 52–3. On Cine Europa, see Martínez Reverte, *La batalla de Madrid*, p. 211.

70 Declaración de Manuel Rascón Ramírez, AHN, FC-Causa General, 1530, Exp. 4, p. 145, 1526, Exp. 5, pp. 196–7; Gibson, *Paracuellos*, p. 49. On the Sección Técnica, see Jesús de Galíndez, *Los vascos en el Madrid sitiado* (Buenos Aires: Editorial Vasca Ekin, 1945) pp. 58–9, 66–7.

71 Declaración de Ramón Torrecilla Guijarro, AHN, FC-Causa General, 1526-3, Exp. 5, pp. 27–8.

72 Declaración de Álvaro Marasa Barasa, AHN, FC-Causa General, 1526-3, Exp. 5, pp. 16–17, 38–40, 124–5; Gibson, *Paracuellos*, pp. 256–9.

73 Galíndez, *Los vascos en el Madrid sitiado*, p. 64.

74 Libro de Actas de la Junta de Defensa de Madrid, Aróstegui and Martínez, *La Junta de Defensa*, pp. 295 ff.

75 Galíndez, *Los vascos en el Madrid sitiado*, pp. 69, 159–60; Manuel Valdés Larrañaga, *De la Falange al Movimiento (1936–1952)* (Madrid: Fundación Nacional Francisco Franco, 1994) pp. 49–52; Raimundo Fernández Cuesta, *Testimonio, recuerdos y reflexiones* (Madrid: Ediciones Dyrsa, 1985) pp. 93–4.

76 Declaración de Luis Martín Buitrago, AHN, FC-Causa General, 1526-2, Exp. 4, p. 21; Galíndez, *Los vascos en el Madrid sitiado*, pp. 58–9, 66–7. On the way the file cards were filled in, *Informaciones*, 10 October 1936.

77 Minute of Ogilvie-Forbes, 15 September 1936, TNA, FO 371/20539 W11376; Aurelio Núñez Morgado, *Los sucesos de España vistos por un diplomático* (Buenos Aires: Talleres Rosso, 1941) pp. 214–22.

78 Minute of Ogilvie-Forbes, 23 November 1936, TNA, FO 371/20551 W17035/16926.

79 Nora Allwork, unpublished diary, Cañada Blanch Centre, London School of Economics, p. 53.

80 Galíndez, *Los vascos en el Madrid sitiado*, pp. 69–70; Gibson, *Paracuellos*, p. 121; Fernández Arias, *La agonía de Madrid*, pp. 63–4.

81 'Murder of 1000 prisoners held by Spanish Government, 15 November 1936', TNA, FO 371/20545 and 20547, quoted Viñas, *El escudo*, pp. 41–2; Schlayer, *Diplomático en el Madrid rojo*, pp. 145–50.

82 Quoted by Tom Buchanan, 'Edge of Darkness: British "Front–line" Diplomacy in the Spanish Civil War, 1936–1937', *Contemporary European History*, Vol. 12, No. 3, 2003, p. 300. On Pérez Quesada, see Joe Robert Juárez, 'Argentine Neutrality, Mediation, and Asylum during the Spanish Civil War', *The Americas*, Vol. 19, No. 4, April 1963, pp. 383–403.

83 Geoffrey Cox, *Defence of Madrid* (London: Victor Gollancz, 1937) p. 183.

84 AHN, FC-Causa General, 1530, Exp. 12, p. 5; Cervera Gil, *Madrid en guerra*, pp. 105–6.

85 Declaración del testigo Melchor Rodríguez García, AHN, FC-Causa General, 1530-2, p. 6; declaración de Gabriel Callejón Molina, AHN, FC-Causa General, 1530-2, p. 32; Alfonso Domingo, *El ángel rojo: la historia de Melchor Rodríguez, el anarquista que detuvo la represión en el Madrid republicano* (Córdoba: Editorial Almuzara, 2009) pp. 172–83; Cervera Gil, *Madrid en guerra*, p. 89.

86 Schlayer, *Diplomático en el Madrid rojo*, pp. 161–2; Domingo, *El ángel rojo*, pp. 183–7.

87 AHN, FC-Causa General, 1530-2/5, pp. 6–7; García Oliver, *El eco de los pasos*, p. 306; Schlayer, *Diplomático en el Madrid rojo*, p. 163; Domingo, *El ángel rojo*, pp. 187–9.

88 Declaraciones de Carlos Mendoza Saenz de Argandoña, José Luis Mendoza Jimeno, Santiago Aliques

Bermúdez, AHN, FC-Causa General, 1530-2, pp. 67, 69, 84.

89 Gibson, *Paracuellos*, pp. 122–6; Cervera Gil, *Madrid en guerra*, pp. 105–6; De la Cierva, *Carrillo miente*, pp. 212–14.

90 Manuel Azaña, *Apuntes de memoria inéditos y cartas 1938–1939–1940* (Valencia: Pre-Textos, 1990) pp. 153–5.

91 *La Voz*, 13 November 1936; *Informaciones*, 13 November 1936; *ABC*, 13 November 1936; *Heraldo de Madrid*, 14 November 1936.

92 *ABC*, 14 November 1936.

93 AHN, FC-Causa General, 1530-2, pp. 7–8, 1526, Exp. 5, pp. 201–3; Eduardo de Guzmán, *El año de la victoria* (Madrid: G. del Toro, 1974) pp. 276–7; Domingo, *El ángel rojo*, pp. 191–6, 201–2; Graham, *The Spanish Republic at War*, p. 194.

94 Aróstegui and Martínez, *La Junta de Defensa*, pp. 90–4; Francisco Largo Caballero, *Mis recuerdos: cartas a un amigo* (Mexico City: Editores Unidos, 1954) pp. 191–2.

95 Galíndez, *Los vascos en el Madrid sitiado*, p. 68.

96 Serrano Poncela al Comité Central del PCE, FPI, AH 63–52, pp. 2–5. In August 1939, he wrote to Fidel Miró of the Libertarian Youth, saying that he could not return to the PSOE lest it damage the movement: Serrano Poncela to Miró, 13 August 1939, FPI, AH 26–28, pp. 4–7. I am immensely grateful to Sandra Souto for drawing my attention to these letters.

97 Gibson, *Paracuellos*, pp. 198–209.

98 Carrillo, *Memorias*, p. 211.

99 Declaración de Ramón Torrecilla Guijarro, AHN, FC-Causa General, 1526-3, Exp. 5, p. 28.

100 AHN, FC-Causa General, 1525-1, pp. 3–4; *La dominación roja*, p. 159.

101 AHN, FC-Causa General, 1530-2, pp. 8 (Melchor Rodríguez), 16 (Eloy de la Figuera); AHN, FC-Causa General, 1526-3, Exp. 5, p. 201 (Cazorla); AHN, FC-Causa General, 1526-3, Exp. 5, p. 198 (Rascón).

102 Galíndez, *Los vascos en el Madrid sitiado*, pp. 132–5.

103 *Informaciones*, 22 December 1936.

104 *Informaciones*, 4, 5 December 1936; *ABC*, 5, 6 December 1936; Javier Rubio, *Asilos y canjes durante la guerra civil española: aspectos humanitarios de una contienda fratricida* (Barcelona: Planeta, 1979) pp. 79–82; Aróstegui and Martínez, *La Junta de Defensa*, pp. 232–3, 303, 319; Galíndez, *Los vascos en el Madrid sitiado*, p. 115; Schlayer, *Diplomático en el Madrid rojo*, pp. 182–3; Enrique Líster, *Nuestra guerra* (Paris: Colección Ebro, 1966) p. 87.

105 On Vázquez Baldominos's role, AHN, FC-Causa General, 1525-1, p. 13. On Grigulevich's role, Evgeny Vorobyov, 'Nachalo boevogo puti Maksa', in Evgeny M. Primakov, Vadim A. Kirpichenko *et al.*, eds, *Ocherki istorii Rossiiskoy vneshnei razvedki*, 6 vols (Moskva: Mezhdunarodnye otnosheniya, 2003–6) III, pp. 152–3, quoted by Volodarsky, 'Soviet Intelligence Services', ch. 3.

106 Domingo, *El ángel rojo*, pp. 197–200.

107 P. Carlos Paramio Roca, Pedro A. García Bilbao and Xulio García Bilbao, *La represión franquista en Guadalajara* (Guadalajara: Foro por la Memoria de Guadalajara, 2010) pp. 32–5.

108 AHN, FC-Causa General, 1530-2, p. 8; Núñez Morgado, *Los sucesos de España*, pp. 285–8; Galíndez, *Los vascos en el Madrid sitiado*, p. 66; Guillermo Cabanellas, *La guerra de los mil días: nacimiento, vida y muerte de la II República española*, 2 vols (Buenos Aires: Grijalbo, 1973) II, pp. 823–6; Gibson, *Paracuellos*, pp. 178–80; Domingo, *El ángel rojo*, pp. 11–27; César Rufino, '¿Conoces

al Ángel rojo?', *El Correo de Andalucía*, 26 April 2008.

109 Domingo, *El ángel rojo*, pp. 25–7, 214.

110 AHN, FC-Causa General, 1526-3, Exp. 5, pp. 202–5 (Fernando Valentí); Domingo, *El ángel rojo*, pp. 202–3, 215–22.

111 *El Alcázar*, 4 January 1977.

112 Ministers in Adolfo Suárez's government demanded an investigation into Paracuellos which must have been extremely cursory since it produced no documentary proof of Carrillo's guilt: Joaquín Bardavío, *Sabado santo rojo* (Madrid: Ediciones UVE, 1980) pp. 130–6.

113 'No fui responsable', *Cambio 16*, 16 January 1977, pp. 12–14; Bardavío, *Sabado santo rojo*, p. 133.

114 Interview with Gibson, *Paracuellos*, pp. 196–7; *El País*, 28 October 2005.

115 Quoted by De la Cierva, *Carrillo miente*, pp. 232–3.

116 Antonio Elorza and Marta Bizcarrondo, *Queridos camaradas: la Internacional Comunista y España, 1919–1939* (Barcelona: Planeta, 1999) p. 379; Ronald Radosh, Mary R. Habeck and Grigory Sevostianov, eds, *Spain Betrayed: The Soviet Union in the Spanish Civil War* (New Haven: Yale University Press, 2001) p. 223. A complete version of this report can be found at pp. 219–33 of *Spain Betrayed* where it is absurdly attributed to Dimitrov, who was in Moscow at the time. On p. 529, Santiago Carrillo is confused with his father Wenceslao.

117 Stoyán Mínev (Stepanov), *Las causas de la derrota de la República española*, ed. Ángel L. Encinas Moral (Madrid: Miraguano Ediciones, 2003) pp. 93, 111–12.

118 Cazorla's wife refers to this: Aurora Arnaiz, *Retrato hablado de Luisa Julián* (Madrid: Compañía Literaria, 1996) p. 113.

119 Ibárruri *et al.*, *Guerra y revolución en España*, II, p. 187.

Chapter 11: Defending the Republic from the Enemy Within

1 Manuel Azaña, *Apuntes de memoria inéditos y cartas 1938–1939–1940* (Valencia: Pre-Textos, 1990) pp. 166–7.

2 Mariano Ansó, *Yo fui ministro de Negrín* (Barcelona: Planeta, 1976) pp. 165–6.

3 Julio Aróstegui and Jesús A. Martínez, *La Junta de Defensa de Madrid* (Madrid: Comunidad de Madrid, 1984) pp. 234; Santiago Carrillo, *Memorias* (Barcelona: Planeta, 1993), p. 210.

4 On Andrés Rodríguez, see Antonio Nadal, *Guerra civil en Málaga* (Málaga: Editorial Arguval, 1984) pp. 90–7; Sergio José Brenes, 'Andrés Rodríguez, concejal comunista en Málaga', *Revista Jábega*, No. 88, 2001, pp. 71–81. The murder of Rodríguez had led to a ferocious gang war. On Trilla, see *La Vanguardia*, 1, 2 August 1936. On Líster and Vidali, see report of André Marty to Comintern Secretariat, 10 October 1936, Ronald Radosh, Mary R. Habeck and Grigory Sevostianov, eds, *Spain Betrayed: The Soviet Union in the Spanish Civil War* (New Haven: Yale University Press, 2001) p. 55.

5 Procedimiento Militar contra José Cazorla Maure, AHN, FC-Causa General, 1525-1, pp. 4–5, 11–14, 25, 31–2; AHN, FC-Causa General, 1526-3, Exp. 5, p. 201. Conesa was executed by the Junta de Casado: *ABC*, 15, 24 March 1939; Luis Español Bouché, *Madrid 1939: del golpe de Casado al final de la guerra civil* (Madrid: Almena Ediciones, 2004) pp. 55, 57, 141.

6 Juan-Simeón Vidarte, *Todos fuimos culpables* (Mexico City: Fondo de Cultura Económica, 1973) p. 392.

7 Manuel Tarín-Iglesias, *Los años rojos* (Barcelona: Planeta, 1985) pp. 92–3.

8 Carmen González Martínez, *Guerra civil en Murcia: un análisis sobre el Poder y los comportamientos colectivos* (Murcia: Universidad de Murcia, 1999) pp. 174–9; José Peirats, *La CNT en la revolución española*, 2nd edn, 3 vols (Paris: Ediciones Ruedo Ibérico, 1971) II, pp. 73–7; Jesús Hernández, *Negro y rojo: los anarquistas en la revolución española* (Mexico City: La España Contemporánea, 1946) pp. 246–8.

9 Jorge Martínez Reverte, *La batalla de Madrid* (Barcelona: Editorial Crítica, 2004) pp. 457–8; Gregorio Gallego, *Madrid, corazón que se desangra* (Madrid: G. del Toro, 1976) pp. 275–6. See also Miguel Iñíguez, *Esbozo de una enciclopedia histórica del anarquismo español* (Madrid: Fundación de Estudios Libertarios Anselmo Lorenzo, 2001) p. 438; Eduardo de Guzmán, *Nosotros los asesinos* (Madrid: G. del Toro, 1976) pp. 101–2.

10 Cazorla's wife recalled the decision as being based on Carrillo's need to organize the JSU conference: Aurora Arnaiz, *Retrato hablado de Luisa Julián* (Madrid: Compañía Literaria, 1996) p. 35.

11 Aróstegui and Martínez, *La Junta de Defensa*, pp. 343–5; Gallego, *Madrid, corazón que se desangra*, pp. 272–5.

12 *Mundo Obrero*, 23, 24, 25 December 1936; *La Voz*, 24 December 1936; *El Socialista*, 24 December 1936; *Claridad*, 25 December 1936; *Heraldo de Madrid*, 25 December 1936; Javier Cervera Gil, *Madrid en guerra: la ciudad clandestina 1936–1939*, 2nd edn (Madrid: Alianza Editorial, 2006) pp. 305–6.

13 *CNT*, 24, 25 December 1936; Gallego, *Madrid, corazón que se desangra*, pp. 276–7; Peirats, *La CNT*, II, pp. 63–6. On false CNTistas in La Mancha, see Pablo

Torres, *Los años oscuros en Miguel Esteban. Represión y fascismo en Castilla-La Mancha. República, Guerra civil y primer franquismo. 1931–1952* (Madrid: Almarabú, 2008) pp. 132–43.

14 *Mundo Obrero*, 26, 27, 29, 31 December 1936, 2 January 1937; *CNT*, 29 December 1936, 1 January 1937; Aróstegui and Martínez, *La Junta de Defensa*, pp. 92–3, 252, 228, 233, 236–8; Julián Zugazagoitia, *Guerra y vicisitudes de los españoles*, 2nd edn, 2 vols (Paris: Librería Española, 1968) I, pp. 219–21; Gallego, *Madrid, corazón que se desangra*, pp. 211–12.

15 Aróstegui and Martínez, *La Junta de Defensa*, pp. 240, 359, 410–16; Procedimiento militar sumarísimo contra José Cazorla Maure, AHN, FC-Causa General, 1525-1, pp. 6, 14–16; Gallego, *Madrid, corazón que se desangra*, pp. 342–3; Alfonso Domingo, *El ángel rojo: la historia de Melchor Rodríguez, el anarquista que detuvo la represión en el Madrid republicano* (Córdoba: Editorial Almuzara, 2009), pp. 217–18.

16 *Frente Libertario*, 18, 23 February 1937; *CNT*, 22 February 1937.

17 *Ahora*, 24 February 1937; *CNT*, 24, 27 February 1937; *Mundo Obrero*, 24 February, 8 March 1937; Jesús de Galíndez, *Los vascos en el Madrid sitiado: memoria del Partido Nacionalista Vasco* (Buenos Aires: Editorial Vasca Ekin, 1945) pp. 158–9; Helen Graham, *The Spanish Republic at War 1936–1939* (Cambridge: Cambridge University Press, 2002) p. 195.

18 *CNT*, 28 February 1937; Aurelio Núñez Morgado, *Los sucesos de España vistos por un diplomático* (Buenos Aires: Talleres Gráficos Argentinos, 1941) pp. 165–8.

19 *ABC*, 2 January 1937; Glicerio Sánchez Recio, *Justicia y guerra en España: los tribunales populares*

(1936–1939) (Alicante: Instituto de Cultura 'Juan Gil-Albert', 1994) pp. 176–9; Juan García Oliver, *El eco de los pasos* (Barcelona: Ruedo Ibérico, 1978) pp. 393–4, 451–2.

20 *CNT*, 17 April 1937; Procedimiento militar sumarísimo contra José Cazorla Maure, AHN, FC-Causa General, 1525-1, pp. 5, 18.

21 Aróstegui and Martínez, *La Junta de Defensa*, pp. 240–1; Gallego, *Madrid, corazón que se desangra*, p. 343; Domingo, *El ángel rojo*, pp. 224–6. On Julián Fernández, see Eduardo de Guzmán, *El año de la Victoria* (Madrid: G. del Toro, 1974) p. 273.

22 *CNT*, 12 March 1937.

23 *Mundo Obrero*, 9 April 1937; Peirats, *La CNT*, II, pp. 69–70; José María Ruiz Alonso, *La guerra civil en la provincia de Toledo: Utopía, conflicto y poder en el sur del Tajo (1936–1939)*, 2 vols (Ciudad Real: Almud, Ediciones de Castilla-La Mancha, 2004) I, pp. 293–4; Francisco Alía Miranda, *La guerra civil en la retaguardia: conflicto y revolución en la provincia de Ciudad Real (1936–1939)* (Ciudad Real: Diputación Provincial, 1994) pp. 121–31, 141–2; Ana Belén Rodríguez Patiño, *La guerra civil en Cuenca (1936–1939)*, Vol. I: *Del 18 de julio a la columna del Rosal* (Madrid: Universidad Complutense, 2003) pp. 182–4; Felix Morrow, *Revolution and Counter-Revolution in Spain* (London: New Park Publications, 1963) p. 75.

24 *Mundo Obrero*, 13 March 1937.

25 *Mundo Obrero*, 14 April 1937; intervention of Cazorla at Junta de Defensa, Aróstegui and Martínez, *La Junta de Defensa*, pp. 445–7. On López de Letona, see Cervera Gil, *Madrid en guerra*, pp. 324, 371–3, 451.

26 On López de Letona and 'the Embassy of Siam', see Procedimiento militar sumarísimo contra José Cazorla Maure, AHN, FC-Causa

General, 1525-1, pp. 17–18; Cervera Gil, *Madrid en guerra*, pp. 324, 371, 373–4. On Verardini, see Ricardo de la Cierva, *1939: agonía y victoria (el protocolo 277)* (Barcelona: Planeta, 1989) p. 103.

27 Julius Ruiz, *Franco's Justice: Repression in Madrid after the Spanish Civil War* (Oxford: Clarendon Press, 2005) p. 103.

28 Cervera Gil, *Madrid en guerra*, pp. 312–16.

29 AHN, FC-Causa General, 1525-1, pp. 5, 17–18; Aróstegui and Martínez, *La Junta de Defensa*, pp. 234–5; *CNT*, 14 April 1937; AHN, FC-Causa General, 1525-1, pp. 5, 18; Cipriano Mera, *Guerra, exilio y cárcel de un anarcosindicalista* (Paris: Ruedo Ibérico, 1976) pp. 131–3.

30 *ABC*, 16 April 1937; AHN, FC-Causa General, 1525-1, p. 18; Aróstegui and Martínez, *La Junta de Defensa*, pp. 440–54.

31 'Una explicación obligada a todo el pueblo antifascista', *CNT*, 17 April 1937.

32 'El ex delegado especial de la Dirección General de Prisiones, compañero Melchor Rodríguez, da cuenta de dos cartas cruzadas entre él y Cazorla', *CNT*, 17 April 1937, p. 4. Procedimiento Militar contra José Cazorla Maure, AHN, FC-Causa General, 1525-1, pp. 31–8.

33 *CNT*, 24 April 1937; Manuel Azaña, diary, 20 May 1937, *Obras completas*, 4 vols (Mexico: Ediciones Oasis, 1966–8) IV, p. 589.

34 *Mundo Obrero*, 26 April 1937.

35 *Mundo Obrero*, 28, 30 April, 14, 15 May 1937.

36 Sánchez Recio, *Justicia y guerra*, p. 21.

37 Ministerio de la Guerra, Estado Mayor Central, *Anuario Militar de España 1936* (Madrid: Imprenta y Talleres del Ministerio de la Guerra, 1936) p. 181.

38 Secretaría general de los Tribunales y Jurados Populares, Registro

General num. 3264, 20 January 1937, in AHN, FC-Causa General, 322-3, Exp. 58, pp. 1–24.

39 Hoja de Servicios del general Ramón Robles Pazos, Archivo Militar General, Segovia; *ABC* (Seville), 8 September 1962, 18 July 1964.

40 For a detailed account of the José Robles case, see Paul Preston, *We Saw Spain Die: Foreign Correspondents in the Spanish Civil War* (London: Constable, 2008) pp. 62–92, and Ignacio Martínez de Pisón, *Enterrar a los muertos* (Barcelona: Seix Barral, 2005) *passim*. On extra-territorial prisons run by the NKVD, see Stanley G. Payne, *The Spanish Civil War, the Soviet Union, and Communism* (New Haven: Yale University Press, 2004) p. 205; Martínez de Pisón, *Enterrar a los muertos*, p. 80.

41 Louis Fischer, *Men and Politics: An Autobiography* (London: Jonathan Cape, 1941) p. 406.

42 Coindreau to Lancaster, 1 June 1937, Robles Papers, MS 47; Dos Passos to Bowers, 21 July 1937, Bowers Papers.

43 Josephine Herbst, unpublished diary, 'Journal Spain', pp. 11–12; Herbst to Bruce Bliven, 30 June 1939, Za Herbst Collection, Beinecke Library, Yale University. Her contemporary diary is much more accurate than her later account, *The Starched Blue Sky of Spain and Other Memoirs* (New York: HarperCollins, 1991). However, it is clear from this later source (pp. 154–5) that it was Pepe Quintanilla who was Dos Passos's informant about Robles.

44 John Dos Passos, letter to the editors of the *New Republic*, July 1939, *The Fourteenth Chronicle: Letters and Diaries* (Boston: Gambit, 1973) p. 527; 'The Fiesta at the Fifteenth Brigade', in John Dos Passos, *Journeys between Wars* (New York:

Harcourt, Brace, 1938) pp. 375–81; John Dos Passos, *Century's Ebb: The Thirteenth Chronicle* (Boston: Gambit, 1975) pp. 90–4.

45 Quintanilla's role is discussed in *Claridad*, 19 April 1937.

46 Articles from *La Batalla* are reproduced in Juan Andrade, *La revolución española día a día* (Barcelona: Editorial Nueva Era/ Publicaciones Trazo, 1979) pp. 41–4 for those of 10 and 12 December 1936.

47 Fischer's warning in Juan Andrade, *Notas sobre la guerra civil: actuación del POUM* (Madrid: Ediciones Libertarias, 1986) p. 13. It is dated as late July but Fischer did not reach Spain until mid-September.

48 On Gerö, see Carles Gerhard, *Comissari de la Generalitat a Montserrat (1936–1939)* (Barcelona: Publicacions de l'Abadia de Montserrat, 1982) pp. xxvi, 570–2, 573–9; Jaume Miravitlles, *Episodis de la guerra civil espanyola* (Barcelona: Editorial Pòrtic, 1972) p. 207.

49 Antonio Elorza and Marta Bizcarrondo, *Queridos camaradas: la Internacional Comunista y España, 1919–1939* (Barcelona: Planeta, 1999) p. 364. A similar, but not identical, text, 'Whatever happens, the final destruction of the Trotskyists must be achieved, exposing them to the masses as a fascist secret service carrying out provocations in the service of Hitler and General Franco, attempting to split the Popular Front, conducting a slanderous campaign against the Soviet Union, a secret service actively aiding fascism in Spain,' is reproduced by Jonathan Haslam, *The Soviet Union and the Struggle for Collective Security 1933–39* (London: Macmillan, 1984), pp. 116 n. 53, 264.

50 Miquel Caminal, *Joan Comorera*, Vol. II: *Guerra i revolució*

(1936–1939) (Barcelona: Editorial Empúries, 1984) pp. 62–72.

51 Burnett Bolloten, *The Spanish Civil War: Revolution and Counterrevolution* (Hemel Hempstead: Harvester Wheatsheaf, 1991) p. 411 (on the basis of an interview with Miguel Serra Pàmies of the PSUC leadership). See also David T. Cattell, *Communism and the Spanish Civil War* (Berkeley: University of California Press, 1955) p. 109; Rudolf Rocker, *Extranjeros en España* (Buenos Aires: Ediciones Imán, 1938) p. 91.

52 Víctor Alba and Marisa Ardevol, eds, *El proceso del POUM: documentos judiciales y policiales* (Barcelona: Editorial Lerna, 1989) p. 21.

53 Ángel Viñas, *El escudo de la República: el oro de España, la apuesta soviética y los hechos de mayo de 1937* (Barcelona: Editorial Crítica, 2007) pp. 488–93; Russian intelligence reports reproduced in Radosh, Habeck and Sevostianov, eds, *Spain Betrayed*, pp. 131–3, 178–84.

54 Josep Sánchez Cervelló, *¿Por qué hemos sido derrotados? Las divergencias republicanas y otras cuestiones* (Barcelona: Flor del Viento, 2006) pp. 119–32.

55 Agustín Guillamón, *The Friends of Durruti Group: 1937–1939* (Edinburgh: AK Press, 1996) pp. 22–45, 57–8; Agustín Guillamón, *Barricadas en Barcelona: la CNT de la victoria de julio de 1936 a la necesaria derrota de mayo de 1937* (Barcelona: Ediciones Espartaco Internacional, 2007) pp. 139–48; García Oliver, *El eco de los pasos*, pp. 420, 443.

56 Josep María Bricall, *Política econòmica de la Generalitat (1936–1939): evolució i formes de la producció industrial* (Barcelona: Edicions 62, 1970) pp. 93–104; Graham, *The Spanish Republic*, pp.

254–6; Pelai Pagès i Blanch, *Cataluña en guerra y en revolución 1936–1939* (Seville: Ediciones Espuela de Plata, 2007) pp. 189–94.

57 Cervelló, *¿Por qué hemos sido derrotados?*, pp. 115–17; Ferran Gallego, *Barcelona, mayo de 1937* (Barcelona: Debate, 2007) pp. 340–9; Josep M. Solé i Sabaté and Joan Villarroya i Font, *La repressió a la reraguarda de Catalunya (1936–1939)*, 2 vols (Barcelona: Publicacions de l'Abadia de Montserrat, 1989) I, pp. 108–9; Graham, *The Spanish Republic*, pp. 261–2; Pierre Broué and Emile Témime, *The Revolution and the Civil War in Spain* (London: Faber & Faber, 1972) pp. 281–2.

58 Ricardo Sanz, *El sindicalismo y la política: los 'Solidarios' y 'Nosotros'* (Toulouse: Imprimerie Dulaurier, 1966) pp. 103–4; Joan Pons i Porta and Josep Maria Solé i Sabaté, *Anarquía y República a la Cerdanya (1936–1939): el 'Cojo de Málaga' i els fets de Bellver* (Barcelona: Publicacions de l'Abadia de Montserrat, 1991) pp. 33–46, 133–41, 154–76; Manuel Benavides, *Guerra y revolución en Cataluña* (Mexico: Ediciones Roca, 1978) pp. 344, 351–62, 371; Joan Pons Garlandí, *Un republicà enmig de faistes* (Barcelona: Edicions 62, 2008) pp. 86–9, 150–4; Miquel Berga, *John Langdon-Davies (1897–1971): una biografia anglo-catalana* (Barcelona: Editorial Pòrtic, 1991) pp. 146–7.

59 Pons i Porta and Solé i Sabaté, *Anarquía y República a la Cerdanya*, pp. 142–54; Gerhard, *Comissari de la Generalitat*, pp. 490–1; Peirats, *La CNT*, II, p. 138; César M. Lorenzo, *Los anarquistas españoles y el poder* (Paris: Ruedo Ibérico, 1972) pp. 90, 215; Grandizo Munis, *Jalones de derrota, promesa de victoria (España 1930–1939)* (Mexico City: Editorial Lucha Obrera, 1948) p. 298.

60 Caminal, *Joan Comorera*, II, p. 120; Gallego, *Barcelona, mayo de 1937*, pp. 379, 413, 430–49; Viñas, *El escudo*, pp. 494–5; Benavides, *Guerra y revolución*, pp. 370–5.

61 Zugazagoitia, *Guerra y vicisitudes*, I, pp. 268, 270–2; Peirats, *La CNT*, II, pp. 138–43; Julio Aróstegui, *Por qué el 18 de julio… y después* (Barcelona: Flor del Viento, 2006) pp. 487–92.

62 Viñas, *El escudo*, pp. 496–500; Guillamón, *Barricadas en Barcelona*, pp. 148–70; Lorenzo, *Los anarquistas españoles*, pp. 217–19.

63 Zugazagoitia, *Guerra y vicisitudes*, I, p. 268.

64 Vidarte, *Todos fuimos culpables*, pp. 658–9; Lorenzo, *Los anarquistas españoles*, pp. 215–17; Pagès, *Cataluña en guerra*, pp. 202–9; Benavides, *Guerra y revolución*, p. 370.

65 Viñas, *El escudo*, pp. 527–33, 537–41; Colonel I. G. Starinov, *Over the Abyss: My Life in Soviet Special Operations* (New York: Ballantine Books, 1995) pp. 131–2; Report by Shtern in Yuri Rybalkin, *Stalin y España: la ayuda militar soviética a la República* (Madrid: Marcial Pons Historia, 2007) pp. 222–4.

66 Manuel Cruells, *Mayo sangriento: Barcelona 1937* (Barcelona: Editorial Juventud, 1970) pp. 45–8; Zugazagoitia, *Guerra y vicisitudes*, I, pp. 271–4.

67 Zugazagoitia, *Guerra y vicisitudes*, I, p. 271; Viñas, *El escudo*, pp. 524–9; John Costello and Oleg Tsarev, *Deadly Illusions* (New York: Crown Publishers, 1993) p. 281.

68 Faupel to Wilhelmsstrasse, 11 May 1937, *Documents on German Foreign Policy*, Series C, Vol. III (London: HMSO, 1959) p. 286; Morten Heiberg and Manuel Ros Agudo, *La trama oculta de la guerra civil: los servicios secretos de Franco 1936–1945* (Barcelona: Editorial Crítica, 2006) pp. 136–9.

69 Azaña, diary, 20 May 1937, *Obras completas*, IV, pp. 575–88, 591–2; Vidarte, *Todos fuimos culpables*, pp. 660–3; Enrique Moradiellos, *Don Juan Negrín López* (Barcelona: Ediciones Península, 2006) pp. 244–7; Graham, *The Spanish Republic*, pp. 298–305; Viñas, *El escudo*, pp. 551–6.

70 *Gaceta de la República*, 4 June 1937; *La Vanguardia*, 6, 8, 9, 10, 12 June 1937; Vidarte, *Todos fuimos culpables*, pp. 670, 675–6, 679–80, 686–8. On Santa Úrsula, see Katia Landau, *Le Stalinisme bourreau de la révolution espagnole* (Paris: Spartacus, 1938) pp. 23–7, reproduced in Marcel Ollivier and Katia Landau, *Espagne: les fossoyeurs de la révolution sociale* (Paris: Spartacus René Lefeuvre, 1975) pp. 12–48. On Burillo, see the remarks on the eve of his execution to Rafael Sánchez Guerra, *Mis prisiones: memorias de un condenado por Franco* (Buenos Aires: Editorial Claridad, 1946) pp. 115–16.

71 *Gaceta de la República*, 28 May 1937; Azaña, diary entry for 29 June 1937, *Obras completas*, IV, p. 638; Juan Negrín, 'Apuntes Barcelona del 1 al 40', Archivo de la Fundación Juan Negrín, Carpeta 2, pp. 21–8; Viñas, *El escudo*, p. 594.

72 Comité Peninsular de la FAI, 'Informe al Pleno de Regionales del Movimiento Libertario sobre la dirección de la guerra y las rectificaciones a que obliga la experiencia', Barcelona, 1938; Diego Abad de Santillán, *Por que perdimos la guerra: una contribución a la historia de la tragedia española*, 2nd edn (Madrid: G. del Toro, 1975) p. 90.

73 Declaración de Teodoro Illera Martín, AHN, FC-Causa General, 1505, Exp. 2, pp. 25–7; Peirats, *La CNT*, II, p. 175; Pagès i Blanch, *Cataluña en guerra*, pp. 218–19.

74 A. de Lizarra, *Los vascos y la República española: contribución a la historia de la guerra civil* (Buenos Aires: Editorial Vasca Ekin, 1944) pp. l02–7.

75 Juan de Iturralde (Father Juan José Usabiaga Irazustabarrena), *La guerra de Franco: los vascos y la Iglesia*, 2 vols (San Sebastián: Publicaciones Clero Vasco, 1978) II, p. 314.

76 Manuel de Irujo, *Un vasco en el Ministerio de Justicia: memorias*, 3 vols (Buenos Aires: Editorial Vasca Ekin, 1976–9) I, *passim*; Hilari Raguer, *La pólvora y el incienso: la Iglesia y la guerra civil española* (Barcelona: Ediciones Península, 2001) pp. 329–31.

77 Galíndez, *Los vascos en el Madrid sitiado*, pp. 114, 135–6, 157–9; Zugazagoitia, *Guerra y vicisitudes*, p. 129; Lizarra, *Los vascos y la República española*, pp. 160–3; Rafael Méndez, *Caminos inversos: vivencias de ciencia y guerra* (Mexico City: Fondo de Cultura Económica, 1987) p. 92.

78 Rosario Queipo de Llano, *De la cheka de Atadell a la prisión de Alacuás* (Valladolid: Librería Santaren, 1939) pp. 37–42, 135–7; Pilar Jaraiz Franco, *Historia de una disidencia* (Barcelona: Planeta, 1981) pp. 128–32; Lizarra, *Los vascos y la República española*, pp. 160–3; Fernando Hernández Holgado, 'Carceleras encarceladas: la depuración franquista de las funcionarias de Prisiones de la Segunda República', *Cuadernos de Historia Contemporánea*, Vol. 27, 2005, pp. 271–290.

79 Raguer, *La pólvora y el incienso*, pp. 171, 178–9; Galíndez, *Los vascos en el Madrid sitiado*, pp. 32–3.

80 Costello and Tsarev, *Deadly Illusions*, p. 267; Evgeny M. Primakov, Vadim A. Kirpichenko *et al.*, eds, *Studies in the History of Russian Foreign Intelligence*, 6 vols (Moskva: Mezhdunarodnye otnosheniya, 2003–6) III, ch. 12, p. 153, quoted by Boris Volodarsky, 'Soviet Intelligence Services in the Spanish Civil War, 1936–1939' (unpublished doctoral thesis, London School of Economics, 2010) p. 147.

81 Carlos M. Rama, 'Camilo Berneri y la revolución española', prologue to Camilo Berneri, *Guerra de clases en España, 1936–1937* (Barcelona: Tusquets Editor, 1977) pp. 31–5; Claudio Venza, 'Prefazione', in Camilo Berneri, *Mussolini alla conquista delle Baleari* (Salerno: Galzerano Editore, 2002) pp. 13–14; Viñas, *El escudo*, p. 546; Heiberg and Ros Agudo, *La trama oculta*, pp. 136–8; Graham, *The Spanish Republic*, pp. 294–6; Bolloten, *The Spanish Civil War*, pp. 453, 875–7; Agustín Souchy *et al.*, *The May Days, Barcelona 1937* (London: Freedom Press, 1987) pp. 40–2; Peirats, *La CNT*, pp. 148–500.

82 Landau, *Le Stalinisme*, pp. 28–44.

83 *Ibid.*, pp. 44–5; Christopher Andrew and Vasili Mitrokhin, *The Sword and the Shield: The Mitrokhin Archive and the Secret History of the KGB* (New York: Basic Books, 1999) p. 441; Volodarsky, 'Soviet Intelligence Services', pp. 202–18. The *Letter of an Old Bolshevik* was compiled by the Menshevik émigré Boris Nikolayevsky on the basis of conversations with Bukharin: Stephen P. Cohen, *Bukharin and the Bolshevik Revolution* (Oxford: Oxford University Press, 1980) p. 366.

84 Orlov to Centre, 27 February 1937, quoted by Costello and Tsarev, *Deadly Illusions*, pp. 265–6, 466.

85 Jesús Hernández, *Yo fui un ministro de Stalin* (Madrid: G. del Toro, 1974) pp. 182–3. I am grateful to Boris Volodarsky for explaining the procedures concerning *liter* operations.

86 Max Rieger, *Espionaje en España* (Madrid: Ediciones Unidad, 1938) pp. 73–131; Georges Soria, *Trotskyism in the Service of Franco: Facts and Documents on the Activities of POUM* (New York: International Publishers, 1938) pp. 5, 12–23.

87 Cervera Gil, *Madrid en guerra*, pp. 250–1, 303–9; Soria, *Trotskyism in the Service of Franco*, pp. 8–11. On Castilla, see 'Andrés Nin: el trotskista que se fue al frío' [interview with Javier Jimenéz], *Cambio16*, No. 305, 16 October 1977, p. 26.

88 Orlov to Moscow Centre, 23 May 1937, quoted by Costello and Tsarev, *Deadly Illusions*, pp. 288–289. See also documentary film by Dolors Genovès, *Especial Andreu Nin: Operació Nikolai*, Catalan TV3, 6 November 1992.

89 'Informe sobre la actuación de la policía en el servicio que permitió el descubrimiento en los meses de abril, mayo y junio de la organización de espionaje de cuyas derivaciones surgieron las detenciones y diligencias instruidas contra elementos destacados del POUM', 28 October 1937, FPI, AH 71–6. The report was discovered by Viñas, *El escudo*, pp. 609–10.

90 Declaración de Fernando Valentí Fernández in Procedimiento Militar contra José Cazorla Maure, AHN, FC-Causa General, 1525-1, pp. 28–30; 'Informe sobre la actuación de la policía', pp. 3–5.

91 On the Fernández Golfín network and its use in the plot against Nin, see Cervera Gil, *Madrid en guerra*, pp. 304–10.

92 'Informe al DGS y al Ministro de la Gobernación', pp. 6–8 of the 'Informe sobre la actuación de la policía', FPI, AH 71–6, reproduced by Viñas, *El escudo*, pp. 690–3.

93 'Andrés Nin: el trotskista que se fue al frío', p. 26. Javier Jimenéz elaborated on these points when interviewed by Dolors Genovès in *Especial Andreu Nin: Operació Nikolai*, Catalan TV3, 6 November 1992.

94 'Informe sobre la actuación de la policía', pp. 8–9. On this particular point, Hernández, *Yo fui un ministro de Stalin*, pp. 140–1, is almost certainly correct. On the reasons why he is generally unreliable, see Herbert Rutledge Southworth, '"The Grand Camouflage": Julián Gorkín, Burnett Bolloten and the Spanish Civil War', in Paul Preston and Ann Mackenzie, eds, *The Republic Besieged: Civil War in Spain 1936–1939* (Edinburgh: Edinburgh University Press, 1996) pp. 260–310, especially pp. 267–8; Julián Gorkín, *El proceso de Moscu en Barcelona: el sacrificio de Andrés Nin* (Barcelona: Aymá S.A. Editora, 1973) pp. 13–14.

95 Gabriel Morón, *Política de ayer y política de mañana (los socialistas ante el problema español)* (Mexico City: Talleres Numancia, 1942) pp. 95–8; Vidarte, *Todos fuimos culpables*, p. 732.

96 Orlov to Moscow Centre, 25 September 1937, quoted by Costello and Tsarev, *Deadly Illusions*, pp. 289, 470.

97 Jaume Miravitlles, *Episodis de la guerra civil espanyola* (Barcelona: Editorial Pòrtic, 1972) pp. 189–90; Andrés Suárez (Ignacio Iglesias), *El proceso contra el POUM: un episodio de la revolución española* (Paris: Ruedo Ibérico, 1974) p. 172.

98 *ABC*, 18 June 1937; Gorkín, *El proceso de Moscu en Barcelona*, pp. 106–120. In Valencia, Nin coincided with the Falangist Raimundo Fernández Cuesta: see Manuel Valdés Larrañaga, *De la Falange al Movimiento (1936–1952)* (Madrid: Fundación Nacional Francisco Franco, 1994) p. 69.

99 'Informe sobre la actuación de la policía', pp. 10–11; Vázquez

Baldominos's orders reproduced in Alba and Ardevol, *El proceso*, pp. 28–33. See also Viñas, *El escudo*, pp. 610–13; Pelai Pagès i Blanch, 'El asesinato de Andreu Nin: más datos para la polémica', *Ebre 38. Revista Internacional de la Guerra Civil 1936–1939*, No. 4, 2010, pp. 57–76.

100 Nin's signed statements after his interrogations reproduced in Alba and Ardevol, *El proceso*, pp. 18–28; Pelai Pagès i Blanch, *Andreu Nin: una vida al servei de la classe obrera* (Barcelona: Laertes, 2009) pp. 307–8.

101 'Informe sobre la actuación de la policía', pp. 11–13; Declaración de Fernando Valentí Fernández in Procedimiento Militar contra José Cazorla Maure, AHN, FC-Causa General, 1525-1, p. 29; witness statements reproduced in Alba and Ardevol, *El proceso*, pp. 36–9. See also Viñas, *El escudo*, pp. 613–17.

102 Hernández, *Yo fui un ministro de Stalin*, pp. 177–82.

103 Payne, *The Spanish Civil War, the Soviet Union*, p. 228.

104 Orlov to Moscow Centre, 24 July 1937, quoted by Costello and Tsarev, *Deadly Illusions*, pp. 291, 470.

105 Costello and Tsarev, *Deadly Illusions*, p. 292. This document is used both in Maria Dolors Genovès, 'Operació Nikolai: l'assassinat d'Andreu Nin', in Borja de Riquer i Permanyer, ed., *Història, política, societat i cultura dels Països Catalans*, Vol. IX: *De la gran esperanza a la gran ensulsiada 1930–1939* (Barcelona: Enciclopèdia Catalana, 1999) pp. 305–7, and in her documentary *Operació Nikolai* where it is attributed to Grigulevich and Pierre is wrongly identified as Ernö Gerö. For the identifications of Bom, Victor and Pierre, see Volodarsky, 'Soviet Intelligence Services', pp. 149–53.

106 Juan Negrín, 'Apuntes Barcelona', pp. 28, 35–41.

107 Declaración de Fernando Valentí Fernández in Procedimiento Militar contra José Cazorla Maure, AHN, FC-Causa General, 1525-1, p. 29; Zugazagoitia, *Guerra y vicisitudes*, I, pp. 291–4; Vidarte, *Todos fuimos culpables*, pp. 727–9; Viñas, *El escudo*, pp. 597–600.

108 Rieger, *Espionaje en España*, pp. 39–44. On the authorship, see Hernández, *Yo fui un ministro de Stalin*, p. 183.

109 Vidarte, *Todos fuimos culpables*, pp. 689–90; Azaña, diary, 29 June, 22 July 1937, *Obras completas*, IV, pp. 638–9, 692; Viñas, *El escudo*, pp. 595–7; Hernández, *Yo fui un ministro de Stalin*, pp. 128–34.

110 Negrín, 'Apuntes Barcelona', pp. 13–14; *ABC*, 20 July 1937; Morón, *Política de ayer*, p. 94.

111 Morón, *Política de ayer*, pp. 99–101; Vidarte, *Todos fuimos culpables*, pp. 732–3.

112 Vidarte, *Todos fuimos culpables*, p. 750.

113 Morón, *Política de ayer*, pp. 102–4; Gregorio Peces-Barba del Brío, 'Las confesiones de un fiscal', *Cuadernos para el Diálogo*, 19 November 1977, pp. 28–9; Causa General, *La dominación roja en España* (Madrid: Ministerio de Justicia, 1945) p. 283; Viñas, *El escudo*, pp. 601–3, 619–24.

114 Gómez Sáiz appointed government representative in Catalonia, *Gaceta*, 4 June 1937. Morón resigns as Sub-Director General de Seguridad, 13 November 1937, *Gaceta de la República*, 14 November 1937.

115 *La Vanguardia*, 13 June 1937; *Gaceta de la República*, 13 June 1937.

116 Azaña, diary, 28 June 1937, *Obras completas*, IV, p. 636; Graham, *The Spanish Republic*, pp. 342–3; Viñas, *El escudo*, p. 591.

117 *Gaceta de la República*, 28 March 1938.

118 *Gaceta de la República*, 7 August 1937; Indalecio Prieto, *Cómo y por*

qué salí del Ministerio de Defensa Nacional: intrigas de los rusos en España (texto taquigráfico del informe pronunciado el 9 de agosto de 1938 ante el Comité Nacional del Partido Socialista Obrero Español) (Mexico City: Impresos y Papeles, S. de R.L., 1940) pp. 76–7; Graham, *The Spanish Republic*, pp. 344–5.

119 Gustavo Durán, *Una enseñanza de la Guerra Española: glorias y miserias de la improvisación de un ejército* (Madrid: Ediciones Júcar, 1980) pp. 95–101; Alexander Orlov, *The March of Time: Reminiscences* (London: St Ermin's Press, 2004) pp. 326–30; Declaración de Pedrero, AHN, FC-Causa General, 1532, Exp. 30, pp. 8, 39.

120 Prieto, *Cómo y por qué*, pp. 78–9; Declaración de Pedrero, AHN, FC-Causa General, 1520-1, pp. 9, 53–7, 65–70, 87, 1532, p. 40.

121 Enrique Líster, *Nuestra guerra* (Paris: Colección Ebro, 1966) p. 125; Hugh Thomas, *The Spanish Civil War* (London: Eyre & Spottiswoode, 1961) p. 778.

122 José Ramón Soler Fuensanta and Francisco Javier López-Brea Espiau, *Soldados Sin Rosto: los servicios de información, espionaje y criptografía en la Guerra Civil española* (Barcelona: Inèdita Editores, 2008) pp. 60–1.

123 Acta de la reunión de la Comisión Nacional de Educación del Soldado de la JSU, el 17 de febrero de 1938, Centro Documental de la Memoria Histórica, Salamanca, sección Político-Social Madrid, Caja 2434, Legajo 4365. I am grateful to Dr Sandra Souto Kustrín for this reference.

124 R. L. Chacón, *Por qué hice las chekas de Barcelona: Laurencic ante el consejo de guerra* (Barcelona: Editorial Solidaridad Nacional, 1939) pp. 10–11, 19–33; Félix Ros, *Preventorio D. Ocho meses en la cheka*, 2nd edn (Madrid: Editorial Prensa Española, 1974) *passim*; Miguel Sabater, *Estampas del cautiverio rojo: memorias de un preso del S.I.M.* (Barcelona: Editorial Librería Religiosa, 1940) pp. 39–51; Francisco Gutiérrez Latorre, *La República del crimen: Cataluña, prisionera 1936–1939* (Barcelona: Editorial Mare Nostrum, 1989) pp. 119–24 and photographs pp. 176–7; Cèsar Alcalà, *Les presons de la República: les txeques a Catalunya* (Barcelona: Editorial Base, 2009) pp. 30–2, 61–2, 75–6, 189–204.

125 Julián Casanova, *Anarquismo y revolución en la sociedad rural aragonesa 1936–1938* (Madrid: Siglo XXI, 1985) pp. 151–263; Joaquín Ascaso, *Memorias (1936–1938): hacia un Nuevo Aragón* (Zaragoza: Prensas Universitarias de Zaragoza, 2006) pp. 24–32, 85–157; Julián Casanova, *De la calle al frente: el anarcosindicalismo en España (1931–1939)* (Barcelona: Editorial Crítica, 1997) pp. 193–4, 232–3.

126 Landau, *Le Stalinisme*, pp. 59–61; Pierre Broué, 'Quelques proches collaborateurs de Trotsky', *Cahiers Léon Trotsky*, No. 1, January 1979.

127 The principal biography of Landau is by Hans Schafranek, *Das Kurze Leben des Kurt Landau: ein Österreichischer Kommunist als Opfer der stalinistischen Geheimpolizei* (Vienna: Verlag für Gesellschaftskritik, 1988).

128 The details of the arrests of the Landaus are recounted in Landau, *Le Stalinisme*, pp. 32–44. See also Volodarsky, 'Soviet Intelligence Services', pp. 232–3.

129 Andrew and Mitrokhin, *The Mitrokhin Archive*, p. 74.

130 *La Vanguardia*, 28 April 1938.

131 John McGovern, *Terror in Spain* (London: Independent Labour Party, 1938) p. 10.

132 Landau, *Le Stalinisme*, pp. 49–50; Irujo, *Un vasco*, I, pp. 20–4, 48–50, 67–70; Lizarra, *Los vascos y la República española*, pp. 111–15, 144–8.

133 Lluís Alegret, *Joan García Oliver: retrat d'un revolucionari anarcosindicalista* (Barcelona: Pòrtic, 2008) pp. 220–2.

134 Elorza and Bizcarrondo, *Queridos camaradas*, p. 379; Radosh, Habeck and Sevostianov, eds, *Spain Betrayed*, p. 223; Larrañaga, *De la Falange al Movimiento*, pp. 67–8.

135 Nadal, *Guerra civil en Málaga*, pp. 417–18, 442–6; José Asensio Torrado, *El general Asensio: su lealtad a la República* (Barcelona: Artes Gráficas CNT, n.d.); Louis Fischer, 'Spain Won't Surrender', *The Nation*, 30 April 1938; Telegram to *The Nation*, New York, 29 April 1938, Louis Fischer Papers, Seeley G. Mudd Manuscript Library, Princeton University, Box 36, MC#024 [henceforth Fischer Papers]; Francisco Largo Caballero, *Mis recuerdos: cartas a un amigo* (Mexico City: Editores Unidos, 1954) pp. 243–5.

136 François Godicheau, 'La Légende noire du Service d'Information Militaire de la République dans la guerre civile espagnole, et l'idée de contrôle politique', *Le Mouvement Social*, No. 201, Vol. 4, 2002, pp. 29–52; Solé and Villarroya, *La repressió a la reraguarda*, I, pp. 246–62, 272–6; Pelai Pagès i Blanch, *La presó model de Barcelona: història d'un centre penitenciari en temps de guerra (1936–1939)* (Barcelona: Publicacions de l'Abadia de Montserrat, 1996) pp. 38–61, 269–302; Sánchez Recio, *Justicia y guerra*, pp. 166–75.

137 AHN, FC-Causa General, 1366-2, Exp. 4, pp. 46, 174–5; Caja 3, Exp. 6, p. 151; Legajo 1378, Caja 1, Exp. 1, pp. 325, 365, 430–5, 464, 521; Justo Martinez Amutio, *Chantaje a un Pueblo* (Madrid: G. del Toro, 1974), pp. 211 f. 228–30.

138 Francesc Badia, *El camps de treball a Catalunya durant la guerra civil (1936–1939)* (Barcelona: Publicacions de l'Abadia de Montserrat, 2001) pp. 113–28; Pagès i Blanch, *La presó model de Barcelona*, pp. 80–90; Sabater, *Estampas del cautiverio rojo*, pp. 190–2; Gutiérrez Latorre, *La República del crimen*, pp. 143–53.

139 Sánchez Recio, *Justicia y guerra*, pp. 181–93.

140 Julius Ruiz, '"Work and Don't Lose Hope": Republican Forced Labour Camps during the Spanish Civil War', *Contemporary European History*, Vol. 18, No. 4, 2009, pp. 419–41.

141 Manuel Tarín-Iglesias, *Los años rojos* (Barcelona: Planeta, 1985) pp. 106–10; Leche to Halifax, 28 June 1938, TNA, FO 371/22619 W9149.

142 Leche to Foreign Office, 24 August 1938, TNA, FO 371/22612, quoted by Peter Anderson, 'The Chetwode Commission and British Diplomatic Responses to Violence behind the Lines in the Spanish Civil War', *European History Quarterly*, forthcoming; Azaña, diary, 12 August 1938, *Obras completas*, IV, p. 888; Tarín-Iglesias, *Los años rojos*, pp. 159, 165–9; Solé i Sabaté and Villarroya i Font, *La repressió a la reraguarda*, I, pp. xvi–xviii, 8, 274–6.

143 Irujo, *Un vasco*, I, pp. 89–91, 250–73.

144 Cowan to FO, 222 August 1938, TNA, FO 371/22612 W1161. On the work of the commission, see Anderson, 'The Chetwode Commission'.

145 TNA, FO 371/22612 W11426.

146 Cowan Memo, 8 November 1938, TNA, FO 371/22615 W16172.

147 Juan Negrín, 'Jornada de Generosidad y Confianza', *La Vanguardia*, 25 December 1938.

148 TNA, FO 371/22613 W12638, W1263. I am grateful to Peter Anderson for drawing my attention to these documents.

149 Chetwode to Halifax, 14 November 1938, Halifax Private Papers, TNA, FO 800/323.

150 *The Times*, 14 February 1939; John Hope Simpson, *Refugees: A Review of the Situation since September 1938* (London, August 1939), p. 56, quoted by Anderson, 'Chetwode Commission'.

151 Chetwode to Halifax 17/04/1939, TNA, FO 425/416 W6162/72/41, quoted by Anderson, 'Chetwode Commission'.

152 *Sesiones de la Diputación Permanente de Cortes. Congreso de los Diputados*, 16 November de 1937, p. 4.

153 Elorza and Bizcarrondo, *Queridos camaradas*, pp. 379–83; Azaña, *Obras completas*, IV, p. 692, 828; Morón, *Política de ayer*, pp. 102–4.

154 *Gaceta de la República*, 1 December 1937; Solé i Sabaté and Villarroya i Font, *La repressió a la reraguarda*, I, pp. 268–73; Cèsar Alcalá, *Las Checas del terror: la desmemoria histórica al descubierto* (Madrid: Libros Libres, 2007) pp. 44–6.

155 Alba and Ardevol, eds, *El proceso*, pp. 357–62, 402–9; Lizarra, *Los vascos y la República española*, pp. 149–54.

156 Gaudioso J. Sánchez Brun, *Instituciones turolenses en el franquismo 1936–1961: personal y mensaje políticos* (Teruel: Instituto de Estudios Turolenses, 2002) pp. 326–7; Amador del Fueyo Tuñón, *Heroes de la epopeya: el Obispo de Teruel* (Barcelona: Editorial Amaltea, 1940) pp. 210–22; Lizarra, *Los vascos y la República española*, pp. 246–7; Indalecio Prieto, *Palabras al viento*, 2nd edn (Mexico City: Ediciones Oasis, 1969) pp. 220–1; Antonio Montero Moreno, *Historia de la persecución religiosa en España 1936–1939* (Madrid: Biblioteca de Autores Cristianos, 1961) pp. 421–7; Jorge Martínez Reverte, *La caída de Cataluña* (Barcelona: Editorial Crítica, 2006) pp. 437–8.

157 Vidarte, *Todos fuimos culpables*, p. 912.

158 Juan Negrín *et al.*, *Documentos políticos para la historia de la República Española* (Mexico City: Colección Málaga, 1945) pp. 25–6; Zugazagoitia, *Guerra y vicisitudes*, II, pp. 241–2.

159 Rafael Méndez, *Caminos inversos: vivencias de ciencia y guerra* (Mexico City: Fondo de Cultura Económica, 1987) pp. l04–6; Indalecio Prieto and Juan Negrín, *Epistolario Prieto y Negrín: puntos de vista sobre el desarrollo y consecuencias de la guerra civil española* (París: Imprimerie Nouvelle, 1939) p. 37; Negrín *et al.*, *Documentos políticos*, pp. 26–7.

160 Enrique Moradiellos, *Juan Negrín López 1892–1956* (Santa Cruz de Tenerife: Parlamento de Canarias, 2005) pp. 131–3; *Actas de la Diputación Permanente. Congreso de los Diputados*, 31 March 1939, p. 9.

161 Louis Fischer, *Men and Politics: An Autobiography* (London: Jonathan Cape, 1941) p. 559.

162 *Epistolario Prieto y Negrín*, pp. 17, 37, 44–5.

163 Minutes of *Congreso de los Diputados, Diputación Permanente*, 31 March 1939, pp. 6, 7, 13.

Chapter 12: Franco's Slow War of Annihilation

1 José Manuel Martínez Bande, *Nueve meses de guerra en el norte*, 2nd edn (Madrid: Editorial San Martín, 1980) pp. 41–50; Pedro Barruso, *Verano y revolución: la Guerra Civil en Gipuzkoa (julio–septiembre de 1936)* (San Sebastian: R&B Editores, 1996) pp. 85–132.

2 Javier Ugarte, 'Represión como instrumento de acción política del Nuevo Estado (Álava, 1936–1939)', *Historia Contemporánea*, No. 35, 2007, pp. 249–71; Marisol Martínez and David Mendaza, *1936: Guerra Civil en Euskal Herria*, Vol. III: *La guerra en Araba: el levantamiento militar en Bizkaia* (Pamplona: Aralar Liburuak, 1999) pp. 48–55, 71–84, 209–11, 234–49; Iñaki Egaña, *Los crímenes de Franco en Euskal Herria 1936–1940* (Tafalla: Editorial Txalaparta, 2009) pp. 69–70, 249.

3 Pedro Barruso Barés, *Violencia política y represión en Guipúzcoa durante la guerra civil y el primer franquismo* (San Sebastián: Hiria Liburuak, 2005) pp. 50–7, 143–6; Iñaki Egaña, *1936: Guerra Civil en Euskal Herria*, Vol. V: *El estatuto de autonomía* (Pamplona: Aralar Liburuak, 1998) pp. 194–5.

4 Barruso Barés, *Violencia política y represión en Guipúzcoa*, pp. 40–111, 153–70 and especially pp. 58–62.

5 El Clero Vasco, *El pueblo vasco frente a la cruzada franquista* (Toulouse: Editorial Egi-Indarra, 1966) pp. 259–72.

6 Jaime del Burgo, *Conspiración y guerra civil* (Madrid: Editorial Alfaguara, 1970) pp. 204–6.

7 Pedro Barruso Barés, 'La represión en las zonas republicana y franquista del País Vasco durante la Guerra Civil', *Historia Contemporánea*, No. 35, 2007, pp. 654–6.

8 *The Times*, 29, 31 August, 1, 2, 4, 5 September 1936; Martínez Bande, *Nueve meses de guerra en el norte*, pp. 64–86.

9 Barruso, *Verano y revolución*, pp. 243–56.

10 Barruso Barés, *Violencia política y represión en Guipúzcoa*, pp. 120–43, 232–40; Mikel Aizpuru, Urko Apaolaza, Jesús Mari Gómez and Jon Ogdriozola, *El otoño de 1936 en Guipúzcoa: los fusilamientos de Hernani* (Irún: Alberdania, 2007) pp. 91–104, 151–83; Iñaki Egaña, *1936: Guerra Civil en Euskal Herria*, Vol. IV: *La guerra en Gipuzkoa* (Pamplona: Aralar Liburuak, 1998) pp. 198–261; Francisco Espinosa Maestre, 'Sobre la represión franquista en el País Vasco', Dialnet, Universidad de la Rioja, http://dialnet.unirioja.es/servlet/articulo?codigo=2914416, p. 5 n. 11; Barruso Barés, 'La represión', pp. 667–9.

11 Jean Pelletier, *Seis meses en las prisiones de Franco: crónica de hechos vividos* (Madrid and Valencia: Ediciones Españolas, 1937) p. 97; Santiago Martínez Sánchez, *Los papeles perdidos del cardenal Segura, 1880–1957* (Pamplona: Ediciones Universidad de Navarra, 2004) pp. 374–93; Barruso Barés, *Violencia política y represión en Guipúzcoa*, pp. 143–53.

12 Alberto Onaindía, *Hombre de paz en la guerra* (Buenos Aires: Editorial Vasca Ekin, 1973) pp. 103–12; Barruso Barés, *Violencia política y represión en Guipúzcoa*, pp. 159–69; Juan de Iturralde (Juan José Usabiaga Irazustabarrena), *La guerra de Franco: los vascos y la Iglesia*, 2 vols (San Sebastián: Publicaciones Clero Vasco, 1978) II, pp. 357–80; Aizpuru et al., *El otoño de 1936*, pp. 200–22.

13 Barruso Barés, *Violencia política y represión en Guipúzcoa*, pp. 171–9.

14 Pelletier, *Seis meses*, pp. 5–26, 34–9, 44–5, 58–71, 94–5, 111–12; Barruso Barés, *Violencia política y represión en Guipúzcoa*, pp. 160–1; Aizpuru et al., *El otoño de 1936*, pp. 187–99; Iturralde, *La guerra de Franco*, II, pp. 343–55; Egaña, *1936: Guerra Civil en Euskal Herria*, V, pp. 190–3.

15 Onaindía, *Hombre de paz*, pp. 172–81.

16 José Luis de la Granja Sainz, *El oasis vasco: el nacimiento de Euskadi en la*

República y guerra civil (Madrid: Editorial Tecnos, 2007) pp. 421–33; José Luis de la Granja Sainz, *República y guerra civil en Euskadi (del Pacto de San Sebastián al de Santoña)* (Bilbao: Instituto Vasco de Administración Pública, 1990) pp. 301–5; Fernando de Meer, *El Partido Nacionalista Vasco ante la guerra de España (1936–1937)* (Pamplona: Ediciones de la Universidad de Navarra, 1992) pp. 163–5, 263–81; Onaindía, *Hombre de paz*, pp. 131–8; Xuan Cándano, *El Pacto de Santoña (1937): la rendición del nacionalismo vasco al fascismo* (Madrid: La Esfera de los Libros, 2006) pp. 45–6.

17 De la Granja Sainz, *República y guerra civil en Euskadi*, pp. 296–301; José Antonio Aguirre y Lecube, *Veinte años de gestión del Gobierno Vasco (1936–1956)* (Durango: Leopoldo Zugaza, 1978) pp. 86–9; George L. Steer, *The Tree of Gernika: A Field Study of Modern War* (London: Hodder & Stoughton, 1938) pp. 110–22.

18 Steer, *Gernika*, p. 159; Bowers to Hull, 30 April 1937, *Foreign Relations of the United States* [henceforth *FRUS*] 1937 (Washington: United States Government Printing Office, 1954) I, p. 291. See the press cutting reproduced in Martínez and Mendaza, *1936: Guerra Civil en Euskal Herria*, III, p. 211.

19 Ugarte, 'Represión como instrumento', p. 259.

20 Steer, *Gernika*, pp. 160–70; Herbert Rutledge Southworth, *Guernica! Guernica!: A Study of Journalism, Propaganda and History* (Berkeley: University of California Press, 1977) pp. 368–9; Jesús Salas Larrazabal, *La guerra de España desde el aire*, 2nd edn (Barcelona: Ariel, 1972) pp. 187–8.

21 Roberto Cantalupo, *Fu la Spagna: Ambasciata presso Franco:*

Febbraio–Aprile 1937 (Milan: Mondadori, 1948) pp. 231–2.

22 Gordon Thomas and Max Morgan-Witts, *The Day Guernica Died* (London: Hodder & Stoughton, 1975) pp. 144, 296; Claude Bowers, *My Mission to Spain* (London: Victor Gollancz, 1954) p. 343.

23 Onaindía to Gomá, 28 April, Gomá to Onaindía, 5 May 1937, Archivo Gomá, *Documentos de la guerra civil*, Vol. V: *Abril–Mayo de 1937*, ed. José Andrés-Gallego and Antón M. Pazos (Madrid: Consejo Superior de Investigaciones Científicas, 2003) pp. 282–4, 357.

24 Del Burgo, *Conspiración*, p. 862.

25 Paul Preston, *Franco: A Biography* (HarperCollins, London, 1993) pp. 239–47.

26 Iturralde, *La guerra de Franco*, II, pp. 372–6; Aizpuru *et al.*, *El otoño de 1936*, p. 221; Francisco Javier Pérez Esteban, 'Represión contra los curas vascos durante la ofensiva de Vizcaya', in Joaquín Rodero, Juan Moreno and Jesús Castrillo, eds, *Represión franquista en el frente norte* (Madrid: Editorial Eneida, 2008) p. 158.

27 *The Times*, 1, 3, 4, 7, 10, 12, 15, 17, 18, 19, 20, 21, 22, 26, 27 May, 1, 4, 7, 12, 14, 15, 16 June 1937; Steer, *Gernika*, pp. 265–316, 322–4, 328–31, 354; Steer to Noel-Baker, 31 May 1937, Noel-Baker Papers, Churchill Archives Centre, Churchill College, Cambridge [henceforth CAC], NBKR, 4x/118; Gilbert to Hull, 29 May 1937, *FRUS 1937*, I, pp. 305–6.

28 Iñaki Egaña, *1936: Guerra Civil en Euskal Herria*, Vol. VII: *Vascos en la guerra fuera de Euskal Herria: represión en Bizkaia* (Pamplona: Aralar Liburuak, 1999) pp. 205–6; Egaña, *Los crímenes de Franco*, pp. 237–40, 248.

29 Barruso Barés, 'La represión', pp. 669–70; Santos Juliá *et al.*, *Víctimas*

de la guerra civil (Madrid: Ediciones Temas de Hoy, 1999) pp. 206–8.

30 Felipe Acedo Colunga, 'Memoria del Fiscal del Ejército de Ocupación', Zaragoza, 15 January 1939 (Archivo del Tribunal Militar Territorial Segundo de Sevilla, doc. sin clasificar, p. 24), quoted by Espinosa Maestre, 'Sobre la represión franquista', pp. 17–20.

31 Ángel David Martín Rubio, *Paz, piedad, perdón … y verdad: la represión en la guerra civil: una síntesis definitiva* (Madrid: Editorial Fénix, 1997) p. 372, suggests 1,778. Egaña, *1936: Guerra Civil en Euskal Herria*, VII, pp. 214–21, 338–52, suggests 903. Barruso Barés, 'La represión', pp. 669–70. See also Egaña, *Los crímenes de Franco*, p. 66; Iturralde, *La guerra de Franco*, II, pp. 285–99.

32 José María Areilza, *Discurso pronunciado por el Alcalde de Bilbao, Sr. D. José María Areilza el día 8 de julio de 1937, en el Coliseo Albia, en función de homenaje al glorioso ejército y milicias nacionales* (n.p., 1937); Egaña, *1936: Guerra Civil en Euskal Herria*, VII, pp. 194–5.

33 Emilio Faldella, *Venti mesi di guerra in Spagna (luglio 1936–febbraio 1938)* (Firenze: Felice Le Monnier, 1939) p. 357; General Vicente Rojo, *España heroica: diez bocetos de la guerra española*, 3rd edn (Barcelona: Ariel, 1975) pp. 91–101; Ramón Salas Larrazábal, *Historia del ejército popular de la República*, 4 vols (Madrid: Editora Nacional, 1973) II, pp. 1215–64; Manuel Aznar, *Historia militar de la guerra de España (1936–1939)* (Madrid: Ediciones Idea, 1940) pp. 430–63; Luis María de Lojendio, *Operaciones militares de la guerra de España* (Barcelona: Montaner y Simón, 1940) pp. 331–44; José Manuel Martínez Bande, *Vizcaya* (Madrid: Editorial San Martín, 1971) pp. 197–204.

34 Jesús Gutiérrez Flóres, *Guerra Civil en Cantabria y pueblos de Castilla*, 2 vols (Buenos Aires: Librosenred, 2006) pp. 23–6.

35 Juan Antonio Cabezas, *Asturias: catorce meses de guerra civil* (Madrid: G. del Toro, 1975) p. 63; Manuel Azaña, *Obras completas*, 4 vols (Mexico City: Ediciones Oasis, 1966–8) IV, p. 846.

36 Gutiérrez Flóres, *Guerra Civil en Cantabria*, pp. 28–9, 36–43; José Luis Ledesma, 'Una retaguardia al rojo: las violencias en la zona republicana', in Francisco Espinosa Maestre, ed., *Violencia roja y azul: España, 1936–1950* (Barcelona: Editorial Crítica, 2010) pp. 217–18.

37 Azaña, *Obras completas*, IV, pp. 782, 784, 846–7; Cándano, *El Pacto de Santoña*, pp. 176–82, 196–205; José Manuel Martínez Bande, *El final del frente norte* (Madrid: Editorial San Martín, 1972) pp. 41–89; Lojendio, *Operaciones militares*, pp. 290–303; Aznar, *Historia militar*, pp. 465–83.

38 Gutiérrez Flóres, *Guerra Civil en Cantabria*, pp. 24–5, 113, 244 (Pérez y García Argüelles), 126–34, 151–74 (executions); Espinosa Maestre, ed., *Violencia roja y azul*, p. 77.

39 Cándano, *El Pacto de Santoña*, pp. 240–53; Alberto Onaindía, *El 'Pacto' de Santoña, antecedentes y desenlace* (Bilbao: Editorial Laiz, 1983) pp. 108–64; Santiago de Pablo, Ludger Mees and José A. Rodríguez Ranz, *El péndulo patriótico: historia del Partido Nacionalista Vasco*, Vol. II: *1936–1979* (Barcelona: Editorial Crítica, 2001) pp. 32–41; Steer, *Gernika*, pp. 386–94; Egaña, *1936: Guerra Civil en Euskal Herria*, VII, pp. 57–87; Martínez Bande, *El final del frente norte*, pp. 89–98; John F. Coverdale, *Italian Intervention in the Spanish Civil War* (Princeton, NJ: Princeton University Press, 1975) pp. 291–4; P. M. Heaton, *Welsh Blockade Runners in the Spanish*

Civil War (Newport, Gwent: Starling Press, 1985) pp. 68, 101–2; Iturralde, *La guerra de Franco*, II, pp. 301–10.

40 Bowers to Hull, 23 October, 13 December 1937, *FRUS 1937*, I, pp. 433, 465–6. A list of those handed over is printed in Egaña, *1936: Guerra Civil en Euskal Herria*, VII, pp. 236–43. See also Juliá *et al.*, *Víctimas*, pp. 205–7.

41 Barruso Barés, 'La represión', pp. 674–81; unpublished manuscript by Balasi Abando de Ereño.

42 Josep Benet, *L'intent franquista de genocidi cultural contra Catalunya* (Barcelona: Publicacions de l'Abadia de Montserrat, 1995) pp. 212–17.

43 Cándano, *El Pacto de Santoña*, pp. 55–8; Barruso Barés, 'La represión', p. 673; Hilari Raguer, *Aita Patxi: prisionero con los gudaris* (Barcelona: Editorial Claret, 2006) pp. 139–50; Pérez Esteban, 'Represión contra los curas vascos', pp. 164–8.

44 Oscar Pérez Solís, *Sitio y defensa de Oviedo*, 2nd edn (Valladolid: Afrodisio Aguardo, 1938) pp. 5–28; Julián Zugazagoitia, *Guerra y vicisitudes de los españoles*, 2nd edn, 2 vols (Paris: Librería Española, 1968) I, pp. 50–4; Matilde de la Torre, *Mares en la sombra: estampas de Asturias*, 2nd edn (Sada-A Coruña: Ediciós do Castro, 2007) pp. 80–97; Cabezas, *Asturias*, pp. 29–31; Guillermo García Martínez, *Los defensores del cerco de Oviedo (19–7–36/17–10–36)* (Oviedo: Autor/Gráficas Careaga, 1994) pp. 25–49; Joaquín Arrarás, *Historia de la cruzada española*, 8 vols, 36 tomos (Madrid: Ediciones Españolas, 1939–43) IV, 15, pp. 141–3.

45 Ledesma, 'Una retaguardia al rojo', pp. 172–3; Cabezas, *Asturias*, pp. 35–6; Miguel Ángel González Muñiz, Javier R. Muñoz *et al.*, *La guerra civil en Asturias*, 2 vols (Gijón and Madrid: Ediciones Júcar, 1986) I, pp. 94–5, 117–27; Ramon Álvarez,

Rebelión militar y revolucion en Asturias: un protagonista libertario (Gijón: Autor/Artes Gráficas NOEGA, 1995) pp. 86–90.

46 Arrarás, *Historia de la cruzada*, VI, 27, pp. 361–3; Joaquín A. Bonet,*¡Simancas! Epopeya de los cuarteles de Gijón* (Gijón: Tipografía Flores, 1939) pp. 181–99; José Manuel Martínez Bande, *Los asedios* (Madrid: Editorial San Martín, 1983) pp. 292–300.

47 Luis de Armiñán, *D. Antonio Aranda Mata General en Jefe de la División de Asturias* (Ávila: Impresora Católica, 1937) p. 31; Pérez Solís, *Sitio y defensa*, pp. 31, 97–9.

48 Webb Miller, *I Found No Peace: The Journal of a Foreign Correspondent* (London: The Book Club, 1937) p. 340.

49 Cabezas, *Asturias*, pp. 31–4; Martínez Bande, *Los asedios*, p. 234; Carmen García García, 'Aproximación al estudio de la represión franquista en Asturias: "paseos" y ejecuciones en Oviedo (1936–1952)', *El Basilisco* (Oviedo), No. 6, July–August 1990, pp. 70–1; Juan Ambou, *Los comunistas en la resistencia nacional republicana (la guerra en Asturias, el País Vasco y Santander)* (Madrid: Editorial Hispamerica, 1978) pp. 333–40; Irene Díaz Martínez, 'La represión franquista en Asturias durante la guerra civil', in Rodero, Moreno and Castrillo, eds, *Represión franquista en el frente norte*, pp. 181–6; González Muñiz, Muñoz *et al.*, *La guerra civil en Asturias*, I, pp. 108–11.

50 González Muñiz, Muñoz *et al.*, *La guerra civil en Asturias*, I, pp. 193–8, 205–8; Díaz Martínez, 'La represión franquista en Asturias', pp. 188–95, 211–14.

51 *ABC* (Seville), 18 October 1936; García Martínez, *Los defensores*, pp. 192–209; Martínez Bande, *Nueve*

meses de guerra en el norte, pp. 110–42.

52 García, 'Aproximación', pp. 71–4; Díaz Martínez, 'La represión franquista en Asturias', pp. 195–200, 214–15; Cabezas, Asturias, pp. 99–102.

53 Ángel Viñas, Guerra, dinero, dictadura: ayuda fascista y autarquía en la España de Franco (Barcelona: Editorial Crítica, 1984) p. 147; Martínez Bande, El final del frente norte, pp. 109–75; Salas Larrazábal, Ejército popular, II, pp. 1470–99; Lojendio, Operaciones militares, pp. 303–26; Aznar, Historia militar, pp. 517–29; Hugh Thomas, The Spanish Civil War, 3rd edn (London: Hamish Hamilton, 1977) pp. 728–31.

54 Azaña, Obras completas, IV, pp. 834, 847–8; Juan Antonio Sacaluga, La resistencia socialista en Asturias 1937–1962 (Madrid: Editorial Pablo Iglesias, 1986) p. 6.

55 Espinosa, ed., Violencia roja y azul, pp. 77, 246.

56 Cabezas, Asturias, pp. 159–86, 196–7, 206–12; Marcelino Laruelo Roa, La libertad es un bien muy preciado: Consejos de Guerra celebrados en Gijón y Camposantos por el ejército nacionalista al ocupar Asturias en 1937: testimonios y condenas (Gijón: En la Estela de Aldebarán, 1999) pp. 185–95, 453–5; Xesús Comoxo, Xesús Costa and Xesús Santos, Rianxo na guerra civil: campo de concentración de prisioneiros de guerra 1937–1939 (Rianxo: Concello de Rianxo, 2003) pp. 32–8.

57 Manuel Suárez Cortina, El fascismo en Asturias (1931–1937) (Gijón: Silverio Cañada, 1981) p. 200; Sacaluga, La resistencia socialista, pp. 5–6; Ronald Fraser, Blood of Spain: The Experience of Civil War 1936–1939 (London: Allen Lane, 1979) pp. 424–6; Luis Miguel Piñera, Posguerra incivil: vencidos y vencedores en Gijón entre 1937 y 1940 (Oviedo: Ayuntamiento de Gijón/KRK Ediciones, 2008) pp. 140–52; Leonardo Borque López, La represión violenta contra los maestros republicanos en Asturias (Oviedo: KRK Ediciones, 2010) pp. 165–242; Rubén Vega García and Begoña Serrano Ortega, Clandestinidad, represión y lucha política: el movimiento obrero en Gijón bajo el franquismo (1937–1962) (Gijón: Ayuntamiento de Gijón, 1998) pp. 17–21.

58 Marta Capín Rodríguez, El Valle de Dios (Madrid: Ediciones MS-CTC, 2004) pp. 177–82, 235–54; La Voz de Asturias, 7 July 2005; Piñera, Posguerra incivil, pp. 138–9.

59 García, 'Aproximación', pp. 74–5; Nicanor Rozada, Relatos de una lucha: la guerrilla y la represión en Asturias (Oviedo: Imprenta Gofer, 1993) pp. 252–3.

60 Eduardo Pons Prades, Las guerras de los niños republicanos (1936–1939) (Madrid: Compañía Literaria, 1997) pp. 126–9.

61 García, 'Aproximación', pp. 76–80.

62 El Comercio Digital, 15 April 2010; María Enriqueta Ortega Valcárcel, La represión en Asturias: ejecutados y fallecidos en la cárcel del coto de Gijón (Avilés: Azucel, 1994) pp. 9–19, 23–49; Laruelo Roa, La libertad, pp. 51–66, 197–203, 209–11; Sacaluga, La resistencia socialista, pp. 7–8; García, 'Aproximación', pp. 81–2.

63 Diario de Burgos, 8 October 1937. I am grateful to Luis Castro who drew this to my attention.

64 Ángela Cenarro Lagunas, Cruzados y camisas azules: los orígenes del franquismo en Aragón, 1936–1945 (Zaragoza: Prensas Universitarias de Zaragoza, 1997) pp. 43–9.

65 Julia Cifuentes Chueca and Pilar Maluenda Pons, El asalto a la República: los orígenes del franquismo

en Zaragoza (1936–1939) (Zaragoza: Institución Fernando el Católico, 1995) pp. 45–61, 171–6; Julián Casanova, Ángela Cenarro, Julita Cifuentes, Maria Pilar Maluenda and María Pilar Salomón, *El pasado oculto: fascismo y violencia en Aragón (1936–1939)*, 3rd edn (Zaragoza: Mira Editores, 2001) pp. 48–65, 243–417 (list of victims in Zaragoza).

66 Cifuentes and Maluenda, *El asalto*, pp. 121–2; Altaffaylla Kultur Taldea, *Navarra 1936: de la esperanza al terror*, 8th edn (Tafalla: Altaffaylla Kultur Taldea, 2004) pp. 690–4; Jesús Vicente Aguirre González, *Aquí nunca pasó nada: La Rioja 1936* (Logroño: Editorial Ochoa, 2007) pp. 926–31; Antonio Hernández García, *La represión en La Rioja durante la guerra civil*, 3 vols (Logroño: Autor, 1982) II, pp. 71, 207–12; Martínez and Mendaza, *1936: Guerra Civil en Euskal Herria*, II, pp. 94–5.

67 *El Siglo*, 6 April 1998; Jesús Pueyo Maisterra, 'Del infierno al Paraíso', unpublished memoirs, pp. 20–1.

68 Víctor Lucea Ayala, *Dispuestos a intervenir en política: Don Antonio Plano Aznárez: socialismo y republicanismo en Uncastillo (1900–1939)* (Zaragoza: Institución Fernando el Católico, 2008) pp. 372–98; Pueyo Maisterra, 'Del infierno al Paraíso', pp. 21–5.

69 Ángela Cenarro, 'La lógica de la guerra, la lógica de la venganza: violencia y fractura social en una comunidad bajoaragonesa, 1939–1940', in Conxita Mir, Jordi Catalán and David Ginard, eds, *Enfrontaments civils: postguerres i reconstruccions*, Vol. II: *Guerra civil de 1936 i franquisme* (Lleida: Associació Recerques i Pagès Editors, 2002), pp. 703–15.

70 Ángela Cenarro Lagunas, *El fin de la esperanza: fascismo y guerra civil en la provincia de Teruel (1936–1939)* (Teruel: Instituto de Estudios Turolenses, 1996) pp. 67–91; Casanova *et al.*, *El pasado oculto*, pp. 183–4, 187–8.

71 Cenarro Lagunas, *El fin de la esperanza*, pp. 71–3, 79–82; Casanova *et al.*, *El pasado oculto*, pp. 175–85.

72 David Alonso Císter, *Verano del 36: la fosa común de la guerra civil de los Llanos de Caudé (Teruel)* (Zaragoza: Mira Editores, 2008) pp. 13–16, 31–155; Emilio Silva and Santiago Macías, *Las fosas de Franco: los republicanos que el dictador dejó en las cunetas* (Madrid: Ediciones Temas de Hoy, 2003) pp. 151–63; Casanova *et al.*, *El pasado oculto*, p. 185.

73 Mantecón to Bergamín, 8 February 1938; Édgar González Ruiz, *Los otros cristeros y su presencia en Puebla* (Puebla: Benemérita Universidad Autónoma de Puebla, 2004) p. 374; Casanova *et al.*, *El pasado oculto*, pp. 185–6, 466, 481. I am grateful to Marco Aurelio Torres H. Mantecón and Édgar González Ruiz for providing me with a copy of Mantecón's letter and to Serafín Aldecoa for his comments on both cases.

74 Amador del Fueyo, *Héroes de la epopeya: el Obispo de Teruel* (Barcelona: Editorial Amaltea, 1940) pp. 86–7.

75 Gaudioso J. Sánchez Brun, *Instituciones turolenses en el franquismo 1936–1961: personal y mensaje políticos* (Teruel: Instituto de Estudios Turolenses, 2002) pp. 336–8; Fueyo, *El Obispo de Teruel*, pp. 110–17.

76 Sánchez Brun, *Instituciones turolenses*, pp. 332–4, 339; Cenarro Lagunas, *El fin de la esperanza*, pp. 150–1.

77 Casanova *et al.*, *El pasado oculto*, p. 182; Cenarro Lagunas, *El fin de la esperanza*, p. 75.

78 'Notas informativas sobre la batalla de Teruel' (assembled by Captain Rogelio Martinez, a Commissar of the Ejército del Este and sent to José Bergamín from Lérida 7 February 1938). I am immensely grateful to Édgar González Ruiz for his kindness in providing me with a copy of these documents. See also González Ruiz, *Los otros cristeros*, p. 375.

79 Vicente García, *Aragón, baluarte de España* (Zaragoza: Librería General, 1938) pp. 188–9; José María Maldonado Moya, *El frente de Aragón: la guerra civil en Aragón (1936–1938)* (Zaragoza: Mira Editores, 2007) pp. 196–200; José Manuel Martínez Bande, *La gran ofensiva sobre Zaragoza* (Madrid: Editorial San Martín, 1973) pp. 57–74.

80 Indalecio Prieto, *La tragedia de España: discursos pronunciados en América del Sur* (Mexico City: Fundación Indalecio Prieto/Sitesa, 1995) pp. 42–3; Marco Aurelio Torres H. Mantecón, *José Ignacio Mantecón: vida y obra de un aragonés en el destierro* (Zaragoza: Editorial Institución Fernando el Católico, 2005) p. 102; 'Notas informativas sobre la batalla de Teruel'; González Ruiz, *Los otros cristeros*, p. 375. I am immensely grateful to Dr Pedro López Peris for his help in reconstructing these events.

81 'Notas informativas sobre la batalla de Teruel'.

82 Cenarro Lagunas, *El fin de la esperanza*, pp. 151–4.

83 Onaindía, *Hombre de paz*, pp. 344–8, 351–72; Prieto, *La tragedia de España*, pp. 42–3; Fueyo, *El Obispo de Teruel*, pp. 162–4; Hilari Raguer, *La pólvora y el incienso: la Iglesia y la guerra civil española* (Barcelona: Ediciones Península, 2001) p. 171.

84 See the letters reprinted in Onaindía, *Hombre de paz*, pp. 373–97.

85 Casanova *et al.*, *El pasado oculto*, pp. 135–50; José María Azpiroz Pascual, *La voz del olvido: la guerra civil en Huesca y la Hoya* (Huesca: Diputación Provincial de Huesca, 2007) pp. 21–6, 30–2; Espinosa Maestre, ed., *Violencia roja y azul*, p. 247.

86 Emilio Casanova and Jesús Lou, *Ramón Acín: la línea sentida* (Zaragoza: Gobierno de Aragón, 2004) pp. 55–62; Azpiroz Pascual, *La voz del olvido*, pp. 128–203.

87 Azpiroz Pascual, *La voz del olvido*, pp. 233–365; Esteban C. Gómez Gómez, *El eco de las descargas: adiós a la esperanza republicana* (Barcelona: Escega, 2002) pp. 143–59, 197–202, 208, 256–60, 491–504; Jeanne Maurín, *Cómo se salvó Joaquín Maurín: recuerdos y testimonios* (Madrid: Ediciones Júcar, 1981) pp. 74–87. On Faustiñana, see Gómez Gómez, *El eco*, pp. 159, 186–7, 194, 209–10, 261–4, 283, 323, 361, 370; Maurín, *Cómo se salvó*, p. 78.

88 Víctor Pardo Lancina, *Tiempo destruido* (Huesca: Gobierno de Aragón, 2009) pp. 136–91; Azpiroz Pascual, *La voz del olvido*, pp. 264–6; Luisa Marco Sola, *Sangre de cruzada: el catolicismo oscense frente a la guerra civil (1936–1939)* (Huesca: Instituto de Estudios Altoaragoneses/Diputación Provincial de Huesca, 2009) pp. 185–8; Casanova *et al.*, *El pasado oculto*, p. 441.

89 Joan Villarroya i Font, *Els bombardeigs de Barcelona durant la guerra civil (1936–1939)*, 2nd edn (Barcelona: Publicacions de l'Abadia de Montserrat, 1999) pp. 79–101, 123–33; Stohrer to Wilhelmstrasse, 23 March 1938, *Documents on German Foreign Policy: Germany*

and the Spanish Civil War 1936–1939, Series C, Vol. III (London: HMSO, 1959) pp. 624–6.

90 Preston, *Franco*, pp. 302–3.

91 Josep M. Solé i Sabaté and Joan Villarroya i Font, *España en llamas: la guerra civil desde el aire* (Madrid: Ediciones Temas de Hoy, 2003) pp. 162–66; Montse Armengou and Ricard Belis, *Ramon Perera: l'home dels refugis* (Barcelona: Rosa dels Vents, 2008) pp. 83–90, 121–6; Mercè Barallat i Barés, *La repressió a la postguerra civil a Lleida (1938–1945)* (Barcelona: Publicacions de l'Abadia de Montserrat, 1991) pp. 39–43, 47–51.

92 Josep Maria Solé i Sabaté, *La repressió franquista a Catalunya 1938–1953* (Barcelona: Edicions 62, 1985) pp. 35–7; Barallat i Barés, *La repressió a Lleida*, pp. 52–5.

93 Benet, *L'intent franquista de genocidi*, pp. 208–12, 217–22; José María Fontana, *Los catalanes en la guerra de España*, 2nd edn (Barcelona: Ediciones Acervo, 1977) p. 322.

94 Hilari Raguer, *Divendres de passió: vida i mort de Manuel Carrasco i Formiguera* (Barcelona: Publicacions de l'Abadia de Montserrat, 1984), pp. 250–78, 334–46, 373–90; Josep Benet, *Manuel Carrasco i Formiguera, afusellat* (Barcelona: Edicions 62, 2009) pp. 84–9, 96–108; Onaindía, *Hombre de paz*, pp. 128–9, 427–9. See also Carrasco's correspondence with his wife written from prison: Manuel Carrasco i Formiguera, *Cartes de la presó*, ed. Hilari Raguer (Barcelona: Publicacions de l'Abadia de Montserrat, 1988).

95 José Manuel Martínez Bande, *La llegada al mar* (Madrid: Editorial San Martín, 1975) pp. 112–13; Benet, *L'intent franquista de genocidi*, pp. 189–99.

96 Barallat i Barés, *La repressió a Lleida*, pp. 69–7; Josep M. Solé i Sabaté and

Joan Villarroya i Font, *L'ocupació militar de Catalunya, març 1938 – febrer 1939* (Barcelona: L'Avenç, 1987) pp. 55–9.

97 General Sagardía, *Del Alto Ebro a las Fuentes del Llobregat: Treinta y dos meses de guerra de la 62 División* (Barcelona: Editora Nacional, 1940) pp. 161–9.

98 Manuel Gimeno, *Revolució, guerra i repressió al Pallars (1936–1939)* (Barcelona: Publicacions de l'Abadia de Montserrat, 1989) pp. 58–77; Solé i Sabaté and Villarroya i Font, *L'ocupació militar*, pp. 63–83.

99 Solé i Sabaté and Villarroya i Font, *L'ocupació militar*, pp. 87–90; Francisco Sánchez Ruano, *Islam y guerra civil española: moros con Franco y con la República* (Madrid: La Esfera de los Libros, 2004) pp. 336–40.

100 Preston, *Franco*, pp. 303–5.

101 Solé i Sabaté, *La repressió franquista*, pp. 36–7; Vicent Gabarda Cebellán, *Els afusellaments al País Valencià (1938–1956)* (Valencia: Edicions Alfons el Magnànim, 1993) p. 74; Vicente Enrique y Tarancón, *Recuerdos de juventud* (Barcelona: Ediciones Grijalbo, 1984) pp. 262–72; Teresa Armengot, Joan Lluís Porcar and Ricard Camil Torres, *La repressió franquista al País Valencià: Borriana i Manises* (Valencia: Tres i Quatre, 2008) pp. 23–41; Joan Lluís Porcar and Teresa Armengot, 'Mort i repressió franquista a Borriana (1938–1950)', in Pelai Pagès i Blanch, ed., *La repressió franquista al País Valencià: primera trobada d'investigadors de la Comissió de la veritat* (Valencia: Tres i Quatre, 2009) pp. 511–22.

102 Fernando Vázquez Ocaña, *Pasión y muerte de la segunda República española* (Paris: Editorial Norte, 1940) pp. 61–2.

103 Antonio D. López Rodríguez, *Cruz, bandera y caudillo: el campo de*

concentración de Castuera (Badajoz: CEDER–La Serena, 2007) pp. 90–107, 226–69; Silva and Macías, *Las fosas de Franco*, pp. 265–9.

104 Juan-Simeón Vidarte, *Todos fuimos culpables* (Mexico City: Fondo de Cultura Económica, 1973) pp. 855–7.

105 Francisco Franco Bahamonde, *Palabras del Caudillo 19 abril 1937–7 diciembre 1942* (Madrid: Ediciones de la Vicesecretaría de Educación Popular, 1943) p. 476.

106 Paul Preston, *Botxins i repressors: els crims de Franco i dels franquistes* (Barcelona: Editorial Base, 2006) pp. l01–13; Josep Cruanyes, *El papers de Salamanca: l'espoliació del patrimoni documental de Catalunya* (Barcelona: Edicions 62, 2003) pp. 16–17, 34–5.

107 José Manuel Martínez Bande, *La campaña de Cataluña* (Madrid: Editorial San Martín, 1979) pp. 41–60; Benet, *L'intent franquista de genocidi*, p. 228.

108 *FRUS 1939*, II, pp. 722–3; Martínez Bande, *Cataluña*, pp. 60–92.

109 Sánchez Ruano, *Islam y guerra civil*, pp. 357–63; Solé i Sabaté and Villarroya i Font, *L'ocupació militar*, pp. 93–108; Núria Bonet Baqué, Amanda Cardona Alcaide and Gerard Corbella López, *Tàrrega 1936–61: aproximació a la repressió, l'exili i la vida cuotidiana* (Tàrrega: Ajuntament de Tàrrega, 2008) pp. 14, 76–7.

110 Franco Bahamonde, *Palabras del Caudillo 1937–1942*, pp. 501–3.

111 Fontana, *Los catalanes en la guerra*, p. 335; Raguer, *La pólvora y el incienso*, p. 375.

112 Josep Recasens Llort, *La repressió franquista a Tarragona* (Tarragona: Publicacions del Cercle d'Estudis Històrics i Socials Guillem Oliver del Camp de Tarragona, 2005) pp. 47–9.

113 Josep Recasens Llort, *La repressió franquista a la comarca de l'Alt Camp (1939–1950)* (Valls: Consell Comarcal de l'Alt Camp/Pagès Editors, 2006) pp. 27–33; Albert Manent i Segimon, *La guerra civil i la repressió del 1939 a 62 pobles del Camp de Tarragona* (Valls: Cossetània Edicions, 2006) *passim*.

114 Fraser, *Blood of Spain*, pp. 481–2.

115 Teresa Pàmies, *Quan érem capitans: memòries d'aquella guerra* (Barcelona: Dopesa, 1974) pp. 149–50.

116 Recounted by Theodor Garriga in an interview broadcast in the Catalunya Ràdio series *Veus de l'exili* in August 2006. See Josep M. Figueres, *Veus de l'exili: vint testimonis de la diàspora catalana* (Valls: Cossetània Edicions, 2007) p. 84.

117 Herbert Matthews, 'Figueras Capital of Loyalist Spain', 'Conflict to Go On', 'Toll of 500 Feared in Figueras Raids', *New York Times*, 28 January, 6, 4 February 1939.

118 Michael Richards, *A Time of Silence: Civil War and the Culture of Repression in Franco's Spain, 1936–1945* (Cambridge: Cambridge University Press, 1998) p. 45.

119 Benet, *L'intent franquista de genocidi*, pp. 129, 235–49.

120 *Ibid.*, pp. 266–7, 339–40.

121 Aram Monfort, *Barcelona 1939: el camp de concentració d'Horta* (Barcelona: L'Avenç, 2008) pp. 28–34; Enric Canals, *Delators: la justicia de Franco* (Barcelona: L'Esfera dels Llibres, 2007) pp. 31–3, 155–7; Julián Casanova, Francisco Espinosa, Conxita Mir and Francisco Moreno Gómez, *Morir, matar, sobrevivir: la violencia en la dictadura de Franco* (Barcelona: Editorial Crítica, 2002) pp. 29–30, 173–9; Joan Sagués, 'Repressió, control i supervivència', in Conxita Mir, Carme Agusti and Josep Gelanch, eds, *Violència i repressió a Catalunya durant el franquisme:*

balanç historiogràfic i perspectives (Lleida: Ediciones de l'Universitat de Lleida, 2001) pp. 87–8.

122 Solé i Sabaté, *La repressió franquista*, pp. 62–7, 95–187; Solé i Sabaté and Villarroya i Font, *L'ocupació militar*, pp. 75–82, 117–30.

123 Casanova *et al*, *Morir, matar, sobrevivir*, pp. 131–7, 159–72; Conxita Mir, *Vivir es sobrevivir: justicia, orden y marginación en la Cataluña rural de posguerra* (Lleida: Editorial Milenio, 2000) pp. 37–58, 128–50, 164–87, 195–202.

124 Estado Español, Ministerio de la Gobernación, *Dictamen de la comisión sobre ilegitimidad de poderes actuantes en 18 de julio de 1936* (Barcelona, 1939) pp. 9–13; Manuel Álvaro Dueñas, '*Por ministerio de la ley y voluntad del Caudillo': la juridición especial de responsabilidades políticas (1939–1945)* (Madrid: Centro de Estudios Políticos y Constitucionales, 2006) pp. 84–121.

Chapter 13: No Reconciliation: Trials, Executions, Prisons

1 Francisco Franco Bahamonde, *Palabras del Caudillo 19 abril 1937–7 diciembre 1942* (Madrid: Ediciones de la Vicesecretaría de Educación Popular, 1943) p. 102.

2 *ABC*, 1 January 1940. Omitted from subsequent compilations of Franco's speeches, the complete text was published at the time as *Mensaje del Caudillo a los españoles: discurso pronunciado por S.E. el Jefe del Estado la noche del 31 de diciembre del 1939* (Madrid: n.p. [Ediciones FE], n.d. [1940]) pp. 16, 19–20.

3 Mónica Lanero Táboas, *Una milicia de la justicia: la política judicial del franquismo (1936–1945)* (Madrid: Centro de Estudios Constitucionales, 1996) pp. 318–19; Manuel Ballbé, *Orden público y militarismo en la España*

constitucional (1812–1983) (Madrid: Alianza Editorial, 1983) pp. 402–9.

4 Emilio Mola Vidal, *Obras completas* (Valladolid: Librería Santarén, 1940) p. 1177.

5 Franco Bahamonde, *Palabras del Caudillo 1937–1942*, p. 343.

6 Ballbé, *Orden público y militarismo*, p. 404; Ramón Serrano Suñer, *Entre el silencio y la propaganda, la Historia como fue: memorias* (Barcelona: Planeta, 1977) pp. 244–8.

7 Josep Cruanyes, *El papers de Salamanca, L'espoliació del patrimoni documental de Catalunya* (Barcelona: Edicions 62, 2003) pp. 16–17, 34–5.

8 Lanero Táboas, *Una milicia de la justicia*, pp. 320–1; Pablo Gil, *La noche de los generales: militares y represión en el régimen de Franco* (Barcelona: Ediciones B, 2004) pp. 143–5; Peter Anderson, *The Francoist Military Trials: Terror and Complicity, 1939–1945* (New York: Routledge/Cañada Blanch Studies, 2010) pp. 53–9.

9 Juan Caba Guijarro, *Por los caminos del mundo* (Móstoles: Talleres CNT-AIT, 1984) p. 15; José Manuel Sabín, 'Control y represión', in Manuel Requena Gallego, ed., *Castilla-La Mancha en el franquismo* (Ciudad Real: Biblioteca Añil, 2003) p. 25.

10 Gil, *La noche de los generales*, pp. 131–8; Pablo Gil Vico, 'Derecho y ficción: la represión judicial militar', in Francisco Espinosa Maestre, ed., *Violencia roja y azul: España, 1936–1950* (Barcelona: Editorial Crítica, 2010), pp. 284–5.

11 Francisco Moreno Gómez, *Córdoba en la posguerra (la represión y la guerrilla, 1939–1950)* (Córdoba: Francisco Baena Editor, 1987) pp. 47–8.

12 Ignacio Arenillas de Chaves, *El proceso de Besteiro* (Madrid: Revista de Occidente, 1976) pp. 402–3.

13 *La Vanguardia Española*, 8 February 1939.

14 Peter Anderson, 'Singling Out Victims: Denunciation and Collusion in the Post-Civil War Francoist Repression in Spain, 1939–1945', *European History Quarterly*, Vol. 39, No. 1, 2009, pp. 18–19.

15 Anderson, *The Francoist Military Trials*, pp. 57–9; Francisco Cobo Romero, *Revolución campesina y contrarrevolución franquista en Andalucía: conflictividad social, violencia política y represión franquista en el mundo rural andaluz 1931–1950* (Granada: Universidad de Córdoba/Universidad de Granada, 2004) pp. 318–19; Julio Prada Rodríguez, *La España masacrada: la represión franquista de guerra y posguerra* (Madrid: Editorial Alianza, 2010) pp. 199–206; Peter Anderson, 'In the Interests of Justice? Grass-roots Prosecution and Collaboration in Francoist Military Trials, 1939–1945', *Contemporary European History*, Vol. 18, No. 1 (2009), pp. 25–44; Enric Canals, *Delators: la justicia de Franco* (Barcelona: L'Esfera dels Llibres, 2007) pp. 29–33; Santiago Vega Sombría, *De la esperanza a la persecución: la represión franquista en la provincia de Segovia* (Barcelona: Editorial Crítica, 2005) pp. 261–2.

16 Antonio Ruiz Vilaplana, *Burgos Justice: A Year's Experience of Nationalist Spain* (London: Constable, 1938) pp. 151–3.

17 Acedo Colunga, 'Memoria del Fiscal del Ejército de Ocupación', analysed by Francisco Espinosa Maestre, *Contra el olvido: historia y memoria de la guerra civil* (Barcelona: Editorial Crítica, 2006) pp. 79–91.

18 Francisco Espinosa Maestre, 'Julio de 1936: golpe militar y plan de exterminio', in Julián Casanova,

Francisco Espinosa, Conxita Mir and Francisco Moreno Gómez, *Morir, matar, sobrevivir: la violencia en la dictadura de Franco* (Barcelona: Editorial Crítica, 2002) pp. 96–102; Espinosa Maestre, *Contra el olvido*, p. 92.

19 Lanero Táboas, *Una milicia de la justicia*, pp. 322, 360–2; Rafael Gil Bracero and María Isabel Brenes, *Jaque a la República (Granada, 1936–1939)* (Granada: Ediciones Osuna, 2009) pp. 225–30, 295–9; Rafael Gil Bracero, 'La justicia nacional y el Tribunal de Responsabilidades Políticas de Granada: las fuentes y primeras conclusiones', in Archivo Histórico Nacional, *Justicia en guerra: jornadas sobre la administración de Justicia durante la Guerra Civil española: instituciones y fuentes documentales* (Madrid: Ministerio de Cultura, 1990) pp. 605–6; María Isabel Brenes Sánchez, 'La represión franquista y la oposición antifranquista en Andalucía Oriental de posguerra: Granada 1939–1959' (unpublished doctoral thesis, Universidad de Granada, 2005) pp. vii–x.

20 According to Wenceslao Carrillo, Minister of the Interior in the Consejo de Defensa Nacional. See the unpublished report by Eustaquio Cañas, 'Marzo de 1939: el último mes', in FPI, ARLF 172-30, p. 28.

21 AHN, FC-Causa General, 1525-1, pp. 2–3, 5–6, 19–25; Aurora Arnaiz, *Retrato hablado de Luisa Julián* (Madrid: Compañía Literaria, 1996) pp. 111–42, 158–9; Melquesidez Rodríguez Chaos, *24 años en la cárcel* (Paris: Colección Ebro, 1968) pp. 27–8, 73–5. *ABC*, 16 February 1940, reported the arrest of Torrecilla, Marasa Barasa, Agapito Sainz and a large group of those implicated in Paracuellos. However,

the interrogation of Torrecilla in the Causa General is dated 11 November 1939.

22 P. Carlos Paramio Roca, Pedro A. García Bilbao and Xulio García Bilbao, *La represión franquista en Guadalajara* (Guadalajara: Foro por la Memoria de Guadalajara, 2010) pp. 32–5, 53–6, 77–9, 89–90.

23 Luis Miguel Sánchez Tostado, *La guerra civil en Jaén: historia de un horror inolvidable* (Jaén: Junta de Andalucía/Colección Memoria Histórica, 2005) pp. 325–30, 519–23, 535–662; *Asociación para la Recuperación de la Memoria Histórica de Jaén* (Jaén: ARMH, 2005) pp. 55–91, 93–128; Francisco Cobo Romero, *Revolución campesina y contrarrevolución franquista en Andalucía: conflictividad social, violencia política y represión franquista en el mundo rural andaluz 1931–1950* (Granada: Universidad de Córdoba/Universidad de Granada, 2004) pp. 318–23.

24 Óscar J. Rodríguez Barreira, *Migas con miedo: prácticas de resistencia al primer franquismo: Almería, 1939–1953* (Almería: Editorial Universidad de Almería, 2008) pp. 71–7; Eusebio Rodríguez Padilla, *La represión franquista en Almería, 1939–1945* (Mojácar: Arráez Editores, 2007) pp. 90–7, 185–6, 198–248, 345, 356–60; Rafael Quiroga-Cheyrouze y Muñoz, *Política y guerra civil en Almería* (Almería: Editorial Cajal, 1986) pp. 244–6, 315–26.

25 Francisco Alía Miranda, *La guerra civil en la retaguardia: conflicto y revolución en la provincia de Ciudad Real (1936–1939)* (Ciudad Real: Diputación Provincial, 1994) pp. 381–92; Espinosa Maestre, ed., *Violencia roja y azul*, p. 77.

26 María Encarna Nicolás Marín, *Instituciones murcianas en el franquismo (1939–1962)* (Murcia: Editora Regional de Murcia, 1982) pp. 505–7; Fuensanta Escudero Andújar, *Dictadura y oposición al franquismo en Murcia: de las cárceles de posguerra a las primeras elecciones* (Murcia: Universidad de Murcia, 2007) pp. 25–61; Fuensanta Escudero Andújar, *Lo cuentan como lo han vivido (República, guerra y represión en Murcia)* (Murcia: Universidad de Murcia, 2000) pp. 123–46, 155–63; Isabel Marín Gómez, *El laurel y la retama en la memoria: tiempo de posguerra en Murcia, 1939–1952* (Murcia: Universidad de Murcia, 2004) pp. 82–99; Espinosa Maestre, ed., *Violencia roja y azul*, p. 77.

27 Manuel Ortiz Heras, *Violencia política en la II República y el primer franquismo: Albacete, 1936–1950* (Madrid: Siglo XXI, 1996) pp. 250–66.

28 Gabarda Cebellán, *Els afusellaments al País Valencià*, pp. 10, 53, 69–81, 201–13; Juan Luis Porcar, *La memòria i les víctimes: repressió franquista a les Comarques de Castelló* (Castellón: Grup per la Recerca de la Memòria Històrica, 2008) pp. 33–42; Miguel Ors Montenegro, 'La represión de guerra y posguerra en Alicante 1926–1939' (unpublished doctoral thesis, Universitat d'Alacant, 1993) p. 48. See also the superb symposium edited by Pelai Pagès i Blanch, *La repressió franquista al País Valencià: primera trobada d'investigadors de la Comissió de la veritat* (Valencia: Tres i Quatre, 2009).

29 Eladi Mainer Cabanes, 'L'exili del coronel Casado amb el Consell de Defensa pel port de Gandia després de la cerca infructuosa d'una pau pactada', in José Miguel Santacreu Soler, ed., *Una presó amb visites al mar: el drama del Port d'Alacant, Març de 1939* (Valencia: Tres i

Quatre, 2008) pp. 115–56; Michael Alpert, *La guerra civil española en el mar* (Madrid: Siglo XX, 1987) pp. 353, 360–2.

30 Juan Martínez Leal, 'El *Stanbrook*: un barco mítico en la memoria de los exiliados españoles', in *Pasado y Memoria. Revista de Historia Contemporánea*, No. 4, 2005, pp. 66–7.

31 *Ibid.*, pp. 67–81; José Miguel Santacreu Soler, 'El bloqueig naval franquista i la sort dels darrers vaixells de l'exili del port d'Alacant', in Santacreu Soler, ed., *Una presó amb visites al mar*, pp. 203–33; Francisco Escudero Galante, *Pasajero 2058: la odisea del Stanbrook* (Alicante: Editorial Club Universitario, 2002) pp. 65–71.

32 Eduardo de Guzmán, *La muerte de la esperanza* (Madrid: G. del Toro, 1973) pp. 196 ff. Rodriguez Chaos, *24 años en la cárcel*, pp. 11–17; Manuel García Corachán, *Memorias de un presidiario (en las cárceles franquistas)* (Valencia: Publicacions de la Universitat de València, 2005) pp. 27–31.

33 Eladi Mainer Cabanes, José Miguel Santacreu Soler and Ricard Camil Torres Fabra, 'El parany dels darrers dies de la guerra al port d'Alacant', in Santacreu Soler, ed., *Una presó amb visites al mar*, pp. 157–95; Ronald Fraser, *Blood of Spain: The Experience of Civil War 1936–1939* (London: Allen Lane, 1979) pp. 502–7.

34 Eduardo de Guzmán, *El año de la victoria* (Madrid: G. del Toro, 1974) pp. 19–23; Juan Caba Guijarro, *Mil gritos tuvo el dolor en el campo de 'Albatera'* (Ciudad Real: Imprenta Angama, 1983) pp. 3–9; Rodriguez Chaos, *24 años en la cárcel*, pp. 18–24; Tomasa Cuevas Gutiérrez, *Cárcel de mujeres (1939–1945)*, 2 vols (Barcelona: Sirocco Books, 1985) II, pp. 87–8.

35 Gabarda Cebellán, *Els afusellaments al Pais Valenciá*, pp. 37–41; Guzmán, *La muerte de la esperanza*, pp. 387–94; Caba Guijarro, *Mil gritos*, pp. 9–13.

36 Guzmán, *El año de la victoria*, pp. 31, 43–6; García Corachán, *Memorias de un presidiario*, pp. 31–3; Javier Navarro Navarro, 'El terror com a epíleg a una guerra: la repressió franquista al País Valenciá: dos testimonis', in Pagès i Blanch, ed., *La repressió franquista al País Valencià*, pp. 307–17.

37 Ramón de las Casas, *Requiem a mis amigos fusilados* (Caracas: Ediciones Surco, 1975) pp. 13–14; Caba Guijarro, *Mil gritos*, pp. 13–16; Guzmán, *El año de la victoria*, pp. 155–82; García Corachán, *Memorias de un presidiario*, pp. 35–42.

38 Julius Ruiz, '"Work and Don't Lose Hope": Republican Forced Labour Camps during the Spanish Civil War', *Contemporary European History*, Vol. 18, No. 4, 2009, pp. 424, 433–5; Juan Martínez Leal and Miguel Ors Montenegro, 'De cárceles y campos de concentración', in 'Dossier: la represión en Alicante (1939–1945)', *Revista Canelobre* (Alicante), Nos. 31–2, 1995, pp. 38–45; Glicerio Sánchez Recio, *Justicia y guerra en España: los tribunales populares (1936–1939)* (Alicante: Instituto de Cultura 'Juan Gil-Albert', 1994) pp. 181–92.

39 Gabarda Cebellán, *Els afusellaments al Pais Valenciá*, pp. 42–4; Guzmán, *El año de la victoria*, pp. 184–9, 195–7, 209–17, 233–4, 249–55; Eduardo de Guzmán, *Nosotros los asesinos* (Madrid: G. del Toro, 1976), pp. 22–4; Caba Guijarro, *Mil gritos*, pp. 17–19.

40 Guzmán, *El año de la victoria*, pp. 54–5, 102–3; Guzmán, *Nosotros los asesinos*, pp. 21–2.

41 Juan M. Molina, *Noche sobre España* (Mexico City: Ediciones de la CNT

de España, 1958) pp. 30–1; Guzmán, *El año de la victoria*, pp. 66–7, 330.

42 A. V. Phillips, *Spain under Franco* (London: United Editorial, 1940) pp. 8–9, 24–5; Gil Vico, 'Derecho y ficción', pp. 251–7; Guzmán, *Nosotros los asesinos*, pp. 14–20, 28–42, 120, 140, 151; Rodriguez Chaos, *24 años en la cárcel*, pp. 33–7; Miguel Núñez, *La revolución y el deseo: memorias* (Barcelona: Ediciones Península, 2002) pp. 103–5.

43 *A la memoria de Ricardo Zabalza* (Mexico City: Federación Española de Trabajadores de la Tierra, 1944) p. 11; Emilio Majuelo, *La generación del sacrificio: Ricardo Zabalza 1898–1940* (Tafalla: Editorial Txalaparta, 2008) pp. 283–337; Guzmán, *Nosotros los asesinos*, pp. 332–4.

44 Sandoval, 'Informe de mi actuación', AHN, FC-Causa General, 1530-1, Exp. 1; Guzmán, *Nosotros los asesinos*, pp. 43, 52, 56–7, 66–7, 79–96; Carlos García Alix, *El honor de las injurias: busca y captura de Felipe Sandoval* (Madrid: T Ediciones/No Hay Penas, 2007) p. 140.

45 Guzmán, *Nosotros los asesinos*, pp. 170–1,184–7, 208, 217.

46 *Ibid.*, pp. 270–1.

47 *Ibid.*, pp. 293–5.

48 *Ibid.*, pp. 285, 292, 299–310; Diego San José, *De cárcel en cárcel* (Sada-A Coruña: Ediciós do Castro, 1988) pp. 65–83; Phillips, *Spain under Franco*, pp. 12–13; Fraser, *Blood of Spain*, p. 508; Josep Subirats Piñana, *Pilatos 1939–1941: prisión de Tarragona* (Madrid: Editorial Pablo Iglesias, 1993) pp. 8–20, 186–243.

49 Summary of MI5 interrogations of Jost, National Archives, 9 July 1945, TNA, KV 2/104 C396445; Rafael García Pérez, *Franquismo y Tercer Reich: las relaciones económicas hispano-alemanas durante la segunda guerra mundial* (Madrid:

Centro de Estudios Constitucionales, 1994) p. 88; Manuel Ros Agudo, *La guerra secreta de Franco* (Barcelona: Editorial Crítica, 2002) pp. 180–1; Ingrid Schulze Schneider, 'La cooperación de la Alemania Nazi en la lucha franquista contra la masonería', in J. A. Ferrer Benimeli, ed., *La masonería en la España del siglo XX*, 2 vols (Toledo: Universidad de Castilla-La Mancha, 1996) pp. 1179–80. Jost was not executed but imprisoned only until 1951: see Helmut Krausnick, Hans Buchheim, Martin Broszat and Hans-Adolf Jacobsen, *Anatomy of the SS State* (London: Collins, 1968) pp. 174, 587.

50 Cruanyes, *El papers de Salamanca*, pp. 42–7; Santiago López García and Severiano Delgado Cruz, 'Víctimas y Nuevo Estado 1936–1940', in Ricardo Robledo, ed., *Historia de Salamanca*, Vol. V: *Siglo Veinte* (Salamanca: Centro de Estudios Salmantinos, 2001) p. 263.

51 Jaime del Burgo, *Conspiración y guerra civil* (Madrid: Editorial Alfaguara, 1970) pp. 260, 552, 631, 703–6; Serrano Suñer, *Memorias*, p. 34; Pedro Sainz Rodríguez, *Testimonio y recuerdos* (Barcelona: Planeta, 1978) pp. 329–30.

52 Cruanyes, *El papers de Salamanca*, pp. 15–16, 47–56; López García and Delgado Cruz, 'Víctimas y Nuevo Estado', p. 264.

53 On Ulibarri's clash with Tusquets, see Javier Domínguez Arribas, 'Juan Tusquets y sus ediciones antisectarias (1936–1939)', in José Antonio Ferrer Benimeli, ed., *La masonería española en la época de Sagasta*, 2 vols (Zaragoza: Gobierno de Aragón, 2007) II, pp. 1167–9; Cruanyes, *El papers de Salamanca*, pp. 234–5.

54 José Luis Rodríguez Jiménez, 'Una aproximación al trasfondo

ideológico de la represión: teoría de la conspiración y policía política franquista', in Jaume Sobrequés, Carme Molinero and Margarida Sala, eds, *Els camps de concentració i el mon penitenciari a Espanya durant la guerra civil i el franquisme* (Barcelona: Museu de'Historia de Catalunya/Editorial Crítica, 2003) pp. 416–18.

55 The principal works, among many others, are: Eduardo Comín Colomer, *La masonería en España: apuntes para una interpretación masónica de la Historia Patria* (Madrid: Editora Nacional, 1944); *La personalidad masónico-comunista de André Marty, 'el carnicero de Albacete'* (Madrid: Ediciones Asmer, 1944); *Ensayo crítico de la doctrina comunista* (Madrid: Ediciones de la Subsecretaría de Educación Popular, 1945); *La República en el exilio* (Barcelona: Editorial AHR, 1957); *Historia secreta de la Segunda República* (Barcelona: Editorial AHR, 1959); *Un siglo de atentados políticos en España* (Madrid: Publicaciones Españolas, 1959); *Historia del Partido Comunista de España*, 3 vols (Madrid: Editora Nacional, 1967); *El 5º Regimiento de Milicias Populares* (Madrid: Editorial San Martín, 1973). In addition, he also wrote many pamphlets in the series 'Temas Españoles'.

56 On the law, see I. Bergudo, J. Cuesta, M. de la Calle and M. Lanero, 'El Ministerio de Justicia en la España "Nacional"', in Archivo Histórico Nacional, *Justicia en guerra*, pp. 273–5.

57 José A. Ferrer Benimelli, 'Franco contra la masonería', *Historia 16*, año II, No. 15, July 1977, pp. 37–51; Luis Suárez Fernández, *Francisco Franco y su tiempo*, 8 vols (Madrid: Fundación Nacional Francisco Franco, 1984) III, pp. 92–100;

Cruanyes, *El papers de Salamanca*, pp. 234–5, 295.

58 José A. Ferrer Benimelli, 'Franco y la masonería', in Josep Fontana, ed., *España bajo el franquismo* (Barcelona: Editorial Crítica, 1986) pp. 260–1; José A. Ferrer Benimelli, *El contubernio judeo-masónico-comunista* (Madrid: Ediciones Istmo, 1982) pp. 297–300.

59 Klaus-Jörg Ruhl, *Franco, Falange y III Reich* (Madrid: Akal, 1986) pp. 54–5; García Pérez, *Franquismo y Tercer Reich*, p. 88; Ros Agudo, *La guerra secreta*, pp. 181–3.

60 Mattieu Séguéla, *Pétain–Franco: les secrets d'une alliance* (Paris: Albin Michel, 1992) pp. 254–5.

61 Marc Ferro, *Pétain* (Paris: Fayard, 1987) pp. 236–7; Jaume Miravitlles, *Gent que he conegut* (Barcelona: Edicions Destino, 1980) pp. 128–9; Séguéla, *Pétain–Franco*, pp. 254–6; Santos Juliá, 'Prólogo', in Julián Zugazagoitia, *Guerra y vicisitudes de los españoles*, 3rd edn (Barcelona: Tusquets Editores, 2001) p. xxiii.

62 Rafael Segovia and Fernando Serrano, eds, *Misión de Luis I. Rodríguez en Francia: la protección de los refugiados españoles julio a diciembre de 1940* (Mexico City: Colegio de México, Secretaría de Relaciones Exteriores/Consejo Nacional de Ciencia y Tecnología, 2000) pp. xiv–xv, 9–40; Geneviève Dreyfus-Armand, *El exilio de los republicanos españoles en Francia: de la guerra civil a la muerte de Franco* (Barcelona: Editorial Crítica, 2001) pp. 140–1.

63 Cipriano de Rivas Cherif, *Retrato de un desconocido* (Barcelona: Ediciones Grijalbo, 1979) pp. 496–7; Francisco Franco Salgado-Araujo, *Mis conversaciones privadas con Franco* (Barcelona: Planeta, 1976) p. 504.

64 Ángel Ossorio y Gallardo, *Vida y sacrificio de Companys* (Buenos

Aires: Editorial Losada, 1943) pp.
261–71; Josep Maria Solé i Sabaté,
'Introducció', Consell de guerra i
condemna a mort de Lluís Companys,
President de la Generalitat de
Catalunya (octubre de 1940)
(Barcelona: Generalitat de
Catalunya, 1999) pp. xix–xxxv;
Josep Benet, La mort del President
Companys (Barcelona: Edicions 62,
1998) pp. 324–50; Josep M. Figueres,
El consell de guerra a Lluís
Companys: President de la
Generalitat de Catalunya (Barcelona:
Edicions Proa, 1997) pp. 147–58;
Manuel Tarín-Iglesias, Los años rojos
(Barcelona: Planeta, 1985) pp.
221–42.

65 Tarín-Iglesias, Los años rojos, pp.
221–2; Benet, La mort, pp. 326–7;
Solé i Sabaté, 'Introducció', Consell
de guerra, p. xxxiii.

66 United Nations, Security Council,
Official Records, First Year: Second
Series, Special Supplement, Report
of the Sub-Committee on the Spanish
Question (New York, June 1946) p.
14; Ros Agudo, La guerra secreta, pp.
183–7; Sir Samuel Hoare,
Ambassador on Special Mission
(London: Collins, 1946) p. 76;
Heleno Saña, El franquismo sin
mitos: conversaciones con Serrano
Suñer (Barcelona: Grijalbo, 1982) p.
118.

67 Hilari Raguer, 'Himmler en
Montserrat', Historia y Vida, No. 158
(1981), pp. 78–85; Jordi Finestres i
Queralt Solé, '1940 Nazis a
Montserrat', Sàpiens, No. 3, January
2003, pp. 22–7.

68 Ros Agudo, La guerra secreta, pp.
187–91; Ramón Garriga, La España
de Franco: las relaciones con Hitler,
2nd edn (Puebla, Mexico: Editorial
Cajica, 1970) pp. 208–9.

69 Rivas Cherif, Retrato, pp. 498–500;
Juliá, 'Prólogo', pp. xxvii–xxxi.

70 Juan Antonio Ramos Hitos, Guerra
civil en Málaga 1936–1937: revisión
histórica, 2nd edn (Málaga: Editorial
Algazara, 2004) pp. 336–42.

71 Benet, La mort, pp. 158–64.

72 Federica Montseny, Mis primeros
cuarenta años (Barcelona: Plaza y
Janés, 1987) pp. 224–39.

73 Séguéla, Pétain–Franco, p. 257;
Mariano Ansó, Yo fui ministro de
Negrín (Barcelona: Planeta, 1976)
pp. 272–9; Manuel Portela
Valladares, Dietario de dos guerras
(1936–1950) (Sada-A Coruña:
Ediciós do Castro, 1988) pp. 178,
185, 195–8.

74 Benet, La mort, pp. 165–75;
Indalecio Prieto, Palabras al viento,
2nd edn (Mexico City: Ediciones
Oasis, 1969) pp. 179–84.

75 Josep Benet, Joan Peiró, afusellat
(Barcelona: Edicions 62, 2008) pp.
60–95, 115–57; José Peiró,
'Presentación', in Juan Peiró,
Trayectoria de la CNT (Gijón:
Ediciones Júcar, 1979) pp. 35–7;
Miravitlles, Gent, p. 129.

76 Marc Baldó and María Fernanda
Mancebo, 'Vida y muerte de Juan
Peset', and Salvador Albiñana,
'Historia de un proceso', in Pedro
Ruiz Torres, ed., Proceso a Juan Peset
Aleixandre (Valencia: Universitat de
València, 2001) pp. 31–63; Benet,
Joan Peiró, afusellat, pp. 207–40. The
entire prison, concentration camp
and trial records of Peset were
published in facsimile as an
appendix to the volume edited by
Pedro Ruiz. The lecture used to
condemn Peset was 'Las
individualidades y la situación en las
conductas actuales'.

77 Alfonso Domingo, El ángel rojo: la
historia de Melchor Rodríguez, el
anarquista que detuvo la represión en
el Madrid republicano (Córdoba:
Editorial Almuzara, 2009) pp.
29–31, 311–46; Raimundo
Fernández Cuesta, Testimonio,
recuerdos y reflexiones (Madrid:
Ediciones Dyrsa, 1985) pp. 95–6;

Leopoldo Huidobro, *Memorias de un finlandés* (Madrid: Ediciones Españolas, 1939) pp. 212–13. I am especially grateful to Alfonso Domingo for sharing with me his research on the trial.

78 Emilio Lamo de Espinosa and Manuel Contreras, *Filosofía y política en Julián Besteiro*, 2nd edn (Madrid: Editorial Sistema, 1990) pp. 115–34; Ignacio Arenillas de Chaves, *El proceso de Besteiro* (Madrid: Revista de Occidente, 1976) pp. 193–5; Enrique Tierno Galván, *Cabos sueltos* (Barcelona: Bruguera, 1981) pp. 26–7, 34; Gabriel Morón, *Política de ayer y política de mañana: los socialistas ante el problema español* (Mexico City: Talleres Numancia, 1942) pp. 142–3; Paul Preston, *¡Comrades! Portraits from the Spanish Civil War* (London: HarperCollins, 1999) pp. 176–92.

79 On the imprisonment and death of Besteiro, see 'Notas de Dolores Cebrián', in Julián Besteiro, *Cartas desde la prisión* (Madrid: Alianza, 1988) pp. 177–202; Andrés Saborit, *Julián Besteiro* (Buenos Aires: Losada, 1967) pp. 301–15.

80 Indalecio Prieto, *Convulsiones de España: pequeños detalles de grandes sucesos*, 3 vols (Mexico City: Ediciones Oasis, 1967–9) III, pp. 334–7.

81 Francisco Largo Caballero, *Mis recuerdos: cartas a un amigo* (Mexico City: Editores Unidos, 1954) pp. 253–6, 267–88; Julio Aróstegui, *Francisco Largo Caballero en el exilio: la última etapa de un líder obrero* (Madrid: Fundación Largo Caballero, 1990) pp. 29, 66–74.

82 Pablo Gil Vico, 'Ideología y represión: la Causa General: evolución histórica de un mecanismo jurídico político del régimen franquista', *Revista de Estudios Políticos*, No. 101, July–September 1998, pp. 159–80. See

also Isidro Sánchez, Manuel Ortiz and David Ruiz, eds, *España franquista: Causa General y actitudes sociales ante la dictadura* (Albacete: Universidad de Castilla-La Mancha, 1993) pp. 11–12; Martínez Leal and Ors Montenegro, 'De cárceles y campos de concentración', p. 36.

83 Gil Vico, 'Derecho y ficción', pp. 251–61.

84 *ABC*, 12 February 1939: 'La justicia de la España Imperial. Una Ley plena de serenidad. Ha sido firmada la ley de Responsabilidades políticas.' The full text in *ABC*, 17, 19 February 1939. See also Sánchez, Ortiz and Ruiz, eds, *España franquista*, pp. 16–17; Bergudo *et al.*, 'El Ministerio de Justicia en la España "Nacional"', pp. 272–3; Juan Carlos Berlinches Balbucid, *La rendición de la memoria: 200 casos de represión franquista en Guadalajara* (Guadalajara: Ediciones Bornova, 2004) pp. 46–62.

85 Manuel Álvaro Dueñas, '*Por ministerio de la ley y voluntad del Caudillo': la jurisdicción especial de responsabilidades políticas (1939–1945)* (Madrid: Centro de Estudios Políticos y Constitucionales, 2006) pp. 68–80, 97–110; Ortiz Heras, *Violencia política*, pp. 393–409; Julián Chaves Palacios, *La represión en la provincia de Cáceres durante la guerra civil (1936–1939)* (Cáceres: Universidad de Extremadura, 1995) pp. 87–91; Elena Franco Lanao, *Denuncias y represión en años de posguerra: el Tribunal de Responsabilidades Políticas en Huesca* (Huesca: Instituto de Estudios Altoaragoneses, 2005) pp. 43–52, 98–119; Vega Sombría, *Segovia*, pp. 179–96; Glicerio Sánchez Recio, *Las responsabilidades políticas en la posguerra española: el partido judicial de Monóvar* (Alicante: Universidad de Alicante, 1984) pp. 6–40; Conxita Mir, Fabià Corretgé,

Judit Farré and Joan Sagués, *Repressió econòmica i franquisme: l'actuació del Tribunal de Responsabilitats Polítiques a la província de Lleida* (Barcelona: Publicacions de l'Abadia de Montserrat, 1997) pp. 63–80; Mercè Barallat i Barés, *La repressió a la postguerra civil a Lleida (1938–1945)* (Barcelona: Publicacions de l'Abadia de Montserrat, 1991) pp. 347–56; Rodríguez Barreira, *Migas con miedo*, pp. 81–101; Berlinches Balbucid, *La rendición*, pp. 97–128; Julius Ruiz, *Franco's Justice: Repression in Madrid after the Spanish Civil War* (Oxford: Clarendon Press, 2005) pp. 131–64.

86 Francesc Vilanova i Vila-Abadal, *Repressió política i coacció econòmica: les responsabilitats polítiques de republicans i conservadors catalans a la postguerra (1939–1942)* (Barcelona: Publicacions de l'Abadia de Montserrat, 1999) pp. 44–51.

87 Josep M. Solé i Sabaté, Carles Llorens and Antoni Strubell, *Sunyol, l'altre president afusellat* (Lleida: Pagès Editors, 1996) pp. 17–23, 80–91, 103–35, 143–7; Vilanova i Vila-Abadal, *Repressió política*, pp. 201–8.

88 Vilanova i Vila-Abadal, *Repressió política*, pp. 75–82.

89 Enrique Suñer, *Los intelectuales y la tragedia española*, 2nd edn (San Sebastián: Editorial Española, 1938) pp. 5–6, 166–7, 171.

90 *Ibid.*, pp. 166–7.

91 *Ibid.*, p. 171.

92 Diego Catalán, *El archivo del romancero: historia documentada de un siglo de historia*, 2 vols (Madrid: Fundación Ramón Menéndez Pidal, 2001) at http://cuestadelzarzal. blogia.com/2010/091301-1.-depuracion-de-menendez-pidal.-fin-de-sus-proyectos-con-una-proyeccion-naciona.php.

93 Franco Lanao, *Denuncias y represión*, pp. 71–2; Mir *et al.*, *Repressió econòmica*, pp. 101–19; Vega Sombría, *Segovia*, p. 183.

94 Álvaro Dueñas, 'Por ministerio de la ley y voluntad del Caudillo', pp. 127–58; Prada Rodríguez, *La España masacrada*, pp. 288–311; Mirta Núñez Díaz-Balart, Manuel Alvaro Dueñas, Francisco Espinosa Maestre and José María García Márquez, *La gran represión: los años de plomo del franquismo* (Barcelona: Flor del Viento, 2009) pp. 124–6, 263–76.

95 José María Iribarren, *Con el general Mola: escenas y aspectos inéditos de la guerra civil* (Zaragoza: Librería General, 1937) p. 253.

96 An Andalusian prisoner interviewed in the CGT documentary DVD directed by Mariano Agudo and Eduardo Montero, *Presos del silencio* (Seville: Intermedia Producciones/ Canal Sur, 2004).

97 Joaquín Maurín, *En las prisiones de Franco* (Mexico City: B. Costa Amic Editor, 1974) pp. 47–8; Carme Molinero, Margarida Sala and Jaume Sobrequés, eds, *Una inmensa prisión: los campos de concentración y las prisiones durante la guerra civil y el franquismo* (Barcelona: Editorial Crítica, 2003) pp. xiii–xxi.

98 Gutmaro Gómez Bravo, *El exilio interior: cárcel y represión en la España franquista 1939–1950* (Madrid: Taurus, 2009) pp. 25–33; Aram Monfort, *Barcelona 1939: el camp de concentració d'Horta* (Barcelona: L'Avenç, 2008) pp. 109–17.

99 Fundación Nacional Francisco Franco, *Documentos inéditos para la historia del Generalísimo Franco*, 4 vols (Madrid: FNFF Azor, 1992) II, 1, pp. 176–9; Alía Miranda, *La guerra civil en la retaguardia*, pp. 385–6; Ortiz Heras, *Violencia política*, pp. 311–12; Marín Gómez, *El laurel y la retama*, pp. 82–5;

Escudero Andújar, *Lo cuentan como lo han vivido*, pp. 125–6.

100 Javier Rodrigo, *Cautivos: campos de concentración en la España Franquista, 1936–1947* (Barcelona: Editorial Crítica, 2005) pp. 26–34, 40–6, 95–107, 193–211; Antonio D. López Rodríguez, *Cruz, bandera y caudillo: el campo de concentración de Castuera* (Badajoz: CEDER-La Serena, 2007) pp. 93–167, 207–24; José Ángel Fernández López, *Historia del campo de concentración de Miranda de Ebro (1937–1947)* (Miranda del Ebro: Autor, 2003) pp. 33–41, 59–67; Juan José Monago Escobedo, *El campo de concentración de Nanclares de la Oca 1940–1947* (Vitoria: Gobierno Vasco, 1998) pp. 39–45; Monfort, *Barcelona 1939*, pp. 118–43.

101 Monfort, *Barcelona 1939*, pp. 149–53; Marín Gómez, *El laurel y la retama*, pp. 90–1; Guzmán, *Nosotros los asesinos*, pp. 285–6; Subirats Piñana, *Pilatos 1939–1941*, p. 1.

102 Isaías Lafuente, *Esclavos por la patria: la explotación de los presos bajo el franquismo* (Madrid: Ediciones Temas de Hoy, 2002) pp. 57–63, 121–9, 135–70; Rafael Torres, *Los esclavos de Franco* (Madrid: Oberón, 2000) pp. 134–45; Javier Rodrigo, *Hasta la raíz: violencia durante la guerra civil y la dictadura franquista* (Madrid: Alianza Editorial, 2008) pp. 138–57.

103 José Luis Gutiérrez Molina, 'Los presos del canal: el Servicio de Colonias Penitenciarias Militarizadas y el Canal del Bajo Guadalquivir (1940–1967)', in Molinero, Sala and Sobrequés, eds, *Una inmensa prisión*, pp. 62–71; Gonzalo Acosta Bono, José Luis Gutiérrez Molina, Lola Martínez Macías and Ángel del Río Sánchez, *El canal de los presos (1940–1962): trabajos forzados: de la represión política a la explotación económica* (Barcelona: Editorial Crítica, 2004) pp. 181–99; José Luis Gutiérrez Casalá, *Colonias penitenciarias militarizadas de Montijo: represión franquista en el partido judicial de Mérida* (Mérida: Editorial Regional de Extremadura, 2003) pp. 15–17, 21–42.

104 Fernando Mendiola Gonzalo and Edurne Beaumont Esandi, *Esclavos del franquismo en el Pirineo: la carretera Igal–Vidángoz–Roncal (1939–1941)* (Tafalla: Editorial Txalaparta, 2007) pp. 171–233; Alía Miranda, *La guerra civil en la retaguardia*, pp. 388–9.

105 *ABC*, 1 April 1940; Fernando Olmeda, *El Valle de los Caídos* (Barcelona: Ediciones Península, 2009) pp. 25, 43, 54–69; Daniel Sueiro, *El Valle de los Caídos: los secretos de la cripta franquista*, 2nd edn (Barcelona: Argos Vergara, 1983) pp. 8–24, 44–73, 118–43, 184–205.

106 José Manuel Sabín, *Prisión y muerte en la España de posguerra* (Madrid: Anaya & Mario Muchnik, 1996) pp. 224–31; Guzmán, *Nosotros los asesinos*, pp. 414–22.

107 José Agustín Pérez del Pulgar, *La solución que España da al problema de sus presos políticos* (Valladolid: Librería Santaren, 1939); Martín Torrent, *¿Qué me dice usted de los presos?* (Alcalá de Henares: Imp. Talleres Penitenciarios, 1942) pp. 98–105; Michael Richards, *A Time of Silence: Civil War and the Culture of Repression in Franco's Spain, 1936–1945* (Cambridge: Cambridge University Press, 1998) pp. 80–4; Gutmaro Gómez Bravo, *La redención de penas: la formación del sistema penitenciario franquista* (Madrid: Los Libros de la Catarata, 2007) pp. 69–97, 147–66; Eugenia Afinoguénova, 'El Nuevo Estado y la propaganda de la Redención de las Penas por el Trabajo en Raza:

anecdotario para el guión de una película de Francisco Franco', *Bulletin of Spanish Studies*, Vol. 84, No. 7, 2007, pp. 889–903.

108 Torrent, *¿Qué me dice usted de los presos?*, pp. 103–21; Ángela Cenarro, 'La institucionalización del universo penitenciario franquista', in Molinero, Sala and Sobrequés, eds, *Una inmensa prisión*, pp. 135–40; Gómez Bravo, *El exilio interior*, pp. 83–6; Sabín, *Prisión y muerte*, pp. 169, 197.

109 Commission Internationale contre le Régime Concentrationaire, *Livre blanc sur le système pénitentiaire espagnol* (Paris: Le Pavois, 1953) pp. 43–7, 205–6. For a brilliant analysis of the work of the Commission, see Ricard Vinyes, 'Territoris de càstig (les presons franquistes, 1939–1959)', in Associació Catalana d'Expresos Polítics, *Notícia de la negra nit: vides i veus a les presons franquistes (1939–1959)* (Barcelona: Diputació de Barcelona, 2001) pp. 43–61. See also Ricard Vinyes, 'El universo penitenciario durante el franquismo', in Molinero, Sala and Sobrequés, eds, *Una inmensa prisión*, pp. 160–2; Gómez Bravo, *El exilio interior*, pp. 24, 76–80; Gómez Bravo, *La redención de penas*, pp. 125–7; Miguel Núñez, *La revolución y el deseo: memorias* (Barcelona: Ediciones Península, 2002) pp. 79–80.

110 Acosta Bono et al., *El canal de los presos*, pp. 214–23; Marín Gómez, *El laurel y la retama*, pp. 99–103; Guzmán, *Nosotros los asesinos*, pp. 388–9; Molina, *Noche sobre España*, pp. 163–8.

111 Eduardo Ruiz Bautista, 'Prisioneros del libro: leer y penar en las cárceles de Franco', in Antonio Castillo and Feliciano Montero, eds, *Franquismo y memoria popular: escrituras, voces y representaciones* (Madrid: Siete Mares, 2003) pp. 118–19; Cenarro,

'La institucionalización', pp. 143–5; Gómez Bravo, *La redención de penas*, pp. 167–75; Juan Antonio Cabezas, *Asturias: catorce meses de guerra civil* (Madrid: G. del Toro, 1975) pp. 234–48.

112 Mavis Bacca Dowden, *Spy-jacked! A Tale of Spain* (Horsham: Gramercy, 1991) pp. 142–3.

113 Cuevas Gutiérrez, *Cárcel de mujeres*, II, p. 66; Tomasa Cuevas Gutiérrez, *Mujeres de la resistencia* (Barcelona: Sirocco Books, 1986) pp. 127–8; Fernando Hernández Holgado, *Mujeres encárceladas: la prisión de Ventas: de la República al franquismo, 1931–1941* (Madrid: Marcial Pons, 2003) pp. 113–20, 138–47.

114 Hernández Holgado, *Mujeres encárceladas*, pp. 158–65; Cuevas Gutiérrez, *Cárcel de mujeres*, II, p. 28; Ángeles García Madrid, *Réquiem por la libertad* (Madrid: Editorial Alianza Hispánica, 2003) pp. 62–3.

115 García Madrid, *Réquiem*, p. 61; Vinyes, 'El universo penitenciario', pp. 164–9; Ricard Vinyes, Montse Armengou and Ricard Belis, *Los niños perdidos del franquismo* (Barcelona: Plaza y Janés, 2002) pp. 68–9, 131; Marín Gómez, *El laurel y la retama*, pp. 181–91; Escudero Andújar, *Lo cuentan como lo han vivido*, pp. 133, 139–40, 154; Escudero Andújar, *Dictadura y oposición*, pp. 58–61; Margarita Nelken, *Las torres del Kremlin* (Mexico City: Industrial y Distribuidora, 1943) pp. 79, 320–1.

116 Pilar Fidalgo, *A Young Mother in Franco's Prisons* (London: United Editorial, 1939) pp. 9–10, 28; Ramón Sender Barayón, *A Death in Zamora* (Albuquerque: University of New Mexico Press, 1989) pp. 134–5, 146–7.

117 Gumersindo de Estella, *Fusilados en Zaragoza 1936–1939: tres años de asistencia espiritual a los reos*

(Zaragoza: Mira Editores, 2003) pp. 62–6, 80–8, 119–21.

118 Cuevas Gutiérrez, *Cárcel de mujeres*, I, pp. 112, 118–21, II, pp. 65, 101, 260–1; García Madrid, *Réquiem*, pp. 32–41, 80–1; Rodriguez Chaos, *24 años en la cárcel*, pp. 65–6; Vinyes, Armengou and Belis, *Los niños perdidos*, pp. 91–2; Hernández Holgado, *Mujeres encárceladas*, pp. 145, 149–53, 246–55.

119 Pura Sánchez, *Individuas de dudosa moral: la represión de las mujeres en Andalucía (1936–1958)* (Barcelona: Editorial Crítica, 2009) pp. 148–9.

120 Hartmut Heine, *La oposición política al franquismo* (Barcelona: Editorial Crítica, 1983) pp. 64–6; Cuevas Gutiérrez, *Cárcel de mujeres*, II, pp. 63–5; García Madrid, *Réquiem*, pp. 81–9; Hernández Holgado, *Mujeres encárceladas*, pp. 230–46; Carlos Fonseca, *Trece rosas rojas: la historia más conmovedora de la guerra civil española* (Madrid: Ediciones Temas de Hoy, 2004) pp. 103–19, 209–34; Giuliana Di Febo, *Resistencia y movimiento de mujeres en España 1936–1976* (Barcelona: Icaria Editorial, 1979) pp. 99–100.

121 Vinyes, Armengou and Belis, *Los niños perdidos*, pp. 67–71, 90–1; Mercedes Núñez, *Cárcel de Ventas* (Paris: Colección Ebro, 1967) pp. 83–4.

122 Vinyes, Armengou and Belis, *Los niños perdidos*, pp. 121–31; Cuevas Gutiérrez, *Cárcel de mujeres*, II, pp. 61–2.

123 Cuevas Gutiérrez, *Cárcel de mujeres*, II, pp. 15–17, 64–6, 92–3; Núñez, *Cárcel de Ventas*, pp. 22–4; García Madrid, *Réquiem*, pp. 90–2; Escudero Andújar, *Lo cuentan como lo han vivido*, pp. 127, 135–8, 140–3; Consuelo García, *Las cárceles de Soledad Real: una vida* (Madrid: Ediciones Alfaguara, 1983) pp. 101–2; Di Febo, *Resistencia*, pp. 33–8; Justo Calcerrada Bravo and

Antonio Ortiz Mateos, *Julia Manzanal 'Comisario Chico'* (Madrid: Fundación Domingo Malagón) pp. 84–99.

124 Núñez, *Cárcel de Ventas*, pp. 64–6.

125 Pilar Fidalgo, *A Young Mother in Franco's Prisons* (London: United Editorial, 1939) p. 31; García, *Las cárceles de Soledad Real*, pp. 127–8; Di Febo, *Resistencia*, p. 36; Vega Sombría, *Segovia*, p. 241.

126 Torrent, *¿Qué me dice usted de los presos?*, pp. 126–32; Ángeles Malonda, *Aquello sucedió así: memorias* (Madrid: Asociación de Cooperativas Farmacéuticas, 1983) p. 103; Ricard Vinyes, *Irredentas: las presas políticas y sus hijos en las cárceles franquistas* (Madrid: Ediciones Temas de Hoy, 2002) pp. 88–9.

127 Vinyes, 'Territoris de càstig', pp. 60–1; Vinyes, *Irredentas*, pp. 74–8; 'Defunciones Cárcel de Mujeres de Saturrarán', http://www.asturiasrepublicana.com/.

128 Antonio Vallejo Nágera, *Higiene de la Raza: la asexualización de los psicópatas* (Madrid: Ediciones Medicina, 1934).

129 Vinyes, *Irredentas*, pp. 49–57.

130 Antonio Nadal Sánchez, 'Experiencias psíquicas sobre mujeres marxistas malagueñas', in *Las mujeres y la guerra civil española* (Madrid: Ministerio de Cultura, 1991) pp. 340–50; Michael Richards, 'Morality and Biology in the Spanish Civil War: Psychiatrists, Revolution and Women Prisoners in Málaga', in *Contemporary European History*, Vol. 10, No. 3, 2001, pp. 395–421; Rodrigo, *Cautivos*, pp. 141–6; Carl Geiser, *Prisoners of the Good Fight: Americans against Franco Fascism* (Westport, Conn.: Lawrence Hill, 1986) p. 154; Antonio Vallejo Nágera, *La locura y la guerra: psicopatología de la guerra española* (Valladolid; Librería

Santarén, 1939) pp. 222–3; Antonio Vallejo and Eduardo Martínez, 'Psiquismo del fanatismo marxista: investigaciones psicológicas en marxistas femeninos delincuentes', *Revista Española de Medicina y Cirugía de Guerra*, No. 9, pp. 398–413; Vinyes, *Irredentas*, pp. 62–70.

131 Antonio Vallejo Nájera, *Eugenesia de la hispanidad y regeneración de la raza española* (Burgos: Talleres Gráficos El Noticiero, 1937) p. 114; Vinyes, *Irredentas*, pp. 58–61.

132 Antonio Vallejo Nájera, *Divagaciones intranscendentes* (Valladolid: Talleres Tipográficos 'Cuesta', 1938) pp. 15–8; Vinyes, Armengou and Belis, *Los niños perdidos*, pp. 36–43; Richards, *A Time of Silence*, pp. 57–9.

133 Carlos Castilla del Pino, *Pretérito imperfecto: autobiografía* (Barcelona: Tusquets, 1997) p. 301.

134 José Luis Mínguez Goyanes, *Onésimo Redondo 1905–1936: precursor sindicalista* (Madrid: Editorial San Martín, 1990) pp. 28–32, 37–8, 150–1; Javier Martínez de Bedoya, *Memorias desde mi aldea* (Valladolid: Ambito Ediciones, 1996) p. 67; Ángela Cenarro Lagunas, *La sonrisa de la Falange: Auxilio Social en la guerra civil y en la posguerra* (Barcelona: Editorial Crítica, 2005) p. 39.

135 Martínez de Bedoya, *Memorias*, p. 112; Cenarro Lagunas, *La sonrisa de la Falange*, pp. 140–3.

136 Diary entry 29 September 1937, Javier Martínez de Bedoya; Mercedes Sanz Bachiller, 'Notas sobre mi trayectoria', unpublished notes written in 1972 (both in Archivo Mercedes Sanz Bachiller); Cenarro Lagunas, *La sonrisa de la Falange*, pp. 82–3.

137 Vinyes, Armengou and Belis, *Los niños perdidos*, pp. 63–77; Vinyes, *Irredentas*, pp. 79–89.

138 Bacca Dowden, *Spy-jacked!*, pp. 185–6.

139 Montse Armengou and Ricard Belis, *El convoy de los 927* (Barcelona: Plaza y Janés, 2005) pp. 251–66, 329–62 (where the correspondence is reproduced); David Wingeate Pike, *Españoles en el holocausto: vida y muerte de los republicanos en Mauthausen* (Barcelona: Mondadori, 2003) pp. 42–7; Montserrat Roig, *Noche y niebla: los catalanes en los campos nazis* (Barcelona: Ediciones Península, 1978) pp. 26–30; Benito Bermejo, *Francisco Boix, el fotógrafo de Mauthausen* (Barcelona: RBA Libros, 2002) pp. 54–9.

140 Armengou and Belis, *El convoy de los 927*, pp. 101–12, 118–29, 138–65; Pike, *Españoles en el holocausto*, pp. 87–95; Mariano Constante, *Yo fui ordenanza de los SS* (Zaragoza: Editorial Pirineo, 2000) pp. 125–36.

141 Armengou and Belis, *El convoy de los 927*, pp. 181–8, 198–210, 263–6.

142 Neus Català, *De la resistencia y la deportación: 50 Testimonios de mujeres españolas* (Barcelona: Ediciones Península, 2000) pp. 19–67; Montse Armengou and Ricard Belis, *Ravensbrück: l'infern de les dones* (Barcelona: Angle Editorial, 2007) pp. 47–5; Roig, *Noche y niebla*, pp. 57–77; Eduardo Pons Prades and Mariano Constante, *Los cerdos del comandante: Españoles en los campos de exterminio nazis* (Barcelona: Argos Vergara, 1978) pp. 39–44, 57–8, 73–6, 97–9, 116–17, 335–6, 347–9.

143 Lope Massaguer, *Mauthausen fin de trayecto: un anarquista en los campos de la muerte* (Madrid: Fundación Anselmo Lorenzo, 1997) pp. 81–6; Prisciliano García Gaitero, *Mi vida en los campos de la muerte nazis* (León: Edilesa, 2005) pp. 62–70. For photographic evidence of the work

in the quarry, see Rosa Toran and Margarida Sala, *Mauthausen: crónica gráfica de un campo de concentración* (Barcelona: Museu d'Història de Catalunya/Viena Edicions, 2002) pp. 198–205; Bermejo, *Francisco Boix*, pp. 186–8, 207; Sandra Checa, Ángel del Río and Ricardo Martín, *Andaluces en los campos de Mauthausen* (Seville: Centro de Estudios Andaluces, 2007) pp. 30–2, 98–9; García Gaitero, *Mi vida*, p. 62.

144 Pike, *Españoles en el holocausto*, pp. 44–5; Antonio Vilanova, *Los olvidados: los exilados españoles en la segunda guerra mundial* (Paris: Ruedo Ibérico, 1969) pp. 200–1; Checa, Del Río and Martín, *Andaluces en los campos de Mauthausen*, pp. 51–7, 222–57; Paramio Roca, García Bilbao and García Bilbao, *La represión franquista en Guadalajara*, pp. 131–2; Sánchez Tostado, *La guerra civil en Jaén*, pp. 665–72; Escudero Andújar, *Dictadura y oposición*, pp. 73–5.

145 *ABC*, 1 April 1964.

146 Francisco Franco, *Discursos y mensajes del Jefe del Estado 1964–1967* (Madrid, 1968) pp. 19–40.

Epilogue: The Reverberations

1 Duilio Susmel, *Vita sbagliata di Galeazzo Ciano* (Milan: Aldo Palazzi Editore, 1962) p. 158.

2 Ramón Serrano Suñer, *Entre el silencio y la propaganda, la Historia como fue: memorias* (Barcelona: Planeta, 1977) pp. 244–8.

3 Carlos Castillo del Pino, *Casa del Olivo: autobiografía (1949–2003)* (Barcelona: Tusquets, 2004) p. 381.

4 Juan Tusquets, *Masones y pacifistas* (Burgos: Ediciones Antisectarias, 1939) p. 257; Antoni Mora, 'Joan Tusquets, en els 90 anys d'un home d'estudi i de combat', Institut d'Estudis Tarraconenses Ramón Berenguer IV, *Anuari 1990–1991 de la Societat d'Estudis d'Història Eclesiàstica Moderna i Contemporània de Catalunya* (Tarragona: Diputació de Tarragona, 1992) pp. 238–9; Ignasi Riera, *Los catalanes de Franco* (Barcelona: Plaza y Janés, 1998) p. 127; Jordi Canal, 'Las campañas antisectarias de Juan Tusquets (1927–1939): una aproximación a los orígenes del contubernio judeo-masónico-comunista en España', in José Antonio Ferrer Benimeli, ed., *La masonería en la España del siglo XX*, 2 vols (Toledo: Universidad de Castilla-La Mancha, 1996) pp. 1208–9.

5 Mora, 'Joan Tusquets', pp. 238–9; Riera, *Los catalanes de Franco*, p. 127; Canal, 'Las campañas antisectarias de Juan Tusquets', pp. 1208–9.

6 Interviews with Lluís Bonada, *Avui*, 28 February 1990, with Mora, 'Joan Tusquets', p. 239, with Joan Subirà, *Capellans en temps de Franco* (Barcelona: Editorial Mediterrània, 1996) p. 36.

7 Esther Tusquets Guillén, *Habíamos ganado la guerra* (Barcelona: Editorial Bruguera, 2007) pp. 153–6, 158–61; Mora, 'Joan Tusquets', p. 234.

8 Arxiu Vidal i Barraquer, *Esglesia i Estat durant la Segona República espanyola 1931/1936*, 4 vols in 8 parts (Monestir de Montserrat: Publicacions de l'Abadia de Montserrat, 1971–90) II, pp. 386, 638, 644–6, III, p. 935; Subirà, *Capellans*, p. 21.

9 Ian Gibson, *El hombre que detuvo a García Lorca: Ramón Ruiz Alonso y la muerte del poeta* (Madrid: Aguilar, 2007) p. 143; Miguel Caballero and Pilar Góngora Ayala, *La verdad sobre el asesinato de García Lorca: historia de una familia* (Madrid: Ibersaf Editores, 2007) p. 309.

10 Juan Manuel Lozano Nieto, *A sangre y fuego: los años treinta en un pueblo andaluz* (Córdoba: Almuzara, 2006) pp. 202, 206–7; Jesús Pueyo Maisterra, 'Del infierno al Paraíso', unpublished memoirs, p. 21.

11 Information supplied by the local chronicler of Fuente de Cantos, Cayetano Ibarra Barroso.

12 Alfonso Domingo, *Retaguardia: la guerra civil tras los frentes* (Madrid: Oberón, 2004) pp. 19, 24–5.

13 Ángel Montoto, 'Salamanca: así fue el terrorismo falangista', *Interviú*, No. 177, 4–18 October 1979, pp. 44–7.

14 Letter reproduced in Enrique de Sena, 'Guerra, censura y urbanismo: recuerdos de un periodista', in Ricardo Robledo, ed., *Historia de Salamanca*, Vol. V: *Siglo Veinte* (Salamanca: Centro de Estudios Salmantinos, 2001) p. 329. Typing errors have been corrected.

15 Gabriel García de Consuegra Muñoz, Ángel López López and Fernando López López, *La represión en Pozoblanco (Guerra Civil y posguerra)* (Córdoba: Francisco Baena, 1989) pp. 132, 136; Francisco Moreno Gómez, *Córdoba en la posguerra (la represión y la guerrilla, 1939–1950)* (Córdoba: Francisco Baena Editor, 1987) p. 96; Francisco Moreno, 'La represión en la posguerra', in Santos Juliá *et al.*,

Víctimas de la guerra civil (Madrid: Ediciones Temas de Hoy, 1999) pp. 312, 332–3.

16 José Casado Montado, *Trigo tronzado: crónicas silenciadas y comentarios* (San Fernando: Autor, 1992) p. 16.

17 Castillo del Pino, *Casa del Olivo*, pp. 372–3.

18 Miguel Angel Mateos, '"Muerte en Zamora": la tragedia de Amparo Barayón', serialized in *La Opinión – El Correo de Zamora*, 3, 4, 5, 6, 7, 8, 24 April 2005; Pilar Fidalgo, *A Young Mother in Franco's Prisons* (London: United Editorial, 1939) p. 22; Ramón Sender Barayón, *A Death in Zamora* (Albuquerque: University of New Mexico Press, 1989) pp. 110, 164–5.

19 *El Caso*, 5 September 1964.

20 Documentación sobre Gonzalo de Aguilera y Munro, remitida a su viuda, Legajo 416, Archivo General Militar de Segovia; *El Adelanto* (Salamanca), 29, 30 August, 1 September 1964; *El Caso*, 5 September 1964; *La Gaceta Regional*, 30 August, 1 September 1964.

21 Testimony to the author, 30 July 1999, of the Cronista de la Ciudad de Salamanca, Dr Salvador Llopis Llopis.

22 Interview of Mariano Sanz González with the Director of the Hospital, Dr Desiderio López, 27 October 1999.

APPENDIX

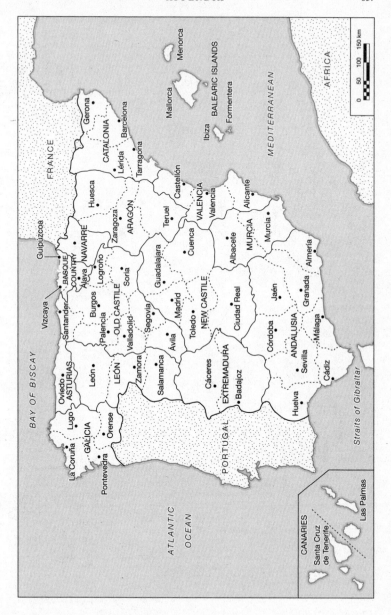

Spain's Regions and Provinces in 1936

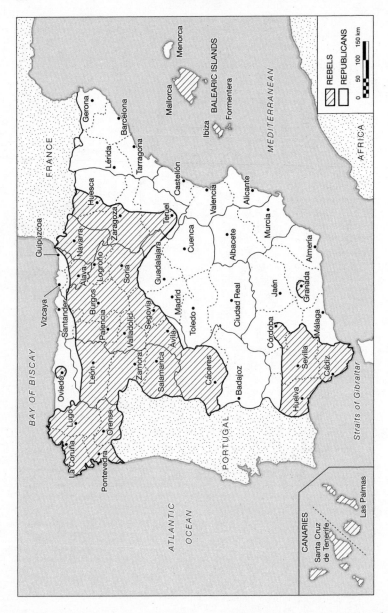

The Division of Spain at the end of July 1936

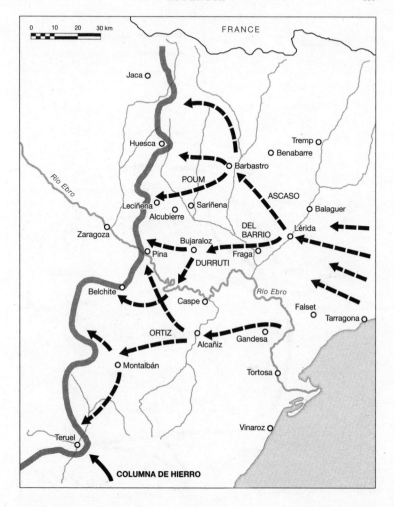

The Catalan 'invasion' of Aragón throughout July and August 1936

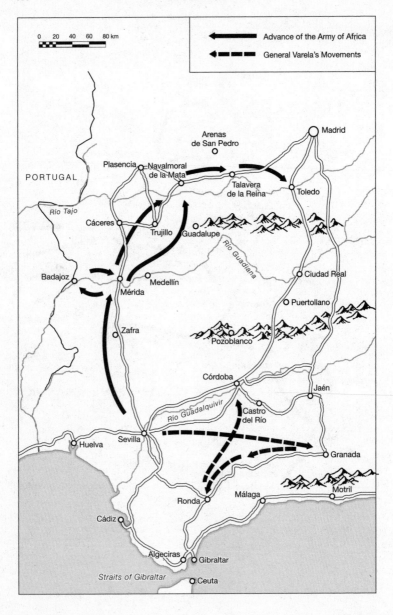

The advance of the Army of Africa from August to October 1936

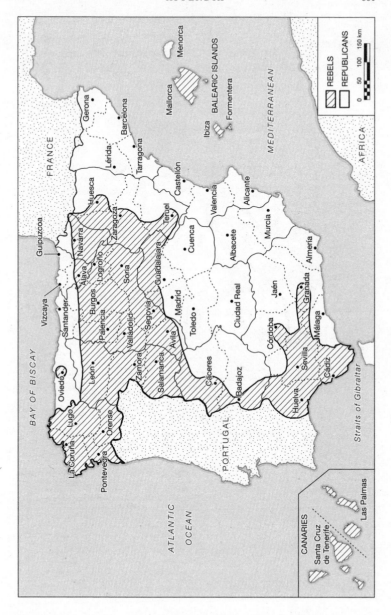

The Division of Spain in September 1936

The Division of Spain in March 1937

The Division of Spain in April 1938

The Division of Spain in February 1939

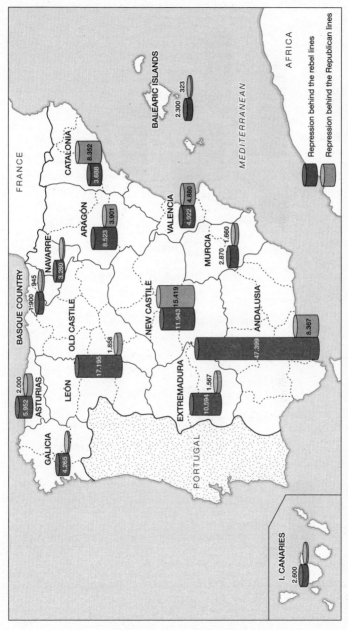

The regions used in the map correspond to the administrative divisions operating in Spain at the time of the Civil War. The total number of victims in the regions of Old Castile and Léon includes data from the provinces that now belong to the autonomous communities of Castile and Léon, La Rioja and Cantabria.

Repression behind the rebel lines

Repression behind the Republican lines

Repression in Spain by Regions and Provinces, 1936–9

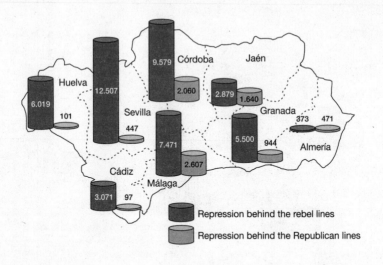

Repression in Andalusia, 1936–9

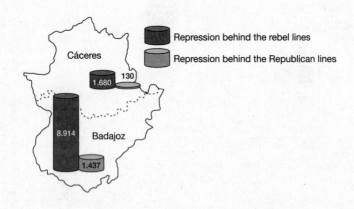

Repression in Extremadura, 1936–9

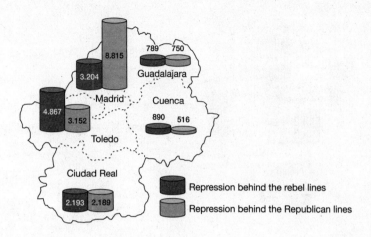

Repression in New Castile, 1936–9

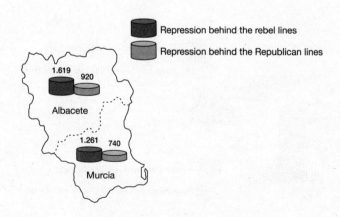

Repression in Murcia, 1936–9

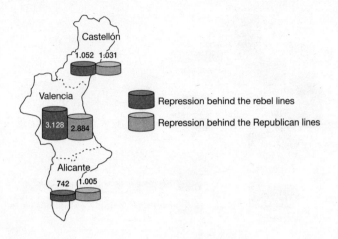

Repression in Valencia, 1936–9

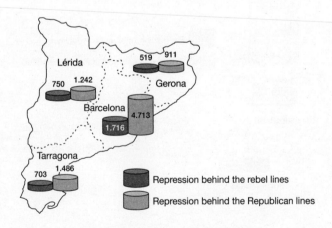

Repression in Catalonia, 1936–9

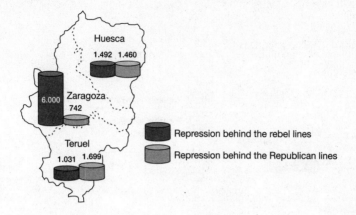

Repression in Aragon, 1936–9

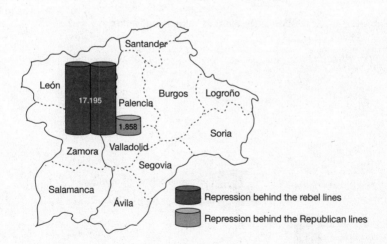

Repression in Old Castile and Léon, 1936–9

The available data for what used to be the regions of Old Castile and Léon are combined without provincial breakdown. The number of victims in these regions includes the data from the provinces that now belong to the autonomous communities of Castile and Léon, La Rioja and Cantabria.

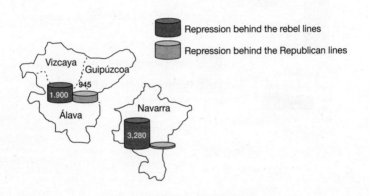

Repression in the Basque Country and Navarre, 1936–9

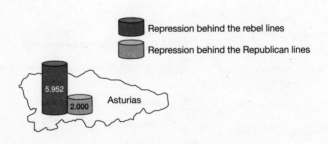

Repression in Asturias, 1936–9

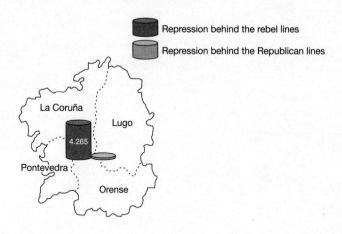

Repression in Galicia, 1936–9

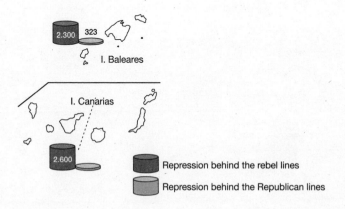

Repression in the Balearic and Canary Islands, 1936–9

INDEX